Conference Record
of the

Seventeenth Annual ACM Symposium on Principles of Programming Languages®

Papers Presented at the Symposium

San Francisco, California
January 17-19, 1990

Sponsored by the

Association for Computing Machinery

Special Interest Group on Automata and Comupuability Theory (SIGACT)
Special Interest Group on Programming Languages (SIGPLAN)

The Association for Computing Machinery
11 West 42nd Street
New York, New York 10036

Copyright © 1990 by the Association for Computing Machinery, Inc. Copying without fee is permitted provided that the copies are not made or distributed for direct commercial advantage, and credit to the source is given. Abstracting with credit is permitted. For other copying of articles that carry a code at the bottom of the first page, copying is permitted provided that the per-copy fee indicated in the code is paid through the Copyright Clearance Center, 27 Congress Street, Salem, MA 01970. For permisssion to republish write to: Director of Publications, Association for Computing Machinery. To copy otherwise, or republish, requires a fee and/or specific permission.

ISBN 0-89791-343-4

Additional copies may be ordered prepaid from:

ACM Order Department　　*Price*
P.O. Box 64145　　　　　　　Members $22.00
Baltimore, MD 21264　　　　　All Others $30.00

ACM Order Number: 549900

WEDNESDAY, JANUARY 17th

Tutorial: 8:00 - 9:15

Introduction to the Lambda Calculus
Henk Barendregt, Nijmegen University

Session 1: 9:30 -- 10:30
Chaired by Andrew Appel

On Laziness and Optimality in Lambda Interpreters: Tools for Specification and Analysis
John Field (Cornell University) 1

An Algorithm for Optimal Lambda Calculus Reduction
John Lamping (Xerox PARC) 16

Session 2: 11:00 -- 12:30
Chaired by Matthias Felleisen

Explicit Substitutions
M. Abadi (DEC SRC), L. Cardelli (DEC SRC),
P.L. Curien (Ecole Normale Superieure), and
J.J. Levy (INRIA Rocquencourt) 31

A Formulae-as-Types Notion of Control
Timothy G. Griffin (Rice University) 47

Implicative Formulae in the Proofs of Computations' Analogy
Andrea Asperti, Gian Luigi Ferrari and Roberto Gorrieri (Universita di Pisa) 59

Session 3: 2:00 -- 3:30
Chaired by Samson Abramsky

Computable Process
Yiannis N. Moschovakis (UCLA) 72

The Chemical Abstract Machine
Gerard Berry (Ecole des Mines de Paris) and
Gerard Boudol (INRIA Sophia-Antipolis) 81

Interaction Nets
Yves Lafont (Ecole Normale Superieure) 95

Session 4: 4:00 -- 5:30
Chaired by Ravi Sethi

Toward a Typed Foundation for Method Specialization and Inheritance
John C. Mitchell (Stanford University) 109

Inheritance is Not Subtyping
William R. Cook, Walter L. Hill and Peter S. Canning (HP Laboratories) 125

A Type System for Smalltalk
Justin O. Graver and Ralph E. Johnson (University of Illinois) 136

THURSDAY, JANUARY 18th

Tutorial: 8:00 - 9:15

    Introduction to Abstract Interpretation
        John Hughes, University of Glasgow

Session 5: 9:30 -- 10:30
Chaired by Paul Hudak

    A Relationship Between Abstract Interpretation and Projection Analysis
        Geoffrey Burn (GEC Hirst Research Center)...151

    On Determining Lifetime and Aliasing of Dynamically
    Allocated Data in Higher-order Functional Specifications
        Alan Deutsch (Ecole Polytechnique)..157

Session 6: 11:00 -- 12:30
Chaired by Saumya Debray

    Small Domains Spell Fast Strictness Analysis
        R.C. Sekar, Shaunak Pawagi, and I.V. Ramarkrishnan (SUNY at Stony Brook)...............169

    An Efficient Hybrid Algorithm for Incremental Data Flow Analysis
        Thomas J. Marlowe and Barbara G. Ryder (Rutgers University).......................................184

    A Finite Presentation Theorem for Approximating Logic Programs
        Nevin Heintze (CMU) and Joxan Jaffar (IBM T.J. Watson Research Center).................197

Session 7: 2:00 -- 4:00
Chaired by Jayadev Misra

    Program Transformation in the Presence of Errors
        John H. Williams, Alexander Aiken, and
        Edward L. Wimmers (IBM Almaden Research Center) 210

    Making Asynchronous Parallelism Safe for the World
        Guy L. Steele, Jr. (Thinking Machines Corporation)...218

    Concurrent Constraint Programming
        Vijay A. Saraswat (Xerox PARC) and Martin Rinard (Stanford University)....................232

    Parallelism in Logic Programs
        Raghu Ramakrishnan (University of Wisconsin-Madison) 246

Session 8: 4:30 -- 6:00
Chaired by Susan Horwitz

    Combining Generational and Conservative Garbage Collection: Framework and Implementations
        Alan Demmers, Mark Weiser, Barry Hayes, Hans Boehm,
        Daniel Bobrow, and Scott Shenker
        (Boehm: Rice University, remainder: Xerox PARC) 261

    Scheduling Time-Critical Instructions on RISC Machines
        Krishna Palem (IBM T.J. Watson Research Center) and
        Barbara Simons (IBM Almaden Research Center) 270

    Automata-Driven Indexing of Prolog Clauses
        R. Ramesh, I.V. Ramakrishnan, and D.S. Warren (SUNY at Stony Brook).....................281

Program Committee Report: 6:00 -- 6:15

FRIDAY, JANUARY 19th

Session 9: 8:00-10:00
Chaired by Jeanne Ferrante

    Fairness and Hyperfairness in Multi-Party Interactions
        Paul C. Attie (University of Texas), Nissim Francez (MCC
        and Technion), and Orna Grumberg (Technion) 292

    Relating Total and Partial Correctness Interpretations of Non-Deterministic Programs
        Carl A. Gunter (University of Pennsylvania) 306

    On Oraclizable Networks and Kahn's Principle
        James R. Russell (Cornell University) 320

    On the Relations Computable by a Class of Concurrent Automata .
        Eugene W. Stark (SUNY at Stony Brook) 329

Session 10: 10:30-12:30
Chaired by Luca Cardelli

    Higher-Order Modules and the Phase Distinction
        Robert Harper (CMU), John C. Mitchell (Stanford University), and
        Eugenio Moggi (University of Edinburgh) 341

    Safe Run-time Overloading
        Francois Rouaix (INRIA Rocquencourt) 355

    Quasi-static Typing
        Satish Thatte (Clarkson University) 367

    Deciding ML Typability is Complete for Deterministic Exponential Time
        Harry G. Mairson (Brandeis University) 382

Author Index

Alexander Aiken 210	Justin O. Graver 136	Shaunak Pawagi 169
Martin Abadi 31	Timothy G. Griffin 47	I. V. Ramakrishnan .169,281
Andrea Asperti 59	Orna Grumberg 292	Raghu Ramakrishnan 246
Paul C. Attie 292	Carl A. Gunter 306	R. Ramesh 281
Gerard Berry 81	Robert Harper 341	Martin Rinard 232
Daniel Bobrow 261	Barry Hayes 261	Francois Rouaix 355
Hans Boehm 261	Nevin Heintze 197	James R. Russell 320
Gerard Boudol 81	Walter L. Hill 125	Barbara G. Ryder 184
Geoffrey Burn 151	Joxan Jaffar 197	Vijay A. Saraswat 232
Peter S. Canning 125	Ralph E. Johnson 136	R. C. Sekar 169
Luca Cardelli 31	Yves Lafont 95	Scott Shenker 261
William R. Cook 125	John Lamping 16	Barbara Simons 270
Pierre-Louis Curien 31	Jean-Jacques Levy 31	Eugene W. Stark 329
Alan Demers 261	Harry G. Mairson 382	Guy L. Steele, Jr. 218
Alan Deutsch 157	Thomas J. Marlowe 184	Satish Thatte 367
Gian Luigi Ferrari 59	John C. Mitchell 109,341	D. S. Warren 281
John Field 1	Eugenio Moggi 341	Mark Weiser 261
Nissim Francez 292	Yiannis N. Moschovakis .. 72	John H. Williams 210
Robert Gorrieri 59	Krishna Palem 270	Edward L. Wimmers 210

v

Forward

The papers in this volume were presented at the Seventeenth Annual ACM SIGACT-SIGPLAN Symposium on Principles of Programming Languages, held January 17-19, 1990 in San Francisco, California.

The program committee received 185 technical summaries, from which it selected 31 for presentation and publication. The submissions were not formally refereed, but were reviewed by the program committee with selected outside assistance. Each summary was assigned to at least three specific members of the committee for review. However, the committee members were strongly encouraged to read more summaries if possible, and ultimately each was read on average by almost four commmittee members. Technical quality, originality, relevance, and clarity were the primary criteria for selection.

The program committee wishes to thank the following individuals for their help in the review process: Martin Abadi, Fran Allen, Hans Boehm, Michael Burke, M. Coffin, Charles Consel, Keith Cooper, Ron Cytron, Bruce F. Duba, Charles Fischer, Mark Hill, S. Hudson, N. Hutchinson, Richard Kelsey, James Larus, David B. MacQueen, S. Manchanda, Bart Miller, John Mitchell, Francesmary Modungo, Raghu Ramakrishnan, Vivek Sarkar, Edith Schonberg, Guri Sohi, Marvin Solomon, Jan Stone, Joe Warren, Willy Zwaenepoel.

Conference Committee

Conference Chair
>Frances E. Allen, *IBM T.J. Watson Research Center*

Registration Chair
>Alex Aiken, *IBM Research Almaden*

Local Arrangements Chair
>Stan Osborne, *San Francisco State University*

Book Exhibit Chair
>Prof. Thomas J. Marlowe, *Seton Hall University*

Program Committee
>Samson Abramsky, *Imperial College*
>Andrew Appel, *Princeton University*
>Luca Cardelli, *DEC Systems Research Center*
>Saumya Debray, *University of Arizona*
>Matthias Felleisen, *Rice University*
>Jeanne Ferrante, *IBM T.J. Watson Research Center*
>Susan Horwitz, *University of Wisconsin-Madison*
>Paul Hudak, **Chair**, *Yale University*
>Jayadev Misra, *University of Texas*
>Ravi Sethi, *AT&T Bell Laboratories*

On Laziness and Optimality in Lambda Interpreters: Tools for Specification and Analysis*

John Field[†]
Cornell University

Abstract

In this paper, I introduce a new formal system, ΛCCL, based on Curien's *Categorical Combinators* [Cur86a]. I show that ΛCCL has properties not possessed by Curien's original combinators that make it particularly appropriate as the basis for implementation and analysis of a wide range of reduction schemes using shared environments, closures, or λ-terms. As an example of the practical utility of this formalism, I use it to specify a simple lazy interpreter for the λ-calculus, whose correctness follows trivially from the properties of ΛCCL.

I then describe a *labeled* variant of ΛCCL, ΛCCL^L, which can be used as a tool to determine the degree of "laziness" possessed by various λ-reduction schemes. In particular, ΛCCL^L is applied to the problem of *optimal* reduction in the λ-calculus. A reduction scheme for the λ-calculus is optimal if the number of redex contractions that must be performed in the course of reducing any λ-term to a normal form (if one exists) is guaranteed to be minimal. Results of Lévy [Lév78,Lév80] showed that for a natural class of reduction strategies allowing *shared* redexes, optimal reductions were, at least in principle, possible. He conjectured that an optimal reduction strategy might be realized in practice using shared closures and environments as well as shared λ-terms. I show, however, using ΛCCL^L, a practical optimal reduction scheme for arbitrary λ-terms using only shared environments, closures, or terms is unlikely to exist.

1 Background

There has been much recent interest in efficient implementations of lazy functional programming languages whose semantics are based on normalizing reduction schemes for the λ-calculus [Pey87,FH88]. Most such implementations have made use of some combination of the notions of *graph reduction* [Wad71,Aug84,Joh84], *environments* [Lan64,HM76, AP81,FW87] or *combinators* [Tur79,Hug84,Joh85]. The first two are means to allow certain redexes to be effectively shared during reduction; the latter can be considered a restricted form of λ-expression for which certain implementation techniques are more efficient.

While all these methods are *normalizing*, that is, guaranteed to yield a normal form[1] if one exists, all end up performing more β-contractions than are absolutely necessary by effectively *copying* redexes. In some cases, this lack of sufficient laziness can result in considerable unnecessary additional computation. Concern for this phenomenon led to the introduction of methods allowing "fully-lazy" reduction [Hug84]. However, J.-J. Lévy's analysis [Lév78,Lév80] made clear that there was a wide range of laziness possible, ranging from profligate (simple leftmost β-reduction without sharing) to optimal, with full-laziness actually somewhere in between. The exact nature of laziness in various implementation has apparently heretofore been something of a mystery[2], and I aim here to give means to analyze this phenomenon more precisely.

This paper presupposes a familiarity with the λ-calculus [Chu41,Bar84,HS86], the de Bruijn λ-calculus [dB72,dB78, Cur86a], and basic ideas from term rewriting systems [HO80, Hue80,Der87]. A brief review of relevant concepts and notation for these subjects is provided in Appendix A. An acquaintance with with Curien's Categorical Combinators [Cur86a,Cur86b,CCM87], and with the work of Lévy on optimality [Lév78,Lév80] would also be useful.

---

*This research was supported by NSF grant DCR 82-02677 and ONR grant N000014-88K-0594.

[†]Author's Address: Department of Computer Science, Cornell University, Upson Hall, Ithaca, NY 14853. Electronic mail: field@cs.cornell.edu.

[1]Technically, implementations of functional languages generally yield *weak head normal forms*.

[2]Peyton Jones [Pey87, p. 400] states that "...it is by no means obvious how lazy a function is, and... we do not at present have any tools for reasoning about this. Laziness is a delicate property of a function, and seemingly innocuous program transformations may lose laziness."

2 Redex Sharing and Environments

Consider the λ-term $M \equiv (\lambda y.(yy))(Iz)$, where $I \equiv \lambda x.x$. It may be reduced to a normal form in any one of three ways:

Example 2.1

$$\sigma_1: M \longrightarrow (Iz)(Iz) \longrightarrow z(Iz) \longrightarrow zz$$
$$\sigma_2: M \longrightarrow (Iz)(Iz) \longrightarrow (Iz)z \longrightarrow zz$$
$$\sigma_3: M \longrightarrow (\lambda y.(yy))z \longrightarrow zz$$

σ_1 is a *leftmost* reduction—one where the leftmost redex is contracted at each step. σ_3 is an *applicative order* reduction, where (informally) the argument part of a redex is reduced to a normal form before the redex is contracted. It is evident that σ_3 reaches the normal form (zz) in the fewest steps. It would clearly be desirable to have an *optimal* reduction strategy—one that always yields a normal form if one exists (i.e., is *normalizing*) and is also guaranteed to do so using the fewest possible redex contractions. Unfortunately, results of Barendregt, et al. [BBKV76], show that no such (recursive) strategy exists. However, we can improve matters considerably by extending the model of reduction a bit.

Note in the example above that the redex (Iz) of M is *copied* in reductions σ_1 and σ_2, since it is substituted for two instances of y. A natural alternative to copying expressions in arguments is to *share* them instead, using a graph-like data structure. The idea is illustrated below:

Example 2.2

$$\sigma_1': (\lambda y.(yy))(Iz) \longrightarrow (\bullet\ \bullet) \longrightarrow (\bullet\ \bullet) \equiv zz$$

σ_1' proceeds from left to right, analogous to σ_1. In this case, however, the redex (Iz) is *shared*, rather than copied, as a result of its substitution for the two instances of variable y. The result of (Iz)'s reduction to z is shared as well. Using this method, the normal form's graph representation is reached after only two reduction steps.

Wadsworth's *graph reduction* algorithm [Wad71] formalizes the idea of Example 2.2. It combines a leftmost redex selection strategy with sharing of argument expressions. However, Wadsworth's algorithm is not *optimal*. If we contract non-leftmost redexes, shorter reductions (still using shared argument expressions) can be achieved, as the following example illustrates: Let $N \equiv (N_1 N_2)$, where $N_1 \equiv \lambda x.(xw)(xz)$ and $N_2 \equiv \lambda y.(Iy)$. Then the following are two graph reductions of N:

Example 2.3

$$\rho_1: N \longrightarrow (\bullet w)(\bullet z) \longrightarrow (Iw)(\bullet z) \longrightarrow w(\bullet z)$$
$$\lambda y.(Iy)\ \lambda y.(Iy)\ \ \ \lambda y.(Iy)$$
$$\longrightarrow w(Iz) \longrightarrow wz$$

$$\rho_2: N \longrightarrow (\bullet w)(\bullet z) \longrightarrow (\bullet w)(\bullet z) \longrightarrow w(\bullet z) \longrightarrow wz$$
$$\lambda y.(Iy)\ \ \ \ \lambda y.y\ \ \ \ \lambda y.y$$

Wadsworth's algorithm performs reduction ρ_1, while ρ_2 reaches the normal form in fewer steps by contracting the shared (Iy) redex inside N_2 before applying it to either w or z (a minimal length reduction can also be achieved without any sharing by contracting the (Iy) redex before N_1 is applied to N_2).

Reducing inner redexes, as in ρ_2, seems to bring about shorter reductions in many cases. Unfortunately, contraction of arbitrary inner redexes can sometimes lead to unnecessarily diverging reductions, as is the case with the applicative order strategy. Wadsworth's scheme reduces only leftmost redexes in order to ensure normalizability (although this is not by any means the only way to do so, see [BKKS87]).

There is evidently a subtle interplay among the issues of efficiency, normalizability, and redex sharing. The quandary is then to find a way to edge closer to the brink of optimality without plunging into the abyss of non-normalizability.

By examining the reductions above, however, we can see that Wadsworth left the door open to further improvements by not taking advantage of all conceivable opportunities for redex sharing. Note in ρ_1 that as N_2 is applied in sequence to w and to z, the inner redex (Iy) is effectively copied (after each substitution for y). If there were some means to *parametrically* share the (Iy) redex while still substituting w and z separately for y, more efficient, and perhaps optimal reductions might still be achievable. This suggests the use of the notions of *environment* and *closure* familiar from implementations of programming languages.

2.1 Reduction Using Environments

A number of reduction schemes for the λ-calculus have been proposed using environments. These include that of Landin [Lan64] using applicative order evaluation, and updated versions devised by Henderson and Morris [HM76] and Aiello and Prini [AP81] to accommodate leftmost evaluation. Each of these systems avoids immediate substitutions for all instances of bound variables in the body of a λ-abstraction after β-contraction, constructing a closure instead.

To be more specific, an environment consists of sets of mappings between variable names and values, or *bindings*. The result of a β-contraction is then a *closure* consisting of the body of the abstraction part of the redex, paired with an environment updated to contain the binding of the abstraction's bound variable to the argument of the redex. The idea is illustrated below:

$$(\lambda x.(xx))N \longrightarrow [(xx), \langle\!\langle x := N \rangle\!\rangle]$$

In general, $[T, E]$ will represent a closure consisting of term T and environment E. An environment is denoted thus:

$$\langle\!\langle B_1, B_2, \ldots \rangle\!\rangle$$

where B_1, B_2, etc. are bindings.

The following example (using the same term as in Example 2.2) shows that sharing of λ-terms can be achieved indirectly through shared bindings:

Example 2.4

$$(\lambda y.(yy))(Iz) \longrightarrow [(yy), \langle\!\langle y := (Iz)\rangle\!\rangle]$$
$$\longrightarrow ([y, \bullet][y, \bullet])$$
$$\!\!\sqcup\!\!\sqcup \langle\!\langle y := (Iz)\rangle\!\rangle$$
$$\longrightarrow ([y, \bullet][y, \bullet]) \cdots \longrightarrow (zz)$$
$$\!\!\sqcup \langle\!\langle y := z\rangle\!\rangle$$

Use of closures obviates copying any part of the body of an abstraction after β-contraction. Wadsworth's scheme, however, copies the parts of the body of an abstraction containing the abstraction's bound variable, in order to avoid incorrect substitutions in pieces of the abstraction's body that might be shared by other terms. By using environments, the body of the abstraction term, and hence any redexes contained therein, have the potential to be shared, avoiding redundant reductions.

Below is another reduction using the term of Example 2.3, showing that shared environments can be used to minimize the number of redex contractions performed in a nominally leftmost strategy: Once again, let $N \equiv (N_1 N_2)$, where $N_1 \equiv \lambda x.(xw)(xz)$ and $N_2 \equiv \lambda y.(Iy)$. Then, using shared environments, we have: (repeated meta-variables such as $\hat{E}$ below correspond to terms or environments shared through graphical data structures)

Example 2.5

$$N \longrightarrow [(xw)(xz), \langle\!\langle x := N_2\rangle\!\rangle] \longrightarrow \cdots$$
$$\longrightarrow (([x, \hat{E}][w, \hat{E}]) [(xz), \hat{E}]),$$
$$\quad\text{where}\quad \hat{E} \equiv \langle\!\langle x := N_2\rangle\!\rangle$$
$$\longrightarrow ((\hat{N}_2 [w, \hat{E}]) [(xz), \hat{E}],$$
$$\quad\text{where}\quad \hat{E} \equiv \langle\!\langle x := \hat{N}_2\rangle\!\rangle, \hat{N}_2 \equiv \lambda y.(Iy)$$
$$\longrightarrow ([\hat{P}, \langle\!\langle y := [w, \hat{E}]\rangle\!\rangle] [(xz), \hat{E}]),$$
$$\quad\text{where}\quad \hat{E} \equiv \langle\!\langle x := \lambda y.\hat{P}\rangle\!\rangle, \hat{P} \equiv (Iy)$$
$$\longrightarrow ([\hat{P}, \langle\!\langle y := [w, \hat{E}]\rangle\!\rangle] [(xz), \hat{E}]),$$
$$\quad\text{where}\quad \hat{E} \equiv \langle\!\langle x := \lambda y.\hat{P}\rangle\!\rangle, \hat{P} \equiv y$$
$$\longrightarrow \cdots$$

Note that the (Iy) redex in N_2 is reduced in a shared environment, *independently* of the substitution for free variable y in closures that refer to N_2.

The question then arises as to whether some *combination* of shared environments, closures, and terms could be used to achieve an optimal reduction scheme, or at least improve on Wadsworth's method. To proceed any further, we will need a more formal system to study reduction using environments and closures.

3 ACCL

In [Cur86a], P.-L. Curien defines a number of equational theories based on Cartesian Closed Categories (CCCs) using terms from the *Pure Categorical Combinatory Logic*, **CCL**. Curien observed that the CCC axioms could model *reduction* in the λ-calculus, i.e., its operational semantics as well as its denotational semantics. Treated as combinators, Curien's axioms have the advantage of avoiding the difficulties with variables and substitution normally encountered in the λ-calculus, and thus has aspects in common with the *de Bruijn λ-calculus* [dB72,dB78].

One set of equational axioms, deemed *Weak Categorical Combinatory Logic*, is the basis for the Categorical Abstract Machine ([CCM87]). However, Curien proposed no system strong enough to simulate arbitrary β-reductions in the λ-calculus that could itself be simulated using only β-reduction. If such a system were available, it would provide an immediate proof of correctness for any reduction scheme for the λ-calculus based on it (since any combinator reduction would correspond to a β-reduction). λ-reduction methods based on Categorical Combinators proposed thus far, such as the Categorical Abstract Machine and schemes by Lins [Lin87], have heretofore required ad-hoc proofs of correctness.

To provide a more sophisticated tool for modeling λ-reduction using environments, I will define a new 2-sorted equational theory, **ACCL**, akin to Curien's theory $CCL\beta$. Its sort structure makes possible proofs of close correspondence between β-reduction and **ACCL** reduction not possible in Curien's original theory. While this modified term structure obscures the elegant categorical origins of Curien's original system, it makes its connection to reduction with environments much more evident.

In the sequel, I will assume that any λ-terms under consideration are actually terms of the de Bruijn λ-calculus, although I will feel free to give examples using named variables.

3.1 Term Structure

Definition 3.1 *The terms of* **ACCL** *are built from a set of variables and constructors over a two-sorted signature. The sorts are as follows:*

— $\mathcal{L}$, *the sort of* lambda-like expressions

— $\mathcal{E}$, *the sort of* environments

The constructors are listed below. Each constructor is given with the sort of the term constructed and the sorts of its argument(s) specified in the corresponding argument positions.

$$\begin{aligned}
\text{Var} &: \mathcal{L} &&\text{(variable reference)}\\
\text{Apply}(\mathcal{L}, \mathcal{L}) &: \mathcal{L} &&\text{(application)}\\
\Lambda(\mathcal{L}) &: \mathcal{L} &&\text{(abstraction)}\\
[\mathcal{L}, \mathcal{E}] &: \mathcal{L} &&\text{(closure)}\\
\emptyset &: \mathcal{E} &&\text{(null environment)}\\
\Box &: \mathcal{E} &&\text{(shift)}\\
\langle \mathcal{E}, \mathcal{L}\rangle &: \mathcal{E} &&\text{(expression list)}\\
\mathcal{E} \circ \mathcal{E} &: \mathcal{E} &&\text{(environment composition)}
\end{aligned}$$

The terms of **ACCL** will be denoted by $\text{Ter}(\mathbf{ACCL})$ and the *closed terms*, those terms containing no variables, by $\text{Ter}_C(\mathbf{ACCL})$.

The following notation (for "de Bruijn" numbers) will be used:

Definition 3.2

$$n! \equiv \begin{cases} \text{Var} & n = 0 \\ [\text{Var}, \Box^n] & n > 0 \end{cases}$$

where

$$\Box^n \equiv \begin{cases} \Box & n = 1 \\ \underbrace{\Box \circ (\Box \circ (\cdots (\Box \circ \Box) \cdots))}_{n \text{ times}} & n > 1 \end{cases}$$

The intuition behind the term structure of ΛCCL is fairly straightforward: Terms of sort $\mathcal{L}$ are analogous to terms in the de Bruijn λ-calculus, after variable numbers are encoded as above. Closures are created by the ΛCCL equivalent of β-contraction. Environments are essentially lists of terms, the association between bound variables and the terms to which they are bound being represented implicitly by position in the list. An environment informally presented as

$$\langle\!\langle x_1 := M_1, x_2 := M_2, \ldots, x_n := M_n \rangle\!\rangle$$

is represented in ΛCCL as

$$\langle\langle\langle \cdots \langle \emptyset, M_n \rangle \cdots \rangle, M_2 \rangle, M_1 \rangle.$$

"$\circ$" allows separate environments to be merged. The only perhaps mysterious term present is "$\Box$", which when composed on the left with an arbitrary environment effects the "shifting" of de Bruijn numbers required when environments are moved inside abstractions, and when composed on the right with an environment causes the outermost piece of the list to be stripped away in the course of variable lookup. All these operations are embodied in the axioms below:

3.2 Axioms

Definition 3.3 *The axioms of ΛCCL are as follows:*

(**Beta**)	$\text{Apply}(\Lambda(A), B) = [A, \langle \emptyset, B \rangle]$
(**AssC**)	$[[A, E_1], E_2] = [A, E_1 \circ E_2]$
(**NullEL**)	$\emptyset \circ E = E$
(**NullER**)	$E \circ \emptyset = E$
(**ShiftE**)	$\Box \circ \langle E, A \rangle = E$
(**VarRef**)	$[\text{Var}, \langle E, A \rangle] = A$
(**DA**)	$[\Lambda(A), E] = \Lambda([A, \langle E \circ \Box, \text{Var} \rangle])$
(**DE**)	$\langle E_1, A \rangle \circ E_2 = \langle E_1 \circ E_2, [A, E_2] \rangle$
(**DApply**)	$[\text{Apply}(A, B), E] = \text{Apply}([A, E], [B, E])$
(**AssE**)	$(E_1 \circ E_2) \circ E_3 = E_1 \circ (E_2 \circ E_3)$
(**NullC**)	$[A, \emptyset] = A$

I define a related equational theory, ECCL, as follows:

Definition 3.4 *The axioms of ECCL are those of ΛCCL without rule Beta.*

It will be useful to consider ΛCCL as the union of two systems intended for different purposes: ECCL, which governs manipulation of environments, and (**Beta**), which models β-reduction.

3.3 ΛCCL as Rewriting System on Closed Terms

By orienting the equations of ΛCCL from left to right, they can be treated as a term rewriting system. The notation $\longrightarrow_{\Lambda\text{CCL}}$ will be used to denote the application of a rule of ΛCCL in some context, i.e., $A \longrightarrow_{\Lambda\text{CCL}} B$ if and only if $A \equiv C[X]$, X may be rewritten to Y using one of the oriented axioms of ΛCCL, and $B \equiv C[Y]$ (contexts are defined in Appendix A. I will use similar notation for ECCL and applications of single rules of ΛCCL, e.g. $\longrightarrow_{(\text{Beta})}$. However, I will restrict myself in the sequel to the *closed terms* of ΛCCL, $\text{Ter}_C(\Lambda\text{CCL})$. Since I am interested in using ΛCCL to model λ-reduction rather than to prove theorems, this restriction will be of no concern. More importantly, in conjunction with the 2-sorted term structure of ΛCCL, the restriction to closed terms makes it possible to prove properties of ΛCCL that did not hold for arbitrary terms of Curien's system CCLβ. I will refer to the formal theories and their corresponding rewriting systems by the same name. The following properties hold of ΛCCL:

Theorem 3.1 *ECCL is noetherian (strongly normalizing).*

Proof We can orient the rules of ECCL by combining the *recursive path ordering* method of Dershowitz and the *lexicographic path ordering* method of Kamin and Lévy (both of which are described in [Der87]) using an extension of Lescanne's notion of *status* [Les84].

We first order the operators of ΛCCL as follows:

$$\emptyset < \Box < \text{Var} < \Lambda(\cdot) < \text{Apply}(\cdot, \cdot) < \langle \cdot, \cdot \rangle < [\cdot, \cdot] = \circ$$

Let A and B be terms of ΛCCL, whose outermost operators are f and g, respectively. We then define the following quasi-ordering such terms:

$$A \equiv f(s_1, \ldots, s_m) \succeq B \equiv g(t_1, \ldots, t_n)$$

if

$$s_i \succeq t, \quad \text{for some} \quad i = 1 \ldots m,$$

or

$$f > g \quad \text{and} \quad s \succ t_j \quad \text{for all} \quad j = 1 \ldots n,$$

or

$$f \equiv g, f \not\equiv \circ, f \not\equiv [\cdot, \cdot], \text{ and}$$
$$\{s_1, \ldots, s_m\} \succeq_M \{t_1, \ldots t_n\}$$

or

$$f \equiv g, f \equiv \circ \text{ or } f \equiv [\cdot, \cdot], \text{ and}$$
$$(s_1, \ldots, s_m) \succeq_* (t_1, \ldots t_n)$$

or

$$f = g, f \equiv \circ, g \equiv [\cdot, \cdot], \text{ and}$$
$$\{s_1, \ldots, s_m\} \succeq_M \{t_1, \ldots t_n\}$$

where $\succeq_M$ is the extension of $\succeq$ to multisets of terms and $\succeq_*$ is the lexicographic extension of $\succeq$ to sequences (see [Der87] for details of these extensions).

Depending on the "status" of *unordered pairs* of operators, either the multiset or lexicographic ordering is used to compare operands. The ordering defined above is a well-quasi-ordering on terms of ΛCCL since it meets Kamin and Lévy's requirements for a *simplification ordering* [KL80]. Generalizations of Lescanne's notion of status were suggested in [Rus87]. Using this ordering, it is straightforward to show that if $A \longrightarrow_{\text{ECCL}} B$, $A \succ B$, and thus that ECCL is noetherian. □

Theorem 3.2 *ECCL is confluent (thus Church-Rossser) on closed terms, i.e.,*

$$A \longrightarrow_{ECCL} B_1 \wedge A \longrightarrow_{ECCL} B_2$$
$$\Longrightarrow (\exists C) \quad B_1 \longrightarrow_{ECCL} C \wedge B_2 \longrightarrow_{ECCL} C$$

Proof We can show **ECCL** confluent by showing critical pairs to be locally confluent [Hue80]. The only problem occurs with the rule pair (**DA**) and (**NullC**), for which we must show

$$(\forall A)(\forall n) \quad [A, \langle\langle\langle \cdots \langle \Box^n, (n-1)!\rangle \cdots \rangle, 1!\rangle, 0!\rangle] \longrightarrow_{ECCL} A$$

and

$$(\forall E)(\forall n) \quad E \circ \langle\langle\langle \cdots \langle \Box^n, (n-1)!\rangle \cdots \rangle, 1!\rangle, 0!\rangle \longrightarrow_{ECCL} E$$

which can be proved for closed terms by a straightforward induction on the structure of A or E. The 2-sorted structure of terms of ΛCCL is essential to this argument. □

We can also have the following

Theorem 3.3 *(Beta) is confluent, i.e.,*

$$A \longrightarrow_{(Beta)} B_1 \wedge A \longrightarrow_{(Beta)} B_2$$
$$\Longrightarrow (\exists C) \quad B_1 \longrightarrow_{(Beta)} C \wedge B_2 \longrightarrow_{(Beta)} C$$

Proof (**Beta**) redexes cannot overlap (i.e., there are no critical pairs), confluence thus follows trivially. □

We can now show ΛCCL confluent by a technique similar to the Tait/Martin-Löf proof of the Church-Rosser property for the λ-calculus. The following reduction relation will be useful:

Definition 3.5

$$\longrightarrow_{Dev} \equiv \longrightarrow_{ECCL} \cdot \longrightarrow_{(Beta)} \cdot \longrightarrow_{ECCL}$$

where '·' denotes relational composition.

$\longrightarrow_{Dev}$ is intended to correspond roughly to the notion of a *development* in the λ-calculus. As usual, $\longrightarrow\!\!\!\!\!\longrightarrow_{Dev}$ represents the reflexive, transitive closure of $\longrightarrow_{Dev}$. I also define the following variant of **ECCL**:

Definition 3.6 *The axioms of BCCL consist of those of ECCL without rule (DApply).*

In order to show ΛCCL confluent, we need the following sequence of lemmas, each represented as a commuting diagram (dotted arrows denote reductions existentially dependent on the arbitrary reductions represented by solid arrows):

Lemma 3.1 *BCCL and (Beta) strongly commute, i.e.,*

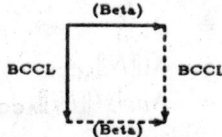

Proof Trivial, since **BCCL** and (**Beta**) have no critical pairs. □

Lemma 3.2 *BCCL and (Beta) commute, i.e.,*

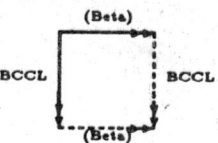

Proof Fill the diagram using lemma 3.1 (by induction on the lengths of the $\longrightarrow\!\!\!\!\!\longrightarrow_{BCCL}$ and $\longrightarrow\!\!\!\!\!\longrightarrow_{(Beta)}$ reductions). □

Lemma 3.3

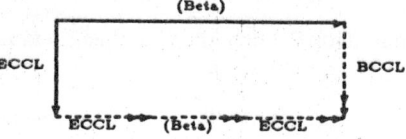

Proof One need only consider the critical pair of Apply([Λ(A), E], [B, E]) and [[A, (∅, B)], E], for which it is easy to show there is a common reduct using the sort of reductions required by the lemma. □

Lemma 3.4

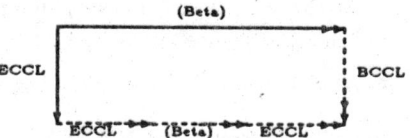

Proof If the **ECCL** rule used is not (**DApply**), then the result follows from lemma 3.2. Otherwise, the (**DApply**) redex in the diagram's premise can also be a (**Beta**) redex. Without loss of generality, assume that some subterm is both a (**Beta**) redex and a (**DApply**) redex, and that it is the first redex contracted in the (**Beta**) reduction. (Since (**Beta**) redexes cannot create other (**Beta**) redexes, redexes in a (**Beta**) reduction can be permuted arbitrarily). We can then construct the desired diagram using lemmas 3.3 and 3.2 as follows:

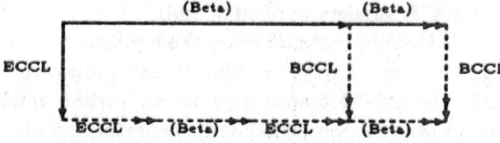

□

Lemma 3.5

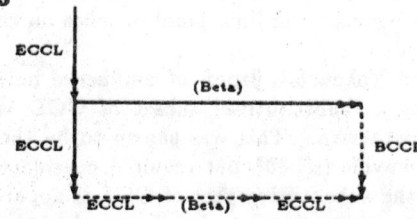

Proof Follows by noetherian induction (see [Hue80]) on the left-hand **ECCL** reduction using lemma 3.4 as a base case. (The rather odd $\longrightarrow_{ECCL}$ appendage in the upper left-hand corner of the diagram is required to provide the appropriate induction hypothesis). □

Lemma 3.6

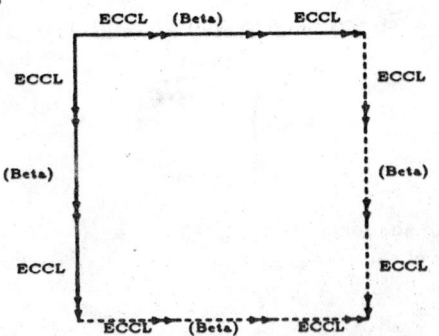

Proof Simple diagram construction using lemma 3.5, theorem 3.2, and theorem 3.3. □

Lemma 3.7 $\longrightarrow_{Dev}$ is confluent on closed terms, i.e.,

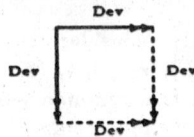

Proof The reductions used in lemma 3.6 are $\longrightarrow_{Dev}$ contractions, and the theorem thus follows by diagram chase. □

Theorem 3.4 ACCL is confluent on closed terms.

Proof $\longrightarrow_{Dev}$ and $\longrightarrow_{ACCL}$ are relationally equivalent. Thus from Lemma 3.7, we must conclude that $\longrightarrow_{ACCL}$ is confluent. □

Theorem 3.4 is a principal result; Curien was unable to exhibit a confluent system strong enough to model arbitrary reductions in the λ-calculus. However, independent work of Hardin [Har87,Har89] and Yokouchi [Yok89] has led to a characterization of *subsets* of Curien's original CCL terms for which confluence of the system CCLβ can be proven. By contrast, the 2-sorted term structure of ACCL rules out the construction of "uninteresting" terms that Hardin and Yokouchi's CCL subsets explicitly omit.

Yokouchi's technique for proving the confluence of CCLβ on subsets of terms is quite similar to the confluence proof given here. Lemma 3.5 was used in an earlier version of this paper to prove a somewhat stronger intermediate result than lemma 3.6; the proof used here was simplified upon observing that Yokouchi's proof of confluence essentially used lemma 3.5 directly, without resort to a more complicated intermediate lemma. Hardin's proof of relies on confluence of the λ-calculus.

Hardin and Yokouchi's proofs of confluence both rely on the fact that a "substitutive" subset of CCL similar to ECCL is noetherian. This was shown to be the case by Hardin and Laville [HL86], but required considerable ingenuity, since the substitutive part of CCL is apparently immune to more conventional techniques used to show termination. The proof that ECCL is noetherian is considerably simplified by its term structure, which in particular admits a distinction between closures and environment not present in CCL.

3.4 Normal Forms

Definition 3.7 *The set of* lambda normal forms *(LNF) is a subset of the terms of* ACCL*, defined inductively as follows:*

$$n! \in LNF$$
$$A \in LNF \implies \Lambda(A) \in LNF$$
$$A \in LNF, B \in LNF \implies Apply(A, B) \in LNF$$

Lambda normal forms are intuitively those terms that "look like" terms of the (de Bruijn) λ-calculus.

Theorem 3.5 *All lambda-like expressions (terms of sort $\mathcal{L}$) of* ACCL *are reducible to a lambda normal form, using the rules of* ECCL*. That is,*

$$(\forall A : \mathcal{L}) \quad (\exists B \in LNF) \text{ s.t. } A \longrightarrow_{ECCL} B$$

Proof Simply note that any term of sort $\mathcal{L}$ that is not in *LNF* contains an ECCL redex. Keep reducing such redexes using rules of ECCL until *LNF* is reached, which must happen eventually since ECCL is noetherian. □

For any term $A : \mathcal{L}$, I will refer to its corresponding term $B \in LNF$ by $lnf(B)$. Since ECCL is confluent and terms in *LNF* are irreducible in ECCL, this normal form is unique.

Definition 3.8 *The set of* partial environment normal forms *(PENF) is a subset of the terms of* ACCL *defined inductively as follows:*

$$\emptyset \in PENF$$
$$\Box^n \in PENF$$
$$E \in PENF \implies \langle E, A \rangle \in PENF$$

Theorem 3.6 *All environments (terms of sort $\mathcal{E}$) of* ACCL *are reducible to a partial environment normal form using the rules of* ECCL*:*

$$(\forall E_1 : \mathcal{E}) \quad (\exists E_2 \in PENF) \text{ s.t. } E_1 \longrightarrow_{ECCL} E_2$$

Proof Once again, we can observe that every term of sort $\mathcal{E}$ that is not in *PENF* must contain an ECCL redex. Such redexes can be reduced until the normal form is reached. □

Terms in *PENF* are not necessarily irreducible in ECCL, thus partial environment normal forms are *not* unique.

3.5 Translation

We can now show state the translation between terms of the de Bruijn λ-calculus and terms of ACCL.

Definition 3.9 *For any term $M \in \lambda^{DB}$, we can define a corresponding term $[\![M]\!]_{ACCL} \in$ ACCL inductively as follows:*

$$[\![i]\!]_{ACCL} = i!$$
$$[\![(\lambda.N)]\!]_{ACCL} = \Lambda([\![N]\!]_{ACCL})$$
$$[\![(N_1 N_2)]\!]_{ACCL} = Apply([\![N_1]\!]_{ACCL}, [\![N_2]\!]_{ACCL})$$

The reverse transformation, $[\![\cdot]\!]_\lambda$, is defined in the obvious way on members of *LNF*.

3.6 Equivalence

I now claim that there is an equivalence between β-reduction and reduction of terms of sort $\mathcal{L}$ in ΛCCL. The following two lemmas are required:

Lemma 3.8 *Let M and N be arbitrary terms of the (de Bruijn) λ-calculus such that $M \longrightarrow_\beta N$. Then $[\![M]\!]_{\Lambda\text{CCL}} \in LNF \longrightarrow_{\Lambda\text{CCL}} [\![N]\!]_{\Lambda\text{CCL}} \in LNF$*

Proof A construction isomorphic to that used by Curien in [Cur86a] to prove a similar result for $\mathbf{CCL}\beta$ suffices, and is omitted here. The ΛCCL equivalent of his construction has the following property:

$$M \longrightarrow_\beta N \Longrightarrow (\exists B) \ [\![M]\!]_{\Lambda\text{CCL}} \longrightarrow_{\text{(Beta)}} B \text{ and } B \longrightarrow_{\text{ECCL}} [\![N]\!]_{\Lambda\text{CCL}}$$

□

Curien's construction yields the following corollary:

Corollary 3.1 *If $A \in LNF$, $C \in LNF$, and there exists B such that $A \longrightarrow_{\text{(Beta)}} B$ and $B \longrightarrow_{\text{ECCL}} C$ then $[\![A]\!]_\lambda \longrightarrow_\beta [\![B]\!]_\lambda$*

Proof Since (Beta) redexes are non-overlapping, we can perform Curien's β-simulation separately on each (Beta) redex contracted in the reduction from A to B, yielding a term in LNF at each stage. Once this process is complete, the resulting term must be C, since ΛCCL is confluent and $C \in LNF$. □

We can now prove the other direction:

Lemma 3.9 *Let $A: \mathcal{L} \longrightarrow_{\Lambda\text{CCL}} B$. Let $\ln f(A) = A'$ and $\ln f(B) = B'$. Then $[\![A']\!]_\lambda \longrightarrow_\beta [\![B']\!]_\lambda$.*

Proof Divide the ΛCCL reduction into subreductions alternating use of ECCL rules and uses of rule (Beta). The proof then reduces to showing that if $A_i \longrightarrow_{\text{(Beta)}} A_{i+1}$, $\ln f(A_i) = A_i'$, $\ln f(A_{i+1}) = A_{i+1}'$, then $[\![A_i']\!]_\lambda \longrightarrow_\beta [\![A_{i+1}']\!]_\lambda$. This can be done using corollary 3.1, which is used in the construction below:

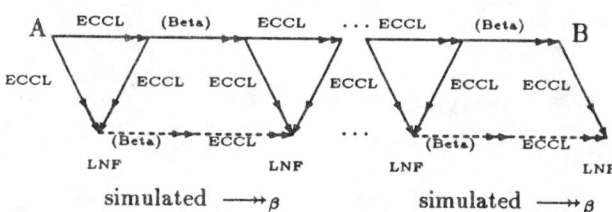

□

We can use the construction of the term above to make the following definition:

Definition 3.10 *Let A be a term of ΛCCL containing a (Beta) redex B. Then the residuals of B (relative to the reduction of A to LNF) are those (Beta) redexes contracted in the proof of lemma 3.9 to simulate β-reduction in $\ln f(A)$. The set of such residuals is denoted by $Resid(B, A)$.*

Putting the results from lemmas 3.8 and 3.9 together yields:

Theorem 3.7 *Given $M \in Ter(\lambda^{DB})$,*

$$M \longrightarrow_\beta N \iff [\![M]\!]_{\Lambda\text{CCL}} \longrightarrow_{\Lambda\text{CCL}} [\![N]\!]_{\Lambda\text{CCL}}$$

This result shows that *any* reduction of a ΛCCL term $A \in LNF$ simulates a reduction in the λ-calculus.

We can now show that in terms of the number of (Beta) contractions performed, ΛCCL is always at least as efficient as the corresponding reduction in the λ-calculus:

Theorem 3.8 *Let $\sigma: A \longrightarrow_{\Lambda\text{CCL}} B$ be a reduction in ΛCCL. Let $\ln f(A) = A'$ and $\ln f(B) = B'$. Let $\rho: [\![A']\!]_\lambda \longrightarrow_\beta [\![B']\!]_\lambda$ be the reduction given by Lemma 3.9. Then the number of β-contractions in ρ is greater than or equal to the number of (Beta) contractions in σ.*

Proof Direct corollary of proof of Lemma 3.9. □

Any reduction scheme for the λ-calculus implemented using ΛCCL would have to perform ECCL reductions as well as (Beta) contractions, but it is not unreasonable to count the former as "overhead," as do many other reduction schemes that manipulate environments as well as contracting β-redexes. One can generally show that in a reasonable reduction scheme, the number of ECCL reductions required is proportional to the number of (Beta) reductions and the size of the initial term.

3.7 Example and Applications

Let $M \equiv \lambda y.((\lambda x.x)y)$. We then have

$$M \longrightarrow_\beta \lambda y.y$$

The equivalent term in ΛCCL after encoding variables, is given by

$$[\![M]\!]_{\Lambda\text{CCL}} \equiv \Lambda(\text{Apply}(\Lambda(0!), 0!)) \equiv \Lambda(\text{Apply}(\Lambda(\text{Var}), \text{Var}))$$

We then have

$$\Lambda(\text{Apply}(\Lambda(\text{Var}), \text{Var}))$$
$$\longrightarrow_{\text{(Beta)}} \Lambda([\text{Var}, \langle \emptyset, \text{Var}\rangle])$$
$$\longrightarrow_{\text{(VarRef)}} \Lambda(\text{Var})$$

and

$$[\![\Lambda(\text{Var})]\!]_\lambda \equiv \lambda y.y$$

In essence, ΛCCL is just a formalization of the informal notions of closure and environment given in the introduction, coupled with a mechanism for indexing environments.

If we treat the axioms of ΛCCL as *transformation rules* on terms, we can note that opportunities for sharing of terms in practical reduction schemes are inherent in the rule. Meta-variables in the axioms may be treated as pointers to terms, and transformations on terms using the axioms as rules should simply copy the corresponding pointer when a meta-variable appears on both sides of the equation, rather than copying the entire term. When a meta-variable is *repeated* on the right side of the equation, as with rules (**DApply**) and (**DE**), the term-pointers corresponding to the repeated variables may safely be set to point to the same term, creating graph-like structures. When any of the rules which contain a single meta-variable on the right side are applied, one has a choice of using *indirection* nodes of some sort or copying the topmost operator of the term.

I will not pursue a formal characterization of sharing here; an informal approach suffices for the purposes of the discussion here. More formal techniques for describing reduction using sharing have been proposed by Staples in [Sta80a,Sta80b,Sta80c,Sta81].

Figure 1 describes an algorithm, $rwhnf()$, that transforms a term of the form $[A, E]$ to the ΛCCL equivalent of weak head normal form, *WHNF*. It is very similar to the interpreters of Henderson and Morris [HM76]) and Aiello and Prini [AP81]. The algorithm is specified using rules of ΛCCL, a recursive redex selection strategy, and shared terms. Since this function simply applies ΛCCL rules to a term in a fixed order, Theorem 3.7 shows it to be correct (i.e., that it effectively performs β-reduction and nothing else). Though the algorithm is not fully-lazy in the sense of Wadsworth, it illustrates the simplicity with which interpreters can be specified using ΛCCL, and functions as a starting point for much more lazy interpreters that can be analyzed using ΛCCL^L.

The normalization properties of reduction schemes using ΛCCL depend on whether or not applications of the rule (**Beta**) are *needed*; this property is discussed below. $rwhnf()$ does indeed turn out to be normalizing.

Given $M \in Ter(\lambda^{DB})$, we construct term $[[[M]]_{\Lambda CCL}, \emptyset] \in Ter(\Lambda CCL)$, and reduce it to $(B \in WHNF) \equiv [[N]]_{\Lambda CCL}$. We thus have $M \twoheadrightarrow_\beta N, N \in whnf$. Figures 2, 3, and 4 are algorithms for normalizing environments (to "partial environment normal form," *PENF*).

The functional *notation* used in the algorithm should be reasonably self explanatory for someone familiar with a language such as ML or Miranda. However, the algorithm should be considered a recursively specified sequence of *transformations* on the term given as argument, not a true function, since no value is to be returned. The **case** statement executes various statements depending on a pattern to be matched. Subpatterns within larger patterns are named using the notation "*subpat:* A". Pattern variables represent pointers to terms, and if a pattern variable appears on the right side of a pattern, the pointer to the term represented by the variable, not the term itself, is copied. ":=" causes a term to be overwritten according to some rule of ΛCCL; only those parts of the overwriting term not named by pattern variables are newly allocated. Statements inside "**seq**...**endseq**" are executed in sequence. $copy(A)$ copies the topmost operator of A; all of A's subterms are referred to by pointers in the new term.

$rwhnf([L, E]: C) \equiv$
    case L **of**
        $Apply(A, B)$: **seq**
            $C := Apply([A, E]: A', [B, E]: B');$
                                          {*rule* **DApply**}
            $rwhnf(A');$
            if $A' \equiv [\Lambda(A''), E']$
            then seq
                $C := [A'', \langle E', B' \rangle];$ {*rule* **Beta′**}
                $rwhnf(C);$
            endseq
            else skip;
        $\Lambda(A)$: **skip**;   {$C \in WHNF$}
        $[L_1, E_1]$: **seq**
            $C := [L_1, E_1 \circ E];$ {*rule* **AssC**}
            $rwhnf(C)$
        endseq;
        $(Var: L_1)$: **seq**   {$C = 0!$}
            $rpenf(E);$ {*transform E to PENF*}
            case E **of**
                $\emptyset: C := L_1;$
                                          {*rule* **NullC**}
                $\square^n$: **skip**;
                      {$E = \square^n$, *thus* $C \in WHNF$}
                $\langle E, A \rangle$: **seq**
                      $rwhnf(A);$
                    $C := copy(A);$
                          {*rule* **VarRef**, $C \in WHNF$}
                  endseq
            endcase
        endseq
    endcase
endfn

Figure 1: Algorithm $rwhnf()$

$rpenf(E) \equiv$
    case E **of**
        $\emptyset$: **skip**;   {$E \in PENF$}
        $\square^n$: **skip**;   {$E \in PENF$}
        $\langle E_1, A \rangle$: $rpenf(E_1);$
        $E_1 \circ E_2$: **seq**
            $rpenf(E_1);$
            $rpenf(E_2);$
            $composeEnvs(E)$
        endseq
    endcase
endfn

Figure 2: Algorithm $rpenf()$

$$\begin{aligned}
&composeEnvs((E_1 \circ E_2)\colon E) \equiv \qquad \{E_1, E_2 \in PENF\}\\
&\quad \textbf{case } E_1 \textbf{ of}\\
&\qquad \emptyset\colon E := E_2; \qquad\qquad \{rule\ \textbf{NullEL}\}\\
&\qquad \Box\colon distribShiftL(E);\\
&\qquad ((\Box\colon E_3) \circ E_4)\colon \textbf{seq}\\
&\qquad\quad E := E_3 \circ ((E_4 \circ E_2)\colon E');\quad \{rule\ \textbf{AssE}\}\\
&\qquad\quad composeEnvs(E');\\
&\qquad\quad distribShiftL(E)\\
&\qquad \textbf{endseq}\\
&\qquad \langle E_3, A\rangle\colon \textbf{seq}\\
&\qquad\quad E := \langle (E_3 \circ E_2)\colon E', [A, E_2]\rangle;\\
&\qquad\qquad\qquad\qquad\qquad\qquad\quad \{rule\ \textbf{DE}\}\\
&\qquad\quad composeEnvs(E')\\
&\qquad \textbf{endseq}\\
&\quad \textbf{endcase}\\
&\textbf{endfn}
\end{aligned}$$

Figure 3: Algorithm $composeEnvs()$

$$\begin{aligned}
&distribShiftL(((\Box\colon E_1) \circ E_2)\colon E) \equiv \quad \{E_2 \in PENF\}\\
&\quad \textbf{case } E_2 \textbf{ of}\\
&\qquad \emptyset\colon E := E_1; \qquad\qquad \{rule\ \textbf{NullER}\}\\
&\qquad \Box^n\colon \textbf{skip}; \quad \{E = \Box^{n+1} \in PENF, n > 0\}\\
&\qquad \langle E_3, A\rangle\colon E := E_3 \qquad \{rule\ \textbf{ShiftE}\}\\
&\quad \textbf{endcase}\\
&\textbf{endfn}
\end{aligned}$$

Figure 4: Algorithm $distribShiftL()$

4 Optimality Criteria

In [Lév78,Lév80], J.-J. Lévy studied the issue of optimal reduction in the λ-calculus in light of the previous work of Wadsworth on graph reduction. Lévy noted that by sharing redexes through graph structures, Wadsworth was essentially contracting multiple β-redexes in *parallel*. Lévy was able to define a natural class of parallel reductions on redexes that are essentially copies of one another, and specify criteria that would have to be satisfied by any optimal parallel reduction of sets such copies. The notion of copy Lévy had in mind was sets of identical terms, modulo substitutions for free variables. Such copies are exactly the terms created by the process of substituting the argument term for multiple instances of the binding variable in the body of a λ-term, and are formally known as *residuals*.

His critical observation was that by examining a term and the reduction that produced it (its "history"), it is decidable which sets of redexes in the term are copies of some redex, or more importantly, *could have been copies* in an alternate reduction (beginning and ending with the same term). He noted that by reducing maximal sets of such copies in parallel, an optimal reduction could be achieved. The question was then whether any practical reduction scheme could be implemented that would ensure that all such copies are shared, and thus for which contraction of a single term would effectively contract all copies. Lévy speculated that some scheme using shared closures, which permit contractions independent of substitutions for free variables (i.e., environments) might allow optimal reduction.

[Lév78] makes use of an extension to the λ-calculus that allows terms to be *labeled*. Such annotations allow specific terms to be "traced" as a reduction progresses, and provides means to compare different reductions. In addition, the labelings are modified during the course of a reduction in such a way that the reduction "history" of a particular term is evident on inspection. An alternative analysis in [Lév80] avoids labelings, and instead allows reductions to be compared using the idea of *meta-reduction*, or reduction *on* reductions to certain canonical forms. The analysis using labels provides a greater intuitive feel for the problem, and, more to the point, will simplify the proofs to follow. Therefore, I will review the analysis using labelings here.

4.1 Lévy's Labeled Lambda Calculus

Lévy's *labeled λ-calculus* was first introduced in [Lév75]. I will use a slightly simplified version proposed by Klop [Klo80], in which an extensive investigation of properties of reductions is made, much of which nicely complements the work of Lévy. A concise summary of Lévy's labeled λ-calculus is given in [Bar84, p. 382, Ex. 14.5.5], and a summary of a number of useful properties is given in [BKKS87, Appendix].

First we must define what constitutes a *label*:

Definition 4.1 *The set of* Lévy-labels, *designated* L, *is defined inductively as follows:*

$$l \in S \implies l \in L$$

$$w, v \in L \implies wv \in L$$
$$w \in L \implies \underline{w} \in L$$

where $S = \{a, b, c, \ldots\}$ *is an infinite set of symbols) and wv is the concatenation of labels w and v.*

An *atomic* label is a label consisting of a single symbol. Note that nested underlinings, e.g. $\underline{ab\underline{c}d}$, may occur.

The set of *labeled* λ-terms consists of the regular λ-terms and terms annotated with labels:

Definition 4.2 *The set of terms in Lévy's labeled λ-calculus, designated $Ter(\lambda^L)$, is defined as follows:*

$$M \in Ter(\lambda) \implies M \in Ter(\lambda^L)$$
$$M \in Ter(\lambda^L), w \in L \implies (M^w) \in Ter(\lambda^L)$$

where x *is an arbitrary variable.*

If M is a meta-variable referring to a labeled term, M^w denotes the concatenation of w to the label of the term to which M refers. I will often refer to terms "with" or "having" label w. A term M *has* label w if M is of the form N^w and N is not of the form P^u for non-null label u. The parentheses surrounding a labeled term will often be omitted for the sake of clarity if no confusion would arise. (If, however, a parenthesized term is *itself* labeled, a formal reduction rule is required to eliminate the parentheses; see below.)

In contexts where a labeled term is expected, unlabeled terms will be treated as having the *null label*, ϵ. We define label concatenation and underlining to behave on the null label as follows:

$$\epsilon w = w$$
$$w\epsilon = w$$
$$\underline{\epsilon} = \epsilon$$

The label of the abstraction part of a redex is called the *degree* of the redex. Thus the degree of the (Ix) redex in $((\lambda x.(I^a x^b)^c)^d z^e)^f$ is a (not c).

The β-contraction rule is now defined for labeled terms as follows:

Definition 4.3 *Labeled β-contraction, denoted by $\longrightarrow_{\beta L}$, is a relation on members of $Ter(\lambda^L)$ defined by:*

$$C[\,((\lambda x.M)^w N)^v\,] \longrightarrow_{\beta L} C[\,(M^{\underline{w}}[x := N^{\underline{w}}])^v\,]$$

where C is an arbitrary context and M and N are arbitrary members of $Ter(\lambda^L)$.

Note that with the null label convention, labeled β-contraction is exactly the same as regular β-contraction on unlabeled terms.

Though the labeled β-contraction rule looks a bit formidable, the idea is quite simple: Whenever a redex is contracted, the underlined form of the label of the redex's abstraction (w) is attached both to the body of the abstraction (M) and to all instances of the argument (N) substituted into the body. Any label attached to the application term (v) is left intact. The attachment to a label of an underlined substring, say ($\underline{w}$), is an indication that the term was effectively generated by contraction of a redex having degree w (this assumes, as I always will, that any labeled reduction has an initial term with no underlined labels). One can thus view labels as a sort of genetic code, in the sense that by knowing the labels of the initial term ("matriarch"?) of a reduction, the lineage of a subsequent term in the reduction may be traced by inspection of the labels.

The formation rules of $Ter(\lambda^L)$ allow multiple labelings of parenthesized terms, which can be created as a resulted of labeled β-contraction. This requires an auxiliary reduction rule for labels:

Definition 4.4 *The* label simplification rule, $\longrightarrow_{\text{lab}}$, *is the following relation on members of $Ter(\lambda^L)$:*

$$C[\,(M^w)^v\,] \longrightarrow_{\text{lab}} C[\,M^{wv}\,]$$

where C is an arbitrary context and M^w is a term of $Ter(\lambda^L)$.

We then have:

Definition 4.5 *Labeled β-reduction, $\longrightarrow\!\!\!\!\!\twoheadrightarrow_{\beta L}$, is the reflexive, transitive closure of ($\longrightarrow_{\text{lab}} \cup \longrightarrow_{\beta L}$), where '$\cup$' denotes relational union.*

The label simplification rule is a technical necessity, but a practical nuisance. Without loss of generality, when referring to a labeled term, I will assume it has been simplified as much as possible using $\longrightarrow\!\!\!\!\!\twoheadrightarrow_{\beta L}$. This assumption is technically justified by the following theorem:

Theorem 4.1 ([Lév75]) $\longrightarrow\!\!\!\!\!\twoheadrightarrow_{\beta L}$ *has the Church-Rosser (confluence) property, i.e.,*

$$M \longrightarrow\!\!\!\!\!\twoheadrightarrow_{\beta L} N_1 \wedge M \longrightarrow\!\!\!\!\!\twoheadrightarrow_{\beta L} N_2$$
$$\implies (\exists P) N_1 \longrightarrow\!\!\!\!\!\twoheadrightarrow_{\beta L} P \wedge N_2 \longrightarrow\!\!\!\!\!\twoheadrightarrow_{\beta L} P$$

Thus labeled λ-reduction is as "well-behaved" as its unlabeled counterpart, and, in a sense, is a strict refinement of the regular λ-reduction. Ignoring the labels, it is simply regular λ-reduction. Depending on the initial labeling, however, it can give a great deal more information about the reduction process.

We can now define transformations from the unlabeled to the labeled world and vice versa:

Definition 4.6 *Let M^l be a term of $Ter(\lambda^L)$. Then the* erasure *of M^l, $Er(M^l)$ is the same term with all the labels erased.*

Definition 4.7 *Let M be a term of $Ter(\lambda)$. Then $M^l \in Ter(\lambda^L)$ is a* labeling *of M iff $Er(M^l) = M$.*

We can also define the erasure of a reduction (overloading the meaning of '$Er()$'):

Definition 4.8 *Let σ^l be a labeled reduction. Then the* erasure *of σ^l, $Er(\sigma^l)$, is the unlabeled reduction obtained by erasing the labels of all the terms in the reduction and replacing all labeled β-contractions by unlabeled β-contractions.*

Finally, we can "lift" reductions on unlabeled terms to their labeled counterparts:

Definition 4.9 *Let M be a term of $\text{Ter}(\lambda)$, M^l be some labeling of M, and $\sigma: M \twoheadrightarrow_\beta N$. Then the lifted reduction $\text{Lift}(\sigma, M^l)$ is defined as the labeled reduction with initial term M^l in which the redexes contracted are the labeled counterparts of those contracted in σ.*

4.2 Optimality

4.2.1 Labels and Residuals

With the machinery of the labeled λ-calculus at hand, certain definitions that are rather complicated without it become straightforward. Labelings can be used to divide all the redexes in a reduction into equivalence classes based on their label. Such equivalence classes are deemed redex *families*:

Definition 4.10 ([Lév78]) *Let*
$$\rho: M \twoheadrightarrow_\beta N$$
be a reduction. Let l be a labeling of M such that each subterm of M^l has a unique atomic label. Let
$$\rho^l: M^l \twoheadrightarrow_{\beta^L} N^l = \text{Lift}(\rho, M^l)$$
be the labeled version of ρ. Then a redex R_j in any term of ρ (not necessarily a redex contracted by ρ) is a member of family class F_w^l iff the corresponding redex R_j^l in ρ^l has degree w.

Rather remarkably, it turns out that family classes can consist not only of sets of redexes that are effectively copies (i.e., residuals) of terms in the current reduction, but also may consist of sets of redexes that are not residuals of any redex in the current reduction, but *would* be residuals in a *different* reduction with the same initial and final terms. Thus labeling makes evident on inspection a property that might seem to require enumeration of all reductions.

4.2.2 Redex Sharing and Parallel Reductions

Having demonstrated the usefulness of the labeled λ-calculus, we can now formalize the notion of *sharing* of terms. Lévy noted that the reduction of a shared redex could be viewed as a *parallel* reduction of all the redexes represented by the shared term in its "flattened," non-graphical form. For instance, in Example 2.2 above, the shared contraction of the (Iz) redex may be viewed as the parallel contraction of the two terms that share it:

Example 4.1
$$\sigma_1'': (\lambda y.(yy))(Iz) \longrightarrow_\beta (Iz)(Iz) \longrightarrow_{\|\beta} zz$$

where '$\longrightarrow_{\|\beta}$' represents parallel β-contraction. Note that parallel β-contraction subsumes ordinary 0 or 1 step β-reduction ($\longrightarrow_{\equiv\beta}$), which is a development of 0 or 1 redexes.

Parallel *reductions* are represented thus:
$$\sigma: M_0 \xrightarrow{C_1}_{\|\beta} M_1 \xrightarrow{C_2}_{\|\beta} \cdots \xrightarrow{C_n}_{\|\beta} M_n$$

where the C_i are the sets of redexes in M_i contracted in parallel at each step.

Defining a consistent notion of parallelism for *overlapping* redexes requires a bit of care. Formally, Lévy defines a parallel reduction as the *complete development* of a set of redexes. See [Lév78] or [Lév80] for more details.

We can now define parallel reductions that reduce entire family classes at once:

Definition 4.11 (Lévy) *A parallel reduction*
$$\sigma: M_0 \xrightarrow{F_{w_1}}_{\|\beta} M_1 \xrightarrow{F_{w_2}}_{\|\beta} \cdots \xrightarrow{F_{w_n}}_{\|\beta} M_n$$
is family-complete iff for each M_i, F_{w_i} is the set of all members of some redex family F_w in M_i.

4.2.3 Call-By-Need Reductions

In order to ensure that an optimal reduction does no unnecessary work (although perhaps does it quite efficiently), we need to ensure that any optimal reduction, like leftmost reduction, reduces no *unneeded* redex. This leads to the following formal definitions:

Definition 4.12 (Lévy) *A redex R in some expression $M \in \text{Ter}(\lambda)$ is needed iff, for all terminating reductions σ with initial term M, either R or one of its residuals is contracted in σ.*

Definition 4.13 (Lévy) *A parallel reduction*
$$\rho: M_0 \xrightarrow{C_1}_{\|\beta} M_1 \xrightarrow{C_2}_{\|\beta} \cdots \xrightarrow{C_n}_{\|\beta} M_n$$
is a call-by-need reduction iff there is at least one needed redex in each C_i.

We now have Lévy's optimality theorem:

Theorem 4.2 ([Lév78,Lév80]) *A parallel reduction*
$$\rho: M \twoheadrightarrow_{\|\beta} N$$
is optimal for the class of all parallel reductions with initial term M if

— ρ is family-complete.

— ρ is call-by-need.

Note that the theorem does not *require* that an optimal strategy use shared redexes—a regular (non-parallel) β-contraction is a degenerate parallel contraction, and if all family classes have one member, a complete reduction requires contraction of only one redex at a time. However, if a fixed redex selection strategy is to be used, some form of sharing is inevitable.

5 Labeled ΛCCL

By analogy with Lévy's labeled λ-calculus, we can define a similarly labeled version of ΛCCL, ΛCCL^L.

Definition 5.1 *The axioms of* ΛCCL^L *are as follows:*

(**Beta**) $\text{Apply}(\Lambda(A)^w, B)^u = [A^{uw}, \langle \emptyset, B^{\underline{w}} \rangle]$
(**AssC**) $[[A, E_1]^u, E_2]^v = [A^{uv}, E_1 \circ E_2]$
(**NullEL**) $\emptyset \circ E = E$
(**NullER**) $E \circ \emptyset = E$
(**ShiftE**) $\Box \circ \langle E, A \rangle = E$
(**VarRef**) $[\text{Var}^u, \langle E, A \rangle]^v = A^{uv}$
(**DA**) $[\Lambda(A)^u, E]^v = \Lambda([A, \langle E \circ \Box, \text{Var} \rangle])^{uv}$
(**DE**) $\langle E_1, A \rangle \circ E_2 = \langle E_1 \circ E_2, [A, E_2] \rangle$
(**DApply**) $[\text{Apply}(A, B)^u, E]^v = \text{Apply}([A, E], [B, E])^{uv}$
(**AssE**) $(E_1 \circ E_2) \circ E_3 = E_1 \circ (E_2 \circ E_3)$
(**NullC**) $[A^u, \emptyset]^v = A^{uv}$
(**DLabel**) $[A, E]^u = [A^u, E]$

Note that the **DLabel** has no analogue in unlabeled ΛCCL. It is the ΛCCL^L equivalent of the the convention allowing the removal of parentheses in multiply-labeled parenthesized terms of λ^L. By analogy with the labeled λ-calculus, the *degree* of a labeled (**Beta**) redex is the label of its abstraction term; e.g., $\text{Apply}(\Lambda(A^u)^w, B^v)^z$ has degree w.

Theorems 3.4, 3.5, 3.9, and 3.7 all apply to ΛCCL^L and λ^L; the proofs are quite similar and are omitted. The translations $[\![\cdot]\!]_{\lambda^L}$ and $[\![\cdot]\!]_{\Lambda\text{CCL}^L}$ are defined in the obvious way analogous to their unlabeled counterparts.

We can now apply Lévy's optimality criteria directly to reductions in ΛCCL, using ΛCCL^L. The idea is to consider each (**Beta**) contraction in a term A as representing a parallel β-contraction on the corresponding λ-term $[\![\text{Inf}(A)]\!]_\lambda$.

We can then make the following definitions:

Definition 5.2 *A reduction* $A \longrightarrow_{\Lambda\text{CCL}} B$ *is λ-optimal if the number of* (**Beta**) *contractions therein is less than or equal the number of parallel β-contractions in an optimal λ-reduction from* $[\![\text{Inf}(A)]\!]_\lambda$ *to* $[\![\text{Inf}(B)]\!]_\lambda$.

Definition 5.3 *A* (**Beta**) *redex B in a term A is λ-needed iff the λ-equivalent of one of B's residuals* $B_i' \in \text{Resid}(B, A)$, $[\![B_i']\!]_\lambda$, *is needed in* $[\![\text{Inf}(A)]\!]_\lambda$ *in the sense of Definition 4.12.*

Theorem 5.1 *Let* $A^l \in \Lambda\text{CCL}^L$ *be a term all of whose subterms have unique labels. Let* $\rho^l: A^l \longrightarrow_{\Lambda\text{CCL}^L} B^l$ *be a* ΛCCL^L *reduction. Then the corresponding unlabeled reduction* $\rho: \text{Inf}(A) \longrightarrow_{\Lambda\text{CCL}} \text{Inf}(B)$ *is λ-optimal if no two* (**Beta**) *redexes in* ρ^l *have the same degree and each* (**Beta**) *redex is λ-needed.*

Proof Follows from Lévy's results on the labeled λ-calculus, the labeled form of Lemma 3.9 and Theorem 3.8.
□

The above theorem gives us the promised tool for analysis of laziness. If we construct a λ-interpreter whose action can be expressed in terms of some application of the rules of ΛCCL, we can determine how close to optimality any such interpreter can come by showing how many (**Beta**) redexes in the corresponding labeled reductions have the same label.

6 Non-Optimality of Reduction with Shared Closures

I can now show that there is no λ-optimal reduction possible in ΛCCL^L, and thus that no reduction scheme that can be expressed using the axioms of ΛCCL is optimal in Lévy's sense. I do so by exhibiting a λ-term for which *every* ΛCCL reduction causes more than one (**Beta**) redex to be contracted in the corresponding labeled form, even when when all terms are shared that are permissible under ΛCCL's rules. The term is as follows:

$$(\lambda x.((xA^d)(xB^e)))(\lambda y.((\lambda z.(z^a t)(z^b u))(\lambda w.y^c v)))$$

where A and B are arbitrary λ-abstractions. Not all subterms are given labels for the sake of clarity.

Space does not permit a complete enumeration of all possible reductions of its corresponding ΛCCL^L translation. However, the crux of the matter is embodied in the following term, which must be produced in any reduction of the ΛCCL equivalent of the term above if no prior (**Beta**) redexes with the same label are to be reduced twice:

$$((\mathbf{[}\bullet, \langle\!\langle y := A^d \rangle\!\rangle\mathbf{]}: C_1)(\mathbf{[}\bullet, \langle\!\langle y := B^e \rangle\!\rangle\mathbf{]}: C_2))$$
$$[((z^a t)(z^b u)), \langle\!\langle z := \lambda w.(y^c v)\rangle\!\rangle]: C_3$$

As before, $\langle\!\langle \cdot \rangle\!\rangle$ represents a ΛCCL environment with the bound variable indicated explicitly. The notation $T:N$ is used to give names to subterms. One is forced here to choose between reducing closure C_3 or one of closures C_1 or C_2. Choosing C_3 yields:

$$((\mathbf{[}\bullet, \langle\!\langle y := A^d \rangle\!\rangle\mathbf{]}: C_1)(\mathbf{[}\bullet, \langle\!\langle y := B^e \rangle\!\rangle\mathbf{]}: C_2))$$
$$((y^c v)(y^c v))$$

which reduces to

$$(((A^{dc} v)(A^{dc} v))(\mathbf{[}\bullet, \langle\!\langle y := B^e \rangle\!\rangle\mathbf{]}: C_2))$$
$$((y^c v)(y^c v))$$

in which two redexes of the form $(A^{dc} v)$ are created, thus yielding a non-optimal reduction (since they have the same degree and are no longer shared).

To avoid the copying that occurs above, one could alternately first reduce closure C_1 (or C_2, for which the argument to follow is symmetric), which would eventually yield a term of the following following form:

$$((\mathbf{[}\bullet, \langle\!\langle z := \lambda w.(A^{dc} v)\rangle\!\rangle\mathbf{]}: C_1')(\mathbf{[}\bullet, \langle\!\langle z := \lambda w.(B^{ec} v)\rangle\!\rangle\mathbf{]}: C_2'))$$
$$((z^a t)(z^b u))$$

which reduces to

$$((\lambda w.\bullet)^a t)((\lambda w.\bullet)^b t)((\lambda w.\bullet)^a t)((\lambda w.\bullet)^b t)$$
$$(A^{dc} v) \qquad (B^{ec} v)$$

The term above has two (actually, two sets) of unshared redexes with the same degree, e.g., $((\lambda w.(A^{dc} v))^a t)$ and

$((\lambda w.(B^{cc}v))^a t)$. If both are needed (which depends on the particular abstractions chosen for A and B, a non-optimal reduction will once again result. In the end, no matter what choice is made, a non-optimal reduction occurs.

The informal observation that shared closures and environments alone are insufficient to implement optimal reduction schemes was also made independently by Curien in [Cur86c]. He did not, however, provide a formal connection (such as that made above using labels) between redex families in the lambda calculus and their equivalents in a formal system using environments, nor was the system he was using as general as the one proposed here.

7 Related Work and Conclusions

A system almost identical to ΛCCL has been independently proposed by Abadi, et.al. [ACCJL89]. Its term structure is isomorphic to that of ΛCCL, and its axioms are the same with two minor exceptions. They propose to use their system to study properties of substitutions, to describe type-checking algorithms, and as the basis for machine-oriented implementations of reduction schemes. They have not, however, proposed a labeled system for the study of the optimality problem.

[AKP84] provides an analysis of the differences between various lazy and fully-lazy λ-interpreters without examining the issue of optimality.

Two schemes, by Staples [Sta82] and, recently, by Lamping [Lam89], have been proposed that claim to implement optimal λ-reduction. Both seem to allow terms to be shared that traditional environment or substitution mechanisms do not allow. However, they are notable for their extreme complexity, and it is not clear that the overhead incurred by these schemes in order to ensure family classes are always shared is not prohibitive.

A practical optimal reduction mechanism might indeed exist for a restricted class of λ-terms, e.g., the so-called "supercombinators" used in functional programming. However, if one believes that ΛCCL is a sufficiently general model of reduction using shared environments or closures, then one must conclude that shared environments, closures, or terms alone are insufficient to achieve optimality in a practical interpreter.

To summarize, I have described a new system of combinators, ΛCCL, with which one can describe a wide variety of reduction methods for the λ-calculus using sharing. I have proved that essentially any reduction in ΛCCL corresponds to β-reduction in the λ-calculus, and thus that λ-reduction schemes using ΛCCL may be proved correct trivially. I have also described a labeled variant of ΛCCL, ΛCCL^L, which can be used as a tool to analyze the degree of laziness present in reduction schemes. I have shown, however, that ΛCCL is insufficient for implementing *optimal* reduction schemes, and thus that more than shared closures, environments, or λ-terms are apparently necessary if optimality is to be achieved at all.

8 Acknowledgements

I would like to thank Tim Teitelbaum for his support, encouragement, and productive discussions during the genesis of these ideas. I am also grateful to Pierre-Louis Curien for his comments on an earlier version of this paper and to Martin Abadi for supplying me with an unpublished version of his joint paper. Finally, I would like to thank especially Jean-Jacques Lévy and Thérèse Hardin for fruitful conversation, providing helpful comments, and pointing me toward related work.

A The Lambda Calculus and Term Rewriting Systems

I will briefly review some of the notation for the lambda-calculus used herein. The conventions used here will generally follow those of [Bar84], to which the reader is referred for details, although a few are taken from [Klo80] or [BKKS87].

A.1 Notation

$C[M]$ denotes a *context* containing M, i.e., $C[M]$ is a λ-term with designated subterm M. M need not be a proper subterm of $C[M]$. Contexts may be defined similarly for other rewriting systems.

$M[x := N]$ denotes the result of substituting N for all free occurrences of x in M.

β-*contraction* is denoted by $\longrightarrow_\beta$.

The reflexive, transitive closure of $\longrightarrow_\beta$, β-*reduction*, is denoted by $\longrightarrow\!\!\!\rightarrow_\beta$.

Other notions of reduction will be defined using analogous notation: if $\longrightarrow_R$ is a relation, then $\longrightarrow\!\!\!\rightarrow_R$ will denote its reflexive, transitive closure, and $=_R$ the induced equivalence.

Since '=' will be reserved to represent equality induced by a reduction relation, I will use '≡' to denote syntactic identity of λ-terms. I will identify on the syntactic level terms that are identical modulo changes of bound variable and avoid the machinery of α-*conversion*, i.e., I will feel free to say

$$\lambda x.x \equiv \lambda y.y$$

(As a practical matter, some reduction schemes will require a mechanism that effectively performs renaming. Such a mechanism will be introduced later).

Reductions, sequences of β-contractions, will be denoted as follows:

$$\sigma: M_0 \xrightarrow{R_1} M_1 \xrightarrow{R_2} M_2 \xrightarrow{R_3} \ldots \xrightarrow{R_n} M_n$$

σ designates the the entire reduction sequence. The M_i are the *terms* of the reduction. The R_i denote the redexes contracted at each step. Where clear from context, the R_i may be omitted. Occasionally, it will be convenient to elide the intermediate terms and denote the entire sequence by $\sigma: M_0 \longrightarrow\!\!\!\rightarrow_\beta M_n$.

A.2 The de Bruijn lambda calculus

The de Bruijn λ-calculus [dB72,dB78] is a variant of the λ-calculus in which variables are replaced by *de Bruijn numbers* denoting their binding depth in the term in which they are contained. This facilitates reduction without concern for variable "capture," which can occur during conventional λ-reduction even when the initial term of a reduction contains no bound variables with the same name. By providing a variable substitution mechanism that appropriately adjusts the de Bruijn numbers of substituted terms, the de Bruijn λ-calculus eliminates the need for α-conversion. The following definitions are from [Cur86a]

Definition A.1 *The set of terms in the de Bruijn λ-calculus, designated $Ter(\lambda^{DB})$, is defined inductively as follows*

$$\begin{aligned} n \in \mathcal{N} &\implies n \in Ter(\lambda^{DB}) \\ M, N \in Ter(\lambda^{DB}) &\implies (MN) \in Ter(\lambda^{DB}) \\ M \in Ter(\lambda^{DB}) &\implies \lambda.M \in Ter(\lambda^{DB}) \end{aligned}$$

where $\mathcal{N}$ is the set of natural numbers.

Definition A.2 *For any $M \in Ter(\lambda)$ such that $FV(M) \subseteq \{x_0, \ldots, x_n\}$, define its de Bruijn translation, $M_{DB(x_0,\ldots,x_n)} \in Ter(\lambda^{DB})$, as follows:*

$$\begin{aligned} x_{DB(x_0,\ldots,x_n)} &= i, \text{ where } i \text{ is minimum s.t. } x = x_i \\ (\lambda y.M)_{DB(x_0,\ldots,x_n)} &= \lambda.M_{DB(y,x_0,\ldots,x_n)} \\ (MN)_{DB(x_0,\ldots,x_n)} &= M_{DB(x_0,\ldots,x_n)} N_{DB(x_0,\ldots,x_n)} \end{aligned}$$

(I will usually write M_{DB} rather than $M_{DB(x_0,\ldots,x_n)}$ when the free variable ordering is irrelevant).

Substitution, β-reduction, and η-reduction can be suitably redefined on λ^{DB} such that

$$M \twoheadrightarrow_{\beta\eta} N \iff M_{DB} \twoheadrightarrow_{\beta\eta} N_{DB}$$

For a concise exposition of the details of β-reduction and the substitution process, see [Cur86a]

References

[ACCJL89] M. Abadi, L. Cardelli, P.-L. Curien, and J.J.-Levy. Explicit substitutions. In *Proc. Seventeenth ACM Symposium on Principles of Programming Languages*, San Francisco, 1989.

[AKP84] Arvind, Vinod Kathail, and Keshav Pingali. Sharing of computation in functional language implementations. In *Proc. International Workshop on High-Level Computer Architecture*, Los Angeles, 1984.

[AP81] Luigia Aiello and Gianfranco Prini. An efficient interpreter for the lambda calculus. *Journal of Computer and System Sciences*, 23:383–424, 1981.

[Aug84] L. Augustsson. A compiler for Lazy ML. In *Proc. ACM Symp. on Lisp and Functional Programming*, Austin, 1984.

[Bar84] H.P. Barendregt. *The Lambda Calculus*, volume 103 of *Studies in Logic and the Foundations of Mathematics*. North-Holland, Amsterdam, 1984.

[BBKV76] H.P. Barendregt, J. Bergstra, J.W. Klop, and H. Volken. Degrees, reductions, and representability in the lambda calculus. Preprint 22, Department of Mathematics, University of Utrecht, The Netherlands, 1976.

[BKKS87] H.P. Barendregt, J.R. Kennaway, J.W. Klop, and M.R. Sleep. Needed reduction and spine strategies for the lambda calculus. *Information and Computation*, 75:191–231, 1987.

[CCM87] G. Cousineau, P.-L. Curien, and M. Mauny. The categorical abstract machine. *Science of Computer Programming*, 8:173–202, 1987.

[Chu41] A. Church. *The Calculi of Lambda Conversion*. Princeton University Press, Princeton, NJ, 1941.

[Cur86a] P.-L. Curien. Categorical combinators. *Information and Control*, 69:188–254, 1986.

[Cur86b] P.-L. Curien. *Categorical Combinators, Sequential Algorithms, and Functional Programming*. Research Notes in Theoretical Computer Science. Pitman, London, 1986.

[Cur86c] P.-L. Curien. De la difficulté d'implémenter le partage optimal au sens de lévy. Unpublished Note, Université de Paris VII, 1986.

[dB72] N.G. de Bruijn. Lambda calculus notation with nameless dummies, a tool for automatic formula manipulation, with application to the church-rosser theorem. *Proc. of the Koninklijke Nederlandse Akademie van Wetenschappen*, 75(5):381–392, 1972.

[dB78] N.G. de Bruijn. Lambda calculus with name-free formulas involving symbols that represent reference transforming mappings. *Proc. of the Koninklijke Nederlandse Akademie van Wetenschappen*, 81(3):348–356, 1978.

[Der87] Nachum Dershowitz. Termination of rewriting. *J. Symbolic Computation*, 3:69–116, 1987.

[FH88] Anthony J. Field and Peter G. Harrison. *Functional Programming*. Addison-Wesley, Wokingham, England, 1988.

[FW87] Jon Fairbairn and Stuart Wray. Tim: A simple, lazy abstract machine to execute supercombinators. In *Proc. Conference on Functional Programming Languages and Computer Architecture*, pages 34–45, Portland, 1987. Springer-Verlag. Lecture Notes in Computer Science 274.

[Har87] Thérèse Hardin. *Résultats de Confluence pour les Règles Fortes de la Logique Combinatoire Catégorique et Liens avec les Lambda-Calculs*. PhD thesis, Université de Paris VII, 1987.

[Har89] Thérèse Hardin. Confluence results for the pure strong categorical logic CCL. λ-calculi as subsystems of CCL. *Theoretical Computer Science*, 65:291–342, 1989.

[HL86] Thérèse Hardin and Alain Laville. Proof of termination of the rewriting system SUBST on CCL. Rapports de Recherche 560, Institut National de Recherche en Informatique et en Automatique, Domaine de Voluceau, Rocquencourt, B.P. 105, 78153 Le Chesnay Cedex, France, August 1986.

[HM76] P. Henderson and J.H. Morris. A lazy evaluator. In *Proc. Third ACM Symposium on Principles of Programming Languages*, pages 95–103, 1976.

[HO80] G. Huet and D.C. Oppen. Equations and rewrite rules: A survey. In R.V. Book, editor, *Formal Language Theory, Perspectives, and Open Problems*, pages 349–405. Academic Press, London, 1980.

[HS86] J.R. Hindley and J.P. Seldin. *Introduction to Combinators and Lambda-Calculus*, volume 1 of *London Mathematical Society Student Texts*. Cambridge University Press, Cambridge, 1986.

[Hue80] G. Huet. Confluent reductions: Abstract properties and applications to term rewriting systems. *Journal of the ACM*, 27(4):797–821, 1980.

[Hug84] R.J.M. Hughes. *The Design and Implementation of Programming Languages*. PhD thesis, Oxford University, September 1984. (PRG-40).

[Joh84] T. Johnsson. Efficient compilation of lazy evaluation. In *Proc. ACM Conf. on Compiler Construction*, Montreal, 1984.

[Joh85] T. Johnsson. Lambda lifting: Transforming programs to recursive equations. In *Proc. Conference on Functional Programming Languages and Computer Architecture*. Springer-Verlag, 1985. Lecture Notes in Computer Science 201.

[KL80] S. Kamin and J.-J. Lévy. Two generalizations of the recursive path orderings. Unpublished note, Department of Computer Science, Univerity of Illinois, Urbana, IL, 1980.

[Klo80] J.W. Klop. *Combinatory Reduction Systems*, volume 127 of *Mathematical Centre Tracts*. Mathematical Centre, Kruislaan 413, Amsterdam 1098SJ, The Netherlands, 1980.

[Lam89] John Lamping. An algorithm for optimal lambda calculus reduction. In *Proc. Seventeenth ACM Symposium on Principles of Programming Languages*, San Francisco, 1989.

[Lan64] P.J. Landin. The mechanical evaluation of expressions. *Computer Journal*, 6:308–320, 1964.

[Les84] Pierre Lescanne. Uniform termination of term rewriting systems. In B. Courcelle, editor, *Ninth Colloquium on Trees in Algebra and Programming*, pages 181–191, Bordeaux, France, 1984. Cambridge University Press.

[Lév75] Jean-Jacques Lévy. An algebraic interpretation of the $\lambda\beta K$-calculus and a labelled λ-calculus. In C. Böhm, editor, *Proc. Symp. on λ-Calculus and Computer Science Theory*. Springer-Verlag, 1975. Lecture Notes in Computer Science 37.

[Lév78] Jean-Jacques Lévy. *Réductions correctes et optimales dans le lambda-calcul*. PhD thesis, Université de Paris VII, 1978. (Thèse d'Etat).

[Lév80] Jean-Jacques Lévy. Optimal reductions in the lambda-calculus. In J.P. Seldin and J.R. Hindley, editors, *To H.B. Curry: Essays on Combinatory Logic, Lambda Calculus, and Formalism*. Academic Press, London, 1980.

[Lin87] R.D. Lins. On the efficiency of categorical combinators as a rewriting system. *Software—Practice and Experience*, 17(8):547–559, August 1987.

[Pey87] S. L. Peyton Jones. *The Implementation of Functional Programming Languages*. Prentice Hall International, Englewood Cliffs, New Jersey, 1987.

[Rus87] Michael Rusinowitch. Path of subterms ordering and recursive decomposition ordering revisited. *J. Symbolic Computation*, 3:117–131, 1987.

[Sta80a] John Staples. Computation on graph-like expressions. *Theoretical Computer Science*, 10:171–185, 1980.

[Sta80b] John Staples. Optimal evaluations of graph-like expressions. *Theoretical Computer Science*, 10:297–316, 1980.

[Sta80c] John Staples. Speeding up subtree replacement systems. *Theoretical Computer Science*, 11:39–47, 1980.

[Sta81] John Staples. Efficient combinatory reduction. *Zeitschr. f. math. Logik und Grundlagen d. Math.*, 27:391–402, 1981.

[Sta82] John Staples. Two-level expression representation for faster evaluation. In *Proc. Second International Workshop on Graph Grammars and Their Applications*, pages 392–404. Springer-Verlag, 1982. Lecture Notes in Computer Science 153.

[Tur79] D.A. Turner. A new implementation technique for applicative languages. *Software—Practice and Experience*, 9:31–49, 1979.

[Wad71] C.P. Wadsworth. *Semantics and Pragmatics of the Lambda-Calculus*. PhD thesis, Oxford University, 1971.

[Yok89] Hirofumi Yokouchi. Church-rosser theorem for a rewriting system on categorical combinators. *Theoretical Computer Science*, 65:271–290, 1989.

An Algorithm for Optimal Lambda Calculus Reduction

John Lamping
Xerox PARC

We present an algorithm for lambda expression reduction that avoids any copying that could later cause duplication of work. It is optimal in the sense defined by Lévy. The basis of the algorithm is a graphical representation of the kinds of commonality that can arise from substitutions; the idea can be adapted to represent other kinds of expressions besides lambda expressions. The algorithm is also well suited to parallel implementations, consisting of a fixed set of local graph rewrite rules.

Overview

The lambda calculus[1] defines beta reduction (reducing the application of a lambda term to an argument) in terms of substitution; each occurrence of the variable bound by the lambda is replaced by a copy of the argument. This can create extra work, since any work needed to simplify the argument must be repeated on each copy.

Lévy[4, 5] has shown that there are lambda expressions for which any order of reduction duplicates work. One example is

$$((\lambda g.(g\ (g\ (\lambda x.x))))$$
$$(\lambda h.((\lambda f.(f\ (f\ (\lambda z.z))))$$
$$(\lambda w.(h\ (w\ (\lambda y.y))))))))$$

which has two redexes, an outer one $((\lambda g\ \ldots)\ \ldots)$, and an inner one $((\lambda f\ \ldots)\ \ldots)$. If the outer redex is reduced first the inner redex will be duplicated, and each copy will have to be reduced. On the other hand, if the inner redex is reduced first, its argument, $(\lambda w.(h\ (w\ (\lambda y.y))))$, will be duplicated, which will cause redundant work later once a value for h is determined. Four copies of the application $(h\ (w\ (\lambda y.y)))$ will ultimately need to be simplified if the inner redex is reduced first, compared to only two copies if the outer redex is reduced first, one for each different value of h.

In general, a tension can occur when a function that is used several times, $(\lambda h\ \ldots)$ in the example above, contains a subfunction that it uses several times, $(\lambda w.(h\ (w\ (\lambda y.y))))$ in the example above. The tension occurs, as in this case, when the subfunction can be simplified given either the value of the argument to the function or the value of the argument to the subfunction. It is possible to simplify each use of the subfunction (to fold it inline) before any of the uses of the function are simplified, so that the work of simplifying each use of the subfunction can be shared among all uses of the function. Alternatively, it is possible to simplify the subfunction (to partial evaluate it) each time the main function is used so that that work of simplifying the subfunction can be shared among all uses of the subfunction. But whichever simplification is done first ends up duplicating the work of the other.

The technique of graph reductions[9] avoids some copying by treating a lambda expression as a tree, which is represented by an acyclic directed graph. Lambda calculus reductions are then modeled by graph operations. Since the lambda expression is represented by a graph, identical subtrees (identical subexpressions) can be represented with a single piece of graph. In particular, reducing a redex doesn't require copying the argument; each use of the argument simply gets a link to the original. This can save work later because one simplification step in a shared section of the graph corresponds to what would be multiple simplifications in the represented lambda expression.

But this only postpones copying by one step. If the lambda term in a redex is represented by a shared section of graph, that section must be copied before the redex can be reduced. Otherwise, the substitution called for by the reduction would affect not only the body of the lambda term in the redex, but also the bodies of the other lambda terms represented by the shared piece of graph. In the example above, graph reduction can reduce the original two redexes without doing any copying, but then it will have to copy in order to reduce any of the newly formed redexes, the applications of the shared functions (λh ...) and (λw.(h (w (λy.y)))). It will duplicate work in doing so.

It is possible to combine graph reduction with the translation of lambda expressions into combinators[8]. Combinator reductions are used to simpify the translated graph instead of the beta conversion rule; a single beta reduction becomes modeled by a series of combinator reductions, each of which is a simple local graph operation. Where a beta reduction on a graph would require copying a function body, the corresponding combinator reductions will be able to avoid copying any subexpressions that don't contain the variable bound by the lambda. This, however, isn't enough to eliminate all duplication of work. In the example, combinator reduction would reduce the outer redex first and then would have to partially copy combinators corresponding to the (λh ...) expression. It would not have to copy the (λf ...) subexpression, because it contains no h, but combinator reduction would have to copy the application ((λf ...) ...), because the argument contains a free h. In copying that application, it duplicates work.

Lévy has given a precise definition of what it would mean to never duplicate work. Given a tree that represents a lambda expression, he defines a system for labelling its links, and defines how the labels should be transformed by lambda reduction. Two links will get the same labelling under these rules if they have a common origin (where having the same origin includes having resulted from copies of a single link or having resulted from reductions of copies of a single redex). Using this labelling, Lévy defines a parallel reduction operation which reduces in one step all redexes having a given label on the link between their application and lambda, thus reducing all copies of a redex in one step. He shows that if this parallel reduction is considered to be a unit step, then no order of reduction duplicates work. From this it follows that normal order parallel reduction is optimal. Lévy did not, however, show how to implement parallel reductions.

Staples[6, 7] has developed an algorithm designed to implement Lévy's parallel reductions, based on using graphical structures to represent partial substitution environments. But his algorithm appears to accumulate structure monotonically as it executes and there doesn't appear to be a bound on the amount of work the algorithm must do for each reduction. Kathail[3] has recently developed an implementation of parallel reductions, but hasn't yet finished a description of it, and so we have not yet been able to compare it to the algorithm presented here.

We have developed an algorithm based on an extension of graph reduction. Ordinary graph reduction makes use of fan-in: several links coming into a single subgraph, each corresponding to a different instance of the subgraph; our algorithm also makes use of fan-out: several links coming out of a single subgraph, each corresponding to a different instance of the subgraph. This algorithm is able to avoid copying in the situations outlined above. More generally, the algorithm will always use a single piece of structure to represent redexes that are equivalent under Lévy's labelling. Although the presentation of the algorithm will be in terms of lambda calculus reductions, the essence of the algorithm is the graphical structure that represents the kinds of commonality that can result from substitution. This is adaptable to other situations involving substitution.

The algorithm consists of a fixed set of graph rewrite rules, which specify local incremental modifications to the graph. The decision of which rule to apply to the graph next and where to apply it is made non-deterministically. No order of rule execution will give incorrect results or generate duplicate beta reductions, but the most efficient implementations would give some rules priority over others. Since the rules operate locally, several rule executions can be done in parallel, on different parts of the graph.

While the algorithm avoids copying, it does not merge identical substructures. That is, if it happens during the course of lambda reduction that two initially different parts of a lambda expression are reduced to identical expressions, the algorithm won't notice that. It will reduce both expressions independently. A facility to notice identical subexpressions could be added to the algorithm, but it wouldn't supplant the algorithm, because the algorithm is able to preserve sharing between subexpressions, like (g (h x)) and (g (h y)), that have no common subexpressions but still have some structure in common.

The rest of this paper illustrates the algorithm in action, gives its rewrite rules, and sketches proofs of its correctness and optimality. The complete rewrite rules of the algorithm appear in figures 3, 4, and 5 at the end of the paper, but are very difficult to understand in isolation. Rather than focus on individual rules, we illustrate the effects of the rules on the graph structure, first with a simplified version of the algorithm, and then with the full algorithm. The simplified version leaves one crucial issue unresolved, which the full algorithm addresses. The paper concludes with the key definitions and lemmas in the proofs of correctness and optimality.

One discouraging note: while both an informal argument and experience with an implementation of the algorithm indicate that the amount of bookkeeping work the algorithm requires for each beta reduction step is proportional to the cost of doing a substitution, we haven't proven this. The difficulty appears to be in correctly formulating the bound.

Simplified Execution Example

Figure 1 illustrates the step by step execution of a simplified version of the algorithm. This section explains what is happening in the figure.

Like graph reduction, the algorithm treats a lambda expression as a tree, which it represents with a rooted graph. Graph A in figure 1 shows the graph the algorithm uses to represent the lambda expression

$$((\lambda g.(g\ (g\ (\lambda x.x))))$$
$$(\lambda h.((\lambda f.(f\ (f\ (\lambda z.z))))$$
$$(h\ (\lambda y.y)))))$$

The nodes in the graph fall into two categories. The ordinary nodes represent parts of a lambda expression. These are the application nodes, written @; lambda nodes, written λx; and variable nodes, written x. The control nodes, on the other hand, don't represent parts of a lambda expression, but instead control how the graph represents a tree. Here, these are the fan nodes, written ▽. This graph resembles the one that a standard graph reduction algorithm would use to represent the same lambda expression. The obvious difference is the two fan nodes, which explicitly show where sharing is occurring.

Throughout figure 1, the thickly drawn link in each graph indicates where the next rule execution occurs. In graph A, this is the topmost application, where the rule which simulates beta reductions (rule I.a in figure 3) will be executed, resulting in graph B. The rule indicates that a subgraph that matches the left hand side of the arrow should be replaced by an instance of the right hand side of the arrow. Node variables, notated like ⓐ, match any node. On the right hand side, they show how the resulting subgraph should be connected with the rest of the graph. This particular rule eliminates nodes and changes connections; other rules will create nodes as well. For a formal semantics of a similar graph rewrite rule system, see Barendregt et al[2].

The rule presumes that all the variable occurrences bound by a given lambda are represented by a single variable node, one variable node per lambda node. This property means that the beta reduction rule doesn't have to do any copying; it can just connect the argument to where the variable was, as illustrated in the figure. The property is first established when a lambda expression is translated into a graph by establishing one variable node for each lambda node, using fan nodes to consolidate the different variable instances bound by a lambda into one variable node.

There is a technical problem in making sure that the variable node matched by the rule is the mate of the lambda node matched by the rule; we resolve this by assuming that there is a link in the graph between the lambda node and its corresponding variable node, indicated in the picture by their common variable name rather than by a line. This also means that the left hand side of the rule is, in fact, connected.

Another execution of rule I.a, this time on the application of the (λf ...) yields graph C, which represents the lambda expression

$$((\lambda h.((h\ (\lambda y.y))$$
$$((h\ (\lambda y.y))$$
$$(\lambda z.z))))$$
$$((\lambda h.((h\ (\lambda y.y))$$
$$((h\ (\lambda y.y))$$
$$(\lambda z.z))))$$
$$(\lambda x.x)))$$

where the subexpression (h (λy.y)) occurs four times, although it occurs only once in the graph.

So far, the algorithm has done nothing different from what graph reduction would do; the next rule execution will change that. The only redexes in the lambda expression are applications of one of the copies of (λh ...). Since those copies are represented by a shared piece of graph, ordinary graph reduction would have to copy the shared piece before it was possible to proceed with a beta reduction.

The algorithm takes the more subtle step that results in graph D. Rule II.c in figure 3 replaces a shared lambda by two lambdas with a shared body; it replaces the variable node paired with the original lambda node with a fan node leading to two variable nodes for the two lambda nodes (ignore the annotation i on the nodes in the rule for the moment). The "upside down" fan node is no different in kind from the other fan nodes; it is just more convenient to draw it in that orientation. The node type is independent of orientation because the graph isn't directed; although application and lambda nodes will always be oriented the same way with respect to the root of the graph, the control nodes can occur in either orientation. The definition of the graph and the operation of the rules only consider which sites of each node are connected to which sites of the other nodes, with no notion of direction. (It would be possible to define an equivalent algorithm on directed graphs, but the distinctions imposed by the directedness of the links would necessitate gratuitously repetitious node types and rules.)

Starting from the perspective of the root of the graph, however, it is natural to superimpose a sense of direction on the graph and to distinguish an "upside down" fan node from a "right side up" fan node. From this theoretical perspective, an "upside down" fan functions as a fan-out, rather than as a fan-in. To see the meaning of a fan-out, first notice that in a graph without fan-outs, every path from the root that follows the superimposed sense of direction to reach an ordinary node represents a path in the lambda expression tree (equivalently, a node in the lambda expression tree, since there is a one-to-one pairing in trees between nodes and paths from the root). The same is true in a graph with fan-outs, except that there is a restriction on the paths. Every fan-out along a path will be paired with some fan-in along the path, and the path must follow the branch out of the fan-out that is marked the same ($\star$ or $\circ$) as the branch it followed into the fan-in. Thus, graph D stands for the lambda expression

$$((\lambda h.((h\ (\lambda y.y)) \\ ((h\ (\lambda y.y)) \\ (\lambda z.z)))) \\ ((\lambda h'.((h'\ (\lambda y.y)) \\ ((h'\ (\lambda y.y)) \\ (\lambda z.z)))) \\ (\lambda x.x)))$$

because the fan-out is paired with the top fan-in, which means that paths from the λh, which go in the $\star$ branch of the top fan-in, must go out the $\star$ branch of the fan-out to the h variable; and correspondingly for paths from the $\lambda h'$.

If, on the other hand, the fan-out were paired with the lower fan-in, the graph would stand for the lambda expression

$$((\lambda h.((h\ (\lambda y.y)) \\ ((h'\ (\lambda y.y)) \\ (\lambda z.z)))) \\ ((\lambda h'.((h\ (\lambda y.y)) \\ ((h'\ (\lambda y.y)) \\ (\lambda z.z)))) \\ (\lambda x.x)))$$

which has an h and h' incorrectly interchanged. Determining which fan-outs pair with which fan-ins is a crucial issue, but that is the issue that is not addressed by this simplified version of the algorithm. The full algorithm uses several additional kinds of control nodes to delimit scopes within which fan-ins and fan-outs can pair. For this simplified explanation, we have omitted those control nodes and the rules that manipulate them. They account for about half of the rule executions of the full algorithm. For the moment, we will assume that the pairing of fan-ins and fan-outs is determined omnisciently.

Finally, it is important to note that the notion of paths is part of an explanation of what lambda expression a graph stands for, not something which the algorithm is directly sensitive to. The algorithm simply does local operations, which are in accord with the bigger picture without being directly cognizant of it.

After the λh node has been split, the beta reduction rule is applicable again. Applying it to reduce the application of $(\lambda h' \ldots)$ results in graph E.

Various rules are applicable at this point; assume that the algorithm turns to the bottom application node in graph E, which represents applications of two different functions: h, and $(\lambda x.x)$. To make progress, it is necessary to duplicate the application node, so the two functions can be reduced separately. This is the only situation where the algorithm duplicates an application node: when the node represents applications of different functions. This stipulation means that an application node is not duplicated unless the resulting nodes will represent different work; it is the key to the optimality of the algorithm. Graph F shows the result of rule IV.e, which duplicates the application; the two new applications get their respective functions and share their common argument. The new graph represents the same lambda expression.

Again, various of the algorithm's rules apply at various points of this graph. Assuming the algorithm chooses to reduce the application of $(\lambda x.x)$, the result is shown in graph G. Next, the rule for duplicating a shared lambda node can be applied to the λy node, giving graph H. In this case, the common body shared between the two new lambda nodes is a single edge. Graph I shows what then happens when the lower fan-out meets its paired fan-in: rule V.b shows how they annihilate each other and connect corresponding links, $\star$ with $\star$ and $\circ$ with $\circ$. This operation leaves the graph representing the same lambda expression as before; the lambda expression tree represented by the middle graph only reflected paths that went through corresponding links of the fans, and those two valid routes are replaced by two links in the right hand graph.

There is still a fan-out meeting a fan-in, but these fans aren't paired with each other, the fan-out is instead paired with the upper fan-in. All four routes going through the two fans contribute to the lambda expression

$$((\lambda h.((h\ (\lambda y.y)) \\ ((h\ (\lambda y.y)) \\ (\lambda z.z)))) \\ ((\lambda y'.y') \\ ((\lambda y'.y') \\ (\lambda z.z))))$$

represented by the graph, so they must all be preserved. Rule V.a shows how the fans should duplicate each other, resulting in graph J, which has a new link for each of the four routes through the two fans in the former graph. The mechanism for deciding whether to use rule V.a or rule V.b will be taken up in the next section.

The algorithm proceeds through the rest of figure 1 using the five rules already illustrated. A few more steps beyond the figure finally result with (λz.z).

Execution Example

One of the key points of the algorithm is that a subpiece of the graph which contains fan-outs can represent different lambda expressions for different paths which reach it. For example, the graph segment

which arose during the simplified example, represents either h or h', depending on the history of the path that reaches it. Any path from the root can be thought of as accumulating a context that records which branches of fan-ins it traversed, so that it knows which branches of fan-outs to take. The context combines with the structure of a piece of graph to determine which lambda expression is represented. Like the notion of paths, this notion of context is not a part of the algorithm, but rather a tool to analyze and understand the algorithm.

The context must not only record which branches of fan-ins were taken, but must organize that information so that it is possible to determine which fan-ins pair with which fan-outs. This section deals with the issue of how to do that.

An obvious idea is to label the fans in the graph, with fans paired if and only if they have identical labels. To see why this scheme isn't adequate, first notice that graphs containing looping paths, for example

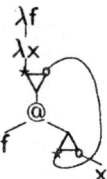

can arise when one instance of a shared expression gets substituted inside another instance of that expression. This graph represents the lambda expression (λf.(λx.(f (f x)))) and is the result, for example, after the algorithm beta reduces

(λf.(λx.((λg.(g (g x)))
(λy.(f y)))))

Looping paths present a problem in situations where a looping path traverses the same fan-in several times before traversing its paired fan-out, such as in the graph segment:

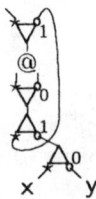

It then becomes necessary to determine which traversal of a fan-in should be paired with a particular traversal of a fan-out. Assume in the graph that the fan-in labeled 0 is paired with the fan-out labeled 0, and similarly for the fans labeled 1. Any legal path that reaches the fan-out labeled 0 will have gone through the fan-in labeled 0 twice. If the traversal of the fan-out should be paired with the second traversal of the fan-in then the graph segment represents the expression ((x y) (x y)). The segment can occur with this interpretation, for example, near the end of the simplification of

(λx.(λy. ((λf.((λh.(h (λp.(h (λq.q)))))
(λl.(((f (λn. (l n))) x) y))))
(λg.(λu.(λv.((g u) (g v))))))))

On the other hand, if the traversal of the fan-out should be paired with the first traversal of the fan-in then the graph segment represents the different expression ((x x) (y y)). The segment can occur with this interpretation, for example, near the end of the simplification of (λx.(λy. ((λf.((λh.(h (λp.(h (λq.p)))))
(λl.(((f (λn. (l n))) x) y))))
(λg.(λu.(λv.((g u) (g v))))))))

The labels on the fans aren't able to distinguish the two cases.

Our solution adds a notion of enclosure to delimit the interaction of fans along paths. Specifically, traversals of fans from different enclosures along a path never pair. Without any intervening enclosures, adjacent identically labeled fans pair, so that the above graph represents the expression ((x y) (x y)). But bracket nodes (to be explained shortly) can be added to the graph:

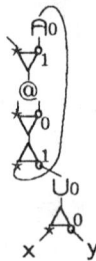

so that the second traversal of the fan-in labeled 0 is enclosed, which makes the fan-out labeled 0 pair the first traversal of the fan-in; the graph represents the expression ((x x) (y y)).

For an explanation of brackets, we return to the example of the previous section. The full algorithm represents the initial lambda expression

$$((\lambda g.(g\ (g\ (\lambda x.x))))$$
$$(\lambda h.\ ((\lambda f.\ f\ (f\ (\lambda z.z)))$$
$$(h\ (\lambda y.y)))))$$

with graph A of figure 2, which is identical to the graph of the simplified example, except that each fan is in its own enclosure, represented in the graph by two new kinds of control nodes, ∪, and ⊎, called bracket nodes, which indicate enclosure boundaries. (For the moment, ignore the difference between the two kinds of bracket nodes and ignore the number next to all control nodes in the graph). The bracketing nodes can be viewed as delimiting enclosures, which indicate how fans pair; or they can be viewed as serving to organize the context and to control its accumulation, which will then determine how fans pair. The two circles on the illustration of graph A are not an actual part of the graph structure, but serve as an aid to visualizing the enclosures (It isn't always possible to illustrate such boundaries on a graph, because brackets enclose segments of paths, not segments of graphs. For the sample execution, the two will coincide, but that wasn't the case in the graph above). The open end of a bracket node points toward the inside of the enclosure it is a part of. From the point of view of a path starting at the root of the graph, a ∩ node looks like an open bracket; crossing it puts the path inside a new enclosure. Similarly, a ⊎ looks a close bracket. As will become apparent later in the example, enclosures can nest or overlap, and a single enclosure can be composed of disjoint regions.

The effect of the brackets on the context accumulated by a path can be deduced by noting that since the fans inside an enclosure cannot pair with fans outside the enclosure, once a path leaves an enclosure its context doesn't reflect any enclosed fans; from outside, it can never matter which branches were taken inside. This requires that the context look like a stack of separate frames or levels, one for each level of nesting of enclosures. Each level of the context records the branches taken through a sequence of fans all at the same level of nesting. An open bracket starts a new level of the context to reflect entering a new enclosure, and a close bracket discards the top level to reflect leaving that enclosure.

The brackets in the initial graph set up a crucial transparency property maintained by the algorithm: if a path segment in the graph corresponds in the lambda expression to going between a lambda and an occurrence of the variable it binds, then the control nodes along the path segment will have no net effect on the accumulated context. The initial bracketing accomplishes this by enclosing each fan, so that the effect of the fan on the context will be discarded. This is fine since, initially, no fan pairs with any other.

The transparency property is needed for the correctness of rule I.a, which simulates beta reduction. Recall that the rule disconnects the argument from the application and reconnects it where the bound variable node was. If the argument were to see different contexts in its new location than it did in its old, it would represent different lambda expressions after the beta reduction than it did before, and the transformation would have been incorrect. But consider any path to the application. The one step extensions of the path to the argument and to the lambda have the same context, since there are no intervening control nodes, and transparency ensures that any extensions of the path corresponding to variable occurrences bound by the lambda have that same context. So after the beta reduction rule runs, any path to the former argument will have the same context as the path in the original expression that represented the argument.

Two applications of rule I.a yield graph B in figure 2 (in this example, we will often show several rule executions at once). At this point, the simplified algorithm would have duplicated the λh node. But now there is a ∪ between the fan and the lambda node. There are a couple of ways of looking at what has to happen, each of which points out a problem.

The immediate goal is to get the ∪ node out of the way, presumably by moving it below the λh node, thus putting the lambda node and fan-in in the same enclosure. But in order to preserve the transparency property, it would also be necessary to add a node above the h node that undoes the effect of the ∪. The problem is that there is no way to undo the irreversible effect of a ∪ node. From the point of view of the context there is no way to know what information the node threw away; from the point of view of enclosures, the enclosure has been closed off and there is no way back in.

One step further ahead of this goal is the need to prepare for the duplication of the λh node. This will require the fan-in to be moved below the λh node and be paired with a fan-out placed where the h variable node is now. For the fans to be paired, they will have to be in the same enclosure. But that enclosure shouldn't include most of the body of the λh, otherwise the fans might incorrectly pair with some other fan inside the body (this isn't a problem in the current graph, but could be in general).

The solution is to have a disconnected enclosure that includes the fan-in and the λh node in one part, and the h node in the other. The first step is rule III.a, which rewrites the ∪ node to a new kind of control node, a conditional bracket, written ⊔, as shown in graph C. A conditional bracket indicates that the area of the graph it encloses might be one component of a disconnected enclosure which has another component in the direction of the link through the bracket. This is indicated with a dashed line in illustrations of enclosures. As in this graph, some of the brackets around a region can be conditional brackets while others are unconditional brackets. Other parts of the enclosure to which the region belongs will never be found in the direction of links that cross unconditional brackets.

A conditional enclosure boundary doesn't necessarily mean that the area of graph it encloses has another component in the direction of the link through the bracket; that is why it is called conditional. For two areas to be part of the same enclosure, they must be at the same level of enclosure nesting and there must be a path segment between them that enters both at conditional brackets. Put negatively, a conditionally enclosed area will never be part of the same enclosure as an unconditionally enclosed area or with an area at a different level of nesting. The rules reflect these principles by having back-to-back conditional brackets cancel each other (rule VII.c), while having a conditional bracket directly enclosed by an unconditional bracket turn into an unconditional bracket (rule VII.d).

In terms of the context, a conditional close bracket suspends a level of context. It says that the level it brackets should be encapsulated, but not thrown away. It acts rather like a closure-forming operator, wrapping the contents of the level it brackets into a capsule which is placed in the newly-uncovered next lower level. Inversely, a conditional open bracket expects to find a capsule as the most recent item of the level, which it opens up to form a new level. On the other hand if there are capsules on a level that a general close bracket discards, the capsules are discarded with everything else.

Changing a general bracket to a conditional bracket changes the contexts accumulated by paths and could thus potentially change the lambda expression represented by a graph, but the algorithm maintains an independence property to preclude that possibility in this case: the top level of the context will never influence which lambda expression is represented by the section of graph below a lambda node. This property means, essentially, that each lambda node has a level of context available for keeping track of different instantiations of the lambdas it represents, which won't interact with the graph below the lambda node. The property is sufficient to ensure the correctness of changing a close bracket above a lambda to a conditional close bracket, since the only difference in context that results from the change is an additional capsule in the top level, which can't affect the lambda expression represented by the graph.

Returning to the example, since the effect of a conditional bracket can be undone, rule II.a can move the conditional bracket below the λh node, putting its reverse above the h node to preserve the transparency of path segments from the λh node to the h node. The result, graph D, has an enclosure that consists of disconnected regions.

Now the lambda node is ready to be duplicated by rule II.c; the fan-out and fan-in would be in the same enclosure, and thus correctly pair with each other. But to stay on the topic of conditional brackets, but we will assume that the algorithm first deals with them some more. The algorithm tries to merge disconnected regions of a single enclosure by moving conditional brackets so that they enclose as large a region as possible; when the disconnected regions meet, the brackets can cancel, merging the regions. From graph D, the two conditional brackets can be propagated over applications by rules IV.b and IV.d, resulting in graph E. In each case a conditional bracket on one branch of the application turns into conditional brackets on each of the other two branches, so that the application becomes included in the enclosed region.

Now two of the conditional brackets have reached unconditional brackets. The conditional brackets are destined to meet and cancel, but there is another enclosure between them. In order for the conditional brackets to meet, at least one of them will have to go through that enclosure. The first step must be to transpose a conditional bracket past an unconditional bracket so that their respective enclosures overlap. But transposing the brackets without adjusting something else would change which close brackets close which open brackets, giving entirely rearranged enclosures, not the desired overlapping enclosures. The solution, implemented by rules VII.f and VII.h (with one more execution of IV.d thrown in) is shown in graph F, where the numbers that are attached to every control node are used to indicate overlapping enclosures.

A control node with a number i interacts with nodes i levels of enclosure removed. Thus the conditional bracket nodes in graph F with number 1 don't form an enclosure with the unconditional brackets they face, but rather with brackets one level of enclosure further out, forming the illustrated regions. Again, the outer two regions are two disconnected components of a single enclosure.

In terms of context, a control node with non-zero number doesn't act on the top level of the context, but rather acts as many levels down in the context as the value of its number (the top level being the 0th). The $⊔_1$ and $⊓_1$ nodes in graph F are acting not at the level of bracketing that directly encloses them, but rather at one level further out. In general, by keeping track of relative offsets of levels, the numbers make it possible to move enclosure boundaries past each other without getting them tangled.

Next, rule II.a moves one of the conditional brackets below the λy node while rule VI.f moves another above a fan-in, giving graph G. Enclosures at deeper levels don't restrict how fans can pair, so moving the level 1 conditional bracket over the fan-in can't affect how the fan is paired.

At this point, the different regions of the single conditional enclosure are touching and rule VII.c can merge them, giving (with the aid of another execution of rule II.a) graph H (The arc near the top of the graph indicates that everything below it is part of an enclosure). Rule VII.c required the conditional brackets to have the same level number; otherwise they would have belonged to different enclosures and should have passed through each other, following rule VII.n. What started in graph D as an enclosure with two disconnected regions has become a single large region. What started back in graph B as independent enclosures have become nested enclosures, preparing the way for lambda reduction while avoiding possible mispairings of fans. The conditional brackets were the instrument of the transformation. In general, conditional enclosure boundaries merge disjoint regions by expanding them until they encounter an enclosing boundary; in this example there was no enclosing boundary so the conditional boundaries expanded to fill the entire surrounding graph structure.

Rule II.c could have been executed any time since graph D. Executing it now gives graph I, which is ready for rule I.b, a version of the beta reduction rule that accomodates a ⋒$_0$ node, giving graph J; the ⋓$_0$ keeps the λx node out of the enclosure. Rule IV.e duplicates the application to give graph K, where a fan-in is facing a fan-out across an enclosure boundary. The enclosure indicates that the fans are not paired, so they should duplicate each other, rather than connect corresponding links. Rule VI.a takes the first step, moving the fan-out inside the enclosure, but incrementing its number to give graph L. Just as with brackets, the number i on the fan indicates that the fan logically belongs i levels of enclosure out. Since the fans now facing each other have different numbers, they belong to different nestings of enclosures, and are thus not paired with each other; they should duplicate each other. All of the enclosure mechanism is ultimately in service of making sure that fans have the right numbers when they meet. Rule V.a does the actual duplication, yielding graph M, then two applications of rule VI.c take the fan-outs back out of the enclosure, yielding graph N. Even though rule VI.c is written upside down compared to the segments it matches in graph M, the rule fires; the graph is undirected, so rules can match in any orientation to the graph as a whole.

Only one other notable thing happens in the execution past graph N. Rule IV.a applies at graph N to move the ⋓$_0$ over the application. This splits the enclosure into two independent enclosures, which would be incorrect if fans in the two enclosures had interacted or if disconnected regions within the two enclosures has been part of one enclosure. This can't happen because a ⋓, called a restricted bracket, is never allowed to be used to bracket a fan from the point or to bracket a conditional bracket from the outside. These restrictions mean that an enclosure can always be split in the vicinity of a restricted bracket, jusifying the use of rule IV.a. The general bracket, ⋃ doesn't have these restrictions, and so the algorithm knows less when it encounters one. For this reason, general brackets are used as little as possible. In fact, they only occur like ⋃$_0$, as close brackets with number 0.

Outline of Proofs

Correctness

First, a quick summary of the algorithm: A legal graph is a rooted undirected graph and contains nodes of only the following types and arities. The ordinary nodes are the lambda nodes, variable nodes, and application nodes:

λx   x   @

The control nodes are the fan nodes, general bracket nodes, restricted bracket nodes, and conditional bracket nodes:

⋀$_i$ ⋃$_0$ ⋓$_i$ ⋓$_i$

As shown, each control node has an associated level number, a non-negative integer, which will always be 0 for general bracket nodes. Finally, there are two periphery node types, the root node and void nodes:

⊕   ⊗

Each graph has one root node, which is its root; each graph presented so far should have had a root node connected to its top node. Void nodes haven't appeared in the examples; they connect to unused parts of a graph. Each arc of a node attaches at a distinguishable site, indicated in the pictures by relative location. In terms of standard graph theory, the nodes are labeled (the label is the node type, including the level number on a control node) and the arcs of a node are ordered.

Running the algorithm consists of encoding of a lambda expression into a graph, which will be described shortly, followed by executing the rewrite rules (then, optionally, reinterpreting the graph as a lambda expression). The rules of figure 3 are the heart of the algorithm. Rules I.a and I.b simulate beta reduction while the other rules of figure 3 get the control nodes out of the way of a potential beta reduction. Only the beta reduction rules change which lambda expression is represented by the graph. The rules in figure 4 eliminate unreachable graph structures (these result from reducing lambdas that have no instance of their bound variable). Those of figure 5 take advantage of special situations to simplify the graph structure, usually getting rid of a control node or two. The algorithm works without the rules of figure 5, but does less bookkeeping work if the rules are available. For example, when an implementation of the algorithm is run on a computation of 6! in the unary representation of Church numerals, it performs only about half as many control rule executions when those rules are available and are given priority. All of the rules that move control nodes move them in a consistent direction; the algorithm can't get into a loop of just shuffling control nodes back and forth. Further, the rules are capable of getting any combination of control nodes out of the way of a potential beta reduction; if a lambda expression has a redex, the algorithm will be able to reduce it. It remains to show that the algorithm correctly simulates beta reduction.

The proof of correctness proceeds by defining the lambda expression represented by a graph and showing that an execution of the beta reduction rule on the graph does, in fact, simulate a collection of beta reductions on the lambda expression, while the remaining rules don't affect the represented lambda expression.

As described earlier, each proper path through the graph corresponds to a path through the lambda expression. A proper path is one which starts at the root and at each fan-out takes the branch corresponding to the branch it took into the paired fan-in. This can be defined precisely by defining the context accumulated by a path and how fan-outs find their matched fan-in in that context. For this discussion, we will use the informal description given in the previous section.

The definition of the tree represented by a graph glossed over the issue of how variables in the represented lambda expression should be named. Equivalently, it ignored the issue of how the scoping of lambdas is represented. Not surprisingly, the control nodes hold the answer. We present some properties relating lambda nodes to control nodes, which legal graphs must obey, show how to establish them in the initial encoding of the lambda expression as a graph, and show how they define how the graph represents scoping. The first three properties have already been mentioned in the examples.

There is a potential for confusion in the following definitions because the names "lambda" and "variable" might refer either to nodes in the graph or to vertices of the represented tree. To avoid ambiguity, we will always use *lambda node* and *variable node* to refer to nodes in the graph and use *lambda* and *variable occurrence* to refer to vertices in the tree.

Property 1 (pairing) *There is a one-to-one pairing between lambda nodes and variable nodes; a variable node represents all variable occurrences bound by all lambdas represented by its paired lambda node and represents nothing else.*

Since one lambda node can represent several lambdas, this property still allows one variable node to represent variable occurrences bound by several lambdas, provided its paired lambda node represents all those lambdas.

The property poses three minor difficulties in translating a lambda expression into a graph. First, it requires every variable to be bound by some lambda; this can be resolved by adding lambdas to the front of the expression to bind any otherwise unbound variables. Second, it presents a problem with expressions where a lambda doesn't bind any variables, for example (λx.(λy.x)). The solution is to go ahead and include variable nodes for all lambda nodes, but to connect unused variable nodes to void nodes. The example would be represented as

$$\begin{array}{cc} \bigcirc & \\ \lambda x & \otimes \\ \lambda y & y \\ x & \end{array}$$

This situation is the way that void nodes are introduced into the graph. Later, if the λy is reduced, the argument will be connected to the ⊗ node and garbage collected by the rules of figure 4. The final problem is that some lambda might bind several variable occurrences; in this case fan-ins are used to collect the references and connect them to the single variable node, as was done in the example.

Property 2 (transparency) *For any proper path segment that represents a sequence of links in the tree from a lambda to a variable occurrence bound by the lambda, the control nodes along the segment will have no net effect on any allowable context for the segment.*

That is, the segment yields the identity transformation on any allowable context. This property can be set up initially by using brackets to encapsulate any fan-ins that were introduced to satisfy the paring property, putting restricted brackets on each branch and general brackets on the points, as was done in the example.

Property 3 (independence) *For any proper path to a lambda node, the make-up of the top level of its context at the lambda node will have no effect on how the path can be extended.*

More operationally, if control nodes that affected only the top level of the context were to be added just above the lambda node, they would not affect the tree represented by the graph. This is the property that justifies rule III.a, converting a general bracket above a lambda node to a conditional bracket.

Property 4 (nesting) *For any proper path segment that represents a sequence of links in the tree from a lambda to a variable occurrence free in the lambda, the context transformation determined by the segment will discard the make-up of the top level of the entering context.*

More operationally, if control nodes that affected only the top level of the context were to be added just above the lambda node, their effects would be discarded by any extension of the path that represents a variable occurrence free in the lambda. This property ensures that beta substitutions preserve the independence property; if an expression is substituted for free a variable inside a lambda, the top level of the context at the lambda won't be visible inside the expression. This property didn't come up in the example, because the example didn't have any free variables inside lambdas.

When initially encoding a lambda expression, this property is established by placing an open restricted bracket just above any lambda that contains free variables and placing one general close bracket just above a variable for each lambda in which the variable is free. This also ends up pairing up the open and close brackets, so as to preserve the transparency property. For example, the expression (λx. (λy. (λz. (x (y z))))) is represented by the graph

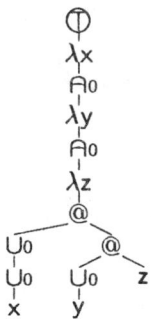

All four properties talk about which lambdas bind which variable occurrences, one in terms of the pairing of lambda nodes with variable nodes and the other three in terms of contexts. In a legal graph, they must agree. The transparency nesting properties are enough to completely determine which lambdas in the tree bind which variable occurrences. Even in a case where a path loops through the same lambda node several times before reaching a bound variable node, they determine which trip through the lambda node represents the lambda that binds the variable occurrence.

To see how the properties determine binding patterns, consider a path to a variable node and the variable occurrence it represents. Of the trips the path makes through lambda nodes, consider the latest one for which the make-up of its top level of context is still available at the variable node. The nesting property implies that the variable occurrence is not free in the lambda represented by that trip, so that lambda or some deeper one must bind the variable occurrence. But all deeper lambdas are represented by later trips through lambda nodes, for which the top level of the context is not available at the variable node. The transparency property implies that lambdas represented by those trips can't bind the variable, so the lambda in question must. In summary, for any path terminating at a variable node, the properties imply that the variable occurrence represented by the path is bound by the lambda represented by the nearest trip through a lambda node for which the make-up of the top level of the accumulated context is still available at the variable node.

We define the names of variables in the tree represented by the graph in accord with the properties. Every lambda in the tree is defined to bind a variable of a different name, and the name of each variable occurrence is then defined to be the same as that of that of lambda that the properties indicate should bind it. This definition assigns all tracking of scoping to the control nodes in the graph. Variable names only appear in the interpretation of the algorithm, not in the algorithm itself. For example, although the definition of beta reduction in the lambda calculus may require substantial renaming to avoid variable capture, the beta reduction rule in the algorithm only needs to change a few links; only the interpretation does renaming. Of course, the algorithm must end up with the same bindings that the lambda calculus would, and it does.

The proof of correctness is an induction, showing that if the graph satisfies the properties, then each rule preserves the properties and each rule preserves the lambda expression represented by the graph, except for the beta substitution rules (I.a and I.b), which simulate beta reductions.

Optimality

The optimality of the algorithm follows from its not duplicating nodes, except when necessary. In particular, application nodes are only duplicated if a fan-out is on their function link and lambda nodes are only duplicated if a fan-in is above them. These are exactly the two situations when a fan node is impeding a potential beta reduction.

The optimality is demonstrated by relating the algorithm's copying with a labelling on lambda expression links that Lévy's defines to specify optimality. Lèvy defines a parallel reduction step consisting of reducing all identically labelled redexes in one step. The task is to show that each beta reduction step of the algorithm corresponds to one of Lèvy's parallel reductions.

It would be nice if any two links in a lambda expression with identical labels under Lévy's labelling were represented by a single link in the graph, but the actual case is slightly more involved. It is possible to define the the *prerequisite chain* of a vertex in the lambda expression, which will be a sequence of links in the lambda expression, all of which must be involved in beta reductions before the vertex can be involved in a beta reduction. Then we can show

Lemma 1 *At any point during the execution of the rules of the algorithm, if two vertices in the tree represented by the graph have prerequisite chains of the same length and if corresponding links in the chains have matching labels, then the chains have the same representation in the graph.*

In the case of redexes, the link from the application to the function is a prerequisite chain by itself, and so the lemma guarantees that all identically labelled redexes will be represented by the same structure in the graph, and thus reduced in a single step.

Lèvy's results then imply that no order of executing the rules of the algorithm will duplicate work. But it is possible that some rule executions might do useless work, that is do beta reductions inside a subexpression that is eventually discarded. The solution is to impose a normal order strategy on the rule execution. An implementation would keep track of part of the graph represents the redex that would be reduced in normal order (this can be done efficiently) and would only execute rules on that part.

Of course, such a strategy reduces the opportunities for parallelism. A parallel implementation of the rules might dispense with normal order to achieve high parallelism at the cost of possibly doing some work that was later discarded. The proof that the rules never duplicate work would still apply to such a system.

Acknowledgments

Jim desRivieres and Jean-Jacques Lévy helped simplify the algorithm. They and Alan Bawden, Pavel Curtis, Dan Friedman, Julia Lawall, and Dan Rabin suggested substantial improvements to earlier drafts.

References

[1] H. P. Barendregt. *The Lambda Calculus : its Syntax and Semantics*, volume 103 of *Studies in logic and the foundations of mathematics*. North-Holland, 1981.

[2] H. P. Barendregt et al. LEAN, an intermediate language based on graph rewriting. *Parallel Computing*, 9:163–177, 1989.

[3] Vinod Kathail. private communication, 1989.

[4] Jean-Jacques Lévy. *Réductions correctes et optimales dans le lambda-calcul.* PhD thesis, Université de Paris, 1978.

[5] Jean-Jacques Lévy. Optimal reductions in the lambda-calculus. In J.P. Seldin and J.R. Hindley, editors, *To H.B. Curry: Essays on Combinatory Logic, Lambda Calculus and Formalism*, pages 159–191. Academic Press, 1980.

[6] John Staples. Efficient evaluation of lambda expressions: a new strategy. Technical Report 23, University of Queensland, Department of Computer Science, St. Lucia, Queensland, 4067, Australia, 1980.

[7] John Staples. Two-level expression representation for faster evaluation. In Hartmut Ehrig, Manfred Nagl, and Grzegorz Rozenberg, editors, *Graph-Grammars and their Application to Computer Science: 2nd International Workshop*. Springer-Verlag, 1982. Lecture Notes in Computer Science 153.

[8] D. A. Turner. A new implementation technique for applicative languages. *Software Practice and Experience*, 9(1), 1979.

[9] C. P. Wadsworth. *Semantics and Pragmatics of the λ-calculus*. PhD thesis, Oxford University , 1971.

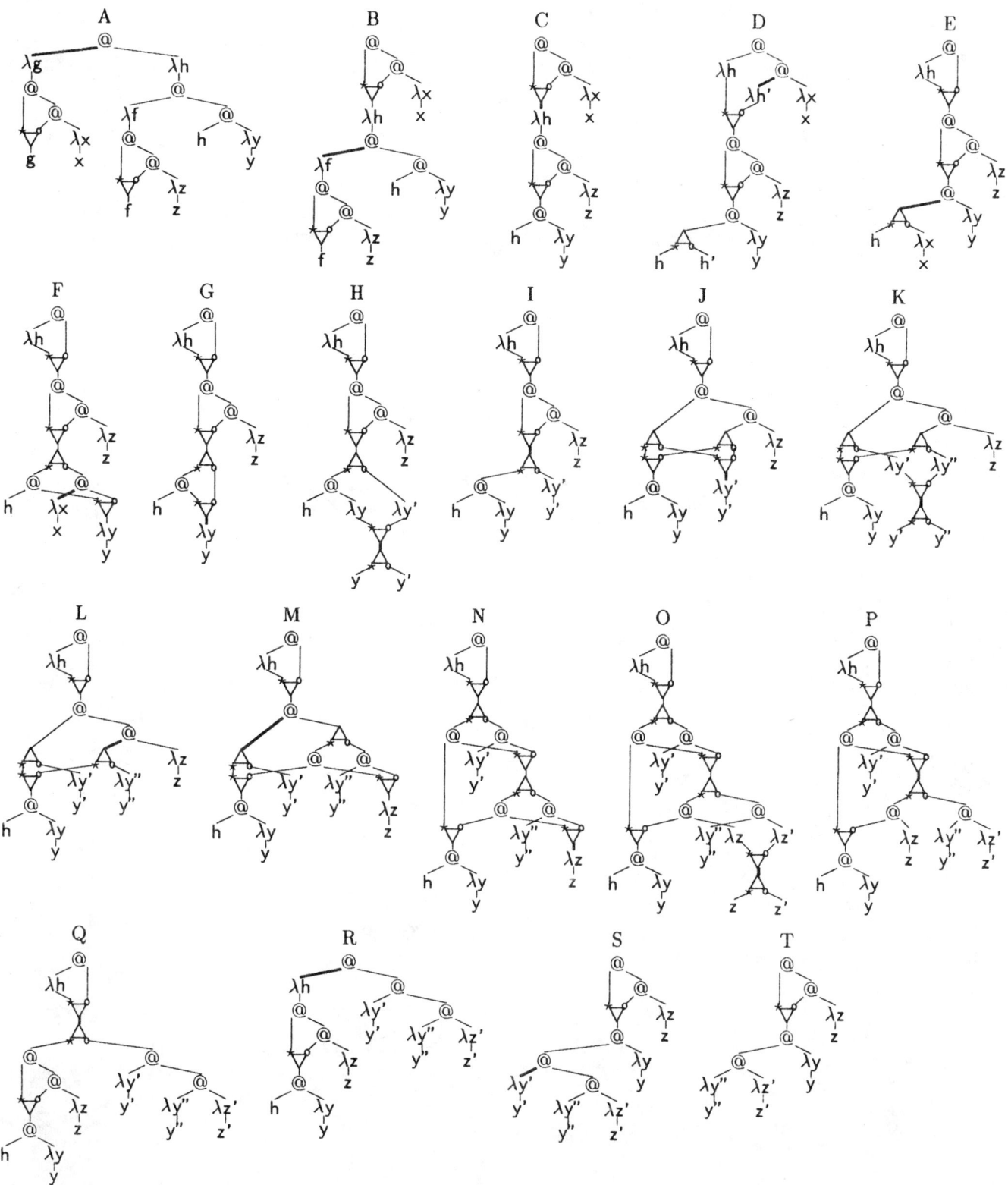

Figure 1: Simplified Execution

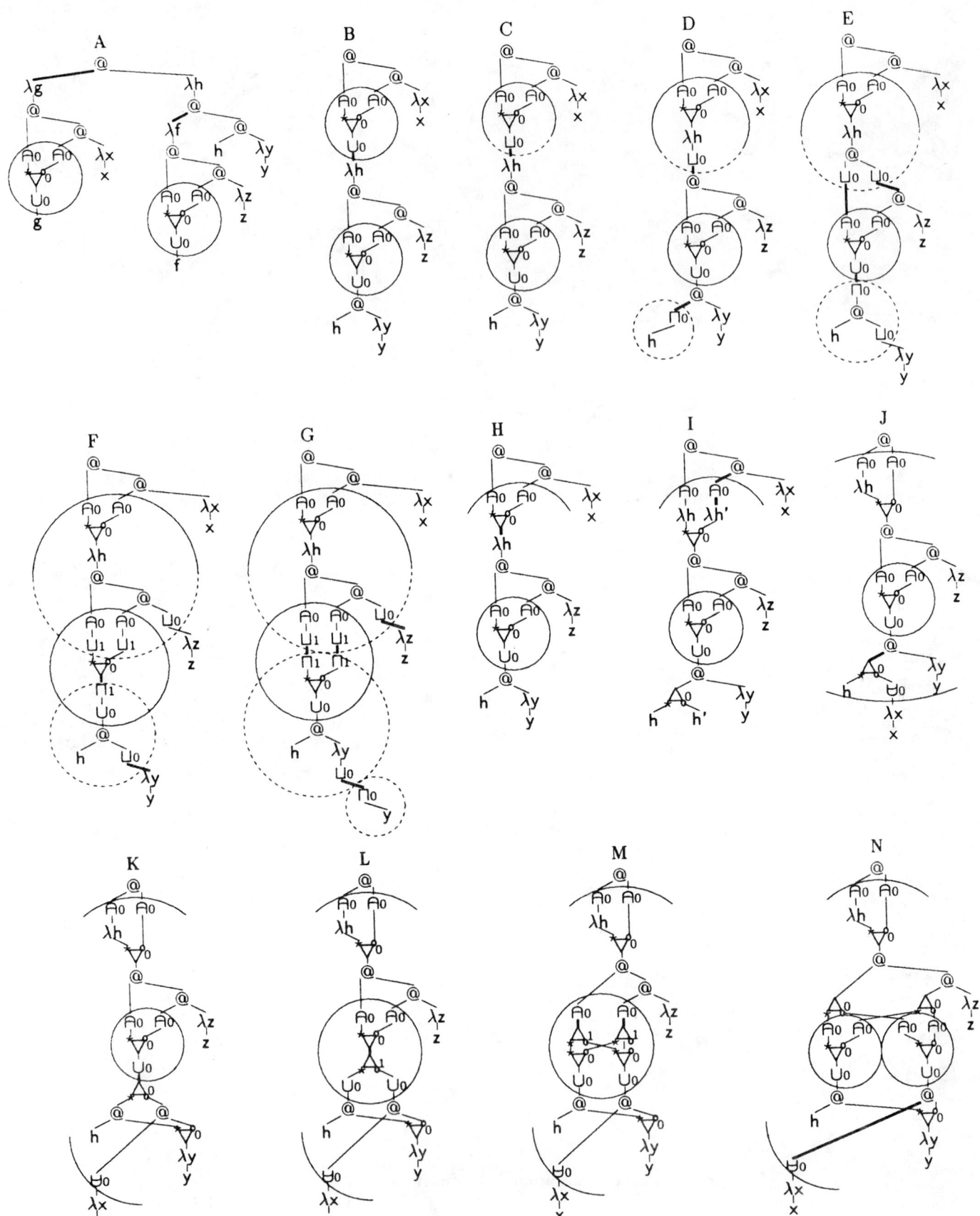

Figure 2: Illustrated Execution

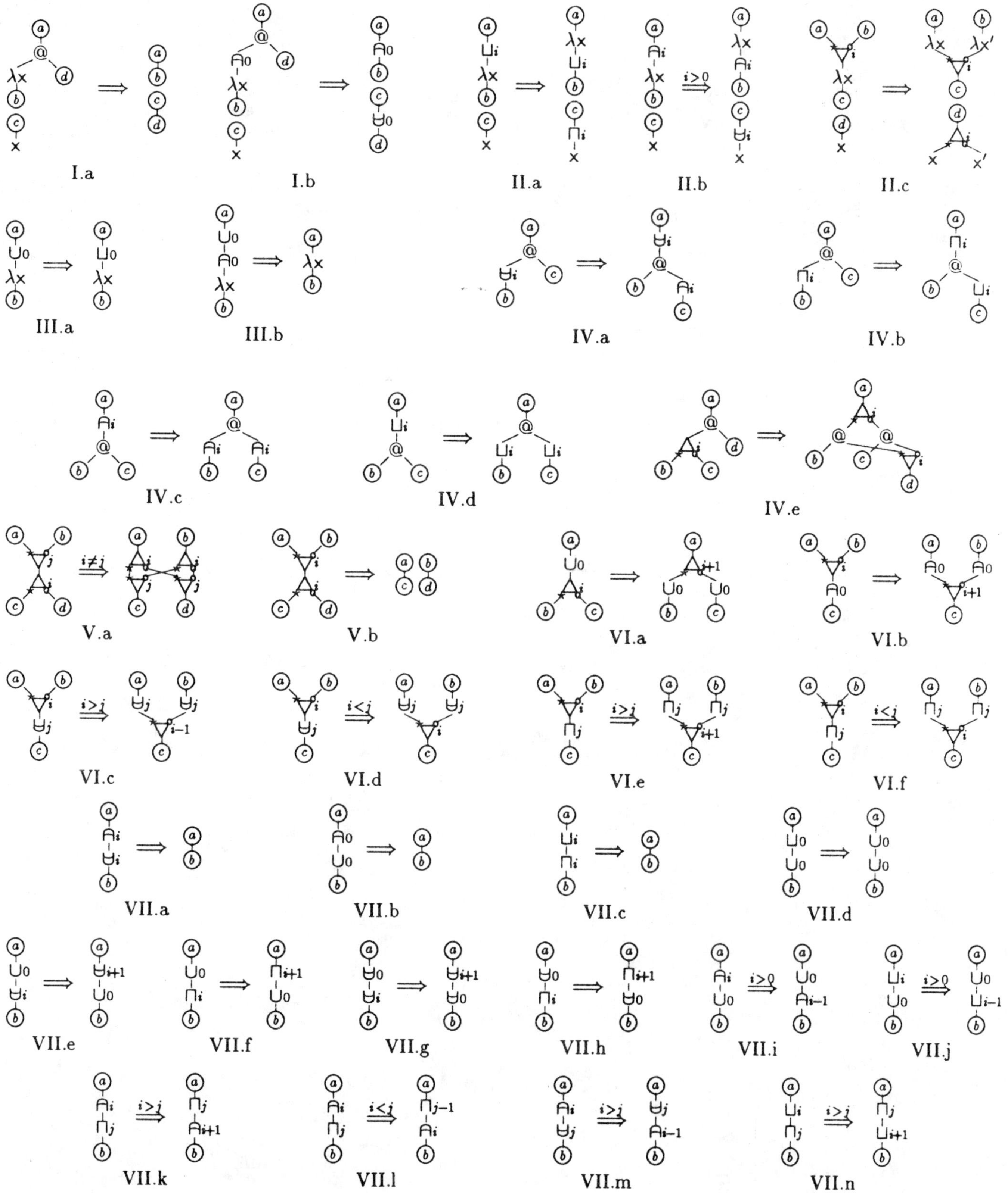

Figure 3: Rules

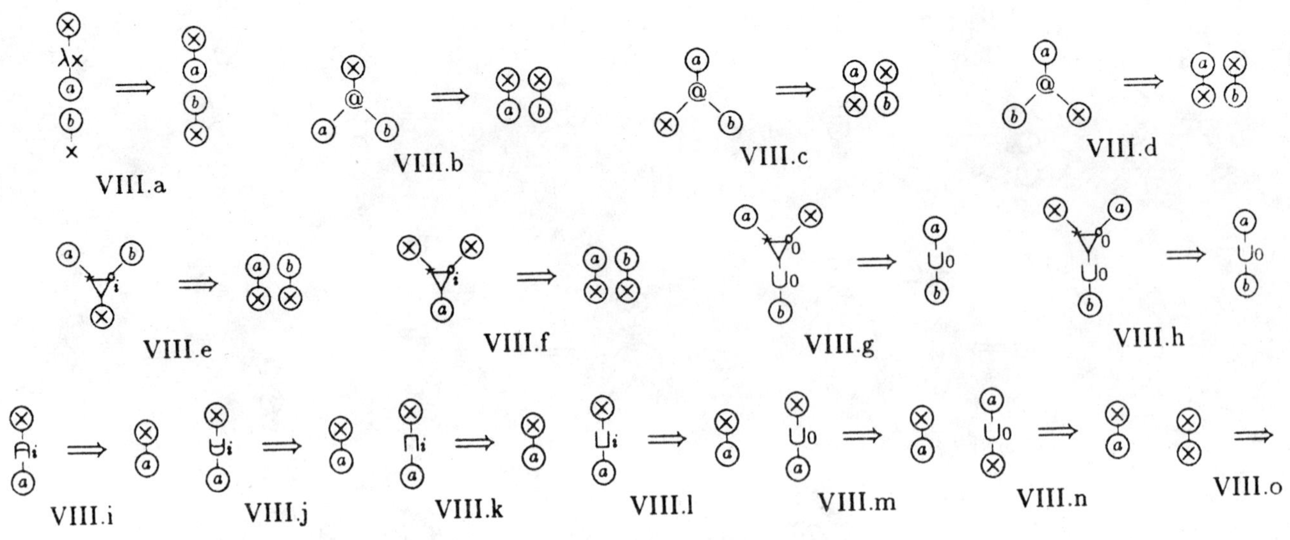

Figure 4: Garbage Collection Rules

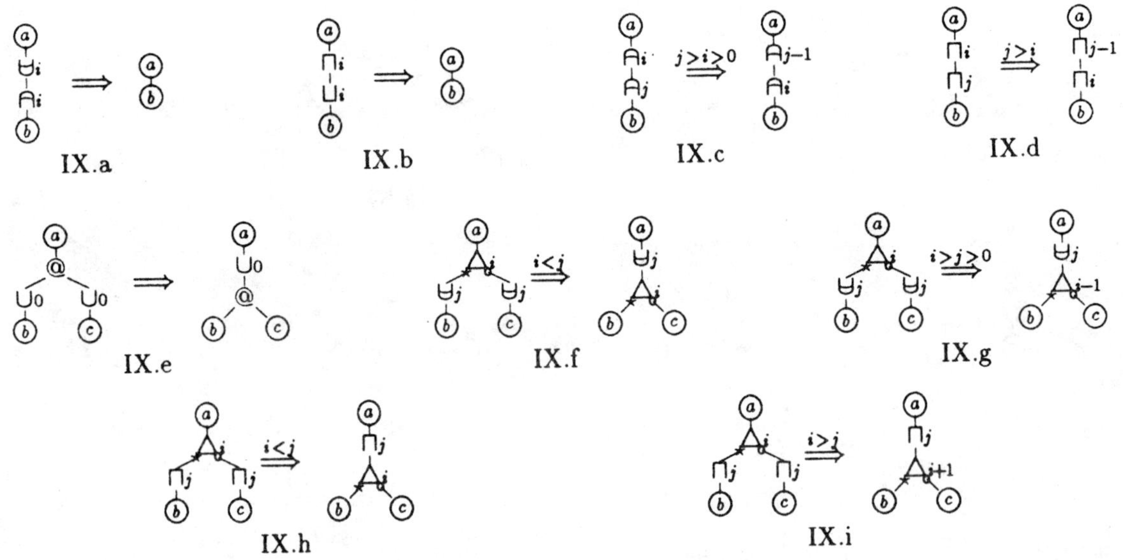

Figure 5: Optimization Rules

Explicit Substitutions

M. Abadi*   L. Cardelli*   P.-L. Curien†   J.-J. Lévy‡

Abstract

The $\lambda\sigma$-calculus is a refinement of the λ-calculus where substitutions are manipulated explicitly. The $\lambda\sigma$-calculus provides a setting for studying the theory of substitutions, with pleasant mathematical properties. It is also a useful bridge between the classical λ-calculus and concrete implementations.

1 Introduction

Substitution is the *éminence grise* of the λ-calculus. The classical β rule,

$$(\lambda x.a)b \to_\beta a\{b/x\}$$

uses substitution crucially though informally. Here a and b denote two terms, and $a\{b/x\}$ represents a where all free occurrences of x are replaced with b. This substitution does not belong in the calculus proper, but rather in an informal meta-level. Similar situations arise in dealing with all binding constructs, from universal quantifiers to type abstractions.

A naive reading of the β rule suggests that the substitution of b for x should happen at once, when the rule is applied. In implementations, substitutions invariably happen in a more controlled way. This is due to practical considerations, relevant in the implementation of both logics and programming languages. The term $a\{b/x\}$ may contain many copies of b (for instance, if $a = xxxx$); without sophisticated structure-sharing mechanisms [13], performing substitutions immediately causes a size explosion.

Therefore, in practice, substitutions are delayed and explicitly recorded; the application of substitutions is independent, and not coupled with the β rule.

---

*Digital Equipment Corporation, Systems Research Center.
†Ecole Normale Supérieure; part of this work was completed while at Digital Equipment Corporation.
‡INRIA Rocquencourt; part of this work was completed while at Digital Equipment Corporation.

Permission to copy without fee all or part of this material is granted provided that the copies are not made or distributed for direct commercial advantage, the ACM copyright notice and the title of the publication and its date appear, and notice is given that copying is by permission of the Association for Computing Machinery. To copy otherwise, or to republish, requires a fee and/or specific permission.

© 1990 ACM 089791-343-4/90/0001/0031 $1.50

The correspondence between the theory and its implementations becomes highly nontrivial, and the correctness of the implementations can be compromised.

In this paper we study the $\lambda\sigma$-calculus, a refinement of the λ-calculus [1] where substitutions are manipulated explicitly. Substitutions have syntactic representations, and if a is a term and s is a substitution then the term $a[s]$ represents a with the substitution s. We can now express a β rule with delayed substitution, called *Beta*:

$$(\lambda x.a)b \to_{Beta} a[(b/x) \cdot id]$$

where $(b/x) \cdot id$ is syntax for the substitution that replaces x with b and affects no other variable ("$\cdot$" represents extension and id the identity substitution). Of course, additional rules are needed to distribute the substitution later on.

The $\lambda\sigma$-calculus is a suitable setting for studying the theory of substitutions, where we can express and prove desirable mathematical properties. For example, the calculus is Church-Rosser and it is a conservative extension of the λ-calculus. Moreover, the $\lambda\sigma$-calculus is strongly connected with the categorical understanding of the λ-calculus, where a substitution is interpreted as a composition [5].

We propose the $\lambda\sigma$-calculus as a step in closing the gap between the classical λ-calculus and concrete implementations. The calculus is a vehicle in designing, understanding, verifying, and comparing implementations of the λ-calculus, from interpreters to machines. Other applications are in the analysis of typechecking algorithms for higher-order languages and in the mechanization of logical systems.

When one considers weak reduction strategies, the treatment of substitutions can remain quite simple—and then our approach may seem overly general. Weak reduction strategies do not compute in the scope of λ's. Then, there arise no nested substitutions or substitutions in the scope of λ's. All substitutions are at the top level, as simple environments. An ancestor of the $\lambda\sigma$-calculus, the $\lambda\rho$-calculus, suffices in this setting [5].

However, strong reduction strategies are useful in general, both in logics and in typechecking higher-order programming languages. In fact, strong reduction strategies are useful in all situations where symbolic matching has to be conducted in the scope of binders. Thus, a general treatment of substitutions is required, where substitutions may occur at the top level and deep inside terms.

In some respects, the $\lambda\sigma$-calculus resembles the calculi of combinators, particularly those of categorical combinators [4]. The $\lambda\sigma$-calculus and the combinator calculi all give full formal accounts of the process of computation, without suffering from unpleasant complications in the (informal) handling of variables. They all make it easy to derive machines for the λ-calculus and to show the correctness of these machines. From our perspective, the advantage of the $\lambda\sigma$-calculus over combinator calculi is that it remains closer to the original λ-calculus.

There are actually several versions of the calculus of substitutions. We start out by discussing an untyped calculus. The main value of the untyped calculus is for studying evaluation methods. We give reduction rules that extend those of the classical λ-calculus and investigate their confluence. We concentrate on a presentation that relies on De Bruijn's numbering for variables [2], and briefly discuss presentations with more traditional variable names.

Then we proceed to consider typed calculi of substitutions, in De Bruijn notation. We discuss typing rules for a first-order system and for a higher-order system; we prove some of their central properties. The typing rules are meant to serve in designing typechecking algorithms. In particular, their study has been of help for both soundness and efficiency in the design of the Quest typechecking algorithm [3].

We postpone discussion of the untyped calculi to section 3 and of the typed calculi to sections 4 and 5. We now proceed with a gentle technical overview.

2 Informal overview

We start with a review of De Bruijn notation, and then preview untyped, first-order, and second-order calculi of substitutions.

2.1 De Bruijn notation

In De Bruijn notation, variable occurrences are replaced with positive integers (called De Bruijn indices); binding occurrences of variables become unnecessary. The positive integer n refers to the variable bound by the n-th surrounding λ binder, for example:

$$\lambda x.\lambda y.xy \quad \text{becomes} \quad \lambda\lambda 21$$

In first-order typed systems, the binder types must be preserved, for example:

$$\lambda x{:}A.\lambda y{:}B.xy \quad \text{becomes} \quad \lambda A.\lambda B.21$$

In second-order systems, type variables too are replaced with De Bruijn indices:

$$\Lambda A.\lambda x{:}A.x \quad \text{becomes} \quad \Lambda\lambda 1.1$$

De Bruijn notation is unreadable, but it leads to simple formal systems. Hence we use indices in inference rules, but variable names in examples.

Classical β reduction and substitution must be adapted for De Bruijn notation. In order to reduce $(\lambda a)b$, it does not suffice to substitute b into a in the appropriate places. If there are occurrences of 2, 3, 4, ... in a, these become "one off," since one of the λ binders surrounding a has been removed. Hence, all the remaining free indices in a must be decremented; the desired effect is obtained with an infinite substitution: the β rule becomes

$$(\lambda a)b \to_\beta a\{b/1, 1/2, 2/3, \ldots\}$$

When pushing this substitution inside a, we may come across a λ term $(\lambda c)\{b/1, 1/2, 2/3, \ldots\}$. In this case, we must be careful to avoid replacing the occurrences of 1 in c with b, since these occurrences correspond to a bound variable and the substitution should not affect them. Hence we must "shift" the substitution. In addition, we must "lift" all the indices of b in order to prevent captures. We obtain $\lambda c\{1/1, b\{2/1, 3/2, \ldots\}/2, 2/3, \ldots\}$.

This informal introduction to De Bruijn notation should suffice to give the flavor of things to come.

2.2 An untyped calculus

We shall study a simple set of algebraic operators that perform all these index manipulations—without $\ldots$'s, even though we treat infinite substitutions that replace all indexes. If s represents the infinite substitution $\{a_1/1, a_2/2, a_3/3, \ldots\}$, we write $a[s]$ for a with the substitution s. A term of the form $a[s]$ is called a *closure*. The change from $\{\}$'s to $[]$'s emphasizes that the substitution is no longer a meta-level operation.

The syntax of the untyped $\lambda\sigma$-calculus is:

Terms $\quad a ::= 1 \mid ab \mid \lambda a \mid a[s]$
Substitutions $\quad s ::= id \mid \uparrow \mid a \cdot s \mid s \circ t$

This syntax of substitutions corresponds to the index manipulations described in the previous section:

- id is the identity substitution $\{i/i\}$ (for all i).

- $\uparrow$ (shift) is the substitution $\{(i+1)/i\}$; for example, $1[\uparrow] = 2$. Thus, we need only the index 1; n+1 is coded as $1[\uparrow^n]$, where $\uparrow^n$ is the composition of n shifts, $\uparrow \circ \ldots \circ \uparrow$. We also write $\uparrow^0$ for id.

- $i[s]$ is the value of the De Bruijn index i in the substitution s, also written $s(i)$ when s is viewed as a function.

- $a \cdot s$ (the cons of a onto s) is the substitution $\{a/1, s(i)/(i+1)\}$; for example,
$$a \cdot id = \{a/1, 1/2, 2/3, \ldots\}$$
$$1 \cdot \uparrow = \{1/1, \uparrow(1)/2, \uparrow(2)/3, \ldots\} = id$$

- $s \circ t$ (the composition of s and t) is the substitution such that $a[s \circ t] = a[s][t]$, hence $s \circ t = \{s(i)/i\} \circ t = \{s(i)[t]/i\}$ and, for example,
$$id \circ t = \{id(i)[t]/i\} = \{t(i)/i\} = t$$
$$\uparrow \circ (a \cdot s) = \{\uparrow(i)[a \cdot s]/i\} = \{s(i)/i\} = s$$

At this point, we have shown most of the algebraic properties of the substitution operations. In addition, composition is associative and distributes over cons (that is, $(a \cdot s) \circ t = a[s] \cdot (s \circ t)$). Moreover, the last example above indicates that $\uparrow \circ s$ is the "rest" of s, without the first component of s; thus, $1[s] \cdot (\uparrow \circ s) = s$.

Using this notation, we can write the *Beta* rule as

$$(\lambda a)b \rightarrow_{Beta} a[b \cdot id]$$

To complement this rule, we can write rules to evaluate 1, for instance

$$1[c \cdot s] \rightarrow c$$

and rules to push substitution inwards, for instance

$$(cd)[s] \rightarrow (c[s])(d[s])$$

In particular, we can derive an intriguing law for the distribution of substitution over λ:

$$(\lambda c)[s] \rightarrow \lambda(c[1 \cdot (s \circ \uparrow)])$$

This law uses all the operators (except id), and suggests that this choice of operators is natural, perhaps inevitable. In fact, there are many possible variations, but we shall not discuss them here.

Explicit substitutions complicate the structure of bindings somewhat. For example, consider the term $(\lambda(1[2 \cdot id]))[a \cdot id]$. We may be tempted to think that 1 is bound by λ, as it would be in a standard De Bruijn reading. However, the substitution $[2 \cdot id]$ intercepts the index, giving the value 2 to 1. Then, after crossing over λ, the index 2 is renamed to 1 and receives the value a. One should keep these complications in mind in examining $\lambda\sigma$ formulas—for example, in deciding whether a formula is closed, in the usual sense.

2.3 A first-order calculus

When we move to a typed calculus, we introduce types both in terms and in substitutions. We assume a set of constant types K. The syntax becomes:

Types	$A ::= K \mid A \rightarrow B$
Environments	$E ::= nil \mid A, E$
Terms	$a ::= 1 \mid ab \mid \lambda A.a \mid a[s]$
Substitutions	$s ::= id \mid \uparrow \mid a{:}A \cdot s \mid s \circ t$

The environments are used in the type inference rules, as is commonly done, to record the types of the free variables of terms. Naturally, in this setting, environments are indexed by De Bruijn indices. The environment $A_1, A_2, \ldots, A_n, nil$ associates type A_i with index i. For example, the axiom for 1 and the rule for λ abstraction are:

$$A, E \vdash 1 : A$$

$$\frac{A, E \vdash b : B}{E \vdash \lambda A.b : A \rightarrow B}$$

In the first-order $\lambda\sigma$-calculus, environments also serve as the "types" of substitutions. We write $s \therefore E$ to say that the substitution s "has" the environment E. For example, the typing rule for cons is:

$$\frac{E \vdash a : A \quad E \vdash s \therefore E'}{E \vdash a{:}A \cdot s \therefore A, E'}$$

The main use of this new notion is in typing closures. Since s provides the context in which a should be understood, the approach is to compute the environment E' of s, and then type a in that environment:

$$\frac{E \vdash s \therefore E' \quad E' \vdash a : A}{E \vdash a[s] : A}$$

2.4 A second-order calculus

When we move to a second-order system, new subtleties appear, because substitutions may contain types, and environments may contain place-holders for types; for example, $Bool{::}\mathrm{Ty} \cdot id \therefore \mathrm{Ty}, nil$.

The typing rules become more complex because types may contain type variables, which must be looked up in the appropriate environments (this problem arises in full generality with dependent types [12]). In particular, the typing axiom for 1 shown above becomes the rule:

$$\frac{E \vdash A :: \mathrm{Ty}}{A, E \vdash 1 : A[\uparrow]}$$

The extra shift is required because A is understood in the environment E in the hypothesis, while it is understood in A, E in the conclusion. An alternative (but heavy) solution would be to have separate index sets for ordinary term variables and for type variables, and to manipulate separate term and type environments as well.

Another instance of this phenomenon is in the rule for λ abstraction, given above. Notice that A must have been proved to be a type in the environment E, while B is understood in A, E in the assumption. Then $A \to B$ is understood in E in the conclusion. This means that the indices of B are "one off" in $A \to B$. The rule for application takes this into account; a substitution is applied to B to "unshift" its indices:

$$\frac{E \vdash b : A \to B \quad E \vdash a : A}{E \vdash b(a) : B[a{:}A \cdot id]}$$

The $B[a{:}A \cdot id]$ part is reminiscent of the rule found in calculi for dependent types, and this is the correct technique for the version of such calculi with explicit substitutions. However, since here we do not deal with dependent types, a will never be substituted in B (B will never contain the index 1). The substitution is still needed to shift the other indices in B.

The main difficulty in our second-order calculus arises in typing closures. The approach described for the first order, while still viable, is not sufficient. For example, if not is the usual negation on $Bool$, we certainly want to be able to type

$$(\lambda 1.not(1))[Bool \cdot id]$$

or, in a more familiar notation,

$$Let\ X = Bool\ in\ \lambda x{:}X.not(x)$$

(We interpret Let via a substitution, not via a λ.) Our strategy for the first-order calculus was to type the substitution, obtaining an environment $(X{::}Ty) \cdot id$, and then type $\lambda x{:}X.not(x)$ in $(X{::}Ty) \cdot id$. Unfortunately, to type this term, it does not suffice to know that X is a type; we must know that X is $Bool$. To solve this difficulty, we have rules to push a substitution inside a term and then type the result. As in calculi with dependent types, the tasks of deriving types and applying substitutions are inseparable.

Finally, as discussed below, surprises arise in writing down the precise rules; for example the rule for typing conses has to be modified. Even the form of the judgement $E \vdash s \therefore E'$ must be reconsidered.

Higher-order calculi (possibly with dependent type constructions) are also of theoretical and practical importance. We do not discuss them formally below, however, for we believe that the main complications arise already at the second order.

3 The untyped $\lambda\sigma$-calculus

In this section we present the untyped $\lambda\sigma$-calculus. We propose a basic set of equational axioms for the $\lambda\sigma$-calculus in De Bruijn notation. The equations induce a rewriting system; this rewriting system suffices for the purposes of computation. We show that the rewriting system is confluent, and thus provides a convenient theoretical basis for more deterministic implementations of the $\lambda\sigma$-calculus. We also consider some variants of the axiom system and treatments using variable names.

As in the classical λ-calculus, actual implementations would resort to particular rewriting strategies. We discuss a normal-order strategy for $\lambda\sigma$ evaluation. Then we focus on a more specialized reduction system, still based on normal order, which provides a suitable basis for abstract $\lambda\sigma$ machines. We describe one machine, which extends Krivine's weak reduction machine [11] with strong reduction.

3.1 The basic rewriting system

The syntax of the untyped $\lambda\sigma$-calculus is the one given in the informal overview,

Terms $\quad a ::= \mathbf{1} \mid ab \mid \lambda a \mid a[s]$
Substitutions $\quad s ::= id \mid \uparrow \mid a \cdot s \mid s \circ t$

Notice that we have not included metavariables over the sorts of terms and substitutions—we consider only closed terms, and this suffices for our purposes. (In De Bruijn notation, the variables $1, 2, \ldots$ are constants rather than metavariables.)

In this notation, we now define an equational theory for the $\lambda\sigma$-calculus, by proposing a set of equations as axioms. When they are all oriented from left to right, the equations become rewrite rules and give rise to a rewriting system. The equations fall into two subsets: a singleton $Beta$, the equivalent of the classical β rule, and ten rules for manipulating substitutions, which we call σ collectively.

$Beta \qquad (\lambda a)b = a[b \cdot id]$

$VarId \qquad \mathbf{1}[id] = \mathbf{1}$

$VarCons \qquad \mathbf{1}[a \cdot s] = a$

$App \qquad (ab)[s] = (a[s])(b[s])$

$Abs \qquad (\lambda a)[s] = \lambda(a[\mathbf{1} \cdot (s \circ \uparrow)])$

$Clos \qquad a[s][t] = a[s \circ t]$

$IdL \qquad id \circ s = s$

ShiftId $\uparrow \circ id = \uparrow$

ShiftCons $\uparrow \circ (a \cdot s) = s$

Map $(a \cdot s) \circ t = a[t] \cdot (s \circ t)$

Ass $(s_1 \circ s_2) \circ s_3 = s_1 \circ (s_2 \circ s_3)$

The equational theory follows from these axioms and rules for replacing equals for equals.

Our choice of presentation is guided by the structure of terms and substitutions. The *Beta* rule eliminates λ's and creates substitutions; the function of the other rules is to eliminate substitutions. Two rules deal with the evaluation of **1**. The next three deal with pushing substitutions inwards. The remaining five express substitution computations. We prove below that the substitution rules always produce unique normal forms; we denote by $\sigma(a)$ the σ normal form of a.

The classical β rule is not directly included, but it can be simulated. The crucial fact is that, if $a_1, \ldots, a_n, \ldots$ is a sequence of consecutive integers after some point, then the meta-level substitution $\{a_1/\mathbf{1}, \ldots, a_n/\mathbf{n}, \ldots\}$ corresponds closely to an explicit substitution:

Proposition 3.1 *If there exist $m \geq 0$ and $p \geq 0$ such that $a_{m+q} = \mathbf{p} + \mathbf{q}$ for all $q \geq 1$, then $a\{a_1/\mathbf{1}, \ldots, a_n/\mathbf{n}, \ldots\} = \sigma(a[a_1 \cdot a_2 \cdot \ldots \cdot a_m \cdot \uparrow^p])$.*

Therefore, the simulation of the β rule consists in first applying *Beta* and then σ until a σ normal form is reached.

As usual, we want a confluence theorem. This theorem will guarantee that all rewrite sequences yield identical results, and thus that the strategies used by different implementations are equivalent:

Theorem 3.2 *Beta + σ is confluent.*

The proof does *not* rely on standard rewriting techniques, as *Beta + σ* does not pass the Knuth-Bendix test (but σ does). We come back to this point below.

Instead, the proof relies on the termination and confluence of σ, the confluence of the classical λ-calculus, and Hardin's interpretation technique [7].

First we show that σ is noetherian (that is, σ reductions always terminate) and confluent.

Proposition 3.3 *σ is noetherian and confluent.*

Since σ is noetherian, let us examine the form of σ normal forms. A substitution in normal form is necessarily in the form $a_1 \cdot (a_2 \cdot (\ldots (a_m \cdot U) \ldots))$ where U is either *id* or a composition $\uparrow \circ (\ldots (\uparrow \circ \uparrow) \ldots)$. A term in normal form is entirely free of substitutions, except in subterms such as $\mathbf{1}[\uparrow^n]$, which codes the De Bruijn index **n+1**. Thus, a term in normal form is a classical λ-calculus term (modulo the equivalence of $\mathbf{1}[\uparrow^n]$ and **n+1**).

In summary, the syntax of σ normal forms is:

Terms $a ::= \mathbf{1} \mid \mathbf{1}[\uparrow^n] \mid ab \mid \lambda a$
Substitutions $s ::= id \mid \uparrow^n \mid a \cdot s$

After these remarks on σ, we can apply Hardin's interpretation technique to show that the full $\lambda\sigma$ system is confluent. First, we review Hardin's method. Let X be a set equipped with two relations R and S. Suppose that R is noetherian and confluent, and denote by $R(x)$ the R normal form of x; that S_R is a relation included in $(R \cup S)^*$ on the set of R normal forms; and that, for any x and y in X, if $S(x,y)$ then $S_R^*(R(x), R(y))$. An easy diagram chase yields that if S_R is confluent then so is $(R \cup S)^*$.

In our case, we take R to be the relation induced by σ, that is, $R(x, y)$ holds if x reduces to y with the σ rules. We take S_R to be classical β conversion, that is, $S_R(x, y)$ holds if y is obtained from x by replacing a subterm of the form $(\lambda a)b$ with $\sigma(a[b \cdot id])$.

Thus two lemmas suffice for proving confluence:

Lemma 3.4 *β is confluent on σ normal forms.*

Lemma 3.5 *If $a \rightarrow_{Beta} b$ then $\sigma(a) \rightarrow_\beta^* \sigma(b)$. If $s \rightarrow_{Beta} t$ then $\sigma(s) \rightarrow_\beta^* \sigma(t)$.*

3.2 Variants

Some subsystems of σ are reasonable first steps to deterministic evaluation algorithms. We can restrict σ in three different ways. The rule *Clos* can be removed. The inference rule

$$\frac{s = s' \quad t = t'}{s \circ t = s' \circ t'}$$

can be removed, and the inference rule for the closure operator can be restricted to

$$\frac{s = s'}{\mathbf{1}[s] = \mathbf{1}[s']}$$

These restrictions (even cumulated) do not prevent us from obtaining σ normal forms and confluence, through the interpretation technique.

Confluence properties suggest a second kind of variant. Although *Beta + σ* is confluent, when we view it as a standard rewriting system on first-order terms it is not even locally confluent. The subtle point is that we have proved confluence on closed $\lambda\sigma$ terms, that is, on terms exclusively constructed from the operators of the $\lambda\sigma$-calculus. In contrast, checking critical pairs involves considering open terms over this signature, with metavariables (that is, variables **x** and **u** ranging over terms and substitutions, different from De Bruijn indexes $1, 2, \ldots$).

Consider, for example, the critical pair:

$$((\lambda a)b)[u] \to^* a[b[u] \cdot u]$$
$$((\lambda a)b)[u] \to^* a[b[u] \cdot (u \circ id)]$$

For local confluence, we would want the equation $(s \circ id) = s$, but this equation is not a theorem of σ. Similar critical pair considerations suggest the addition of four new rules:

Id	$a[id] = a$
IdR	$s \circ id = s$
VarShift	$1 \cdot \uparrow = id$
SCons	$1[s] \cdot (\uparrow \circ s) = s$

These additional rules are well justified from a theoretical point of view. However, confluence on closed terms can be established without them, and they are not computationally significant. Moreover some of them are admissible (that is, every closed instance is provable). More precisely Id and IdR are admissible in σ, and $SCons$ is admissible in $\sigma + VarShift$.

We should particularly draw attention to the last rule, $SCons$. It expresses that a substitution is equal to its first element appended in front of the rest. This rule is reminiscent of the surjective-pairing rule, which deserved much attention in the classical λ-calculus. Klop has showed that surjective pairing destroys confluence for the λ-calculus [10].

Similarly, we conjecture that our system is not confluent when we have metavariables for both terms and substitutions. (Local confluence still holds.) The following term, inspired by Klop's counterexample [10], seems to work as a counterexample to confluence:

$$Y(Y(\lambda \lambda \mathbf{x}[1[\mathbf{u} \circ (1 \cdot id)] \cdot (\uparrow \circ (\mathbf{u} \circ ((21) \cdot id)))]))$$

where Y is a fixpoint combinator, **x** is a term metavariable, and **u** is a substitution metavariable.

The reader may wonder what thwarts the techniques used in the last subsection. The point is that in Lemma 3.5, our reduction to the classical substitution lemma depended on the syntax of substitutions in normal form, which is not so simple any more (the syntax allows in particular expressions of the form $\mathbf{u} \circ (1 \cdot id)$, as in the claimed counterexample).

We can go half way in adding metavariables. If we add only term metavariables, the syntax of substitution σ normal forms is unchanged. This protects us from the claimed counterexample. There are two additional cases for term σ normal forms:

Terms $\quad a ::= 1 \mid 1[\uparrow^n] \mid ab \mid \lambda a \mid \mathbf{x} \mid \mathbf{x}[s]$

We believe that confluence can be proved in this case by the interpretation technique. Confluence on normal forms would be obtained through an encoding of the normal forms in the λ-calculus extended with constants, which is known to be confluent (**x** becomes a constant; $\mathbf{x}[s]$ becomes a constant applied to the elements of s).

3.3 The $\lambda\sigma$-calculus with names

Let us discuss a more traditional formulation of the calculus, with variable names $x, y, z, \ldots$, as a small digression. Two ways seem viable.

In one approach, we consider the syntax:

Terms $\quad a ::= x \mid ab \mid \lambda x.a \mid a[s]$
Substitutions $\quad s ::= id \mid (a/x) \cdot s \mid s \circ t$

The corresponding theory includes axioms such as:

Beta	$(\lambda x.a)b = a[(b/x) \cdot id]$
Var1	$x[(a/x) \cdot s] = a$
Var2	$x[(a/y) \cdot s] = x[s] \quad (x \neq y)$
Var3	$x[id] = x$
Abs	$(\lambda x.a)[s] = \lambda y.(a[(y/x) \cdot s])$
	(y occurs in neither a nor s)

The rules correspond closely to the basic ones presented in De Bruijn notation. The Abs rule does not require a shift operator, but involves a condition on variable occurrences. (The side condition could be weakened.) The consideration of the critical pairs generated by the previous rules immediately suggests new rules, for example:

$$(a/x) \cdot ((b/y) \cdot s) = (b/y) \cdot ((a/x) \cdot s) \quad (x \neq y)$$

These are unpleasant rules. The given rule destroys the existence of substitution normal forms. Intuitively, we may take this as a hint that this calculus with names does not really enjoy nice confluence features. In this respect, the calculus in De Bruijn notation seems preferable.

There is an alternative solution, with the shift operator. The syntax is now:

Terms $\quad a ::= x \mid ab \mid \lambda x.a \mid a[s]$
Substitutions $\quad s ::= id \mid \uparrow \mid (a/x) \cdot s \mid s \circ t$

In this notation, intuitively, $x[\uparrow]$ refers to x after the first binder. The equations are the ones of the $\lambda\sigma$-calculus in De Bruijn notation except for:

Beta	$(\lambda x.a)b = a[(b/x) \cdot id]$
Var1	$x[(a/x) \cdot s] = a$
Var2	$x[(a/y) \cdot s] = x[s] \quad (x \neq y)$
Var3	$x[id] = x$
Abs	$(\lambda x.a)[s] = \lambda x.(a[(x/x) \cdot (s \circ \uparrow)])$

This framework may be useful for showing the differences between dynamic and lexical scopes in programming languages. The rules here correspond to lexical binding, but dynamic binding is obtained by erasing the shift operator in rule *Abs*.

3.4 A normal-order strategy

As usual, we want a complete rewriting strategy—a deterministic method for finding a normal form whenever one exists. Here we study normal-order strategies (the leftmost-outermost redex is chosen at each step). Completeness follows from the completeness of the normal-order strategy for the λ-calculus.

The normal-order algorithm naturally decomposes into two parts: a weak normal-order algorithm, for obtaining weak head normal forms, and recursive calls on this algorithm. In our setting, weak head normal forms are defined as follows:

Definition 3.6 *A weak head normal form (whnf for short) is a $\lambda\sigma$ term of the form λa or $\mathbf{n}a_1 \cdots a_m$.*

We write $\xrightarrow{n}_\beta$ for the usual (one step) weak normal-order β reduction in the λ-calculus, and write $\xrightarrow{n}$ for the (one step) weak normal-order $Beta + \sigma$ reduction in the $\lambda\sigma$-calculus. Clearly, $\xrightarrow{n}_\beta$ and $\xrightarrow{n}$ are related:

Proposition 3.7 *If $a \xrightarrow{n} b$ then either $\sigma(a) \xrightarrow{n}_\beta \sigma(b)$ or $\sigma(a)$ and $\sigma(b)$ are identical. The $\xrightarrow{n}$ reduction of a terminates (with a weak head normal form) iff the $\xrightarrow{n}_\beta$ reduction of $\sigma(a)$ terminates.*

Corollary 3.8 $\xrightarrow{n}$ *is a complete strategy.*

We can also define a system $\xrightarrow{wn}$, which incorporates some slight optimizations (present also in our abstract machine, below). In $\xrightarrow{wn}$, the rule

$$((\lambda a)[s])b \xrightarrow{wn} a[b \cdot s]$$

replaces the rules

$$(\lambda a)b \xrightarrow{n} a[b \cdot id]$$

$$(\lambda a)[s] \xrightarrow{n} \lambda(a[1 \cdot (s \circ \uparrow)])$$

The new rule is an optimization justified by the σ reduction steps

$$((\lambda a)[s])b \xrightarrow{n\,*} a[(1 \cdot (s \circ \uparrow)) \circ (b \cdot id)] \rightarrow^* a[b \cdot s]$$

which is not allowed in $\xrightarrow{n}$.

Both $\xrightarrow{n}$ and $\xrightarrow{wn}$ are weak in the sense that they do not reduce under λ's. In addition, $\xrightarrow{wn}$ is also weak in the sense that substitutions are not pushed under λ's. In this respect, $\xrightarrow{wn}$ models environment machines—while $\xrightarrow{n}$ is closer to combinator reduction machines.

We do not exactly get weak head normal forms—for instance, $\xrightarrow{wn}$ does not reduce even $(\lambda 11)(\lambda 11)$ or $(1[(\lambda 11) \cdot id])(\lambda 11)$. This motivates a syntactic restriction which entails no loss of generality: we start with closures, and all conses have the form $a[s] \cdot t$. Under this restriction, we cannot start with $(\lambda 11)(\lambda 11)$, but instead have to write $((\lambda 11)(\lambda 11))[id]$, which has the expected, nonterminating behavior. We obtain:

Proposition 3.9 *If $a \xrightarrow{wn} b$ then either $\sigma(a)$ and $\sigma(b)$ are identical or $\sigma(a) \xrightarrow{n}_\beta \sigma(b)$. The $\xrightarrow{wn}$ reduction terminates (with a term of the form $(\lambda a)[s]$ or $\mathbf{n}a_1 \ldots a_m$) iff the $\xrightarrow{n}_\beta$ reduction of $\sigma(a)$ terminates.*

3.5 Towards an implementation

As a further refinement, we adapt $\xrightarrow{wn}$, to manipulate only expressions of the forms $a[t]$ and $s \circ t$. The substitution t corresponds to the "global environment," whereas substitutions deeper in a or s correspond to "local declarations." In defining our machine, we take the view that the linear representation of a can be read as a sequence of machine instructions acting on the graph representation of t.

In this approach, some of the original rules are no longer acceptable, since they do not yield expressions of the desired forms. For example, the reduct of the *App* rule, $(a[s])(b[s])$, is not a closure. In order to reduce $(ab)[s]$, we have to reduce $a[s]$ to a weak head normal form first. In the machine discussed below, we use a stack for storing $b[s]$.

The following reducer $whnf()$ embodies these modifications to $\xrightarrow{wn}$. The reducer takes a pair of arguments, the term a and the substitution s of a closure, and returns another pair, of one of the forms $(\mathbf{n}a_1 \cdots a_m, id)$ and $(\lambda a', s')$. To compute $whnf()$, the following axioms and rules should be applied, in the order of their listing. We proceed by cases on the structure of a, and when a is $\mathbf{n}$ by cases on the structure of s, and when s is a composition $t \circ t'$ by cases on the structure of t.

$$whnf(\lambda a, s) = (\lambda a, s)$$

$$\frac{whnf(a,s) = (\lambda a', s')}{whnf(ab,s) = whnf(a', b[s] \cdot s')}$$

$$\frac{whnf(a,s) = (a', id) \quad (a' \text{ not an abstraction})}{whnf(ab,s) = (a'(b[s]), id)}$$

$$whnf(\mathbf{n}, id) = (\mathbf{n}, id)$$

$$whnf(\mathbf{n}, \uparrow) = (\mathbf{n+1}, id)$$

$$whnf(\mathbf{1}, a[s] \cdot t) = whnf(a, s)$$

$$whnf(\mathbf{n+1}, a \cdot s) = whnf(\mathbf{n}, s)$$

$$whnf(\mathbf{n}, s \circ s') = whnf(\mathbf{n}[s], s')$$

$$whnf(\mathbf{n}[id], s) = whnf(\mathbf{n}, s)$$

$$whnf(\mathbf{n}[\uparrow], s) = whnf(\mathbf{n+1}, s)$$

$$whnf(\mathbf{1}[a \cdot s], s') = whnf(a, s')$$

$$whnf(\mathbf{n+1}[a \cdot s], s') = whnf(\mathbf{n}[s], s')$$

$$whnf(\mathbf{n}[s \circ s'], s'') = whnf(\mathbf{n}[s], s' \circ s'')$$

$$whnf(a[s], s') = whnf(a, s \circ s')$$

A simple extension of the rules yields normal forms:

$$\frac{whnf(a, s) = (\lambda a', t)}{nf(a, s) = \lambda(nf(a', \mathbf{1} \cdot (t \circ \uparrow)))}$$

$$\frac{whnf(a, s) = (\mathbf{n}(a_1[s_1]) \ldots (a_m[s_m]), id)}{nf(a, s) = \mathbf{n}(nf(a_1, s_1)) \ldots (nf(a_m, s_m))}$$

The precise soundness property of $whnf()$ is:

Proposition 3.10 *Given a and s, $whnf(a,s) = (a', s')$ is provable if and only if $\sigma(a'[s'])$ is the weak head normal form of $\sigma(a[s])$.*

The last step we consider is the derivation of a transition machine from the rules for $whnf()$. One basic idea is to implement the recursive call on $a[s]$ during the evaluation of $(ab)[s]$ by using a stack to store the argument $b[s]$. Thus, the stack contains closures.

The following table represents an extension of Krivine's abstract machine [11, 5]. The first column represents the "current state," the second one represents the "next state." Each line has to be read as a transition from a triplet (Subst, Term, Stack) to a triplet of the same nature. To evaluate a program a in the global environment s, the machine is started in state $(s, a, \langle \rangle)$, where $\langle \rangle$ is the empty stack. The machine repeatedly uses the first applicable rule. The machine stops when no transition is applicable any more. These termination states have one of the forms $(id, \mathbf{n}, a_1 \cdot \ldots \cdot a_m)$ and $(s, \lambda a, \langle \rangle)$, which represent $\mathbf{n} a_1 \cdots a_m$ and $(\lambda a)[s]$, respectively.

The machine can be restarted when it stops, and then we have a full normal form λ reducer.

Subst	Term	Stack	Subst	Term	Stack
$\uparrow$	$\mathbf{n}$	S	id	$\mathbf{n+1}$	S
$a[s] \cdot t$	$\mathbf{1}$	S	s	a	S
$a \cdot s$	$\mathbf{n+1}$	S	s	$\mathbf{n}$	S
$s \circ s'$	$\mathbf{n}$	S	s'	$\mathbf{n}[s]$	S
s	ab	S	s	a	$b[s] \cdot S$
s	λa	$b \cdot S$	$b \cdot s$	a	S
s	$\mathbf{n}[id]$	S	s	$\mathbf{n}$	S
s	$\mathbf{n}[\uparrow]$	S	s	$\mathbf{n+1}$	S
s'	$\mathbf{1}[a \cdot s]$	S	s'	a	S
s'	$\mathbf{n+1}[a \cdot s]$	S	s'	$\mathbf{n}[s]$	S
s''	$\mathbf{n}[s \circ s']$	S	$s' \circ s''$	$\mathbf{n}[s]$	S
s'	$a[s]$	S	$s \circ s'$	a	S

Specifically, when the machine terminates with the triplet $(s, \lambda a, \langle \rangle)$, we restart it in the initial state $(\mathbf{1} \cdot (s \circ \uparrow), a, \langle \rangle)$, and when the machine terminates with the triplet $(id, \mathbf{n}, a_1[s_1] \cdot \ldots \cdot a_n[s_n] \cdot \langle \rangle)$, we restart n copies of the machine in the states $(s_1, a_1, \langle \rangle), \ldots, (s_n, a_n, \langle \rangle)$.

The machine is correct:

Proposition 3.11 *Starting in the state $(s, a, \langle \rangle)$, the machine terminates in $(id, \mathbf{n}, a_1 \cdot \ldots \cdot a_m)$ iff $whnf(a, s) = (\mathbf{n} a_1 \ldots a_m, id)$, and it terminates in $(s, \lambda a, \langle \rangle)$ iff $whnf(a, s) = (\lambda a, s)$.*

By now, we are far away from the wildly nondeterministic basic rewriting system of Section 3.1. However, through the derivations, we have managed to keep some understanding of the successive refinements and to guarantee their correctness. In great part, this has been possible because the $\lambda\sigma$-calculus is more concrete than the λ-calculus, and hence an easier starting point.

4 First-order theories

In the previous section, we have seen how to derive a machine that can be used as a sensible implementation of the untyped $\lambda\sigma$-calculus, and in turn of the untyped λ-calculus. Different implementation issues arise in typed systems. For typed calculi, we need not just an execution machine, but also a typechecker. As will become apparent when we discuss second-order systems, explicit substitutions can also help in deriving typecheckers. Thus, we want a typechecker for the $\lambda\sigma$-calculus.

At the first order, the typechecker does not present much difficulty. In addition to the usual rules for a classical system L1, we must handle the typechecking of substitutions. Inspection of the rules of L1 shows that this can be done easily, since the rules are deterministic.

In this section we describe the first-order typed $\lambda\sigma$-calculus. We prove that it preserves types under reductions, and that it is sound with respect to the λ-calculus. We move on to the second-order calculus in the next section. We start by recalling the syntax and the type rules of the first-order λ-calculus with De Bruijn's notation.

Types	$A ::= K \mid A \to B$
Environments	$E ::= nil \mid A, E$
Terms	$a ::= \mathbf{n} \mid \lambda A.a \mid ab$

Definition 4.1 (Theory L1)

(L1-var) $\qquad A, E \vdash \mathbf{1} : A$

(L1-varn) $\qquad \dfrac{E \vdash \mathbf{n} : B}{A, E \vdash \mathbf{n+1} : B}$

(L1-lambda) $\qquad \dfrac{A, E \vdash b : B}{E \vdash \lambda A.b : A \to B}$

(L1-app) $\qquad \dfrac{E \vdash b : A \to B \quad E \vdash a : A}{E \vdash ba : B}$

We do not include the β rule, because we now focus on typechecking—rather than on evaluation.

The first-order $\lambda\sigma$-calculus has the syntax:

Types	$A ::= K \mid A \to B$
Environments	$E ::= nil \mid A, E$
Terms	$a ::= \mathbf{1} \mid ab \mid \lambda A.a \mid a[s]$
Substitutions	$s ::= id \mid \uparrow \mid a{:}A \cdot s \mid s \circ t$

The type rules come in two groups, one for giving types to terms, and one for giving environments to substitutions. The two groups interact through the rule for closures.

Definition 4.2 (Theory S1)

(S1-var) $\qquad A, E \vdash \mathbf{1} : A$

(S1-lambda) $\qquad \dfrac{A, E \vdash b : B}{E \vdash \lambda A.b : A \to B}$

(S1-app) $\qquad \dfrac{E \vdash b : A \to B \quad E \vdash a : A}{E \vdash ba : B}$

(S1-clos) $\qquad \dfrac{E \vdash s \therefore E' \quad E' \vdash a : A}{E \vdash a[s] : A}$

(S1-id) $\qquad E \vdash id \therefore E$

(S1-shift) $\qquad A, E \vdash \uparrow \therefore E$

(S1-cons) $\qquad \dfrac{E \vdash a : A \quad E \vdash s \therefore E'}{E \vdash a{:}A \cdot s \therefore A, E'}$

(S1-comp) $\qquad \dfrac{E \vdash s'' \therefore E'' \quad E'' \vdash s' \therefore E'}{E \vdash s' \circ s'' \therefore E'}$

In S1, we include neither the *Beta* nor the σ axioms.

Clearly, typechecking is decidable in S1. We proceed to show that S1 is sound. As a preliminary, we prove two lemmas. The first lemma relies on the notion of σ normal form, which was defined in the previous section. We use a modified version of the σ rules for typed terms; four of the rules change.

VarCons $\quad \mathbf{1}[a{:}A \cdot s] = a$

Abs $\quad (\lambda A.a)[s] = \lambda A.(a[\mathbf{1}{:}A \cdot (s \circ \uparrow)])$

ShiftCons $\quad \uparrow \circ (a{:}A \cdot s) = s$

Map $\quad (a{:}A \cdot s) \circ t = a[t]{:}A \cdot (s \circ t)$

The typed version of σ enjoys the properties of the untyped version.

A term in σ normal form is typeable in S1 iff it is typeable in L1, and σ reduction $\to_\sigma$ preserve typings:

Lemma 4.3 *For all a in σ normal form, $E \vdash_{S1} a{:}A$ iff $E \vdash_{L1} a{:}A$.*

Lemma 4.4 (Subject reduction) *If $a \to_\sigma a'$ and $E \vdash_{S1} a{:}A$, then $E \vdash_{S1} a'{:}A$. Similarly, if $s \to_\sigma s'$ and $E' \vdash_{S1} s \therefore E''$, then $E' \vdash_{S1} s' \therefore E''$.*

Together, the two lemmas give us soundness:

Proposition 4.5 (Soundness) *If $E \vdash_{S1} a{:}A$ then $E \vdash_{L1} \sigma(a){:}A$.*

One may wonder whether a completeness result holds, as a converse to our soundness result. Unfortunately, the answer is no. For instance, if L1 gives a type to a but not to b, then S1 cannot give a type to $\mathbf{1}[a \cdot b \cdot id]$, while L1 gives a type to $\sigma(\mathbf{1}[a \cdot b \cdot id])$, that is, to a. However, if L1 gives types to a and b, then S1 gives a type to $\mathbf{1}[a \cdot b \cdot id]$. Conversely, if S1 gives a type to $\mathbf{1}[a \cdot b \cdot id]$, then L1 gives types to a and b.

These observations suggest a reformulation of the soundness and completeness claim. Informally, one would like to show that S1 can give a type to a term iff L1 can give a type to the normal forms of the term and of some subterms that σ normalization discards.

5 Second-order theories

Type rules and typecheckers are also needed for second-order calculi. Unfortunately, the situation is more complex than at the first order, because types include binding constructs (quantifiers). These interact with substitutions in the same subtle ways in which λ interacts with substitutions. (We have no equivalent of β reduction here, but this too reappears in higher-order typed systems.)

In implementing a typechecker (or proofchecker) for the second or higher orders, we face the same concerns of efficient handling of substitution and correctness of implementation that pushed us from the untyped λ-calculus to the untyped $\lambda\sigma$-calculus. It is nice to discover that we can apply the same concept of explicit substitutions to tackle typechecking problems as well.

In order to carry out this plan, we must first obtain a second-order system with explicit substitutions, which already incurs several difficulties. Then we must refine the system, and obtain an actual typechecking algorithm. During this enterprise, we should keep in mind the goal of deriving an algorithm that is correct and close to a sensible implementation by virtue of handling substitutions explicitly.

Second-order theories are considerably more complex than untyped or first-order theories, both in number of rules and in subtlety. The complication is already apparent in the De Bruijn formulation of the ordinary second-order λ-calculus (L2, below). The complication intensifies in the second-order $\lambda\sigma$-calculus (S2) because of unexpected difficulties. (We mentioned some of them in the overview.)

We begin with a description of L2, then we define S2 and prove that it is sound with respect to L2. Unlike L1, L2, and even S1, the new system S2 is not deterministic. Therefore, we also define a second-order typechecking algorithm S2alg, and prove that it is sound with respect to S2.

The syntax and the type rules for the second-order λ-calculus are:

Types $\qquad A ::= \mathbf{n} \mid A \to B \mid \forall A$
Environments $\quad E ::= nil \mid A, E \mid Ty, E$
Terms $\qquad a ::= \mathbf{n} \mid \lambda A.a \mid \Lambda a \mid ab \mid aB$

Definition 5.1 (Theory L2)

(L2-nil) $\qquad \vdash nil \text{ env}$

(L2-ext) $\qquad \dfrac{\vdash E \text{ env} \quad E \vdash A :: Ty}{\vdash A, E \text{ env}}$

(L2-ext2) $\qquad \dfrac{\vdash E \text{ env}}{\vdash Ty, E \text{ env}}$

(L2-tvar) $\qquad \dfrac{\vdash E \text{ env}}{Ty, E \vdash \mathbf{1} :: Ty}$

(L2-tvarn) $\qquad \dfrac{E \vdash \mathbf{n} :: Ty \quad E \vdash A :: Ty}{A, E \vdash \mathbf{n+1} :: Ty}$

(L2-tvarn2) $\qquad \dfrac{E \vdash \mathbf{n} :: Ty}{Ty, E \vdash \mathbf{n+1} :: Ty}$

(L2-tfun) $\qquad \dfrac{E \vdash A :: Ty \quad A, E \vdash B :: Ty}{E \vdash A \to B :: Ty}$

(L2-tgen) $\qquad \dfrac{Ty, E \vdash B :: Ty}{E \vdash \forall B :: Ty}$

(L2-var) $\qquad \dfrac{E \vdash A :: Ty}{A, E \vdash \mathbf{1} : A\{\uparrow\}}$

(L2-varn) $\qquad \dfrac{E \vdash \mathbf{n} : B \quad E \vdash A :: Ty}{A, E \vdash \mathbf{n+1} : B\{\uparrow\}}$

(L2-varn2) $\qquad \dfrac{E \vdash \mathbf{n} : B}{Ty, E \vdash \mathbf{n+1} : B\{\uparrow\}}$

(L2-lambda) $\qquad \dfrac{A, E \vdash b : B}{E \vdash \lambda A.b : A \to B}$

(L2-Lambda) $\qquad \dfrac{Ty, E \vdash b : B}{E \vdash \Lambda b : \forall B}$

(L2-app) $\qquad \dfrac{E \vdash b : A \to B \quad E \vdash a : A}{E \vdash b(a) : B\{a{:}A \cdot id\}}$

(L2-App) $\qquad \dfrac{E \vdash b : \forall B \quad E \vdash A :: Ty}{E \vdash b(A) : B\{A{::}Ty \cdot id\}}$

We now move on to the S2 system, with the following syntax:

Types $\qquad A ::= \mathbf{1} \mid A \to B \mid \forall A \mid A[s]$
Environments $\quad E ::= nil \mid A, E \mid Ty, E$
Terms $\qquad a ::= \mathbf{1} \mid \lambda A.a \mid \Lambda a \mid ab \mid aB \mid a[s]$
Substitutions $\quad s ::= id \mid \uparrow \mid a{:}A \cdot s \mid A{::}Ty \cdot s \mid s \circ t$

In the previous section, we have seen how to formulate a first-order $\lambda\sigma$-calculus (S1) by adding one closure rule and a group of substitution rules to the first-order λ-calculus (L1). In S1, the task of deriving types can be separated from the task of applying substitutions. As indicated in the informal overview, this approach does not extend to S2. The rules of S2 described below are structured in such a way that substitutions are automatically pushed inside terms during typechecking. The unfortunate side effect is a small explosion in the number of rules. We do not include an analogue for S1-clos (in fact, we conjecture that it is admissible).

S2 is formulated with equivalence judgments, for example judgments of the form $E \vdash a \sim b : A$. This judgment means that a and b are equivalent terms of type A in the environment E. We can recover the standard judgments, with definitions such as

$$E \vdash a : A \ =_{def} \ E \vdash a \sim a : A$$

In S2, equivalence judgments are needed because it is not always possible to prove directly $E \vdash a : A$, but only $E \vdash b : A$ for a term b that is σ-equivalent to a (as in the example above). Formally, in order to prove $E \vdash a \sim a : A$, we first prove $E \vdash a \sim b : A$, and then use symmetry and transitivity. Similarly, it is not always possible to prove directly $E \vdash a : A$, but instead $E \vdash a : B$ for a type B that is σ-equivalent to A—then we "retype" a from B to A.

We have seen in section 2 how the typing axiom for **1** has to be modified. Similar considerations show that the rule for conses, S1-cons, needs to be modified as well, and suggest the following, tentative rule:

$$\frac{E \vdash a \sim b : A[s] \qquad E \vdash s \sim t \therefore E'}{E \vdash A[s] \sim B[t] :: \mathrm{Ty}}$$
$$E \vdash a{:}A \cdot s \sim b{:}B \cdot t \therefore A, E'$$

Note that, in the hypothesis, we require that a have type $A[s]$ rather than A: the reason is that A is well-formed in E' rather than in E. Furthermore, we require that s and t be equivalent substitutions of type E', but in truth their type is irrelevant. This suggests a new approach: we deal with judgments of the form

$$E \vdash s \sim t \ \mathrm{subst}_p$$

where p records the length $|E'|$ of E'.

In fact, we could hardly do more than keep track of the lengths of substitutions. As the following example illustrates, the type of a substitution cannot be determined satisfactorily. In the tentative rule above, let $E = nil$, $s = t = Bool{::}\mathrm{Ty} \cdot id$, $a = b = true$, and $A = \mathbf{1}$ and $B = Bool$. We obtain

$$nil \vdash true{:}\mathbf{1} \cdot s \sim true{:}Bool \cdot t \therefore \mathbf{1}{::}\mathrm{Ty}, nil$$

where we would more naturally expect $Bool{::}\mathrm{Ty}, nil$. The information that **1** is $Bool$ is not found in the environment: s has to be used to check that **1** is indeed $Bool$. It seems thus that the type of a substitution cannot be intrinsically defined.

With these explanations in mind, the reader should be able to approach the rules of the theory S2.

Definition 5.2 (Theory S2) *See appendix 7.*

S2 is sound, in the following sense:

Proposition 5.3 (Soundness)

1. *If $E \vdash_{S2} a \sim b : A$
   then $\sigma(E) \vdash_{L2} \sigma(a) : \sigma(A)$ and $\sigma(a) = \sigma(b)$.*

2. *If $E \vdash_{S2} A \sim B :: \mathrm{Ty}$
   then $\sigma(E) \vdash_{L2} \sigma(A) :: \mathrm{Ty}$ and $\sigma(A) = \sigma(B)$.*

3. *If $\vdash_{S2} E \sim E'$ env
   then $\vdash_{L2} \sigma(E)$ env and $\sigma(E) = \sigma(E')$.*

4. *If $E \vdash_{S2} s \sim s' \ \mathrm{subst}_p$ then for some m and n*

   - $\sigma(s) = G_1 \cdot \ldots \cdot G_m \cdot \uparrow^n$ and $\sigma(s') = G'_1 \cdot \ldots \cdot G'_m \cdot \uparrow^n$,
   - *for all $q \leq m$, either $G_q = G'_q = A :: \mathrm{Ty}$ and $\sigma(E) \vdash_{L2} A :: \mathrm{Ty}$ for some A, or $G_q = a{:}A$, $G'_q = a{:}A'$, $\sigma(A[\uparrow^q \circ s]) = \sigma(A'[\uparrow^q \circ s'])$, and $\sigma(E) \vdash_{L2} a : \sigma(.1[\uparrow^q \circ s])$ for some a, A, and A',*
   - $p = m + |E| - n$.

As for S1, we speculate that the soundness claim for S2 can be strengthened, and that a converse completeness result then holds.

We now provide a typechecking algorithm S2alg for the second-order calculus. The algorithm is formulated as a set of rules, for easy comparison with S2.

For terms that are not closures, S2alg and L2 operate identically. However, these are the least interesting cases: an actual implementation would manipulate only closures (as in subsection 3.5). In order to typecheck a term $a[s]$, the strategy is to analyze simpler and simpler components of a while accumulating more and more complex substitutions in s. When we reach an index, we extract the relevant information from the substitution or from the environment.

Informally, the algorithmic flow of control for each rule is: start with the given parts of the conclusion, recursively do what the assumptions on top require, accumulate the results, and from them produce the unknown parts of the conclusion. For example, if we want to type a in the environment E, we select an inference rule of S2alg by inspecting the shape of its conclusion. Then we move on to the assumptions of this rule, recursively; we solve the typing problems presented by each of them, and collect the results to produce a type for the original term a.

Some of the rules involve tests for type equivalence; two auxiliary "reduction" judgments are used:

$$E \vdash s \leadsto s' \quad subst_p \quad \text{and} \quad E \vdash A \leadsto A' :: \text{Ty}$$

In these judgments, s' and A' are in a sort of weak head normal form, namely: s' is never a composition and if A' is a closure then it has the form $1[\uparrow^n]$.

Definition 5.4 (S2alg) *See appendix 8.*

To show that S2alg really defines an algorithm, we first notice that only one rule can be applied bottom-up in each situation. For the judgments $E \vdash A::\text{Ty}$ and $E \vdash A \leadsto A'::\text{Ty}$, we test applicability by cases on A; when $A = B[s]$, by cases on B; and when $B = 1$ by cases on the reduction of s. For $E \vdash a : A$, we proceed by cases on a; when $a = b[s]$, by cases on b; and when $b = 1$ by cases on the reduction of s. For $E \vdash s \; subst_p$, we proceed by cases on s, and when $s = t \circ u$ by cases on t. For $E \vdash s \leadsto s' \; subst_p$, we proceed by cases on s; when $s = t \circ u$, by cases on t; and when $t = \uparrow$ by cases on the reduction of u. Finally, $E \vdash A \leadsto B :: \text{Ty}$ is handled by cases on the reductions of A and B.

The following invariants can be used to show that the algorithm considers all the cases that may arise when the input terms are well typed:

- If $E \vdash s \leadsto s' \; subst_p$ then s' has one of the forms id, $\uparrow^n$, $a{:}A \cdot t$, and $A{::}\text{Ty} \cdot t$.

- If $E \vdash A \leadsto A' :: \text{Ty}$ then A' has one of the forms 1, $1[\uparrow^n]$, $B \to C$, and $\forall B$.

Finally, the algorithm always terminates, with success or failure, because every rule either reduces the size of terms or moves terms towards a normal form. The algorithm S2alg is sound with respect to S2. For example, if $E \vdash_{S2alg} A :: \text{Ty}$ then we can prove $E \vdash_{S2} A \sim A :: \text{Ty}$. We conjecture that the algorithm is also complete, in the sense that for example if $E \vdash_{S2} A \sim A' :: \text{Ty}$ then $E \vdash_{S2alg} A :: \text{Ty}$.

6 Conclusion

The usual presentations of the λ-calculus discreetly play down the handling of substitutions. This helps in developing the metatheory of the λ-calculus, at a suitable level of abstraction. We hope to have demonstrated the benefits of a more explicit treatment of substitutions, both for untyped systems and typed systems. The theory and the manipulation of explicit substitutions can be delicate, but useful for correct and efficient implementations.

Acknowledgements We have benefited from discussions on untyped systems with P. Crégut, T. Hardin, E. Muller, and A. Suárez, and from C. Hibbard's editorial help.

7 Appendix: Theory S2

7.1 Type equivalence

$$\frac{E \vdash A \sim B :: \text{Ty}}{E \vdash B \sim A :: \text{Ty}}$$

$$\frac{E \vdash A \sim B :: \text{Ty} \quad E \vdash B \sim C :: \text{Ty}}{E \vdash A \sim C :: \text{Ty}}$$

$$\frac{\vdash E \; env}{\text{Ty}, E \vdash 1 \sim 1 :: \text{Ty}}$$

$$\frac{E \vdash A \sim A' :: \text{Ty} \quad A, E \vdash B \sim B' :: \text{Ty}}{E \vdash A \to B \sim A' \to B' :: \text{Ty}}$$

$$\frac{\text{Ty}, E \vdash B \sim B' :: \text{Ty}}{E \vdash \forall B \sim \forall B' :: \text{Ty}}$$

$$\frac{\vdash E \; env}{E \vdash 1[id] \sim 1 :: \text{Ty}}$$

$$\frac{E \vdash 1 :: \text{Ty} \quad E \vdash A :: \text{Ty}}{A, E \vdash 1[\uparrow] \sim 1[\uparrow] :: \text{Ty}}$$

$$\frac{E \vdash 1 :: \text{Ty}}{\text{Ty}, E \vdash 1[\uparrow] \sim 1[\uparrow] :: \text{Ty}}$$

$$\frac{E \vdash 1[\uparrow^n] :: \text{Ty} \quad E \vdash A :: \text{Ty}}{A, E \vdash 1[\uparrow^{n+1}] \sim 1[\uparrow^{n+1}] :: \text{Ty}}$$

$$\frac{E \vdash 1[\uparrow^n] :: \text{Ty}}{\text{Ty}, E \vdash 1[\uparrow^{n+1}] \sim 1[\uparrow^{n+1}] :: \text{Ty}}$$

$$\frac{E \vdash A{::}\text{Ty} \cdot s \; subst_p}{E \vdash 1[A{::}\text{Ty} \cdot s] \sim A :: \text{Ty}}$$

$$\frac{E \vdash s \sim s' \; subst_p \quad E \vdash 1[s'] :: \text{Ty}}{E \vdash 1[s] \sim 1[s'] :: \text{Ty}}$$

$$\frac{E \vdash A[s] \to B[1{:}A.(s \circ \uparrow)] :: \text{Ty}}{E \vdash (A \to B)[s] \sim A[s] \to B[1{:}A \cdot (s \circ \uparrow)] :: \text{Ty}}$$

$$\frac{E \vdash \forall(B[1 :: \text{Ty} \cdot (s \circ \uparrow)]) :: \text{Ty}}{E \vdash (\forall B)[s] \sim \forall(B[1{::}\text{Ty} \cdot (s \circ \uparrow)]) :: \text{Ty}}$$

$$\frac{E \vdash A[s \circ t] :: \text{Ty}}{E \vdash A[s][t] \sim A[s \circ t] :: \text{Ty}}$$

$$\frac{E \vdash A \sim B :: \text{Ty} \quad \vdash E \sim E' \; env}{E' \vdash A \sim B :: \text{Ty}}$$

7.2 Term equivalence

$$\frac{E \vdash a \sim b : A}{E \vdash b \sim a : A}$$

$$\frac{E \vdash a \sim b : A \quad E \vdash b \sim c : A}{E \vdash a \sim c : A}$$

$$\frac{E \vdash A :: \mathrm{Ty}}{A, E \vdash 1 \sim 1 : A[\uparrow]}$$

$$\frac{E \vdash A \sim A' :: \mathrm{Ty} \quad A, E \vdash b \sim b' : B}{E \vdash \lambda A.b \sim \lambda A'.b' : A \rightarrow B}$$

$$\frac{\mathrm{Ty}, E \vdash b \sim b' : B}{E \vdash \Lambda b \sim \Lambda b' : \forall B}$$

$$\frac{E \vdash b \sim b' : A \rightarrow B \quad E \vdash a \sim a' : A}{E \vdash b(a) \sim b'(a') : B[a:A \cdot id]}$$

$$\frac{E \vdash b \sim b' : \forall B \quad E \vdash A \sim A' :: \mathrm{Ty}}{E \vdash b(A) \sim b'(A') : B[A::\mathrm{Ty} \cdot id]}$$

$$\frac{E \vdash 1 : A}{E \vdash 1[id] \sim 1 : A}$$

$$\frac{E \vdash 1 : A \quad E \vdash B :: \mathrm{Ty}}{B, E \vdash 1[\uparrow] \sim 1[\uparrow] : A[\uparrow]}$$

$$\frac{E \vdash 1 : A}{\mathrm{Ty}, E \vdash 1[\uparrow] \sim 1[\uparrow] : A[\uparrow]}$$

$$\frac{E \vdash 1[\uparrow^n] : A \quad E \vdash B :: \mathrm{Ty}}{B, E \vdash 1[\uparrow^{n+1}] \sim 1[\uparrow^{n+1}] : A[\uparrow]}$$

$$\frac{E \vdash 1[\uparrow^n] : A}{\mathrm{Ty}, E \vdash 1[\uparrow^{n+1}] \sim 1[\uparrow^{n+1}] : A[\uparrow]}$$

$$\frac{E \vdash a:A \cdot s \; \mathrm{subst}_p}{E \vdash 1[a:A \cdot s] \sim a : A[s]}$$

$$\frac{E \vdash s \sim s' \; \mathrm{subst}_p \quad E \vdash 1[s'] : A}{E \vdash 1[s] \sim 1[s'] : A}$$

$$\frac{E \vdash \lambda A[s].b[1:A \cdot (s \circ \uparrow)] : B}{E \vdash (\lambda A.b)[s] \sim \lambda A[s].b[1:A \cdot (s \circ \uparrow)] : B}$$

$$\frac{E \vdash \Lambda(b[1::\mathrm{Ty} \cdot (s \circ \uparrow)]) : B}{E \vdash (\Lambda b)[s] \sim \Lambda(b[1::\mathrm{Ty} \cdot (s \circ \uparrow)]) : B}$$

$$\frac{E \vdash (b[s])(a[s]) : A}{E \vdash b(a)[s] \sim (b[s])(a[s]) : A}$$

$$\frac{E \vdash (b[s])(A[s]) : B}{E \vdash b(A)[s] \sim (b[s])(A[s]) : B}$$

$$\frac{E \vdash a[s \circ t] : A}{E \vdash a[s][t] \sim a[s \circ t] : A}$$

$$\frac{E \vdash a \sim b : A \quad E \vdash A \sim B :: \mathrm{Ty}}{E \vdash a \sim b : B}$$

$$\frac{E \vdash a \sim b : A \quad \vdash E \sim E' \; env}{E' \vdash a \sim b : A}$$

7.3 Substitution equivalence

$$\frac{E \vdash s \sim t \; \mathrm{subst}_p}{E \vdash t \sim s \; \mathrm{subst}_p}$$

$$\frac{E \vdash s \sim t \; \mathrm{subst}_p \quad E \vdash t \sim u \; \mathrm{subst}_p}{E \vdash s \sim u \; \mathrm{subst}_p}$$

$$\frac{\vdash E \; env}{E \vdash id \sim id \; \mathrm{subst}_{|E|}}$$

$$\frac{E \vdash A :: \mathrm{Ty}}{A, E \vdash \uparrow \sim \uparrow \; \mathrm{subst}_{|E|}}$$

$$\frac{\vdash E \; env}{\mathrm{Ty}, E \vdash \uparrow \sim \uparrow \; \mathrm{subst}_{|E|}}$$

$$\frac{E \vdash s \sim t \; \mathrm{subst}_p \quad E \vdash A[s] \sim B[t] :: \mathrm{Ty} \quad E \vdash a \sim b : A[s]}{E \vdash a:A \cdot s \sim b:B \cdot t \; \mathrm{subst}_{p+1}}$$

$$\frac{E \vdash A \sim B :: \mathrm{Ty} \quad E \vdash s \sim t \; \mathrm{subst}_p}{E \vdash A::\mathrm{Ty} \cdot s \sim B::\mathrm{Ty} \cdot t \; \mathrm{subst}_{p+1}}$$

$$\frac{E \vdash s \sim s' \; \mathrm{subst}_p}{E \vdash id \circ s \sim s' \; \mathrm{subst}_p}$$

$$\frac{E \vdash \uparrow \; \mathrm{subst}_p}{E \vdash \uparrow \circ id \sim \uparrow \; \mathrm{subst}_p}$$

$$\frac{E \vdash s \sim s' \; \mathrm{subst}_p \quad E \vdash a : A[s]}{E \vdash \uparrow \circ (a:A \cdot s) \sim s' \; \mathrm{subst}_p}$$

$$\frac{E \vdash s \sim s' \; \mathrm{subst}_p \quad E \vdash A :: \mathrm{Ty}}{E \vdash \uparrow \circ (A::\mathrm{Ty} \cdot s) \sim s' \; \mathrm{subst}_p}$$

$$\frac{E \vdash s \sim s' \; \mathrm{subst}_{p+1}}{E \vdash \uparrow \circ s \sim \uparrow \circ s' \; \mathrm{subst}_p}$$

$$\frac{E \vdash a[t]:A \cdot (s \circ t) \; \mathrm{subst}_p}{E \vdash (a:A \cdot s) \circ t \sim a[t]:A \cdot (s \circ t) \; \mathrm{subst}_p}$$

$$\frac{E \vdash A[t]::\mathrm{Ty} \cdot (s \circ t) \; \mathrm{subst}_p}{E \vdash (A::\mathrm{Ty} \cdot s) \circ t \sim A[t]::\mathrm{Ty} \cdot (s \circ t) \; \mathrm{subst}_p}$$

$$\frac{E \vdash s \circ (t \circ u) \; \mathrm{subst}_p}{E \vdash (s \circ t) \circ u \sim s \circ (t \circ u) \; \mathrm{subst}_p}$$

$$\frac{E \vdash s \sim t \; \mathrm{subst}_p \quad \vdash E \sim E' \; env}{E' \vdash s \sim t \; \mathrm{subst}_p}$$

7.4 Environment equivalence

$$\frac{\vdash E \sim E' \ env}{\vdash E' \sim E \ env}$$

$$\frac{\vdash E \sim E' \ env \quad \vdash E' \sim E'' \ env}{\vdash E \sim E'' \ env}$$

$$\vdash nil \sim nil \ env$$

$$\frac{\vdash E \sim E' \ env \quad E \vdash A \sim B :: Ty}{\vdash A, E \sim B, E' \ env}$$

$$\frac{\vdash E \sim E' \ env}{\vdash Ty, E \sim Ty, E' \ env}$$

8 Appendix: Algorithm S2alg

8.1 Inference for types

$$\frac{\vdash E \ env}{Ty, E \vdash 1 :: Ty}$$

$$\frac{E \vdash A :: Ty \quad A, E \vdash B :: Ty}{E \vdash A \to B :: Ty}$$

$$\frac{Ty, E \vdash B :: Ty}{E \vdash \forall B :: Ty}$$

$$\frac{Ty, E \vdash s \leadsto id \ subst_p}{Ty, E \vdash 1[s] :: Ty}$$

$$\frac{E \vdash 1 :: Ty \quad E \vdash A :: Ty}{A, E \vdash 1[\uparrow] :: Ty}$$

$$\frac{E \vdash 1 :: Ty}{Ty, E \vdash 1[\uparrow] :: Ty}$$

$$\frac{E \vdash 1[\uparrow^n] :: Ty \quad E \vdash A :: Ty}{A, E \vdash 1[\uparrow^{n+1}] :: Ty}$$

$$\frac{E \vdash 1[\uparrow^n] :: Ty}{Ty, E \vdash 1[\uparrow^{n+1}] :: Ty}$$

$$\frac{E \vdash s \leadsto A::Ty \cdot t \ subst_p}{E \vdash 1[s] :: Ty}$$

$$\frac{E \vdash s \leadsto \uparrow^n \ subst_p \quad E \vdash 1[\uparrow^n] :: Ty}{E \vdash 1[s] :: Ty}$$

$$\frac{E \vdash A[s] :: Ty \quad A[s], E \vdash B[1 : A \cdot (s \circ \uparrow)] :: Ty}{E \vdash (A \to B)[s] :: Ty}$$

$$\frac{Ty, E \vdash B[1::Ty \cdot (s \circ \uparrow)] :: Ty}{E \vdash (\forall B)[s] :: Ty}$$

$$\frac{E \vdash A[s \circ t] :: Ty}{E \vdash A[s][t] :: Ty}$$

8.2 Inference for terms

$$\frac{E \vdash A :: Ty}{A, E \vdash 1 : A[\uparrow]}$$

$$\frac{E \vdash A :: Ty \quad A, E \vdash b : B}{E \vdash \lambda A.b : A \to B}$$

$$\frac{Ty, E \vdash b : B}{E \vdash \Lambda b : \forall B}$$

$$\frac{E \vdash b : A \to B \quad E \vdash a : A}{E \vdash b(a) : B[a:A \cdot id]}$$

$$\frac{E \vdash b : \forall B \quad E \vdash A :: Ty}{E \vdash b(A) : B[A::Ty \cdot id]}$$

$$\frac{A, E \vdash s \leadsto id \ subst_p}{A, E \vdash 1[s] : A[\uparrow]}$$

$$\frac{E \vdash 1 : A \quad E \vdash B :: Ty}{B, E \vdash 1[\uparrow] : A[\uparrow]}$$

$$\frac{E \vdash 1 : A}{Ty, E \vdash 1[\uparrow] : A[\uparrow]}$$

$$\frac{E \vdash 1[\uparrow^n] : A \quad E \vdash B :: Ty}{B, E \vdash 1[\uparrow^{n+1}] : A[\uparrow]}$$

$$\frac{E \vdash 1[\uparrow^n] : A}{Ty, E \vdash 1[\uparrow^{n+1}] : A[\uparrow]}$$

$$\frac{E \vdash s \leadsto a:A \cdot t \ subst_p}{E \vdash 1[s] : A[t]}$$

$$\frac{E \vdash s \leadsto \uparrow^n \ subst_p \quad E \vdash 1[\uparrow^n] : A}{E \vdash 1[s] : A}$$

$$\frac{A[s], E \vdash b[1 : A \cdot (s \circ \uparrow)] : B}{E \vdash (\lambda A.b)[s] : A[s] \to B}$$

$$\frac{Ty, E \vdash b[1::Ty \cdot (s \circ \uparrow)] : B}{E \vdash (\Lambda b)[s] : \forall B}$$

$$\frac{E \vdash b[s] : A \to B \quad E \vdash a[s] : A'}{E \vdash A \leftrightarrow A' :: Ty}$$
$$\frac{}{E \vdash (b(a))[s] : B[a[s] : A \cdot id]}$$

$$\frac{E \vdash b[s] : \forall B \quad E \vdash A[s] :: Ty}{E \vdash (b(A))[s] : B[A[s]::Ty \cdot id]}$$

$$\frac{E \vdash a[s \circ t] : A}{E \vdash a[s][t] : A}$$

8.3 Inference for substitutions

$$\frac{\vdash E \ env}{E \vdash id \ subst_{|E|}}$$

$$\frac{E \vdash A :: Ty}{A, E \vdash \uparrow \ subst_{|E|}}$$

$$\frac{\vdash E \ env}{Ty, E \vdash \uparrow \ subst_{|E|}}$$

$$\frac{E \vdash a : B \quad E \vdash s \ subst_p \quad E \vdash A[s] \leftrightarrow B :: Ty}{E \vdash a : A \cdot s \ subst_{p+1}}$$

$$\frac{E \vdash A :: Ty \quad E \vdash s \ subst_p}{E \vdash A::Ty \cdot s \ subst_{p+1}}$$

$$\frac{E \vdash s \ subst_p}{E \vdash id \circ s \ subst_p}$$

$$\frac{E \vdash s \ subst_{p+1}}{E \vdash \uparrow \circ s \ subst_p}$$

$$\frac{E \vdash a[t] : A \cdot (s \circ t) \ subst_p}{E \vdash (a : A \cdot s) \circ t \ subst_p}$$

$$\frac{E \vdash A[t] :: Ty \cdot (s \circ t) \ subst_p}{E \vdash (A :: Ty \cdot s) \circ t \ subst_p}$$

$$\frac{E \vdash s \circ (t \circ u) \ subst_p}{E \vdash (s \circ t) \circ u \ subst_p}$$

8.4 Substitution reduction

$$\frac{\vdash E \ env}{E \vdash id \leadsto id \ subst_{|E|}}$$

$$\frac{E \vdash A :: Ty}{A, E \vdash \uparrow \leadsto \uparrow \ subst_{|E|}}$$

$$\frac{\vdash E \ env}{Ty, E \vdash \uparrow \leadsto \uparrow \ subst_{|E|}}$$

$$\frac{E \vdash A[s] :: Ty \quad E \vdash a : B \quad E \vdash B \leftrightarrow A[s] :: Ty \quad E \vdash s \ subst_p}{E \vdash a : A \cdot s \leadsto a : A \cdot s \ subst_{p+1}}$$

$$\frac{E \vdash A :: Ty \quad E \vdash s \ subst_p}{E \vdash A::Ty \cdot s \leadsto A::Ty \cdot s \ subst_{p+1}}$$

$$\frac{E \vdash s \leadsto s' \ subst_p}{E \vdash id \circ s \leadsto s' \ subst_p}$$

$$\frac{E \vdash s \leadsto id \ subst_{p+1}}{E \vdash \uparrow \circ s \leadsto \uparrow \ subst_p}$$

$$\frac{E \vdash s \leadsto \uparrow^n \ subst_{p+1}}{E \vdash \uparrow \circ s \leadsto \uparrow^{n+1} \ subst_p}$$

$$\frac{E \vdash s \leadsto a : A \cdot s' \ subst_{p+1} \quad E \vdash s' \leadsto s'' \ subst_p}{E \vdash \uparrow \circ s \leadsto s'' \ subst_p}$$

$$\frac{E \vdash s \leadsto A::Ty \cdot s' \ subst_{p+1} \quad E \vdash s' \leadsto s'' \ subst_p}{E \vdash \uparrow \circ s \leadsto s'' \ subst_p}$$

$$\frac{E \vdash a[t] : A \cdot (s \circ t) \ subst_p}{E \vdash (a : A \cdot s) \circ t \leadsto a[t] : A \cdot (s \circ t) \ subst_p}$$

$$\frac{E \vdash A[t]::Ty \cdot (s \circ t) \ subst_p}{E \vdash (A::Ty \cdot s) \circ t \leadsto A[t]::Ty \cdot (s \circ t) \ subst_p}$$

$$\frac{E \vdash s \circ (t \circ u) \leadsto v \ subst_p}{E \vdash (s \circ t) \circ u \leadsto v \ subst_p}$$

8.5 Type reductions

$$\frac{\vdash E \ env}{Ty, E \vdash 1 \leadsto 1 :: Ty}$$

$$\frac{E \vdash A :: Ty \quad A, E \vdash B :: Ty}{E \vdash A \rightarrow B \leadsto A \rightarrow B :: Ty}$$

$$\frac{Ty, E \vdash B :: Ty}{E \vdash \forall B \leadsto \forall B :: Ty}$$

$$\frac{Ty, E \vdash s \leadsto id \ subst_p}{Ty, E \vdash 1[s] \leadsto 1 :: Ty}$$

$$\frac{E \vdash s \leadsto \uparrow^n \ subst_p \quad E \vdash 1[\uparrow^n] :: Ty}{E \vdash 1[s] \leadsto 1[\uparrow^n] :: Ty}$$

$$\frac{E \vdash s \leadsto A::Ty \cdot s' \ subst_p \quad E \vdash A[s'] \leadsto B :: Ty}{E \vdash 1[s] \leadsto B :: Ty}$$

$$\frac{E \vdash A[s] :: Ty \quad A[s], E \vdash B[1 : A \cdot (s \circ \uparrow)] :: Ty}{E \vdash (A \rightarrow B)[s] \leadsto A[s] \rightarrow B[1 : A \cdot (s \circ \uparrow)] :: Ty}$$

$$\frac{Ty, E \vdash B[1::Ty \cdot (s \circ \uparrow)] :: Ty}{E \vdash (\forall B)[s] \leadsto \forall(B[1::Ty \cdot (s \circ \uparrow)]) :: Ty}$$

$$\frac{E \vdash A[s \circ t] \leadsto B :: Ty}{E \vdash A[s][t] \leadsto B :: Ty}$$

8.6 Type equivalence

$$\frac{E \vdash A \rightsquigarrow 1 :: Ty \quad E \vdash A' \rightsquigarrow 1 :: Ty}{E \vdash A \leftrightarrow A' :: Ty}$$

$$\frac{E \vdash A \rightsquigarrow B \rightarrow C :: Ty \quad E \vdash A' \rightsquigarrow B' \rightarrow C' :: Ty \quad E \vdash B \leftrightarrow B' :: Ty \quad B, E \vdash C \leftrightarrow C' :: Ty}{E \vdash A \leftrightarrow A' :: Ty}$$

$$\frac{E \vdash A \rightsquigarrow \forall B :: Ty \quad E \vdash A' \rightsquigarrow \forall B' :: Ty \quad Ty, E \vdash B \leftrightarrow B' :: Ty}{E \vdash A \leftrightarrow A' :: Ty}$$

$$\frac{E \vdash A \rightsquigarrow 1[\uparrow^n] :: Ty \quad E \vdash A' \rightsquigarrow 1[\uparrow^n] :: Ty}{E \vdash A \leftrightarrow A' :: Ty}$$

8.7 Inference for environments

$$\vdash nil \;\; env$$

$$\frac{\vdash E \;\; env \quad E \vdash A :: Ty}{\vdash A, E \;\; env}$$

$$\frac{\vdash E \;\; env}{\vdash Ty, E \;\; env}$$

References

[1] H.P. Barendregt, *The Lambda Calculus: Its Syntax and Semantics*, North Holland, 1985.

[2] N. De Bruijn, Lambda-calculus Notation with Nameless Dummies, a Tool for Automatic Formula Manipulation, Indag. Mat. 34, pp. 381–392, 1972.

[3] L. Cardelli, Typeful Programming, SRC Report No. 45, Digital Equipment Corporation, 1989.

[4] H.P. Curry and R. Feys, *Combinatory Logic*, Vol. 1, North Holland, 1958.

[5] P.-L. Curien, The $\lambda\rho$-calculi: An Abstract Framework for Closures, unpublished (preliminary version printed as LIENS report, 1988).

[6] P.-L. Curien, *Categorical Combinators, Sequential Algorithms and Functional Programming*, Pitman, 1986.

[7] T. Hardin, Confluence Results for the Pure Strong Categorical Combinatory Logic, to appear in Theoretical Computer Science, 1988.

[8] T. Hardin, A. Laville, Proof of Termination of the Rewriting System SUBST on CCL, Theoretical Computer Science 46, pp. 305–312, 1986.

[9] G. Huet, D.C. Oppen, Equations and Rewrite Rules: A Survey, in *Formal Languages Theory: Perspectives and Open Problems* (R. Book, editor), pp. 349–393, Academic Press, 1980.

[10] J.W. Klop, *Combinatory Reduction Systems*, Math. Center Tracts 129, Amsterdam, 1980.

[11] J.-L. Krivine, unpublished.

[12] P. Martin-Löf, *Intuitionistic Type Theory*, notes by G. Sambin of a series of lectures given in Padova in 1980, Bibliopolis, 1984.

[13] C.P. Wadsworth, *Semantics and Pragmatics of the Lambda Calculus*, Dissertation, Oxford University, 1971.

A Formulae-as-Types Notion of Control

Timothy G. Griffin*
Department of Computer Science
Rice University
Houston, TX 77251-1892

Abstract

The programming language Scheme contains the control construct `call/cc` that allows access to the current continuation (the current control context). This, in effect, provides Scheme with first-class labels and jumps. We show that the well-known formulae-as-types correspondence, which relates a constructive proof of a formula α to a program of type α, can be extended to a typed Idealized Scheme. What is surprising about this correspondence is that it relates *classical* proofs to typed programs. The existence of computationally interesting "classical programs" — programs of type α, where α holds classically, but not constructively — is illustrated by the definition of conjunctive, disjunctive, and existential types using standard classical definitions. We also prove that all evaluations of typed terms in Idealized Scheme are finite.

1 Introduction

The formulae-as-types correspondence [10,18,8], also referred to as the propositions-as-types correspondence and as the Curry/Howard isomorphism, relates a constructive proof of a formula α to a program of type α. This correspondence has been restricted to constructive logic because it is widely believed that,

---

*This work was supported in part by DARPA grant CCR-87-20277. The author's current address: *Departamento de Ciência da Computação, IMECC – UNICAMP, Caixa Postal 6065, 13801 Campinas SP, Brazil.* email: griffin@bruc.ansp.br

Permission to copy without fee all or part of this material is granted provided that the copies are not made or distributed for direct commercial advantage, the ACM copyright notice and the title of the publication and its date appear, and notice is given that the copying is by permission of the Association for Computing Machinery. To copy otherwise, or to republish, requires a fee and/or specific permission.

in general, classical proofs lack computational content. This paper shows, however, that the formulae-as-types correspondence *can* be extended to classical logic in a computationally interesting way. It is shown that classical proofs posses computational content when the notion of computation is extended to include explicit access to the current control context.

This notion of computation is found in the programming language Scheme [16], which contains the control construct `call/cc`[1] that provides access to the current continuation (the current control context). This, in effect, provides Scheme with first-class labels and jumps, and allows for programs that are more efficient than purely functional programs. The formulae-as-types correspondence presented in this paper is based on a typed version of *Idealized Scheme* — a typed ISWIM containing an operator $\mathcal{C}$ similar to `call/cc` — developed by Felleisen *et al* [3,2,4] for reasoning about Scheme programs.

Section 2 reviews ISWIM and its extension to Idealized Scheme (IS) with the control operator $\mathcal{C}$ of Felleisen *et al*. Roughly speaking, the evaluation of $\mathcal{C}(M)$ abandons the current control context and applies M to a procedural abstraction of this context.

A typed version of Idealized Scheme is presented in Section 3 together with a formulae-as-types correspondence between typed terms and natural deduction proofs for classical implicational logic. Types include the type $\perp$, which corresponds to the proposition "false." The type $\alpha \to \perp$ is abbreviated as $\neg \alpha$ ("not α"). An application of $\mathcal{C}$ is typed as follows. If M is of type $\neg\neg\alpha$, then $\mathcal{C}(M)$ is of type α. This rule corresponds to the classical inferrence rule for elimination of double negation.

Section 4 demonstrates that there are computationally interesting typed IS programs of type α, where α holds classically, but not constructively. It is shown that if conjunctive, disjunctive, and existential types are defined using standard classical definitions, then

---

[1] `call/cc` abbreviates `call-with-current-continuation`.

the operations of pairing, projection, injection, and analysis by cases can be defined using $\mathcal{C}$.

There are many equivalent ways of defining classical logic. For example, in place of double negation elimination, classical logic is often defined by adding the law of the excluded middle, $\alpha \vee \neg \alpha$, to constructive logic. Section 5 shows that the law of the excluded middle can be given an operational interpretation that is computationally equivalent to that of $\mathcal{C}$.

In Section 6 it is shown that the well-known cps (continuation passing style) transform corresponds to an embedding of classical into constructive logic. Section 7 uses a modified cps transform to prove that all evaluations of well-typed IS programs are finite.

2 From ISWIM to Idealized Scheme

Landin's ISWIM [11,12] is a call-by-value language whose core syntax is made up of expressions of the λ-calculus,

$$N ::= x \mid NN \mid \lambda x.N$$

where x ranges over an infinite set of variables. The operational semantics of ISWIM was defined by Landin in terms of the SECD-machine. Plotkin [14] showed that this definition is equivalent[2] to the (partial) function eval_v:

1. $\text{eval}_v(V) = V$,
2. $\text{eval}_v(MN) = \text{eval}_v(Q[V/x])$ if $\text{eval}_v(M) = \lambda x.Q$ and $\text{eval}_v(N) = V$.

Each V represents a *value*, where values are defined to be variables or λ-abstractions. Throughout this paper the metavariables V, V_1, V_2, ... will range over values. The notation $M[N/x]$ denotes the usual capture-avoiding substitution of N for all free occurrences of x in M.

An expression of the form $(\lambda x.M)V$ is called a β_v-redex. The function eval_v reduces at each step the leftmost-outermost β_v-redex not inside the scope of a λ-abstraction. Felleisen *et al* [3,4] have formalized this evaluation order in terms of *evaluation contexts*. ISWIM evaluation contexts E are defined inductively as

$$E ::= [\,] \mid EN \mid VE,$$

where $[\,]$ represents a "hole." If E is an evaluation context, then $E[M]$ denotes the term that results from placing M in the hole of E. It is not difficult to show that any closed term M is either a value or can be written in a *unique* way as $M = E[R]$, where R is a β_v-redex. Moreover, R is the leftmost-outermost β_v-redex of M that is not inside of a λ-abstraction. The notation $M \propto E[R]$ means that $E[R]$ is this unique representation of M. For example, if $E_0 = (\lambda x.M)[\,]$ and $E_1 = [\,]$, then

$$(\lambda x.M)V = E_0[V] \propto E_1[(\lambda x.M)V].$$

The unique representation of any non-value in terms of an evaluation context and a β_v-redex gives rise to the context rewrite rule

$$E[(\lambda x.M)V] \mapsto_{\beta_v} E[M[V/x]], \qquad (\mapsto_{\beta_v})$$

whose reflexive, transitive closure $\mapsto^*_{\beta_v}$ is equivalent to eval_v.

Lemma 1 $\text{eval}_v(M) = V$ iff $M \mapsto^*_{\beta_v} V$.

In other words, $\mapsto_{\beta_v}$ can be taken as defining an abstract operational semantics for ISWIM. An ISWIM term M *evaluates* to V if and only if $M \mapsto^*_{\beta_v} V$.

The notation of evaluation contexts gives a clear picture of the manner in which subterms are evaluated during the evaluation of a term. (The notation $\mapsto^k_{\beta_v}$ denotes a k-fold application of the $\mapsto_{\beta_v}$ rule.)

Lemma 2 1. If $E[M] \mapsto^k_{\beta_v} E[N]$, then $M \mapsto^k_{\beta_v} N$.

2. If $E[M] \mapsto^*_{\beta_v} V$, then there is a value V_0 such that $E[M] \mapsto^* E[V_0] \mapsto^*_{\beta_v} V$.

Thus, at any point i in an evaluation sequence

$$M_0 \mapsto_{\beta_v} M_1 \mapsto_{\beta_v} \cdots \mapsto_{\beta_v} M_i \mapsto_{\beta_v} \cdots$$

if $M_i = E[N]$, for a non-value N, then E must "wait" for N to evaluate to a value before the evaluation sequence can continue with computations involving subterms of E. That is, E represents *the rest of the computation that remains to be done after N is evaluated*. The context E is called the *continuation* (or *control context*) of N at this point in the evaluation sequence. The notation of evaluation contexts allows, as we shall see below, a concise specification of the operational semantics of operators that manipulate continuations (indeed, this was its intended use [3,2,4,1]).

The programming language Scheme [16] contains `call/cc`, a control construct that provides programs with direct access to a procedural abstraction representing the current continuation (the current control context). Felleisen *et al* [3,2,4,1] have presented an extension to ISWIM called Idealized Scheme[3], or IS,

---
[2]This paper ignores constants and their evaluation.

[3]This paper treats only the assignment-free sublanguage of Idealized Scheme.

which incorporates two constructs that manipulate control contexts. IS expressions are defined by extending the grammar of ISWIM as follows:

$$N ::= \cdots \mathcal{A}(N) \mid \mathcal{C}(N).$$

The operators $\mathcal{A}$ and $\mathcal{C}$ are called, respectively, *abort* and and *control*. In IS, any closed term M is either a value, or can be written in a unique way as $M = E[R]$, where R is either a β_v-redex, $R = \mathcal{A}(N)$, or $R = \mathcal{C}(N)$.

Informally, the evaluation of $\mathcal{A}(M)$ throws away the current control context and continues with the evaluation of M. This is expressed with a context rewrite rule, where the definition of evaluation contexts has been extended to IS expressions in the obvious way, as

$$E[\mathcal{A}(M)] \mapsto_\mathcal{A} M \qquad (\mapsto_\mathcal{A})$$

The operational semantics of $\mathcal{C}(M)$ can be described informally as follows. As with $\mathcal{A}$, the evaluation of $E[\mathcal{C}(M)]$ abondons the control context E. The term M is then applied to a procedural abstraction of the abandoned control context. If this procedure is invoked with a value V in any context E_1, then E_1 is abandoned and evaluation resumes with $E[V]$. This is expressed with the rule,

$$E[\mathcal{C}(M)] \mapsto_\mathcal{C} M\lambda z.\mathcal{A}(E[z]). \qquad (\mapsto_\mathcal{C})$$

The operator $\mathcal{A}$ can be defined in terms of $\mathcal{C}$ as

$$\mathcal{A}(M) \stackrel{\text{def}}{=} \mathcal{C}(\lambda d.M),$$

where d is a dummy variable not free in M, since

$$\begin{aligned} E[\mathcal{A}(M)] &= E[\mathcal{C}(\lambda d.M)] \\ &\mapsto_\mathcal{C} (\lambda d.M)\lambda z.\mathcal{A}(E[z]) \\ &\mapsto_{\beta_v} M \end{aligned}$$

Therefore, $\mathcal{A}(M)$ will be treated as a defined construct, and the rules $\mapsto_{\beta_v}$ and $\mapsto_\mathcal{C}$ will be treated as defining the operational semantics of IS. The notation $\mapsto_u$ denotes the union of the two evaluation rules.

The operational semantics of $\mathcal{C}$ differs from that of `call/cc` in that $\mathcal{C}$ need not return to the location of its use. If a version of `call/cc` were to be added to IS, say $\mathcal{K}$, then it would have the evaluation rule

$$E[\mathcal{K}(M)] \mapsto_\mathcal{K} E[M\lambda z.\mathcal{A}(E[z])]. \qquad (\mapsto_\mathcal{K})$$

However, this addition is not necessary since an operator computationally equivalent to $\mathcal{K}$ can be defined as

$$\mathcal{K}_d(M) \stackrel{\text{def}}{=} \mathcal{C}(\lambda k.k(Mk)). \qquad (\mathcal{K}_d)$$

One use of $\mathcal{K}_d$ is in the implementation of a "catch/throw" mechanism similar to that of Common Lisp [17]. Think of the evaluation of $E_0[\mathcal{K}_d(\lambda j.M)]$ as a "catch" that labels the current context with the name j. If j is never invoked, or "thrown to" during the evaluation of M, then this expression returns "normally." If, on the other hand, an application of j, such as $E_1[jV]$, is encountered during the evaluation of M, then the value V is "thrown back to" the location labeled by j. That is, the context E_1 is abandoned and evaluation resumes with $E_0[V]$. The following illustrates how this is accomplished with the evaluation rules of Idealized Scheme. If $Q = \lambda z.\mathcal{A}(E_0[z])$, then

$$\begin{aligned} E_0[\mathcal{K}_d(\lambda j.M)] &\mapsto_\mathcal{C} (\lambda k.k((\lambda j.M)k))Q \\ &\mapsto_{\beta_v} Q((\lambda j.M)Q) \\ &\mapsto_{\beta_v} Q(M[Q/j]) \end{aligned}$$

If $M[Q/j] \mapsto^*_{\beta_v} V$, then the evaluation returns "normally" with

$$\begin{aligned} &\mapsto^*_{\beta_v} QV \\ &\mapsto_\beta \mathcal{A}(E_0[V]) \\ &\mapsto_\mathcal{A} E_0[V] \\ &\cdots \quad \cdots \end{aligned}$$

If, on the other hand, a value is eventually thrown, then

$$\begin{aligned} Q(M[Q/j]) &\mapsto^*_{\beta_v} E_1[QV] \\ &\mapsto_{\beta_v} E_1[\mathcal{A}(E_0[V])] \\ &\mapsto_\mathcal{A} E_0[V] \\ &\cdots \quad \cdots \end{aligned}$$

showing that the context E_1 is abandoned and that evaluation continues with V in the restored context E_0.

3 Formulae-as-types for IS

This section develops a typed version of Idealized Scheme (IS_t) together with a formulae-as-types correspondence between IS_t expressions and a system of natural deduction for classical implicational logic. The evaluation of typed terms requires a minor modification to the operational semantics of IS.

Define type expressions α as

$$\alpha ::= t \mid \alpha \to \alpha',$$

where t is a member of a set of atomic types. Type expressions will also be read as propositions (formulae), with $\alpha \to \beta$ representing "α implies β."

The syntax of ISWIM is modified so that variables are tagged with a type expression: x^α and $\lambda x^\alpha.M$.

Typed ISWIM, written as $ISWIM_t$, is defined in the same way as the simply-typed λ-calculus. A variable x^α has type α; if M has type $\alpha \to \beta$ and N has type α, then MN has type β; if M has type β, then $\lambda x^\alpha.M$ has type $\alpha \to \beta$. The notation M^α means that M has type α.

First, the Curry-Howard isomorphism between $ISWIM_t$ terms and natural deduction proofs for minimal logic (**M**) is presented. The reader is referred to Prawitz [15], Stenlund [18], and Girard [8], for a complete treatment. Second, the correspondence is extended to IS_t with a logically consistent typing for $\mathcal{C}$.

Natural deduction derivations (proofs) Σ are tree-structured objects whose leaves contain formulae representing assumptions and whose nodes represent the application of inference rules. A derivation Σ with conclusion α is written as

$$\begin{array}{c} \Sigma \\ \alpha \end{array}$$

The system **M** of natural deduction derivations is generated from assumptions α, the inference rule for $\to$-elimination ($\to E$, or *modus ponens*)

$$\frac{\begin{array}{cc} \Sigma_1 & \Sigma_2 \\ \alpha \to \beta & \alpha \end{array}}{\beta}$$

and the inference rule for $\to$-introduction ($\to I$)

$$\frac{\begin{array}{c} [\alpha] \\ \Sigma \\ \beta \end{array}}{\alpha \to \beta}$$

The notation

$$\begin{array}{c} \alpha \\ \Sigma \\ \beta \end{array}$$

means that there are zero or more undischarged occurrences of the assumption α in the derivation Σ, while the notation

$$\begin{array}{c} [\alpha] \\ \Sigma \\ \beta \end{array}$$

means that some of these assumptions have been discharged (made unavailable).

For each derivation Σ there is a corresponding $ISWIM_t$ term M of type α, which is defined by induction on the structure of Σ. Assume that the assumptions of Σ are divided into a disjoint collection of sets, each associated with a unique variable. An assumption α corresponds to the variable x^α, where x is the variable associated with the set for α. If

$$\begin{array}{c} \Sigma_1 \\ \alpha \to \beta \end{array}$$

corresponds to the term $M^{\alpha \to \beta}$ and

$$\begin{array}{c} \Sigma_2 \\ \alpha \end{array}$$

corresponds to the term N^α, then

$$\frac{\begin{array}{cc} \Sigma_1 & \Sigma_2 \\ \alpha \to \beta & \alpha \end{array}}{\beta}$$

corresponds to $(MN)^\beta$. If

$$\begin{array}{c} \alpha \\ \Sigma \\ \beta \end{array}$$

corresponds to M^β, then

$$\frac{\begin{array}{c} [\alpha] \\ \Sigma \\ \beta \end{array}}{\alpha \to \beta}$$

corresponds to $(\lambda x^\alpha.M)^{\alpha \to \beta}$, provided that the set of discharged assumptions is the set associated with the variable x.

We will now extend the correspondence between typed terms and proofs to IS by finding a logically consistent typing for $\mathcal{C}$. Let us start by looking at the $\mapsto_\mathcal{C}$ rule

$$E[\mathcal{C}(M)] \mapsto_\mathcal{C} M \lambda z.\mathcal{A}(E[z]). \qquad (\mapsto_\mathcal{C})$$

Let α and β be arbitrary types. Suppose that E is of type β and that the hole in E is expecting a term of type α. It seems reasonable to give the term $\lambda z.\mathcal{A}(E[z])$ the type $\alpha \to \beta$ since for any value V of type α,

$$(\lambda z.\mathcal{A}(E[z]))V \mapsto^+_u E[V],$$

which is of type β. Therefore, since both sides of the $\mapsto_\mathcal{C}$ rule are of type β, M must have type $(\alpha \to \beta) \to \beta$. We then arrive at the following typing rule for $\mathcal{C}(M)$: if M has type $(\alpha \to \beta) \to \beta$, then $\mathcal{C}(M)$ has type α.

It follows from this derivation that if N is a closed term of type β, then $\mathcal{A}(N) = \mathcal{C}(\lambda d.N)$ can be given *any* type α. Therefore, if we want a type system that is logically consistent when types are read as propositions, β must be a proposition that has no proof (otherwise every proposition is provable). Assume that the set of atomic types contains the type $\bot$, which represents an empty type, or the proposition "false." Define $\neg\alpha$ (read "not α") as

$$\neg\alpha \stackrel{\text{def}}{=} \alpha \to \bot, \qquad (\neg\alpha).$$

We then arrive at a logically consistent typing for $\mathcal{C}(M)$: if M has type $\neg\neg\alpha$, then $\mathcal{C}(M)$ has type α. This will be the typing used for typed Idealized Scheme, which is written as IS_t. Such an instance of $\mathcal{C}(M)$ will often be written as $\mathcal{C}^\alpha(M)$ in order to make explicit the type of the term.

From a logical perspective, $\mathcal{C}^\alpha(M)$ correponds to the *classical* proof rule for double negation elimination ($\bot_c$)

$$\frac{\begin{array}{c}\Sigma\\ \neg\neg\alpha\end{array}}{\alpha}$$

if $M^{\neg\neg\alpha}$ corresponds to the derivation Σ. The system **C** is defined to be **M** extended with the $\bot_c$ rule.

Note that $\mathcal{A}(M)$ now corresponds to the constructive rule for $\bot$-elimination ($\bot_e$)

$$\frac{\begin{array}{c}\Sigma\\ \bot\end{array}}{\alpha}$$

which can be derived in **C**. The notation $\mathcal{A}^\alpha(M)$ indicates that this term has type α. The constructive system **J** is defined to be **M** extended with the $\bot_e$ rule.

There is one problem with this typing of IS. The $\mapsto_c$ rule applies only when the entire expression $E[\mathcal{C}(M)]$ is of type $\bot$, and since there are no closed terms of this type, the rule is useless! To rectify this problem, a minor modification is made to the operational semantics of IS. The basic idea is as follows. Instead of evaluating an expression M^α with the $\mapsto_u$ rules, the expression $\mathcal{C}(\lambda k^{\neg\alpha}.kM)$ is evaluated with the rules of $\mapsto_u$ being applied only inside of the expression $\mathcal{C}(\lambda k.\cdots)$. The rules now make "type sense" since the body of the λ-expression is of type $\bot$.

Formally, define the operational semantics $\mapsto_t$ as the union of the following rules.

$$\mathcal{C}(\lambda k.E[(\lambda x.M)V]) \quad \mapsto_{t\beta_v} \quad \mathcal{C}(\lambda k.E[M[V/x]])$$

$$\mathcal{C}(\lambda k.E[\mathcal{C}(M)]) \quad \mapsto_{tC} \quad \mathcal{C}(\lambda k.M\lambda z.\mathcal{A}(E[z]))$$

$$\mathcal{C}(\lambda k.kV) \quad \mapsto_{C_e} \quad V$$

The last rule is subject to the proviso that k is not free in V. This rule merely allows for the removal of the outermost $\mathcal{C}$ at the end of some computations. An expression is in $\mapsto_t$ normal form if none of these rules apply.

Definition 1 (evaluation of typed terms) *A closed IS_t expression M^α evaluates to Q if*

$$\mathcal{C}^\alpha(\lambda k^{\neg\alpha}.kM) \mapsto_t^* Q$$

and Q is in $\mapsto_t$ normal form.

That $\mapsto_t$ is only a minor modification to the $\mapsto_u$ semantics is stated in the following lemma.

Lemma 3 *If $\mathcal{C}(\lambda k.kM) \mapsto_u^* V$, then $\mathcal{C}(\lambda k.kM) \mapsto_t^* Q$, where Q is either V, $\mathcal{C}\lambda k.kV'$, or $\mathcal{C}\lambda k.V'$, and $V = V'[\lambda x.\mathcal{A}(x)/k]$.*

In other words, the only type violation of the system $\mapsto_u$ is the replacement of the top-level continuation k with $\lambda x.\mathcal{A}(x)$.

The types of "classical programs" cannot be given the same operational interpretation as the types of "constructive programs." A program M corresponding to a constructive proof of $\alpha \to \beta$ takes inputs of type α to outputs of type β. This is no longer the case with classical programs since the evaluation of an expression need not return to the point of its evaluation but may "jump" to some other evaluation context. In the type system presented here, the distinction between a "returning expression" and a "jumping expression" cannot be made by inspecting an expression's type. Thus, if M is a classical program of type $\alpha \to \beta$ and N is a classical program of type α, we know only that if the application of M to N returns to the current control context, then it will return with a (classical) value of type β. Note that the evaluation of either M, N, or the application of M to N could result in a jump.

4 Conjunctive, disjunctive, and existential types

This section demonstrates that there are computationally interesting IS_t terms of type α, where α holds in classical, but not constructive, logic. It is shown that if conjunctive and disjunctive types are defined using standard classical definitions, then the operations of pairing, projection, injection, and analysis by cases can be defined using $\mathcal{C}$. The section concludes by pointing out that if IS_t types are extended with universal types $\forall x^t.\alpha(x)$, then existential types $\exists x^t.\alpha(x)$ can be defined in IS_t.

That the connectives for conjunction and disjunction cannot be defined in constructive (implicational) logic is related, via the Curry/Howard correpondence, to the fact that pairing, projection, injection, and analysis by cases are not definable in the simply typed λ-calculus. It is well known, however, that the connectives for conjunction and disjunction can be defined *classically* in terms of negation and implication as

$$\alpha \wedge \beta \stackrel{\text{def}}{=} \neg(\alpha \to \neg\beta),$$

$$\alpha \vee \beta \stackrel{\text{def}}{=} \neg\alpha \to \beta.$$

The remainder of the section proceeds as follows. The introduction and elimination rules for $\wedge$ and $\vee$ are derived in the classical system **C** and the computational properties of the IS_t terms corresponding to these derived rules are investigated. It is shown that these terms can be used for pairing, projection, injection, and analysis by cases.

The $\wedge$-introduction rule

$$\frac{\begin{matrix}\Sigma_1 & \Sigma_2 \\ \alpha & \beta\end{matrix}}{\alpha \wedge \beta} \quad (\wedge I)$$

can be derived in **C** as

$$\frac{\dfrac{[\alpha \to \neg\beta] \quad \overset{\Sigma_1}{\alpha}}{\neg\beta} \quad \overset{\Sigma_2}{\beta}}{\dfrac{\bot}{\neg(\alpha \to \neg\beta)}}$$

If M^α and N^β are IS_t terms corresponding to the derivations Σ_1 and Σ_2, then the IS_t term

$$\langle M, N \rangle \stackrel{\text{def}}{=} \lambda f^{\alpha \to \neg\beta}.fMN$$

of type $\alpha \wedge \beta$ corresponds to the derived $\wedge$-introduction rule.

The two rules for $\wedge$-elimiantion

$$\frac{\overset{\Sigma}{\alpha_1 \wedge \alpha_2}}{\alpha_i} \quad (\wedge E_i),$$

can be derived in **C** as

$$\frac{\dfrac{\overset{\Sigma}{\neg(\alpha_1 \to \neg\alpha_2)} \quad \dfrac{[\alpha_i] \quad [\neg\alpha_i]}{\dfrac{\bot}{\neg\alpha_2}}}{\dfrac{\bot}{\dfrac{\neg\neg\alpha_i}{\alpha_i}}}}$$

If the term M of type $\alpha \wedge \beta$ corresponds to the derivation to Σ, then the IS_t term

$$\pi_i(M) \stackrel{\text{def}}{=} \mathcal{C}(\lambda j^{\neg \alpha_i}.M \lambda x_1^{\alpha_1}.\lambda x_2^{\alpha_2}.jx_i)$$

of type α_i corresponds to the derived rule for $\wedge$-elimination.

Computationally, the terms $\langle M, N\rangle$ and π_i represent operations of pairing and projection. The derivations of the computational properties of these terms are carried out with the $\mapsto_u$ rules, with the understanding that typed terms are to be evaluated using the $\mapsto_t$ rules. This is done only to avoid the notational clutter of wrapping around each term the expression $\mathcal{C}(\lambda k.\cdots)$.

Let $Q = \lambda z.\mathcal{A}(E[z])$, then

$$\begin{aligned}E[\pi_1(\langle M_1, M_2\rangle)] &\mapsto_\mathcal{C} & \langle M_1, M_2\rangle(\lambda x_1.\lambda x_2.Qx_i) \\ &\mapsto_{\beta_v} & (\lambda x_1.\lambda x_2.Qx_i)M_1 M_2\end{aligned}$$

Now, if both M_1 and M_2 evaluate to values V_1 and V_2, respectively, then the evaluation has the form

$$\begin{aligned}\mapsto_u^+ & \quad (\lambda x_1.\lambda x_2.Qx_i)V_1 M_2 \\ \mapsto_{\beta_v} & \quad (\lambda x_2.Qx_i[V_1/x_1])M_2 \\ \mapsto_u^+ & \quad (\lambda x_2.Qx_i[V_1/x_1])V_2 \\ \mapsto_\beta & \quad QV_i \\ \mapsto_\beta & \quad \mathcal{A}(E[V_i]) \\ \mapsto_\mathcal{A} & \quad E[V_i] \\ \vdots & \quad \vdots\end{aligned}$$

Thus, the evaluation of $E[\pi_i(\langle M_1, M_2\rangle)]$ forces both M_1 and M_2 to be evaluated to values V_1 and V_2 at the top-level before V_i is thrown back to the context E. Note, however, that in general the terms M_i need not return. As a special case, if the evaluation starts with a pair of values, then we have

$$E[\pi_i(\langle V_1, V_2\rangle)] \mapsto_u^+ E[V_i].$$

This should be campared to adding operators for pairing and projection to $ISWIM_t$ together with the evaluation rule

$$E[\pi_i(\langle M_1, M_2\rangle)] \mapsto_{\pi_i} E[M_i]. \qquad (\mapsto_{\pi_i})$$

If $E[\pi_i(\langle M_1, M_2\rangle)] \mapsto_{\pi_i} E[M_i]$, then M_i must evaluate to a value V_i before the evaluation can continue with subterms of E (by an extension of Lemma 2, Section 2, with the appropriate definition of evaluation contexts). The classical definition requires, however, that *both* M_1 and M_2 are evaluated to values.

Turning to disjunction, the introduction rule

$$\frac{\overset{\Sigma}{\alpha_1}}{\alpha_1 \vee \alpha_2} \quad (\vee I_1),$$

can be derived in **C** in such a way that if M^α corresponds to the derivation Σ, then

$$\text{inj}_1(M) \stackrel{\text{def}}{=} \lambda k^{\neg \alpha_1}.\mathcal{A}^{\alpha_2}(kM)$$

is a IS_t term of type $\alpha_1 \vee \alpha_2$ corresponding to the derived rule for $\vee I_1$. The introduction rule

$$\frac{\begin{array}{c}\Sigma\\ \alpha_2\end{array}}{\alpha_1 \vee \alpha_2} \quad (\vee I_2),$$

can be derived in **C** in such a way that if the term M of type α_2 corresponds to the derivation Σ, then

$$\mathrm{inj}_2(M) \stackrel{\text{def}}{=} \lambda k^{\neg \alpha_1}.M$$

is of type $\alpha_1 \vee \alpha_2$ corresponding to the derived $\vee I_2$-rule. Finally, the $\vee$-elimination rule

$$\frac{\begin{array}{ccc}\Sigma & [\alpha_1]\\ & \Sigma_1 & [\alpha_2]\\ \alpha_1 \vee \alpha_2 & \delta & \Sigma_2\\ & & \delta\end{array}}{\delta} \quad (\vee E).$$

can be derived in **C** in such a way that the term

$$\mathrm{case}(M, F_1, F_2) \stackrel{\text{def}}{=} \mathcal{C}(\lambda j^{\neg \delta}.j(F_1(M \lambda a.j(F_1 a))))$$

of type δ corresponds to the derived rule when $F_i = \lambda x_i^{\alpha_i}.M_i$ correspond to the derivations

$$\frac{\begin{array}{c}[\alpha_i]\\ \Sigma_i\\ \delta\end{array}}{\alpha_i \to \delta}$$

for $i \in \{1, 2\}$.

Computationally, the terms $\mathrm{inj}_i(M)$ and $\mathrm{case}(M, F_1, F_2)$ represent operations of injection and case analysis. Let $Q = \lambda z.\mathcal{A}(E[z])$, then

$$E[\mathrm{case}(\mathrm{inj}_1(N_1), F_1, F_2)] \mapsto_u^+ (\lambda a.Q(F_1 a))N_1,$$

and

$$E[\mathrm{case}(\mathrm{inj}_2(N_2), F_1, F_2)] \mapsto_u^+ Q(F_2 N_2)$$

are easy to derive using the $\mapsto_u$ rules. Suppose that N_i evaluates to V_i. If $F_i V_i$ evaluate to a value V_i', then in both cases evaluation can be continued as

$$\begin{array}{rl}\mapsto_u^+ & QV_i'\\ \mapsto_{\beta_v} & \mathcal{A}(E[V_i'])\\ \mapsto_{\mathcal{A}} & E[V_i']\\ \vdots & \vdots\end{array}$$

Thus, the result of applying F_i to V_i is evaluated at the top-level to a value V_i' before this value is thrown back to the context E. Again, the evaluation of this application need not return.

Suppose that IS_t types are extended with universal types, $\forall x.\alpha$, where x ranges over integer terms. In logical terms, this corresponds to extending the propositional calculus to a first-order predicate calculus. It is assumed that types (propositions) have been extended to include predicates such as equality. If M has type $\forall x.\alpha$ and n is an integer expression, then Mn has type $\alpha[n/x]$. If x is not free in any type of a free variable of M^α, then $\lambda x.M$ has type $\forall x.alpha$.

Existential types can now be defined with the standard classical definition,

$$\exists x.\alpha \stackrel{\text{def}}{=} \neg \forall x.\neg \alpha(x).$$

Define the terms

$$P_1 \stackrel{\text{def}}{=} \lambda x.\lambda w^{\alpha(x)}.\lambda f^{\forall y.\neg \alpha(y)}.fxw$$

of type $\forall x.(\alpha(x) \to \exists y.\alpha(y))$, and

$$P_2 \stackrel{\text{def}}{=} \lambda p^{\exists x.\alpha(x)}.\lambda f^{\forall x.(\alpha(x) \to \beta)}.\mathcal{C}(\lambda j^{\neg \beta}.p(\lambda x.\lambda w.j(fxw)))$$

of type $\exists x.\alpha(x) \to (\forall x.(\alpha(x) \to \beta)) \to \beta$. These terms represent operators for computing with (weak) existential types (see, for example, [10]). For an integer value n, V_1 of type $\alpha[n/x]$, and V_2 of type $\forall x.(\alpha(x) \to \beta)$, the evaluation

$$E[P_2(P_1 n V_1) V_2] \mapsto_u^+ Q(V_2 n V_1)$$

can be derived with $Q = \lambda z.\mathcal{A}(E[z])$. If $V_2 n V_1$ evaluates to a value V, then this value is thrown back to the context E.

5 The excluded middle

There are many equivalent ways of defining classical logic. For example, in place of double negation elimination, classical logic is often defined by adding the law of the excluded middle, $\alpha \vee \neg \alpha$, to constructive logic. This section shows that the law of the excluded middle can be given an operational interpretation that is computationally equivalent to that of $\mathcal{C}$.

For any α, the law of the excluded middle can be derived in **C** as

$$\frac{[\neg(\alpha \vee \neg \alpha)] \quad \dfrac{\dfrac{[\neg(\alpha \vee \neg \alpha)] \quad \dfrac{[\alpha]}{\alpha \vee \neg \alpha}}{\bot}}{\dfrac{\neg \alpha}{\alpha \vee \neg \alpha}}}{\dfrac{\bot}{\dfrac{\neg \neg(\alpha \vee \neg \alpha)}{\alpha \vee \neg \alpha}}}$$

This derivation corresponds to the IS_t term

$$c^\alpha \stackrel{def}{=} \mathcal{C}(\lambda j^{\neg(\alpha \vee \beta)}.j(\text{inj}_2(\lambda a^\alpha.j(\text{inj}_1(a)))))$$

of type $\alpha \vee \neg\alpha$. It is then easy to derive, using the $\mapsto_u$ rules, an evaluation rule for c,

$$E[c] \mapsto_c E[\text{inj}_2(\lambda a.Q(\text{inj}_1(a)))],$$

where $Q = \lambda z.\mathcal{A}(E[z])$. (As in the previous section, notational clutter is avoided by using the $\mapsto_u$ evaluation rules.)

Alternatively, suppose that typed constants c^α are added to an extended ISWIM, which contains injections and analysis by cases. Note that this corresponds to an alternative formalization of classical logic in which the double negation elimination rule can be derived as

$$\cfrac{\alpha \vee \neg\alpha \quad [\alpha] \quad \cfrac{\cfrac{\neg\neg\alpha \quad [\neg\alpha]}{\bot}}{\overline{\alpha}}}{\alpha}$$

This derivation corresponds to the derived version of $\mathcal{C}$,

$$\mathcal{C}_c^\alpha(M) \stackrel{def}{=} \text{case}(c^\alpha, \lambda a^\alpha.a, \lambda k^{\neg\alpha}.\mathcal{A}^\alpha(Mk)),$$

where M corresponds to Σ. Suppose that $\mapsto_c$ is taken as a primitive evaluation rule and evaluation contexts include contexts of the form $\text{case}(E, M_1, M_2)$. Then the evaluation rule for $\mathcal{C}_c$ can be derived as

$$E[\mathcal{C}_c(M)] \mapsto_{c_c} M\lambda z.Q'(\text{inj}_1(z)), \quad (\mapsto_{c_c})$$

where $Q' = \lambda z.\mathcal{A}(E[\text{case}(z, \lambda a.a, \lambda k.\mathcal{A}(Mk))])$. Note that $\mapsto_{c_c}$ is computationally equivalent to the $\mapsto_c$ rule, since for any context E_1,

$$E_1[(\lambda z.Q'(\text{inj}_1(z)))V] \mapsto^+ E[V].$$

Similar results can be obtained for other formalizations of classical logic. For example, suppose classical logic is defined as **J** extended with Peirce's law

$$\cfrac{\Sigma}{\cfrac{(\alpha \to \beta) \to \alpha}{\alpha}}$$

This rule can be put into correspondence with a typed version of $\mathcal{K}$ (see Section 2 for the definition of $\mathcal{K}$) as follows. If M is a term of type $(\alpha \to \beta) \to \alpha$, then $\mathcal{K}_\beta^\alpha(M)$ has type α. Now $\mathcal{C}$ can then be defined as

$$\mathcal{C}^\alpha(M) \stackrel{def}{=} \mathcal{K}_\bot^\alpha(\lambda j^{\neg\alpha}.\mathcal{A}^\alpha(Mj)),$$

which corresponds to the derivation of double negation elimination using $\bot_e$ and Peirce's law. The $\mapsto_c$ rule can then be derived with the rules $\mapsto_{\beta_v}$, $\mapsto_\mathcal{A}$, and $\mapsto_\mathcal{K}$.

6 The cps transform is a logical embedding

A common approach to providing a semantics for a language that contains labels and jumps is via a translation to a language that explicitly represents continuations as functions. Such a translation is often called a *continuation passing style* transformation, or simply a *cps* transformation. A cps transform $\overline{M}$ for untyped λ-expressions was introduced by Fischer [7] and extended to expressions containing $\mathcal{C}$ by Felleisen *et al* [3]. A slightly modified cps transform is defined here as

$$\overline{x} = \lambda k.kx,$$
$$\overline{\lambda x.M} = \lambda k.k(\lambda x.\overline{M}),$$
$$\overline{MN} = \lambda k.\overline{M}(\lambda m.\overline{N}(\lambda n.mnk)),$$
$$\overline{\mathcal{C}(M)} = \lambda k.\overline{M}(\lambda m.m(\lambda z.\lambda d.kz)\lambda x.\mathcal{A}(x)).$$

This definition differs from the one in [3] in the last clause, where we use $\lambda x.\mathcal{A}(x)$ rather than $\lambda x.x$.

Although the cps transform is defined for untyped expressions, it defines a transformation on typed expressions as well. Assume there is a distinguished type o, and define the transformation α^* on types as

$$t^* = t,$$
$$(\alpha \to \beta)^* = \alpha^* \to (\beta^* \to o) \to o.$$

Theorem 4 *[cps as a typed transform] If M is an IS_t expression of type α, then $\overline{M}$ has type $(\alpha^* \to o) \to o$.*

This fact simply extends a result of Meyer and Wand [13] from simply-typed terms to typed terms containing $\mathcal{C}$.

An *embedding* of classical implicational logic (**C**) into constructive implicational logic (**J**) is defined to be a translation of formulae α' such that if there is a classical proof of α, then there is a constructive proof of α', where α is classically equivalent to α'. It is interesting to note that if we take $\mathcal{A}$ to be a basic construct, then the cps transform corresponds to such an embedding.

For **S** being **J** or **C**, let $\Gamma \vdash_\mathbf{S} \alpha$ represent the assertion that there exists an **S**-derivation for α, all of whose undischarged assumptions are in the set of formulae Γ. Let $\Gamma^* = \{\alpha^* \mid \alpha \in \Gamma\}$. Theorem 4 can now be restated in terms of proofs.

Theorem 5 (cps as a proof transform) *If Σ is a proof of $\Gamma \vdash_\mathbf{C} \alpha$ corresponding to M, then there exists a proof $\overline{\Sigma}$ of $\Gamma^* \vdash_\mathbf{J} (\alpha^* \to o) \to o$ that corresponds to $\overline{M}$.*

If $o = \bot$, then it is easy to check that for all α,

$$\vdash_C \alpha \leftrightarrow \neg\neg\alpha^*,$$

and so the translation corresponds to an embedding[4].

7 Evaluations are finite

In this section it is shown that all computations with well-typed IS_t terms are finite.

Theorem 6 (finite evaluation) *The evaluation of any well-typed IS_t term M^α is finite.*

The method of proof involves a translation of IS_t terms M to simply-typed λ-terms M' so that any infinite evaluation sequence starting from M induces an infinite β-reduction sequence starting from M'. Then, since there are no infinite β-reductions in the simply-typed λ-calculus (see, for example, [9]) there can be no infinite evaluations of IS_t terms.

An obvious candidate for this translation is the cps transform of the previous section. However, as mentioned in Plotkin [14], the cps transform $\overline{M}$ introduces many "bookkeeping" redexes. These bookkeeping redexes prevent the direct use of the cps transform as the desired translation. To overcome this problem, a modified cps transform $\overline{\overline{M}}$ is defined that contracts many of the bookkeeping redexes, that is, $\overline{M} \to_\beta^* \overline{\overline{M}}$. This modified cps transform will serve as the translation described above.

For the purposes of this proof the operator $\mathcal{A}$ will be taken as primitive and the evaluation rules of IS_t will include the rule

$$\mathcal{C}(\lambda k.E[\mathcal{A}(M)]) \mapsto_{t\mathcal{A}} \mathcal{C}(\lambda k.M). \qquad (\mapsto_{t\mathcal{A}})$$

Clearly, there is no loss of generality in this assumption.

Define $\Psi(x^\alpha) = x^{\alpha^*}$, and $\Psi(\lambda x^\alpha.M) = \lambda x^{\alpha^*}.\overline{\overline{M}}$. Define

$$\overline{\overline{M}} \stackrel{\text{def}}{=} \lambda k.(M:k),$$

for k not free in M. Given a term M of type α, and a value V of type $\alpha^* \to o$, define the term $M : V$ of type o, by induction on M (it is assumed that types are chosen appropriately and that new variables are chosen to avoid capture):

1. $V_1 : V_0 = V_0 \Psi(V_1)$
2. $V_1 V_2 : V_0 = \Psi(V_1)\Psi(V_2)V_0$
3. $V_1 N : V_0 = N : \lambda n.\Psi(V_1)nV_0$

---
[4] The author has not been able to find this embedding mentioned in the literature of proof theory.

4. $MV_1 : V_0 = M : \lambda m.m\Psi(V_1)V_0$
5. $MN : V_0 = M : (\lambda m.N : (\lambda n.mnV_0))$
6. $\mathcal{A}(M) : V_0 = M : \lambda x.\mathcal{A}(x)$
7. $\mathcal{C}(M) : V_0 = M : \lambda m.m(\lambda z.\lambda k.V_0 z)\lambda x.\mathcal{A}(x)$
8. $\#\mathcal{C}(\lambda j.M) : V_0 = (M : \lambda x.\mathcal{A}(x))[(\lambda z.\lambda k.V_0 z)/j]$

The special symbol $\#$ will be used to mark the top-level of a term. This definition was based on Plotkin's definition of $M : V$ in [14]. However, the $M : V$ defined here reduces more redexes and is extended to the language of IS.

The relation $\to_\beta$ denotes the usual notion of β reduction, while $\to_\beta^+$ and $\to_\beta^*$ denote the transitive, and transitive, reflexive closures, respectively, of $\to_\beta$.

Lemma 7 *For all M, $\overline{M} \to_\beta^* \overline{\overline{M}}$.*

Therefore, if M has type α, then $\overline{\overline{M}}$ has type $(\alpha^* \to o) \to o$. The following lemma states that every $\mapsto_t$ evaluation step from a term M induces zero or more $\to_\beta$ steps on the term $\overline{\overline{\#M}}$.

Lemma 8 *1. If $M_0 \mapsto_{t\beta_v} M_1$, then $\overline{\overline{\#M_0}} \to_\beta^+ \overline{\overline{\#M_1}}$.*

2. If $M_0 \mapsto_{t\mathcal{C}} M_1$, then $\overline{\overline{\#M_0}} \to_\beta^* \overline{\overline{\#M_1}}$.

3. If $M_0 \mapsto_{t\mathcal{A}} M_1$, then $\overline{\overline{\#M_0}} = \overline{\overline{\#M_1}}$.

The proof of this lemma will require the following lemmas, which are stated without proof.

Lemma 9 *For all evaluation contexts E, terms M, and values V*

$$E[M] : V = M : V^E$$

where V^E is defined by induction on E as

1. $V^{[\,]} = V$,
2. $V^{E_1 N} = (\lambda m.N : (\lambda n.mnV))^{E_1}$,
3. $V^{E_1 V'} = (\lambda m.m\Psi(V')V)^{E_1}$,
4. $V^{V'E_1} = (\lambda n.\Psi(V')nV)^{E_1}$.

Lemma 10 *For all M, values V,*

$$\overline{\overline{M}}[\Psi(V)/x] = \overline{\overline{M[V/x]}}.$$

The proof of Lemma 8 uses the abbreviations

$$\begin{aligned}
A &\stackrel{\text{def}}{=} \lambda x.\mathcal{A}(x), \\
M^\circ &\stackrel{\text{def}}{=} \lambda k_0.M[J(k_0)/k], \\
J(V) &\stackrel{\text{def}}{=} \lambda z.\lambda d.Vz \\
&\quad (z,d \text{ not free in } V).
\end{aligned}$$

Proof of Lemma 8. For the first part of the lemma, suppose

$$\begin{aligned}
M_0 &= \mathcal{C}(\lambda k.E[(\lambda x.M)V]), \\
M_1 &= \mathcal{C}(\lambda k.E[M[V/x]]).
\end{aligned}$$

Looking at the left-hand side, we have

$$\begin{aligned}
\overline{\overline{\#M_0}} &= (E[(\lambda x.M)V] : A)^\circ \\
&= ((\lambda x.M)V : A^E)^\circ \\
&= ((\lambda x.\overline{\overline{M}})\Psi(V)A^E)^\circ \\
&\to_\beta (\overline{\overline{M}}[\Psi(V)/x]A^E)^\circ \\
&= (\overline{\overline{M[V/x]}}A^E)^\circ \\
&= ((\lambda k_1.M[V/x] : k_1)A^E)^\circ \\
&\to_\beta (M[V/x] : A^E)^\circ.
\end{aligned}$$

Now, turning to the right-hand side,

$$\begin{aligned}
\overline{\overline{\#M_1}} &= (E[M[V/x]] : A)^\circ \\
&= (M[V/x] : A^E)^\circ,
\end{aligned}$$

which is equal to the left-hand side. For the second part of the lemma, suppose

$$\begin{aligned}
M_0 &= \mathcal{C}(\lambda k.E[\mathcal{C}(N)]), \\
M_1 &= \mathcal{C}(\lambda k.N\lambda z.\mathcal{A}(E[z])).
\end{aligned}$$

First, note that

$$\begin{aligned}
\Psi(\lambda z.\mathcal{A}(E[z])) &= \lambda z.\overline{\overline{\mathcal{A}(E[z])}} \\
&= \lambda z.\lambda d.(\mathcal{A}(E[z]) : d) \\
&= \lambda z.\lambda d.(E[z] : A) \\
&= \lambda z.\lambda d.(z : A^E) \\
&= \lambda z.\lambda d.A^E z \\
&= J(A^E)
\end{aligned}$$

Looking at the left-hand side, we have

$$\begin{aligned}
\overline{\overline{\#M_0}} &= (E[\mathcal{C}(N)] : A)^\circ \\
&= (\mathcal{C}(N) : A^E)^\circ \\
&= (N : \lambda m.mJ(A^E)A)^\circ.
\end{aligned}$$

Turning to the right-hand side, there are two cases to consider. Suppose N is not a value, then

$$\begin{aligned}
\overline{\overline{\#M_1}} &= (N\lambda z.\mathcal{A}(E[z]) : A)^\circ \\
&= (N : \lambda m.m\Psi(\lambda z.\mathcal{A}(E[z]))A)^\circ \\
&= (N : \lambda m.mJ(A^E)A)^\circ,
\end{aligned}$$

and the left- and right-hand sides are equal. Suppose, on the other hand, that N is a value. Looking at the left-hand side, we have

$$\begin{aligned}
\overline{\overline{\#M_0}} &= (N : \lambda m.mJ(A^E)A)^\circ \\
&= ((\lambda m.mJ(A^E)A)\Psi(N))^\circ \\
&\to_\beta (\Psi(N)J(A^E)A)^\circ,
\end{aligned}$$

while on the right we have

$$\begin{aligned}
\overline{\overline{\#M_1}} &= (N\lambda z.\mathcal{A}(E[z]) : A)^\circ \\
&= (\Psi(N)\Psi(\lambda z.\mathcal{A}(E[z]))A)^\circ \\
&= (\Psi(N)J(A^E)A)^\circ,
\end{aligned}$$

which is equal to the left-hand side. Finally, for the third part of the lemma, suppose

$$\begin{aligned}
M_0 &= \mathcal{C}(\lambda k.E[\mathcal{A}(N)]), \\
M_1 &= \mathcal{C}(\lambda k.N).
\end{aligned}$$

On the left we have

$$\begin{aligned}
\overline{\overline{\#M_0}} &= (E[\mathcal{A}(N)])^\circ \\
&= (\mathcal{A}(N) : A^E)^\circ \\
&= (N : A)^\circ,
\end{aligned}$$

which is equal to $\overline{\overline{\#M_1}}$. □

Lemma 11 *All sequences of $\mapsto_\mathcal{C}$ steps are finite.*

Proof. Any sequence of $\mapsto_\mathcal{C}$ steps must have the form

$$\begin{aligned}
M_0 &\propto E_1[\mathcal{C}(M_1)] &&\mapsto_\mathcal{C} M_1V_1 \\
&\propto E_2[\mathcal{C}(M_2)]V_1 &&\mapsto_\mathcal{C} M_2V_2 \\
&\cdots \cdots && \cdots \cdots \\
&\propto E_i[\mathcal{C}(M_i)]V_{i-1} &&\mapsto_\mathcal{C} M_iV_i \\
&\cdots \cdots && \cdots \cdots
\end{aligned}$$

for some sequence of values $V_1, V_2, \cdots$, and some sequence of terms $M_1, M_2, \cdots$. This sequence must be finite since each M_{i+1} is a proper subterm of M_i and all terms have finite depth. □

By essentially the same argument we can prove the following lemma.

Lemma 12 *All evaluation sequences composed only of applications of the $\mapsto_{t\mathcal{C}}$ and $\mapsto_{t\mathcal{A}}$ rules are finite.*

We can now prove the main result of this section.

Proof of Theorem 6. Let M be a typed IS term of type α. Suppose there is an infinite evaluation sequence

$$\mathcal{C}\lambda k^{\neg\alpha}.M_0 \mapsto_t \mathcal{C}\lambda k^{\neg\alpha}.M_1 \mapsto_t \cdots$$

where $M_0 = kM$. Let $N_i = \mathcal{C}\lambda k.M_i$ and $Q_i = \overline{\overline{\#N_i}}$. Then, by Lemma 8,

$$Q_0 \to_\beta^* Q_1 \to_\beta^* \cdots$$

where $Q_i = Q_{i+1} = \cdots = Q_{i+j}$ is possible only when the evaluation subsequence from Q_i to Q_{i+j} is composed only of $\mapsto_{tC}$ and $\mapsto_{tA}$ steps. Since each such subsequence is finite by Lemma 12, it must be possible to find an infinite subsequence

$$Q_0 \to_\beta^+ Q_1' \to_\beta^+ Q_2' \to_\beta^+ \cdots$$

However, since Q_0 is well-typed (of type $(\alpha^* \to o) \to o$), this contradicts the well-known fact that simply typed λ-terms are strongly normalizing. Therefore, there cannot exist an infinite evaluation sequence starting from M. □

8 Conclusion

This paper has shown that a formulae-as-typed correspondence can be defined between classical propositional logic and a typed Idealized Scheme containing a control operator similar to Scheme's call/cc. It should be noted, however, that the paper merely presents a *formal* correspondence between classical logic and Idealized Scheme. At this point there still remains the question: Why should there be any correspondence at all? Whether or not there is a "deeper reason" underlying the correspondence is unclear at this time.

[Note: Shortly before the publication deadline for this conference the work of Andrzej Filinski [6,5] was brought to my attention. His work may provide a "deeper reason," for the correspondence described in this paper. However, due to the lack of time, I have been unable to investigate this thoroughly. Filinki defines the Symmetric Lambda Calculus (SLC), which gives a symmetric treatment of values and continuations. He then develops a categorical model of this language in which values and continuations are dual notions. Classical types for control operators seem to arise naturally in this setting.]

9 Acknowledgments

I'm indebted to Matthias Felleisen for introducing me to call/cc, for spending many hours patiently explaining his work in this area, and for his comments on drafts of this paper. I would like to thank Bob Harper for his comments on drafts of this paper and for bringing the work of Andrzej Filinski to my attention.

References

[1] M. Felleisen. *The calculi of λ_v-CS conversion: a syntactic theory of control and state in imperative higher-order programming languages*. PhD thesis, Indiana University, 1987. Technical Report No. 226.

[2] M. Felleisen and D. Friedman. Control operators, the secd-machine, and the λ-calculus. In *Formal Description of Programming Concepts III*, pages 131–141, North-Holland, 1986.

[3] M. Felleisen, D. Friedman, E. Kohlbecker, and B. Duba. Reasoning with continuations. In *Proceedings of the First Symposium on Logic in Computer Science*, pages 131–141, IEEE, 1986.

[4] M. Felleisen, D. Friedman, E. Kohlbecker, and B. Duba. A syntactic theory of sequential control. *Theoretical Computer Science*, 52(3):205–237, 1987.

[5] A. Filinski. Declarative continuations: an investigation of duality in programming language semantics. In *Summer Conference on Category Theory and Computer Science, Manchester, UK*, Springer-Verlag, 1989. to appear in the Lecture Notes in Computer Science.

[6] A. Filinski. *Declarative Continuations and Categorical Duality*. Master's thesis, University of Copenhagen, Copenhagen, Denmark, August 1989. DIKU Report 89/11, Computer Science Department.

[7] M. J. Fischer. Lambda calculus schemata. In *Proc. ACM Conference on Proving Assertions About Programs*, pages 104–109, 1972. SIGPLAN Notices 7.1.

[8] J. Girard, P. Taylor, and Y. Lafont. *Proofs and Types*. Volume 7 of *Cambridge Tracts in Computer Science*, Cambridge University Press, 1989.

[9] R. J. Hindley and J. Seldin. *Introduction to Combinators and λ-Calculus*. London Mathematical Society Student Texts, Cambridge University Press, 1986.

[10] W. Howard. The formulae-as-types notion of construction. In J. P. Seldin and J. R. Hindley, editors, *To H. B. Curry: Essays on Combinatory Logic, Lambda-Calculus, and Formalism*, pages 479–490, Academic Press, NY, 1980.

[11] P. Landin. The mechanical evaluation of expressions. *Computer Journal*, 6(4), 1964.

[12] P. Landin. The next 700 programming languages. *Commun. ACM*, 9(3):157–166, 1966.

[13] A. R. Meyer and M. Wand. Continuation semantics in typed lambda-calculi (summary). In R. Parikh, editor, *Logics of Programs*, pages 219–224, Springer-Verlag, 1985. Lecture Notes in Computer Science, Volume 193.

[14] G. Plotkin. Call-by-name, call-by-value and the λ-calculus. *Theoretical Computer Science*, 1:125–159, 1975.

[15] D. Prawitz. *Natural Deduction*. Almquist and Wiksell, 1965.

[16] J. Rees and W. Clinger. The revised[3] report on the algorithmic language scheme. *SIGPLAN Notices*, 21(12):37–79, 1986.

[17] G. L. Steele. *Common Lisp: The Language*. Digital Press, Bedford, MA, 1984.

[18] S. Stenlund. *Combinators, Lambda-Terms and Proof Theory*. D. Reidel, Dordrecht, Holland, 1972.

Implicative Formulae in the "Proofs as Computations" Analogy

Andrea Asperti, Gian Luigi Ferrari, Roberto Gorrieri
Università di Pisa, Dipartimento di Informatica
Corso Italia 40, I - 56125 Pisa Italy
asperti {giangi, gorrieri}@di.unipi.it

ABSTRACT

In [As87] a correspondence between the subset of Linear Logic [Gi86] involving the conjunctive tensor product only and Place/Transition Petri Nets [Rei85] is established. In this correspondence, formulae are regarded as distributed states and provable sequents are computations in the net. Developing this idea, Martì-Oliet and Meseguer [MaM89] have suggested that all the other computations of Linear Logic, which do not have an immediate correspondence with Petri Nets, should be regarded as "gedanken" or idealized processes, providing a richer language for the specification and the study of properties of distributed computations. In this paper we apply this program to the fundamental connective of linear implication. We prove that the introduction of linear implication allows us to observe the net at a lower, more decentralized level of atomicity, where the preemption of each resource needed for the firing of a transition is represented as a separate move. We give a conservative theorem relating computations at different levels of abstraction. The categorical semantics establishes a tight correspondence among Petri nets, monoidal closed categories and tensor theories, reminiscent of the well known relation among functional languages, cartesian closed categories and intuitionistic logic [LS86]. The identification of computations in the categorical model naturally suggests the generalisation of the notion of process [DMM89] at the lower level of atomicity.

1. INTRODUCTION

Petri Nets [Pet62] are the first and maybe the most popular formalism for specifying and modelling distributed activities. A Petri Net is defined as a set of places which can contain tokens, a set of transitions and a flow relation connecting places and transitions. A place in the net is interpreted as a resource type, a token in the place as an instance of the resource associated to the place, and a transition as an activity which consumes resources and produces other resources in accordance with the flow relation.

In [As87] it is proved that a net N can be regarded as a theory in the language of Linear Logic [Gi86], involving only the connective of tensor product $\otimes$, which plays the role of conjunction (see also [GG89, MaM89]). Linear Logic is a logical calculus where a particular care is devoted to the introduction and deletion of hypothesis during the deductive process, with the effect that formulae look like resources subject to a limited use. The main idea of the relation between tensor theories and Petri Nets is that an atomic formula A can be thought of as a token in a place named A, and a tensor formula $A_1 \otimes ... \otimes A_n$ as a marking i.e. a distribution of tokens on the places $A_1,...,A_n$. The proof of a sequent of the form $A_1,..., A_n \vdash B$ is then a computation from the marking $A_1 \otimes ... \otimes A_n$ to B. A specific net is described by a set of external axioms (a tensor theory) and the dynamic behaviour of the net is

Research partially supported by Joint Collaboration Contract ST2J-0374-C(EDB) of EEC and by Esprit Basic Research Actions, project 3011 CEDISYS.

described by the inference rules of the propositional tensor fragment. It is easily proved that a net computation corresponds to a proof in the tensor fragment, and conversely every proof has an associated computation on the net.

The expressive power of full Linear Logic is far beyond the expressive power of Petri Nets. In this respect, [MaM89] suggests that all the computations of Linear Logic which do not have an immediate correspondence with Petri Nets should be regarded as *gedanken* or *idealized* processes, providing a richer language for the specification and the study of net properties. They also develop a few examples involving the two additive connectives of conjunction and disjunction, relating them to situations of internal and external nondeterminism (see also [GG89] on this subject).

In this paper we pursue their program, studying the fundamental connective of linear implication. We suggest to look at an implicative formula (e.g. $B \rightarrow C$) as a sort of non-concluded distributed state of a given computation, where some resources (B) are needed to properly terminate with the production of other resources (C). We prove that this approach enables one to observe the system at a lower, more decentralized level of atomicity: indeed we can observe, as a separate move, the preemption of every resource needed for the firing of a transition. In other words, if a place A is a pre-condition of more than one transition, then each token in A can autonomously decide in which transition to be involved, reaching an intermediate state where it can only wait for the tokens taking part to the selected transition. This behavior, not allowed in classical Petri Net Theory, represents a sort of more decentralized description of distributed computations. However, a serious problem arises: the possibility of deadlock. For instance, suppose to have two transitions t: $A, B \vdash C$ and t': $A, B \vdash D$; from the state $A \otimes B$ it can happen that t preempts the token in A and t' the token in B, yielding the deadlock state $(B \rightarrow C) \otimes (A \rightarrow D)$. Deadlock situations and strategies for controlling the decentralized execution of net specifications can be formally understood and profitably studied in the proof theoretic setting of the implicative fragment of Linear Logic.

The main result we prove about the introduction of linear implication is that it is conservative with respect to the class of *concluded* derivations. If a sequent $\Gamma \vdash A$ is provable in a tensor theory T with the implicative fragment of the logic and A does not contain the connective of implication, then there exists a derivation of $\Gamma \vdash A$ within the pure tensor fragment. Moreover the two derivations have the same (categorical) semantics, that is they describes the same process. This result nicely relates the two different levels of atomicity from which we can observe the behaviour of the net.

The paper is organized as follows. Section 2 introduces the tensor fragment, while its categorical semantics is investigated in Section 3. Section 4 settles the correspondence between tensor theories, Petri nets, and monoidal categories. Section 5 studies the fragment extended with linear implication and introduces the notions of *concluded computation* and *deadlock*. Moreover the semantics in monoidal closed categories naturally suggests the right generalization of the notion of process [DMM89]. Finally, in Section 6 the relation between the different levels of atomicity is established as a corollary of a weaker version of Gentzen's Hauptsatz.

2. THE TENSOR FRAGMENT OF LINEAR LOGIC

Linear Logic [Gi86] is essentially a Gentzen Calculus of Sequents (see [Pr65]) without weakening and contraction rules, and with a duplication of the usual logical connectives of conjunction and disjunction, naturally suggested by the lack of such structural rules. This means that neither useless premises can be freely added during the inference, nor different occurrences of the same formula in the premises can be identified: each hypothesis is "used" once and only once. In this sense, logical formulae loose their abstract, platonistic countenance of truth values, or types, gaining the more concrete nature of "resources" or "states". Moreover, any step of logical deduction modifies the state of its premises. This is very appealing for computer science applications, and in particular for concurrent computations since it puts emphasis on dynamics.

The Tensor Fragment is the part of linear logic in which the only logical connective is the conjunctive multiplicative tensor $\otimes$. This subcalculus has (formally) an intuitionistic nature, since only one formula can appear in the right hand side of a sequent. The *alphabet* of the fragment is given by atomic propositions and by the tensor $\otimes$. A *formula* is either an atomic proposition or the product $A \otimes B$ of two formulae. An intuitionistic *sequent* has the syntactic structure $\Gamma \vdash B$ where Γ is a finite (possibly empty) list of formulae, and B is another formula. The *inference rules* of the calculus formalize the process of construction of complex proofs by means of simpler ones.

$$(Ax) \quad A \vdash A$$

$$(exc, l) \quad \frac{\Gamma \vdash A}{\Gamma' \vdash A} \quad \Gamma' \text{ permutation of } \Gamma$$

$$(cut) \quad \frac{\Gamma_1 \vdash A \quad A, \Gamma_2 \vdash B}{\Gamma_1, \Gamma_2 \vdash B}$$

(A is called *cut formula*)

$$(\otimes, l) \quad \frac{\Gamma, A, B \vdash C}{\Gamma, A \otimes B \vdash C}$$

$$(\otimes, r) \quad \frac{\Gamma_1 \vdash A \quad \Gamma_2 \vdash B}{\Gamma_1, \Gamma_2 \vdash A \otimes B}$$

A *derivation* D is a tree of sequents satisfying the following conditions:

- the topmost sequents of D are logical axioms
- every sequent in D except the lowest one (the root) is an upper sequent of an inference whose lower sequent is also in D.

The root sequent is also called *final* sequent.

A *tensor theory* T is a set of sequents, playing the role of extra logical axioms. If T is a tensor theory, a *T-derivation* D is a derivation where the topmost sequents can be in T. A *marked* tensor theory Th is a pair ‹ A, T ›, where A is a formula and T is a tensor theory. When considering marked theories, we are interested in all the derivations of the theory having A as l.h.s. of their final sequents.

3. CATEGORICAL SEMANTICS

The categorical semantics of full Linear Logic has been mostly developed by Lafont [La88] and Seely [Se87], with contributions of several other people ([DP89], [MaM89], see also [AL90] for an updated account). In particular, a model for the tensor fragment is a Symmetric Monoidal Category, whose relevance in Concurrency Theory has been emphasized in [DMM89].

Definition 3.1 (*Symmetric Monoidal Categories*)
A Symmetric Monoidal Category is a category C with a functor $\otimes: C \times C \to C$ (called tensor product), and an object **1** such that:
1) assoc: $X \otimes (Y \otimes Z) \cong (X \otimes Y) \otimes Z$
2) ins: $X \cong 1 \otimes X$
3) exch: $X \otimes Y \cong Y \otimes X$

are natural isomorphisms, called *structural isomorphisms*. Moreover these isomorphisms must satisfy the well-known MacLane-Kelly coherence equations [ML71]. When the structural isomorphisms are actually identities, i.e. 1)-3) above are equations, the monoidal category is called *strict*.

Definition 3.2 (*The Categorical Interpretation*)
Given a tensor theory T and a symmetric monoidal category C, the categorical interpretation I of T over C associates every atomic formula A in T with an object I(A) of the category. The interpretation I is then inductively extended to all the formulas by $I(A \otimes B) = I(A) \otimes I(B)$, and to sequences $\Gamma = A_1, ..., A_n$ by $I(\Gamma) = I(A_1) \otimes ... \otimes I(A_n)$. Every provable sequent $\Gamma \vdash A$ is interpreted as a morphism $f: I(\Gamma) \to I(A)$. In particular I fixes the interpretation for the extra-logical axioms, while every logical axiom $A \vdash A$ is interpreted as the identity morphism of I(A). The interpretation of the provable sequents is inductively defined on the derivation tree, according to the following rules.

(Ax) $\quad id_A : A \vdash A$

(exc) $\dfrac{f: A \otimes B \vdash C}{f \circ exch : B \otimes A \vdash C}$

(cut) $\dfrac{f: B \vdash A \quad g: A \otimes C \vdash D}{g \circ f \otimes id_C : B \otimes C \vdash D}$

($\otimes$, r) $\dfrac{f: A \vdash B \quad g: C \vdash D}{f \otimes g : A \otimes C \vdash B \otimes D}$

Notice that there is no interpretation for ($\otimes$, l) rule since the comma in the left hand side of the sequent is already identified with $\otimes$.

Fixed a theory T, there exists an obvious monoidal category C(T) freely generated by T. For many respects, it is easier to work in this free category, than in the original logic framework. The most important advantage is that it is simpler to handle arrows of the category than derivations of the logic. Another drawback of the logic formalization, which disappears at the categorical level, is the annoying syntactic distinction between the comma in the l.h.s. of a sequent and the connective of tensor product. In the following, we shall often make a blend use of notations in the two frameworks, prefixing each sequent in a derivation with its associated term in the category.

4. TENSOR THEORIES AND PETRI NETS

The analogy between formulae and states (proofs and computations), and its possible application to the theory of Petri Nets was pointed out by the first author [As87], and has been recently revisited and extended in [MaM89] and [GG89]. Any formula of a tensor fragment can be interpreted as representing the distributed state of a system, describing its individual components; for instance the formula $A \otimes B$, where A and B are atomic, represents a state whose individual components are A and B. In other words, an atomic formula can be understood as a *token* in a place, and any formula as a *distribution* of tokens in the net places. A sequent $\Gamma \vdash A$ describes a computation starting from the state Γ and ending in the state represented by the formula A. The deductive engine of the tensor fragment provides the tools to represent the dynamic behaviour: the ($\otimes$, r) rule describes the parallel execution of computations and the cut rule their sequential composition.

Now we introduce the classical definition of Petri Nets. By Petri Nets we mean Place/Transition Petri Nets [Rei85].

Definition 4.1 (*Place Transition Petri Nets*)
A Petri Net N is a quadruple (S, T, F, M_0) where:
- S is a non empty set of places,
- T is a set of transitions, $S \cap T = \emptyset$,
- F is a multiset relation over $(S \times T) \cup (T \times S)$ called the *causal dependency relation*,
- M_0 is a non-empty multiset of places, called the *initial marking*

The causal dependency relation (also called *flow relation*) can be interpreted as a function from $(S \times T) \cup (T \times S)$ to the set **N** of natural numbers. Also markings can be interpreted as functions from S to **N**. For simplicity, a marking M is usually represented as $\{n_1 s_1, ..., n_p s_p\}$

where the natural number $n_i > 0$ indicates the number of the occurrences (*tokens*) of the place s_i in M.

For any transition t its preset is defined as the multiset over S given by $pre(t)(s) = F(s,t)$. Similarly, the postset $post(t)(s) = F(t,s)$. The dynamic behaviour of P/T Nets is defined by the *token game*. Each firing of a transition removes its preset and produces its postset.

Definition 4.2 (*The Token Game*)
Let N be a net, and let M be a marking. A transition t is *enabled* at M if $pre(t)(s) \leq M(s)$. If t is enabled at M, then the *firing* of t ($M - t \rightarrow M'$) transforms M in M': $M'(s) = M(s) - pre(t)(s) + post(t)(s)$.

Definition 4.3 (*Firing Sequence and Reachable Marking*)
Let N be a net, and let M_0 be the initial marking of N. A *firing sequence* is a sequence ($M_0, t_1, M_1, ..., t_n, M_n$) such that $M_0 - t_1 \rightarrow M_1 ... t_n \rightarrow M_n$. M_n is called *reachable* from M_0.

Let A^n indicate the tensor n-power i.e the formula $A \otimes A \otimes ... \otimes A$ where the atomic formula A occurs n times. Let A be a formula, $\mu(A)$ denotes the multiset of the atomic formulae occurring in A; this operation is obviously extended to sequences of formulae via multiset union.

Definition 4.4 (*Marking-formulae*)
Given a marking $M = \{n_1 s_1, ..., n_p s_p\}$ the associated (marking-)formula is $\otimes M = s_1^{n_1} \otimes ... \otimes s_p^{n_p}$.

Definition 4.5 (*Petri Net Theories*)
Given a Petri Net $N = (S, T, F, M_0)$ the marked tensor theory associated with N is the pair $Th(N) = \langle \otimes M_0, Th \rangle$ where Th is the set of the extra logical axioms, defined in the alphabet S of atomic formulae, as follows: for any $t \in T$, $t: \Gamma \vdash A$ is an axiom in Th where $pre(t) = \mu(\Gamma)$ and $post(t) = \mu(A)$.
The formula $\otimes M_0$ is called initial formula of $\langle \otimes M_0, Th \rangle$.

A tensor theory provides the logic counterpart of Petri Nets; in fact a net is uniquely characterized by the preset and the postset of its transitions. The deductive engine of the tensor fragment provides the tools to represent the dynamic behaviour.

Theorem 4.6
Given a net N, M_n is reachable from M_0 if and only if $\otimes M_0 \vdash A$ is a provable sequent in the tensor theory Th(N) and $\mu(A) = M_n$.

The proof (straightforward) of the last theorem settles a constructive correspondence between firing sequences and derivations.

Interpreting the functor $\otimes$ as parallel composition and $\cdot$ as sequential composition, the equational nature of the categorical semantics, developed in Section 3, imposes some relevant identifications among computations. In addition to the basic categorical equations:

$(f \cdot g) \cdot h = f \cdot (g \cdot h)$ *associativity of composition*
$id \cdot f = f = f \cdot id$ *identity is an idle computation*

we have:

$(f \otimes g) \cdot (f' \otimes g') = (f \cdot f') \otimes (g \cdot g')$ *functoriality of* $\otimes$

This law describes one of the basic property about concurrency: the parallel composition of two given independent computations $f \cdot f'$ and $g \cdot g'$ has the same effect of the computation whose steps are the parallel composition $f \otimes g$ and $f' \otimes g'$. As an interesting instance of this law, consider the following example. Given two computations $t_1: A \vdash B$, $t_2: C \vdash D$, we have:

$(id_C \otimes t_1) ; (t_2 \otimes id_B) = t_1 \otimes t_2 = (t_2 \otimes id_A) ; (id_D \otimes t_1)$

that is the well-known property that the concurrent execution of two independent transitions t_1 and t_2, is equivalent to their execution in any order.

If the symmetric monoidal category C is strict, we have the law:

$f \otimes g = g \otimes f$ *commutativity of* $\otimes$

which states the intuitive fact that parallel composition is commutative. These interesting laws were first pointed out by Meseguer and Montanari [MM88] which gave a characterization of Petri Nets as monoidal categories. This approach to an algebraic description of Petri Nets as monoids has been further investigated in [DMM89], where the above outlined notion of computations suggested by the equation of monoidal categories (called *commutative processes* in [DMM89]) is compared with the well-known notion of *process* [GR83]. They prove that commutative processes are the least abstract model which is more abstract than both firing sequences and processes (see also [BD87]).

Remark From a proof-theoretic perspective, it would be interesting to single out which is, in a class of equivalent proofs, the more reduced, i.e. the proof with only the strictly necessary cuts. Since the cut rule corresponds to sequential composition, Gunter and Gehlot [GG89] point out that this requirement can be restated in concurrency theory as follows: among all the equivalent computations, which is the maximally concurrent? In the categorical approach this problem can be solved in a natural way by appropriately "orienting" the semantic equations given above (with some care to the associativity of the composition). The simplicity of this solution is due to the fact that it is much simpler to work with terms than with derivation trees. This result, based on a suggestion of Montanari, will be the object of a forthcoming paper.

5. DECENTRALIZED COMPUTATIONS AND LINEAR IMPLICATION

In this section, we enrich the tensor fragment with the introduction of the linear implication connective. The Linear Logic rules for implication are:

Definition 5.1 (*Linear Implication*)

$$(\rightarrow, r) \quad \frac{\Gamma, A \vdash B}{\Gamma \vdash A \rightarrow B}$$

$$(\rightarrow, l) \quad \frac{\Gamma_1 \vdash A \quad B, \Gamma_2 \vdash C}{A \rightarrow B, \Gamma_1, \Gamma_2 \vdash C}$$

In the categorical semantics, the connective of linear implication $\rightarrow$ is interpreted as the right adjoint to the tensor product $\otimes$, that is as a bifunctor $\rightarrow: C \times C \rightarrow C$ such that there exists a natural isomorphism

(1) $\Lambda : C[c \otimes a, b] \cong C[c, a \rightarrow b]$.

Monoidal Categories where the tensor product $\otimes$ has a right adjoint are called *Monoidal Closed*.

Property 5.2 (*Monoidal closed categories*)
The existence of the adjunction in (1) is equivalently characterized as follows:
for all objects a, b, c in C :
- an object $a \rightarrow b$
- a morphism $eval_{a,b}: (a \rightarrow b) \otimes a \rightarrow b$
   (evaluation map, i.e. modus ponens)
- for every object c an operation
   $\Lambda_c : C[c \otimes a, b] \rightarrow C[c, a \rightarrow b]$

such that for all morphisms $f: c \otimes a \rightarrow b$, $h: c \rightarrow (a \rightarrow b)$, the following equations hold:
   β) $eval_{a,b} \circ (\Lambda_c(f) \otimes id_a) = f$
   η) $\Lambda_c(eval_{a,b} \circ h \otimes id_a) = h$

Definition 5.3 (*The Categorical Interpretation*)
The categorical interpretation of linear implication is defined as follows:

$$(\rightarrow, r) \quad \frac{f: C \otimes A \vdash B}{\Lambda_c(f): C \vdash A \rightarrow B}$$

$$(\rightarrow, l) \quad \frac{f: D \vdash A \quad g: B \otimes E \vdash C}{g \circ (eval_{A,B} \circ (id_{A \rightarrow B} \otimes f)) \otimes id_E : (A \rightarrow B) \otimes D \otimes E \vdash C}$$

A formula without $\rightarrow$ represents a state where all the activated transitions, if any, have been terminated; a formula containing the linear implication represents an intermediate, non-concluded state of a computation. The introduction of the connective of implication allows us to have a finer vision of the computations. Each sequent of a tensor theory T represents an atomic move; the implication rules allow us to break it down into a computation of simpler moves.

Definition 5.4 (*Concluded and Open Sequents*)
A sequent $\Gamma \vdash A$ is *concluded* iff A does not contain any occurrence of the implication connective; it is *open* otherwise

Example 5.5
Consider the transition $t: A, B \vdash C$, and suppose to be in the state A. In the pure multiplicative fragment, no computation was possible other than the idle move $A \vdash A$. On the contrary, in the implicative fragment, we have also the computation $\Lambda(t): A \vdash B \to C$, where t locally gets the only available resource A, reaching the non concluded state $B \to C$. When B becomes available, from $B \to C$ by modus ponens we obtain C. This is described by the following derivation D:

$$\frac{\dfrac{A, B \vdash C}{A \vdash B \to C} \qquad \dfrac{B \vdash B \quad C \vdash C}{B \to C, B \vdash C} \text{ (modus ponens)}}{A, B \vdash C}$$

Intuitively, this computation is equivalent to the direct firing of t, that is to the trivial derivation $D' = A, B \vdash C$. The derivation D' and D can be naïvely represented in terms of the two nets as illustrated below according to their well-known graphical representation.

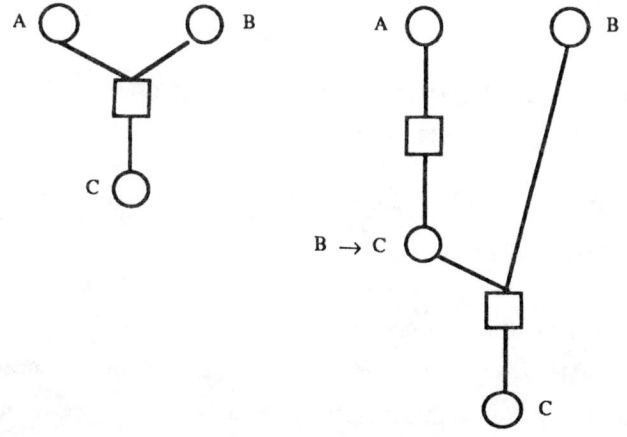

The property of linear implication informally outlined above is further stressed by the categorical semantics. In fact the β-equation

$$\text{eval}_{B,C} \circ (\Lambda_A(f) \otimes \text{id}_B) = f: A \otimes B \vdash C$$

expresses the fact that a computation $f: A \otimes B \vdash C$ regarded as an atomic step, is equivalent to a sequence of simpler *consecutive* steps, namely the preemption of a by f, and the conclusion of the open computation $\Lambda_A(f)$ when b becomes available.

Example 5.6
Suppose to have two transitions $f: C \otimes A \vdash B$, $g: D \vdash A$, and to start with an initial marking $C \otimes D$. This is a possible computation:

$$\text{eval}_{A,B} \circ (\Lambda_C(f) \otimes g) : C \otimes D \vdash B$$

Looking for C and A, f finds only C and preempts it, yielding the open state $A \to B$. At the same time g produces A from D. Now the open computation $\Lambda_C(f)$ can be concluded with the production of B. Another possible strategy for the execution of f and g is the following:

$$f \circ \text{id}_C \otimes g: C \otimes D \vdash B$$

which can be read as follows: first g is fired, while C stays idle; then the pair $C \otimes A$ evolves into B by f. The previous computations are identified by the equational theory:
$\text{eval}_{A,B} \circ (\Lambda_C(f) \otimes g) = \text{eval}_{A,B} \circ (\Lambda_C(f) \otimes \text{id}_A \circ \text{id}_C \otimes g)$
    by the functoriality of $\otimes$
$= (\text{eval}_{A,B} \circ \Lambda_C(f) \otimes \text{id}_A) \circ \text{id}_C \otimes g$ by associativity
$= f \circ \text{id}_C \otimes g$ by β

The introduction of the linear implication increases the potential non determinism of the system; as a consequence some computations have to be properly understood as unsuccessful. A typical example is provided by the two transitions $t: A, B \vdash C$ and $t': A, B \vdash D$, in the initial state $A \otimes B$, when t preempts the token in A and t' the token in B, yielding the state $(B \to C) \otimes (A \to D)$. In this case both the transitions cannot terminate. This situation is known under the name of *deadlock*.

65

Definition 5.7 (*Conclusive Sequent and Deadlock*)
Given a tensor theory T, a sequent $\Gamma \vdash A$ is *T-conclusive* iff there exist a concluded T-derivation $A\vdash A'$. A sequent $\Gamma \vdash A$ which is not (T)-conclusive is called a *(T-) deadlock*.

Example 5.8 (*The Dining Philosophers*).
The Dining Philosophers can be represented by the following theory T (we consider the case of three philosophers t_1, t_2, t_3 and three forks C_1, C_2, C_3):

$t_1: C_1, C_2 \vdash C_1 \otimes C_2$,
$t_2: C_2, C_3 \vdash C_2 \otimes C_3$,
$t_3: C_3, C_1 \vdash C_3 \otimes C_1$

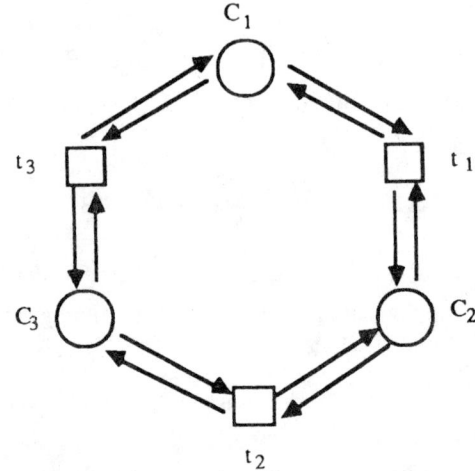

The following are examples of computations:
(a) $(id_{C_1} \otimes t_2) \circ (t_1 \otimes id_{C_3}) : C_1, C_2, C_3 \vdash C_1 \otimes C_2 \otimes C_3$,
(b) $id_{C_1} \otimes \Lambda(t_1 \circ exch) \otimes \Lambda(t_3)$:
$C_1, C_2, C_3 \vdash C_1 \otimes (C_1 \rightarrow (C_1 \otimes C_2)) \otimes (C_1 \rightarrow (C_3 \otimes C_1))$,
(c) $\Lambda(t_1) \otimes \Lambda(t_2) \otimes \Lambda(t_3)$:
$C_1, C_2, C_3 \vdash (C_1 \rightarrow C_3 \otimes C_1) \otimes (C_2 \rightarrow C_1 \otimes C_2) \otimes (C_3 \rightarrow C_2 \otimes C_3)$

The sequent (a) is concluded: it represents the computation where the first and second philosopher have eaten the one after the other. The sequent (b) is conclusive: here the first and third philosopher have respectively taken at the same time the fork at their left and their right; now they are competing for the fork C_1. Finally (c) is a deadlock: all the philosophers have taken the fork at their right.

As a remark, notice that a distributed implementation of a Petri net specification can be achieved by the definition of strategies of deduction in the implicative fragment which avoid the occurrence of deadlock situations, namely by means of a metalevel deduction system which provides a guideline to the application of the rules in the derivation. This topics will be further investigated elsewhere.

Example 5.9
Consider the transitions $f: A \vdash B$, $g: C \vdash D$, $h: D \vdash E$.
The computations:

$f \otimes (h \circ g): A \otimes C \vdash B \otimes E$
$eval \circ \Lambda(f \otimes h) \otimes g : A \otimes C \vdash B \otimes E$

are semantically equivalent, as
$eval \circ \Lambda(f \otimes h) \otimes g = eval \circ \Lambda(f \otimes h) \otimes id \circ id \otimes g =$
$= f \otimes h \circ id \otimes g = (f \circ id) \otimes (h \circ g) = f \otimes (h \circ g)$

The second computation can be read as follows. From the state $A \otimes C$, the transition f could fire; instead, the decision to execute a parallel transition $f \otimes h$ is taken, and A is preempted waiting for the availability of D. This is described in the computation $\Lambda(f \otimes h)$ leading from A to the open state $D \rightarrow (B \otimes E)$. At the same time g produces D from C, and the whole computation can terminate with the parallel firing of f and h. The interesting fact is that in

$eval \circ \Lambda(f \otimes h) \otimes g : A \otimes C \vdash B \otimes E$,

the production of E seems to depend from D (consider the subcomputation $\Lambda(f \otimes h): A \vdash D \rightarrow (B \otimes E)$). This dependence does not exist in the computation $f \otimes (h \circ g): A \otimes C \vdash B \otimes E$. We are now able to observe a richer class of dependencies. These dependences are *temporal dependencies* since they are originated by the execution strategy; they can be eliminated in every equivalent computation where the transitions are executed as atomic moves (see Corollary 6.4).

6. CONCLUDED COMPUTATIONS: THE OPEN CUT ELIMINATION THEOREM.

In this section we relate computations at a different level of atomicity. We prove that any concluded computation is equivalent to a computation where every transition is executed as an atomic move. This follows as a corollary of a weak version of Gentzen's Hauptsatz. Note that we need to prove anew this result since a consequence of the introduction of "external" axioms, is the failure of the general Gentzen's Hauptsatz.

Definition 6.1 (*open formulae*)

A formula is an *open formula*, if it contains a subformula whose main connective is the implication. A *open cut* (*o-cut*) is a cut whose cut formula is open. A *o-cut free derivation* is a derivation which contains no open cuts.

Theorem 6.2. (*The o-cut Elimination Theorem*)

Let T be a tensor theory, and let D be a T-derivation of the sequent $\Gamma \vdash A$ in the implicative fragment. Then there exists a o-cut free derivation D' of the same sequent. Moreover the final sequents associated with D and D' have the same categorical semantics

The previous theorem is easily obtained from the following lemma, by induction on the number of the o-cut rules occurring in the derivation D. The proof of the lemma can be found in the appendix.

Lemma 6.3

Let T be a set of axioms which only contain atomic formulas, and let D be a T-derivation of the sequent $\Gamma \vdash A$ which contains only one o-cut rule occurring as the last inference. Then there exists a o-cut free derivation D' of the same sequent. Moreover the final sequents associated with D and D' have the same categorical semantics.

Corollary 6.4

Let T be a tensor theory, and let D be a T-derivation of the concluded sequent $\Gamma \vdash A$ in the implicative fragment. Then there exists a T-derivation D' of the same sequent $\Gamma \vdash A$ in the tensor fragment. Moreover the final sequents of D and D' have the same categorical semantics.

Proof By the o-cut elimination theorem we know that there exists a o-cut free T-derivation D of $\Gamma \vdash A$. However, in a o-cut free derivation every open formula which has been introduced at same stage of the derivation will definitively appear as a subformula in some formula of the final sequent (subformula property). Since no such formula appear in $\Gamma \vdash A$, no one has been introduced, and no application of $(\rightarrow, r)$ and $(\rightarrow, l)$ can be in D.

Acknowledgements

The authors would like to thank P. Degano, G. Longo, S. Martini, J. Meseguer and U. Montanari for the stimulating discussions on the topics of this paper.

REFERENCES

[AL90] Asperti A., Longo G., Categories, Types and Structures. Book, to appear MIT Press, 1990.

[As87] Asperti A., *A Logic for Concurrency*, Technical Report, Dipartimento di Informatica, Univ. Pisa, 1987.

[BD87] Best E., Devillers R., *Sequential and Concurrent Behaviour in Petri Net Theory*, Theoretical Computer Science, **55**, 1987.

[DP87] De Paiva V., *The Dialectica Categories*, in AMS Conference on Categories in Computer Science and Logic, (Gray-Scedrov Eds.) Boulder, 1987.

[DMM89] Degano P., Montanari U., and Meseguer J., *Axiomatizing Net Computations and Processes*, in Proc. Logics in Computer Science '89, Asilomar, 1989.

[GG89] Gunter C., Gehlot V., *Nets as Tensor Theories*, in Proc. 10th International Conference on Application and Theory of Petri Nets, Bonn, 1989.

[Gi86] Girard J. Y., *Linear Logic*, Theoretical Computer Science, **50**, 1986

[GR83] Goltz U., Reisig W., *The Non Sequential Behaviour of Petri Nets*, Information and Computation, **57**, 1983.

[La88] Lafont Y., *The Linear Abstract Machine*, Theoretical Computer Science, **59**, 1988.

[LS86] Lambek J., Scott P.J., *Introduction to Higher Order Categorical Logic*, Cambridge Univertsity Press, 1986.

[ML71] Mac Lane S., *Categories for the Working Mathematicians*, Springer-Verlag, 1971.

[MaM89] Martì-Olitet N., Meseguer J., *From Petri Nets to Linear Logic*, to appear in Proc. Third Conference on Category Theory and Computer Science, Manchester, 1989.

[MM88] Meseguer J., Montanari U., *Petri Nets are Monoids: A New Algebraic Foundation for Net Theory*, In Proc Logics in Computer Science '88, 1988 (full version to appear in *Information and Computation*).

[Pe62] Petri C.A., *Kommunication mit Automaten*, Schriften des Institutes fur Instrumentelle Mathematik, Bonn 1962.

[Pr65] Prawitz D., *Natural Deduction: A Proof-Theoretic Study*, Almqvist and Wiksell, Stockholm, 1965.

[Rei85] Reisig W., *Petri Nets: An Introduction*, Springer Verlag, 1985.

[Se87] Seely R., *Linear Logic, *-Autonomous Categories and Cofree Coalgebras*, in AMS Conference on Categories in Computer Science and Logic, (Gray-Scedrov Eds.) Boulder, 1987.

APPENDIX: Proof of Lemma 6.3

We define two scales for measuring the complexity of a proof: the *rank* and the *grade*.

A path in a derivation D from a leaf to the root is called a *thread*. Given a thread T and an occurrence of a formula A in the final sequent of T, we call *rank* of A in T the number of consecutive sequents in T, counting upward, which contain the same occurrence of the formula A. The rank of every thread is at least 1. Given a derivation D with only one o-cut as last inference, we call a thread a left (right) thread if it contains the left (right) upper sequent of the cut. The left (right) rank of a derivation D is the maximum among the ranks of the left (right) threads in D. The rank of a derivation D is the sum of its left and right ranks. The rank of a derivation is at least 2.

The *grade* of a formula A (denoted by $g(A)$) is the number of logical symbols contained in A. The grade of a cut is the grade of the cut formula. When a derivation D has only one cut as the last inference, we define the grade of D (denoted by $g(D)$) to be the grade of this cut.

We prove the lemma by double induction on the grade g and rank r of the derivation D. The proof is subdivided in two main cases, namely $r=2$ and $r>2$.

Case 1: r = 2

We distinguish cases according to the forms of the proofs of the upper sequents S_1 and S_2 of the cut rule.

1.1) S_1 or S_2 is an axiom. This case is not possible, since by hypothesis we only consider axioms with atomic formulae.

1.2) S_1 or S_2 is the lower sequent of a cut rule. Impossible, since $r=2$.

1.3) both S_1 and S_2 are the lower sequents of logical inferences. Since the left and right rank of D is 1, the cut formulae on each side are the principal formulas of the logical inferences.

We use induction on the grade, reducing the proof to another proof with cuts of lesser grade. We distinguish two cases according to the outermost logical symbol of A.

($\rightarrow$) the derivation D has the structure:

$$\dfrac{\dfrac{\Gamma, A \vdash B}{\Gamma \vdash A \rightarrow B} \qquad \dfrac{\Gamma_1 \vdash A \quad B, \Gamma_2 \vdash C}{A \rightarrow B, \Gamma_1, \Gamma_2 \vdash C}}{\Gamma, \Gamma_1, \Gamma_2 \vdash C}$$

where by assumption the proofs ending with $\Gamma, A \vdash B$, $\Gamma_1 \vdash A$ or $\Gamma_2, B \vdash C$ do not contain any o-cut. Then consider the following derivation, and note that both the cuts have lesser grade than the original one:

$$\dfrac{\dfrac{\dfrac{\Gamma_1 \vdash A \quad \Gamma, A \vdash B}{\Gamma, \Gamma_1 \vdash B} \quad \Gamma_2, B \vdash C}{\Gamma_2, \Gamma, \Gamma_1 \vdash C}}{\text{exchanges}}$$
$$\Gamma, \Gamma_1, \Gamma_2 \vdash C$$

($\otimes$) The derivation has the structure:

$$\dfrac{\dfrac{\Gamma_1 \vdash A \quad \Gamma_2 \vdash B}{\Gamma_1, \Gamma_2 \vdash A \otimes B} \qquad \dfrac{\Gamma, A, B \vdash C}{\Gamma, A \otimes B \vdash C}}{\Gamma, \Gamma_1, \Gamma_2 \vdash C}$$

where by assumption the proofs ending with $\Gamma_1 \vdash A$, $\Gamma_2 \vdash B$ and $\Gamma, A, B \vdash C$ do not contain any o-cut.
Consider the derivation:

$$\dfrac{\Gamma_1 \vdash A \qquad \Gamma, A, B \vdash C}{\Gamma, \Gamma_1, B \vdash C}$$

This proof contains at most an o-cut as its last inference. Furthermore the grade of the cut formula is less than $g(A \otimes B)$. By induction hypothesis, we have then a o-cut free derivation D" of $\Gamma, \Gamma_1, B \vdash C$. Then we have:

$$\dfrac{\Gamma_2 \vdash B \qquad \Gamma, \Gamma_1, B \vdash C}{\Gamma, \Gamma_1, \Gamma_2 \vdash C}$$

Again this proof contains at most one o-cut as its last inference and the grade of the cut formula is less than $g(A \otimes B)$. By induction hypothesis, we have then a requested o-cut free derivation D" of $\Gamma, \Gamma_1, B \vdash C$.

Case 2: r > 2

The induction hypothesis is that we can eliminate the cut from every derivation D' which contains only one cut as the last inference, and which satisfies either $g(D')<g(D)$, or $g(D')=g(D)$ and $rank(D')<rank(D)$.
There are two main cases, namely: $rank_r(D)>1$; $rank_l(D)>1$ (and $rank_r(D) = 1$).

2.1) $rank_r(D) > 1$

we distinguish several subcases according to the logical inference whose lower sequent is S_2.

2.1.1) the sequent S_2 is the lower sequent of a cut rule. The derivation D has three possible structures:

2.1.1.1)

$$\dfrac{\Gamma \vdash A \qquad \dfrac{\Gamma_1, A, \Gamma_2 \vdash C \qquad \Delta_1, C, \Delta_2 \vdash B}{\Delta_1, \Gamma_1, A, \Gamma_2, \Delta_2 \vdash B}}{\Delta_1, \Gamma_1, \Gamma, \Gamma_2, \Delta_2 \vdash B}$$

Where by hypothesis, C cannot be a open formula.
Consider the derivation

$$\dfrac{\Gamma \vdash A \qquad \Gamma_1, A, \Gamma_2 \vdash C}{\Gamma_1, \Gamma, \Gamma_2 \vdash C}$$

the grade of D' is the same of D, namely g(A). Moreover the two derivations have the same left rank, while $\text{rank}_r(D') = \text{rank}_r(D)-1$, thus we can apply the induction hypothesis, obtaining a o-cut free derivation of $\Gamma_1, \Gamma, \Gamma_2 \vdash C$. Then with a cut of C we obtain:

$$\frac{\Gamma_1, \Gamma, \Gamma_2 \vdash C \qquad \Delta_1, C, \Delta_2 \vdash B}{\Delta_1, \Gamma_1, \Gamma, \Gamma_2, \Delta_2 \vdash B}$$

2.1.1.2)

$$\frac{\Gamma \vdash A \qquad \dfrac{\Gamma_1 \vdash C \qquad \Delta_1, A, \Delta_2, C, \Delta_3 \vdash B}{\Delta_1, A, \Delta_2, \Gamma_1, \Delta_3 \vdash B}}{\Delta_1, \Gamma, \Delta_2, \Gamma_1, \Delta_3 \vdash B}$$

analogous to 2.1.1.1)

2.1.1.3)

$$\frac{\Gamma \vdash A \qquad \dfrac{\Gamma_1 \vdash C \qquad \Delta_1, C, \Delta_2, A, \Delta_3 \vdash B}{\Delta_1, \Gamma_1, \Delta_2, A, \Delta_3 \vdash B}}{\Delta_1, \Gamma_1, \Delta_2, \Gamma, \Delta_3 \vdash B}$$

analogous to 2.1.1.1)

2.1.2) the sequent S_2 is the lower sequent of an exchange rule. The derivation has the structure:

$$\frac{\Gamma \vdash A \qquad \dfrac{\Delta_1, A, \Delta_2 \vdash B}{\Gamma_1, A, \Gamma_2 \vdash B}}{\Gamma_1, \Gamma, \Gamma_2 \vdash B}$$

where Δ_1, Δ_2 is a permutation of Γ_1, Γ_2. The derivation D'

$$\frac{\Gamma \vdash A \qquad \Delta_1, A, \Delta_2 \vdash B}{\Delta_1, \Gamma, \Delta_2 \vdash B}$$

has the same grade of D, namely g(A). Moreover the two derivations have the same left rank, while $\text{rank}_r(D') = \text{rank}_r(D) - 1$, thus we can apply the induction hypothesis, obtaining a o-cut free derivation of $\Delta_1, \Gamma, \Delta_2 \vdash B$. With an exchange rule we than obtain the requested proof of $\Gamma_1, \Gamma, \Gamma_2 \vdash B$.

2.1.3) the sequent S_2 is the lower sequent of a logical inference J. In this case the principal formula of the inference cannot be the cut formula. We distinguish several cases according to the J rule:

2.1.3.1) $J = (\rightarrow, r)$

The derivation D has the structure:

$$\frac{\Gamma \vdash A \qquad \dfrac{\Gamma_1, A, \Gamma_2, B \vdash C}{\Gamma_1, A, \Gamma_2 \vdash B \rightarrow C}}{\Gamma_1, \Gamma, \Gamma_2 \vdash B \rightarrow C}$$

Consider the derivation D':

$$\frac{\Gamma \vdash A \qquad \Gamma_1, A, \Gamma_2, B \vdash C}{\Gamma_1, \Gamma, \Gamma_2, B \vdash C}$$

D' has the same grade of D, namely g(A). Moreover the two derivations have the same left rank, while $\text{rank}_r(D')= \text{rank}_r(D)-1$, thus we can apply the induction hypothesis, obtaining a o-cut free derivation of $\Gamma_1, \Gamma, \Gamma_2, B \vdash C$. With an application of $(\rightarrow, r)$ we than obtain the requested proof of $\Gamma_1, \Gamma, \Gamma_2 \vdash B \rightarrow C$.

2.1.3.2) $J = (\rightarrow, l)$. Similarly

2.1.3.3) $J = (\otimes, r)$

The derivation D has two possible structures, namely:

$$\frac{\Gamma \vdash A \qquad \dfrac{\Gamma_1, A, \Gamma_2 \vdash B \qquad \Delta \vdash C}{\Gamma_1, A, \Gamma_2, \Delta \vdash B \otimes C}}{\Gamma_1, \Gamma, \Gamma_2, \Delta \vdash B \otimes C}$$

and

$$\frac{\Delta \vdash B \quad \Gamma_1, A, \Gamma_2 \vdash C}{\Gamma \vdash A \quad \Delta, \Gamma_1, A, \Gamma_2 \vdash B \otimes C}$$
$$\Delta, \Gamma_1, \Gamma, \Gamma_2 \vdash B \otimes C$$

We treat only the first case, the other one being completely analogous.

Consider the derivation D'

$$\frac{\Gamma \vdash A \quad \Gamma_1, A, \Gamma_2 \vdash B}{\Gamma_1, \Gamma, \Gamma_2 \vdash B}$$

D' has the same grade of D, namely g(A). Moreover the two derivations have the same left rank, while $\text{rank}_r(D')= \text{rank}_r(D)-1$, thus we can apply the induction hypothesis, obtaining a o-cut free derivation of $\Gamma_1, \Gamma, \Gamma_2 \vdash B$. With an application of $(\otimes, r)$ we than obtain:

$$\frac{\Gamma_1, \Gamma, \Gamma_2 \vdash B \quad \Delta \vdash C}{\Gamma_1, \Gamma, \Gamma_2, \Delta \vdash B \otimes C}$$

2.1.3.4) $J = (\otimes, 1)$. Similarly.

2.2) $\text{rank}_l(D) > 1$ (and $\text{rank}_r(D) = 1$)

This case is proved in the same way as 2.1 above.

This completes the proof of Lemma 6.3 and hence of the o-cut-elimination theorem.

Computable processes

Yiannis N. Moschovakis*
Department of Mathematics, UCLA
ynm@math.ucla.edu

October 23, 1989

Abstract

In this paper we study concurrent, asynchronous processes and functions on them which can be programmed using the (full) unfair or the fair merge operations. The main result is a normal form theorem for these (relatively) "computable process functions" which implies that although they can be very complex when viewed as classical set-functions, they are all "loosely implementable" in the sense of Park [7]. We also announce a variation and a substantial strengthening of the main "transfer principle" of [4] which have applications to the semantics and logic of programming languages with interactive (deterministic) or concurrent (non-deterministic) constructs.

1 Introduction

Suppose 0, 1 are *atomic acts* which induce transition functions on a set of states and we define the *non-deterministic process* C by the recursion

$$C = (0 \text{ or } 1) \text{ next } C.$$

No matter how we make precise the notion of process, this C is so simple that it is ultimately identified with the set of all infinite sequences of 0's and 1's, the classical Cantor set. It is natural to think of C as a *computable process* since it is defined by such an elementary recursion, but this brings up a question: the members of C are arbitrary binary sequences and most of them cannot be individually computed. The same problem comes up with the process

$$M = par(\bar{0}, \bar{1}),$$

---
*During the preparation of this paper the author was partially supported by an NSF Grant.

where $\bar{a}$ is the constant, infinite sequence $aaa\cdots$ and *par* denotes the *fair merge* of two sequences. Some (like Dijkstra in [3]) reject M altogether on the grounds that it involves *unbounded non-determinism*, but those who accept the fair merge as a meaningful programming construct would also tend to consider M computable. Viewed as a set, it contains all the infinite sequences in C which are not eventually constant, almost all of them of course not individually computable.

In [7] Park argues that we should understand such non-deterministic definitions *loosely*. "Noone requires of a correct implementation for parallelism that there be an appropriate sense in which *all* scheduling algorithms be possible in it, only that there be one such scheduling algorithm, and if fairness be required that the scheduler be fair." So we may consider M implementable since it has at least one computable member, e.g. the alternating sequence of 0's and 1's. Now the existence of implementations is obviously important, but it will hardly do as a single criterion for computability: noone would call an arbitrary set of binary sequences computable simply because it may happen to have a computable member.

On the other hand, we cannot identify C or M with some subset of their computable members, we need *all* their members. When we want to deduce properties of some program which calls M, we cannot be assured that M will be implemented by a computable "merger", only that the sequence which will be delivered will be fair; it may be that some piece of hardware is doing the merging, non-computably. In fact, we tend to call non-deterministic processes like C and M "computable" primarily because they are defined by seemingly simple and intuitive programming constructs. The fact that they have computable members is a formal consequence of such definitions (however trivial for these examples) and not the basic reason for thinking of them as computable.

A main aim of this paper is to define *computable processes* and *computable process functions* in the context of the game-theoretic modeling of concurrent, asynchronous systems introduced in [4].[1] We will characterize these ob-

---
[1] Similar modelings of concurrent, asynchronous systems in terms

jects in the cases where we take as given the full (unfair) merge, the fair merge in the sense of Park (as above) and the richer *state-depended fair merge* which is most natural in the context of our concurrency theory. The results imply that these notions are very robust and provide some considerable justification for our choice of definitions.

A second aim is to discuss the relevance of the results in [4] and this paper to the following central problem in the theory of programming languages with non-deterministic constructs. Suppose we are given (the syntax of) a programming language $\mathcal{L}$ and a deterministic semantics for it, i.e. we know how to assign meanings to the programs of $\mathcal{L}$ when we are given deterministic interpretations for the "non-logical" symbols of $\mathcal{L}$. We want to define non-deterministic semantics for $\mathcal{L}$ which still make sense when some of the non-logical symbols are assigned non-deterministic interpretations, e.g. when a function symbol is interpreted by some merge operation. To be useful, such new semantics must satisfy the following two conditions:

1. The new meaning of a program E is (essentially) the same as the old meaning when all the symbols which occur in E are assigned deterministic interpretations.

2. The logic of the language does not change: i.e. if two programs E_1 and E_2 are assigned the same meaning in all deterministic interpretations, then they are also assigned the same meaning in all non-deterministic interpretations.

We meet the same problem at a simpler, deterministic stage, when we start with "closed" (non-interactive) semantics for some $\mathcal{L}$ and we want to extend them conservatively to "interactive", though still deterministic interpretations. Such vague questions can be made precise for specific languages and given semantics for them and we will answer them for some special, "toy" examples in Section 2. In Section 3 we will state the main results of this paper about computable process functions and in Section 4 we will discuss briefly continuing work on this project.

Like those of [4], the results announced here are proved by a general technique which "reduces" process recursion to least-fixed-point recursion and which requires the prior development of some considerable technical machinery, not easy to explain in a short abstract. We will save the proofs for the full versions of these two papers, now in preparation.

---

of games have also been presented recently in [1], [9] and (apparently) they have antecedents in older work of Lamport. In addition to [7] and [8], the question of computability in connection with "multiprogramming" is also raised in [2].

2 Introducing interaction and non-determinism

Consider the language $\mathcal{L}$ whose expressions are defined by the recursion

$$E ::\equiv x \mid f(x_1, \ldots, E_n) \mid E_0 \text{ where } \{x_1 = E_1, \ldots, E_n\},$$

where x is any variable (from a fixed, infinite set), f is any function symbol (from a fixed set of function symbols, each with an assigned non-negative arity) and the last construct denotes mutual recursion. We will consider three kinds of simple denotational semantics for $\mathcal{L}$ on structures of the form

$$\mathcal{A} = (\text{States}, \iota, \text{Acts}, skip, \mathcal{F}) \qquad (1)$$

where the following hold:[2]

1. States is some set of *states* which contains the *initial state* ι.

2. Acts is some set of *atomic acts*, with each $a \in$ Acts inducing a total transition function $s \mapsto sa$ on States. The special "delay" act $skip$ satisfies $s\,skip = s$ for every state.

3. A *history* is a finite sequence of acts $h = a_1 a_2 \cdots a_n$ which acts on States in the obvious way,

$$sh = (\cdots(sa_1)a_2)\cdots)a_n;$$

a state s' is **accessible** from s is there exists a history h such that $s' = sh$, and we assume that every state is accessible from ι.

4. $\mathcal{F}$ is an assignment of an n-ary "function" to each n-ary function symbol. The kind of these functions will depend on the semantics.

In the typical case the state is a store of variables and buffers and the acts include assignments, sending and receiving messages, etc.

We will also consider the richer language

$$\mathcal{L}^*(\mathsf{A}) = \mathcal{L}(\mathsf{A}, \text{next}, \text{cond}_\mathsf{R})$$

which depends on an additional set A of *act symbols*. The expressions of $\mathcal{L}^*(\mathsf{A})$ are defined by accepting each

$$\mathsf{do}(a) \equiv a, \qquad (a \in \mathsf{A} \cup \{skip\})$$

---

[2] The structures of [4] had an added compatibility relation on acts and the richer language of that paper had typed expressions, the types controlling the state dependence and "potential" side effects of the meaning of expressions. Both of these features are useful for the faithful modeling of some important examples of concurrent programs, but they do not change the mathematics of the situation and it is best for the present purposes to keep matters simple.

I	s_0	s_1	s_2	s_3	$\ldots$
II	(a_0, w_0)	(a_1, w_1)	(a_2, w_2)	(a_3, w_3)	
State : ι	$s_0 a_0$	$s_1 a_1$	$s_2 a_2$	$s_3 a_3$	$\ldots$

Figure 1: The game.

as a prime expression and adding two more formation rules,

$$(E, M) \mapsto E \text{ next } M,$$
$$(E, M) \mapsto \text{cond}_R(E, M).$$

Structures for $\mathcal{L}^*(A)$ are exactly as in (1), but now Acts is a function which associates with each act symbol $a \in A$ a transition function on States.

A. Procedure semantics. As usual, a *stream of acts* is either a finite sequence of the form $(a_1, a_2, \ldots, a_n, \mathbf{1})$ where $n > 0$, each a_i is an act and $\mathbf{1}$ is a special *termination indicator* (a *convergent stream*), or a finite or infinite sequence of acts (a *divergent stream*). Each convergent stream u induces a transition function on the states $s \mapsto su$, by acting as a history. The *concatenation* $u * v$ of two strings is defined so that if u is divergent then $u * v = u$ and if u is convergent, then we obtain $u * v$ by concatenating u and v as sequences and then removing the first $\mathbf{1}$. A **procedure** is a function

$$\alpha : \text{States} \to \text{Streams}.$$

The set Π of procedures inherits a natural partial ordering from the initial segment relation on streams,

$$\alpha \leq \beta \iff (\forall s)[\alpha(s) \text{ is an initial segment of } \beta(s)].$$

A **procedure function** of n arguments is any monotone and continuous function

$$\phi : \Pi^n \to \Pi$$

and a **procedure structure** is one where $\mathcal{F}$ assigns procedure functions to the function symbols of $\mathcal{L}$.

Examples of procedure functions are the constants (0-ary and state independent)

$$do(a) = \lambda(s)(a, \mathbf{1}), \quad (a \in \text{Acts}), \tag{2}$$

sequential execution

$$\alpha \text{ next } \beta = \lambda(s)[\alpha(s) * \beta(s\alpha(s))], \tag{3}$$

and the *conditionals*

$$cond_R(\alpha, \beta) = \lambda(s) \begin{cases} \alpha(s), & \text{if } R(s), \\ \beta(s), & \text{otherwise,} \end{cases} \tag{4}$$

one for each relation R on the states. Notice that in the definition of *next* the state $s\alpha(s)$ is defined when needed as an argument to β, i.e. when $\alpha(s)$ is a convergent stream.

To interpret the expressions of $\mathcal{L}$ in a procedure structure, we let the variables vary over procedures and we interpret the recursion construct by the taking of simultaneous least-fixed-points; for $\mathcal{L}^*(A)$, we additionally interpret the expressions a, E next M and $\text{cond}_R(E, M)$ by the procedure functions in (2), (3) and (4) for some R. In this way, for each procedure structure $\mathcal{A}$, each expression E and each n-tuple of variables $\vec{x}$ which includes all the free variables of E, we obtain an n-ary procedure function ϕ_E, the function defined by E. Two expressions E, M in $\mathcal{L}$ or $\mathcal{L}^*(A)$ are **procedure equivalent** if on every procedure structure and for every $\vec{x}$ they are assigned in this way the same function $\phi_E = \phi_M$.

With this simple denotational semantics, $\mathcal{L}$ is a barebones command language, $\mathcal{L}^*(A)$ a bit richer. Both languages allow full recursion, however, so that on structures with a usable conditional and a reasonably rich state which makes possible some value passing, $\mathcal{L}^*(A)$ can be a "complete" command language.

B. Behavior semantics. As in [4], we associate with each structures $\mathcal{A}$ the *game of interaction* $G = G(\mathcal{A})$, where player II represents some computing agent or program fragment and player I represents everybody else—*the world*.[3] A *run* of G (pictured in Figure 1) is played in stages, with I and II exchanging moves at the n'th stage so that they may alter *the state* g_n initially set by $g_{-1} = \iota$. At stage n, I plays first some state s_n which must be accessible from g_{n-1}; II then responds with a pair (a_n, w_n) of an act a_n and an *indicator* $w_n = \partial$ or $w_n = \mathbf{1}$ and the new state is set $g_n = s_n a_n$; if the indicator $w_n = \mathbf{1}$, the run ends, otherwise we proceed to the next stage $n+1$. No one wins or loses this game. The point of introducing it is that the game imagery allows for natural, intuitive definitions of various concepts whose precise specifications may be quite complex.

A **behavior** is a partial strategy for II in the game G, i.e. (formally) a partial function

$$\sigma : \text{States}^* \to \text{Acts} \times \{\partial, \mathbf{1}\}$$

---

[3] This is a simplified version of the game in [4], appropriate for the present case where we allow only one act execution at a time.

I	s_0	s_1	s_2	s_3
$\sigma:$ II	(a_0, ∂)	(a_1, ∂)	$(a_2, 1)$	
σ next $\tau:$ II	(a_0, ∂)	(a_1, ∂)	(a_2, ∂)	$\tau(s_3)$

Figure 2: Sequential composition.

on non-empty sequences of states, except that we identify behaviors which agree on all legal partial runs of the game. The set $\mathsf{B} = \mathsf{B}(\mathcal{A})$ of behaviors carries the natural partial ordering of partial-function-inclusion, with the totally undefined behavior $\emptyset$ at the bottom. If ω is a (total) *strategy for player* I and $\sigma \in \mathsf{B}$, then

$$\omega \star \sigma = a_0, a_1, \ldots$$

is the stream of acts "executed" (by player II) in the run of the game where I plays by ω and II responds by σ—terminated with $\mathbf{1}$ if II ever plays $(a_n, \mathbf{1})$.

An n-ary **behavior function** is any monotone, continuous function

$$F : \mathsf{B}^n \to \mathsf{B}$$

and a **behavior structure** is one where $\mathcal{F}$ assigns behavior functions to the function symbols of the language. For example, the behavior function which models *execution of an act* a is the constant

$$do(a) = a = \lambda(\overline{s}(n))(a, \mathbf{1}), \qquad (5)$$

where by notational convention,

$$\overline{s}(n) = s_0, \ldots, s_n.$$

In Figure 2 we have indicated the first few moves of player II by the *sequential composition* σ next τ, with the shown assumptions about the values of σ. We also have a natural conditional for each relation R on the states,

$$cond_R(\sigma, \tau) = \lambda(\overline{s}(n)) \begin{cases} \sigma(\overline{s}(n)), & \text{if } R(s_0), \\ \tau(\overline{s}(n)), & \text{otherwise.} \end{cases} \qquad (6)$$

Behaviors are the natural denotations of deterministic, interactive programs. Suppose, for example that the state has an integer variable X and consider the closed expression *checkzero* defined by the recursion

$$checkzero = \begin{cases} skip, & \text{if } X = 0, \\ skip \text{ next } checkzero, & \text{otherwise.} \end{cases}$$

The procedure assigned to *checkzero* checks the state once, terminates immediately if $X = 0$ and idles forever if $X \neq 0$; the behavior assigned to *checkzero* is the function on sequences of states such that for each $\overline{s}(n) = (s_0, \ldots, s_n)$,

$$checkzero(\overline{s}(n)) = \begin{cases} (skip, \mathbf{1}), & \text{if } (\exists i \leq n) X(s_i) = 0, \\ (skip, \partial), & \text{otherwise.} \end{cases}$$

In a "closed environment" where *checkzero* is the only program being executed both denotations will produce the same sequence of states, but it makes sense to "play" the behavioral denotation in a natural way against a world where other agents are changing the state and it will still have the desired effect, i.e. idle until X becomes 0 and then quit.

We define the semantics of $\mathcal{L}$ and $\mathcal{L}^*(\mathsf{A})$ on behavior structures, by letting the variables vary over behaviors and (again) interpreting the recursion construct by the taking of least fixed points; in $\mathcal{L}^*(\mathsf{A})$ we also interpret the constant function symbols with the behavioral conditional, act and sequential execution defined by (6), (5), and Figure 2. The definition associates with each expression E and list of variables $\vec{x}$ a behavior function F_E. We call E and M **behavior equivalent** if on every behavior structure and for every $\vec{x}$, $F_E = F_M$.

With each procedure α we can associate the behavior

$$\iota(\alpha) = \lambda(\overline{s}(n)) \begin{cases} (\alpha(s_0)(n), \mathbf{1}), & \text{if } \alpha(s_0)(n+1) \simeq 1, \\ (\alpha(s_0)(n), \partial), & \text{otherwise,} \end{cases}$$

which checks out only the first state it sees and then blindly plays the moves dictated by α. Conversely, with each behavior σ we can associate the procedure

$$\iota^{-1}(\sigma) = \lambda(s)[\omega_s \star \sigma],$$

where ω_s is the strategy for I which begins the game with the state s and then just repeats at each stage the state it sees. Obviously

$$\iota^{-1}(\iota(\alpha)) = \alpha,$$

but the composition in the opposite order is not the identity because the map ι^{-1} "loses information." Using these maps we can lift faithfully procedure functions to behavior functions, setting (in the case of a procedure function of one variable)

$$\phi^\iota(\sigma) = \iota(\phi(\iota^{-1}(\sigma))).$$

thm 2.1 *Let $\mathcal{A}^\iota$ be the behavior structure associated with a procedure structure $\mathcal{A}$ by replacing each procedure function ϕ in $\mathcal{A}$ by the corresponding behavior function ϕ^ι. For every expression E of $\mathcal{L}^*(\mathsf{A})$, if ϕ_E and F_E are the functions associated with E in $\mathcal{A}$ and $\mathcal{A}^\iota$ respectively, then for all procedures $\alpha_1, \ldots, \alpha_n$,*

$$\phi_E(\alpha_1, \ldots, \alpha_n) = \iota^{-1}(F_E(\iota(\alpha_1), \ldots, \iota(\alpha_n)));$$

as a consequence, $\mathcal{L}^*(A)$-expressions which are behavior equivalent are also procedure equivalent.

Conversely, if two $\mathcal{L}^*(A)$-expressions are procedure equivalent, then they are also behavior equivalent. ⊣

The first of these assertions is fairly trivial. The second assertion is quite simple for $\mathcal{L}$-expressions but requires a bit of work for expressions in the richer language $\mathcal{L}^*(A)$.

C. Process semantics. Non-deterministic processes in a structure $\mathcal{A}$ are modeled in [4] by **players**, i.e. non-empty sets of behaviors.

One of the basic premises of [4] is that (non-deterministic) *process transformations* can be modeled by functions on the set $\mathcal{P}$ of players which are determined by their "implementations", and one is tempted (at first) to take as the (abstract) implementations of

$$f : \mathcal{P} \to \mathcal{P}$$

all behavior functions

$$F : \mathsf{B} \to \mathsf{B}$$

such that

$$\sigma \in x \implies F(\sigma) \in f(x).$$

But if f is defined by the recursion

$$f(x) = x \text{ next } f(x), \qquad (7)$$

then, quite obviously

$$f(x) = \{\sigma_0 \text{ next } \sigma_1 \text{ next } \cdots \mid \sigma_0, \sigma_1, \ldots \in x\}$$

and the most natural implementation of f is the "infinitary" operation

$$F(\sigma_0, \sigma_1, \sigma_2, \ldots) = \sigma_0 \text{ next } \sigma_1 \text{ next } \sigma_2 \cdots.$$

In general, an **infinitary behavior function** (of n arguments) is any monotone, continuous operation

$$F : (N \to \mathsf{B})^n \to \mathsf{B}, \quad (N = \{0, 1, \ldots\}),$$

and we call F an *abstract implementation* of a player function

$$f : \mathcal{P}^n \to \mathcal{P}$$

if for every n-tuple of players $\vec{x} = x_1, \ldots, x_n$ and sequences of behaviors $\vec{p} = p_1, \ldots, p_n$,

$$[p_1 : N \to x_1, \ldots, p_n : N \to x_n] \implies F(\vec{p}) \in f(\vec{x}).$$

A set I of such abstract implementations *determines the values of* f, if for all $\vec{x}, \vec{p}$ as above,

$$f(\vec{x}) = \{F(\vec{p}) \mid p_1 : N \to x_1, \ldots, p_n : N \to x_n, F \in I\}.$$

The idea is to model process transformations with player functions whose values are determined by *some* set of their abstract implementations, but there is an extra wrinkle: it is useful to adopt an *intensional approach* and *identify* a process function with a specific determining set of abstract implementations, suitably closed as follows.

For every function $\pi : N \to N$ and every $p : N \to \mathsf{B}$, let

$$p^\pi(i) = p(\pi(i))$$

and for each infinitary behavior function G (of two arguments, for simplicity) and $\pi, \rho : N \to N$, put

$$G^{\pi,\rho}(p, q) = G(p^\pi, q^\rho).$$

We call F *reducible* to G if there exist $\pi, \rho : N \to N$ such that $F = G^{\pi,\rho}$. An **intensional player function** (**ipf**) is any set f of infinitary behavior functions which is closed under this notion of reducibility, and the *player values* of f are given by

$$f(\vec{x}) = \{F(\vec{p}) \mid p_1 : N \to x_1, \ldots, p_n : N \to x_n, F \in f\}.$$

A set $I \subseteq f$ generates an ipf f, if

$$f = \{F \mid F \text{ is reducible to some } G \in I\},$$

i.e. f is the closure of I under reducibility. It is easy to verify that each I which generates f determines the values of f as above. Most often we define ipf's by specifying a simple generating set for them.

A **process structure** now is one where $\mathcal{F}$ assigns ipf's (of the appropriate arity) to the function symbols of the language. Using the operations on ipf's defined in [4]—and in particular the key interpretation of definition by recursion—we can assign to each process structure $\mathcal{A}$, each expression E of $\mathcal{L}$ and each list of variables $\vec{x}$ which includes all the free variables of E, a process function f_E; two expressions E, M are **process equivalent** if we have $f_E = f_M$, on every $\mathcal{A}$.

To interpret behavior semantics into process semantics, set for each behavior σ

$$\jmath(\sigma) = \{\sigma\},$$

and with each behavior function F (binary, for simplicity), associate the ipf $F^\jmath$ whose abstract implementations are all functions reducible to $\lambda(p, q)F(p(0), q(0))$. This gives, in particular, natural ipf interpretations $do(a)^\jmath$, $next^\jmath$ and $cond_R^\jmath$ of act execution, sequential execution and the conditionals and allows us to extend the definition os process semantics to the expressions of $\mathcal{L}^*(A)$.

The first conservation result for this interpretation is an exercise in ipf recursion.

thm 2.2 *Let $\mathcal{A}^\jmath$ be the process structure associated with a behavior structure $\mathcal{A}$ by replacing each behavior function*

F in $\mathcal{A}$ by the corresponding ipf $F^\jmath$. For every expression E of $\mathcal{L}^*(\mathsf{A})$, if F_E and f_E are the functions associated with E in $\mathcal{A}$ and $\mathcal{A}^\jmath$ respectively, then for all behaviors $\sigma_1,\ldots,\sigma_n$,

$$F_E(\sigma_1,\ldots,\sigma_n) = \jmath^{-1}(f_E(\jmath(\sigma_1),\ldots,\jmath(\sigma_n))).$$

As a consequence, $\mathcal{L}^*(\mathsf{A})$-expressions which are process equivalent are also behavior equivalent. ⊣

The second conservation theorem we need is a strengthening of the main result (8.1) of [4] and requires some work.

thm 2.3 Transfer Principle. *Behavior equivalent $\mathcal{L}$-expressions are also process equivalent.* ⊣

Limitations of the Transfer Principle. The identity
$$\mathsf{cond}_R(x,\ x) = x \qquad (8)$$
is valid in behavior semantics, because whatever conditional $cond_R$ interprets cond_R, we have $R(s_0)$ or $\neg R(s_0)$ for every state, and hence for every behavior σ,

$$cond_R(\sigma,\ \sigma) = \sigma.$$

On the other hand, in process semantics, the ipf interpretation of the left-hand-side of (8) includes the state-dependent abstract implementation
$$F(p) = \lambda(\overline{s}(n)) \begin{cases} p(0)(\overline{s}(n)), & \text{if } R(s_0), \\ p(1)(\overline{s}(n)), & \text{otherwise}, \end{cases}$$

while every abstract implementation of the identity ipf $\lambda(x)x$ interpreting the right-hand-side is state-independent. Thus *the Transfer Principle 2.3 does not hold for expressions of $\mathcal{L}^*(\mathsf{A})$*. Notice that this simple counterexample does not involve recursion, but depends on the well-known "algebraic" difficulties that crop up when we introduce conditionals in a non-deterministic setting. We will discuss it briefly in the last section.

Leaving this obstruction aside for the moment, the upshot of these results is that in deriving properties of programs expressible in $\mathcal{L}$, we may interpret expressions using the simplest of semantics which allow us to describe the properties we care about. Later on we may need to use more complex semantics, when we combine these expressions with others in which interactive or non-deterministic constructs occur; we are assured that the meanings of expressions is preserved (modulo the trivial "liftings" $\imath, \jmath$) and that every valid identity (true in all interpretations of the semantics we assumed) which we may have used in our derivations will retain its validity as we switch semantics.

3 Computable process functions

To make clear the intended meaning of our results, in this section we will often say *process* rather than *player* and *process function* instead of *intensional player function*. In effect we will be assuming that our mathematical modeling of these intuitive notions is faithful.

def 3.1 A process function f on a structure $\mathcal{A}$ is **computable**, if it is definable on $\mathcal{A}$ by some expression E of $\mathcal{L}$, i.e. $f = f_E$ in the sense of **C** above.

Since we are interested in characterizing the computability of "true" (non-deterministic) process functions like the fair merge, we will factor out the mundanely computable behavior functions by means of the following definition.

def 3.2 A behavior structure $\mathcal{A}$ as in (1) is **manageable, complete** if it satisfies the following hypotheses:

1. There exist fixed (non-repetitive) enumerations $\mathsf{States} = \{S_0, S_1, \ldots\}$ and $\mathsf{Acts} = \{A_0, A_1, \ldots\}$ and a fixed recursive function $exec : N \times N \to N$, so that
$$S_i A_j = S_{exec(i,j)}.$$

2. For each state s, there are infinitely many distinct states which are accessible from s.

3. Every recursive behavior function is in $\mathcal{A}$—i.e. it is assigned to some function symbol by $\mathcal{F}$.

The first two hypotheses certainly hold in the standard example where the state is a finite (or effectively enumerable) store of variables and buffers.[4] They allow us to "identify" states and acts with integers, but also (using standard recursive codings) to identify finite sequences of states with integers, behaviors with (special) partial functions on N to N, etc. Thus we can talk about *recursive behavior functions* in the third hypothesis, and these certainly include act execution, sequential execution, conditionals based on recursive conditions on the state, etc.[5]

We will characterize computability in *expanded structures* of the form $(\mathcal{A}, \mathcal{F}^*)$, obtained by adding to a manageable, complete behavior structure $\mathcal{A}$ some set $\mathcal{F}^*$ of ipf's, e.g. the various merges. Formally we should write $(\mathcal{A}^\jmath, \mathcal{F}^*)$, which is a "proper" process structure, but the conservation results of Section 2 insure that the distinction is only notational.

---

[4] The second hypothesis is not really needed for most of the results, but it simplifies the statement of "non-triviality" theorems; ditto for the assumption that there are infinitely many distinct acts.

[5] We want to avoid issues of language design here. It is quite obvious that we could enrich the language $\mathcal{L}$ with a few simple constructs so that the third hypothesis becomes a theorem.

I	s_0	s_1	s_2	s_3	s_4
μ:	1	0	1	1	0
$\mu[\sigma_0, \sigma_1]$: II	$\sigma_1(s_0)$	$\sigma_0(s_1)$	$\sigma_1(s_0, s_2)$	$\sigma_1(s_0, s_2, s_3)$	$\sigma_0(s_1, s_4)$

Figure 3: Action of binary merger.

A *merger* on a structure $\mathcal{A}$ is any (total) function $\mu :$ States$^* \to \{0, 1\}$. Given behaviors σ_0, σ_1 in $\mathcal{A}$, $\mu[\sigma_0, \sigma_1]$ is the (conjunctive) *merged behavior* of σ_0, σ_1, defined (roughly) by decreeing that in a certain stage of the game it calls σ_0 or σ_1 accordingly as μ gives the value 0 or 1. Rather than give the formal definition which is somewhat technical, we indicate in Figure 3 the first few moves of the play by $\mu[\sigma_0, \sigma_1]$ for given values of μ. (The picture does not indicate that if some σ_i first plays some $(a_n, \mathbf{1})$ when it is called, then from that stage on $\mu[\sigma_0, \sigma_1]$ calls the other behavior σ_{1-i} independently of the value of μ.) A merger μ is *state independent* if its values depend only on the stage of the game and not what has been played, i.e. for some $\nu : N \to \{0, 1\}$ and all sequences of states,

$$\mu(s_0, \ldots, s_n) = \nu(n);$$

a merger μ is *fair* if for every σ_0, σ_1 and every infinite run of the game by $\mu[\sigma_0, \sigma_1]$, each σ_i either plays some $(a_n, \mathbf{1})$ at some stage when it is called, or is called infinitely often.

We define the (full, unfair) *merge*, the *parkmerge* and the *fairmerge* process functions by the equations

$$\begin{aligned}
merge(x, y) &= \{\mu[p(0), q(0)] \mid \\
&\quad p : N \to x, \, q : N \to y, \\
&\quad \mu \text{ any merger}\}, \\
parkmerge(x, y) &= \{\mu[p(0), q(0)] \mid \\
&\quad p : N \to x, \, q : N \to y, \\
&\quad \mu \text{ any fair, state--} \\
&\quad \text{independent merger}\}, \\
fairmerge(x, y) &= \{\mu[p(0), q(0)] \mid \\
&\quad p : N \to x, \, q : N \to y, \\
&\quad \mu \text{ any fair merger}\}.
\end{aligned}$$

Of course we must read these equations as definitions of ipf's, so that (for example) *merge* is the ipf generated by the set of abstract implementations

$$F_\mu(p, q) = \mu[p(0), q(0)], \quad (\mu \text{ any merger}),$$

and it is easy to check that its abstract implementations are precisely all functions of the form

$$F_{\mu,k,l}(p, q) = \mu[p(k), q(l)], \quad (k, l \in N, \mu \text{ any merger}).$$

Another simple process function obviously related to *merge* is *binary disjunction*, which using the same convention is defined by

$$x \text{ or } y = \{r(0) \mid r \in x \cup y\}.$$

We use the name *parkmerge* for Park's *fairmerge*, his terminology being more appropriate in our context for the full, state dependent fair merge operation.

If F is a monotone, continuous operation of the type

$$F : (N \to \mathbf{B})^n \times (N \to N) \to \mathbf{B}, \quad (9)$$

then for each $\delta \in (N \to N)$ the function

$$F_\delta : (N \to \mathbf{B})^n \to \mathbf{B}$$

is an infinitary behavior function of n arguments. A process function f is *defined recursively from a set O of total, number-theoretic functions*, if there exists a recursive function(al) F as in (9) such that f is generated by the set

$$I = \{F_\delta \mid \delta \in O\}.$$

Notice that if f is defined recursively from O via the recursive functional F, then its values are given by

$$f(\vec{x}) = \{F(\vec{p}, \delta) \mid p_1 : N \to x_1, \ldots, p_n : N \to x_n, \delta \in O\},$$

i.e. intuitively, we can compute each $f(\vec{x})$ if we are "given" arbitrary calls to behaviors in the process arguments and an "oracle" $\delta \in O$. The definition makes sense for functions with 0 arguments, i.e. processes: a process x is defined recursively from the set of oracles O if there is a recursive $F : (N \to N) \to \mathbf{B}$ such that

$$x = \{F(\delta) \mid \delta \in O\}. \quad (10)$$

thm 3.3 Main Result. *Fix a manageable, complete behavior structure $\mathcal{A}$.*

(1) The computable process functions of $(\mathcal{A}, merge)$ are the same as the computable process functions of $(\mathcal{A}, or)$; a process function f is computable in $(\mathcal{A}, merge)$ if and only if f is defined recursively from the Cantor set $C = (N \to \{0, 1\})$.

(2) A process function f is computable in the expanded structure $(\mathcal{A}, parkmerge)$ if and only if f is defined recursively from the full Baire space $(N \to N)$.

(3) A process function f is computable in the expanded structure $(\mathcal{A}, fairmerge)$ if and only if it is defined recursively from the set of wellfounded trees

$$WF = \{\delta : N \to \{0,1\} \mid$$
$$(\forall \alpha : N \to N)(\exists n)[\delta(\overline{\alpha}(n)) = 1]\},$$

where $\overline{\alpha}(n)$ is the integer code of the finite sequence $(\alpha(0), \ldots, \alpha(n-1))$.

(4) In each of these cases the set of computable process functions does not change if we further expand the structure by functions which are defined recursively by the specified set of oracles.

(5) For each of the structures in (1)–(3), every computable process function has a recursive abstract implementation and every computable process contains a recursive behavior. ⊣

It is easiest to read off some of the consequences of this theorem for the case of total processes, which may be identified with subsets of the Baire space $N \to N$ since all their members are totally defined behaviors. Recall the logical classification of analytical subsets of Baire space by how many and what kind of quantifiers we need to define them beginning with a recursive relation R, cf. [6, 5]. In this summary table of definitions, i varies over N and Greek letters vary over the Baire space $N \to N$:

$$\begin{array}{llll} \Pi_1^0 & \delta \in x & \Longleftrightarrow & (\forall i) R(\delta, i) \\ \Sigma_1^1 & \delta \in x & \Longleftrightarrow & (\exists \alpha)(\forall i) R(\delta, \alpha, i) \\ \Sigma_2^1 & \delta \in x & \Longleftrightarrow & (\exists \alpha)(\forall \beta)(\exists i) R(\delta, \alpha, \beta, i) \end{array}$$

The *dual classes* to these are defined by taking the negations of these forms and they are denoted by interchanging Σ and Π, e.g. the class of complements of Π_1^0 sets is Σ_1^0. It is known that each of these classes is proper, i.e. none of them is included in its dual.

We will characterize the total processes computable in the full (unfair) *merge* in terms of two natural notions.

def 3.4 A **direct observable** of a behavior σ is a finite sequence

$$obs = s_0, \sigma(s_0), s_1, \sigma(s_0, s_1), \ldots, s_n, \sigma(s_0, \ldots, s_n)$$

which is a legal initial part of the game of interaction, i.e. all the terms of the sequence are defined and I's partial play $(s_0, \ldots, s_n)$ satisfies the condition of accessibility. An **ideal observable** of σ is any finite set of its direct observables.

The **direct** and **ideal** observables of a process x are the direct and ideal observables of the behaviors in x.

Notice that every ideal observable of a behavior σ is the restriction $\sigma \upharpoonright \Delta$ of σ to a finite set Δ of sequences of states which is closed under initial segments (a *tree*) and such that σ is defined on every member of Δ. For each process x and finite tree of state sequences Δ, we let

$$idobs_x(\Delta) = \{\sigma \upharpoonright \Delta \mid \sigma \in x, \ (\forall \bar{s}(n) \in \Delta)\sigma(\bar{s}(n)) \downarrow\}$$

be the set of *ideal observables of x on Δ*.

The direct observables of a process x are the facts about x that we can learn by direct "experimentation" or "testing", i.e. by adopting the role of player I (the external world) in the game of interaction, trying all legal moves and recording the responses of x. The ideal observables may also be viewed as facts about x which can be learned by testing, but we must be allowed some questionable "backtracking" (or "undoing") moves in the game, where (playing as I) we can "change our mind", take back a state s_i and replace it by s_i' after recording x's response to s_i. We will not analyze here any further the various notions of *observational equivalence* between behaviors and processes and their relation to the extensive literature on this notion in the now standard modelings of concurrent systems by Milner (CCS) and Hoare (CSP).

def 3.5 A process x is **effectively dense in itself** if from (a canonical listing of) each ideal observable $\Theta = \sigma \upharpoonright \Delta$ of x we can effectively find a recursive behavior $\sigma' \in x$ which realizes Θ in the sense that $\Theta = \sigma' \upharpoonright \Delta$.

thm 3.6 *Let $\mathcal{A}$ be a fixed, manageable, complete behavior structure. A total process x is computable in $(\mathcal{A}, merge)$ if and only if it is computable in $(\mathcal{A}, or)$, if and only if the following conditions hold:*

(1) As a subset of Baire space, x is Π_1^0 and effectively dense in itself.

(2) For each finite tree Δ, the set of ideal observables $idobs_x(\Delta)$ is finite, and we can effectively find (from Δ) a canonical listing of it.

It follows, in particular, that x is an "effectively compact" set. ⊣

We do not have a similar, complete characterization of computable, total processes for the more complex merges, but we can say something about them.

thm 3.7 *Let $\mathcal{A}$ be a fixed manageable, complete behavior structure.*

(1) If a total process x is computable in the expanded structure $(\mathcal{A}, parkmerge)$, then x is effectively dense in itself and for each tree Δ the set of ideal observables $idobs_x(\Delta)$ is recursively enumerable; as a subset of Baire space, x is Σ_1^1, possibly in $\Sigma_1^1 \setminus \Pi_1^1$.

(2) If a total process x is computable in the expanded structure $(\mathcal{A}, fairmerge)$, then x is effectively dense in itself and for each tree Δ the set of its ideal observables $idobs_x(\Delta)$ is recursively enumerable; as a subset of Baire space x is Σ_2^1, possibly in $\Sigma_2^1 \setminus \Pi_2^1$. ⊣

The upshot of these results is that total processes which are computable in either of the fair merges are very effective in the "loose" sense of Park; at the same time, they can be terribly complex when we view them "extensionally" (as subsets of Baire space), even including for the full state-depended *fairmerge* proper Σ_2^1 sets.

4 Continuing work

The most obvious problem left open in [4] and this paper is the extension of this work to languages richer than $\mathcal{L}$ and $\mathcal{L}^*(A)$, for example the natural strengthenings of these languages which allow value passing and the introduction of higher types. The characterizations of computability appear to extend quite trivially when we introduce value passing and (most likely) will also go through relatively unscathed in higher types. The Transfer Principle, on the other hand, already fails for $\mathcal{L}^*(A)$, but it may be that the counterexample (8) suggests the direction in which we should look for a remedy.

Notice that although (8) fails as an intensional identity between process functions, its two sides are *observationally equivalent* under any reasonable definition of "direct observation" for processes, including "infinitary experiments" which test and observe the behavior of a process forever: for example, for every strategy ω for player I in the game of interaction and every player x, quite trivially

$$\omega \star \text{cond}_R(x, x) = \omega \star x.$$

Perhaps we can show that behavior equivalent expressions in fairly rich structures are observationally equivalent in the appropriate process semantics, with a natural, rigorous definition of observational equivalence which is appropriate for the present modeling of non-deterministic processes by players. In any case, it will be useful to develop such a theory of observational equivalence so that we can bring this work into the mainstream of current research on concurrent systems.

A more "mathematical" interesting problem is the characterization of total processes computable in *parkmerge* and *fairmerge* left incomplete in **3.7**. For example, by **3.3**, a set $x \subseteq \mathcal{B}$ is a computable, total process of $(\mathcal{A}, parkmerge)$ exactly when x is a *recursive image* of Baire space, but which Σ_1^1 sets can be so represented? Classical descriptive set theory and its modern effective version have many methods for dealing with *pre-images* of definable pointclasses, but I was unable to find a single interesting fact about *images* in the standard reference [5], other than the trivial facts used in the proof of **3.7**. It would be best to find a characterization of these special Σ_1^1 sets in terms of notions that have algorithmic significance (as in **3.6**), but even an abstract, mathematical characterization may be interesting.

References

[1] M. Abadi, L. Lamport and P. Wolper, Realizable and unrealizable specifications of reactive systems, Proceedings of the 1989 ICALP, to appear.

[2] M. Broy, A theory for nondeterminism, parallelism, communication, and concurrency, *Th. Computer Science 45* (1986), 1-61.

[3] E. W. Dijkstra, *A discipline of programming*, Prentice-Hall, 1976.

[4] Y. N. Moschovakis, A game-theoretic modeling of concurrency, Proceedings of the fourth annual symposium on *Logic in Computer Science*, pp. 154-163, IEEE Computer Society Press, 1989.

[5] Y. N. Moschovakis, *Descriptive set theory*, Studies in Logic, North Holland, 1980.

[6] H. Rogers, Jr., *Theory of recursive functions and effective computability*, McGraw-Hill, NY, 1967.

[7] D. Park, On the semantics of fair parallelism, Proc. Copenhagen Winter School, *Springer LNCS 104* (1980), 504-526.

[8] D. Park, The "fairness" problem and nondeterministic computing networks, *Foundations of Comp. Sc. IV*, 33-162, Mathematisch Centrum, Amsterdam 1983.

[9] A. Pnueli and R. Rosner, On the synthesis of a reactive module, Proceedings of the 1989 ICALP, to appear.

The Chemical Abstract Machine

Gérard Berry*

Ecole des Mines
Sophia-Antipolis
06560 Valbonne, France

Gérard Boudol

INRIA
Sophia-Antipolis
06560 Valbonne, France

Abstract

We introduce a new kind of abstract machine based on the chemical metaphor used in the Γ language of Banâtre & al. States of a machine are chemical solutions where floating molecules can interact according to reaction rules. Solutions can be stratified by encapsulating subsolutions within membranes that force reactions to occur locally. We illustrate the use of this model by describing the operational semantics of the TCCS and CCS process calculi. We also show how to extract a higher-order concurrent λ-calculus out of the basic concepts of the chemical abstract machine.

1 Introduction

We present the notion of a *Chemical Abstract Machine*, suited to model asynchronous concurrent computations. We show that chemical abstract machines can "implement" known models of concurrent computation such as algebraic process calculi [18,6] and a concurrent λ-calculus similar to the one presented in [7].

Abstract machines are widely used in the classical theory of sequential computations. Turing Machines or Random Access Machines are primary tools within the theories of recursive functions and computational complexity. The SECD machine [17] and the Categorical Abstract Machine [10] are used to study and implement the λ-calculus, while the SMC machine [19] may be used to describe the semantics of usual imperative constructs.

---

*presently at LIX, Ecole Polytechnique, 91 128 Palaiseau, France
  Work supported by the french Programme de Recherches Coordonnées C^3.

The situation is much less clear in the field of concurrent programming. Models such as Petri Nets, Communicating Automata, or Data Flow Networks can be considered as abstract machines, but certainly they lack expressive power. More expressive models such as Algebraic Process Calculi [18,6] are intended to be specification formalisms for distributed systems rather than abstract machines. Implementation models of Concurrent Programming Languages such as CSP [16] are conceptually based on standard sequential machine models augmented with scheduling facilities, not on specific abstract machines.

Most available concurrency models are based on architectural concepts, e.g. networks of processes communicating by means of ports or channels. Such concepts convey a rigid geometrical vision of concurrency. Our chemical abstract machine model is based on a radically different paradigm, which originated in the Γ language of Banâtre and Le Metayer [2,3]. These authors pointed out that parallel programming with control threads is more difficult to manage than sequential programming, a fact that contrasts with the common expectation that parallelism should ease program design. They argued that a high-level parallel programming methodology should be liberated from control management. A similar idea motivates the UNITY model of Chandy and Misra [9]. Then they proposed a model where the concurrent components are freely "moving" in the system and communicate when they come in contact.

Intuitively, the state of a system is like a *chemical solution* in which floating *molecules* can interact with each other according to *reaction rules*; a *magical mechanism* stirs the solution, allowing for possible contacts between molecules. In chemistry, this is the result of Brownian motion, but we don't insist on any particular mechanism, this being an implementation matter not studied here, see [2,9]. The solution transformation process is obviously truly parallel: any number of reactions can be performed in parallel, provided that they involve disjoint sets of molecules. Notice that the tuple space model of Linda [8] is based on very similar concepts and bears the same degree of potential parallelism, as well as the sets of assignments used in UNITY [9].

Let us give a simple but striking example from [2,3]. Assume the solution is originally made of all integers from 2 to n, along with the rule that any integer destroys its multiples. Then the solution will end up containing the prime numbers between 2 and n. See [2,3] for more examples and for implementation techniques.

Technically, a Γ program is defined by the structure of the molecules it handles and by a set of reaction rules. Solutions are represented by *multisets* of molecules: this accounts for the associativity and commutativity of parallel composition, that is the implicit stirring mechanism. The reaction rules are multiset rewritings.

We keep the same basic notions for chemical abstract machines. We elaborate on the original Γ language by presenting molecules in a systematic way as terms of algebras and refining the classification of rules. Some molecules do not exhibit interaction capabilities; those which are ready to interact are called *ions*. A solution can be *heated* to break complex molecules into smaller ones up to ions. Conversely, a solution can be *cooled* to rebuild heavy molecules from components. Furthermore, to deal with abstraction and hierarchical programming, we allow a molecule to contain a subsolution enclosed in a *membrane*, which can be somewhat *porous* to allow communication between the encapsulated solution and its environment.

The chemical abstract machines all obey a simple set of structural laws. Each particular machine is given by adding a set of simple rules that specify how to produce new molecules from old ones. Unlike the inference rules classically used in structural operational semantics, the specific rules have no premises and are purely local.

In this paper, we concentrate on the descriptive power of chemical abstract machines. The strength of the model lies in the membrane notion. Membranes make it possible to build chemical abstract machines that have the power of classical process calculi or that behave as concurrent generalizations of the lambda-calculus.

To familiarize the reader with our concepts, the next section presents a simple machine for a subset of CCS. Section 3 gives some formal definitions. In Section 4, we treat the full TCCS [13] calculus and indicate how to handle other process calculi. Section 5 is devoted to a concurrent lambda-calculus similar to that of [7]. We conclude in section 6.

2 Handling a Subset of CCS

Our first illustrative example is a fragment CCS^- of Milner's process calculus CCS [18], containing the most basic operators 0 (inaction), '.' (prefixing), and '|' (parallel), as well as the restriction operator '\' to make the example non-trivial.

Let $\mathcal{N} = \{a, b, \ldots\}$ be a set of *names* and $\mathcal{L} = \{a, \overline{a} \mid a \in \mathcal{N}\}$ be the set of *labels* built on $\mathcal{N}$. We use the symbols α, β, etc., to range over labels, with $\overline{\overline{\alpha}} = \alpha$. The CCS^- agents p, q, etc., are given by the syntax:

$$p ::= 0 \mid \alpha.p \mid (p \mid p) \mid p \backslash a$$

2.1 The Semantics of TCCS

Process calculi semantics are usually defined by inference rules in Plotkin's structural operational semantics style, called SOS for short. Milner's original rules involve an additional τ label representing internal communication. This happens to be quite unnatural with respect to abstract machine executions, where internal transitions should not be visible to the user. We prefer to use the De Nicola – Hennessy TCCS rules [13] that define two kinds of transitions between agents: the *internal* transitions $p \to p'$ and the *labelled* transitions $p \xrightarrow{\alpha} p'$. Intuitively, $p \to p'$ means that p can become p' by executing an internal action, and $p \xrightarrow{\alpha} p'$ means that p can offer its environment to accept the action α and then become p'.

Both transitions systems are defined in a structural way: the behavior of an agent is deduced from the behaviors of its components. Since internal communications generate internal transitions, the inference systems for $\to$ invokes the one for $\xrightarrow{\alpha}$:

$$\alpha.p \xrightarrow{\alpha} p$$

$$\frac{p \to p'}{p \mid q \to p' \mid q \text{ and } q \mid p \to q \mid p'}$$

$$\frac{p \xrightarrow{\alpha} p'}{p \mid q \xrightarrow{\alpha} p' \mid q \text{ and } q \mid p \xrightarrow{\alpha} q \mid p'}$$

$$\frac{p \xrightarrow{\alpha} p' \quad q \xrightarrow{\overline{\alpha}} q'}{p \mid q \to p' \mid q'}$$

$$\frac{p \to p'}{p \backslash a \to p' \backslash a}$$

$$\frac{p \xrightarrow{\alpha} p' \quad \alpha \notin \{a, \overline{a}\}}{p \backslash a \xrightarrow{\alpha} p' \backslash a}$$

2.2 Basic Chemistry: Concurrency and Communication

We now take the chemical abstract machine point of view, limiting us to internal transitions of restriction-free agents in this section. Restriction and external communication will be treated in the next section.

Instead of composing their behaviors, we make the agents or *molecules* directly react with each other within a *solution*, that is a multiset $S = \{\!| p, q, \ldots |\!\}$. There are only two basic rules:

parallel:
$$p \,|\, q \rightleftharpoons p, q$$

reaction:
$$a.p, \overline{a}.q \to p, q$$

The rules apply to molecules present in the solution; they do not apply inside molecules.

The first rule is reversible. It says that any molecule of the form $p\,|\,q$ that floats in the solution can be *heated up* (symbol $\rightharpoonup$) to decompose it into its components p and q, and conversely that any pair p, q of molecules can be *cooled down* (symbol $\leftharpoondown$) to rebuild a compound molecule $p\,|\,q$. The comma ',' appearing in the right-hand side expresses that the heating and cooling rule respectively yield and take a pair of molecules.

The reaction rule deals with *ions*, i.e. molecules of the form $\alpha.p$. Since α is the ion's communication capability, we call it its *valence*. Whenever two complementary ions float in the solution, they can react with each other and release their bodies in the solution. The valences simply vanish. Unlike the parallel rule, the reaction rule is irreversible.

To execute an agent p, we start from the solution $S_0 = \{\!| p |\!\}$. Heating the solution exhibits the potential communications, which can then be performed using the reaction rule. Notice that a *hot* solution obtained by heating an agent as much as possible contains only ions. Conversely, any solution obtained by transitions from S_0 can be *frozen* by cooling rules into a solution $\{\!| q |\!\}$ consisting of a single CCS$^-$ term, or into the empty solution, analogous to the term 0.

To see the chemical abstract machine at work, let us consider an execution of the agent $a.b.0\,|\,\overline{a}.0\,|\,\overline{b}.0$.

$$\begin{array}{rl}
& \{\!| a.b.0\,|\,\overline{a}.0\,|\,\overline{b}.0 |\!\} \\
\stackrel{*}{\rightharpoonup} & \{\!| a.b.0, \overline{a}.0, \overline{b}.0 |\!\} \quad \text{(parallel)} \\
\to & \{\!| b.0, 0, \overline{b}.0 |\!\} \quad \text{(reaction)} \\
\to & \{\!| 0, 0, 0 |\!\} \quad \text{(reaction)}
\end{array}$$

The final solution $\{\!| 0, 0, 0 |\!\}$ only contains the inert molecule 0. It is natural to clean it up by using the following rule, which says that 0 evaporates when heated:

inaction cleanup:
$$0 \to$$

A last cleaning step yields the empty solution $\{\!||\!\}$.

Generally speaking, chemical executions are non-deterministic. For example, in the solution $\{\!| a.0, \overline{a}.b.0, \overline{a}.c.0 |\!\}$, the $a.0$ ion can react with any of the two others ions, yielding either $\{\!| b.0, \overline{a}.c.0 |\!\}$ or $\{\!| \overline{a}.b.0, c.0 |\!\}$ after cleanup.

The reader will appreciate the simplicity of the chemical executions compared to the sequence of proofs and simplifications involved in the SOS semantics. The use of the structural rules for '$|$' is factored throughout an execution by the heating process, since we directly chain reactions by keeping the solution hot. The SOS evaluation involves structural rules at *each* computation step.

In fact, the simplification comes from the abandon of the rigid algebraic syntax. Chemical concurrency is *naturally* associative and commutative, since multisets are intrinsically unordered. The notion of syntactic position disappears even for the standard syntactic parallel construct '$|$': it is impossible to know whether $\{\!| p, q |\!\}$ was obtained by heating $\{\!| p\,|\,q |\!\}$ or $\{\!| q\,|\,p |\!\}$. On the contrary, the SOS semantics need to first introduce behaviors to recover concurrency out of the fixed syntax, then to define what it means for processes to be equivalent, and finally to *prove* equivalences such as $p\,|\,q \sim q\,|\,p$. SOS also involves inference rules with non-trivial premises, which are certainly more complex than the naive cham rewrite rules.

Furthermore, we treat structural simplifications in the same way as reactions: to suppress a 0, we simply evaporate it. In SOS semantics, one needs to prove that $p\,|\,0$ is equivalent to p, and one performs transitions and simplifications in separate steps and by separate techniques.

However, the notion of behavior that underlies the SOS semantics has advantages. In particular, $p \stackrel{\alpha}{\to} p'$ also tells that p can perform an α when requested by some *external* observer, thus defining at once how an agent communicates with its environment. We must define the same notion in our setting.

A solution should be able to perform a visible α action whenever it contains an ion $\alpha.p$. This ion should then export the α valence and become p. One could imagine to let it disintegrate into p and emit an α-particle to the environment. However, such a technique would violate Milner's most useful principle, which states that there should be no difference in nature between internal and external communications. The right solution is to make the observer *react* with the valence of any molecule of the solution. This requires a richer machinery developped in the next section.

2.3 More Advanced Chemistry: Membranes and Airlocks

Consider a restriction agent $p\backslash a$ floating in a solution. If p is already of the form $\alpha.q$, $\alpha \notin \{a, \overline{a}\}$, we can build a new ion by the following simple rule:

restriction ion:

$$(\alpha.p)\backslash a \rightleftharpoons \alpha.(p\backslash a) \quad \text{if } \alpha \notin \{a, \overline{a}\}$$

But this does not work if p is compound. In this case, p should be able to freely perform internal reactions and to also propose communications to other ions floating in the main solution, using its own ions of unrestricted valences. To let p evolve on its own, we put it in a new local solution contained within a *membrane* $\{\!|\,.\,|\!\}$:

restriction membrane:

$$p\backslash a \rightleftharpoons \{\!|\,p\,|\!\}\backslash a$$

The new subsolution obeys the same rules as the global solution. To realize global communications, we need to make the membrane *porous* to valences. A first simple idea would be to use an heavy ion formation rule such as:

$$\{\!|\,\alpha.p,\ p_1,\ p_2,\ldots p_n\,|\!\} \to \alpha.\{\!|\,p,\ p_1,\ p_2,\ldots p_n\,|\!\}$$

We reject such a rule for two reasons. First, it does not involve only simple molecules as did previous rules; on the contrary, it involves finding an ion within a solution, which is neither simple nor general. Second, it is irreversible, since the information of where α comes from is lost. If a wrong valence is chosen, the heavy ion can stay forever in the main solution, like a *precipitate*. Consider for example $\{\!|\,a.0,\ \{\!|\,\overline{a}.0,\ b.0\,|\!\}\backslash c\,|\!\}$ when choosing b: we are stuck with the inert solution $\{\!|\,a.0,\ b.(\{\!|\,\overline{a}.0,\ 0\,|\!\}\backslash c)\,|\!\}$.

The technique we propose is in two steps. First, we introduce a new mechanism at the general chemical machine level: the *airlock* mechanism. It extracts any molecule from a solution (not necessarily an ion), puts the rest of the solution within a membrane, and isolates the extracted molecule within an airlock attached to the membrane. The airlock construct is written $m \triangleleft S$ where m is the isolated molecule and S the remaining solution; it is a *single* molecule. The reversible (meta) rule is:

airlock:

$$\{\!|\,m, m_1, m_2, \ldots, m_n\,|\!\} \rightleftharpoons \{\!|\,m \triangleleft \{\!|\,m_1, m_2, \ldots m_n\,|\!\}\,|\!\}$$

The solution $\{\!|\,m_1, m_2, \ldots m_n\,|\!\}$ contained in the new molecule is allowed to freely continue internal reactions (see the formal definitions in the next section).

Second, we build an heavy ion from any ion in the airlock, using the rule:

heavy ion:

$$(\alpha.p) \triangleleft S \rightleftharpoons \alpha.(p \triangleleft S)$$

In this way, we guarantee reversibility by preserving the attachment between α and p. A restriction molecule can propose several valences in succession to its environment until a communication takes place.

Let us give a simple example of communication involving an heavy ion:

$$\begin{array}{rll}
& \{\!|\,a.0\,|\,(\overline{a}.p\,|\,q)\backslash b\,|\!\} & \\
\xrightarrow{*} & \{\!|\,a.0,\ \{\!|\,\overline{a}.p,\ q\,|\!\}\backslash b\,|\!\} & \text{(par., restr. membr.)} \\
\to & \{\!|\,a.0,\ \{\!|\,(\overline{a}.p)\triangleleft\{\!|\,q\,|\!\}\,|\!\}\backslash b\,|\!\} & \text{(airlock)} \\
\to & \{\!|\,a.0,\ \{\!|\,\overline{a}.(p\triangleleft\{\!|\,q\,|\!\})\,|\!\}\backslash b\,|\!\} & \text{(heavy ion)} \\
\to & \{\!|\,a.0,\ (\overline{a}.(p\triangleleft\{\!|\,q\,|\!\}))\backslash b\,|\!\} & \text{(restr. membrane)} \\
\to & \{\!|\,a.0,\ \overline{a}.((p\triangleleft\{\!|\,q\,|\!\})\backslash b)\,|\!\} & \text{(restriction ion)} \\
\to & \{\!|\,0,\ (p\triangleleft\{\!|\,q\,|\!\})\backslash b\,|\!\} & \text{(reaction)} \\
\to & \{\!|\,\{\!|\,p\triangleleft\{\!|\,q\,|\!\}\,|\!\}\backslash c\,|\!\} & \text{(restr. membrane)} \\
\to & \{\!|\,\{\!|\,p,\ q\,|\!\}\backslash c\,|\!\} & \text{(airlock)}
\end{array}$$

Notice how we guarantee reversibility by putting or removing membranes. Once the heavy ion $\overline{a}.(p\triangleleft\{\!|\,q\,|\!\})$ has been constructed, it is not possible to put back p into q's solution, since the airlock molecule is not contained within a membrane. It is not possible to build such a membrane, since the membrane rule cannot be applied inside an ion.

The airlock technique makes it now easy to define what it means for an external observer to *observe* a solution. If the solution is reduced to a single ion, then the observer can pick up the ion's valence and release its body. More precisely, let S, S' denote solutions. We set $S \xrightarrow{\alpha} S'$ if there exist a molecule m such that $S \xrightarrow{*} \{\!|\,\alpha.m\,|\!\}$ and $\{\!|\,m\,|\!\} \xrightarrow{*} S'$. For example, one has

$$\{\!|\,a.0,\ b.0\,|\!\} \xrightarrow{a} \{\!|\,b.0\,|\!\}$$

taking $m = 0 \triangleleft \{\!|\,b.0\,|\!\}$.

The relation between this new kind of behavior and the standard TCCS one will be precisely stated in section 4.

3 Formal Definitions

3.1 Chemical Abstract Machines

A *chemical abstract machine* or *cham* $\mathcal{C}$ is specified by defining *molecules* m, m', etc., *solutions* S, S', etc., and *transformation rules*. Molecules are terms of algebras, with specific operations for each cham. Solutions are finite multisets of molecules, written $\{\mid m_1, m_2, \ldots, m_k \mid\}$. Furthermore, in each cham, any solution S can itself be be considered as a single molecule and can therefore appear as a *subsolution* of another molecule. The corresponding $\{\mid . \mid\}$ operator is called the *membrane* operator. For instance, if 0 and $+$ are the molecule building operations, then 0, $0+0$, $0+\{\mid 0 \mid\}$, and $\{\mid 0, \{\mid 0+0, 0 \mid\} \mid\}$ are molecules, the latter also being a solution.

The transformation rules have the form

$$m_1, m_2, \ldots, m_k \to m'_1, m'_2, \ldots m'_l$$

where the m_i and m'_j are molecules. As usual, the rules will be presented by means of *rule schemata*, the actual rules being the instances of these schemata. To avoid "multiset matching", we require the subsolutions appearing in rule schemata to be either a single solution variable S that generates all solutions, or of the form $\{\mid m \mid\}$ where m is a single molecule.

To state how reaction rules apply to solutions, we need some notation. The multiset union of S and S' is written $S \uplus S'$. As in the λ-calculus [4], we use the context notation $C[\,]$ to denote a molecule with a hole $[\,]$ in which to place other molecule.

The transformation rules determine a *transformation relation* $S \to S'$ between solutions, according to the following three laws:

- **The Reaction Law.** An instance of the right-hand-side of a rule can replace the corresponding instance of its left-hand-side. If

$$m_1, m_2, \ldots, m_k \to m'_1, m'_2, \ldots m'_l$$

is a rule and $M_1, M_2, \ldots, M_k, M'_1, M'_2, \ldots, M'_l$, are instances of the m_i's and the m_j's, then

$$\{\mid M_1, M_2, \ldots, M_k \mid\} \to \{\mid M'_1, M'_2, \ldots M'_l \mid\}$$

- **The Chemical Law.** Reactions can be performed freely within any solution:

$$\frac{S \to S'}{S \uplus S'' \to S' \uplus S''}$$

- **The Membrane Law.** A subsolution can evolve freely in any context:

$$\frac{S \to S'}{\{\mid C[S] \mid\} \to \{\mid C[S'] \mid\}}$$

The chemical and membrane laws are the only ones to involve premisses. They factor what is usually called "structural rules" in particular calculi. All other laws and rules are purely local.

Some chams, but not all of them, use the additional *airlock* construct. An airlock is a molecule of the form $m \triangleleft S$ where m is a molecule and S is a solution. Airlocks are built and suppressed by the following reversible law:

- **The Airlock Law**

$$\{\mid m \mid\} \uplus S \leftrightarrow \{\mid m \triangleleft S \mid\}$$

A cham is an intrinsically parallel machine: one can simultaneously apply several rules to a solution provided that no molecule is involved in more than one rule; one can also transform subsolutions in parallel. In this paper, we only study the expressive power of chams; it does not depend on using parallel evaluation, since a non-conflicting parallel application of rules is equivalent to any sequence of the individual rules. See [2] for a practical use of parallel reductions.

3.2 A Classification of Rules

We usually distinguish between three kinds of rules: *heating rules* $\rightharpoonup$, *cooling rules* $\rightharpoondown$, and *reaction rules* $\to$. The distinction is merely a matter of taste. As a rule of thumb, we present all structural rules as heating rules, possibly paired with inverse cooling rules. Heating rules decompose a single molecule into simpler ones, and cooling rules recompose a compound molecule from its components. We generally write the heating and cooling rules together, using the symbol $\rightleftharpoons$. We say that a solution is *hot* (resp. *frozen*) if no heating (resp. cooling) rule applies to it. In the sequel, we shall always consider that the transitions given by the airlock law are heating and cooling ones.

The reflexive, symmetric, and transitive closure of $(\rightharpoonup \cup \rightharpoondown)$ is written $\stackrel{*}{\rightleftharpoons}$. According to our conventions, it usually represents structural equivalence.

The reaction rules usually involve several molecules. These molecules are often in a particular form in which they cannot be heated further; we call them *ions*. A solution is *inert* if no reaction rule applies to it, nor to any solution obtained by heating it.

4 Process Calculi Chams

In this section, we finish the treatment of the TCCS process calculus, we establish the semantical equivalence between the cham semantics and the original structural semantics, and we briefly indicate how to handle other process calculi.

4.1 The Full TCCS Calculus

We finish the description of the TCCS calculus [13] and of its SOS semantics. We have already seen the inaction '0', parallel '|', prefixing '.', and restriction '\' operators. We now add the remaining operators: the relabelling operator '[.]', the two sum operators '$\oplus$' (internal sum) and '$[\!]$' (external sum), and the fixpoint definition $\texttt{fix}_i(\vec{x} = \vec{p})$, which is a shorthand for:

$$\texttt{letrec } x_1 = p_1 \text{ and } \ldots \text{ and } x_n = p_n \text{ in } x_i$$

The final syntax is as follows:

$$p ::= 0 \mid \alpha.p \mid (p \mid q) \mid p \backslash a \mid p[\phi]$$
$$\mid p \oplus q \mid p [\!] q \mid \texttt{fix}_i(\vec{x} = \vec{p})$$

We give the semantics of the new operators. A relabelling is a mapping $\phi : \mathcal{N} \mapsto \mathcal{L}$, extended to labels by setting $\phi(\overline{\alpha}) = \overline{\phi(\alpha)}$. The relabelling operator takes an agent p and a relabelling ϕ and produces a new agent $p[\phi]$ that behaves like p except that all its visible actions are relabelled by ϕ:

$$\frac{p \to p'}{p[\phi] \to p'[\phi]}$$

$$\frac{p \xrightarrow{\alpha} p'}{p[\phi] \xrightarrow{\phi(\alpha)} p'[\phi]}$$

Sums represent non-deterministic choices. There are several possible sums, see [13] for an extensive discussion. The simplest sum is the internal sum $\oplus$, which non-deterministically chooses a component:

$$p \oplus q \to p$$
$$p \oplus q \to q$$

In an external sum $p [\!] q$, the agents p and q can freely perform internal actions and can also propose communications to the environment. The choice is made only when such a communication is performed:

$$\frac{p \to p'}{p [\!] q \to p' [\!] q \quad \text{and} \quad q [\!] p \to q [\!] p'}$$

$$\frac{p \xrightarrow{\alpha} p'}{p [\!] q \xrightarrow{\alpha} p' \quad \text{and} \quad q [\!] p \xrightarrow{\alpha} p'}$$

Finally, the fixpoint operation is a simple unfolding. Let $p[\vec{q}/\vec{x}]$ denote the result of the simultaneous substitution of the q_i to the x_i in p:

$$\texttt{fix}_i(\vec{x} = \vec{p}) \to p_i[\texttt{fix}(\vec{x} = \vec{p})/\vec{x}]$$

4.2 Handling the New Operators

We first explain how to handle the new operators. Then we give the exact syntax of molecules and the complete set of rules of the TCCS cham.

The relabelling operator can be handled just as the restriction operator, by building a membrane and exporting relabelled names as heavy ion valences. Internal sum is handled by the same rules as in the SOS semantics; since the rules are not structural, we call them reaction rules and not heating rules. The fixpoint expansion rule is also as in the SOS semantics, and it is clearly a heating rule. See the exact rules in the rule summary below.

External sum needs more care. Since the summands p and q should each be able to freely perform internal transitions, we open one membrane for each of them. We therefore introduce a new *molecule pairing* operator $<.,.>$ and the expansion rule:

$$p [\!] q \rightleftharpoons <\{\!|p|\!\}, \{\!|q|\!\}>$$

Assume that the left subsolution S produces an ion $\alpha.m$ and that we want to export α. Then we can give S the form $\{\!| \alpha.n |\!\}$, either by taking $n = m$ if S only contains the given ion, or by building an airlock $(\alpha.m) \triangleleft S_1$ and then an heavy ion $\alpha.(m \triangleleft S_1)$. To export the valence, we can use the rule:

$$<\{\!|\alpha.n|\!\}, S'> \to \alpha. <n, S'>$$

However, as discussed in section 2, we must be careful to avoid precipitates and to make the above rule reversible. The reverse cooling rule must recognize that the valence belongs to n and not to S' when it is given a pair $<n, S'>$. Furthermore, once the α valence is consumed by some reaction, we are left with a pair $<n, S'>$ that we must transform into n to realize the summand selection; we need a cooling rule of the form:

$$<n, S'> \to n$$

Here again, we must recognize which is n and which is S'.

We can use several techniques to solve this problem. The one we choose is to tag the internal pair when the heavy ion is built to directly remember the valence attachment. The rules for the left-hand-side choice are:

$$<\{\!|\alpha.m|\!\}, S> \rightleftharpoons \alpha.(l :<m, S>)$$
$$l :<m, m'> \to m$$

The rules for the right-hand-side choice are symmetric with a label r.

An alternative technique would be to always force n to be an airlock, noticing that a solution $\{\!|\,\alpha.m\,|\!\}$ containing a single ion can always be heated into $\{\!|\,\alpha.(m\triangleleft\{\!|\,|\!\})\,|\!\}$, and to use the following rules:

$$<\{\!|\,\alpha.(m\triangleleft S)\,|\!\}, S'> \rightleftharpoons \alpha.<m\triangleleft S, S'>$$
$$<m\triangleleft S, S'> \rightharpoonup m\triangleleft S$$

This technique would decrease the number of molecule constructors, but is rather *ad-hoc* and we don't use it here. This discussion might look a bit tedious, but it shows two things: first, designing a cham has much to do with standard programming; second, the external sum operator is not very natural in concurrent abstract machines.

Let us give a simple external sum evaluation example:

$$\{\!|\,a.\overline{b}.0\,|\,((\overline{a}.0\,|\,b.0)\,|\!|\,q)\,|\!\}$$
$$\stackrel{*}{\rightharpoonup}\ \{\!|\,a.\overline{b}.0,\ <\{\!|\,\overline{a}.0,\ b.0\,|\!\},\{\!|\,q\,|\!\}>\,|\!\}$$
$$\stackrel{*}{\rightharpoonup}\ \{\!|\,a.\overline{b}.0,\ <\{\!|\,\overline{a}.(0\triangleleft\{\!|\,b.0\,|\!\})\,|\!\},\{\!|\,q\,|\!\}>\,|\!\}$$
$$\stackrel{*}{\rightharpoonup}\ \{\!|\,a.\overline{b}.0,\ \overline{a}.l:<0\triangleleft\{\!|\,b.0\,|\!\},\{\!|\,q\,|\!\}>\,|\!\}$$
$$\rightharpoonup\ \{\!|\,\overline{b}.0,\ l:<0\triangleleft\{\!|\,b.0\,|\!\},\{\!|\,q\,|\!\}>\,|\!\}$$
$$\rightharpoonup\ \{\!|\,\overline{b}.0,\ 0\triangleleft\{\!|\,b.0\,|\!\}\,|\!\}$$
$$\rightharpoonup\ \{\!|\,\overline{b}.0,\ 0,\ b.0\,|\!\}$$

Notice the last step: when an airlock $m\triangleleft S$ floats in a solution, one can cool it down and release m and all the molecules of S in the containing solution. This requires to use both the airlock law and the chemical law.

4.3 The Complete TCCS Cham

We summarize the syntax and rules of the final TCCS cham.

Syntax

Agents:

$$p ::= 0\ |\ \alpha.p\ |\ (p\,|\,q)\ |\ p\backslash a\ |\ p[\phi]$$
$$|\ p\oplus q\ |\ p\|q\ |\ \mathtt{fix}_i(\vec{x}=\vec{p})$$

Molecules:

$$m ::= p\ |\ \alpha.m\ |\ m\backslash a\ |\ m[\phi]\ |\ S\ |\ m\triangleleft S$$
$$|\ <m,m>\ |\ l:<m,m>\ |\ r:<m,m>$$

Notice that parallel and sums are agent operators, not molecules operators.

Rules

parallel:
$$p\,|\,q \rightleftharpoons p,\ q$$

reaction:
$$a.m,\ \overline{a}.n \rightarrow m,\ n$$

restriction membrane:
$$m\backslash a \rightleftharpoons \{\!|\,m\,|\!\}\backslash a$$

restriction ion:
$$(\alpha.m)\backslash a \rightleftharpoons \alpha.(m\backslash a)\quad \text{if } \alpha\notin\{a,\overline{a}\}$$

relabelling membrane:
$$m[\phi] \rightleftharpoons \{\!|\,m\,|\!\}[\phi]$$

relabelling ion:
$$(\alpha.m)[\phi] \rightleftharpoons \phi(\alpha).(m[\phi])$$

$\oplus$*-left:*
$$p\oplus q \rightarrow p$$

$\oplus$*-right:*
$$p\oplus q \rightarrow q$$

$\|$*-expansion:*
$$p\|q \rightleftharpoons <\{\!|\,p\,|\!\},\{\!|\,q\,|\!\}>$$

left $\|$-ion:
$$<\{\!|\,\alpha.m\,|\!\}, S> \rightharpoonup \alpha.l:<m,S>$$

right $\|$-ion:
$$<S,\{\!|\,\alpha.m\,|\!\}> \rightharpoonup \alpha.r:<S,m>$$

left projection:
$$l:<m,m'> \rightharpoonup m$$

right projection:
$$r:<m,m'> \rightharpoonup m'$$

fixpoint:
$$\mathtt{fix}_i(\vec{x}=\vec{p}) \rightarrow p_i[\mathtt{f\vec{i}x}(\vec{x}=\vec{p})/\vec{x}]$$

Additional Cleanup Rules

inaction cleanup:
$$0 \rightharpoonup$$

restriction cleanup:
$$\{\!|\,|\!\}\backslash a \rightharpoonup$$

relabelling cleanup:
$$\{\!|\,|\!\}[\phi] \rightharpoonup$$

4.4 Comparing the Cham and SOS

We define labeled transitions as explained in section 2.

Definition: Given a solution S, we write $S \xrightarrow{\alpha} S'$ if there exists a molecule m' such that $S \xrightarrow{*} \{\!|\, \alpha.m' \,|\!\}$ and $\{\!|\, m' \,|\!\} \xrightarrow{*} S'$.

Remember that the structural equivalence $\rightleftharpoons^*$ between solutions is the reflexive, symmetric, and transitive closure of the heating and cooling relations. In the sequel, we shall neglect the cleanup rules and consider only the reversible heating/cooling rules. Then $S \rightleftharpoons^* S'$ if and only if there exists a sequence of heating or cooling steps from S to S'.

The following result shows that the cham differs from the original TCCS calculus only in the number of internal steps involved in computations. As far as labelled transitions are concerned, the solution $\{\!|\, p \,|\!\}$ can do whatever the term p can do, and it cannot do more.

Theorem: Let p be a TCCS agent.

1) If $p \to p'$ in TCCS, then $\{\!|\, p \,|\!\} \xrightarrow{*} \{\!|\, p' \,|\!\}$ in the TCCS cham. If $p \xrightarrow{\alpha} p'$ in TCCS, then $\{\!|\, p \,|\!\} \xrightarrow{\alpha} \{\!|\, p' \,|\!\}$; more precisely, there exists a molecule m' such that $\{\!|\, p \,|\!\} \to \{\!|\, \alpha.m' \,|\!\}$ and $\{\!|\, m' \,|\!\} \rightleftharpoons^* \{\!|\, p' \,|\!\}$.

2) If $\{\!|\, p \,|\!\} \to S'$, then there exists a TCCS agent p' such that $S' \rightleftharpoons^* \{\!|\, p' \,|\!\}$. If $\{\!|\, p \,|\!\} \xrightarrow{\alpha} S'$, then there exists a TCCS agent p' such that $p \xrightarrow{\alpha} p'$ and $S' \rightleftharpoons^* \{\!|\, p' \,|\!\}$.

Sketch of proof: To prove 1), one shows how to perform given TCCS derivations by chaining cham transitions. The proof is by induction on the size of p and by cases on the form of the given TCCS transition. We show two typical cases.

First if $p = p_1 | p_2 \to p'_1 | p'_2 = p'$ with $p_1 \xrightarrow{\alpha} p'_1$ and $p_2 \xrightarrow{\overline{\alpha}} p'_2$ for some α, by induction, there exist m'_1 and m'_2 such that $\{\!|\, p_1 \,|\!\} \xrightarrow{*} \{\!|\, \alpha.m'_1 \,|\!\}$, $\{\!|\, m'_1 \,|\!\} \rightleftharpoons^* \{\!|\, p'_1 \,|\!\}$, $\{\!|\, p_2 \,|\!\} \xrightarrow{*} \{\!|\, \overline{\alpha}.m'_2 \,|\!\}$, and $\{\!|\, m'_2 \,|\!\} \rightleftharpoons^* \{\!|\, p'_2 \,|\!\}$. We build the following transformation sequence:

$$\begin{aligned}
& \{\!|\, p \,|\!\} \\
= \ & \{\!|\, p_1 | p_2 \,|\!\} \\
\to \ & \{\!|\, p_1, p_2 \,|\!\} & (parallel) \\
\xrightarrow{*} \ & \{\!|\, \alpha.m'_1, \overline{\alpha}.m'_2 \,|\!\} & (cham\ laws) \\
\to \ & \{\!|\, m'_1, m'_2 \,|\!\} & (reaction) \\
\rightleftharpoons^* \ & \{\!|\, p'_1, p'_2 \,|\!\} & (cham\ laws) \\
\to \ & \{\!|\, p'_1 | p'_2 \,|\!\} & (parallel) \\
= \ & \{\!|\, p' \,|\!\}
\end{aligned}$$

which shows the required property of p.

Assume now $p = q \setminus a \xrightarrow{\alpha} q' \setminus a = p'$, with $\alpha \notin \{a, \overline{a}\}$. By induction, there exists n' such that $\{\!|\, q \,|\!\} \to \{\!|\, \alpha.n' \,|\!\}$ and $\{\!|\, n' \,|\!\} \rightleftharpoons^* \{\!|\, q' \,|\!\}$. Let $m' = n' \setminus a$. We build the execution sequence:

$$\begin{aligned}
& \{\!|\, p \,|\!\} \\
= \ & \{\!|\, q \setminus a \,|\!\} \\
\to \ & \{\!|\, \{\!|\, q \,|\!\} \setminus a \,|\!\} & (restriction\ membrane) \\
\xrightarrow{*} \ & \{\!|\, \{\!|\, \alpha.n' \,|\!\} \setminus a \,|\!\} & (cham\ laws) \\
\to \ & \{\!|\, (\alpha.n') \setminus a \,|\!\} & (restriction\ membrane) \\
\to \ & \{\!|\, \alpha.(n' \setminus a) \,|\!\} & (restriction\ ion) \\
= \ & \{\!|\, \alpha.m' \,|\!\}
\end{aligned}$$

Furthermore, one has:

$$\begin{aligned}
& \{\!|\, m' \,|\!\} \\
= \ & \{\!|\, n' \setminus a \,|\!\} \\
\to \ & \{\!|\, \{\!|\, n' \,|\!\} \setminus a \,|\!\} & (restriction\ membrane) \\
\rightleftharpoons^* \ & \{\!|\, \{\!|\, q' \,|\!\} \setminus a) \,|\!\} & (cham\ laws) \\
\to \ & \{\!|\, q' \setminus a \,|\!\} & (restriction\ membrane) \\
= \ & \{\!|\, p' \,|\!\}
\end{aligned}$$

which shows the required property of p.

Proving 2) is harder and we just sketch of the proof architecture. The properties of $\to$ and $\xrightarrow{\alpha}$ are proved together by induction on the number of irreversible rules applied in the given derivations.

If this number is 0, then the property of $\to$ is obvious with $p' = p$. To prove the property of $\xrightarrow{\alpha}$, we use a lemma about ion formation.

The lemma shows how ions $a.m$ can be formed in arbitrary subsolutions using only heating and cooling rules. The valences of such ions always come from label positions in TCCS terms that yield observable transitions. Furthermore, the ion bodies are kept untouched in the heating-cooling process. More formally, assume $\{\!|\, p \,|\!\} \rightleftharpoons^* C[\alpha.m]$ where the ion $\alpha.m$ floats in some subsolution. Then one can cool down $C[\alpha.m]$ into $C'[\alpha.q]$ by using only ion cooling rules, in such a way that $\alpha.q$ is exactly a subexpression of the original agent $p = C_1[\alpha.q]$, with the additional properties $p \xrightarrow{\alpha} C_1[q]$ in TCCS and $\{\!|\, C_1[q] \,|\!\} \rightleftharpoons^* \{\!|\, C'[q] \,|\!\}$.

Now if $\{\!|\, p \,|\!\} \rightleftharpoons^* \{\!|\, \alpha.m' \,|\!\}$, one can use the lemma to show that p has the form $C[\alpha.q]$ with $C[q] \rightleftharpoons^* m'$. This show the required property of $\xrightarrow{\alpha}$, taking $p' = C[q]$.

Assume now that the number of irreversible transitions in a given derivation is strictly positive. The derivation can be put in the form $S \xrightarrow{*} S_1 \rightarrow S_2 \xrightarrow{*} S'$ with $S \stackrel{*}{\rightleftharpoons} S_1$ and where $S_1 \rightarrow S_2$ is irreversible. The only difficult case is the one where the transition form S_1 to S_2 is a reaction. By a slight extension of the lemma to two-hole contexts, one can show that $p = C[\alpha.q][\overline{\alpha}.r]$, $p \rightarrow p' = C[q][r]$ in TCCS, and $\{|\ p'\ |\} \stackrel{*}{\rightleftharpoons} C'[q][r]$ with $S_1 \stackrel{*}{\rightleftharpoons} C[\alpha.q][\overline{\alpha}.r]$ and $S_2 \stackrel{*}{\rightleftharpoons} C[q][r]$. The global induction hypothesis applies to p' and gives the final result.

4.5 Handling Other Process Calculi

In Milner's original calculus CCS, there is no notion of an internal unlabelled transition. The special label τ is used to report transitions provoked by internal communications. The sum $p + q$ is defined by the following rule: i:

$$\frac{p \xrightarrow{\alpha} p'}{p+q \xrightarrow{\alpha} p' \text{ and } q+p \xrightarrow{\alpha} p'}$$

n which one can take $\alpha = \tau$. Therefore, a summand can be chosen either by an external communication or by an internal one.

To simulate CCS by a cham, we abandon the simple reaction rule of TCCS and replace it by the following rule:

τ-reaction:

$$a.m,\ \overline{a}.n \rightarrow \tau.(m\,|\,n)$$

Since a τ-ion can neither be heated nor interact with another molecule, the only thing it can do is to traverse all membranes up to the external observer. An observation by this observer consumes the τ valence, and frees the ion body that can be heated to release the parallel components. With this new definition of reaction, the rules of + are simply the above rules of [].

Notice that performing an internal communication is more than just building a τ: the communication is really performed only when the final observer accepts it by *consuming* this τ. Therefore, the machine's behavior can no longer be defined independently of the observation process. Furthermore, the τ-reaction rule reduces the potential parallelism of the execution machine to a bare minimum. The simulation of CCS is rather unsatisfactory. We don't believe that CCS can be "implemented" in a more natural way, which is an indication that τ and + might not be good *programming* primitives. This is quite well-known to CCS simulator implementors.

Given a CCS agent p, we can show that the solution $\{|\ p\ |\}$ is in *weak bisimulation* with the agent p w.r.t. our definition of observation. Strong bisimulation can also be obtained by making the τ-reaction rule reversible, that is by allowing the machine to *undo* all its internal operations. The details are beyond the scope of this paper.

Handling other process calculi raises no particular problem. For example, the reader can easily write a natural cham for MEIJE [6], which is universal among the labelled process calculi. This tells that the cham formalism have basically the same power as the SOS one w.r.t. process calculi.

5 A Concurrent λ-calculus

5.1 Generalizing the λ-calculus

Algebraic process calculi model concurrency but have a limited expressive power compared to the λ-calculus, where one is able to express all possible combinators and to code many types of data. On the other hand, the λ-calculus is intrinsically sequential [4,5] and cannot handle even the weakest form of concurrency. Building new calculi that combine both abilities is a goal of primary importance [7,21]. In [7], we introduced such a tentative concurrent lambda-calculus called the γ-calculus. We could describe the (lazy) evaluation in this calculus by means of a cham. However, our formalism itself suggests a simpler, and perhaps better calculus of the same kind. To introduce this new calculus, let us first say a few words about the λ- and γ-calculi. Some familiarity with the λ-calculus will be assumed. We just recall the syntax:

$$M ::= x \mid (\lambda x.M) \mid (MM)$$

where x stands for any variable. We are interested here in the *lazy* evaluation of λ-terms (following [1]), that is the reflexive and transitive closure of the relation $M \triangleright M'$ inductively given by

$$(\lambda x.M)N \triangleright M[N/x]$$

$$M \triangleright M' \Rightarrow MN \triangleright M'N$$

Intuitively, a λ-calculus redex $(\lambda x.M)N$ is like a valued CCS communication of the form $\lambda x.M \mid \overline{\lambda}(N)$, since both yield $M[N/x]$ as a result. Hence one could imagine treating the lambda-calculus as a CCS-like process calculus where agents are communicable values, λ becoming a particular label. In such a calculus, functional application should appear as a particular parallel combination of two agents, the function and its argument, and β-reduction should be just a particular case of communication. However, the above simple redex translation would not take care of the non-associative character of application and would not treat double applications correctly. Consider, for instance, the λ-term $((\lambda x.\lambda y.M)N)P$. The translation would be $\lambda x.\lambda y.M \,|\, \overline{\lambda}(N) \,|\, \overline{\lambda}(P)$. The associative/commutative character of concurrency would make the arguments N and P interchangeable, which is clearly wrong. Thomsen solved this problem in [21] using the CCS operators of restriction and renaming. However in his higher order calculus, β-reduction is performed in two steps, involving an intermediary state which does not represent a λ-term. Then the λ-calculus is not exactly a sub-calculus of Thomsen's CHOCS calculus.

Another solution was presented in [7] using two concurrency operators: an interleaving operator '$|$' and a binary communication operator '$\odot$'. Communications arise as follows: in a term $(M \odot N)$, all '$|$' concurrent components of M can communicate with all concurrent components of N, up to termination of M or N, termination being written as a special symbol 1. Then the $\odot$ operator disappears by application of the simplification rule $(M \odot 1) = (1 \odot M) = M$, and λ-application can be represented by $(M \odot \overline{\lambda}(N))$. For instance, the above double application works in the following way (assuming x, y not free in N):

$$\begin{aligned}
& ((\lambda x.\lambda y.M \odot \overline{\lambda}(N)) \odot \overline{\lambda}(P)) && \\
\rightarrow\ & ((\lambda y.M[N/x] \odot 1) \odot \overline{\lambda}(P)) && \text{(communication)} \\
=\ & ((\lambda y.M[N/x]) \odot \overline{\lambda}(P)) && \text{(simplification)} \\
\rightarrow\ & (M[N/x][P/y] \odot 1) && \text{(communication)} \\
=\ & M[N/x][P/y] && \text{(simplification)}
\end{aligned}$$

A cham describing this calculus would treat the terms $\lambda x.M$ and $\overline{\lambda}(N)$ as ions, but the interpretation of the concurrency operators of this calculus would be somewhat unnatural. In a cham, the parallelism is always commutative and associative and allows for communication, while $(M \,|\, N)$ disallows communication and $\odot$ is non-associative. As a matter of fact, the cham framework indicates another possibility for representing properly the λ-application, by means of an encapsulated parallel combination of the function and its argument.

5.2 The γ-calculus

The key idea of our new higher-order concurrent calculus is to *internalize* the concepts of the chemical abstract machine within the syntax. Let us review these concepts:

- *solutions*: these are built by heating a parallel combination of molecules. Therefore the corresponding syntactic construct is parallel composition $(M \,|\, N)$. Since solutions are multisets of possibly interacting processes, this operator allows communication.

- *membrane*: encapsulating a subsolution within a membrane forces reactions to occur locally. Here we will introduce a corresponding *localization* construct $\langle M \rangle$.

- *reactions*: basically, these occur when opposite ions float inside the same solution. We shall distinguish two kinds of reactive molecules, the *negative* ones, or receptors, and the *positive* ones, or emitters.

Typically, a receptor in the λ-calculus is an abstraction $\lambda x.M$. To emphasize the ion character, we shall denote such an atomic receptor $x^- M$, and an atomic emitter sending the value M will be denoted M^+. Therefore the syntax of our calculus is:

$$M ::= x \,|\, x^- M \,|\, (M)^+ \,|\, (M \,|\, M) \,|\, \langle M \rangle$$

where x stands for any variable. As usual we shall omit (or add) some parentheses in writing the terms, which will be called processes or sometimes agents. In what follows we shall call this concurrent calculus the γ-calculus, superseding the one proposed in [7].

To formalize the execution mechanism, we need a syntactic notion of *stable* state. Basically, a stable term is made out of ions of the same valence (either positive or negative), and will therefore represent an inert solution. Formally, the syntax for pure emitters or receptors and for stable terms is given by:

$$\begin{aligned}
E &::= M^+ \,|\, (E \,|\, E) \,|\, \langle E \rangle \\
R &::= x^- M \,|\, (R \,|\, R) \,|\, \langle R \rangle \\
W &::= E \,|\, R
\end{aligned}$$

Now we give the γ-cham describing the (lazy) evaluation of terms. The molecules are given by the following grammar:

$$U ::= M \,|\, S \,|\, (U \,|\, U) \,|\, \langle U \rangle$$

where M stands for any term and S for any solution (i.e. finite multiset of molecules). The transformation rules are:

solution:
$$U \,|\, V \rightleftharpoons U, V$$

membrane:
$$\langle U \rangle \rightleftharpoons \{\!|\, U \,|\!\}$$

hatching:
$$\langle W \rangle \rightleftharpoons W$$

β-reaction:

$$x^- M, N^+ \to M[N/x]$$

where U, V stand for molecules, M, N for terms and W for any stable term. Note that the reaction rule, which is the only irreversible rule, embodies communication. The power of the calculus is essentially due to the rules concerning the membrane construct. This should not be confused with CCS restriction: if a membrane encloses a stable state (i.e. emitter or receptor), then it may vanish. The hatching rule conveniently replaces the termination equations concerning the cooperation operator of [7] (in our calculus, a "cooperation" operator would be $\langle M \mid N \rangle$). In what follows we shall use the notation $M \xrightarrow{*} N$ as an abbreviation for $\{\!|M|\!\} \xrightarrow{*} \{\!|N|\!\}$.

This γ-calculus contains the λ-calculus, since we may now define the application (MN) as the combination $\langle M \mid N^+ \rangle$. Let us see this point in some detail; we define a translation θ from the set of λ-terms to the set of terms given by the grammar:

$$M ::= x \mid x^- M \mid \langle M \mid M^+ \rangle$$

The translation is as follows:

$$\theta(x) = x$$
$$\theta(\lambda x.M) = x^- \theta(M)$$
$$\theta(MN) = \langle \theta(M) \mid \theta(N)^+ \rangle$$

Then we may show that there is a close correspondence between lazy evaluation of λ-terms and evaluation in the γ-cham of their translation. More precisely, it is easy to prove that

$$M \triangleright^* M' \Leftrightarrow \theta(M) \xrightarrow{*} \theta(M')$$

and, moreover, that each intermediate state in the evaluation of $\theta(M)$ cools down to a λ-term. For instance, the above double application works as follow:

$$\begin{aligned}
& \langle \langle x^- y^- M \mid N^+ \rangle \mid P^+ \rangle \\
\xrightarrow{*} & \{\!|\{\!|x^- y^- M, N^+|\!\}, P^+|\!\} \quad \text{(membrane, solution)} \\
\to & \{\!|\{\!|y^- M[N/x]|\!\}, P^+|\!\} \quad \text{(reaction)} \\
\to & \{\!|y^- M[N/x], P^+|\!\} \quad \text{(hatching)} \\
\to & \{\!|M[N/x][P/y]|\!\} \quad \text{(reaction)}
\end{aligned}$$

Since the λ-calculus is embedded in our γ-calculus, one can define arbitrary combinators such as a "replicator", D, that satisfies $(DM) \xrightarrow{*} M \mid (DM)$ for all M, or a "killer", U, that satisfies $(UM) \xrightarrow{*} U$. This is easy using standard fixpoint combinators. Moreover, our concurrent γ-calculus is more powerful than the λ-calculus. The most important non λ-definable object that can now be constructed is the *internal choice* (or more accurately *join*) operator. To see this, let us denote by K and F the two cancellators, i.e., respectively $\lambda x.\lambda y.x$ and $\lambda x.\lambda y.y$ (in our syntax $x^- y^- x$ and $x^- y^- y$). Then the choice operator is defined by

$$\oplus =_{\text{def}} \langle K \mid K^+ \mid F^+ \rangle$$

This operator may be evaluated either into K, like (KK)F, or into F, like (KF)K, therefore one easily sees that $\oplus MN \xrightarrow{*} M$ and $\oplus MN \xrightarrow{*} N$. Clearly such a combinator is not λ-definable since it does not preserve the Church-Rosser property.

As in [7], we extend our syntax by defining *concurrent abstractions*, that is sets of negative valences. More precisely, we define receptors of the form $[x_1 \mid \cdots \mid x_n]^- M$ where $x_1, \ldots, x_n$ are distinct variables. Such a term is able to receive n unordered values, to be substituted for these variables in M. Obviously these terms can be incorporated in our calculus with an additional rule:

choice:

$$[x_1 \mid \cdots \mid x_n]^- M \to x_i^- [\cdots \mid x_{i-1} \mid x_{i+1} \mid \cdots]^- M$$

Concurrent abstractions do not add power to the original calculus, since we can also define an atomic receptor $[x_1 \mid \cdots \mid x_n]^- M$ as a choice among all possible permutations $x_{i_1}^- \cdots x_{i_n}^- M$. For instance, using an infix notation for the choice:

$$[x \mid y]^- M =_{\text{def}} x^- y^- M \oplus y^- x^- M$$

The concurrent abstraction feature allows us to define combinators in a very compact way. For instance, the choice operator can be redefined by $\oplus = [x \mid y]^- x$, that is a parallel variant of the usual cancellator K.

We can also define a "parallel or", which is a parallel variant of the usual "left-sequential or" (cf. [7]). Let us see this point in some detail. It is known (see [4]) that $K = x^- y^- x$ and $F = x^- y^- y$ can be regarded as the truth values, respectively true and false. Then one may define a combinator for disjunction, namely $V = x^- y^- (xK)y$. This combinator is such that VKX reduces to K and VFX reduces to X. However, VXK (that is "X or true") cannot be in general reduced to K without evaluating X. For instance if, as usual, Ω denotes the non-terminating term $\Delta\Delta$ (where $\Delta = x^- (xx)$ is the duplicator) then the evaluation of $V\Omega K$ does not terminate. This is why V is "left-sequential". Moreover from Berry's sequentiality theorem (see [4]), one can show that there is no λ-definable combinator representing *parallel disjunction*, that is a combinator O such that both OKX

and OXK reduce to K, without evaluating X (and obviously OFF reduces to F). This combinator exists in the γ-calculus and is represented by:

$$O = [x \mid y]^{-}(xK)y$$

that is a parallel variant of the left-sequential disjunction (or equivalently a choice between left-sequential disjunction V and right-sequential disjunction $y^{-}x^{-}(xK)y$, see [10]).

5.3 Semantics

It seems fair to say that we have not yet established that "parallel disjunction is γ-definable". This is a semantic statement, so we would have first to define an equivalence relation $\simeq$ on γ-terms such that (using an infix notation for the "parallel disjunction" combinator O):

$$K \, O \, \Omega \simeq K \simeq \Omega \, O \, K$$

and

$$\Omega \, O \, \Omega \simeq \Omega$$

In [7] it was proposed to adapt the notion of observational bisimulation $\approx$ of CCS [18] (see also [21]), to serve as the semantic equivalence. We could define this notion here (with the idea that x^{-} is an input guard and M^{+} an output action), but this does not seem to be a good choice. For instance we would have $(K \, O \, \Omega) \not\approx K$ since $(K \, O \, \Omega)$ may be reduced to ΩKK, a term without any communication capability, which is certainly different from K.

As a matter of fact, observational bisimulation has often been criticized for being too discriminating, and weaker "extensional" equivalences have been proposed (for a survey, see [12] and [15]). For instance Darondeau in [11] argued that "a semantics which stems from more sophisticated observers [than programs] is not really extensional". In other words, the semantics of processes should be derived from their observation by means of *program contexts* $C[]$. These program contexts may be regarded as *tests* over processes, and there is a natural way to define an associated *testing equivalence* (cf. [14]): two process are equivalent if they pass the same tests. This is the kind of semantical equality we propose for our γ-calculus. However, we shall not follow [11] and [14] for what concerns the result of experiments. To report the success of a test we shall use, as in [1], the simplest operational information, namely *convergence*, that is existence of a normal form: the agent M pass the test $C[]$ if $C[M]$ converges.

Formally, an agent M is said to converge, in notation $M \Downarrow$, if and only if there exists an *inert* solution S such that

$$\{\!|M|\!\} \stackrel{*}{\rightarrow} S$$

Then the definition of the testing preorder (on closed terms) is exactly the one of Morris' preorder (cf. [4], exercise 16.5.5, and [1]), that is:

$$M \sqsubseteq N \Leftrightarrow_{\text{def}} \forall C.\ C[M]\Downarrow \Rightarrow C[N]\Downarrow$$

As usual the associated equivalence $\simeq$ is given by

$$M \simeq N \Leftrightarrow_{\text{def}} M \sqsubseteq N \ \&\ N \sqsubseteq M$$

Let us see an example, showing that testing allows to distinguish divergent terms in the γ-calculus (unlike the lazy λ-calculus). We still use MN to abbreviate application, that is $\langle M \mid N^{+} \rangle$. As we saw, the typically divergent λ-term is $\Omega = \Delta\Delta$ where Δ is the duplicator $x^{-}(xx)$. It might be observed that $P = \langle \Delta \mid \Delta^{+} \rangle$ is also a divergent term, since it can only be evaluated into Ω. Similarly, we can define a "triplicator" $\Upsilon = x^{-}((xx)x)$, and it is easy to see that $Q = \langle \Upsilon \mid \Upsilon^{+} \rangle$ is again a divergent term. Now there is a test separating P and Q, namely

$$C = \langle\langle [\cdot] \mid z^{-}(F)^{+}\rangle \mid \Omega^{+}\rangle$$

(recall that $F = x^{-}y^{-}y$, hence $FM \stackrel{*}{\rightarrow} I = y^{-}y$). It is not difficult to see that $C[P]$ diverges, whereas $C[Q] \stackrel{*}{\rightarrow} I$, therefore $P \not\simeq Q$.

We shall not investigate here the properties of the testing preorder. A first step would be to prove a generalization of the well-known "context lemma" (cf. [10]), showing that observers of the form

$$\langle \cdots \langle [\cdot] \mid R_1 \rangle \cdots \mid R_k \rangle$$

are enough to test the agents, that is

$M \sqsubseteq N \Leftrightarrow \forall k\ \forall R_1, \ldots, R_k.$
$\quad \langle \cdots \langle M \mid R_1 \rangle \cdots \mid R_k \rangle\Downarrow \Rightarrow \langle \cdots \langle N \mid R_1 \rangle \cdots \mid R_k \rangle\Downarrow$

Such a result would allow us to give a simple proof of the desired properties of the parallel-or combinator.

6 Conclusion

Unlike other models, the Γ [2] and cham models handle (true) concurrency as *the* primitive built-in notion. What the cham model adds to Γ is the structure of molecules as terms and the notion of a subsolution. The CCS and TCCS implementations give a simple operational vision of these calculi. Inference rules are replaced by standard rewrite rules. The difference between internal and external transitions is made obvious and so are the well-known difficulties with sums considered as programming primitives. More powerful "universal" process calculi such as MEIJE [6] can be handled as well. The concurrent λ-calculus fully exploits the ability of going back and forth between terms and solutions. It can be viewed as a direct extension of the lazy λ-calculus of [1].

Of course, this is still a preliminary work. Other concurrent computation paradigms should also be modelled; we think in particular of modelling process handling in operating systems, and of providing a cham for the new calculus of mobile processes proposed by Milner & al. in [20]. The theory of machine executions should also be fully developed.

Acknowledgments

We are indebted to Ilaria Castellani, Philippe Darondeau, Matthew Hennessy, Robin Milner and Serge Yoccoz for helpful discussions about this work and previous versions of the paper.

References

[1] Samson Abramsky. The lazy λ-calculus. In D. Turner, editor, *Declarative Programming*, Addison Wesley, 1988.

[2] Jean-Pierre Banâtre, Anne Coutant, and Daniel Le Metayer. A parallel machine for multiset transformation and its programming style. In *Future Generation Computer Systems 4*, pages 133–144, North-Holland, 1988.

[3] Jean-Pierre Banâtre and Daniel Le Metayer. *A New Computational Model and Its Discipline of Programming*. Technical Report INRIA Report 566, 1986.

[4] Henk Barendregt. *The Type-Free Lambda-Calculus. Studies in Logic Volume 103*, North-Holland, 1981.

[5] Gérard Berry. Séquentialité de l'evaluation formelle des λ-expressions. In B. Robinet, editor, *Program Transformations 3rd International Colloquium on Programming*, pages 67–80, DUNOD, Paris, 1978.

[6] Gérard Boudol. Notes on algebraic calculi of processes. In K. Apt, editor, *Logic and Models of Concurrent Systems*, NATO ASI Series F13, 1985.

[7] Gérard Boudol. Towards a lambda-calculus for concurrent and communicating systems. In *TAPSOFT 1989, Lecture Notes in Computer Science 351*, pages 149–161, Springer-Verlag, 1989.

[8] Nicholas Carriero and David Gelerntner. Linda in context. *Communications of the ACM*, 32(4):444–458, 1989.

[9] Mani Chandy and Jayadev Misra. *Parallel Program Design, a Foundation*. Addison-Wesley, 1988.

[10] Pierre-Louis Curien. *Categorical Combinators, Sequential Algorithms, and Functional Programming. Research Notes in Theoretical Computer Science*, Pitman, London, John Wiley & Sons, New York, Toronto, 1986.

[11] Philippe Darondeau. About fair asynchrony. *Theoretical Computer Science*, 37:305–336, 1985.

[12] Rocco De Nicola. Extensional equivalences for transition systems. *Acta Informatica*, 24:211–237, 1987.

[13] Rocco De Nicola and Matthew Hennessy. CCS without τ's. In *TAPSOFT 87, Lecture Notes in Computer Science 249*, pages 138–152, Springer-Verlag, 1987.

[14] Rocco De Nicola and Matthew Hennessy. Testing equivalences for processes. *Theoretical Computer Science*, 34:83–133, 1984.

[15] Matthew Hennessy. Observing processes. In *Linear Time, Branching Time and Partial Orders in Logics and Models for Concurrency, Lecture Notes in Computer Science 354*, pages 173–200, Springer-Verlag, 1989.

[16] C.A.R. Hoare. *Communicating Sequential Processes*. Prentice Hall, 1985.

[17] Peter Landin. The mechanical evaluation of expressions. *Computer Journal*, 6:308–320, 1964.

[18] Robin Milner. *Communication and Concurrency. International Series in Computer Science*, Prentice Hall, 1989.

[19] Robin Milner. *Program Semantics and Mechanized Proofs*, pages 3–44. Mathematical Center Tracts 82, Amsterdam, 1976.

[20] Robin Milner, Joachim Parrow, and David Walker. *A Calculus of Mobile Processes*. Technical Report ECS-LFCS-89-85, LFCS, Edinburgh University, 1989.

[21] Bengt Thomsen. A calculus of higher-order communicating systems. In *Proc. 16th ACM Annual Symposium on Principles of Programming Languages*, pages 143–154, 1989.

Interaction Nets

Yves Lafont
CNRS
Laboratoire d'Informatique de l'Ecole Normale Supérieure *

Abstract

We propose a new kind of programming language, with the following features:

- a simple graph rewriting semantics,

- a complete symmetry between constructors and destructors,

- a type discipline for deterministic and deadlock-free (microscopic) parallelism.

Interaction nets generalise Girard's *proof nets* of linear logic and illustrate the advantage of an *integrated logic* approach, as opposed to the *external* one. In other words, we did not try to design a logic describing the behaviour of some given computational system, but a programming language for which the type discipline is already (almost) a logic.

In fact, we shall scarcely refer to logic, because we adopt a naïve and pragmatic style. A typical application we have in mind for this language is the design of interactive softwares such as editors or window managers.

1 Principles of Interaction

Throughout this text, *net* means *undirected graph with labelled vertices*, also called *agents*. For each label, also called *symbol*, a finite set of *ports* has been fixed:

*Address: 45 rue d'Ulm, 75230 Paris Cedex 05, France. Electronic mail: lafont@dmi.ens.fr

We shall consider rewrite rules :

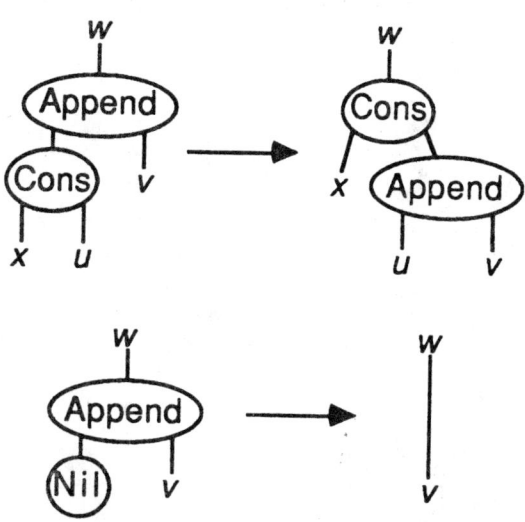

Here, rewriting is just a convenient language to express a very concrete notion of *interaction*, which we shall make precise by requiring some properties of rules. The first one is in fact imposed by our option of nets (as opposed to trees or directed graphs):

1. (linearity)

   Inside a rule, each variable occurs exactly twice, once in the left member and once in the right one.

Consequently, explicit duplication and erasing symbols are required for algorithms such as *unary multiplication* (figure 1).

To express our second constraint, we must first distinguish a *principal port* for each symbol:

2. (binary interaction)

Agents interact through their principal port only, which means that left members of rules are restricted to the following form:

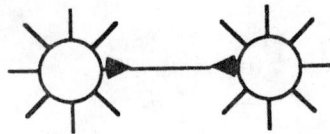

Indeed the rules for *append* satisfy our constraint:

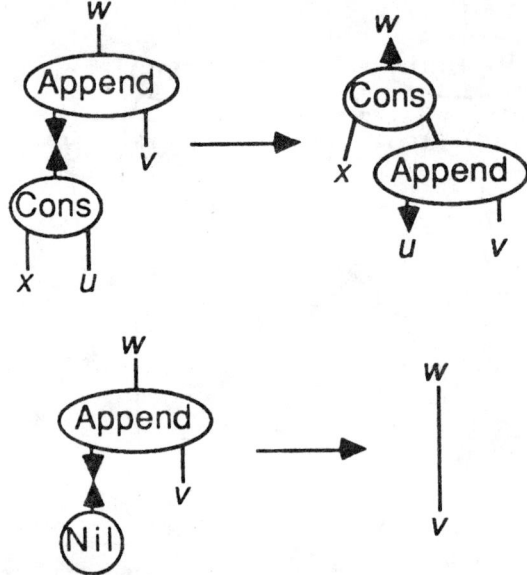

But for example, *unary maximum* cannot be expressed as follows:

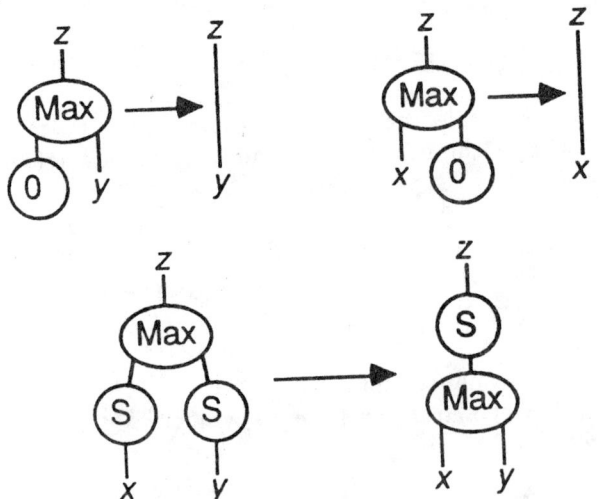

An extra symbol is needed (figure 2). In other words, we have to choose which argument is looked first (local sequentiality), and algorithms such as *parallel or* are excluded.

A pair of agents which are connected by their principal port is called *alive*, because some rule — maybe several, maybe none — is supposed to reduce it. Clearly, a third constraint is necessary to ensure deterministic computation:

3. (no ambiguity)

There is *at most one* rule for each pair of distinct symbols S, T, and no rule for S, S.

The three conditions are enough to get the following (easy) property:

Proposition 1 *(strong confluence)*
 If $\mathcal{N}$ reduces in one step to $\mathcal{P}$ and $\mathcal{Q}$, with $\mathcal{P} \neq \mathcal{Q}$, then $\mathcal{P}$ and $\mathcal{Q}$ reduce in one step to a common $\mathcal{R}$.

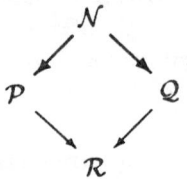

Indeed, by conditions 2 and 3, rules apply to disjoint pairs of agents, and cannot interfere with each other. Usual complications are avoided by condition 1. In fact, interactions are purely *local* and can be performed concurrently: proposition 1 expresses that the relative order of concurrent reductions is completely irrelevant.

So far, nothing ensures that all alive pairs of agents are reducible, but it is a reasonable requirement, and indeed, it will be the case of *typed* nets. Consequently, if the right member of a rule contains some alive pair, we should be able to reduce it, and the following condition is natural:

4. (optimisation)

Right members of rules contain no alive pair.

Even with this extra condition, termination is not ensured. The simplest counterexample is the *turnstile* (figure 3).

To illustrate the flexibility of nets for programming, we exhibit two simple examples: *concatenation of difference-lists* and *polish parsing*.

Concatenation of lists is performed in *linear time* with respect to its first argument. *Constant time* concatenation is possible with *difference-lists*: the idea consists in plugging the front of the second argument at the end of the second one. This requires two steps (figure 4) with an extra symbol, as in the case of *unary maximum*.

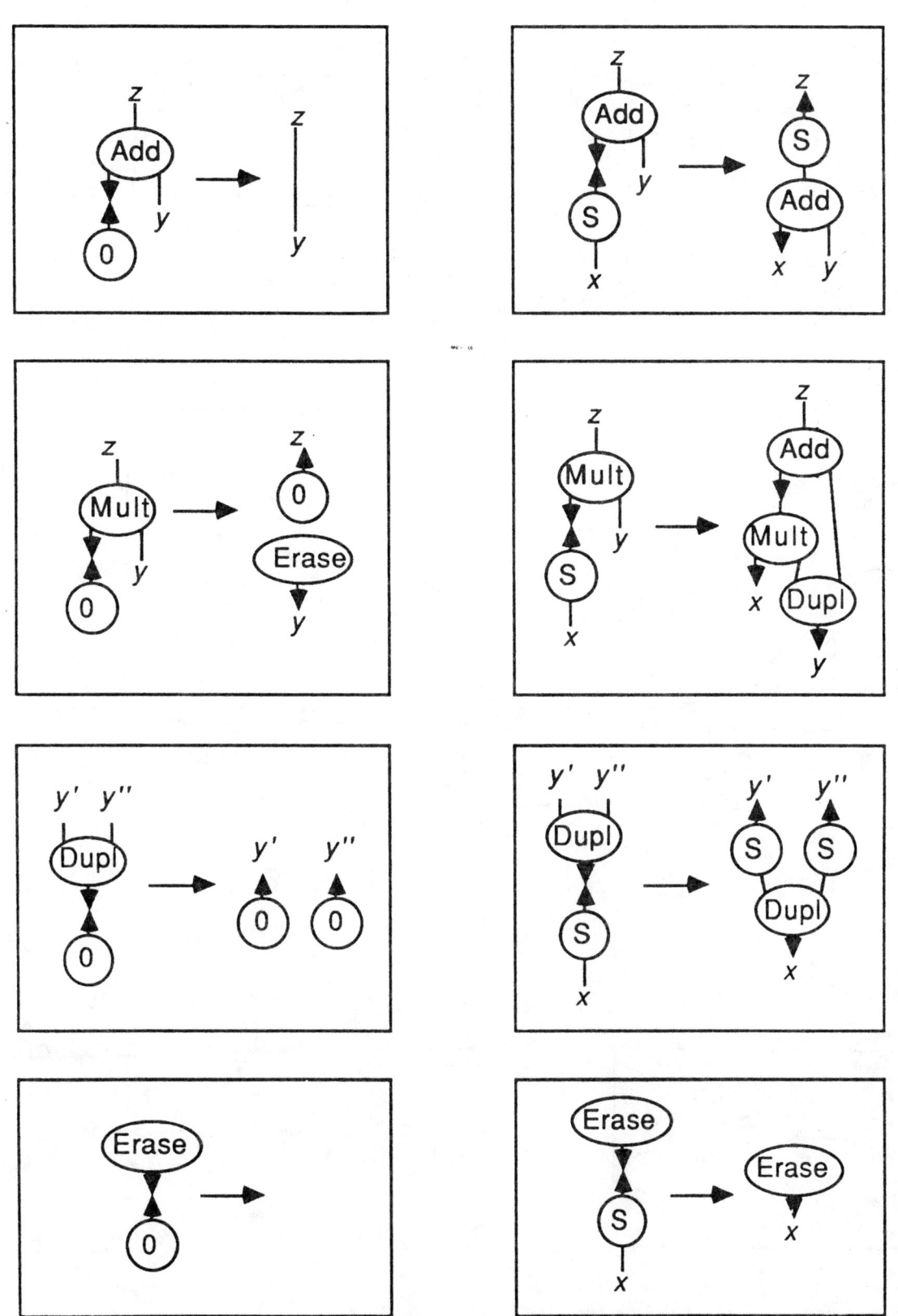

Figure 1: explicit duplication and erasing for unary multiplication

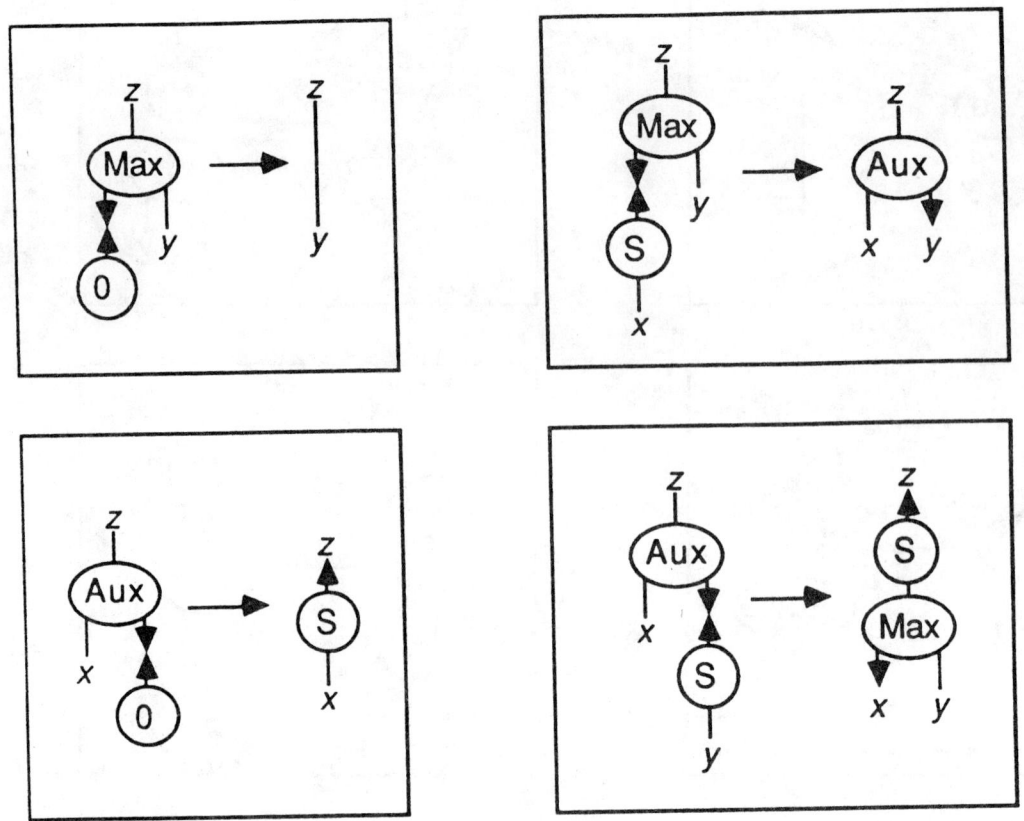

Figure 2: extra symbol for unary maximum

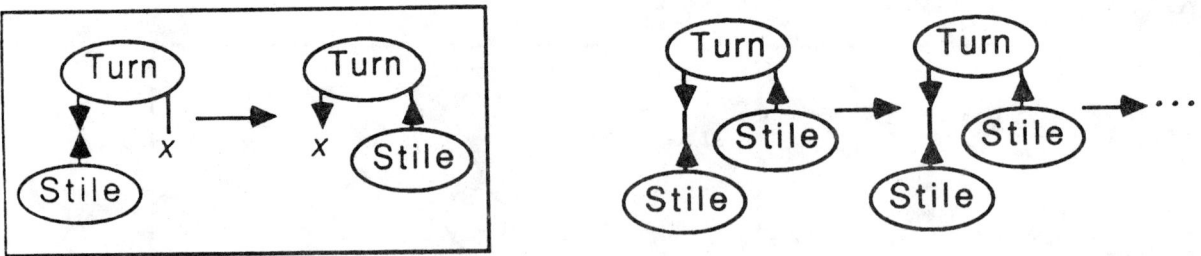

Figure 3: infinite computation with turnstile

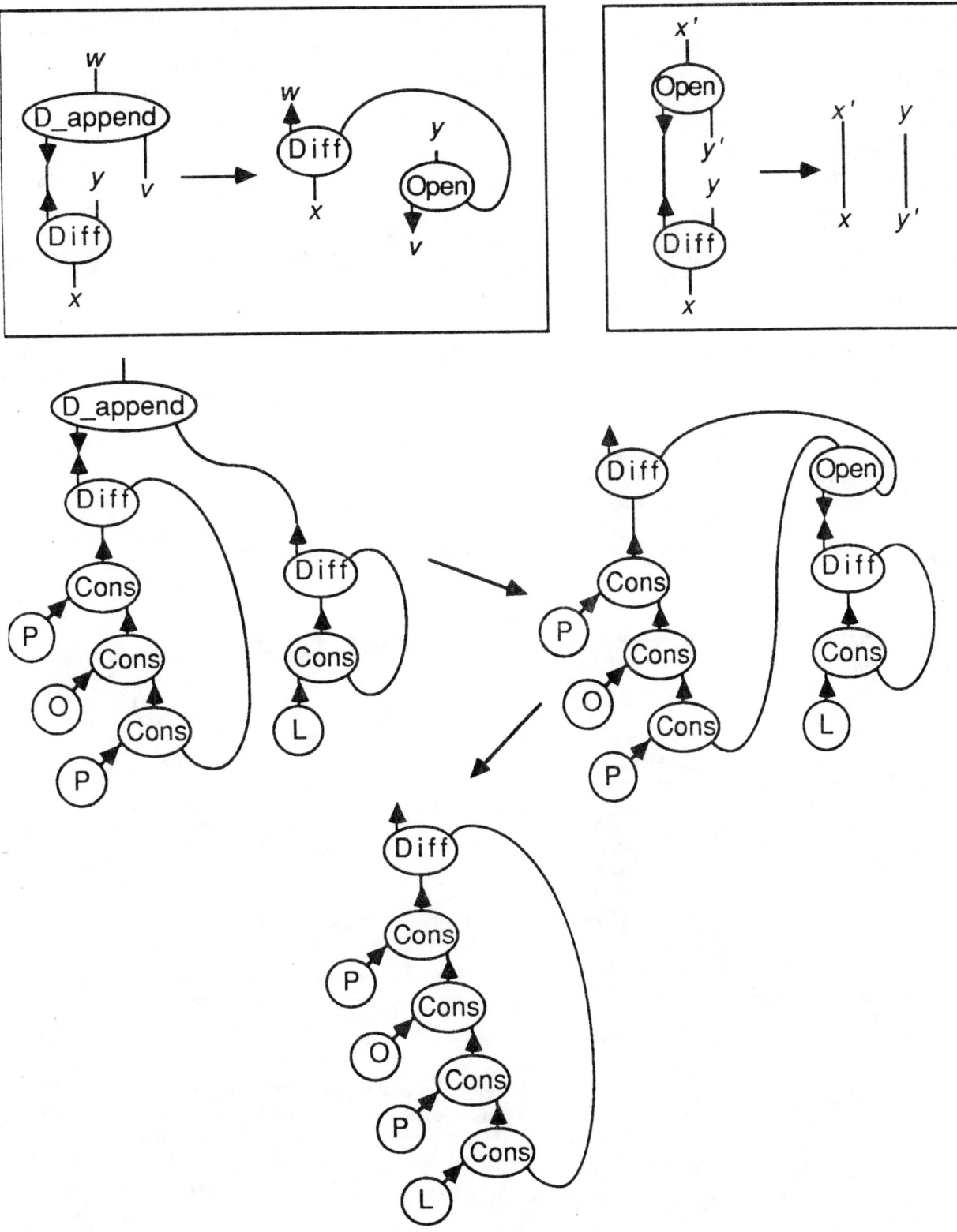

Figure 4: concatenation of difference-lists

Our second example is a parser for very simple arithmetic expressions in polish notation:

$$expression: \quad + \; expression \; expression$$
$$\qquad\qquad | \; 1$$

The parser takes an infinite stream of symbols as input, and returns a tree as well as a new stream (the rest) as outputs (figure 5).

Finally, note that the expressive power of interaction nets is not limited: *Turing machines* or *SK-reduction*, for example, can be easily simulated within interaction nets.

2 A Type Discipline

We are going to strengthen the conditions of section 1 so that for each alive pair of agents, some rule applies. Introducing rules for all pairs of symbols is not conceivable: how the devil would Cons interact with Nil, or Parse with Append? Moreover this would be inconsistent with condition 3. So we are led to limit valid configurations by means of *typing*.

We introduce *constant types* atom, list, nat, d_list, stream, tree, ... For each symbol, ports must be typed as input (τ^-) or output (τ^+):

A net is *well typed* if inputs are connected to outputs of the same type. A rule is well typed if:

- symbols in the left member *match*, which means that their principal ports have opposite types,
- the right member is well typed (the types of variables being given by the left member).

So we have new conditions for typed interaction:

5. (typing)

    Rules are well typed.

6. (completeness)

    There is a rule for each pair of matching symbols.

All examples in section 1 are easily typed. The choice of an input/output denomination is purely conventional: it does not matter if you call input what I call output, and conversely, but we must agree on matching. In other words, the notions of *constructor* (symbol with a positively typed principal port, like Cons) and *destructor* (symbol with a negatively typed principal port, like Append) are symmetrical in our system.

So far, typing ensures *local correctness* of computations, but we shall see that a notion of *global correctness* is necessary to prevent *deadlock*.

Proposition 2 *(stopping cases)*

Let $\mathcal{N}$ be well typed, finite, nonempty, with free variables $x_1, \ldots, x_n$. If $\mathcal{N}$ is irreducible then one of the following conditions holds:

i) some x_i is connected to a principal port, or to another variable,

ii) $\mathcal{N}$ contains a vicious circle:

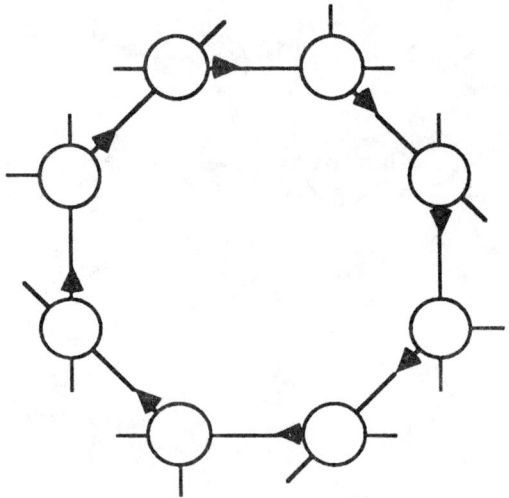

Indeed, starting from any point, you can follow principal ports until you reach a variable, or you loop! Case (i) simply means that $\mathcal{N}$ is ready to interact with its environment, but case (ii) is pathological. In fact, by condition 2, we have clearly:

Proposition 3 *(deadlock)*

A vicious circle stays forever.

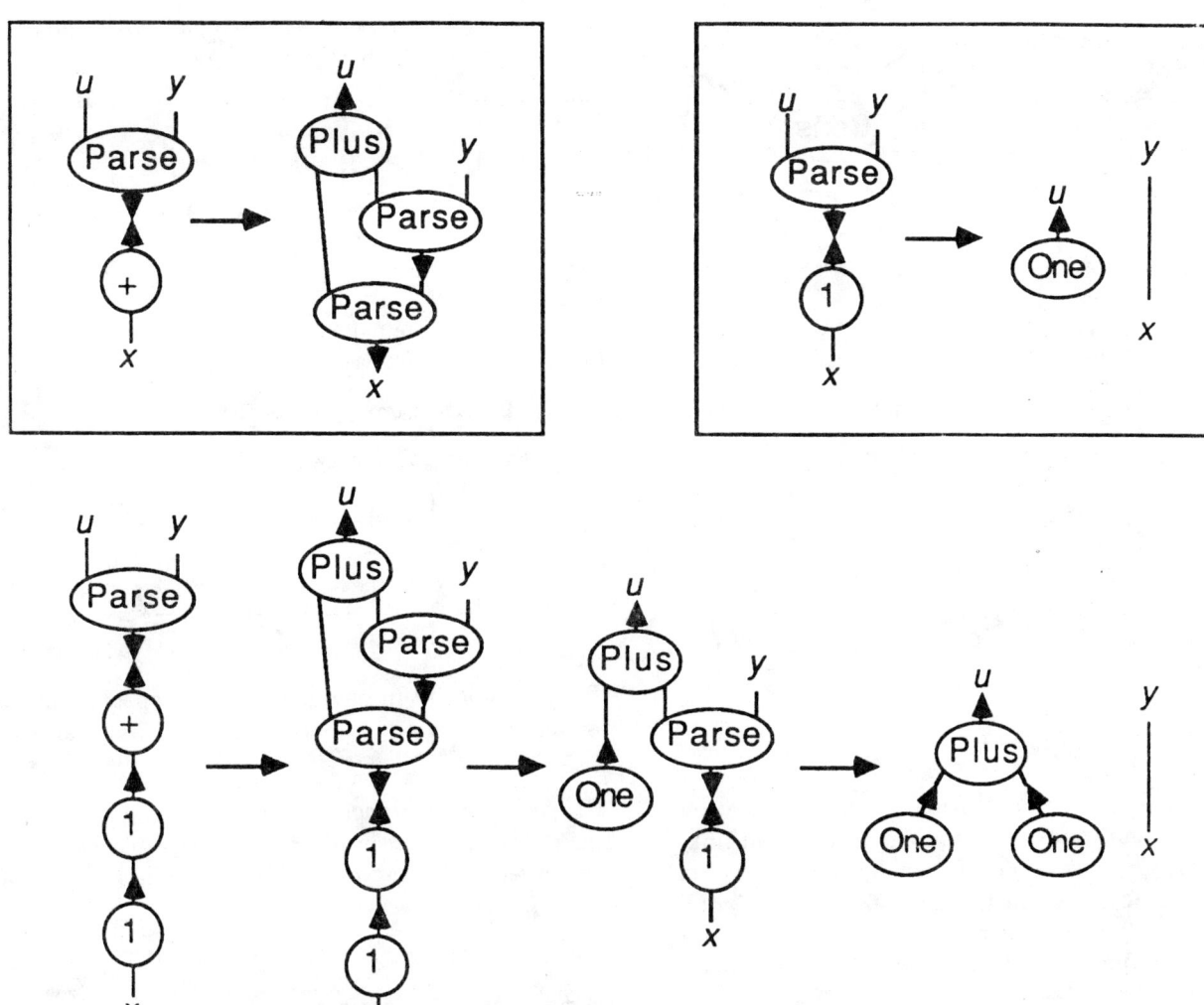

Figure 5: polish parsing

The trouble with vicious circles is that they can appear unexpectedly during a computation:

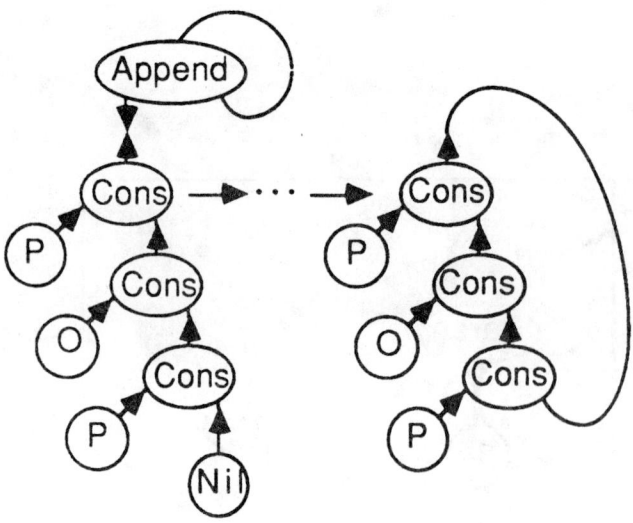

By the way, we should also consider the degenerated case:

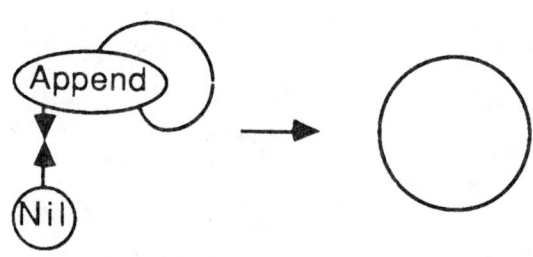

We need some **extra** condition to prohibit creation of such configurations. Forbidding cycles is unthinkable, because our examples (figures 8, 4 and 11) would collapse, but it is possible to distinguish between good and bad cycles. For that purpose, we assume that a *partition* on auxiliary ports is given for each symbol:

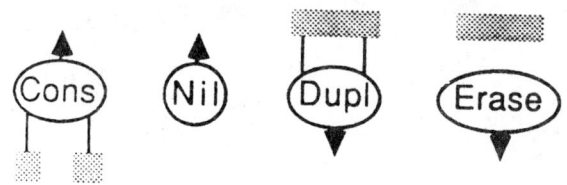

A net is called *simple* if it can be obtained by using only the following operations:

- LINK (an edge):

- CUT (a single connection between two nets):

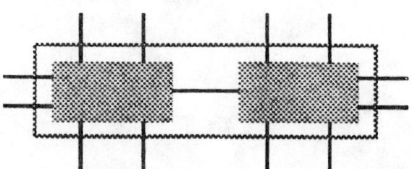

- GRAFT (connecting a new agent with nets, according to its partition):

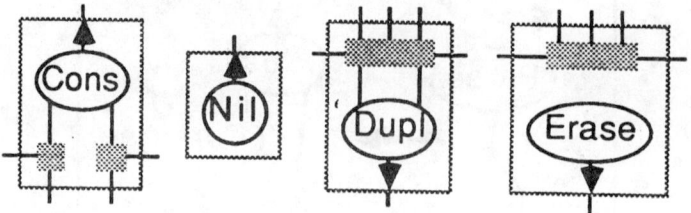

We also introduce a larger class of *semi-simple* nets by allowing two extra operations:

- EMPTY (an empty net)
- MIX (juxtaposing two nets):

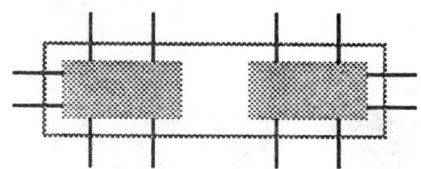

To get some intuition, consider the special case of symbols with *discrete* partitions (all classes are singletons):

Proposition 4 *(topological interpretation)*
In the discrete case, a net is simple when it is a connected graph without cycle, and it is semi-simple when it has no cycle.

In the general case, a straightforward induction gives:

Proposition 5 *(static correctness)*
A semi-simple net (and so, a simple one) contains no vicious circle.

Of course, the converse is false: we are not just worried about actual deadlocks but about potential ones.

A rule is *simple* if, when variables have been grouped according to partitions in the left members, the right member becomes simple (figure 7). With a suitable choice of partitions for symbols (figure 6) all rules in this paper are actually simple[1].

---

[1] As far as deadlock is concerned, *semi-simple* rules could be allowed, but the author has no interesting example. In fact, it is still not clear which concept, *simplicity* or *semi-simplicity*, should be used

102

The following result is essentially an adaptation of the *cut elimination theorem* for multiplicative linear logic (see appendix):

Proposition 6 *(invariance)*
Simple nets are closed under reduction by simple rules.

So our last constraint is:

7. (simplicity)

   Rules are simple.

With this condition, proposition 5 and 6 have the following consequence:

Proposition 7 *(dynamic correctness)*
A simple net will never deadlock.

3 A Programming Language

In this section, we describe a *concrete syntax* for interaction programming. A program contains three parts:

- *type* declaration (a list of identifiers),
- *symbol* declaration (identifiers with typing and partitions),
- interaction rules (the core of the program).

For each symbol, the type of its principal port is given first:

$$\textbf{symbol} \quad \begin{aligned}&\text{Cons} : \text{list}^+ ; \text{atom}^-, \text{list}^- \\ &\text{Nil} : \text{list}^+ \\ &\text{Append} : \text{list}^- ; \text{list}^-, \text{list}^+\end{aligned}$$

Non-discrete partitions are specified by means of curly brackets.

$$\textbf{symbol} \quad \begin{aligned}&\text{Dupl} : \text{nat}^- ; \{\text{nat}^+, \text{nat}^+\} \\ &\text{Erase} : \text{nat}^- ; \{\}\end{aligned}$$

Notation for rules is a bit disconcerting, but very natural. Consider the following example:

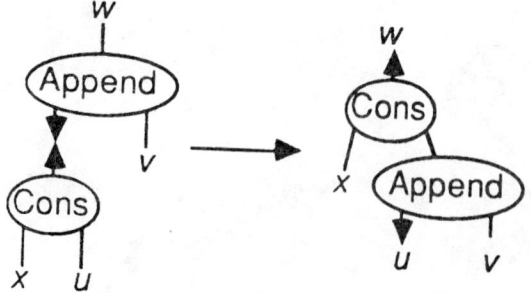

We join variables between left and right members:

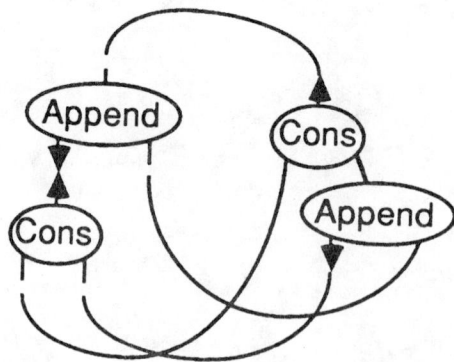

Putting principal ports up and auxiliary ones down, we obtain two trees with links between leafs:

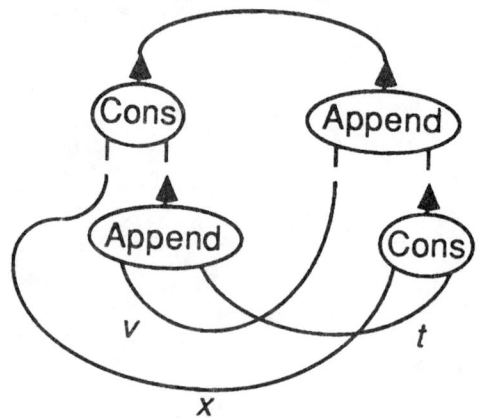

So interaction is written as follows:

$$\text{Cons}\,[x, \text{Append}(v,t)] \quad)\!(\quad \text{Append}\,[v, \text{Cons}(x,t)]$$

Note that the left and right sides of $)\!($ have nothing to do with the left and right members of the initial rule. It requires a bit of training to become acquainted with this syntax (figures 8, 9, 10 and 11).

This language can be implemented efficiently on a sequential machine. Basically, nets are encoded by means of cells and pointers, and alive pairs are stored in a stack. Because of the linearity, there is no need for a *garbage collector* (as in [Lafont88a]).

Here we described only the kernel of our language, but it should be interfaced with external devices such as keyboards or displays: for example, the output of a keyboard can be seen as an infinite stream of agents with characters as symbols (as in figure 5). Furthermore some extensions such as *polymorphic typing* and *modularity* are certainly needed to get a high level programming language.

```
        type   nat

     symbol   0 : nat⁺
              S : nat⁺; nat⁻
              Add : nat⁻; nat⁻, nat⁺
              Mult : nat⁻; nat⁻, nat⁺
              Dupl : nat⁻; {nat⁺, nat⁺}
              Erase : nat⁻; {}
              Max : nat⁻; nat⁻, nat⁺
              Aux : nat⁻; nat⁻, nat⁺
```

$$0 \quad)(\quad \text{Add } [y, y]$$
$$\text{S } [\text{Add}(y, t)] \quad)(\quad \text{Add } [y, \text{S}(t)]$$

$$0 \quad)(\quad \text{Mult } [\text{Erase}, 0]$$
$$\text{S } [\text{Mult}(y', \text{Add}(y'', z))] \quad)(\quad \text{Mult } [\text{Dupl}(y', y''), z]$$

$$0 \quad)(\quad \text{Dupl } [0, 0]$$
$$\text{S } [\text{Dupl}(x', x'')] \quad)(\quad \text{Dupl } [\text{S}(x'), \text{S}(x'')]$$

$$0 \quad)(\quad \text{Erase}$$
$$\text{S } [\text{Erase}] \quad)(\quad \text{Erase}$$

$$0 \quad)(\quad \text{Max } [y, y]$$
$$\text{S } [x] \quad)(\quad \text{Max } [\text{Aux}(x, z), z]$$

$$0 \quad)(\quad \text{Aux } [x, \text{S}(x)]$$
$$\text{S } [y] \quad)(\quad \text{Aux } [\text{Max}(y, t), \text{S}(t)]$$

Figure 8: unary arithmetics

type   atom, list

symbol P : atom$^+$
              O : atom$^+$
              L : atom$^+$
              Cons : list$^+$; atom$^-$, list$^-$
              Nil : list$^+$
              Append : list$^-$; list$^-$, list$^+$

Cons $[x, \text{Append}(v, t)]$ $\rangle\langle$ Append $[v, \text{Cons}(x, t)]$
                  Nil $\rangle\langle$ Append $[v, v]$

Figure 9: lists

---

type   list, d_list

symbol Diff : d_list$^+$; {list$^-$, list$^+$}
              D_append : d_list$^-$; d_list$^-$, d_list$^+$
              Open : d_list$^-$; list$^-$, list$^+$

Diff $[x, y]$ $\rangle\langle$ D_append $[\text{Open}(t, y), \text{Diff}(x, t)]$
Diff $[x, y]$ $\rangle\langle$ Open $[y, x]$

Figure 10: difference-lists

---

type   stream, tree

symbol + : stream$^+$; stream$^-$
              1 : stream$^+$; stream$^-$
              Plus : tree$^+$; tree$^-$, tree$^-$
              One : tree$^+$
              Parse : stream$^-$; {tree$^+$, stream$^+$}

+ $[\text{Parse}(v, \text{Parse}(w, y))]$ $\rangle\langle$ Parse $[\text{Plus}(v, w), y]$
              1 $[x]$ $\rangle\langle$ Parse $[\text{One}, x]$

Figure 11: parsing

Conclusion

Our proposal can be compared with existing programming paradigms. As in *functional programming*, we have a strong type discipline and a deterministic semantics based on a Church-Rosser property, but the functional paradigm (like intuitionistic logic) assumes an essential asymmetry between inputs and outputs, which is incompatible with parallelism and unconvenient for writing interactive softwares.

Our rules are clearly reminiscent of clauses in *logic programming*, especially in the use of variables (see the example of difference-lists), and our proposal could be related to PARLOG or GHC. There are also some similarities with *data-flow languages* and the CCS-CSP family, but as far as we know, the concepts of *principal port* (which is critical for determinism) and *semi-simplicity* (which prevents deadlock) has never been considered in such systems.

In the appendix, we explain how this work relates to linear logic. Our first contribution was much more in the lineage of functional programming, with an emphasis on questions of lazyness and memory allocation [Girafont,Lafont88a]. On the other hand, [Lafont87] can be considered as an embryo of interaction nets, although the right framework was not discovered at that time. The first idea of generalising multiplicative connectors of linear logic appears in [Girard88] (partitions are considered in [Regnos]) and led to the *Geometry of interaction* [Girard89,Girard89a].

We are now working on a true implementation of the language to develop real examples in a practical programming environment.

Appendix: Linear Logic

Let us write $\vdash A_1, \ldots, A_n$ if there is a *simple* net with free variables $x_1, \ldots, x_n$ of types $A_1, \ldots, A_n$. By definition of *simplicity*, we have the following rules:

$$\frac{\vdash \Gamma, A, B, \Delta}{\vdash \Gamma, B, A, \Delta} \text{EXCHANGE}$$

$$\frac{}{\vdash A, A^{op}} \text{LINK} \qquad \frac{\vdash A, \Gamma \quad \vdash A^{op}, \Delta}{\vdash \Gamma, \Delta} \text{CUT}$$

The exchange rule expresses that the order of variables is irrelevant (simple nets are not necessarily planar graphs). So far, those are rules of *linear logic* [Girard87] (see also in [Giraflor] for a short introduction) but here we have plenty of *logical rules* corresponding to the symbol declaration part of our programs, for example:

$$\frac{\vdash \text{atom}^+, \Gamma \quad \vdash \text{list}^+, \Delta}{\vdash \text{list}^+, \Gamma, \Delta} \text{Cons} \qquad \frac{}{\vdash \text{list}^+} \text{Nil}$$

$$\frac{\vdash \text{list}^+, \Gamma \quad \vdash \text{list}^-, \Delta}{\vdash \text{list}^-, \Gamma, \Delta} \text{Append}$$

$$\frac{\vdash \text{nat}^-, \text{nat}^-, \Gamma}{\vdash \text{nat}^-, \Gamma} \text{Dupl} \qquad \frac{\vdash \Gamma}{\vdash \text{nat}^-, \Gamma} \text{Erase}$$

Basically, interaction consists in *cut elimination*:

$$\frac{\dfrac{}{\vdash \text{list}^+} \text{Nil} \quad \dfrac{\vdash \text{list}^+, \Gamma \quad \vdash \text{list}^-, \Delta}{\vdash \text{list}^-, \Gamma, \Delta} \text{Append}}{\vdash \Gamma, \Delta} \text{CUT}$$

$$\downarrow$$

$$\frac{\vdash \text{list}^+, \Gamma \quad \vdash \text{list}^-, \Delta}{\vdash \Gamma, \Delta} \text{CUT}$$

The concrete syntax Nil $\rangle\langle$ Append $[v,v]$ is of course more concise!

By adding *polymorphic typing*, we integrate "official" rules of linear logic such as:

$$\frac{\vdash A, \Gamma \quad \vdash B, \Delta}{\vdash A \otimes B, \Gamma, \Delta} \text{Times}$$

but not the following one:

$$\frac{\vdash A, \Gamma \quad \vdash B, \Gamma}{\vdash A \& B, \Gamma} \text{With}$$

Indeed, our proposal generalises the so-called *multiplicative* fragment of linear logic, for which the notion *proof net* works very well, but with very limited dynamics (everything reduces in linear time). On the contrary, our type system does not ensure termination, although it would be interesting to isolate terminating subsystems.

References

[Girard87] J.Y. Girard, Linear logic, *TCS* **50** (1987) 1-102.

[Girard88] J.Y. Girard, Multiplicatives, in *Rendiconti del seminario matematico dell'università e politecnico di Torino*, special issue on logic and computer science (1988).

[Girard89] J.Y. Girard, Towards a geometry of interaction, in *Conference on categories, computer science and logic*, Contempory Mathematics, *AMS* **92** (1989).

[Girard89a] J.Y. Girard, Geometry of interaction 1: interpretation of system F, in *ASL meeting* (North-Holland, Padova, 1989).

[Girafont] J.Y. Girard & Y. Lafont, Linear Logic and Lazy Computation, in *TAPSOFT '87, vol. 2*, *LNCS* **250** (Springer-Verlag, Pisa) 52-66.

[Giraflor] J.Y. Girard, Y. Lafont, P. Taylor, *Proofs and Types*, Cambridge Tracts in Theoretical Computer Science (Cambridge University Press, 1989).

[Lafont87] Y. Lafont, Linear Logic Programming, in *Workshop on Programming Logic* (Göteborg, 1987) 209-220.

[Lafont88] Y. Lafont, Logiques, Catégories et Machines, thèse de doctorat (Université de Paris VII, 1988).

[Lafont88a] Y. Lafont, The Linear Abstract Machine, *TCS* **59** (1988) 157-180.

[Regnos] V. Danos & L. Régnier, The structure of multiplicatives, typescript (1988).

Toward a typed foundation for method specialization and inheritance

John C. Mitchell [*]
Department of Computer Science
Stanford University
jcm@cs.stanford.edu

Abstract

This paper discusses the phenomenon of *method specialization* in object-oriented programming languages. A typed function calculus of objects and classes is presented, featuring method specialization when methods are added or redefined. The soundness of the typing rules (without subtyping) is suggested by a translation into a more traditional calculus with recursively-defined record types. However, semantic questions regarding the subtype relation on classes remain open.

1 Introduction

In spite of the increasing popularity of object-oriented programming, several issues do not seem to be well understood. In particular, although preliminary formal semantics have been proposed [Kam88, Red88, Yel89], there is neither an accepted basis for reasoning about basic issues such as program transformation or optimization, nor a sound basis for flexible typing disciplines. This paper presents a typed function calculus with simple forms of "objects" and "classes" which illustrate an essential feature of inheritance we call method specialization. To give some insight into the connection between this calculus and previous formal analysis, we also give a translation of objects and classes into records and recursively-defined

---

[*] Supported in part by an NSF PYI Award, matching funds from Digital Equipment Corporation, the Powell Foundation, and Xerox Corporation, and NSF grant CCR-8814921.

record types. This clarifies some of the challenges involved in giving compositional, typed semantics to realistic object-oriented languages.

Apart from typing and mathematical semantics, the basic calculus used in this paper is relatively straightforward. The main idea is to provide a functional (*i.e.*, side-effect free) form of "prototyping," or "delegation" [Bor86, Lie86, LTP86, US87] so that one object may be created by inheriting methods from another. For simplicity, we treat methods and instance variables uniformly; methods may be replaced, and therefore instance variables may be regarded as methods that return a constant value. The set of messages an object will answer, and the types of their results, are specified by a form of type we call a class. One class will be considered a subclass (or subtype) of another if every object of the first is guaranteed to behave properly when considered as an element of the second class. Thus, in our view, classes are types whose elements are objects, and inheritance is a mechanism for constructing one object from another. The subclass relation is determined by behavioral characteristics of objects rather than program declarations. While this may not be the predominant view of object-oriented programming, it is consistent with at least one important practical view and it is a convenient model for our purposes.

Method specialization, which is described in some detail in Section 2, is achieved by treating objects as collections of functions, each representing a method of the object. When a method is invoked, the appropriate function is applied to the object itself. In other words, instead of using a special symbol *self* to allow a method to refer to the object to which it belongs, we use the first argument of the method. This approach is also used directly in T [RA82, AR88], which we were not aware of when we first began experimenting with this idea, and in the implementation of Modula 3 [CDG+88, CDJ+89]. The main point of the paper is not to promote this view of objects, but to develop typing rules for methods which usefully reflect the way they are inherited.

One long-term goal is to develop a flexible, polymorphic typing discipline which could prevent such common run-time errors as *message not understood*. This is not an easy task, as illustrated by the vagaries of the early proposals for typing in Smalltalk [BI82, Suz81] and the subtle bugs surrounding *like self* [Coo89b] in the more recent language Eiffel [Mey88]. Another reason to develop typing rules is that in giving types, we are forced to specify exactly what kind of value is defined by each kind of expression in the language. This seems quite valuable when we consider substitution equivalence, which is critical to understanding or reasoning about transformation and optimization.

The calculus presented in this paper owes much to the recent line of work on record calculi with subtyping, beginning with Cardelli's 1984 paper [Car88]. A number of influential typing ideas, including bounded quantification, were sketched out in [CW85], and summarized in [DT88]. More recently, type inference techniques been presented in [Wan87], followed up by [Sta88, JM88, Rém89, Wan89]. From an untyped, denotational point of view, the primary studies seem to be Cook's thesis [Coo89a], which highlights method specialization, and the denotational semantics presented in [Kam88, Red88, Yel89]. The general perspective of this paper has developed from a tutorial presentation at the 1988 OOPSLA conference with Luca Cardelli [CM88], a subsequent joint paper [CM89], and numerous conversations with members of the ABEL group at HP Labs (Peter Canning, William Cook, Walt Hill and Walter Olthoff).

2 Method specialization

An important phenomena that seems essential to object-oriented programming will be referred to as *method specialization*. Although there is really only one basic idea, it will be helpful to separate method specialization into two forms, one involving the addition of methods, and the other involving method replacement, or "overriding." Both forms may be illustrated using example classes of points (*c.f.* [CW85, JM88]). The class *point* contains objects that have x, y and *move* methods. If points have integer coordinates, then the functionality of point objects may be summarized by the signature,

$$\textbf{class } point \textbf{ methods}$$
$$x : int, \, y : int,$$
$$move : int \times int \rightarrow point$$

which we will regard as the type of all objects having x, y, and *move* methods of the indicated functionality. Note that we allow methods to return functions, which reduces method parameterization to ordinary function application. A more specialized class of points are the colored points, which have an additional method returning their color

$$\textbf{class } colored\_point \textbf{ methods}$$
$$x : int, \, y : int, \, c : color,$$
$$move : int \times int \rightarrow colored\_point$$

and an appropriately revised type of *move* method. In a language such as Smalltalk [GR83], we might first define a *point* class and use *point* objects in writing a graphics package. Later, after upgrading to a color display, we might define the subclass of *colored_point*'s and use these instead. In a delegation- or prototype-based language such as Self, we might use a similar programming technique, although we would define the basic point methods in a prototype point, instead of a class declaration. An important aspect of object-oriented languages in general is that much of the code we write for *point*'s may be used directly on *colored_point*'s, eliminating what could otherwise be a significant amount of reprogramming.

When we define *colored_point* 's, either as a subclass (as in Smalltalk) or by prototyping (as in Self), the *move* method is *specialized* as it is inherited. In particular, the type of *move* changes when it is inherited. If we send the *move* message to a point, along with integer "displacements" δ_x and δ_y, we obtain a point with modified x and y coordinates. However, when we send the *move* message to a colored point, we obtain a colored point instead of an uncolored point. While this will be completely familiar to anyone who has written a program in an object-oriented language, it is worth noting that it is difficult to simulate this behavior within traditional typed languages such as Pascal and Ada; the typing constraints interfere (see [DCBA89], for example). In particular, the correct behavior of *move* on colored points cannot be simulated using only a "conversion" function mapping *colored_point* to *point* (*c.f.* [BL88, BTCGS89]). If we convert a *colored_point* p to a *point* p' and then send the *move* message to p', we obtain a *point* instead of a *colored_point*.

A more complex form of method specialization occurs when a method is overridden. To give an example, we need one method which depends on another. Let us assume we have another class of points, each having a method *slide* which moves the point one unit up and to the right.

> **class** *sl_point* **methods**
> $x : int, y : int,$
> $move : int \times int \rightarrow sl\_point,$
> $slide : sl\_point$

Since we have a *move* method, the natural implementation of *slide* is to send *move* with argument $\langle 1, 1 \rangle$. We now get an interesting form of method specialization if we replace *move* in some object (or subclass) which inherits *slide*. One subclass of *sl_point* might be the class *dir_point* of directed points which have x, y coordinates and a direction, say an angle *theta*.

> **class** *dir_point* **methods**
> $x : int, y : int, theta : real,$
> $move : int \times int \rightarrow dir\_point,$
> $slide : dir\_point$

Let us assume that when we move a directed point, we wish to maintain its orientation toward some position on the perimeter of some bounding box, such as the boundary of the window or screen on which it is displayed. To achieve this behavior, we would redefine the *move* method to calculate a new direction whenever the x and y coordinates are altered. However, *slide* may be inherited directly from sliding points, because of the following phenomenon. With *slide* implemented by invoking *move*, the inherited *slide* method will invoke the more specialized *move* method associated with directed points. In other words, when *slide* is inherited by *dir_point*, this method is specialized in accordance with the *move* method on directed points, even though *slide* was declared as part of *sl_point*. This kind of behavior is relatively easy to implement. However, from a mathematical point of view, this form of specialization seems to be a fairly complex operation on functions.

While method specialization is very useful in a variety of programming situations, method specialization seems to complicate static analysis. In particular, let us say two expressions are *substitution equivalent* (or observationally congruent) if we may substitute one for the other any place inside any program, without changing the overall program behavior. This is an important relation in any language, since it characterizes the local program transformations or optimizations that may be applied safely in any context. In a Pascal-like language, it is relatively easy to state a simple condition guaranteeing substitution equivalence of two procedures: if both return the same results and have the same side-effects, for all possible values of the input parameters, then either may be substituted for the other in any program. However,

looking only at a single method body in an object-oriented language, it is difficult to see whether a simple local transformation could change the behavior of the entire program. The novice might suspect, for example, that in-line substitution of a method body might preserve program meaning. However, if we replace the reference to *move* in the method body of *slide* by in-line code, this would change the way that *slide* works when inherited by directed points. Specifically, if *slide* does not refer to *move*, then overriding *move* has no effect on the behavior of *slide*.

3 Method specialization and natural transformation

There is a simple and intuitive connection between method specialization and natural transformation. We will illustrate the main idea using an elementary view of objects resembling [Car88]. Although the formal development of the paper does not depend on this section, the correspondence will hopefully gives some insight into the typing rules of the calculus presented in Section 4. For the remainder of this section, we will use *simple object* to mean a record of some type, and *simple method* to mean a certain kind of function on simple objects. A *simple class* is therefore a record type.

At the risk of overdoing a single example, let us consider simple classes of cartesian points. The most basic is the class *simple_point* whose elements are simple objects (records) with integer x and y components. Using the notation of [CM89], we may write this record type as follows[1].

$$simple\_point ::= \langle\!\langle x : int, y : int \rangle\!\rangle$$

It is also useful to consider a simple class of colored points

$$simple\_col\_point ::= \langle\!\langle x : int, y : int, c : color \rangle\!\rangle$$

Writing $<:$ for the subtype relation, we have $simple\_col\_point <: simple\_point$ by accepted subtyping rules explained in [Car88, CM89] and summarized in Appendices A and B.

A function which moves points as in Section 2 should change the x and y coordinates of any record with integer x and y fields, and preserve any additional components, such as $c : color$. If we define *simple_move* as a function from *simple_point* to *simple_point*, then we may apply *simple_move* to any

---

[1] In [CM89], a record type may be written by enclosing a list of labels (or field names) and types within double angle brackets $\langle\!\langle , \rangle\!\rangle$, as described in Appendix A.

simple object of any subtype of *simple_point* (see rule (*subsum*) in Appendix B). However, this always gives us a *simple_point*, rather than an element of a subtype such as *simple_col_point*. In order to get a map from *simple_col_point* to *simple_col_point*, and similarly for any other type of records with $x:int$, $y:int$ and additional components, *simple_move* must be a function of a more complicated type. The correct functionality in this case corresponds to a natural transformation.

Since natural transformations are maps between functors over categories, it might seem that we should now introduce a lot of categorical machinery. However, by working within a calculus that has the appropriate form of polymorphic functions, we may define functors and natural transformations using syntactic expressions of the calculus. In doing so, we consider the types of the calculus as objects (in the categorical sense of the word) of a category. There are two choices of morphisms. One might be the class of morphisms given by closed function expressions (or, equivalently, open expressions with exactly one free variable; see [MS89]). However, the more appropriate category seems to be the preorder given by the provable subtyping assertions of our calculus. We will be primarily concerned with subcategories of this category which consist of all subtypes of a given type. Since these categories are preorders, a functor is determined by a function F from subtypes of some A to types such that whenever $s <: t <: A$, we have $Fs <: Ft$. In type systems based on [CW85], the "kind" $\forall s <: A.T$ is the collection of all functions which map every subtype s of A to a type (element of the kind T of all types). It is a helpful notational convention to use a double colon "::" for kind membership and reserve the single colon for types. Using this notation, the functors we consider are given by type functions $F :: \forall s <: A.T$. Rather than explain the general idea in any more detail (*c.f.* [Rey84, RP89]), we will illustrate the approach by the example at hand. It is hoped that the main ideas will be immediately clear to those familiar with category theory, and still reasonably accessible to those without.

To consider *simple_move* as a natural transformation, we must generalize *simple_point* from a type to a functor. The codomain of the functor we want should be the collection of subtypes of *simple_point*, since *simple_move* acts as a function on each subtype of *simple_point*. Using record type expressions of [CM89], we may define the map

$$F ::= \lambda R <: \langle\!\langle\rangle\!\rangle \backslash x\, y . \langle\!\langle R \,|\, x:int, y:int\rangle\!\rangle$$

from subtypes of $\langle\!\langle\rangle\!\rangle \backslash x\, y$ to record types, which is explained below. It is easy to verify that F is a functor. In words, this type function maps any type R of records without x and y fields to the type $\langle\!\langle R \,|\, x:int, y:int\rangle\!\rangle$ of all records obtained by adding integer x and y fields to some record from R. In more detail, $\langle\!\langle\rangle\!\rangle$ is the type of all records, and (consequently) $\langle\!\langle\rangle\!\rangle \backslash x\, y$ is the type of all records without x or y fields. The constraint that formal parameter R of F must be a subtype of $\langle\!\langle\rangle\!\rangle \backslash x\, y$ first implies that the domain of F is the collection of all subtypes of $\langle\!\langle\rangle\!\rangle \backslash x\, y$, and second guarantees that the type expression $\langle\!\langle R \,|\, x:int, y:int\rangle\!\rangle$ is well-formed, since in the [CM89] calculus we may only add fields to records which are known not to already have these fields. The range of the functor F is the collection of all subtypes of *simple_point* which are obtained by adding new fields[2]. Thus F is a functor on the subcategory of our language whose objects are record types without x and y fields and whose morphisms are given by the subtyping preorder on these types.

The natural extension of *simple_move* to a map on arbitrary types of the form $\langle\!\langle R \,|\, x:int, y:int\rangle\!\rangle$ is the polymorphic function

$$\begin{aligned}
&simple\_move ::= \\
&\quad \lambda R <: \langle\!\langle\rangle\!\rangle \backslash x\, y. \\
&\quad\quad \lambda a : \langle\!\langle R \,|\, x:int, y:int\rangle\!\rangle . \\
&\quad\quad\quad \langle a\backslash x\, y \,|\, x = a.x + 1,\ y = a.y + 1\rangle.
\end{aligned}$$

In words, the first parameter of this function may be any type R which is a subtype of $\langle\!\langle\rangle\!\rangle \backslash x\, y$, which means that R may be any type of records without x and y fields. The second parameter is a record a of type $\langle\!\langle R \,|\, x:int, y:int\rangle\!\rangle$. Since R may be arbitrary, we know that a has integer x and y fields, but do not know what other fields this record might have. The record expression $a\backslash x\, y$ denotes the result of removing x and y fields from a, and the form $\langle r \,|\, x = M, y = N\rangle$ is used to extend a record r by adding x and y fields with values M and N, respectively. Thus the function body $\langle a\backslash x\, y \,|\, x = a.x + 1,\ y = a.y + 1\rangle$ defines a record a' which is identical to a, but with x and y fields each incremented by 1. An elementary calculation within the record calculus shows that *simple_move* defines a natural transformation. This means that if $R <: S$,

---

[2]In general, a subtype of *simple_point* may have the form $\langle\!\langle R \,|\, x:\sigma, y:\tau\rangle\!\rangle$ where $R <: \langle\!\langle\rangle\!\rangle \backslash x\, y$ and both σ and τ are subtypes of *int*. However, since arbitrary subtypes of *int* may not be closed under addition, the appropriate types to use in discussing the functionality of *simple_move* have the form $\langle\!\langle R \,|\, x:int, y:int\rangle\!\rangle$. Put another way, we wish to describe the functionality of *simple_move* using a functor whose range is the collection of all types which are closed under *simple_move*. When we apply *simple_move* to a simple object of some arbitrary subtype $\langle\!\langle R \,|\, x:\sigma, y:\tau\rangle\!\rangle$, the best our type system can do is guarantee that the result has "more generous" type $\langle\!\langle R \,|\, x:int, y:int\rangle\!\rangle$.

and consequently

$$\langle\!\langle R \,|\, x:int, y:int\rangle\!\rangle <: \langle\!\langle S \,|\, x:int, y:int\rangle\!\rangle$$

are two subtypes of *simple_point*, and if we begin with any element r of the smaller subclass $\langle\!\langle R \,|\, x:int, y:int\rangle\!\rangle$, the following two computations yield the same result. The first applies *move* to r, and then "converts" r to the larger subclass $\langle\!\langle S \,|\, x:int, y:int\rangle\!\rangle$ according to the subtyping assertion $R <: S$. The second computation converts r to the larger subclass before applying *move*. The fact that these two give the same result seems to capture the intuitive property that however we specialize *simple_move* on subclasses, it should respect the behavior of *simple_move* on *simple_point*'s.

It is worth mentioning that the view of methods as natural transformations not only gives us a reasonable "default" for specializing a method to subclasses with additional properties, but allows for the possibility of "redefining" methods in any way that is consistent with our interpretation of subtyping. However, within the framework of "simple objects," we have no linguistic or semantic mechanism for redefining methods. This leads us to include methods as components of objects, as we do in the next section.

4 Classes and objects

4.1 Class types

In the record calculus of [CM89], a record type determines a finite map from field names to types. Since the type of an object would naturally be a list of method names and their types, it is expedient to use record field names as method names, and define class types using record types. As a consequence of using the type expressions of [CM89], we get variables ranging over finite maps with certain method names guaranteed *not* to be in their domain. This is exactly what we need in order to type methods on objects (*c.f.* [JM88]). While it is certainly possible to define class types without mentioning records, it is convenient to use the following formation rule.

$$\frac{\Gamma, t :: T \triangleright R <: \langle\!\langle\rangle\!\rangle}{\Gamma \triangleright \mathbf{class}\, t.\{R\} :: T}$$

In words, if R is any record type expression, possible containing a free type variable t, then $\mathbf{class}\, t.\{R\}$ is a type. The type variable t is bound in $\mathbf{class}\, t.\{R\}$ If R is an explicit record type of the form $\langle\!\langle \ldots \rangle\!\rangle$, then it is convenient to omit the angle brackets from the corresponding **class** type expression. For example, the class of points may be written

$$point ::= \mathbf{class}\, t.\{x:int, y:int, move:int \times int \to t\}$$

In words, the type expression for *point* defines the class t with methods $x:int, y:int$ and $move:int \times int \to t$.

4.2 Operations on objects

An object is a value which accepts messages. The simplest object is the "empty" object, which accepts no messages at all. We will write $\{\}$ for the empty object, and $o \Leftarrow m$ for the result of sending message m to object o. Since the result of sending a message may be a function (from objects to objects, for example), there is no special syntax for message parameters.

In addition to sending a message, there are two basic operations on objects, adding a method and replacing a method. Suppose o is an object accepting messages $m_1, \ldots, m_k$ and that we want to extend o to an object o' accepting an additional message n. We begin by choosing a "method body" e, which must be a function; the result of sending message n to the new object o' will be the result of the application eo' of method body e to object o'. A reasonable syntax for the object obtained by extending o with method body e for n might be

$$\mathbf{extend}\, o\, \mathbf{with}\, n = e$$

Using the syntax $o \Leftarrow n$ for sending message n to o, we could then evaluate message send by a rule such as

$$(\mathbf{extend}\, o\, \mathbf{with}\, n = e) \Leftarrow n$$
$$= e(\mathbf{extend}\, o\, \mathbf{with}\, n = e)$$

Since e is passed the entire object as a parameter, the method body may send any other message $m_1, \ldots, m_k$ to the object, or send the message n if desired. In this way, recursion and "self-reference" become inherent parts of our object model.

There is a minor technical difficulty with the simple syntax presented above. Suppose we send a message m_i to the object o' above. This is not the "most recently added" method, but a method implemented in the "old" object o. The method body for m_i is therefore designed to be applied to some object that does not have an n method, but only methods among $m_1, \ldots, m_k$. Therefore, before we apply the appropriate method body to o', we must somehow alter the method body to accept an argument with additional methods. As a "bookkeeping" mechanism for keeping the types of methods straight, we will use a syntax for objects that indicates, for each method, the list of methods that were known at the time this method was added. Specifically, if o is an object accepting messages $m_1, \ldots, m_k$, we will write $\{o \mid n(m_1, \ldots, m_k, n) = e\}$ for the result of extending o with method body e for n. The equational rules for manipulating object expressions will allow us to "update" the types of method bodies to account for methods added later (see Table 2 and related discussion).

If we replace a method, then we write $\{o \leftarrow m_i(m_1, \ldots, m_k) = e\}$ for the object obtained from o by redefining m_i to be e. Since an object containing a method e may later be altered by adding or replacing methods, our typing rules must guarantee that e makes sense for any object obtained in this way.

4.3 Typing rules for objects

The first typing rule specifies that the empty object belongs to the class which does not promise any methods.

$$\frac{\Gamma \text{ context}}{\Gamma \triangleright \{\} : \text{class}\, t.\{\}}$$

In words, if Γ is a well-formed context (designating types for variables; see Appendix B), then we have the *judgement* $\Gamma \triangleright \{\} : \text{class}\, t.\{\}$ asserting that in context Γ, the expression $\{\}$ has type $\text{class}\, t.\{\}$.

The next rule describes method addition, which is relatively complicated. There are two main features of this rule. The first is that a method must be a function applicable to the object obtained by adding this method, and that the type of the result of sending a message is the type of this function application. The second overall objective is to guarantee that the method will make sense for all "future" objects constructed from this one. In intuitive terms, we require that a method have the polymorphic type of a "natural transformation" on the "functor" which produces extensions of the present class. (Technically, it is worth noting that that the "functor" is actually a map from types to types which does not always seem to respect the subtyping preorder.) If we begin with an object o of type $\text{class}\, t.\{m_1 : \sigma_1, \ldots, m_k : \sigma_k\}$, then every object obtained by adding or redefining methods will have a type of the form $\text{class}\, t.\{Ft \mid m_1 : \sigma_1, \ldots, m_k : \sigma_k\}$, where F is a function from types to record types such that Ft never involves the names $m_1, \ldots, m_k$ of methods of o. Since the types of "future" objects are characterized by type functions, we want any method we add to o to define a natural transformation on a functor whose domain is a category of maps from types to types. (The morphisms of this category correspond to the point-wise subtyping preorder on $T \Rightarrow T$ described in Appendix B). In a notation following [CM89], we require that the new method body have a type of the form

$$\forall F <: (\lambda t :: T.\langle\!\rangle \backslash m_1 \ldots m_k n).$$
$$[\text{class}\, t.\{Ft \mid m_1 : \sigma_1, \ldots, m_k : \sigma_k, n : \tau\}/t](t \to \tau)$$

where the constraint $F <: (\lambda t :: T.\langle\!\rangle \backslash m_1 \ldots m_k n)$ guarantees that the function F from types to types always produces a record type without $m_1 \ldots m_k n$, and the square brackets in the subexpression $[\ldots/t](t \to \tau)$ indicate substitution. In words, the new method body must be a polymorphic function which, for any "possible future" type $\text{class}\, t.\{Ft \mid m_1 : \sigma_1, \ldots, m_k : \sigma_k, n : \tau\}$, maps objects of this type to some result type possibly depending on the type of objects involved. The formal rule, which is illustrated by example in Section 4.4, appears at the top of Table 1. Reading the rule in words, we begin with an object e_1 which has methods $m_1, \ldots, m_k$ and wish to add another method n implemented using method body e_2. For this to make good sense, e_2 must be a function which, for any addition methods Ft, makes sense on an object of type $\text{class}\, t.\{Ft \mid m_1 : \sigma_1, \ldots, m_k : \sigma_k, n : \tau\}$, where τ is the type of result of sending message n to the new object. The constraint at the binding occurrence of F is that for any argument t, the type Ft must be a subtype of $\langle\!\rangle \backslash m_1 \ldots m_k$. This is a formal way of saying that Ft may be any finite function from field names to types "containing" t which does not associate a type to any $m_1, \ldots, m_k, n$.

The rule for replacing one method by another is similar, but somewhat less complicated. If we begin with an object $e_1 : \text{class}\, t.\{m_1 : \sigma_1, \ldots, m_k : \sigma_k\}$ and wish to replace m_i, then we need an alternate method body with the type required to produce a result of type σ_i. While it seems reasonable to allow the new method body to have a type corresponding to some subtype of σ_i, we will make the simplifying assumption that the new method returns the same type of result as the old. The formal rule which accomplishes appears in Table 1.

Since we may only add methods one-at-a-time, the reader may wonder whether it is possible to define an object with two mutually recursive methods, m and n, for example. It is generally possible to do this, but in a fuller development of the calculus it would probably be worthwhile to use more general rules allowing simultaneous addition of several methods. There is no technical problem in doing this, but the typing rules become more difficult to read.

The typing rule for message send specifies that

$$\text{(add meth)} \quad \frac{\Gamma \triangleright e_1 : \mathbf{class}\, t.\{m_1 : \sigma_1, \ldots, m_k : \sigma_k\}}{\Gamma \triangleright e_2 : \forall F <: (\lambda t :: T.\langle\!\langle\rangle\!\rangle \backslash m_1 \ldots m_k n).[\mathbf{class}\, t.\{Ft \mid m_1 : \sigma_1, \ldots, m_k : \sigma_k, n : \tau\}/t](t \to \tau)}{\Gamma \triangleright \{e_1 \mid n(m_1, \ldots, m_k, n) = e_2\} : \mathbf{class}\, t.\{m_1 : \sigma_1, \ldots, m_k : \sigma_k, n : \tau\}}$$

$$\text{(ovw meth)} \quad \frac{\Gamma \triangleright e_1 : \mathbf{class}\, t.\{m_1 : \sigma_1, \ldots, m_k : \sigma_k\}}{\Gamma \triangleright e_2 : \forall F <: (\lambda t :: T.\langle\!\langle\rangle\!\rangle \backslash m_1 \ldots m_k).[\mathbf{class}\, t.\{Ft \mid m_1 : \sigma_1, \ldots, m_k : \sigma_k\}/t](t \to \sigma_i)}{\Gamma \triangleright \{e_1 \leftarrow m_i(m_1, \ldots, m_k) = e_2\} : \mathbf{class}\, t.\{m_1 : \sigma_1, \ldots, m_k : \sigma_k\}}$$

$$\text{(class } E) \quad \frac{\Gamma \triangleright e : \mathbf{class}\, t.\{m_1 : \sigma_1, \ldots, m_k : \sigma_k\}}{\Gamma \triangleright e \Leftarrow m_i : [\mathbf{class}\, t.\{m_1 : \sigma_1, \ldots, m_k : \sigma_k\}/t]\sigma_i}$$

$$\{o \mid m(m_1, \ldots, m_k) = e\} \Leftarrow m \;=\; e\,(\lambda t :: T.\langle\!\langle\rangle\!\rangle)\,\{o \mid m(m_1, \ldots, m_k) = e\}XS$$

Table 1: Typing and evaluation rules for objects.

the result of sending the message has whatever type is specified. The formal rule (**class** E) appears in Table 1. To illustrate (**class** E) by example, a object representing a number, with its own addition method (as described in [GR83], for example) might be defined by an expression with type $e : \mathbf{class}\, t.\{val : num, plus : t \to t\}$. Sending the addition message to this object produces a function from this class to itself

$$e \Leftarrow plus : \mathbf{class}\, t.\{val : num, plus : t \to t\}$$
$$\to \mathbf{class}\, t.\{val : num, plus : t \to t\}$$

Therefore, $e \Leftarrow plus\; e$ produces another object of the same class.

The evaluation rules for objects compute the result of message send by applying the appropriate method to the object itself. The equational axiom at the bottom of Table 1 is based on this idea, with type application to the constant "empty record type" function used to make the application type correct. The corresponding axiom for a redefined method is similar.

There are several equational axioms for manipulating object expressions, most of them following the pattern of record axioms explained in [CM89]. One nontrivial axiom allows us to permute the order of methods. In general, an object which has been extended twice will have the form

$$\{\{o \mid n(m_1, \ldots, m_k, n) = e\} \mid n'(m_1, \ldots, m_k, n, n') = e'\}$$

Note that the method body e does not assume the object has a method named n', since the second method was added later. However, e' assumes a method named n. The equational axiom for exchanging the order of methods is given in Table 2, where the change in method body accounts for the presence of n'. Intuitively, this type manipulation is related to the fact that a natural transformation must be applied to the type of an argument before it is applied to the argument itself. However, in our calculus, we do not have a basic operation that returns the type of an expression. Therefore, we must "precompute" the type of a method argument incrementally as we build the object itself.

4.4 An example

As an example, we will show how to define an object of class *point*. Recall that a point has x, y and *move* methods. We will define a point whose x and y methods are constant functions, returning integer coordinates x_0 and y_0. The *move* method will return a function which, given a pair of integers, returns a point with x and y coordinates altered accordingly. We begin by adding polymorphic constant functions (as methods) to the empty object $\{\} : \mathbf{class}\, t.\{\}$. Since we will also use constant functions in the definition of *move*, it is helpful to introduce the following general form for methods returning constant methods,

$$c\_meth_{\bar{m}, \bar{\sigma}}[e] \;::=\; \lambda F <: (\lambda t :: T.\langle\!\langle\rangle\!\rangle \backslash \bar{m}).$$
$$\lambda x : (\mathbf{class}\, t.\{Ft \mid \bar{m} : \bar{\sigma}\}).e$$

for any sequence $\bar{m}$ of method names, sequence $\bar{\sigma}$ of corresponding types, and expression e not containing F or x free. (If $\bar{m} = m_1 \ldots m_k$ and $\bar{\sigma} = \sigma_1 \ldots \sigma_k$, we write $\bar{m} : \bar{\sigma}$ for $m_1 : \sigma_1, \ldots, m_k : \sigma_k$.) For any integer

$$\frac{\Gamma \triangleright \{\{o \mid n(\bar{m}, n){=}e\} \mid n'(\bar{m}, n, n'){=}e'\} : \text{class}\, t\,.\{Ft \mid n : \tau, n' : \tau'\}}{\Gamma \triangleright \{\{o \mid n(\bar{m}, n){=}e\} \mid n'(\bar{m}, n, n'){=}e'\} = \begin{array}{l} \{\{o \mid n'(\bar{m}, n, n'){=}e'\} \mid n(\bar{m}, n, n){=} \\ \lambda G <: (\lambda t :: T.\langle\!\langle\rangle\!\rangle \backslash \bar{m}nn').e\,(\lambda t :: T.\langle\!\langle Gt \mid n' : \tau'\rangle\!\rangle)\} \end{array}} \quad n' \text{ not among } \bar{m},$$

Table 2: Equational rule for permuting methods.

expression e without F or x free, the constant function $c\_meth_{\bar{m},\bar{\sigma}}[e]$ has the following "bounded polymorphic type."

$$\forall F <: (\lambda t :: T.\langle\!\langle\rangle\!\rangle \backslash \bar{m}).$$
$$(\text{class}\, t.\{Ft \mid \bar{m} : \bar{\sigma}\}) \to int$$

Therefore, by the object extension rule, the object

$$\{\{\} \mid x(x) = c\_meth_{x,int}[x_0]\}$$

with method x returning the integer coordinate x_0 has type $\text{class}\, t.\{x : int\}$. This object may be extended with a constant y method returning integer coordinate y_0.

$$p_{xy} ::= \{\{\{\} \mid \quad x(x) \quad = \quad c\_meth_{x,int}[x_0] \\ \quad\quad\quad\} \mid \quad y(x,y) \quad = \quad c\_meth_{(xy),(int\,int)}[y_0] \\ \quad\quad\}$$

This gives us an object with two integer methods.

It it useful to make several observations about the object $p_{x,y}$. First, note that the first method added, x, "expects" to be passed an object with only one method, while the second method expects both x and y. This is indicated by the lists of method names in the object expression. If we send the message y to $p_{x,y}$, the the result may be computed directly using the equational rule at the bottom of Table 1. However, if we send the x message, then we must first permute the order of methods using the equational rule on Table 2. This rule changes the type of the method body for x so that the function may be applied to any object with at least the two methods x and y. We now continue the example by adding a $move$ method to $p_{x,y}$.

The move method for $p_{x,y}$ will be a polymorphic function of type

$$\forall F <: (\lambda t :: T.\langle\!\langle\rangle\!\rangle \backslash x\,y\,move).$$
$$\text{class}\, t.\{Ft \mid x : int, y : int, move : int \times int \to t\}$$
$$\to int \times int \to$$
$$\text{class}\, t.\{Ft \mid x : int, y : int, move : int \times int \to t\}$$

since $move$ must map any object with x, y, $move$ and additional methods to another object of the same type. An appropriate method body for $move$ is given at the top of Table 3. This function takes any object with x, y and $move$ methods and replaces the x and y methods by constant functions returning new coordinates. Note that the new coordinates are calculated by sending x and y messages to the object and incrementing the results. We obtain a point object by adding this method to the object p_{xy}

$$pt ::= \{p_{xy} \mid move(x, y, move) = move\_meth\}$$

To complete the example, we will compute the value of $pt \Leftarrow move$ in Table 3. Thus $pt \Leftarrow move$ is a function which, given a displacement $d : int \times int$, returns an object which is identical to pt, but with x and y coordinates incremented by the first and second components of d.

One very important fact about this calculation is that if we had a more "specialized" kind of point pt', with any number of additional methods, the same calculation would give us a new point identical to pt', but with x and y methods replaced by constant functions returning new coordinates. It is exactly this uniform behavior of methods, guaranteed by the typing rules, that allows us to inherit $move$ from pt and use it on extensions of pt.

5 A translation of objects into records

The object and class expressions introduced in the previous section may be interpreted in the calculus with records and recursive type definitions summarized in Appendix B, in the sense that under an appropriate syntactic translation, all of the typing and equational rules for objects are derived rules of the record calculus. Although we have not studied the semantics of the target record calculus when recursive type declarations are allowed [CM89], the calculus is close enough to other systems so that semantic soundness seems very likely (see [BTCGS89]). However, as outlined in Section 6, this translation does not respect the natural subtyping relation on classes. Thus a semantic account of class subtyping remains an open problem.

The translation into records is syntax-directed, proceeding by induction on the formation of an ex-

$$move\_meth ::= \lambda F <: (\lambda t :: T.\langle\!\langle\rangle\!\rangle \backslash x\, y\, move).$$
$$\lambda o : \mathbf{class}\, t.\{Ft \mid x:int,\, y:int,\, move:int \times int \to t\}.$$
$$\lambda d:int \times int.$$
$$\{\{o \Leftarrow x(x,y,move)=c\_meth[(o \Leftarrow x) + fst\, d]\}$$
$$\Leftarrow y(x,y,move)=c\_meth[(o \Leftarrow y) + snd\, d]\}$$

$$pt \Leftarrow move \;=\; \{p_{xy} \mid move(x,y,move) = move\_meth\} \Leftarrow move$$
$$= (move\_meth)\,(\lambda t :: T.\langle\!\langle\rangle\!\rangle)\, pt$$
$$= \lambda d:int \times int.$$
$$\{\{pt \leftarrow x(x,y,move)=c\_meth[(pt \Leftarrow x) + fst\, d]\}$$
$$\leftarrow y(x,y,move)=c\_meth[(pt \Leftarrow y) + snd\, d]\}$$

Table 3: *Move* method body and example calculation.

pression. The translation of an object is essentially a record containing the methods of the object. More precisely, we translate the empty object to the empty record, and $\{e_1 \mid m(m_1,\ldots,m_k,m)=e_2 : F\}$ to the record expression $\langle Trans_{m:F}(e_1) \mid m=e_2\rangle$, where $Trans_{m:F}$ is a translation which makes sure that the type of each method in e is "adjusted" to take the presence of the additional method into account. A class type expression $\mathbf{class}\,t.\{m_1:\sigma_1,\ldots,m_k:\sigma_k\}$ may be interpreted as the recursive type expression

$$\mu t.\langle\!\langle m_1 : t \to \sigma_1, \ldots, m_k : t \to \sigma_k \rangle\!\rangle$$

Note however that we may select components directly from a record of this type, whereas message send only gives us "indirect" access to the methods of an object. This is the main reason why the translation of objects into records does not respect the natural subtype ordering on class types. The translation becomes slightly more complicated in the presence of record type variables (which must also be translated), but is essentially routine given the development of [CM89]. Details are omitted from this conference paper.

6 Subtyping

The subtype relation on classes is relatively subtle. However, since ordinary bounded quantification is not the only way to define polymorphic functions over all classes of a certain form [CCH+89], our ability to write useful programs is not as dependent on the subtyping relation as might at first appear. By analogy with record types, one might think that if one class type is obtained from another by adding methods, this should be a subclass. However, consider the classes

$$A ::= \mathbf{class}\,t.\{x:int,\, y:int,\, plus:t \to t\}$$
$$B ::= \mathbf{class}\,t.\{x:int,\, plus:t \to t\}$$

Should we consider $A <: B$? The bottom line is that we may only adopt $A <: B$ if, in any context, any expression of type B could safely be replaced by an expression of type A. But consider the expression $o \Leftarrow plus\, o$, where $o:B$. If the *plus* method for some $o':A$ is implemented by using both x and y methods, then it certainly does not make sense to replace the first occurrence of o by $o':A$. Thus $A <: B$ is unsound. On the other hand, it certainly seems reasonable that any class of the form

$$\mathbf{class}\,t.\{\ldots,\, print:string,\ldots\}$$

should be a subtype of $printable ::= \mathbf{class}\,t.\{print:string\}$. This would be useful, for example, in writing a print queue which collects *printable* objects and prints each one in turn (each using its own *print* method).

This example raises an important issue regarding the difference between the natural subtyping relation on classes and subtyping on recursive record types. For example, a class with print method might be interpreted, under the translation mentioned above, as the recursive record type

$$R ::= \mu t.\langle\!\langle x:t \to \sigma,\, print:t \to string \rangle\!\rangle$$

while the class *printable* would be interpreted as

$$printable\_rcd ::= \mu t.\langle\!\langle print:t \to string \rangle\!\rangle$$

Under the accepted notion of subtyping for recursive record types (see Appendix B), we do *not* have

$R <:\ printable\_rcd$. (This is similar to the $A <:\ B$ example above.) This illustrates that in semantic models of the calculus of objects and classes, it is important to take seriously the fact that methods may not be selected from objects, only applied to the object itself. For without this consideration, the expected subtyping relation on classes cannot be semantically justified.

7 Conclusion

We have developed a preliminary function calculus with objects and classes, and justified the typing rules by translation into a more commonly studied calculus which is believed sound. Although we may explain method specialization using the more familiar framework of recursively-defined record types, semantic justification of reasonable subtyping rules seems a difficult open problem.

The calculus of objects and classes is presented using record type expressions from the record calculus of [CM89]. This is convenient when it comes to translating objects into records, but from a programming point of view it seems unnecessarily complex. In future work, it might be useful to simplify the language to those type expressions that are absolutely necessary to program realistic object-oriented examples, and eliminate records in favor of objects.

The main long-term objectives of this work are to provide a basis for reasoning about object-oriented programming languages, and to design flexible polymorphic type systems. In future work, it seems worthwhile to consider languages with different sets of basic operations, in hopes that we could more easily guarantee that the meanings of expressions have the types outline here, without requiring as much type information in the syntax itself. Although type inference algorithms might help, it seems more useful to take up the connection with natural transformations in earnest and define a language in which application of natural transformation is a basic operation. Or, since many of the type functions do not induce functors (*i.e.*, do not respect subtyping), a treatment based on presheaf categories seems more promising. This might alleviate much of the complication and could lead to a more elegant language. Another research direction is to try to adapt the typing concepts presented here to a prototyping-based language such as Self. It is hoped that some of the optimizations achieved through dynamic typing in [CU89], for example, could be guaranteed by a static typing discipline along the lines suggested here.

Acknowledgements: I am grateful to Luca Cardelli of DEC Systems Research Center and the members of the ABEL group at HP Laboratories (Peter Canning, William Cook, Walt Hill and Walter Olthoff) for many discussions. Thanks also to Eugenio Moggi, Gordon Plotkin and Andre Scedrov for their comments and insight.

References

[AR88] N. Adams and J. Rees. Object-oriented programming in Scheme. In *Proc. ACM Symp. Lisp and Functional Programming Languages*, pages 277–288, July 1988.

[BI82] A.H. Borning and D.H. Ingalls. A type declaration and inference system for Smalltalk. In *ACM Symp. Principles of Programming Languages*, pages 133–141, 1982.

[BL88] K. Bruce and G. Longo. A modest model of records, inheritance and bounded quantification. In *Third IEEE Symp. Logic in Computer Science*, pages 38–51, 1988.

[BMM89] K. B. Bruce, A. R. Meyer, and J. C. Mitchell. The semantics of second-order lambda calculus. *Information and Computation*, 1989. (to appear).

[Bor86] A.H. Borning. Classes versus prototypes in object-oriented languages. In *ACM/IEE Fall Joint Computer Conf.*, pages 36–40, 1986.

[BTCGS89] V. Breazu-Tannen, T. Coquand, C.A. Gunter, and A. Scedrov. Inheritance and explicit coercion. In *Fourth IEEE Symp. Logic in Computer Science*, page (to appear), 1989.

[Car86] L. Cardelli. Amber. In *Combinators and Func. Programming*, pages 21–47. Springer-Verlag LNCS 242, 1986.

[Car88] L. Cardelli. A semantics of multiple inheritance. *Information and Computation*, 76:138–164, 1988. Special issue devoted to *Symp. on Semantics of Data Types*, Sophia-Antipolis (France), 1984.

[CCH+89] P. Canning, W. Cook, W. Hill, J. Mitchell, and W. Olthoff. F-bounded quantification for object-oriented programming. In *Functional Prog. and Computer Architecture*, 1989. To appear.

[CDG+88] L. Cardelli, J. Donahue, L. Galssman, M. Jordan, B. Kalsow, and G. Nelson. Modula-3 report. Technical Report SRC-31, DEC systems Research Center, 1988.

[CDJ+89] L. Cardelli, J. Donahue, M. Jordan, B. Kalsow, and G. Nelson. The Modula-3 type system. In *Sixteenth ACM Symp. Principles of Programming Languages*, pages 202–212, 1989.

[CM88] L. Cardelli and J.C. Mitchell. Semantic methods for object-oriented languages. Unpublished OOPSLA tutorial, 1988.

[CM89] L. Cardelli and J.C. Mitchell. Operations on records. In *Math. Foundations of Prog. Lang. Semantics*, 1989. To appear.

[Coo89a] W.R. Cook. *A Denotational Semantics of Inheritance*. PhD thesis, Brown University, 1989.

[Coo89b] W.R. Cook. A proposal for making Eiffel type-safe. In *European Conf. on Object-Oriented Programming*, pages 57–72, 1989.

[CU89] C. Chambers and D. Ungar. Customization: Optimizing compiler technology for Self, a dynamically-typed object-oriented programming language. In *SIGPLAN '89 Conf. on Programming Language Design and Implementation*, pages 146–160, 1989.

[CW85] L. Cardelli and P. Wegner. On understanding types, data abstraction, and polymorphism. *Computing Surveys*, 17(4):471–522, 1985.

[DCBA89] A. DiMaio, C. Cardingno, R. Bayan, and C. Atkinson. Dragoon: an Ada-based object-oriented language. In *Proc. Ada-Europe Conference*, 1989. To appear.

[DT88] S. Danforth and C. Tomlinson. Type theories and object-oriented programming. *ACM Computing Surveys*, 20(1):29–72, 1988.

[Gir71] J.-Y. Girard. Une extension de l'interpretation de Gödel à l'analyse, et son application à l'élimination des coupures dans l'analyse et la théorie des types. In J.E. Fenstad, editor, *2nd Scandinavian Logic Symposium*, pages 63–92. North-Holland, 1971.

[Gir72] J.-Y. Girard. Interpretation fonctionelle et elimination des coupures de l'arithmetique d'ordre superieur. Theses D'Etat, Universite Paris VII, 1972.

[GR83] A. Goldberg and D. Robson. *Smalltalk-80: The language and its implementation*. Addison Wesley, 1983.

[JM88] L. Jategaonkar and J.C. Mitchell. ML with extended pattern matching and subtypes. In *Proc. ACM Symp. Lisp and Functional Programming Languages*, pages 198–212, July 1988.

[Kam88] S. Kamin. Inheritance in smalltalk-80: a denotational definition. In *ACM Symp. Principles of Programming Languages*, pages 80–87, 1988.

[Lie86] H. Lieberman. Using prototypical objects to implement shared behavior in object-oriented systems. In *Proc. ACM Symp. on Object-Oriented Programming: Systems, Languages, and Applications*, pages 214–223, October 1986.

[LTP86] W.R. LaLonde, D.A. Thomas, and J.R. Pugh. An exemplar based Smalltalk. In *Proc. ACM Symp. on Object-Oriented Programming: Systems, Languages, and Applications*, pages 322–330, October 1986.

[Mey88] B. Meyer. *Object-Oriented Software Construction*. Prentice-Hall, 1988.

[Mit84] J.C. Mitchell. Coercion and type inference (summary). In *Proc. 11-th ACM Symp. on Principles of Programming Languages*, pages 175–185, January 1984.

[MPS86] D. MacQueen, G Plotkin, and R. Sethi. An ideal model for recursive polymorphic types. *Information and Control*, 71(1/2):95–130, 1986.

[MS89] J.C. Mitchell and P.J. Scott. Typed lambda calculus and cartesian closed categories. In *Proc. Conf. Computer Science and Logic June 14-20, 1987, Univ. Colorado Boulder*, volume 92 of *Contemporary Mathematics*, pages 301-316. Amer. Math. Society, 1989.

[RA82] J. Rees and N. Adams. T, a dialect of Lisp, or lambda: the ultimate software tool. In *Proc. ACM Symp. Lisp and Functional Programming Languages*, pages 114-122, August 1982.

[Red88] U.S. Reddy. Objects as closures: Abstract semantics of object-oriented languages. In *Proc. ACM Symp. Lisp and Functional Programming Languages*, pages 289-297, July 1988.

[Rém89] D. Rémy. Typechecking records and variants in a natural extension of ML. In *16-th ACM Symposium on Principles of Programming Languages*, pages 60-76, 1989.

[Rey84] J.C. Reynolds. Polymorphism is not set-theoretic. In *Proc. Int. Symp. on Semantics of Data Types, Sophia-Antipolis (France), Springer LNCS 173*, pages 145-156. Springer-Verlag, 1984.

[RP89] J.C. Reynolds and G.D. Plotkin. On functors expressible in the polymorphic lambda calculus. *Information and Computation*, page to appear, 1989.

[Sta88] R. Stansifer. Type inference with subtypes. In *Proc. 15-th ACM Symp. on Principles of Programming Languages*, pages 88-97, January 1988.

[Suz81] N. Suzuki. Inferring types in Smalltalk. In *ACM Symp. Principles of Programming Languages*, pages 187-199, 1981.

[US87] D. Ungar and R.B. Smith. Self: The power of simplicity. In *Proc. ACM Symp. on Object-Oriented Programming: Systems, Languages, and Applications*, pages 227-241, 1987.

[Wan87] M. Wand. Complete type inference for simple objects. In *Proc. 2-nd IEEE Symp. on Logic in Computer Science*, pages 37-44, 1987. Corrigendum in *Proc. 3-rd IEEE Symp. on Logic in Computer Science*, page 132, 1988.

[Wan89] M. Wand. Type inference for record concatenation and simple objects. In *Proc. 4-nd IEEE Symp. on Logic in Computer Science*, pages 92-97, 1989.

[Yel89] P.M. Yelland. First steps towards fully-abstract semantics for object-oriented languages. In *European Conf. on Object-Oriented Programming*, pages 347-367, 1989.

A Summary of Cardelli-Mitchell record operations

A.1 Introduction

This appendix contains an intuitive summary of the record operations presented in [CM89]. The general idea of [CM89] is to extend a polymorphic type system with a notion of subtyping at all types. Record types are then introduced as specialized type constructions with some specialized subtyping rules.

A.2 Record values

A record value is essentially a finite map from labels to values, where the values may belong to different types. Syntactically, a record value is a collection of fields, where each field is a labeled value. To capture the notion of a map, the labels in a given record must be distinct. Hence the labels can be used to identify the fields, and the fields should be regarded as unordered. This is the notation we use:

$\langle \rangle$ the empty record.
$\langle x = 3, y = true \rangle$ a record with two fields, labeled x and y, and equivalent to $\langle y = true, x = 3 \rangle$.

There are three basic operations on record values, *extension*, *restriction*, and *extraction*. These have the following basic properties.

Extension $\langle r | x = a \rangle$ adds a field of label x and value a to a record r, provided a field of label x is not already present. This restriction will be enforced statically by the type system. The additional brackets placed around the operator help to make the examples more readable; we also write $\langle r | x = a | y = b \rangle$ for $\langle \langle r | x = a \rangle | y = b \rangle$.

Restriction $r \backslash x$ removes the field of label x, if any, from the record r. We write $r \backslash xy$ for $(r \backslash x) \backslash y$.

Extraction $r.x$ extracts the value corresponding to the label x from the record r, provided a field having

$$\begin{array}{rcll}
\langle\langle x = 3\rangle | y = true\rangle & = & \langle x = 3, y = true\rangle & \text{extension} \\
\langle x = 3, y = true\rangle\backslash y & = & \langle x = 3\rangle & \text{restriction (canceling y)} \\
\langle x = 3, y = true\rangle\backslash z & = & \langle x = 3, y = true\rangle & \text{restriction (no effect)} \\
\langle x = 3, y = true\rangle . x & = & 3 & \text{extraction} \\
\langle\langle x = 3\rangle | x = 4\rangle & & \text{invalid extension} \\
\langle x = 3\rangle . y & & \text{invalid extraction}
\end{array}$$

Table 4: Example record expressions

that label is present. This restriction will be enforced statically by the type system.

We have chosen these three operations because they seem to be fundamental constituents of more complex operations. Some examples are given in Table 4.

Some additional operators may be defined in terms of the ones above.

Renaming $r[x \leftarrow y] \stackrel{\text{def}}{=} \langle r\backslash x | y = r.x\rangle$ changes the name of a record field.

Overriding $\langle r \leftarrow x = a\rangle \stackrel{\text{def}}{=} \langle r\backslash x | x = a\rangle$. If x is present in r, replace its value with one of a possibly unrelated type, otherwise extend r with $x = a$ (compare with [Wan89]). Given adequate type restrictions, this can be seen as an updating operator, or a method overriding operator. We write $\langle r \leftarrow x = a, y = b\rangle$ for $\langle\langle r \leftarrow x = a\rangle \leftarrow y = b\rangle$.

It is clear that any record may be constructed from the empty record using extension operations. In fact, it is convenient to regard the syntax for a record of many fields as an abbreviation for iterated extensions of the empty record, *e.g.*,

$$\langle x = 3, y = true\rangle \stackrel{\text{def}}{=} \langle\langle\langle\rangle | x = 3\rangle | y = true\rangle.$$

This approach to record values allows us to express the fundamental properties of records using combinations of simple operators of fixed arity, as opposed to *n*-ary operators. Hence we never have to use schemas with ellipses, such as $\langle x_1 = a_1, ..., x_n = a_n\rangle$, in our formal treatment.

Since $r\backslash x = r$ whenever r lacks a field of label x, we may write $\langle x = 3, y = true\rangle$ using any of the following expressions:

$$\begin{array}{rcl}
\langle\langle\rangle | x = 3 | y = true\rangle & = & \langle\langle\langle\rangle\backslash x | x = 3\rangle\backslash y | y = true\rangle \\
& = & \langle\langle\rangle, x = 3, y = true\rangle
\end{array}$$

The latter forms match a similar definition for record types, given in the next section.

A.3 Record types

In describing operations on record values, we made positive assumptions of the form "a field of label x must occur in record r" and negative assumptions of the form "a field of label x must not occur in record r". These constraints will be verified statically by the type system. To accomplish this, record types must convey both positive and negative information. Positive information describes the fields that members of a record type must have, while negative information describes the fields the members of that type must not have. Within these constraints, the members of a record type may or may not have additional fields or lack additional fields. It is worth emphasizing that both positive and negative constraints restrict the elements of a type, hence increasing either kind of constraint will lead to smaller sets of values. The smallest amount of information is expressed by the "empty" record type $\langle\!\langle\rangle\!\rangle$. The "empty" record type is empty only in that it places no constraints on its members – every record has type $\langle\!\langle\rangle\!\rangle$, since all records have at least no fields and lack at least no fields. Some examples are given in Table 5.

As with record values, we have three basic operations on record types.

Extension $\langle\!\langle R | x : A\rangle\!\rangle$ This type denotes the collection obtained from R by adding x fields with values in A in all possible ways (provided that none of the elements of R have x fields). More precisely, this is the collection of those records $\langle r | x = a\rangle$ such that r is in R and a is in A, provided that a positive type field x is not already present in R (this will be enforced statically). We sometime write $\langle\!\langle R | x : A | y : B\rangle\!\rangle$ for $\langle\!\langle\langle\!\langle R | x : A\rangle\!\rangle | y : B\rangle\!\rangle$.

Restriction $R\backslash x$ This type denotes the collection obtained from R by removing the field x (if any) from all its elements. More precisely, this is the collection of those records $r\backslash x$ such that r is in R. We write $R\backslash xy$ for $(R\backslash x)\backslash y$.

Extraction $R.x$ This is the type associated to label

$\langle\!\langle\rangle\!\rangle$	the type of all records. Contains, e.g., $\langle\rangle$ and $\langle x=3\rangle$.
$\langle\!\langle\rangle\!\rangle\backslash x$	the type of all records which lack a field labeled x. E.g., $\langle\rangle$, $\langle y=true\rangle$, *but not* $\langle x=3\rangle$.
$\langle\!\langle x:Int, y:Bool\rangle\!\rangle$	the type of all records which have at least fields labeled x and y, with values of types *Int* and *Bool*. E.g., $\langle x=3, y=true\rangle$, $\langle x=3, y=true, z=str\rangle$ but not $\langle x=3, y=4\rangle$, $\langle x=3\rangle$.
$\langle\!\langle x:Int\rangle\!\rangle\backslash y$	the type of all records which have at least a field labeled x of type *Int*, and no field with label y. E.g., $\langle x=3, z=str\rangle$, but not $\langle x=3, y=true\rangle$.

Table 5: Example record type expressions.

$\langle\!\langle\langle\!\langle x:Int\rangle\!\rangle\backslash y\|y:Bool\rangle\!\rangle$	=	$\langle\!\langle x:Int, y:Bool\rangle\!\rangle$	extension
$\langle\!\langle x:Int, y:Bool\rangle\!\rangle\backslash y$	=	$\langle\!\langle x:Int\rangle\!\rangle\backslash y$	restriction (canceling y)
$\langle\!\langle x:Int, y:Bool\rangle\!\rangle\backslash z$	=	$\langle\!\langle x:Int, y:Bool\rangle\!\rangle\backslash z$	restriction (no effect)
$\langle\!\langle x:Int, y:Bool\rangle\!\rangle.x$	=	Int	extraction
$\langle\!\langle\langle\!\langle\rangle\!\rangle\|x:Bool\rangle\!\rangle$		invalid extension	
$\langle\!\langle x:Int\rangle\!\rangle.y$		invalid extraction	

Table 6: Record type extension examples

x in R, provided R has such a positive field. This provision will be enforced statically. Again, several derived operators can be defined from these.

Renaming $R[x, y] \stackrel{\text{def}}{=} \langle\!\langle R\backslash x|y = R.x\rangle\!\rangle$ changes the name of a record type field.

Overriding $\langle\!\langle R \leftarrow x:A\rangle\!\rangle \stackrel{\text{def}}{=} \langle\!\langle R\backslash x|x:A\rangle\!\rangle$ if a type field x is present in R, replaces it with a field x of type A, otherwise extends R. Given adequate type restrictions, this can be used to override a method type in a class signature (i.e. record type) with a more specialized one, to produce a subclass signature.

One crucial formal difference between these operators on types and the similar ones on values is that $\langle\!\langle\rangle\!\rangle\backslash y \neq \langle\!\langle\rangle\!\rangle$, since records belonging to the "empty" type may have y fields, whereas $\langle\rangle\backslash y = \langle\rangle$. In forming record types, one must always make a field restriction before a type extension, as illustrated by example in Table 6.

It helps to read the examples in terms of the collections they represent. For example, the first example for restriction says that if we take the collection of records that have x and y (and possibly more) fields, and remove the y field from all the elements in the collection, then we obtain the collection of records that have x (and possibly more) but no y. In particular, we do not obtain the collection of records that have x and possibly more fields, because those would include y.

The way positive and negative information is formally manipulated is actually easier to understand if we regard record types as abbreviations, as we did for record values:

$$\langle\!\langle x:Int, y:Bool\rangle\!\rangle \stackrel{\text{def}}{=} \langle\!\langle\langle\!\langle\langle\!\langle\rangle\!\rangle\backslash x|x:Int\rangle\!\rangle\backslash y|y:Bool\rangle\!\rangle$$

Then, when considering $\langle\!\langle y:Bool\rangle\!\rangle\backslash y$, we actually have $\langle\!\langle\langle\!\langle\rangle\!\rangle\backslash y|y:Bool\rangle\!\rangle\backslash y$. If we allow the outside positive and negative y labels to cancel, we are still left with $\langle\!\langle\rangle\!\rangle\backslash y$. The inner y restriction reminds us that y fields have been eliminated from records of this type.

A.4 Subtyping

The subtyping rules for record types are essentially that every record type is a subtype of $\langle\!\langle\rangle\!\rangle$, and the subtyping relation respects the type operations of extension, restriction and extraction. Writing $A <: B$ for *A is a subtype of B*, we have the following examples.

$\langle\!\langle x:Int, y:Bool\rangle\!\rangle <: \langle\!\langle\rangle\!\rangle$	
$\langle\!\langle R\|x:A\rangle\!\rangle <: \langle\!\langle S\|x:A\rangle\!\rangle$	if $R <: S <: \langle\!\langle\rangle\!\rangle\backslash x$
$R\backslash x <: S\backslash x$	if $R <: S <: \langle\!\langle\rangle\!\rangle$
$R.x <: S.x$	if $R <: S <: \langle\!\langle x:A\rangle\!\rangle$

In general, a record type R will be a subtype of another record type S if every positive constraint (labeled field) associated with R is also a positive constraint imposed by S, and similarly for negative constraints (fields required to be absent). There are some subtleties. For example, $\langle\!\langle R\backslash x | x : Int \rangle\!\rangle$ is not necessarily a subtype of R, and *never* a subtype of $R\backslash x$, even though this might seem consistent with the point of view expressed in [Car88], for example.

B Summary of full typed calculus

B.1 Overview

The basic calculus we use is a higher-order typed lambda calculus, in the general style of Girard's F_ω [Gir71, Gir72] and many subsequent systems. In addition to function types and polymorphism, we will use recursive type definitions, subtyping and a relatively elaborate form of record types and operations. All of this is quite "standard," in the sense of being syntactically familiar to type theorists, with the exception of the record calculus and subtyping. The main subtyping notions are primarily due to Cardelli [Car88, CW85], with some remnants of [Mit84]. The record calculus with subtyping is explored in some depth in [CM89], although certain semantic and pragmatic questions remain. While many of the syntactic aspects of this calculus will be familiar, the reader should not take this as an indication that the semantics are well-understood. In particular, the combination of record operations, subtyping and recursive types poses a number of mathematical challenges However, it seems that the bulk of the the problems here have been identified and discussed in the literature (see, for example, [BTCGS89, BL88, CM89]). Due to space limitations, we will only summarize the basic parts of the calculus.

B.2 Kinds

The types and type-producing functions of the calculus are characterized by *kinds*, following [Gir72, MPS86, BMM89]; kinds are called *orders* in [Gir72] and some subsequent work. The kinds consist of the base kind T, the kind of all types, and kinds of functions over T. Since we wish to consider type constructors defined only on subtypes of some type A, for example, we will allow "dependent" kinds of the form $\forall s <: A .. \kappa_1$, where $A :: \kappa_2$. While we could also introduce product kinds $\kappa_1 \times \kappa_2$, we have no immediate need for them in this paper. We write "κ kind" if κ is a well-formed kind expression.

B.3 Contexts

Free variables are given types or kinds using *contexts*, which are ordered lists of assumptions about variables. We write "Γ context" if Γ is a well formed context. The basic rules for context are standard, with $\emptyset$ context. We write $v :: \kappa$ to indicate that v has kind κ, and $x : \tau$ to indicate that x has type τ. Kinded variables are added to contexts using the rule

$$\frac{\Gamma \text{ context}, \quad \kappa \text{ kind}}{\Gamma, v :: \kappa \text{ context}} \quad v \notin Dom(\Gamma).$$

We omit the analogous rule for typed variables.

Since subtyping is a basic notion of the calculus, we may assert in a context that a fresh type variable denotes a subtype of a given type. It is also useful to have "subtyping" at higher kinds, with the intuitive meaning that $<:$ on kind $\kappa_1 \Rightarrow \kappa_2$ is the pointwise ordering

$$F <:_{\kappa_1 \Rightarrow \kappa_2} G \quad \text{iff} \quad \forall v : \kappa_1 . fv <:_{\kappa_2} gv.$$

We generally omit subscripts from the subtype relation.

Subtyping assumptions are added to contexts according to the rule

$$\frac{\Gamma \triangleright A :: \kappa}{\Gamma, U <: A \text{ context}}.$$

B.4 Subtyping

The main typing rule associated with subtyping is called *subsumption*.

$$(subsum) \quad \frac{\Gamma \triangleright e : \sigma, \quad \Gamma \triangleright \sigma <: \tau}{\Gamma \triangleright e : \tau}$$

This rule lets us apply a function $f : \sigma \to \tau$ to an argument $x : \sigma'$, whenever $\sigma' <: \sigma$, for example.

B.5 Function Types

We have ordinary function types, formed according to the typing rule

$$(\to) \quad \frac{\Gamma \triangleright A :: T, \quad \Gamma \triangleright B :: T}{\Gamma \triangleright A \to B :: T}$$

and polymorphism over all kinds, as in F_ω.

$$(\forall) \quad \frac{\Gamma, v :: \kappa \triangleright A :: T}{\Gamma \triangleright \forall v :: \kappa . B :: T}$$

In addition, as in [CW85], we have bounded polymorphism.

$$(\forall\ bdd) \quad \frac{\Gamma, u <: A \triangleright B :: T}{\Gamma \triangleright \forall u <: A . B :: T}$$

Introduction and elimination rules defining terms of these types are standard and omitted.

We do not seem to need the so-called F-bounded polymorphism of [CCH+89], since most useful cases seem to be handled by ordinary bounded quantification over kind $T \Rightarrow T$. (We have not done a thorough study of this point, and it may eventually be necessary to introduce F-bounded polymorphism.)

B.6 Record Types

The "empty" or "universal" record type is written $\langle\!\langle\rangle\!\rangle$, following [CM89].

$$\frac{\Gamma \text{ context}}{\Gamma \triangleright \langle\!\langle\rangle\!\rangle :: T}$$

This type contains all records.

Additional types of records are formed by adding constraints of the form $x : \tau$, which assert that all elements of this type must have an x component of type τ, and constraints of the form $\backslash x$, which assert that no elements of this type may have an x component.

$$\frac{\Gamma \triangleright R <: \langle\!\langle\rangle\!\rangle \backslash x, \quad \Gamma \triangleright A :: T}{\Gamma \triangleright \langle\!\langle R | x : A \rangle\!\rangle :: T}$$

$$\frac{\Gamma \triangleright R <: \langle\!\langle\rangle\!\rangle}{\Gamma \triangleright R \backslash x : T}$$

In [CM89], if R is a type of records, with every record guaranteed to have an x component, then $R.x$ is the type of all x components of records from R. However, we do not seem to need type expressions of the form $R.x$ in this paper.

Using equational rules, which we omit, every record type of the pure calculus may be simplified to the form

$$\langle\!\langle R \backslash x_1 \backslash x_2 \ldots | y_1 : A_1 | \ldots \rangle\!\rangle$$

where R is either the empty record type $\langle\!\langle\rangle\!\rangle$, a record type variable, or an application beginning with a variable of some functional kind. It is convenient to write $\langle\!\langle x_1 : A_1, \ldots, x_k : A_k \rangle\!\rangle$ for $\langle\!\langle \langle\!\langle\rangle\!\rangle \backslash x_1 \backslash x_2 \ldots | x_1 : A_1 | \ldots | x_k : A_k \rangle\!\rangle$.

B.7 Record Subtyping

Every record type is a subtype of the type $\langle\!\langle\rangle\!\rangle$ containing all records. Moreover, subtyping respects record type extension and restriction.

$$\frac{\Gamma \triangleright R <: S <: \langle\!\langle\rangle\!\rangle \backslash x, \quad \Gamma \triangleright A <: B}{\Gamma \triangleright \langle\!\langle R | x : A \rangle\!\rangle <: \langle\!\langle S | x : B \rangle\!\rangle}$$

$$\frac{\Gamma \triangleright R <: S <: \langle\!\langle\rangle\!\rangle}{\Gamma \triangleright R \backslash x <: S \backslash x}$$

A derived rule is is that from $\Gamma \triangleright \sigma_1 <: \tau_1, \ldots, \Gamma \triangleright \sigma_k <: \tau_k$ we may derive that $\langle\!\langle m_1 : \sigma_1, \ldots, m_k : \sigma_k, n_1 : \rho_1, \ldots, n_\ell : \rho_\ell \rangle\!\rangle$ is a subtype of $\langle\!\langle m_1 : \tau_1, \ldots, m_k : \tau_k \rangle\!\rangle$, which may be familiar from [Car88].

B.8 Recursive Types

Recursive types will be used to describe records which contain methods applicable to the records themselves. Rather than write recursive types in the common programming language form

$$tree = leaf + \langle\!\langle l : tree, r : tree \rangle\!\rangle$$

we will use the more concise syntax

$$\mu t . leaf + \langle\!\langle l : t, r : t \rangle\!\rangle.$$

The formation rule for record types is

$$\frac{\Gamma, v :: T \triangleright \sigma :: T}{\Gamma \triangleright \mu v :: T . \sigma :: T}$$

and the natural subtyping rule for record types [Car86, BTCGS89] is

$$\frac{\Gamma, (s <: t) \triangleright \sigma <: \tau, \quad \Gamma \triangleright t :: T}{\Gamma \triangleright (\mu v :: T . \sigma) <: (\mu v :: T . \tau)}$$

The usual term formation rules associated with recursive types are

$$(\mu \, I) \quad \frac{\Gamma \triangleright e : [\mu v :: T . \sigma / t]\sigma}{\Gamma \triangleright abs \, e : \mu v :: T . \sigma}$$

$$(\mu \, E) \quad \frac{\Gamma \triangleright e : \mu v :: T . \sigma}{\Gamma \triangleright rep \, e : [\mu v :: T . \sigma / t]\sigma}$$

where *abs* and *rep* are names for the isomorphism between $\mu v :: T . \sigma$ and $[\mu v :: T . \sigma / t]\sigma$. For simplicity of notation, we will omit *abs* and *rep* from expressions.

Inheritance Is Not Subtyping

William R. Cook Walter L. Hill Peter S. Canning

Hewlett-Packard Laboratories

P.O. Box 10490 Palo Alto CA 94303-0969

Abstract

In typed object-oriented languages the subtype relation is typically based on the inheritance hierarchy. This approach, however, leads either to insecure type-systems or to restrictions on inheritance that make it less flexible than untyped Smalltalk inheritance. We present a new typed model of inheritance that allows more of the flexibility of Smalltalk inheritance within a statically-typed system. Significant features of our analysis are the introduction of polymorphism into the typing of inheritance and the uniform application of inheritance to objects, classes and types. The resulting notion of *type inheritance* allows us to show that the type of an inherited object is an inherited type but not always a subtype.

1 Introduction

In strongly-typed object-oriented languages like Simula [1], C++ [28], Trellis [25], Eiffel [19], and Modula-3 [9], the inheritance hierarchy determines the conformance (subtype) relation. In most such languages, inheritance is restricted to satisfy the requirements of subtyping. Eiffel, on the other hand, has a more expressive type system that allows more of the flexibility of Smalltalk inheritance [14], but suffers from type insecurities because its inheritance construct is not a sound basis for a subtype relation [12].

In this paper we present a new typed model of inheritance that supports more of the flexibility of Smalltalk inheritance while allowing static type-checking. The typing is based on an extended polymorphic lambda-calculus and a denotational model of inheritance. The model contradicts the conventional wisdom that inheritance must always make subtypes. In other words, we show that incremental change, by implementation inheritance, can produce objects that are not subtype compatible with the original objects. We introduce the notion of *type inheritance* and show that an inherited object has an inherited type. Type inheritance is the basis for a new form of polymorphism for object-oriented programming.

Much of the work presented here is connected with the use of self-reference, or recursion, in object-oriented languages [3, 4, 5]. Our model of inheritance is intimately tied to recursion in that it is a mechanism for incremental extension of recursive structures [11, 13, 22]. In object-oriented languages, recursion is used at three levels: objects, classes, and types. We apply inheritance uniformly to each of these forms of recursion while ensuring that each form interacts properly with the others. Since our terminology is based on this uniform development, it is sometimes at odds with the numerous technical terms used in the object-oriented paradigm. Our notion of object inheritance subsumes both delegation and the traditional notion of class inheritance, while our notion of class inheritance is related to Smalltalk metaclasses.

Object inheritance is used to construct objects incrementally. We show that when a recursive object definition is inherited to define a new object, a corresponding change is often required in the type of the object. To achieve this effect, polymorphism is introduced into recursive object definitions by abstracting the type of *self*. Inheritance is defined to specialize the inherited definition to match the type of the new object being defined. A form of polymorphism developed for this purpose, called F-bounded polymorphism [3], is used to characterize the extended types that may be created by inheritors.

Class inheritance supports the incremental definition of classes, which are parameterized object definitions. A class is recursive if its instances use the class to create new instances. When a class is inherited to define a new class, the inherited creation operations are updated to create instances of the new class. Since class recursion is also related to recursion in the object types, the polymorphic typing of inheritance is extended to cover class recursion. We also introduce a generalization of class inheritance that allows modification of instantiation parameters.

A final application of inheritance is to the definition of recursive types. Type inheritance extends a recursive record type to make a new type with similar recursive structure but more fields. Because of an interaction between function subtyping and recursion, an inherited type is not necessarily a subtype of the type from which it was derived. This is a second sense in which inheritance is not subtyping. Type inheritance is useful for constructing the types of objects produced by object inheritance. In addition, F-bounded polymorphic functions can be applied to the types of objects that inherit from a given object definition and then to objects of that type; objects with different inherited types are prevented from being mixed together.

The typed model of inheritance is directly relevant to the analysis and design of programming languages. It indicates how object-oriented languages could be extended to support more flexible forms of inheritance while retaining static typing. Several other theories of typed inheritance have also been proposed [15, 20, 30]. A preliminary comparison reveals a similarity of approach. However, the models are based on a wide range of theoretical foundations, and more research is required to resolve the differences.

The next section surveys terminology and background on objects, types, and inheritance for our model of object-oriented programming. The following three sections are organized to address the use of inheritance for the three kinds of recursion found in object-oriented programs. Section 3 examines the relationship between object recursion and type recursion, and introduces a polymorphic typing of inheritance to allow more flexibility in the presence of recursive types. Section 4 introduces recursive classes with instantiation parameters and extends inheritance to allow modification of parameters by subclasses. Section 5 defines a notion of inheritance for types and demonstrates its connection to object inheritance. Section 6 illustrates these features with a practical programming example. Section 7 applies the model to the analysis of object-oriented languages and compares it to other models of typed inheritance.

2 Background

2.1 A Typed Record Calculus

A typed polymorphic lambda-calculus with records is used to describe the typing of inheritance. The language is functional and explicitly typed; no provision is made for imperative constructs or type inference. Imperative constructs, which support mutable object state, are not included because they do not affect the analysis of inheritance. An untyped version of the calculus is used to introduce new constructs before giving a typed presentation.

2.2 Records

A record is a finite mapping of labels to values. A record with fields $x_1, \ldots, x_n$ and associated values $v_1, \ldots, v_n$ is written $\{x_1 = v_1, \ldots, x_n = v_n\}$. If the values have type $\sigma_1, \ldots, \sigma_n$ then the record has type $\{x_1 : \sigma_1, \ldots, x_n : \sigma_n\}$. Selecting the a component of a record r is given by $r.a$.

Cardelli [6, 8] identified record subtyping as an important form of polymorphism in object-oriented programming. The main idea is that if a record r has fields $x_1 : \sigma_1, \ldots, x_k : \sigma_k$ and also $x_{k+1} : \sigma_{k+1}, \ldots, x_\ell : \sigma_\ell$, then a record r' with fields $x_1 : \sigma_1, \ldots, x_k : \sigma_k$ can be constructed from r by omitting fields. Therefore, any record with type $\{x_1 : \sigma_1, \ldots, x_k : \sigma_k, \ldots, x_\ell : \sigma_\ell\}$ can be coerced into a record of type $\{x_1 : \sigma_1, \ldots, x_k : \sigma_k\}$. The general form of this coercion allows the field values to be coerced as well:

$$\frac{\sigma_1 \leq \rho_1, \ldots, \sigma_k \leq \rho_k,}{\{x_1 : \sigma_1, \ldots, x_k : \sigma_k, \ldots, x_\ell : \sigma_\ell\} \leq \{x_1 : \rho_1, \ldots, x_k : \rho_k\}}$$

In our model, record types indicate exactly what fields a record contains. This differs from Cardelli, who uses a *subsumption* model in which a record type represents all records that have at least the specified fields. We do not use subsumption because it complicates the problem of record combination.

2.3 Record Combination

The language supports a simple record combination operator, **with**, that joins two records. The typing of **with** is defined by a typed introduction rule.

$$\frac{e_1 : \{x_1 : \sigma_1, \ldots, x_j : \sigma_j, x_{j+1} : \tau_1, \ldots, x_k : \tau_{k-j}\}}{e_2 : \{x_{j+1} : \sigma_{j+1}, \ldots, x_n : \sigma_n\} \quad (k \leq n)}{e_1 \text{ with } e_2 : \{x_1 : \sigma_1, \ldots, x_n : \sigma_n\}}$$

If there are common fields, $x_{j+1}, \ldots, x_k$, they may have different types in the two records. The conflict is resolved by taking the value from e_2. An analogous operator, $+$, is defined on record types. The evaluation rule performs the corresponding operation on record values. The operator **with** is well-behaved because our types are exact specifications of the fields in a record. If subsumption were allowed, the actual value of e_2 could have more fields than mentioned in its type. According to the evaluation rule, these fields would take precedence over the fields in e_1 resulting in a unsound typing.

Our record combination operator is simpler than the ones proposed by Rémy [23] and Wand [29, 30]. The simply typed version of **with** is sufficient for the analysis in this paper.

2.4 Recursive Types

The notation for a recursive type defined by $T = F[T]$ is $\mu t.F[t]$. A recursive type is equal to its infinite expansion. One step in this expansion is given by the *unrolling* rule:

$$\mu t.F[t] = F[\mu t.F[t]]$$

One recursive subtype is a subtype of another if their infinite expansions are in a subtype relation. An induction rule is used to specify the subtype relation [7].

$$\frac{\Gamma,\ s \leq t\ \vdash\ \sigma[s] \leq \tau[t]}{\Gamma\ \vdash\ \mu s.\ \sigma[s] \leq \mu t.\ \tau[t]}$$

To illustrate, the types T_1 and T_2 are subtypes of T. These subtypes do not have the same pattern of recursion as T. T_3 is not a subtype of T, even though it has the same recursive structure, because of the contravariance [6] of the function type in the b field.

$$T = \mu t.\{a: int, c: t, b: t \rightarrow t\}$$
$$T_1 = \{a: int, c: T, b: T \rightarrow T, d: bool\}$$
$$T_2 = \mu t.\{a: int, c: t, b: T \rightarrow t, d: bool\}$$
$$T_3 = \mu t.\{a: int, c: t, b: t \rightarrow t, d: bool\}$$

2.5 Polymorphism

Subtype-bounded polymorphism [10] allows functions to be written that operate uniformly over all subtypes of a given type. A bounded polymorphic function is defined by the expression $\Lambda t \leq \sigma.\ e$. If assuming $t \leq \sigma$ gives e type τ, then the polymorphic function has type $\forall t \leq \sigma.\tau$. For recursive types, however, there are forms of structural similarity not captured by subtyping, as illustrated above. The types that have the *recursive structure* of $T = \mu t.F[t]$ are those that satisfy the constraint $t \leq F[t]$. In the example above, $F[t] = \{a: int, c: t, b: t \rightarrow t\}$. Of types T_1, T_2 and T_3, only T_3 satisfies the constraint $T_3 \leq F[T_3]$. F-bounded polymorphism [3], written $\forall t \leq F[t].\sigma$, supports parametric quantification over the recursive types that share the recursive structure specified by F. Examples demonstrating the use of F-bounded polymorphism in typing functions involving recursive types are given in [3].

2.6 Objects

As in [5, 11, 22, 31], we represent objects as records whose fields contain methods. The methods of an object may refer to each other, so objects are naturally viewed as mutually recursive definitions. The traditional interpretation of mutual recursion from denotational semantics is as a fixed point of a function on environments of identifiers. For example, an object handling messages $m_1, \ldots, m_j$ by methods $e_1, \ldots, e_j$ is a fixed point of the function P.

$$P = \lambda(self).\ \{m_1 = e_1, \ldots, m_j = e_j\}. \qquad (1)$$

The expressions $e_1, \ldots, e_j$ may contain references to *self*; for example, to call the m method with argument 3 one would write *self*.$m(3)$. The function P is a definition of the object $\mathbf{Y}(P)$. The type of an object is a record type, and is often a recursive record type [2, 3, 4, 5, 24]. Recursion in object types is associated, for example, with a method that simply returns the pseudovariable *self*.

While our language does not support mutable object state, lexically bound variables can be used to parameterize objects (see Section 4.1). If mutable variables were supported, any pattern of shared state among different objects could be defined, including those characteristic of delegation systems [18]. To simplify the presentation, some methods are simple values instead of functions; if state were introduced then lambda-abstractions would be required on all methods to delay evaluation.

2.7 Inheritance

An untyped, compositional model of inheritance based on the fixed-point function, $\mathbf{Y}$, was developed independently by Cook [11, 13] and Reddy [22]. Given a definition, P, of a *parent* recursive value $\mathbf{Y}(P)$ and a self-referential modifier M, one may construct a *child* value $\mathbf{Y}(\lambda(s).\ M(s)(P(s)))$. This example illustrates inheritance as an operation on recursive definitions.

Inheritance allows a new object definition to be derived from an existing one where self-reference in the inherited object definition is unified with self-reference in new methods.

$$C = \lambda(self).\ P(self)\ \text{with} \atop \{m'_1 = e'_1, \ldots, m'_k = e'_k\} \qquad (2)$$

The use of the pseudovariable *super* to refer directly to parent methods is also supported in the model. This generalization is illustrated in Section 6.

A simple typing of inheritance is easily derived by adding type-constraints to the basic inheritance model [11]. If P has type $\sigma \rightarrow \sigma$ for some σ, then the object $\mathbf{Y}(P)$ has type σ. If the modifier has type $\tau \rightarrow \sigma \rightarrow \tau$ to produce an object of type τ from one of type σ, then $\lambda(s).\ M(s)(P(s))$ has type $\tau \rightarrow \tau$ and its fixed point is an object of type τ. The significant constraint introduced by inheritance is that τ must be a subtype of σ for the application $P(s)$ to be type-correct.

3 Object Inheritance

3.1 Problems in the Simple Typing of Inheritance

In this section we illustrate some problems in using the simple typing of inheritance to define objects with recursive types. One problem arises because the simple typing of inheritance does not always provide the most precise type possible. Consider a simple object definition with a method i returning the value 5 and a method id that returns the object itself.

$$P = \lambda(self).\ \{i = 5, id = self\}$$

The object $\mathbf{Y}(P)$ has type $\sigma = \mu t.\{i : int, id : t\}$, thus the simple typing of inheritance gives P the type $\sigma \to \sigma$. A child C is defined by inheriting P and adding a single boolean field b.

$$C = \lambda(self).\ P(self)\ \mathbf{with}\ \{b = true\}$$

In the simple typing of inheritance, $\mathbf{Y}(C)$ has type $\sigma + \{b : bool\}$, or $\tau_1 = \{i : int, id : \sigma, b : bool\}$. Note that τ_1 is not directly recursive in the type of the id method.

Expanding C to eliminate $P(self)$ and combine records gives an equivalent expression.

$$C_1 = \lambda(self).\ \{i = 5, id = self, b = true\}$$

$\mathbf{Y}(C_1)$ has type $\tau_2 = \mu t.\{i : int, id : t, b : bool\}$. Since $\tau_2 < \tau_1$ the simple typing has resulted in less precise type for the inherited object than is possible.

A more serious problem occurs when attempting to use contravariant [6] recursive types. Consider a new object definition with an equality method instead of an identity method.

$$P' = \lambda(self).\ \{i = 5, eq = \lambda(o).(o.i = self.i)\}$$

Although several typings for $\mathbf{Y}(P')$ are possible, the one that expresses eq as a binary method is recursive in the type of the eq method.

$$\sigma' = \mu t.\{i : int, eq : t \to bool\}$$

Now C' can be defined, by inheriting P' while adding a b field and redefining eq.

$$\begin{aligned}C' = \lambda(self).\ & P'(self)\ \mathbf{with} \\ \{\ & b = true, \\ & eq = \lambda(o).(o.i = self.i\ \text{and} \\ & \qquad\qquad o.b = self.b) \\ \}\end{aligned}$$

Before examining possible typings for C, consider the object it defines. The object $\mathbf{Y}(C')$ has a recursive type, τ'_2.

$$\tau'_2 = \mu t.\{i : int, b : bool, eq : t \to bool\}$$

The simple typing of C' fails because $\tau'_2 \not\leq \sigma'$. Simple types cannot be assigned to the definition of C' because P' of type $\sigma' \to \sigma'$ cannot be applied to $self$ which has type τ'_2 as required by the inheritance. It is important to note that in an untyped framework this use of inheritance is meaningful, but the type system is simply not expressive enough to describe the relevant constraints. The simple typing of inheritance, with its subtype assumption, cannot give a typing for this example.

3.2 Polymorphism and Inheritance

To overcome these problems we introduce polymorphism directly into the mechanism of inheritance. This is motivated by observing the type-dependency within a recursive definition: the type of object created depends on the type of $self$. We provide a more flexible typing by abstracting the type of $self$ and replacing type recursion by type-dependency. The type recursion is reintroduced when the object is constructed. Let $F[t] = \{m_1 : \sigma_1, \ldots, m_j : \sigma_j\}$ be a type function defining a recursive type $\sigma = \mu t.F[t]$. An object with methods e_i of type σ_i is defined by an expression in which the type of $self$ is polymorphic.

$$\begin{aligned} P : & \forall t \leq F[t].t \to F[t] \\ P = & \Lambda\ t \leq F[t].\ \lambda(self : t). \\ & \{m_1 = e_1, \ldots, m_j = e_j\} \end{aligned} \qquad (3)$$

The F-bounded constraint $t \leq F[t]$ is central to the model. It provides information about the methods defined by the object denoted by $self$. For example, if $F[t] = \{m : t \to t, n : t\}$, the n method could return $self.m(self)$. Of course, the exact type t is unknown — it is supplied by inheritors to indicate the type of the complete object into which the methods in P are being incorporated.

Object instantiation must now include the type of the object being created, as in $\mathbf{Y}(P[\sigma])$. The simple typing is recovered by forming $P[\sigma] : \sigma \to F[\sigma]$, which, by unrolling, is equal to $\sigma \to \sigma$.

For inheritance, it is necessary to define a type $\tau = \mu s.G[s]$ such that $G[t] \leq F[t]$. Any type satisfying $t \leq G[t]$ also satisfies $t \leq F[t]$.

The typing of inheritance involves defining a new polymorphic function that specializes its parent to the appropriate type before modifying its methods.

$$\begin{aligned} C : & \forall t \leq G[t].t \to G[t] \\ C = & \Lambda\ t \leq G[t].\ \lambda(self : t). \\ & P[t](self)\ \mathbf{with}\ \{m'_1 = e'_1, \ldots, m'_k = e'_k\} \end{aligned} \qquad (4)$$

The fields m'_i must be assigned values as specified in $G[t]$. The use of $P[t]$ is type-correct because $G[t] \leq F[t]$. The simple record combination operator, $\mathbf{with}$, is sufficient because it is applied to values whose types are constant. Although it might seem reasonable to abstract over P to produce an *abstract subclass*, or *wrapper* [21], the resulting function cannot be assigned a useful type without a more expressive record combination operator.

To illustrate the polymorphic typing of inheritance, the examples from Section 3.1 are combined into a single construct.

$$P = \Lambda\, t \leq F[t].\, \lambda(self:t).$$
$$\{\ i = 5,$$
$$id = self,$$
$$eq = \lambda(o:t).(o.i = self.i)\ \}$$

The type function $F[t] = \{i:int, id:t, eq:t\rightarrow bool\}$ specifies the recursive type of the objects, and P has type $\forall t \leq F[t].t \rightarrow F[t]$.

The inheriting definition adds a method b and redefines the equality method.

$$C = \Lambda\, t \leq G[t].\, \lambda(self:t).$$
$$P[t](self)\ \textbf{with}$$
$$\{\ b = true,$$
$$eq = \lambda(o:t).(o.i = self.i\ \text{and}$$
$$o.b = self.b)$$
$$\}$$

The new object has type $\tau = \mu t.G[t]$.

$$G[t] = \{i:int, id:t, b:bool, eq:t\rightarrow bool\}$$

The polymorphic application $P[t]$ is valid because $t \leq G[t]$ and $G[t] \leq F[t]$ imply $t \leq F[t]$. Despite this relationship between G and F, their fixed points are not in a subtype relation.

4 Class Inheritance

4.1 Classes

A class is a parameterized object definition. In the previous section we used simple classes that were just descriptions of a single object. A more sophisticated notion of class includes instantiation parameters so that multiple objects, called the *instances* of the class, may be created. In this interpretation classes are functions that create object specifications. Classes may be inherited to define other classes.

A class is recursive if its instances use the class to make new instances. When a method using class recursion is inherited, the recursive use of the class is modified so that the method constructs subclass instances instead. Smalltalk is a good illustration of class recursion and inheritance: an object can determine the class that created it with the expression *self class*. To create a new instance like itself an object sends its class a *new* message: *self class new*. In Smalltalk, *new* messages are handled by metaclasses, which support specialization of object creation by inheritance.

A recursive class is defined using fixed points, just as objects are fixed points of mutually recursive method specifications. For objects, the functional argument represented *self*, to which recursive messages are sent. For classes, the argument represents the class to use in constructing new instances. This argument is called *myclass*. The general untyped form of a recursive class definition has two levels of recursion, *myclass* and *self*.

$$\mathcal{P} = \lambda(myclass).\,\lambda(x).\,\lambda(self).$$
$$\{m_1 = e_1, \ldots, m_j = e_j\}$$

The argument x represents the instantiation parameter. The class recursion variable, *myclass*, is used in the expressions e_i to construct new instances of the class. Let $P = \mathbf{Y}(\mathcal{P})$ be the class associated with the class definition $\mathcal{P}$. An object is instantiated with parameter a by applying the class to a and then taking the fixed point: $\mathbf{Y}(P(a))$. The complete equation for making an instance from a recursive class definition involves a double fixed point: $\mathbf{Y}(\mathbf{Y}(\mathcal{P})(a))$. Two applications of the fixed-point function are used because class recursion and object recursion are independent.

In the child class definition, $\mathcal{P}$ is passed a new value for *myclass* so that the inherited methods m_i create instances of $\mathcal{C}$, not instances of $\mathcal{P}$.

$$\mathcal{C} = \lambda(myclass).\,\lambda(x).\,\lambda(self).$$
$$\mathcal{P}(myclass)(x)(self)\ \textbf{with}$$
$$\{m'_1 = e'_1, \ldots, m'_k = e'_k\}$$

4.2 Typed Class Inheritance

The typing of class recursion uses the same technique of polymorphism introduced in Section 3.2. Although the scope of class-level recursion contains the scope of object recursion, the polymorphism associated with the type of *self* must be moved outside of the class recursion variable.

$$\mathcal{P} : \forall t \leq G[t].(\alpha\rightarrow(t\rightarrow t))\rightarrow(\alpha\rightarrow(t\rightarrow F[t]))$$
$$\mathcal{P} = \Lambda\, t \leq F(t).\,\lambda(myclass:\alpha\rightarrow(t\rightarrow t)). \quad (5)$$
$$\lambda(y:\alpha).\,\lambda(self:t).$$
$$\{m_1 = e_1, \ldots, m_k = e_k\}$$

Note that *myclass* produces values of type $t\rightarrow t$ rather than $t\rightarrow F[t]$ as in the final result-type of $\mathcal{P}$. This allows the fixed point of *myclass* to be used without complete knowledge of the final binding of t. The objects created by this class definition have type $\sigma = \mu t.F[t]$. Instantiation of a class definition with polymorphic typing, $P = \mathbf{Y}(\mathcal{P}[\sigma])$, involves binding the type argument the instance type and then taking the fixed point. The class P has type $\alpha\rightarrow(\sigma\rightarrow\sigma)$.

The typing of an inheriting class definition is straightforward.

$$C : \forall t \leq G[t].(\alpha \rightarrow (t \rightarrow t)) \rightarrow (\alpha \rightarrow (t \rightarrow G[t]))$$
$$C = \Lambda\, t \leq G(t) \,.\, \lambda(myclass : \alpha \rightarrow (t \rightarrow t)).$$
$$\lambda(x : \alpha) \,.\, \lambda(self : t).$$
$$\mathcal{P}[t](myclass)(x)(self) \quad (6)$$
$$\text{with } \{m'_1 = e'_1, \ldots, m_k = e'_k\}$$

4.3 Changing Instantiation Parameters

Class inheritance is complicated by the common need to change the form of the instantiation parameters of the subclass to be of some type β. The problem is that the inherited definition expects a value of *myclass* with type $\alpha \rightarrow (t \rightarrow t)$, but the subclass definition of *myclass* has type $\beta \rightarrow (t \rightarrow t)$. Unless $\alpha \leq \beta$, the types will not match. This condition is too restrictive: it is common for the subclass to require more information, not less.

The difference between the initialization parameters is bridged by two translation functions. The first translation, $Q : \beta \rightarrow \alpha$, converts child parameters to the form required by the parent class. The second translation, $T : \alpha \rightarrow \beta$, converts parent parameters to the form required by the child so that uses of *myclass* in parent methods will construct child instances. With these translation functions, the inheritance construct supports modification of instantiation parameters.

$$C : \forall t \leq G[t].(\beta \rightarrow (t \rightarrow t)) \rightarrow (\beta \rightarrow (t \rightarrow G[t]))$$
$$C = \Lambda\, t \leq F(t) \,.\, \lambda(myclass : \beta \rightarrow (t \rightarrow t)).$$
$$\lambda(y : \beta) \,.\, \lambda(self : t). \quad (7)$$
$$\mathcal{P}[t](myclass \circ T)(Q(y))(self)$$
$$\text{with } \{m'_1 = e'_1, \ldots, m'_k = e'_k\}$$

T and Q are defined in a context in which y and *self* are bound. The context is particularly relevant in the case of T, since the additional information required for subclass instantiation is often computed from *self*.

5 Type Inheritance

As an operation on recursive definitions, inheritance can also be applied to recursively defined record types. Let $F[t] = \{x_1 : \sigma_1, \ldots, x_n : \sigma_n\}$ be a type function defining a recursive record type $\sigma = F[\sigma]$. Type inheritance allows the definition F to be modified to define a new type. A definition that inherits F has the form

$$G[t] = F[t] + \{x'_1 : \sigma'_1, \ldots, x'_n : \sigma'_n\}$$

G defines the type $\tau = G[\tau]$, a child of σ. Note that $G[t]$ need not be a subtype of $F[t]$ because the field types may be changed. The replacement of field types during type inheritance is analogous to the replacement of field values (methods) during object inheritance.

There is a close connection between type inheritance and class/object inheritance. In the polymorphic typing defined in Section 3.2, the type function G which specifies the type of the inheriting object may be expressed by inheriting F. The types of methods $m'_1, \ldots, m'_k$ that are changed can be identified in a type-function R for which $G[t] = F[t] + R[t]$ Thus the type of an inherited object is an inherited type.

The properties of types of inherited objects are analogous to those of subtypes. The constraint imposed by object inheritance, $G[t] \leq F[t]$, ensures that inherited objects can be used as arguments to F-bounded polymorphic functions just as values of subtypes can be used as arguments to subtype-bounded polymorphic functions. Thus F-bounded polymorphism is useful in object-oriented programming for writing functions that work uniformly over the subclasses of a class.

6 Example

The following example illustrates the recursive structure of objects, classes and types, and the typing of inheritance given in Sections 3 and 4. The class definition exhibits both object and class recursion, and gives an example of typed class inheritance. The type of the objects created from the inherited class is defined using the type inheritance operation described in Section 5. For a more complete discussion of a version of this example and the informal object-oriented notation used below, see [4].

A type *Point* specifies the interface of movable planar points. When a point is moved it returns a new point at the new location.

interface *Point*
    x : *Real*
    y : *Real*
    move(Real, Real) : *Point*
    equal(Point) : *Boolean*

More formally, *Point* is the fixed point of a type function derived from the interface definition.

$$F[t] = \{\; x : Real,$$
$$y : Real,$$
$$move : Real \times Real \rightarrow t,$$
$$equal : t \rightarrow Boolean\; \}$$

Type inheritance can be used to extend the recursive type *Point*.

interface *ColorPoint* **inherits** *Point*
    color : *Color*

Type inheritance is explained as extension of type functions in Section 5. *ColorPoint* is the fixed point of G.

$$G[t] = F[t] + \{color : Color\}$$

ColorPoint $\not\leq$ *Point* because the equality method is contravariant. Intuitively, a *ColorPoint* can't be used where a *Point* is expected because it does not make sense to compare *Points* and *ColorPoints* for equality. The problem is that *Points* do not have color. The system could also have been designed to allow the comparison, but then the *ColorPoint* equality method could not determine the color of its argument.

On the other hand, *ColorPoint* does have the same recursive structure as *Point*: *ColorPoint* $\leq F[ColorPoint]$ and for all t, $G[t] \leq F[t]$. These are exactly the constraints required by inheritance.

The class *cart_point* implements objects of type *Point*. It has two initialization parameters, x and y, that specify the location of the point in cartesian coordinates.

class *cart_point* (x:Real, y:Real)
 implements *Point*
 method x : *Real*
  return x
 method y : *Real*
  return y
 method *move(dx:Real, dy:Real)* : *Point*
  return new *myclass(self.x + dx, self.y + dy)*
 method *equal(p:Point)* : *Boolean*
  return *(self.x = p.x)* and *(self.y = p.y)*

Instances of *cart_point* are recursive because they send messages to *self*. The class *cart_point* is also recursive because the *move* method uses *myclass* to create a new point at a given distance from itself. Both the *equal* method and the *move* method involve the type *Point* in association with object recursion, so there is an opportunity to encode these types so that they may be specialized. The definition above is easily translated into the format of Equation 5.

$\mathcal{P} = \Lambda\, t \leq F[t]\,.\,\lambda(myclass : (Real \times Real) \to (t \to t))$.
 $\lambda(x : Real, x : Real)\,.\,\lambda(self : t)$.
  $\{\; x = x,$
   $y = y,$
   $move = \lambda(dx : Real, dy : Real)$.
    $\mathbf{Y}(myclass(self.x + dx, self.y + dy)),$
   $equal = \lambda(o : t)$.
    $(self.x = o.x)\;$ and $\;(self.y = o.y)$
  $\}$

Instances of *cart_point* have type *Point*. The class associated with this definition is

$$cart\_point = \mathbf{Y}(\mathcal{P}[Point])$$

To illustrate, consider the point at location $(2,5)$. Of course, the object has an infinite expansion, so it can only be written using fixed points.

$p\;=\;\mathbf{Y}(cart\_point(2,5))$
 $=\;\mathbf{Y}(\mathbf{Y}(\mathcal{P}[Point])(2,5))$
 $=\;\{\; x = 2,$
   $y = 5,$
   $move = \lambda(dx : Real, dy : Real)$.
    $\mathbf{Y}(cart\_point(2 + dx, 5 + dy)),$
   $equal = \lambda(o : t)$.
    $(2 = o.x)\;$ and $\;(5 = o.y)\,\}$

Using inheritance, a new class *color_point* is defined. Instances of *color_point* have an additional method *color* that is defined using an additional instantiation parameter for the class. The equality method is redefined so that two points are equal only if their colors match.

class *color_point* (x:Real, y:Real, c:Color)
 implements *ColorPoint*
 inherit *cart_point(x,y)*
  translating new *myclass(x′, y′)*
   to new *myclass(x′, y′, self.color)*
 method *color* : *Color*
  return c
 method *equal(p:ColorPoint)* : *Boolean*
  return *super.equal(p)* and
   (self.color = p.color)

The class *color_point* inherits *cart_point* and indicates the two translations. The first translation is given by *cart_point(x,y)*; it indicates how to instantiate the inherited point class. The second translation is more explicit; it indicates how recursive calls within *cart_point* are to be translated to construct *color_point* objects. In this example the moved point simply retains its color. It is also possible to define an arbitrary computation of the new color from the point's position and previous color. The modified *equal* method uses *super* to invoke the original notion of equality and add a new constraint. The treatment of *super* simply involves an additional let variable.

$\mathcal{C} = \Lambda\, t \leq G[t]\,.$
 $\lambda(myclass : (Real \times Real \times Color) \to (t \to t))$.
  $\lambda(x : Real, y : Real, c : Color)$.
   $\lambda(self : t)$.
  let $super = \mathcal{P}[t](\lambda(x′, y′)\,.\,myclass(x′, y′, c))$
    $(x, y)(self)$
  in $super$ **with** $\{\; color = c$
    $equal = \lambda(o : t)$.
     super.equal(o) and
      (self.color = o.color)
   $\}$

Most of the work occurs in the value bound to *super*. First, the parent class definition is applied to t, a polymorphic type variable constrained by $t \leq G[t]$. This polymorphic application is legal because $\mathcal{P}$ accepts any type $t \leq F[t]$ and we know that $G[t] \leq F[t]$. The result is applied to a translated form of the class recursion variable *myclass*. Recursive class instantiation in *cart_point* are translated to construct colored points. Finally, the parent component is initialized by x and y, and *self* is bound to interpret method recursion properly.

Instances of *color_point* and *cart_point* cannot be intermixed in a program because their types are not subtype compatible (they cannot be compared for equality). However, it is possible to write F-bounded polymorphic functions that operate uniformly over either *Points* or *ColorPoints*.

7 Related Type Systems for Inheritance

7.1 Eiffel

Eiffel is based on an identification of classes with types and of inheritance with subtyping. Within this context, however, Eiffel is able to express many of the constructs described in this paper. The correspondence is not complete, because the identification of inheritance and subtyping makes Eiffel's type system insecure [12].

In Eiffel, the pseudovariable *Current* is used instead of *self* to indicate object recursion. Class recursion and a form of type inheritance are expressed by the type expression *Like Current*, which refers to the current class. That is, it denotes the class in which it appears or into which it is inherited. *Like Current* acts somewhat like the type variable t in the polymorphic typing of inheritance. The following code illustrates its use to implement the example from Section 3.2.

```
class P feature
    i : Integer is 5;
    id : Like Current is Current
    eq(other : Like Current) : Boolean is
        begin
            Result := (other.i = Current.i)
        end
end P

class C inherit P redefine eq feature
    b : Integer is 5;
    eq(other : Like Current) : Boolean is
        begin
            Result := (other.i = Current.i)
                and (other.b = Current.b)
        end
end P
```

This code illustrates the problem of assuming that subclasses are subtypes. With this assumption, one can assign an instance c of class C to a variable $v:P$, $v:=c$. It is then legal to send the *eq* message to v with parameter p of class P. However, $v.eq(p)$ cannot execute properly because p does not have a b attribute. A modified conformance rule that eliminates this problem was proposed in [12].

Like Current also allows Eiffel to express class recursion. For example, the following *clone* method always creates an instance of the same class as the receiver of the message because it uses *Like Current* for the class. Unfortunately, Eiffel has no way to translate instantiation parameters uniformly.

```
class Copier feature
    clone : Like Current is
    local
        temp : Like Current;
    begin
        temp.Create;
        Result := temp;
    end
end
```

The typed model of inheritance presented in this paper provides a formal model in which Eiffel may be explained. It also indicates why Eiffel's type-system is insecure and how the language may be corrected and extended.

7.2 Other Languages

Like Eiffel, most other strongly-typed object-oriented languages, including Modula-3, C++, Trellis and Simula, are based on the identification of classes and types. Their subtype relations are based on their inheritance hierarchies. Unlike Eiffel, these languages are type-safe because they restrict inheritance to satisfy subtyping. In Modula-3, C++ and Simula, the types of methods may not be changed. Trellis allows the types to be changed according to the rules for function subtypes.

None of the languages provide support for class inheritance, as we define it. It can be simulated manually by defining a method in a root class P called *mynew* which simply executes **new** P. If *mynew* is redefined manually in each subclass C to return **new** C, then class inheritance can be achieved by always using *mynew* instead of **new**. Except in Trellis, the typing does not work correctly because *mynew* must have result-type P in all classes.

Simula and C++ are interesting because they provide mechanisms for translating the subclass instantiation parameters into a form appropriate for instantiation of the parent. This mechanism is explained by the Q translation introduced in Section 4.3.

7.3 Mitchell

Mitchell [20] has developed a typed object model based on extensible records and self-application. Object types are defined by a special **class** notation.

$$T = \text{class } t \ \{m_1 : \sigma_1, \ldots, m_k : \sigma_k\}$$

Objects of type T are similar to records of functions representing methods, except that record component selection is replaced by a *message send* operation. The methods are polymorphic functions with an additional hidden argument. The polymorphism, over a domain of type functions, is used to specialize method types, while the extra argument represents *self*. They are both bound by the message sending operator, $\Leftarrow$, which binds the polymorphic argument to an empty type function, and binds the argument *self* to the object itself. Thus recursion in objects is implemented by self-application.

$$o \Leftarrow m \ = \ o.m[\lambda(t :: TYPE).\ \{\ \}](o)$$

A new object may be created by replacing methods or adding new methods in an existing object. Recursion in the types of existing methods are adjusted during extension.

There is a close relationship between Mitchell's work and the model presented in this paper. Although expressed in a different framework, the polymorphic typing of methods achieves the same effect. One advantage of Mitchell's framework is that the type of the *self* argument of each method can be different, giving a more precise typing of methods. Our system has the advantage of simplicity: it does not require special **class** types, extensible records, quantification of type functions, etc.

The systems also differ in their basic object models. Mitchell uses extensible objects, self-application, and a form of delegation [18, 27], while we use records, fixed points, inheritance, and recursive classes. In the models this difference manifests itself in the relative order of record construction and *self* abstraction. In our system, polymorphism (F-bounded) and *self* occur outside the record of methods, requiring type application and a fixed-point function to create an object, which is a simple record. Mitchell places the polymorphism (over type functions) and *self* within each method of an object and binds them during message passing.

Since record formation and *self* abstraction are independent, it appears that the two systems are isomorphic at the value level. Even so, there are tradeoffs. One advantage of the delegation system is that classes and objects are unified. However, class recursion does not seem to be supported, since all object creation is done by extending existing objects. This makes it difficult to construct objects with hidden state, as is possible with recursive classes. Our system has the advantage of a uniform treatment of inheritance on objects, classes and types. A formal investigation of relationship between the models may provide useful insights into implementation techniques and possible extensions.

7.4 Wand

Wand [29, 31] and Remy [23] have developed a type-inference scheme for dealing with records and record extension. Wand's system also allows recursive types. Record types are total functions from labels to a union of *present* and *absent* fields. The system uses ML-style parametric polymorphism instead of record subtype polymorphism: a record type has the form $\Pi[l_i : f_i]\rho$, where l_i are the explicitly defined fields and f_i is either $present(\tau)$ or *absent*. The *record extension variable* ρ represents any additional fields the record may have. In these systems there is no notion of subtyping; there is only parametric polymorphism. In a recent manuscript, Wand [30] proposes a type-inference rule in the style of ML for object inheritance with recursive types. With first-order extension variables and recursive types, his system can express F-bounded polymorphism. Thus his system can type the examples given in this paper.

A practical drawback to using first-order polymorphism to implement record subtype polymorphism is that records and record functions cannot be passed as arguments and then used with subtype polymorphism; the first-order constraint requires that the types be bound when the record is passed. A more serious problem arises in the presence of recursive types. In a traditional type-system with record subtypes, a subtype of a recursive type may have different fields at each level of unrolling in its infinite expansion. If restricted to first-order quantification, the extension variables in a recursive type cannot be instantiated at each level of unrolling. To achieve the effect of record subtyping, quantifiers would have to be included in the scope of recursion.

These problems could be solved by introducing explicit quantification, at the cost of making type-inference much more complex. A detailed comparison of Wand's type-inference approach based on record extension and our explicitly-typed approach with F-bounded polymorphism is an important topic for future research.

7.5 TS

The TS project [15, 16, 17] has recognized that inheritance does not necessarily produce subtypes. To type-check existing Smalltalk programs, which may contain ad-hoc combinations of code, their system copies the text of methods from parent to child before type-checking. These inherited method expressions are type-checked in their new context and may have very different types than they did in the parent class. As a result, a particular expression may be type-checked many times, depending on the depth of the inheritance hierarchy. They also perform type inference, using ML-style unification and first-order polymorphism.

The polymorphic typing of inheritance presented here supports a somewhat more abstract notion of typed inheritance, since a single (polymorphic) type must be assigned to a class. Our polymorphic typing of inheritance uses only the type of the parent, not its method expressions; the type of an inherited method may change but only according to its polymorphic typing. The polymorphic typing provides a degree of encapsulation not found in TS, but TS can type-check some programs that do not have polymorphic typings.

8 Conclusion

We present a typed model of inheritance that preserves more of the flexibility of inheritance in untyped object-oriented languages. Our typing applies to both object and class inheritance. In addition, a notion of inheritance for types is introduced. Type inheritance is analogous to subtyping, but is useful for object-oriented programming because inherited objects have inherited types, not subtypes.

Previously, typed languages allow either modification of instantiation parameters (Simula and C++) or provide class inheritance (Eiffel), but not both. Smalltalk provides both but is untyped. Our model provides a explicit higher-order formalism in which class inheritance, inheritance over recursive types, and modification of instantiation parameters are all supported.

Acknowledgement

We would like to thank Luca Cardelli, David Chase, Jim Donahue, John Mitchell and Benjamin Pierce for the discussions on this work. We would also like to thank Alan Snyder for his support and inspiration [26].

References

[1] G. M. Birtwistle, O.-J. Dahl, B. Myhrhaug, and K. Nygaard. *SIMULA Begin*. Auerbach, 1973.

[2] A. H. Borning and D. H. Ingalls. A type declaration and inference system for Smalltalk. In *Proc. of Conf. on Principles of Programming Languages*, pages 133–141, 1982.

[3] P. Canning, W. Cook, W. Hill, J. Mitchell, and W. Olthoff. F-bounded polymorphism for object-oriented programming. In *Proc. of Conf. on Functional Programming Languages and Computer Architecture*, pages 273–280, 1989.

[4] P. Canning, W. Cook, W. Hill, and W. Olthoff. Interfaces for strongly-typed object-oriented programming. In *Proc. ACM Conf. on Object-Oriented Programming: Systems, Languages and Applications*, pages 457–467, 1989.

[5] P. Canning, W. Hill, and W. Olthoff. A kernel language for object-oriented programming. Technical Report STL-88-21, Hewlett-Packard Labs, 1988.

[6] L. Cardelli. A semantics of multiple inheritance. In *Semantics of Data Types, LNCS 173*, pages 51–68. Springer-Verlag, 1984.

[7] L. Cardelli. Amber. In *Combinators and Functional Programming Languages, LNCS 242*, pages 21–47, 1986.

[8] L. Cardelli. Structural subtyping and the notion of power type. In *Conf. Rec. ACM Symp. on Principles of Programming Languages*, pages 70–79, 1988.

[9] L. Cardelli, J. Donahue, M. Jordan, B. Kaslow, and G. Nelson. The Modula-3 type system. In *Conf. Rec. ACM Symp. on Principles of Programming Languages*, pages 202–212, 1989.

[10] L. Cardelli and P. Wegner. On understanding types, data abstraction, and polymorphism. *Computing Surveys*, 17(4):471–522, 1985.

[11] W. Cook. *A Denotational Semantics of Inheritance*. PhD thesis, Brown University, 1989.

[12] W. Cook. A proposal for making Eiffel type-safe. In *Proc. European Conf. on Object-Oriented Programming*, pages 57–70. BCS Workshop Series, 1989. Also in *The Computer Journal*, 32(4):305–311, 1989.

[13] W. Cook and J. Palsberg. A denotational semantics of inheritance and its correctness. In *Proc. ACM Conf. on Object-Oriented Programming: Systems, Languages and Applications*, pages 433–444, 1989.

[14] A. Goldberg and D. Robson. *Smalltalk-80: the Language and Its Implementation*. Addison-Wesley, 1983.

[15] J. Graver. *Type-Checking and Type-Inference for Object-Oriented Programming Languages*. PhD thesis, University of Illinois, 1989.

[16] R. Johnson and J. Graver. A user's guide to Typed Smalltalk. Technical Report UIUCDCS-R-88-1457, University of Illinois, 1988.

[17] R. Johnson, J. Graver, and L. Zurawski. TS: An optimizing compiler for Smalltalk. In *Proc. ACM Conf. on Object-Oriented Programming: Systems, Languages and Applications*, 1988.

[18] H. Lieberman. Using prototypical objects to implement shared behavior in object-oriented systems. In *Proc. ACM Conf. on Object-Oriented Programming: Systems, Languages and Applications*, pages 214–223, 1986.

[19] B. Meyer. *Object-Oriented Software Construction*. Prentice-Hall, 1988.

[20] J. C. Mitchell. Towards a typed foundation for method specialization and inheritance. In *Proc. of Conf. on Principles of Programming Languages*, 1989.

[21] D. Moon. Object-oriented programming with Flavors. In *Proc. ACM Conf. on Object-Oriented Programming: Systems, Languages and Applications*, pages 1–9, 1986.

[22] U. S. Reddy. Objects as closures: Abstract semantics of object-oriented languages. In *Proc. ACM Conf. on Lisp and Functional Programming*, pages 289–297, 1988.

[23] D. Rémy. Typechecking records and variants in a natural extension of ML. In *Conf. Rec. ACM Symp. on Principles of Programming Languages*, pages 77–88, 1989.

[24] J. Reynolds. User-defined data types and procedural data structures as complimentary approaches to data abstraction. In *New Advances in Algorithmic Languages*. INRIA, 1975.

[25] C. Schaffert, T. Cooper, B. Bullis, M. Kilian, and C. Wilpolt. An introduction to Trellis/Owl. In *Proc. ACM Conf. on Object-Oriented Programming: Systems, Languages and Applications*, pages 9–16, 1986.

[26] A. Snyder. Inheritance and the development of encapsulated software components. In B. Shriver and P. Wegner, editors, *Research Directions in Object-Oriented Programming*, pages 165–188. MIT Press, 1987.

[27] L. A. Stein. Delegation is inheritance. In *Proc. ACM Conf. on Object-Oriented Programming: Systems, Languages and Applications*, pages 138–146, 1987.

[28] B. Stroustrup. *C++*. Addison-Wesley, 1987.

[29] M. Wand. Complete type inference for simple objects. In *Proc. IEEE Symposium on Logic in Computer Science*, pages 37–44, 1987.

[30] M. Wand. Type inference for objects with instance variables and inheritance, 1989. manuscript.

[31] M. Wand. Type inference for record concatenation and multiple inheritance. In *Proc. IEEE Symposium on Logic in Computer Science*, pages 92–97, 1989.

A Type System for Smalltalk

Justin O. Graver
University of Florida

Ralph E. Johnson
University of Illinois at Urbana-Champaign

Abstract

This paper describes a type system for Smalltalk that is type-safe, that allows most Smalltalk programs to be type-checked, and that can be used as the basis of an optimizing compiler.

1 Introduction

There has been a lot of interest recently in type systems for object-oriented programming languages [CW85, DT88]. Since Smalltalk was one of the earliest object-oriented languages, it is not surprising that there have been several attempts to provide a type system for it [Suz81, BI82]. Unfortunately, none of the attempts have been completely successful [Joh86]. In particular, none of the proposed type systems are both type-safe and capable of type-checking most common Smalltalk programs. Smalltalk violates many of the assumptions on which most object-oriented type systems are based, and a successful type system for Smalltalk is necessarily different from those for other languages.

We have designed a new type system for Smalltalk. The biggest difference between our type system and others is that most type systems for object-oriented programming languages equate classes with types and subclassing with subtyping [Suz81, BI82, SCB*86, Str86, Mey88]. In our type system, types are based on classes (i.e. each class defines a type or a family of types) but subclassing has no relationship to subtyping. This is because Smalltalk classes inherit implementation and not specification.

Our type system uses discriminated union types and signature types to describe inclusion polymorphism and describes functional polymorphism (sometimes called parametric polymorphism, see [DT88]) using bounded universal quantification. It has the following features:

- automatic case analysis of union types,

- effective treatment of side-effects by basing the definition of the subtype relation on equality of parameterized types, and

- type-safety, i.e. a variable's value always conforms to its type.

Because the type system uses class information, it can be used for optimization. It has been implemented as part of the TS (Typed Smalltalk) optimizing compiler [JGZ88].

2 Background

Smalltalk [GR83] is a pure object-oriented programming language in that everything, from integers to text windows to the execution state, is an object. In particular, classes are objects. Since everything is an object, the only operation needed in Smalltalk is message sending. Smalltalk uses run-time type-checking. Every message send is dynamically bound to an implementation depending on the class of the receiver. This unified view of the universe makes Smalltalk a compact yet powerful language.

Smalltalk is extremely extensible. Most operations are built out of a small set of powerful primitives.

For example, control structures are all implemented in terms of blocks, which are the Smalltalk equivalent of closures. Smalltalk's equivalent to if-then-else is the ifTrue:ifFalse: message, which is sent to a boolean object with two block arguments. If the receiver is an instance of class True then the "true block" is evaluated. Similarly, if the receiver is an instance of class False then the "false block" is evaluated. Looping is implemented in a similar way using recursion. These primitives can be used to implement case statements, generators, exceptions, and coroutines[Deu81].

Smalltalk has been used mostly for prototyping and exploratory development. It is ideal for these purposes because Smalltalk programs are easy to change and reuse, and Smalltalk comes with a powerful programming environment and large library of generally useful components. However, it has not been used as much for production programming. This is partly because it is hard to use for multi-person projects, partly because it is hard to deliver application programs without the large programming environment, and partly because it is not as efficient as languages like C. In spite of these problems, the development and maintenance of Smalltalk programs is so easy that more and more companies are developing applications with it.

A type system can help solve Smalltalk's problems. Type information makes programs easier to understand and can be used to automatically check interface consistency, which makes Smalltalk better suited for multiperson projects. However, our main motivation for type-checking Smalltalk is to provide information needed by an optimizing compiler. Smalltalk methods (procedures) tend to be very small, making aggressive inline substitution necessary to achieve good performance. Type information is required to bind methods at compile-time. Although some type information can be acquired by dataflow analysis of individual methods [CUL89], explicit type declarations produce better results and also make programs more reliable and easier to understand. From this point of view, the type system has been quite successful, because the TS compiler can make Smalltalk programs run nearly as fast as C programs.

It is important that a type system for Smalltalk not hurt Smalltalk's good qualities. In particular, it must not hinder the rapid-prototyping style often used by Smalltalk programmers. Exploratory programmers try to build programs as quickly as possible, making localized changes instead of global reorganization. They often use explicit run-time checks for particular classes (evidence that code is in the wrong class) and create new subclasses to reuse code rather than to organize abstraction (evidence that a new abstract

```
class Change:
    values
        ↑Array with: self class with: self parameters
    parameters
        self subclassResponsibility

class ClassRelatedChange:
    parameters
        ↑className

class MethodChange:
    parameters
        ↑Array with: className with: selector

class OtherChange:
    parameters
        ↑self text
```

Figure 1: Change and its subclasses.

class is needed) [JF88]. Although conscientious programmers remove these improprieties from finished programs, we wanted a type system that would allow them, since they are often important intermediate steps in the development process. Thus, a static type system for Smalltalk must be as flexible as the traditional dynamic type-checking.

In an untyped object-oriented language like Smalltalk, classes inherit only the implementation of their superclasses. In contrast, most type systems for object-oriented programming languages require classes to inherit the specification of their superclasses [BI82, Car84, CW85, SCB*86, Str86, Mey88], not just the implementation [Suz81, Joh86]. A class specification can be an explicit signature [BHJL86], the implicit signature implied by the name of a class [SCB*86], or a signature combined with method pre- and post-conditions, class invariants, etc. [Mey88]. Inheriting specification means that the type of methods in subclasses must be subtypes of their specifications in superclasses.

Since Smalltalk is untyped, only implementation is inherited. This makes retrofitting a type system difficult. Since specification inheritance is a logical organization, many parts of the Smalltalk inheritance hierarchy conform to specification inheritance, but there is nothing in the language that requires or enforces this. Thus, it is common to find classes in the Smalltalk-80 class library that inherit implementation and ignore specification.

Dictionary is a good example of a class that inherits implementation but not specification; it is a subclass of Set. A Dictionary is a keyed lookup table that is implemented as a hash table of <key, value> pairs. Dictionary inherits the hash table implementation from Set, but applications using Sets would behave quite differently if given Dictionaries instead.

Abstract classes, a commonly used Smalltalk programming technique, provide other examples where classes inherit implementation but not specification. Consider the method definitions shown in Figure 1. These (and other) classes are used to track changes made to the system. The abstract class Change defines the values method in terms of the parameters method. The implementation of the values method is inherited by the subclasses of Change. The result of sending the values message depends on the result of sending the parameters message, which is different for each class in Figure 1. Hence, the specification of the values method is also different for each of the classes.

A class-based type system with explicit union types works for an implementation inheritance hierarchy and greatly simplifies optimization, but is not very flexible when it comes to adding new classes to the system. To regain some of the flexibility we incorporate type-inference and signatures. This gives us both flexibility and the ability to optimize.

A type system suitable for an optimizing Smalltalk compiler must also have parameterized types. It is difficult to imagine a (non-trivial) Smalltalk application that does not use Collections. The compiler must be able to associate the type of objects being added to a Collection with the type of objects being removed from it. Without parameterized types, all Collections are reduced to homogeneous groups of generic objects. Furthermore, due to the potentially imperative side-effects of any operation, a special imperative definition of subtyping for parameterized types is used (see Section 3.1).

The type system must also be able to describe the functional and inclusion polymorphism exhibited by many Smalltalk methods. Functional polymorphism can be described, in the usual manner, with (implicit) bounded universal quantification of type variables. Inclusion polymorphism can be described with explicit union types or signatures.

For a detailed discussion of these issues see [Gra89].

3 Types

The abstract and concrete syntax for type expressions is shown in Figure 2 (abstract syntax on the left and concrete syntax on the right). In the concrete syntax grammar terminals are underlined, (something)* represents zero or more repetitions of the something, and (something)+ represents one or more repetitions of the something. Each of the type forms will be described in detail in the following sections.

We use the abstract syntax in inference rules and the concrete syntax in examples. Type expressions are denoted by s, t, and u. Type variables are denoted by p (abstract syntax) or by P (concrete syntax). Lists (tuples) of types are denoted by $\vec{t} = <t_1, t_2, \ldots, t_n>$. The empty list is denoted by $<>$ and $t \cdot \vec{t}$ is the list $<t, t_1, t_2, \ldots, t_n>$. Similar notation is used for lists of type variables. C denotes a class name and m denotes a message selector.

Strictly speaking, a type variable is not a type; it is a place holder (or representative) for a type. We assume that all free type variables are (implicitly) universally quantified at an appropriate level. For example, the local type variables of a method type are assured to be universally quantified over the type of the method; the class type parameters of a class are assumed to be universally quantified over all type definitions in the class. We also assume that all type variables are unique (i.e. have unique names) and are implicitly renamed whenever a type containing type variables is conceptually instantiated. For example, the local type variables of a method type are renamed each time the method type is "used" at a call site. We do use explicit range declarations for type variables to achieve bounded universal quantification (see Sections 3.5 and 3.6). Given these assumptions, we treat type variables as types.

3.1 Subtyping

The intuitive meaning of the subtype relation $\sqsubseteq$ is that if $s \sqsubseteq t$ then everything of type s is also of type t. The subtyping relation for our type system can be formalized as a set of type inference rules (as in [CW85]). C is a set of inclusion constraints for type variables. The notation $C.p \sqsubseteq t$ means to extend the set C with the constraint that the type variable p is a subtype of the type t. The notation $C \vdash s \sqsubseteq t$ means that from C we can infer $s \sqsubseteq t$. A horizontal bar is logical implication: if we can infer what is above it then we can infer what is below it.

The following are basic inference rules.

$$C \vdash t \sqsubseteq Anything$$

	$t ::=$		$Type ::=$
(object type)	$C(\vec{t})$		$ClassName \ (\underline{of:} \ Type)^*$
(block type)	$\mid \vec{t} \to t$		$\mid \underline{Block} \ (\underline{of:} \ Type)^* \ \underline{returns:} \ Type$
(union type)	$\mid t + t$		$\mid Type \underline{+} Type$
	$\mid (t)$		$\mid \underline{(} Type \underline{)}$
(signature type)	$\mid < m, \vec{t} \to t >^*$		$\mid \underline{understands:} \ ((MsgName$
			$\qquad (\underline{of:} \ Type)^{\underline{+}} \underline{returns:} \ Type)^*\underline{)}$
	$\mid (t)$		$\mid \underline{(} Type \underline{)}$
(type variable)	$\mid p$		$\mid P$
($\top$)	$\mid Anything$		$\mid \underline{Anything}$
($\bot$)	$\mid Nothing$		$\mid \underline{Nothing}$

Figure 2: The abstract and concrete syntax of types.

$$C \vdash Nothing \sqsubseteq t$$

$$C.p \sqsubseteq t \vdash p \sqsubseteq t$$

$$C.t \sqsubseteq p \vdash t \sqsubseteq p$$

$$C \vdash p \sqsubseteq p$$

The following rules are used for the type parameter lists of object types (see Section 3.2) and for the argument type lists for block types (see Section 3.4).

$$C \vdash <> \sqsubseteq <>$$

$$\frac{C \vdash s \sqsubseteq s' \quad C \vdash \vec{t} \sqsubseteq \vec{t}'}{C \vdash s \cdot \vec{t} \sqsubseteq s' \cdot \vec{t}'}$$

Subtyping is reflexive, transitive, and antisymmetric.

$$C \vdash t \sqsubseteq t$$

$$\frac{C \vdash s \sqsubseteq t \quad C \vdash t \sqsubseteq u}{C \vdash s \sqsubseteq u}$$

$$\frac{C \vdash s \sqsubseteq t \quad C \vdash t \sqsubseteq s}{C \vdash s = t}$$

3.2 Object Types

Some variables contain only one kind of object. For example, all Characters[1] have an instance variable that contains a SmallInteger ASCII value. Other variables can contain different kinds of objects. For example, a Set can contain SmallIntegers, Characters, Arrays, Sets, and so on. Each class has a set of zero or more type variables called *class type parameters* that can be used in type expressions to specify the types of instance variables. These are the only type variables that can appear in type declarations for instance variables.

An *object type* is a class name together with a possibly empty list of types. The type list of an object type provides values for the class type parameters defined for the corresponding class. Thus, the size of the type list that may accompany a class name is fixed by the corresponding class definition. For example, the classes SmallInteger and Character have zero class type parameters, so SmallInteger and Character are valid object types. The classes Array and Set each have one class type parameter, so *Array of: SmallInteger* and *Set of: (Array of: Character)* are valid object types.

Due to the imperative nature of Smalltalk [GR83, Joh86] and because of the antimonotonic ordering of function types [DT88] we define subtyping for object types as equality, i.e. one object type is included in another if and only if they are equal (Cardelli also takes this approach for "updatable" objects in [Car85]). (Recall that C is a set of inclusion constraints and C is a class name.)

$$\frac{C \vdash \vec{s} = \vec{t}}{C \vdash C(\vec{s}) \sqsubseteq C(\vec{t})}$$

3.3 Union Types

The type system defined so far cannot describe an Array containing both Characters and SmallIntegers. In Smalltalk, a variable can contain many different kinds of objects over its lifetime. Thus, a type can be a nonempty "set" of object types (or other types). An example of a *union type* is

(Array of: SmallInteger) + (Array of: Character)
+ (Array of: (SmallInteger + Character)).

---

[1] The phrase "a SomeClass" refers to an instance of class SomeClass. The phrase "class SomeClass" refers to the class itself.

Here, the plus operator is read as "or," so a variable of the above type could contain an Array whose elements are all SmallIntegers, all Characters, or a mixture of the two.

Our type system does not use the subclass relation on classes to induce the subtype relation on types. Instead, type inclusion is based on discriminated union types. An object type t is included in a union type u only if t is included in one of u's elements.

$$\frac{C \vdash s \sqsubseteq t}{C \vdash s \sqsubseteq t + u}$$

A union type u is included in a union type u' only if each element of u is included in u'.

$$\frac{C \vdash s \sqsubseteq u \quad C \vdash t \sqsubseteq u}{C \vdash s + t \sqsubseteq u}$$

Some examples are:

$Character \sqsubseteq Character + SmallInteger$
$Array\ of:\ SmallInteger \sqsubseteq$
$(Array\ of:\ SmallInteger) + (Array\ of:\ Character)$
$Array\ of:\ SmallInteger \not\sqsubseteq$
$Array\ of:\ (SmallInteger + Character)$

Note that our type system does not reflect class inheritance. Even though Integer is a subclass of Number, Integer is not a subtype of Number. However, we can specify the type of all subclasses of Number by listing them, i.e. $Integer + Float + Fraction$.[2]

3.4 Block Types

Blocks (function abstractions) are treated differently from other objects. A *block type* consists of the name *Block*, a possibly empty list of types for block arguments, and a return type. For example,

$Block\ of:\ (Array\ of:\ Character)\ of:\ SmallInteger$
$returns:\ Character$

represents the type of a block with two arguments, and *Block returns: SmallInteger* represents a block with no arguments. Block types differ from object types in several ways. Unlike object types, there is no class Block. Types beginning with the name *Block* can have different sized argument type lists.

A block type u is included in a block type u' only if the return type of u is included in the return type

---

[2]Common union types such as *Integer + Float + Fraction* and *True + False* are presently abbreviated using the global variables *NumberType* and *BooleanType*, respectively. Another approach is to use the object type of an abstract class (classes such as Number, Collection, and Boolean that provide an implementation template for subclasses but have no instances of their own) to automatically denote the union of the types of all its non-abstract subclasses.

SequenceableCollection subclass: #OrderedCollection
    instanceVariables: 'firstIndex <*SmallInteger*>
                      lastIndex <*SmallInteger*>'
   classVariables: ''
   typeParameters: 'ElementType'
   poolDictionaries: ''
   category: 'Sequenceable-Collections'

Figure 3: Class definition for OrderedCollection.

---

of u' and if each argument type of u' is included in the corresponding argument type of u (this is the standard antimonotonic subtype relation for function types [MS82]).

$$\frac{C \vdash \vec{s}\,' \sqsubseteq \vec{s} \quad C \vdash t \sqsubseteq t'}{C \vdash \vec{s} \to t \sqsubseteq \vec{s}\,' \to t'}$$

For example,

$Block\ returns:\ Character$
$\sqsubseteq Block\ returns:\ (Character + SmallInteger)$

$Block\ of:\ (Float + SmallInteger)\ returns:\ SmallInteger$
$\sqsubseteq Block\ of:\ Float\ returns:\ (Character + SmallInteger).$

3.5 Typed Class Definitions

All instance variables and class variables must have their types declared. Each class defines a set of type variables called class type parameters, which may be used to specify the types of instance and class variables.

Figure 3 shows the definition of OrderedCollection, which is a subclass of SequenceableCollection. Note that the type of each instance variable is declared when the variable is declared and that angle brackets are used to set off type expressions from the regular Smalltalk code.

A class definition defines an "object type" in which the type list is the list of class type parameters (appearing in the same order as in the class definition). The type defined by the above class definition would be

OrderedCollection of: ElementType.

The scope of the class type parameter *ElementType* is limited to the method and variable definitions in class OrderedCollection (the same scope as a class variable). Class type parameters are inherited by subclasses, just like instance and class variables. Any use of the OrderedCollection type outside of this scope

```
{  localTypeVariables: <P1> <P2>
   receiverType: <Self>
   arguments: arg1 <arg1Type> arg2 <arg2Type>
   temporaries: temp <tempType>
   blockArguments: blkArg <blkArgType>
   returnType: <Self> }

message selector and argument names
      "comment stating purpose of message"

      | temporary variable names |
      statements
```

Figure 4: Template for typed methods.

must "instantiate" its class type parameter to a type constant (like *Character*) or to a locally known type variable. Thus, the above type actually defines a family of object types.

The *range* (upper bound for type instantiation) of a class type parameter may be restricted by including an optional range type declaration. A class type parameter may only be instantiated to a type that is a subtype of its range type. The range declaration of a class type parameter is syntactically identical to the type declaration for a variable. In the above example, if we wished to restrict the elements of OrderedCollections to be Characters, the typeParameters: field would be declared as 'ElementType <Character>'. If the range declaration of a class type parameter is omitted it is assumed to be *Anything*.

3.6 Typed Method Definitions

The types of method arguments, temporary variables, and block arguments can be explicitly declared or inferred by the TS type-inference mechanism [Gra89]. The only difference between a typed method and an untyped method is that the typed method has type declarations. Type declarations must precede any part of the method definition. A typed method template is shown in Figure 4. The arguments for the fields arguments:, temporaries:, and blockArguments: are lists of identifier <type> declaration pairs. The arguments for the receiverType: and returnType: fields are single type declarations. The arguments for the localTypeVariables: field are capitalized identifiers. The range of a type variable can be restricted by using the range: modifier. For example, the local type variable declaration <P range: (Integer + Character)> declares *P* to be a type variable that can be associated with any of the types *Integer*, *Character*, or *Integer* + *Character*. Local type variables are instantiated during type-checking to types determined by the types of actual arguments at a call site. Local type variables will usually, though not necessarily, correspond to the class type parameters of some class.

The do: method for SequenceableCollection is shown in Figure 5 as an example of a typed method definition. Notice that certain fields of the type declarations have been omitted. The syntax rules for type declarations are fairly liberal. Fields can occur in any order. All fields except receiverType: and returnType: can have multiple occurrences. The smallest type declaration for a method is "{}."

Self represents the type of the pseudo-variable self (and super). Unfortunately, the class of self is different in each class that inherits a method, so *Self* must differ, too. Thus, each method is type checked for each class that inherits it by replacing *Self* with the type appropriate for the inheriting class. In the absence of a receiverType: declaration (which is over 99% of the time), *Self* defaults to the object type for the class in which the method is being compiled. Otherwise, *Self* is replaced with the type given in the receiverType: declaration. A legal receiverType: must be a subtype of the default value of *Self*.

Returning to the example of Figure 5, SequenceableCollection has one class type parameter called *ElementType*, so the type substituted for *Self* will be *SequenceableCollection of: ElementType*. The argument aBlock is a block that takes one argument of type *ElementType* and returns an object of unknown type *P*. When do: is envoked in another method definition both *ElementType* and *P* will be associated with actual receiver and argument types. The temporary variables index and length have values dependent on the size of Collections. In Smalltalk implementations with 30+ bit SmallIntegers, the possible size of any Collection is well within the range of SmallIntegers.[3] There is no explicit return statement in the method so it implicitly returns self.

Type declarations and typed methods introduce the notions of message and method types. A *message type* consists of a message selector, a receiver type, a list of argument types, and a return type. A *method type* consists of a message type and a set of constraints on the type variables used in the message

---

[3]Smalltalk defines infinite precision integer arithmetic using the classes LargeNegativeInteger, SmallInteger, and LargePositiveInteger (the three subclasses of class Integer). SmallIntegers are essentially machine integers; instances of the Large-Integer classes are more complex.

```
{ localTypeVariables: <P>
  arguments: aBlock <Block of: ElementType returns: P>
  temporaries: index <SmallInteger> length <SmallInteger>
  returnType: <Self> }

do: aBlock
    "Evaluate aBlock for each of the receiver's elements."

    | index length |
    index ← 0.
    length ← self size.
    [(index ← index + 1) <= length]
        whileTrue: [aBlock value: (self at: index)]
```

Figure 5: The do: method for SequenceableCollection.

type. A method type denotes the type of a method relative to a specific class of receivers. Therefore, *Self* should already have been expanded and should never appear in a method type. The type of the above method is denoted by

$<SequenceableCollection\ of:\ ElementType>$
$\quad do:\ <Block\ of:\ ElementType\ returns:\ T>$
$\quad \uparrow <SequenceableCollection\ of:\ ElementType>$.

Message types use the same notation. Local range constraints on type variables are shown enclosed in braces following the return type of a method type. For example,

$<Object>$ foo: $<P>\ \uparrow<P>$
$\{<P> \sqsubseteq <Integer + Character>\}$.

Subtyping for message types, although complicated by type variables (see [Gra89]), is essentially the same as for block types, with the added condition that the selectors must be equal.

3.7 Metaclass Method Definitions

In regular class method definitions the type *Self* refers to the type of the receiver. It is useful to extend this notion to be able to refer to the type of the class of the receiver. This is done by using the *Self class* type specification.

Similarly, when defining methods in a metaclass it is useful to be able to refer to the type of instances of the metaclass. This is done by using the *InstanceType* type specification. For example, Figure 6 shows the typed method definition of new: for the Set metaclass.

```
{ receiverType: <Self>
  arguments: anInteger <SmallInteger>
  returnType: <InstanceType> }

new: anInteger
    "Answer a new instance of size anInteger."

    ↑(super new: (anInteger max: 1)) setTally
```

Figure 6: The new: method in Set class.

4 Type-Checking

Type-checking is specified using inference rules similar to those used to describe subtyping. Besides a set of type constraints $\mathcal{C}$, we need a set of assumptions $\mathcal{A}$ about the types of variables. The notation $\mathcal{A}.v : t$ means to extend the set $\mathcal{A}$ with the assumption that variable v has type t. The notation $\mathcal{C}, \mathcal{A} \vdash e : t$ means that from the constraints $\mathcal{C}$ and assumptions $\mathcal{A}$ we can infer that an expression e has type t. If a type can be inferred for an expression the expression is *type-correct*. The following rule describes the essence of subtyping:

$$\frac{\mathcal{C}, \mathcal{A} \vdash e : s \quad \mathcal{C} \vdash s \sqsubseteq t}{\mathcal{C}, \mathcal{A} \vdash e : t}$$

4.1 Basic Type-Checking

A method is type-correct if each of its statements is type-correct and if the type of the expression in each return statement is a subtype of the declared return type of the method. Type-checking an expression requires knowing the types of its subexpressions.

The types of all variables are declared.

$$C, \mathcal{A}.v : t \vdash v : t$$

The types of the pseudo-variables true, false, and nil are constants.

$$\vdash \underline{\text{true}} : True$$

$$\vdash \underline{\text{false}} : False$$

$$\vdash \underline{\text{nil}} : UndefinedObject$$

The type of a literal (constant) is inferred from its class.

$$\vdash n : Integer$$

$$\vdash \$c : Character$$

etc.

If this type is not general enough then an explicit type declaration can be used to supply the "correct" type [Gra89].

An assignment statement $v \leftarrow e$ is type-correct if both v and e are type-correct (variables are trivially type-correct) and if the type of e is a subtype of the type of v. The type of an assignment statement $v \leftarrow e$ is the type of e.

$$\frac{C, \mathcal{A} \vdash v : s \quad C, \mathcal{A} \vdash e : t \quad C \vdash t \sqsubseteq s}{C, \mathcal{A} \vdash (v \leftarrow e) : t}$$

A statement sequence $e_1 \ldots e_n$ is type-correct if each statement in the sequence is type-correct. The type of a statement sequence is the type of the last statement in the sequence.

$$\frac{C, \mathcal{A} \vdash e_1 : t_1 \quad \ldots \quad C, \mathcal{A} \vdash e_n : t_n}{C, \mathcal{A} \vdash (e_1 \ldots e_n) : t_n}$$

The type of a block is inferred from the declared types of its arguments and the inferred type of its statement list.

$$\frac{C, \mathcal{A}.\vec{y} : \vec{t} \vdash e : u}{C, \mathcal{A} \vdash [\vec{y} \mid e] : \vec{t} \rightarrow u}$$

An additional inference rule for blocks is given in Section 4.2.

A return statement $\uparrow e$ is type-correct if e is type-correct and if the type of e is a subtype of the declared return type of the method. The set of assumptions $\mathcal{A}$ contains a special variable returnValue whose type is the declared return type of the method being type-checked. The only place a return statement can appear is as the last statement in the statement list of a method or a block. The types of the top-level statements in the statement list of a method can be ignored. The type of a block will always be checked for inclusion within some block type. To afford the maximum freedom to such blocks, the type given to return statements is the special type $Nothing$, which is included in any type.

$$\frac{C, \mathcal{A} \vdash \underline{\text{returnValue}} : t \quad C, \mathcal{A} \vdash e : t}{C, \mathcal{A} \vdash (\uparrow e) : Nothing}$$

Due to the simplicity of Smalltalk, the only remaining kind of expression is the message send. Type-checking a message send involves looking up one or more method types. The message send is type-correct if, for each method type, there exists a mapping of type variables to types such that, under this mapping, the type of each actual argument is a subtype of the corresponding formal argument. The type of a message send is the union of the return types of each of these method types, evaluated in their respective type assignment environments.

Let H be a hierarchy of typed class definitions and $H < C, m >$ be the definition in class C for method m, i.e.

$$H < C, m > = \vec{p} \sqsubseteq \vec{u} \, C(\vec{s}) \, m \, \vec{y} : \vec{t} \uparrow u \, \vec{z} : \vec{t}' e$$

where $\vec{p} \sqsubseteq \vec{u}$ are local type variables with range declarations, $C(\vec{s})$ is the type of the receiver, $\vec{y} : \vec{t}$ are typed arguments, u is the return type, $\vec{z} : \vec{t}'$ are the typed temporaries, and e is the method body. The notation

$$C(\vec{s}) \cdot \vec{t} \rightarrow u \mid \vec{p} \sqsubseteq \vec{u}$$

denotes a method type where $C(\vec{s})$ is the receiver type, $\vec{t}$ is the list of argument types, u is the return type, and $\vec{p} \sqsubseteq \vec{u}$ are range constraints. For notational convenience, we use the following inference rule to extract method types from method definitions.

$$\frac{H < C, m > = \vec{p} \sqsubseteq \vec{u} \, C(\vec{s}) \, m \, \vec{y} : \vec{t} \uparrow u \, \vec{z} : \vec{t}' e}{\vdash < C, m >_d : C(\vec{s}) \cdot \vec{t} \rightarrow u \mid \vec{p} \sqsubseteq \vec{u}}$$

The notation $\vdash < C, m >_d : t$ means it can be inferred that t is the declared method type of the method invoked when sending the message m to an instance of class C.

In the following inference rule for message sends, $e : C(\vec{s})$ signifies that the type of the receiver is an object type, $\vec{e} : \vec{t}$ denotes the typed arguments, and $e \, m \, \vec{e}$ denotes a message send.

$$C, \mathcal{A} \vdash e : C(\vec{s}) \quad C, \mathcal{A} \vdash \vec{e} : \vec{t}$$

$$C, \mathcal{A} \vdash < C, m >_d : C(\vec{s}') \cdot \vec{t}' \rightarrow u' \mid \vec{p} \sqsubseteq \vec{u}$$

$$\frac{\mathcal{C}.(\vec{p} \sqsubseteq \vec{u}).(C(\vec{s}) \sqsubseteq C(\vec{s}\,')).(\vec{t} \sqsubseteq \vec{t}\,') \vdash u' \sqsubseteq u}{\mathcal{C}, \mathcal{A} \vdash (e\ m\ \vec{e}) : u}$$

Message sends to receivers with union types are handled by an inference rule in Section 4.2.

Consider, for example, the message send anArray at: 2, where the type of the variable anArray is *Array of: Character*. Let the method type associated with the method that would be invoked if the at: message were sent to an Array be

$$<Array\ of:\ P>\ at:\ <SmallInteger>\ \uparrow <P>.$$

The inference rule for message sends produces a set of inclusion equations

$P \sqsubseteq Anything$	(range of P)
$Array\ of:\ Character \sqsubseteq Array\ of:\ P$	(receiver type)
$SmallInteger \sqsubseteq SmallInteger$	(argument type)

whose solution is

$$P \sqsubseteq Character.$$

In general, there may not be a unique solution to a given set of inclusion equations. How to deal with (avoid) multiple solutions is discussed in [Gra89]. If no solution exists then there is a type error somewhere.

An inference rule is also needed to type-check method definitions. Recall that the abstract definition for a method m looks like

$$\vec{p} \sqsubseteq \vec{u}\ C(\vec{s})\ m\ \vec{y} : \vec{t} \uparrow u\ \vec{z} : \vec{t}\,'e.$$

If, by adding type declarations appropriately to $\mathcal{C}$ and $\mathcal{A}$, it can be inferred that e has type u then it can be inferred that the definition of m is type-correct and is of type

$$C(\vec{s}) \cdot \vec{t} \rightarrow u\ |\ \vec{p} \sqsubseteq \vec{u}.$$

This is expressed in the following inference rule where self : $C(\vec{s})$ is the implicit type of the pseudo-variable self and returnValue is a special variable used for type-checking return statements.

$$H<C,m> = \vec{p} \sqsubseteq \vec{u}\ C(\vec{s})\ m\ \vec{y} : \vec{t} \uparrow u\ \vec{z} : \vec{t}\,'e$$

$$\frac{\mathcal{C}.\vec{p} \sqsubseteq \vec{u}, \mathcal{A}.\underline{self} : C(\vec{s}). \vec{y} : \vec{t}.\ \underline{returnValue} : u.\ \vec{z} : \vec{t}\,' \vdash e : u}{\mathcal{C}, \mathcal{A} \vdash <C,m> : C(\vec{s}) \cdot \vec{t} \rightarrow u\ |\ \vec{p} \sqsubseteq \vec{u}}$$

Note that $<C,m>: t$ denotes the true inferred type of a method m for class C, which must be included in the declared method type $<C,m>_d : t'$.

4.2 Case Analysis

Type-checking Smalltalk programs frequently requires case analysis of a union type. Even though the type of a variable may be a union type when its use throughout an entire method is considered, its type in any particular use can be considered an object type (or one of several object types). This reflects the fact that a variable may reference only one object at a time. It is therefore more precise, when type-checking an expression containing a variable with a union type, to type-check the expression separately for each type in the union type. The type of the expression is then the union of the separate result types.

$$\frac{\mathcal{C}, \mathcal{A}.v : s \vdash e : u \quad \mathcal{C}, \mathcal{A}.v : t \vdash e : u}{\mathcal{C}, \mathcal{A}.v : s+t \vdash e : u}$$

Case analysis is useful when used with the following rule: a block whose body is type-incorrect has type *IllegalBlock*. (i.e. if no better type can be inferred for a block then it can always be inferred to be *IllegalBlock*)

$$\mathcal{C}, \mathcal{A} \vdash [\vec{y}\ |\ e] : IllegalBlock$$

Thus, a type-incorrect block will not necessarily cause the containing method to be type-incorrect. This rule, combined with case analysis and the definitions of the normal Smalltalk control structures, provides automatic type discrimination, as shown in the next example.

The typed method definition of controlToNextLevel for class Controller is shown in Figure 7. The notNil message is defined to return an object of type *True* for all classes except UndefinedObject, for which it is defined to return an object of type *False*. If the type of aView is assumed to be *View* then the type of the expression aView notNil is *True*. The ifTrue: method defined for class True has a type

$$<True>\ ifTrue:\ <Block\ returns:\ P>\ \uparrow <P>$$

where P is a local type variable for the method. Since the type of aView is *View*, the controller and startUp messages are type-correct and P can be mapped to the return type for the actual block argument.

On the other hand, if the type of aView is assumed to be *UndefinedObject* then the type of the expression aView notNil is *False*. Class False defines the ifTrue: method to have type

$$<False>\ ifTrue:\ <P>\ \uparrow <UndefinedObject>$$

so objects of type *False* accept ifTrue: messages with an argument of any type. The method has this type because it ignores its arguments and simply returns

```
{ temporaries: aView <View + UndefinedObject>
  returnType: <Self> }

controlToNextLevel
    "Pass control to the next control level, that is, to the Controller of a subView
    of the receiver's view if possible. The receiver finds the subView (if any)
    whose controller wants control and sends that controller the startUp message."

    | aView |
    aView ← view subViewWantingControl.
    aView notNil ifTrue: [aView controller startUp]
```

Figure 7: The controlToNextLevel method for class Controller.

nil. Since the type of aView is *UndefinedObject*, the controller message is undefined; the body of the block is illegally typed and the block's type is *IllegalBlock*. However, P can be mapped to *IllegalBlock*, so the block can legally be an argument of the ifTrue: message for class False. Thus, the entire method ControlToNextLevel is type-correct.

4.3 Inheritance

One way that inheritance complicates type-checking is that the type of a method for a subclass that inherits it is slightly different from its type in the class that defines it. For example, the type of the receiver is different, and the type of the returned value will be different when the receiver is returned. This problem is solved by referring to the type of the receiver as *Self* and expanding *Self* to the type of the receiver in each subclass. *Self* is not a type, but instead is "macro-expanded" to a type at compile-time.

Abstract classes provide another way in which the type of a method can change when it is inherited. Consider the method definitions shown in Figure 1. The values method is defined in class Change and inherited by the other classes. The return type of values depends on the return type of parameters, which is different for each class. The types of the different parameters methods are

$<Change>$ parameters $\uparrow<Change>$
$<ClassRelatedChange>$ parameters $\uparrow<Symbol>$
$<MethodChange>$ parameters $\uparrow<Array\ of:\ Symbol>$
$<OtherChange>$ parameters $\uparrow<String>$

where the types in "receiver position" are receiver types and the types following the "↑" are return types. Thus, the values method must be recompiled in the context of each subclass of Change to compute its correct return type for that context.

Another way in which abstract classes show that Smalltalk classes inherit implementation, not specification, is that some methods cannot be executed by all of the classes that inherit them. For example, class Collection has a number of methods that use the add: message, such as addAll:, but it does not implement or inherit the add: message itself. Instead, add: is implemented by the various subclasses of Collection. Some of its subclasses, such as Array, do not implement add: and thus cannot use methods like addAll:. Smalltalk relies on run-time type-checking and the "does not understand" error to detect when an undefined message is sent to an object. Our type system detects all such cases at compile-time.

These problems are solved by retype-checking methods in each subclass that inherits them. The method definition (defined in terms of *Self*) is inherited and *Self* is expanded to refer to the current class as described in section 3.6. We assume that the hierarchy of typed class definitions H (see Section 4.1) contains not only the user declared method definitions for a class, but also any methods that can be meaningfully (i.e. type-correctly) inherited by a class. If H_0 is a partial function from $<C,m>$ pairs to method definitions representing user declared methods then H is derived by extending H_0 to include definition points for inherited methods. In other words, if $H_0<C,m>$ is a user defined method then $H<C',m>$ has the same definition provided that C' is a subclass of C and $H_0<C',m>$ is not defined. There are many possible H function. A type-correct H is one in which, for all method types derivable from H, the declared type of $H<C,m>$

is the same as the type inferred by type-checking.

$$\frac{(\vdash <C,m>_d: t) \Longrightarrow (C, \mathcal{A} \vdash <C,m>: t)}{\vdash C, \mathcal{A}}$$

Strictly speaking, if every method definition in $\vec{H}$ must type-check then certain methods in abstract classes must be removed in order to have a type-correct H (e.g. the addAll: method in class Collection).

In practice, inherited methods are type-checked upon demand, i.e. when code is first compiled that might cause that method to be invoked. Array can then be a legitimate subclass of Collection; no inherited code that invokes add: will be type-correct.

The benefits of delaying type-checking of inherited methods is that a method is only retype-checked for every subclass that actually inherits it, and that this type-checking is spread out over a large amount of time. A new class does not require any of the methods that it inherits to be type-checked when it is created. Adding a new method to a superclass does not require type-checking it for every subclass that inherits it, nor does adding a new variable. However, changing the type of a method or variable might require a lot of computation to ensure that each of its uses is still type-correct.

4.4 Specific Receivers

Some classes have methods that can be executed by only a subset of their instances. For example, the whileTrue: message should be sent only to blocks that return Booleans. We can specify this by using the receiverType: field in the type declaration of the method definition as shown in Figure 8. Recall that if this field is omitted then *Self* defaults to the object type for the class in which the method is being compiled. Although whileTrue: is nearly the only method in the Smalltalk-80 class library that needs to declare a specific receiver, it is easy to imagine other methods that would need this feature, such as a summation method in Collection.

4.5 Signature Types

A *signature type* is a type (i.e. a set of object and block types) specified by a set of message types. An object type (or block type) t is included in a signature type s if, for each message type $m \in s$, a message of type m sent to an object of type t is type-correct. In other words, an object type is in a signature type if it "understands each message in the signature."

$$\frac{C, \mathcal{A} \vdash e: t \quad C, \mathcal{A} \vdash \vec{e}: \vec{t} \quad C, \mathcal{A} \vdash (e\ m\ \vec{e}): u}{C, \mathcal{A} \vdash t \sqsubseteq <<m, t \cdot \vec{t} \to u>>}$$

```
{ localTypeVariables: <P>
  receiverType: <Block returns: (True + False)>
  arguments: aBlock <Block returns: P>
  returnType: <UndefinedObject> }

whileTrue: aBlock
    ↑self value
        ifTrue:
            [aBlock value.
             self whileTrue: aBlock]
```

Figure 8: whileTrue: for class BlockContext.

$$\frac{C, \mathcal{A} \vdash t \sqsubseteq <<m, t \cdot \vec{t} \to u>> \quad C, \mathcal{A} \vdash t \sqsubseteq <<m', t' \cdot \vec{t'} \to u'>>}{C, \mathcal{A} \vdash t \sqsubseteq <<m, t \cdot \vec{t} \to u>, <m', t' \cdot \vec{t'} \to u'>>}$$

The message types in a signature type may have occurrences of *Self* to denote the type represented by the signature. Receiver types of *Self* may be omitted. When an object type is being checked for inclusion in a signature type *Self* is instantiated to the object type.

A signature type includes object types belonging to classes not yet created. Thus, signature types contain an infinite number of object types. In fact, the type specified by an empty signature contains every possible object type, since every object type understands every message type in the signature.

$$C, \mathcal{A} \vdash t \sqsubseteq <>$$

Since signature types specify the largest possible types, procedures that use them exhibit the most polymorphism and so are the most flexible. However, use of signature types prevents the compiler from performing some important kinds of optimizations, since they do not provide enough information about the class of the receiver to allow compile-time binding of message sends.

A signature type is specified by a special kind of type declaration.

$$<understands:\ \#(tm1\ tm2\ \ldots)>$$

Here, the *tm*'s are strings containing message type specifications. An example will be given shortly. Signature types may also be used to restrict the range of type variables. A local type variable with a signature range would have a declaration of the form

$$<P\ understands:\ \#(tm1\ tm2\ \ldots)>.$$

```
{   receiverType: <Self>
    arguments: anObject <understands: #('= <ElementType> ↑<False + True>')>
    temporaries: tally <SmallInteger>
    blockArguments: each <ElementType>
    returnType: <SmallInteger> }

occurrencesOf: anObject
    "Answer how many of the receiver's elements are equal to anObject."

    | tally |
    tally ← 0.
    self do: [:each | anObject = each ifTrue: [tally ← tally + 1]].
    ↑tally
```

Figure 9: The occurrencesOf: method in class Collection.

Since such declarations may be recursive, complex mutually recursive signature types can be built.

As an example, consider the occurrencesOf: method for class Collection shown in Figure 9. The only restriction placed on the type of the argument anObject is that its corresponding class (or classes) must implement (or inherit) an = (equality) message that will take an argument of type *ElementType* and return a boolean. It is helpful to compare the use of the do: message in this example with its definition in Figure 5.

Type-checking a message send to a receiver whose type is a signature type is straightforward since all relevant type information is contained in the signature type.

$$\frac{\mathcal{C}, \mathcal{A} \vdash e : < \ldots < m, \vec{t}\,' \to u' > \ldots >}{\mathcal{C}, \mathcal{A} \vdash \vec{e} : \vec{t} \quad \mathcal{C}.\vec{t} \sqsubseteq \vec{t}\,' \vdash u' \sqsubseteq u}{\mathcal{C}, \mathcal{A} \vdash (e\ m\ \vec{e}) : u}$$

5 Beyond Signatures

The type system described so far, with explicit union types, case analysis, and signature types, is quite powerful. However, there are still some methods that elude type-checking.

Although Smalltalk is a typeless language, it is possible to discriminate between classes of objects and provide a simple kind of explicit run-time type-checking. An example is the isLookupKey message whose implementation is shown in Figure 10. Messages like isLookupKey can be used in a method to "type-check" an argument before sending it a message that it might not understand.

A example of this style of programming is the = (equality) message shown in Figure 11. Equality must be defined between any two objects and should not be subject to run-time errors. This style of implementation meets both of these criteria. The problem is how to type-check such a method.

The type of this method can be roughly stated as follows. An argument must understand the isLookupKey message. If an argument responds to this message with true then it must also understand the key message and the method will (presumedly) return an object of type *True + False*, otherwise the method returns an object of type *False*.

In general, the type of a polymorphic method like = is complicated, but its type for a specific use is simple and easy to understand. Thus, type-checking a method defers some of the type-checking for a method until its invocations are type-checked. It doesn't matter when a method is type-checked, only that type-checking is completed before any code that invokes the method is executed.

When a send of = to a LookupKey needs to be type-checked, the code in Figure 11 is substituted for the call. The types of the actual arguments then replace those of the formal arguments, allowing both definition and use information to be used in type-checking. This usually permits the = method to be type-checked completely. If not, then type-checking for the method that sends = must also be deferred. This static analysis technique has proven useful for type-inference as well as for type-checking [Gra89].

```
class Object:

    isLookupKey
        ↑false


class LookupKey:

    isLookupKey
        ↑true
```

Figure 10: Implementation of isLookupKey.

```
= aLookupKey

    aLookupKey isLookupKey
        ifTrue: [↑self key = aLookupKey key]
        ifFalse: [↑false]
```

Figure 11: = (equality) in class LookupKey.

6 Type Safety

A type system can only be shown correct relative to a formal definition of the language. This section outlines a proof of correctness for the type system relative to Kamin's denotational semantics of Smalltalk [Kam88].

Usually a type is described as a set of objects. Type safety then means that the value of an expression is always contained in its type. However, our types are not sets of objects, so a different definition of type safety is needed. We will define type safety by assigning an object type to each object and then showing that the value of an expression always is assigned a type contained in the expression's type.

The type of an object depends not only on its current state but also on its past and future states. Thus, it may not be possible to decide whether an object is in a particular type, though it is often possible to show that it is not. For example, a Set is never in *Array of: Character*, and a Set containing Characters is not in *Set of: SmallInteger*. However, it is not easy to tell whether a Set containing only Characters is in *Set of: (SmallInteger + Character)*—it all depends on whether or not the Set is referenced by a variable that *requires* it to contain only Characters.

Definition 1 (Object/type consistency) *An object o is consistent with a mapping from objects to types ξ, relative to a class hierarchy H, and a state ψ, if*

1. $\xi(o) = \mathtt{C}(\vec{t})$,

2. *the class of o is C, and*

3. *for each instance variable x_i of o, let t_i be the declared type of x_i with type variables replaced by the types given in $\xi(o)$. Then the type of the object referred to by x_i is a subtype of t_i.*

If each object had a type assigned to it then we could check whether an object was consistent with its type by checking whether its class was consistent with its type and whether the types assigned to the values of its instance variables were included in the declared types of its instance variables. This assignment would be consistent if every object was consistent with the type assigned to it. Although this type-assignment might not be unique, any consistent type-assignment could be thought of as describing the types of all objects. These ideas are formalized in Definition 1.

A state is consistent with a type-assignment ξ if every object in the state is consistent with ξ.

Proposition: *If a type-correct program is in a state that is consistent with a type assignment ξ then any succeeding state will be consistent with ξ.*

The only way that a consistent type-assignment can become inconsistent is if the state changes. This is because the type-assignment itself is constant and, in Kamin's semantics, objects never change and the class hierarchy does not change. Thus, we can prove the proposition by showing that ξ is maintained as an invariant every place where the state can be changed.

There are two ways that the state changes in Kamin's semantics. The first is when a variable changes its value. This happens in an assignment statement and in assigning arguments to formal parameters when evaluating a method or block.

The second way that the state changes is when a new object is created. The type of some new objects, such as new blocks, are known in advance so the new object will always be of the correct type. Unfortunately, problems occur with the new primitive and when creating a new context to evaluate a method. This is because instance variables of new objects and local variables of new contexts are both initialized to nil, but the types of these variables usually do not include *UndefinedObject*. Thus, until the variables are initialized, their value is not consistent with their type. We ensure type-safety by requiring all variables whose types do not include *UndefinedObject* to be assigned before they are read, and use flow analysis to check this. Thus, we will change the statement of the proposition slightly.

Type-Safety Theorem: *If a type-correct program is in a state that is consistent with a type assignment ξ except for unassigned variables, and if a variable is always assigned before it is read, then any succeeding state will be consistent with ξ.*

Proof: In a type-correct program, the type of the expression of an assignment statement must be included in the type of the variable, so, if each expression returns a value that is consistent with its type then assignment statements maintain the consistency of the type-assignment. Once a variable is assigned, its value will have a type that is included in the type of the variable. Thus, if the value of any expression has a type that is included in the type of the expression then whenever a variable v is read, the type of the value of v will be consistent with the type of v.

The theorem is proved by structural induction on the number of message sends in the evaluation of an expression. The base case is where there are no message sends. Since there are no message sends there can only be assignment statements, whose right-hand sides are literals or variables. The variables either are type-consistent or will be assigned before they are read, so the assignment statements will all maintain the consistency of the type-assignment.

The induction step is to assume that any expression that can be evaluated in $n-1$ message sends (or less) is type-safe and to prove that evaluating an expression

$$\text{rcv k1: exp}_1 \text{ k2: exp}_2 \ldots \text{km: exp}_m$$

that requires n message sends is type-safe. Since an expression must be type-checked before it can be evaluated, we know that the types of the argument expressions to the k1:k2:...km: message are included in the types of the formal parameters of the method that is invoked. Evaluating any $\exp_i$ will take less than n message sends, so each argument is consistent with its corresponding type. When the new context is created and the method is executed, the formal parameters of the method will be bound to objects whose type is included in the type of the parameter. Methods also create temporary variables, but they are unassigned, so invoking a method maintains the consistency of the type-assignment (except for unassigned variables).

We assumed that the expression involves n message sends. One of them is the k1:k2:...km: message, so evaluating the body of the method will involve less than n message sends. Thus, every expression evaluation in it will result in an object whose type is included in the type of the expression that produced it. In particular, the type of the object returned from the method will be included in the type of the expression in the return statement, and, according to the type-checking rules for the return statement, the type of the expression in a return statement must be included in the declared return type of the method. Thus, the type of the object returned as a result of the k1:k2:...km: message will be included in the return type of the method.

The type of

$$\text{rcv k1: exp}_1 \text{ k2: exp}_2 \ldots \text{km: exp}_m$$

is the union of the return types of a number of methods, but it certainly includes the return type of the method that was invoked. Thus, the result of the expression, which is the object being returned by the method, has a type that is included in the type of the expression. ∎

Type-safety also depends on all the primitives being given correct types. Since primitives are written in a language other than Smalltalk, it is impossible to reason about them within the framework presented here. A few primitives are inherently unsafe. These are primarily used by the debugger. Most of the primitives have simple types, however.

7 Conclusion

Our type system for Smalltalk is type-safe. It has been implemented in Smalltalk and used in the TS optimizing compiler for Smalltalk [JGZ88]. It has been able to solve most type-checking problems in the standard Smalltalk-80 class hierarchy. Thus, it is correct, useful, and usable.

Our type system is also unique. It differs from other type systems for object-oriented programming languages by acknowledging that only implementation is inherited, not specification, and by handling case analysis of union types automatically.

Our type system is more complicated than other type systems for object-oriented programming languages. Whether this complication is justified depends partly on whether a new language is being defined or whether a type system is being defined for Smalltalk. Current Smalltalk programming practice requires a type system like ours.

Acknowlegements

This research was supported by NSF contract CCR-8715752, by the AT&T ISEP grant, and by an equipment grant from Tektronix.

References

[BHJL86] Andrew Black, Norman Hutchinson, Eric Jul, and Henry Levy. Object structure in the Emerald system. In *Proceedings of OOPSLA '86*, pages 78–86, November 1986. printed as SIGPLAN Notices, 21(11).

[BI82] A. H. Borning and D. H. H. Ingalls. A type declaration and inference system for Smalltalk. In *Conference Record of the Ninth Annual ACM Symposium on Principles of Programming Languages*, pages 133–139, 1982.

[Car84] Luca Cardelli. A semantics of multiple inheritance. In *Semantics of Data Types, Lecture Notes in Computer Science, n. 173*, pages 51–67, Springer-Verlag, 1984.

[Car85] Luca Cardelli. Amber. In *Combinators and Functional Programming Languages, Proceedings of the 13th Summer School of the LITP*, Le Val d'Ajol, Vosges (France), May 1985.

[CUL89] Craig Chambers, David Ungar, and Elgin Lee. An efficient implementation of Self, a dynamically-typed object-oriented language based on prototypes. In *Proceedings of OOPSLA '89*, pages 49–70, October 1989. printed as SIGPLAN Notices, 24(10).

[CW85] Luca Cardelli and Peter Wegner. On understanding types, data abstraction, and polymorphism. *Computing Surveys*, 17(4):471–522, December 1985.

[Deu81] L. Peter Deutsch. Building control structures in the Smalltalk-80 system. *Byte*, 6(8):322–347, August 1981.

[DT88] Scott Danforth and Chris Tomlinson. Type theories and object-oriented programming. *Computing Surveys*, 20(1):29–72, March 1988.

[GR83] Adele Goldberg and David Robson. *Smalltalk-80: The Language and its Implementation*. Addison-Wesley, Reading, Massachusetts, 1983.

[Gra89] Justin Graver. *Type-Checking and Type-Inference for Object-Oriented Programming Languages*. PhD thesis, University of Illinois at Urbana-Champaign, 1989.

[JF88] Ralph E. Johnson and Brian Foote. Designing reusable classes. *Journal of Object-Oriented Programming*, 1(2):22–35, 1988.

[JGZ88] Ralph E. Johnson, Justin O. Graver, and Lawrence W. Zurawski. TS: An optimizing compiler for Smalltalk. In *Proceedings of OOPSLA '88*, pages 18–26, November 1988. printed as SIGPLAN Notices, 23(11).

[Joh86] Ralph E. Johnson. Type-checking Smalltalk. In *Proceedings of OOPSLA '86*, pages 315–321, November 1986. printed as SIGPLAN Notices, 21(11).

[Kam88] Samuel Kamin. Inheritance in Smalltalk-80: A denotational definition. In *Conference Record of the Fifteenth Annual ACM Symposium on Principles of Programming Languages*, pages 80–87, 1988.

[Mey88] Bertrand Meyer. *Object-oriented Software Construction*. Prentice Hall, 1988.

[MS82] David MacQueen and Ravi Sethi. A higher order polymorphic type system for applicative languages. In *ACM Symposium of LISP and Functional Programming*, pages 243–252, 1982.

[SCB*86] Craig Schaffert, Topher Cooper, Bruce Bullis, Mike Kilian, and Carrie Wilpolt. An introduction to Trellis/Owl. In *Proceedings of OOPSLA '86*, pages 9–16, November 1986. printed as SIGPLAN Notices, 21(11).

[Str86] Bjarne Stroustrup. *The C++ Programming Language*. Addison-Wesley Publishing Co., Reading, MA, 1986.

[Suz81] Norihisa Suzuki. Inferring types in Smalltalk. In *Conference Record of the Eighth Annual ACM Symposium on Principles of Programming Languages*, pages 187–199, 1981.

A Relationship Between Abstract Interpretation and Projection Analysis (Extended Abstract)*

G L Burn

Department of Computing
Imperial College
180 Queens Gate
London SW7 2BZ
United Kingdom

Abstract

Abstract interpretation and projection analysis are two techniques for finding out information about lazy functional programs. Two typical uses of these techniques are speeding up sequential implementations, and the introduction of parallelism into parallel implementations.

Our main result is the proof of a relationship between a certain class of projections and a certain class of abstract interpretations.

One of the claims of projection analysis is that it can find out information about head-strictness, whilst abstract interpretation cannot. We show that there are at least two intuitive notions of head-strictness, and that one of them can be determined using abstract interpretation.

1 Introduction

A number of analyses have been developed which find out information about programs. The methods that have been developed fall broadly into two classes, those based on the ideas of abstract interpretation (e.g. [8, 4, 7, 6, 2]), and those based on projections (e.g. [9]), although some work has been done on inverse image analysis ([5]).

The analysis techniques have mostly been applied to finding out information about the definedness of functions. This information has then been used to make more efficient implementations of functional programs. For example, the information can be used to compile code that builds less closures when executing a program on a sequential machine. On a parallel machine, it has been used to indicate which parts of a functional program can be evaluated in parallel.

When abstract interpretation and projection analysis are applied to the problem of finding out definedness information about functions, the results are intuitively very similar. The main theorem of this paper, Theorem 3.1, gives a formal relationship between abstract interpretation and projection analysis. This gives us another piece of information to help decide which analysis technique is the more useful.

Wadler and Hughes cite the fact that projection analysis can determine information about *head-strictness* as one of their main reasons for developing the technique [9, p. 388]. We show that there are at least two different notions of head-strictness. Although the notions are overlapping, each is able to determine information the other cannot. One type of head-strictness can be determined by abstract interpretation and projection analysis. Unfortunately Theorem 3.1 does not tell us whether or not the notion of head-strictness defined in [9] can be determined using abstract interpretation.

For simplicity of exposition, we will give all of our results in terms of functions of one argument; they can easily be generalised. We will use the framework for abstract interpretation from [2] when discussing abstract interpretation.

2 Some Preliminary Definitions, Facts and Lemmata

The main theorem of this paper relies on a number of definitions, facts and lemmata, given in this section. Some of the definitions are standard, some are taken from [9] or from [2], and some are new to this paper. In

---

*Research partially funded by ESPRIT Project 415: Parallel Architectures and Languages for AIP - A VLSI-Directed Approach. This work was completed whilst the author was working at the GEC Hirst Research Centre, East Lane, Wembley, Middx HA9 7PP, United Kingdom.

the full version of this paper, proofs of the lemmata will be given. The main theorem states a general relationship between abstract interpretations satisfying certain constraints, and a class of projections. As an example of the use of this theorem, we will show the relationship between abstract interpretation and projections for lists. The definitions of the abstract domains and projections are given in Section 2.2.

2.1 General Definitions and Results

For each type, a domain which contains all of the elements of that type must be given. In [2], two domains are given for each type. If σ is a type, then D_σ^{st} is the domain which is the standard interpretation of the type. This is the domain in which the normal semantics of an expression of that type is given a value. The domain for the abstract interpretation of the type is denoted by D_σ^{ab}.

In order to capture the concept of a function *needing* to evaluate an argument (to a certain extent), Wadler and Hughes introduced a new domain element called $\mathbf{7}$, which was less defined than $\bot$. Adding new domain element in this way can be formalised using domain *lifting*.

Definition 2.1

If σ is a type, then we denote the lifted type by $lift\ \sigma$.

The function *lift* can be applied to domains and functions*. If D_σ^I is the I-interpretation (either the standard or abstract interpretation) of the type σ, then $lift\ D_\sigma^I$ is the I-interpretation of the type $lift\ \sigma$. If D is a domain, then the elements of $lift\ D$ are $\{\bot_{lift\ D}\} \bigcup \{<0,d> | d \in D\}$. The ordering on the domain is defined by :

$$\begin{array}{lll} \bot_{lift\ D} & \sqsubseteq d & \forall d \in (lift\ D) \\ <0,\ d> & \sqsubseteq <0,\ d'> & \text{iff } d \sqsubseteq d' \end{array}$$

If $f : \sigma \to \tau$, then $lift\ f : lift\ \sigma \to lift\ \tau$, where $lift\ f$ is defined by :

$$\begin{array}{ll} (lift\ f)\ \bot_{lift\ D_\sigma^I} & = \bot_{lift\ D_\tau^I} \\ (lift\ f)\ <0,d> & =<0,\ f\ d> \end{array}$$

Definition 2.2

- A function α is a *projection* if it is idempotent and less than the identity, that is, $\alpha \circ \alpha = \alpha$, and $\alpha \sqsubseteq ID$, where ID is the identity function.

---
*$lift$ is a functor over the category of domains.

- A projection $\alpha : lift\ \sigma \to lift\ \sigma$ is *lift-strict* if

$$\alpha\ <0, \bot_{D_\sigma^I}> = \bot_{lift\ D_\sigma^I}.^\dagger$$

The greatest lift-strict projection is STR, defined by

$$\begin{array}{lll} STR\ \bot_{lift\ D_\sigma^I} & = & \bot_{lift\ D_\sigma^I} \\ STR\ <0, \bot_{D_\sigma^I}> & = & \bot_{lift\ D_\sigma^I} \\ STR\ u & = & u \text{ if } <0, \bot_{D_\sigma^I}> \sqsubset u \end{array}$$

For any projection $\alpha : lift\ \sigma \to lift\ \sigma$, the corresponding lift-strict projection is $STR \circ \alpha$. For any projection $\alpha : \sigma \to \sigma$, where σ is not a lifted domain, the corresponding lift-strict projection is $STR \circ (lift\ \alpha)$. The lift-strict projection corresponding to a projection α will be denoted by α^S.[‡] Clearly, if α is a lift-strict projection, then $\alpha^S = \alpha$.

- A projection $\alpha : \sigma \to \sigma$ is a *smash* projection if either $\alpha\ u = \bot_{D_\sigma^I}$ or $\alpha\ u = u$.

Definition 2.3

- If α is a projection, f a function and $f \circ \alpha = f$, then we will say that f is α-*strict* in its argument.

- If α and β are projections, f a function and $\beta \circ f \circ \alpha = \beta \circ f$, then we will say that f is α-strict in a β context, and write it $f : \beta \Rightarrow \alpha$.

Given a strict abstraction map for each base type, the theory of [2, Chapters 2 and 5] defines abstraction and concretisation maps for all types. An abstraction map, abs_σ, sends a value in the standard interpretation of the type σ to its representation in the abstract domain. Concretisation is a sort of inverse to abstraction, roughly returning the "set" of elements which abstract to something less than or equal to the value being concretised. We will write the concretisation map for the type σ as $Conc_\sigma$. The abstraction map for the type $\sigma \to \tau$ is given below, because we will need it for defining the abstract interpretation of a projection.

Definition 2.4

$$abs_{\sigma \to \tau}\ f = \lambda \bar{s}. \bigsqcup \{abs_\tau\ f\ s\ |\ s \in Conc_\sigma(\bar{s})\}^\circ$$

([2, Proposition 2.3.3]) where $\bigsqcup$ is the least upper bound operator and $^\circ$ is the Hoare powerdomain closure operator (which is an inconsequential technicality for this paper).

[†]In [9], such projections are simply called *strict*. However, we feel that this is a confusing use of terminology, especially when projections are recast into a world using lifted domains.

[‡]This is different from the convention of [9], where lift-strict projections are primed.

Notation If u is some value, then we will denote the abstract interpretation of u by $\overline{u}$.

Definition 2.5

If α is a projection of type $\sigma \to \sigma$, then we define its abstract interpretation by
$$\overline{\alpha} = abs_{\sigma \to \sigma} \alpha$$

Definition 2.6

A function f is *bottom-reflecting* ($\perp$-*reflecting*) if $f\ u = \perp$ implies $u = \perp$, that is, $\perp$ is the only value which f may map to $\perp$.

If all the abstraction maps for the base types are $\perp$-reflecting, then abstraction is $\perp$-reflecting for all types [2, Lemma 2.4.4].

Important Restriction We will only consider $\perp$-reflecting abstraction maps.

Definition 2.7

Suppose that α is a projection of type $\sigma \to \sigma$. Then an abstract domain point $\overline{u} \in D_\sigma^{ab}$ and a projection $\alpha : \sigma \to \sigma$ are *related* if $\forall u \in Conc_\sigma(\overline{u})$, $\alpha\ u = \perp_{D_\sigma^{st}}$, and $\forall u \notin Conc_\sigma(\overline{u})$, $\alpha\ u = u$. Note that such an α is also a smash projection.

Lemma 2.8

Suppose that a projection $\alpha : \sigma \to \sigma$ is related to $\overline{u}$. Then $\overline{\alpha}\ \overline{u} = \perp_{D_\sigma^{ab}}$, and for all $\overline{u'}, \overline{u'} \sqsupseteq \overline{u}, \overline{u'} \neq \overline{u}$, $\overline{\alpha}\ \overline{u'} \neq \perp_{D_\sigma^{ab}}$.

Lemma 2.9

If $f : \beta \Rightarrow \alpha$, and α is a lift-strict projection, then β is also a lift-strict projection.

Fact 2.10

For all types σ, $Conc_\sigma \perp_{D_\sigma^{ab}} = \{\perp_{D_\sigma^{st}}\}$ [2, Lemma 2.4.7, Fact 5.5.3].

The standard interpretation semantic function is denoted by E^{st}, and the semantic function for the abstract interpretation is denoted by E^{ab}. Throughout the paper, when we refer to a function f, we will generally be referring to its standard interpretation.

Fact 2.11

If $f : \sigma \to \tau$ and $abs \circ \rho^{st} \sqsubseteq \rho^{ab}$ and $(E^{ab}\ [\![f]\!]\ \rho^{ab})\ \overline{s} = \overline{t}$, then for all $s \in Conc_\sigma\ \overline{s}$, $(E^{st}\ [\![f]\!]\ \rho^{st})\ s \in Conc_\tau\ \overline{t}$ [2, Theorem 2.7.1, Theorem 5.6.3].

Fact 2.12

$\overline{f \circ g} \sqsubseteq \overline{f} \circ \overline{g}$ [2, Proposition 2.6.1].

2.2 An Application : Lists

We are interested in the five projections ID, T, H, H_B, and $T \circ H$, and their lift-strict versions. ID is the identity function, and T, H, and H_B will be defined below; T and H were originally defined in [9].[§] If A is some type, then we are interested in *Alists*, which are lists of elements of type A.

Definition 2.13

$$T\ u = \begin{cases} \perp & \text{if } u \in \{D_A^{st\ *}.\perp_{D_{Alist}^{st}}\} \bigcup \{D_A^{st\ \omega}\} \\ u, & \text{otherwise} \end{cases}$$

$$\begin{aligned}
H\ \perp_{D_{Alist}^{st}} &= \perp_{D_{Alist}^{st}} \\
H\ cons\ \perp_{D_A^{st}}\ e &= \perp_{D_{Alist}^{st}} \\
H\ cons\ u\ e &= cons\ u\ (H\ e),\ u \neq \perp_{D_A^{st}} \\
H\ nil &= nil
\end{aligned}$$

$$\begin{aligned}
H_B\ \perp_{D_{Alist}^{st}} &= \perp_{D_{Alist}^{st}} \\
H_B\ cons\ \perp_{D_A^{st}}\ e &= \perp_{D_{Alist}^{st}} \\
H_B\ cons\ u\ e &= cons\ u\ e,\ u \neq \perp_{D_A^{st}} \\
H_B\ nil &= nil
\end{aligned}$$

Both H and H_B capture notions of head-strictness. Intuitively, a function being H-strict means that, if it needs to evaluate the list, then it needs to evaluate the head as well, and the tail of the list is in an H-strict context, whilst being H_B-strict means that, if it needs to evaluate the list, then it needs to evaluate the head as well. The relationship between H and H_B is discussed further in Section 5.

We use the abstract domain shown in Figure 1 for the abstract interpretation of lists. With this domain we distinguish lists which have an undefined head from those which do not, in order to capture the intuitive notion that a function is head-strict if it returns returns $\perp$ when applied to a list with an undefined head. If we coalesce the points 1 and 2, and the points 3, 4 and 5, then we get the abstract domain of [10].

We now define the abstraction map for lists of elements of type A.

Definition 2.14

[§]There is an error in the definition of T in [9]. In order for T to be continuous, it must map infinite lists to $\perp$, as above, but this is not the case in their definition.

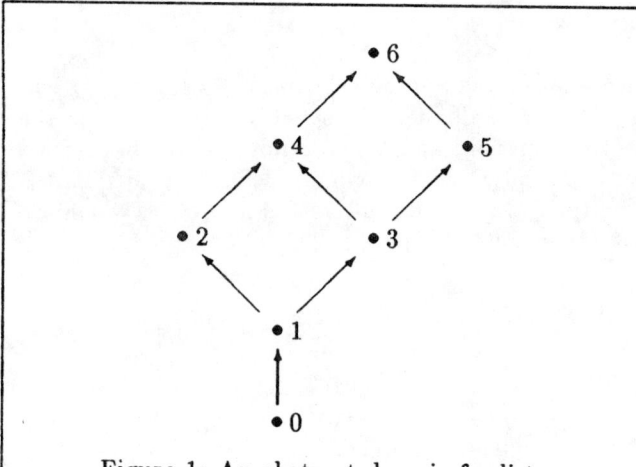

Figure 1: An abstract domain for lists

If $u \in D^{st}_{Alist}$, $abs_{Alist}\ u$ has the value:

0   if $u = \bot_{D^{st}_{Alist}}$
1   if $u \in \{\bot_{D^{st}_A}.D^{st}_A{}^*.\bot_{D^{st}_{Alist}}\} \bigcup \{\bot_{D^{st}_A}.D^{st}_A{}^\omega\}$
2   if $u \in \{(D^{st}_A - \bot_{D^{st}_A}).D^{st}_A{}^*.\bot_{D^{st}_{Alist}}\}$
           $\bigcup\{(D^{st}_A - \bot_{D^{st}_A}).D^{st}_A{}^\omega\}$
3   if $u \in \{\bot_{D^{st}_A}.D^{st}_A{}^*.nil\}$
4   if $u \in \{(D^{st}_A - \bot_{D^{st}_A}).D^{st}_A{}^*.\bot_{D^{st}_A}.D^{st}_A{}^*.nil\}$
5   if $u \in \{\bot_{D^{st}_A}.(D^{st}_A - \bot_{D^{st}_A})^*.nil\}$
6   if $u \in \{(D^{st}_A - \bot_{D^{st}_A})^*.nil\}$

This abstraction map is clearly strict, continuous and $\bot$-reflecting, as required by the theory.

Fact 2.15

The projection ID is related to 0, $ID^S (= STR)$ is related to $<0, 0>$, T is related to 2, T^S is related to $<0, 2>$, $T \circ H$ is related to 4, $(T \circ H)^S$ is related to $<0, 4>$, H_B is related to 5, and H_B^S is related to $<0, 5>$.

3 The Main Theorem

The main theorem of this paper states a strong relationship between abstract interpretations using $\bot$-reflecting abstraction maps and projection analyses using smash projections.

Theorem 3.1

Suppose that $f : \sigma \to \tau$, that $\overline{u}$ is related to $\alpha : \sigma \to \sigma$ and that $\overline{v}$ is related to $\beta : \tau \to \tau$. Then

1. *$f : \beta \Rightarrow \alpha$ and f strict implies $\overline{f}\,\overline{u} \sqsubseteq \overline{v}$.*
2. *$\overline{f}\,\overline{u} \sqsubseteq \overline{v}$ implies $f : \beta \Rightarrow \alpha$.*

Proof

1. Suppose f is strict and $f : \beta \Rightarrow \alpha$. Then $\beta \circ f = \beta \circ f \circ \alpha$ implies

$$\begin{aligned}\overline{\beta}\,(\overline{f}\,\overline{u}) &\sqsubseteq \overline{\beta}\,(\overline{f}\,(\overline{\alpha}\,\overline{u})) & \text{Fact 2.12}\\ &= \overline{\beta}\,(\overline{f}\,\bot_{D^{ab}_\sigma}) & \text{Lemma 2.8}\\ &= \overline{\beta}\,\bot_{D^{ab}_\tau} & \text{since } f \text{ is strict}\\ &= \bot_{D^{ab}_\tau} & \text{Lemma 2.8.}\end{aligned}$$

Therefore, since β is related to $\overline{v}$, by Lemma 2.8, we have that $\overline{f}\,\overline{u} \sqsubseteq \overline{v}$.

2. Suppose $\overline{f}\,\overline{u} \sqsubseteq \overline{v}$. Then there are two cases to consider.

- $u \in Conc_\sigma(\overline{u})$:

$$\begin{aligned}\overline{\beta}\,(f\,u) &\sqsubseteq \overline{\beta}\,(\overline{f}\,\overline{u}) & \text{Fact 2.12}\\ &\sqsubseteq \overline{\beta}\,\overline{v} & \text{assumption}\\ &= \bot_{D^{ab}_\tau} & \text{Lemma 2.8}\end{aligned}$$

Therefore $\beta\,(f\,u) = \bot_{D^{st}_\tau}$ (by Fact 2.10), and since $\beta \circ f \circ \alpha \sqsubseteq \beta \circ f$, $\beta\,(f\,(\alpha\,u)) = \bot_{D^{st}_\tau}$. Hence $\forall u \in Conc_\sigma(\overline{u}), (\beta \circ f \circ \alpha)\,u = (\beta \circ f)\,u\ (= \bot_{D^{st}_\tau})$.

- $u \notin Conc_\sigma(\overline{u})$: This is trivial, for in this case $\alpha\,u = u$.

$\square$

Unfortunately there is an asymmetry in the theorem, which cannot be removed. If $f : \beta \Rightarrow \alpha$ and f is not strict, then it is not necessarily true that $\overline{f}\,\overline{u} \sqsubseteq \overline{v}$. For example, if $\alpha = T$ and $\beta = ID$, then the function f, defined below, is $f : ID \Rightarrow T$, and not strict, but $\overline{f}\,2 = 6$, not 0 (which is related to ID).

$$f\ xs = [\ ]$$

It is also not necessarily true that $\overline{f}\,\overline{u} \sqsubseteq \overline{v}$ implies that f is strict. This can be seen by considering the function f defined below, which is not strict.

$$f\ xs = append\ [\ ]\ xs$$

We can only conclude that a function is strict if there exists a $\overline{u}$ such that $\overline{f}\,\overline{u} \sqsubseteq \bot$.

There are two major questions left unanswered by Theorem 3.1. Firstly, part 1 of the theorem indicates that some functions may be α-strict in a β-strict context, but not strict. Is this information useful to an implementation? If it is not, then abstract interpretation and projection analysis can be used interchangeably when the particular abstract interpretation and projections are related. We show in the next section that it is useful to know that $f : \beta \Rightarrow \alpha$ when f is not strict. Secondly, the projection H is not a smash projection. What is the relationship between H_B and H?

4 Non-strict Projections

The function f defined below is like the *length* function, but it is non-strict in its first argument because it only evaluates it when its second argument is non-zero; it is T-strict (in an ID-strict context), but not strict, in its first argument. It is easily seen that this is useful information for an implementation. Intuitively, the sequential pragmatics associated with a function being T-strict say that in an application of the function, if the argument is evaluated, then the whole structure of the list has to be evaluated. Therefore, code can be generated which initially creates a closure for the argument expression. If the closure is evaluated, then the whole of the structure of the list can be evaluated without creating any closures for the tails. (The companion paper, [3], formalises this notion and gives compilation rules.) If the information that f is T-strict but not strict is ignored, then the evaluation of an application of f will have to create closures for all of the tails of the list.

$$f\ xs\ y = \quad if\ y = 0\ then\ 0$$
$$\quad else\ if\ (null\ xs)\ then\ 0$$
$$\quad else\ 1 + (f\ (tl\ xs)\ y)$$

Therefore, it is useful to know that a non-strict function f is α-strict in a β-strict context. In fact, there is an exact characterisation for what it means to be α-strict in a β-strict context, but not strict, which has a nice interpretation in terms of an implementation (see [3]).

5 Head Strictness

Because of the fact that $H \sqsubseteq H_B$, we have the following two theorems.

Theorem 5.1

If f is H_B-strict, then it is not necessarily true that f is H-strict.

Proof

The function f defined below is H_B-strict but not H-strict.

$$f\ xs = (hd\ xs) + (length\ xs)$$

□

Theorem 5.2

If $f : H_B \Rightarrow \alpha$ and $f : H \Rightarrow \beta$, then it is not necessarily true that $\alpha \sqsubseteq \beta$.

Proof

Consider the function *append*, defined by :

$$append\ [] \quad ys = ys$$
$$append\ (x : xs)\ ys = x : (append\ xs\ ys)$$

The function *append* is H-strict but not strict in its second argument in an H-strict context ([9, p. 403]), but is only ID-strict in its second argument in an H_B-strict context.

□

Theorems 5.1 and 5.2 tell us that it is useful to have the information from both H and H_B, because each is able to give information the other is not. The two types of head-strict projection cannot be dispensed with in an implementation either; that H_B is needed, can be seen from the example in Theorem 5.1, and the need for the pragmatics for H can be seen from the function f defined below.

$$f\ [\,] \quad = \quad [\,]$$
$$f\ (x : xs) \quad = \quad if\ x = 0\ then\ [\,]$$
$$\quad else\ if\ (null\ xs)\ then\ [\,]$$
$$\quad else\ f\ xs$$

Informally, the sequential pragmatics for the argument to an H-strict function, which is being evaluated, is to create a *cons* with an evaluated head and whose tail is in an H-strict context, whilst H_B does not do anything to the tail. In the above example, using the pragmatics associated with H will cause all of the evaluated *cons* cells to be created with evaluated heads, whilst the pragmatics associated with H_B will only cause this to happen for the first *cons*. In a companion paper, [3], we formalise these intuitions in a more general framework.

6 Conclusion

In this paper we have shown that there is a strong relationship between abstract interpretations using $\bot$-reflecting abstraction maps and smash projections. In fact, projections give us strictly more information because the abstract interpretation result always implies the projection result, but the reverse implication is only true when the function in question is also strict. We showed in Section 4 that this extra information is useful in an implementation. Of course, there are other sorts of projections and abstraction maps, and it is not clear if there is any more general relationship between the two analysis techniques, or their relative power.

We have also introduced a second notion of head-strictness, besides the one in [9]. Although they are overlapping notions, we showed that each is able to find out information that the other is not. This means that both are useful in doing the analysis of a program and in the implementation.

There are however two ways that abstract interpretation is more powerful than the current state-of-the-art in projection analysis. Firstly, abstract interpretation is able to find out information about higher-order functions, see [4, 2, 6] for example. Secondly, the definition of the abstract interpretation can be implemented exactly, that is, the abstract interpretation is like a set of rules which can be impelmented exactly. However, determining the exact projection transformers for a function is probably equivalent to the halting problem. It is unclear from the inference rules for determining projection transformers, given in [9], just how much information is lost in the process. It is also unclear how comparitively efficient implementations of the two analysis techniques are.

In the companion paper, [3], we show how the information from projection analysis can be used to make more efficient implementations on sequential machines, or to introduce parallelism for a parallel machine. This work builds on the concepts of *evaluators* and *evaluation transformers* introduced in [2, 1].

There are obviously strong relationships between abstract interpretation and projection analysis, and inverse image analysis [5]. We have yet to investigate the relationship between the first two and the third.

7 Acknowledgements

I would like to thank the following people for their help. Phil Wadler and I had extensive discussions about head-strictness. John Hughes suggested that I should use lifting to make the presentation of the results clearer. Serendipitously, the theory is now more sound. Chris Hankin made some helpful comments on various drafts of this work. David Lester and I have had a number of discussions on the subject matter of this paper.

This work was partially funded by ESPRIT Project 415 - Parallel Architectures and Languages for AIP - A VLSI-Directed Approach.

References

[1] G. L. Burn. Evaluation transformers – A model for the parallel evaluation of functional languages (extended abstract). In G. Kahn, editor, *Proceedings of the Functional Programming Languages and Computer Architecture Conference*, pages 446–470. Springer-Verlag LNCS 274, September 1987.

[2] G.L. Burn. *Abstract Interpretation and the Parallel Evaluation of Functional Languages*. PhD thesis, Imperial College, University of London, March 1987.

[3] G.L. Burn. Using projection analysis in executing lazy functional programs. Draft Manuscript, July 1989.

[4] G.L. Burn, C.L. Hankin, and S. Abramsky. Strictness analysis of higher-order functions. *Science of Computer Programming*, 7:249–278, November 1986.

[5] P. Dybjer. Inverse image analysis. In *Proceedings of the 14th International Colloquium on Automata, Languages and Programming*, Karlsruhe, Germany, July 1987. Springer-Verlag LNCS 267.

[6] P Hudak and J Young. Higher order strictnesss analysis in untyped lambda calculus. In *Proceedings of 12th ACM Symposium on Principles of Programming Languages*, pages 97–109, January 1986.

[7] D Maurer. Strictness computation using special lambda-expressions. In H Ganzinger and N.D. Jones, editors, *Proceedings of the Workshop on Programs as Data Objects*, pages 136–155, DIKU, Copenhagen, Denmark, 17-19 October 1985. Springer-Verlag LNCS 217.

[8] A. Mycroft. *Abstract Interpretation and Optimising Transformations for Applicative Programs*. PhD thesis, University of Edinburgh, Department of Computer Science, December 1981. *Also* published as CST-15-81.

[9] P. Wadler and R. J. M. Hughes. Projections for strictness analysis. In G. Kahn, editor, *Proceedings of the Functional Programming Languages and Computer Architecture Conference*, pages 385–407. Springer-Verlag LNCS 274, September 1987.

[10] P.L. Wadler. Strictness analysis on non-flat domains (by abstract interpretation over finite domains). In S. Abramsky and C.L. Hankin, editors, *Abstract Interpretation of Declarative Languages*, chapter 12, pages 266–275. Ellis Horwood Ltd., Chichester, West Sussex, England, 1987.

On determining lifetime and aliasing of dynamically allocated data in higher-order functional specifications

ALAIN DEUTSCH*
ICSLA Team
Laboratoire d'Informatique de l'Ecole Polytechnique (LIX)
91128 Palaiseau Cedex - France.
deutsch@poly.polytechnique.fr

Abstract

We present a static analysis method for determining aliasing and lifetime of dynamically allocated data in lexically scoped, higher-order, strict and polymorphic languages with first class continuations. The goal is validate program transformations that introduce imperative constructs such as destructive updatings, stack allocations and explicit deallocations in order to reduce the run-time memory management overhead. Our method is based on an operational model of higher order functional programs from which we construct statically computable abstractions using the abstract interpretation framework. Our method provides a solution to a problem left open [Hudak 86] : determining isolation of data in the case of higher order languages with structured data.

1 Introduction

Functional specifications are a powerful description tool. They are used in denotational specifications, functional languages and specification languages. Our goal is to implement efficiently functional specifications on conventional sequential computers. However, such specifications lack control over memory management : there are no means of controlling assignment and deallocation of heap allocated data structures such as tuples, sums, partial applications, arrays, numbers and continuations. Because of this, functional programs tend to be much slower than their imperative equivalents. As destructive updating operations have constant time and space cost, it is desirable to transform applicative updatings into imperative updatings (as shown in [Aasa, Holmstrom & Nilsson 88]).

We have developed a method for detecting opportunities to automatically transform applicative constructs into imperative constructs such as destructive updatings of composite objects (such as partial applications, arrays, complex numbers or continuations ...), bounded-extent allocations (for instance stack allocations) and explicit deallocations (i.e compile-time garbage collection). In order to validate these program transformations, two classes of informations are computed. The *liveness* of data structures is used to control bounded-extent allocations. The *isolation* of data structures controls the introduction of destructive operations. These informations are themselves computed from safe approximations of the possible states of an abstract machine simulating the execution of programs from which we compute approximate informations about *reachability* of data. These informations can be used even in the case of imperative languages, as the introduction of explicit deallocation commands in a programming language renders the language unsafe, as a program may deallocate a valid reference. Compile-time determination of liveness of data may be used to check that deallocations are safe. This method is an application of the formal framework of abstract interpretation [Cousot & Cousot 79,Cousot 81].

1.1 Related work

Several methods have been proposed to reduce the run-time cost of heap management :

Lifetime analyses have been proposed in [Barth 77,Hughes 87,Ruggieri & Murtagh 88]. These analyses are used to validate the replacement of indefinite extent allocations by bounded-extent allocations. [Hughes 87] describes a method suitable for higher-order purely functional programs with structured data, based on a combination of a forward analysis and a backward analysis (to determine transmission properties of procedures). [Chase 88] discusses the safety of such transformations.

Appel has shown in [Appel 87] that garbage collection can be faster that stack allocation. An example of this is provided by the Standard ML [Appel 89] garbage collector which is sufficiently efficient to allow the heap allocation of the entire run-time stack. In such a context it is probably not worthwhile to transform heap allocations into stack allocations. Unfortunately such a technique is not always usable, as it requires assignments not to be frequent, which is not the case with imperative languages or lazy languages (because of the need to update delay closures).

Another approach consists in replacing dynamic alloca-

---

*This work has been partly funded by the Greco de Programmation du CNRS

tions by static allocations, for example by replacing local variables by global variables [Raoult & Sethi 84, Raoult & Sethi 85, Schmidt 85, Kastens & Schmidt 86, Sestoft 89].

An alternative approach to the elimination of temporary data is symbolic composition, as proposed in [Wadler 88]. Given an expression $f(g(x))$, this method computes at compile time a procedure f_g such that $f(g(x)) = f_g(x)$, but which is less space consuming whenever the value of $g(x)$ is temporary. Although limited to first order linear programs, this approach has the advantage of improving also the time complexity of programs by eliminating multiple traversal of data structures.

Sharing analyses for purely functional languages have been proposed in : [Schwartz 78, Inoue, Seki & Yagi 88, Bloss 89, Jones & Le Metayer 89]. The goal of these analyses is to validate program transformations such as introduction of destructive updatings and explicit deallocations. [Schwartz 78] describes a verification system for user-supplied sharing declarations in a first order language without side-effects. Sharing is directly described by abstract values, and this can cause information to be lost across procedure calls. [Inoue, Seki & Yagi 88] presents a method to perform compile-time garbage collection of temporary results in a functional, lexically-scoped, strict, first order language with dynamically allocated data. It is based on the combination of an analysis that detects newly allocated cells and a transmission analysis. These analyses compute informations relative to a prespecified regular pattern (for example linearly linked lists), but have a cost linear in the size of the program. [Bloss 89] describes a method for determining isolation of data in the case of a lazy, first order language with flat arrays using path analysis. [Jones & Le Metayer 89] extends [Schwartz 78]. Rather than relying on user-supplied declarations, this method computes sharing information and is based on the combination of two backward analyses (transmission and necessity of data) and a forward analysis. The language is a lexically-scoped, strict, first order language with dynamically allocated data. Abstract values are made finite by a depth-limiting technique similar to that of [Jones & Muchnick 81].

Several sharing analyses for non-purely functional languages have been described. The method reported in [Cousot & Cousot 77b] is an alias analysis that computes at each program point a partition of the program variables into disjoint collections such that if two variables belong to distinct collections, then they cannot refer to the same record (even indirectly). [Jones & Muchnick 81, Jones & Muchnick 82] describe several methods to perform data flow analysis of languages with dynamic allocation and structured data. These methods are forward data flow analyses that compute descriptions of the possible structure of the values of variables in a first order list-processing language with destructive updating and dynamic allocation. The analysis of [Jones & Muchnick 81] computes at each program point a set of abstract stores. Each abstract store is a graph which is k-limited : no path from the roots has length $> k$. The method reported in [Jones & Muchnick 82] computes a single data description per program point. Recursively defined structures are approximated by the set of program points that allocated them, plus a retrieval function that maps program points to structure components. [Jones 81] describes a method to perform data and flow analysis of λ-terms under call-by-value and call-by-name. This is done by constructing a function that simulates the states reachable during the interpretation of a λ-term using a SECD like machine. [Coutant 86] describes an alias analysis for first order imperative languages. [Hudak 86] describes a method to compute approximations of reference counts of dynamically allocated data in a lexically-scoped, strict, first-order applicative language with dynamically allocated flat arrays. The analysis computes at each program point a set of pairs of environments mapping variables to (abstract) locations and stores mapping locations to approximate reference counts. [Neirynck, Panangaden & Demers 87] presents an alias analysis for a strict, higher-order language with side-effects, scalar data and bounded-extent allocation of mutable cells containing scalars. [Stransky 88] describes a general method to perform abstract interpretation of dynamically scoped, strict, first order languages with dynamically allocated mutable data. It computes for each program point an abstract environment and an abstract store represented by a graph. [Larus & Hilfinger 88] presents a method to determine aliasing of structured data in the case of a strict, lexically-scoped, first order language with dynamically allocated mutable data. It computes at each program point a graph modeling the set of possible stores than can arise. [Horwitz, Pfeiffer & Reps 89] describes a method for determining data dependences between program statements in a language with dynamically allocated data. It is an extension of [Jones & Muchnick 81].

[Weihl 80, Shivers 88] describe control-flow and call-graph estimation methods for languages with procedure parameters or first class procedures. These methods could be used to extend a first order analysis. But the resulting call graph could be too conservative in the case of programs which make intensive use of higher-order procedures. Moreover, in order to flow analyse a procedure call, we need to known what procedure is involved, but also its environment, so that a call graph is not sufficient.

A static analysis for a higher-order language with first class continuations was described in [Jouvelot & Gifford 89]. It is not based on abstract interpretation but on effect checking. This method can be used to detect stack allocability of objects, and relies to some extent on user supplied declarations. It does not however achieve the effect of sharing analysis.

Our goal is to develop a semantically based sharing and lifetime analysis method applyable to lexically-scoped, strict, higher-order languages with dynamically allocated data.

1.2 Overview

Section 2 recalls the framework of abstract interpretation. Section 3.1 describes a typical functional language which will be the subject of the discussion. This language will be described by means of an operational, state-transition based semantics that captures store-level details such as sharings. Liveness and isolation of data structures will be formulated by means of predicates on the set of reachable states (section 3.3). In this framework we construct an abstract semantics (section 4). We then construct approximate isolation predicates defined on approximate states (section 5). A summary of the correctness proof is then presented (section 6). We then conclude by a presentation of some results and possible extensions.

2 Preliminaries

2.1 Notations

If $f \in D_1 \to D_2$ and $S \in \wp(D_1)$, then $f(S)$ denotes $\{f(x) \mid x \in S\}$. If $D = D_1 + D_2$, then the injection functions are (by abuse of overloading) $D_1 \in D_1 \to D$ and $D_2 \in D_2 \to D$. If $s \in D^*$ and $d \in D$, then $d::s$ denotes $\langle d \rangle \S s$; $\{x_1 \mapsto y_1, \ldots, x_n \mapsto y_n\}$ is the function than maps x_1 to $y_1 \ldots$ and in the context were a total function is required, any $v \notin \{x_1, \ldots, x_n\}$ to $\bot$. If $s \in D^*$, then $(x \in s) \Leftrightarrow \exists n \in [1, \|s\|] : x = s \downarrow n$. Variables denoting sets or sequences are often starred, such as s^*. If f is a partial function, then $x \to_f y \Leftrightarrow x \in Dom(f) \wedge f(x) = y$. If $\to$ is a relation, then $\to^*$ is its reflexive, transitive closure, $post(\to)(S) = \{y \mid x \in S \wedge x \to y\}$, $pre(\to)(S) = \{x \mid y \in S \wedge x \to y\}$. If $f : A \to A$ is a continuous function, A a complete lattice, $x \in A$ and $x \sqsubseteq f(x)$, then $luisfx$ is the least fixed point of f greater than x [Cousot 78, 2.7.0.1]. If $X \in \wp(A)$, and $\sqsubseteq$ is a partial ordering of A, then $\downarrow X = \{x' \mid x \in X \wedge x' \sqsubseteq x\}$.

2.2 Definition and Construction of Abstract Interpretations

We briefly recall the framework of abstract interpretation as defined by [Cousot & Cousot 79, Nielson 85].

The *standard semantics* (operational or denotational) of a program $[\![P]\!]$ is typically defined by a mapping $\mathcal{M}$ from states to states :

$$\mathcal{M}[\![P]\!] \in State \to State$$

As we wish to express properties w.r.t the set of all reachable states, the $\mathcal{M}$ function is extended point to point to sets of states, thus providing the *static semantics* (or collecting semantics) :

$$\mathcal{M}_S[\![P]\!] \in \wp(State) \to \wp(State)$$

An *abstract semantics* is defined by a triple $\langle State^\#, \mathcal{M}^\#, \langle \alpha, \gamma \rangle \rangle$, where $\langle State^\#, \sqsubseteq \rangle$ is a complete lattice that abstracts sets of states and $\mathcal{M}^\#$ is an abstraction of $\mathcal{M}_S$. The relationship between $\langle \wp(State), \subseteq \rangle$ and $\langle State^\#, \sqsubseteq \rangle$ is defined by the *pair of adjoined functions* $\langle \alpha, \gamma \rangle$: both α and γ are required to be monotonic and to satisfy [Cousot & Cousot 79, 5.3.0.1, 5.3.0.4] :

$$\begin{aligned} \alpha &\in \wp(State) \to State^\# \\ \gamma &\in State^\# \to \wp(State) \\ id &\sqsubseteq \gamma \circ \alpha \\ \alpha \circ \gamma &\sqsubseteq id \end{aligned}$$

$\mathcal{M}^\#$ is a *correct upper approximation* of $\mathcal{M}_S$ iff for all P [Cousot & Cousot 79, 7.1.0.2] :

$$\alpha \circ \mathcal{M}_S[\![P]\!] \circ \gamma \sqsubseteq \mathcal{M}^\#[\![P]\!] \tag{1}$$

How is $State^\#$ constructed ? It is possible to invent $State^\#$, and then the pair of adjoined functions. Another approach consists in inducing $State^\#$ from the structure of $State$. Indeed $State$ is constructed from basic operators such as $\times, +, \to$ as well as basic sets such as $\mathbb{N}$ and $\mathbb{B}$. For each such operator, it is possible to define several abstraction (and concretization) functionals varying in cost and precision. These functionals synthesize new abstraction (concretization) functions from existing ones.

2.3 Constructing Abstraction Functions

In this section we describe useful abstraction functions and abstraction functionals that will be used to construct abstract domains form concrete ones. Most of these abstraction functions were given in [Cousot & Cousot 79] and [Nielson 85]. The concretization functions are not described explicitly, since they are determined by the abstraction functions provided these are surjective complete-$\sqcup$-morphisms [Cousot & Cousot 79, 5.3.0.5].

We begin with (almost) simplest abstraction function: α_2 maps the empty set on $\bot$, any non empty set on $\top$.

$$\begin{aligned} \alpha_2(\emptyset) &= \bot \\ \alpha_2(\{e_1, \ldots\}) &= \top \end{aligned}$$

The less informative abstraction function α_1 maps any set onto $\bot$:

$$\alpha_1(S) = \bot$$

Another useful abstraction, α_c, maps any singleton set onto itself. It is used for constant propagation.

$$\begin{aligned} \alpha_c(\emptyset) &= \bot \\ \alpha_c(\{x\}) &= x \\ \alpha_c(\{x_1, x_2, \ldots\}) &= \top \end{aligned}$$

Given a lifted set $A_\bot$, we may want to abstract sets of elements. We have two orderings : an ordering on the elements, and the inclusion ordering. As the element ordering is simple, we can define an abstraction that preserves both orderings as follows :

$$\alpha_\bot(\alpha) = \lambda S.\alpha(S \setminus \{\bot\})$$

There are several methods to abstract a set of pairs $\wp(A \times B)$. First of all the independent attribute method that treats members of A and B separately. Given two abstraction functions $\alpha_A \in \wp(A) \to A^\#$, $\alpha_B \in \wp(B) \to B^\#$, $\alpha_{\times I}$ computes an abstraction function mapping sets of pairs to (strict) pairs of abstractions.

$$\begin{aligned} \alpha_{\times I}(\alpha_A, \alpha_B) &\in \wp(A \times B) \to (A^\# \times B^\#) \\ \alpha_{\times I}(\alpha_A, \alpha_B) &= \lambda S.\langle \alpha_A\{a | \langle a,b \rangle \in S\}, \alpha_B\{b | \langle a,b \rangle \in S\} \rangle \end{aligned}$$

The abstract domain $A^\# \times B^\#$ can be constructed using the smash product. This identifies elements having the same meaning (through the induced concretization function γ) : for instance : $\gamma(\langle \bot, x \rangle) = \gamma(\langle x, \bot \rangle) = \gamma(\bot) = \emptyset$.

However this abstraction ignores the relations between members of A and B. To obtain better precision, the relational method can be used :

$$\begin{aligned} \alpha_{\times R}(\alpha_A, \alpha_B) &\in \wp(A \times B) \to \wp(A^\# \times B^\#) \\ \alpha_{\times R}(\alpha_A, \alpha_B) &= \lambda S.\{\langle \alpha_A\{a\}, \alpha_B\{b\} \rangle | \langle a,b \rangle \in S\} \end{aligned}$$

An intermediate approach consists in recording for each value of $\alpha_A(a)$ the abstraction of the set of corresponding B values [Cousot & Cousot 79]. This uses the isomorphism between $\wp(A \times B)$ and $A \to \wp(B)$.

$$\alpha_{\times E}(\alpha_A, \alpha_B) \in \wp(A \times B) \to (A^\# \to B^\#)$$
$$\alpha_{\times E}(\alpha_A, \alpha_B) = \lambda S. \bigsqcup \{\alpha_A\{a\} \mapsto \alpha_B\{b\} \mid \langle a, b\rangle \in S\}$$

More generally, we may want to reduce the cardinality of a set of abstract values $\wp(A^\#)$. This can be done by means of a surjective function $f \in A \to B$ that extracts from an abstract value a distinctive information (the tokens of [Jones & Muchnick 82]) :

$$\alpha_=(f, \alpha) \in \wp(A) \to (B \to A^\#)$$
$$\alpha_=(f, \alpha)(S) \bigsqcup \{f(x) \mapsto \alpha\{x\} \mid x \in S\}$$

All these abstraction functions are useful, depending on the degree of precision needed[1]

F.Nielson has proposed to abstract $\wp(A+B)$ by $A^\# + B^\#$ [Nielson 85, p.181] :

$$\alpha_{+N}(\alpha_A, \alpha_B) \in \wp(A+B) \to A^\# + B^\#$$
$$\alpha_{+N}(\alpha_A, \alpha_B) =$$
$$\lambda S. A^\#(\alpha_A\{x \mid A(x) \in S\}) \sqcup B^\#(\alpha_B\{x \mid B(x) \in S\})$$

However, this abstraction can be insufficiently precise : consider a polymorphic language. Then the values of a polymorphic variable can be of several monomorphic types, and α_{+N} would abstract these values to $\top$. A more precise abstraction consists in abstracting $\wp(A+B)$ by $A^\# \times B^\#$ [Cousot & Cousot 79, 10.1.0.4], based on the isomorphism $\wp(A+B) \simeq (\wp(A) \times \wp(B))$, the abstraction function is then:

$$\alpha_{+C}(\alpha_A, \alpha_B) \in \wp(A+B) \to (A^\# \times B^\#)$$
$$\alpha_{+C}(\alpha_A, \alpha_B) =$$
$$\lambda S. (\alpha_A\{x \mid A(x) \in S\}, \alpha_B\{x \mid B(x) \in S\})$$

Because of the isomorphism $A^* \simeq (A^0 + A^1 + \cdots)$, it is possible to define an abstraction functional for $\wp(A^*)$ using the abstractions for sums and products :

$$\alpha_*(\alpha_+, \alpha_\times, \alpha_A) = \alpha_+(\alpha_2, \alpha_A, \alpha_\times(\alpha_A, \alpha_A), \ldots)$$

However because A^* is isomorphic to an unbounded sum of products its abstraction through α_* and $\alpha_{\times C}$ would result in an infinite product. Using the isomorphism $A^\infty \simeq (\mathbb{N} \to A)$ and specializing α_* w.r.t α_{+C} and α_{+N} yields :

$$\alpha_{*C}(\alpha_\times, \alpha_A) \in \wp(A^*) \to (\mathbb{N} \to B^\#)$$
$$\alpha_{*C}(\alpha_\times, \alpha_A)(S) =$$
$$\bigsqcup \{\|s\| \mapsto \alpha_\times(\alpha_A, \ldots, \alpha_A)\{s\} \mid s \in S\}$$

$$\alpha_{*N}(\alpha_\times, \alpha_A) \in \wp(A^*) \to B^\#$$
$$\alpha_{*N}(\alpha_\times, \alpha_A)(S) =$$
$$\begin{cases} \bot & S = \emptyset \\ x & \alpha_{*C}(\alpha_\times, \alpha_A)(S) = \{n \mapsto x\} \\ \top & \text{otherwise} \end{cases}$$

---

[1]Example. Let α_s be the abstraction function that associates to each set of naturals its sign.

$$\begin{aligned} S &= \{\langle -1, -1\rangle, \langle 0, 0\rangle, \langle 1, 1\rangle, \langle -1, 1\rangle\} \\ \alpha_{\times I}(\alpha_s, \alpha_s)(S) &= \langle \top, \top\rangle \\ \alpha_{\times R}(\alpha_s, \alpha_s)(S) &= \{\langle -, -\rangle, \langle 0, 0\rangle, \langle +, +\rangle, \langle -, +\rangle\} \\ \alpha_{\times E}(\alpha_s, \alpha_s)(S) &= \{- \mapsto \top, 0 \mapsto 0, + \mapsto +\} \end{aligned}$$

A more approximate abstraction can be defined by identifying all elements of the sets of sequences :

$$\alpha_\bullet(\alpha) \in A^* \to A^\#$$
$$\alpha_\bullet(\alpha)(S) = \bigsqcup \{x \mid s \in S \wedge x \in s\}$$

Sets of partial functions can be abstracted by monotone maps. To ensure monotonicity we use the following function :

$$mon(f) = \bigsqcup \{x' \mapsto f(x') \mid x' \sqsubseteq x\}$$

Now a set of functions can be abstracted by :

$$\alpha_\to(\alpha_A, \alpha_B) \in \wp(A \to B) \to mon(A^\# \to B^\#)$$
$$\alpha_\to(\alpha_A, \alpha_B)(F) =$$
$$mon\left(\bigsqcup \{\alpha_A\{x\} \mapsto \alpha_B\{f(x)\} \mid f \in F \wedge x \in Dom(f)\}\right)$$

The abstract equivalent of application is application, the abstract equivalent

of updating is :

$$upd^\#(f, x, y) = f \sqcup \bigsqcup \{x' \mapsto y \mid x' \sqsubseteq x\}$$

Whenever the target of α_A (say $A^\#$) is such that any element is equal to the union of a finite number of atoms (an atom is a minimal, non $\bot$ element), and provided α_A is totally strict (α_A is strict and $\alpha_A(x) = \bot \Leftrightarrow x = \bot$), a more approximate version of $\alpha_\to$ can be given. Indeed we can restrict the domain of α_A to the atoms of $A^\#$. Let $D_{A^\#}(a)$ be the atomic decomposition of $a \in A^\#$:

$$\alpha_{\to'}(\alpha_A, \alpha_B) \in \wp(A \to B) \to (A^\# \to B^\#)$$
$$\alpha_{\to'}(\alpha_A, \alpha_B)(F) =$$
$$\bigsqcup \{x' \mapsto \alpha_B\{f(x)\} \mid f \in F \wedge x \in Dom(f) \wedge$$
$$x' \in D_{A^\#}(\alpha_A\{x\})\}$$

The abstract equivalent of application is no more application but the union of the images of the decomposition :

$$apply'^\# \langle f, x\rangle = \bigsqcup f(D_{A^\#}(x))$$
$$upd'^\# \langle f, x, y\rangle = f \sqcup \bigsqcup \{x' \mapsto y \mid x' \in D_{A^\#}(x)\}$$

Generally $\alpha_{\to'}(\alpha_A, \alpha_B)(F)$ is less precise than $\alpha_\to(\alpha_A, \alpha_B)(F)$, unless α_A maps atoms to atoms, in which case they are equivalent in precision.

PROPOSITION 1 *If $\alpha_A \in \wp(A) \to A^\#$ and $\alpha_B \in \wp(B) \to B^\#$ are abstraction functions, α_A is totally strict, and every element of $A^\#$ is the union of a finite number of atoms, then $\alpha_{\to'}(\alpha_A, \alpha_B)$ is an abstraction function from $\wp(A \to B)$ to $mon(A^\# \to B^\#)$.*

3 Concrete Semantics

3.1 Operational Semantics

Rather than directly analyzing a high level language, we consider a language suited to the implementation of functional

$$
\begin{aligned}
I &\in Cmd \\
C &\in Cst \\
P &\in Pgm \\
L &\in Lab \\
N &\in Num \\
Pr &\in Prim = \{+,=,\text{inject},\text{tuple},\text{cc},\text{array}\ldots\} \\
P &\to I_{L_1},\ldots,I_{L_n} \\
I &\to \text{Dup}(N) \mid \text{Cst}(C) \\
&\mid \text{Case}(L_1,\ldots,L_n) \mid \text{Jump}(L) \mid \text{Apply} \mid \text{Return} \\
&\mid \text{Closure}(L,N) \mid \text{Stop} \mid \text{Prim}(Pr)
\end{aligned}
$$

Figure 1: Syntax

languages (as in [Hecht 77, Nielson 85, Stransky 88] with other languages). This language is a variant of the SECD machine [Landin 64] not dissimilar to the FAM [Cardelli 84], to the Ponder abstract machine [Fairbairn & Wray 86] and to the abstract machine of [Nielson & Nielson 86]. The syntax of the language is shown at figure 1. Note that it is possible to translate arbitrary programs into this language using for instance the two level semantics approach of [Nielson & Nielson 88]. Given a language L defined by its denotational semantics, we can analyse L programs by translating their TML denotations into our language.

Commands operate on states consisting of a value stack, a store, a reference to a continuation and a program counter. Stacks are represented by sequences of values, stores by finite mappings from locations (Loc) to stored values (Sv) and continuations by states not comprising stores. Expressible values (Ev) are either scalar objects (integers, ...) or reference to sharable objects such as sums, tuples, partial applications (closures) and continuations. Ev also contains a least element Ω which denotes undefined values. This induces a partial order on $State$.

$$
\begin{aligned}
State &= Lab \times Stk \times Store \times Cont \\
Stk &= Ev^* \\
Store &= Loc \to Sv \\
Cont &= Loc_\Omega \\
Ev &= (Int + Unit + Loc)_\Omega \\
Sv &= Sum + Tup + Cls + Cnt + Vec \\
Sum &= \mathbb{N} \times Ev \\
Tup &= Ev^* \\
Cls &= Lab \times Ev^* \times \mathbb{N} \\
Cnt &= Lab \times Stk \times Cont \\
Vec &= Ev^*
\end{aligned}
$$

A program P is a sequence of labeled commands. The Dup(n) command pushes the nth stack value on top of stack, Cst(C) pushes a constant, Case($L_1,\ldots,L_n$) branches to L_t, where t is the tag of the sum object on top of the stack, and pushes the untagged sum value, Jump(L) transfers control (only forward, so that no loops can be constructed without Apply), Apply applies a procedure to an argument. If the procedure is a closure, then the application may result either in the construction of a new closure (a partial application), or in an effective application. If the procedure is a continuation, then the current local state is discarded. Closure(L,N) constructs a closure object of order N of the procedure starting at label L, Stop halt the machine and Prim(Pr) perform various data operations such as arithmetic ($+,-,\ldots$), tuple construction and component selection (tuple$_1$,tuple$_2$,...,select$_1$,...), sum injection (inject$_1$,inject$_2$,...), array creation, selection, destructive and applicative updating (array,sel,upd,fupd). The cc primitive captures the current procedure continuation, which is sufficiently powerful to model the Scheme call/cc construct [Haynes & Friedman 87].

The meaning of a program will be defined by the partial state transition function τ mapping states to states (see figure 2). The meaning of constants is defined by the auxiliary function K. Primitive operations are defined by P.

$$
\begin{aligned}
K &\in Cst \to Ev \\
P &\in (Prim \times Ev^* \times State) \to Ev \times Store
\end{aligned}
$$

New store locations are allocated by the *new* function. The exact structure of Loc is left unspecified yet, for instance whole states may be used as locations (although this would require domains rather than sets). Indeed the common usage of integers (or time stamps) as locations is related : to each location uniquely corresponds a state (not considering garbage collection).

$$ new \in State \to Loc $$

We outline some typical primitive definitions :

$$
\begin{aligned}
P[\![\text{tuple}_n]\!]v'^*\langle L,v^*,\sigma,\kappa\rangle &= \\
\langle Loc(\ell),\sigma[\ell \mapsto Tup(v'^*)]\rangle &\text{ where } \ell = new\langle L,v^*,\sigma,\kappa\rangle \\
P[\![\text{inject}_n]\!]\langle v\rangle\langle L,v^*,\sigma,\kappa\rangle &= \\
\langle Loc(\ell),\sigma[\ell \mapsto Sum\langle n,v\rangle]\rangle &\text{ where } \ell = new\langle L,v^*,\sigma,\kappa\rangle \\
P[\![+]\!]\langle Int(v_1),Int(v_2)\rangle\langle L,v^*,\sigma,\kappa\rangle &= \langle Int(v_1+v_2),\sigma\rangle \\
P[\![+]\!]\langle \Omega,\_\rangle\langle L,v^*,\sigma,\kappa\rangle &= \langle \Omega,\sigma\rangle \\
P[\![+]\!]\langle \_,\Omega\rangle\langle L,v^*,\sigma,\kappa\rangle &= \langle \Omega,\sigma\rangle \\
P[\![\text{cc}]\!]\langle\rangle\langle L,v^*,\sigma,\kappa\rangle &= \langle Cont(\kappa),\sigma\rangle
\end{aligned}
$$

Now the meaning of a program P in the initial configuration $c_0 = \langle L,v^*,\sigma,\kappa\rangle$ is defined as the (possibly infinite) sequence of states $\langle c_0, \tau(c_0), \tau(\tau(c_0))\ldots\rangle$ whose last element (if the sequence is finite) is either an exit state or an error state.

3.2 Static Semantics

We now define the static semantics as the point to point extension of τ to sets of states [Cousot & Cousot 77a] :

$$
\begin{aligned}
State_S &= \wp(State) \\
\tau_S(c_S) &= post(\to_\tau)(c_S)
\end{aligned}
$$

Given a set of initial states Φ, the set of its immediate successors is defined by $post(\to_\tau^*)(\Phi)$ which by [Cousot 81, 10-4] can be computed as $M_S(\Phi)$:

$$ M_S(c_S) = luis\ (\tau_S \cup id)\ c_S \qquad (2) $$

3.3 Exact Isolation Predicates

The M_S function computes the (possibly infinite) set of successors of the initial states. From it, we can now provide a

$$\tau \in State \rightarrow State$$
$$\tau(s) =$$
case s **of**
$$\langle [\![\mathtt{Dup}(n)]\!]_L, v^*, \sigma, \kappa \rangle \rightarrow \langle L+1, (v^* \downarrow n)::v^*, \sigma, \kappa \rangle$$
$$\langle [\![\mathtt{Cst}(C)]\!]_L, v^*, \sigma, \kappa \rangle \rightarrow \langle L+1, (K[\![C]\!])::v^*, \sigma, \kappa \rangle$$
$$\langle [\![\mathtt{Case}(L_1, \ldots, L_n)]\!]_L, Loc(\ell)::v^*, \sigma[\ell \mapsto Sum\langle i,v\rangle], \kappa \rangle \rightarrow \langle L_i, v::v^*, \sigma[\ell \mapsto Sum\langle i,v\rangle], \kappa \rangle$$
$$\langle [\![\mathtt{Jump}(L')]\!]_L, v^*, \sigma, \kappa \rangle \rightarrow \langle L', v^*, \sigma, \kappa \rangle$$
$$\langle [\![\mathtt{Apply}]\!]_L, v::Loc(\ell)::v^*, \sigma[\ell \mapsto Cls\langle L', v'^*, 1\rangle], \kappa \rangle \rightarrow$$
$$\quad \langle L', v::v'^*, \sigma[\ell \mapsto Cls\langle L', v'^*, 1\rangle, \ell' \mapsto Cnt\langle L+1, v^*, \kappa\rangle], \ell' \rangle \text{ where } \ell' = new(s)$$
$$\langle [\![\mathtt{Apply}]\!]_L, v::Loc(\ell)::v^*, \sigma[\ell \mapsto Cls\langle L', v'^*, n+1\rangle], \kappa \rangle \rightarrow$$
$$\quad \langle L+1, Loc(\ell')::v^*, \sigma[\ell \mapsto Cls\langle L', v'^*, n+1\rangle, \ell' \mapsto Cls\langle L', v::v'^*, n\rangle], \kappa \rangle \text{ where } \ell' = new(s)$$
$$\langle [\![\mathtt{Apply}]\!]_L, v::Loc(\ell)::v^*, \sigma[\ell \mapsto Cnt\langle L', v'^*, \kappa'\rangle], \kappa \rangle \rightarrow \langle L', v::v'^*, \sigma[\ell \mapsto Cnt\langle L', v'^*, \kappa'\rangle], \kappa' \rangle$$
$$\langle [\![\mathtt{Return}]\!]_L, v::v^*, \sigma[\kappa \mapsto Cnt\langle L', v'^*, \kappa'\rangle], \kappa \rangle \rightarrow \langle L', v::v'^*, \sigma[\kappa \mapsto Cnt\langle L', v'^*, \kappa'\rangle], \kappa' \rangle$$
$$\langle [\![\mathtt{Closure}(L', n)]\!]_L, v^*, \sigma, \kappa \rangle \rightarrow \langle L+1, Loc(\ell)::v^*, \sigma[\ell \mapsto Cls\langle L', \langle\rangle, n\rangle], \kappa \rangle \text{ where } \ell = new(s)$$
$$\langle [\![\mathtt{Prim}(P)]\!]_L, v_1::\cdots v_{arity[\![P]\!]}::v^*, \sigma, \kappa \rangle \rightarrow \langle L+1, v::v^*, \sigma', \kappa \rangle \text{ where } \langle v, \sigma' \rangle = P[\![P]\!]\langle v_1,..,v_{arity[\![P]\!]}\rangle s$$

Figure 2: The state transition function τ

---

semantic characterization of isolation : an expressible value v is isolated if it is not accessible : a value is accessible if there are no valid paths from active areas (stack and continuation) to the location referred to by v. This provides a definition of isolation as a property which we now make more precise :

DEFINITION 1 (ACCESSIBILITY) *A location $\ell \in Loc$ is accessible from a value v through the store σ iff $\pi_{Ev}(v, \ell, \sigma)$, where :*

$$\pi_{Ev}(v, \ell, \sigma) = (v \in Loc) \vee \pi_{Loc}((v|Loc), \ell, \sigma)$$
$$\pi_{Loc}(\ell_1, \ell_2, \sigma) = (\ell_1 = \ell_2) \vee \bigvee_{v \in S(\sigma(\ell_1))} \pi_{Ev}(v, \ell_2, \sigma)$$
$$\pi_{Cont}(\kappa, \ell, \sigma) = (\kappa \neq \Omega) \wedge \pi_{Loc}(\kappa, \ell, \sigma)$$

and $S(sv)$ are the directly accessible sons of sv :

$$\begin{aligned} S &\in Sv \rightarrow Ev^* \\ S(Sum\langle t,v\rangle) &= \langle v \rangle \\ S(Tup\langle v^*\rangle) &= v^* \\ S(Cls\langle L, v^*, n\rangle) &= v^* \\ S(Cnt\langle L, v^*, \ell\rangle) &= \langle Loc(\ell)::v^*\rangle \\ S(Vec\langle v^*\rangle) &= v^* \end{aligned}$$

The active parts of a state are those that will be used in a future computation. We will define the restriction of a state c to its active parts as the least state equivalent to c. Two states can be defined as equivalent either if both fail to terminate, or if both produce identical outputs. We assume the existence of a function $output \in State \rightarrow Out$ that selects from a state the output computed so far (we could be more precise by adjoining an output store to $State$).

DEFINITION 2 (STATE EQUIVALENCE) *Two states $c_1, c_2 \in State^2$ are equivalent iff $c_1 \approx c_2$, where :*
$$c_1 \approx c_2 \Leftrightarrow ((c_1 \rightarrow_\tau^* c_1' \not\rightarrow_\tau) \wedge (c_2 \rightarrow_\tau^* c_2' \not\rightarrow_\tau) \wedge (output(c_1') = output(c_2')))$$

In the case of programs with partial output, this definition would not be suitable, as non terminating programs with different outputs would be considered as equivalent. A revised definition would be : given two computation traces $\langle c_1, \ldots \rangle$ and $\langle c_2, \ldots \rangle$, for each c_i there must exists a state c_j such that $output(c_i) = output(c_j)$ (if τ preserves the order of output). In this way, all non-terminating programs would not be considered as equivalent.

Now we can define the restriction of a state c_1, as the least defined state c_2 that is still equivalent to c_1 :

DEFINITION 3 (STATE RESTRICTION) *Given a state $c \in State$, the smallest state equivalent to c is $\mathcal{R}(c)$, where :*

$$\mathcal{R} \in State \rightarrow State$$
$$\mathcal{R}(c) = \sqcap\{c' \mid c' \sqsubseteq c \wedge c' \approx c\}$$

The $\mathcal{R}$ function is a lower closure operator (i.e a reductive projection). Another use of projections in semantic analysis was reported in [Launchbury 87] in the context of binding time analysis.

DEFINITION 4 (ISOLATION) *The n-th stack value is always isolated in the context L if given an initial description $\Phi \in States$, $(I (\mathcal{R}(\mathcal{M}_S(\Phi))) L n)$ holds, where :*

$$I \in State_S \rightarrow Lab \rightarrow \mathbb{N} \rightarrow \mathbb{B}$$
$$I \ c_S \ L \ n \Leftrightarrow$$
$$(\forall \langle L, v^*, \sigma, \kappa \rangle \in c_S(L)), v = (v^* \downarrow n) \wedge v \in Loc \wedge$$
$$\neg \pi_{Cont}(\kappa, (v|Loc), \sigma) \wedge$$
$$\bigwedge_{1 \leq i \leq \|v^*\| \wedge i \neq n} \neg \pi_{Ev}((v^* \downarrow i), (v|Loc), \sigma)$$

4 Abstract Semantics

4.1 Partitioning the States

The first step consists in partioning sets of states by program point [Cousot & Cousot 77a]. To each program point is associated the set of all corresponding states. The correspondence between $State_S$ and $State_P$ is immediate and is based on the isomorphism $\wp(A \times B) \simeq A \rightarrow \wp(B)$:

$$State_P = Lab \rightarrow \wp(Stk \times Store \times Dump)$$
$$\tau_P \in State_P \rightarrow State_P$$
$$\tau_P(c_P) = \bigsqcup\{\tau_{P1}\langle L, v^*, \kappa, \sigma \rangle \mid$$
$$\qquad L \in Dom(c_P) \wedge \langle v^*, \sigma, \kappa \rangle \in c_P(L)\}$$
$$\tau_{P1}(c) = \{L' \mapsto \{\langle v'^*, \sigma', \kappa'\rangle\} \mid c \rightarrow_\tau \langle L', v'^*, \sigma', \kappa'\rangle\}$$

The meaning of a whole program, given a description of the initial states $\Phi \in State_P$ is $M_P(\Phi)$ where :

$$M_P(c_P) = \textit{luis}\,(\tau_P \cup id)\,c_P \qquad (3)$$

The next step is to construct appropriate abstractions of $State_P$. More precisely, we need to construct abstraction functions for each component of $State_P$: (sets of) value stacks, stores and continuations.

4.2 Abstracting Local Stacks

As the language does not allow loops (jump commands can only skip forward), local stacks have finite heights. Furthermore we assume that the set of all stacks obtainable at a given point have the same height. Thus the $\alpha_{\bullet N}$ is sufficient :

$$\begin{aligned}
\alpha_{Stk} &\in \wp(Stk) \to Stk^{\#} \\
\alpha_{Stk} &= \alpha_{\bullet N}(\alpha_{\times I}, \alpha_{Ev}) \\
Stk^{\#} &= \alpha_{Stk}(\wp(Stk)) = (Ev^{\#\,*})_{\bot}^{\top}
\end{aligned}$$

Assuming that abstract operations are doubly strict, the abstractions of concatenation and projection are concatenation and projection.

4.3 Abstracting Stored Values

Stored values are abstracted using the standard abstraction functionals :

$$\begin{aligned}
\alpha_{Sum} &= \alpha_{\times E}(id, \alpha_{Ev}) \\
Sum^{\#} &= \mathbb{N} \to Ev^{\#} \\
\alpha_{Tup} &= \alpha_{\bullet C}(\alpha_{\times I}, \alpha_{Ev}) \\
Tup^{\#} &= \mathbb{N} \to Ev^{\#\,*} \\
\alpha_{Cls} &= \alpha_{\times E}(id, \alpha_{\times I}(\alpha_{\bullet N}(\alpha_{\times I}, \alpha_{Ev}), \alpha_c)) \\
Cls^{\#} &\simeq Lab \to (\mathbb{N} \times Ev^{\#\,*}) \\
\alpha_{Cnt} &= \alpha_{\times E}(id, \alpha_{\times I}(\alpha_{Stk}, \alpha_{Cont})) \\
Cnt^{\#} &\simeq Lab \to (Stk^{\#} \times Cont^{\#}) \\
\alpha_{Vec} &= \alpha_{\bullet}(\alpha_{Ev}) \\
Vec^{\#} &= Ev^{\#} \\
\alpha_{Sv} &= \alpha_{+C}(\alpha_{Sum}, \alpha_{Tup}, \alpha_{Cls}, \alpha_{Vec}) \\
Sv^{\#} &= Sum^{\#} \times Tup^{\#} \times Cls^{\#} \times Cnt^{\#}
\end{aligned}$$

The corresponding abstract injection operations are defined as follows :

$$\begin{aligned}
Sum^{\#}\langle t, v \rangle &= \langle \{t \mapsto v\}, \bot, \bot, \bot, \bot \rangle \\
Tup^{\#}(v^*) &= \langle \bot, \{\|v^*\| \mapsto v^*\}, \bot, \bot, \bot \rangle \\
Cls^{\#}\langle L, n, v^* \rangle &= \langle \bot, \bot, \{L \mapsto \langle n, v^* \rangle\}, \bot, \bot \rangle \\
Cnt^{\#}\langle L, v^*, \kappa \rangle &= \langle \bot, \bot, \bot, \{L \mapsto \langle v^*, \kappa \rangle\}, \bot \rangle \\
Vec^{\#}(v) &= \langle \bot, \bot, \bot, \bot, v \rangle
\end{aligned}$$

The projection operations are :

$$\begin{aligned}
Sum^{\#-1}(S) &= \{\langle t, v \rangle \mid v = (S \downarrow 1)(t)\} \\
Tup^{\#-1}(S) &= \{v^* \mid v^* = (S \downarrow 2)(n)\} \\
Cls^{\#-1}(S) &= \{\langle L, n, v^* \rangle \mid \langle n, v^* \rangle = (S \downarrow 3)(L)\} \\
Cnt^{\#-1}(S) &= \{\langle L, v^*, \kappa \rangle \mid \langle v^*, \kappa \rangle = (S \downarrow 4)(L)\} \\
Vec^{\#-1}(S) &= \{S \downarrow 5\}
\end{aligned}$$

4.4 Abstracting Locations

Until now, the structure of Loc has not been specified. Let us suppose that each concrete $\ell \in Loc$ is a tuple representing the state in which ℓ has been allocated. That is, a location is composed of a label, a stack, a store and a dump. The new function is then : $new(s) = s$.

The lattice of abstract locations can be constructed using one of the abstraction functionals for products. As we wish precise approximation of locations, we use the relational abstraction function :

$$\alpha_{Loc} = \alpha_{\times R}(\alpha_{Lab}, \alpha'_{Stk}, \alpha'_{Store}, \alpha'_{Cont})$$

Now several definitions of $\langle \alpha_{Lab}, \alpha'_{Stk}, \alpha'_{Store}, \alpha'_{Cont} \rangle$ are suitable.

For instance using $\langle id, \alpha_1, \alpha_1, \alpha_1 \rangle$ would distinguish locations by birth point : all objects allocated at a given program point are referenced by the same abstract location. In this case we have (using simplification isomorphisms) :

$$Loc^{\#} \simeq \wp(Lab)$$

This precisely models the approximation method of [Jones 81, p.389] and [Jones & Muchnick 82] later used by [Ruggieri & Murtagh 88, Mogensen 87]. Extensions of this method [Hudak 86, Stransky 88, Larus & Hilfinger 88] use more precise abstractions taking into account other state components such as continuations or initial cell values. They can be described by a suitable choice of the abstraction functions. For example the family of approximations proposed in [Hudak 86] can be modeled by $\alpha_{Cont}^{\prime n}$, where n is the order of approximation and :

$$\begin{aligned}
\alpha_{Cont}^{\prime n}(S) = \\
\{\langle L_i \mid i \in [1, n] \wedge Cnt^{\#}\langle L_{i, -}, \ell_{i+1} \rangle \in \sigma(\ell_i)\rangle \mid \\
\langle \sigma, \ell_1 \rangle \in S\}
\end{aligned}$$

In that case :

$$Loc^{\#} \simeq \wp(Lab^{n+1})$$

In the case of programs with recursive data structures such as trees, these abstractions may fail to detect unsharings. This is because the abstractions chosen for locations identify data that have different structures. For instance a non convergent binary tree and a convergent binary tree can be approximated in the same way. Storeless methods representing directly sharing information [Schwartz 78, Inoue, Seki & Yagi 88, Jones & Le Metayer 89] are more precise in these cases. But unfortunately they are less precise across procedure calls, and are not appropriate for languages with side-effects.

4.5 Abstracting Stores

A set of stores can be abstracted using the $\alpha_{\to}$ abstraction function. However, as abstract locations are sets, we can use the $\alpha_{\to'}$ abstraction, since each element of a power set is the union of atoms (in this case singleton sets), and that

$$\tau''^{\#} \in Lstate^{\#} \to \wp(Lstate^{\#})$$
$$\tau''^{\#}(s) =$$
case s **of**
$\quad \langle [\![\texttt{Dup}(n)_L]\!], v^*, \sigma, \kappa \rangle \to \{\langle L+1, (v^* \downarrow n)::v^*, \sigma, \kappa \rangle\}$
$\quad \langle [\![\texttt{Cst}(C)_L]\!], v^*, \sigma, \kappa \rangle \to \{\langle L+1, (K^{\#}[\![C]\!])::v^*, \sigma, \kappa \rangle\}$
$\quad \langle [\![\texttt{Case}(L_1,\ldots,L_n)_L]\!], v::v^*, \sigma, \kappa \rangle \to \{\langle L_i, v'::v^*, \sigma, \kappa \rangle \mid \langle i, v' \rangle \in Sum^{\#-1}(apply'^{\#}\langle \sigma, Loc^{\#-1}(v)\rangle)\}$
$\quad \langle [\![\texttt{Jump}(L')_L]\!], v^*, \sigma, \kappa \rangle \to \{\langle L', v^*, \sigma, \kappa \rangle\}$
$\quad \langle [\![\texttt{Apply}_L]\!], v::v'::v^*, \sigma, \kappa \rangle \to$
$\qquad \{\langle L', v::v'^*, upd'^{\#}\langle \sigma, \ell', Cnt\langle L+1, v^*, \kappa\rangle\rangle, \ell'\rangle \mid$
$\qquad\quad \langle L', n, v'^* \rangle \in Cls^{\#-1}(apply'^{\#}\langle \sigma, Loc^{\#-1}(v')\rangle) \wedge n = 1 \wedge \ell' = new^{\#}(s)\} \cup$
$\qquad \{\langle L+1, Loc^{\#}(\ell)::v^*, upd'^{\#}\langle \sigma, \ell, Cls^{\#}\langle L', n-1, v::v'^*\rangle\rangle, \kappa\rangle \mid$
$\qquad\quad \langle L', n, v'^* \rangle \in Cls^{\#-1}(apply'^{\#}\langle \sigma, Loc^{\#-1}(v')\rangle) \wedge n > 1 \wedge \ell' = new^{\#}(s)\} \cup$
$\qquad \{\langle L', v::v'^*, \sigma, \kappa' \rangle \mid \langle L', v'^*, \kappa' \rangle \in Cnt^{\#-1}(apply'^{\#}\langle \sigma, Loc^{\#-1}(v')\rangle)\}$
$\quad \langle [\![\texttt{Return}_L]\!], v::v^*, \sigma, \kappa \rangle \to \{\langle L', v::v'^*, \sigma, \kappa'\rangle \mid \langle L', v'^*, \kappa'\rangle = Cnt^{\#-1}(apply'^{\#}\langle \sigma, Loc^{\#-1}(\kappa)\rangle)\}$
$\quad \langle [\![\texttt{Closure}(L', N)_L]\!], v^*, \sigma, \kappa \rangle \to \{\langle L+1, Loc^{\#}(\ell), upd'^{\#}\langle \sigma, \ell, Cls^{\#}\langle L', N, \langle\rangle\rangle\rangle, \kappa\rangle \mid \ell = new^{\#}(s)\}$
$\quad \langle [\![\texttt{Stop}_L]\!], v^*, \sigma, \kappa \rangle \to \{\langle L, v^*, \sigma, \kappa \rangle\}$
$\quad \langle [\![\texttt{Prim}(Pr)_L]\!], v_1::\cdots v_{arity[\![Pr]\!]}::v^*, \sigma, \kappa \rangle \to \{\langle L+1, v::v^*, \sigma', \kappa\rangle \mid \langle v, \sigma' \rangle = P^{\#}[\![Pr]\!]\langle\langle v_1,\ldots, v_{arity[\![Pr]\!]}\rangle, s\rangle\}$
$\quad \langle L, v^*, \sigma, \kappa \rangle \to \{\langle L, v^*, \sigma, \kappa \rangle\}$

$$\tau'^{\#} \in Lstate^{\#} \to State^{\#}$$
$$\tau'^{\#}(s) = \{L \mapsto \{\rho^{\#}\langle v^*, \sigma, \kappa\rangle \mapsto \langle v^*, \sigma, \kappa\rangle\} \mid \langle L, v^*, \sigma, \kappa\rangle \in \tau''^{\#}(s)\}$$

$$\tau^{\#} \in State^{\#} \to State^{\#}$$
$$\tau^{\#}(c) = \bigsqcup \{\tau'^{\#}\langle L, v^*, \sigma, \kappa\rangle \mid L \in Dom(c) \wedge \langle t, \langle v^*, \sigma, \kappa\rangle\rangle \in c(L)\}$$

Figure 3: The abstract function $\tau^{\#}$

α_{Loc} is totally strict :

$$\alpha_{Store} = \alpha_{\to'}(\alpha_{Loc}, \alpha_{Sv})$$
$$Store^{\#} = Loc^{\#} \to Sv^{\#}$$

4.6 Abstracting Values

How can a set of values $\{v_1, \ldots\} \in \wp(Ev)$ be approximated? $\wp(Ev)$ is a set of sum objects. As the language we are analyzing is polymorphic, several instances of a variable may be bound to values of different types. Thus we use the α_{+C} abstractor. Furthermore as a value can be undefined (the Ω value), we use the α_{Ω} abstraction :

$$\alpha_{Ev} = \alpha_{\Omega}(\alpha_{+C}(\alpha_{Int}, \alpha_{Unit}, \alpha_{Loc}))$$
$$\alpha_{Int} = \alpha_2$$
$$\alpha_{Unit} = \alpha_2$$
$$Ev^{\#} = 2 \times 2 \times Loc^{\#}$$

Note that the choice of α_{Int} is arbitrary. For instance we could have chosen an abstraction suitable for constant propagation or range estimation.

The abstract injection and projection functions are :

$$Int^{\#}(n) = \langle n, \bot, \bot \rangle \qquad Int^{\#-1}(v) = v \downarrow 1$$
$$Unit^{\#}(u) = \langle \bot, u, \bot \rangle \qquad Unit^{\#-1}(v) = v \downarrow 2$$
$$Loc^{\#}(\ell) = \langle \bot, \bot, \ell \rangle \qquad Loc^{\#-1}(v) = v \downarrow 3$$

4.7 Abstracting continuations

As procedure continuations are represented by locations, we can use the same abstraction as for locations, lifted by α_{Ω} :

$$\alpha_{Cont} = \alpha_{\Omega}(\alpha_{Loc})$$
$$Cont^{\#} = Loc^{\#}$$

4.8 Abstracting States

Abstract states can be constructed following two approaches. It is first possible to consider the set of possible triples of abstract stacks, abstract stores and abstract continuations using $\alpha_{\times R}$. This corresponds to the relational method: the analysis would determine relations between stack components (see for instance [Jones & Muchnick 81, Hudak 86, Horwitz, Pfeiffer & Reps 89]). However a fully relational analysis can have a cost exponential in the size of the program, as each n-way conditional with m predecessors can yield nm successors. We can use the independent attribute method (as in [Jones & Muchnick 82, Stransky 88, Larus & Hilfinger 88]), by ignoring relations between stacks, stores and continuations using $\alpha_{\times I}$.

$$\alpha_{State} = \lambda S.(\alpha_{\times I}(\alpha_{Stk}, \alpha_{Store}, \alpha_{Cont}) \circ S)$$
$$State^{\#} = \alpha_{State}(State_P) \qquad (4)$$
$$= Lab \to Stk^{\#} \times Store^{\#} \times Cont^{\#} \qquad (5)$$

Alternatively, the analysis can be made more precise by using a limited form of relational analysis [Sharir & Pnueli 81, Jones & Muchnick 82, Stransky 88, Mogensen 89]. In this case we have :

$$\alpha_{State} = \lambda S.(\alpha_{=}(\rho, \alpha_{\times R}(\alpha_{Stk}, \alpha_{Store}, \alpha_{Cont})) \circ S)$$

$$State^{\#} = Lab \to (T \to (Stk^{\#} \times Store^{\#} \times Cont^{\#})) \quad (6)$$

where $\rho \in (Stk \times Store \times Cont) \to T$. The precision of the analysis will now depend on the choice of the ρ function. Setting $\rho = \lambda \langle v^*, \sigma, \kappa \rangle.\top$ yields the non relational analysis (5). Setting $T = \mathbb{N}_\perp^*$ and ρ as a function that extracts from the stack the tags of the sum objects directly accessible would yield a semi relational scheme ([Cousot & Cousot 79, 10.2.0.2]). We have found in practice that choosing a ρ that extracts from the current continuation the set of successive return points yields quite precise results ($T = \wp(Lab)$) :

$$\rho \in (Stk \times Store \times Cont) \to \wp(Lab)$$
$$\rho \langle v^*, \sigma, \kappa_1 \rangle =$$
$$\{L_{i+1} \mid \kappa_i \in Dom(\sigma) \wedge \langle L_{i+1}, v^*_{i+1}, \kappa_{i+1} \rangle = \sigma(\kappa_i)\}$$

The abstraction $\rho^{\#}$ of ρ can be derived directly.

A further abstraction can be defined in order to get a smaller domain. We can ignore relations between stores and program points, thus yielding a single global store (the retrieval function of [Jones & Muchnick 82]) :

$$State^{\#} = Store^{\#} \times (Lab \to Stk^{\#} \times Cont^{\#}) \quad (7)$$

In any case the order on $State^{\#}$ is consistent both with the subset ordering on $State$ (because abstraction functions preserve order) and to the element ordering on $State$ (by definition of α_{Ev}) :

PROPOSITION 2 $\forall (C_1, C_2) \in State_P^2, (\forall L \in Lab, \forall c_1 \in C_1(L), \exists c_2 \in C_2(L) : c_1 \sqsubseteq_{State} c_2) \Rightarrow \alpha_{State}(C_1) \sqsubseteq_{State^{\#}} \alpha_{State}(C_2)$

4.9 Abstracting the Transition Function

The abstract equivalent of the transition function τ is shown at figure 3. The $\tau'^{\#}$ function computes the successors of an abstract state. The following auxiliary functions are used :

$$Lstate^{\#} = Lab \times Stk^{\#} \times Store^{\#} \times Cont^{\#}$$
$$new^{\#} \in Lstate^{\#} \to Loc^{\#}$$
$$K^{\#} \in Cst \to Ev^{\#}$$

The exact definition of primitives depends on the definition of the corresponding abstraction functions. For instance :

$$new^{\#} \langle L, v^*, \sigma, \kappa \rangle = \{L\}$$
$$p^{\#}[\![\text{tuple}_n]\!] v'^* \langle L, v^*, \sigma, \kappa \rangle =$$
$$\langle Loc^{\#}(\ell), upd'^{\#} \langle \sigma, \ell, Tup^{\#}(v'^*) \rangle \rangle$$
$$\text{where } \ell = new^{\#} \langle L, v^*, \sigma, \kappa \rangle$$
$$p^{\#}[\![+]\!] \langle v_1, v_2 \rangle \langle L, v^*, \sigma, \kappa \rangle =$$
$$\langle Int^{\#}(Int^{\#-1}(v_1)) +^{\#} (Int^{\#-1}(v_2)), \sigma \rangle$$
$$p^{\#}[\![cc]\!] v'^* \langle L, v^*, \sigma, \kappa \rangle = \langle Loc^{\#}(\kappa), \sigma \rangle$$

The approximate analysis of a whole program given the abstract initial conditions Φ is $M^{\#}(\Phi)$ where :

$$M^{\#}(c) = luis (\tau^{\#} \sqcup id) c \quad (8)$$

4.10 Abstracting the restriction function $\mathcal{R}$

The restriction of a state to its necessary components is in essence a backward problem. Thus a precise solution requires a backward analysis that computes from an abstract state the smallest necessary predecessors (w.r.t $\sqsubseteq_{State^{\#}}$) compatible with the descendants of the initial states. More precisely, we look for a monotonic function $\tau_B^{\#}$ such that given a set of initial states Φ, a correct upper approximation of the initial states $\Phi^{\#}$ and a concrete state $s \in State$ (with $\wp(State) \simeq State_P$) :

$$\alpha_{State}(\mathcal{R}[pre(\to_r)(s) \cap \downarrow post(\to_r^*)(\Phi)]) \subseteq \quad (9)$$
$$\tau_B^{\#}(\Phi^{\#})(\alpha_{State}\{s\})$$

The $\tau_B^{\#}$ function itself is constructed with the help of an auxiliary function $B^{\#} \in Lstate^{\#} \times Lstate^{\#} \to Lstate^{\#}$, which given an abstract state c and one of its abstract successors c', computes a restriction of c sufficient to generate c'. The $B^{\#}$ function is directly derived from the $\tau'^{\#}$ function and is not shown here.

Then the approximate analysis of a whole program given the abstract entry states $\Phi \in State^{\#}$ and the abstract exit states $\Psi \in State^{\#}$ is $M_B^{\#}(\Phi, \Psi)$:

$$M_B^{\#}(\Phi, \Psi) = luis (\tau_B^{\#}(M^{\#}(\Phi)) \sqcup id) \Psi \quad (10)$$

Rather than providing explicitly an abstraction of $\mathcal{R}$, we have provided a backward analysis, which restricts the result of the forward analysis by computing backward the minimal states necessary to meet an output specification.

4.11 Correctness

In this section we provide a summary of the correctness proof of our abstract interpretation. We refer to [Deutsch 89] for details. The proof consists in showing that the abstract functions are correct approximations of their static counterparts.

First, we show that α_{State} is a correct abstraction function.

PROPOSITION 3 α_{State} is a complete-$\sqcup$-morphism.

DEFINITION 5 An abstract state $c \in State^{\#}$ is a correct upper approximation of $c_P \in State_P$ by α_{State} iff $\alpha_{State}(c_P) \sqsubseteq c$

We next show that $\tau^{\#}$ is a correct upper approximation of τ_P: given a correct upper approximation of a state c_P, $\tau^{\#}$ computes a correct upper approximation of $\tau_P(c_P)$. This will allow us to prove that $M^{\#}$ is a correct upper approximation of M_S. We give a lemma stating the correctness of $\tau'^{\#}$ w.r.t τ_{P1}.

PROPOSITION 4 $\tau'^{\#}$ is safe : for all $c_P \in State_P$, for all $c \in State^{\#}$ such that c is a correct upper approximation of c_P:

$$\forall L \in Dom(c_P),$$
$$\forall \langle v^*, \sigma, \kappa \rangle \in c_P(L),$$
$$\forall \langle v^{\#*}, \sigma^{\#}, \kappa^{\#} \rangle = c(L),$$
$$\alpha_{State}(\tau_{P1}\langle L, v^*, \sigma, \kappa \rangle) \sqsubseteq \tau'^{\#}\langle L, v^{\#*}, \sigma^{\#}, \kappa^{\#} \rangle$$

PROOF : *By enumeration of the possible commands.* □

PROPOSITION 5 $M^\#$ *is a correct upper approximation of* M_P.

PROOF : *First show that $\tau^\#$ is a correct upper approximation of τ_P. Then let $f_1(c_P) = c_P \cup \tau_P(c_P)$ and $f_2(c) = c \sqcup \tau^\#(c)$. Let $Q(c_P,c) \Leftrightarrow \alpha_{State}(c_P) \sqsubseteq c$, then we show that $Q(luis f_1 c_P, luis f_2 c)$ by fixed point induction (Q is an inclusive predicate). From this we deduce that $\alpha_{State} \circ M_P \sqsubseteq M^\# \circ \alpha_{State}$ [Cousot 81, Theorem 10-25].* □

PROPOSITION 6 $M_B^\#$ *is safe : for all $\Phi \in State_P$, let $\Psi \in State_P$ be the exit states reachable from Φ, then :*
$\alpha_{State}(\mathcal{R}(M_P(\Phi))) \sqsubseteq M_B^\#(\alpha_{State}(\Phi), \alpha_{State}(\Psi))$

5 Approximate Isolation Predicates

Isolation of data is detected by performing a post analysis on the abstract states. We define a monotone (w.r.t implication ordering on $\mathbb{B}$) approximate isolation predicate $I^\# \in State^\# \rightarrow Lab \rightarrow \mathbb{N} \rightarrow \mathbb{B}$. It must be related to I by the following property :

$$I^\#(\alpha_{State}(c_P)) \, L \, n \Rightarrow I(c_P) \, L \, n \qquad (11)$$

DEFINITION 6 (ACCESSIBILITY ESTIMATES)
$$\pi^\#_{Ev}(v, \ell_1, \sigma, L) = \bigvee_{\ell_2 \in Loc^{\#-1}(v)} \pi^\#_{Loc}(\ell_2, \ell_1, \sigma, L)$$
$$\pi^\#_{Loc}(\ell, \ell, \sigma, L) = tt$$
$$\pi^\#_{Loc}(\ell_1, \ell_2, \sigma, \{\ell_1\} \cup L) = ff$$
$$\pi^\#_{Loc}(\ell_1, \ell_2, \sigma, L) = \bigvee_{v^* \in S^\#(\sigma(\ell))} \bigvee_{v \in v^*} \pi^\#_{Ev}(v, \ell, \sigma, \{\ell\} \cup L)$$
$$\pi^\#_{Cont}(\kappa, \ell, \sigma) = \pi^\#_{Ev}(Loc^\#(\kappa), \ell, \sigma, \emptyset)$$

The $S^\#$ function extracts from an abstract storable value the set of sequences of abstract expressible values simultaneously accessible :

$$S^\# \in Sv^\# \rightarrow \wp(Ev^{\#*})$$
$$S^\#(sv) = \{\langle v \rangle \mid \langle \_, v \rangle \in Sum^{\#-1}(sv)\} \cup$$
$$\{v^* \mid v^* \in Tup^{\#-1}(sv)\} \cup$$
$$\{v^* \mid \langle \_, \_, v^* \rangle \in Cls^{\#-1}(sv)\} \cup$$
$$\{Loc^\#(\ell)::v^* \mid \langle \_, v^*, \ell \rangle \in Cnt^{\#-1}(sv)\}$$
$$\{v \mid v \in Vec^{\#-1}(sv)\}$$

DEFINITION 7 (ISOLATION ESTIMATES) *The $I^\#$ function is defined as follows:*

$$I^\# \in State^\# \rightarrow Lab \rightarrow \mathbb{N} \rightarrow \mathbb{B}$$
$$I^\# c \, L \, n \Leftrightarrow$$
$$\forall \langle t \rangle \langle v^*, \sigma, \kappa \rangle = c(L) \wedge \ell \in Loc^{\#-1}(v^* \downarrow n) \wedge$$
$$\neg \pi^\#_{Cont}(\kappa, \ell, \sigma) \wedge \bigwedge_{1 \leq i \leq \|v^*\| \wedge i \neq n} \neg \pi^\#_{Ev}(v^* \downarrow i, \ell, \sigma, \emptyset)$$

PROPOSITION 7 $I^\#$ *provides safe isolation estimates : the property (11) is satisfied by $I^\#$.*

6 Results

6.1 Implementation

A preliminary prototype has been implemented in ML. This includes the analyser as well as a compiler for a subset of ML. The analyser itself implements the $M^\#$ and $M_B^\#$ functions. The crucial efficiency point is the order in which the program points are processed during the iteration. Classical data flow analysers perform a pre-analysis in order to determine a node listing from the dependencies between program points [Kennedy 76]. But we can not do so, because the control flow is not a priori available, as our language comprises higher-order procedures. Several evaluation orders have been tried. The most efficient we have experimented consists in locally iterating each procedure in turn until global stabilization. But more work is required to find a formal solution.

6.2 Examples

As an example, we show the analysis of a continuation-based denotational-like specification of a call by value λ-calculus with constants and a call/cc-like construct (figure 4). After a straightforward translation into our language (syntactic domains replaced by disjoint sum types, lambda-lifting,...), the analysis correctly recognizes that the continuations are non-isolated (possibly shared) with the base semantics. But if the equation corresponding to *cwcc* is suppressed, then the continuations are shown to be isolated just before application, and may thus be discarded during invocation. Indeed we have tried our method on a specification of a full core Scheme similar to that of [Rees & Clinger 86]. As with the last example, our analysis correctly recognizes that the continuations can be deallocated before invocation if the call/cc construct is suppressed. Moreover, the store component is shown to be isolated before updates (i.e : single-threaded). The example arrays programs of [Aasa, Holmstrom & Nilsson 88] have been successfully analysed.

6.3 Extensions

The work reported here is a first attempt to solve the problem of sharing determination for higher-order languages ; more work is needed to provide more precise abstractions for structured data.

Although we have considered the case of a low-level language, we could probably reformulate our work without much change in the case of higher level, expression oriented languages.

We have considered the case of a language with lexically scoped names. However, many languages support constructs which introduce dynamically scoped names, for instance the exception mechanisms of ML or ADA. The method proposed in [Stransky 88] could be used to handle such constructs.

We have not discussed how the isolation informations can be used to transform programs. Work this area is reported in [Ruggieri & Murtagh 88, Inoue, Seki & Yagi 88, Jones & Le Metayer 89].

Although we have discussed a specific problem, several other problems can be solved in an uniform manner using our analysis. For instance the problem of detecting sharing of partial applications [Goldberg 87] can be solved by examining the abstract states corresponding to applications. We

Syntax
$$V \in Var$$
$$C \in Cst$$
$$E \in Exp$$
$$E \to V|C|\lambda V.E|(E_1\ E_2)|(cwcc\ E)$$

Domains
$$e \in Ev = D + P + K \quad values$$
$$D = Cst \quad constants$$
$$P = K \to K \quad procedures$$
$$\kappa \in K = Ev \to Ev \quad continuations$$
$$\rho \in U = Var \to Ev \quad environments$$

Valuations
$$apply \in Ev \to K \to K$$
$$apply(Dc)\kappa = \lambda v.\bot$$
$$apply(Pf)\kappa = f(\kappa)$$
$$apply(K\kappa')\kappa = \kappa'$$

$$\mathcal{E} \in Exp \to U \to K \to Ev$$
$$\mathcal{E}[\![V]\!]\rho\kappa = \kappa(\rho[\![V]\!])$$
$$\mathcal{E}[\![C]\!]\rho\kappa = \kappa[\![C]\!]$$
$$\mathcal{E}[\![\lambda V.E]\!]\rho\kappa = \kappa(\lambda\kappa'v.\mathcal{E}[\![E]\!](\rho[\![V]\!] \mapsto v])\ \kappa')$$
$$\mathcal{E}[\![(E_1\ E_2)]\!]\rho\kappa = \mathcal{E}[\![E_1]\!]\rho(\lambda v.\mathcal{E}[\![E_2]\!]\rho\ (apply\ v\ \kappa))$$
$$\mathcal{E}[\![(cwcc\ E)]\!]\rho\kappa = \mathcal{E}[\![E]\!]\rho(\lambda v.apply\ v\ \kappa\ (K\kappa))$$

Figure 4: Example specification of a λ-language with call/cc

---

can then derive propositions such as : every partial application of procedure f to k arguments is not shared. In order to extend our analysis to languages with call by need, we could formulate the semantics of a lazy language using explicit representations of delayed expressions as self-modifying procedural thunks. Our analysis method may prove sufficiently powerful to handle such cases.

7 Conclusion

We have presented a formal method for statically estimating sharings and lifetimes of dynamically allocated data in a higher order language with first class continuations. Our method is based on the abstract interpretation of a suitable language defined by an operational semantics that explicits details such as storage allocation and sharing. An exact formulation of the problem was given, then a simulation method that computes a superset of the reachable states has been constructed. The correctness of this simulation was established following the abstract interpretation proof method.

References

[Aasa, Holmstrom & Nilsson 88] A. Aasa, S. Holmström, and C. Nilsson. An efficiency comparison of some representations of purely functional arrays. *BIT*, 28:490–503, 1988.

[Appel 87] A. Appel. Garbage collection can be faster than stack allocation. *Information Processing Letters*, (25):275–279, Jun. 1987.

[Appel 89] A. Appel. Simple generational garbage collection and fast allocation. *Software Practice and Experience*, 19(2):171–183, Feb. 1989.

[Barth 77] J.M. Barth. Shifting garbage collection overhead to compile time. *CACM*, 20(7):513–518, Jul. 1977.

[Bloss 89] A. Bloss. Update analysis and the efficient implementation of functional aggregates. In *Conference on Functional Programming Languages and Computer Architecture*, pages 26–38, ACM Press, London, Sep. 1989.

[Cardelli 84] L. Cardelli. Compiling a functional language. In *Symposium on LISP and Functional Programming*, pages 208–209, ACM, 1984.

[Chase 88] D.R. Chase. Safety considerations for storage allocation optimizations. In *SIGPLAN'88 Conference on Programming Language Design and Implementation*, pages 1–9, Atlanta, Jun. 1988.

[Cousot & Cousot 77a] P. Cousot and R. Cousot. Abstract interpretation : a unified lattice model for static analysis of programs by construction of approximation of fixpoints. In *4th Annual ACM Symposium on Principles of Programming Languages*, pages 238–252, Los Angeles, Jan. 1977.

[Cousot & Cousot 77b] P. Cousot and R. Cousot. Static determination of dynamic properties of generalized type unions. *SIGPLAN Notices*, 12(3):77–94, Mar. 1977.

[Cousot & Cousot 79] P. Cousot and R. Cousot. Systematic design of program analysis frameworks. In *6th Annual ACM Symposium on Principles of Programming Languages*, pages 269–282, 1979.

[Cousot 78] P. Cousot. *Méthodes itératives de construction et d'approximation de points fixes d'opérateurs monotones sur un treillis, analyse sémantique de programmes*. Thèse d'état, Mar. 1978. Université scientifique et médicale de Grenoble.

[Cousot 81] P. Cousot. *Program Flow Analysis: Theory and Applications*, chapter Semantic foundations of program analysis, pages 303–342. Prentice-Hall, 1981.

[Coutant 86] D. Coutant. Retargetable high-level alias analysis. In *13th Annual ACM Symposium on Principles of Programming Languages*, pages 110–118, Jan. 1986.

[Deutsch 89] A. Deutsch. *On determining lifetime and aliasing of dynamically allocated data in higher-order functional specifications (extended version)*. Research Report LIX/RR/89/(to appear), Ecole Polytechnique, 91128 Palaiseau, France, 1989.

[Fairbairn & Wray 86] J. Fairbairn and S.C. Wray. Code generation techniques for functional languages. In *Conference Record of the 1986 ACM symposium on LISP and Functional Programming*, pages 94–104, Aug. 1986.

[Goldberg 87] B. Goldberg. Detecting sharing of partial applications in functional programs. In G. Kahn, editor, *Functional Programming Languages and Computer Architecture*, pages 408–425, Springer Verlag, Sep. 1987. Volume 274 of *Lecture Notes on Computer Science*.

[Haynes & Friedman 87] C.T. Haynes and D.P. Friedman. Embeding continuations in procedural objects. *ACM Transactions on Programming Languages and Systems*, 9(4):582–598, Oct. 1987.

[Hecht 77] M.S. Hecht. *Flow Analysis of Computer Programs*. Elsevier North-Holland, New York, 1977.

[Horwitz, Pfeiffer & Reps 89] S. Horwitz, P. Pfeiffer, and T. Reps. Dependence analysis for pointer variables. In *Conference on Programming Language Design and Implementation*, pages 28–40, Jun. 1989. Volume 24 of *SIGPLAN Notices*.

[Hudak 86] P. Hudak. A semantic model of reference counting and its abstraction. In *Conference Record of the 1986 ACM symposium on LISP and Functional Programming*, pages 351–363, Aug. 1986.

[Hughes 87] J. Hughes. Backward analysis of functional programs. In D. Bjørner, A.P. Ershov, and N.D Jones, editors, *Proc. Workshop on Partial Evaluation and Mixed Computation*, pages 155–169, North-Holland, Denmark, Oct. 1987.

[Inoue, Seki & Yagi 88] K. Inoue, H. Seki, and H. Yagi. Analysis of functional programs to detect run-time garbage cells. *ACM Transactions on Programming Languages and Systems*, 10(4):555–578, Oct. 1988.

[Jones & Le Metayer 89] S.B. Jones and D. Le Métayer. Compile-time garbage collection by sharing analysis. In *Conference on Functional Programming Languages and Computer Architecture*, pages 54–74, ACM Press, London, Sep. 1989.

[Jones & Muchnick 81] N.D. Jones and S. Muchnick. *Program Flow Analysis: Theory and Applications*, chapter Flow Analysis and Optimization of Lisp-like structures, pages 102–131. Prentice-Hall, New Jersey, 1981.

[Jones & Muchnick 82] N.D. Jones and S. Muchnick. A flexible approach to interprocedural data flow analysis and programs with recursive data structures. In *9th Annual ACM Symposium on Principles of Programming Languages*, pages 66–74, ACM Press, 1982.

[Jones 81] N.D. Jones. Flow analysis of lambda expressions. In *Symposium on Functional Languages and Computer Architecture*, pages 376–401, Chalmers University of Technology, Goteborg, Sweden, Jun. 1981.

[Jouvelot & Gifford 89] P. Jouvelot and D.K. Gifford. Reasoning about continuations with control effects. In *Conference on Programming Language Design and Implementation*, pages 218–226, ACM Press, Jun. 1989.

[Kastens & Schmidt 86] U. Kastens and M. Schmidt. Lifetime analysis for procedure parameters. In G. Goos and J. Hartmanis, editors, *European Symposium on Programming*, pages 53–69, Springer Verlag, Mar. 1986. Volume 213 of *Lecture Notes on Computer Science*.

[Kennedy 76] K.W. Kennedy. Node listings applied to data flow analysis. In *3th Annual ACM Symposium on Principles of Programming Languages*, pages 10–21, Jan. 1976.

[Landin 64] J. Landin. *The Mechanical Evaluation of Expressions*. Volume 6, Computer Journal, Jan. 1964.

[Larus & Hilfinger 88] J.R. Larus and P.N. Hilfinger. Detecting conflicts between structure accesses. In *SIGPLAN'88 Conference on Programming Language Design and Implementation*, pages 21–34, ACM, Jun. 1988.

[Launchbury 87] J. Launchbury. Projections for specialisation. In D. Bjørner, A.P. Ershov, and N.D. Jones, editors, *Workshop on Partial Evaluation and Mixed Computation*, pages 299–315, North Holland, Oct. 1987.

[Mogensen 87] T.Æ. Mogensen. Partially static structures in a self-applicable partial evaluator. In D. Bjørner, A.P. Ershov, and N.D. Jones, editors, *Workshop on Partial Evaluation and Mixed Computation*, pages 325–347, North Holland, Oct. 1987.

[Mogensen 89] T.Æ. Mogensen. Binding time analysis for polymorphically typed higher-order languages. In *Proc. TAPSOFT*, pages 298–312, Springer Verlag, 1989. Volume 352 of *Lecture Notes on Computer Science*.

[Neirynck, Panangaden & Demers 87] A. Neirynck, P. Panangaden, and A.J. Demers. Computation of aliases and support sets. In *14th Annual ACM Symposium on Principles of Programming Languages*, pages 274–283, 1987.

[Nielson & Nielson 86] H.R. Nielson and F. Nielson. Semantics directed compiling for functional languages. In *Annual ACM Conference on Lisp and Functional Programming*, pages 249–257, Aug. 1986.

[Nielson & Nielson 88] F. Nielson and H.R. Nielson. Two-level semantics and code generation. *Theoretical Computer Science*, 56(1):59–133, Jan. 1988.

[Nielson 85] F. Nielson. Expected forms of data flow analyses. In H. Ganziger and N.D. Jones, editors, *Programs as Data Objects*, pages 172–191, Springer Verlag, 1985. Volume 217 of *Lecture Notes on Computer Science*.

[Raoult & Sethi 84] J.C. Raoult and R. Sethi. The global storage needs of a subcomputation. In *11th Annual ACM Symposium on Principles of Programming Languages*, pages 149–157, ACM Press, 1984.

[Raoult & Sethi 85] J.C. Raoult and R. Sethi. *On Finding Stacked Attributes*. Technical Report 206, LRI, Université Paris-Sud, 91405 Orsay, France, Feb. 1985.

[Rees & Clinger 86] J. Rees and W Clinger. Revised^3 report on the algorithmic language scheme. *SIGPLAN Notices*, 21(12):37–79, Dec. 1986.

[Ruggieri & Murtagh 88] C. Ruggieri and T. Murtagh. Lifetime analysis of dynamically allocated objects. In *15th Annual ACM Symposium on Principles of Programming Languages*, pages 285–293, 1988.

[Schmidt 85] D. Schmidt. Detecting global variables in denotational specifications. *ACM Transactions on Programming Languages and Systems*, 7(2):299–310, Apr. 1985.

[Schwartz 78] J. Schwartz. Verifying the safe use of destructive operations in applicative programs. In B. Robinet, editor, *Transformations de programmes : 3^e colloque international sur la programmation*, pages 394–410, Dunod, Paris, mar. 1978.

[Sestoft 89] P. Sestoft. Replacing function parameters by global variables. In *Conference on Functional Programming Languages and Computer Architecture*, pages 39–53, ACM Press, London, Sep. 1989.

[Sharir & Pnueli 81] M. Sharir and A. Pnueli. *Program Flow Analysis: Theory and Applications*, chapter Two approaches to interprocedural data flow analysis, pages 189–234. Prentice-Hall, 1981.

[Shivers 88] O. Shivers. Control flow analysis in scheme. In *Conference on Programming Language Design and Implementation*, pages 164–174, Jun. 1988.

[Stransky 88] I. Stransky. *Analyse sémantique de structures de données dynamiques avec application au cas particulier de langages LISPiens*. PhD thesis, Université de Paris-Sud, Orsay, France, Jun. 1988.

[Wadler 88] P. Wadler. Deforestation: transforming programs to eliminate trees. In *European Symposium On Programming*, Springer Verlag, 1988. Volume 300 of *Lecture Notes on Computer Science*.

[Weihl 80] W.E. Weihl. Interprocedural data flow analysis in the presence of pointers, procedure variables, and label variables. In *7th Annual ACM Symposium on Principles of Programming Languages*, pages 83–94, 1980.

Small Domains Spell Fast Strictness Analysis

R.C. Sekar*, Shaunak Pawagi and I.V. Ramakrishnan*
Dept. of Computer Science,
SUNY at Stony Brook, NY 11794

Abstract

Use of strictness analysis in parallel evaluation and optimization of lazy functional languages is well known. The first formal treatment of strictness analysis appeared in Mycroft's seminal work which however dealt only with flat domains. Unlike flat domains, strictness analysis on non-flat domains involves determining how a function transforms a demand (degree of strictness) on its output into a demand on its arguments. Solutions to this problem in its full generality require large domains and appear both complex and expensive to implement. However, only two kinds of demands arise naturally in lazy normalization of terms, viz., *e*-demand (normal form needed) and *d*-demand (root stable or head normal form needed). Based on this observation, we identify three useful forms of strictness for non-flat domains - *ee*, *dd* and *de*. Each of these three forms of strictness play an important role in evaluation of functional programs. Specifically, *ee* strictness is used for transforming call-by-need to call-by-value and *dd* strictness is useful in repairing violations of *strong sequentiality* of equational programs as well as in a critical optimization step used in rewriting implementations of such languages. We present intuitively simple methods to compute them. Our methods are computationally efficient as they are based on small domains (1 point for *ee* and *dd* and 2 points for *de*). They are powerful enough to extract all useful strictness information in practice and are general enough to handle functions defined by rewrite rules. We are able to reason about all user defined data types within a single framework and also handle polymorphism.

---

*Partially supported by NSF grant CCR-8805734

Permission to copy without fee all or part of this material is granted provided that the copies are not made or distributed for direct commercial advantage, the ACM copyright notice and the title of the publication and its date appear, and notice is given that copying is by permission of the Association for Computing Machinery. To copy otherwise, or to republish, requires a fee and/or specific permission.

© 1990 ACM 089791-343-4/90/0001/0169 $1.50

1 Introduction

Use of strictness analysis in parallel evaluation and optimization of lazy functional languages is well known. The first formal treatment of strictness analysis appeared in Mycroft's seminal research [Myc80]. His work however only dealt with first order functions on *flat domains* such as integers and subsequently a lot of research has gone into handling higher order functions on such domains.(See [Burn85,Hud86] for example.) Strictness analysis on *non-flat domains* (such as lists) is an important topic of current research. Unlike flat domains, a data object in *non-flat domains* could be in several "stages" of evaluation, e.g., a list could be fully evaluated or some of its heads may be evaluated or only the outer structure of the list may be evaluated. Different functions may demand their arguments in different stages of evaluation. Secondly the strictness of most functions is *context-dependent*, i.e., it may be 'safe' to evaluate an argument of a function in some contexts and it may be unsafe in others. Any satisfactory solution to strictness analysis must address these two issues.

Hughes [Hug85], Wadler [Wad87], Lindstrom [Lin86] and Hall [Hall87] pioneered the study of strictness analysis on non-flat domains. They clarified what it means to do strictness analysis on non-flat domains and gave a precise formulation of the problem. Their methods use large domains as they reason about many contexts a function is likely to be evaluated in. Hence they appear (justifiably) complex and expensive to implement. Moreover some of them only deal with monomorphic languages while others use different domains for different data types and therefore must be capable of automatically synthesizing these domains and modifying the analysis procedures for each user defined data type. Thus the development of a *simple* and *efficient* method for strictness analysis on non-flat domains that can uniformly deal with all user defined data objects, polymorphism and that is also extensible to higher-order functions has remained an open problem. We address this problem in this paper.

1.1 Overview

We develop a method for strictness analysis of functions using a constructor-based term rewriting system (TRS). In such a system, a function is defined by a set of oriented equations (called *rewrite rules*) of the form $l \rightarrow r$ where the left hand side (lhs) l and right hand side (rhs) r are terms that may contain variables. Almost all programs written in functional languages such as LML[Aug84], Miranda[Tur85], HOPE[Burs80] and O'Donnell's equational logic[OD85] constitute such a TRS. The evaluation of functions in a TRS proceeds by repeated replacements (also called reductions) of *redexes* (a redex is an instance of a left hand side) in the input term by the corresponding right hand side till the *normal form* of the term (which contains no redexes) is obtained.

Our approach to strictness analysis is based on how a function transforms a *demand* (i.e., required degree of evaluation) on its output into a demand on its arguments. Although several kinds of demands are possible, only two kinds arise naturally in lazy normalization of terms. These are *e*-demand or *normal form* demand and *d*-demand or *head normal form* demand. (A term t is in head normal form if no reduction is performed at its root in any sequence of reductions leading to its normal form.) Based on this observation, we identify three useful forms of strictness: *ee*, *dd* and *de* strictness. These forms of strictness specify respectively

- which e_i are needed in *normal* form in order to normalize $f(e_1, ..., e_n)$
- which e_i are needed in *head normal* form to *head normalize* $f(e_1, ..., e_n)$
- which e_i are needed in *normal* form to *head normalize* $f(e_1, ..., e_n)$

Each of these three forms of strictness play an important role in evaluation of functional programs. For instance, *ee*-strictness is used in transforming call-by-need to call-by-value (and consequently in automatic extraction of parallelism) and *dd*-strictness is used for enlarging the class of equational programs that admit lazy evaluation. Thus it is appropriate to view each of these three analysis as serving independent objectives.

ee analysis is the most important contribution of this paper. Most functions used in programs appear to be *ee* in all their arguments[1]. For example, in fig.1 this is true of all functions except *if* and *length*. Primitive functions such as $*$ and $+$, as well as some defined functions like *sumtree* and *sequence* are *de* in their arguments. *Split* is *de* in its first argument. Functions such as *reverse*, *length*, *merge* etc. are *dd* in their arguments.

We assume a normal form demand on the output of the program, unlike [Hall87] who assumes only a (weaker) stream demand (i.e., all the heads of the output are needed but not the tails). It may appear that normal form assumption will pose problems in handling streams. But we argue (see section 4.3) that stream behavior (viz., incremental output) is readily achievable in a parallel implementation using normal form demand. Furthermore we also argue that stream strictness assumption results in very few transformations of call-by-need's to call-by-value unless some form of termination analysis is incorporated into the analysis procedure. Since termination analysis is a very difficult problem, many of the call-by-need's that are transformed under the normal form assumption are not so transformed under stream demand.

1.2 Salient Features of our Method and Related Results

- Our method treats pattern matching directly. Therefore unlike previous methods we do not handle constructs such as *if* and *case* separately nor do we need to translate equational programs into these constructs for strictness analysis.

- Our method is simple and computationally efficient. Unlike previous approaches which introduce big domains (such as ten points in [Wad87], infinite in [Hall87]) our *ee* and *dd* analyses require only single point domains whereas our *de* analysis requires a two point domain. Use of small domains makes our analysis simple (to follow) and also computationally efficient since the search for fixpoints is considerably speeded up. On the other hand big domains entail considerable penalties at run time. In particular, if there are n points in a domain and k arguments to a function then at run time we have to maintain a table of nk words for this function. The table specifies in what context each of the k arguments should be evaluated corresponding to each of the n contexts in which the function is likely to be evaluated. Alternatively, we can have n versions of the function instead of the table[2]. In contrast, our method requires at most k bits of storage.

- Our analysis procedures are very effective in practice. Table 1 shows the % of functions evaluated

---

[1] This is not just a coincidence and the reasons will be evident in section 3.

[2] If the number of contexts that arise in the program being analyzed is n' and $n' < n$ then there needs to be only $n'k$ entries in the table or n' versions.

$$if(true, x, y) \rightarrow x$$
$$if(false, x, y) \rightarrow y$$
$$append(x:xs, y)^3 \rightarrow x:append(xs, y)$$
$$append(nil, y) \rightarrow y$$
$$reverse(x:xs) \rightarrow append(reverse(xs), x:nil)$$
$$reverse(nil) \rightarrow nil$$
$$length(x:xs) \rightarrow 1 + length(xs)$$
$$length(nil) \rightarrow 0$$
$$sumtree(node(l,r)) \rightarrow sumtree(l) + sumtree(r)$$
$$sumtree(leaf(val)) \rightarrow val$$
$$qs(x:xs) \rightarrow qs1(split(xs, x, nil, nil))$$
$$qs(nil) \rightarrow nil$$
$$split(x:xs, y, u, v) \rightarrow if(x > y, split(xs, y, x:u, v),$$
$$split(xs, y, u, x:v))$$
$$split(nil, y, u, v) \rightarrow tuple(u, y, v)$$
$$qs1(tuple(x, y, z)) \rightarrow append(qs(x), y:qs(z))$$
$$sequence(x, y) \rightarrow if(x < y,$$
$$x:sequence(x+1, y), nil)$$

Figure 1: Examples

Examples	%age evaluated using call-by-value	%age of parallelism extracted
Matrix[4] multiplication	100	100
Quicksort	100	100
Mergesort	100	100
Sumtree	100	100
N queens	100	100
Factorial	100	100
Determinant Evaluation	100	100
Numerical Integration	100	100
FFT	100	100
Recursive Doubling	100	100

Table 1: Efficacy of ee-analysis. Programs given in appendix

by call-by-value and % of available parallelism extracted by ee analysis on many commonly used programs.

- Our analysis procedures are independent of data types and consequently handle all user-defined data types and polymorphism uniformly. Unlike our method, previous methods used different domains for different data types. Therefore these methods must be capable of automatically synthesizing these domains and suitably modifying the analysis procedure for each user-defined data type. Furthermore, some of the previous approaches [Wad87] are limited to monomorphic languages.

- We present a very effective linear-time heuristic (in the size of the program) for detecting functions that are ee-strict on all their arguments. It succeeds on all the examples in fig.1 (except length and split) and almost all the functions used in the programs for the examples in table 1. The same heuristic also computes Mycroft's $f^\#$ within the same time bounds and since most functions on flat domains are also strict on all their arguments, fast strictness analysis on such functions can now be done.

This paper is organized into seven sections and an appendix. Section 2 contains all the technical details of ee, dd and de analyses. Our method extends Mycroft's work (on flat domains) naturally to non-flat domains. Hence it should be possible to carry over the enhancements made to Mycroft's method to our method also. For instance, we mention in passing in section A of appendix how to extend our method to higher-order functions along lines suggested by Clack and Peyton Jones for extending Mycroft's method (to handle such functions on flat domains) [Cla85]. In Section 3 we show that all the three forms of strictness (ee, dd and de) have distinct intuitive meanings and are related to identifiable properties of the program. Specifically, ee-strictness is related to "non-erasing" property of functions and dd is related to the property of sequentiality of equational programs. Section 4 contains a linear time (in the size of the program) heuristic for ee analysis that is very useful in practice. In this section we also discuss the difficult problems that need to be tackled for satisfactorily handling stream strictness (which is a consequence of not assuming e-demand on the output of a function). Section 5 discusses applications of ee- and de- strictness in parallelism extraction and use of dd-strictness in optimization of equational programs and repairing violations of strongly sequentiality. Comparison with related work appears in section 6 followed by concluding remarks in section 7. Programs for the examples in table 1 appear in section B of appendix.

Notations

In a constructor-based TRS all the functors are partitioned into two disjoint sets $\mathcal{F}$ and $\mathcal{C}$ such that only the

---
[3]: is an infix operator standing for cons.
[4] %age evaluated by call-by-value figure for these cases is given when n(size of input) tends to infinity.

outermost symbol of every lhs is in $\mathcal{F}$ while the rest are in $\mathcal{C}$. For a term t, $\mathcal{V}(t)$ is the set of variables in it. We assume that $\mathcal{V}(r) \subseteq \mathcal{V}(l)$ for every rule $l \to r$. A *substitution* maps variables to terms. By $t[u \leftarrow v]$ we refer to the term obtained from t by replacing the subterm u in t by v. An *instance* $t\beta$ of a term t is obtained by replacing x by $\beta(x)$ for each variable x in t. A *redex* in term u is an occurrence of an instance of an lhs. A term t is in *normal form*(NF) if it contains no redexes. By $t \to u$ we mean that u is obtained by replacing a redex $l\beta$ in t by $r\beta$, where $[l \to r]$ is a rewrite rule. The reflexive and transitive closure of $\to$ is denoted by $\to^*$. A term t is in *head normal form*(HNF) if there is no t' such that $t \to^* t'$ and t' contains a redex at the root. f, g, h refer to function symbols, c to constructor symbols, x, y, z, u, v to variables and s, t, e to arbitrary terms.

2 Technical Details

As in [Lin86] we associate strictness with the notion of *demand propagation*, i.e., how a demand on the output of a function is transformed into demands on its arguments. A *demand* specifies the extent to which a term t needs to be evaluated. We consider the following two demands:

1. e or *exhaustive* demand: t is required in NF.
2. d demand: t is required in HNF.

There is a natural ordering on demands based on their strength, and is given by $e > d$. Note that our notation differs from that of Lindstrom [Lin86], where d and d^e denote d and e respectively.

A function f is a *de* propagator (i.e., *de* strict) on its ith argument if in every sequence of reductions that takes any term $f(s_1, s_2, ..., s_n)$ to its HNF, s_i is normalized. (For dd replace 's_i is normalized' by 's_i is head normalized' and for ee replace 'HNF' by 'NF'.)

In order to analyze ee-, dd- and de-strictness of functions[5], we associate three non-standard interpretations f^{ee}, f^{dd} and f^{de} with each function f. These map f to a boolean formula on its arguments $x_1, ..., x_n$. f transforms an a-demand on $t = f(s_1, ..., s_n)$ to a b-demand on s_i if $f^{ab}(x_1, ..., x_n) = 0$ whenever $x_i = 0$ ($a, b \in \{e, d\}$). For instance, if $f^{ee}(x_1, x_2, x_3) = x_1 \wedge (x_2 \vee x_3)$, then to normalize t we need to normalize s_1 and one of s_2 and s_3. Not that in flat domains d and e demands coincide and hence we expect f^{ee} and f^{dd} coincide with $f^\#$ of Mycroft. It is pleasing to note that this is indeed the case.

We now proceed to to describe the analysis procedures for f^{ee}, f^{dd} and f^{de}. Only ee analysis is described in detail whereas the other two are briefly sketched as they are quite similar to ee. In all these analyses we assume that f is defined by pattern match through the following equations:

$$f(t_1^1, ..., t_n^1) \to e_1$$
$$\vdots \quad \vdots$$
$$f(t_1^h, ..., t_n^h) \to e_h$$

2.1 ee Analysis

For a term t, t^{ee} is a boolean formula on the variables in t which specifies those variables in it that are e-demanded in order to normalize t. Herein e-demand on a variable implies that any term substituting for it needs to be normalized. More precisely, let $t^{ee} = (x_{11} \wedge x_{12} \wedge \cdots \wedge x_{1r_1}) \vee (x_{21} \wedge \cdots \wedge x_{2r_2}) \vee \cdots \vee (x_{n1} \wedge \cdots \wedge x_{nr_n})$, where x_{ij}'s denote variables in t. We relate t^{ee} to the strictness property of t as follows.

Definition 1 (Strictness Property) *In every sequence of rewrites that takes any ground instance s of t (i.e., $s = t\beta$) to its NF, all the terms in one of the sets $\{\beta(x_{11}), ..., \beta(x_{1r_1})\}, ..., \{\beta(x_{n1}), ..., \beta(x_{nr_n})\}$ must be normalized.*

Any nonvariable term t is an instance of either $c(x_1, ..., x_n)$ or $f(x_1, ..., x_n)$. If we are given $[c(x_1, ..., x_n)]^{ee}$ and $[f(x_1, ..., x_n)]^{ee}$ (abbreviated as c^{ee} and f^{ee}), and the following rule for computing the strictness of an instance, then we can compute the strictness of arbitrary terms.

<u>**Rule of Substitution**</u> $[t\beta]^{ee} = t^{ee}[x_{ij} \leftarrow [\beta(x_{ij})]^{ee}]$
Proof: Let t^{ee} be as before and $[\beta(x_{ij})]^{ee} = \bigvee_{k=1}^{m_{ij}} Y_k^{ij}$, where $Y_k^{ij} = \bigwedge_{l=1}^{p_{ijk}} y_{kl}^{ij}$. Here y_{kl}^{ij}'s are variables in $\beta(x_{ij})$. From the strictness property of t we know that in order to normalize any ground instance $s = t\beta\sigma$, all terms in one of $\{\beta(x_{11})\sigma, ..., \beta(x_{1r_1})\sigma\}, ..., \{\beta(x_{n1})\sigma, ..., \beta(x_{nr_n})\sigma\}$ need to normalized. Let φ_i denote the strictness of $t\beta$, considering only cases when all the terms in $\{\beta(x_{i1})\sigma, ..., \beta(x_{ir_i})\sigma\}$ must be normalized. Then $[t\beta]^{ee}$, which is found by considering all possible cases is given by $\varphi_1 \vee \cdots \vee \varphi_n$. Now φ_i is obtained as follows. Let $\mathcal{Y}_k^{ij} = \{\sigma(y_{k1}^{ij}), ..., \sigma(y_{kp_{ijk}}^{ij})\}$. Note that in order to normalize $\beta(x_{ij})\sigma$, all terms in one of $\mathcal{Y}_1^{ij}, ..., \mathcal{Y}_{m_{ij}}^{ij}$ must be normalized. Therefore in order to normalize all of $\{\beta(x_{i1})\sigma, ..., \beta(x_{ir_i})\sigma\}$, all terms in one of $\mathcal{Y}_1^{i1}, ..., \mathcal{Y}_{m_{i1}}^{i1}$ and all terms in one of $\mathcal{Y}_1^{i2}, ..., \mathcal{Y}_{m_{i2}}^{i2}$ and $\cdots$ need to be normalized. Therefore $\varphi_i = (\bigvee_{k=1}^{m_{i1}} Y_k^{i1}) \wedge (\bigvee_{k=1}^{m_{i2}} Y_k^{i2}) \wedge \cdots$. It can be easily seen that $t^{ee}[x_{ij} \leftarrow [\beta(x_{ij})]^{ee}] = \varphi_1 \vee \cdots \vee \varphi_n$. ∎

Now we derive the equations to compute x^{ee}, c^{ee} and f^{ee}. For the variable case, its substitution is to be normalized and hence $x^{ee} = x$. For the case $c(x_1, ..., x_n)$,

---
[5] Among the four possible propagators ed is very weak and is not considered in this paper.

the NF of its instance $c(s_1,...,s_n)$ is obtained only by normalizing each of $s_1,...,s_n$. Hence c^{ee} is the conjunction of x_i's. Note that if $rank(c) = 0$ then $c^{ee} = 1$. In order to compute f^{ee} observe that any instance $f(s_1,...,s_n)$ (of $f(x_1,...,x_n)$) can be rewritten into only one of $e_1,...,e_k$. Therefore f^{ee} is a disjunction of e_j^{ee}, for $j = 1,...,k$. However, f^{ee} is a formula on $x_1,...,x_n$ and these variables differ from those in e_j. Hence we need a function g_j that transforms a formula on the variables in e_j into one on $x_1,...,x_n$. Thus

$$x^{ee} = x \qquad (1)$$

$$[c(x_1,...,x_n)]^{ee} = x_1 \wedge \cdots \wedge x_n \qquad (2)$$

$$[f(x_1,...,x_n)]^{ee} = \bigvee_{j=1}^{k} g_j(e_j^{ee}) \qquad (3)$$

The following equations applied in the order in which they are given, specify each g_j. Here φ's and ϕ's stand for arbitrary boolean formulae in disjunctive normal form (DNF) and φ with a subscript stands for conjunction.

$$g_j(\psi \vee \varphi) = g_j(\psi) \vee g_j(\varphi) \qquad (4)$$

$$g_j(\varphi_1) = (\bigwedge_{i \mid t_i^j \text{ contains no variables}} x_i) \wedge g_j(\varphi_1) \qquad (5)$$

$$g_j(x_{i1} \wedge \cdots \wedge x_{ir_i} \qquad (6)$$

$$\wedge \varphi_1) = x_i \wedge g_j(\varphi_1) \qquad (7)$$

$$g_j(\varphi_1) = 1, \text{ otherwise.} \qquad (8)$$

The justification for these equations is as follows. If $f(s_1,...,s_n)$ is rewritten by the jth equation then $s_i = t_i^j \beta$. If t_i^j contains variables $x_{i1},...,x_{ir_i}$ and all these are e-demanded to normalize e_j, then s_i must be normalized. This is because all nonvariable symbols in t_i^j are constructors, and so s_i will be in NF if each of $\beta(x_{i1}),...,\beta(x_{ir_i})$ are in NF. Hence x_i appears in $g_j(e_j^{ee})$ if $x_{i1} \wedge \cdots \wedge x_{ir_i}$ appears in e_j^{ee} (and hence (7)). By the same argument, if t_i^j consists entirely of constructors (no variables), s_i must be normalized to match it and hence x_i is e-demanded (and hence (5)). Otherwise we cannot say anything about the demand on x_i and thus it does not appear in f^{ee} (and hence (8)).

The above equations directly compute f^{ee} if f is non-recursive. In case of recursive functions we use the following fix point iteration procedure. Let $f, h, ...$ denote all functions in the program[6]. Define $f^{ee,0} = \bigwedge_{j=1}^{n} x_j$ ($h^{ee,0}$ etc. are defined analogously). $f^{ee,i+1}$ is defined to be $\bigvee_{j=1}^{k} g_j(e_j^{ee}[f^{ee} \leftarrow f^{ee,i}, h^{ee} \leftarrow h^{ee,i}, ...])$. The limit of the sequence $f^{ee,0}, f^{ee,1}, ...$ is defined to

be f^{ee}. Before proceeding to prove the existence of such a limit and the correctness of our method, we illustrate how the above equations are used to compute strictness of $reverse$ (see fig.1) We assume that ap (abbreviation for $append$) has already been analyzed and $ap^{ee}(x, y) = x \wedge y$. Since rv (abbreviation for $reverse$) is recursive we use fix point iteration, starting with $rv^{ee0}(x_1) = x_1$.

$$\begin{aligned} rv^{ee1}(x_1) &= g_1([ap(rv(x_{12}), x_{11} : nil)]^{ee}) \vee g_2(nil^{ee}) \\ &= g_1(ap^{ee}([rv(x_{12})]^{ee}, [x_{11} : nil]^{ee}) \vee g_2(1) \\ &= g_1([rv(x_{12})]^{ee} \wedge [x_{11} : nil]^{ee}) \vee g_2(1) \\ &= g_1((rv^{ee0}([x_{12}]^{ee})) \wedge x_{11}) \vee g_2(1) \\ &= g_1(x_{12} \wedge x_{11}) \vee g_2(1)^7 \\ &= x_1 \vee x_1 = x_1 \\ &= x_1 \end{aligned}$$

A fix point has been reached, showing that $rv^{ee}(x_1) = x_1$.

Now we proceed to show that f^{ee} can be effectively computed. The first step is to show that g_j's are monotonic on boolean functions. Note that our definition of g_j is based on the DNF *representation* of a boolean function, which is not unique. Hence we need to show that g_j is indeed a function on boolean functions.

Lemma 1 g_j *is a function that maps boolean functions with variables* $x_{11},...,x_{1r_1},...,x_{nr_n}$ *to a boolean function with variables* $x_1,...,x_n$.

Proof: This lemma is established by showing that all DNF's that are equivalent are mapped onto equivalent formulas by g_j. First, note that the boolean formulas do not contain $\neg$ and hence there is a unique minimal DNF if the absorption law $(\varphi_1 \wedge \psi_1) \vee \varphi_1 = \varphi_1$ is used to minimize a DNF. In other words, any DNF representing a function can be rewritten into any other DNF representing the same function by successive applications of the absorption law (i.e., either by replacing $(\varphi_1 \wedge \psi_1) \vee \varphi_1$ into φ_1 or vice versa). Hence it suffices to show that $g_j((\varphi_1 \wedge \psi_1) \vee \varphi_1) = g_j(\varphi_1)$, which, by (4), reduces to showing $g_j(\varphi_1 \wedge \psi_1) \vee g_j(\varphi_1) = g_j(\varphi_1)$. Suppose $g_j(\varphi_1)$ can be reduced to φ_1' by repeated application of (7) followed by an application of (8). The same series of reductions using (7) can be performed on $g_j(\varphi_1 \wedge \psi_1)$ to yield $\varphi_1' \wedge g_j(\psi_1')$. Now $(\varphi_1' \wedge g_j(\psi_1')) \vee \varphi_1' = \varphi_1' = g_j(\varphi_1)$ and this completes the proof. ∎

Corollary 1 g_j's are monotonic.

If φ and ψ are in DNF then the formula $\varphi \vee \psi$ is in DNF and therefore equation 4 can be applied to yield $g_j(\varphi \vee \psi) = g_j(\varphi) \vee g_j(\psi)$. This implies g_j's are monotonic.

---

[6]For notational simplicity we list all the functions in a program as $f, h, ..$

[7]From definition of $reverse$, $g_1(x_{11} \wedge x_{12}) = x_1$ (by (7)) and $g_2(1) = x_1$ (by (5)).

Now we show that f^{ee} can be effectively computed.

Lemma 2 $f^{ee,i+1} \geq f^{ee,i}$.

Proof: We prove a stronger result, i.e., $f^{ee,i+1} \geq f^{ee,i}, h^{ee,i+1} \geq h^{ee,i}$ etc., where $\geq$ stands for the natural ordering on the lattice of boolean formula (given by $\varphi \geq \psi$ iff $\varphi \vee \psi = \varphi$). The proof of this lemma is by induction. For basis we need to show that $f^{ee,1} \geq f^{ee,0}$. Note that $f^{ee,1} > 0$ since all $g_j(\varphi) > 0$ for any φ. Therefore $f^{ee,1} \geq x_1 \wedge \cdots \wedge x_n = f^{ee,0}$ since 0 is the only boolean formula less than $x_1 \wedge \cdots \wedge x_n$. For the induction step, assume that $f^{ee,i+1} \geq f^{ee,i}$ for all $i < m$. Let ψ_l denote the formula $\bigvee_{j=1}^{k} g_j(e_j^{ee}[f^{ee} \leftarrow f^{ee,l-1}, h^{ee} \leftarrow h^{ee,l-1}, ...])$. Note that ψ_{m+1} is obtained from ψ_m by replacing $f^{ee,m-1}, h^{ee,m-1}, ...$ by $f^{ee,m}, h^{ee,m}, ...$ Since g_j's are monotonic on the lattice of boolean formulas and $f^{ee,m} \geq f^{ee,m-1}, h^{ee,m} \geq h^{ee,m-1}$, etc. (by induction hypothesis), we have $\psi_{m+1} = f^{ee,m+1} \geq \psi_m = f^{ee,m}$. ∎

Corollary 2 f^{ee} *can be effectively computed.*

Follows from the fact that the domain of boolean functions is finite and hence the ascending chain $f^{ee,0}, f^{ee,1}, ...$ reaches a limit after a finite number of steps.

2.1.1 Proof of Safety

The previous approaches to strictness analysis using abstract interpretation used methods based on denotational semantics. Specifically, the concrete interpretation domain is a lattice and the meaning of recursive functions is their least fixed point. The same holds in the abstract interpretation domain. The safety proof in such a case involves showing that the mapping from concrete to abstract interpretation domain is preserved under composition and least fixed point operation. In contrast, we do not assume that the language is given a denotational semantics. In fact, our focus is on languages with semantics based on equational logic. We establish safety by directly showing that f^{ee} correctly specifies the arguments of f that are normalized in *any* reduction sequence that takes any term $f(\cdots)$ to its NF.

We first consider only nonrecursive programs.

Theorem 1 *For nonrecursive programs, the procedure to compute t^{ee} is sound with respect to definition 1 (strictness property).*

Proof: In order to do this we must show that the equations for x^{ee}, c^{ee}, f^{ee} and the rule of substitution are correct. Having already done so for substitution rule, we now consider the remaining three cases.

Case 1: x^{ee}: Correctness in this case is obvious.

Case 2: c^{ee}: Any instance $c(s_1, ..., s_n)$ of $c(x_1, ..., x_n)$ can be normalized only by normalizing $s_1, ..., s_n$ and hence the correctness of c^{ee}.

Case 3: f^{ee}: In this case, the proof proceeds as follows. We divide all paths to NF into several groups. Within each group we specify the subterms that must be normalized when any path in that group is taken. Then a boolean formula can be associated with each group that captures this information. The disjunction of the boolean formulas for each group will then specify the subterms to be normalized in any path to NF, and hence the strictness of f.

Let $s = f(s_1, ..., s_n)$ be an arbitrary instance of $f(x_1, ..., x_n)$.

$Group_1$: s is in HNF: In this case the NF can be reached only by normalizing each of $s_1, ..., s_n$. Therefore $f^{ee} = x_1 \wedge \cdots \wedge x_n$ in this case.

$Group_2$: s is not in HNF: In any reduction sequence of s to NF, s reduces to an instance $s' = f(s'_1, ..., s'_n)$ of some lhs, where $s_i \rightarrow^* s'_i$. This group can now be subdivided into k groups depending on which of the k rules defining f is applicable.

$Group_{2,j}$: jth rule matches s': In this case $s' = f(t_1^j, ...t_n^j)\sigma$ and is rewritten into e_j. Assume that e_j^{ee} is already known (this holds for nonrecursive programs) and is given by $\varphi_1 \vee \cdots \vee \varphi_m$. Now this group can be further divided into m groups depending on whether the subterms normalized are substitutions for variables in one of $\varphi_1, \varphi_2, \cdots \varphi_m$.

$Group_{2,j,l}$: subterms corresponding to φ_l are normalized. Now consider a t_i^j that contains variables $x_{i1}, ..., x_{ir_i}$. If $\varphi_l = x_{i1} \wedge \cdots \wedge x_{ir_i} \cdots$, then all subterms $\sigma(x_{iq}), 1 \leq q \leq r_i$ are normalized on any path in this group and hence $s'_i = t_i^j \sigma$ is normalized. Thus s_i is normalized on any path in this group. Now consider those t_i^j's that contain no variables. The s'_i's are in NF and thus s_i's are again normalized on these paths. Thus equations (7) and (5) correctly specify the boolean formula that identifies the subterms to be normalized in any path in this group.

Equation (4) corresponds to taking a disjunction over all groups within $Group_{2,j}$, and (3) corresponds to disjunction over all groups within $Group_2$. Finally, we take the disjunction over $Group_1$ and $Group_2$ to get $(\bigvee_{j=1}^{k} g_j(e_j^{ee})) \vee (x_1 \wedge \cdots \wedge x_n) = \bigvee_{j=1}^{k} g_j(e_j^{ee})$ (since $g_j(e_j^{ee}) > 0$ and 0 is the only formula less than $(x_1 \wedge \cdots \wedge x_n)$). This establishes the correctness of f^{ee}, assuming that we already know e_j^{ee}. In case of nonrecursive functions, f^{ee} can be computed bottom up, and this completes the proof. ∎

Now we need to extend the proof of correctness to recursive functions. First we define *depth* of a sequence of reductions $t_1 \rightarrow t_2 \rightarrow \cdots \rightarrow t_r$ as follows. Label all occurrences of $f, h, ...$ in t_1 with 0. Every time a redex

$f(\cdots)$ (or $h(\ldots),\ldots$) with label i is to be rewritten into an $e_j\beta$, label all occurrences of $f,h,\ldots$ in e_j with $i+1$ before rewrite. (Note that the occurrences of $f,h,\ldots$'s within β are not relabelled.) Now depth of $t_1 \to \cdots \to t_r$ is the maximum label assigned to any occurrence of a function symbol in $t_1,\ldots,t_r$. Intuitively, the labelling process counts the "number of times" a function symbol is rewritten.

We now define nonrecursive approximations to f that behave exactly like f on reduction sequences whose depth is bounded. Let $f^0, h^0, \ldots$ be constructors. Now f^{i+1} is defined by the equations

$$f^{i+1}(t_1^j,\ldots,t_n^j) \to e_j[f \leftarrow f^i, h \leftarrow h^i,\ldots], 1 \le j \le k$$

$h^{i+1},\ldots$ are defined analogously. Observe the close parallel between the definitions of $f^{ee,i}$ and f^i. In order to show that the f^i's "behave" like f, we define $strip(t)$ as the term obtained from t by replacing every $f^i, h^i,\ldots$ for all i by $f, h,\ldots$ respectively and $affix(t,i)$ as the term obtained by replacing $f, h,\ldots$ by $f^i, h^i, \ldots$.

Lemma 3 *For all sequences $t_1 \to \cdots \to t_n$ of depth less than l there exists a corresponding sequence $affix(t_1,l) = t'_1 \to \cdots \to t'_n$ where $strip(t'_i) = t_i$.*

Proof: By induction on n. It is routine and omitted.

Lemma 4 $f^{ee,i} = [f^i]^{ee}$.

Proof: By induction on i. For the basis f^0 is a constructor and hence $[f^0]^{ee} = x_1 \wedge \cdots \wedge x_n = f^{ee,0}$. Assume inductively that $f^{ee,m} = [f^m]^{ee}$ for all $m < i$. Now $[f^i]^{ee} = \bigvee g_j([e_j[f \leftarrow f^{i-1}, h \leftarrow \cdots]]^{ee})$, which is the same as $\bigvee g_j(e_j^{ee}[f^{ee} \leftarrow (f^{i-1})^{ee},\ldots]) = f^{ee,i}$. The proof now follows from induction hypothesis. ∎

Theorem 2 *The fix point iteration procedure computes f^{ee} correctly for recursive functions.*

Proof: The proof proceeds by showing that for every sequence that takes any instance $f(s_1,\ldots,s_n)$ to its NF, the subterms that need to be normalized are correctly specified by f^{ee}. Pick any sequence $\Gamma = t_1 \to t_2 \to \cdots \to t_n$ that normalizes $f(s_1,\ldots,s_n)$. Let i be the smallest integer such that $[f^i]^{ee} = f^{ee}$. The existence of such an i follows from corollary 2 and lemma 4. Let $l = max(1 + \text{depth of } \Gamma, i)$. By lemma 3 there exists a sequence $\Gamma' = t'_1 \to t'_2 \to \cdots \to t'_n$ where $affix(t_1,l) = t'_1$ and $strip(t'_i) = t_i$. Note that there is a one to one correspondence between subterms of t_i and subterms of t'_i. Therefore s_i (in t_1) is normalized whenever its corresponding subterm in t'_1 is normalized. From theorem 1, $[f^l]^{ee} = f^{ee}$ correctly specifies the subterms in t'_i normalized in Γ' and hence f^{ee} correctly specifies the subterms of t_1 normalized in Γ. Since no assumption was made about Γ or $s_1,\ldots,s_n$, the above holds for all reduction sequences leading to NF of any term $f(s_1,\ldots,s_n)$ and this concludes the proof. ∎

2.2 dd Analysis

To define t^{dd} observe that if the term is just the variable x, then there is a d-demand on it and hence $t^{dd} = x$. If it has a constructor at its root, then it is already in HNF and hence there is no demand on its subterms. The definition of t^{dd} when $t = f(s_1,\ldots,s_n)$ is quite similar to that of t^{ee}. Thus we have

$$x^{dd} = x \quad (9)$$
$$[c(x_1,\ldots,x_n)]^{dd} = 1 \quad (10)$$
$$[f(x_1,\ldots,x_n)]^{dd} = \bigvee_{j=1}^{k} g_j(e_j^{dd}) \quad (11)$$

The justification for forming the disjunction (over the k cases) is the same as for ee analysis. Now we define g_j as follows. Observe that when $f(s_1,\ldots,s_n)$ is rewritten by the jth equation and t_i^j is a nonvariable term, s_i needs to be root stabilized in order to match t_i^j. If t_i^j is a variable that is d-demanded in e_j, then also s_i needs to be root stabilized. This leads us to the following equations to define g_j.

$$g_j(\varphi) = \left(\bigwedge_{\substack{i \mid t_i^j \text{ is a} \\ \text{nonvariable}}} x_i\right) \wedge g_j(\varphi) \quad (12)$$

$$g_j(\varphi_1 \vee \varphi_2) = g_j(\varphi_1) \vee g_j(\varphi_2) \quad (13)$$
$$g_j(\varphi_1 \wedge \varphi_2) = g_j(\varphi_1) \wedge g_j(\varphi_2) \quad (14)$$
$$g_j(x_{i1}) = x_i, \text{ if } t_i^j \text{ is a variable} \quad (15)$$
$$g_j(x_{il}) = 1, \text{ if } t_i^j \text{ is a nonvariable} \quad (16)$$

In equation (16) the variable x_{il} is dropped since x_i is already known to be d-demanded by equation 12. By this definition, for the function $sequence$, $g_1(x_{11} \wedge x_{21}) = x_1 \wedge x_2$ and for $reverse$, $g_1(x_{11} \wedge x_{12}) = x_1$.

We illustrate how to compute f^{dd} for the if rule. Extensions to recursive functions is done using fixpoint iteration as before.

$$\begin{aligned} if^{dd}(x_1,x_2,x_3) &= [g_1(x_{21}^{dd}) \wedge x_1] \vee [g_2(x_{31}^{dd}) \wedge x_1] \\ &= (x_2 \wedge x_1) \vee (x_3 \wedge x_1) = \\ &= x_1 \wedge (x_2 \vee x_3) \end{aligned}$$

2.3 de Analysis

If the term t is just a variable x, then there is only d-demand on it but no e-demand and hence $t^{de} = 1$. If a term $c(s_1,\ldots,s_n)$ is d-demanded, then, since it is already in root stable form, there is no demand on its subterms $s_1,\ldots,s_n$. A function f may transform the d-demand on its output to a e-demand on some of its arguments (as specified by f^{de}) and d-demand on some others (as specified by f^{dd}). Hence the demand on the subterms of $f(s_1,\ldots,s_n)$ can be computed by propagating these *transformed demands* through the arguments.

This leads us to the following definition of t^{de}. A slight notational modification is needed here since the equation defining f^{de} deals with two different forms of strictness unlike the previous definitions. We therefore define $[f(s_1,...,s_n)]^{de}$ directly rather than from $f(x_1,...,x_n)$ as was done for ee and dd analysis.

$$x^{de} = 1 \quad (17)$$
$$[c(s_1,...,s_n)]^{de} = 1 \quad (18)$$
$$[f(s_1,...,s_n)]^{de} = f^{de}(s_1^{ee},...,s_n^{ee}) \quad (19)$$
$$= \wedge f^{dd}(s_1^{de},...,s_n^{de}) \quad (20)$$

where f^{de} is defined as follows:

$$f^{de}(x_1,...,x_n) = \bigvee_{j=1}^{k} g_j(e_j^{de}) \quad (21)$$

Here g_j is defined as in ee analysis. We illustrate de analysis through the example $sumtree$. In the following st is used to abbreviate $sumtree$. Note that $g_1(x_{11} \wedge x_{12}) = x_1$ and $g_2(1) = x_1$. Starting with $st^{de0} = x_1$ and assuming $+^{de}(x,y) = x \wedge y$ and $st^{ee} = x_1$, we have

$$st^{de1}(x_1) = g_1([st(x_{11}) + st(x_{12})]^{de}) \vee g_2(nil^{de})$$
$$= g_1([st(x_{11})]^{ee} \wedge [st(x_{12})]^{ee}) \wedge$$
$$\text{(second term)}) \vee x_1$$
$$= g_1(st^{ee,0}(x_{11}) \wedge st^{ee,0}(x_{12})) \vee x_1$$
$$= g_1(x_{11} \wedge x_{12}) \vee x_1$$
$$= x_1 \vee x_1 = x_1$$

and thus $sumtree$ is de in its argument. In step 2 of the above derivation the second term ($+^{dd}(s_1^{de},...,s_n^{de})$) in the definition of f^{de} was skipped because the de-strictness of $sumtree$ can be inferred even if we assume it to be 1.

Extensions to Higher Order Functions:
Our method can be extended to deal with higher order functions. We suggest how this can be done in section A of appendix. A formal treatment of this extension is beyond the scope of this paper.

3 Underlying Intuition

As mentioned earlier ee, dd and de strictness have distinct intuitive meanings related to identifiable properties of programs. We discuss this in the following.

3.1 Nonerasing TRS and ee-strictness

A function is nonerasing in its ith argument if it does not discard portions of this argument without even examining them. More precisely, ith argument t_i can be rewritten into a $t'_i \sigma_i$ such that every constructor symbol in t'_i participates in a match against a nonvariable symbol of an lhs and the substitutions σ_i appear unchanged in the normal form of $f(t_1,...,t_n)$. We refer to t'_i as a *skeleton* and σ_i as a *body*. The function can be thought of as *consuming* the skeleton and *conserving* the body. For example, in the case of $append(1:1+1:3:nil,1:2*1:nil) = 1:2:3:1:2:nil$, we have $t'_1 = x:y:z:nil$, $\sigma_1 = \{x=1, y=1+1, z=3\}$, $t'_2 = u$ and $\sigma_2 = \{u = 1:2*1:nil\}$.

Suppose that a term $t = f(t_1,...,t_n)$ is to be normalized and we know that f is nonerasing in its ith argument. Since each of the terms in the substitution σ_i appears in the normal form of t, each of them needs to be normalized. Note that in order to evaluate f, t_i has to be evaluated at least to the extent of yielding its skeleton. When the skeleton of t_i is evaluated and each term in its body is in normal form, t_i will be in normal form. Therefore t_i can be safely normalized before evaluating f. Thus a nonerasing function transforms an e-demand on its output to an e-demand on its arguments.

Constructors such as *cons* serve as 'tuple' operators and their effect is just to 'enclose' data items. We need to be able to utilize this information if our strictness analysis is to be effectively applied for algebraic data types. *The concept of nonerasing (or ee-strictness) precisely captures this effect of 'enclosing'*[8]. Just as most functions on flat domains are strict in their arguments, most functions on non-flat domains are ee-strict and the effectiveness of our methods is largely because of this fact. Intuitively, erasing functions are likely to occur rarely since such a function discards parts of its argument without even examining them.

3.2 Sequentiality and dd-strictness

The concept of sequentiality [Huet79] is related to directionality of a normalization algorithm. The normalization algorithm can be *lazy* and *deterministic* only if the TRS used in normalization is sequential. Given that a lazy evaluation procedure rewrites only those redices that *need* to be rewritten in order to reach NF, this means that we should be able to identify at least one needed redex in any term. Observe that a redex in a term t is needed if an e-demand at the root of t results in a d-demand at the root of the redex.

In general, functions such as $length$ that are dd-strict but not ee-strict occur (although not frequently). While normalizing terms whose root symbol is such a function only a d-demand can be assumed on its arguments. Since any term could appear in these argument positions, we conclude that a system is sequential if a d-

---

[8]For terms with constructor roots, the skeleton is just a variable and its body is the whole term

demand on the root of every term (that is reducible) results in a d-demand on one of the redices in it.

Huet and Levy [Huet79], O'Donnell [OD85] and Thatte [That84] have developed methods for computing needed redices in *strongly sequential* systems and its restricted variants. All these methods correspond to approximating the term $\bigvee_{j=1}^{k} g_j(e_j^{dd})$ by the first term on the rhs of equation 12 (i.e., $\bigwedge_{i|t_i^j}$ is a nonvariable x_i). However their analysis procedure reasons about all *partial redices* (a term t is a partial redex if there exists an lhs which is an instance of t), whereas we reason only about those of the form $f(x_1, ..., x_n)$. Despite this, dd-analysis described in this paper is useful for repairing violations of strong sequentiality in many cases (see section 5).

3.3 *de*-strictness

It appears that functions on non-flat domains are rarely *de*-strict. On the other hand, since d- and e-demands coincide on flat-domains, most functions on flat-domains are *de*-strict. A function f is *de*-strict if it "consumes" all its input before any term with f as root can be reduced to its head normal form. Since the root of a term in head normal form can be output, head normalizing can be thought of as producing (incremental) output. This leads us to the following characterization of a *de*-strict function: the skeletons of its arguments are their normal forms and these are fully consumed before the function produces any output.

A *de*-strict function such as *split* produces its output bottom-up, i.e., the leaves of the output term are produced first and the root appears last. (This characterization holds vacuously for *sumtree* also since its output is a term with a single node.) For functions whose outputs are lists, this means that these lists are produced in the reverse order. This justifies why *de*-strict functions on non-flat domains are rare in practice.

4 Pragmatics

We now discuss the practical implications of our methods. The applications of our analysis procedures (for parallel evaluation, sequentiality repair and a critical optimization step for TRS implementations) are discused in the following section.

4.1 How Effective are Our Methods?

Table 1 illustrates the efficacy of *ee*-analysis. Situations where it might fail arise in the context of erasing functions such as *length*. It would appear that such functions may benefit from an analysis that infers that *length* needs to evaluate the outer structure of its input list without fully evaluating the elements of the list. However, this analysis would be useful only if the argument to *length* is not already evaluated. It is possible to ensure that the list will be fully evaluated if it is also used by an *ee*-strict function under *e*-demand. It will be quite surprising if a list is referenced exclusively by functions that discard parts of it **without even examining** them! Hence a finer grain analysis may not yield any more useful strictness information than *ee*-analysis.

4.2 Linear Time Heuristics for *ee*-analysis

The time complexity of the analysis method presented earlier is exponential in the number of arguments to a function [Hud86]. However, we can employ efficient heuristics to test if a function is *ee*-strict in all its arguments. In this section we describe such a heuristic that requires time proportional to the size of the program. In those cases when this heuristic fails we resort to the method in section 2. This heuristic also computes Mycroft's $f^\#$ within the same time bounds. In the following, we assume that if f and h are not mutually recursive and f calls h, then the analysis of h is done prior to that of f [Myc80]. We also assume that the wordsize (typically 32 or 64 bits) is larger than the number of variables in an lhs (typically 2 or 3).

Fixpoint iteration is used to compute f^{ee} for recursive functions, starting with $f^{ee,0}$ being *ee*-strict in all its arguments. If f^{ee} is indeed *ee*-strict in all its arguments, then $f^{ee} = f^{ee,1}$ and there needs to be just a single iteration. If this iteration (as well as checking that $f^{ee,1} = x_1 \wedge \cdots \wedge x_n$) can be done in time proportional to the sizes of the rhs involved, we have an algorithm whose time complexity is linear in the size of the program.

Recall $f^{ee}(x_1, ..., x_n) = \bigvee_{j=1}^{k} g_j(e_j^{ee})$, and so $f^{ee,1} = \bigwedge_{i=1}^{n} x_i$ iff $g_j(e_j^{ee}) = \bigwedge_{i=1}^{n} x_i$ for every j. This in turn implies that if $x_{11}, ..., x_{nr_n}$ are all the variables in the lhs of the jth equation defining f then e_j^{ee} must be $\bigwedge_{i=1}^{n} \bigwedge_{j=1}^{r_i} x_{ij}$. We need to test if this is the case for each e_j in time proportional to the size of e_j. In order to do this, we compute an approximation to e_j^{ee} by substituting an approximation of h^{ee} for each function or constructor h that appears in e_j. This approximation, denoted by h^{ne}, is the set of arguments that are not erased by h, i.e., those arguments in which h is *ee*-strict. For the occurrences of f in e_j, $f^{ne} = \{x_1, ..., x_n\}$. The following equations compute the approximation e_j^{ne}.

$$\begin{aligned} x^{ne} &= \{x\} \\ [c(s_1, ..., s_n)]^{ne} &= s_1^{ne} \cup \cdots \cup s_n^{ne} \end{aligned}$$

$$[h(s_1,...,s_n)]^{ne} = \bigcup_{h \text{ is } ee \text{ strict in } x_i} s_i^{ne} \quad \text{if } h \neq if$$
$$= s_1^{ne} \cup (s_2^{ne} \cap s_3^{ne}) \quad \text{if } h = if$$

If the sets s_i^{ne} are represented by bitvectors then union and intersection operations can be done in constant time. It is immediate from the above definition that the number of such operations is bounded by the number of edges in the tree representation of e_j. This implies that e_j^{ne} can be computed in time proportional to the size of e_j. Since checking if $e_j^{ne} = \{x_{11},...,x_{nr_n}\}$ can be done in constant time with the bitvector representation, we have the desired linear algorithm.

If $f_1,...,f_l$ are mutually recursive then they have to be analyzed simultaneously using the above procedure. If there is at least one f_i such that $f_i^{ne} \neq \{x_1,...,x_{rank(f_i)}\}$, then we cannot conclude anything about the ee-strictness of any of $f_1,...,f_l$. We say that the above heuristic fails in such cases. In practice such failures do not occur very often. For instance, this method succeeds in all examples in fig.1 (except *length* and *split*) and those in table 1.

4.3 Appropriateness of Stream Strictness (or the Case for e-demand)

Note that assuming e-demand at the root may pose difficulties in handling programs that diverge after producing some output, e.g., after generating the first few elements of a list. For instance, suppose we want to normalize $f(g(list))$, where f is ee-strict and $g(list)$ diverges after producing some output. A sequential implementation that uses our ee analysis will never evaluate f since f will be applied only after completely evaluating $g(list)$. Hence no output will be produced. In contrast observe that this is not the case in a parallel implementation since evaluation of f proceeds in parallel with that of g and hence f will "consume" all the output produced by g, thus producing the initial part of the output.

Programs that diverge after producing some output must be aborted abnormally through user intervention. Clearly, such scenarios seldom arise with programs that are used very often and it is precisely such programs that warrant the extra compile time effort spent in optimization using strictness analysis. Thus our simple e-demand assumption is quite acceptable even for sequential evaluation in most cases.

Nevertheless, the only demand that assures nonterminating programs do produce some output is *stream demand*, i.e., "all the heads of the output stream are needed" [Hall87]. Suppose head normalizing a subterm t of the input term leads to a nonterminating computation. Further suppose that t is the first such subterm.

Then stream demand requires that the portions of the term above and to the left of t be output. This poses an important and difficult problem with stream strictness. Unless some form of termination analysis is performed, very few call-by-need's can be transformed into call-by-value and consequently very little parallelism is extracted.

For illustration, consider the *quicksort* example in fig.1. When $qs(l)$ is evaluated under stream demand assumption, call-by-value can be used only in evaluating the first argument of *split*. This is possible since *split* is *de* on this argument and hence even to produce the head of the output list, the whole of the input list is to be normalized. After splitting, the term gets rewritten into $append(qs(l_1), qs(l_2))$. When stream demand is assumed, $qs(l_2)$ needs to be evaluated only if $qs(l_1)$ terminates and outputs a finite list l_1'. This implies that unless we know that qs terminates on input l_1, it is not safe to evaluate $qs(l_2)$ before *append* – which means that without knowing this we cannot use call-by-value for the second argument of *append*. In addition no significant parallelism can be exploited since $qs(l_1)$ and $qs(l_2)$ cannot be evaluated in parallel.

Proving termination in the presence of recursive functions is based on establishing a well-founded ordering in which each rhs is strictly less than the corresponding lhs. Coming up with the ordering often requires insight into the problem being solved and is difficult to automate except in trivial cases. For instance, in the *quicksort* example, termination depends on showing that the lengths of both lists output by *split* is strictly less than that of its input list. Termination of many other functions such as *factorial*, *matmult*, *mergesort* are also equally difficult to establish. Given this complexity and the insight needed to come up with the ordering, it seems unlikely that such a procedure can be automated. Hence we discuss how much useful strictness information can be found under stream strictness assumption without termination analysis.

Without such termination analysis, we can evaluate only the first element of qs, apply *append* on this element to output it, generate the next element and so on. Observe that this process is not too different from usual lazy evaluation, viz., head normalize $qs(l_1)$, then head normalize *append*, and then evaluate the first element. Consequently, most call-by-needs transformed under normal form demand appear not to be transformed under this demand. This means that no significant parallelism can be exploited under stream strictness assumption. For instance, in the examples given in table 1, it uses call-by-value only for *sum*, *split* and *fac*. It exploits parallelism in *fac* only, and fails to exploit any parallelism in others. Furthermore, in most examples (such as *quicksort*, *mergesort*) evaluation under stream demand assumption results in about the same number of suspensions and resumptions of function evaluations as normal lazy evaluation. Based on the above discussion, it therefore appears that performing strictness analysis under stream demand will not be very useful.

5 Applications

In this section we outline the applications of our analysis methods. We discuss in some detail applications unique to our methods and mention the others in passing.

5.1 Parallel Evaluation: Use of *ee* and *de*-analysis

The use of strictness analysis for enhancing parallelism in functional programs is well known [Cla85]. The essential idea is that if a function is known to require some of its arguments in normal form, they can be normalized in parallel. Our strictness analysis methods are thus useful for automatic extraction of parallelism implicit in a functional program.

In addition to increasing parallelism, strictness analysis also improves the efficiency of parallel normalization in two ways. Firstly, we realize the advantages of call-by-value over call-by-need [Myc80]. Secondly, it reduces interprocessor communication considerably. Consider the term $sum(sequence(n))$ where the sum node is in processor p_1 and $sequence(n)$ is in p_2. If strictness analysis is used, p_1 communicates with p_2 asking it to normalize $sequence(n)$ and pass the result back. Thus communication is limited to a single normalization request and another to pass the result back. On the other hand, without strictness analysis, p_1 will ask p_2 to only head normalize $sequence(n)$. This will ultimately result in n communications for head normalization requests and another n to pass the results back. This shows that in a parallel environment the gains of strictness analysis are very substantial.

5.2 Applications of *dd*-analysis

5.2.1 Optimization for Term Rewriting Implementations

Robert Strandh pointed out a potential source of inefficiency in the term rewriting implementation of an equational language [Str87]. The rhs of the equations are typically large terms and contain subterms which may ultimately be "thrown away". Consider for example the rhs $if(t_1, t_2, t_3)$ where one of t_2 or t_3 will always be discarded. The computation involved in creating such subterms is thus wasted. Very often, an rhs has several nested levels of if, thus wasting much of the effort spent in creating it.

In order to remedy these problems, Strandh proposed to transform the input program into another where the depth of rhs are uniformly reduced to 2. This bounds the computation wasted in creating portions of the term that are ultimately discarded. The reduction in depth was achieved by introducing new functions that "abbreviate" some of the subterms. For instance, the function f given by

$$f(x,y) \to x * if(x^2 > y^2, h(y), i(y))$$

is transformed into

$$\begin{aligned} f(x,y) &\to x * f_1(x,y) \\ f_1(x,y) &\to if(f_2(x,y), h(y), i(y)) \\ f_2(x,y) &\to f_3(x) > f_4(y) \\ f_3(x) &\to x^2 \\ f_4(y) &\to y^2 \end{aligned}$$

The idea of uniformly decreasing the depth of rhs seems quite arbitrary. While it may be an adequate solution for most practical cases it is not intuitively satisfactory. Note that in the above example, only $h(y)$ or $i(y)$ can be discarded. Since these terms cannot be abbreviated further, there is no need to transform the above equation. By introducing unnecessary abbreviations, the computational effort has actually *increased* through the extra rewrites. If it is possible to discover which subterms cannot be discarded, i.e., will always be subjected some degree of evaluation, then we can avoid introducing abbreviations for such subterms. This is indeed possible through dd-analysis, as described below.

When a rewrite is performed, there is a d-demand at the root of the rewritten part of the term. If this d-demand is transformed into a d-demand at the root of a subterm, then that subterm will be subjected to at least one level of evaluation and hence the subterm need not be abbreviated. Otherwise the subterm is abbreviated. If this criterion is used then the equation defining f is not transformed at all. This is what we expect in the case of f. *This transformation is critical for efficient implementation and dd-analysis tells us exactly when to transform.*

5.2.2 Sequentiality Repair

Another application of dd-analysis is in repairing violations of *strong sequentiality* of equational programs. Consider the term $merge(f(t_1), f(t_2))$, where at least one of $f(t_1)$ and $f(t_2)$ is to be head normalized in order for any of the equations defining $merge$ to match, but we cannot find which one. Hence the system is not strongly sequential. The only safe way to handle such constructs is to first fork off *parallel* processes each attempting to head normalize one argument, wait till one of them succeeds and then kill the other processes. There are obvious overheads associated with such a parallel strategy.

Observe that *merge* is *dd* in both its arguments and hence both $f(t_1)$ and $f(t_2)$ can be safely head normalized in $merge(f(t_1), f(t_2))$ before attempting any evaluation of *merge*. There is no need to fork parallel processes and no effort is wasted. Thus by performing *dd*-analysis we are able to give sequential normalization algorithms even for systems that are not strongly sequential.

6 Comparison with Related Work

Hughes [Hug85] was the first to address strictness analysis for non-flat domains. His method was based on an analysis of the context in which an expression is evaluated. However, his methods were not completely intuitive and the analysis requires algebraic manipulation techniques that do not seem mechanizable.

The notion of demand propagation we use is similar to that of Lindstrom [Lin86]. His demand patterns include not only $\{e, d\}$, but also recursively formed pairs of them. His method is based on abstract interpretation of a class of function graphs [Kel80] over this domain of demand patterns. However, his approach is quite complex and appears quite expensive to implement. Although he is able to reason about intermediate levels of strictness, his methods are not powerful enough to conclude that in order to normalize $append(x, y)$, both x and y can be normalized before evaluating *append*.

Hall and Wise [Hall87] use strictness patterns (which resemble demand patterns of Lindstrom) to annotate programs with strictness information. Unlike us, they create several versions of a function depending on the context in which it is invoked, but no satisfactory means of controlling the number of versions (by merging versions that are similar) is presented. Also, they can extract strictness information even from a list in which every other element is strict. They do not assume a normal form demand at the root of the term being normalized, but only that all heads of the output stream are needed. The implications of this were discussed in section 4.3.

Wadler and Hughes [Wad87] base strictness analysis on context analysis. They can reason about some intermediate levels of strictness (such as head strictness and tail strictness for lists), but still restrict their analysis to a finite number of contexts (which correspond to some "simple" strictness patterns of Hall). Unfortunately, their method does not reason adequately through user defined functions. For instance, in the definition $cond(x, y, z) = if(x, y, z)$, they cannot conclude that *cond* is strict in one of y or z. For this reason they give special treatment to *if* and *case* constructs, assuming that the user is unlikely to define functions like *cond*.

All the above approaches, unlike our methods, use large domains. Moreover some of them are restricted to monomorphic languages while the others use different domains for different data types and therefore must automatically synthesize these domains and modify the analysis for each user defined data type. Although, unlike them, we do not reason about intermediate levels of strictness, we do not seem to lose any power because of it. Our methods are still able to transform call-by-need into call-by-value in most cases in practice.

7 Conclusion

In this paper we presented a new approach for strictness analysis of equational (or functional) programs on non-flat domains. Our approach is simpler and more intuitive than previously known methods. It is also more general in its ability to handle function definitions by pattern match, polymorphism and all user defined data types. It is computationally efficient and has little run time overhead. Although our approach appears quite powerful in practice, it would an interesting problem to generalize our method to reason about intermediate levels of strictness also.

Acknowledgement

We thank Prof. Prateek Mishra for his valuable comments and suggestions on preliminary versions of this paper.

References

[Aug84]   L. AUGUSTSSON, A compiler for Lazy ML, *Proc. of the 1984 LISP and Functional Programming Conference.*

[Burn85]   BURN, G.L., C.L. HANKIN AND S. ABRAMSKY, Theory and Practice of Strictness Analysis for Higher Order Functions, *Workshop on Programs as Data Objects*, edited by N. JONES AND H. GAZINGER, *Springer-Verlag LNCS 217, 1985.*

[Burs80]   BURSTALL, MACQUEEN AND SANELLA,

HOPE: An Experimental Applicative Language, *Proc. of 1st Int. LISP Conf., 1980.*

[Cla85] C. CLACK AND S.L. PEYTON JONES, Strictness Analysis — a Practical Approach, *Functional Programming and Computer Architecture, Springer-Verlag LNCS 201, 1985, pp. 35-49.*

[Cou77] COUSOT, P. AND R. COUSOT, Abstract Interpretation: A Unified Lattice Model for Static Analysis of Programs by Construction or Approximation of Fixpoints, *Symp. on Principles of Programming Languages, 1977.*

[Fut85] KOKICHI FUTATSUGI, JOSEPH A. GOGUEN, JEAN-PIERRE JOUANNAUD, AND JOSE MESEGUER, Principles of OBJ2, *Proc. 12th ACM Symposium on Principles of Programming Languages, 1985.*

[Hall87] CORDELIA V. HALL AND DAVID S. WISE, Compiling Strictness into Streams, *14th ACM Symp. on Principles of Programming Languages, 1987, pp. 132-143.*

[HD82] HOFFMAN, C. AND O'DONNELL, M., Programming with Equations, *ACM Transactions on Programming Languages and Systems, 1982, pp. 83-112.*

[Hud86] P. HUDAK AND J. YOUNG, Higher Order Strictness Analysis for Untyped Lambda Calculus, *13th ACM Symp. on Principles of Programming Languages, 1986, pp. 97-109.*

[Huet79] HUET, G. AND LEVY, J.J., Computations in Nonambiguous Linear Term Rewriting Systems, *Tech. Rep. No. 359(1979), INRIA, Le Chesney, France.*

[Hug85] R.J.M. HUGHES, Strictness Detection in non-flat Domains, *Workshop on Programs as Data Objects,* edited by N. JONES AND H. GAZINGER, *Springer-Verlag LNCS 217, 1985.*

[Kel80] KELLER, R.M, Semantics and Applications of Function Graphs, *Technical Report UUCS-80-112, Univ. of Utah, 1980.*

[Kuo89] KUO, T.M. AND P. MISHRA, Strictness Analysis: A Type Inference Perspective, *Conference on Functional Programming and Computer Architecture, 1989 (to appear).*

[Lin86] GARY LINDSTROM, Static Evaluation of Functional Programs, *Proc. of SIGPLAN'86 Symp. on Compiler Construction, SIGPLAN Notices 21, 7, 1986, pp. 196-206.*

[Mar87] C. MARTIN AND C. HANKIN, Finding Fixed Points in Finite lattices, *Conf. on Functional Programming Languages and Computer Architecture, 1987.*

[Myc80] ALAN MYCROFT, The Theory and Practice of Transforming Call-by-need into Call-by-value, *International Symposium on Programming, Springer LNCS 83, 1980.*

[OD77] M.J. O'DONNELL, Computing in Systems described by Equations, *Springer LNCS 58, 1977.*

[OD85] O'DONNELL. M.J., Equational Logic as a Programming Language, *MIT Press 1985.*

[OD87] M.J. O'DONNELL, Term-Rewriting Implementation of Equational Logic Programming, *Rewriting Techniques and Applications, Springer-Verlag LNCS 256, 1987, pp. 1-12.*

[Sek89] R.C. SEKAR, SHAUNAK PAWAGI AND I.V. RAMAKRISHNAN, Transforming Strongly Sequential Rewrite Systems with Constructors for Efficient Parallel Execution, *3rd Int. Conf. on Rewriting Techniques and Applications 1989.*

[Str87] ROBERT STRANDH, Optimizing Equational Programs, *Rewriting Techniques and Applications, Springer-Verlag LNCS 256, 1987, pp. 13-24.*

[That84] SATISH THATTE, Demand driven Evaluation with Equations, *Technical Report CRL-TR-34-84, University of Michigan Computing Research Laboratory, Ann Arbor.*

[Tur85] D.A. TURNER, Miranda: A non-strict Functional Language with Polymorphic Types, *Functional Programming Languages and Computer Architecture, Springer-Verlag LNCS 201, 1985, pp. 1-16.*

[Wad87] PHILIP WADLER AND R.J.M. HUGHES, Projections for Strictness Analysis, *3rd Int. Conf. on Functional Programming and Computer Architecture, 1987.*

Appendix

A Higher Order Functions

We suggest how *ee*-analysis can be extended to deal with higher order functions. This extension follows similar lines along which Mycroft's method was extended to higher order functions [Burn85]. The development here is quite intuitive and is illustrated through an example.

Consider the function *map* defined as follows:

$$map(h, x_{21} : x_{22}) \rightarrow h(x_{21}) : map(h, x_{22})$$
$$map(h, nil) \rightarrow nil$$

where h is a function variable.

$$map^{ee} = g_1([h(x_{21}) : map(h, x_{22})]^{ee}) \vee g_2(nil^{ee})$$
$$= g_1(h^{ee}(x_{21}) \wedge map^{ee}(h, x_{22})) \vee x_2$$

Now note that h^{ee} is unknown when we use fix point iteration procedure to compute map^{ee}. Checking equality of $map^{ee,i}$ and $map^{ee,i+1}$ under such circumstances is a difficult problem. (Progress in this direction is reported in [Mar87].) However, h^{ee} can be only one of x_1 and 1. Let us denote $map^{ee,i}[h^{ee} \leftarrow \varphi]$ by $map^{ee,i}(\varphi)$. Now if $map^{ee,i}(1) = map^{ee,i+1}(1)$ and $map^{ee,i}(x_1) = map^{ee,i+1}(x_1)$, then we can conclude that $map^{ee,i} = map^{ee,i+1}$. Based on this observation, we compute map^{ee} as follows.

$$map^{ee,1} = g_1(h^{ee}(x_{21}) \wedge h \wedge x_{22}) \vee x_2$$
$$map^{ee,1}(1) = h \vee x_2$$
$$map^{ee,1}(x_1) = g_1(x_{21} \wedge x_{22} \wedge h) \vee x_2 = x_2$$
$$map^{ee,2} = g_1(h^{ee}(x_{21}) \wedge$$
$$[g_1(h^{ee}(x_{22,1}) \wedge h \wedge x_{22,2}) \vee x_{22}]) \vee x_2$$
$$map^{ee,2}(1) = g_1(g_1(h \wedge x_{22,2})) \vee x_2 = h \vee x_2$$
$$map^{ee,2}(x_1) = g_1(x_{21} \wedge [g_1(x_{22,1} \wedge h \wedge x_{22,2}) \vee x_{22}])$$
$$\vee x_2$$
$$= g_1(x_{21} \wedge x_{22}) \vee x_2 = x_2$$

A fixpoint has been reached. The analysis shows that *map* is *ee*-strict in its second argument if its first argument is an *ee*-strict function.

B Programs for Examples in Table 1

1. Matrix Multiplication

Input: Two matrices, first is a list whose elements are rows and the second is a list whose elements are columns.

Output: The product matrix, which is list of its rows.

$$matmult(x : xs, y) \rightarrow rowmult(x, y) :$$
$$matmult(xs, y)$$
$$matmult(nil, y) \rightarrow nil$$
$$rowmult(x, y : ys) \rightarrow dotmult(x, y) :$$
$$rowmult(x, ys)$$
$$rowmult(x, nil) \rightarrow nil$$
$$dotmult(x : xs, y : ys) \rightarrow x * y + dotmult(xs, ys)$$
$$dotmult(nil, nil) \rightarrow nil$$

2. Mergesort

$$mergesort(x : y : z) \rightarrow mergesort1($$
$$split(x : y : z, nil, nil))$$
$$mergesort(x : nil) \rightarrow x : nil$$
$$split(x : y : xs, z, w) \rightarrow split(xs, x : z, y : w)$$
$$split(x : nil, z, w) \rightarrow \langle x : z, w \rangle$$
$$split(nil, z, w) \rightarrow \langle z, w \rangle$$
$$mergesort1(\langle z, w \rangle) \rightarrow merge(mergesort(z),$$
$$mergesort(w))$$
$$merge(x : xs, y : ys) \rightarrow if(x > y, y : merge(x : xs, ys)$$
$$x : merge(xs, y : ys))$$
$$merge(x, nil) \rightarrow x$$
$$merge(nil, y) \rightarrow y$$

3. Numerical Integration

numint uses trapezoidal rule to evaluate the integral of a function f from Xlo to Xhi, with $deltaX$ being the distance between successive points. *numint* partitions the interval Xlo to Xhi recursively into smaller intervals till the size of the interval is less than $deltaX$, whence the area of the corresponding trapezoid is computed. $eval(f, x)$ gives the value of f at x.

$$numint(f, Xlo, Xhi, deltaX) \rightarrow$$
$$if(Xhi - Xlo > deltaX,$$
$$numint(f, Xlo, (Xlo + Xhi)/2, deltaX)$$
$$+ numint(f, (Xlo + Xhi)/2, Xhi, deltaX),$$
$$(Xhi - Xlo) * (eval(f, Xlo) + eval(f, Xhi))/2)$$

4. N Queens

Partitions the search space (consisting of all possible placings of n pieces on a $n \times n$ chess borad) recursively till the space consists of just a single spacing. The validity of this placing is then checked using *check* and if so, the placing is output using *gen*. Note *check* and *gen* are not specified here, as they are not of much relevance to the parallelism aspect.

$nqueens\_all\_soln(n) \to nqueens(0, n^n - 1, n)$
$nqueens(lpos, hpos, n) \to$
$\quad if(lpos < hpos,$
$\quad\quad append(nqueens(lpos, \lfloor(lpos + hpos)/2\rfloor, n),$
$\quad\quad\quad nqueens(\lfloor(lpos + hpos)/2\rfloor + 1, hpos, n)),$
$\quad if(check(lpos, n), gen(lpos, n), nil))$

5. Factorial

$fac(x, y) \to$
$\quad if(x < y, fac(x, \lfloor(x + y)/2\rfloor) * fac(\lfloor(x + y)/2\rfloor + 1, y), x)$

6. Recursive Doubling (also known as Path Compression)

Input: a term $f(ptr(f(ptr(...f(last(finval), t_n)...), t_2), t_1)$. This term actually denotes a string of processors, with the ith f standing for the ith 'processor' with its local data item t_i and a link to next processor $ptr(...)$.

output: A term denoting the input processors, each with a direct pointer to *finval*.

Remarks: A naive algorithm for this takes $O(n)$ time, where n is the number of f's. The parallel algorithm given below takes only $O(\log n)$ time. Such a parallel algorithm forms the heart of many parallel algorithms. In the output term h's denote processors. Actually, each f, g and h should be identified as a processor in different states of computation. The doubling is done as follows. f outputs its link and changes itself into a g. Using the link output by the processor to which g is linked, g links itself to the processor linked to the processor to which it was originally linked.

$f(ptr(x), y) \to ptr(x) : g(ptr(x), y)$
$f(last(x), y) \to last(x) : h(last(x), y)$

$g(((x : y) : u) : v, w) \to f(u, w)$
$g((last(x) : y) : u, w) \to f(last(x), w)$
$g(last(x) : y, w) \to f(last(x), w)$

7. Determinant Evaluation

det evaluates the determinant of the input matrix by Gauss elimination. From its input matrix (first argument), *elim* selects the first row whose first entry is nonzero (this row is known as pivot row). It then uses *rowselim* to eliminate the first entry of the succeeding rows with the pivot row. Now, the determinant is given by the product of the first entry of the pivot row and the determinant of the matrix obtained by deleting the first column and the pivot row.

$det(x) \to elim(x : y, nil)$
$det(nil) \to 1$

$elim((x : y) : u : v, w) \to$
$\quad if(x \neq 0,$
$\quad\quad x * det(append(rowselim(x, y, u : v), w)),$
$\quad elim(u : v, y : w))$
$elim((x : y) : nil, w) \to x * det(y : w)$

$rowselim(x, y, (u : us) : v : vs) \to$
$\quad subtract(u/x, y, us) : rowselim(x, y, v : vs)$
$rowselim(x, y, (u : us) : nil) \to$
$\quad subtract(u/x, y, us) : nil$

$subtract(elimfac, y : y_1 : ys, z : z_1 : zs) \to$
$\quad (z - y * elimfac) : subtract(elimfac, y_1 : ys, z_1 : zs)$
$subtract(elimfac, y : nil, z : nil) \to$
$\quad z - y * elimfac : nil$

8. FFT

fft takes 3 arguments. *inp* is a list of N points and w is a root of unity. Using *split*, it partitions this list into lists of evn and odd points. The FFTs of these lists are combined using *half* to produce the first and second halves of the output list. The i_{th} element of the output of *half* is $x_i + fac * w^i * y_i$, where x_i and y_i are the i_{th} elements of its first and second argument lists and *fac* is its fourth argument.

$fft(N, inp, w) \to$
$\quad if(N = 1, inp, fft1(N, w, split(inp, nil, nil)))$

$split(x : y : z, u, v) \to split(z, x : u, y : v)$
$split(nil, u, v) \to \langle reverse(u), reverse(v) \rangle$

$fft1(N, w, \langle b, c \rangle) \to$
$\quad append(half(fft(N/2, b, w^2), fft(N/2, c, w^2), 0, 1),$
$\quad\quad half(fft(N/2, b, w^2), fft(N/2, c, w^2), 0, -1))$

$half(x : xs, y : ys, i, fac) \to$
$\quad (x + w^i * y * fac) : half(xs, ys, i + 1, fac)$
$half(nil, nil, i, fac) \to nil$

An Efficient Hybrid Algorithm for Incremental Data Flow Analysis

Thomas J. Marlowe[1] (marlowe@paul.rutgers.edu)
Barbara G. Ryder (ryder@aramis.rutgers.edu)
Department of Computer Science, Rutgers University

0. Abstract

Our exhaustive and incremental *hybrid* data flow analysis algorithms, based on iteration and elimination techniques, are designed for incremental update of a wide variety of monotone data flow problems in response to source program changes. Unlike previous incremental iterative methods, this incremental algorithm efficiently computes *precise* and *correct* solutions. We give theoretical results on the imprecision of *restarting iteration* for incremental update by fixed point iteration which provided motivation for our algorithm design. Described intuitively, the main algorithm idea is to factor the data flow solution on strong connected components of the flow graph into local and external parts, solving for the local parts by iteration and propagating these effects on the condensation of the flow graph to obtain the entire data flow solution. The incremental hybrid algorithm re-performs those algorithm steps affected by the program changes.

1. Introduction

Data flow analysis information provides semantic descriptions of program behavior useful in software testing, debugging and maintenance, especially of large software systems [21, 24, 19]. This information is also essential to ensure correctness of source code optimization and parallelization, that is, vectorization and concurrentization [1, 3, 5]. Maintaining data flow information about the *current state* of a system can be costly, both because of the large size of the system under analysis and the need to obtain updated information about an altered system relatively quickly. *Incremental analysis* techniques seek to avoid recalculation of data flow information *from scratch*; using knowledge of the former data flow solution and source changes introduced, these methods *update* this solution to reflect the effects of the program changes.

Existing incremental iterative methods have utilized *restarting iteration* as a solution technique; that is, fixed point iteration [14] has obtained a problem solution, the program is altered *slightly*, and iteration is resumed starting at the old fixed point [6]. For some program changes, this technique applied naively will not obtain the same solution as a *from scratch* iteration; we characterize this behavior as *imprecise* (see below).

We offer iteration-based data flow analysis algorithms which use ideas from elimination methods [26], namely a graph decomposition, thereby suggesting the title *hybrid* algorithm. The resulting algorithms extend ideas in [15] and [31]. Our algorithms handle a large class of data flow problems, including not only the classical bitvector problems (i.e., Reaching Definitions, Live Uses of Variables, Available Expressions, Very Busy Expressions [1, 14]), but other distributive problems such as Forward Bound Set[2] and Aliasing [10], and some monotone problems, although provably not Constant Propagation. Our incremental algorithm is precise and efficient for edits affecting the control structure of the program, *structural edits*, and those which do not, *non-structural edits* [24].

The hybrid algorithms use the strong component decomposition of a flow graph. They rely on factoring the

---

[1]Also of Department of Mathematics and Computer Science, Seton Hall University, So. Orange, NJ 07079.

[2]Forward Bound Set calculates the set of global, local or formal variables possibly associated on call chains with some formal f and reports these at the procedure declaring f. This is related to the Bound Set problem [4, 11] which only reports formal to formal associations along call chains and reports them at the procedure containing the initiating call site.

data flow solution on each region into external and internal parts which are solved for separately on the region. The external part, captured in a *representative problem* depending only on local information within that region, represents information external to a strong component which arrives at its head node. The internal part is solved by straight-forward fixed point iteration. Central to the method is determination of the appropriate representative problem for each data flow problem. At present, this is not a mechanical operation, however we do present a general approach to building representative problems and outline a number of examples. Our techniques apply most easily to forward data flow problems on reducible flow graphs, but can be extended naturally to backward problems, or to programs with multiple entry points, and to flow graphs with irreducible or unreachable regions [16].

In the remainder of this abstract, we first define ideas relevant to incremental iterative algorithms. Second, we describe our hybrid algorithm in its exhaustive and incremental versions, as applied to Reaching Definitions. Examples of both versions of the algorithm are given. Third, we present the notion of *problem invariants* and show how they aid in defining representative problems. Finally, we discuss related work and future directions.

Data Flow Frameworks: An instance of a forward data flow framework can be specified by a tuple

$$D = <G, L, F, M, \eta>,$$

where G is a rooted digraph $<V,E,\rho>$,[3] L is a semilattice, F is a space of functions mapping L into L, M is a mapping of edges E of G into F, and η is an element of L [17]. Intuitively, G is the (intraprocedural or interprocedural) flow graph with root at ρ, L a lattice of solutions, M the assignment of transition functions to edges, and η is the entry solution at ρ; F is usually not represented explicitly. M can be thought of as specifying a system of $|V|$ equations [26] or a single vector-valued equation. L is usually taken to be a meet semilattice, in which case the data flow solution S corresponding to the given tuple is the maximum fixed point (MFP) of M. An iterative algorithm for S uses an *initial safe estimate X*, and an iterative (scheduling) scheme I, such as worklist or round robin [14].[4] In a meet semilattice a *safe solution* will be *below* the *MFP*, but an *initial safe estimate* will usually be *above* it; the key point is that iteration initialized at a safe estimate will converge to the *MFP*. Changes in a program induce changes in G, or L, or M, or a combination of these. For example, in Reaching Definitions adding a definition changes L and M, while adding a program loop changes G; in Forward Bound Set, changing the parameters of a call affects only M. *Projection*, that is, changes to L and corresponding changes to M, requires, for most incremental algorithms, work linear in the size of the flow graph.

After projection, however, an incremental iterative algorithm must still solve the changed problem, iterating from an initial safe estimate. We say the algorithm can *restart iteration* if the old solution is a safe initial estimate; otherwise, all or part of the solution must be *reinitialized* to a safe initial value. In [25], we show that restarting for a meet-semilattice problem is safe whenever (modulo changes in the solution space by projection), the new solution lies below the old. We can show that for distributive problems, the old solution S is unsafe if and only if there is a vertex at which S is not greater than the new solution S', and that the effect of a sequence of edges drives this *inconsistency* to a

---

[3] G can be a multigraph.

[4] For most problems, whether an algorithm converges to S is independent of I.

vertex through which it is preserved along an infinite sequence of closed paths. We have a similar result for monotone functions; these results are provably sharp [16]. However, our safe restarting condition is not useful, since it requires knowledge of the new solution. Further, even with this condition, projection and reinitialization still yield an average update cost at least linear in the size of the flow graph.

Incremental Algorithms: An *incremental algorithm* I for a data flow problem P takes a solution S to an initial instance P of P and a change ΔP, and produces a solution S' to $P+\Delta P$. Ideally, the complexity of the algorithm should depend only on the size of ΔP, and the size of its effect on the solution, but this can rarely be achieved. A more realistic hope is that in some sense the average complexity will be significantly less than the cost of finding the solution *from scratch* by a good exhaustive algorithm E.

An incremental algorithm I is *correct* if the resulting solution s' is a *safe solution* for $P+\Delta P$, (i.e., $s' \leq S'$ and *precise* if $S'=s'$. I is *efficient* if the complexity of I is much less than the complexity of E whenever both ΔP and the change in the solution, ΔS, are both much smaller than $|P|$:
$|\Delta P|, |\Delta S| \leq \leq |P| \rightarrow$
$Complexity[I(P, S(P), \Delta P)) < < Complexity[E(P+\Delta P)]$.
at least in some on-the-average sense.

Without projection, incremental iterative algorithms cannot be correct, since some changes do change L. Without reinitialization, they will be correct (if they halt) but not precise. With projection and reinitialization, existing incremental iterative algorithms are inefficient since they involve average overhead at least linear in the size of the flow graph. We seek a family of algorithms which recovers efficiency by *limiting* the extent of projection and reinitialization in either the frequency, the extent in the flow graph, or the extent in the solution structures.

Hybrid Algorithms: We have designed exhaustive and incremental *hybrid* algorithms, based on a decomposition of the flow graph into strong components. We call these decompositions *balanced* if the size of the condensation and the size of the largest component are much less than the size of the original flow graph.[5] Our algorithms rely on a corresponding *factorization* of the lattice into an *internal factor* capturing data flow within a region, and a *representative problem*, which, although expressible in terms of local information, is sufficient to capture local effects by and on external information. The global solution is recovered from these two, and is represented explicitly at component head nodes and exit nodes only. For balanced decompositions, the incremental hybrid algorithm is both precise and efficient for a class of edits which includes arbitrary structural and non-structural changes.[6]

2. The Exhaustive Hybrid Algorithm

In its broadest outline, the exhaustive hybrid algorithm consists of structure construction and factorization, iterative solution of internal information, and propagation of that information to other regions. Factorization allows graceful incrementalization. On regions where there is no local edit and no structural change, we expect the internal solution to remain unchanged; effects on the external solution need merely to be propagated. At the cost of using a different lattice representation for each region, maintaining structure information, and increasing the cost of a data flow solution calculation by a constant factor,

---
[5]Components are required to be single-entry. This follows from, but does not require, reducibility.

[6]In [16] we show how to aggregate acyclic subgraphs of the flow graph into single-entry regions and use them in our algorithm to control the size of the flow graph condensation to achieve balanced decompositions.

we obtain demonstrable savings in space and time. In this section, we describe the exhaustive hybrid algorithm as used for solving Reaching Definitions.

The Local Problem: The key idea is that definitions of a variable external to a region are treated identically by edits within the region [12, 31]. Let G be decomposed into regions $\{R_i\}$ so that each R_i is single-entry and the condensation relative to the R_i is acyclic. Let R be one of these regions, with head node $h(R)$. Let $IntDefs$ be the set of *internal* definitions generated in R, and $ExtDefs$ all other (*external*) definitions: $Defs = IntDefs \oplus ExtDefs$. Further, suppose the index of R_i is its topological label, and that each region can be reached from the root node ρ (which must lie in R_1). Finally, assume at least one external definition of each variable reaches the head node of each (non-root) region.

Theorem 2.1: Given a region R_i, a vertex v in R_i, and a variable x, let $Ext(x,R_i)$ be the set of external definitions of x reaching $h(R_i)$. Then for any vertex v of R_i, either every d in $Ext(x,R_i)$ reaches v, or no external definition of x does. Further, the former occurs if and only if there is an x-def-clear path from $h(R_i)$ to v.
Proof: See [16]. ■

The *Restricted Reaching Definitions* problem for R has as its flow graph the *local graph for* R, consisting of R with an artificial root node ρ' adjoined as unique predecessor of the head node $h(R)$. Its lattice is the power set of internal definitions, $2^{IntDefs}$, and its flow functions are the restriction of the flow functions of the original Reaching Definitions problem on the edges of R to the subset $IntDefs$; the value at ρ' is $\emptyset$ and no definitions are generated or preserved there. Solving the Restricted Reaching Definitions problem correctly for internal definitions, gives no direct information on the flow of external definitions in R.

We can, however, iterate throughout R one additional bit of information per *local variable*, that is, a variable with a definition in R. We can think of these bits as either virtual definitions of each variable at ρ' or as a distinct lattice, 2^{Vars} with *May Be Preserved*, initialized to $\underline{1}$ at ρ'; their flow functions are obvious. If the variable x is local to R, then it will be preserved at v if and only if definitions of x are preserved there; if x is non-local, it will be preserved throughout R. We call this problem on $Vars$ the *representative problem*; it summarizes external definition reaching information. By Theorem 2.1, the fixed point for this problem completely determines Reaching Definitions in R for external definitions.

Combining Local Solutions: The two separate problems, the restricted problem, (i.e., internal definitions reaching) and the representative problem (i.e., external definitions reaching), together form the *Local Reaching Definitions* problem for R, LRD_R. Their solutions can be combined and sent to successor regions to yield a correct solution for the global Reaching Definitions problem for G.

Theorem 2.2: Let $\underline{D}$ be an instance of Reaching Definitions with flow graph G. Suppose LRD_R has been correctly solved on R, and that the set of external definitions $Ext(R) = \cup Ext(x,R)$ reaching $h(R)$ is correct. Then for every v in R,

$$RD(v) = (LRD_R(v) \cap IntDefs)$$
$$\cup (\cup \{Ext(x,R) | x \in LRD_R(v)\})$$
$$\cup (\cup \{Ext(x,R) | x \text{ not local to } R\}).$$

In particular, knowing the sets $Ext(x,R)$, we can determine the set of definitions reaching the bottom of each region exit w in R, and thus those reaching the head node of each successor region Q from outside. The combination of restricted, representative, and head-node external information to give the global solution constitutes a *solution function*. Solution function expansion at exit nodes, and the meet at successor head nodes, gives *propagation*. Once local problems are solved, propagation occurs *on the condensed graph*; no further iteration is required.

We now have all the machinery we need to describe our exhaustive algorithm; in fact, its correctness follows from the results of the last two sections.

Phases of the Exhaustive Hybrid Algorithm: [16]

1. Construct flow graph.
2. Find the strong components of the flow graph.
3. Find a topological order for the components.
4. Determine local information (variables, definitions, flow functions, etc.).
5. Set up the global lattice (however, setup storage for global solutions and flow functions only at region headers and exits)
6. Set up the local lattices.
7. Iterate to local solutions.
8. In topological order on the components, propagate the solution.

The first four phases of the algorithm are usually performed during earlier analysis, and phases 1, 4, and 5 are required in any iterative algorithm. Phase 7 (iteration) cannot (for Reaching Definitions) be more costly for the hybrid algorithm than for standard iteration. Further, the complexity of phases 1 (flow graph construction) and 4 (local information) depends linearly on the size of the programs and on the size of the resulting flow graph. Standard graph algorithms for strong components and topological sort are linear in the size of the graph analyzed, which for phase 2 is the flow graph, and for phase 3 the condensed graph.

The costs of phases 5 and 6 (global and local set-up) cannot be greater than twice the set-up cost for standard iteration, and will almost always be less, depending on the relative sizes of global and local problems, and of the flow graph and its condensation. The cost of phase 8 (propagation) is also linear in the size of the condensed graph.

Assuming that both the condensed graph and the largest region are much smaller than the original flow graph, or that local lattices are much smaller than the global lattice, the hybrid algorithm will be more efficient than standard iterative solution, both in time and in space, by a factor of up to $n^{1/2}$, where n is the number of nodes in the flow graph [16].

Example: Figure 7-1 shows an intermediate portion of the flow graph of a large procedure, which, conveniently, breaks down into small connected components, as shown in Figure 7-2, which also shows the (strong component) condensation. The edges coming into $a1$ and $b1$ come from possibly different regions above them; there may in fact be several such edges in each case.

The condensation has as a possible topological order (A,B,C,D). In Figure 7-3 we show the local problem for region A, and, in Figure 7-4, its solution.[7] Thus, external definitions of x reach everywhere, and those of y reach only $a1$ and $a2$. Propagation through exit nodes gives as the exit term for (total solution at the *bottom* of) $a4$:

$Exit(a4) = ExtDefs(x,A) \cup \{(x,a3)\}, \{(y,a4)\}$,

and at $a5$:

$Exit(a5) = ExtDefs(x,A) \cup \{(x,a3)\}, \{(y,a2),(y,a4)\}$.

Figure 7-5 now shows the corresponding unexpanded exit solutions for each of the regions (where x stands for $Ext(x,\_)$), and then illustrates propagation by giving the expansion for Reaching Definitions at node headers and exits. Note that what is specified is the value of

---

[7]As in our discussion of the local problem, we will use ρ' for the entry node to every region.

$RD \cap ExtDefs$ at the top of the header nodes, and the value (contributed to successor headers) of Reaching Definitions at the *bottom* of exit nodes.

3. The Incremental Hybrid Algorithm

Using the terminology of [22], we say a region R is MODIFIED by an edit if local information or structure is changed in R; AFFECTED if the value of the solution changes in R, or if it is MODIFIED; and INFLUENCED if it is the successor of some AFFECTED region, or the target of an added or deleted inter-region edge. Finally, a region is NEW if it is created by the edit, possibly by the split or merger of former regions.

The incremental hybrid algorithm applied to Reaching Definitions involves possible update in each of the exhaustive algorithm phases. When a definition is added or deleted, the local problem changes in the MODIFIED region, requiring a *local projection* and a possible reinitialization. In addition, projection in the global problem is required at all region headers and exits. Local problems must be created and initialized in NEW regions. Iteration is required only in MODIFIED and NEW regions. Propagation, initialized at the successors of MODIFIED and NEW regions, and targets of inter-region edge changes, restores the correct solution; this propagation is limited to INFLUENCED regions.

The information needed to construct an incremental algorithm is not just the set of invariants or the representative problem, but also the change classification, that is, what type of edits will occur, and what phases will be invoked by each change.

We have in [16] detailed analyses of the effects of various changes, following the classification scheme of Figure 3-1. The complexity of an update is a function of the number of atomic edits involved, the size of the largest region, the size of the condensed graph, and the maximum number of definitions and variables in a region, but is otherwise *independent of the size of the flow graph*. Our incremental algorithm is precise; for programs with a reducible balanced decomposition, it is *efficient*.[8]

Figure 3-1: Types of Changes for Incremental Hybrid Algorithm

Non-structural
   1. Add a definition
   2. Delete a definition
Structural
   3. Add an edge
      (1) intra-region edge
      (2) forward in toporder
      (3) backward in toporder
         (a) merges components
         (b) other
      (4) creates irreducibility
         (must be inter-region edge)
      (5) removes unreachability
         (must be inter-region edge)
   4. Delete an edge
      (1) intra-region edge
         (a) splits the component
         (b) other
      (2) forward in toporder
      (3) removes irreducibility
         (must be intra-region edge)
      (4) creates unreachable region(s)
   5. Add a node (of degree one)
   6. Delete a node (of degree one)
   7. Merge basic blocks
   8. Split a basic block

In summary the incremental hybrid algorithm involves the following steps:

1. Examine the edit, determining the type and location of each change.
2. Update the flow graph and local information

---

[8] We can handle irreducible regions by embedding them in "IMPROPER" regions; we remain efficient if the resulting decomposition is balanced [16].

(in response to local edits).
3. Update the region decomposition and the topological order.
4. Update representative and restricted problems as necessary in any MODIFIED or NEW region (project and reinitialize; change local lattices), and change region entry and exit (and if necessary exit edge) solution data structures.
5. Iterate to a solution in any MODIFIED or NEW regions.
6. Using the topological order, propagate from MODIFIED, NEW or AFFECTED regions, or from the target of added or deleted inter-region edges, to their INFLUENCED neighbors.

Standard precise incremental iterative algorithms appear in [20, 6]. Such standard algorithms will also need our phases 1 and 2 (classify and interpret changes), with essentially the same complexity. For a single edit, phase 3 (update local problems) has cost proportional to the size of the largest region plus the size of the condensed graph, and phase 6 (propagation) depends on the size of the condensed graph, with cost dominated by the cost of maintaining the priority queue of INFLUENCED regions. This cost will often be sublinear in condensed graph size, as we anticipate frequent early termination.

Finally, phase 4 (local problem update) has cost proportional to the size of the MODIFIED or NEW region plus size of the condensed graph, and phase 5 (iteration) has cost proportional to the size of the MODIFIED or NEW region; average cost for standard precise incremental iteration is proportional to flow graph size. We may retrieve additional savings from use of local problems and from early termination.

If the condensed graph and the largest region are much smaller than the size of the flow graph, and edge addition does not frequently join distant regions, then the incremental hybrid algorithm will be more efficient than standard precise incremental iteration, possibly by factors exceeding $n^{1/2}$.

Example: Our examples of incremental updates for our Reaching Definitions Algorithm refer to the flow graph of Figure 7-2, and modify the exhaustive solution there. For ease of reference, the changes are independent; each is made to the original flow graph.

1. **Add a definition of y at $b2$.**

   Project in B (and at region headers and exits), and reinitialize definitions of y (and the variable y bit) in B. Then iterate (in B). The exit solution at $b3$ is unchanged, so STOP.

2. **Add a definition of x at $a1$.**

   Project in A (and at region headers and exits), and reinitialize definitions of x (and the variable x bit) in A. Then iterate (in A).
   The exit terms (at node bottom) at $a4, a5$ change, so must propagate.
   Propagate $a5$ to $b1$; change exit term at $b3$.
   Propagate $a4, b3$ to $c1$; exit term at $c3$ doesn't change; STOP.
   D is still on the queue. Propagate $a4$ to $d1$; exit term at $d2$ doesn't change; STOP.
   Queue is now empty.

3. **Delete edge $(a3, a1)$.**

   Doesn't disconnect A, so no structure changes. No projection; reinitialize in A, just the definitions of y and the definition of x at $a3$, since no other definitions crossed that edge. Iterate in A. No changes in exit terms, so STOP.

4. **Add edge $(b2, c1)$.**

   No changes to *any* local problem, except that $b2$ is now a *region exit node*. Set up space for exit term storage, and compute the exit term for $b2$.
   Propagate to $c1$, changing the solution (B's external definitions of y now reach C).
   Compute the exit term for $c3$; it changes.
   Continue propagation below C.

5. Add edge $(d2, a2)$.

Changes strongly connected components; A and D now merge.
Formulate a local problem for the new region and solve. (Can use existing information for initial estimate.)
Changes exit term at $a4, a5$, but not at $d2$.
Propagate from $a5$ to $b1$; entry solution changes, so propagate to exit term $b3$, which also changes.
Propagate from $a4, b3$ to $c1$; entry solution changes. However, exit term at $c3$ does not. STOP.

4. Invariants and Representative Problems

Extending the hybrid methods described previously to arbitrary data flow problems requires being able to factor those problems into appropriate local problems and to propagate solutions on the condensation of the flow graph. Our incremental algorithm involves a *change classification* scheme to limit the amount of work required in response to each type of change, in addition to structure update and factorization information.

Let P be an instance of a data flow problem whose flow graph G has been decomposed as above. The *Restricted Problem* for P on region R is the instance of P which would be formulated for the local graph, G_R, with the same local information; intuitively, the Restricted Problem expresses effects of information internal to R. The global solution at $h(R)$ will also involve information arriving on incoming edges from flow graph predecessor regions. The possible *external solution information* must be accounted for in solving the global problem within R, and in propagating the solution to R's successors. We wish to *represent* that information using *only* information local to R; however, this specifies in general only the *form* of the information arriving at $h(R)$, not the particular data items (e.g., variables rather than definitions); these must somehow be encoded in a *Representative Problem*. Finally, we need a *Solution Function* to allow us to recover the global problem solution at exit nodes of R from Restricted and Representative Problem solutions there, and the external information arriving at $h(R)$. (We give a glossary of terminology in Figure 7-6.)

The key to generating representative problems and solution functions is to determine a class of *invariants* depending only on region information, yet sufficient to encode external solution elements. (The term *invariant* reflects the lack of external dependence; the same set of invariants will suffice regardless of changes to the program external to and preserving the region.) Specifically, we want a map $Inv: Ext(R) \rightarrow Invariants(R)$, which partitions possible arriving external data into equivalence classes, so that members of a given class behave identically under edits within the region. In Reaching Definitions, for example, each external definition (of a variable appearing in the region) is associated with that variable; Theorem 2.1 ensures the equivalence class condition. In Section 5, we give invariants for a wide variety of data flow problems. The technique extends, with some modification, to backward problems and more general flow graph decompositions [16].

Important questions are:

1. What is the general form of an individual datum arriving at the header node? (For example, in Reaching Definitions, it is the name of an external definition of some program variable.)

2. Is there any dependence of that information on data associated with the head node $h(R)$? (In Reaching Definitions, there is not. For Forward Bound Set, however, a datum is a pair (a, b), where b is *a formal of* $h(R)$, the flow graph being the *call graph* of the program.)

3. Is there ever an identification of data in the external problem with data in the restricted

problem? (In Reaching Definitions, no. For Available Expressions, however, instances of the same expression, one inside and another outside R, will be identified.)

4. Can we iterate in the representative problem, without identifying each datum by the invariant to which it is associated? If we do need to label information, we will treat each labelled problem (except the restricted problem) as a *representative problem factor*. If information local to R can affect not just the values for the representative problem, but also the set of problem factors, we will say the problems *strongly interact*. (Examples of these effects occur in Aliasing [16]; we need to keep track of which alias pairs/sets at the head node result in a given pair in the representative problem.)[9]

5. Examples of Invariants

Most data flow problems can be seen as either essentially set-theoretic, with functions given by union and intersection on a power-set lattice, such as Reaching Definitions, or transitive-closure-like, with individual data represented by ordered pairs and transition functions involving composition. The approaches to finding invariants differ somewhat for these two cases. We present here one problem of each type; in [16] we handle other problems, including the alias algorithms of [18, 10, 12] and several graph problems (e.g., shortest paths). The sets of invariants presented here are naive; our algorithms will typically use optimizations. The aim here is rather to show how sets of invariants arise naturally from consideration of problem properties.

Available Expressions (a set problem): Each datum is an expression, specified by a pair of variables and an operator. An expression is killed by a definition of either of its variables. There is no head node information reflected in arriving external information, but data instances of the same binary expression will be identified; if one is inside and the other outside R, this will identify internal and external instances. The set of pairs of variables is part of the invariant set, and *represents* all expressions which do not also occur internally. Possible duplications are handled by including in the invariants a copy of the set of internal expressions; each internal expression represents possible external occurrences of itself.

Forward Bound Set (a closure problem): We assume flat code and single-entry regions; more general cases are discussed in [16]. Recall that the Forward Bound Set Problem reports at the location of f the set of pairs $<g,f>$, where g is any variable (*global, local, or formal*) bound along a call chain to f. Incoming information consists of pairs (a,b), where b is a formal parameter of $h(R)$ (since all call chains originating outside R must pass through $h(R)$). Also, all pairs with second component b (a formal of $h(R)$) create similar pairs (a,c) as b is bound to c. The only interaction between external and internal problems can come at $h(R)$, or through multiple instances of globals (both inside and outside of R) used as actual parameters. However, the first case is already accounted for, and, since globals can occur only in the first component of a pair, the second case also causes no difficulty. The set of invariants is the set of parameters of the head node.

6. Related Work

Incremental iterative algorithms have been proposed by [13, 9, 11] where restarting is always used, and thus imprecision introduced. Precise incremental iterative algorithms, using change classification and reinitialization,

---

[9]In non-distributive problems, the effect of a set of external data elements is not in general the meet of the effects of the individual elements, and factor interactions are thus more complicated. Also, for general problems, update complexity depends on the number of representative problem factors as well as the factors given above for Reaching Definitions.

were apparently first proposed in [20]; Pollock's algorithms were stated for bitvector problems, but can clearly be extended to arbitrary data flow problems. A survey of these works is found in [6].

Use of the strong component decomposition to guide iteration was proposed in [15], for exhaustive iteration only. Other graph decompositions, such as intervals, are routinely used in elimination algorithms, both exhaustively [2, 29, 26] and incrementally [4, 8, 24, 27]; in [16], we consider their use in incremental iteration. The incremental elimination algorithms of [8] do not handle edits which introduce irreducibilities; those of [4, 24, 27] handle even smaller classes of edits. Also, structure update appears to be more difficult and costly for these decompositions than for strong components.

Strong component structure also guides the exhaustive and incremental algorithms of [7, 31]. Both of these are less general than our algorithm; [31] applies to a limited class of problems (all of which are factorable); the algorithms of [7] cover at least the distributive problems, but only those edits which neither change the strong component decomposition nor require reinitialization.

An incremental algorithm based on the path algebra methods of [30] can be found in [23]. Like elimination algorithms, it uses fine flow graph structure; it is precise only for distributive problems, and in any case is not designed to be practical.

The idea of combining aspects of iteration and elimination has also arisen as a method of handling irreducibilities in elimination algorithms [4, 28], and as a general technique in [7], but is not used incrementally, nor as systematically or with as great an average-case gain in complexity as in our hybrid algorithm.

Finally, incremental attribute grammar algorithms have been developed, beginning with [22]; this development is essentially orthogonal to our own.

In summary, on the one hand, the hybrid algorithm appears to allow efficient and precise incremental solution of a variety of data flow problems, avoiding the often higher solution update costs of iteration and the PVT method, and the complicated structure update and summary flow function information of elimination and path algebra methods. On the other, we believe that the algorithms of [20] and [8] can be made to handle at least the same class of edits and problems we cover. We intend to explore these issues through empirical comparison of the three algorithms.

7. Conclusions and Future Work

We have presented an exhaustive and an incremental hybrid iteration-elimination data flow analysis algorithm, applicable to general monotone frameworks. We have explained how the incremental version of the algorithm, which handles source code changes for a wide variety of data flow problems, is *precise*, *correct* and *efficient*, unlike previous incremental iterative methods. We have discussed the lattice factorization that underlies our approach and discussed several specific problem examples.

Future work includes empirical profiling of our hybrid incremental method versus reinitialization techniques for restarting iteration. We also wish to study the appropriateness of using our hybrid technique rather than elimination-based incremental methods for specific classes of problems. We will empirically observe the nature of strong component decompositions of actual program flow graphs and call graphs. This will aid us in further developing the notion of *acyclic regions*, to help achieve balanced decompositions [16].

Figure 7-1: A Portion of an Intraprocedural Flow Graph

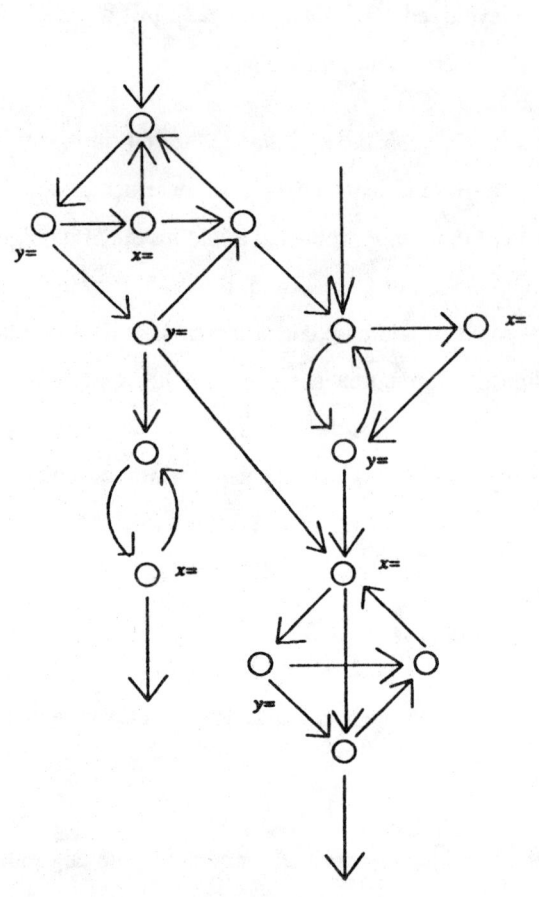

Figure 7-2: Regions and Condensation for The Flow Graph of Figure 7-1

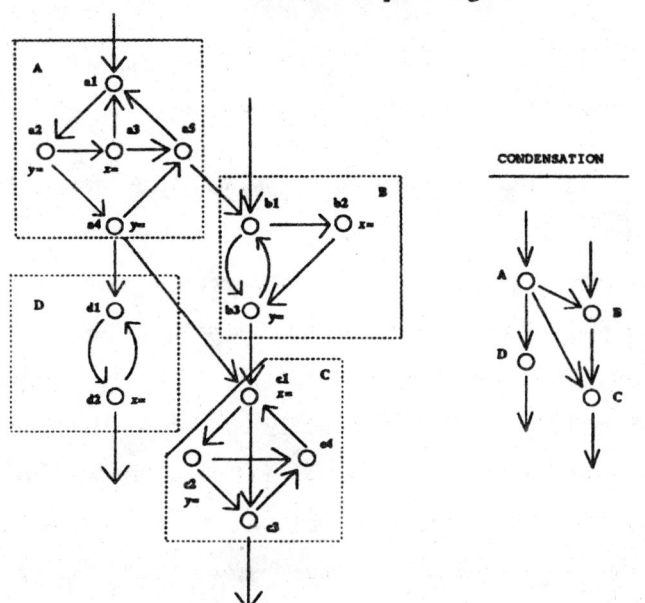

Figure 7-3: The Local Problem for Region A

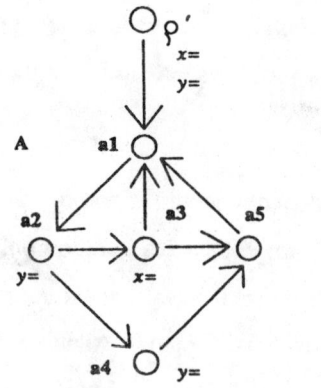

Definitions at ρ' are equivalent to variable bits.

Figure 7-4: Solution of the local problem

$LRD(a1) = \{(x,\rho'), (y,\rho'),$
$(x,a3), (y,a2), (y,a4)\}$

External defs of x reach everywhere; y reach $a1, a2$ only

$LRD(a2) = \{(x,\rho'), (y,\rho'),$
$(x,a3), (y,a2), (y,a4)\}$

Exits at $a4, a5$

$LRD(a3) = \{(x,\rho'), (x,a3), (y,a2)\}$

Exit Terms:

$LRD(a4) = \{(x,\rho'), (x,a3), (y,a2)\}$

$a4: Defs(x) = ExtDefs \cup \{a3\}$
$Defs(y) = \{a4\}$

$LRD(a5) = \{(x,\rho'), (x,a3),$
$(y,a2), (y,a4)\}$

$a5: Defs(x) = ExtDefs \cup \{a3\}$
$Defs(y) = \{a2, a4\}$

Figure 7-5: Propagation for the Problem of Figure 7-1

Local Solutions at Bottom of Node Exits

$a4: \{(x,\rho'), (x,a3), (y,a4)\}$
$a5: \{(x,\rho'), (x,a3), (y,a2), (y,a4)\}$
$b3: \{(x,\rho'), (x,b2), (y,b3)\}$
$c3: \{(x,c1), (y,\rho'), (y,c2)\}$
$d2: \{(x,d2), (y,\rho')\}$

Propagation

$ExtDefs(a1) = \{(x,e1), (y,e2)\}$ from regions above A
$ExitTerm(a4) = \{(x,e1), (x,a3), (y,a4)\}$
$ExitTerm(a5) = \{(x,e1), (x,a3), (y,a2), (y,a4)\}$

$ExtDefs(b1) = \{(x,e1), (x,e3), (x,a3), (y,e4), (y,a2), (y,a4)\}$
                       $(x,e3)$ and $(y,e4)$ incoming edge;
                       others from $a5$
$ExitTerm(b3) = \{(x,e1), (x,e3), (x,a3), (x,b2), (y,b3)\}$

$ExtDefs(c1) = \{(x,e1), (x,e3), (x,a3), (x,b2), (y,a2), (y,a4), (y,b3)\}$
                       Union of Exit Terms for $a4$ and $b3$
$ExitTerm(c3) = \{(x,c1), (y,a2), (y,a4), (y,b3), (y,c2)\}$

$ExtDefs(d1) = \{(x,e1), (x,a3), (y,a4)\}$ from $a4$
$ExitTerm(d2) = \{(x,d2), (y,a4)\}$

Figure 7-6: Terminology for Problem Factorization

restricted problem	expresses solution contribution from within R alone.
external solution information	expresses information outside R.
invariants	an encoding of external information as locally visible information.
distinct data instances	no datum can occur both in restricted problem and externally.
identified data instances	a datum may occur both in R and externally.
representative problem	a data flow problem on the set of invariants, capturing data flow effects in R on external information.
representative problem factor	a portion of the representative problem, specified by a subset of invariants, which can be solved independently.
strong interaction	local information can affect the set of representative problem factors.
local problem	the problem which must be solved for each region; comprises the restricted and representative problems.
external entry information	external information arriving at $h(R)$ along inter-region edges.
solution map	a reverse correspondence between invariants and global information, giving a global value at region exits depending on local problem information at the exit node and external entry information at the corresponding region header.
exit term	the value at the bottom of an exit node which contributes to the (data flow) solution at successor region head nodes; determined by the *solution map* and the effect of the (node-dependent) transition function.
exit edge term	analogous to *exit term* for problems in which transition functions are edge-dependent; there is one for each edge out of the region.
propagation	moving from region to region by a combination of solution at region exits and global propagation on inter-region edges; equivalently, by evaluating exit terms (or exit edge terms) at taking meets; computes *external entry information*.

References

[1] A.V. Aho, R. Sethi, J.D. Ullman.
Compilers: principles, techniques, and tools.
Addison-Wesley, Reading, MA, 1986.

[2] F.E. Allen, J. Cocke.
A program data flow analysis procedure.
Communications of the ACM 19:137-147, 1977.

[3] R. Allen, K. Kennedy.
Automatic translation of FORTRAN programs to vector form.
ACM Transactions on Programming Languages and Systems 9(4):491-542, 1987.

[4] M. Burke.
An interval analysis approach toward exhaustive and incremental interprocedural data flow analysis.
Technical Report RC 12702, IBM Thomas J. Watson Research Center, Yorktown Heights, N.Y., July, 1987.

[5] M. Burke, R. Cytron.
Interprocedural dependence analysis and parallelization.
In *Proceedings of the ACM SIGPLAN Symposium on Compiler Construction*, pages 162-175. June, 1986.
SIGPLAN Notices, Vol 21, No 6.

[6] M. Burke, B.G. Ryder.
Incremental iterative data flow analysis algorithms.
Laboratory for Computer Science Research Technical Report LCSR-TR-96, Rutgers University, New Brunswick, N.J., 1987.

[7] J. Cai, R. Paige.
Program derivation by fixed point computation.
Science of Computer Programming 11(3):197-261, April, 1989.

[8] M. Carroll, B. Ryder.
Incremental data flow update via attribute and dominator updates.
In *Conference Record of the Fifteenth Annual ACM Symposium on Principles of Programming Languages*, pages 274-284. Association for Computing Machinery - SIGPLAN, January, 1988.

[9] K.D. Cooper.
Interprocedural data flow analysis in a programming environment.
PhD thesis, Department of Mathematical Sciences, Rice University, 1983.

[10] K. Cooper.
Analyzing aliases of reference formal parameters.
In *Conference Record of the Eleventh Annual ACM Symposium on Principles of Programming Languages*, pages 281-290. June, 1984.

[11] K. Cooper, K. Kennedy.
Efficient computation of flow insensitive interprocedural summary information.
In *Conference Record of the Eleventh Annual ACM Symposium on Principles of Programming Languages*, pages 247-258. June, 1984.
SIGPLAN Notices, Vol. 19, No. 6.

[12] K. Cooper, K. Kennedy.
Fast interprocedural alias analysis.
In *Conference Record of the Sixteenth Annual ACM Symposium on Principles of Programming Languages*, pages 49-59. January, 1989.

[13] V. Ghodssi.
Incremental analysis of programs.
PhD thesis, Dept. of Computer Science, Central Florida University, 1983.

[14] M.S. Hecht.
Flow analysis of computer programs.
Elsevier North-Holland, Amsterdam, Neth., 1977.

[15] S. Horwitz, A. Demers, T. Teitelbaum.
An efficient general iterative algorithm for data-flow analysis.
Acta Informatica 24(6):679-694, 1987.

[16] T.J. Marlowe.
Incremental iteration and data flow analysis.
PhD thesis, Department of Computer Science, Rutgers University, 1989.

[17] T.J. Marlowe, B.G. Ryder.
Properties of data flow frameworks: A unified model.
Acta Informatica, 1989.
to appear.

[18] E.W. Myers.
A precise interprocedural data flow algorithm.
In *Conference Record of the Eighth Annual ACM Symposium on Principles of Programming Languages*, pages 219-230. Association for Computing Machinery - SIGPLAN, January, 1981.

[19] L. Pollock, M.L. Soffa.
INCROMINT - An INCRemental Optimizer for Machine Independent Transformations.
In *Proceedings of SOFTFAIR II - A Second Conference on Software Development Tools, Techniques and Alternatives*, pages 162-171. December, 1985.

[20] L. Pollock, M.L. Soffa.
An incremental version of iterative data flow analysis.
IEEE Transactions on Software Engineering 15(12), December, 1989.

[21] S. Rapps, E. Weyuker.
Selecting software test data using data flow information.
IEEE Transactions on Software Engineering SE-11(4):367-375, April, 1985.

[22] T. Reps.
Optimal-time incremental semantic analysis for syntax-directed editors.
In *Conference Record of the Ninth Annual ACM Symposium on Principles of Programming Languages*, pages 169-176. Association for Computing Machinery - SIGPLAN, January, 1982.

[23] B. Rosen.
A lubricant for data flow analysis.
SIAM Journal of Computing 11(3):493-511, 1982.

[24] B.G. Ryder, M. Carroll.
An incremental algorithm for software analysis.
In *Proceedings of the ACM SIGSOFT/SIGPLAN Software Engineering Symposium on Practical Software Development Environments*, pages 171-179. Association for Computing Machinery, December, 1986.
SIGPLAN Notices, vol 21, 1, January 1987.

[25] B.G. Ryder, T.J. Marlowe, M.C. Paull.
Conditions for incremental iteration: examples and counterexamples.
Science of Computer Programming 11(1):1-15, October, 1988.

[26] B.G. Ryder, M.C. Paull.
Elimination algorithms for data flow analysis.
ACM Computing Surveys 18(3):277-316, September, 1986.

[27] B.G. Ryder, M.C. Paull.
Incremental data flow analysis algorithms.
ACM Transactions on Programming Languages and Systems 10(1):1-50, January, 1988.

[28] J.T. Schwartz, M. Sharir.
A design for optimizations of the bitvectoring class.
Courant Computer Science Report 17, New York University, New York, N.Y., 1979.

[29] R.E. Tarjan.
Fast algorithms for solving path problems.
Journal of the ACM 28(3):594-614, 1981.

[30] R.E. Tarjan.
A unified approach to path problems.
Journal of the ACM 28(3):576-593, 1981.

[31] F.K. Zadeck.
Incremental data flow analysis in a structured program editor.
In *Proceedings of the ACM SIGPLAN Symposium on Compiler Construction*, pages 132-143. June, 1984.
SIGPLAN Notices, Vol 19, No 6.

A Finite Presentation Theorem for Approximating Logic Programs

(Extended Abstract)

Nevin Heintze
School of Computer Science
Carnegie Mellon University
Pittsburgh, PA 15213

Joxan Jaffar
IBM T.J. Watson Research Center
PO Box 218
Yorktown Heights, NY 10598

Summary

The notion of cartesian closure on a set of unifiers has been used to define approximations of the least models of logic programs. Such approximations, often called types, are not known to be recursive. In this paper, we use cartesian closure to define a similar, but more accurate, approximation. The main result proves that our approximation is not only recursive, but that it can be finitely represented in the form of a cyclic term graph. This explicit representation can be used as a starting point for logic program analyzers.

1 Introduction

The problem at hand is: given a logic program, obtain an approximation of its meaning, that is, obtain an approximation of its least model. The definition of the approximation should be declarative (so that results can be proved about soundness and relative completeness); the approximation should be accurate (so that it is meaningful in program analysis), and finally, the approximated meaning should be a recursive set.

The meaning of a logic program is defined using the fundamental notions of unification (representing the primitive computation step) and that of collecting unifiers (representing non-determinism). To define an approximation to this meaning, it suffices to define the corresponding notions of approximate unification and that of approximate collection of unifiers. The relevant area in logic programming is that of type inference, in which there are two main approaches. In one, the approximation is based on ignoring pointwise dependencies between two sets of values in two different argument positions[1]. The other approach is based on abstract interpretation; approximation here is based on treating several values as one abstract value.

In [8], [9] and [12], which exemplify the first approach, one can view that regular unification is used (there is no abstraction on the underlying domain), but that the collection of unifiers is approximated by means of a *cartesian closure* operator which enlarges collections of unifiers. Considering unifiers as equations, a collection of unifiers defines a relation (tuples). One can now view that the cartesian closure operator augments a collection of unifiers in such a way that the resulting relation is the (tuple-)cartesian closure of the original relation. For example, the operator augments the two unifiers $[X/a, Y/b], [X/c, Y/d]$ with $[X/a, Y/d], [X/c, Y/b]$.

Intuitively, using cartesian closure corresponds to reasoning about a program using its variables

---

[1] This approximation is also important, for efficiency reasons, in imperative languages [6].

as ranging over sets as opposed to individual values. It is for this reason, in fact, that the induced approximation is used to formalize types in logic programs. This is despite the fact that there are no known algorithms for inferring such types. That is, the approximate meanings of programs are not known to be recursive.

The approach using abstract interpretation, on the other hand, deals with an abstraction of the underlying domain which then induces an approximation of unifiers and collections of unifiers which is *finitary*[2,3]. (See, for example, [2].) The approximate meaning of a program, therefore, is automatically recursive. Its accuracy is not directly comparable to that of cartesian closure based approximations; it is, however, limited[4] by the essentially finite bound on the number of different states between which the approximate reasoning can discriminate.

In this paper, we define an approximation based only on cartesian closure. We then show that it is more accurate than other approximations which are based on cartesian closure. Our main result proves that our approximation to any program is recursive. Because our approximation is perfectly accurate for programs whose head atoms are linear (no two occurrences of the same variable), and whose body atoms each contain at most one distinct variable which appears elsewhere in the rule, we obtain a new subclass of logic programs which is decidable. This strengthens the result of [1] which used a main result of [10] to prove, amongst other results, that unary logic programs are decidable. The most important aspect of our proof, however, is that it is constructive: it provides an algorithm to represent the approximate meaning in the form of a cyclic term graph. This explicit representation can then be used as a starting point for logic program analyzers.

---

[2]This need not mean a finite abstract domain.

[3]For efficiency reasons, many abstract interpretation algorithms, e.g. [3], also use cartesian closure.

[4]Abstract interpreters have been useful, however, for inferring *runtime* properties.

2 Background & Related Work

The meaning of a logic program may be defined as the least fixpoint of the function T_P which maps from and into interpretations. This function may be defined as follows[5]:

$$T_P(\mathcal{I}) \stackrel{def}{=} \left\{ H\beta : \begin{array}{l} H \longleftarrow \tilde{B} \in P, \text{ and} \\ \beta \in \{\theta : \tilde{B}\theta \subseteq \mathcal{I}\} \end{array} \right\}$$

where θ ranges over all substitutions which are ground with respect to $var(P)$, the variables in P. Our definition of the approximate meaning of a program will be defined using a similar function.

A *set-substitution* α is like an ordinary substitution except that variables are mapped into sets of terms as opposed to terms. Furthermore, $X\alpha = \{X\}$ except for a finite number of variables. Now define an approximation operator $\mathcal{A}_{\tilde{X}}$ which takes as input a nonempty collection Θ of substitutions which are ground w.r.t. the (possibly empty set of) variables $\tilde{X}$. It outputs a single set-substitution α such that for every variable X, $X\alpha$ is:

$$\begin{cases} \{t : X/t \text{ appears in some } \theta \in \Theta\} & \text{if } X \in \tilde{X}; \\ \{X\} & \text{if } X \notin \tilde{X}. \end{cases}$$

We say that $\mathcal{A}_{\tilde{X}}$ is undefined when applied to an empty set. Our approximation to the meaning of a logic program P can now be formalized by an adaptation of T_P above. Let $\tilde{X}$ denote $var(P)$; then:

$$\mathcal{T}_P(\mathcal{I}) \stackrel{def}{=} \left\{ a : a \in H\alpha \begin{array}{l} \text{where} \\ H \longleftarrow \tilde{B} \in P, \text{ and} \\ \alpha = \mathcal{A}_{\tilde{X}}(\{\theta : \tilde{B}\theta \subseteq \mathcal{I}\}) \\ \text{is defined.} \end{array} \right\}.$$

Thus while the least fixpoint of T_P, call it $T_P \uparrow \omega$, is the exact meaning of P, the least fixpoint of $\mathcal{T}_P$, call it $\mathcal{T}_P \uparrow \omega$, is our approximation of the meaning of P. Clearly $\mathcal{T}_P \uparrow \omega \supseteq T_P \uparrow \omega$ for any P, and so our approximation is conservative.

Take, for example, the program following pro-

---

[5]The symbol $\sim$ groups atoms or terms into a possibly empty sequence or set, depending on context.

gram P:

```
p(a, b).
p(b, a).
q(X, Y) ←— p(X, Y).
```

Here $T_P(\emptyset)$, call it $\mathcal{I}$, is simply $\{p(a,b), p(b,a)\}$. To compute $T_P(\mathcal{I})$, we first note that $\{\theta : p(X,Y)\theta \subseteq \mathcal{I}\}$ contains two substitutions $[X/a, Y/b]$ and $[X/b, Y/a]$. Applying $\mathcal{A}_{X,Y}$ to this collection, we obtain the set substitution $\alpha = [X/\{a,b\}, Y/\{a,b\}]$ which, when applied to the head atom $q(X,Y)$, gives rise to $\{q(a,a), q(a,b), q(b,a), q(b,b)\}$. Thus $T_P(\mathcal{I}) = \{p(a,b), p(b,a), q(a,a), q(a,b), q(b,a), q(b,b)\}$, and this, in fact, equals $\mathcal{T}_P \uparrow \omega$. In contrast, $T_P \uparrow \omega$ contains only four elements.

In the literature, the following cartesian closure operator $\star$ has been used over sets of terms and atoms rather than sets of substitutions: for any set S of ground terms or atoms,

$$S^\star \stackrel{def}{=} \begin{array}{l} \{c : c \text{ is a constant in } S\} \cup \\ \{f(t_1, \ldots, t_n) : t_i \in (f_{(i)}^{-1}(S))^\star\} \end{array}$$

where f ranges over the function and predicate symbols in S, and $f_{(i)}^{-1}(S) \stackrel{def}{=} \{t_i : f(t_1, \cdots, t_n) \in S\}$ denotes a projection of S. The work on types [12], for example, deals with the following function:

$$Y_P(\mathcal{I}) \stackrel{def}{=} \left\{ H\beta : \begin{array}{l} H \leftarrow \tilde{B} \in P, \text{ and} \\ \beta \in \{\theta : \tilde{B}\theta \subseteq \mathcal{I}\} \end{array} \right\}^\star$$

and so the approximate meaning of the program P is the least fixpoint of Y_P, call it $Y_P \uparrow \omega$. It is easy to see that Y_P is less accurate than $\mathcal{T}_P$. For example, program P consisting of just two facts p(a, b) and p(b, a) is such that $Y_P \uparrow \omega = \{p(a,a), p(a,b), p(b,a), p(b,b)\} \supset \mathcal{T}_P \uparrow \omega$ whereas $\mathcal{T}_P \uparrow \omega = T_P \uparrow \omega$. The decidability of $Y_P \uparrow \omega$ was left open.

The earlier work in [8] associates to a program, not a function, but a formula in which variables range over sets. The approximate meaning of a program is then given by a certain model of these formulas. It turns out that this model is essentially a fixpoint of Y_P. The accuracy of the program approximation that this model defines is therefore bounded by $Y_P \uparrow \omega$. In [8] and in a subsequent paper [9], algorithms were presented for solving subclasses of these set based formulas. The solvability problem for the general class was left open.

We conclude this section by illustrating the differences between Y_P, $\mathcal{T}_P$ and T_P. Consider the following program P:

```
p(f(a, b)).
p(f(b, a)).
r(X)    ←— p(f(X, X)).
s(f(Y, Z)) ←— p(f(Y, Z)).
```

Here $Y_P \uparrow \omega$ is

$$\left\{ \begin{array}{l} p(f(a,a)), p(f(a,b)), p(f(b,a)), p(f(b,b)) \\ r(a), r(b) \\ s(f(a,a)), s(f(a,b)), s(f(b,a)), s(f(b,b)) \end{array} \right\}$$

while $\mathcal{T}_P \uparrow \omega$ is

$$\left\{ \begin{array}{l} p(f(a,b)), p(f(b,a)) \\ s(f(a,a)), s(f(a,b)), s(f(b,a)), s(f(b,b)) \end{array} \right\}$$

and $T_P \uparrow \omega$ is

$$\left\{ \begin{array}{l} p(f(a,b)), p(f(b,a)) \\ s(f(a,b)), s(f(b,a)) \end{array} \right\}.$$

In general, we have $Y_P \uparrow \omega \supseteq \mathcal{T}_P \uparrow \omega \supseteq T_P \uparrow \omega$ for any program P.

3 A Closed Form for Fixpoints

Our first step toward a finite representation of $\mathcal{T}_P \uparrow \omega$ will be a quantified formula whose least model equals $\mathcal{T}_P \uparrow \omega$. Before we define this formula, we require some preliminary definitions.

Consider the denumerable alphabets Σ of function symbols, Π of predicate symbols, and $\mathcal{V}$ of variables. Let HB and HU respectively denote the Herbrand universe and base associated with these alphabets. A *HB-set expression* is defined to be either:

- a special variable, not in $\mathcal{V}$, of the form Υ_p where $p \in \Pi$ (call these the *type variables*), or
- of the form $p(t_1, \ldots, t_n)$ where $p \in \Pi$ and $t_1, \ldots, t_n$ are HU-set expressions, or
- of the form $t \cup s$ or $t \cap s$ where t and s are HB-set expressions.

A HU-*set expression* is defined to be either:

- a variable X in $\mathcal{V}$, or a special constant of the form $\bot$ or $\top$, or
- of the form $f(t_1, \ldots, t_n)$ where $f \in \Sigma$ and $t_1, \ldots, t_n$ are HU-set expressions, or
- of the form $t \cup s$ or $t \cap s$ where t and s are HU-set expressions.

Finally, a *set expression* is either a HB-set expression or a HU-set expression.

A *set constraint* is of the form $s = t$ where either both s and t are HB-set expressions or both s and t are HU-set expressions[6]. An *interpretation* $\mathcal{I}$ maps each type variable into HB and each variable in $\mathcal{V}$ into HU. $\mathcal{I}$ can be extended, in an obvious way, to map set expressions as follows. If t is:

- the special constant $\bot$, then $\mathcal{I}(t)$ is $\emptyset$;
- the special constant $\top$, then $\mathcal{I}(t)$ is HU;
- a constant symbol c, then $\mathcal{I}(t)$ is $\{c\}$;
- $f(t_1, \ldots, t_n)$ where $n \geq 1$ and $f \in \Pi \cup \Sigma$, then $\mathcal{I}(t)$ is
  $\{f(s_1, \cdots, s_n) : s_1 \in \mathcal{I}(t_1), \cdots, s_n \in \mathcal{I}(t_n)\}$;
- $u \cup s$ or $u \cap s$, then $\mathcal{I}(t)$ is $\mathcal{I}(u) \cup \mathcal{I}(s)$ or $\mathcal{I}(u) \cap \mathcal{I}(s)$ respectively.

This mapping, in turn, induces a mapping from collections $\mathcal{C}$ of set constraints into $\{true, false\}$ in the obvious way. If $\mathcal{I}(\mathcal{C})$ is *true*, we say that $\mathcal{I}$ is a *model* of $\mathcal{C}$.

Let P be an arbitrary program and denote its rules by $R_1, \cdots, R_N$, $1 \leq N$. We assume that rules are written so that they do not share variables. Let

---

[6] The solvability problem for set constraints is open. A decision procedure for a restricted class appears in [5].

Π_P denote the predicate symbols in P. Let $P|_p$ denote the subset of rules in P defining the relation p. Let R_i be of the form $H_i \longleftarrow \tilde{B}_i$, $1 \leq i \leq N$. We are now in a position to define, for each program P, a formula which represents the approximate meaning of P. This formula is comprised of two main parts. The first part is a collection of set equations, $\mathcal{C}$, and is defined as follows:

$$\bigwedge_{p \in \Pi_P} \Upsilon_p = \bigcup_{i:R_i \in P|_p} H_i.$$

That is, each equation in $\mathcal{C}$ equates a type variable Υ_p and the union of the head atoms in $P|_p$.

The second part of our formula is a conjunction of several subformulas, one for each rule in P. Consider the following collection $\mathcal{D}_i$ of pairs corresponding to a rule R_i in P:

$$\{(p(\tilde{t}), \Upsilon_p) : p(\tilde{t}) \text{ is a body atom in } R_i\}.$$

The subformula corresponding to R_i, call it $\mathcal{F}(\mathcal{D}_i)$, will be defined in terms of the pairs $\mathcal{D}_i$. Before we formally define $\mathcal{F}(\mathcal{D}_i)$, consider some example programs. Let P be

```
p(a).
p(b).
q(X) <--- p(X).
```

so that $\mathcal{C}$ is $\Upsilon_p = p(a) \cup p(b) \wedge \Upsilon_q = q(X)$, $\mathcal{D}_1 = \mathcal{D}_2 = \emptyset$, and $\mathcal{D}_3$ is the singleton $\{(p(X), \Upsilon_p)\}$. In this example, if $\mathcal{F}(\mathcal{D}_1)$ and $\mathcal{F}(\mathcal{D}_2)$ are simply *true* and $\mathcal{F}(\mathcal{D}_3)$ is the set equation $p(X) = \Upsilon_p$, then the formula

$$\mathcal{C} \wedge \mathcal{F}(\mathcal{D}_1) \wedge \mathcal{F}(\mathcal{D}_2) \wedge \mathcal{F}(\mathcal{D}_3)$$

captures $T_P \uparrow \omega$ in the sense that its least model (in which $X = \{a, b\}$) is equal to $T_P \uparrow \omega$. In general, however, obtaining a subformula $\mathcal{F}(\mathcal{D}_i)$ by simply making the pairs $\mathcal{D}_i$ into set equations will not be appropriate. Suppose P were

```
p(a).
p(b).
r(a).
r(c).
q(X) <-- p(X), r(X).
```

Then $\mathcal{C}$ is $\Upsilon_p = p(a) \cup p(b) \wedge \Upsilon_r = r(a) \cup r(c) \wedge \Upsilon_q = q(X)$, $\mathcal{D}_1 = \mathcal{D}_2 = \mathcal{D}_3 = \mathcal{D}_4 = \emptyset$, and $\mathcal{D}_5 = \{(p(X), \Upsilon_p), (q(X), \Upsilon_q)\}$. For this example, an appropriate formulation of the subformulas $\mathcal{F}(\mathcal{D}_1)$, $\mathcal{F}(\mathcal{D}_2)$, $\mathcal{F}(\mathcal{D}_3)$ and $\mathcal{F}(\mathcal{D}_4)$ is simply that they are each *true*, and an appropriate formulation of $\mathcal{F}(\mathcal{D}_5)$ is

$$X = \{x : (p(x) \in \Upsilon_p \wedge r(x) \in \Upsilon_r)\}.$$

The least model of the formula $\mathcal{C} \wedge \mathcal{F}(\mathcal{D}_1) \wedge \mathcal{F}(\mathcal{D}_2) \wedge \mathcal{F}(\mathcal{D}_3) \wedge \mathcal{F}(\mathcal{D}_4) \wedge \mathcal{F}(\mathcal{D}_5)$ (in which $X = \{a\}$) thus captures $T_P \uparrow \omega$.

The above two examples only had only one variable in the body atoms. Now suppose P were

```
p(a, b).
p(c, d).
q(X,Y) <-- p(X,Y).
```

then $\mathcal{C}$ is $\{\Upsilon_p = p(a,b) \cup p(c,d) \wedge \Upsilon_q = q(X,Y)\}$, $\mathcal{D}_1 = \mathcal{D}_2 = \emptyset$, and $\mathcal{D}_3 = \{(p(X,Y), \Upsilon_p)\}$. As above, the subformulas $\mathcal{F}(\mathcal{D}_1)$ and $\mathcal{F}(\mathcal{D}_2)$ can each be assigned *true*. An appropriate formulation of $\mathcal{F}(\mathcal{D}_3)$ is a conjunction of two equations:

$$X = \{x : \exists y \, (p(x,y) \in \Upsilon_p)\},$$
$$Y = \{y : \exists x \, (p(x,y) \in \Upsilon_p)\}$$

so that the least model of our formula $\mathcal{C} \wedge \mathcal{F}(\mathcal{D}_1) \wedge \mathcal{F}(\mathcal{D}_2) \wedge \mathcal{F}(\mathcal{D}_3)$ (in which $X = \{a,c\}$ and $Y = \{b,d\}$) captures $T_P \uparrow \omega$.

In general, $\mathcal{D}_i$ will be a collection of pairs of the form $\{(a_1, s_1), \cdots, (a_m, s_m)\}$ such that for all $1 \leq j \leq m$,

- a_j is an atom or term, and
- s_j is a set expression.

Letting $\mathcal{V} = \{X_1, \cdots, X_k\}$ denote the variables in $a_1, \cdots, a_m$, we define $\mathcal{F}(\mathcal{D}_i)$ to be[7] the conjunction, over $1 \leq j \leq k$, of:

$$X_j = \left\{ x_j : \exists x_1 ... x_{j-1} x_{j+1} ... x_k \begin{pmatrix} a_1 \mu \in s_1 \\ \vdots \\ a_m \mu \in s_m \end{pmatrix} \right\}$$

where $x_1, \cdots, x_k$ are new variables, and μ denotes the renaming substitution $[X_1/x_1, \cdots X_k/x_k]$.

An *interpretation* and *model* of such a formula are defined by extending, in the obvious way, the definitions given in section 2 for an interpretation and a model of set equations.

We are now in position to define formally, given a program P, a formula whose least model characterizes the desired set $T_P \uparrow \omega$. In order to keep this definition as simple as possible, we assume that programs have no ground atoms in the head of any non-fact rule; call such restricted programs *non-degenerate*. To see that no generality is in fact lost, consider a program P which contains such offending rules. Rewrite P into P' by adding a new variable, as an extra argument in the first position, to every atom in P. Clearly $T_P \uparrow \omega$ can be easily extracted from $T_{P'} \uparrow \omega$ by simply ignoring the first argument of all atoms in the latter set. We shall deal with degenerate programs at the end of this paper.

Let $R_1, \cdots, R_N$ denote the rules in the rules in P, and we now define that the formula corresponding to P is

$$\mathcal{C} \wedge \mathcal{F}(\mathcal{D}_1) \wedge \cdots \wedge \mathcal{F}(\mathcal{D}_N)$$

where $\mathcal{C}$ is

$$\bigwedge_{p \in \Pi_P} \Upsilon_p = \bigcup_{i: R_i \in P|_p} H_i$$

and each $\mathcal{D}_i$, $1 \leq i \leq N$, is the collection of pairs

$$\{(p(\tilde{t}), \Upsilon_p) : p(\tilde{t}) \text{ is a body atom in } P\} \cup$$
$$\{(X, \top) : X \text{ appears in } H_i \text{ but not in } \tilde{B}_i\}.$$

---

[7] If $\mathcal{D}_i$ is empty, then $\mathcal{F}(\mathcal{D}_i)$ is simply *true*.

For example, consider the program:

```
p(a, b).
p(b, a).
q(X, W) <-- p(X, X).
r(Y, Z) <-- p(Y, Z).
```

$\mathcal{C}$ is $\Upsilon_p = p(a,b) \cup p(b,a) \wedge \Upsilon_q = q(X,W) \wedge \Upsilon_r = r(Y,Z)$, $\mathcal{D}_1$ is $\emptyset$, $\mathcal{D}_2$ is $\emptyset$, $\mathcal{D}_3$ is $\{(p(X,X),\Upsilon_p), (W,\top)\}$ and $\mathcal{D}_4$ is $\{(p(Y,Z),\Upsilon_p)\}$. The formula $\mathcal{C} \wedge \mathcal{F}(\mathcal{D}_1) \wedge \mathcal{F}(\mathcal{D}_2) \wedge \mathcal{F}(\mathcal{D}_3) \wedge \mathcal{F}(\mathcal{D}_4)$ is therefore given by:

$$
\begin{aligned}
(4a) \quad \Upsilon_p &= p(a,b) \cup p(b,a), \\
(4b) \quad \Upsilon_q &= q(X,W), \\
(4c) \quad \Upsilon_r &= r(Y,Z), \\
(4d) \quad X &= \left\{ x : \exists w \begin{pmatrix} p(x,x) \in \Upsilon_p \\ w \in \top \end{pmatrix} \right\}, \\
(4e) \quad W &= \left\{ w : \exists x \begin{pmatrix} p(x,x) \in \Upsilon_p \\ w \in \top \end{pmatrix} \right\}, \\
(4f) \quad Y &= \{ y : \exists z \, (p(y,z) \in \Upsilon_p) \}, \\
(4g) \quad Z &= \{ z : \exists y \, (p(y,z) \in \Upsilon_p) \}.
\end{aligned}
$$

where equations (4a), (4b) and (4c) arise from the definition of $\mathcal{C}$, equations (4d) and (4e) arise from $\mathcal{D}_3$, and equations (4f) and (4g) arise from $\mathcal{D}_4$. The one and only model for this formula is given by

$$
\begin{aligned}
\Upsilon_p &= \{p(a,b), p(b,a)\}, \\
\Upsilon_q &= \emptyset, \\
\Upsilon_r &= \{r(a,a), r(b,b), r(a,b), r(b,a)\}, \\
X &= \emptyset, \\
W &= \emptyset, \\
Y &= \{a,b\}, \\
Z &= \{a,b\}.
\end{aligned}
$$

In what follows, we shall abbreviate the sequence $\mathcal{D}_1, \cdots, \mathcal{D}_N$, where N denotes the number of rules in the program, by $\tilde{\mathcal{D}}$, and the formula $\mathcal{F}(\mathcal{D}_1) \wedge \cdots \wedge \mathcal{F}(\mathcal{D}_N)$ by $\mathcal{F}(\tilde{\mathcal{D}})$. Where $\mathcal{I}$ is a model of a collection of set equations, we write $\mathcal{I}_{\Upsilon_P}$ to denote the subset of HB defined by the union of $\mathcal{I}(\Upsilon_p)$ over all the type variables Υ_p associated with P. We now formally state that the models of the formula $\mathcal{C} \wedge \mathcal{F}(\tilde{\mathcal{D}})$ correspond to the fixpoints of T_P.

Main Lemma 1
Let P be a non-degenerate logic program. Then
(a) $\mathcal{I}$ is a model of $\mathcal{C} \wedge \mathcal{F}(\tilde{\mathcal{D}})$ implies that $\mathcal{I}_{\Upsilon_P}$ is a fixpoint of T_P;
(b) $\mathcal{I}'$ is a fixpoint of T_P implies that there is a model $\mathcal{I}$ of $\mathcal{C} \wedge \mathcal{F}(\tilde{\mathcal{D}})$ such that $\mathcal{I}_{\Upsilon_P} = \mathcal{I}'$. □

4 A Simplification Algorithm for Set Constraints

We shall deal with the formula $\mathcal{F}_P(\tilde{\mathcal{D}})$ in the next section. In this section, we describe an algorithm, called $SIMPLIFY$, which inputs a collection of set constraints in the form $\{X_1 = s_1, X_2 = s_2, \cdots X_n = s_n\}$ where the X_i are distinct variables and the s_i are set expressions, into an equivalent system written in a form such that the least model is apparent.

For simplicity, we assume that the set expressions s_i are in disjunctive normal form w.r.t. $\cup$ and $\cap$. We write $DNF(s)$, where s is a set expression, to denote the equivalent expression obtained by applying the usual distributive operation on $\cap$ over $\cup$ so that the result is in DNF. Clearly such a function is easily implementable. We tacitly assume that the symbols $\cup$ and $\cap$ are associative, commutative and idempotent. Thus, for example, we may regard $s \cap (t \cap u)$ and $(s \cap t) \cap u$ as identical expressions. We shall also assume that the set expression s_i are not deeply nested[8]. We lose no generality because we can rewrite any conjunction $\mathcal{C}$ of set equations by exhaustively applying the following transformation: if $\mathcal{C}$ contains a subexpression $f(t_1, \cdots, t_n)$ where t_i, $1 \leq i \leq n$, is not a variable, then replace that occurrence of t_i by a new variable X and add to $\mathcal{C}$ the equation $X = t_i$. Clearly the resulting collection is equivalent to the original collection and is not deeply nested.

We now define formally the input and output format of the $SIMPLIFY$ algorithm.

---
[8]The term nesting means encapsulation within the scope of a function or predicate symbol.

Definition 1 (Normal Form) *A collection of set equations C is in* normal form *if it is (a) not deeply nested, (b) of the form $X_1 = s_1$, $X_2 = s_2$, $\cdots$, $X_n = s_n$ where the X_i, $1 \leq i \leq n$, are distinct, and (c) the s_i, $1 \leq i \leq n$, are set expressions.* □

Given a collection $C = \{X_1 = s_1, X_2 = s_2, \cdots, X_n = s_n\}$ of set equations in normal form, we refer to the variables $X_1, \cdots, X_n$ as the *solved variables* of C. We write $lhs(C)$ to denote the set of variables on the left-hand-sides of equations in C, and we write $rhs(C)$ to denote the set of expressions appearing in the right-hand-sides. We write $rhs(C)|_X$ to denote

$$\begin{cases} s & \text{if } X = s \text{ appears in } C; \\ X & \text{otherwise.} \end{cases}$$

Definition 2 (Solved Form) *A normal form collection of set equations C is in* solved form *if it is of the form:*

$$X_1 = s_{1,1} \cup s_{1,2} \cup \cdots \cup s_{1,m_1}$$
$$\vdots$$
$$X_n = s_{n,1} \cup s_{n,2} \cup \cdots \cup s_{n,m_n}$$

where for each $1 \leq i \leq n$ and $1 \leq j \leq m_i$, the set expression $s_{i,j}$ is either (a) a constant, or (b) of the form $f(Y_1, \cdots, Y_n)$ where f is an n-ary function or predicate symbol and each $Y_i, 1 \leq i \leq n$, is a variable, or (c) a non-solved variable, or (d) of the form $X \cap s$ where X is a non-solved variable. □

Where $X = s_1 \cup \cdots \cup s_n$ is an equation in a solved form collection C, we write $crhs(C)$ to denote the subset of the expressions in $rhs(C)$ which fall into cases (a) and (b) above. Similarly, we define $crhs(C)|_X$ to be subset of the expressions in $rhs(C)|_X$ which fall into cases (a) and (b) above.

Despite the above seemingly complicated definition of solved form, the main property that is required from constraints C in solved form is simply that its least model (and it is easy to show this exists) can be immediately extracted. More specifically, the least model of C can be expicitly presented by replacing all occurrences of non-solved variables by $\bot$ (since in the least model they are the empty set) and simplifying appropriately. What will remain is a collection in the following form:

Definition 3 (Explicit Form) *A collection of set equations C is in* explicit form *if it is of the form:*

$$X_1 = s_{1,1} \cup s_{1,2} \cup \cdots \cup s_{1,m_1}$$
$$\vdots$$
$$X_n = s_{n,1} \cup s_{n,2} \cup \cdots \cup s_{n,m_n}$$

where for $1 \leq i \leq n$, the X_i are distinct variables, and for each $1 \leq j \leq m_i$, the set expression $s_{i,j}$ is either (a) a constant, or (b) of the form $f(Y_1, \cdots, Y_n)$ where f is an n-ary function or predicate symbol and each $Y_i, 1 \leq i \leq n$, is a solved variable. □

For example, let the solved form collection C be

$$X = f(Y) \cup a,$$
$$Y = g(X) \cup (h(X) \cap Z).$$

We may describe the least model of C, which is:

$$X = \{a, fg(a), \cdots (fg)^n(a), \cdots\},$$
$$Y = \{g(a), gfg(a), \cdots (gf)^n g(a), \cdots\}$$

by the explicit form:

$$X = f(Y) \cup a,$$
$$Y = g(X).$$

We may also construct the following term graph as an alternative representation:

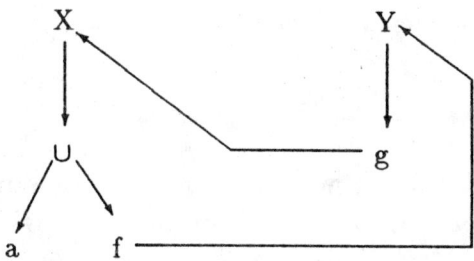

We now present the *SIMPLIFY* algorithm which is essentially a controlled sequence of applications of a number of transformations. Consider first the following two transformation steps on a collection C in normal form:

Transformation 1 (C-Substitute) If C contains two distinct equations $X = s$, $Y = t$ such that s contains an un-nested occurrence of the variable Y, then replace that occurrence of Y by t and apply DNF appropriately.

Transformation 2 (Cycle-Removal) If C contains the equation $X = s$, such that s contains an un-nested occurrence of the variable X, then replace that occurrence of X by a new variable.

Essentially, the result of repeatedly applying these transformations is that C will contain no un-nested solved variables on the right-hand-sides. While these two transformations serve to the implement obvious notion of substitution, there are two noteworthy points: first, they cannot be applied in an arbitrary order, and second, the latter transformation is not intuitive.

We next subject C to the following three transformations.

Transformation 3 (Intersection Clash) If C contains an occurrence of the expression $t \cap s$ where t and s have distinct outermost symbols, replace that occurrence by $\bot$.

Transformation 4 (Intersect^n Simplification) If C contains an occurrence of the expression $t \cap \bot$ or $t \cap \top$, then replace that occurrence by $\bot$ or t respectively.

Transformation 5 (Intersection Distribution) If C contains an occurrence of the expression $f(X_1, \cdots, X_n) \cap f(Y_1, \cdots, Y_n)$, then replace that occurrence by $f(V_1, \cdots, V_n)$, and add the constraint $V_i = DNF(rhs(C)|_{X_i} \cap rhs(C)|_{Y_i})$, $1 \leq i \leq n$, where the V_i are new variables.

---

input a normal form collection C;
1. **rename** each variable X in C into $V_{\{X\}}$;
2. **for** each solved variable X in C **do**
3.   **exhaustively-apply**
        transformation 2 to C;
4.   **exhaustively-apply**
        transformation 1 using X to C;
    endfor
5. **repeat**
6.   **exhaustively-apply**
        transformations 3 and 4 to C;
7.   **if** transformation 5 is applicable to C
        that is, C contains a subexpression
        of the form
        $f(V_{S_1}, V_{S_2}, \cdots, V_{S_n}) \cap f(V_{T_1}, V_{T_2}, \cdots, V_{T_n})$
8.   **then**
        replace the above subexpression by
        $f(V_{S_1 \cup T_1}, \cdots, V_{S_n \cup T_n})$;
9.   **for each** $i : 1 \leq i \leq n$ **do**
10.   **if** $V_{S_i \cup T_i}$ is non-solved **then**
11.   add to C the equation
            $V_{S_i \cup T_i} = DNF(rhs(C)|_{V_{S_i}} \cap rhs(C)|_{V_{T_i}})$;
          endif
        endfor
    endif
12. **until** none of transformations 3, 4 and 5 is applicable to C;
    rename each variable $V_{\{X\}}$, $X \in \mathcal{V}$, into X;
    output C;

Figure 1: **SIMPLIFY**

The entire $SIMPLIFY$ algorithm is presented in figure 1.

The correctness of the individual transformations, and the fact that we obtain a solved form upon termination of $SIMPLIFY$, can be easily verified. Termination, however, cannot be guaranteed if these transformations were applied in an arbitrary order. (For example we can apply the intersection distribution transformation to the constraint $X = f(X) \cap f(X)$ forever.) To obtain termination, we showed, in [4], that the number of new variables which need to be introduced by the intersection transformation can be bounded by $2^{|\mathcal{V}|}$ where $\mathcal{V}$ denote the variables in C. The details are lengthy and hence omitted.

In summary,

Lemma 1 *Let C denote a normal form collection of set constraints. Then the $SIMPLIFY$ algorithm, when input with C, outputs a collection C_s of set constraints such that*

- *C_s is equivalent to C, and*
- *C_s is in solved form.* □

5 The Main Result

In section 3, we defined, corresponding to a given program P, a formula consisting of a normal form collection C of set equations, and a formula $\mathcal{F}(\tilde{\mathcal{D}})$ where $\tilde{\mathcal{D}}$ is a family of collections of pairs. We now present our main algorithm which inputs such a formula and performs a finite number of reduction steps

$$C, \tilde{\mathcal{D}} \Longrightarrow C^{(0)}, \tilde{\mathcal{D}}^{(0)} \Longrightarrow \ldots \Longrightarrow C^{(n)}, \tilde{\mathcal{D}}^{(n)}$$

and finally obtains a collection of solved form set equations $C^{(n)}$ such that the least model of $C^{(n)}$ is the same as the least model of the formula $C \wedge \mathcal{F}(\tilde{\mathcal{D}})$. The essence of the algorithm is that it progressively transfers information about the least model we seek from $\tilde{\mathcal{D}}^{(i)}$ to $C^{(i)}$, $0 \leq i \leq n$. In the final step, therefore, $C^{(n)} \wedge \mathcal{F}(\tilde{\mathcal{D}}^{(n)})$ will be such that all the desired information will be in $C^{(n)}$.

The basis of this algorithm, as for the $SIMPLIFY$ algorithm described previously, is a group of transformations. Each transformation below takes two items as input: (a) a collection of set equations C and (b) a family $\tilde{\mathcal{D}} = \{\mathcal{D}_1, \cdots, \mathcal{D}_N\}$ of collections of pairs. Each transformation outputs two items: (a) a family $\tilde{\mathcal{D}}'$ of collections of pairs, and (b) a collection δ of set equations in normal form. If a transformation is applied on C and $\tilde{\mathcal{D}}$ to obtain $\tilde{\mathcal{D}}'$ and δ, we write

$$C, \tilde{\mathcal{D}} \Longrightarrow \tilde{\mathcal{D}}', \delta$$

and we say that a transformation was, in the *context* of C, *applied* on $\tilde{\mathcal{D}}$ to obtain the the new family $\tilde{\mathcal{D}}'$ and an *extracted collection* δ of set equations.

Transformation 6 ($\tilde{\mathcal{D}}$-Substitution) *If $\tilde{\mathcal{D}}$ contains an un-nested occurrence of a solved variable Y in the right-hand-side of a pair, then replace the occurrence by $rhs(C)|_Y$ and apply DNF appropriately. Output the resulting $\tilde{\mathcal{D}}$, and $\delta = \emptyset$.* □

Transformation 7 (Clash) *If $\mathcal{D}_j \in \tilde{\mathcal{D}}$ contains a pair $(f(t_1, \cdots, t_n), g(s_1, \cdots, s_m))$ where $f \neq g$, or a pair $(s, \bot)$, then output $\tilde{\mathcal{D}} - \{\mathcal{D}_j\}$ and $\delta = \{Y_1 = \bot, \cdots, Y_k = \bot\}$ where $Y_1, \cdots, Y_k$ are the variables in the left-hand-sides of $\mathcal{D}_j$.* □

Transformation 8 (Cancellation) *If $\tilde{\mathcal{D}}$ contains a pair $(f(s_1, \cdots, s_n), f(t_1, \cdots, t_n))$, then replace the pair by the pairs $(s_1, t_1), \cdots, (s_n, t_n)$. Output the resulting $\tilde{\mathcal{D}}$ and $\delta = \emptyset$.* □

Define the function $NONEMPTY(C, s)$, where C is a collection of set equations in solved form and s is a set expression, to be *true* iff $C \models s \neq \emptyset$. Clearly applying $NONEMPTY$ to (C, s) is equivalent to applying it to

$$(SIMPLIFY(C \cup \{X = s\}), X)$$

where X is a new variable. Thus the problem of implementing the function $NONEMPTY$ can be reduced to the problem of determining if a given variable is always non-empty in a given solved form. Such a test, detailed in [4], can be easily implemented.

Transformation 9 (Compaction) *If $\mathcal{D}_j \in \tilde{\mathcal{D}}$ is of the form $(\tilde{X}, \tilde{\Phi})$ and if $NONEMPTY(C, s_{Y_i})$ for all $1 \leq i \leq k$ where*

- *$\tilde{X}$ is a family of variables, and $var(\tilde{X}) = \{Y_1, \cdots, Y_k\}$;*
- *the notation s_Y, where Y ranges over $Y_1, \cdots, Y_k$, denotes the set expression $\phi_1 \cap \cdots \cap \phi_m$ such that $(Y, \phi_1), \cdots, (Y, \phi_m)$ are the pairs in $\mathcal{D}_j$ of the form (Y, ϕ),*

then output $\tilde{\mathcal{D}} - \{\mathcal{D}_j\}$ and $\delta = \{Y_1 = s_{Y_1}, \cdots, Y_k = s_{Y_k}\}$. ☐

Transformation 10 (Union) If $\mathcal{D}_j \in \tilde{\mathcal{D}}$ is of the form $\{(s, t_1 \cup t_2), (\tilde{\Psi}, \tilde{\Phi})\}$ then

- let $Y_1, \cdots, Y_k$ be the variables in s and $\tilde{\Psi}$;

- let $Y_1', \cdots, Y_k', Y_1'', \cdots, Y_k''$ be distinct new variables and let η_1 and η_2 denote the renaming substitutions $[Y_1/Y_1', \cdots, Y_k/Y_k']$ and $[Y_1/Y_1'', \cdots, Y_k/Y_k'']$;

- let $\tilde{\mathcal{D}}'$ be $\tilde{\mathcal{D}} - \{\mathcal{D}_j\} \cup \{\mathcal{D}_j', \mathcal{D}_j''\}$ where
$\mathcal{D}_j' = \{(s\eta_1, t_1), (\tilde{\Psi}\eta_1, \tilde{\Phi})\}$ and
$\mathcal{D}_j'' = \{(s\eta_2, t_2), (\tilde{\Psi}\eta_2, \tilde{\Phi})\}$, and

- let δ be
$\{Y_1 = Y_1\eta_1 \cup Y_1\eta_2, \cdots, Y_k = Y_k\eta_1 \cup Y_k\eta_2\}$;

and output $\tilde{\mathcal{D}}'$ and δ. ☐

Transformation 11 (Intersection) If $\mathcal{D}_j \in \tilde{\mathcal{D}}$ contains a pair $(s, t_1 \cap t_2)$, then replace that pair by the two pairs $(s, t_1), (s, t_2)$. Output the resulting $\tilde{\mathcal{D}}$ and $\delta = \emptyset$. ☐

Whenever one of the above transformations is applied on $\tilde{\mathcal{D}}$ in the context of $\mathcal{C}$ to obtain δ and $\tilde{\mathcal{D}}'$, we write $\mathcal{C}, \tilde{\mathcal{D}} \xrightarrow{tf} \tilde{\mathcal{D}}, \delta$ to indicate by tf the particular transformation used. We say that $\tilde{\mathcal{D}}$ is *closed* under a transformation if that transformation is not applicable to $\tilde{\mathcal{D}}$.

Intuitively, these transformations fall into three classes. The cancel, union and intersection transformations simplify the collections $\mathcal{D}_j$ independently of $\mathcal{C}$. The substitution transformation, on the other hand, modifies $\mathcal{D}_j$ using $\mathcal{C}$. The clash and compact transformations perform the essential work of transferring information to $\mathcal{C}$ by augmenting it with new constraints. Crucial to the termination, correctness and completeness of this system of transformations is the synchronization between the compaction transformation, which contains a semantic condition, and the others (but

```
function REDUCE(C, D̃) {
     Δ := ∅;
1.   repeat {
2.      while (the substitution transformation
                 is applicable to C, D̃) do {
             C, D̃ ──subs──▶ D̃, δ
             Δ := Δ ∪ δ;
        }
3.      while (the union or intⁿ transformation
                 is applicable to C, D̃) do {
             C, D̃ ──union──▶ D̃, δ  or
             C, D̃ ──intersect──▶ D̃, δ  accordingly;
             Δ := Δ ∪ δ;
        }
4.      while (the cancel or clash transformation
                 is applicable to C, D̃) do {
             C, D̃ ──cancel──▶ D̃, δ  or
             C, D̃ ──clash──▶ D̃, δ  accordingly;
             Δ := Δ ∪ δ;
        }
5.      while (the compaction transformation
                 is applicable to C, D̃) do {
             C, D̃ ──compact──▶ D̃, δ
             Δ := Δ ∪ δ;
        }
     } until (no transfⁿ is applicable to C, D̃);
6.   return (D̃, Δ);
}
```

Figure 2: **REDUCE**

mainly the substitution transformation). Specifically, while the semantic condition ensures correctness, we need to prove that it is indeed satisfied when necessary.

We are now in a position to define, in figure 2, the reduction step of our algorithm. This step is described in the form of a function whose essential operation is an exhaustive application of the above transformations in the context of a fixed collection $\mathcal{C}$ of set constraints. For the sake of simpler proofs, however, we have restricted the order in which transformations may be applied.

Our main algorithm can now be described in figure 3. In [4], we proved, in two main parts, that

Figure 3: Main Algorithm

```
       input an non-degenerate logic program P;
1.     construct C, D̃ as defined in section 3;
2.     rewrite C into normal form;
3.     C^(0) := SIMPLIFY(C);
4.     V_0 := var(C^(0));
       i := 0;
5.     repeat {
6.        (D̃^(i+1), Δ) := REDUCE(C^(i), D̃^(i));
7.        C^(i+1) := SIMPLIFY(C^(i) ∪ Δ);
          i := i + 1;
8.     } until
          (crhs(C^(i+1))|_X = crhs(C^(i))|_X
          for all X ∈ V_0);
       output  C^(i);
```

Figure 4: Final Algorithm

```
       input an arbitrary logic program P;
1.     rewrite P by systematically replacing each
          atom p(t_1, ..., t_n), n ≥ 0, by the atom
          p(Z, t_1, ..., t_n), where Z is a new variable
          each time, and call the result P';
2.     input P' to the main algorithm,
          and let the output be C';
3.     rewrite C' by systematically replacing each
          atom p(t_1, t_2, ..., t_{n+1}), n ≥ 1, by the atom
          p(t_2, ..., t_{n+1}), and call the result C;
4.     simplify C into explicit form;
       output  C;
```

$REDUCE(\mathcal{C}, \tilde{\mathcal{D}})$ terminates. The proof that the main algorithm terminates then followed.

Lemma 2 (Termination of REDUCE)
(a) Each of the four while-loops terminates.
(b) The main repeat-loop terminates. □

Main Lemma 2 (Termination)
The main algorithm terminates. □

The next property that is required of these transformations is that they are correct. This notion of correctness has two aspects. First, we require that the transformations preserve the least model. That is

Lemma 3 (Partial-Correctness of Transformations)
If $\mathcal{C}, \tilde{\mathcal{D}} \Longrightarrow \tilde{\mathcal{D}}', \delta$, then $\mathcal{C} \wedge \mathcal{F}(\tilde{\mathcal{D}})$ is equivalent to $(\mathcal{C} \cup \delta) \wedge \mathcal{F}(\tilde{\mathcal{D}}')$.

While this is relatively easy to show for the substitution, clash, cancel and intersection transformations the proofs for the compaction and union transformations are more involved. In the case of the compaction transformation, this is because there is a non-trivial transfer of information from $\mathcal{D}_j$ to $\mathcal{C}$. In the case of the union transformation, this is because the transformation itself is complicated.

The second aspect of the correctness argument is more involved. Essentially, it consists of establishing an invariant that is preserved by each transformation application. The purpose of this invariant is to show that upon termination, we have actually computed the least fixpoint of $\mathcal{T}_P$. In other words, this invariant, in conjunction with the termination condition

$$crhs(\mathcal{C}^{(n+1)})|_X = crhs(\mathcal{C}^{(n)})|_X \text{ for all } X \in \mathcal{V}_0,$$

must imply that the least model of $\mathcal{C}^{(n)}$ is equivalent to the least model of the original formula $\mathcal{C} \wedge \mathcal{F}(\tilde{\mathcal{D}})$. A major complication is that the least model of $\mathcal{C}^{(n)}$ is in general not a model of the final formula $\mathcal{C}^{(n)} \wedge \mathcal{F}(\tilde{\mathcal{D}}^{(n)})$. The details are left to [4].

Before formally stating the main result, we present, in figure 4, a simple extension to the main algorithm to deal with arbitrary programs. This algorithm formalizes the comments made in section 3 concerning degenerate programs.

We now state the main result of this paper which is that the final algorithm computes an explicit representation of $\mathcal{T}_P \uparrow \omega$ for an arbitrary program P.

Theorem: Let P be an arbitrary logic program input to the final algorithm. Then

- the final algorithm terminates, returning a formula $\mathcal{C}$;
- $\mathcal{C}$ is a collection of set equations in explicit form, and
- where $\mathcal{I}$ is the least model of $\mathcal{C}$, $\mathcal{I}|_{\Upsilon_P} = T_P \uparrow \omega$.

□

6 Conclusion

Using the notion of cartesian closure on a collection of unifiers we defined an approximation to the meaning of a logic program. We argued that our approximation is more accurate than similar approximations in the literature, and this literature primarily being that on type inference in logic programming. The main result, that our approximation of a program is a recursive and finitely presentable set, was then presented in the form of an algorithm which has two parts.

The first part of our algorithm, called $SIMPLIFY$, was a decision procedure for a class of set equations, that is, set equations in normal form. Earlier related work is that of Reynolds [11] and Jones and Muchnick [7], the latter being an independent treatise of work similar to the former. In these works, the set expressions were allowed to contain projection functions, but they were not allowed to contain the intersection function (these works were not concerned with problem of shared variables inherent in logic programs). Thus their transformations mainly served to eliminate occurrences of projection functions while ours mainly served to eliminate occurrences of the intersection function[9].

The second and main part of our algorithm is also based upon a group of transformations. When used directly, these transformations do not always lead to a terminating computation. The key aspect of the main algorithm, therefore, is in its controlled use of the transformations. This is realized by the function REDUCE each of whose invocations performed transformations local to a fixed collection of set equations. The main loop in the main algorithm then ensured that REDUCE is invoked sufficiently often.

We finally note that two important practical issues have yet to be addressed: the first is efficiency; second, our algorithm does not, in general, return a *minimal* representation of $T_P \uparrow \omega$. Early investigations into the former issue reveal that our algorithm will be practical when applied to a large class of programs. The latter issue can be dealt with by algorithms similiar to those used for minimizing finite-state automata.

Acknowledgements

The authors are grateful to Saumya Debray, Thom Fruehwirth, Michael Maher, Peter Stuckey and Eyal Yardeni who reviewed the complete version of this paper.

References

[1] D. Angluin and D.N. Hoover, "Regular Prefix Relations" *Mathematical Systems Theory* 17, pp 167 - 191, 1984.

[2] M. Bruynooghe, "A Practical Framework for the Abstract Interpretation of Logic Programs", revised version of report CW-62, Dept. Comp. Sci., K.U. Leuven, 33 pages, October 1987.

[3] M. Bruynooghe and G. Janssens, "An Instance of Abstract Interpretation integrating Type and Mode Inference", *Proceedings 5th Int. Conf. on Logic Programming*, K.A. Bowen and R.A. Kowalski (eds), MIT Press, pp 669 - 683, August 1988.

[4] N.C. Heintze and J. Jaffar, "A Finite Presentation Theorem for Approximating Logic Programs", forthcoming CMU and IBM Research Report, 56 pages, October 1989.

[5] N.C. Heintze and J. Jaffar, "A Decision Procedure for a Class of Herbrand Set Constraints", forthcoming CMU and IBM Research Report, 40 pages, October 1989.

---

[9] In [5], we deals with *both* projection and intersection.

[6] N.D. Jones and S.S. Muchnick, "Complexity of Flow Analysis, Inductive Assertion Synthesis, and a Language due to Dijkstra", in *Proceedings 20th Conference on Foundations of Computer Science*, pp 185 - 190, also in, *Program Flow Analysis: Theory and Applications*, N.D. Jones and S.S. Muchnick (eds), Prentice-Hall, 1981.

[7] N.D. Jones and S.S. Muchnick, "Flow Analysis and Optimization of LISP-like Structures", *Proceedings 6th ACM Symposium on Principles of Programming Languages*, pp 244 - 256, 1979.

[8] P. Mishra, "Toward a Theory of Types in PROLOG", *Proceedings 1st IEEE Symposium on Logic Programming*, Atlantic City, pp 289 - 298, 1984.

[9] P. Mishra and U.S. Reddy, "Declaration-free Type Checking", *Proceedings 12th ACM Symposium on Principles of Programming Languages*, New Orleans, pp 7 - 21, 1985.

[10] M.O. Rabin, "Decidability of Second-order Theories and Automata on Infinite Trees", *Transactions of the American Math. Society 141*, pp 1 - 35, 1969.

[11] J.C. Reynolds, "Automatic Computation of Data Set Definitions", *Information Processing 68*, North-Holland, pp 456 - 461, 1969.

[12] E. Yardeni and E.Y. Shapiro, "A Type System for Logic Programs", in *Concurrent PROLOG: Collected Papers*, Vol. 2, MIT Press, pp 211 - 244, 1987.

Program Transformation in the Presence of Errors

Alexander Aiken   John H. Williams   Edward L. Wimmers

IBM Almaden Research Center
650 Harry Rd.
San Jose, CA 95120
email: *lastname*@ibm.com

Abstract

Language designers and implementors have avoided specifying and preserving the meaning of programs that produce errors. This is apparently because being forced to preserve error behavior severely limits the scope of program optimization, even for correct programs. However, preserving error behavior is desirable for debugging, and error behavior must be preserved in any language that permits user-generated exceptions.

This paper presents a technique for preserving the power of general program transformations in the presence of a rich collection of distinguishable error values. This is accomplished by introducing an annotation, "Safe", to mark occurrences of functions that cannot produce errors. Succinct and general algebraic laws can be expressed using Safe, giving program transformations in a language with many error values the same power and generality as program transformations in a language with only a single error value.

1 Introduction

A laudable trend of the past two decades has been the increased use of denotational semantics to guide the design and implementation of programming languages. Semantics-driven language design has produced cleaner and simpler languages and provided more precise standards for testing the correctness of language implementations.

An apparent exception to this trend is the treatment of error handling. All too often, errors are considered to be outside the pale of the denotational semantics; if anything is specified about error behavior, it is usually through some *ad hoc* mechanism. Some language features—such as strong typing—reduce the negative impact of such a design but cannot avoid it completely; runtime errors exist in every language and must be handled in an implementation.

Many languages simply omit errors altogether from their formal semantic specification. For example, early Fortran implementations were free to report errors as the implementor saw fit, and transformations to improve performance could change the behavior of error-producing programs. This approach is still taken with some modern languages, e.g., Haskell [HWA*88] and Miranda [Tur85], where strong typing and lazy evaluation lessen the need for error recovery and exception handling.

Other languages include errors in the domain of values and provide some mechanism for computing with (or recovering from) errors, but the formal specification allows considerable variation in the behavior of implementations. For example, in [Ste84] Steele writes:

> "The definition of Common Lisp ... explicitly requires the interpreter and compiler to impose identical semantics on *correct* programs *so far as possible*." (emphasis added)

Indeed, in one Common Lisp implementation, taking the car of an atom produces a run time error when interpreted but returns the current package when compiled!

One study of program transformations carefully accounts for the fact that many common optimizations do not preserve error behavior by giving a precise, denotational treatment of such transformations [CF89]. In this approach, errors are considered to approximate other values, and program transformations are lifting operations that can (possibly) make programs more defined. Another approach [Hen81]

> "...examines the optimization difficulties imposed by common exception handling facili-

ties [and] proposes restrictions on these mechanisms that make the optimization of programs possible."

Why have language designers and implementors avoided specifying and preserving the meaning of errors? The answer appears to be that not preserving error behavior increases the power and effectiveness of transforming correct programs, i.e., the "important" programs. For instance, substituting s2 (which selects the second element of a sequence) for s1 ∘ t1 (which selects the first element of the tail of a sequence) may improve a program's running time, but a programmer who hadn't used the primitive s2 and was unaware of its existence would be confused by the run-time error message "s2 incorrectly applied to a non-sequence argument."

If the language designer opts for language clarity and ease of debugging by making a semantic distinction between t1 errors and s2 errors, then the general transformation becomes invalid, and some weaker version must be substituted, perhaps in the form of a set of rules identifying particular contexts in which the replacement is valid. This can be a significant loss, since identifying such contexts in general requires knowledge of the entire program. Thus, including errors as semantic objects in order to make a language easier to use appears to weaken the generality and power of the language's program transformations.

This paper presents a technique for preserving the power of general program transformations in the presence of a rich collection of distinguishable error values. This is accomplished by introducing an annotation, "Safe", to mark occurrences of functions that cannot produce errors. Succinct and general algebraic laws can be expressed using Safe, thereby giving program transformations in a language with many error values the same power and generality as program transformations in a language with only a single error value (such as FP [Bac78]). In fact, the Safe mechanism accomplishes much more. It actually strengthens equational reasoning by providing a sufficient condition on a program context $E(\cdot)$ and functions f and g, such that $E(f) \equiv E(g)$ even if $f \not\equiv g$.

The Safe mechanism is presented in the context of the functional language FL [BWW86], but it should be applicable to any language whose program transformations can be expressed equationally. Section 2 describes enough of FL to illustrate the technique and prove its soundness. Section 3 introduces the Safe mechanism and gives a simple example illustrating that having just two distinguishable errors causes as much loss of algebraic generality as having arbitrarily many different kinds of errors. This shows that it is not possible through careful language design to make a gradual trade-off between the expressiveness of error reporting and algebraic generality. Section 3 also contains the Substitutability Theorem, which provides a criterion for proving the soundness of transformations involving Safe. Some examples of optimization using Safe are given in Section 4. Section 6 concludes with suggestions for further work.

2 An Overview of FL

FL [BWW86] is the result of an effort to design a practical functional language based on FP [Bac78]. Figure 1 gives the subset of FL needed to understand the laws and examples that follow. Some features of the language are ignored altogether; in particular, input/output functions and syntactic sugar are omitted. A definition of each function is given only for some arguments; for all other arguments, the function f returns an error value f_{err} (e.g., $s1:0 \equiv s1_{err}$).[1] The evaluation order is leftmost-innermost; thus, in $[f, g]:x$, $f:x$ is evaluated and then $g:x$ is evaluated.

In designing FL, it was recognized that one of the deficiencies of FP is that it has a single error message ⊥ (or *Wrong!*) for all exceptional circumstances. Error messages and exception handling are an integral part of FL; as in the current version of Standard ML [HMT89], errors are first class values rather than the special results of functions that fail to produce values. Semantically, error values in FL are treated differently than ordinary values. All functions are strict with respect to errors; that is, $f: x_{err} \equiv x_{err}$ for any function f and error value x_{err}. Sequence construction is also strict with respect to errors; a sequence collapses to the leftmost error

---

[1] In fact, FL functions produce more informative errors than just the name of the function, but this countable set of errors is sufficient to illustrate the technique.

$$
\begin{aligned}
\text{f:x} &\quad \text{denotes function application}\\
\langle x_1,\ldots,x_n\rangle &\quad \text{denotes sequence construction}\\
(\text{f}\circ\text{g})\text{:x} &= \text{f:}(\text{g:x})\\
[\text{f}_1,\ldots,\text{f}_n]\text{:x} &= \langle \text{f}_1\text{:x},\ldots,\text{f}_n\text{:x}\rangle\\
(\text{p}\to\text{q};\text{r})\text{:x} &= \begin{cases} \text{p:x} & \text{if p:x} \in \mathcal{E}_{FL}\\ \text{r:x} & \text{if p:x} = \underline{\text{false}}\\ \text{q:x} & \text{otherwise}\end{cases}\\
\bar{\text{x}}\text{:y} &= \text{x}\\
\alpha\text{:f:}\langle x_1,\ldots,x_n\rangle &= \langle \text{f:}x_1,\ldots,\text{f:}x_n\rangle\\
+\text{:}\langle x_1,\ldots,x_n\rangle &= x_1+\ldots+x_n\\
\text{si:}\langle x_1,\ldots,x_n\rangle &= x_i\\
\text{tl:}\langle x_1,x_2,\ldots,x_n\rangle &= \langle x_2,\ldots,x_n\rangle\\
\text{rev:}\langle x_1,\ldots,x_n\rangle &= \langle x_n,\ldots,x_1\rangle\\
\text{al:}\langle x,\langle y_1,\ldots,y_n\rangle\rangle &= \langle x,y_1,\ldots,y_n\rangle\\
\text{distl:}\langle x,\langle y_1,\ldots,y_n\rangle\rangle &= \langle\langle x,y_1\rangle,\ldots,\langle x,y_n\rangle\rangle\\
\text{id:x} &= \text{x}\\
\text{dom:f} &= \text{s1}\circ[\text{id},\text{f}]\\
\text{mkerr:"string"} &= \text{stringerr}\\
\text{catch:}\langle \text{f},\text{g}\rangle\text{:x} &= \begin{cases} \text{g:}\langle x,y\rangle & \text{if f:x} = Err(y)\\ \text{f:x} & \text{otherwise}\end{cases}
\end{aligned}
$$

Figure 1: A subset of FL.

it contains. This behavior is justified by the intended use of errors in FL: errors represent a situation in which something extraordinary has happened, and therefore an error should persist until caught or until it escapes from (and becomes the result of) the program. Some of the semantic treatment of errors can be seen in the recursive domain equations for FL:

$$
\begin{aligned}
\mathcal{D}_{FL} &= \mathcal{D}_{FL}^+ \cup \mathcal{E}_{FL}\\
\mathcal{D}_{FL}^+ &= A \cup \textit{Seqs}(\mathcal{D}_{FL}^+) \cup (\mathcal{D}_{FL}^+ \to \mathcal{D}_{FL})\\
&\quad \textit{(the ordinary values)}\\
\mathcal{E}_{FL} &= \textit{Err}(\mathcal{D}_{FL}^+) \cup \{\bot\}\\
&\quad \textit{(the error values)}
\end{aligned}
$$

In these equations, A is the set of atoms, *Seqs* is sequence construction, and *Err* is error construction. The ordering on $\mathcal{D}_{FL}^+$ is the standard one; in $\mathcal{E}_{FL}$, $Err(x) \leq Err(y) \Leftrightarrow x \leq y$ and $\bot \leq x$ for all x.

3 The Safe Mechanism

One of the principles underlying FL is that a programming language should have a rich algebra useful for reasoning about and optimizing programs. Errors have a great impact on the algebra; for example, if two expressions can produce distinct errors, then the order of evaluation of the expressions usually cannot be changed without changing the error produced. Even with errors, however, there are many general identities that hold between FL programs; as usual, $\text{f} \equiv \text{g}$ means that f and g denote the same semantic value.

$$
\begin{aligned}
\text{f}\circ\text{id} &\equiv \text{f} & (1)\\
\text{id}\circ\text{f} &\equiv \text{f} & (2)\\
[\text{f}_1,\ldots,\text{f}_n]\circ\text{g} &\equiv [\text{f}_1\circ\text{g},\ldots,\text{f}_n\circ\text{g}] & (3)\\
\text{f}\circ(\text{p}\to\text{q};\text{r}) &\equiv \text{p}\to\text{f}\circ\text{q};\text{f}\circ\text{r} & (4)\\
(\text{p}\to\text{q};\text{r})\circ\text{f} &\equiv \text{p}\circ\text{f}\to\text{q}\circ\text{f};\text{r}\circ\text{f} & (5)
\end{aligned}
$$

These laws hold because the order of application of the component functions is unchanged.

However,

$$[\text{g},\text{f}] \equiv \text{rev}\circ[\text{f},\text{g}] \qquad (6)$$

which is a law in FP, is not valid for all FL functions f and g; if f produces $\bot$ and g produces tlerr, then [g, f] produces tlerr, but rev ∘ [f, g] produces $\bot$. This example shows there cannot be a gradual trade-off of expressiveness of error reporting for generality of program transformations. Having two errors is as limiting as having arbitrarily many, since the existence of just one error distinguishable from $\bot$ is sufficient to invalidate any "law" that does not preserve the order of evaluation of its constituent functions. However, it is true that

$$[g, f] \equiv \mathbf{rev} \circ [f, g] \text{ if neither side makes an error} \quad (7)$$

That is, there are *contexts* in which $[g, f]$ can be substituted for $\mathbf{rev} \circ [f, g]$. There are many other examples of rewrite rules that are correct provided neither side produces an error, and including them greatly enhances the power of a program transformation system. The following informal examples illustrate the notion of "rewriting in context", i.e., using rules whose validity depends on the context in which they are applied. In these examples, an occurrence of a function f is annotated as being "safe" (written $S(f)$), if it is known that that occurrence is guaranteed not to produce an error when applied to a non-error value; the notation $f \mapsto g$ simply indicates that f is rewritten to g. (N.B. For now, $S(f)$ is an extralinguistic notion; the phrase "annotating f with $S(f)$" has no more semantic content than the phrase "painting f green".)

Consider the program $\mathbf{rev} \circ [\tilde{\ }0, \tilde{\ }1]$. Since the two constant functions cannot produce an error unless applied to an error, neither can the construction of the two constant functions. Thus the program can be rewritten:

$$\mathbf{rev} \circ [\tilde{\ }0, \tilde{\ }1] \mapsto$$
$$\mathbf{rev} \circ [S(\tilde{\ }0), S(\tilde{\ }1)] \mapsto$$
$$\mathbf{rev} \circ S([\tilde{\ }0, \tilde{\ }1])$$

Now note that because the argument to reverse is safe, the order of evaluation of the elements of the sequence must be irrelevant, so the application of $\mathbf{rev}$ can be eliminated. As a last step, the annotation S can be dropped:

$$\mathbf{rev} \circ S([\tilde{\ }0, \tilde{\ }1]) \mapsto$$
$$S([\tilde{\ }1, \tilde{\ }0]) \mapsto$$
$$[\tilde{\ }1, \tilde{\ }0]$$

This rewriting sequence is correct in the sense that the final program is equivalent to the original program; i.e., $\mathbf{rev} \circ [\tilde{\ }1, \tilde{\ }0] \equiv [\tilde{\ }1, \tilde{\ }0]$. At this point, however, the safe mechanism is informal, and it is easy to make mistakes. Consider the program $\mathbf{rev} \circ [\mathtt{distl}, \mathtt{tl} \circ \mathtt{al}]$. Because $\mathtt{al}$ follows $\mathtt{distl}$ in the order of evaluation, and because $\mathtt{al}$ produces an error for exactly the same arguments as $\mathtt{distl}$, $\mathtt{al}$ can be marked safe.

$$\mathbf{rev} \circ [\mathtt{distl}, \mathtt{tl} \circ \mathtt{al}] \mapsto \mathbf{rev} \circ [\mathtt{distl}, \mathtt{tl} \circ S(\mathtt{al})]$$

Next notice that if $\mathtt{al}$ is error-free, then $\mathtt{tl}$ always succeeds and returns the second component of the original argument. Therefore $S(s2)$ can be substituted for $\mathtt{tl} \circ S(\mathtt{al})$.

$$\mathbf{rev} \circ [\mathtt{distl}, \mathtt{tl} \circ S(\mathtt{al})] \mapsto \mathbf{rev} \circ [\mathtt{distl}, S(s2)]$$

At this point, one might suppose that $\mathbf{rev}$ can be eliminated as in the previous example, since only one of the functions in the sequence to be reversed can produce an error and therefore the evaluation order of the elements of the sequence is irrelevant:

$$\mathbf{rev} \circ [\mathtt{distl}, S(s2)] \stackrel{?}{\mapsto} [S(s2), \mathtt{distl}]$$

Now, however, something has gone wrong: $\mathbf{rev} \circ [\mathtt{distl}, \mathtt{tl} \circ \mathtt{al}] \neq [s2, \mathtt{distl}]$, because $\mathbf{rev} \circ [\mathtt{distl}, \mathtt{tl} \circ \mathtt{al}]: 3$ produces $\mathtt{distlerr}$, whereas $\mathbf{rev} \circ [s2, \mathtt{distl}]: 3$ produces $s2_{\mathtt{err}}$ (which isn't even mentioned in the original program). The fact that intuition can fail on such a small and simple example is strong motivation to provide a precise formalism for stating and verifying these transformations.

A first step towards formalizing the rewrite rules is to express qualified laws such as (7) equationally. One way to do this is to force both sides to produce some identical "don't care" value for all arguments not in the domain of interest. In the following definition of $\mathtt{Safe}$, $\perp$ plays the role of the "don't care" value.

Definition 3.1 (Safe) For every FL function f, $\mathtt{Safe}{:}f$ denotes the function:

$$\mathtt{Safe}{:}f{:}x = \begin{cases} x & \text{if } x \in \mathcal{E}_{\mathrm{FL}} \\ \perp & \text{if } f{:}x \in \mathcal{E}_{\mathrm{FL}} \\ f{:}x & \text{otherwise} \end{cases}$$

For convenience, $\mathtt{Safe}{:}f$ is often abbreviated $S{:}f$. With this definition of $\mathtt{Safe}$, Law (7) can be expressed as:

$$S{:}[g, f] \equiv S{:}(\mathbf{rev} \circ [f, g]) \quad (8)$$

Moreover, many other useful laws are expressible:

$$f \equiv S{:}f \circ \text{dom}{:}f \tag{9}$$
$$f \circ S{:}(\text{dom}{:}f) \equiv S{:}f \tag{10}$$
$$S{:}f \circ S{:}g \equiv S{:}(f \circ g) \tag{11}$$
$$S{:}p \to S{:}q; S{:}r \equiv S{:}(p \to q; r) \tag{12}$$
$$[f, g] \equiv [f, g \circ S{:}(\text{dom}{:}f)] \tag{13}$$
$$[S{:}f_1, \ldots, S{:}f_n] \equiv S{:}[f_1, \ldots, f_n] \tag{14}$$
$$\text{rev} \circ S{:}[f_1, \ldots, f_n] \equiv S{:}[f_n, \ldots, f_1] \tag{15}$$
$$S{:}(s1 \circ t1) \equiv S{:}s2 \tag{16}$$
$$\text{catch}{:}\langle S{:}f, g\rangle \equiv S{:}f \tag{17}$$
$$\text{catch}{:}\langle f, g\rangle \circ S{:}(\text{dom}{:}h) \equiv \text{catch}{:}\langle f \circ S{:}(\text{dom}{:}h), g\rangle \tag{18}$$

Note that some of the informal $\mapsto$ steps have been captured as equivalences; e.g., Laws (14) and (15). Unfortunately, others cannot be expressed as equivalences. For example, the rule $t1 \circ S{:}(a1) \mapsto S{:}(s2)$ cannot be written as $t1 \circ S{:}a1 \equiv s2$, since $(t1 \circ S{:}a1){:}\langle 1, 2, 3\rangle \equiv \text{a1err}$ whereas $s2{:}\langle 1, 2, 3\rangle \equiv 2$; nor could it be $t1 \circ S{:}a1 \equiv S{:}s2$, for the same reason.

The difficulty is that $\equiv$ is a symmetric relation, whereas the desired property is inherently asymmetric: $t1 \circ S{:}a1$ can be rewritten to $S{:}s2$, because in any program in which $t1 \circ S{:}a1$ could appear, the function $S{:}s2$ produces the same result. Thus, at least some of the desired rewrite rules $f \mapsto g$ are valid only when f appears in a "good" context; i.e., in one which enforces the condition that $S{:}f$ cannot produce $\bot$. The following definitions develop the relation $\rhd$ (read "rewrites in context to"), which both captures this asymmetry and defines a set of contexts in which such rewrite rules can be applied.

Definition 3.2

1. The set of *simple expressions* is the smallest set of FL functions such that:
   - $s1, t1, \text{rev}, a1, \text{dist1}, \text{id}, \tilde{\ }a$ for all atoms a, and mkerr are simple expressions.
   - If $e_1, \ldots, e_n$ are simple expressions, then $e_1 \circ e_2$, $[e_1, \ldots, e_n]$, $(e_1 \to e_2; e_3)$, $\text{dom}{:}e_1$, $\text{catch}{:}\langle e_1, e_2\rangle$, $\text{Safe}{:}e_1$, and $\alpha{:}e_1$ are simple expressions.

2. E is a *simple context* iff $E(f)$ is a simple expression for every simple expression f.

Since only the language processor introduces and manipulates Safe expressions, and since transformations preserve the meaning of expressions, the transformations need to work only for expressions that can be written without Safe.

Definition 3.3 A simple expression f is *user-definable* iff there exists a simple expression u with no occurrences of Safe such that $f \equiv u$.

Definition 3.4 Let f, g be simple expressions. $f \rhd g$ iff for every simple context E such that $E(f)$ is user-definable, $E(f) \equiv E(g)$.

This definition of $\rhd$ allows the expression of a large number of "in-context" transformations. Note that (22) is a correct version of the incorrect rewriting step discussed above.

$$t1 \circ S{:}a1 \quad \rhd \quad s2 \tag{19}$$
$$S{:}f \quad \rhd \quad f \tag{20}$$
$$\text{dom}{:}(S{:}f) \quad \rhd \quad \text{id} \tag{21}$$
$$\text{rev} \circ [S{:}f, g] \quad \rhd \quad [g, S{:}f] \tag{22}$$
$$\alpha{:}f \circ \alpha{:}(S{:}g) \quad \rhd \quad \alpha{:}(f \circ S{:}g) \tag{23}$$
$$\text{dom}{:}(S{:}(\alpha{:}f)) \quad \rhd \quad \alpha{:}(S{:}(\text{dom}{:}f)) \tag{24}$$

There is one nagging problem. Definition 3.4 provides little assistance in establishing that $f \rhd g$, because it requires reasoning about all possible contexts. The purpose of the Substitutability Theorem (given below) is to provide a sufficient condition that is easier to check. The following definition gives this condition; the idea is that f should rewrite to g if f and g agree wherever f does not return the "don't care" value.

Definition 3.5 $f \leq_s g$ iff $f{:}x \equiv g{:}x$ whenever $f{:}x \not\equiv \bot$.

The following two lemmas precisely capture the properties of simple expressions that are needed to make the technique of "in-context substitutions" work.

Lemma 3.6 If E is a simple context and $f \leq_s g$, then $E(f) \leq_s E(g)$.

Lemma 3.7 If e is a user-definable simple expression, then $e{:}x \not\equiv \bot$ whenever $x \not\equiv \bot$.

The Substitutability Theorem reduces the problem of verifying that $f \rhd g$ to the easier problem of checking that $f \leq_s g$ in the case where $E(f)$ is a user-definable simple expression.

Theorem 3.8 (Substitutability Theorem)
If f and g are simple expressions and $f \leq_s g$, then $f \triangleright g$.

Proof: Let E be a simple context and assume that $E(f)$ is user-definable. By Lemma 3.6, $E(f) \leq_s E(g)$. By Lemma 3.7, $E(f): x \not\equiv \bot$ if $x \not\equiv \bot$. Together these facts imply that $E(f): x \equiv E(g): x$ if $x \not\equiv \bot$. By strictness, $E(f): \bot \equiv \bot \equiv E(g): \bot$. Therefore, $E(f) \equiv E(g)$. □

Using the Substitutability Theorem, transformations (19)-(24) are easily verified. Note that the proof of the Substitutability Theorem depends only on Lemmas 3.6 and 3.7; therefore, this approach works with any extension of the simple expressions that preserves these two Lemmas. Also note that pure identities, such as transformations (1)-(17), apply to *all* expressions, not merely the simple expressions.

4 Using Safe

This section shows the usefulness of Safe with a few short examples illustrating the elimination of function calls, the use of Safe in code generation, the optimization of exception handling, and the use of in-context laws. Recall that $\text{dom}: f: x$ is $f: x$ if $f: x$ is an error value and x otherwise (see Figure 1). The examples use the following laws involving dom:

$$\text{dom}: \text{id} \equiv \text{id} \tag{25}$$
$$\text{dom}: [f_1, \ldots, f_n] \equiv \text{dom}: f_n \circ \ldots \circ \text{dom}: f_1 \tag{26}$$
$$\text{dom}: \text{al} \circ \text{dom}: \text{distl} \equiv \text{dom}: \text{distl} \tag{27}$$
$$S: (\text{dom}: \text{tl}) \equiv S: (\text{dom}: \text{sl}) \tag{28}$$

In the first example, nothing is known about f, but the fact that id is a total function allows the construction of the two functions to be reversed.

$$\begin{aligned}
&\text{rev} \circ [f, \text{id}] \\
\equiv\ & \text{rev} \circ S: [f, \text{id}] \circ \text{dom}: [f, \text{id}] && \text{by 9} \\
\equiv\ & S: [\text{id}, f] \circ \text{dom}: [f, \text{id}] && \text{by 15} \\
\equiv\ & S: [\text{id}, f] \circ \text{dom}: \text{id} \circ \text{dom}: f && \text{by 26} \\
\equiv\ & S: [\text{id}, f] \circ \text{id} \circ \text{dom}: f && \text{by 25} \\
\equiv\ & S: [\text{id}, f] \circ \text{dom}: f && \text{by 2} \\
\equiv\ & S: [\text{id}, f] \circ \text{dom}: f \circ \text{id} && \text{by 1} \\
\equiv\ & S: [\text{id}, f] \circ \text{dom}: f \circ \text{dom}: \text{id} && \text{by 25} \\
\equiv\ & S: [\text{id}, f] \circ \text{dom}: [\text{id}, f] && \text{by 26} \\
\equiv\ & [\text{id}, f] && \text{by 9}
\end{aligned}$$

This transformation is an optimization, because the end result eliminates the application of rev. Note, however, that the intermediate steps are not necessarily optimizations, because they involve computing some values twice; in particular, f could be arbitrarily expensive to compute. The law $f \equiv S: f \circ \text{dom}: f$ is very useful for introducing safe functions, but if the added dom cannot be discharged, then the resulting program could be less efficient than the original program. In the worst case, using Law 9 could result in a program that computes f once very slowly to preserve errors and then once again to produce the result!

The next example illustrates that there are intermediate cases where dom cannot be completely discharged but the result is still a useful optimization. Section 6 contains further discussion of the problem of discharging dom.

$$\begin{aligned}
& \text{rev} \circ [\text{distl}, \text{al}] \\
\equiv\ & \text{rev} \circ S: [\text{distl}, \text{al}] \circ \text{dom}: [\text{distl}, \text{al}] && \text{by 9} \\
\equiv\ & S: [\text{al}, \text{distl}] \circ \text{dom}: [\text{distl}, \text{al}] && \text{by 15} \\
\equiv\ & S: [\text{al}, \text{distl}] \circ \text{dom}: \text{al} \circ \text{dom}: \text{distl} && \text{by 26} \\
\equiv\ & S: [\text{al}, \text{distl}] \circ \text{dom}: \text{distl} && \text{by 27} \\
\equiv\ & [S: \text{al}, S: \text{distl}] \circ \text{dom}: \text{distl} && \text{by 14}
\end{aligned}$$

In this case, the end result is an optimization not only because the application of rev is eliminated, but also because dom: distl permits the rest of the program to be executed without checking the arguments of any of the functions. The use of Safe makes it easy for a code generator to take advantage of this fact. When a primitive is marked as safe, a code generator can produce a version of the primitive that does not check its argument; in this example, both al and distl can run unchecked.

The following example presents a more substantial optimization (similar to loop-jamming optimizations for imperative languages [ASU86]) and illustrates the use of in-context laws:

$$\begin{aligned}
& [\alpha: \text{sl}, \alpha: + \circ \alpha: \text{tl}] \\
\equiv\ & [\alpha: \text{sl}, \alpha: + \circ \alpha: \text{tl} \circ S: (\text{dom}: (\alpha: \text{sl}))] && \text{by 13} \\
\equiv\ & [\alpha: \text{sl}, \alpha: + \circ \alpha: \text{tl} \circ \alpha: (S: (\text{dom}: \text{sl}))] && \text{by 24} \\
\equiv\ & [\alpha: \text{sl}, \alpha: + \circ \alpha: (\text{tl} \circ S: (\text{dom}: \text{sl}))] && \text{by 23} \\
\equiv\ & [\alpha: \text{sl}, \alpha: + \circ \alpha: (\text{tl} \circ S: (\text{dom}: \text{tl}))] && \text{by 28} \\
\equiv\ & [\alpha: \text{sl}, \alpha: + \circ \alpha: (S: \text{tl})] && \text{by 10} \\
\equiv\ & [\alpha: \text{sl}, \alpha: (+ \circ S: \text{tl})] && \text{by 23}
\end{aligned}$$

Even though the second, third, and last steps use in-context transformations, these steps are actually equivalences, because they occur in simple contexts. Since the first and last lines are equivalent they can be substituted freely one for the other in any program. Note that this shows that it is not necessary that the entire program be simple for an in-context law to apply—it is sufficient that in-context laws be used within simple sub-expressions.

The final example illustrates how Safe is used to optimize exception handling. Suppose a programmer defines a function newtl that returns the empty sequence whenever tl would return an error. A simple definition of newtl is catch:⟨tl,[]⟩. Now, if newtl appears in a context where it always gets an argument in the proper domain of tl, newtl can be transformed to S:tl as follows:

$$
\begin{aligned}
&\text{newtl} \circ \text{S:(dom:tl)} \\
\equiv\ &\text{catch:}\langle\text{tl},[]\rangle \circ \text{S:(dom:tl)} &&\text{by def. of newtl} \\
\equiv\ &\text{catch:}\langle\text{tl} \circ \text{S:(dom:tl)},[]\rangle &&\text{by 18} \\
\equiv\ &\text{catch:}\langle\text{S:tl},[]\rangle &&\text{by 10} \\
\equiv\ &\text{S:tl} &&\text{by 17}
\end{aligned}
$$

5 Related Work

Safety analysis bears some resemblance to *projection analysis* [WH87]. Both techniques deal with manipulating "annotations". For projection analysis, these annotations are projections; for safety analysis, the annotation is the function Safe. Many of the techniques for manipulating the annotations are also similar; however, safety analysis and projection analysis are addressed at two different problems. Projection analysis is primarily concerned with determining (in a lazy system) whether a function is strict in its arguments, and gives a nice way of addressing that problem. Safety analysis (as presented here for a strict language) is concerned not only with determining when a function is "safe" but also with trying to use that fact to facilitate other source-level optimizations.

6 Conclusions and Future Work

The Safe mechanism resolves the tension between the desire to make functional programs run fast through optimization and the desire to have a language in which it is easy to write and debug programs. This tension is perhaps at a maximum in FL, because no distinction is made between user-generated exceptions and system-generated errors—both are legitimate error values. Thus, it would be disastrous for an FL compiler to fail to preserve the error behavior of a program; on the other hand, preserving errors creates problems for optimization. Safe solves this dilemma by providing a way to express the program transformations of a language with a single error value in a language with many error values.

The transformations involving Safe are useful only if Safe functions can be introduced by a compiler. While it remains to be proven that Safe enables large scale optimization in practice, one practical problem is readily apparent from the examples in this paper. As noted in Section 4, it is desirable to introduce Safe without using the law $f \equiv \text{S:}f \circ \text{dom:}f$, which requires computing f twice. In this law, dom:f ensures that the *type* of S:f is such that S:f cannot produce an error. Thus, discharging dom:f is a type inference problem—a type inference algorithm can check whether f is safe before Law 9 is applied, and if f is safe the dom need not be introduced.

It would strengthen the theoretical treatment if the restriction of in-context laws to simple expressions could be removed. While this is not critical from a practical point of view—the class of simple expressions covers many commonly occurring situations—the added generality may help clarify the semantic role of Safe and add some power to the algebra.

7 Acknowledgements

The congenial atmosphere of the FL group (John Backus, Thom Linden, Peter Lucas, and Paul Tucker) contributed significantly to this work. It is also a pleasure to thank Luca Cardelli, Robert Cartwright,

David Chase, Jim Donahue, Joe Halpern, Paul Hudak, Matthias Felleisen, Phil Wadler, Jennifer Widom, and the members of IFIP WG 2.8 for their helpful comments and suggestions. In particular, Joe Halpern's persistent critiques greatly improved the presentation of Section 3.

References

[ASU86] A. V. Aho, R. Sethi, and J. D. Ullman. *Compilers: Principles, Techniques, and Tools.* Addison-Wesley, 1986.

[Bac78] J. Backus. Can programming be liberated from the von Neumann style? A functional style and its algebra of programs. *Communications of the ACM*, 21(8):613–641, August 1978.

[BWW86] J. Backus, J. H. Williams, and E. L. Wimmers. *The FL Language Manual.* Technical Report RJ 5339 (54809), IBM, 1986.

[CF89] R. Cartwright and M. Felleisen. The semantics of program dependence. In *Proceedings of the 1989 Conference on Programming Language Design and Implementation*, June 1989.

[Hen81] J. Hennessy. Program optimization and exception handling. In *Proceedings of the 1981 Symposium on Principles of Programming Languages*, January 1981.

[HMT89] R. Harper, R. Milner, and M. Tofte. *The Definition of Standard ML—Version 3.* Technical Report ECFS-LFCS-89-81, Laboratory for Foundations of Computer Science, University of Edinburgh, 1989.

[HWA*88] P. Hudak, P. Wadler, Arvind, B. Boutel, J. Fairbairn, J. Fasel, J. Hughes, T. Johnsson, D. Kieburtz, S. P. Jones, R. Nikhil, M. Reeve, D. Wise, and J. Young. *Report on the Functional Programming Language Haskell.* Technical Report DCS/RR-666, Yale University, December 1988.

[Ste84] G. L. Steele. *Common Lisp: The Language.* Digital Press, 1984.

[Tur85] D. A. Turner. Miranda: A non-strict functional language with polymorphic types. In *Proceedings of the IFIP International Conference on Functional Programming and Computer Architecture*, Springer Verlag Lecture Notes in Computer Science no. 201, 1985.

[WH87] P. Wadler and R. J. M. Hughes. Projections for strictness analysis. In *Proceedings of the Symposium on Functional Programming Languages and Computer Architecture*, pages 385–407, Springer Verlag Lecture Notes in Computer Science no. 274, September 1987.

Making Asynchronous Parallelism Safe for the World

Guy L. Steele Jr.

Thinking Machines Corporation
245 First Street
Cambridge, Massachusetts 02142

gls@think.com

Abstract: We need a programming model that combines the advantages of the synchronous and asynchronous parallel styles. Synchronous programs are determinate (thus easier to reason about) and avoid synchronization overheads. Asynchronous programs are more flexible and handle conditionals more efficiently.

Here we propose a programming model with the benefits of both styles. We allow asynchronous threads of control but restrict shared-memory accesses and other side effects so as to prevent the behavior of the program from depending on any accidents of execution order that can arise from the indeterminacy of the asynchronous process model.

These restrictions may be enforced either dynamically (at run time) or statically (at compile time). In this paper we concentrate on dynamic enforcement, and exhibit an implementation of a parallel dialect of Scheme based on these ideas. A single successful execution of a parallel program in this model constitutes a proof that the program is free of race conditions (for that particular set of input data).

We also speculate on a design for a programming language using static enforcement. The notion of distinctness is important to proofs of noninterference. An appropriately designed programming language must support such concepts as "all the elements of this array are distinct," perhaps through its type system.

This parallel programming model does not support all styles of parallel programming, but we argue that it can support a large class of interesting algorithms with considerably greater efficiency (in some cases) than a strict SIMD approach and considerably greater safety (in all cases) than a full-blown MIMD approach.

1 Introduction

Models of parallel computation largely fall into two categories that may be loosely characterized as "synchronous" versus "asynchronous" or even more loosely as "SIMD" versus "MIMD" models. Each category provides for many processes, each operating on data (either its own data, globally shared data, or both).

In a typical synchronous program, there is a single thread of control; control is active at only one point in the program text at a time. All processes execute the same instruction at the same time (possibly conditionally, so that at any given time each process either executes the current instruction or else sits idle for that instruction). The primary programming concern is to organize the computation, subject to this constraint, so that most of the processes can perform useful work most of the time. Typically one organizes the data to be processed into arrays whose elements may be processed in parallel. Programming languages supporting this model include APL [16, 10], Fortran 8X [38, 4], MPP Pascal [23], Connection Machine Lisp [32, 39], and C* [25]. Hardware architectures supporting this model include Illiac IV [5], the Goodyear MPP [23], the ICL DAP [7], Non-Von [29], and the Connection Machine system [13].

In a typical asynchronous program, there are many threads of control; control may be active at many points in the program text simultaneously. At any given time each process may be executing a different instruction. The primary programming concern is to organize communication among the processes. The problems of communication are largely of two kinds: mutual exclusion problems (where some scarce resource cannot be shared simultaneously by all the processes that may need it) and producer-consumer problems (where one process produces a computational result that another process needs). Typically one organizes a problem around control structures that solve these communication problems rather than around data structures *per se*. There are numerous hardware multiprocessor architectures supporting this paradigm, and also many programming languages. Worthy of mention are specific techniques for communication such as semaphores [6], monitors [15], message-passing, and pipes; such programming languages as Concurrent Pascal, Modula-2 [40], Occam, and Multilisp [12, 11]; and such hardware architectures as the Denelcor HEP [17], the Inmos Transputer, the BBN Butterfly [26], the Caltech Hypercube [28], and multicomputers such as those manufactured by Sequent, Alliant, and Encore.

Each model has certain advantages and disadvantages. The synchronous approach has a certain simplicity. Because control is at exactly one place in the program text, it is not necessary to consider a potentially exponential number of process interactions. That makes it much easier to reason about the behavior of programs. A primary drawback of synchronous models is the need to organize computations so that every process does the same thing at the same time. Frequently it is the case that every process needs to execute a block of code B at the same time, but the most natural coding of B requires the use of conditional control structures. A simple if-then-else control structure reduces average processor utilization to 50%, because during execution of the then part the processes that need to execute the else part must idle, and vice versa. Nested conditionals can in principle reduce processor utilization exponentially (though in practice conditionals are usually not nested very deeply). In the case where there are more processes than hardware processors, dynamic load-balancing at the architectural level can alleviate this problem; nevertheless, effective use of a synchronous model requires the programmer to restrict the use of conditionals.

The asynchronous approach to parallelism has complementary properties. Conditional control structures are not a problem because processes can execute instructions independently. Reasoning about programs (including the construction of correctness arguments) can be profoundly more difficult, as we have argued elsewhere [32]. The difficulty stems from the indeterminacy (some would say "nondeterminism" but that is an abuse of terminology) of the asynchronous model; the same program may be executed in many different ways, depending on the relative speeds of the various processes. This unpredictability makes communication difficult; insteading of wasting cycles because of conditionals, processes may waste time on busy-waiting or other overheads associated with communication. Again, dynamic load-balancing at the architectural level can alleviate this problem, in the case where there are more processes than hardware processors. Nevertheless, effective use of an asynchronous model requires the programmer to restrict the use of communication mechanisms and to design the program so that it will operate correctly despite the unpredictability of execution order. (For a further discussion of the advantages and disadvantages of determinacy, see the discussion by Halstead [12].)

We wish to develop a programming paradigm that has some of the advantages of each of these categories: the simplicity of reasoning and ease of communication of the SIMD approach, and the processor utilization and flexibility of control structure afforded by the MIMD approach.

One example of such a hybrid is the use of vectorizing Fortran compilers that accept ordinary "serial" Fortran 77 code and perform the analysis necessary to break the program into more or less independent fragments (typically the successive iterations of a loop) that can then be executed on different hardware processors. The Alliant Fortran compiler [3, 2] is one instance of this approach.

Two other current trends may be noted. The array primitives of Fortran 8x are adequate for expressing algorithms suitable for vector and SIMD computers, but a new standards committee has grown out of a group known as the Parallel Computing Forum because of a perceived need to provide other means of expressing parallelism in Fortran. Briefly put, SIMD isn't enough. On the other hand, a well-designed and widely respected support environment for asynchronous multicomputers, the crystalline operating system CrOS III for hypercube computers [8], consists largely of library routines that discipline the space of execution behaviors by providing operations typical of the SIMD style of computation. Briefly put, MIMD is too much; we need to develop conventional modes of use.

Here we propose a fairly restrictive, perhaps draconian, set of conventions. We design a programming model that is explicitly MIMD in feel and flavor, while placing severe restrictions on the use of side effects. The unpredictability of the MIMD approach is thereby rendered harmless—the restrictions are so designed that it is impossible for the unpredictability of the order of program execution to have an effect on the external behavior of the program. In other words, running the same program twice will always produce the same results. One consequence of this is that "accidental" global deadlock cannot occur; if a program fails to terminate, then it would have failed to terminate no matter what execution order was chosen for the individual operations of the processes.

The practical effect is that asynchronously executing processes are forbidden to communicate with one another. Parallel processes (threads) may read shared data, but such data must have been computed before they were spawned; and they may cooperatively contribute to collective results, but such results may be used only after the parallel threads that computed them have been terminated (thereby synchronizing them). At first glance this sounds like SIMD, but it provides greater freedom because the reading of shared data or the writing of results need not be simultaneous or even particularly coordinated; parallel threads are free to pursue widely varying control paths in pursuit of their assigned subtasks. Our approach may be regarded simply as a stylistic discipline that may be imposed on any MIMD programming system; but our purpose is moreover to propose specific linguistic and implementation mechanisms to enforce this style. Alternatively, the approach may be regarded as a prescription for enriching SIMD methodology without losing its benefits.

Our aim is to find a strategy for writing parallel programs that will work well on a variety of parallel architectures, thereby promoting program portability.

2 Our Process Model

We assume a set of control threads executing within a shared memory space, and that threads may be freely created and destroyed. Program execution begins with a single thread of control. A thread may perform arbitrary functional computations. At any time it may also

- terminate itself, in which case it ceases to exist and cannot be resumed.

- spawn a set of threads; these new threads are called *siblings* of one another, and *children* of the spawning thread.[1]

- perform an operation on shared memory; such operations may include (but are not limited to) reading, writing, incrementing, and bitwise-ORing-into.

When a process P spawns a set of child threads then execution of P is suspended and all the children begin execution asynchronously and in parallel. Execution of P is resumed if and when all its children have terminated themselves.

Therefore all the threads of control in existence at any point in time[2] are organized as a tree. Threads at interior nodes are in a state of suspension. Threads at the leaves are active, and execute all asynchronously with respect to one another. We do not necessarily assume that computational effort is distributed fairly among all the active threads; if one active thread fails to terminate, then it may be that no other thread makes progress.

The interleaving of operations on shared memory performed by threads executing in parallel is not predictable. Operations on shared memory are assumed to behave as if serialized. (We realize that in positing this assumption we are relying on the existence of another synchronization mechanism to perform this serialization efficiently and at a low level. This is all right because our purpose here is not to invent a new synchronization mechanism that is *primitive*, but rather one that presents certain properties to the user.)

There is no loss of generality in requiring that a parent thread be suspended while its children execute, and that all child threads be destroyed before the parent may be resumed. To get the effect of a parent thread P executing in parallel with various children $p_1, p_2, \ldots, p_n$ one merely writes the program so as to spawn an additional child thread p_0 whose task is to continue the computation that would have been performed by the parent thread. To get the effect of suspending the children $p_1, p_2, \ldots, p_n$ of a process P, executing P for a time, and then resuming $p_1, p_2, \ldots, p_n$, one merely writes the program so that p_1 through p_n terminate themselves; note that the requirement is only that the threads of control themselves be destroyed, and not any associated state information (such as control stacks), and therefore P can subsequently spawn new children $p'_1, p'_2, \ldots, p'_n$ whose tasks are to continue the computations that would have been performed by $p_1, p_2, \ldots, p_n$. As we shall see, the requirements are imposed purely to allow a simple description of forbidden side effects in the next section.

In this model the various threads of control can communicate only through side effects on the shared memory. In the next section we place restrictions on the use of side effects so as to effectively prohibit their use for synchronization purposes. Therefore the only means of process synchronization is termination. More specifically, a set of siblings can be known all to have reached specific points in their execution only if those points are termination points, in which case the parent thread can know that they have all terminated because it, the parent, has resumed execution.

It is not difficult to invent a syntax for spawning threads; the familiar **parbegin-parend** or **doacross** are quite adequate. The new idea here is not in the hierarchical organization of threads, but in the restrictions on their behavior.

---

[1] It would be more accurate to call them *littermates* rather than *siblings*, because we wish to describe a relationship that holds between two children that are part of the same spawn set but not between two children that are spawned at different times. I also briefly considered using the term *whelp* in place of *spawn*, so as not to mix the metaphors. Eventually I came to my senses, and have adhered to more familiar terminology.

[2] For simplicity, I speak of time as if there were a single absolute global clock. I realize that a relativistic interpretation of time may be more appropriate in a distributed system, as in the work of Lamport [21]. A proper formulation of our process model would speak of slices through space-time rather than of points in time.

3 Forbidden Side Effects

In our process model the order in which operations on shared memory are performed is not predictable. Our goal is to restrict the use of side effects in such a way that that this unpredictability cannot affect the externally visible behavior of a program.

We say that thread P is *responsible* for performing an operation E if E is directly performed by thread Q and Q is a descendant of P (possibly P itself).

We say that two operations E_1 and E_2 are *not causally related* if there are two sibling threads p_1 and p_2 such that p_1 is responsible for E_1 and p_2 is responsible for E_2. (If two such operations *are* causally related according to this definition, then one necessarily precedes the other in the serialization ordering.)

An operation E on shared memory may alter the state of the memory, and may also make some part of the memory state available to the thread that executes it. We write

$$E(M) \to M' \Rightarrow V$$

to indicate that E, operating on memory state M, alters the memory state to M' and returns value V. We also write simply $E(M) \to M'$ if E alters the state but returns no value (we may regard it as returning some fixed constant value), or $E(M) \Rightarrow V$ if E returns a value but does not alter the memory state.

Two operations E_1 and E_2 are said to *commute with respect to a memory state M* if the order in which they are performed does not matter. That is, if

$$E_1(M) \to M_a' \Rightarrow V_{1a}$$
$$E_2(M_a') \to M_a'' \Rightarrow V_{2a}$$

and

$$E_2(M) \to M_b' \Rightarrow V_{2b}$$
$$E_1(M_b') \to M_b'' \Rightarrow V_{1b}$$

then E_1 and E_2 commute with respect to M if and only if $M_a'' = M_b''$, $V_{1a} = V_{1b}$, and $V_{1a} = V_{1b}$. (Note that it is not required that $M_a' = M_b'$.)

The minimal restriction that guarantees that the unpredictability of ordering will not affect the behavior of a program is then that, for any possible serialization order for the operations performed by a program, any two consecutive operations of the program that are not causally related must commute with respect to the memory state that precedes the first. (Note that exchanging such consecutive operations produces another possible serialization order.)

It is convenient, however, to impose a more restrictive condition that does not depend on the details of particular run-time memory states, to limit the amount of effort required the check the condition (either at compilation time or run time). We say that two operations E_1 and E_2 *commute* if they commute with respect to all possible memory states (and, if appropriate, all possible arguments to the operations). Our condition is then simply that any two operations that are not causally related must commute.

4 Operations

We divide the shared memory into disjoint regions called *cells* (to suggest, at least to those conversant with the terminology of Lisp-like languages, that each such region might be a single program variable). A reasonable set of operations might then be "read cell C" and "write cell C" for every cell C. In this case two operations commute if they refer to different cells or if both are read operations. Note that two write operations on the same cell are considered not to commute; actually, they do commute if they write the same value, but for our purposes we treat the value to be written as an argument to the operation rather than an integral part of it, and therefore deem two write operation on the same cell not to commute because they do not commute for all possible arguments. This decision is not essential, however.

Note that cells cannot be used for interprocess synchronization. One might imagine, for example, that a thread P could write 0 into a cell C and then spawn two threads p_1 and p_2, with the intention that p_1 should busy-wait until the value of C is 1, and that p_2 will eventually write 1 into C. However, such a sequence of events would be forbidden. In order to busy-wait, p_1 must read cell C; such an operation does not commute with the writing of C by p_2. (Indeed, the fact that a read does not commute with a write is the entire point of the busy-waiting technique.)

There are many other operations that may usefully be regarded as primitive. One is the set of operations "add a value to cell C." Unlike write operations, add operations on the same cell do commute: it doesn't matter whether one first adds 2 to C and then 4, or first 4 and then 2; either way the net result is to add 6 to C. (We deal here only with integer addition, and ignore all quibbles about the nonassociativity of floating-point addition.) Note that this operation is assumed to return no value. Two instances of a fetch-and-add type of operation on the same cell would not commute, because the two executing processes might receive different values under different execution orders. Observe also that the operation "add to C" must be regarded as atomic if two instances of it are to commute; two instances of a non-primitive implementation of the form "$read(C) \Rightarrow V$; $write(C, A + V)$" would not commute.

More generally, two instances of any atomic operation of the form $C := F(C, A)$ will commute with respect to the same cell C provided that $F(F(x,y),z) =$

$F(F(x,z),y)$ for all x, y, and z. Such operations F of course include all familiar operations that are commutative and associative, such as logical AND, OR, and exclusive OR operations, multiplication, GCD, and set union. An example of an appropriate noncommutative operation is the adjoining of an element to a set. Note that the Lisp operation **cons** is *not* suitable; the order of the elements in the resulting list would be unpredictable.

At this point we make another oversimplification. We assume that all the operations are partitioned into equivalence classes. Operations on the same cell in the same class must commute, and operations on the same cell in different classes are assumed not to commute. (To see why this is an oversimplification, consider the three classes of operations on cells containing complex numbers:

(a) multiply C by 2
(b) multiply C by i
(c) replace C with its complex conjugate

Members of classes (a) and (b) commute, as do members of (a) and (c); but members of (b) and (c) do not commute, and so class (a) cannot be merged with either of the other classes. One can handle complicated situations such as this, but we ignore these complications here.) Note that each individual write operation is in a class by itself. Operations on different cells are assumed always to commute.

5 Dynamic Trapping of Forbidden Side Effects

The restriction that any two side effects must either be causally related or commute can in principle be checked either at compile time (static checking) or run time (dynamic checking). In this section we consider a technique for dynamic checking. We make no attempt at recovery from such an error; if the restriction is violated then the entire program is aborted.

To every cell we add some state information that summarizes the history of the operations on that cell. When an operation is performed on the cell, the history information is updated and perhaps extended. Unfortunately, the size of the history information is not fixed, but proportional to the maximum depth in the process tree of any thread that has operated on the cell. This is ameliorated by the fact that the method prunes history information when threads are terminated.

More specifically, the state information for a cell is an ordered tuple of pairs

$$\langle (p_1, e_1), (p_2, e_2), \ldots, (p_m, e_m) \rangle$$

where every p_j is either (an identifier for) a thread or else the special marker $*$, and every e_j is either (an identifier for) an operation class or else the special marker $*$. The meaning of a pair (p_j, e_j) is that thread p_j (whose depth in the tree is in fact j, the root thread being at depth 0) is responsible for an operation e_j on the cell. In each case, $*$ means that more than one thread or operation class has been involved.

Every thread also has associated with it a set of cells, the *responsibility set*. A cell is in the set if that thread is responsible for some operation performed on that cell and there is no surviving child of that thread that is also responsible for that same operation.

Suppose then that a specific thread q at depth k performs an operation e upon cell C, whose state information is

$$\langle (p_1, e_1), (p_2, e_2), \ldots, (p_m, e_m) \rangle$$

Let $q_k = q$, and let the ancestors of q be called $q_{k-1}, \ldots, q_1$ where q_1 is a child of the root of the process tree. Then the cell's state information is updated as follows:

for every j $(1 \leq j \leq k)$ **do**
  if $j > m$ **then**
    add the pair (q_j, e) as pair j of the state tuple
  else if $e = e_j$ **then**
    if $q_j \neq p_j$ **then**
      replace p_j with $*$ in pair j of the state tuple **fi**
  else if $q_j = p_j$ **then**
    if $e \neq e_j$ **then**
      replace e_j with $*$ in pair j of the state tuple **fi**
  else abort the program
  fi fi fi
od

Moreover, cell C is added to the responsibility set of q.

When a thread is terminated, all the cells in its responsibility set are added to its parent's responsibility set.

Suppose a thread q at depth k spawns some children. When all children have been terminated and q is about to be resumed, all cells in the responsibility set for q must be pruned; that is, the history tuple for each such cell is truncated to retain only the first k pairs.

Claim: the program will be aborted by the safety check if and only if the program contains any two operations on the same cell that are not causally related and are not of the same operation class.

Proof sketch for $\rightarrow$: the program is aborted by the safety check shown above in the case where $j \leq m$, $e \neq e_j$, and $q_j \neq p_j$. Now the meaning of the pair (p_j, e_j) in the state tuple is that some thread p_j has executed operation e_j on the cell in question. The nearest common ancestor of q and p_j is necessarily p_a for some $a < j$ (possibly p_0, the root of the process tree). Because we have taken p_a to be the *nearest* common ancestor, $p_{a+1} \neq q_{a+1}$. Now if p_{a+1} and q_{a+1} belonged to different spawn sets, p_{a+1} must have belonged to the earlier spawn set, and on termination of all the threads of that spawn set the cell history would have been pruned to depth a, eliminating all pairs of greater depth, including (p_j, e_j). But this contradicts the assumption that the safety check aborted on inspecting pair (p_j, e_j); therefore p_{a+1} and q_{a+1} belong to the same spawn set and are siblings. It follows that the operation(s) represented by the pair (p_j, e_j) and the operation that prompted the safety check are not causally related, and because $e \neq e_j$ they are not of the same operation class.

Proof sketch for ←: if operations E_1 and E_2 are not causally related then there are siblings p_1 and p_2 (call their depth j) responsible for them. Without loss of generality assume E_1 occurs first as seen by C. If no pruning of the state of C to a depth $< j$ occurs between E_1 and E_2 then E_2 will abort. If such a pruning does occur, then there must be a third operation E_3 that caused C to be in the responsibility set of some thread p_3. This operation E_3 must differ in class from one of E_1 and E_2 (whichever it is, call it E_{12}) and is not causally related to either. Furthermore the siblings responsible for E_{12} and E_3 are at a depth less than j, so we have reduced the problem to a similar one of lesser depth. By induction on the depth of responsible siblings we must eventually find two events without a pruning to a lesser depth between them.

6 Efficient Encodings of Cell State

There is a simple encoding of the cell state information as a bit vector. If we are willing to delay the checking of restrictions from cell-update time to history-pruning time, then the overhead directly associated with a cell operation can be reduced to a single bitwise inclusive OR operation. It is likely that for many programs the bit-vector will fit into 32 or 64 bits; in this case the overhead may be simply one or two OR instructions.

The idea is to assign a distinct nonzero bit pattern to each of a set of n siblings in such a way that the OR of any two patterns is different from any of the assigned patterns. One way to do this is to use patterns of length $2 \log(n + 1)$ (all logarithms here are base 2); the pattern for sibling number j is formed by expressing j in binary and then replacing each 0 by 01 and each 1 by 10. One can do better by using a k-out-of-m code; each pattern is of length m, and has exactly k 1-bits. It is easy to see that the OR of any two distinct patterns will have more than k 1-bits, and so is distinct from any of the assigned patterns. One gets the maximal number of patterns, of course, when $k = \lfloor \frac{m}{2} \rfloor$. This encoding requires only a number of bits q satisfying $q - (\log q)/2 \approx \log n - (\log(2/\pi))/2$. (This follows easily from Stirling's formula $n! \approx n^n e^{-n} \sqrt{2\pi n}$.) Instead of requiring double the number of bits for a binary representation, only a small number of bits need be added. For example, a 16-out-of-32 code provides more than 2^{29} patterns, needing only 3 bits more than a pure binary encoding. Similarly, a 52-out-of-104 code provides more than 2^{100} patterns, so for all practical purposes no more than 4 extra bits are ever needed.

The operation classes may be similarly encoded. (A write operation may be encoded as a pattern that is all 1-bits; this works out to have the right properties.)

Consider then a state tuple

$$\langle (p_1, e_1), (p_2, e_2), \ldots, (p_m, e_m) \rangle$$

The bit-vector encoding of this tuple is simply the result of concatenating of encodings $[p_1][e_1][p_2][e_2]\ldots[p_m][e_m]$ where $[x]$ means the bit-pattern assigned to x.

The tricky thing about this encoding is that, for example, p_1 and its sibling p'_1 may spawn different numbers of children, and so the tails of bit vectors associated with such children may not have the same format at all. Nevertheless the encoding works. (Proof sketch: if tails of two different formats are ever OR'ed into a state tuple bit-vector, then for the pair j before the format divergence the value of p_j must be $*$. If e_j is also $*$, the program will be aborted, so suppose it is e. The garbling of formats in the tails may indeed make it impossible to detect certain pairs of conflicting operations as early as they might be, but for any such pair of operations at least one will not be of operation class e, and therefore a conflict will eventually be detected and the program aborted at that time.)

This encoding is particularly attractive for hardware that includes a combining memory switch. The Ultracomputer [27] has a "fetch-and-add" memory switch that allows many processes simultaneously (that is, in one memory cycle) to add a value to the same memory location. A similar switch providing a combining bitwise OR operation can handle this state update operation quite nicely. (The Connection Machine model CM-2 [37] does in fact support such a combining operation.)

Another encoding of state tuples is quite compact but requires somewhat more processing per operation. This encoding has four components: a thread id, an operation id, and three counters capable of holding values from 0 to the length of the largest state tuple ever to be encoded. The key observation is that the following constraints hold in any valid state tuple:

$$(p_j = *) \wedge (j > k) \rightarrow (p_k = *)$$

(because siblings cannot have a common descendant)

and
$$(e_j = *) \wedge (j < k) \rightarrow (e_k = *)$$

(because if any thread is responsible for more than one type of operation on a cell then all its ancestors are also responsible). Therefore a state tuple consists of three segments: a prefix, in which every p_i is a thread id and every e_i is $*$; a middle, in which every p_i is a thread id and every e_i is the same operation id e; and a suffix, in which every p_i is $*$ and every e_i is the same e as in the middle. If we assume that from any thread id we can recover its ancestor without too much trouble, then we can encode a state vector as p_j (for the largest j such that $p_j \neq *$), e, and three counts. The counts could be the lengths of the three segments, but the running totals of these lengths may be more convenient, so that one has the length of the prefix, the length of the prefix and middle together, and the length of the entire state tuple.

If there are fewer than 256 operation types, if a thread id can be represented in 32 bits, and if one is willing to restrict the depth of process nesting to 255, then this encoding of the state tuple will fit neatly into 64 bits. These are not unreasonable assumptions for the next few years.

The choice of encoding provides tradeoffs between memory, speed of cell events, and the speed of thread termination.

7 Static Enforcement of Safe Side Effects

It should be possible to design a programming language that statically enforces constraints on side effects. We have sketched out such a design (and coded a few sample programs in it) but it is not complete. Global variables cause considerable difficulties. We believe that the best approach is to build on the excellent work of Gifford, Lucassen, et al., on the design of FX-87 [9].

Just as there are certain kinds of programs that are easier to express in a dynamically typed language than a statically typed language, so there are certain algorithms that are difficult to express under static effect checking. One is the parallel radix-enumeration sort, in which for each bit of the key, two parallel sum-prefix operations are performed, one for keys with a 0-bit and one for keys with a 1-bit. These sum-prefix operations calculate distinct indices for each key; the keys are then simultaneously stored into the new places indicated by the corresponding indices. The problem is that for the storing operation there ought to be a separate thread for each key, but it requires a nontrivial proof, probably beyond the capabilities of any simple static effect-checking system, to show that no two keys are stored into the same location. Nevertheless we are optimistic that a language with static checking may be useful for expressing many interesting parallel algorithms.

We suspect that two ideas are particularly important to the design of a language suitable for this style of programming. One is declaring or deducing that the values stored in an array are all distinct, particularly in the case of an array of subscripts or pointers. The other is a rich set of combining assignment operations, possibly user-defined. The methods of Parker [22] are relevant here; where simple writes into shared memory would be forbidden by our model, one may use updates that combine to make a result "more and more defined" within some partial order.

It may also be possible to design a static effect-checking system with carefully controlled loopholes. Every use of a loophole should require of the programmer a proof that any indeterminacy allowed by the loophole does not affect the net behavior of the program as required by the problem specification. It may also be possible to automatically *mask* the use of such loopholes in the same manner that FX-87 can automatically mask certain side effects.

8 Implementation Status

As a demonstration, we have implemented an interpreter for a dialect of Scheme [36, 35, 1, 24] that does dynamic checking of the side effect restriction. (A stripped-down copy of this interpreter, written in Common Lisp [30, 31], appears in the Appendix to this paper.) This toy dialect includes constants, lexically scoped variables, if, begin, lambda, let (which is purely syntactic sugar), label, and function calls. Primitive functions include all the usual side-effect-free Common Lisp operations on numbers, characters, and lists.

Parallelism is introduced through map, which in this interpreter must be implemented as a special form rather than as a function. The form (map f x) applies the function f to every element of the list x, and returns a list of the results. (More generally, f may take any number of arguments n, and the form looks like (map f x_1 x_2 ... x_n).) The many applications of f are performed by separate threads, spawned by the thread that executes the map form. The trivial variant maplist is also supported.

The only side effects permitted are on cells. The function cell creates a cell, initialized to a given value; the functions read-cell, write-cell, and add-cell operate on cells. (This toy dialect does not address the problem of I/O, but it is easy in principle to treat streams of characters as cells permitting such operations as "read character" and "write character.") The routine cell-update handles the updating of state information.

Note that in this implementation the operation class unique is handled specially in order to deal properly with write operations.

(Explicit occurrences of the operations cell-read and cell-write make code rather bulky. In a full compiler-based language implementation one would expect cells to be syntactically invisible. The compiler would determine which variables or array elements might be accessed by more than one thread and automatically introduce state tuples and the operations upon them.)

The interpreter is written in a continuation-passing style [34, 33]; routines whose names begin with "@" take continuations. Such continuations require one argument, namely the value resulting from an evaluation, application, or other operation.

The use of continuations allows the interpreter to implement a crude round-robin timesharing system. A queue of processes is maintained in the form of a list of continuations. (Continuations in the queue take no arguments.) A process-swap may occur every time @eval is entered. The routine @map adds many processes to the queue. Termination consists merely in completing execution of the application for which a thread was created; when all the children have terminated, the list of results is sent to the original continuation of the map form. The loop in routine try and the cookie named *dismiss* deal with the possibility that the underlying Common Lisp implementation does not implement iterative tail-recursion.

A few sample programs have been tested in this language, including a 30-line program to compute the sum-prefix of a list of numbers by the method of pointer-jumping, shown here in a pseudo-Algol notation [14]:

for all k **in parallel do**
    $chum[k] := next[k]$
    while $chum[k] \neq null$ **do**
        $value[chum[k]] := value[k] + value[chum[k]]$
        $chum[k] := chum[chum[k]]$
    od
od

(The index k ranges over all the cells of the linked list; the *next* operation is the same as the Lisp cdr.) The error checking has been verified by perturbing the sample programs into plausible but incorrect variants. The sum-prefix program and one incorrect variant are included in the Appendix.

It is illuminating to consider what sorts of effects declarations would be required to demonstrate the correctness of the sum-prefix program in a framework similar to that of FX-87. Note first that the functions map and maplist execute a function many times simultaneously; therefore the function must either be pure (having no side effects) or perform side effects that do not interfere with one another; the latter is possible only if the side effects are somehow linked to distinct argument values. Therefore there must be a way to indicate that the elements of a list are distinct, and a way to specify FX-87 memory regions as a function of such distinct elements.

For example, the code fragment

```
(cell-write (car chum)
            (+ (cell-read (car chum)) v))
```

is legitimate only because it can be proved that each of the threads that has a non-nil value for its chum in fact has a value distinct from all the others, and furthermore that the cells that are the car components of all those non-nil chums are distinct; it follows that none of these cells will be accessed by more than one thread, and therefore the code may read and then write without intermediate synchronization. On the other hand, it is necessary to synchronize between the reading of the values and the read/write of the chums, because those two sets of cells are not disjoint (and so the members of their union are not distinct). The erroneous version of the sum-prefix program contains exactly this mistake, and execution of this version of the interpreter results in a trap by the safety check in routine cell-update.

FX-87 provides a way (the runion operator) to treat several regions collectively as a single region; a simple extension would allow the user to speak of indexed arrays of regions and to treat the union of all the regions in an array as a single region. This would suffice for expressing the idea that each element of a list belongs to a different region, and that side effects on different elements of a list therefore do not interfere with one another.

9 Comparison with Other Work

Kruskal et al. [18] discuss sets of compatible memory-update operations in the context of designing a memory switch that can perform many operations simultaneously. At various intermediate stages the switch can combine multiple operations on the same memory location into a single operation. They combine noncommuting operations by arbitrarily choosing a particular serialization. This is convenient for the designer because he is free to choose from many possible serializations the one having the simplest implementation in the switch. Such a hardware switch could just as easily provide an error signal on detecting noncommuting operations, and so could provide dynamic enforcement for the programming model presented here.

Lamport has discussed hardware and software solutions to the problem of designing multiprocessor systems that are provably correct [20, 19].

Myrias Corp. manufactures an asynchronous parallel computer system that is quite similar in some respects to the technique outlined here. A parallel DO construct causes threads to be spawned, each executing the body for a different value of the index variable. Logically these threads share the memory space of the parent thread but with copy-on-write access, supported in the usual manner by the operating system through the use of memory-management-unit page tables. It may be that more than one child thread writes to the same page of the parent's memory space; in this case each child thread gets its own copy to work with. When the threads have all terminated, the various copies of a given page are reconciled and merged back into the parent thread's memory space.

The work of Gifford, Lucassen, *et al.* on FX-87 is mostly closely related to the programming-language aspects of this work. That language effectively has a serial semantics, but is strongly typed not only with respect to types of the usual sort but also with respect to side effects. From this information the language implementation can better determine which program fragments can safely be scheduled for parallel execution. What we have called *cells* could be identified with the *regions* of FX-87, which are the minimal units of side-effect checking. Regions may be single variables or megabytes of complex data structures. Associating our state tuples to relatively large regions would make the space overhead negligible. On the other hand, algorithms that rely on permuting array elements often require regions to be logically divided into many fine-grained subregions over at least part of the program text.

There have been many other programming languages designed for asynchronous parallel execution. Most provide tools that make it possible for the programmer, with some cleverness, to skirt the problems of indeterminacy. I know of no other language design, however, whose primary design goal is to entirely prevent the user from running afoul of the indeterminacy of the asynchronous execution model.

10 Conclusions

We wish to construct a parallel programming system that has the benefits of both the synchronous and asynchronous modes of computation. Our programming model may be viewed either as a loosening of the requirement of strict synchrony typical of of the SIMD style or as the imposing of fairly severe restrictions on *laissez-faire* asynchrony. We believe it is appropriate to enforce these restrictions linguistically, by means of new data types, additional compiler analysis, and/or run-time safety checks. We do not claim that all interesting or useful parallel programs can be rendered in this model, and the range of applicability is an open question. Nevertheless, we believe that this approach could enhance portability of parallel programs by reducing the semantic gap between different parallel hardware architectures.

11 Acknowledgments

I would like to thank W. Daniel Hillis and Sheryl Handler of Thinking Machines Corporation for their encouragement and support.

References

[1] Abelson, Harold, and Sussman, Gerald Jay, with Sussman, Julie. *Structure and Interpretation of Computer Programs*. MIT Press (Cambridge, Massachusetts, 1985).

[2] Abu-Sufah, Walid, and Malony, Allen D. Vector processing on the Alliant FX/8 multiprocessor. In Hwang, Kai, Jacobs, Steven M., and Swartzlander, Earl E., editors, *Proc. 1986 International Conference on Parallel Processing*. IEEE Computer Society (August 1986), 559–566.

[3] *FX/FORTRAN Programmer's Handbook*. Alliant Computer Systems Corporation (Acton, Massachusetts, May 1985).

[4] *Draft Proposed Revised American National Standard Programming Language Fortran*, ANSI X3.9-198x, draft S8, Version 112 edition. American National Standards Institute, Inc. (Washington, D. C., 1989).

[5] Bouknight, W. J., Denenberg, Stewart A., McIntyre, David E., Randall, J. M., Sameh, Amed H., and Slotnick, Daniel L. The ILLIAC IV system. *Proceedings of the IEEE 60*, 4 (April 1972).

[6] Dijkstra, Edsger W. The structure of "THE"-multiprogramming system. *Communications of the ACM 11*, 5 (May 1968), 345.

[7] Flanders, P. M., et al. Efficient high speed computing with the Distributed Array Processor. In *High Speed Computer and Algorithm Organization*. Academic Press (1977), 113–127.

[8] Fox, Geoffrey C., Johnson, Mark A., Lyzenga, Gregory A., Otto, Steve W., Salmon, John K., and Walker, David W. *General Techniques and Regular Problems*. Volume I of *Solving Problems on Concurrent Processors*. Prentice-Hall (Englewood Cliffs, New Jersey, 1988).

[9] Gifford, David K., Jouvelot, Pierre, Lucassen, John M., and Sheldon, Mark A. *FX-87 Reference Manual*. MIT/LCS/TR 407. MIT Laboratory for Computer Science (Cambridge, Massachusetts, September 1987).

[10] Gilman, Leonard, and Rose, Allen J. *APL: An Interactive Approach*, second edition. Wiley (New York, 1976).

[11] Halstead, Robert H., Jr. Implementation of Multilisp: Lisp on a multiprocessor. In *Proc. 1984 ACM Symposium on Lisp and Functional Programming*. ACM SIGPLAN/SIGACT/SIGART (Austin, Texas, August 1984), 9–17.

[12] Halstead, Robert H., Jr. Multilisp: A language for concurrent symbolic computation. *ACM Transactions on Programming Languages and Systems* 7, 4 (October 1985), 501–538.

[13] Hillis, W. Daniel. *The Connection Machine*. MIT Press (Cambridge, Massachusetts, 1985).

[14] Hillis, W. Daniel, and Steele, Guy L., Jr. Data parallel algorithms. *Communications of the ACM* 29, 12 (December 1986), 1170–1183.

[15] Hoare, C.A.R. Monitors: an operating system structuring concept. *Communications of the ACM* 17, 10 (October 1974), 549–557.

[16] *APL\360 User's Manual*. International Business Machines Corporation (August 1968).

[17] Kowalik, Janusz S., editor. *Parallel MIMD Computation: HEP Supercomputer and Its Applications*. Scientific Computation Series. MIT Press (Cambridge, Massachusetts, 1985).

[18] Kruskal, Clyde P., Rudolph, Larry, and Snir, Mark. Efficient synchronization on multiprocessors with shared memory. *ACM Transactions on Programming Languages and Systems* 10, 4 (October 1988), 579–601.

[19] Lamport, Leslie. How to make a multiprocessor computer that correctly executes multiprocess programs. *IEEE Transactions on Computers* C-28, 9 (September 1979), 690–691.

[20] Lamport, Leslie. Proving the correctness of multiprocess programs. *IEEE Transactions on Software Engineering* SE-3, 3 (March 1977), 125–143.

[21] Lamport, Leslie. Time, clocks, and the ordering of events in a distributed system. *Communications of the ACM* 21, 7 (July 1978), 558–565.

[22] Parker, D. Stott. Partial order programming. In *Proceedings of the Sixteenth Symposium on Principles of Programming Languages*. Association for Computing Machinery (Austin, January 1989), 260–268.

[23] Potter, J. L., editor. *The Massively Parallel Processor*. Scientific Computation Series. MIT Press (Cambridge, Massachusetts, 1985).

[24] Rees, Jonathan, Clinger, William, et al. Revised[3] report on the algorithmic language Scheme. *ACM SIGPLAN Notices* 21, 12 (December 1986), 37–79.

[25] Rose, John R., and Steele, Guy L., Jr. C*: An extended C language for data parallel programming. In Kartashev, Lana P., and Kartashev, Steven I., editors, *Proc. Second International Conference on Supercomputing*. Volume II. International Supercomputing Institute (Santa Clara, California, May 1987), 2–16.

[26] Schmidt, Gary E. The Butterfly parallel processor. In Kartashev, Lana P., and Kartashev, Steven I., editors, *Proc. Second International Conference on Supercomputing*. Volume I. International Supercomputing Institute (Santa Clara, California, May 1987), 362–365.

[27] Schwartz, J. T. Ultracomputers. *ACM Transactions on Programming Languages and Systems* 2, 4 (October 1980), 484–521.

[28] Seitz, C. The cosmic cube. *Communications of the ACM* 28, 1 (January 1985), 22–33.

[29] Shaw, David Elliot. *The NON-VON Supercomputer*. Technical Report. Department of Computer Science, Columbia University (New York, August 1982).

[30] Steele, Guy L., Jr., Fahlman, Scott E., Gabriel, Richard P., Moon, David A., and Weinreb, Daniel L. *Common Lisp: The Language*. Digital Press (Burlington, Massachusetts, 1984).

[31] Steele, Guy L., Jr., et al. *Common Lisp: The Language*, second edition. Digital Press (Bedford, Massachusetts, 1990).

[32] Steele, Guy L., Jr., and Hillis, W. Daniel. Connection Machine Lisp: Fine-grained parallel symbolic processing. In *Proc. 1986 ACM Conference on Lisp and Functional Programming*. ACM SIGPLAN/SIGACT/SIGART (Cambridge, Massachusetts, August 1986), 279–297.

[33] Steele, Guy Lewis, Jr. *LAMBDA: The Ultimate Declarative*. AI Memo 379. MIT Artificial Intelligence Laboratory (Cambridge, Massachusetts, November 1976).

[34] Steele, Guy Lewis, Jr., and Sussman, Gerald Jay. *LAMBDA: The Ultimate Imperative*. AI Memo 353. MIT Artificial Intelligence Laboratory (Cambridge, Massachusetts, March 1976).

[35] Steele, Guy Lewis, Jr., and Sussman, Gerald Jay. *The Revised Report on SCHEME: A Dialect of LISP*. AI Memo 452. MIT Artificial Intelligence Laboratory (Cambridge, Massachusetts, January 1978).

[36] Sussman, Gerald Jay, and Steele, Guy Lewis, Jr. *SCHEME: An Interpreter for Extended Lambda Calculus*. AI Memo 349. MIT Artificial Intelligence Laboratory (Cambridge, Massachusetts, December 1975).

[37] *Connection Machine Model CM-2 Technical Summary*. Thinking Machines Corporation (Cambridge, Massachusetts, April 1987).

[38] Wagener, Jerrold L. Status of work toward revision of programming language Fortran. *ACM FORTEC Forum* 3, 2 (May 1984), 1–42.

[39] Wholey, Skef, and Steele, Guy L., Jr. Connection Machine Lisp: A dialect of Common Lisp for data parallel programming. In Kartashev, Lana P., and Kartashev, Steven I., editors, *Proc. Second International Conference on Supercomputing*. Volume III. International Supercomputing Institute (Santa Clara, California, May 1987), 45–54.

[40] Wirth, Niklaus. *Programming in Modula-2*. Springer-Verlag (Berlin, 1982).

Appendix: A Parallel Dialect of Scheme

```
(defstruct closure body vars env)
(defun build-closure (lambda-exp env)
  (make-closure :body (caddr lambda-exp) :vars (cadr lambda-exp) :env env))

(defstruct procid parent responsibility-set)
(defun build-procid (parent)
  (make-procid :parent parent :responsibility-set '()))

(defvar *queue* '())
(defvar *dismiss* (list '*dismiss*))
(defun enqueue (thunk) (setq *queue* (nconc *queue* (list thunk))))
(defun queueswap (thunk) (enqueue thunk) (dismiss))
(defun dismiss () (assert (not (null *queue*))) *dismiss*)

(defun try (exp)
  (setq *queue* '())
  (do ((v (@eval exp '() (build-procid nil) #'identity) (funcall (pop *queue*))))
      ((not (eq v *dismiss*)) (assert (null *queue*)) v)
    (assert (not (null *queue*)))))

(defun @eval (exp env procid cont)
  (queueswap
    #'(lambda ()
        (cond ((atom exp)
                (cond ((symbolp exp) (funcall cont (lookup exp env)))
                      (t (funcall cont exp))))
              (t (case (car exp)
                   (QUOTE (funcall cont (cadr exp)))
                   (BEGIN (@evlis (cdr exp) env procid
                            #'(lambda (ls) (funcall cont (car (last ls))))))
                   ((MAP MAPLIST)
                    (@eval (cadr exp) env procid
                       #'(lambda (fn)
                            (@evlis (cddr exp) env procid
                               #'(lambda (args) (@map (car exp) fn args procid cont))))))
                   (IF (@eval (cadr exp) env procid
                         #'(lambda (val)
                             (@eval (if val (caddr exp) (cadddr exp))
                                env procid cont))))
                   (LAMBDA (funcall cont (build-closure exp env)))
                   (LET (@eval '((lambda ,(mapcar #'car (cadr exp))
                                   ,@(cddr exp))
                                 ,@(mapcar #'cadr (cadr exp)))
                           env procid cont))
                   (LABEL (let ((newenv (acons (cadr exp) 'UNDEFINED env)))
                            (@eval (caddr exp) newenv procid
                               #'(lambda (val)
                                   (rplacd (car newenv) val)
                                   (funcall cont val)))))
                   (t (@eval (car exp) env procid
                        #'(lambda (fn)
                            (@evlis (cdr exp) env procid
                               #'(lambda (args)
                                   (@apply fn args procid cont)))))))))))
```

```
(defun @evlis (exps env procid cont)
  (if (null exps)
      (funcall cont '())
      (@eval (car exps) env procid
             #'(lambda (val)
                 (@evlis (cdr exps) env procid
                         #'(lambda (rest) (funcall cont (cons val rest))))))))

(defun lookup (s env)
  (let ((x (assoc s env)))
    (cond (x (cdr x))
          ((fboundp s) (list 'primop s))
          (t (symbol-value s)))))

(defun @map (kind fn args procid cont)
  (let ((n (reduce #'min (mapcar #'length args))))
    (let ((result (make-list n)))
      (do ((r result (cdr r))
           (a args (mapcar #'cdr a)))
          ((some #'null a) (dismiss))
        (let ((argset (ecase kind (MAP (mapcar #'car a)) (MAPLIST a)))
              (slot r))
          (enqueue
            #'(lambda ()
                (let ((newprocid (build-procid procid)))
                  (@apply fn argset
                          newprocid
                          #'(lambda (val)
                              (rplaca slot val)
                              (setq n (- n 1))
                              (setf (procid-responsibility-set procid)
                                    (append (procid-responsibility-set newprocid)
                                            (procid-responsibility-set procid)))
                              (cond ((zerop n)
                                     (reset-cells procid)
                                     (funcall cont result))
                                    (t (dismiss)))))))))))))

(defun depth (procid)
  (if (null procid) 0 (+ 1 (depth (procid-parent procid)))))

(defun reset-cells (procid)
  (let ((n (depth procid)))
    (dolist (cell (procid-responsibility-set procid))
      (when (> (length (cell-state cell)) n)
        (setf (cell-state cell)
              (nthcdr (- (length (cell-state cell)) n)
                      (cell-state cell)))))))

(defun @apply (fn args procid cont)
  (cond ((primop-p fn) (funcall cont (apply (primop-fn fn) args)))
        ((cellop-p fn) (funcall cont (apply (cellop-fn fn) procid args)))
        (t (@eval (closure-body fn)
                  (pairlis (closure-vars fn) args (closure-env fn))
                  procid
                  cont))))
```

```
(defun primop-p (x) (and (not (atom x)) (eq (car x) 'primop)))
(defun primop-fn (x) (cadr x))

(defun cellop-p (x) (and (not (atom x)) (eq (car x) 'cellop)))
(defun cellop-fn (x) (cadr x))

(defvar cell-read '(cellop $cell-read))
(defvar cell-write '(cellop $cell-write))
(defvar cell-add '(cellop $cell-add))
(defvar cell-logior '(cellop $cell-logior))

(defstruct cell contents state)

(defun cell (initval)
  (make-cell :contents initval :state '()))

(defun $cell-read (procid x)
  (cell-update x procid 'read)
  (cell-contents x))

(defun $cell-write (procid x newval)
  (cell-update x procid 'unique)         ;writes are mutually exclusive
  (setf (cell-contents x) newval)
  x)

(defun $cell-add (procid x newval)
  (cell-update x procid 'add)
  (setf (cell-contents x) (+ (cell-contents x) newval))
  x)

(defun $cell-logior (procid x newval)
  (cell-update x procid 'logior)
  (setf (cell-contents x) (logior (cell-contents x) newval))
  x)

(defun cell-update (x procid op)
  (let* ((s (cell-state x))
         (n (- (depth procid) (length s))))
    (cond ((plusp n)
           (setq s (nconc (make-list n) s))
           (setf (cell-state x) s))
          ((minusp n)
           (setq s (nthcdr (- n) s))))
    (do ((p procid (procid-parent p))
         (q s (cdr q)))
        ((null p))
      (cond ((null (car q)) (rplaca q (cons p op)))
            ((and (eq (cdar q) op) (not (eq op 'unique)))
             (unless (eq (caar q) p) (rplaca (car q) t)))
            ((eq (caar q) p)
             (unless (eq (cdar q) op) (rplacd (car q) t)))
            (t (error "Conflicting side effects"))))
    (push x (procid-responsibility-set procid))))
```

```
;;; An algorithm for computing the sum-prefix of a list of numbers.
(let ((cells (maplist (lambda (x) (cons (cell (car x)) (cell '?)))
                      list-to-be-scanned)))
  (begin
   (maplist (lambda (x) (cell-write (cdar x) (cadr x))) cells)
   ((label loop
           (lambda ()
             (begin (print (map (lambda (x) (cell-read (car x))) cells))
                    (if (null (cell-read (cdar cells)))
                        (map (lambda (x) (cell-read (car x))) cells)
                        (let ((values (map (lambda (x) (cell-read (car x)))
                                           cells)))
                          (let ((newchums
                                 (map (lambda (x v)
                                        (let ((chum (cell-read (cdr x))))
                                          (if chum
                                              (begin
                                               (cell-write (car chum)
                                                           (+ (cell-read (car chum)) v))
                                               (cell-read (cdr chum)))
                                              nil)))
                                      cells
                                      values)))
                            (begin
                             (map (lambda (x n) (cell-write (cdr x) n))
                                  cells
                                  newchums)
                             (loop)))))))))))

;;; An erroneous version of the same algorithm (see text).
(let ((cells (maplist (lambda (x) (cons (cell (car x)) (cell '?)))
                      list-to-be-scanned)))
  (begin
   (maplist (lambda (x) (cell-write (cdar x) (cadr x))) cells)
   ((label loop
           (lambda ()
             (begin (print (map (lambda (x) (cell-read (car x))) cells))
                    (if (null (cell-read (cdar cells)))
                        (map (lambda (x) (cell-read (car x))) cells)
                        (let ((newchums
                               (map (lambda (x)
                                      (let ((chum (cell-read (cdr x))))
                                        (if chum
                                            (begin
                                             (cell-write (car chum)
                                                         (+ (cell-read (car chum))
                                                            (cell-read (car x))))

                                             (cell-read (cdr chum)))
                                            nil)))
                                    cells)))
                          (begin
                           (map (lambda (x n) (cell-write (cdr x) n))
                                cells
                                newchums)
                           (loop)))))))))
```

Concurrent Constraint Programming

Vijay A. Saraswat
Xerox PARC

Martin Rinard
Stanford University

(Extended Abstract)

Abstract

This paper presents a new and very rich class of (concurrent) programming languages, based on the notion of computing with *partial information*, and the concommitant notions of consistency and entailment.[1] In this framework, computation emerges from the interaction of concurrently executing agents that communicate by placing, checking and instantiating constraints on shared variables. Such a view of computation is interesting in the context of programming languages because of the ability to represent and manipulate partial information about the domain of discourse, in the context of concurrency because of the use of constraints for communication and control, and in the context of AI because of the availability of simple yet powerful mechanisms for controlling inference, and the promise that very rich representational/programming languages, sharing the same set of abstract properties, may be possible.

To reflect this view of computation, [Sar89] develops the cc family of languages. We present here one member of the family, $cc(\downarrow,\rightarrow)$ (pronounced "cc with Ask and Choose") which provides the basic operations of blocking Ask and atomic Tell and an algebra of behaviors closed under prefixing, indeterministic choice, interleaving, and hiding, and provides a mutual recursion operator. $cc(\downarrow,\rightarrow)$ is (intentionally!) very similar to Milner's CCS, but for the radically different underlying concept of communication, which, in fact, provides a general—and elegant—alternative approach to "value-passing" in CCS. At the same time it adequately captures the framework of committed choice concurrent logic programming languages. We present the rules of behavior for cc agents, motivate a notion of "visible action" for them, and develop the notion of c-trees and reactive congruence analogous to Milner's synchronization trees and observational congruence. We also present an equational characterization of reactive congruence for Finitary $cc(\downarrow,\rightarrow)$.

1 Introduction

Almost since its inception, computing science has been dominated by a view of computation based on the von Neumann memory model. Following [Dij76] we may say that in this view, the state of the system is specified by a *store*, which is a vector V of n variables of interest, and a *valuation* assigning to each variable in V a fully-formed (completely known) value in its domain. Thus each store describes a point in the n-dimensional *state space* for the system, obtained by taking the product of all possible values for the variables X_i. Let us define a *constraint* to be a subset of the state space, that is, a set of valuations. When designing a (possibly non-deterministic) algorithm, we are concerned with specifying a mechanism, such that when it is initiated in a store that satisfies a given constraint (the "pre-condition") it terminates in a store that satisfies another given constraint (the "post-condition"). Hence in any formal notation ("programming language") used to describe such algorithms, some basic operations are necessary to transform one store to another. In imperative programming languages, the basic operations executed by an agent are *Read*, which obtains the value of some variable in the store, and *Write* (or assignment) which translates the store parallel to some axis by *changing* the value of some variable (possibly based on applying some functions to the values obtained from prior reads).

One way to describe the notion of *constraint program-*

---

[1] The class is founded on the notion of "constraint logic programming" [JL87,Mah87], fundamentally generalizes concurrent logic programming, and is the subject of the first author's dissertation [Sar89], on which this paper is substantially based.

ming as presented here is to contrast it with the view presented above. The fundamental difference is that in constraint programming the store is itself a constraint, a set of valuations which provides *partial information* about the possible values for the given variables. The basic operations an agent may execute are *Ask* (instead of read), which checks whether or not the store *entails* a given constraint (that is, whether every valuation permitted by the store is permitted by the constraint), and *Tell* (instead of write), which adds a given constraint to the store, provided that the resultant store is *consistent* (that is, permits at least one valuation—note that the set of valuations corresponding to a conjunction of two constraints is the intersection of the set of valuations of each conjunct). Thus, a basic step does not change the value of a variable, but may rule out certain values that were previously possible; we say that the store is *monotonically refined*, since at any step of the computation, the set of possible values for the variable is contained in the set of possible values at any prior step. As above, an algorithm in this framework is designed in such a way that when it is initiated in a store that satisfies (entails) a given constraint, the pre-condition, it terminates in a store that satisfies (entails) another given constraint, the post-condition. In this way, the entire constraint programming framework is based on extremely general notions of partial information, with its concommitant notions of consistency and entailment.

A fundamental consequence of this radically different view of the store—which, incidentally, one may regard as the essence of (definite clause) logic programming—is that it enables a simple, elegant but very powerful paradigm for concurrent computation. Briefly, one may imagine multiple agents of the kind described above, executing concurrently in a shared store. Synchronization is achieved through a *blocking* Ask: an agent may block if it attempts to ask whether a constraint is entailed by the given store, and it is not yet so; it remains blocked until such time as (if ever) some other concurrently executing agents add constraints to the store such that the resulting store is strong enough to either entail the query or its negation.

The development of this notion of *concurrent constraint programming* is the subject of this paper, and the dissertation [Sar89] on which it is based. Conceptually, the notion provides a theoretical footing for the intuitive, pre-theoretic visions about computing with constraints, evidenced in some of the work of such people as Sutherland, Sussman, Steele, Borning and some of their colleagues. Further, a coherent development of this notion leads to a synthesis and extension of some of the work on *concurrent logic programming*, which has occupied a number of researchers for the better part of this decade, and the more recent notion of *constraint logic programming* due to [JL87,Mah87]. Their union properly generalizes both: the former because its basic concepts of communication and synchronization are now seen to be applicable in a far more general setting, and the latter because it introduces a simple but powerful framework for control where earlier there was none. More generally, a major promise of this approach is that it will enable a very simple treatment of thorny issues in the semantics of concurrent, non-deterministic programming languages, and that, too, in the context of a versatile and expressive computational framework.

The rest of this paper is as follows. We flesh out the basic framework in more detail, and introduce the $cc(\downarrow, \rightarrow)$ family of languages. We discuss a wide number of constraint systems with respect to which the languages in the cc family may be instantiated, and their computational relevance. We discuss the notion of observation for the cc languages, and present characterizations for reactive equality and reactive congruence for these languages.

2 The basic framework

In general, we construe a constraint system to be any system of partial information that supports the notions of consistency and entailment. As such this notion is very weak, and can be used to capture a very broad class of interesting computational systems. For the present, we shall be content with a very simple class of first-order constraint systems:

Definition 2.1 A *simple first-order constraint system* is a quadruple $\mathcal{C} = \langle \Sigma, \mathcal{A}, \mathtt{Var}, \Phi \rangle$ where Σ is a many-sorted first-order vocabulary, with associated set of sorts S and ranking function ρ, $\mathcal{A}$ is a Σ-structure, $\mathtt{Var}$ is an S-sorted set of *object-variables* and Φ, the set of *admissible constraints*, is some non-empty subset of $(\Sigma, \mathtt{Var})$-formulas, closed under conjunction. □

In order to execute programs in a concurrent constraint language, the implementation needs to ensure only that Ask (entailment) and Tell (consistency) operations can be performed on admissible constraints, with respect to a store which is itself a conjunction of admissible constraints. However, when presenting the "reactive" semantics for these languages in Section 4, we will find it necessary to apply these operations (and the operation that determines if a constraint is true for all valuations) on an extended set of constraints which is also closed under implication, and existential and universal quantification. Hence *reasoning* about programs using this semantics may require a more sophisticated constraint system than is necessary to implement these programs.

The most popular constraint system in use in (concurrent) constraint/logic programming languages is the system that we call Herbrand.[2] It interprets a given vocabulary Σ over the free Σ-algebra. The constraints permitted are possibly existentially quantified conjunctions of equalities. Consistency in such a system can be checked by executing the (first-order) unification algorithm, and entailment by executing (a variation of) the matching algorithm.[3] More examples of computationally interesting constraint systems will be given in Section 3.

In the following, the many-sorted nature of a constraint system is not important, and we shall implicitly assume that various operations "preserve sorts". As usual, an $\mathcal{A}$-valuation is a mapping from Var to the domain of $\mathcal{A}$. In what follows, we will ambiguously regard a constraint c as denoting the possibly infinite set of valuations which realizes the constraint. Thus two constraints will be deemed equal if they yield the same set of valuations, even though their syntactic presentations may be different. (For example, if we interpret the operations and relations $\times, +, <$ in the standard manner, over the integers, the constraints $X \times X + Y \times Y = 25 \wedge 0 < X < Y$ and $X = 3 \wedge Y = 4$ will be deemed identical.) In the following, for any syntactic object χ (e.g., constraint) we shall use the notation $\mathbf{var}(\chi)$ to refer to the set of variables in χ. Further, if V is a finite subset of $\mathbf{var}(\chi)$, and $\mathbf{var}(\chi) \setminus V = X$, we shall use the notation $\delta V.c$ to refer to the constraint $\exists X.c$, which may be thought of as "projecting" out the information on the "hidden variables" X. Finally, we use the notation $(\exists)(c)$ to refer to the existential closure of c, that is, to $\delta \emptyset.c$.

2.1 The basic operations on store-as-constraint

Given that the store is a pool of partial information about the variables of interest, what sort of interesting basic operations can be defined on it?

We have already mentioned Ask and Tell. An "Ask c" operation succeeds if c is entailed by the store, fails if it is not, and suspends until it can either succeed or fail. A "Tell c" operation succeeds iff the conjunction of the store and c is consistent, and the store is atomically augmented with c if it is. (Note that both Ask and Tell are are *stable* operations, in the following sense. If at any stage in the past, the store successfully answered c, then the current store will successfully answer c; and

if at some stage in the past some agent had succeeded in (atomically) telling c to the store, then it is always possible to tell c in the current store. Hence Ask-and-Tell languages possess the following stable property: if an agent executes an Ask or Tell at some stage of the computation, then at all subsequent stages it will be able to re-execute the same Ask or Tell.[4])

We mention in passing that work on concurrent logic programming [Ued85,CG86,Str89] has yielded some operations which may be simplified and generalized in this setting as refinements of atomic Tell. In order to model distributed programming languages, it turns out to be convenient to conceptualize not a *single* shared store, but to imagine that multiple agents are executing concurrently at different sites, each with its own local store. Atomic publication now corresponds to the publication of a constraint *simultaneously* at all sites. In general this operation can be rather expensive, and the more "loosely coupled" notion of *eventual publication* has been found to be very useful [Ued85,Sar89]:[5] namely, the constraint being published is added at the local site, and will be communicated to other sites asynchronously and over time. Computation will abort in case during this propagation an inconsistency is discovered. Hence eventual publication may be regarded as an "unsafe" approximation to atomic publication, motivated from efficiency concerns. The nice surprise of [Ued86] is that in many situations eventual publication can be used safely and predictably.[6]

Drawing on an early version of Parlog [CG86], [FT89a] loosens the requirements of publication even further, as not to require any consistency-checking at run-time.[7] Their ":=" operator is an instantiation, over a given constraint system, of the following more basic and more general operator. The Initialization operator takes a constraint $c(X, \bar{Y})$ and a variable X, sus-

---

[2] Though per [Dav83] there may be some justification for calling it Skolem.

[3] In fact, [Mah88] shows that checking the consistency of arbitrary first-order constraints in this setting is decidable.

[4] This property of the language was used with great effect in [SWKS88] to define the notion of a "live global snapshot" in this setting, and to show that it could be obtained with a very simple protocol. Such a snapshot can be used to determine whether a network of such agents satisfies some stable property.

[5] [Ued86] discusses in detail the property of "antisubstitutability" that unification in GHC satisfies. The notion of eventual publication was extracted from this analysis in [Sar88,Sar89].

[6] In retrospect, perhaps eventual and atomic publication should have been called local and global publication. But the terminology is now well-established, and we shall stick with it. The local/global distinction also gives rise to two versions of Ask, with different implementation costs: one which checks whether the constraint is entailed from the local store and another which checks if the constraint is entailed in every store.

[7] In the case of *Strand*, which is defined over a slightly restricted subset of the Herbrand constraint system, this implies that no unification needs to be done at run-time.

pends until the store σ entails $\exists X.c$, and then succeeds iff $C \models \delta X.\sigma$ (ignoring c). On success, c is added to the store, without checking for consistency, which is guaranteed. In some settings [FT89a], these conditions can be checked very efficiently. (However, it must be kept in mind that if this operation is executed on the local store—as opposed to being executed at all sites simultaneously—it could still lead to computation being aborted, because of the asynchronous nature of inter-site communication.)

Some "unstable" basic operations (Check, Inform, Instantiate) of use in specialized situations are also discussed in [Sar89]. However, by far the most fundamental operations are Ask and (various approximations to) Tell, and it is on the Ask-and-Tell language $cc(\downarrow,\rightarrow)$ that we shall focus in this paper.

2.2 Building up more complex programs from simpler ones

Hitherto, we have examined in some detail a novel view of the store with two operations on it, Ask and Tell. Turning a blind eye to the connection with logic programming for a moment, it is interesting to speculate on the question: in what ways may these basic "Read" and "Write" operations be combined into more complex behaviors? That is, what are the combinators on agents one may wish to provide in order to obtain a reasonable (concurrent) programming language?

At this level of generality, this question has been asked and answered in earlier work by Milner [Mil83]:

> In a definitive calculus there should be as few operators or combinators as possible, each of which embodies some distinct and intuitive idea, and which together give completely general expressive power ... If we disregard the recursion construction (some such construction is essential for defining infinite behaviour) we have reduced our combinators to the following four, with manifestly distinct roles:
>
> 1. Product, *for combining agents concurrently ...;*
> 2. Action, *a combinator representing the occurrence of a single indivisible event;*
> 3. Summation, *the disjunctive combination of agents, allowing alternate courses of action;*
> 4. Restriction, *for delimiting the interface through which an agent interacts with others.*

Indeed the $cc(\downarrow,\rightarrow)$ languages have precisely these four combinators, though the definition of restriction is quite different in flavor because of the different underlying communication mechanism. (In fact, the cc framework does define other combinators, for non-deterministic choice, user-defined atomic transactions, reconciliation etc [Sar89]. However, most of these combinators are of use in the more general setting of (concurrent) indeterministic *and* non-deterministic ("backtracking") languages, which Milner was quite definitely not addressing. In this paper we confine our attention to $cc(\downarrow,\rightarrow)$, which does not allow non-deterministic choice.)

In the following, we use the meta-variables $A, A_1, \ldots$ to range over the set of agents, $b, b_1, \ldots$ to range over the basic actions, $X, X_1, \ldots$ to range over object-variables, $p, p_1, \ldots$ to range over procedure names, and R to range over parameter lists (lists of object-variables). In addition, we use the notation $\bar{\chi}$, for some meta-syntactic variable χ to stand for some finite, comma-separated list of the form $(\chi_1, \ldots, \chi_n)$.

The set of agent expressions may be defined inductively by the little grammar:[8]

$$\mathtt{A}::= \mathtt{nil} \mid \mathtt{stop} \mid c\downarrow \rightarrow A \mid c\star \rightarrow A \qquad (1)$$
$$\mid A + A \mid A \parallel A \mid \exists X.A$$
$$\mid pR \mid (\mathtt{fix}_j\bar{p}R\bar{A})R$$

Programs must satisfy the syntactic condition that the length of parameter lists for any procedure is identical to the length of the list of actual arguments. (*Finitary* $cc(\downarrow,\rightarrow)$ is $cc(\downarrow,\rightarrow)$ without recursion.)

Intuitively, an agent can execute the basic action $c\downarrow$ in a store σ if σ entails c; otherwise the agent is suspended. An agent can execute the basic action $c\star$ in σ if σ accepts c, that is, if $\sigma \wedge c$ is consistent; otherwise it cannot progress. The agent $b \rightarrow A$ (for b some basic action) can behave like the agent A, provided that it can do the basic action b first. $A_1 \parallel A_2$ behaves like A_1 and A_2 executing in parallel, so that their basic actions are interleaved. $A_1 + A_2$ is the agent that may behave either like A_1 or like A_2, but the choice must be made when either A_1 or A_2 executes its first step. (Thus the choice may be influenced by the environment, unlike Hoare's "internal non-determinism".) $\exists X.A$ (read: "A, with X restricted") behaves like A, except that the variable X is "bound" in A and must be replaced at run-time with a new variable "local" to A that is, "renamed apart" from any other variable in the environment.[9] As a con-

---

[8] In actual programming languages in the cc family, we also introduce a binary sequential operator (":") which allows the generation of composite basic actions (to be executed atomically) from other simple and composite atomic actions. However, at least when the only basic operators allowed are Ask and Tell, the addition of such an operator does not increase the expressiveness of the language, and we omit it from discussion here.

[9] Such dynamic renaming can usually be implemented effi-

sequence, X is also *hidden* in A, in the sense that the environment cannot influence A through X, and A cannot influence the environment by posting constraints on X. This is the natural notion of hiding in cc languages since variables serve as the conduit for communication between concurrently executing agents. Next, pR is a procedure call on p, with the argument list R (a list of object-variables). $(\mathtt{fix}_j \bar{p} \bar{R} \bar{A}) R'$ is the agent A_j, with its formal parameters R_j replaced by R', and with occurrences of the procedure variables $\bar{p}$ "bound" by the given declaration.

Finally, nil is the agent that has no behaviors. The primitive stop agent is necessary because we would like to distinguish successful termination of the system from unsuccessful termination. Intuitively, a stop agent executes a special visible action $c\checkmark$ indicating termination, where c is a projection of the current store, and then behaves like nil. However, the rules of behaviors of other agents are defined in such a way that agents $(A_1 \parallel A_2)$ can so indicate successful termination only when both A_1 and A_2 have; similarly for other combinators.

Example 2.1 (nrev/2 in this syntax) The usual "naive reverse" program may be written as:

```
(fix₁(nrev, append)((X₁, X₂)(X₁, X₂, X₃))
 ((null(X₁)↓ → (X₁ = X₂)⋆ → stop
  + cons(X₁)↓
     → ∃X₃.∃X₄.((X₄ = [car(X₁)], X₃ = cdr(X₁))⋆
          → ∃X₅.(nrev(X₃, X₅)
               ‖ append(X₅, X₄, X₂)))),
  (null(X₁)↓ → (X₃ = X₂)⋆ → stop
  + cons(X₁)↓
     → ∃X₄.∃X₅.(car(X₃) = car(X₁),
          X₄ = cdr(X₁), X₅ = cdr(X₃))⋆
          → append(X₄, X₂, X₅))))(A, B).
```

In the above, the constraints null, cons etc are used with their obvious interpretation. Intuitively, this agent expects its environment to constrain its first argument (**A**) to be a list, over time, and in return, it will constrain its second argument (**B**) to be the reverse of its first argument.

In reality such a program is written, with obvious shorthand, as:

---

ciently in distributed systems, without the kind of global knowledge that might seem necessary. Indeed, its effect is to provide a distributed, uniform, virtual name-space across all sites participating in the computation.

```
(fix₁(nrev, app)((X₁, X₂)(X₁, X₂, X₃))
 ((null(X₁)↓ → (X₁ = X₂)⋆ → stop
  + cons(X₁)↓ → ∃X₅.(nrev(cdr(X₁), X₅)
                ‖ append(X₅, [car(X₁)], X₂))),
  (null(X₁)↓ → (X₃ = X₂)⋆ → stop
  + cons(X₁)↓ →(car(X₃) = car(X₁))⋆
          → append(cdr(X₁), X₂, cdr(X₃)))
))(A, B).
```

And this, in turn, is not too far from the "Ask-tell" clausal syntax—closer to conventional logic programming syntax—employed in [Sar88]:

```
nrev(X₁, X₂) ← null(X₁) : (X₁ = X₂) | stop.
nrev(X₁, X₂) ← cons(X₁) : true |
    nrev(cdr(X₁), X₅), append(X₅, [car(X₁)], X₂).
append(X₁, X₂, X₃) ← null(X₁) : (X₂ = X₃) | stop.
append(X₁, X₂, X₃) ← cons(X₁) : car(X₁) = car(X₃) |
    append(cdr(X₁), X₂, cdr(X₃)).
```

□

Programs in the "algebraic" syntax introduced above may readily be translated to programs in the usual "clausal" syntax for logic programming languages, and vice versa. (We take it to be a strength of Milner's analysis that it is applicable even to the seemingly unrelated context of (concurrent) constraint programming languages.) Nevertheless we prefer to work in this paper with the algebraic notation which is more convenient for the task at hand, and it makes the connections with CCS/CSP more obvious. Indeed the algebraic notation presented above may well be regarded as abstract syntax for the concrete "clausal" syntax of logic programming.

2.3 The behavior of $cc(\downarrow, \rightarrow)$ agents

To define the behaviors of agents in this language, we employ an indexed labelled transition system, with set of configurations (also called *processes*) $(P, Q \ldots \in) \Gamma = \{\langle A, \sigma \rangle \mid \sigma \text{ consistent}\}$ and the set of labels $(\lambda \in) \Lambda$ (defined below) and indexed by $\{V \subseteq_f \mathtt{Var}\}$, the set of finite sets of variables. Formally, a store σ consists of a constraint and a set of variables; $c : V$ represents the store with constraint c and set of variables V. We require that $\mathbf{var}(c) \subseteq V$ for all stores $c : V$, and extend some operations on constraints to operations on stores in the following manner:

$$
\begin{aligned}
c:V \Rightarrow c' &\equiv c \Rightarrow c' : V \cup \mathbf{var}(c') \\
c' \Rightarrow (c:V) &\equiv c' \Rightarrow c : V \cup \mathbf{var}(c') \\
c:V \Rightarrow c':V' &\equiv c \Rightarrow c' : V \cup V' \\
c:V \wedge c' &\equiv c \wedge c' : V \cup \mathbf{var}(c') \\
c' \wedge (c:V) &\equiv c' \wedge c : V \cup \mathbf{var}(c') \\
c:V \wedge c':V' &\equiv c \wedge c' : V \cup V' \\
\mathcal{C} \models c:V &\equiv \mathcal{C} \models c \\
\forall X.c:V &\equiv \forall X.c \\
\exists X.c:V &\equiv \exists X.c
\end{aligned}
$$

The relation $V \vdash P \xmapsto{\lambda} Q$ is to be read as: "P is observed to take the action λ, on the visible variables V, and then behave like Q". In this section we define a *transformational* semantics, which is adequate to capture the behavior of the program executed in isolation from its environment. (In Section 4, we will consider which basic actions taken by an agent should be considered visible.) Hence the only observation allowed is the observation of a constraint c on successful termination of the store. This corresponds to the usual situation in logic programming languages when a user interacts with the system by executing an agent and waiting for the "answer bindings" (here: constraints) to be printed on the screen. Hence we set $\Lambda = \{\tau\} \cup \{c\sqrt{}\}$, where we take τ to stand for the "silent" action, indicating that the process has made internal progress.

The transition relation is defined inductively in the usual SOS style. A basic action can be executed when the relevant conditions are satisfied:

$$
\frac{\mathcal{C} \models (\exists)(\sigma \wedge c)}{V \vdash \langle c\star \to A, \sigma\rangle \xmapsto{\tau} \langle A, \sigma \wedge c\rangle} \quad \frac{\mathcal{C} \models \sigma \Rightarrow c}{V \vdash \langle c\downarrow \to A, \sigma\rangle \xmapsto{\tau} \langle A, \sigma\rangle} \quad (2)
$$

(From now on, we shall write $P \xmapsto{\lambda} Q$ for the assertion $V \vdash P \xmapsto{\lambda} Q$ whenever each assertion in a transition rule uses the same index V.) The definition of interleaving and choice are standard. Note that we use "Milner's choice", as opposed to Hoare's internal and external indeterministic choices [BHR84]. It turns out to be much more convenient to implement, and all concurrent logic programming languages implement this version of choice:

$$
\frac{\langle A_1, \sigma\rangle \xmapsto{\lambda} \langle A_1', \sigma'\rangle \quad (\lambda \neq c\sqrt{} \text{ for some } c)}{\begin{aligned}\langle A_1 \parallel A_2, \sigma\rangle &\xmapsto{\lambda} \langle A_1' \parallel A_2, \sigma'\rangle \\ \langle A_2 \parallel A_1, \sigma\rangle &\xmapsto{\lambda} \langle A_2 \parallel A_1', \sigma'\rangle \\ \langle A_1 + A_2, \sigma\rangle &\xmapsto{\lambda} \langle A_1', \sigma'\rangle \\ \langle A_2 + A_1, \sigma\rangle &\xmapsto{\lambda} \langle A_1', \sigma'\rangle\end{aligned}} \quad (3)
$$

The axioms for successful termination are equally straightforward:

$$
\frac{\begin{aligned}\langle A_1, c:V\rangle &\xmapsto{c\sqrt{}} \langle \mathtt{nil}, c:V\rangle \\ \langle A_2, c:V'\rangle &\xmapsto{c\sqrt{}} \langle \mathtt{nil}, c:V'\rangle\end{aligned}}{\begin{aligned}\langle A_1 \parallel A_2\rangle &\xmapsto{c\sqrt{}} \langle \mathtt{nil}, c:V \cup V'\rangle \\ \langle A_1, \sigma\rangle &\xmapsto{c\sqrt{}} \langle \mathtt{nil}, \sigma\rangle \\ \langle A_1 + A_2, \sigma\rangle &\xmapsto{c\sqrt{}} \langle \mathtt{nil}, \sigma\rangle \\ \langle A_2 + A_1, \sigma\rangle &\xmapsto{c\sqrt{}} \langle \mathtt{nil}, \sigma\rangle\end{aligned}} \quad (4)
$$

Next we consider the behaviors of $\exists X.A$.

$$
\frac{\langle A[Y/X], c:V' \cup \{Y\}\rangle \xmapsto{\lambda} Q \quad Y \notin V'}{V \vdash \langle \exists X.A, c:V'\rangle \xmapsto{\lambda} Q} \quad (5)
$$

The axiom for mutual recursion is the usual "stay one step ahead of the execution" one, modified in the obvious way to allow parameter transmission. As is conventional, we use the notation $A[\mathtt{fix}\bar{p}\bar{R}\bar{A}/\bar{p}]$ to indicate the agent obtained by simultaneously replacing all occurrences of p_i in A by $\mathtt{fix}_i\bar{p}\bar{R}\bar{A}$ and renaming bound (object and procedure) variables to avoid capture. In the following rule, R_j is presumed to be some list of variables $\bar{X}$.

$$
\frac{\langle A_j[\bar{Y}/\bar{X}][\mathtt{fix}\bar{p}\bar{R}\bar{A}/\bar{P}], \sigma\rangle \xmapsto{\lambda} Q}{\langle (\mathtt{fix}_j\bar{p}\bar{R}\bar{A})\bar{Y}, \sigma\rangle \xmapsto{\lambda} Q} \quad (6)
$$

Finally, the single axiom for **stop** is evident—in store σ **stop** can make a single transition, publishing the constraint $\delta V.\sigma$ (the store projected onto the visible variables):

$$
V \vdash \langle \mathtt{stop}, \sigma\rangle \xmapsto{\delta V.\sigma \sqrt{}} \langle \mathtt{nil}, \sigma\rangle \quad (7)
$$

nil has no behaviors.

The *computations* of a process are defined in the standard way, as sequences of transitions. Terminating computations may yield answers. The *set of answers* of a process P, $SS(P)$ is the set:

$$
SS(P) = \{c \mid \mathbf{var}(P) \vdash P(\xmapsto{\tau})^\star \xmapsto{c\sqrt{}} Q, \} \text{ for some } Q
$$

where we use the notation $P\mathcal{R}_1\mathcal{R}_2 Q$ to indicate relational composition , "$\star$" is the Kleene star.

2.4 Comparison with previous work

$cc(\downarrow, \to)$, as we have sketched it above, is essentially a "committed choice" concurrent logic programming language, parameterized over the embedded constraint system, and with the operations of blocking Ask and atomic Tell. Indeed, all the major concurrent logic programming languages neatly fit into the cc/Herbrand framework. Flat Parlog [Gre87] and Flat GHC [Ued86] are revealed as Eventual Herbrand, that is, as cc languages over the Herbrand constraint system, with Blocking Ask and Eventual Tell operations. **FCP**($\downarrow$, $|$) [Sar85] (modulo a minor adjustment discussed in [Sar87a]) is revealed as Atomic Herbrand, that is, the cc language over Herbrand, with Blocking Ask and Atomic Tell operation. Strand, the first commercially available programming language in this framework [Str89], is the cc language with Blocking Ask and Initialize basic operations, over a slightly simplified version of Herbrand.[10]

The treatment of the transformational semantics for the cc languages is based on [Sar89]. It considerably simplifies and generalizes the treatment of "flat" languages in [Sar87b], besides presenting it in an algebraic setting. The relationship of this work with some more recent work on the semantics of concurrent logic programming languages is discussed in Section 4.

[Mah87] first suggested, in the context of the design of the language ALPS (which may be thought of as being a cleaner "logical" variant of FGHC) how the synchronization condition for FGHC could be modelled logically. This paper was very influential in our development of the concurrent constraint programming framework. [Sar88] first presented the Ask and Tell metaphor, but it concentrated on showing how a number of synchronization mechanisms in concurrent logic programming languages could be expressed in this constraint-based setting. [Sar89] developed the concurrent constraint programming framework as presented here. The debts of this work to Milner's development of CCS are obvious.

More generally, from a concurrent programming point of view, there are tantalizing connections with the UNITY work [CM88]. cc languages are essentially non-deterministic transition systems over partially defined stores. The focus in this paper (and in [Sar89]), is to show that very sophisticated and usable programming languages emerge provided that the notion of communication and synchronization is suitably enriched.

3 Constraint systems

Concurrent logic programming languages, which have been thoroughly studied in the last few years, are currently the most well-developed exemplars of the power of constraint-based communication. Many programming idioms for these languages have been discovered, which deal, for example, with incomplete messages (messages whose responses can automatically—and efficiently—be routed back to the receiver), recursive doubling (technique for path-shortening), short circuits (used for the detection of stable properties of networks [SWKS88]), producer consumer synchronization, many-to-one communication using bags, techniques for modelling agents with mutable local state, etc. Note that these languages already have the power to communicate embedded ports in messages, without having to resort to infinite summations, as has variously been proposed for CCS. Further, these idioms allow the natural expression of fine-grained concurrency. Many of these idioms are discussed in the literature in such places as [Sha83], [Kah89], [FT89b], [Sar89], [Gre87], [Ued86] etc.

However, Herbrand is not the only kind of constraint system based on trees which is useful in this setting. For example [Sar89] shows that with a suitable choice of vocabulary, it is possible to get fixed-width arrays, extensible arrays, infinite arrays along two dimensions, records, "feature-structures" [AK84,Smo88] etc. in very natural ways.

More generally, constraint-based systems are endemic in AI. They range from systems based on Boolean algebras in use in knowledge representation systems with sophisticated inheritance schemes,[11] to systems arising from the so-called "hybrid reasoning" approach in AI, to explicitly tailored systems used in various vision algorithms [MR88], to discrete constraint systems [DvH+88] used in various search problems, to propositional caculus based constraint sytems used in conjunction with various kinds of "truth maintenance systems" to control problem-solvers, to constraint systems used in qualitative reasoning about the physical world, and so on.

Of course the use of constraint systems in traditional algebra and geometry settings is already well-known, and has been exploited in the constraint programming setting in [JLL].

We end with a few slogans which capture the flavor of constraint-based communication. These slogans are expanded on in much more depth in [Sar89].

Constraints specify partial information. Agents do not synchronize only on the availability of complete information about objects (variables). Two or more agents may simultaneously produce non-redundant pieces of information about the same variable.

Communication is additive. Only constraints that are consistent with previously placed constraints can

---

[10] We remark in passing that Flat Concurrent Prolog is not covered by the cc framework. We are not concerned however (on the contrary!) since that language was, in retrospect, a rather poorly designed language, with a very obscure synchronization mechanism. (The arcane details may be found in [Sar89].) Indeed, Shapiro and his colleagues have now moved over to Atomic Herbrand, essentially abandoning Flat Concurrent Prolog [KYSK88].

[11] Indeed, [Sar89] borrowed the Ask and Tell terminology from [BFL85]!

be added to the system. Once a constraint is added to the system, it stays forever. This leads to the stability of the Ask and Tell operations.

Constraints are types. The types-as-sets view makes types monadic constraints. More sophisticated type systems allow inheritance (implicational hierarchies), type specialization (conjunctions) and classification (exclusive disjunctions). The constraints view provides a coherent conceptual framework for a much richer space of type specifications, including multiadic types.

Communication channels may be embeddable. In the Herbrand constraint system, variables may be communicated in messages between agents with the same ease as data.

Communication is open. Whenever an agent places a constraint on a variable, any agent with access to that variable is affected. There is no a priori distinction betwen producers and consumers. In order to be affected by the environment, an agent does not need to know *how* the communication occurred: who generated it, when was it generated, etc.

4 Abstract semantics for cc($\downarrow, \rightarrow$) languages

In Section 2 we gave an operational semantics for cc($\downarrow, \rightarrow$), which associates with each agent the set of "answers" obtained by running the agent. However, such a semantics is obviously not compositional, since not enough information is stored with the semantic objects. In this section we take the first steps towards identifying the basic ideas that must be used in the semantic modelling of the cc($\downarrow, \rightarrow$) languages. We introduce the notion of "visible variables" of an agent—the set of variables that form the interface between the agent and its "environment"—and analyze the notion of "visible actions" for a cc($\downarrow, \rightarrow$) agent, axiomatize it in the standard SOS style, define c-trees to be the derivation trees obtained by "unrolling" the one-step transition relation, introduce two "bisimulation" equivalences on c-trees from which we derive two congruences (with respect to cc($\downarrow, \rightarrow$) combinators), axiomatize these congruences for Finite cc($\downarrow, \rightarrow$), and argue that one of them is the "finest reasonable" congruence on cc($\downarrow, \rightarrow$) agents.

4.1 Visible actions and reactive semantics

Let the "environment" in which an agent is executed be an abstraction of the rest of the computational system— including concurrently executing agents—with which the agent must interact to complete its computation. In order to interact, an agent must have certain variables— the *visible variables*—in common with its environment. A basic action is said to be a *visible action* if the agent's capability to engage in that action may be influenced by the environment. Thus a visible Tell action is an action that imposes "new" constraints (i.e., constraints which are not yet known to have been imposed) on the visible variables, and a visible Ask action is one which checks whether some new constraints have been imposed on the visible variables. Note that a visible action is not something that is "directly seen" by another agent— rather it is a step in the agent's own computation which could have been influenced by the action of some other agent. Such circumspection is necessary in understanding this concept because communication in cc languages is very indirect, and hence the concepts developed in the CCS/CSP framework—in which an event is observable if the environment can synchronously engage in it—may not be directly relevant.

In the following, we analyze this problem in detail. We define the (indexed) *reactive transition system*, over the set of configurations $\Gamma_r = \Gamma = \{\langle A, \sigma \rangle \mid \sigma \text{ consistent}\}$ (indexed as before by $\{V \subseteq_f \text{Var}\}$) and the set of labels $\Lambda_r = \Lambda \cup \{c\downarrow, c\star\}$ extended to include the basic actions. The interpretation of the transition $V \vdash P \xrightarrow{c\star} Q$ is that the process P may in one step add the new information c (in the visible variables V) to the store, and then behave like Q. Similarly, the interpretation of $V \vdash P \xrightarrow{c\downarrow} Q$ is: in order to progress, P must assume that the environment supplies a constraint at least as strong as c (in the visible variables), where c is information new to the store.

Let us now consider the axioms for $\longrightarrow$. Suppose an agent engages in the basic action $c\star$ in the store σ. Clearly, this action is invisible to the environment if $\mathcal{C} \models \sigma \Rightarrow \delta V.(\sigma \wedge c)$, where V is the set of visible variables. For, any action that the environment can engage in before the agent executes this action, it can engage in after the agent executes this action. (Note that c may add information on "non-visible" variables, but this can never be detected directly by the environment.) Even though the agent has made progress, the ability of the environment to progress has not been affected in any way; hence the agent has made *silent* progress. We thus have the axiom:

$$\frac{\mathcal{C} \models (\exists)(\sigma \wedge c) \quad \mathcal{C} \models (\sigma \Rightarrow \delta V.(\sigma \wedge c))}{V \vdash \langle c\star \rightarrow A, \sigma \rangle \xrightarrow{\tau} \langle A, \sigma \wedge c \rangle} \quad (8)$$

Otherwise, if the constraint can in fact be published (that is, is consistent with the store) then progress by the agent has resulted in new information being added to the store. The information added is the same as that added by any other agent engaging in a basic action $c'\star$ which is identical to $c\star$ (as far as the set of visible variables V is concerned) in the context of σ, i.e., is such that $\delta V.(\sigma \wedge c) \iff \delta V.(\sigma \wedge c')$. Subsequent to this action, the environment is prohibited from engaging in any action inconsistent with $\delta V.(\sigma \wedge c)$; hence we say that the agent has engaged in the visible action $\delta V.(\sigma \wedge c)\star$:

$$\frac{\mathcal{C} \models (\exists)(\sigma \wedge c) \quad \mathcal{C} \not\models \sigma \Rightarrow \delta V.(\sigma \wedge c)}{V \vdash \langle c\star \to A, \sigma \rangle \xrightarrow{\delta V.(\sigma \wedge c)\star} \langle A, \sigma \wedge c \rangle} \quad (9)$$

Similar considerations apply if an agent engages in the action $c \downarrow$. If the store σ is such that $\mathcal{C} \models \sigma \Rightarrow c$, then the agent has made silent progress; for, no (consistent) action taken by the environment can either influence this progress or be influenced by it. Assume now that $\mathcal{C} \not\models (\sigma \Rightarrow c)$. Let X be the set of variables in the store less the visible variables V. Now it is possible for the agent to progress iff it is possible for the environment to supply some new constraint c'_0 on V such that when conjoined with σ, it entails c. Hence c'_0 must satisfy the properties:

1. $\mathcal{C} \models (\exists)(\sigma \wedge c'_0)$, and,

2. $\mathcal{C} \models c'_0 \Rightarrow (\sigma \Rightarrow c)$.

If there is a constraint c'_0 on the variables V which satisfies these properties, then the weakest such constraint is: $c_0 \equiv \forall X.(\sigma \Rightarrow c)$. [12] Hence we say that if $\mathcal{C} \not\models \sigma \Rightarrow c$, and $\mathcal{C} \models (\exists)(\sigma \wedge c_0)$, an agent $c \to A$ may, in store σ, engage in the new visible action $\delta V.(\sigma \wedge c_0) \downarrow$. The resulting store, $\sigma \wedge c_0$ is exactly strong enough to entail c. Thus we have the axioms:

$$\frac{\mathcal{C} \models (\exists)(\sigma \wedge c) \quad \mathcal{C} \models \sigma \Rightarrow c}{V \vdash \langle c \downarrow \to A, \sigma \rangle \xrightarrow{\tau} \langle A, \sigma \rangle} \quad (10)$$

$$\frac{\begin{array}{c}\mathcal{C} \not\models \sigma \Rightarrow c \\ c' : V \sqcup X \equiv \sigma \quad c_0 \equiv \forall X.(\sigma \Rightarrow c) \\ \mathcal{C} \models (\exists)(\sigma \wedge c_0)\end{array}}{V \vdash \langle c \downarrow \to A, \sigma \rangle \xrightarrow{\delta V.(\sigma \wedge c_0)\downarrow} \langle A, \sigma \wedge c_0 \rangle} \quad (11)$$

The axioms for **stop**, choice, interleaving, the restriction operation and recursion (Rules 3,4, 5, 6 and 7) remain unchanged. This rounds up the list of axioms that $\longrightarrow$ satisfies.

4.2 Derivation trees

The above rules implicitly define the tree of actions that a cc agent engages in (obtained by "unrolling" the one step "$\xrightarrow{\lambda}$" relation, indexed by V, the set of free variables of the agent). Such trees, which we shall call c-trees, play the same fundamental role for cc that synchronization trees play for CCS. In brief, c-trees are trees whose arcs are labelled with elements of Λ^r and which satisfy the conditions:

- if an arc is not labelled with τ then the constraint labelling it is consistent and strictly stronger than any constraint labelling an ancestor arc, and,

- if the arc entering a node is labelled with $c\sqrt{}$ then the node has no outgoing arcs.

If two agents have the same c-tree, then they have the same success set; in fact the success set can be obtained in an obvious way by considering the "ask-free" branches of the c-tree.

Next we consider when two agents may be said to have c-trees that are "similar":

Definition 4.1 A relation $\sim$ on processes is a *rigid V-bisimulation* iff for all processes P and Q such that $P \sim Q$, if $V \vdash P \xrightarrow{\lambda} P'$ then $V \vdash Q \xrightarrow{\lambda} Q'$ and $P' \sim Q'$, and vice versa. $\square$

Definition 4.2 (Reactive equality) Two agents A and A' in free variables V and V' respectively are said to be *reactively equal* (written $A \simeq A'$) iff there exists a rigid $(V \cup V')$-bisimulation $\sim$ such that $\langle A, \emptyset : V \cup V' \rangle \sim \langle A', \emptyset : V \cup V' \rangle$. Two processes P and Q are *reactively equal on* V (written $V \vdash P \simeq Q$) iff there exists a rigid V-bisimulation $\sim$ such that $P \sim Q$. $\square$

The theory of bisimulation has been explored in a number of places e.g. [Mil84] and is mathematically very attractive.

Theorem 4.1 *Reactive Equality is a congruence for Finitary* $cc(\downarrow, \to)$. *That is, if* $A_1 \simeq A'_1$ *and* $A_2 \simeq A'_2$ *then:*

$$\begin{array}{ll} b \to A_1 \simeq b \to A'_1 & A_1 \parallel A_2 \simeq A'_1 \parallel A'_2 \\ A_1 + A_2 \simeq A'_1 + A'_2 & \exists X.A_1 \simeq \exists X.A'_1 \end{array}$$

The congruence proofs for the various cases consist of constructing a relation containing the appropriate processes, and then using several key lemmas (some of which are given below), to show that this relation is a bisimulation.[13]

First we need some definitions. Say that two constraint c, c' are V-*identical* iff $\mathcal{C} \models \delta V.c \iff \delta V.c'$. (From now on we shall abuse notation and write $c_1 = c_2$

---

[12] There may be no such constraint because it may not be possible to answer c from σ given that only a V-constraint can be added to σ. For example, if σ is **true**, c is Y=1, and V is any set of variables which does not contain Y.

[13] Detailed proofs of this result and others in this paper may be found in [SRng].

to mean that $\mathcal{C} \models c_1 \iff c_2$.) For a constraint c and store σ, say that c *extends* σ *on* V iff $\mathcal{C} \models (\exists)(\sigma \wedge c)$ and if X is the set of variables occurring in σ less V, then $\mathcal{C} \models c \iff \exists X.c$. Thus c may constrain variables other than the non-visible ones of σ.

Let $P \equiv V \vdash \langle A, \sigma \rangle \xrightarrow{\lambda_1} Q$ and $P' \equiv V \vdash \langle A, \sigma' \rangle \xrightarrow{\lambda_2} Q'$ be two transitions. We say they *correspond* iff each is generated from the same subterm of A. This notion can be generalized in the obvious way if the agents in P and P' are not identical but are variants of each other.

Lemma 4.2 (Anti-augmentation lemma)
If $V \vdash \langle A, \sigma \wedge d \rangle \xrightarrow{\lambda_1} \langle A_1, \sigma_1 \rangle$ and d extends σ on V, then there exists a corresponding transition $V \vdash \langle A, \sigma \rangle \xrightarrow{\lambda_2} \langle A_1, \sigma_2 \rangle$, where $\sigma_1 = \sigma_2 \wedge d$.

Lemma 4.3 Let $V \vdash \langle A, \sigma \wedge d \rangle \xrightarrow{\lambda_1} \langle A_1, \sigma_1 \rangle$ be a transition, where d extends σ on V. Let $V \vdash \langle A, \sigma \rangle \xrightarrow{\lambda_2} \langle A_1, \sigma_2 \rangle$ be a corresponding transition. Then, for any agent A', store σ' V-identical to σ, and constraint d' V-identical to d and extending σ' on V, if $V \vdash \langle A', \sigma' \rangle \xrightarrow{\lambda_2} \langle A'_1, \sigma'_2 \rangle$ then we must have $V \vdash \langle A', \sigma' \wedge d' \rangle \xrightarrow{\lambda_1} \langle A'_1, \sigma'_2 \wedge d' \rangle$.

Lemma 4.4 (Augmentation lemma for $\simeq$)
Let $V \vdash \langle A, \sigma \rangle \simeq \langle A', \sigma' \rangle$, where σ, σ' are V-identical. Let d, d' be two constraints such that d extends σ on V, d' extends σ' on V, and d is V-identical to d'. Then $V \vdash \langle A, \sigma \wedge d \rangle \simeq \langle A', \sigma' \wedge d' \rangle$.

We give an equational characterization of reactive equality for Finitary $cc(\downarrow,\rightarrow)$ in Table 1.

Theorem 4.5 *The laws $(A1)$-$(A8')$ and $(B1)$-$(B8)$ are complete for reactive equality for Finitary $cc(\downarrow,\rightarrow)$.*

We prove the theorem by defining a normal form, showing that each agent is related to its normal form by equational reasoning using the given laws, and showing that bisimilar agents have identical normal forms. The normal form of an agent differs from its c-tree only in that some branches of the normal form may terminate in **stop**, whereas corresponding branches of the c-tree terminate in a label of the form $c\sqrt{}$.

Each agent can be converted to its normal form by using $(A8')$ and $(B1)$ to "push down" $\parallel$ constructs, and $(B5)$-$(B8)$ to push down constructs of the form $\exists X$. $(B2)$ and $(B3)$ propagate constraints down the tree, ensuring that each branch of the tree has the correct labels, while $(B4)$ trims inconsistent branches and converts each Ask and Tell that adds no new information to the visible variables into a τ.

Law $(B6b)$ deserves futher explanation. Because applying this law hides any information about X in c from

Generic laws for reactive equality are given below. They are applicable when the index set $I = \emptyset$, since we take **nil** to be the zero for disjunction. All the laws numbered An are from [Mil84]. We use the notation $[b]$ to refer to b's constraint.

$(A1)\quad x + (y + z) = (x + y) + z$

$(A2)\quad x + y = y + x$

$(A3)\quad x + x = x$

$(A4)\quad x + \mathtt{nil} = x$

$(A8')\quad u \parallel v = \Sigma_{i \in I} b_i \rightarrow (A_i \parallel v)$
$ + \Sigma_{j \in J} b'_j \rightarrow (u \parallel A'_j)$
where $u = \Sigma_{i \in I}(b_i \rightarrow A_i)$
and $v = \Sigma_{j \in J}(b'_j \rightarrow A'_j)$

The following laws are specific to $cc(\downarrow,\rightarrow)$. The term τ is to be thought of as shorthand for the basic operation $\mathtt{true}\star$.

$(B1)\quad \mathtt{stop} \parallel A = A = \mathtt{stop} \parallel A$

$(B2)\quad b \rightarrow ((c \downarrow \rightarrow A') + A) =$
$ b \rightarrow ((([b] \wedge c) \downarrow \rightarrow A') + A)$
$ b \rightarrow ((c \star \rightarrow A') + A) =$
$ b \rightarrow ((([b] \wedge c) \star \rightarrow A') + A)$

$(B3)\quad b \rightarrow ((c \downarrow \rightarrow A') + A) =$
$ b \rightarrow ((([b] \Rightarrow c) \downarrow \rightarrow A') + A)$
$ b \rightarrow ((c \star \rightarrow A') + A) =$
$ b \rightarrow ((([b] \Rightarrow c) \star \rightarrow A') + A)$

$(B4)\quad \dfrac{\mathcal{C} \models \neg[b]}{(b \rightarrow A = \mathtt{nil})} \qquad \dfrac{\mathcal{C} \models [b]}{(b \rightarrow A = \tau \rightarrow A)}$

$(B5)\quad \exists X.\Sigma_{i \in I}(b_i \rightarrow A_i) = \Sigma_{i \in I} \exists X.(b_i \rightarrow A_i)$

$(B6a)\quad \exists X.(c \star \rightarrow \mathtt{stop}) = (\exists X.c) \star \rightarrow \exists X.\mathtt{stop}$

$(B6b)\quad \dfrac{\begin{array}{l}\forall i \in I. \mathcal{C} \models c_i \Rightarrow c \\ \forall j \in J. \mathcal{C} \models c \vee c'_j \\ \forall j \in J.\ \exists X.((c \wedge \forall X.c'_j) \star \rightarrow A'_j) = \\ (((\exists X.c) \wedge \forall X.c'_j) \star \rightarrow \exists X.A'_j)\end{array}}{\exists X.(c \star \rightarrow A) = (\exists X.c) \star \rightarrow \exists X.A}$
where $A = (\ \Sigma_{i \in I} c_i \star \rightarrow A_i +$
$ \Sigma_{j \in J} c'_j \downarrow \rightarrow A'_j)$

$(B7)\quad \exists X.\mathtt{stop} = \mathtt{stop}$

$(B8)\quad \exists X.(c \downarrow \rightarrow A) = (\forall X.c) \downarrow \rightarrow \exists X.A$

Table 1: Axiomatization of Reactive Equality

A, we must ensure that this information has been propagated to A before applying the law. The first clause of the law's antecedent makes sure that each c_i can be written as $c \wedge c'$ for some c', which guarantees that the information can be propagated through A_i. The second clause ensures that each c'_j can be written as $c \Rightarrow c'$ for some c', which guarantees that $(B8)$ will produce the correct Ask when the $\exists X$ is pushed down. Note, however, that c'_j does not contain the information in propagatable form. Therefore, the third clause makes sure that this information has been propagated to A'_j by verifying that $(B8)$ can be legally applied to $\exists X.c'_j \downarrow \to A'_j$ in the given context. Think of $(B6b)$ as a one step rule with lookahead.

4.3 Identifying c-trees

Reactive equality can be coarsened further—exactly as in CCS— by taking into consideration the interpretation of "τ" as indicative of silent, internal progress.

Definition 4.3 If $\lambda \neq \tau$ and
$$V \vdash \langle A, \sigma \rangle (\xrightarrow{\tau})^* \langle A_1, \sigma_1 \rangle \xrightarrow{\lambda} \langle A_2, \sigma_2 \rangle (\xrightarrow{\tau})^* \langle A', \sigma' \rangle$$
then $V \vdash \langle A, \sigma \rangle \stackrel{\lambda}{\Longrightarrow} \langle A', \sigma' \rangle$.
If $V \vdash \langle A, \sigma \rangle (\xrightarrow{\tau})^* \langle A', \sigma' \rangle$ then $V \vdash \langle A, \sigma \rangle \Longrightarrow \langle A', \sigma' \rangle$.
□

Definition 4.4 A relation $\sim$ on processes is a V-bisimulation iff for all processes P and Q such that $P \sim Q$, if $V \vdash P \stackrel{\lambda}{\Longrightarrow} P'$ then $V \vdash Q \stackrel{\lambda}{\Longrightarrow} Q'$ and $P' \sim Q'$, and vice versa, and if $V \vdash P \Longrightarrow P'$ then $V \vdash Q \Longrightarrow Q'$ and $P' \approx Q'$, and vice versa. □

Definition 4.5 (Reactive equivalence) Two agents A and A' in free variables V and V' respectively are said to be *reactively equivalent* (written $A \approx A'$) iff there exists a $(V \cup V')$-bisimulation $\sim$ such that
$\langle A, \emptyset : V \cup V' \rangle \sim \langle A', \emptyset : V \cup V' \rangle$.

Two processes P and Q are V-bisimilar (written $V \vdash P \approx Q$) iff there exists a V-bisimulation $\sim$ such that $P \sim Q$. □

Reactive equivalence for cc is the counterpart for observational equivalence for cc, under the assumption that the interactions of the agent with the store are observed. Since this is not the usual notion of observation for cc processes (see, e.g. the discussion of "visible" actions in Section 4.1), we have avoided the use of the phrase "observational equivalence". However, as was the case in CCS, reactive equivalence is not a congruence for cc and for precisely the same reason: it is not respected by "+" contexts. We have:

Theorem 4.6 *Reactive equivalence is preserved by the prefixing, hiding and interleaving operations.*

The laws characterizing reactive congruence for Finitary cc are the laws in Table 1 and:

$(A5) \quad A + \tau \to A = \tau \to A$
$(A6) \quad b \to (A_1 + \tau \to A_2) =$
$\qquad\qquad b \to (A_1 + \tau \to A_2) + b \to A_2$
$(A7) \quad b \to \tau \to A = b \to A$

Table 2: Laws characterizing reactive congruence for Finitary cc

The proof of this theorem is similar to the proof of Theorem 4.1 with the exception that the lemmas must be applied to the multiple "$\xrightarrow{\lambda}$" transitions that make up a single "$\stackrel{\lambda}{\Longrightarrow}$", instead of only a single "$\xrightarrow{\lambda}$" transition.

Define reactive congruence for cc to be the largest congruence contained in reactive equivalance. For Finitary cc($\downarrow, \to$), it can be characterized merely by adding the appropriate "τ-laws" from CCS. (See Table 2.)

Theorem 4.7 *The laws $(A1)$–$(A8')$ and $(B1)$–$(B8)$ are complete for reactive congruence for Finitary cc($\downarrow, \to$).*

The key idea here is to use the laws $(B1)$–$(B8)$ and $(A8')$ to convert agents to labelled trees. Once this is done, Milner's proofs [Mil84] go through essentially unchanged.

Reactive congruence—the largest congruence contained in reactive equivalence—seems the finest interesting congruence for cc($\downarrow, \to$) agents. Certainly two agents that are bisimilar have the final set of observables. Bisimulation has elegant mathematical properties, and is similar to ideas on "corresponding derivations" used in logic programming [Llo84].

It is known that bisimulation congruence is too fine a congruence for CCS for "reasonable" notions of testing [BIM88]. Research by many people in the last several years has established a number of coarser congruences—such as simulation, ready simulation, refusal congruence, failures congruence etc.—and has succeeded in tying these notions to reasonable notions of testing. We believe that it will be possible to coarsen reactive congruence for cc in a fashion similar to that done for CCS. Similarly, we believe that it will be possible to extend the notions of testing for cc to take account of the richer scenarios suggested for example in [Abr89]. However we believe it will be considerably harder to tie such testing notions to the corresponding congruences in cc because of the contextual nature of communication. We look forward to considerable work in this area in the near future.

4.4 Comparisons with other work

Recently [GMS89] have proposed a notion of "reactive behaviors". A reactive behavior is just the notion of input-output record which one of us introduced in [Sar85], generalize to our setting of concurrent constraint languages: it corresponds to a "trace" of visible actions, with all information about silent transitions and hidden branches removed. They present a rather limited "full abstraction" result for $cc(\downarrow,\rightarrow)$ that ignores the subtleties associated with hidden branching. [dBK88] explores a denotational semantics based on metric domains for the Herbrand instantiation of $cc(\downarrow,\rightarrow)$. (In fact they consider "deep guards" as well, and also point out connections with the semantics of imperative concurrent languages.) Connections with some of the other work on the semantics of concurrent logic programming languages are made in [Sar89].

5 Future work, and conclusions

Within the context of concurrent logic programming research, the notion of concurrent constraint programming and the cc languages, as developed in [Sar89] and summarized here, promise to have a fundamental impact. The realization that the synchronization mechanisms which had earlier been defined in very *ad hoc*, messy ways had nothing to do with unification, substitutions, idempotence etc.—those were mere implementation details—has cleared the way for the definition and implementation of simpler, conceptually cleaner and more powerful languages. At the semantic end, it is now obvious how the technically very convoluted results in [Sar85], [GCLS88] and [UF88] can be dramatically simplified and generalized. Indeed, we are confident that the concurrent logic programming field will be subsumed by, and merge into, the more fundamental and general concurrent constraint programming field.

With the connection between cc and CCS/CSP intuitively clear, we foresee an explosion of work in this field in the future. Perhaps the best tack would be to proceed in the "specification-oriented" framework set up by [OH86] for relating various models with each other. We look forward to the presentation of such models for cc and the clarification of their relationships in the near future. However, it seems that a prime target has to be the development of a denotational semantics which is fully abstract with respect to the standard notion of observation for logic programs (that is, observe the "success set", possibly with deadlock and divergence). This was attempted in [GCLS88] but for an artificially powerful language, which does not lie in the $cc(\downarrow,\rightarrow)$ framework.

We conclude with a quotation from [Hen88]:

As this avenue of research is developed to include languages with more sophisticated features we will require a more sophisticated mathematical framework, and it is unlikely that this will be found in the existing literature. I give two examples to illustrate the point. ...As a second example, we could take the language in Hoare 1978 or the full version of CCS in Milner 1980. Here values are passed along the channels so that the actions are no longer uninterpreted. Rather, the port names now act as variable binders in the same way as λ-abstraction in the λ-calculus. An adequate semantic treatment of these languages would therefore require a mathematical framework of Σ-domains which supports equational theories, variable binders, and, presumably, equational theories incorporating these binders.

Concurrent constraint programming may well provide an alternate simple, elegant, and practical framework for the development of these ideas. The framework we have presented above already caters for a very sophisticated and useful form of communication and synchronization. Indeed, the promise of the present approach is that it will enable the construction of concrete, implemented, practical languages which provide very rich facilities for communication and which seem destined to be widely used in the future, and which are at the same time theoretically simple and admit elegant semantic treatment.

Acknowledgements. There are too many debts that the first author owes to too many people for him to even think of acknowledging them here. He has tried to make amends in the preface to [Sar89].

References

[Abr89] S. Abramsky. Tutorial on concurrency. Presented at 1989 POPL, January 1989.

[AK84] Hassan Ait-Kaci. *A lattice theoretic approach to computation based on a calculus of partially ordered type structures*. PhD thesis, University of Pennsylvania, Computer and Information Science Department, 1984.

[BFL85] Ronald J. Brachman, Richard E. Fikes, and Hector J. Levesque. *Readings in Knowledge Represenation*, chapter KRYPTON: A functional approach to Knowledge Representation, pages 411 - 429. Morgan Kaufmann Publishers, 1985.

[BHR84] S.D. Brookes, C.A.R. Hoare, and A.W. Roscoe. A Theory of Communicating Sequential Processes. *Journal of the Association for Computing Machinery*, 31(3):560–599, July 1984.

[BIM88] Bard Bloom, Soren Istrail, and Albert R. Meyer. Bisimulation can't be traced: Preliminary report. In *Proceedings of the ACM Symposium on Principles of Programming Languages*, pages 229–239, 1988.

[CG86] K. L. Clark and S. Gregory. Parlog: parallel programming in logic. *TOPLAS*, 8(1):1–49, January 1986.

[CM88] Mani Chandy and Jay Misra. *Parallel Program Design—A foundation*. Addison Wesley, 1988.

[Dav83] Martin Davis. *Automation of Reasoning: Classical papers on computational logic*, chapter The prehistory and early history of automated deduction. Springer Verlag, 1983.

[dBK88] J.W. de Bakker and J.N. Kok. Uniform abstraction, atomicity and contractions in the comparative semantics of Concurrent Prolog. In *Proceedings of the Fifth Generation Computer Systems Conference*, December 1988.

[Dij76] E. W. Dijkstra. *A Discipline of Programming*. Prentice-Hall, 1976.

[DvH+88] M. Dincbas, P. van Hentenryck, H. Simonis F. Berthier. The constraint logic programming language CHIP. In *Proceedings of the FGCS Conference*, November 1988.

[FT89a] Ian Foster and Steve Taylor. Strand: A practical parallel programming language. In *North American Logic Programming Conference*, 1989.

[FT89b] Ian Foster and Steve Taylor. *Strand: New concepts in parallel programming*. Prentice Hall, 1989.

[GCLS88] Rob Gerth, Mike Codish, Yossi Lichtenstein, and Ehud Shapiro. A fully abstract denotational semantics for Flat Concurrent Prolog. In *LICS 88*, 1988.

[GMS89] Haim Gaifman, Michael J. Maher, and Ehud Shapiro. Reactive behavior semantics for concurrent constraint logic programs. In *North American Logic Programming Conference*, October 1989. To appear.

[Gre87] S. Gregory. *Parallel Logic Programming in Parlog*. International Series in Logic Programming. Addison-Wesley, 1987.

[Hen88] Matthew Hennessy. *Algebraic theory of processes*. MIT Press, 1988.

[JL87] Joxan Jaffar and Jean-Louis Lassez. Constraint logic programming. In *Proceedings of the SIGACT-SIGPLAN Symposium on Principles of Programming Languages*, pages 111–119. ACM, January 1987.

[JLL] J. Jaffar, J.-L. Lassez, and C. Lassez. Constraint logic programming: Tutorial. IEEE SLP 87 Tutorial.

[Kah89] Kenneth Kahn. Objects – a fresh look. In *Proceedings of the European Conference on Object-Oriented Programming*, pages 207–224. Cambridge University Press, July 1989.

[KYSK88] S. Kliger, E. Yardeni, E. Shapiro, and K. Kahn. The language **FCP**(:,?). In *Conference on Fifth Generation Computer Systems*, December 1988.

[Llo84] J.W. Lloyd. *Foundations of Logic Programming*. Symbolic Computation series. Springer Verlag, 1984.

[Mah87] Michael Maher. Logic semantics for a class of committed-choice programs. In *4th International Conference on Logic Programming*. MIT Press, May 1987.

[Mah88] Michael Maher. Complete axiomatizations of the algebras of finite, rational and infinite trees. Technical report, IBM T.J. Watson Research Center, 1988.

[Mil83] Robin Milner. Calculi for synchrony and asynchrony. *Theoretical Computer Science*, 25:267–310, 1983.

[Mil84] Robin Milner. Lectures on a calculus for communicating systems. In S. Brookes, A. Roscoe, and G. Winskell, editors, *Seminar on Concurrency*, LNCS 197, 1984.

[MR88] Alan Mackworth and Ray Reiter. The logic of depiction. Technical report, University of British Columbia, October 1988.

[OH86] E.-R. Olderog and C.A.R. Hoare. Specification-oriented semantics for communicating processes. *Acta Informatica*, 23:9–66, 1986.

[Sar85] Vijay A. Saraswat. Partial correctness semantics for cp($\downarrow$,|, &). In *Proceedings of the FSTTCS Conference*, number 206, pages 347–368. Springer-Verlag, December 1985.

[Sar87a] Vijay A. Saraswat. Compiling **CP**($\downarrow$, |, &) on top of Prolog. Technical Report CMU-CS-87-174, Computer Science Department, Carnegie Mellon University, October 1987.

[Sar87b] Vijay A. Saraswat. The concurrent logic programming language **CP**: definition and operational semantics. In *Proceedings of the SIGACT-SIGPLAN Symposium on Principles of Programming Languages*, pages 49–62. ACM, January 1987.

[Sar88] Vijay A. Saraswat. A somewhat logical formulation of CLP synchronization primitives. In *Proceedings of LP 88*. MIT Press, August 1988.

[Sar89] Vijay A. Saraswat. *Concurrent Constraint Programming Languages*. PhD thesis, Carnegie-Mellon University, January 1989. Also to be published by MIT Press, 1989.

[Sha83] Ehud Shapiro. A subset of Concurrent Prolog and its interpreter. Technical Report CS83-06, Weizmann Institute, 1983.

[Smo88]   Gert Smolka. A feature logic with subsorts. Technical Report Lilog Report 33, IBM Deutschland, May 1988.

[SRng]   Vijay A. Saraswat and Martin Rinard. Concurrent constraint programming. Technical report, Xerox PARC, forthcoming.

[Str89]   Strand Software Technologies Inc. *Strand 88 Users Manual*, June 1989.

[SWKS88] Vijay A. Saraswat, David Weinbaum, Ken Kahn, and Ehud Shapiro. Detecting stable properties of networks in concurrent logic programming languages. In *Proceedings of the Seventh Annual ACM Symposium on Principles of Distributed Computing (PODC 88)*, pages 210–222, August 1988.

[Ued85]   K Ueda. Guarded horn clauses. Technical Report TR-103, ICOT Technical report, June 1985.

[Ued86]   K. Ueda. *Guarded Horn Clauses*. PhD thesis, University of Tokyo, 1986.

[UF88]   K. Ueda and K. Furukawa. Tranformation rules for GHC programs. In *3d International Conference on Fifth Generation Computer Systems*, 1988.

Parallelism in Logic Programs

Raghu Ramakrishnan
Computer Sciences Department
University of Wisconsin-Madison, WI 53706, U.S.A.
raghu@cs.wisc.edu

1 Introduction

We consider the parallel evaluation of logic programs. This has been the subject of much research in the logic programming and, recently, the deductive database communities. We review this work, and observe that there is a commonly used measure of parallelism based on a top-down evaluation paradigm of identifying subgoals and answers. To formalize this intuition, we propose a simple abstract model of computation that makes precise the tension between the objectives of restricting the computation on the one hand and extracting parallelism on the other. In essence, if a subgoal is restricted by bindings generated in the solution of another, the latter subgoal must be solved first. This precedence is reflected in our model of computation by the choice of *sideways information propagation graphs*, or sips, which, informally, describe the order in which the literals in the body of a rule are to be solved.

Our thesis is that parallel evaluation methods can be viewed as implementing a choice of sips, a choice that determines the set of goals and facts that must be evaluated. Two evaluation methods that implement the same sips can then be compared to see which obtains a greater degree of parallelism, and we provide a formal measure of parallelism to do this. It is important to understand what is and — more importantly, perhaps — what is not implied by the statement that evaluation method $\mathcal{M}$ is "more parallel in our model" than evaluation method $\mathcal{N}$. First, our model only allows comparison of methods that fit the sip paradigm of computation, which is that some choice of sips for the rules in the logic program is implemented by the evaluation method. In Section 3, we show that most proposed methods for parallel evaluation of logic programs do fit this paradigm; in Section 7 we consider some methods that do not. Second, we compare the parallelism obtained by methods when they use the same sips. Thus, informally, $\mathcal{M}$ is more parallel than $\mathcal{N}$ if for every choice of sips, it succeeds in obtaining as much or more parallelism. Similarly, when we say that an evaluation method is "most parallel in our model", this does not mean that a faster parallel method cannot be found for a given problem. It does mean that once we choose to represent a problem — any problem — as a particular logic program and make a choice of sips, then the evaluation method obtains as much or more parallelism than any other method for evaluating the program according to the sips. Third, our model implicitly assumes that there are enough resources to work on all identified subcomputations in parallel, and therefore ignores implementation overheads and resource constraints. Any real evaluation method (or at least an implementation of it) must contend with the problem of mapping a computation onto the available resources, and in doing so must often sacrifice either restriction or parallelism. This aspect of the computation is not captured by our abstract model; however, it clearly affects results obtained using the model.

An important result that we establish is that transforming a program using the Magic Templates algorithm [Ra88] and then evaluating the fixpoint bottom-up provides a "most parallel" implementation for a given choice of sips, provided that there are no resource constraints. We emphasize a fundamental difference between this approach and top-down, process-oriented evaluation methods: whereas

---

*This work was supported in part by an IBM Faculty Development Award, a David and Lucile Packard Foundation Fellowship in Science and Engineering and NSF grant IRI-8804319.

a top-down evaluation method proceeds by creating processes to solve subgoals, the bottom-up approach proceeds by applying rules to facts to produce new facts. Indeed, the bottom-up method has no inherent notion of a "process", nor of a "goal", although we will establish a correspondence between certain facts generated in the bottom-up evaluation of a rewritten program (as per the Magic Templates algorithm) and goals generated in top-down evaluation methods, and refer to these facts as goals. This distinction is significant in terms of implementation overhead.

A number of other issues must be considered when comparing a bottom-up memoing method with top-down methods. These include relative implementation overheads and flexibility, and the use of memoing for multiple query optimization, incremental evaluation, and termination detection. While an investigation of these issues is beyond the scope of this paper, we discuss their impact in the full version.

The abstract model also allows us to establish several results comparing other proposed parallel evaluation methods in the logic programming and deductive database literature, thereby showing some natural, and sometimes surprising, connections. This suggests that our model does indeed capture the informal notion of parallelism that is used in parallel logic programming. Our results shed light on the limits of the sip paradigm of computation, which we extend in the process.

The paper is organized as follows. Following preliminary definitions in Section 2, we survey some proposed parallel evaluation methods for logic programs in Section 3. In Section 4, we develop a model of computation that allows us to view a class of evaluation methods based on sips at an abstract level, and a measure of parallelism that can be used to compare them. The class includes all the methods surveyed in Section 3, and several others as well. In Section 5, we present a bottom-up evaluation method based on rewriting a program, according to the Magic Templates algorithm, and evaluating the fixpoint of the rewritten program bottom-up. In Section 6, we compare the parallelism obtained using several proposed parallel evaluation methods. We consider the limitations of sips in Section 7, and discuss possible extensions. We then discuss some practical considerations in Section 8 and present our conclusions in Section 9.

2 Preliminaries

The language considered in this paper is that of Horn logic, and we assume the standard definitions of *term*, *definite clause*, etc. We also refer to a vector of terms as a *tuple*, and denote it by the use of an overbar, e.g., $\bar{t}$. Following the syntax of Edinburgh Prolog, definite clauses (rules) are written as

$$p :- q_1, \ldots, q_n.$$

read declaratively as q_1 and q_2 and ... and q_n implies p. A logic program is a pair $\langle P, Q \rangle$ where P is a set of predicate definitions and Q is the *input*, which consists of a query, or goal, and possibly a set of facts for "database predicates" appearing in the program. We follow the convention in deductive database literature of separating the set of rules with non-empty bodies (the set P) from the set of facts, or unit clauses, which appear in Q and are called the *database*. P is referred to as the *program*, or the set of rules. The meaning of a logic program is given by its least Herbrand model [vEK76].

A substitution is an idempotent mapping from the set of variables of the language under consideration to the set of terms, that is, the identity mapping at all but finitely many points. A substitution σ is *more general* than a substitution θ if there is a substitution φ such that $\theta = \varphi \circ \sigma$. Substitutions are denoted by lower case Greek letters θ, σ, ϕ, etc. Two terms t_1 and t_2 are said to be *unifiable* if there is a substitution σ such that $\sigma(t_1) = \sigma(t_2)$; σ is said to be a *unifier* of t_1 and t_2. Note that if two terms have a unifier, they have a most general unifier that is unique upto renaming of variables.

3 A Survey of Proposed Parallel Evaluation Methods

We discuss several proposed parallel evaluation methods, focusing on the parallelism that is realized, that is, what subgoal computations are allowed to proceed in parallel. The survey in this section motivates our development of an abstract model of computation to compare the parallelism in different methods. We develop the model in the next section; it abstracts the behaviour of a class of methods called "sip-methods". The methods discussed in this section all fall into this class, unless otherwise noted.

One of the objectives of this paper is to identify the similarities and differences in proposed parallel evaluation methods, both top-down and bottom-up, and to this end, we provide a uniform and sufficiently detailed description of the major approaches. While the relationship between bottom-up and top-down evaluation methods has recently been studied widely in the deductive database community, the more complicated nature of parallel evaluation methods has made the connections harder to see. Indeed, it has been remarked that the work on parallel evaluation in the logic programming community, typically top-down methods, is not likely to be useful in the context of bottom-up parallel evaluation [CW89]. We think that on the contrary much can be gained by a careful study of the literature of both top-down and bottom-up approaches. There is a strong relationship between the structure of top-down and bottom-up computations, as demonstrated in [Br89, Ra88, Se89] and also [BMSU86, BeR87, Ul89b, Ul89a, Vi89, KL86, KL88], etc. While the details of an implementation of a top-down method would differ considerably from that of a bottom-up method, we believe that many ideas, such as schemes for structure-sharing, are likely to work in either approach.

The parallelism in logic programs is often broadly classified into *And-*, *Or-* and *Stream* parallelism. And-parallelism refers to the parallel solution of subgoals generated from literals in the same rule body. Or-parallelism refers to the parallel evaluation of different rules that unify with a given goal. Stream-parallelism refers to the eager processing by a subgoal (the "consumer") of an argument value, such as a list, that is being constructed by another subgoal (the "producer"). We will restrict our attention to the first two, since the last typically forces us to consider additional properties of the computation such as determinacy and structure-sharing in some detail. Most of the methods that we discuss in this section proceed by identifying subgoals and creating processes to solve them. However, there has been some work on achieving similar results through bottom-up fixpoint evaluation, and we discuss this work as well.

3.1 The And-Or Tree Model

An And-Or tree for a logic program has the query as the root node, which is an Or-node. An Or-node is always labeled with a goal, and has one child And-node per rule whose head unifies with this label. The label of a child And-node is the corresponding rule with the unifying substitution applied to it. The unifying substitution is used to label the arc from the parent Or-node to this And-node. An And-node has at most one child Or-node per body literal in its label. The label of a child Or-node is a variant of the corresponding body literal.

The And-Or model presented in [Co83] builds And-Or trees by generating a process for each node in a top-down order. The query is the root node. The children of an Or-node are generated as described above. We now describe how the children of an And-node are generated: A child Or-node is created for the left-most body literal in the label of the And-node. The arc to the Or-node is labeled with the identity substitution. For each answer, which can be viewed as a substitution σ, to the Or-node corresponding to a body literal, an Or-node is generated for the next body literal. If the path from the And-node to the first Or-node is labeled with θ, the label of the second Or-node is the corresponding body literal with the substitution $\sigma\theta$ applied to it. This substitution is used to label the arc to it.

At any time, an And-node has at most one child Or-node per body literal in the label. Solutions to Or-nodes are saved as they are generated, and And-nodes are solved by generating all combinations of children through backtracking.

Much work has been done on this model; in particular, the ordering could be a partial order and sibling Or-nodes corresponding to different body literals could be generated simultaneously. In general, this creates problems if these children share variables. Therefore sibling Or-nodes are generated simultaneously only if they do not share variables. Since a variable that is shared between the corresponding literals could be bound to a ground term by a preceding Or-node, detecting such opportunities for solving the children of an And-node in parallel is a difficult problem. Several researchers have addressed this issue, e.g., [De84, CDD85]. Another area of research has been to identify intelligent ways to backtrack past predecessor nodes when a node fails (i.e., to recognize that alternative solutions to these predecessors would not enable the given node to succeed, and thus avoid generating further solutions to them.) Conery also suggested schemes for dynamically re-ordering the nodes in the And-Or tree [Co83]; these cannot always be described as sip-methods, and this is discussed further in Section 7.

An important restriction of the And-Or model is to simply avoid Or-parallelism by generating the children And-nodes of an Or-node one at a time. This restriction ensures the property that every variable instance in the computation has a unique binding at any time. (With Or-parallelism, recall that an Or-node saves multiple answers; these provide multiple bindings for the variables that appear in it.) This typically results in the loss of much parallelism, but reduces implementation overhead (e.g. [De84, HR89]).

3.2 Full Or-Parallelism

Full Or-parallelism is best understood in terms of *SLD-trees*. The SLD-tree for a logic program has the query as the root node. Every node in the tree is a conjunction of goals. A node has one child for each resolvent obtained by resolving one of the goals in the node with some rule in the program. The leaves are empty nodes. The conjunction of substitutions along a path from the root to a leaf, applied to the query, yields an answer.

Full Or-parallelism consists of exploring each branch of the SLD-tree in parallel, as initially proposed in [CH83]. Thus, if we have a node "$p1(5, X), p2(X, Y)$" and two rules "$p1(U, V) :- q1(U, V).$" and "$p1(W, Z) :- q2(W, Z).$", there are two children for this node: "$q1(5, V), p2(V, Y)$" and "$q2(5,Z),p2(Z,Y)$". This leads to an unnecessary duplication of effort — with no real gain in parallelism — in the repeated solution of the goal $p2(Z, Y)?$.

A solution to this problem is to solve $q1(5, V)?$ and $q2(5, Z)?$ in parallel, and to then solve the $p2$ goal for each binding of the first argument in parallel. We describe the solution in the general case in terms of a modified And-Or tree, with the only difference being that at any time, an And-node could have more than one child Or-node corresponding to a given body literal. As before, for the left-most body literal in its label, an And-node has one child Or-node per rule whose head unifies with it, and the arc to this Or-node is labeled with the unifying substitution. The Or-nodes for every other body literal are generated as follows: When a child Or-node for the ith body literal returns an answer, which can be viewed as a substitution σ for the variables in it, this is composed with the substitution, say θ, on the arc to this Or-node and the resulting substitution $\theta\sigma$ is applied to the $i + 1$st body literal in the label of the And-node. This results in a goal, generated from the $i + 1$st literal, and one child Or-node is created with this label. The arc from the And-node to this Or-node is labeled with the substitution $\theta\sigma$.

This is indeed how the Or-parallel model proposed in [CH83] is implemented, as described in [CH84]. In essence, rules are solved left to right, and for each goal, all rules with which it unifies are solved in parallel. Notice that, except for the root, each Or-node is created in response to the answer to another Or-node; the creation of And-nodes can be avoided by directly creating tokens for all the Or-nodes that are its leftmost children. Thus, with each Or-node in the tree, we can associate a set of Or-nodes that were generated because of answers to it. Let us call this the set of successors. The computation proceeds by creating "tokens" in a top-down order for each Or-node in the modified And-Or tree. A token contains enough information to generate tokens for all its successors. (In particular, this includes information about the label of the parent And-node; this is achieved by means of a "continuation", and we refer the reader to [CH84] for details.)

Note that there is no And-parallelism; a rule is always solved from left to right.

3.3 The Reduce-Or Model

Kalé observed that many of the proposed evaluation methods were either incomplete or did not extract all available parallelism, or both. This was the motivation for the development of the Reduce-Or evaluation model. It is in effect a combination of the And-Or and the fully Or-parallel models as we have described them.

The model is essentially the fully Or-parallel model extended to solve And-nodes according to a partial order, rather than a total left to right order, thereby also exploiting And-parallelism. The only change concerns the generation of the children Or-nodes of an And-node. A partial order is associated with each rule (and thus, any And-node that it labels). Consider an And-node, and the associated partial order over the body literals of the label. A node with no predecessors is treated like a left-most literal in the fully Or-parallel model — one Or-node is generated for each rule that unifies with it, and the arc to this Or-node is labeled with the unifying substitution. Consider a body literal p with predecessors $p_1, \ldots, p_k$ in the partial order. Let $\theta_i, i = 1, \ldots, k$ be an answer substitution for p_i, and let the composition $\theta = \theta_1, \ldots, \theta_k$ be consistent. Then, an Or-node is generated for the goal $p\theta$, and the arc from the And-node to this Or-node is given the label $p\theta$. Kalé does not insist that sibling Or-nodes that correspond to different body literals and that are generated in parallel should contain no shared variables. Instead, any conflicts are resolved by explicitly composing answer substitutions for all the body literals, one per literal. In effect, this corresponds to taking a join on the body of a rule to generate an answer fact for the head predicate.

We conclude this discussion of top-down methods by formally defining And- and Or- parallel steps in terms of And-Or trees.

Definition 3.1 An *And-parallel step* is the simultaneous generation of two goals that correspond to different body literals in the label of an And-node.

Definition 3.2 An *Or-parallel step* is the simultaneous generation of goals $g_1, \ldots, g_k$ from a given goal g by unifying g with the heads of two different rules and generating $g_1, \ldots, g_k$ by instantiating body literals with no predecessors. The generated goals must not all be obtained from just one of the rules.

We assume that once a goal is "generated", it can be processed immediately. (In effect, a goal is considered to be generated when its processing begins.)

3.4 Bottom-Up Methods

The literature on bottom-up evaluation is extensive, and we do not propose to cover it in detail here. We refer the reader to surveys and expositions presented in [BaR86, Br89, NR89, Ul89a]. We note that while most of this literature deals with the implementation of *Datalog*, which is a subset of logic programs without function symbols, recent proposals treat full logic programs [Ra88, Se89]. We will examine one of these proposals ([Ra88]) in detail later. The following brief discussion should be supplemented by consulting Section 5.

The fundamental operation in bottom-up approaches is the application of a rule to a set of facts to generate new facts, which is similar to the use of the T_P operator to construct the least fixpoint model [vEK76]. An obvious drawback is that all consequences of the program are generated, not just the facts relevant to processing the given query. From our presentation of the top-down methods, it is clear that these methods restrict the computation by propagating bindings from the query as the construct the And-Or trees in top-down order. The essential idea in most bottom-up methods is to combine a top-down generation of goals with a bottom-up generation of facts. In general, this requires that all generated goals and facts should be retained and the process repeated iteratively until no new goals and facts are generated.

Most of the proposed methods use a top-down control strategy to generate goals, e.g., [DW87, Lo85, Vi89]. Some use a graph structure over the rules of the program for this purpose, e.g., [KL86, KL88, vG86]. It has been shown however, that this can be achieved through source-to-source program transformations, and this is the approach that we will pursue [BMSU86, RLK86, BeR87, Ra88, Se89]. We believe that this has significant advantages to offer in terms of uniformity, overheads, and implementation alternatives.

4 A Computation Model

We consider how the evaluation of a logic program can be formalized at an abstract level in a way that allows us to make precise the degree of parallelism. We emphasize that the model we develop in this section is not an execution model, in that it does not specify how to evaluate a program, and should not be confused with execution models such as And-Or models or the Reduce-Or Process Model. Rather, it is a formal model in which we can abstractly represent computations that correspond to execution of a logic program using some execution model (i.e., evaluation method).

We begin by observing that while the semantics of a logic program is purely declarative in that it does not depend on how the program is evaluated or on any concept of a program state, there is a natural notion of state associated with any execution of a logic program.

The following definitions provide a starting point, and are subsequently refined: The *state* of a program execution is a pair $\langle \mathcal{F}, \mathcal{G} \rangle$, where $\mathcal{F}$ and $\mathcal{G}$ are sets of facts and goals, respectively. The *initial state* is defined by $\mathcal{F}$ = set of given facts in the program (the *EDB*, in database terminology, or the set of rules with empty bodies), and $\mathcal{G}$ = the initial query. A *computation* is a progression from the initial state to a final state, in which $\mathcal{F}$ contains all facts in the answer to the query, through a sequence of transitions from one state to another.

To complete our model of computation, we must define the notion of a state transition. Intuitively, we seek to describe a single step of computation. To do this, we must make explicit certain assumptions about the class of evaluation methods that we consider, and we do this in the following subsection.

4.1 Sip-Method

The class of evaluation methods that we consider proceed by generating subgoals and facts (that are solutions to some of the subgoals), using the logic program $\langle P, Q \rangle$. In order to account for the restrictions placed upon the sets of goals and facts that can be generated at any given time by different evaluation methods, we will assume a "hidden state" $\mathcal{H}$. At any point in the computation, the state is a triple $\langle \mathcal{F}, \mathcal{G}, \mathcal{H} \rangle$. A new fact or goal can be generated by the use of a rule in P on $\mathcal{F} \cup \mathcal{G}$, subject to restrictions imposed by the hidden state and the evaluation method.

Initially, the set of facts $\mathcal{F}$ consists of the *EDB* facts in Q. The set of goals $\mathcal{G}$ contains the given query, also in Q. (The hidden state $\mathcal{H}$ is assumed to be properly initialized.) New facts can be generated as follows.

Consider a rule: $r : p :\!\!- q_1, \ldots, q_n$.
We can generate a new fact $p\theta$ by applying a substitution θ such that for $i = 1, \ldots, n$:

1. there is a fact d_i in $\mathcal{F}$ and a substitution σ_i such that $q_i\theta = d_i\sigma_i$, and
2. there is a goal $c?$ in $\mathcal{G}$ and a substitution σ_0 such that $p\theta = c\sigma_0$.

In most evaluation methods, only the substitution $\phi = mgu(\langle p, q_1, \ldots, q_n\rangle, \langle c, d_1, \ldots, d_n\rangle)$ is applied, since applications of other substitutions only generate facts that are subsumed by the fact $p\phi$. We will assume this in the rest of this paper, and also make a similar assumption in the following description of how goals can be generated. The effect of the hidden state $\mathcal{H}$ and the evaluation method $\mathcal{M}$ — which we do not specify in further detail — is to allow only a subset of the above new facts to be generated. Generated facts are added to $\mathcal{F}$; further, a (newly generated or previously known) fact $f \in \mathcal{F}$ can be discarded if it is subsumed by another fact in $\mathcal{F}$. The cost of detecting that a fact is subsumed may sometimes override the gains, and some methods do not discard such facts; we will not require this as part of our definition of sip methods. However, not discarding subsumed facts may lead to unnecessary derivations of new facts.

To specify how goals can be generated, we must introduce the notion of a *sideways information passing*, or sip, graph. We define a sip graph for a rule to be a partial ordering of the body literals.[1] New goals are generated by invoking a rule, in a top-down sense, with some known goal. Further, they literals in the body of a rule are solved in some order, more generally a partial order. Each literal is solved by generating a subgoal from it and then obtaining solutions to this subgoal. In generating a subgoal from a literal, the goal with which the rule was invoked and the solutions obtained to literals that precede the given literal in the sip partial order are all used to bind variables and thereby restrict the new subgoal. Thus, to generate a subgoal from a literal q_k, we need the goal with which the rule was invoked, and the facts (solutions) corresponding to literals that precede it in the sip order.

Formally:

Let the predecessors of q_k be the literals $q_i, \ldots, q_j$, let $c \in \mathcal{G}$ and $\{d_i, \ldots, d_j\} \subseteq \mathcal{F}$, and
let $\theta = mgu(\langle p, q_i, \ldots, q_j\rangle, \langle c, d_i, \ldots, d_j\rangle)$.
Then, we can generate the goal $q_k\theta?$.

Generated goals are added to $\mathcal{G}$, and as for facts, subsumed goals can be discarded. The effect of the hidden state $\mathcal{H}$ and the evaluation method $\mathcal{M}$ is again to allow only a subset of the new goals to be generated. Henceforth, we will refer to the above operations as simply "applying a rule" (in a given state, according to a given evaluation method) to generate a fact or a goal. In a given state, we will in general be able to apply several rules simultaneously to produce new goals and facts. Indeed, the same rule could be applied to produce several new goals and facts from the sets $\mathcal{F}$ and $\mathcal{G}$. Thus, a state transition can add a set of facts or goals, each of which can be generated by a single application of a rule to $\mathcal{F} \cup \mathcal{G}$.

We now summarize our description of sip-methods.

Definition 4.1 Sip-Method
Consider a logic program $\langle P, Q\rangle$ and a choice of sips for the rules in P. A *sip-method* is defined to be an evaluation method that generates only facts and goals that can be generated from Q by applying the rules in P in some order according to the chosen sips under the assumption of a hidden state that disallows the generation of no fact or goal. A *subsumption-checking sip-method* is one that discards subsumed facts and goals as soon as possible. A *complete (resp. subsumption-checking) sip-method* is one that computes maximal sets of facts and goals, as per the definition of a (resp. subsumption-checking) sip-method.

The maximal sets of goals and facts that may be computed are independent of the details of the evaluation method (and the associated encoding of the hidden state), and are determined by the program and the sips. If the evaluation method is to guarantee all answers that follow from the least Herbrand model semantics, all these goals and facts must be generated, since it is otherwise possible to construct inputs such that some answer is not generated. This motivates the definition of complete sip-methods; we note that not all proposed evaluation methods are complete.

While a broad class of evaluation methods can be viewed as sip-methods, it is important to note that methods that allow "coroutining" — the computation of two goals is interleaved, and typically, the bindings generated by each are used to restrict the other — cannot be considered sip-methods. We pursue this point further in Section 7.

4.2 A Summary of Our Model of Computation

We now present the formal definitions of states, transitions and computations.

Definition 4.2 Consider a program $\langle P, Q\rangle$.

---
[1] We will assume that the choice of sips is made for us — making a good choice is a hard problem, and orthogonal to the results in this paper.

- The *state* of a program execution is a triple $\langle \mathcal{F}, \mathcal{G}, \mathcal{H} \rangle$, where $\mathcal{F}$ and $\mathcal{G}$ are sets of facts and queries, respectively, and $\mathcal{H}$ denotes a hidden component of the state.

- The *initial state* is defined by $\mathcal{F}$ = set of given facts in the program (the EDB, in database terminology, or the set of rules with empty bodies), and $\mathcal{G}$ = the initial query.

- A *state transition* according to evaluation method $\mathcal{M}$ in state $\mathcal{S}_1 = \langle \mathcal{F}_1, \mathcal{G}_1, \mathcal{H}_2 \rangle$ changes the state to $\mathcal{S}_2 = \langle \mathcal{F}_2, \mathcal{G}_2, \mathcal{H}_2 \rangle$, and is denoted as $\mathcal{S}_1 \vdash_\mathcal{M} \mathcal{S}_2$.
  $\mathcal{F}_2 = \mathcal{F}_1 \cup \{f | f$ is a fact that can be generated from $\mathcal{F}_1 \cup \mathcal{G}_1$ in hidden state $\mathcal{H}_1$ according to method $\mathcal{M}$ by a single rule application.$\}$
  $\mathcal{G}_2 = \mathcal{G}_1 \cup \{g | g$ is a goal that can be generated from $\mathcal{F}_1 \cup \mathcal{G}_1$ in hidden state $\mathcal{H}_1$ according to method $\mathcal{M}$ by a single rule application.$\}$
  Note that $\cup$ can lead to facts or goals being discarded because they are now subsumed. Further, we assume that the hidden state $\mathcal{H}_2$ is obtained by suitably updating $\mathcal{H}_1$ to reflect the behaviour of $\mathcal{M}$.

- A *final state* is a state such that no new facts or goals can be generated and no rule applications change the hidden state.

- A *computation sequence* according to method $\mathcal{M}$ is a progression from the initial state to a final state, through a sequence of state transitions according to $\mathcal{M}$ from one state to another.

The *length* of a computation sequence is the number of state transitions in it.

According to our model, in a given state, there is a unique transition according to a given evaluation method, and thus a unique computation sequence for a given program and choice of sips. This essentially reflects the most optimistic situation, where all possible generations of new goals and facts are carried out simultaneously at each step, and makes the assumption that there are no resource constraints. It is worth remarking that the sets $\mathcal{F}$ and $\mathcal{G}$ may not change in a state transition, and only the hidden state $\mathcal{H}$ is updated. This corresponds to the situation that all the facts and goals that can be generated are previously known, and the only effect of generating them is to possibly make them visible in some subcomputations where they were not visible earlier. The details are germane to how $\mathcal{H}$ is to be updated; we do not consider this updating process in our abstraction of a computation.

In subsequent sections, we denote the hidden state as T for evaluation methods in which all goals and facts are visible to all computations. However, in the following example, we simply omit the hidden state, for simplicity, with the understanding that it is manipulated appropriately by the evaluation method and influences the generation of the computation sequence.

Example 4.1 We now present an example that illustrates our model of computation by listing the computation sequences in our model for execution according to several different evaluation methods. We use the following program; the only rule with a body that contains more than one literal is the first, and we assume that the chosen sip leaves the first two literals relatively unordered but before the third.

$p(X, Y) :- b1(X), b2(Y), b3(X, Y, Z).$
$p(X, Y) :- b4(X, Y).$
$b1(5).$
$b2(6). \ b2(7).$
$b3(5, 6, 8). \ b3(5, 7, 9).$
$b4(1, 2).$
$p(U, V)?$

We mark goals by a terminal "?", and represent the sets $\mathcal{F}$ and $\mathcal{G}$ as a single set of goals and facts. For brevity we use the notation "$\cup\{\ldots\}$" to denote a state in a computation sequence that is obtained by adding the set between $\{$ and $\}$ to the set in the previous state in the sequence (and updating the hidden state, which is not shown).

Prolog Prolog is a left-to-right evaluation method that does not exploit any parallelism. Its computation sequence is:
$\{p(U,V)?\} \vdash \cup\{b1(X)?\} \vdash \cup\{b1(5)\} \vdash \cup\{b2(Y)?\}$
$\vdash \cup\{b2(6)\} \vdash \cup\{b3(5,6,Z)?\}$
$\vdash \cup\{b3(5,6,8)\}$
$\vdash \cup\{p(5,8)\} \vdash \cup\{b2(7)\} \vdash \cup\{b3(5,7,Z)?\}$
$\vdash \cup\{b3(5,7,9)\} \vdash \cup \{p(5,9)\} \vdash \cup\{b4(X,Y)?\}$
$\vdash \cup\{b4(1,2)\} \vdash \cup\{p(1,2)\}$

Note that the goal $b2(Y)?$ is generated a second time after backtracking. We do not see this in the above sequence since its only effect in our model is to affect the hidden state; the set of known facts and goals is unaffected by the re-derivation of a previously known goal.

Ciepielewski-Haridi This is a fully Or-parallel method proposed in [CH83]. It does not exploit any And-parallelism.
$\{p(U,V)?\} \vdash \cup\{b1(X)?, b4(X,Y)?\} \vdash \cup$
$\{b1(5), b4(1,2)\} \vdash \cup\{p(1,2), b2(Y)?\} \vdash \cup$
$\{b2(6), b2(7)\} \vdash \cup\{b3(5,6,Z)?, b3(5,7,Z)?\}$
$\vdash \cup\{b3(5,6,8), b3(5,7,9)\} \vdash \cup\{p(5,8), p(5,9)\}$

Observe that the parallelism has resulted in a much shorter computation sequence. There is no And-parallelism since in no one transition do we add goals corresponding to different body literals.

DeGroot This is an And-parallel method that exploits no Or-parallelism, and was proposed in [De84].
$\{p(U,V)?\} \vdash \cup\{b1(X)?, b2(Y)?\} \vdash \cup\{b1(5), b2(6)\} \vdash \cup\{b3(5,6,Z)?\} \vdash \cup\{b3(5,6,8)\} \vdash \cup\{p(5,8)\} \vdash \cup\{b2(7)\} \vdash \cup\{b3(5,7,Z)?\} \vdash \cup\{b3(5,7,9)\} \vdash \cup\{p(5,9)\} \vdash \cup\{b4(X,Y)?\} \vdash \cup\{b4(1,2)\} \vdash \cup\{p(1,2)\}$

Conery This is a method that attempts to realize both And- and Or- parallelism, and is one of the methods proposed in [Co83].
$\{p(U,V)?\} \vdash \cup\{b1(X)?, b2(Y)?\} \vdash \cup\{b1(5), b2(6), b2(7)\} \vdash \cup\{b3(5,6,Z)?\} \vdash \cup\{b3(5,6,8)\} \vdash \cup\{p(5,8)\} \vdash \cup\{b3(5,7,Z)?\} \vdash \cup\{b3(5,7,9)\} \vdash \cup\{p(5,9)\} \vdash \cup\{b4(X,Y)?\} \vdash \cup\{b4(1,2)\} \vdash \cup\{p(1,2)\}$

Notice that in this method, the two $b3$ goals are sequentialized.

Reduce-Or This is also a method that exploits both And- and Or- parallelism, and is proposed in [Ka87a]. It identifies all the available parallelism in this example.
$\{p(U,V)?\} \vdash \cup\{b1(X)?, b2(Y)?, b4(X,Y)?\} \vdash \cup\{b1(5), b2(6), b2(7), b4(1,2)\} \vdash \cup\{p(1,2), b3(5,6,Z)?, b3(5,7,Z)?\} \vdash \cup\{b3(5,6,8), b3(5,7,9)\} \vdash \cup\{p(5,8), p(5,9)\}$ □

4.3 A Measure of Parallelism

We now describe how the parallelism allowed by two evaluation methods can be compared.

Definition 4.3 Given two evaluation methods $\mathcal{M}_1$ and $\mathcal{M}_2$, we say that $\mathcal{M}_1$ is *more parallel than* $\mathcal{M}_2$ if and only if for every choice of a program $\langle P,Q \rangle$ and a set of sips S, the computation sequence according to $\mathcal{M}_1$ is no longer than the computation sequence according to $\mathcal{M}_2$.

By definition, our measure of parallelism will not allow us to compare computations that use different choices of sips, since the measure is defined in terms of a property that must hold for every choice of sips (and programs).

We remark that the length of a computation sequence corresponds to the time taken by the algorithm. For example, if we consider bottom-up fixpoint computation of a (rewritten) program, this length is equal to the number of *stages* or *iterations*.

We now present a result that is useful for proving that one method is more parallel than another.

Theorem 4.1 $\mathcal{M}_1$ *is more parallel than* $\mathcal{M}_2$ *if the following holds for every program* $\langle P,Q \rangle$ *and choice of sips* $\mathcal{S}$:

Let $\mathcal{F}_{1_i}$ and $\mathcal{G}_{1_i}$ denote the set of facts and goals in the state of the computation sequence S_1 according to $\mathcal{M}_1$ at Step i, and let $\mathcal{F}_{2_i}$ and $\mathcal{G}_{2_i}$ denote the corresponding sets for the computation sequence S_2 according to $\mathcal{M}_2$. For all i less than or equal to the length of S_1, $\mathcal{F}_{2_i} \subseteq \mathcal{F}_{1_i}$ and $\mathcal{G}_{2_i} \subseteq \mathcal{G}_{1_i}$.

The theorem does not hold in the only-if direction because we can choose arbitrary hidden states. Typically, considering methods in the literature, the only-if direction also holds. However, it is difficult to identify abstract conditions on hidden states that allow us to prove the claim in the only-if direction.

We identify two extreme classes of methods.

Definition 4.4 An evaluation method is said to be *maximally parallel* if no other method that implements the same choice of sips is more parallel in our abstract model of computation.

Definition 4.5 An evaluation method is said to be *sequential* if it is not more parallel in our abstract model of computation than any other method that implements the same choice of sips.

5 Bottom-Up Evaluation

The bottom-up approach that we consider is to take the program $\langle P,Q \rangle$, rewrite P according to the choice of sips, and to then evaluate the fixpoint by a bottom-up iteration.

To keep this paper self-contained, we present brief descriptions of the rewriting and iteration phases in this section.

5.1 The Magic Templates Rewriting

We present a simplified version of the algorithm, tailored to the case that sips are just partial orderings of the body literals in a rule, and that a single sip is associated with a rule, for all goals that invoke this rule. The reader is referred to [Ra88] for a more general algorithm capable of implementing more sophisticated sip choices, and also for a detailed discussion of bottom-up fixpoint computation in the presence of non-ground facts.

The idea is to compute a set of auxiliary predicates that contain the goals. The rules in the program are then modified by attaching additional literals that act as filters and prevent the rule from generating irrelevant tuples.

Definition 5.1 The Magic Templates Algorithm

We construct a new program P^{mg}. Initially, P^{mg} is empty.

1. Create a new predicate $magic\_p$ for each predicate p in P. The arity is that of p.

2. For each rule in P, add the *modified version* of the rule to P^{mg}. If rule r has head, say, $p(\bar{t})$, the modified version is obtained by adding the literal $magic\_p(\bar{t})$ to the body.

3. For each rule r in P with head, say, $p(\bar{t})$, and for each literal $q_i(\bar{t}_i)$ in its body, add a *magic rule* to P^{mg}. The head is $magic\_q_i(\bar{t}_i)$. The body contains all literals that precede q_i in the sip associated with this rule, and the literal $magic\_p(\bar{t})$.

4. Create a *seed* fact $magic\_q(\langle\bar{c}\rangle)$ from the query.

Example 5.1 Consider the following program.

$sg(X,Y) := flat(X,Y).$
$sg(X,Y) := up(X,U), sg(U,V), down(V,Y).$
$sg(john, Z)?$

For a choice of sips that orders body literals from left to right, as in Prolog, the Magic Templates algorithm rewrites it as follows:

$sg(X,Y) := magic\_sg(X,Y), flat(X,Y).$
$sg(X,Y) :=$
    $magic\_sg(X,Y), up(X,U), sg(U,V), down(V,Y).$

$magic\_sg(U,V) :=$
    $magic\_sg(X,Y), up(X,U).$
$magic\_sg(john, Z).$

□

We have the following results characterizing the transformed program P^{mg} with respect to the original program P, from [Ra88].

Theorem 5.1 [Ra88]
$\langle P, Q \rangle$ *is equivalent to* $\langle P^{mg}, Q \rangle$ *with respect to the set of answers to the query.*

Definition 5.2 Let us define the *Magic Templates Evaluation Method* as follows:

1. Rewrite the program $\langle P, Q \rangle$ according to the choice of sips using Magic Templates.

2. Evaluate the fixpoint of the rewritten program.

Theorem 5.2 [Ra88] *The Magic Templates Evaluation Method is a complete sip-method.*

The careful reader will notice that some joins are repeated in the bodies of rules defining magic predicates and modified rules. The *supplementary* version of the rewriting algorithm essentially identifies these common sub-expressions and stores them (with some optimizations that allow us to delete some columns from these intermediate, or supplementary, relations). We refer the reader to [BeR87] for details, with the remark that the variant is similar to the basic Magic Templates algorithm with respect to parallelism.

The problem of mapping a bottom-up fixpoint computation onto a fixed set of processors has received attention lately [WS88, CW89, Do89, GST89]. While considering this work is beyond the scope of this paper, we remark that the interaction of the techniques used in this work and the Magic Templates algorithm remains little understood and is an area for further study.

6 Comparing Methods

We now present some results characterizing the parallelism obtained by some proposed evaluation methods, using the abstract model of computation and measure of parallelism developed in Section 4.

We remark that in this section, positive results, of the form that one method is more parallel than another, are typically proved by an induction on the height of derivation trees for the program. Negative results, of the form that some degree of parallelism cannot (always) be achieved by a method, are typically established by considering an example and proving that the claim holds on this program. Several proofs are omitted from this extended abstract due to space constraints.

Our first result provides strong evidence in favor of the Magic Templates approach to parallel evaluation. We show that rewriting a program using the Magic Templates algorithm and then computing the fixpoint bottom-up realizes all the parallelism allowed by the choice of sips.

Theorem 6.1 Parallelism of Magic Templates

The Magic Templates evaluation method is maximally parallel.

Proof (Sketch) Let us denote the bottom-up fixpoint evaluation of the rewritten program as $\mathcal{M}$. We show that if there is a transition $\langle \mathcal{F}_1, \mathcal{G}_1, \mathcal{H}_1 \rangle \vdash_S \langle \mathcal{F}_2, \mathcal{G}_2, \mathcal{H}_2 \rangle$ according to a sip-method S that uses the same sips chosen for the rewriting algorithm, then there is a transition $\langle \mathcal{F}_1, \mathcal{G}_1, \mathbf{T} \rangle \vdash_\mathcal{M} \langle \mathcal{F}_2, \mathcal{G}_2, \mathbf{T} \rangle$. The proof proceeds by induction on the length of computations. As a basis, the initial state is always of the form $\langle \mathcal{F}, \mathcal{G}, \mathbf{T} \rangle$. The induction relies on the structure of rules defining "magic" predicates, and the fact that the hidden state for a bottom-up computation is always $\mathbf{T}$ since all goals and facts are visible (in the form of facts, the distinction no longer being significant) to all subcomputations. □

We remarked in Section 4 that the length of the computation sequence for an evaluation method (in our abstract model) corresponds to the time taken by the method. We have the following corollary.

Corollary 6.1 *Consider a logic program $\langle P, Q \rangle$. Let P^{mg} be the program obtained by applying the Magic Templates transformation to P. The length of the computation sequence (in our abstract model) for the bottom-up fixpoint evaluation of $\langle P^{mg}, Q \rangle$ is less than or equal to the length of the computation sequence for any sip-method on the same program and sips.*

Next, we consider similar results for other proposed evaluation methods. Let us define a *memoing* method to be one that maintains a copy of all generated goals and facts. The next theorem indicates that memoing methods achieve more parallelism since they avoid recomputing goals.

Theorem 6.2 Power of Memoing

No non-memoing method is maximally parallel.

Proof (Sketch) We show that the bottom-up evaluation of $\langle P^{mg}, Q \rangle$, a memoing method, obtains more parallelism on the following program $\langle P, Q \rangle$:

$p(X,Y) :- q1(X,Z), q2(Z,Y).$
$q1(X,Y) :- b(X,Y).$
$q2(X,Y) :- q1(X,Z), q3(Z,Y).$
$q3(X,Y) :- b(X,Y).$
$b(5,5).$
$p(5,U)?$

Intuitively, when the goal $q1(5, Z)?$ is generated a second time, in Rule 3, the solution $q1(5,5)$ has already been generated. Bottom-up evaluation can use this solution directly at the next step to identify the goal $q3(5, Y)?$. On the other hand, without memoing, we must re-solve this goal (generating the subgoal $b(5, Z)?$ and the facts $b(5,5), q1(5,5)$ in subsequent steps) before we can identify the goal $q3(Z, Y)?$. □

The difference in the program used in the above proof can be significant if the computation of the goal $q1(5, Z)?$ is expensive. The following result shows that the length of the computation sequence according to a non-memoing method may not even be polynomial in the length of the computation sequence according to bottom-up (memoing) evaluation of the rewritten program. This is not surprising if we require that both methods use the same sip: Consider the well-known Fibonacci program. It is easy to see that the bottom-up method is polynomial and that the non-memoing method is exponential in terms of the number of inferences. If we choose a left-to-right sip for the recursive rule, the computation is made sequential, and the difference in the number of inferences directly translates into a difference in the length of the computation sequence. The following result is stronger in that it is independent of the choice of sips. That is, there are programs such that the difference cannot be bridged by any choice of sips for the non-memoing method.

Theorem 6.3 *Consider a logic program $\langle P, Q \rangle$. Let the length of the computation sequence (in our abstract model, for some choice of sips) of the bottom-up evaluation of $\langle P^{mg}, Q \rangle$ be m, and let the length for computation according to a non-memoing method for some choice of sips be n. In general, the function g such that $n = g(m)$ is at least exponential, independent of the choice of sips for the non-memoing method.*

Since evaluation under the Reduce-Or model does not do memoing, the previous theorems show that it is not maximally parallel, and that the length of a computation may be exponentially longer than that of a computation according to the Magic Templates method.

Kalé discusses the parallelism obtained by several methods in [Ka87b], but without reference to a precise measure of parallelism, and the following theorems may be viewed as formalizations of the discussion in that paper.

Theorem 6.4 *Evaluation according to the Reduce-Or Model is maximally parallel relative to the class of methods that do not do any memoing.*

Theorem 6.5 *Evaluation according to a non-memoing method that exploits only And- or Or- parallelism, but not both, is strictly less parallel than evaluation according to the Reduce-Or process model.*

Proof (Sketch) The proof is similar to that of Theorem 6.2. We consider examples from [Ka87b], and show that the computation sequences for such methods are longer than the corresponding sequences according to the Reduce-Or model. □

Our next result illustrates a limitation of our measure of parallelism, which is that it does not allow us to compare certain pairs of evaluation methods.

Theorem 6.6 *Consider a method whose allowed transitions contain no Or-parallel steps, and one whose allowed transitions contain no And-parallel steps. Let both methods be more parallel than a sequential method. Then, neither method is more parallel than the other.*

6.1 Methods That Sacrifice Restriction for Parallelism

We present a result that indicates why we chose a definition of a sip-method that differs from the definition in [Ra88]. It also illustrates the trade-off between restricting search and parallelizing the computation.

Let us relax our definition of a sip-method in this subsection to also include methods that compute a set of the facts and goals, say $\mathcal{F}_1$ and $\mathcal{G}_1$, such that $ground(\mathcal{F} \cup \mathcal{G}) \subseteq ground(\mathcal{F}_1 \cup \mathcal{G}_1)$, where $\mathcal{F}$ and $\mathcal{G}$ are the sets that must be computed according to the definition of a sip-method in Section 4. This allows us to consider methods that are not sip-optimal, in that they do not eliminate all computation that is irrelevant according to the sips. As an extreme example, the bottom-up evaluation of the original program can be seen to implement any choice of sips (extremely inefficiently), since we can view it as generating a goal containing a vector of n distinct variables for each n-ary predicate, and obtaining all solutions. Thus, every possible goal with predicate name p is an instance of this most general goal for p. Intuitively, this allows us to work on all relevant goals immediately, but at the cost of additionally working on irrelevant goals. From the proof of Theorem 6.3, it is easy to see that any irrelevant computation can be made arbitrarily complex, even non-terminating, and thus the unrestricted computation sequence could be much longer than a restricted computation sequence. Thus, bottom-up evaluation of the original program is not necessarily more parallel than another evaluation method, by our measure of parallelism. This is pertinent when we wish to compute all answers and terminate, or if (as is likely) resources are limited. However, termination is in general undecidable, and even the restricted computation may not terminate. If resources are (effectively) unlimited, and we are only interested in obtaining answers as soon as possible, then, it might be worth evaluating the fixpoint of the original program without rewriting it to restrict the computation. This is justified by the following simple proposition.

Proposition 6.7 *Consider a logic program $\langle P, Q \rangle$. Let C_1 be the computation sequence in our abstract model for bottom-up fixpoint evaluation of this program, and let C_2 be the computation sequence for some other evaluation method, for some choice of sips. If a goal or fact appears at Step n in C_2, then it is subsumed by some fact that appears in C_1 at Step m, for some $m \leq n$.*

6.2 A Note on Magic Templates

The above results lead us to the following observation.

Remark: A claim such as Theorem 6.1 cannot be made for any other evaluation method that we are aware of. (It is possible to extend some of the methods so that such a claim holds.)

Such a remark is tedious to prove given the number of proposed methods, and so we simply offer an informal justification. First, from Theorem 6.2 it follows that we need only consider memoing methods as candidates. Of these, Alexander Templates [Se89] is the only one (other than Magic Templates) that is capable of dealing with non-ground facts. Examples are readily found where dealing with such facts is necessary to restrict search as per the sips we consider. Alexander Templates, like Magic Templates, rewrites the program and then evaluates the fixpoint, but it cannot deal with And-parallelism since it only allows left-to-right sips.

We note that this remark should be read with all the limitations of sip-methods and our measure of parallelism in mind; nevertheless, we believe that it is significant. First, as Kalé observes [Ka87a], identifying the available parallelism is a useful first step; it remains to consider efficient realizations. In this, we believe that the Magic Templates method offers considerable flexibility since it frees us from the constraints imposed by maintaining a network of processes and associated binding environments. We consider this point further in Section 8.

7 More On Sip-Methods

We have restricted out attention to evaluation methods that are sip-methods. This has allowed a fundamental separation of concerns: the sips specify the order in which rules are to be evaluated, that is, how bindings are to be propagated in order to restrict the computation, and the evaluation method implements this decision (a step that includes some choice of a control strategy). Not all proposed evaluation methods qualify as sip-methods. We now consider behaviour that cannot be captured by sip-methods, and attempt to extend our definition of sips, simultaneously indicating the necessary changes to the Magic Templates method. These extensions preserve the essential separation of concerns in the sip paradigm of computation. There are certain evaluation methods, however, whose behaviour we cannot capture even with the extended definitions of sips. We examine this and observe that there are some fundamental limitations to the sip paradigm; this implies that certain top-down methods cannot be mimicked by rewriting followed by fixpoint evaluation.

7.1 Multiple Sips Per Rule

Let us return to the survey in Section 3, and the discussion of And-Or trees. We made the assumption that for each And-node, there was a unique partial order that determined by the associated label. That is, each rule in the program has a unique partial ordering according to which the body literals are to be solved in any invocation of the rule. We could relax this assumption in several ways. Consider the set of possible goals with predicate name p. We could partition this set into several — preferably, but not necessarily, non-intersecting — subsets. For each rule defining p, for each such subset, we could choose a sip that indicates the order in which body literals are to be solved when the this must be done for each subset of goals.

One way to partition the set of goals is by means of a compile-time analysis that indicates which argument positions we expect to be bound. This leads to a notion of "bound" and "free" arguments, similar to "input" and "output" modes, that has been proposed and used by a number of researchers. We note that [Ra88] incorporates such an analysis into the Magic Templates algorithm. Recall that the algorithm adds a modified rule and a set of magic rules for each rule in the original program. If we wish to use a different ordering of body literals for goals in different subsets, in essence a modified rule and magic rules must be added for each subset.

All of the methods in Section 3 choose sips at compile time.

7.2 Dynamic Sips

It is possible that the choice of the order in which the body literals are to be solved is made at run-time when the rule is invoked. We briefly outline one way to incorporate this into the Magic Templates algorithm. The crux of the problem is that for each rule, we may wish to choose a different partial order at run-time for each goal. Noting that there are only a finite number of different partial orders over a finite set, we could simply generate modified and magic rules corresponding to each partial order. Now, we must determine which group of modified and magic rules is to be used for solving a given goal. To do this, we observe that the goal is described in these rules by a magic literal in the body, say $mp(\bar{t})$. We now add an additional literal $classify_{r\_s}(\bar{t})$ to the body. The s subscript denotes the subset of goals, and the corresponding choice of sips or partial ordering, for which this (modified or magic) rule was generated. If $p(\bar{t})$? is a generated goal, $classify_{r\_s}(\bar{t})$ must be true for some s (since it must be a member of one of the subsets of goals that we consider).

In effect, we have taken advantage of the finite number of partial orders to rewrite the program at compile time. However, we have abandoned a static classification of goals based on a compile-time analysis, such as "bound" and "free" arguments, in favor of a dynamic classification. We remark that this is not necessarily a win; our objective here is to examine the limits of the sip paradigm of computation, which we believe is essentially reached with the above formulation of dynamic sips.

7.3 Limitations of the Sip Paradigm

These limitations are seen when we examine evaluation methods that re-order goals in And-Or trees dynamically, but they can also be observed with a static ordering. Let us return to the discussion of And-Or trees, and consider And-nodes again. Let p and q be two body literals in the label of an And-node. Let $p1$ and $p2$ be body literals in a descendant And-node of p, and similarly $q1$ and $q2$ for q. A sip-method, even one that uses the dynamic sip selection of the previous subsection, must either order both $p1$ and $p2$ ahead of both $q1$ and $q2$, order the q's ahead of the p's, or leave the p's unordered relative to the q's. In particular, an evaluation method that requires the following solution order is not a sip-method: $p1, q1, p2, q2$.

This limitation arises, of course, because the sip mechanism only allows us to order goals that arise as body literals in a single rule. All subgoals of these goals must respect the above order. The sip formalism does not allow us to consider the resolvent that is the set of all subgoals and then pick an arbitrary order.

This is precisely what committed choice languages such as Parlog [CG86] and Concurrent Prolog [Sh86], the *freeze* primitive in Nu-Prolog [Na87], and some other proposed methods, e.g. in [Co83], achieve by dynamically suspending and starting goals. The ordering is controlled typically by variable annotations that, for example, suspend a goal until one of its variables is instantiated [CG86, Sh86, Na87]; it can also be controlled by a sophisticated run-time scheduler [Co83]. Methods that use annotations typically sacrifice completeness. Completely unrestricted dynamic re-ordering carries a high run-time overhead. Nevertheless, there may be situations where such approaches perform better than any sip-method. In particular, they permit coroutining.

8 Pragmatics

We briefly discuss several practical considerations.

8.1 Overheads

There are a number of important differences in the overheads associated with top-down and bottom-up evaluation. Top-down evaluation uses a recursive control strategy. A sequential implementation such as Prolog uses stacks to manage goals. Parallel methods generate a new process each goal, which carries a significant overhead on most systems. (Token based methods, e.g. [CH84], have their own additional overheads such as managing shared environments.) Bottom-up methods do not create a process per goal, but they recover the connections between facts and goals by explicit additional joins. This is typically also done by top-down methods that do memoing and aim to exploit both And- and Or- parallelism; however, significant optimization is possible in methods that only exploit a limited form of And-parallelism that results in a single binding for each variable at any point in the execution.

In this paper, we have assumed that the resources are sufficient to exploit all available parallelism. In the case that resources are limited, as is likely, the actual parallelism obtained will be curtailed by how efficiently the computation can be mapped onto the resources.

8.2 Load Sharing in Bottom-up Evaluation

The problem of mapping a bottom-up fixpoint computation onto a fixed set of processors has received attention lately. While considering this work is beyond the scope of this paper, we remark that the interactions of the techniques used in this work and the Magic Templates algorithm remain little understood and suggest an area for further study. We direct the interested reader to [WS88, CW89, Do89, GST89].

8.3 Some Added Advantages of Memoing

The remarks in this subsection apply equally to top-down and bottom-up methods that do memoing. As we have already seen, memoing offers gains in terms of avoiding redundant computation and increased parallelism. It also offers other important advantages:

1. *Multiple Query Optimization* Multiple queries may be seen as providing multiple "seeds" for the Magic Templates algorithm. Redundancy is avoided as before, whether it arises in the computation of one of the queries alone, or whether it arises due to common subcomputations in different top-level queries. In either case, some goal is generated more than once, and can be discarded after the first time, as before, if we have memoed the goal and solutions to it.

2. *Incremental Evaluation* If we wish to re-evaluate a query after adding some facts or rules to the program, the memoed results of the previous evaluation naturally enable us to avoid much recomputation. In the context of the Magic Templates algorithm, all memoed results can be taken to be assertions. Re-evaluation after deletions is more difficult, but some analysis of the affected predicates may allow us to retain many of the memoed relations.

3. *Improved Termination Properties* It is possible that memoing makes the difference between termination and non-termination. For example, consider the following program:

$$t(X,Y) :- t(X,Z), b(Z,Y).$$
$$t(X,Y) :- b(X,Y).$$
$$t(5,Y)?$$

This is a program on which Prolog will not terminate, repeatedly generating the goal $t(5,Z)?$, but memoing enables us to recognize that the goal has been generated before, and thereby devise modifications to Prolog that do terminate (e.g., see [Vi89]). In fact, this causes Prolog to be incomplete. We note that memoing is not essential for completeness; the Reduce-Or model [Ka87a] is complete, although it does not memoing. This is essentially because all paths are explored in parallel, and so even if some paths are non-terminating — and will never produce new solutions — all paths that do produce solutions are considered. However, the Reduce-Or computation will not terminate on this program. Memoing methods, including Magic Templates, terminate on it.

9 Conclusions

The main contributions of this paper are: (1) an abstract model of computation that allows us to make precise the degree of parallelism that is obtained by several proposed evaluation methods, (2) comparisons between methods based on this model, including the result that the Magic Templates algorithm is maximally parallel in this model, and (3) a discussion of the limitations of the abstract model, and in particular, the limitations of the sip paradigm on which the model is based.

In summary, we believe that our results provide strong motivation for a careful study of parallel evaluation of logic programs based on rewriting and subsequent fixpoint evaluation, as well as a sound basis for comparisons of parallelism in various logic program evaluation methods.

10 Acknowledgements

Conversations with Catriel Beeri, Sanjay Kalé, Michael Kifer, Jeff Naughton, Divesh Srivastava and S. Sudarshan have influenced this paper. I thank them for their generous input.

References

[BMSU86] F. Bancilhon, D. Maier, Y. Sagiv and J.D. Ullman, Magic Sets and Other Strange Ways to Implement Logic Programs. In *Proc. ACM Symposium on Principles of Database Systems*, pages 1-15, Boston, Massachusetts, March 1986.

[BaR86] F. Bancilhon and R. Ramakrishnan, An Amateur's Introduction to Recursive Query Processing Strategies. In *Proc. ACM SIGMOD International Conference on Management of Data*, pages 16-53, Washington, D.C., 1986. Revised and reprinted in *Readings in AI and Databases*, Eds. M. Brodie and J. Mylopoulos, pages 376-430, 1988.

[BeR87] C. Beeri and R. Ramakrishnan, On the Power of Magic. In *Proc. ACM Symposium on Principles of Database Systems*, pages 269-283, San Diego, California, March 1987.

[Br89] F. Bry, Query Evaluation in Recursive Databases: Bottom-up and Top-Down Reconciled. *ECRC TR IR-KB-64, April 1989.*

[CDD85] J.-H. Chang, A.M. Despain and D. DeGroot, AND-Parallelism of Logic Programs Based on A Static Data Dependency Analysis. In *Digest of Papers, Compcon 85, IEEE Computer Society, Feb. 1985.*

[CH83] A. Ciepielewski and S. Haridi, A Formal Model for Or-Parallel Execution of Logic Programs. In *Information Processing 83*, pages 299-305, North-Holland, Sept. 1983.

[CH84] A. Ciepielewski and S. Haridi, Control of Activities in the Or-Parallel Token Machine In *Proc. IEEE Symposium on Logic Programming, Atlantic City, Feb. 1984.*

[CG86] K.L. Clark and S. Gregory, Parlog: Parallel Programming in Logic. In *Transactions on Programming Languages*, pages 1-49, January 1986.

[CW89] S.R. Cohen and O. Wolfson, Why a Single Parallelization Strategy is Not Enough in Knowledge Bases. In *Proc. ACM Symposium on Principles of Database Systems*, pages 200-216, Philadelphia, Pennsylvania, March 1989.

[Co83] J. Conery, The And-Or Process Model for Parallel Interpretation of Logic Programs. *Ph.D. thesis, TR 204, Univ. of California, Irvine, June 1983.*

[De84] D. DeGroot, Restricted And-Parallelism. In *Proc. Intl. Conf. on Generation Computer Systems, ICOT, 1984.*

[DW87] S.W. Dietrich and D.S. Warren, Extension Tables: Memo Relations in Logic Programming. In *Proc. IEEE Symposium on Logic Programming, San Francisco, Sept. 1987.*

[Do89] G. Dong, On Distributed Processing of Datalog Queries by Decomposing Databases. In *Proc. ACM SIGMOD International Conference on Management of Data*, pages 26-35, Portland, 1986.

[EKM82] N. Eisinger, S. Kasif, J. Minker, Logic Programming: A Parallel Approach. In *Proc. First Logic Programming Conference, 1982.*

[GST89] S. Ganguly, A. Silberschatz, S. Tsur, A Framework for the Parallel Processing of Datalog Queries. *Manuscript.*

[HR89] M. Hermenegildo and F. Rossi, On the Correctness and Efficiency of Independent And-Parallelism in Logic Programms. In *Proc. N. American Conference on Logic Programming, pages 369-389, Cleveland, 1989.*

[Ka87a] L.V. Kalé, Parallel Execution of Logic Programs: The Reduce-Or Process Model. In *Proc. Intl. Conference on Logic Programming, pages 616-632, Melbourne, May 1987.*

[Ka87b] L.V. Kalé, Completeness and Full Parallelism of Parallel Logic Programming Schemes. In *Proc. IEEE Symposium on Logic Programming, pages 125-133, San Francisco, Sept. 1987.*

[KL86] M. Kifer and E. Lozinskii, A Framework for an Efficient Implementation of Deductive Databases. In *Proc. Advanced Database Symposium, Tokyo, 1986.*

[KL88] M. Kifer and E. Lozinskii, Sygraf: Implementing Logic Programs in a Database Style. In *Trans. on Software Engineering, pages 922-935, July 1988.*

[Lo85] E. Lozinskii, Evaluating Queries in Deductive Databases by Generating. In *Proc. Intl. Joint Conf. on Artificial Intelligence, pages 173-177, 1985.*

[Na87] L. Naish, Parallelizing Nu-Prolog. *Dept. of Computer Science, Univ. of Melbourne, TR 17, 1987.*

[NR89] J. Naughton and R. Ramakrishnan, A Unified Approach to Logic Program Evaluation. *Technical Report, Computer Sciences Department, Univ. of Wisconsin, Madison, 1989.*

[Po81] G.H. Pollard, Parallel Execution of Horn Clause Programs. *Ph.D. thesis, Imperial College of Science and Technology, Univ. of London, 1981.*

[Ra88] R. Ramakrishnan, Magic Templates: A Spellbinding Approach to Logic Programs. In *Proc. Intl. Conference on Logic Programming, pages 140-159, Seattle, Washington, August 1988.*

[RLK86] J. Rohmer, R. Lescoeur and J.M. Kerisit, The Alexander Method, a Technique for the Processing of Recursive Axioms in Deductive Databases. In *New Generation Computing, 4, 3, pages 273-285, 1986.*

[Se89] H. Seki, On the Power of Alexander Templates. In *Proc. 8th ACM SIGMOD-SIGACT Symposium on Principles of Database Systems, pages 150-159, 1989.*

[Sh86] E. Shapiro, Concurrent Prolog: A Progress Report. In *IEEE Computer, pages 44-58, August 1986.*

[Ul89a] J.D. Ullman, Principles of Database and Knowledge-Base Systems, Volumes 1 and 2. *Computer Science Press, 1989.*

[Ul89b] J.D. Ullman, Bottom-Up Beats Top-Down for Datalog, In *Proc. 8th ACM SIGMOD-SIGACT Symposium on Principles of Database Systems, pages 140-149, 1989.*

[vG86] A. van Gelder, A Message Passing Framework for Logical Query Evaluation. In *Proc. ACM SIGMOD International Conference on Management of Data, pages 16-53, Washington, D.C., 1986.*

[vEK76] M. van Emden and R. Kowalski, The Semantics of Predicate Logic as a Programming Language. In *JACM 28, no. 4, pages 733-742, Oct. 1976.*

[Vi89] L. Vieille, Recursive Query Processing: The Power of Logic To appear in *Theoretical Computer Science, 1989.*

[WS88] O. Wolfson and A. Silberschatz, Sharing the Load of Logic Program Evaluations. In *Proc. 7th ACM SIGMOD-SIGACT Symposium on Principles of Database Systems, 1988.*

Combining Generational and Conservative Garbage Collection: Framework and Implementations

Alan Demers
Mark Weiser
Barry Hayes
Hans Boehm
Daniel Bobrow
Scott Shenker

Xerox Palo Alto Research Center
Palo Alto, Ca 94304

SUMMARY

Two key ideas in garbage collection are *generational collection* and *conservative pointer-finding*. Generational collection and conservative pointer-finding are hard to use together, because generational collection is usually expressed in terms of copying objects, while conservative pointer-finding precludes copying. We present a new framework for defining garbage collectors. When applied to generational collection, it generalizes the notion of younger/older to a partial order. It can describe traditional generational and conservative techniques, and lends itself to combining different techniques in novel ways. We study in particular two new garbage collectors inspired by this framework. Both these collectors use conservative pointer-finding. The first one is based on a rewrite of an existing trace-and-sweep collector to use one level of generation. The second one has a single parameter, which controls how objects are partitioned into generations; the value of this parameter can be changed dynamically with no overhead. We have implemented both collectors and present measurements of their performance in practice.

I. Introduction

Garbage collectors fall into two general classes: reference-counting and tracing. In this paper we consider only tracing collectors. A tracing garbage collector works by starting with a root set of memory objects, following the pointers found there to other memory objects that should be preserved, and so on recursively, until all objects accessible from the roots have been found. Inaccessible objects are garbage and can be reclaimed.

Garbage collection has a colorful past. It is considered essential by some programming subcultures, such as those from a Lisp heritage, and is considered superfluous or dangerous by other subcultures, such as those from a systems programming or real-time background. However, there has been some use of garbage collection in systems programming [Rovner85] [Weiser89] [Cardelli88], and even real-time constraints are possible [Baker78] [Appel88]. In general, interest in garbage collection is growing.

Garbage collection is almost never shared among multiple language implementations. Instead, every language with garbage collection does it differently, even idiosyncratically, because collection usually depends on implementation assumptions about the uses of pointers. There is, however, a technique for identifying pointers that is nearly language-independent. This technique, called *conservative pointer-finding*, identifies a superset of the true pointers, in effect by treating every word of a memory object as if it *might* possibly contain a pointer [Boehm88]. Conservative pointer-finding precludes copying objects—when an object is copied, every pointer to that object must be updated to refer to the new location, but conservative pointer-finding cannot distinguish pointers from integers.

so updating them is not safe.

One can combine partially conservative with partially copying collection [Bartlett88]. Other techniques, such as calling language-dependent pointer-finding routines during the trace (which we do), further relieve the problems of conservative pointer knowledge.

A key method for achieving high performance garbage collection is to concentrate reclamation effort on recently allocated objects. This technique, a version of which was used as early as 1975 in the SITBOL collector [Hanson77] [Ripley78], has come to be known as "generational collection", because it classifies objects by how old they are [Lieberman83]. Generational collectors have always been copying collectors, partly because copying results in more compact storage (and thus fewer total pages in use), but primarily because generations have always been defined and implemented in terms of different memory spaces segregated by object ages. Since generational collection has become widely known, almost all new implementations use this technique [Unger84] [Moon84] [Sobalvarro88] [Courts87] [Wilson89]. It has substantial performance benefits, and is compatible with real-time performance requirements.

Conservative collection has great potential for being the foundation of a language-independent system of collection, but precludes copying in the general case. Generational collection is extremely important for high-performance collection, but seems to require copying of objects. Combining the two is the challenge we took on, and the result is two-fold: first, a better theoretical framework for understanding garbage collection in general, and generational collection in particular; second, several new implementations of garbage collectors based on this theoretical framework. Although our framework applies to previous generational collectors as well, the new ones we have implemented all have the property that they use conservative pointers and so do not copy. Partially copying collectors, in the style of Bartlett, are also possible, but we haven't done them.

II. Collector Theory

Storage model and partial garbage collection

We fix on a model of computer storage in which there is a countably infinite set O of *objects*, with a distinguished *root object* $r \in O$.

1: Definition. A *storage state* S is a pair $\langle AS, P \rangle$, where AS, the *allocated set*, is a finite subset of O, and $P \subseteq O \times O$, the *points-to relation*, is a reflexive binary relation on O. □

2: Definition. A storage state is *valid* if it satisfies the following invariants:

$I_0 : r \in AS$.
$I_1 : ((\langle a, b \rangle \in P) \land (a \in AS)) \Rightarrow (b \in AS)$.
$I_2 : ((\langle a, b \rangle \in P) \land (a \notin AS)) \Rightarrow (b = a)$. □

Reflexivity of P is required for technical reasons. Since the garbage collectors described below are essentially computing the reflexive transitive closure P^*, the assumption that P is reflexive has no effect on their operation.

3: Remark. In any valid storage state, all objects reachable from the root are allocated; that is, $P^*(r) \subseteq AS$. □

The client program, or *mutator*, repeatedly makes changes to the storage state. The only assumption we make about these changes is that they preserve validity.

The *garbage collector*, which runs repeatedly and atomically with respect to the mutator, *reclaims* selected objects by deleting them from AS; the collector is *valid* if it accomplishes this without changing P on allocated objects and without violating the invariants. Formally,

4: Definition. A *garbage collection* of storage state $\langle AS, P \rangle$ is a a storage state $\langle AS', P' \rangle$ such that

$AS' \subseteq AS$, and
$(a \in AS') \Rightarrow (P'(a) = P(a))$.

The collection is *valid* if

$(\langle AS, P \rangle \text{ valid}) \Rightarrow (\langle AS', P' \rangle \text{ valid})$.

A *(valid) garbage collector* is a function mapping storage states to (valid) garbage collections. □

Stated in these terms, a garbage collector is completely characterized by the strategy it uses to choose AS', the set of *retained* objects. Clearly, choosing AS' to be exactly the *reachable* set $P^*(r)$ yields a valid collection. We call this collection *precise*, because of the following:

5: Lemma. If $\langle AS', P' \rangle$ is a valid garbage collection of $\langle AS, P \rangle$, then

$AS' = P^*(AS') \supseteq P^*(r)$. □

A collection that retains a proper superset of $P^*(r)$ is called *partial* (since it reclaims only part of the unreachable memory). As we discuss below, there can be compelling practical reasons for building a valid partial garbage collector rather than a precise one.

Not every superset of $P^*(r)$ yields a valid partial collection according to our theory. By Lemma 5 above, we require that the retained set AS' be closed under P. It is possible to argue that *every* tracing collector must identify a "reachable" set that is closed under P. However, one can imagine building a collector that does not reclaim all the objects it identifies as unreachable (e.g. because some of them are on nonresident pages). Our theory would not apply to such a collector. In addition, the theory says nothing about running time, which is in any event implementation-dependent. The theory does enable us to determine formally sets of objects that can be collected and sets of objects that may safely be ignored during a collection.

We can characterize those supersets of $P^*(r)$ that yield valid partial collections with the help of the following:

6: Definition. Let $\langle AS, P \rangle$ and $\langle AS, Q \rangle$ be valid storage states. Then $\langle AS, Q \rangle$ is a *pointer augmentation* of $\langle AS, P \rangle$ if $Q \supseteq P$. □

7: Theorem. Let $\langle AS, P \rangle$ be a valid storage state. $AS' \subseteq AS$ yields a valid garbage collection iff $AS' = Q^*(r)$, where $\langle AS, Q \rangle$ is a pointer augmentation of $\langle AS, P \rangle$. □

This theorem states that, for the class of garbage collectors we are considering, every valid partial collection is equivalent to a precise collection on a pointer augmentation of the true state.

Posets, embeddings and pointer augmentation

Here we define an embedding of a storage state in a partially-ordered set. We argue that any pointer augmentation can be induced by an appropriately-chosen embedding. By Theorem 7 above, every valid partial collection is equivalent to a pointer augmentation plus a precise collection. Combining these results, we are assured that one can fully explore the space of valid partial garbage collections by exploring the space of embeddings.

8: Definition. A *pointed partially ordered set*, (hereafter *poset*), is a triple $\langle D, \geq, \perp \rangle$, where D is a nonempty set, $\geq$ is a reflexive, transitive and antisymmetric relation on D, and $\perp \in D$ such that $\forall x \in D \; x \geq \perp$. □

9: Definition. Let $D = \langle D, \geq, \perp \rangle$ be a poset, and let $S = \langle AS, P \rangle$ be a valid storage state. An *embedding* of S into D is a pair $\langle F, A \rangle$ of functions from O into D such that
$$\forall a, b \in O \; \langle a, b \rangle \in P \Rightarrow F(a) \geq A(b).$$
An embedding $\langle F, A \rangle$ determines an *induced points-to relation* $P_{F,A}$ on O by
$$\langle a, b \rangle \in P_{F,A} \text{ iff } F(a) \geq A(b)$$
$$\wedge ((a = b) \vee ((a \in AS) \wedge (b \in AS))).$$
The embedding is said to be *lossless* if $P_{F,A} = P$. □

A natural correspondence between embeddings and pointer augmentations is given by the following two lemmas. Lemma 10 states that every embedding induces a pointer augmentation; lemma 11 states that every pointer augmentation is induced by some embedding.

10: Lemma. Let $S = \langle AS, P \rangle$ be a valid storage state, and let $\langle F, A \rangle$ be an embedding of S in poset $D = \langle D, \geq, \perp \rangle$. Then $\langle AS, P_{F,A} \rangle$ is a pointer augmentation of $\langle AS, P \rangle$, and $\langle F, A \rangle$ is a lossless embedding of $\langle AS, P_{F,A} \rangle$ in D. □

11: Lemma. Let $S = \langle AS, P \rangle$ be a valid storage state, and let $S' = \langle AS, P' \rangle$ be a pointer augmentation of S. Then there exists a poset $D = \langle D, \geq_D, \perp_D \rangle$ and an embedding $\langle F, A \rangle$ of S in D such that $P_{F,A} = P'$. That is, $\langle F, A \rangle$ is a lossless embedding of S' in D. □

Pointer augmentations can be performed directly on embeddings with the aid of the following:

12: Definition. Let $D = \langle D, \geq_D, \perp_D \rangle$ and $E = \langle E, \geq_E, \perp_E \rangle$ be posets. A function h from D to E is a *homomorphism* from D to E if it is strict and monotonic. □

13: Lemma. Let $D = \langle D, \geq_D, \perp_D \rangle$ and $E = \langle E, \geq_E, \perp_E \rangle$ be posets, and let h be a homomorphism from D to E. Let $S = \langle AS, P \rangle$ be a valid storage state, and $\langle F, A \rangle$ an embedding of S in D. Then $\langle h \circ F, h \circ A \rangle$ is an embedding of S in E with $P_{h \circ F, h \circ A} \supseteq P_{F,A} \supseteq P$. □

In the above lemma, $\langle AS, P_{h \circ F, h \circ A} \rangle$ is a pointer augmentation of $\langle AS, P \rangle$. Further, $\langle AS, P_{h \circ F, h \circ A} \rangle$ is losslessly embedded in E by $\langle h \circ F, h \circ A \rangle$. Thus, a homomorphism on the range of an embedding induces a pointer augmentation. As before, we can prove something very close to the converse:

14: Lemma. Let $S = \langle AS, P \rangle$ be a valid storage state. There exists a poset $D = \langle D, \geq_D, \perp_D \rangle$, called a *canonical poset* for S, and a lossless embedding $\langle F, A \rangle$ of S in D, called a *canonical* embedding for S, with the following property. For any pointer augmentation $S' = \langle AS, P' \rangle$, there exists a poset $D' = \langle D', \geq_{D'}, \perp_{D'} \rangle$ and a homomorphism h from D to D' such that $\langle h \circ F, h \circ A \rangle$ is a lossless embedding of S' in D'.

Proof (sketch): To construct a canonical embedding for storage state $S = \langle AS, P \rangle$, we let
$$D = \{\perp_D\} \cup (O \times \{0, 1\}),$$
and let $\geq_D$ be the reflexive closure of the relation
$$\{\langle \langle a, 0 \rangle, \langle b, 1 \rangle \rangle \mid \langle a, b \rangle \in P\}.$$
It is easy to verify that $\geq_D$ so defined is transitive and antisymmetric, so $D = \langle D, \geq_D, \perp_D \rangle$ is a poset. It is also easy to verify that the pair of functions $\langle F, A \rangle$ given by
$$F(a) = \langle a, 0 \rangle \qquad A(a) = \langle a, 1 \rangle$$
is a lossless embedding of S in D. Now if $S' = \langle AS, P' \rangle$ is any pointer augmentation of S, the identity function on $(O \times \{0, 1\})$ yields the required homomorphism between the canonical posets for S and S'. □

Thus, any pointer augmentation on a storage state S can be induced by a suitably chosen homomorphism on the canonical embedding for S.

Constructing partial collectors from embeddings

In practice, there are two basic reasons to build a partial collector rather than a precise one. First, the actual points-to relation may be unavailable. This comes about in languages like C, where the typing system provides too little information to identify all the pointers, making it necessary to use a conservative pointer-finding strategy. Second, some easily-identified subset of the allocated objects may be richer in collectable objects than the entire allocated set. In that case, collecting from only that subset can reclaim a large fraction of the unreachable objects at substantially less cost than a full collection. This is the basis of generational collection schemes. The savings that result can be dramatic on machines with virtual memory — a well-designed generational collector can cause far fewer page faults than a full collector. Either of these sources of imprecision, or their combination, can be expressed in a natural way as the pointer augmentation induced by an embedding.

It is straightforward to express conservative pointer-finding: the conservative points-to relation is simply a pointer augmentation of the true points-to relation, and so by Lemma 11 can be expressed as the induced points-to relation of an embedding. Our storage model disallows pointers to unallocated objects, and the conservative pointer-finding collectors described below do the same — roughly, a bit pattern is not treated as a pointer unless its value is the address of an allocated object.

Describing a generational garbage collector is only slightly more involved. Informally, a generational collector works by partitioning the allocated objects into *threatened* objects, which are candidates for collection, and *immune* objects, which will not be collected. Optionally, the collector may then be able to identify efficiently a set of objects called the *bystanders*, which are guaranteed not to contain pointers into the threatened set. The identified bystander set need not include *all* objects without pointers into the threatened set, but it is advantageous to identify as many bystanders as possible, since the collector does not need to trace through bystanders.

For a garbage collection described by an embedding, immune and bystander sets are easily identified as follows. Let $S = \langle AS, P \rangle$ be a valid storage state, let $D = \langle D, \geq, \perp \rangle$ be a poset, and let $\langle F, A \rangle$ be an embedding of S in D. Consider the collection described by $\langle F, A \rangle$, that is, the precise collection on $\langle AS, P_{F,A} \rangle$. The immune set consists of all allocated objects in $A^{-1}(\perp)$. Similarly, the bystander set consists of all allocated objects in $F^{-1}(\perp)$. To see this, consider the points-to relation $P_{F,A}$. The pairs in this relation that are of interest to us are the ones between allocated objects, since these are the only ones that affect the reachable set. By Definition 9, if a and b are allocated objects and $b \in A^{-1}(\perp)$, then $\langle a, b \rangle \in P_{F,A}$. That is, every allocated object in $A^{-1}(\perp)$ is pointed to by every allocated object. In particular, every allocated object in $A^{-1}(\perp)$ is directly pointed to by the root object r. Thus, no such object can be collected, and we can identify $AS \cap A^{-1}(\perp)$ as the immune set. Again by Definition 9, if $a \in F^{-1}(\perp)$ and $\langle a, b \rangle \in P_{F,A}$ then $b \in A^{-1}(\perp)$. That is, the only nontrivial pointers from objects in $F^{-1}(\perp)$ go to allocated objects in $A^{-1}(\perp)$. Since there are no pointers from objects in $F^{-1}(\perp)$ to objects in the threatened set (which is given by $AS - A^{-1}(\perp)$), we can identify $AS \cap F^{-1}(\perp)$ as the bystander set.

To describe generational garbage collection, we would like to be able first to choose an immune set and then to introduce a pointer augmentation that determines exactly the chosen immune set. Here we describe a useful family of immune sets for which this process is particularly easy.

15: Definition. An *ideal* in a poset $D = \langle D, \geq, \perp \rangle$ is a nonempty downward-closed subset of D. □

As before, we begin with an embedding $\langle F, A \rangle$ of storage state S in poset D. We choose an ideal $I \subseteq D$ such that $AS \cap A^{-1}(I)$ is the desired immune set. Define the function h from D to D by

$$h(x) = \begin{cases} \perp & x \in I \\ x & \text{otherwise} \end{cases}$$

Clearly h yields a homomorphism from D to D. Thus, by Lemma 13, $\langle AS, P_{h \circ F, h \circ A} \rangle$ is a pointer augmentation of $\langle AS, P_{F,A} \rangle$, and $\langle h \circ F, h \circ A \rangle$ is a lossless embedding of $\langle AS, P_{h \circ F, h \circ A} \rangle$ into D. Straightforward computation yields

$$P_{h \circ F, h \circ A} = P_{F,A} \cup \{ \langle a, b \rangle \mid a \in AS \land b \in AS \land b \in (h \circ A)^{-1}(\perp) \}.$$

That is, $P_{h \circ F, h \circ A}$ consists exactly of $P_{F,A}$ augmented by pointers from all allocated objects to the objects in the chosen immune set. A precise garbage collection of $\langle AS, P_{h \circ F, h \circ A} \rangle$ is the best one possible, given the choice of immune set, in the following sense: for any valid collection $\langle AS', P' \rangle$ of $\langle AS, P_{F,A} \rangle$,

$$AS' \supseteq (AS \cap A^{-1}(I)) \Rightarrow$$
$$AS' \supseteq (P_{h \circ F, h \circ A})^*(r).$$

That is, any valid collection of $\langle AS, P_{F,A} \rangle$ that retains all the chosen immune objects must retain all the objects in $(P_{h \circ F, h \circ A})^*(r)$.

Combining collection strategies

Here we show how the collections described by two different embeddings can be combined in a natural way by combining the embeddings.

16: Definition. Let $D_1 = \langle D_1, \leq_1, \perp_1 \rangle$ and $D_2 = \langle D_2, \leq_2, \perp_2 \rangle$ be posets. The *(strict) Cartesian product* $D_1 \times D_2$ is the poset $D = \langle D, \leq, \perp \rangle$ where

$$D = \{\perp\} \cup \{ \langle x_1, x_2 \rangle \mid x_1 \in D_1 - \{\perp_1\} \land x_2 \in D_2 - \{\perp_2\} \},$$

$\perp \leq \perp$,

$\perp \leq \langle x_1, x_2 \rangle$, and

$\langle x_1, x_2 \rangle \leq \langle y_1, y_2 \rangle$ iff $x_1 \leq_1 y_1 \land x_2 \leq_2 y_2$.

Below we use the notational convention that pairing is a strict operation; i.e., that

$$\langle x_1, \perp \rangle = \langle \perp, x_2 \rangle = \langle \perp, \perp \rangle = \perp. \quad \square$$

17: Definition. Let $f : S \to D$ and $g : S \to E$ be functions; we define $f \otimes g : S \to D \times E$ by

$$(f \otimes g)(x) = \langle f(x), g(x) \rangle \quad \forall x \in S. \quad \square$$

18: Remark. If $f(x) = \perp$ or $g(x) = \perp$ then $(f \otimes g)(x) = \perp$. In particular,

$$(f \otimes g)^{-1}(\perp) = f^{-1}(\perp) \cup g^{-1}(\perp). \quad \square$$

19: Lemma. Let $S = \langle AS, P \rangle$ be a valid storage state; let $\langle F, A \rangle$ and $\langle F', A' \rangle$ be embeddings of S into D and D', respectively. Then $\langle F \otimes F', A \otimes A' \rangle$ is an embedding of S into $D \times D'$. Further,

$$P_{F \otimes F', A \otimes A'} = P_{F,A} \cap P_{F',A'}$$
$$\cup \{ \langle a, b \rangle \mid (a \in AS) \land (b \in AS) \land ((A \otimes A')(b) = \perp) \}. \quad \square$$

The last term in the expression for $P_{F \otimes F', A \otimes A'}$ above arises from strictness of the pairing operation. Intuitively, $P_{F \otimes F', A \otimes A'}$ consists of $P_{F,A} \cap P_{F',A'}$ augmented by pointers from all allocated objects to the objects in the union of the immune sets determined by A and by A'. Thus, a precise collection of $\langle AS, P_{F \otimes F', A \otimes A'} \rangle$ has the effect of using the union of the immune sets together with all the pointer information available from $P_{F,A}$ and $P_{F',A'}$.

Taking the Cartesian product of two embeddings in this way is a particularly powerful tool for defining a generational collector. For example, let $\langle F, A \rangle$ be an embedding of S into poset D that induces the most accurate points-to information available. Without loss of generality, assume that $A^{-1}(\perp) = \emptyset$. (It is easy to exclude $\perp$ from the range of A, by adding a new bottom element and "lifting" D if necessary). Let $\langle F', A' \rangle$ be an embedding of S into D' such that $(AS \cap A'^{-1}(\perp))$ is the desired immune set. Consider the precise collection of $\langle AS, P_{F \otimes F', A \otimes A'} \rangle$. For all threatened objects the induced points-to relation $P_{F \otimes F', A \otimes A'}$ is at least as accurate as $P_{F,A}$. The immune and threatened sets, however, are determined entirely by $P_{F',A'}$. Thus, we can make $\langle F', A' \rangle$ as simple (and as easy to compute) as we desire without losing any of the pointer information encoded in $\langle F, A \rangle$.

III. Introduction to Practice

We have implemented two collectors described by the theory presented above. For each collector, we first explain its operation in terms of an intuitive partial order and A and F functions. We then summarize the implementation and present some performance numbers to indicate that the theory leads to practical new strategies.

Both our implementations use total orders, rather than strictly partial orders. We believe there are important uses of partial orders, but our first order of business was to show that our theory led to new and practical collectors in more conventional domains, and this led us to generational collection, where the natural partial order is linear time.

Both our implementations use a trick of implementation of A's and F's motivated by temporal causality of pointers, as follows: A pointer written at time t cannot point to an object allocated at time $t' > t$. Therefore, if $F(a)$ is the time at which a last had a pointer written to it, and $A(b)$ is the time of allocation of b, then the invariant

$$\forall\, a, b \in O\ \langle a, b\rangle \in P \Rightarrow F(a) \geq A(b)$$

is true by causality. Naturally this is not as precise as possible, since the pointer written at time $F(a)$ might have been to an object with allocation time well before $F(a)$. On the other hand, standard virtual memory support, such as page write-protection or dirty bits, is sufficient to enable us to maintain the invariant.

Another practical issue in our implementations is using summary, per-"card", information rather than per-object information. A card is a single contiguous region of memory together with information about the objects contained in that region. There are usually several cards per physical page of memory. Cards are used to reduce the per-object overhead of information like A and F, by storing the information only once per card. We use the term "card pollution" to refer to the imprecision that results from maintaining information on a per-card rather than a per-object basis. For example, when keeping A and F values per card, the invariant $\forall\, a, b \in O\ \langle a, b\rangle \in P \Rightarrow F(a) \geq A(b)$ requires that $A(c)$ be the minimum A, and $F(c)$ be the maximum F, for all the objects on card c. Pollution then results as $A(c)$ gets smaller than max($A(a)$) for all a on c, and as $F(c)$ gets larger than min($F(a)$) for all a on c.

One basic technique to avoid pollution is to remove cards from use by the allocator when their objects have lasted for a few generations. This keeps max(A) from growing. It also has an indirect effect on F pollution by avoiding turnover of objects on the card, and so keeping the F values stable and not growing to point to objects with later birthdays. Each collector below has its own scheme for avoiding pollution.

IV. Collector I

As one experiment, we modified an existing trace-and-sweep collector (a descendant of the one described in [Boehm88]) to be generational. The strategy for a partial collection can be described in terms of the following embedding of the storage state. Consider the poset $B = \langle \{0,1\},\ \geq,\ 0\rangle$, with the intuition that 0 represents "old" objects, allocated before the last collection, and 1 represents "new" objects. We define $A(a) = 1$ if a was allocated since the last collection, and 0 otherwise; $F(a) = 0$ if it is known that a has not been altered since the last collection, and 1 otherwise. By the causality argument above, this definition of A's and F's preserves our invariants, and so is a legitimate embedding. Poset B has only one interesting ideal, namely $\{0\}$. As discussed in Section II above, the immune set associated with this embedding, $A^{-1}(0)$, consists of all objects allocated before the last collection.

The actual collection strategy used by Collector I is described by the Cartesian product of the above embedding with an embedding for conservative pointer-finding. We now show that this strategy allows a simple and efficient implementation.

Sticky Mark Bits

Collector 1 may be viewed as a modification of a conventional mark-sweep collector, in which we sometimes neglect to reset the mark bits between collections. In this way, every object that survived the last collection has its mark bit set, and thus the mark bit can also be interpreted as the A value of the object corresponding to the poset B. Therefore we dubbed this approach "sticky mark bit" collection.

The algorithm for a full garbage collection in a conventional mark-sweep collector can be expressed as follows:

    1. Clear all mark bits.
    2. Mark all objects reachable from the roots.
    3. Reclaim all unmarked objects.

The algorithm for a partial garbage collection is only slightly different. We attempt to reclaim only those objects allocated since the last collection (i.e., not marked by it). Thus, for partial collections, we do not perform step 1. This implicitly establishes the A values corresponding to the poset B. The bystanders are those objects with F value of 0, that is, those objects that have not been altered since the last collection. These do not need to be considered. We assume that all other immune objects are reachable, and treat then as additional roots. This is implemented by replacing step 1 by:

    1'. Mark from all modified marked objects.

As in Collector II below, we have no way of identifying modified objects other than through the paging hardware. Thus step 1' must be implemented as:

    1''. Mark from all marked objects on dirty cards.

This is the only substantial difference between full and partial collections. In practice it is important to intersperse partial collections with full collections, since a significant number of short-lived objects will survive a single collection.

We can state A and F more precisely now in terms of our implementation: Every object has two properties: $M(a)$ is true if a is marked, and $D(a)$ is true if a is on a page that has been dirtied. Then the following mapping expresses A and F values in terms of the information maintained by the algorithm:

$$M(a) \Rightarrow A(a) = 0$$
$$\sim M(a) \Rightarrow A(a) = 1$$
$$M(a) \wedge D(a) \Rightarrow F(a) = 1$$
$$M(a) \wedge \sim D(a) \Rightarrow F(a) = 0$$
$$\sim M(a) \Rightarrow F(a) = 1$$

Results from Collector I

We replaced the standard garbage collector and allocator in Ibuki Common Lisp [IBUKI87] with our Collector I, using a card size of 4096 bytes. We measured collection times for the Boyer benchmark from the Gabriel benchmarks [Gabriel85], and for the Ibuki Common Lisp compiler compiling its two largest modules of about 1000 lines each. The heap size was fixed at 2.5M, and full trace-and-sweep was performed just before measurement began. The tests were performed on a Sun-3/260 with 24MB ram. All programs fit in real memory, and the machine was essentially unloaded during the tests. Measured times are in seconds of Unix user+system time.

We compared collection times for two different collection policies:

> **Policy 1**: All collections are full trace-and-sweep, triggered when the heap is full.
>
> **Policy 2**: A partial collection is triggered after approximately every 100 Kbytes of allocation. Such collections ignore cards that are more than 3/4 full. A full collection is triggered when all cards are more than 3/4 full.

Under both policies, the sweep phase is deferred almost entirely until allocation time. This may save some time, since some cards are never swept, and it always reduces garbage collection pauses. Dirty bits are simulated by checksumming cards. We excluded the deferred sweep time and the (substantial) checksumming overhead from the measurements.

For the Boyer benchmark under policy 1, a typical run took 3 collections, with a total time of 8.5 seconds. (About 2.7 additional seconds were spent sweeping during allocation.) Essentially the full heap of more than 600 pages was touched during every collection.

Under policy 2 there were typically 30 partial collections, plus an average of 1.4 full collections. An average of only 42 cards were touched per partial collection. Total collection time per iteration was 21.5 seconds (plus about 3.2 seconds delayed sweep overhead). The new collector was therefore slower in cpu time, but it touched far fewer pages during most collections. For applications running in limited physical memory, this advantage would certainly outweigh the increase in cpu time. Also, garbage collection pauses were reduced from about 3 seconds (under policy 1) to about 1/2 second, and thus would have been unnoticeable on a slightly faster machine.

The number of remaining full collections is relatively high in this example, since the heap becomes close to full. One explanation is that the heap is sufficiently full that even a complete collection may free only a third of the heap. We would also no doubt benefit from collecting slightly less frequently, thus reducing the number of short-lived objects that "accidentally" survive until the next full collection. This would also substantially reduce the required cpu time. We observed that if we also postpone partial collections until the heap fills up, we incur only about a 40% cpu time overhead, but still keep the number of pages touched in a partial collection down to about half.

For the compilation benchmark we obtained similar performance results. Policy 1 resulted in an average of 2.8 collections per benchmark iteration, with a garbage collection time of 7.3 seconds. Policy 2 reduced the number of full collections to exactly one per iteration, but added 26 partial collections. Total collection time went up to 20.7 seconds. About 57 cards were touched by each partial collection.

V. Collector II.

Our second collector, rather than using a single bit for time, uses the integers starting at zero. CurrentTime increases by one each collection. Rather than implicit A and F functions as in Collector I, we use explicit A and F functions related to object birthdays: $A(a)$ is the time at which a was first created, and $F(a)$ is the latest creation time of any object directly pointed to by a.

For efficiency, A and F values are maintained per-card rather than per-object, as discussed above. The A-value of a card is set when the card is used for the first time and never altered until the card is completely empty. The F-value is computed by remembering its value when we are scanning the pointers on the card during a collection. To maintain the F-values, cards with a valid F-value are write-protected. When a write occurs on a physical page, we turn off the protection and remember that the cards on that page no longer have valid F-values. At the next collection these cards will be considered to point into the threatened cards and so will be rescanned, recomputing their F-values.

A collection begins with the identification of a *threatening boundary* (TB), which is simply an integer between 0 and currentTime. Objects on cards with A-values strictly less than TB are immune; objects on cards with F-values strictly less than TB are bystanders. Thus, TB=0 does a full trace-and-sweep. TB>0 does a generational collection back some distance into the past.

To reduce card pollution, Collector II removes a card from consideration for allocation when it is three-fourths full and its A-value is two generations old. If it later becomes half full, it is again available for use by the allocator. To reduce paging overhead, Collector II also uses a version of trace-queueing, described in Section VI.

Results from Collector II

Measurements of Collector II used the same setup and benchmarks as measurements of Collector I, with the exception that cards were reduced to 512 bytes. Measurements of Collector II were done on a Sun-4/260, a faster machine than the Sun 3, with a significantly different architecture. Therefore, no direct comparison should be made between the times given in the previous section and those in this section.

We compared collection times for two different collection policies:

> **Policy 1**: Trace-and-Sweep. TB always 0, collect when heap is three-fourths full.

> **Policy 2**: Generational. TB = currentTime-1, collect every 100k bytes allocated.

For Boyer, the generational collector did 31 collections, using a total time for all GC's of 43 seconds. It touched on the average only 57 physical pages per collection. By comparison, the trace-and-sweep collector did 11 collections totalling 75 seconds of GC time, and touched an average of 285 physical pages per collection. Generational wins on every count.

For the compiler, our generational collector was more typical of generational schemes: it used more cpu, but touched fewer pages. It did 24 collections, using a total GC time of 46 seconds, touching an average of 126 physical pages at each collection. The trace-and-sweep collector ran only 4 times, using a total time of 29 seconds, touching an average of 430 pages at each collection.

The above numbers indicate that this collector is on the right track. The generational version of Collector II touches far fewer pages than the full trace-and-sweep version. Particularly remarkable is the use of less cpu time for generational collection than for full trace-and-sweep, at least in the Boyer benchmark. This is not usually true of generational collectors, which tend to trade cpu-time for a smaller working set. Overall, Collector II's times are still much slower than the normal Ibuki system, and slower than Collector I, but we have done none of the usual system tuning one needs in a production quality collector and allocator. We believe our collection times can be improved by a factor of 2-10 by some straightforward performance tuning.

VI. Other Fancy Tricks

There are many other tricks to making our collector implementations effective. Below we discuss four which are of particular interest: parallelism, trace queueing, lifetime prediction and application hints.

Parallelism

To reduce the pauses that result from garbage collections over large sets of objects, we have built an experimental implementation of Collector II in which tracing of the heap is incremental. The basic technique is to make a virtual snapshot of the heap when the collector starts. We do this by simulating a kind of "copy-on-write" behavior—we write-protect the entire heap and copy pages as they are written by the application program during parallel collection. This is similar to techniques suggested by Shaw [Shaw87]. It takes only 3 milliseconds on a Sun-4 to take the write fault, copy the page, and unprotect it. In practice we have seen a maximum of only 20 page faults per second of application time (during the Ibuki compiler), although of course a much worse "toy" application is easy to construct.

Now when the collector is invoked it finds all of the pointers from the stack, registers, global data, and non-threatened cards into threatened cards. These pointers are remembered for tracing later. All cards are then write-protected, starting the virtual snapshot, and control is given back to the mutator. Objects allocated after the start of a parallel collection are not considered for collection.

Tracing now occurs incrementally during allocations. At each allocation request a single card of the heap is traced. Pointers off the card are saved for later. Notice that there is an upper bound on the time each allocation will take, and the expense of a large garbage collection can be amortized over a longer time.

Trace Queueing

It is a goal of generational collection to keep the size of the set of objects being traced small, thereby keeping collections short and unintrusive. Unfortunately, generational collection also allows accumulation of old but unreachable objects. In a long-lived program, such as an operating system, it is necessary occasionally to collect the entire heap. While this large collection is running, performance of the mutator degrades, but the program can continue running with no *a priori* limits on storage imposed by the collector.

If done naively, full collections can degrade mutator performance beyond usability. The problem arises in systems with virtual memory when the number of pages accessed by the collector is much larger than the number of available pages of physical memory. A naive depth-first trace of all live objects accesses nonresident pages frequently and repeatedly. Consequently, the collector generates a large number of page faults, swapping out the mutator's working set.

The trace of the heap must keep track of all objects that have been reached but not yet explored. A simple depth-first search keeps these unexplored objects on a stack and explores the object on the top of the stack when it finds itself at a leaf. Instead, the collector can partition the unexplored objects into buckets based on their addresses, and choose to explore objects that are already in memory whenever possible.

We implement trace queueing in Collector I by bucket-sorting the stack of references to be explored. In Collector II we trace all of the references on a single card at each allocation request. This gives the desired locality on the trace and a form of pseudo-parallelism. There is an upper bound on the time each allocation will take, since the collector is accessing only one card.

Trace queueing can cause unexpected performance penalties. For instance, the anomalous fact that Collector II uses less cpu time for generational collections than for full trace-and-sweep is largely explained by the greater number of off-page pointers followed during full trace-and-sweep. Turning off page queueing resulted in collection times more nearly proportional to the number of bytes actually traced by each collector.

Lifetime Prediction

With a copying collector, all new objects are allocated in a new space, and those surviving collection are copied to a different area. This results in a high density of live objects in memory. A non-copying collector, however, does not have this advantage. Objects that will soon die are allocated alongside objects that will be tenured. This natural intermingling of objects of different lifetimes results in fragmentation of the tenured storage. Allocating new objects in the holes in tenured storage fills the holes, but collecting those new objects is inefficient.

If we can predict object lifetimes in advance, then we can allocate long-lived and short-lived objects on separate cards. A reasonable predictor of object lifetimes is the allocation site. Static lifetime prediction algorithms typically rely on this assumption [Hudak86]. However, it is not clear exactly what constitutes an allocation site. The value of the program counter at the point of call to the memory allocation routine is a bad choice — many LISP systems perform essentially all allocation from inside a routine implementing "cons." We need to identify the allocation site by information that simultaneously is cheap to compute and is a reasonable summary of the entire call stack. The stack pointer is a plausible candidate.

We built a modification of collector I that used the 11 low-order bits of the stack pointer to summarize the allocation site. It tracks lifetimes of a few objects, namely those that are the first allocation from a site and those that initiate allocation from a new card. If more than 3/4 of the tracked objects from a site survive the first collection, it declares the site to be long-lived. Cards that are more than half (but less than 3/4) full are reserved for allocations from such sites.

This scheme can be successful. On contrived test programs that exhibited exceptionally clean "generational" behavior, it eventually led to accumulation of a majority of all the long-lived objects on separate cards. This in turn led to significantly faster collection times, since the cards that were actually being examined by the collector contained few surviving objects. As a result, total collection times decreased to essentially those for the nongenerational collector.

Unfortunately, the success of the method is both machine- and application-dependent. It failed on a Sun 4, for example: on that processor, nearly every activation record has size exactly 96 bytes, so the stack pointer value contains little information.

On the compiler benchmark the strategy appeared to be marginally successful at concentrating long-lived objects, but not successful enough to show a performance improvement. Precise comparisons are difficult, since the partial collector effectively retires pages once they are 1/2 instead of 3/4 full. Nevertheless, at least the number of collections did not increase. On the Boyer benchmark some performance degradation was observed. However, given that this is a theorem proving benchmark, it is perhaps not surprising that object lifetime prediction is hard.

Application Hints

Our Collector II can accept hints from the application in the form of advice about TB values. For instance, the application can remember currentTime just before performing some storage-intensive operation. Then, when the operation is done, the application can request a collection back to the remembered time, which will reclaim the temporary objects created for that operation.

To test this idea, we made a run of Collector II compiling the two large lisp modules, with the following change: before compiling the first module currentTime was remembered, and between compiling the two modules a collection was done with TB of the remembered time. Total collection time was cut from 46 to 35 seconds — still not as good as the trace-and-sweep (29 seconds) but much closer. Fascinating but not unexpected, the number of physical pages accessed during that collection in the middle was still only 129 pages, about the same as all the other generational collections. So with the right hints, at no loss of working set, collection time can be greatly improved.

VI. Conclusions

Our theory describes a large space of interesting garbage collectors. It is also a predictive theory — so far, it has led us to two unique implementations of generational collectors with reasonable performance. There is much work to do to apply the theory to more kinds of collectors, and to explore further the space of implementations, particularily to take full advantage of the flexibility of partial orders.

VII. Acknowledgements

Hans Boehm was partially supported by DARPA/NSF grant CCR 87-20277. Barry Hayes was partially supported by the Northern California Chapter of ARCS Foundation, Inc., and by DARPA contract N000014-87-K-0828.

References

[Appel88] A. Appel, J. Ellis, and K. Li. Real-time Concurrent Garbage Collection on Stock Multiprocessors. *Proceedings of the SIGPLAN '88 Conference on Programming Language Design and Implementation*, SIGPLAN Notices 23,7 (July 88), pp. 11-20.

[Baker78] Henry G. Baker, Jr. List Processing in Real Time on a Serial Computer, *Communications of the ACM* 21, 4 (April 1978), pp. 280-294.

[Bartlett88] Joel F. Bartlett. *Compacting Garbage Collection with Ambiguous Roots*. Western Research Laboratory Research Report 88/2, Digital Equipment Corp., February 1988.

[Boehm88] Hans-Juergen Boehm and Mark Weiser. Garbage Collection in an Uncooperative Environment. to appear in *Software: Practice and Experience*. 1988.

[Cardelli88] Luca Cardelli, James Donahue, Lucille Glassman, Mick Jordan, Bill Kalsow and Greg Nelson. *Modula-3 Report*. Olivetti Research Center Technical Report ORC-1, 1988.

[Courts87] Bob Courts. Improving Locality of Reference in a Garbage-Collecting Memory Management System. Internal TI memo, November 1987.

[Fitzgerald86] Robert Fitzgerald and Richard Rashid. The Integration of Virtual Memory Management and Interprocess Communication in Accent. *ACM Transactions on Computer Systems*. Vol. 4, No. 2. pp. 147-177, May 1986.

[Gabriel85] Richard Gabriel. *Performance and Evaluation of Lisp Systems*. MIT Press, 1985.

[Hanson77] David R. Hanson. Storage Management for an Implementation of SNOBOL4. *Software: Practice and Experience*. Vol. 7, No. 2. pp. 179-192, March 1977.

[Hudak86] Paul Hudak. A Semantic Model of Reference Counting and its Abstraction. *Proceedings of the 1986 Conference on Lisp and Functional Programming*. pp. 351-363, Aug. 1986.

[IBUKI87] IBUKI Common Lisp, IBLC Release 01/01. IBUKI, Mountain View, Ca, 1987.

[Lieberman83] Henry Lieberman and Carl Hewitt. A Real-Time Garbage Collector Based on the Lifetimes of Objects. *Communications of the ACM*, Vol. 26, No. 6, pp. 419-429, June 1983.

[Moon84] David A. Moon. Garbage Collection in a Large Lisp System. *ACM Symposium on Lisp and Functional Languages*, August 1984.

[Ripley78] G. David Ripley, Ralph E. Griswold, David R. Hanson. Performance of Storage Management in an Implementation of SNOBOL4. *IEEE Transactions on Software Engineering*, SE-4, No. 2, pp. 130-137, March 1978.

[Rovner85] Paul Rovner. On Adding Garbage Collection and Runtime Types to a Strongly-Typed, Statically-Checked, Concurrent Language. Xerox PARC Report CSL-84-7, 1985.

[Shaw87] Robert A. Shaw. *Improving Garbage Collector Performance in Virtual Memory*. Computer Systems Laboratory Technical Report: CSL-TR-87-323, Stanford University, March 1987.

[Sobalvarro88] Patrick G. Sobalvarro. *A Lifetime-based Garbage Collector for LISP Systems on General-Purpose Computers*. Bachelors Thesis, Electrical Engineering and Computer Science, Massachusetts Institute of Technology. September 1988.

[Unger84] David Unger. Generation Scavenging: A Nondisruptive High Performance Storage Reclamation Algorithm. in *ACM SIGSOFT/SIGPLAN Practical Programming Environments Conference*, 157-167, April 1984.

[Weiser89] Mark Weiser, Alan Demers, and Carl Hauser. The Portable Common Runtime Approach to Interoperability. *Proceedings 13th ACM Symposium on Operating System Principles*, December 1989.

[Wilson89] Paul R. Wilson. A Simple Bucket-Brigade Advancement Mechanism for Generation-Based Garbage Collection. *SIGPLAN Notices*, 24:5, May 1989.

Scheduling Time-Critical Instructions on RISC Machines

Krishna V. Palem [*] Barbara B. Simons [†]

Abstract

An instruction or a set of instructions can be considered time critical if their execution is required to free up a resource. Time critical instructions might be used to make shared resources such as registers more quickly available for reuse; or they might be used for real time computations, portions of which are critical for the operation of some piece of equipment. In this paper we present a polynomial time algorithm for optimally scheduling instructions with or without time critical constraints on RISC machines such as the IBM 801, the Berkeley RISC machine, and the HP Precision Architecture. We also show that in the absence of time critical constraints, the greedy algorithm always produces a schedule for a target machine with multiple identical pipelines that has a length less than twice that of an optimal schedule. The behavior of the greedy algorithm is of interest because, as we show, the instruction scheduling problem becomes NP-hard for arbitrary length pipelines, even when the basic block of code being input consists of only several independent streams of straight-line code, and there are no time-critical constraints. Finally, we present the first correct proofs that the problem becomes NP-hard even for small pipelines, no time-critical constraints, and input of several independent streams of straight-line code if there is only a single register or if there is a bus constraint.

1 Introduction

Many code optimization problems for parallel and pipelined machines can be modeled as deterministic scheduling problems. Typically, these scheduling problems involve rearranging generated object code that is derived from a single basic block of source code[*]. The object code instructions have deterministic behavior and often require a single unit of execution time on the CPU [15,22,23]. A fast algorithm for rearranging the object code in a basic block to minimize execution time can improve the quality and efficiency of the code generated by the compiler. In addition, it is frequently necessary to guarantee that time critical instructions are completed early in the schedule. For example, the early execution of certain instructions might help to minimize spillage induced by register allocation.

To illustrate, assume that instruction s_i initializes a value which is subsequently referenced by instructions $s'_1, s'_2, \ldots, s'_k$. Suppose that s_i is given an early deadline and that $s'_1, s'_2, \ldots, s'_k$ are given somewhat later, but still early, deadlines. Then if a schedule satisfies the deadline constraints, the register that is used to store the value initialized by s_i will be available for other use no later than the

---

[*]IBM Research Division, T.J. Watson Research Center, P. O. Box 704, Yorktown Heights, NY 10598, (914) 789-7846, kpalem@ibm.com.

[†]IBM Research Division, Almaden Research Center, 650 Harry Road, San Jose, CA 95120, (408) 927-1785, simons@ibm.com.

---

[*]Techniques, such as *trace scheduling* [8] and *global compaction* [1,18], can be used to increase the size of the input to the scheduling algorithm.

latest deadline that is assigned to $s'_1, s'_2, \ldots, s'_k$.

We present a fast algorithm that takes a basic block of code as its input and constructs an optimum schedule satisfying time critical constraints for two problem classes. (It also constructs an optimal schedule for the same problem classes if there are no time critical constraints). One of these classes models machines such as the IBM 801 [23,24], the Berkeley RISC [15], and the HP Precision Architecture [10]. We also show that in the absence of time critical constraints the greedy algorithm produces a schedule for target machines with multiple identical pipelines that has a length which is less than twice that of an optimal schedule. Therefore, the greedy algorithm can be used as a fast heuristic for producing good (but not necessarily optimal) schedules for a wide range of target machines.

This paper contains three NP-completeness results. The first shows that the problem of producing schedules with minimum overall completion time is NP-hard if the depth of the pipeline grows as part of the input, even when the basic block of code being input consists of only several independent streams of straight-line code, and these instructions have no time-critical constraints. The other two results demonstrate how the introduction of resource constraints can make a problem become NP-complete. In particular, the instruction scheduling problem is NP-hard for a single small-depth pipeline, even if the inputs are only independent streams of straight-line code without time critical constraints, provided there is only a single register or a bus constraint[†] on the instruction scheduler. A weaker NP-completeness result for the instruction scheduling problem in the presence of register constraints is claimed in [13], but their result appears to be flawed.

2 Description of the Model

We consider target machines in which every machine instruction requires one cycle of CPU time. If the operands of the instruction are derived from on-chip registers, then such instructions are fetched, decoded, and executed in one cycle. In contrast, some instructions, such as LOADs and STOREs,

---

[†]The bus contention problem was brought to our attention as an open problem at the Workshop on Programming Languages and Compilers for Parallel Computing, Cornell Univ., Aug, 1988.

require additional cycles due to latencies introduced by memory access.

We use the standard directed acyclic graph (DAG) representation of basic blocks [13]. Each node in the DAG corresponds to an instruction and each edge corresponds to a dependence. An instruction cannot be executed until all of its predecessors are completed. Furthermore, if an instruction, say a LOAD, requires additional time to complete, instructions that depend on that load must be delayed until the entire LOAD has been completed. The additional delay, which is represented as a weight on the appropriate out-edges from the LOAD to its immediate descendents, is called an *inter-instructional latency*, or *latency* for short. The value of the latency is the additional delay beyond the unit of time required by the CPU.

Figure 1 shows a simple DAG, all the edges of which have latency 1, and two possible schedules for that DAG. Schedule S_1 illustrates how unnecessary idle time can be introduced if the nodes are scheduled in a suboptimal order. Clearly, schedule S_2, which completes execution earlier than S_1, is preferable. The idle time in schedule S_1 could have been introduced either at compile-time by explicitly introduced no-ops, or at run-time if the target machine has hardware interlocks. Therefore, depending on the machine, the problem is either to minimize the number of idle cycles caused by no-ops produced by the compiler or to minimize the number of cycles during which the interlocks are activated.

In addition, the input might contain time critical instructions. Such an instruction has associated with it a non-negative integer which is called a *deadline*. In this case, the problem is to construct a schedule in which all instructions are completed by their deadlines. A schedule in which all the nodes are completed by their deadlines is called a *feasible* schedule for the given instance. An instruction which is completed after its deadline is said to be *tardy*. If instructions are allowed to be tardy, the corresponding optimization problem consists of constructing a schedule in which the maximum tardiness is minimized.

2.1 Some definitions

Assume we have a set of instructions that either form a basic block or have been obtained using a form of trace scheduling. The problem input is a

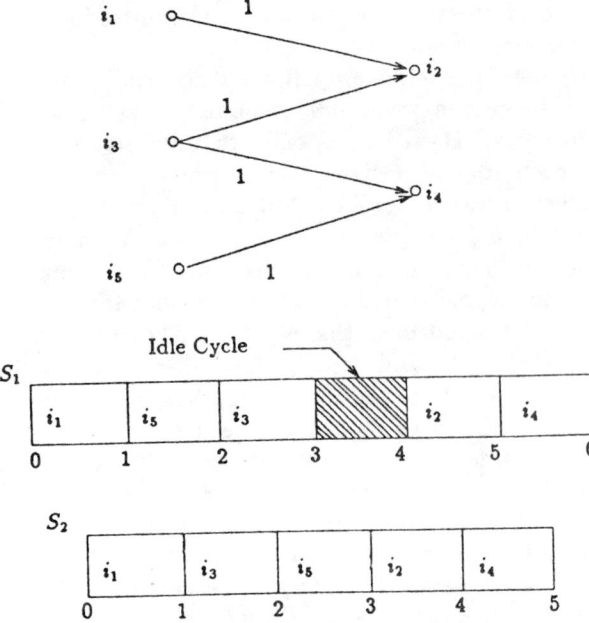

Figure 1: A DAG with two possible schedules

DAG $G = (N, E)$, where each node $i \in N$ corresponds to one of the instructions, and each edge $(i,j) \in E$ corresponds to a dependence. In addition, each edge has a non-negative integer weight $w(i,j)$, which is the latency of edge (i,j). Finally, if a node i has to be completed by a certain time t, then i has a *deadline* $d(i) = t$.

Formally, a schedule S is specified by a start time $S(i)$ and a machine $M(i)$ from the set $1, 2, \ldots, m$ of identical processors in the target machine such that:

1. For $i, j \in N, i \neq j$, and $M(i) = M(j)$, $|S(i) - S(j)| \geq 1$. (No two nodes are executed simultaneously on the same machine).
2. $S(j) \geq S(i) + w(i,j) + 1$ for $(i,j) \in E$. (The earliest start time of a node depends on the start time, processing time, and latency of its predecessors).

If there are no deadlines, then the goal of the algorithm is to construct a schedule with *minimum completion time*, that is $\max_i \{S(i) + 1\}$ is minimized; if there are deadlines, then the goal is to construct a *feasible* schedule, namely one in which every node is completed by its deadline. If for some assignment of deadlines there is no feasible schedule, then the algorithm should return that information. As we show in section 4.1.2, if the rank algorithm, defined below, constructs a feasible schedule for a problem instance with deadlines, it also constructs a minimum completion time schedule for an instance of the same type of problem without deadlines.

2.2 Relationship to pipeline scheduling

The pipeline model studied in this paper is more general than the classical or standard notion of a pipeline machine. A *standard pipeline machine of length k* is a machine with k unit length stages for which an instruction which enters the first stage of the pipeline at time t exits from the last stage at time $t + k$. A new instruction can enter the pipeline at times $t+1, t+2, \ldots$. In this model the start time of an instruction is at least k units greater than that of any instruction on which it depends. Also, as many as k instructions may be in the pipeline simultaneously. The model of a standard pipeline is a special case of the latency model in which all the latencies are $k - 1$.

A generalization of the standard pipeline model is obtained by allowing an instruction to exit the pipeline at some stage prior to the last stage. An instance of this problem can be represented by having identical latencies on all the out-edges of a node but allowing different nodes to have different values on their out-edges. For the algorithms in this paper, we consider only the most general version of the model, namely one in which different out-edges of the same node can have different latencies.

2.3 Compiler construction issues

We briefly discuss the interaction between the scheduler and other stages of optimization in the compiler, particularly register allocation. If the register allocation phase precedes the scheduling phase, then by forcing instructions to use the same register, the register allocator can create dependencies between instructions that are not otherwise dependent. Consequently, unnecessary hazards can be introduced. This problem can be caused by any shared resource that is allocated at compile time. Another example in which unnecessary hazards could be introduced is a target machine with a single shared bus for data transfer that is used to fetch and store data *and* instructions from memory.

There are different approaches for handling the interaction between the scheduler and the register allocator. In the approach used by Hennessy and Gross [12,13], the instruction scheduler is explicitly constrained by hazards that are introduced by the register allocator and by memory access. Gibbons and Muchnick [10] deal with register allocation by introducing edges in the DAG to prevent instructions that share registers from overlapping. Register allocation is handled in the PL.8 compiler [3] by having the instruction scheduler preceded by a first register allocation phase and succeeded by a second register allocation phase. In the first phase the allocation is done for a target machine with an unbounded number of registers. After instruction scheduling, register allocation for the actual target machine is performed, and hazards are eliminated by appropriately introduced *spill code*. The latter two approaches obviate the need for the scheduler to explicitly deal with constraints introduced by register allocation, other than those encoded into the input DAG.

We assume that the compiler designer has employed a technique such as that in [10] or [3]. Consequently, the problem of instruction scheduling is separated from that of register allocation. Similar approaches can be used to separate the scheduler from constraints introduced by other shared resources, such as a bus. For a more detailed discussion see [2].

3 Previous work

In [3,4,5,6,9,10,12,13,14,16,17,19] various aspects of instruction scheduling for pipeline machines are studied. A survey of deterministic scheduling results for pipelined machines is contained in [16]. Some of these results can be found in more detail in [6,9,17]. In [19], Palem characterizes a general sufficient condition for pipelined scheduling problems to be solvable in polynomial time, and shows that some new problems, as well as several previously known polynomially solvable scheduling problems, satisfy this condition.

We have already discussed the approach taken for the PL.8 compiler [3]. Hennessy and Gross [12,13] present a heuristic that runs in time $O(n^4)$, where n is the number of nodes in the DAG, and report performance results for their heuristic on the MIPS machine [14]. There is no analysis of the worst case performance of the heuristic. Gibbons and Muchnick [10] describe a heuristic for the case in which the latencies are 0 or 1 with the substantially improved running time of $O(n^2)$. Although they report good performance for the heuristic, they, too, do not do a worst case analysis of the quality of the schedules produced by their heuristic. Bernstein and Gertner [4] give an algorithm for optimally scheduling an arbitrary graph with latencies of 0 or 1 on a single processor. Since their algorithm uses transitive reduction as a preprocessing step, the running time of their algorithm is either that of transitive reduction[‡] or $O(n^2)$, if preprocessing costs are ignored. Their algorithm does not handle time critical nodes. In [5], Bernstein, Rodeh and Gertner analyze the worst case behavior of the greedy algorithm for a target machine with a single pipeline. In section 5 we present a generalization of that result to the multiple pipeline or processor case.

4 The rank algorithm

A standard technique for instruction scheduling is to use a greedy algorithm that always schedules a node whenever there is at least one available node. If there are more nodes available than processors, nodes are chosen arbitrarily. (See section 5 for a definition of the greedy algorithm). The problem with such an approach is that it does not take into consideration any of the graph structure, in prioritizing nodes[§]. The rank algorithm, defined below, uses information about the latencies between a node i and each of i's successors, as well as the deadline of node i, to compute the *rank* of i, written $rank(i)$. Once the ranks are all computed, the algorithm constructs a list based on the ranks which it then schedules greedily. The rank algorithm constructs a feasible single processor schedule, whenever such a schedule exists, for an arbitrary input DAG if all the latencies are either 0 or 1 and some or all of the nodes have preassigned deadlines. Although the rank algorithm is not guaranteed to find

---

[‡]The running time is either $O(ne)$, where e is the number of edges in the DAG, or the running time of matrix multiplication.

[§]The *highest level first* algorithm, which is a more sophisticated version of the greedy algorithm, is also frequently used. However, the highest level first algorithm is not guaranteed to solve even simple cases of the instruction scheduling problem, as illustrated in schedule S_1 of figure 1.

a feasible schedule if the latencies are greater than 1, or if there is more than one pipeline in the target machine, we conjecture that its behavior as a heuristic is quite good in the general case.

4.1 The algorithm

1. Compute the *ranks* of all the nodes.
2. Construct *list*, which is an ordered list of nodes in *non-decreasing* order of their ranks.
3. Apply the greedy scheduling algorithm to *list*. If some node is not scheduled to complete by its rank, halt in failure.

4.1.1 Computing the ranks

We first discuss the rank computation assuming that there are no deadlines, and then show how to easily extend the computation to handle deadlines. The *weighted length* of a path p is the sum of its constituent edge latencies and the number of nodes in p, excluding its endpoints. Let $\mathbf{w}^+(i,j)$ denote the weighted length of the longest path from node i to its successors j.

The rank of node i can be computed when $\mathbf{w}^+(i,j)$ and $rank(j)$ have been computed for all nodes j that are successors of i. In the absence of deadlines, we assume that the overall completion time of the schedule is some large integer D. Initially, all nodes are assigned a rank of D, and D remains the rank of all nodes that have no successors. A node with no successors is called a *sink*.

Let i be a node whose successors' ranks have all been computed. We construct a sorted list sw of the successor set of node i. The nodes in sw are sorted in non-increasing order by the $\mathbf{w}^+$ values, i.e. if $\mathbf{w}^+(i,j) > \mathbf{w}^+(i,p)$, then node j occurs before node p in sw. Let sw_q be all the nodes j in sw for which $\mathbf{w}^+(i,j) = q$. Because sw is sorted, the nodes in sw_q are contiguous in sw.

We next sort each segment sw_q by non-increasing order of ranks. Let swr be the resulting list. The nodes in swr are all the successors of node i stored in the non-increasing order based on $\mathbf{w}^+$; all the nodes with the same $\mathbf{w}^+$ value are further sorted by their ranks.

We refer to each possible integer time at which a node can start as a *time step*. A schedule for a target machine with m processors can be represented by a matrix in which each row represents one of the processors of the target machine, and each column represents a time step. A *slot* is a single entry in the matrix, and represents a specific time step on a specific processor.

To compute $rank(i)$, we select nodes in the order in which they appear in swr, starting at the beginning of swr. Each time we select a node j, we "backward schedule" j by scheduling it in the latest available (idle) slot which completes no later than $rank(j)$. In particular, we schedule j in the time step ending at the largest D' such that:

1. $D' \leq rank(j)$ and,
2. the number of nodes that occur before j in swr and have been assigned this time step is strictly less than m.

The rank of i with respect to j equals $D' - \mathbf{w}^+(i,j) - 1$. The 1 represents the processing time of j; equivalently, $D'-1$ is the start time of node j. The rank of i with respect to j gives the latest time that node i can finish if node j is to be completed by its rank. We compute the rank of i with respect to each of its successors; $rank(i)$ is the smallest of these values.

If there are deadlines, the modification to the rank computation is straightforward. Let $d(i)$ be the deadline assigned to node i. If i has no pre-assigned deadline, set $d(i) = D$, where D is some very large integer. (As before, D represents the maximum overall completion time of the schedule). Then the rank of i with respect to j is redefined to be $\min\{d(i), D' - \mathbf{w}^+(i,j) - 1\}$, where, as before, D' is the completion time of node j in the backward schedule. Infeasibility of a schedule is determined as soon as the greedy algorithm fails to schedule some node to start before its rank.

4.1.2 Correctness of the ranks

Below we present the key theorem and proof for the rank algorithm. It shows that no node can be completed later than its rank if all the nodes are completed by their deadlines. (Nodes with no pre-assigned deadlines are given the default deadline D). Note that the proof is entirely general, and holds for any number of processors and any latencies.

Theorem 1 *Let G be a DAG and S a schedule for G in which every node is completed by its deadline. Then every node i in S is completed no later than $rank(i)$.*

Proof. The proof is an induction on the number of nodes in the successor set of i. If i is a sink node, then the theorem follows trivially from the definition of rank.

Suppose that i is not a sink node and assume that the induction assumption holds for successors of i. If $rank(i) = d(i)$, then the theorem obviously holds. So assume that $rank(i) = D' - \mathbf{w}^+(i,j') - 1$, and let j' be the first node scheduled in the backwards schedule in the time step ending at D'. If $D' = rank(j')$, then the result follows immediately from the assumption that the ranks of all the successors of i satisfy the theorem, together with the definition of $\mathbf{w}^+(i,j')$.

Now assume that $D' < rank(j')$, and let $S_{backward}$ with completion time $T_{backward}$ be the backwards schedule as it exists immediately after the insertion of j'.

Case 1. There are no idle slots in the time steps ending at $D'+1, D'+2, \ldots, T_{backward}$. Then $rank(j) \leq T_{backward}$, for $j \in S_{backward}$, since otherwise some node would be completed later than $T_{backward}$. From the order in which nodes are placed in $S_{backward}$ we get $\mathbf{w}^+(i,j) \geq \mathbf{w}^+(i,j')$, $j \in S_{backward}$. The theorem follows from a simple pigeon hole argument.

Case 2. There is some idle slot in the time steps ending at $D'+1, D'+2, \ldots, T_{backward}$. Let t be the completion time of the smallest valued (earliest) such time step containing an idle slot. Since $S_{backward}$ is constructed greedily, it follows that all nodes in time steps with completion time less than t have rank less than t. Also, all these time steps have no idle slots. Therefore, all nodes scheduled in time steps prior to t must be completed prior to t and have a $\mathbf{w}^+$ value at least as great as $\mathbf{w}^+(i,j')$. The theorem again follows from a pigeon hole argument. ∎

The following lemma is used below. If I is a problem instance, then I_δ is defined to be the problem instance that is obtained by adding δ to every preassigned deadline of I. If a node has no preassigned deadline, then it is given the preassigned deadline of $D+\delta$ (rather than D). We also define $rank(i)$ to be the ranks computed for instance I, and $rank_\delta(i)$ to be the rank of node i in I_δ.

Lemma 2 *Let I and I_δ be as defined above. Then $rank(i) = rank_\delta(i) + \delta$.*

Proof. The proof follows directly from the definition of rank. ∎

Corollaries 3 and 4 show that the rank algorithm can be used to solve the minimum tardiness problem, as well as the minimum completion time problem in the absence of deadlines.

Corollary 3 *Assume that the rank algorithm constructs a feasible schedule for a problem instance if one exists. Then if the rank algorithm is allowed to run to completion for an infeasible instance, it constructs a minimum tardiness schedule.*

Proof. If a problem instance I is infeasible, then there exists a sufficiently large δ such that when δ is added to all the deadlines, the corresponding problem instance I_δ is feasible. Since by assumption the rank algorithm constructs a feasible schedule if one exists, the smallest δ for which a feasible schedule can be constructed is the value of the minimum tardiness. It follows from lemma 2 that *list* is the same for both I and I_δ. Therefore, the same schedule is constructed for both problem instances. ∎

Corollary 4 *Suppose the rank algorithm constructs a minimum tardiness schedule for a problem instance if one exists. Then the rank algorithm also constructs a minimum completion time schedule both for inputs in which all nodes have the same preassigned deadlines and for inputs in which no nodes have a preassigned deadline.*

Proof. The proof follows from the technique of giving each node the same number D as a deadline and then applying corollary 3. ∎

4.1.3 The running time of the rank algorithm

For the running time analysis we assume that the input DAG is a connected graph. We also assume that the input DAG is a transitively closed graph, where the *transitive closure* of a graph $G = (N, E)$ is a graph $G' = (N, E')$ which consists of all the nodes from G together with an edge from i to j if there is a path in G from i to j. Otherwise, the transitive closure is automatically computed during the computation of the $\mathbf{w}^+$ values. The computation of all the $\mathbf{w}^+$ values takes time $O(en)$. Given the $\mathbf{w}^+$ values, constructing the lists sw and swr

involves sorting the various successor sets. Since each edge in the transitively closed graph is used for processing the rank of only one node, the total time required for sorting all the sets sw and swr is $O(e' \log n)$, where e' is the number of edges in the transitive closure of G. Once the list swr has been constructed, the backward scheduling step of the rank computation is performed. This step can be implemented efficiently using the UNION-FIND algorithm [25]. The time required for applying the UNION-FIND algorithm is $O(e'\alpha(e'))$, where $\alpha(\cdot)$ is the inverse of Ackermann's function, and e' is the number of edges in the transitive closure of G. (For all practical purposes, the value of the inverse Ackermann function can be assumed to be a very small integer). Finally, using heaps the greedy algorithm implementation runs in time $O(n \log n)$. Summarizing¶:

Theorem 5 *The running time for the rank algorithm is $O(en)$ if the $\mathbf{w}^+$ values are not part of the input, or $O(e' \log n)$ otherwise.*

4.1.4 Optimality of the rank algorithm

The more important class of problems for which the rank algorithm constructs an optimal schedule is the class of arbitrary DAGs in which the latencies are either 0 or 1, the deadlines are arbitrary, and there is a single machine ($m = 1$). As noted earlier, this class models many different RISC machines.

Theorem 6 *Let $G = (N, E)$ be a DAG, the edges of which have latencies of either 0 or 1 and the nodes of which have arbitrary deadlines. Then the rank algorithm constructs a feasible schedule for G whenever one exists, and determines that there is no feasible schedule otherwise.*

Proof. Assume for contradiction that the rank algorithm fails to construct a feasible schedule for G, but there is a feasible schedule for G. Let S_{rank} be the partial schedule that had been constructed by the greedy scheduling algorithm, and let i be the first node that had not been scheduled by its rank. Since the rank algorithm halts in failure only when it encounters a node that has not been completed by its rank, all the nodes in S_{rank} are scheduled to complete by their ranks.

¶If the number of edges in the input DAG is considerably smaller than the number of nodes, the running time could be less.

Backtrack over S_{rank} examining the contents of each time step until the first of the following three events occurs:

1. a node j is encountered such that $rank(j) < rank(i)$
2. an empty slot is encountered
3. all of S_{rank} has been examined.

Suppose the first condition holds, namely node j is encountered with $rank(j) < rank(i)$. Let t be the time step at which j is scheduled and let Σ be the set of nodes scheduled in time steps $t+1, t+2, \ldots, rank(i)$ together with node i itself. (Node j is not included in Σ).

The node scheduled in time step $t-1$ must be a predecessor of all the nodes in Σ, since otherwise one of those nodes would have been scheduled at time step t. Let j' be the node scheduled at time step $t-1$. If $k \in \Sigma$ is an immediate successor of j', then $w(j, k) = 1$, since otherwise the greedy algorithm would schedule node k at time t. Therefore, for all successors k' of j' we have $\mathbf{w}^+(j', k') \geq 1$. Consequently, by the pigeon hole principle together with the definition of rank, $rank(j) < t - 1$. This contradicts the assumption that all the nodes in S_{rank} were completed by their ranks.

If the second condition holds, namely an idle slot is encountered, then the argument is the same as above.

If the last condition holds, then S_{rank} has no idle time, and all the nodes in S_{rank} have rank no greater than $rank(i)$. Consequently, by theorem 1 and the pigeon hole principle, there is no feasible schedule for the problem instance. ∎

Another class of graphs for which the rank algorithm constructs a feasible schedule whenever one exists is called *monotone interval-orders*. For this problem class the number of processors in the target machine can be arbitrary, and the latencies and deadlines can assume arbitrary integer values.

An *interval-order* graph is a DAG $G = (N, E)$, where N is a set of closed intervals in the real line. The edges of G are derived from the order between these intervals as follows. For $i, j \in N$, $(i, j) \in E$ if and only if for any pair of numbers x and y, if $x \in i$ and $y \in j$, then $x < y$. Each edge has a latency, and each node has a deadline, both of which are arbitrary non-negative integers. The following lemma is from [21].

Lemma 7 *Let $G = (N, E)$ be an interval-order graph. Then for $i, j \in N$, either all the predecessors of i are also predecessors of j or all predecessors of j are also predecessors of i.*

A *monotone* interval-order graph is one in which, given any pair of edges (i, j) and (i, j'), $w(i, j) \geq w(i, j')$ whenever the predecessors of j' are also predecessors of j.

Theorem 8 *Let $G = (N, E)$ be a monotone interval-order graph with arbitrary latencies and deadlines, and assume that there are $m \geq 1$ machines. Then the rank algorithm constructs a feasible schedule for G whenever one exists, and determines that there is no feasible schedule otherwise.*

Proof. As in theorem 6, assume for contradiction that the rank algorithm fails to construct a feasible schedule for G, but there is a feasible schedule for G. Let S_{rank} be the partial schedule that had been constructed by the greedy scheduling algorithm and let i be the first node that had not been scheduled by its rank. For $j \in S_{rank}$, $S_{rank}(j)$ is the start time of j. Clearly, $rank(j) > S_{rank}(j)$ for all nodes in S_{rank} except i. We consider the following three cases.

Case 1. There are precisely m nodes with ranks bounded above by $rank(i)$ scheduled at each of the times $0, 1, \ldots, rank(i)$. Then by a simple pigeon hole argument together with theorem 1, there does not exist any feasible schedule.

Case 2. There is either an idle slot or some node with rank greater than $rank(i)$ scheduled at time $rank(i) - 1$. Then i must have a predecessor, say j, such that $S_{rank}(j) + \mathbf{w}^+(j, i) + 1 \geq rank(i)$. Otherwise, i would have been scheduled to start at time $rank(i) - 1$. From the definition of rank we get that $rank(j) \leq S_{rank}(j)$, contradicting the assumption that any node in a slot smaller than $rank(i)$ has a start time less than its rank.

Case 3. There is some time $t' < rank(i) - 1$ such that there is either an idle slot or some node with rank greater than $rank(i)$ scheduled at time t'. Let t be the largest such time, and let Σ be the set of nodes with start times of $\{t+1, t+2, \ldots, rank(i) - 1\}$ together with node i. Clearly, $|\Sigma| = (rank(i) - t - 1) \times m + 1$. Any node $i' \in \Sigma$ must have a predecessor j such that $S_{rank}(j) + \mathbf{w}^+(j, i') + 1 > t$. Otherwise, i' would have been assigned start time t. We say that j is a *constraining node of i'*.

Let $k \in \Sigma$ be the node in Σ with the smallest sized predecessor set, i.e. $|pred(k)| \leq |pred(k')|$, for $k, k' \in \Sigma$. Since G is an interval-order, it follows from lemma 7 that $pred(k) \subseteq pred(k')$, for $k, k' \in \Sigma$. Lemma 7 also implies that for every node $j' \in pred(k)$, j' is a predecessor of all the nodes in Σ. Let $j \in pred(k)$ be a constraining node for k. Then, because G is a monotone interval order, $\mathbf{w}^+(j, k') \geq \mathbf{w}^+(j, k)$ for $k' \in \Sigma$ and j is a constraining node for all $k' \in \Sigma$. But now the rank computation for j gives the finish time of node j to be greater than $rank(j)$, contradicting the assumption that i is the first node with this property. ∎

5 The greedy algorithm

One approach that is frequently used in scheduling algorithms is to first create an ordered list of the nodes and to then apply the *greedy algorithm*. The algorithm schedules instructions as soon as they become eligible, while giving priority to the eligible nodes that appear earliest on the list. Such a strategy can make a bad decision only when there are more instructions available for scheduling at a particular time than there are processors on which to schedule them. In this section we describe the greedy scheduling algorithm and show that any schedule constructed greedily from an arbitrary list does not do too badly when compared with the best possible schedule.

5.1 The greedy scheduling algorithm

The input to the greedy algorithm is an ordered list of the nodes in a DAG G, latencies, which can be any non-negative integer less than k, and m, the number of processors in the target architecture. The greedy algorithm scans the list repeatedly, choosing up to m nodes on each scan to be scheduled. A node is eligible to be chosen if all of its predecessors in G have been scheduled on an earlier scan and the relevant latency constraints have been satisfied. At the end of the scan, the chosen nodes are deleted from the list, and new nodes become eligible. The process is repeated until the list is empty.

By using a heap, the greedy algorithm can be implemented in $O(e + n \log n)$, where e is the number of edges in the input DAG and n is the number of nodes. In this implementation the nodes are inserted into the heap as soon as they are eligible to be scheduled. To adhere to the original order of the list, the key used for the heap is the location of the node in the list.

Theorem 9 *Let $G = (N, E)$ be an arbitrary DAG with arbitrary latencies between 0 and k. Then the greedy algorithm constructs a schedule for G on a target machine with m processors that is guaranteed to be no more than a factor of $2 - 1/m(k+1)$ worse than optimal.*

Proof. We first consider a schedule, called S_∞, constructed by the greedy algorithm for the given DAG G with the assumption that we have as many processors as we can use at our disposal. (Note that since there are only n nodes, we can never use more than n processors). Since we have as many processors as we need, it follows that the only delay in S_∞ comes from constraints that are intrinsic to G, namely the edges and the latencies, and therefore S_∞ has the minimum possible completion time for G. Let S_∞^t denote all the nodes that are scheduled to start at time t in S_∞. We use l_∞ to denote the total number of such non-empty time steps in S_∞; that is, l_∞ is the number of time steps in S_∞ that have at least one node scheduled in them. Let T_∞ be the completion time of schedule S_∞.

S_{greedy}, with completion time T_{greedy}, denotes an arbitrary schedule produced by the greedy algorithm. We use S_∞ to bound the amount of idle time in S_{greedy}. We represent S_{greedy} as a matrix in which each row represents one of the processors and each column represents a time step; $slot(i, j)$ denotes the entry in the ith row and jth column, $1 \leq i \leq m, 1 \leq j \leq T_{greedy}$. (Note that for a single machine, the above matrix has a single row and therefore, i can be omitted). We say that $slot(i, j)$ is *active* provided there is a node scheduled to start at time j on machine i; $slot(i, j)$ is idle otherwise. The following lemma bounds the total amount of idle time in S_{greedy}:

Lemma 10 *The total number of idle slots in S_{greedy} is bound above by $(T_\infty - l_\infty)m + l_\infty(m - 1)$.*

Proof. Follows from a straightforward induction on the non-empty time steps S_∞^t for increasing t. ∎

If ν is the total number of slots in S_{greedy}, then since each column of the matrix has m slots,

$$T_{greedy} = \nu/m. \qquad (1)$$

From lemma 10 and the fact that each active slot in S_{greedy} contains at least one node, we have:

$$\begin{aligned} \nu &\leq n + m(T_\infty - l_\infty) + (m-1)l_\infty \\ &\leq n + mT_\infty - l_\infty. \end{aligned} \qquad (2)$$

Combining 1 and 2, we get

$$T_{greedy} \leq 1/m(n - l_\infty) + T_\infty. \qquad (3)$$

Since the maximum latency on any edge in the input DAG is k, we get

$$T_\infty \leq l_\infty(k+1) \qquad (4)$$

or,

$$T_\infty/(k+1) \leq l_\infty. \qquad (5)$$

Substituting 5 in 3, we have:

$$\begin{aligned} T_{greedy} &\leq 1/m(n - T_\infty/(k+1)) + T_\infty \\ &\leq n/m + T_\infty(1 - 1/(m(k+1))). \end{aligned} \qquad (6)$$

Substituting

$$T_{opt} \geq n/m \qquad (7)$$

and

$$T_{opt} \geq T_\infty \qquad (8)$$

in 6, we get

$$T_{greedy} \leq T_{opt} + T_{opt}(1 - 1/(m(k+1))) \qquad (9)$$

or,

$$T_{greedy}/T_{opt} = 2 - 1/(m(k+1)). \qquad (10)$$

While the completion time of a greedy schedule is within a factor of 2 of the completion time of an optimal schedule, the quality of the greedy schedule can degrade as the number of processors in the target machine, as well the latencies, increase. There are examples in [16] for which a schedule constructed by the greedy algorithm can be arbitrarily close to the bound of above theorem, thereby showing that the bound it tight.

6 NP-completeness results

All of the NP-completeness reductions use a DAG which is a set of chains. A *chain* is a subgraph that consists of only a simple path, namely every node has at most one in-edge and one out-edge, and the graph is connected. Since a chain is very simple graph (for example, a chain is also a tree), these are very strong negative results. The proofs are omitted.

6.1 Registers

If there is only a single processor and a single register on the target machine, and some, but not necessarily all, of the nodes are preassigned to the register, then constructing a minimum completion time schedule is NP-complete. To the best of our knowledge, ours is the first correct proof that the addition of register constraints can transform a version of the instruction scheduling problem for which polynomial time algorithm exists (from theorem 6) into an NP-complete problem.

We define a *register constraint* as follows. For node i let w_{max} be the maximum latency for all edges (i, j). If i references a register, then no other node can reference that register until at least w_{max} time units after the completion of instruction i [13].

Theorem 11 *Let $G = (N, E)$ be a DAG which is a set of chains for which the latencies are all equal to 1 and there is only one register. The problem of determining if there is a single machine schedule for G having a completion time no greater than D, for some given D, is NP-complete.*

6.2 Bus constraints

We now consider the case in which the target machine has a single processor, with the memory and the processor connected by a single bus. We ignore any register constraints. If an instruction does not involve a memory access, then it is completed in a single cycle; if it does require a memory access, then it uses two cycles. Because the memory access is performed on the second cycle, two instructions that access memory can be pipelined. However, if we execute an instruction that does not perform a memory access (e.g. a register-register instruction) during the second cycle of a memory access instruction, then both instructions complete execution at the same time, resulting in contention for the bus. In this situation, we say that a *bus hazard* has occurred. Note that we are interested in proving a negative result, we have assumed a particularly simple execution mode for the target machine. In particular, the only form of pipelining that is allowed is when the first cycle of a LOAD or STORE instruction is allowed to overlap the second cycle of another such instruction.

There are several ways to avoid a bus hazard. An architectural solution is to introduce bus-contention hardware that avoids conflicts by serializing the requests. A software solution might be to introduce no-ops during a post-pass scan. In both approaches the additional constraint introduced by the shared bus is transparent to the instruction scheduler.

Alternatively, we could try to expand the scheduling algorithm to include bus hazards. For this case, the instruction scheduling problem would be generalized to include the constraint that no two instructions can *finish* simultaneously.

Theorem 12 *Let $G = (N, E)$ be a DAG which is a set of chains for which the latencies are only 0 or 1. The problem of determining if there is a single machine schedule for G having a completion time no greater than D, for some given D, in which no two instructions complete simultaneously is NP-complete.*

6.3 Arbitrary latencies

Hennessy and Gross [13] have shown that the instruction scheduling problem is NP-complete for *arbitrary* DAG's with latency constraints of 0 and two other values. Our result shows that even if the DAG is restricted to being a set of chains, the problem remains NP-complete.

Theorem 13 *Let $G = (N, E)$ be a DAG which is a set of chains for which the latencies can be 0 or two other values. The problem of determining if there is a single machine schedule for G having a completion time no greater than D, for some given D, is NP-complete.*

7 Acknowledgement

We thank Dave Alpern, Paul Hudak, Mary Van Deusen, Mark Wegman, and Kenny Zadeck for helpful discussions and suggestions. We are also grateful to David Bernstein for pointing out an error in an earlier draft and for several useful comments.

References

[1] A. Aiken and A. Nicolau, "Loop Quantization: An Analysis and Algorithm", *Technical Report No. 87-821*, Cornell University, (March, 1987).

[2] F. Allen, B. Rosen, and K. Zadeck (eds), "Optimization in Compilers", MIT Press, to appear.

REFERENCES

[3] M. Auslander and M. Hopkins, "An Overview of the PL.8 Compiler", *Proc. ACM SIGPLAN Symposium on Compiler Construction,* (1982), 22-31.

[4] D. Bernstein and I. Gertner, "Scheduling Expressions on a Pipelined Processor with a Maximal Delay of One Cycle", *ACM TOPLAS,* Vol. 11, No. 1, (Jan, 1989), 57-66.

[5] D. Bernstein, M. Rodeh, and I. Gertner, "Approximation algorithms for scheduling arithmetic expressions on pipelined machines", *Journal of Algorithms,* 10, (March 1989), 120-139.

[6] J. Bruno, J.W. Jones III, and K. So, "Deterministic scheduling with pipelined processors", *IEEE Trans. Computers,* C-29, (1980), 308-316.

[7] J. Ellis, *Bulldog: a compiler for VLIW architectures,* The MIT Press, Cambridge, MA, (1986).

[8] J.A. Fisher, "Trace Scheduling: A Technique for Global Microcode Compaction", *IEEE Trans. on Computers,* Vol. C-30, No. 7, (July, 1981) 478-490.

[9] H. Gabow, "Scheduling UET Systems on Two Uniform Processors and Length Two Pipelines", *SIAM J. Comp,* 17, (1988), 810-829.

[10] P. Gibbons and S. Muchnick, "Efficient Instruction Scheduling for Pipelined Architecture", *Proc. of the ACM Symp. on Compiler Construction,* Palo Alto, CA, (June, 1986), 11-16.

[11] R. L. Graham, "Bounds for Certain Multiprocessor Anomalies", *Bell System Technical Journal,* 45, (1966), 1563-1581.

[12] J. Hennessy and T. Gross, "Code Generation and Reorganization in the Presence of Pipeline Constraints", *Proc. Ninth POPL,* Albuquerque, N.M., (Jan. 1982), 120-127.

[13] J. Hennessy and T. Gross, "Postpass Code Optimization of Pipeline Constraints", *ACM TOPLAS,* 5, (1983), 422-448.

[14] J. Hennessy, N. Jouppi, J. Gill, F. Baskett, A. Strong, T. Gross, C. Rowen, and J. Leonard, "The MIPS Machine", *Proc. IEEE Coupcon,* San Francisco, CA, (Feb. 1982), 2-7.

[15] G. Katavenis, *Reduced Instruction Set Computer Architecture for VLSI,* MIT Press, Cambridge, MA, (1984).

[16] E. Lawler, J.K. Lenstra, C. Martel, B. Simons, and L. Stockmeyer, "Pipeline Scheduling: A Survey", *Technical Report,* RJ 5738, IBM Research Division, San Jose, CA., (1987).

[17] J. Y-T Leung, O. Vornberger, and J. Witthoff, "On some variants of the bandwidth minimization problem", *SIAM J. Comput.,* 13, (1984), 650-667.

[18] A. Nicolau, "Loop Quantization or Unwinding Done Right", *Proc. 1st International Conference on Supercomputing,* Springer-Verlag Lecture Notes in Computer Science), (June, 1987), 294-308.

[19] K. Palem, "On the Complexity of Precedence Constrained Scheduling", CS-TR-86-10, Department of Computer Sciences, The University of Texas, Austin, Tx, 1986.

[20] K. Palem and B. Simons, "Algorithms for Optimal Instruction Scheduling on Pipelines", *Confidential Technical Report,* RJ 6592, IBM Research Division, San Jose, CA, (1988).

[21] C. Papadimitriou and M. Yannakakis, "Scheduling interval-ordered tasks", *SIAM J. Comput.,* 8, (1979), 405-409.

[22] D. Patterson, "Reduced Instruction Set Computers", *CACM,* 28, (1985), 8-21. The MIT Press, Cambridge, MA, (1986).

[23] G. Radin, "The 801 Minicomputer", *IBM J. Res. Dev.* 27, (1983), 237-246.

[24] R. Simpson, "The IBM RT Personal Computer", *Byte,* Extra Edition, (1986), 43-78.

[25] R. E. Tarjan, "Efficiency of a good but not linear set union algorithm", *J. ACM,* 22, (April 1975), 215-225.

Automata-Driven Indexing of Prolog Clauses [†]

R. Ramesh
Department of Computer Science
University of Texas at Dallas
Richardson, TX 75083.

I.V. Ramakrishnan and D.S. Warren
Department of Computer Science
State University of New York at Stony Brook
Stony Brook, NY 11794.

Abstract

Indexing Prolog clauses is an important optimization step that reduces the number of clauses on which unification will be performed and can avoid the pushing of a choice point. It is quite desirable to increase the number of functors used in indexing as this can considerably reduce the size of the filtered set. However this can cause an enormous increase in running time if indexing is done naively. This paper describes a new technique for indexing that utilizes all the functors in a clause-head. More importantly, in spite of using all the functors, this technique is still able to quickly select relevant clause-heads at run time. This is made possible primarily by a finite-state automaton that guides the indexing process. The automaton is constructed at compile time by preprocessing all the clause-heads.

1 Introduction

The fundamental computational step in execution of Prolog programs is the selection and unification of clause-heads with goal. A successful unification results in the creation of several subgoals and each of these in turn must be unified with additional clause-heads. This process continues until either all the subgoals created are satisfied by the facts or one of them fails to unify with any clause-head. Thus the repeated selection of unifiable clause-heads is an important operation critical to the efficiency of Prolog program execution. Developing techniques to significantly enhance the speed of this selection process is therefore a problem of practical importance to Prolog compilation and execution technology.

[†]Research partially supported by NSF grant CCR-8805734

Fast selection techniques that have been proposed, typically first filter the clause-heads to form a (presumably small) set that are likely to unify and then perform unification on each of the filtered clause-head in this set. These techniques can be broadly grouped into two classes.

The techniques in the first group basically index on the outermost functor of one or more arguments in the clause-head. A hash table is built on these functors which is then accessed for retrieving the filtered set of clause-heads. This approach is quite popular as seen by its use in the WAM (warren abstract machine)[12], Quintus Prolog [9], Stony Brook Prolog [11] and several other Prolog systems [2,13]. The problems with this approach are that firstly it fails to distinguish between distinct clause-heads that do not differ in the functor of the argument indexed on. For instance, by indexing on the outermost functor of the first argument it fails to distinguish $p(f(a,b),c)$ from $p(f(a,c),d)$. Secondly, if the goal has a variable corresponding to the argument indexed on then again it will fail to distinguish between clause-heads. These two situations can sometimes be handled by allowing the programmer to specify the indexing argument. The selection process now is no longer transparent and to write efficient programs the programmer must be aware of the indexing method used in the Prolog system and organize the program to exploit it effectively.

The second group of techniques transforms every clause into a binary codeword by first transforming each of its argument into a codeword and then OR'ing all of them together. The filtered set is obtained by searching for the goal's codeword among the codewords for clause-heads. This technique has been studied in [10]. The problem with this method is that such an encoding is an imperfect representation of a clause-head. Specifically, important structural information in clause-heads is lost in the transformation process. Thus, although $p(a,b)$ and $p(b,a)$ are structurally dissimilar, yet they are assigned the same code. Note that this method is well-suited for database applications where arguments are atomic. However, Prolog clauses are complex structures containing variables. Known transformation techniques for dealing with them are quite ad hoc and result in significant loss of structural information quite critical for filtering.

Increasing the number of symbols used in indexing can result in reducing the size of the filtered set. But doing so can increase running time if indexing is done naively. A 'good' indexing technique therefore should be able to utilize all the (non-variable) symbols in clause-heads without losing significant structural information and have good run time performance. In this paper we address the important problem of designing such a technique.

1.1 Brief Overview and Related Results

We describe a new technique for indexing Prolog clause-heads. Unlike known techniques it utilizes all the non variable symbols in clause-heads for indexing. Furthermore even structurally different clause-heads containing the same functors (such as $p(a,b)$ and $p(b,a)$) are distinguished. In our approach each clause-head is transformed into a set of strings by doing a left-to-right preorder traversal and removing nodes labelled with variables. Thus $f(a, g(X, b))$ is transformed into fag and b. Observe that the *clause-head strings* so obtained contain all the non variable symbols in its head. As each function symbol is assumed to have unique arity in Prolog implementations, these strings also retain the head's structure, i.e., we can reconstruct the clause-head given its preorder sequence.

Given a goal we perform a series of complex string matching steps involving clause-head strings and goal strings. The outcome of these steps are then correlated to obtain the filtered set. These string matching steps require repeated inspection of goal strings and therefore performing each such step independently is inefficient. Hence we construct a finite-state automaton (based on the clause-head strings) and use it to guide our indexing process. The information embodied in the states of the automaton is now used to avoid reinspection of sequences of symbols in goal strings and thereby improve the performance of our technique. The following are some important features of our technique.

- The finite-state automaton is constructed at compile time by preprocessing all the clause-heads.
- Selecting a clause-head at run time is accomplished within time (in the worst case) proportional to the number of variables in the clause-head and goal.
- Time to construct the automaton (at compile time) and its space requirements are both quadratic in the size of the clause-heads (in the worst case). Both can be made linear by increasing the constant in the running time of clause selection and we briefly outline how this is accomplished.

- An important aspect of our technique is that a selected clause-head will unify with the goal if they are both *linear* (i.e., each variable is restricted to at most one occurrence). In other words among the selected clause-heads only those that have repeated variables may fail to unify. Often clause selection in typical Prolog programs involves linear terms only. This fact can be gainfully exploited by our technique to obtain the unifier during the indexing process. In contrast, known methods do this by performing unification on each clause-head in their filtered set (which is at least as large as the one constructed by our technique). Unification of each such clause-head requires time proportional to the sum of its size and that of the goal (using known linear-time unification algorithms in [8]).

- Our technique generalizes the known methods of indexing on functors of specified arguments. It is also transparent to the programmer who need no longer organize the program to effectively exploit the indexing method used by the compiler.

Finally, we also discuss another indexing technique (that also utilizes all the functors in a clause-head) for a machine model in which we can perform bit-string operations of union and intersection in constant time. This technique is of practical importance as long as the number of clause-heads with the same predicate name does not exceed the wordsize.

This paper is organized as follows. In the following section issues related to compiling clause-heads for fast indexing are identified. Based on these issues we describe their compilation into a finite-state matching automaton in section 3. The clause-heads are selected based on the outcome of scanning the goal with the automaton at run time. A method to do this scan efficiently is outlined in section 4. A variant of the indexing technique that results in reducing the space requirements of the automaton is described in section 5. In section 6 we describe another indexing technique using bit string operations. Concluding remarks appear in section 7.

1.2 Notations

A *term* is either a variable or an expression of the form $f(t_1, t_2, \ldots, t_n)$ where f is a functor of arity $n \geq 0$ and $t_1, t_2, \ldots, t_n$ in turn are also terms.

We adopt the standard Prolog convention of using capital letter for the first symbol in a variable name. Thus $f(a, g(X, b)$ is a term with X as the variable, f and g

```
begin
  fail:=false;
  repeat
    If G(p_g) and R(p_r) are both functors
      then begin
        If G(p_g)≠ R(p_r) then fail=true
        else begin p_g:=p_g + 1; p_r:=p_r + 1 end
      end else
        if one of them is a variable, say G(p_g), then
          begin p_g:=p_g + 1;
            advance p_r to node immediately
            following the subtree rooted at R(p_r)
          end
  until (fail=false) or
    (G and R are completely scanned)
end.
```

Fig. 1: Selection Algorithm

as functors of arity 2 and a and b as functors of arity 0. A *term tree* is the standard tree representation of a term (see fig.2).
A term is *linear* if each variable in it occurs only once.

2 Issues in Selecting Clause-Heads

We first identify issues involved in indexing clause-heads (called **rules** from now on) through a simple selection algorithm.

2.1 Simple Selection Algorithm

Our selection algorithm uses all those nodes in the goal and rule that do not occur within variable substitutions when the two are unified. Specifically, it selects a rule if and only if it unifies with the goal after uniquely renaming multiple occurrences of variables in both the rule and goal. (Note that such renaming makes them both linear terms.)

The structure of rules selected by our selection algorithm is described by the following intuitive picture. First superpose the goal and rule trees at their roots. Next mark all those nodes that fall on variables. The rule is selected if and only if after deleting all such marked nodes and their subtrees, the two trees are isomorphic.

Fig.1 is an outline of such a selection algorithm. The rule and goal trees are traversed in preorder and stored in arrays R and G respectively. Two pointers, p_r and p_g, are used to scan R and G respectively. The rule is selected if upon termination $fail$ is false. The trouble with this selection algorithm is that its running time is proportional to the number of nodes in the goal and rule trees (in the worst case). Note that within this time bound we can in fact unify them using well known linear-time unification algorithms (such as [8,6]).

We now examine issues related to improving considerably the running time of our simple selection algorithm.

2.2 Improving Running Time

Observe that our simple selection algorithm cycles between two phases - *match* and *skip*. In each step the phase is first determined and then the computation appropriate to that phase is performed. Transition between phases occurs as follows. If the algorithm is in match phase and the nodes currently being compared are both functors then it continues to remain in the same match phase. On the other hand a new match phase is entered if it is currently in a skip phase and the nodes being compared are again functors. Finally, it enters a new skip phase whenever one of the nodes being compared is a variable. The computations performed in the two phases are as follows. If the pair of functor symbols compared in a match phase are identical then p_g and p_r are both incremented by one. A mismatch on the other hand, results in the rule being discarded. For the skip phase, suppose (without loss of generality) p_g points to a node labelled with a variable, say X, and p_r to some node, say v. Then p_g is advanced by one whereas p_r skips the entire subtree rooted at v and advances to the node immediately following the last node in the skipped subtree in preorder. We say that the subtree at v is the *substitution* computed for X.

Note that the total number of distinct phases the algorithm goes through is proportional to the *number of substitutions computed* which in the worst case is at most equal to the total number of variables in both the goal and rule. Also note that each skip phase can be accomplished in $O(1)$ time by keeping a pointer with every node v (in arrays G and R) to the node that appears last in the preorder traversal of the subtree rooted at v. Observe that if we can accomplish each match phase also in $O(1)$ time then the worst case running time of our selection algorithm is proportional to the number of substitutions computed. We now examine issues related to doing the match phase in $O(1)$ time.

2.3 String Matching Operations

The computation performed in a match phase is basically comparing pairs of functor symbols in succession. If we can compare this entire sequence of functor pairs in $O(1)$ time then the match phase requires only

$O(1)$ time. Towards this objective we examine below the kinds of string matching questions that can possibly arise in a match phase. We will denote the string of functors separating two consecutive variables in the goal's (rule's) preorder as *goal (rule) strings* (see fig.2 below).

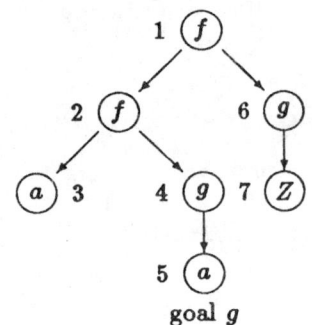

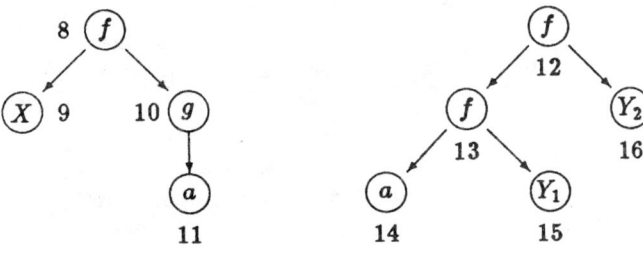

Fig. 2

Observe that the two variables, for which substitutions are computed in the skip phases immediately preceding and succeeding a match pahse, are either both rule variables (such X_i, X_{i+1} in fig.3(a)) or are both goal variables (such as Y_j, Y_{j+1} in fig.3(c)) or one is a goal variable and the other a rule variable (such as X_i, Y_{j+1} in fig.3(b) and Y_j, X_{i+1} in fig.3(d)). In fig.3 α and β denote rule and goal strings respectively and the preorder traversals of the rule and goal are stored in arrays R and G respectively. The pair of arrows leaving a variable mark the two ends (in R or G as appropriate) of the subtree computed as its substitution (such as a and b for X_i in fig.3(a)).

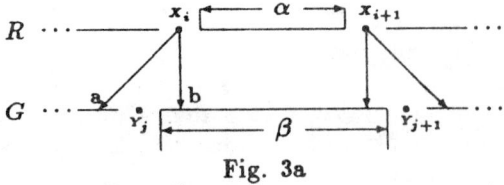

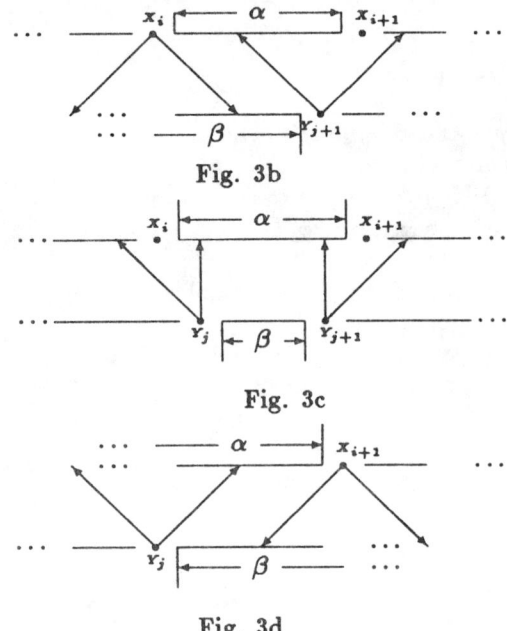

Each of these four situations gives rise to a different string matching question in the match phase as follows.

1. Does α (rule string) occur in β (goal string)? (Fig.3(a)).
2. Does a prefix of α match a suffix of β? (Fig.3(b)).
3. Does β (goal string) occur in α (rule string)? (Fig.3(c)).
4. Does a prefix of β match a suffix of α? (Fig.3(d)).

Observe that these four questions are a special case of the generic question - Does the prefix of a rule (goal) string occur in a goal (rule) string? We now show how to compile the rule strings into a finite-state automaton that at run time will enable us to answer these questions in $O(1)$ time.

3 Compiling Automata

Central to our technique is a finite-state automaton constructed from the rule strings. Such an automaton was first conceived by Knuth, Morris and Pratt [5] for recognizing instances of a single keyword string in a text string. Aho and Corasick [1] extended it to handle multiple keyword strings. This automaton is a trie in which each node denotes a state. From each state the automaton either makes a *goto* transition or a *failure* transition depending on whether the next symbol in the input extends the keyword prefix matched so far. Fig.4(a) is such an automaton for the three rule strings generated from the rules in fig.2

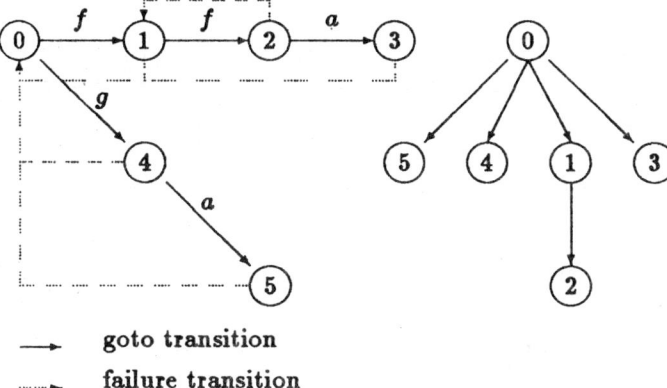

- → goto transition
- ⋯▸ failure transition

Fig. 4a: Automaton   Fig. 4b: Fail Tree

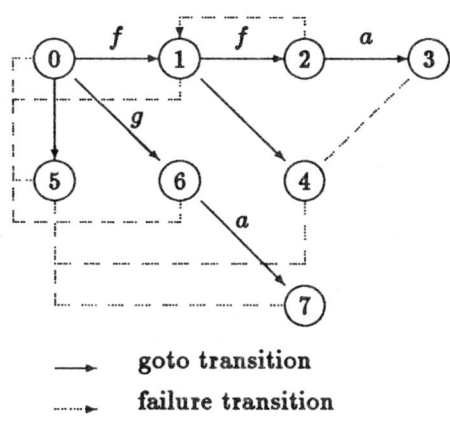

- → goto transition
- ⋯▸ failure transition

Fig. 4c: Automaton

Time required to construct this automaton is linear in the size of the keywords and if the alphabet set is fixed then the space required by it is also linear in the size of the keywords [1]. The following two properties of the automaton form the basis of our compilation.

1. Every prefix of a keyword string is represented by a state in the automaton.
2. If the *failstate* of i is j (i.e., the failure transition from i goes to j) then j represents the longest proper suffix of the string represented by i. (We say state i *represents* string σ if the path in the automaton from its start node to i spells σ. Thus state 2 in fig.4(a) represents ff.)

The main problem with this automaton is that (as is) it is only able to tell whether an entire keyword string occurred in the input text. This is all that is needed for rule selection when the goal is *ground* as in functional/equational programming. However recall that in the presence of variables in the goal we need to know whether a prefix of a rule (goal) string occurs in a goal (rule) string.

We first extend the automaton to handle such questions. The rule strings generated from the clause-heads of the Prolog program form the keywords of this automaton. At run time the automaton scans the symbols of the goal tree in preorder. Suppose we want to know whether the prefix α of a rule string, say r_i, matches the substring β of goal (see fig.5(a)).

Let s_β denote the state of the automaton after reading the last symbol in β. Let s_α be the state representing α. (Recall property (1).) Then,

Theorem 1 α *matches* β *iff* s_α *is reachable from* s_β *through zero or more failure transitions only.*

The proof of the theorem follows from property (1). Details are omitted.

Observe that each state has a unique fail state. So by deleting all the goto transitions and reversing the directions on failure transitions we obtain the *fail tree* of the automaton. (Fig.4(b) is the fail tree for the automaton in fig.4(a).) To each node in this fail tree we assign its preorder number (*pre*) and the number of descendants (*nd*) in its subtree. Note that all this preprocessing is done at compile time. For α to match β, s_α must be an ancestor of s_β in the fail tree (i.e., verify $pre(s_\alpha) \leq pre(s_\beta) \leq pre(s_\alpha) + nd(s_\alpha)$). Since this can be verified in $O(1)$ time we can therefore answer in $O(1)$ time whether a prefix of a rule string occurs in a goal string.

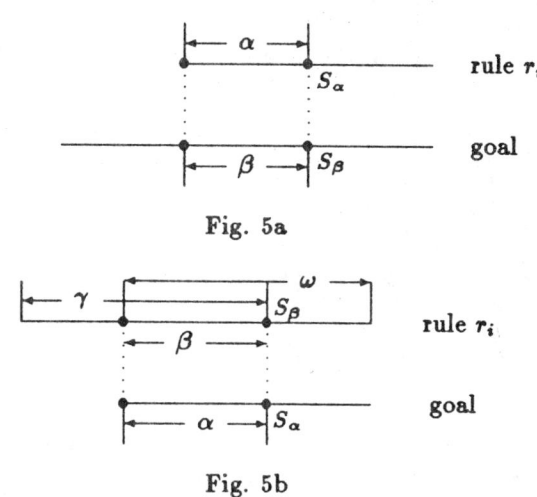

Fig. 5a

Fig. 5b

Now we extend the automaton to answer whether a prefix α of goal string matches a substring β of a rule string (see fig.5(b)). s_α is the state of the automaton on scanning α and s_β is the state corresponding to prefix γ of rule string. Note that the goal strings are not available at compile time. As the automaton is constructed without these strings we can no longer guarantee that every prefix of a goal string will be represented by a state in the automaton. Hence theorem 1 is no longer useful to answer questions related to prefixes of goal strings. Specifically, even if α does not match β, s_α can still be an ancestor of s_β in the fail tree. For instance, the automaton in fig.4(a) ends up in state 1 upon scanning the prefix gf of a goal string. Now observe that even though 1 is an ancestor of 2 in the fail tree, gf does not occur in the rule string ffa. The problem is that s_α is an ancestor of s_β even if a suffix of α occurs in β (such as f in the above example). To overcome this we must ensure that if a prefix of a goal string matches a substring of a rule string then that substring is a prefix of some keyword in the automaton. (Obviously if the automaton was constructed using the goal strings also then this is easily ensured.) However note that we do not need to represent every prefix of a goal string in the automaton. We need only those that match substrings of rule strings. Based on this important observation we now show how this can be accomplished using rule strings only!

In fig.5(b) suppose α matches β. Now observe that β is a prefix of ω which in turn is a suffix of a rule string. Thus all we need to do now is to make every suffix of a rule string into a keyword of the automaton. (Thus, in addition to the rule strings in fig.2 we now insert their suffixes a, fa also into the automaton, in fig.4(a), as its keywords. Fig.4(c) is the resulting automaton.) Finally, note that even after doing so s_α will be an ancestor of s_β if any suffix of α occurs in β. We can eliminate such possibilities by

Theorem 2 α *matches* β *iff* s_α *is an ancestor of* s_β *and depth*(s_α) *in the goto tree*[1] $= |\alpha|$.

The theorem's condition is again verifiable in $O(1)$ time. Thus all string matching questions can be answered in $O(1)$ time.

Finally note that the size of the all the keywords inserted into the automaton (rule strings and all their suffixes) can now become quadratic in the size of the rule strings (in the worst case).

4 Scanning Goal

To begin our selection we have to first scan the goal tree in preorder with the automaton and store its state transitions in an array. Clearly, for efficiency reasons we should not inspect regions of goal that occur within a variable substitution of every rule. For example, in fig. 2 the goal's subtree $g(a)$ occurs inside substitutions for X (in rule 1) as well as Y_1 (in rule 2).

We now outline the essential ingredients involved in avoiding inspection of such subtrees during selection. The main idea is to inspect the goal on demand only to the extent needed to perform a string match. Rules are in two states - *active* and *suspended*. Initially all

---
[1]The *goto tree* of the automaton is obtained by removing all its failure transitions.

location	1
node labels	f
state	1

Fig. 6a

location	1	2	3
node labels	f	f	a
state	1	2	3

Fig. 6b

location	1	2	3	4
node labels	f	f	a	?
state	1	2	3	?

Fig. 6c

location	1	2	3	4	5
node labels	f	f	a	?	g
state	1	2	3	?	6

Fig. 6d

of them are active. To begin with we pick any active rule and inspect the first few functors of the goal (in preorder) that are necessary to perform the first string match involving the selected rule. Suppose the skip phase immediately following the match phase is *triggered* by a rule variable[2]. We then suspend this rule on that node in the goal tree that immediately follows the skipped subtree in preorder. In general a rule, say r_i, is suspended only when the skip phase is triggered by r_i's variable and there are nodes in the skipped subtree that have not been inspected. A suspended rule is reactivated whenever the node, on which it is suspended, is either inspected in order to perform a string match step on behalf of an active rule or it becomes the root of a substitution. In case all rules become suspended then we reactivate the rule that is suspended on the node farthest from the root of the goal tree. The algorithmic details are a bit involved and are omitted. We illustrate this scanning process on the goal and rules in fig.2 using the automaton in fig.4(c).

Initially, r_1 and r_2 are active. States 1 and 7 represent the first and second strings of r_1 respectively (f and ga) and state 3 represents the only string (ffa) of r_2. To begin with we can choose any rule, say r_1. Before we can match its first string we have to scan the goal. As the length of this string is 1, we inspect only one goal symbol which in this case is its first symbol. (The inspected symbols of the goal are stored in an array.)

The first string match step of r_1 succeeds as the state representing its first string and the state of the automaton on reading the first goal symbol are the same (fig.6(a) shows the contents of the goal array on inspecting its first symbol). The next phase is a skip (triggered by X). The subtree rooted at 2 in the goal is skipped

---
[2]A skip phase is said to be triggered by a rule (goal) variable if in this phase a substitution is computed for the rule (goal) variable.

and r_1 is suspended on node 6 in the goal tree. Following this we choose the next active rule (r_2) and perform its first string matching step. To do this we need to scan the goal further as the symbols inspected so far (which is 1) is shorter than that required to perform this step. We scan two more symbols (see fig.6(b)).

The first string match of r_2 succeeds as the state representing its first string ffa is the same as that in the 3rd entry of the goal array. In the following skip phase, triggered by Y_1, the subtree at 4 is skipped. Following this r_2 is also suspended at node 6. Now note that both rules are suspended. This means that the subtree at 4 occurs inside variable substitutions of both rules. Therefore we need not inspect any symbols within this subtree. In the array this is represented by a dummy variable (see fig.6(c)).

At this point both are suspended on the same node. So we can activate any one, say r_2. (In general we choose the rule suspended on a node farthest from root.) For r_2 the step to be performed now is compute Y_2's substitution. In this skip phase the subtree at 6 is skipped. r_1 now is reactivated as the node on which it was suspended (node 6) has become the root of a substitution. Following this skip phase r_2 is selected as there is no node in the goal tree that follows the subtree at 6 in preorder.

Since r_1 is the only active rule left we begin its second string match. To do this we have to inspect the symbols in nodes 6 and 7 (see fig.6(d)). Since 7 is labelled with the variable Y we therefore stop the scan and perform the match. Notice that for inspecting these two nodes state 0 was used as initial state of the automaton. This is because the symbols inspected in this scan constitute a different goal string. The preceding goal string terminated before the dummy variable. Observe that the second string matching step of r_1 involves matching the prefix g of rule string ga with the goal string g. This also is successful as the state of the automaton on inspecting node 6 of the goal (state 6) also represents the prefix g of the rule string ga. In the following skip phase, triggered by Z (goal variable), the subtree rooted at node 11 in r_1 is skipped. As this is the last node in r_1's preorder it also is selected.

4.1 Coarse Filtering

The selection algorithm (described so far) regards every rule as a likely candidate for inclusion in the filtered set and so processes each of them separately. Thus it will unnecessarily examine a rule even if the functor symbol at its root differs from that of the goal's root. In contrast note that an indexing technique that is based on hashing the root functor symbol, will not even examine such rules.

We now modify the selection algorithm to avoid such needless computations. Specifically, we first construct a coarsely filtered set of rules such that the first string of every rule in this set is either a prefix of the goal's first string or vice versa. (Note that the first string in every rule always begins with the root's functor symbol.) More importantly, rules that do not belong to this set are not looked at during its construction.

Let g_1 denote the goal's first string. Let $S_1 = \{r \mid$ the first string of r is a prefix of $g_1\}$ and $S_2 = \{r \mid g_1$ is a prefix of the first string of $r\}$. The following is a description of the ideas underlying the construction of the coarsely filtered set $S_1 \bigcup S_2$. But first we need the following concept. We say that A is the *primary accepting* state of a keyword string α if it is both an accepting state for α and represents α. For instance in fig. 4(a), both 1 and 2 are the accepting states of the rule string f. But only state 1 is its primary accepting state.

Suppose $r \in S_1$ and its first string β matches a prefix α of g_1. Since β is a keyword string of the automaton, one of its accepting states is a primary accepting state. Now note that the path from the start state to this primary accepting state spells out β. This implies that α can be entirely scanned by the automaton without making any failure transitions. Based on this observation S_1 can be constructed as follows. The automaton scans the symbols in g_1 (from left to right) and makes transitions. It continues scanning these symbols as long as it makes only goto transitions. During such a scan if the automaton makes a goto transition to the primary accepting state of β then rule r is included in S_1.

For constructing S_2, suppose $r \in S_2$ and g_1 is a prefix of its first string β. Once again the automaton can scan g_1 entirely without making any failure transitions. Let A denote the state of the automaton on completely scanning g_1 without making any failure transitions. If g_1 is a prefix of β then the primary accepting state of β must be a descendant of A in the goto tree. Therefore S_2 will consist of only those rules such that the primary accepting states of their first strings are descendants of A in the goto tree.

During compilation we maintain the following information. With each state A, we keep a set C_A of all those rules for which A is the primary accepting state of their first strings. (Note that all rules in C_A should have identical first strings.) We also maintain another set D_A of rules such that the primary accepting states of their first strings are descendants of A in the goto tree.

At run time the automaton starts off by reading the symbols in g_1. It continues scanning them as long as it makes only goto transitions. During this scan if it enters an accepting state A then the rules in C_A are added to S_1. The scanning process is suspended when either g_1 is completely scanned without making any failure transitions or a failure transition occurs before all the symbols in g_1 have been read. In the former case, if B is the state of the automaton on completely scanning g_1 then $S_2 = D_B$ whereas in the latter case $S_2 = \emptyset$. In either case construction of the coarsely filtered set is now complete. We resume the scan of the goal strings from where it was suspended and proceed with the selection algorithm as described earlier. However we now need to examine the rules in the coarse set only. Note that we have already completed the first match phase for all these rules. So this step can be now be skipped by the selection algorithm.

Finally some remarks about efficiency. Suppose there are n rules in a Prolog program. If only m of these rules are included in the coarsely filtered set then computing this set at run time requires at most $O(m)$ time over and above the time required to scan g_1. We have thus managed to exclude the remaining $n - m$ rules without even examining them.

5 Selection using Linear Space

Recall that the space needed for the automaton can become quadratic in the size of the rules. We now briefly outline modifications to our selection algorithm that will reduce quadratic space to linear at the expense of increasing the constant in its running time.

Notice that the same automaton was used to handle the two generic string matching questions, namely, occurrences of prefixes of rule strings in goal strings and vice versa. Recall that to answer the former question we only need the rule strings in the automaton (and not their suffixes) and therefore in such a case the automaton requires only linear space. The idea now is not to use the automaton for dealing with the latter question, viz., prefixes of goal strings in rule strings but to use a *suffix tree* instead.

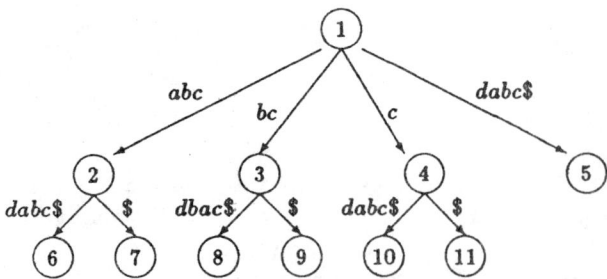

Fig 7: Suffix tree for $abcdabc$

A suffix tree of a string s is a trie in which each root-to-leaf path spells out a distinct suffix of s. Fig.7 is the suffix tree for string $s = abcdabc$. We preprocess all the rule strings and build a suffix tree. Such a tree requires space linear in the size of the rules[7]. In addition to scanning the goal strings with the automaton we now scan them with the suffix tree also. While scanning with the suffix tree its nodes serve as states and the edges as goto transitions. A boolean flag (initialized to false) is maintained with each goal symbol. This flag is set to true if a successful transition is made upon inspecting the goal symbol with the suffix tree. In such a case the node number (from which a transition is made) is also stored with the inspected symbol. To verify whether a prefix α of the goal string matches the substring β of a rule string (see fig.5(b)) we proceed as follows. Suppose $\beta = \alpha$. Then let s_α denote the node reached in the suffix tree upon scanning α. Observe that β is a prefix of a suffix ω. Therefore the root-to-leaf path in the suffix tree that spells out ω must pass through s_α. All we need to do now is verify whether the leaf node of this root-to-leaf path occurs in the subtree rooted at s_α. This again can be done in $O(1)$ time.

Finally, note that each rule string appears twice - once in the automaton and once in suffix tree. However observe that every rule corresponding to a ground fact gives rise to only one rule string. Selecting a fact only involves verifying whether goal strings occur in the fact's rule string. This can be easily answered using the suffix tree alone. So rule strings corresponding to ground facts need not be a part of the automaton. This can result in considerable savings in both space required and running time of applications that deal with voluminous amount of ground facts such as Prolog databases.

6 Indexing Technique using Bit Strings

We now describe another indexing technique suitable for a machine model in which bit string operations of union and intersection are done in constant time. As long as the number of rules with the same predicate name does not exceed the wordsize then this method is of practical importance. (Thus it is not appropriate for important applications such as Prolog databases as they typically involve voluminous number of rules with the same head symbol.)

Each rule tree is again preprocessed into a trie and the tries of all the rules are then merged. The trie for a rule tree is constructed as follows. First we assign a integer label to every edge in the tree. Specifically, if a node v is labelled with a functor f of arity k then v has k subtrees and the edge leading into the ith subtree is labelled i. Next we remove the variable names from all those nodes labelled with variables. Finally every node labelled with a functor symbol is split into two nodes connected by an edge that is labelled with the original node label. (See trie for rule r_1 in fig.8(a).) The tries for all the rules are then merged together by a process similar to that used in the construction of the automaton in section 3. (Fig.8(b) is the trie for r_1 and r_2). The space required for the trie is linear in the size of the rules.

Let t_i denote the trie for rule r_i and T the trie obtained by merging all the t_i's together. With each node v in T we maintain two sets S_v and M_v. We include r_i in S_v if the path from the root of T to v is a proper prefix of a root-to-leaf path in t_i. If they are identical then r_i is included in M_v instead of S_v (see fig.8(b)).

The goal is scanned in conjunction with T in a recursive fashion. Each recursive call has three parameters - the node u in goal currently being inspected, a node v in T and a set S of rules whose root-to-leaf paths have been successfully matched so far. For the very first recursive call u is the root of the goal tree, v is the root of T and S consists of all the rules whose tries have been merged to form T. The call begins by inspecting the label of u. Suppose u is labelled with a variable then this call returns successfully with S as the set of rules selected at this point. On the other hand if u is labelled with a functor symbol and there is no edge leaving v that is labelled with this functor symbol then it means that prefixes of root-to-leaf paths of rules in S_v that have been matched so far cannot be extended any further and are to be removed from S. Therefore this call returns with $S = S \cap \overline{S_v}$ where $\overline{S_v}$ is set compliment of S_v. Suppose there is an edge from v to w that has the same functor label then we descend to w in T as we have now been able to extend prefixes of root-to-leaf paths of some of the rules in S. Note that these rules must also be present in S_w. However S_w may also have rules that are not in S. Moreover for some rules in S their root-to-leaf paths might have terminated at v. Such rules must be present in M_v. Therefore we create two new sets $S_1 = S \cap S_w$ and $M_1 = S \cap M_v$. Note that for any rule in S_1 we have matched only a prefix of a root-to-leaf path and in order to complete this match we must scan the goal further. To do this we initiate a number of recursive calls as follows. Observe that w has the same number of children as v and the edges leaving w are all labelled with integers. Let $w_1, w_2, \ldots, w_l$ and $u_1, u_2, \ldots u_l$ denote the children of w and u respectively. We then initiate l recursive calls with u_i, w_i, S_1 as the input to the ith call. On returning from this call S_1 is updated to become $S_1 \cap S_i$. Finally, on returning from the lth recursive call S is updated to become $S_1 \cup M_1$. When the first recursive call initiated at the root of the goal is complete then S denotes the set of selected rules. Notice that by associating a bit per rule set intersection and union can be done in $O(1)$

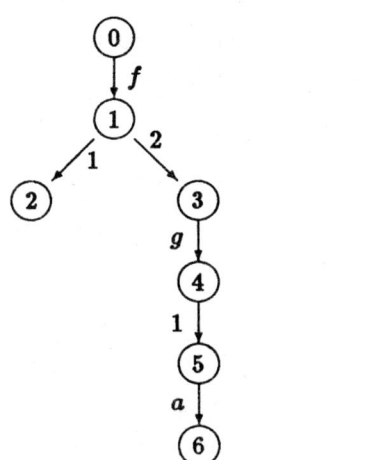

Fig. 8a: trie for r_1

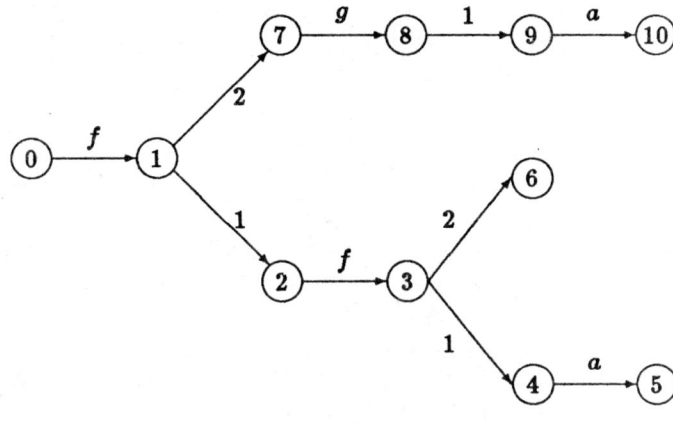

$S_1 = \{r_1, r_2\}$ $M_1 = M_3 = M_4 = \emptyset$
$S_2 = S_3 = S_4 = \{r_2\}$ $M_8 = M_9 = \emptyset$
$S_5 = S_6 = S_6 = \emptyset$ $M_2 = M_{10} = \{r_1\}$
$S_7 = S_8 = S_9 = \{r_1\}$ $M_5 = M_6 = M_7 = \{r_2\}$

Fig. 8b

time. In such a case the running time is bounded by the number of recursive calls which in turn is proportional to the size of the goal. However this method does not compute substitutions for variables.

Lastly we briefly mention a modification to the method when set unions and intersections cannot be performed using bit strings. For every rule, S_v has a count of the number of path strings in the rule that passes through v. Similarly M_v has a count of the number of path strings that terminate on v. We associate a counter with every rule. While scanning, this counter gets updated to reflect the number of path strings of the rule that have been matched so far. Upon completion of the scan a rule is selected if its counter value equals the number of path strings in it. An idea similar to this was used in [4] for doing tree pattern matching. Observe that selecting a rule will now require time proportional to the number of leaves in it. In contrast, recall that in our first indexing method a rule is selected in time proportional to the number of substitutions computed and this number is *always less than or equal* to the number of leaves in the rule.

7 Concluding Remarks

In this paper we described an automata-driven indexing technique for Prolog that selects rules quickly at run time. Although we compile all the rule strings in this technique, in practice we can choose the appropriate strings to index on a few arguments only. Thus our technique generalizes known techniques that index on functors. For instance, most existing Prolog implementations index on the outermost functor of specified argument(s), say the ith argument. This involves building hash tables that groups all the rules with the same outermost functor in the ith argument into a single set. To index only on the ith argument using our technique we proceed as follows. As part of compilation we first transform every rule so that its ith argument becomes the first argument. We perform a similar transformation on the goal (prior to execution). Next we construct the coarse filter based on the transformed rules and goal. However we now suspend the scan on examining the second symbol in the goal's first string. This corresponds to the outermost symbol in the goal's i^{th} argument before transformation. If A is the state of the automaton upon reading the second symbol then $S_2 = D_A$ and $S_1 \bigcup S_2$ at this point is exactly the set of rules in the hash table corresponding to the outermost symbol in the goal's i^{th} argument.

We also described another efficient indexing technique that is useful in situations where the number of rules with the same root symbol does not exceed a word-size. This can be of practical importance for small Prolog programs.

References

[1] A.V. Aho and M.J. Corasick, Efficient String Matching: An Aid to Bibliographic Search, CACM, Vol 18 No. 6, June 1975, pp. 333-340.

[2] K.L. Clark and F.G. McCabe, The Control Facilities in IC-PROLOG, Expert Systems in Micro Electronic Age, Ed. D. Michie, Edinburg University Press, 1979.

[3] B. Demoen, A. Marien and A. Callebaut, Indexing Prolog Clauses, To appear in North American Conference in Logic Programming, Cleveland, Oct 1989.

[4] C.M. Hoffmann and M.J. O'Donnell, Pattern Matching in Trees, JACM 29, 1, 1982 pp. 68-95.

[5] D.E. Knuth, J.H. Morris and V.R. Pratt, Fast Pattern Matching in Strings, SIAM Journal of Computing Vol 6, No 2, 1977, pp. 323-350.

[6] A. Martelli and U. Montanari, An Efficient Unification Algorithm, ACM TOPLAS, Vol 4, No. 2, Apr 1982, pp. 258-282.

[7] E. M. McCreight, A Space-Economical Suffix Tree Construction Algorithm, Journal of ACM, Vol 23, No. 2, April 1976, pp. 263-272.

[8] M.S. Paterson and M.N. Wegman, Linear Unification, Journal of Computer System and Science, Vol 16, No. 2, April 1978, pp. 158-167

[9] Quintus Prolog Users Guide, Quintus Computer Systems Inc., Mountain View, California.

[10] K. Ramamohanarao and J. Shepherd, A Superimposed Codeword Indexing Scheme for Very Large Prolog Databases, Proceedings of the Third International Conference on Logic Programming, Jul 1986, Lecture Notes on Computer Science, Vol. 225, Springer Verlag pp. 569-576.

[11] S.K. Debray, The SB-Prolog System, Version 2.3.2: A User Manual, Technical Report 87-15, Department of Computer Science, University of Arizona, Toucson, Dec 1987.

[12] D.H.D. Warren, An Abstract Prolog Instruction Set, Technical Note 309, SRI International.

[13] D.H.D. Warren, Implementing Prolog - Compiling Predicate Logic Programs, D.A.I Research Reports 39, 40, University of Edinburg, 1977.

[14] M.J. Wise and D.M.W. Powers, Indexing PROLOG Clauses via Superimposed Code Words and Field Encoded Words, Proceedings of the IEEE Conference on Logic Programming, Jan 1984, pp. 203-210.

Fairness and Hyperfairness in Multi-party Interactions[†]

(Extended Abstract)

Paul C. Attie[1]   Nissim Francez[2,3]   Orna Grumberg[3]

1. Department of Computer Sciences, The University of Texas at Austin, USA
2. Microelectronics and Computer Technology Corporation, Austin, Texas, USA
3. Computer Science Department, Technion, Haifa, Israel

Abstract

In this paper, a new fairness notion is proposed for languages with *multi-party interactions* as the sole interprocess synchronization and communication primitive. The main advantage of this fairness notion is the elimination of starvation occurring solely due to race conditions (i.e., ordering of independent actions). Also, this is the first fairness notion for such languages which is fully-adequate with respect to the criteria presented in [AFK88]. The paper defines the notion, proves its properties, and presents examples of its usefulness.

1 Introduction

Fairness is one of the most important classes of *liveness* properties employed by languages for nondeterministic, concurrent and distributed programs and by their underlying models of computation. This importance stems from the semantic intricacies of constructs in such languages, which makes the verification of typical progress properties (e.g., eventual response to a request for service) difficult. Fairness properties at the language level (e.g., an action that is sufficiently often enabled is eventually executed) are used to verify that programs written in that language satisfy their progress specification.

In this paper, we are interested in formulating a fairness notion appropriate for concurrent programs expressed in programming languages with *multi-party interactions* as their primitive construct for interprocess synchronization and communication. A multi-party interaction is more abstract and higher level than the more commonly used point-to-point communication which is usually expressed by message-passing primitives such as *send* and *receive* (either asynchronous, or *CSP*-like handshaking) or by remote procedure calls (e.g., *ADA*-like *rendezvous*). A single multi-party interaction hides (in more than one way) the details of its implementation by several point-to-point communication operations. Among other things, the ordering of point-to-point communication operations is abstracted away, and so high level designs can be produced which do not contain such low level details. Several such multi-party interaction constructs have been proposed,

---

[†]The work started during a summer visit of the second author to the Software Technology Program of the Microelectronics and Computer Technology Corporation, and continued at the Technion, where the part of the second author was partially supported by the Fund for the Promotion of Research in the Technion, and also by MCC/STP. The first author was supported throughout by a grant from MCC/STP.

e.g., *scripts* [FHT86], *joint actions* [BKS83], *shared actions* [RM87], *compacts* [Ch87] and *teams* and *interactions* [Fo87]. In addition, the *handshakes* in Hoare's algebraic version of CSP [Ho85] are also multi-party synchronizations, though this fact is not stressed there. It is our view that such constructs will become more frequently used as more and more complicated concurrent programs are designed, especially since many implementations of multi-party interactions have appeared [BKS84,BKS88,Ba87,CM87,CM88].

We deal with both serialized and overlapping semantics. In serialized semantics, interaction execution is atomic, i.e., one interaction is executed at a time, and parallelism is modeled by the nondeterministic interleaving of interaction executions. In overlapping semantics, interaction execution has finite (nonzero) duration, so executions of non-conflicting interactions can overlap in time. Parallelism is modeled by the nondeterministic interleaving of interaction fragments, which, roughly speaking, are events that represent the start and finish of interaction executions. As is well known by now for binary interactions (i.e., interactions with exactly two participants) [GFK84,BKS84,BKS85,AFK88,Fr86], natural fairness properties, which are satisfied in a *serialized* execution (one interaction at a time), need not hold in an *overlapping* execution. This also holds, of course, for general multi-party interactions.

A *conspiracy* occurs if, from a certain stage in a computation, an interaction is never enabled for execution because conflicting interactions intermittently engage some of the needed participants. This situation occurs in both serialized and overlapping semantics. What is needed is a fairness notion that prevents this behavior whenever it is due solely to "race conditions", i.e., whenever its prevention involves delaying some interactions and proceeding with independent, non-conflicting interactions (this is made more precise in the sequel). In this paper, we formulate such a fairness notion for multi-party interactions. Our notion also satisfies the three semantic criteria posed in [AFK88] for fairness notions, (namely *feasibility, liveness enhancement*, and *equivalence robustness*, which are briefly explained in this paper) and is the first fairness notion for multi-party interactions that does so (to our knowledge). The existence of such a fairness notion was presented as an open problem by Pnueli [Pn86]. This problem is positively solved in this paper, though it is not clear at this time whether the solution is the most general one.

The rest of the paper is organized as follows. Section 2 presents a mini-language, an abstraction of Raddle [Fo87], in terms of which *hyperfairness*, the fairness notion proposed for multi-party interactions, is defined. Both its serialized and overlapping semantics are given. In Section 3 hyperfairness is defined, and examples are presented, which rely on hyperfairness for their required liveness properties. In Section 4 an *explicit scheduler* transformation [AO83,OA88] for hyperfairness is proposed and proven to be *faithful*, i.e., it generates all and only hyperfair computations of a given program. Section 5 presents our conclusions.

2 The Language IP (Interacting Processes)

In this section we present a simple mini-language, called *IP (Interacting Processes)*, first introduced in [Fr89]. The language is an abstraction and simplification of programming languages containing the multi-party interaction, and is suitable for focusing on fair conflict-resolutions among interactions, omitting other features found in similar, but more elaborate languages. Its main feature is the usage of multi-party interactions as *guards*, thereby generalizing both Dijkstra's original guarded commands language [Dij76], which has only boolean guards, and CSP [Ho78], which uses synchronous binary communication operations as guards. Further results regarding the proof-theory (of partial-correctness) of multi-party interactions, expressed via the IP language, are reported in [Fr89].

A program $P :: [\ P_1 \| \ldots \| P_n\ ]$ consists of a *concurrent composition* of $n \geq 1$ (fixed n) *processes*, having *disjoint* local states (i.e., no shared variables). A *process* P_i, $1 \leq i \leq n$, consists of a statement S, where S may take one of the following forms:

dummy statement - *skip*: A statement with no effect on the state.

assignment - $x := e$: The variable x is local to P_i and e is an expression over P_i's local state.

interaction - $a\,[\bar{v} := \bar{e}]$: Here a is the *interaction name* and $\bar{v} := \bar{e}$ is an optional parallel assignment constituting a *local interaction body*. Process P_i is a *participant* of interaction a. All variables in $\bar{v}$ are local to P_i and pairwise distinct. The expressions $\bar{e}$ may involve variables *not local* to P_i (belonging to other participants of interaction a). The participants of interaction a, denoted PA_a, is the set of all processes that syntactically refer to a. Interaction a is *readied* by process P_i, if control of P_i has reached a point where executing a is one of the possible continuations. Interaction a is *enabled* if and only if *all* of its participants have readied it. It can be executed only if it is enabled. Thus, an interaction synchronizes all of its participants. Execution of an interaction consists of the parallel execution of the local interaction bodies contained in all participant processes. Variables within $\bar{e}$ return the value that they held immediately before execution of interaction a. Upon termination of a local interaction body a participating process resumes its local thread of control (i.e., no synchronization at the end of an interaction). Note that if the body $\bar{v} := \bar{e}$ is empty (so the interaction appears as $a\,[\,]$) for some participating process, the effect of the interaction on that process is pure synchronization.

sequential composition - $S_1; S_2$: First S_1 is executed. If and when it terminates, S_2 is executed. We freely use $S_1; \ldots ; S_k$ for any $k \geq 2$.

nondeterministic selection -

$[\,\bigcup_{k=1,m} B_k; a_k\,[\bar{v}_k := \bar{e}_k] \to S_k\,]$: Here $B_k; a_k\,[\bar{v}_k := \bar{e}_k]$ is a *guard*, composed of two parts. The part B_k is a boolean expression over the local state of P_i. The part $a_k\,[\bar{v}_k := \bar{e}_k]$ is an *interaction guard*. S_k is any statement. When a nondeterministic selection statement is evaluated in some state, the k'th guard is *open* if B_k is true in that state (note that the interaction a_k is *readied* by P_i at that state). The guard is *enabled* if and only if it is open and the interaction a_k is enabled. Executing the statement involves the following steps: evaluation of all boolean parts to determine the collection of open guards. If this collection is empty the statement *fails*. Otherwise an enabled guard is passed (simultaneously with the execution of all the other matching local interaction bodies of a_k in the other participating parties) and then S_k is executed. In case there are open guards, but none is enabled, execution is *blocked* (possibly forever) until some open guard is enabled.

nondeterministic iteration -

$*[\,\bigcup_{k=1,m} B_k; a_k\,[\bar{v}_k := \bar{e}_k] \to S_k\,]$: Similar to the nondeterministic selection, but execution terminates once no open guards exist, and execution of the whole statement is repeated after each execution of a guarded command.

Note that nested concurrency is excluded by the above definition, since it is orthogonal to the issue under investigation. We now turn to formal definitions of the operational semantics, based on Plotkin's transition scheme [Pl83]. We define two different semantics: *serialized* and *overlapping* (compare with a similar distinction in [BKS85] and [GFK84]). The former is better suited for correctness-proofs, while the latter captures better the behavior induced by typical implementations. The difference between the serialized and overlapping semantics is, that in the former each program action is represented by a single transition, while in the latter every program action is represented by a number of transitions (referred to as *action fragments*), one causing the effect of the program action on the state, the rest releasing the participants. The proposed hyperfairness handles conspiracies under both semantic definitions. Throughout we assume some *interpretation* over which computations occur, and leave it implicit.

2.1 Serialized Semantics

The central characteristic of this semantics is that local actions and interactions take place one at a time. A *configuration* $<[S_1\|\ldots\|S_n], \sigma>$ consists of a concurrent program and a global state. The global state is a mapping from program variables to values in the domain of the interpretation. A configuration represents an intermediate stage in a computation where S_i is the rest of the program that process P_i has still to execute (sometimes referred to as its syntactic continuation), while σ is the *current* state at that stage. We stipulate (for facilitating the definition) an *empty* continuation E (not a program in the language) satisfying the identities $S; E = E; S = S$ for every S. A configuration $<[E\|\ldots\|E], \sigma>$ is a *terminal* configuration. For a state σ, we use the usual notions of a *variant* $\sigma[c/x]$

and $\sigma[\bar{c}/\bar{x}]$, obtained from σ by changing the value of x to c ($\bar{x}$ to $\bar{c}$, respectively) and preserving the values of all other variables. We use $\sigma(e)$ to denote the value of an expression e in a state σ. We use PA_a to denote the set of all processes that participate in interaction a, i.e., all processes which contain a construct "$a[\bar{v} := \bar{e}]$" within their body. We now define the (*serialized*) transition relation "$\rightarrow$" among configurations. Note that the transitions given by "$\rightarrow$" are atomic.

$$< [S_1 \| \ldots \|S_i\| \ldots \|S_n], \sigma > \rightarrow$$
$$< [S_1 \| \ldots \|E\| \ldots \|S_n], \sigma > \quad (1)$$

for any $1 \leq i \leq n$, iff $S_i = skip$, or
$S_i = *[\bigsqcup_{j=1,n_i} B_j; a_j[\bar{v}_j := \bar{e}_j] \rightarrow T_j]$ and $\neg \bigvee_{j=1,n_i} B_j$ holds in σ.

$$< [S_1 \| \ldots \|S_i\| \ldots \|S_n], \sigma > \rightarrow$$
$$< [S_1 \| \ldots \|E\| \ldots \|S_n], \sigma[\sigma(e)/x] > \quad (2)$$

for any $1 \leq i \leq n$, iff $S_i = (x := e)$.

$$< [S_1\|..\|S_{i_1-1}\|S_{i_1}\|S_{i_1+1}\|..\|S_{i_k-1}\|S_{i_k}\|S_{i_k+1}\|..\|S_n], \sigma >$$
$$\rightarrow$$
$$< [S_1\|..\|S_{i_1-1}\|S'_{i_1}\|S_{i_1+1}\|..\|S_{i_k-1}\|S'_{i_k}\|S_{i_k+1}\|..\|S_n], \sigma' > \quad (3)$$

iff the following holds: There is an interaction a with a set of participants $PA_a = \{i_1, \ldots, i_k\}$ (for some $1 \leq k \leq n$), and for every $i \in PA_a$ one of the following conditions holds:

(a) $S_i = a[\bar{v}_i := \bar{e}_i]$ and $S'_i = E$

(b) $S_i = [\bigsqcup_{j=1,n_i} B_j; a_j[\bar{v}_j := \bar{e}_j] \rightarrow T_j]$ and there exists some j, $1 \leq j \leq n_i$, s.t. B_j holds in σ, $a_j = a$ and $S'_i = T_j$

(c) $S_i = *[\bigsqcup_{j=1,n_i} B_j; a_j[\bar{v}_j := \bar{e}_j] \rightarrow T_j]$ and there exists some j, $1 \leq j \leq n_i$, s.t. B_j holds in σ, $a_j = a$, $S'_i = T_j; S_i$.

Finally, for all these cases, $\sigma' = \sigma[\sigma(\bar{e})/\bar{v}]$, with $\bar{v} = \bigcup_{i \in PA_a} \bar{v}_i$, $\bar{e} = \bigcup_{i \in PA_a} \bar{e}_i$, where $\cup$ denotes a union operation which is ordered by process index.

For any $1 \leq i \leq n$, if
$$< [S_1 \| \ldots \|S_i\| \ldots \|S_n], \sigma > \rightarrow$$
$$< [S'_1\| \ldots \|S'_i\| \ldots \|S'_n], \sigma' >$$
then
$$< [S_1;T_1\| \ldots \|S_i;T_i\| \ldots \|S_n;T_n], \sigma > \rightarrow$$
$$< [S'_1;T_1\| \ldots \|S'_i;T_i\| \ldots \|S'_n;T_n], \sigma' > \quad (4)$$

where some of the S'_i may be identical to the corresponding S_i. Note that this serialized semantics does impose synchronization at the end of an interaction. For this semantics, we now define the following notions.

Definitions:

(1) A (*serialized*) *computation* π of P on σ is a maximal (finite or infinite) sequence of configurations C_i, $i \geq 0$, such that:
(a) $C_0 = <P, \sigma>$.
(b) For all $i \geq 0$, if C_i is not the last configuration in π, then $C_i \rightarrow C_{i+1}$.

(2) The computation π *terminates* iff it is finite and its last configuration is terminal; π *deadlocks* iff it is finite and its last configuration is *not* terminal.

(3) An interaction a is *enabled* in a configuration C iff C has one of the forms in clause (3) of the definition of '$\rightarrow$' and all the conditions are satisfied for a.

(4) Two interactions a_1 and a_2 are in *conflict* in a configuration C iff both interactions are enabled in C and they have non-disjoint set of participants, i.e., $PA_{a_1} \cap PA_{a_2} \neq \emptyset$.

(5) Two interactions a_1 and a_2 are *independent* iff $PA_{a_1} \cap PA_{a_2} = \emptyset$., i.e., they have no common participant.

(6) Two computations are equivalent iff they differ only in the order in which independent interactions are executed.

(7) The *interaction trace* of a computation is the sequence of interaction names of the interactions that were executed in the computation. Often, the interaction trace suffices to uniquely identify a computation.

2.2 Overlapping Semantics

The main characteristic of this semantics is that it is *not* an interleaving of actions. Rather, actions have (unspecified) *duration*, so that an action can start while another action is in progress (obviously, a non-conflicting one). This is still represented as an interleaving of so called atomic *action fragments* which are of a finer grain of atomicity then that of program actions.

In order to allow the treatment of this semantics within the same transitional framework, we augment a configuration with an additional boolean array (of size n, the number of processes), called the *readiness* state and denoted by ρ. If $\rho[i] = true$, $1 \leq i \leq n$, in a configuration C, this means that process P_i is currently ready to engage in an action (either local or with other participants); otherwise, P_i is *engaged* in some action. In our semantics, the "real" local-state transformation is instantaneous and resets the readiness bit of the acting process(es). However, a participating process can not engage in any other action (including a local one), until another transition, setting the readiness bit, has taken place. Also, in this semantics participants of an interaction are synchronized upon entrance, but are not synchronized upon exit of the interaction. We denote the resulting transition relation by '$---\rightarrow$'. Its defining clauses are similar to the ones in the serialized case, with the following changes.

(a) A state transformation transition can only take place if the readiness bits of all participants are *true*.

(b) In the resulting configuration, the readiness bits of all participants are *false*.

(c) The following atomic transition is added
$< [S_1 ||..|| S_n], \sigma, (\rho[1], .., \rho[i-1], false, \rho[i+1], .., \rho[n]) >$
$---\rightarrow$
$< [S_1 ||..|| S_n], \sigma, (\rho[1], .., \rho[i-1], true, \rho[i+1], .., \rho[n]) >$
for every $1 \leq i \leq n$.

An *overlapping* computation π of P is defined similarly to the serialized case, except that the transition $---\rightarrow$ replaces $\rightarrow$, and the following conditions are added:

(a) In the initial configuration $\rho[i] = true$ for all $1 \leq i \leq n$.

(b) In a terminal configuration $\rho[i] = true$ for all $1 \leq i \leq n$.

(c) In an infinite computation, $\rho[i] = true$ infinitely-often, for every $1 \leq i \leq n$ (i.e., every action terminates within a finite time).

Likewise, the concepts of deadlock, termination and conflict are defined similarly to the serialized case.

We say that process P_i *readies* an interaction a in a configuration C iff P_i satisfies one of the conditions imposed in (a) - (c) in clause (3) of the definition of '$\rightarrow$' and $\rho[i] = true$. We denote this property by $ready_i(a)$. The interaction a is *enabled* in a configuration C iff it is jointly readied in C by all its participants, i.e., $\bigwedge_{i \in PA_a} ready_i(a)$ holds in C.

Note again that the difference between the serialized and overlapping semantics is, that in the former each program action is represented by a single transition, while in the latter every program action is represented by a number of transitions (referred to as *action fragments*), one causing the effect of the program action on the state, the rest releasing the participants. The notion of independence is naturally extended also to action fragments and their representing transitions.

To simplify the notation, we refer only to programs in a normal form similar to the one defined in [ABC87] for CSP programs. In this form, each process consists of one main nondeterministic iteration (after some initialization assignments). The interaction-bodies serving as guards in these iterations are referred to as *top-level* interaction-bodies.

3 Fairness and Hyperfairness for Multi-Party Interactions

We briefly review known fairness notions for multi-party interactions and then suggest a new fairness notion, called *hyperfairness*, having some desirable properties which the previous notions lack. The main additional advantage is that the property of *conspiracy resistance* (to be explained below) is exploited.

Following the distinctions made in [FdR80,KdR83,BKS85,GFK84] (see also [Fr86], chapter

level/subject	Unconditional	Weak	Strong
Process	In an infinite computation every process interacts infinitely often (in any interaction). See remark 1.	In an infinite computation every continuously enabled process interacts infinitely often. See remark 2.	In an infinite computation every infinitely-often enabled process interacts infinitely often.
Group	In an infinite computation every interacting group interacts infinitely often (in any of its mutual interactions). See remarks 1 and 3.	In an infinite computation every continuously enabled interacting group interacts infinitely often.	In an infinite computation every infinitely-often enabled interacting group interacts infinitely often.
Interaction	In an infinite computation every (specific) interaction occurs infinitely often. See remark 1.	In an infinite computation every continuously enabled interaction occurs infinitely often.	In an infinite computation every infinitely-often enabled interaction occurs infinitely often.

Table 1: Fairness notions for multi-party interactions

5), the classification of fairness notions for multi-party interactions presented in [AFK88] is along two orthogonal directions.

(a) *The subject of fairness*: a process, a (fixed) group of processes and a *specific* interaction among a group of processes.

(b) *The level of fairness*: The three common levels are unconditional, weak and strong, which differ in the enabledness conditions required to guarantee eventual execution of the subject action. See [Fr86] for a detailed description of these levels and other variants of fairness. We summarize this classification for the *IP* language in Table 1.

Remarks on Table 1:

(1) This notion is only meaningful in a context where processes (resp. groups, interactions) are always enabled.

(2) A process is enabled if (any) one of its actions is enabled.

(3) Note that a given interacting group may have several different interactions which have that group as the set of participants.

As noted in [AFK88], none of the fairness notions in Table 1 are fully adequate (in a sense defined there and reviewed in the next section) for multi-party interactions. We now propose a fairness notion that *is* adequate.

The main idea can be informally described as follows. A *conspiracy* (w.r.t. an interaction a) occurs if PA_a can be partitioned into two (disjoint) subsets $PA_a^i \cup PA_a^p$, such that all members of PA_a^i are continuously ready to participate in the interaction a, while members of PA_a^p ready a infinitely-often, but *not at the same time*, i.e., not in the same configuration. Thus, in such an infinite computation a is *not* infinitely-often enabled, and need not eventually occur by any of the previously mentioned fairness notions. If the conspiracy is due to the inherent semantics of the program (e.g., see table 5), then there is no way to guarantee the enablement of interaction a. If, however, the conspiracy is due to the interleaving of independent actions, or action fragments, (e.g., see table 2) then it should be possible to control the scheduling in such a way as to eventually cause the enablement of a. This is exactly the behavior which hyperfairness enforces, as described in the succeeding paragraphs.

We wish to ensure that if the members of PA_a^p can infinitely often ready a independently of PA_a^i and of each other, then a will eventually be executed. This is achieved as follows. It is convenient to use one of the well known fairness notions (given in Table 1 above) to ensure actual execution. What remains then, is to ensure that the enabledness condition of this "underlying" fairness notion is met. Since members of PA_a^p ready a independently of PA_a^i and of each other, they can be successively "frozen" in a state in which they ready a (thereby joining PA_a^i), and when they are all "frozen" there, a is enabled. If a is enabled sufficiently often, the underlying fairness notion will ensure the eventual execution of a. In this paper, we chose the underlying fairness notion to be strong interaction fairness, and in the sequel, we use "fairness" to denote strong interaction fairness, unless otherwise stated. We now turn to a formal presentation of these ideas.

Definition (Pnueli).
(1) A process P_i is *insistent* on an interaction a from a certain point in a computation π iff it continuously readies a in π from that point onwards.

(2) A process P_i is *persistent* on an interaction a in a computation π iff it readies a infinitely-often in π.

Definition.
Let P be a program in normal form, a an interaction in P, and A an arbitrary subset of PA_a. The (a, A)-*derived* program $P_{a,A}$ is obtained from P by replacing with *false* the local guard of every top level interaction body b (where $b \neq a$) in every process $P_i \in A$.

In other words, when any processes in A has a continuation from the top level, it is prevented from participating in any interaction other than a.

Definition (Conspiracy Resistance).
An interaction a is *conspiracy resistant* in a program P iff for every fair computation π the following condition holds:

Let π_1 be a finite prefix of π with final configuration $C = <S, \sigma>$, and let PA_a^i be the set of all the participants of a that ready a in C. Then, for every fair computation π_2 of the (a, PA_a^i)-derived program S_{a,PA_a^i} (starting in state σ), there exists a participant $P_j \in (PA_a - PA_a^i)$ such that P_j eventually readies a along π_2.

We refer to this as each process in PA_a^i being a-*frozen*, and to P_j as *independently readying* the interaction a. Thus, conspiracy-resistance may be achieved whenever the participants of a can ready a *independently* of each other. The implied independence manifests itself by the fact that a-freezing an arbitrary subset of the participants of a does not prevent the eventual readiness for a of yet another participant. A scheduler that gradually "freezes" more and more participants of interaction a once such participants ready a ensures the eventual enabledness of a. Note that in the above definition $PA_a^i = \emptyset$ is possible. We now come to the definition of our central notion.

Definition (Hyperfairness).
Let P be an IP program in which every top-level interaction is conspiracy-resistant. Then, an infinite computation π of P is *hyperfair* iff the following condition is met:

π is fair and every top-level interaction is infinitely-often enabled in π. Furthermore, every finite computation of P is hyperfair.

If P is an IP program in which not every top-level interaction is conspiracy-resistant, then every computation π of P is hyperfair.

It is important to notice an essential difference between the fairness notions considered so far on the one hand, and hyperfairness on the other hand. The former imply eventual execution if an appropriate enabledness condition is satisfied. Hyperfairness implies eventual enablement (and subsequent execution due to the underlying fairness) if the condition of conspiracy resistance is satisfied. Note that enablement and conspiracy resistance are different types of conditions. An enablement condition for a particular interaction a of a particular program P may hold in some computations (π) of P but not in others, i.e., it is a function of a, P, and π, whereas conspiracy resistance is not a property of individual computations, i.e., it is a function only of a and P.

With any of the previous fairness notions, if a (top level) interaction a does not satisfy the enabledness condition, e.g., if a is never enabled along a computation π, then π is vacuously fair with respect to a. However, this is not the case with hyperfairness. If all top level interactions are conspiracy resistant, then π is not hyperfair with respect to interaction a *because a* is not enabled at any point of π. Note that if a different underlying fairness notion were used, e.g., weak interaction fairness, then a different hyperfairness notion would be required, namely one that ensures the required enabledness conditions for weak interaction fairness. We now present several examples which illustrate hyperfairness.

$PHIL :: [p_1 \| \ldots \| p_n \| f_1 \| \ldots \| f_n]$ where

$$p_i :: s_i :=' t';$$
$$*[\ s_i =' t' \rightarrow s_i :=' h'$$
$$[]$$
$$s_i =' h'; \ get\text{--}forks_i\ [s_i :=' e'] \rightarrow give\text{--}forks_i\ [s_i :=' t']$$
$$],$$

$$f_i :: *[\ get\text{--}forks_i\ [\,] \rightarrow give\text{--}forks_i\ [\,]$$
$$[]$$
$$get\text{--}forks_{i+1}\ [\,] \rightarrow give\text{--}forks_{i+1}\ [\,]$$
$$].$$

Table 2: A starvation free solution of the dining philosophers problem in hyperfair IP

Example 1 (dining philosophers). A typical problem which can be solved by the introduction of hyperfairness is the famous *dining philosophers* problem. A solution formulated in the *IP* language is presented in Table 2. In this example, when the i'th philosopher p_i is *hungry* ($s_i = 'h'$) it can *eat* ($s_i = 'e'$) by interacting in the three-party interaction $get\text{--}forks_i$ (together with the i'th fork f_i and the i–1-th fork f_{i-1}). In this and all other dining philosopher examples, all operations on indices are cyclic. After p_i finishes eating, it becomes *thinking* ($s_i = 't'$) by interacting with the same forks once again in the $give\text{--}forks_i$ interaction.

This program displays conspiratorial behavior. Let $n = 4$ (i.e., 4 philosophers) and suppose that p_2 is in a *hungry* state and waits (insistently!) for the interaction $get\text{--}forks_2$ to be executed. In order for that interaction to be enabled, it has to be readied simultaneously by both fork-processes f_1 and f_2. Consider the following interaction trace π of a serialized computation

$$\pi = get\text{--}forks_1\ get\text{--}forks_3\ (give\text{--}forks_1\ get\text{--}forks_1$$
$$give\text{--}forks_3\ get\text{--}forks_3\ )^\omega$$

It is clear that $get\text{--}forks_2$ is never enabled in π because $get\text{--}forks_1$ and $get\text{--}forks_3$ alternately engage f_1 and f_2 respectively. Note that the conspiracy against $get\text{--}forks_2$ in π is due to "unfortunate" scheduling which prevents f_1 and f_2 from readying $get\text{--}forks_2$ simultaneously. This is an example of conspiracy occurring in the serialized semantics, since π is a serialized computation. Now p_i is insistent on $get\text{--}forks_i$ (once $s_i = 'h'$), and the two fork processes f_i and f_{i-1} ready $get\text{--}forks_i$ independently of each other and of p_i, so the interaction $get\text{--}forks_i$ (for every $1 \leq i \leq n$) is conspiracy-resistant. As all top level interactions are conspiracy resistant, by hyperfairness, $get\text{--}forks_i$ must be enabled infinitely often, and so π will be excluded as an illegal (i.e., not hyperfair) computation. Note that in the interaction trace of the equivalent computation

$$\pi' = get\text{--}forks_1\ get\text{--}forks_3\ (give\text{--}forks_1\ give\text{--}forks_3$$
$$get\text{--}forks_1\ get\text{--}forks_3\ )^\omega$$

in which the $get\text{--}forks_1$ interaction is commuted with the independent $give\text{--}forks_3$ interaction, no conspiracies occur, and $get\text{--}forks_2$ is infinitely often enabled (it is enabled immediately after $get\text{--}forks_3$ has been executed). But π' is also not hyperfair, because $get\text{--}forks_2$ is infinitely often enabled but never executed, and so π' is not fair.

Example 2 (dining philosophers with fork cleaning). In the previous example, the two forks readied the $get\text{--}forks_i$ interaction unconditionally. Here is a somewhat strengthened example (Table 3), where the forks have boolean conditions and additional interactions with a *cleaning* process c, which interacts with a non-clean fork to clean it. Here $clean\text{--}test_i$ represents some hidden condition, returning a boolean value representing the state of cleanliness of a fork. It is easy to see that the $get\text{--}forks_i$ interactions are still conspiracy-

$PHIL :: [p_1 \| \ldots \| p_n \| f_1 \| \ldots \| f_n \| c]$ where

$p_i :: \ldots$ as before $\ldots$

$f_i :: clean_i := true;$
$\quad *[\ clean_i;\ get-forks_i\ [\ ] \to give-forks_i\ [clean_i := clean-test_i]$
$\quad\quad []$
$\quad\quad clean_i;\ get-forks_{i+1}\ [\ ] \to give-forks_{i+1}[clean_i := clean-test_i]$
$\quad\quad []$
$\quad\quad \neg clean_i;\ cleaning_i\ [clean_i := true] \to skip$
$\quad\ ],$

$c :: \{cleaning\ service\} * [\ \underset{i=1,n}{[]}\ cleaning_i\ [\ ] \to skip]$

Table 3: Dining philosophers with a cleaning service

resistant. This property follows from the structure of process c, which is ready to interact with any fork. However, the $cleaning_i$ interactions are *not* conspiracy-resistant! To see that, consider a configuration C in which the fork-process f_i is clean (i.e., $clean_i = true$ holds), while f_{i-1} and f_{i+1} are dirty (i.e. $\neg clean_{i-1}$ and $\neg clean_{i+1}$ hold). Clearly, $c \in PA^i_{cleaning_i},$[‡] in C, since it readies $cleaning_i$. Let π_2 be a continuation from C, along which c is "frozen" on $cleaning_i$. Then, c will never clean any of f_{i-1} and f_{i+1}, preventing p_{i-1} and p_i from eating and f_i from getting dirty, thereby readying the $cleaning_i$ interaction. Thus, $cleaning_i$ is not conspiracy-resistant due to the failure of f_i to ready it independently of c. Hence, a hyperfair scheduler which freezes c like this could cause a deadlock (e.g., if all forks except f_i are dirty, and c is $cleaning_i$-frozen, then no interaction is enabled and the system is deadlocked).

Example 3 (dining philosophers with a diligent cleaner). The example in Table 4 displays a conspiracy-resistant fork-cleaning interaction. It is not surprising, that achieving this end involves a "harder-working" cleaning process. In order to prevent the mutual-dependency of readying the $cleaning$ interaction, the cleaning-process c keeps track of the cleanliness state of all forks, and readies $cleaning_i$ only if f_i is dirty. Thus,

---

[‡]note that the superscript i denotes "insistence" while the sub-subscript i is an index over $1 \ldots n$

when c is $cleaning_i$-frozen, f_i is dirty and so $cleaning_i$ is enabled. Therefore, the situation in the previous example is avoided.

Example 4 (dining philosophers with vicious forks). Finally, we present (Table 5) another variant of the dining philosophers problem in which the $get-forks_i$ interactions are *not* conspiracy-resistant and hyperfairness does not help. In this example, the neighbor forks f_i, f_{i-1} interact among themselves in a $switch_i$ interaction and thus coordinate their readiness to participate in the $get-forks_i$ interaction, i.e., the l_i boolean in f_i and the r_{i-1} boolean in f_{i-1} are never simultaneously true, and so the $get-forks_i$ interaction is never enabled. Hence conspiracy is inherent in the program semantics, and is not due to race conditions. The program for p_i is as in Table 2.

4 Properties of Hyperfairness

In this section we analyze hyperfairness in terms of the (briefly reviewed here) criteria of feasibility, equivalence robustness, and liveness enhancement, which are posed and formally defined in [AFK88].

Feasibility: Any fairness assumption excludes some of the otherwise admissible computations (the "unfair" ones). A necessary property of a fairness assumption

$PHIL :: [p_1\|\ldots\|p_n\|f_1\|\ldots\|f_n\|c]$ where

$p_i :: \ldots$ as before $\ldots$

$f_i :: \ldots$ as in Table 3 $\ldots$

$c ::$ {diligent cleaner} $c_1 := true; \ldots c_n := true;$
$\quad *[\; \underset{i=1,n}{[]} \; c_i \wedge c_{i-1}; \; get\text{-}forks_i \,[\,] \rightarrow skip$
$\quad\quad \underset{i=1,n}{[]} \; give\text{-}forks_i \,[c_i := clean\text{-}test_i; \; c_{i-1} := clean\text{-}test_{i-1}] \rightarrow skip$
$\quad\quad \underset{i=1,n}{[]} \; \neg c_i; \; cleaning_i \,[c_i := true] \rightarrow skip \;]$

Table 4: Dining philosophers with a diligent cleaning service

$PHIL :: [p_1\|\ldots\|p_n\|f_1\|\ldots\|f_n]$ where

$p_i :: \ldots$ as before $\ldots$

$f_i :: l_i := true; \; r_i := true; \; c_i := true; \; sw_i := true;$
$\quad *[\; l_i; \; get\text{-}forks_i \,[\,] \rightarrow give\text{-}forks_i \,[\,]$
$\quad\quad []$
$\quad\quad r_i; \; get\text{-}forks_{i+1} \,[\,] \rightarrow give\text{-}forks_{i+1} \,[\,]$
$\quad\quad []$
$\quad\quad switch_i \,[c_i := \neg c_i; \; sw_i := (c_i = sw_i); \; l_i := (c_i \wedge sw_i)] \rightarrow skip$
$\quad\quad []$
$\quad\quad switch_{i+1} \,[r_i := (c_{i+1} \wedge \neg sw_{i+1})] \rightarrow skip$
$\quad\;].$

Table 5: Dining philosophers with vicious forks

is that for every program some (finite or infinite) fair computation does exist (in other words, not all computations are excluded). Without this requirement, no scheduler could correctly treat the fairness and produce one of the fair computations. Moreover, since any reasonable scheduler cannot 'predict' the possible continuations at each point of the computation, it should be possible to extend every partial computation to a fair one.

Equivalence robustness: Concurrent systems are often modeled by means of interleaving (atomic) actions. However, the order of execution of *independent* actions in such an interleaving is arbitrary. Thus two execution sequences which are identical up to the order of independent actions are equivalent. This leads to the second criterion: a fairness assumption is *equivalence robust* if it respects this equivalence. That is, for two equivalent infinite sequences either both are fair according to the given definition, or both are unfair.

Liveness Enhancement: All models of parallel computation assume a fundamental liveness property that an action will eventually be executed in some process if the system is not deadlocked. A justification for adding an additional liveness requirement in the form of a fairness notion, is that there exists a program which has some liveness property which it would not have without the fairness notion. This criterion is termed *liveness enhancement* in order to emphasize that additional liveness properties will hold for some programs. Some fairness notions cannot force a communication to occur in a model if it did not have to occur under the fundamental liveness property. These notions are not liveness enhancing for that model.

A fairness notion is *fully adequate* iff it is feasible, equivalence-robust and liveness enhancing. The main result in this section is the establishment of the full adequacy of hyperfairness. *Feasibility* is established by presenting an *explicit scheduler* ([AO83]) for hyperfairness and proving its *faithfulness*. This is done below. *Liveness enhancement* follows from the examples in Section 3. *Equivalence robustness* is established by the following lemma.

Lemma: hyperfairness is equivalence robust.
Proof: Let π_1, π_2 be the interaction traces of two equivalent computations of program P. If P contains a top level interaction that is not conspiracy resistant, then every computation of P is hyperfair and we are done. Thus we now assume that every top level interaction of P is conspiracy resistant. We now establish (π_1 is hyperfair implies π_2 is hyperfair), which establishes the lemma. By definition of hyperfairness, we have that π_1 is (strongly) fair and every top level interaction is infinitely often enabled in π_1. Hence, by definition of strong fairness, every top level interaction is executed infinitely often along π_1. As π_1 and π_2 are equivalent, and therefore contain the same interaction events, every top level interaction is executed infinitely often along π_2 as well, thus π_2 is strongly fair. Also, every top level interaction must be infinitely often enabled along π_2 (in order to be infinitely often executed), hence π_2 is hyperfair. □

4.1 An explicit scheduler for hyperfairness

Let P be a typical IP program in normal form. Let $a_1, \ldots, a_m$, for some $m \geq 0$, be an enumeration of all the top-level interactions in P. With each interaction a_j we associate a *priority variable* z_j (as in [AO83]). We now define a hyperfair scheduler H for IP. It is represented as an additional process, running in parallel with $P_i, 1 \leq i \leq n$, and having access to all of their local states, including the control positions. The priority variables z_i are local to H. We skip here the somewhat tedious task of representing the combined program in IP.

The (index of the) interaction with the highest priority is chosen by H and preserved in a local variable MIN:

$$MIN \stackrel{def.}{=} \min\{k \mid z_k = \min\{z_l \mid l = 1, \ldots, m\}\}.$$

In every process P_i, $1 \leq i \leq n$, the following modification is made: in the top level nondeterministic iteration, the local guard B_j^i (guarding a top level interaction a_j in P_i) is strengthened to:

$$B_j^i \wedge (i \in PA_{MIN} \Rightarrow (j = MIN \vee \neg B_{MIN}^i)).$$

Thus, a participant of a_{MIN} does not ready any other interaction once it readies a_{MIN} (is indeed a_{MIN}-frozen), until a_{MIN} is enabled. When a_{MIN} is enabled,

$$H :: z_1 :=?, \ldots; z_n :=?; \textit{compmin};$$
$$[\underset{j=1,n}{[]} j = MIN \rightarrow [\bigwedge_{i \in PA_{get-forks_j}} ready_i(get\text{-}forks_j) \rightarrow \forall k \neq j : z_k := z_k - 1; z_j :=?; \textit{compmin}$$
$$[]$$
$$\neg \bigwedge_{i \in PA_{get-forks_j}} ready_i(get\text{-}forks_j) \rightarrow skip\,]$$
$$].$$

Table 6: Hyperfair scheduler for dining philosophers example

the following update of the z_i variables takes place. First, $z_{MIN} :=?$, (this denotes the assignment of an arbitrary positive integer to z_{MIN}) and for $k \neq MIN$, $z_k := z_k - 1$, after which MIN is redetermined, and all strengthened local guards are reevaluated. In order to avoid an extra level of indexing, we assume here that each process has at most one interaction-body for each interaction a_j, $1 \leq j \leq m$.

It is important to note that the hyperfair scheduler H really acts in conjunction with a given scheduler (call it F) for the underlying fairness notion. The real task of H (under the assumption that all the interactions in the program P are conspiracy-resistant) is to force a situation where each interaction is sufficiently-often enabled, and therefore eventually scheduled by F. However, if some top level interactions in P are not conspiracy-resistant, H will not guarantee the enabledness of any interaction and a conspiracy may occur. In this case, the combined execution may end in a deadlock (see example 2, previous section). Thus, the implementation should employ a deadlock-detection procedure, and remove all the restrictions imposed by H if deadlock ever occurs, as this would indicate that at least one top level interaction is not conspiracy resistant, and in this case, hyperfairness guarantees nothing. We now state and prove the main theorem expressing the required properties of H.

Theorem (faithfulness of H):

For every $P \in IP$, if all top-level interactions in P are conspiracy-resistant in P, then:

(a) The restriction of every infinite fair computation of P under H (to variables of P) is a computation of P along which every top-level interaction is infinitely-often enabled (i.e., is a hyperfair computation).

(b) Every fair computation of P along which every top-level interaction is infinitely-often enabled (i.e., every hyperfair computation), can be extended (by assigning values to the $\bar{z}$ variables) to an infinite computation of P under H.

The proof (given in the full paper) is structured similarly to the ones in [AO83]. In proving (a), we show that once an interaction is chosen as MIN, its conspiracy-resistance guarantees its eventual enabledness. Given that, it is shown that if there is a conspiracy-resistant interaction a_i not enabled from some point onwards, this means that other interactions serve as the current MIN and are repeatedly enabled, decreasing z_i until $MIN = i$ has to hold. In proving (b), the values assigned to each z_i keep track, roughly speaking, of the number of interactions that are executed until the next time a_i is enabled.

As a simple example, consider again the dining philosophers program in Table 2. As the $get\text{-}forks$ interactions have no boolean part in their guards, p_i is insistent on $get\text{-}forks_i$ once $s_i = 'h'$ holds. The $get\text{-}forks_i$ interactions are conspiracy-resistant, and we have H of the form shown in table 6. Here $compmin$ is the program section

$$MIN := \min\{k \mid z_k = \min\{z_l \mid l = 1, \ldots, n\}\}.$$

Due to the conspiracy-resistance of $get\text{-}forks_{MIN}$ and the modifications of the processes as above, $get\text{-}forks_{MIN}$ will eventually be enabled. The underlying fairness will eventually select it for execution, implying the non-starvation of p_{MIN}. Since every $get-forks_i$ interaction is eventually selected as MIN, no philosopher starves.

5 Conclusions

In this paper, a fairness notion fully-adequate for multi-party interactions, called *hyperfairness* is presented. It guarantees that top-level *conspiracy-resistant* interactions, in which each participant infinitely-often readies the interaction independently of all other participants, are infinitely-often enabled, and by the underlying fairness are also infinitely-often executed. Thus hyperfairness eliminates computations where the reason for an interaction a being never enabled is simply "unfortunate" scheduling, as opposed to the case where the reason is inherent in the program semantics, in which case no fairness notion can guarantee the eventual enablement (and subsequent execution) of a.

Though conspiracy-resistance is a rather strong property, it does occur quite often when the processes are loosely coupled in the sense that there is no strong causal dependence in sequences of consecutive interactions in which a process participates. The dining philosophers problem is a typical situation where conspiracy-resistance holds. We defer the issue of presenting a formal proof-rule for proving conspiracy-resistance to another occasion.

We believe that the study of subtle liveness properties of multi-party interaction is crucial to their understanding. A first step towards this end is proposed in this paper.

Acknowledgements

We wish to thank Shmuel Katz for useful discussions related to the definition of conspiracy-resistance and its connection to equivalence robustness. Thanks are also due to Leslie Lamport who detected an error in the definition of conspiracy resistance in an earlier draft.

References

[ABC87] K.R. Apt, L. Bouge, Ph. Clermont: "Two normal form theorems for CSP programs", IPL 26, 1987, pp. 165-171.

[AFK88] K.R. Apt, N. Francez, S. Katz: "Appraising Fairness in Distributed Languages", Distributed Computing 2:226-241, August 1988. Also: proc. 14th ACM-POPL symposium, Munich, Germany, Jan. 1987.

[AO83] K.R. Apt, E.-R. Olderog: "Proof Rules and Transformations Dealing With Fairness", Science of Computer Programming 3, pp. 65-100, 1983.

[Ba87] R. Bagrodia: "A Distributed Algorithm to Implement N-Party Rendezvous", TR, Dept. of Computer Science, Univ. of Texas at Austin, June 1987.

[BKS83] R.J.R. Back, R. Kurki-Suonio: "Decentralization of Process Nets With Centralized Control", Distributed Computing 3:73-87, 1989. Also: proc. 2nd ACM-PODC, Montreal, Canada, August 1983.

[BKS84] R.J.R. Back, R. Kurki-Suonio: "Cooperation in distributed systems using symmetric multiprocess handshaking", TR A34, Abo Akademi, 1984.

[BKS85] R.J.R. Back, R. Kurki-Suonio: "Serializability in Distributed Systems With Handshaking", TR 85-109, CMU, 1985.

[BKS88] R.J.R. Back, R. Kurki-Suonio: "Distributed cooperation with action systems", ACM-TOPLAS 10,4: 513-554, October 1988

[Ch87] A. Charlesworth: "The Multiway Rendezvous", ACM-TOPLAS 9, 2: 350-366, July 1987.

[CM87] K.M. Chandy, J. Misra: "Synchronizing Asynchronous Processes - the Committee-Coordination Problem", TR, Dept. of Computer Science, Univ. of Texas at Austin, 1987.

[CM88] K.M. Chandy, J. Misra: **Parallel Program Design: A Foundation**, (chapter 14), Addison Wesley, 1988.

[Dij76] E.W. Dijkstra: **A Discipline of Programming**, Prentice-Hall, 1976.

[FdR80] N. Francez, W.P. de Roever: "Fairness in Communicating Processes", unpublished memo, Computer Science Dept., Utrecht University, July 1980.

[FHT86] N. Francez, B.T. Hailpern, G. Taubenfeld: "SCRIPT - A Communication Abstraction Mechanism and Its Verification", Science of Computer Programming 6,1, pp. 35-88, Jan. 1986.

[Fo87] I.R. Forman: "On the Design of Large Distributed Systems", TR STP-098-86 (Rev. 1.0), MCC, Austin, TX, Jan. 1987. A preliminary version presented at the First International Conf. on Computer Languages, Miami, FL, October 1986.

[Fr86] N. Francez: **Fairness**, Springer-Verlag, 1986.

[Fr89] N. Francez: "Cooperating proofs for distributed programs with multi-party interactions", IPL Vol. 32, No. 5, pp. 235-242, September 1989.

[GFK84] O. Grumberg, N. Francez, S. Katz: "Fair Termination of Communicating Processes", 3rd ACM-PODC Conference, Vancouver, BC, Canada, August 1984.

[Ho78] C.A.R. Hoare: "Communicating Sequential Processes", CACM 21,8, pp. 666-678, August 1978.

[Ho85] C.A.R. Hoare: **Communicating Sequential Processes**, Prentice-Hall, 1985.

[KdR83] R. Kuiper, W.P. de Roever: "Fairness Assumptions for CSP in a Temporal Logic Framework", proc. TC.2 Working Conference on Formal Description of Programming Concepts, Garmisch Partenkirchen (D. Biorner, ed.), North Holland, 1983.

[OA88] E.-R. Olderog, K.R. Apt: "Transformations Realizing Fairness Assumptions for Parallel Programs", ACM-TOPLAS 10,3: 420-455, July 1988.

[Pl83] G.D. Plotkin: "An Operational Semantics for CSP", TC.2 working group conference on the formal description of programming concepts, Garmisch Partenkirchen, (D. Biorner, ed.), North Holland, 1983.

[Pn86] A. Pnueli: lecture notes of CS395T, "Specification and Verification of Reactive Systems", Univ. of Texas at Austin, fall 1986 (notes taken by Charlie Richter).

[RM87] S. Ramesh, H. Mehndiratta: "A methodology for developing distributed programs", IEEE-TSE vol. SE-13, 8: 967-976, August 1987.

RELATING TOTAL AND PARTIAL CORRECTNESS INTERPRETATIONS OF NON-DETERMINISTIC PROGRAMS

Carl A. Gunter

University of Pennsylvania
Department of Computer and Information Sciences
Philadelphia, PA 19104 U.S.A.
gunter@cis.upenn.edu

Abstract

The purpose of this paper is to discuss the relationship between the interpretations of non-deterministic programs using the upper (total correctness) powerdomain on the one hand and the lower (partial correctness) powerdomain on the other. It is shown that there is a close semantic relationship between these two interpretations which suggests the formulation of a new operator called the *mixed powerdomain*. It is shown that the mixed powerdomain has many pleasing domain-theoretic and algebraic properties. The mixed powerdomain is closely related to new powerdomains which have been recently investigated as mathematical models of partial information in databases. Some of the basic intuitions captured by such structures may have uses for the specification of non-deterministic computations. The paper includes a sample non-deterministic programming language and a semantics using the mixed powerdomain.

1 Introduction.

The literature on the denotational semantics of non-deterministic programs has focused on the use of three operators known as the *upper*, *lower* and *convex* powerdomains (sometimes also known as the Smyth, Hoare and Plotkin powerdomains respectively). Each of the three powerdomains reflects a different attitude about what the semantics is trying to capture about the meaning of a program. However, it is my goal in this paper to explore the idea that there is a fourth view of program meaning which is not fully captured by these three operators. In particular, I will present a kind of generalization of the convex powerdomain called the *mixed* powerdomain. The mixed powerdomain generalizes the convex powerdomain by allowing the "total correctness component" of program meaning to differ from the "partial correctness component" of program meaning. Structures based on a closely related intuition have been found useful in research on mathematical models of partial information in databases [BDW88, BO86, BJO89] and it is my belief that some of the results that have been uncovered there may be relevant in the study of the semantics of non-deterministic programs. (Just as the research on powerdomains has influenced this research on databases.)

A *powerdomain* is a "computable" analog of the powerset operator. They were introduced in the 1970's as a tool for providing semantics for programming languages with non-determinism. For such applications, the powerset operator was unsatisfactory for basically the same reasons that the full function space was unusable for the semantics of certain features of sequential programming languages (such as higher-order procedures and dynamic scoping). In the full powerset, there are *too many* sets and this causes problems for the solution of recursive domain equations. Hence, such applications call for a more parsimonious theory of subsets, based on a concept of non-deterministic computability.

The study of powerdomains has revealed many interesting connections between the semantics of programming languages and traditional topics of mathematical research in topology and category theory as well as ideas from logic. It is the goal of this paper to exploit some of the intuitions learned from these lines of research. The seminal work on powerdomains and their application in programming language semantics was G. Plotkin's paper [Plo76] on what is often called the *Plotkin powerdomain*. Subsequent research by M. B. Smyth [Smy78] led to the discovery of two similar constructions often called the *Smyth* and *Hoare* powerdomains. These three powerdomains have been used widely in programming language theory, and they have also sparked a body of theoretical research into their properties and relationships to similar constructions in Mathematics. Smyth [Smy83] demonstrated a close connection between the Smyth and Hoare powerdomains and the concepts of upper and lower semi-continuity respectively. He also found that the Plotkin powerdomain was related to what is known as the *Vietoris construction* from topology. This research led Smyth to suggest the names for the three powerdomains which I will use below: upper (Smyth), lower (Hoare) and convex (Plotkin). The categorical significance of the powerdomains was demonstrated by Hennessy and Plotkin [HP79] who proved that each of the three can be seen as a left adjoints to appropriate forgetful functors. There has also been progress on understanding the powerdomains from the point of view of logic. Winskel [Win85] showed how each of the three powerdomains can be characterized using modal formulas under an interpretation in terms of non-deterministic computations. Abramsky has highlighted many useful connections between domains, topology and logic in his work on "domains in logical form" [Abr88, Abr87, Abr89] where he gives a thorough treatment of the logic of the convex powerdomain.

This body of research has several benefits. First of all it provides us with much more perspective on why the upper, lower and convex powerdomain constructions are "natural" and, of course, we are benefited by a deeper understanding of the mathematical properties of the operators themselves. Such an understanding can assist us, for example, in finding good axioms for programs which can be given a powerdomain semantics. For this paper, the basic mathematical theory of powerdomains—in particular, their logical properties—suggest new constructions which carry intuitions which are not fully captured by the upper, lower and convex operators. The theory for these latter operators provides a standard for properties which must be proved for any new construction. In this paper I will show that many of these properties can be proved for the new operator which I will present.

This paper is divided into five sections. After this introductory discussion the second section defines a PCF-like programming language with a non-deterministic choice operator. The denotational semantics for the language using powerdomains is described. It is argued that there is an intuitive relationship between meanings of programs given using partial and total correctness interpretations which can be partly captured by a binary relation between the upper and lower powerdomains. This binary relation can itself be viewed as a powerdomain called the *mixed* powerdomain. The third section discusses the domain-theoretic properties of the mixed powerdomain in some detail. It is shown that the mixed powerdomain can be extended to a continuous functor $\mathcal{M}$ which can appear in recursive domain equations. It is shown that $\mathcal{M}$ is distinct from the convex (Plotkin) powerdomain but, like the convex powerdomain, does not preserve the bounded completeness property of Scott domains. It is shown that the upper and lower powerdomains can be embedded into the mixed powerdomain, while the convex powerdomain is isomorphic to an easy-to-understand subdomain. On the other hand the mixed powerdomain is isomorphic to a simple subdomain of the lattice of Scott open subsets of the convex powerdomain. The fourth section introduces the concept of a mix algebra and shows how the mixed powerdomain can be characterized in terms of mix algebras. An open problem concerning the algebraic properties of the emptyset in powerdomains is discussed in this context and it is shown that the emptyset can be cleanly accommodated using the ideas for the mixed powerdomain. The fifth section discusses an extension of the programming language given in the second section by adding a second flavor of non-deterministic choice. An operational semantics for this new construct is defined and discussed. It is then shown how the idea embodied in the now construct and its operational semantics can be captured denotationally using the mixed powerdomain.

2 Powerdomain semantics for a simple non-deterministic programming language.

In this section, I will describe a simple programming language similar to the language PCF of Plotkin [Plo77] but including a (boundedly) non-deterministic choice primitive. A semantics using a "generic" powerdomain is then given to illustrate how the specific choice of powerdomain need not affect the form of the semantic equations (although the meanings of programs will depend on the choice of certain domains and operators). I will then discuss the question of how the semantics using the upper and lower powerdomains could be related. The main goal of the section is to motivate a relation $\bowtie$ between upper and lower powerdomains of a domain D which which has the property that the interpretation of a expression in one powerdomain must be in the $\bowtie$ relation with the interpretation in the other powerdomain. It will be shown that this relation is preserved by basic powerdomain operations.

The abstract syntax for the *raw terms* of our sample language is given as follows:

$$
\begin{aligned}
x &\in \text{Variable} \\
z &\in \text{IntegerNumeral} \\
s &::= \text{int} \mid \text{bool} \mid s \to s \mid \\
e &::= z \mid \text{plus} \mid \text{times} \mid \text{negation} \mid \\
&\quad \text{true} \mid \text{false} \mid \text{andalso} \mid \text{not} \mid \\
&\quad \text{equals} \mid \text{lessthan} \mid \\
&\quad x:s \mid \lambda x:s.\,e \mid e(e) \mid \\
&\quad \mu x:s.\,e \mid \text{if } e \text{ then } e \text{ else } e \mid e \text{ or } e
\end{aligned}
$$

The symbols x and z range over syntactic classes of *variables* and *integer numerals* respectively. The *type expressions* are those of the simple typed lambda-calculus with two base types **integer** and **boolean**. The language of expressions is basically the simple typed lambda calculus with recursion $\mu x:s.\,e$, a branching construct **if** e **then** e **else** e, and a collection of basic operations. What makes the language particularly of interest here is the fact that it also includes a non-deterministic branching construct e_1 **or** e_2.

We will give a semantics to derivable sequents of the form $H \vdash e : s$ where e is a raw term and H is a *type context* $x_1:s_1,\ldots,x_n:s_n$ where the variables x_i are distinct and include all of the free variables of e. A program of the language will be a term $e:s$ with no free variables such that $\vdash e:s$ is derivable in the calculus which will now be described. First of all, the basic constants have types assigned as follows:

$$
\begin{aligned}
H &\vdash z : \text{int} \\
H &\vdash \text{plus} : \text{int} \to (\text{int} \to \text{int}) \\
H &\vdash \text{times} : \text{int} \to (\text{int} \to \text{int}) \\
H &\vdash \text{negation} : \text{int} \to \text{int} \\
H &\vdash \text{true} : \text{bool} \\
H &\vdash \text{false} : \text{bool} \\
H &\vdash \text{andalso} : \text{bool} \to (\text{bool} \to \text{bool}) \\
H &\vdash \text{not} : \text{bool} \to \text{bool} \\
H &\vdash \text{equals} : \text{int} \to (\text{int} \to \text{bool}) \\
H &\vdash \text{lessthan} : \text{int} \to (\text{int} \to \text{bool})
\end{aligned}
$$

Functions such as addition have been written in "curried" form to make the semantic functions a bit simpler to define. Types for the expressions of the calculus must be derived from the following axiom and rules:

$$H, x:s, H' \vdash x:s$$

$$\frac{H, x:s \vdash e:t}{H \vdash \lambda x:s.\,e : s \to t}$$

$$\frac{H \vdash e : s \to t \qquad H \vdash e' : s}{H \vdash e(e') : t}$$

$$\frac{H, x:s \vdash e:s}{H \vdash \mu x:s.\,e : s}$$

$$\frac{H \vdash e : \text{bool} \qquad H \vdash e' : s \qquad H \vdash e'' : s}{H \vdash \text{if } e \text{ then } e' \text{ else } e'' : s}$$

$$\frac{H \vdash e : s \qquad H \vdash e' : s}{H \vdash e \text{ or } e' : s}$$

The following rules define our intended operational semantics for the most interesting constructs in the calculus:

$$\lambda x.\,e \Rightarrow \lambda x.\,e$$

$$\frac{e \Rightarrow \lambda x.\,e'' \qquad e' \Rightarrow c' \qquad [c'/x]e'' \Rightarrow c}{e(e') \Rightarrow c}$$

$$\frac{e_1 \Rightarrow \text{true} \qquad e_2 \Rightarrow c}{\text{if } e_1 \text{ then } e_2 \text{ else } e_3 \Rightarrow c}$$

$$\frac{e_1 \Rightarrow \text{false} \qquad e_3 \Rightarrow c}{\text{if } e_1 \text{ then } e_2 \text{ else } e_3 \Rightarrow c}$$

$$\frac{e_1 \Rightarrow c}{e_1 \text{ or } e_2 \Rightarrow c} \qquad \frac{e_2 \Rightarrow c}{e_1 \text{ or } e_2 \Rightarrow c}$$

$$\frac{[\mu x.\,e/x]e \Rightarrow c}{\mu x.\,e \Rightarrow c}$$

Note that the function applications are evaluated in applicative order and evaluation is non-deterministic because of the last two rules.

I will now outline a semantics using powerdomains for the language just presented. Let P be a powerdomain operator. Types are given a meaning as domains as follows:

- $\text{int}^* = P(\mathbb{Z}_\perp)$ where $\mathbb{Z}$ is the discrete poset of integers.

- $\text{bool}^* = P(\mathbb{B}_\perp)$ where $\mathbb{B}$ is a discrete poset with two elements tt and ff.

- $(s \to t)^* = P((\sigma \multimap t^*)_\perp)$ where $P(\sigma) \equiv s^*$.

Because of the choice construct e_1 or e_2, every program has a set of possible values that may result from its evaluation.

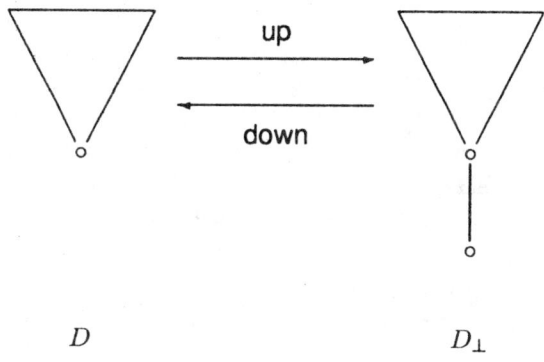

Figure 1: The lift of a cpo.

Hence, each type must be interpreted as a powerdomain of values. Given domains D and E, I have written $D \multimap E$ for the domain of strict ($\bot$-preserving) continuous functions and $D_\bot$ for the *lift* of D obtained by adding a new least element. The interpretation of functions as (sets of) lifted strict functions reflects the operational rules for the evaluation of lambda-expressions and applications as given above.

For example, the interpretation **plus*** of the addition function is a the singleton element

$$\{|\mathsf{up}(\lambda n : \mathbb{Z}_\bot. \{|\mathsf{up}(\lambda m : \mathbb{Z}_\bot. \{|m+n|\})|\})|\}$$

in the domain

$$(\mathbf{int} \to (\mathbf{int} \to \mathbf{int}))^*$$
$$= P((\mathbb{Z}_\bot \multimap P((\mathbb{Z}_\bot \multimap P(\mathbb{Z}_\bot))_\bot))_\bot)$$

The brackets $\{| \cdot |\}$ represent the singleton operation associated with the powerdomain and the function ext extends a function $f : D \to P(E)$ to a function $\mathsf{ext}(f) : P(D) \to P(E)$. The map up is a non-strict continuous function which takes a value to the corresponding value in the lifted domain. There is a function down which goes in the opposite direction. Figure 1 provides an illustration. The reason that the interpretation of a lambda-expression is lifted is to insure that the interpretation will not identify the terminating program $\lambda x : s. \bot$ with the non-terminating program $\bot$.

In general, the interpretation of a sequent $H \vdash e : s$ is a function which assigns to each H-environment ρ a value $[\![H \vdash e : s]\!]\rho$ in s^*. An H-environment is a function which assigns to each variable x_i in the context $H = x_1 : s_1, \ldots, x_i : s_i, \ldots x_n : s_n$ an element $\rho(x_i)$ of the domain s_i^*. So, for example, we have

$$[\![H \vdash \mathbf{plus} : \mathbf{int} \to (\mathbf{int} \to \mathbf{int})]\!]\rho = \mathbf{plus}^*$$

for any context H and H-environment ρ. For an expression e with no free variables, we may write $[\![e : s]\!]$ rather than $[\![\emptyset \vdash e : s]\!]\rho$. The semantic function on the sequents is defined by induction on structure of terms as follows:

- Interpretation for variables:

$$[\![H, x : s, H' \vdash x : s]\!]\rho = \rho(x)$$

- The interpretation for lambda-terms:

$$[\![H \vdash \lambda x : s. e : s \to t]\!]\rho$$
$$= \{|\mathsf{up}(\lambda d : \sigma. [\![H, x : s \vdash e : t]\!]\rho[\{|d|\}/x])|\}$$

where $P(\sigma) \equiv s^*$.

- The interpretation for function application:

$$[\![H \vdash e(e') : t]\!]\rho = \mathsf{ext}(F)[\![H \vdash e : s \to t]\!]\rho$$

where $F : (s^* \multimap t^*)_\bot \to t^*$ is defined by

$$F(f) = \mathsf{ext}(\mathsf{strict}(\mathsf{down}(f)))[\![H \vdash e' : s]\!]\rho.$$

with

$$\mathsf{strict}(f)(x) = \begin{cases} f(x) & \text{if } x \neq \bot \\ \bot & \text{if } x = \bot \end{cases}$$

- The interpretation for recursion:

$$[\![H \vdash \mu x : s. e : s]\!]\rho = \bigvee_{i=0}^{\infty} d_i$$

where $d_0 = \{|\bot|\} \in s^*$ and $d_{i+1} = [\![H, x : s \vdash e : s]\!]\rho[d_i/x]$.

- The interpretation for branching:

$$[\![H \vdash \mathbf{if}\ e\ \mathbf{then}\ e'\ \mathbf{else}\ e'' : s]\!]\rho$$
$$= \mathsf{ext}(f)[\![H \vdash e : \mathbf{bool}]\!]\rho$$

where $f : P(\mathbb{B}_\bot \to s^*$ is given by

$$f(x) = \begin{cases} \{|\bot|\} & \text{if } x = \bot \\ [\![H \vdash e' : s]\!]\rho & \text{if } x = tt \\ [\![H \vdash e'' : s]\!]\rho & \text{if } x = ff \end{cases}$$

- Finally, the interpretation for non-deterministic choice:

$$[\![H \vdash e\ \mathbf{or}\ e' : s]\!]\rho = [\![H \vdash e : s]\!]\rho \uplus [\![H \vdash e' : s]\!]\rho$$

where $\uplus$ is the union operation for the powerdomain.

Naturally, there are some theorems that need to be proved about the relationship between the denotational semantics using the powerdomain and the operational semantics of the language. What these relationships are will depend on the choice of powerdomain. The statment and proof of such results would probably be a tractable and interesting research problem (I know of very few such results in the literature for anything other than the convex powerdomain) but it is not my purpose to explore any such result for the upper and lower powerdomains in this paper. However, I will return to this topic for the new powerdomain introduced in the next section. My reason for writing things out in this way was to illustrate that the semantics can be given in terms of the three basic powerdomain operators: singleton $\{|\cdot|\}$, union $\uplus$ and extension ext. Given a domain D, let $\mathcal{U}D$ and $\mathcal{L}D$ be the upper and lower powerdomains of D respectively (I will give precise definitions of these below). Each of the two powerdomains will have its own associated singleton, union and extension operators. Hence, we can assume that the semantic function $[\![\cdot]\!]$ takes the choice of powerdomain P as a parameter. Let $[\![\cdot]\!]^\sharp$ and $[\![\cdot]\!]^\flat$ be notations for the semantic functions on our language in terms of the upper and lower powerdomains respectively. (The notation is meant to be mnemonic: the *sharp* symbol $\sharp$ is used for the *upper* powerdomain and the *flat* symbol $\flat$ for the *lower* powerdomain.)

Although the upper and lower powerdomains give rise to different interpretations of our language, it is reasonable to expect that there is a close relationship between $[\![e:s]\!]^\sharp$ and $[\![e:s]\!]^\flat$. Naturally, some relationship should follow from the appropriate theorems matching the operational semantics of the language with the two respective powerdomain semantics. However, is it possible to formulate a purely semantic relationship between these $[\![\cdot]\!]^\sharp$ and $[\![\cdot]\!]^\flat$?

Let us consider a few examples before proceeding to a full collection of rigorous definitions. The interpretation of the type of integers using the upper powerdomain is essentially the set of all finite subsets of $\mathbb{Z}$ together with a set $\{\bot\}$. The interpretation of the type of integers using the lower powerdomain is the set of *all* subsets of $\mathbb{Z}$ together with $\{\bot\}$. One of the primary differences between the interpretations will be the fact that $s \uplus^\sharp \{\bot\} = \{\bot\}$ whereas $s \uplus^\flat \{\bot\} = s$ (using an obvious notation for the unions in the two powerdomains). Suppose, for example, that $[\![e : \mathbf{int}]\!]^\sharp = \{1, 2\}$. From this, we expect that e never diverges but may yield 1 or 2 as the result of its evaluation; so we will also have $[\![e : \mathbf{int}]\!]^\flat = \{1, 2\}$. On the other hand, if $[\![e : \mathbf{int}]\!]^\flat$ is the set of all even integers, then e may perform arbitrarily long evaluations and may therefore also diverge. Thus $[\![e : \mathbf{int}]\!]^\sharp = \{\bot\}$. Is there a way to make these arguments which does not appeal to the intended operational semantics, but instead uses some basic semantic relationship between the two interpretations? What I would like is a relation $\bowtie$ on $\mathcal{U}(\mathbf{int}) \times \mathcal{L}(\mathbf{int})$ such that $[\![e : \mathbf{int}]\!]^\sharp \rho \bowtie [\![e : \mathbf{int}]\!]^\flat \rho$ for any program e of integer type. For integers, it is possible to show that the least relation $\bowtie$ such that

- $s \bowtie s$ for any finite $s \subseteq \mathbb{Z}$, and

- $\{\bot\} \bowtie t$ for any $t \subseteq \mathbb{Z}$

has this property.

In order to carry this discussion further and generalize the relation $\bowtie$ to general types, it is essential to provide some rigorous definitions. A *pre-order* is a set A together with a binary relation $\gtrsim$ which is reflexive and transitive (but not necessarily anti-symmetric). We sometimes write $x \lesssim y$ when $y \gtrsim x$. Given a pre-ordering A, we define three pre-orderings on finite non-empty subsets $\mathcal{P}_f^* A$ of A as follows. Suppose $u, v \in \mathcal{P}_f^* A$, then

- $u \gtrsim^\sharp v$ iff for every $x \in u$ there is a $y \in v$ such that $x \gtrsim y$,

- $u \gtrsim^\flat v$ iff for every $y \in v$ there is a $x \in u$ such that $x \gtrsim y$,

- $u \gtrsim^\natural v$ iff $u \gtrsim^\sharp v$ and $u \gtrsim^\flat v$

It is easy to check that each of these relations is, in fact, a pre-ordering. These are called the *upper*, *lower* and *convex* orderings respectively. Given a pre-order A and $x \subseteq A$, let $\downarrow x = \{b \in A \mid b \lesssim a \text{ for some } a \in x\}$. A subset $x \subseteq A$ is an *ideal* if it is directed and $x = \downarrow x$. For a pre-order A, let $\mathsf{idl}(A)$ be the domain (*i.e.* algebraic cpo) of ideals on A, ordered by subset inclusion. For any domain D, let KD be the basis of compact elements of D. The *upper powerdomain* $\mathcal{U}D$ is defined to be the domain of ideals $\mathsf{idl}((KD)^\sharp)$. The *lower powerdomain* $\mathcal{L}D$ is $\mathsf{idl}((KD)^\flat)$ and the *convex powerdomain* is $\mathsf{idl}((KD)^\natural)$.

Recall the following definitions for the singleton and union operations on the upper and lower powerdomains:

$$\{|x|\}^\sharp = \{u \mid \exists a \in u.\, a \in x\}$$
$$\{|x|\}^\flat = \{u \mid \forall a \in u.\, a \in x\}$$
$$r \uplus^\sharp s = \{w \mid u \cup v \gtrsim^\sharp w \text{ for some } u \in r \text{ and } v \in s\}$$
$$r \uplus^\flat s = \{w \mid u \cup v \gtrsim^\flat w \text{ for some } u \in r \text{ and } v \in s\}$$

In general, I will put in the superscripts only to emphasize the types of the operations—usually the type will be clear from the context. In addition to these operations, we must define how the extension operation ext used in the semantic equations earlier are defined for each of the powerdomains.

Theorem 1 *Let D and E be domains. For any continuous $f : D \to \mathcal{U}E$, the map $\hat{f} : \mathcal{U}D \to \mathcal{U}E$ given by*

$$\hat{f}(r) = \bigsqcup \{f(a_1) \uplus^\sharp \cdots \uplus^\sharp f(a_n) \mid \{a_1, \ldots, a_n\} \in r\}$$

is the unique continuous, $\uplus^\sharp$-preserving function which completes the following diagram:

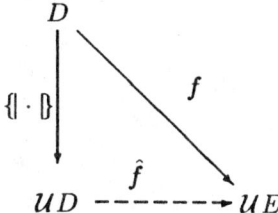

Theorem 2 *Let D and E be domains. For any continuous $f : D \to \mathcal{L}E$, the map $\check{f} : \mathcal{L}D \to \mathcal{L}E$ given by*

$$\check{f}(r) = \bigcup \{f(a_1) \uplus^\flat \cdots \uplus^\flat f(a_n) \mid \{a_1, \ldots, a_n\} \in r\}$$

is the unique continuous, $\uplus^\flat$-preserving function which completes the following diagram:

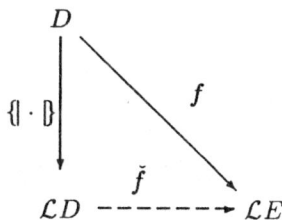

We now express the desired relationship between upper and lower powerdomains:

Definition: For any domain D, define a binary relation $\bowtie$ on $\mathcal{U}D \times \mathcal{L}D$ by $r \bowtie s$ iff for every $u \in r$ and $v \in s$, there is a $v' \in s$ such that $u \lesssim^\sharp v'$ and $v \lesssim^\flat v'$. ∎

The relation is actually more intuitive than its technical definition suggests. This intuition is best understood through some of the results which will be offered in the next section. For the purposes of this section, we simply prove that the $\bowtie$ relationship is preserved by the basic powerdomain operators which were used to build of the meanings of programs in our sample programming language above.

Proposition 3 *Let D and E be domains. Then*

1. *$\{|x|\}^\sharp \bowtie \{|x|\}^\flat$ for each $x \in D$.*

2. *if $r, r' \in \mathcal{U}D$ and $s, s' \in \mathcal{L}D$ and $r \bowtie r'$ and $s \bowtie s'$, then $r \uplus^\sharp r' \bowtie s \uplus^\flat s'$.*

3. *if $f : D \to \mathcal{U}E$ and $g : D \to \mathcal{L}E$ satisfy $f(x) \bowtie g(x)$ for each $x \in D$, then $\hat{f}(r) \bowtie \check{g}(s)$ whenever $r \bowtie s$.* ∎

Proof: 1. Suppose $u \in \{|x|\}^\sharp$ and $u \in \{|x|\}^\flat$. Let $w = (u \cap x) \cup v$. Since $w \subseteq x$ and x is an ideal, there is an $a \in x$ such that $b \lesssim a$ for each $b \in w$. Now $\{a\} \in \{|x|\}^\flat$ and $u \lesssim^\sharp \{a\}$ and $v \lesssim^\flat \{a\}$.

2. Suppose $u \in r \uplus^\sharp r'$ and $v \in s \uplus^\flat s'$. By the definitions of the union operations in the respective powerdomains, there are elements $p \in r$, $p' \in r'$, $q \in s$, and $q' \in s'$ such that $u \lesssim^\sharp p \cup p'$ and $v \lesssim^\flat q \cup q'$. Since $r \bowtie s$, there is a $w \in s$ such that $p \lesssim^\sharp w$ and $q \lesssim^\flat w$. Similarly, since $r' \bowtie s'$, there is a $w' \in s'$ such that $p' \lesssim^\sharp w'$ and $q' \lesssim^\flat w'$. Now, $p \cup p' \lesssim^\sharp w \cup w'$ and $q \cup q' \lesssim^\flat w \cup w'$ so $u \lesssim^\sharp w \cup w'$ and $v \lesssim^\flat w \cup w'$. Since $w \cup w' \in s \uplus s'$, we are done.

3. Let $u \in \hat{f}(r)$ and $v \in \check{g}(s)$. By the definitions of $\hat{f}$ and $\check{g}$, there are sets $u' = \{a_1, \ldots, a_n\} \in r$ and $v' = \{b_1, \ldots, b_m\} \in s$ such that

$$u \in f(a_1) \uplus^\sharp \ldots \uplus^\sharp f(a_n)$$
$$v \in g(b_1) \uplus^\flat \ldots \uplus^\flat g(b_m)$$

Since $r \bowtie s$, there is a $w = \{c_1, \ldots, c_l\} \in s$ such that $u' \lesssim^\sharp w$ and $v' \lesssim^\flat w$. Thus $u \in r' = f(c_1) \uplus^\sharp \ldots \uplus^\sharp f(c_l)$ and $v \in s' = g(c_1) \uplus^\flat \ldots \uplus^\flat g(c_l)$. But $f(c_i) \bowtie g(c_i)$ for each $i \leq l$, so $r' \bowtie s'$ by part (2) above. Now $u \in r'$ and $v \in s'$ so there is some $w' \in s'$ such that $u \lesssim^\sharp w'$ and $v \lesssim^\flat w'$. But $s' \subseteq \check{g}(s)$ so we are done. ∎

3 The mixed powerdomain.

In this section we study in some detail the subset $\bowtie$ of $\mathcal{U}D \times \mathcal{L}D$. What we will show is that this subset can itself be viewed as a powerdomain having many of the pleasing properties of the upper, lower and convex powerdomains but distinct from each of these.

Definition: Let $\langle A, \succsim \rangle$ be a pre-order. A *mix* (on A) is a pair $(u, v) \in \mathcal{P}_f^* A \times \mathcal{P}_f^* A$ of finite non-empty sets such that $v \succsim^\sharp u$. Define $\mathcal{M}^0 A$ to be the set of mixes on A under the pre-order given by taking $(u, v) \succsim (u', v')$ iff $u \succsim^\sharp u'$ and $v \succsim^\flat v'$. As with other pre-orders, we write $x \precsim y$ if $y \succsim x$. We also write $x \approx y$ if $x \precsim y$ and $x \succsim y$. The *mixed powerdomain* $\mathcal{M}D$ is the domain of ideals $\mathrm{idl}(\mathcal{M}^0 KD)$. ∎

As aside on uniformity of notation, we might have written $A^{(\sharp,\flat)}$ for $\mathcal{M}^0 A$ by analogy to the notations $A^\sharp$ and $A^\flat$. Similarly, $\succsim^{(\sharp,\flat)}$ would be another possible notation for $\succsim$.

A closely related structure known as the *sandwiches powerdomain* has been studied in the setting of databases:

Definition: A *sandwich* is a pair $(u, v) \in \mathcal{P}_f^* A \times \mathcal{P}_f^* A$ such that there is a set $w \in \mathcal{P}_f^* A$ such that $w \succsim^\sharp u$ and $w \succsim^\flat v$. The *sandwich powerdomain* of a domain D is the ideal completion of the set of sandwiches over KD under the ordering $(u, v) \succsim (u', v')$ iff $u \succsim^\sharp u'$ and $v \succsim^\flat v'$. ∎

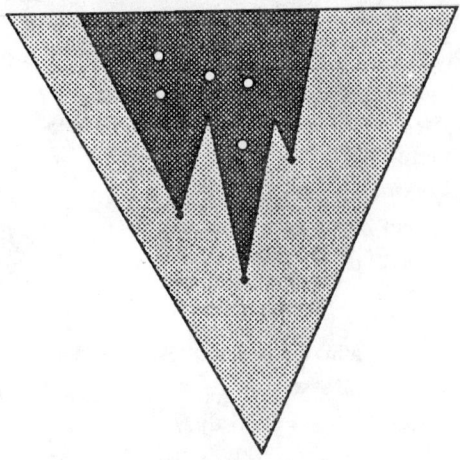

Figure 2: *A mixed powerdomain element (u,v) is illustrated above. The elements of the set u are indicated as closed circles (dots). They determine a shaded upper set within which the elements of v must lie. The elements of v are represented as open circles.*

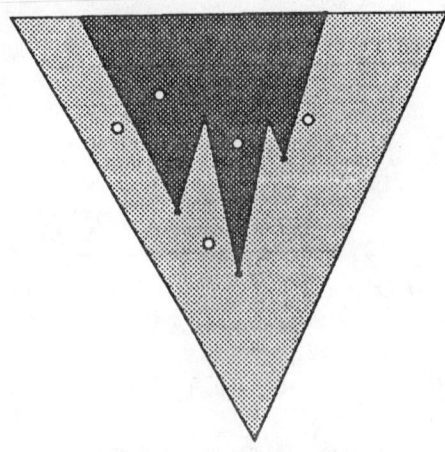

Figure 3: *A sandwich (u,v) is illustrated above. The elements of the set u are indicated as closed circles (dots). They determine a shaded upper set. The elements of v are represented as open circles; each element of v is required to have an upper bound in the shaded region.*

Obviously, any mix is a sandwich. Moreover, sandwiches have a number of pleasing properties that make them an interesting possible alternative to the convex powerdomain. For example, the sandwich powerdomain of a bounded complete domain (sometimes called a "Scott domain") is again a bounded complete domain.

However, the following proposition partially motivates our interest in mixes:

Proposition 4 *For any domain D, $\mathcal{M}D$ is isomorphic to the subset $\bowtie$ of $\mathcal{U}D \times \mathcal{L}D$.* ∎

Does the $\bowtie$ relation really enjoy the nice technical properties that the usual powerdomain operators do? The answer to this question is "yes". In this section I will sketch some of the results which show this. I will try to keep the discussion as self-contained as possible, but the reader will need to know some domain theory in order to follow. Most of the necessary background can be found in [SP82], [Gun87] and [GS88]. Proofs and technical details of the results about the mixed powerdomain can be found in [Gun89].

The first step is to show how to define a continuous mixed powerdomain functor on the category of domains (*i.e.* algebraic cpo's and continuous functions). This functor will take finite posets to finite posets, and hence it cuts down to a continuous functor on bifinite domains[1] which is the largest (and most robust) cartesian closed category of domains. In the next section, we will look at domains that have a bottom element; this will be explicitly stated when it is needed.

The following lemma is a quite useful way to define functions between algebraic cpo's:

---
[1] Bifinite domains are called "profinite domains" in [Gun87].

Lemma 5 *Let A be a pre-order and suppose E is a domain. If $f : A \to E$ is monotone, then there is a unique continuous function f' which completes the following diagram*

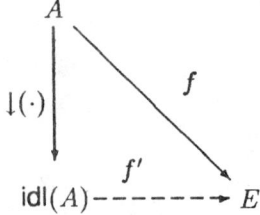

In particular, a continuous function $f : D \to E$ between domains D and E is uniquely determined by its restriction to KD. ∎

Now, recall that $\mathcal{M}D = \mathsf{idl}(\mathcal{M}^0(KD))$ and suppose $f : D \to E$ is a continuous function between domains D and E. For any $x \in \mathcal{M}(D)$ we define $\mathcal{M}(f)(x)$ to be the set of pairs $(u', v') \in \mathcal{M}^0(KE)$ such that there is a pair $(u,v) \in x$ for which

$$(f^*(u), f^*(v)) \succsim (u', v')$$

where $f^*(u)$ and $f^*(v)$ are the images of u and v respectively under the function f. It can be shown that this makes sense and $\mathcal{M}(f)$ is a continuous function from $\mathcal{M}D$ into $\mathcal{M}E$. Suppose $g : E \to F$ is another continuous function, then it is also possible to show that $\mathcal{M}(g \circ f)(x) = \mathcal{M}(g)(\mathcal{M}(f)(x))$. Since $\mathcal{M}(\mathsf{id}_D) = \mathsf{id}_{\mathcal{M}(D)}$, where id_D and $\mathsf{id}_{\mathcal{M}(D)}$ are the identity maps on D and $\mathcal{M}(D)$ respectively, it follows that $\mathcal{M}$ is an endofunctor on the category of domains and continuous functions. Indeed, we have the following

Lemma 6 *If $f \leq g$, then $\mathcal{M}(f) \leq \mathcal{M}(g)$. If M is a directed subset of $D \to E$, then $\mathcal{M}(\bigvee M) = \bigvee \mathcal{M}(M)$.* ∎

Hence, the methods discussed in [SP82] can be used to show that $\mathcal{M}$ defines a continuous functor on domains (with continuous functions or embeddings).

Now that the mixed powerdomain has been established as a continuous functor on bifinite domains, we may conclude that it can be used in any of the domain equations that are used with other powerdomains. This leaves a shopping list of questions about its technical similarity with the other operators:

1. Is the mixed powerdomain also closed on smaller categories, such as the bounded complete algebraic cpo's (Scott domains)?

2. Are the other powerdomains embedded in the mixed powerdomain?

3. Do any of the topological and freeness theorems that hold for the upper, lower and convex powerdomains have an analog that holds for the mixed powerdomain?

4. Can the mixed powerdomain be used for the semantics of non-deterministic programming languages?

I will provide at least a partial answer to each of these questions.

Perhaps the most striking property of the mixed powerdomain is an anomaly which it shares with the convex powerdomain: *it does not preserve the property of bounded completeness*. For example, the poset displayed in Figure 4 is bounded complete, but its mixed powerdomain is not.[2] This fact, and other similarities between the mixed and convex powerdomains make it natural to ask whether these operators might actually be *isomorphic*. Given a preorder A, it is clear that there is a nice monotone map from $A^\natural$ into $\mathcal{M}^0 A$ defined by $u \mapsto (u, u)$. This map is an *order-embedding*, i.e. for each $u, v \in A^\natural$,

$$u \lesssim^\natural v \text{ iff } (u, u) \precsim (v, v).$$

Could this be an isomorphism? Let me attempt an intuitive answer to this question before actually providing a rigorous proof. Consider the *truth value cpo* T displayed in Figure 5. It has three elements, t for true, f for false and 0 (i.e. $\bot$) for truth value "unknown". The upper and lower powerdomains of T are also displayed there with equivalent elements identified and representatives of the equivalence classes tagging the nodes. In the upper powerdomain, the set $\{t, f\}$ is a partial description with three possible "refinements". In the lower powerdomain, the set $\{t\}$ can be

[2]The example is due to Peter Buneman.

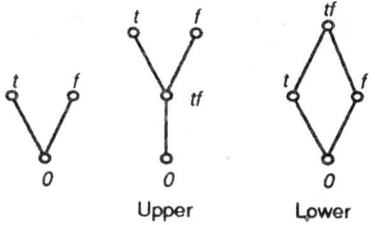

Figure 5: *Upper and lower powerdomains of the truth value cpo.*

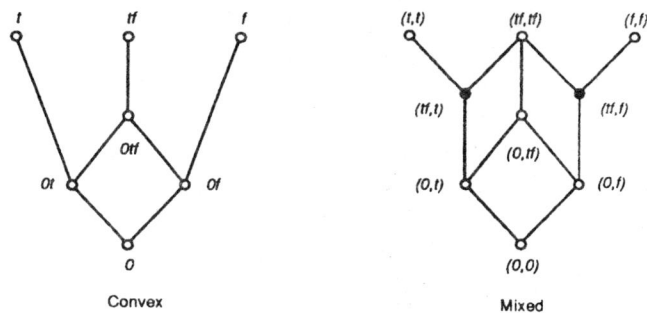

Figure 6: *The convex and mixed powerdomains of the truth value cpo are not isomorphic. The order-embedded image of the convex powerdomain in the mixed powerdomain is indicated with open circles in the figure on the right. The two points not in the image of this order-embedding are indicated with closed circles.*

seen as a partial element with two possible refinements. The mixed powerdomain element $(\{t, f\}, \{t\})$ can be seen as a partial element which has three possible refinements, namely itself (which I'm counting as a refinement for now) and the total mixed elements $(\{t\}, \{t\})$ and $(\{t, f\}, \{t, f\})$. These last two elements are *total* descriptions of the sets $\{t\}$ and $\{t, f\}$. I claim that there is no counterpart to this partial description in the convex powerdomain. The only potential candidate is the set $\{0, t\}$, but the order-embedded element $(\{0, t\}, \{0, t\})$ is strictly less less than $(\{t, f\}, \{t\})$ in the mixed powerdomain and has the partial element $(0, \{t, f\})$ as a refinement, whereas this element is incomparable to $(\{t, f\}, \{t\})$. The reader may find it helpful to go through this discussion while looking at the Hasse diagrams of the convex and mixed powerdomains of T which appear in Figure 6. In any case, it is clear from the pictures (which are my rigorous proof) that these posets are not isomorphic since the convex powerdomain has 7 elements whereas the mixed powerdomain has 9.

To use the mixed powerdomain for the semantics of programming languages, it is essential to define a collection of auxiliary functions such as those ordinarily associated with the powerset operation. There are two such operations which are of primary interest. The *mixed powerdo-*

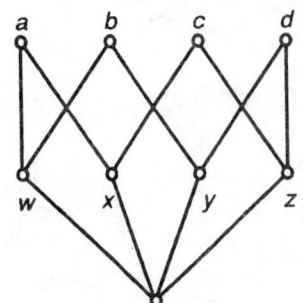 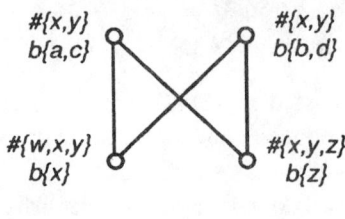

Figure 4: *The four elements indicated in the picture on the right show that the mixed powerdomain of the bounded complete domain pictured on the left is not bounded complete. The two mixes at the bottom have no least upper bound, since the two mixes indicated above them are minimal upper bounds.*

main union is a function $\uplus : \mathcal{M}^0 A \times \mathcal{M}^0 A \to \mathcal{M}^0 A$. If $u = (u^\sharp, u^\flat)$ and $v = (v^\sharp, v^\flat)$ are elements of $\mathcal{M}^0 A$, their union is defined as follows:

$$u \uplus v = (u^\sharp \cup v^\sharp, u^\flat \cup v^\flat).$$

To see that this makes sense, we must first show that $u \uplus v$ is an element of the mixed powerdomain of A. Suppose $x \in u^\flat \cup v^\flat$. If $x \in u^\flat$, then there is an element $x' \in u^\sharp$ such that $x' \lesssim x$ because $u^\sharp \lesssim^\sharp u^\flat$. Since a similar fact holds for elements of $v^\flat$, it follows that $u \uplus v$ is indeed an element of $\mathcal{M}^0 A$. To see that the union is also monotone, suppose $v \gtrsim w$ for some $w \in \mathcal{M}^0 A$. To show that $u \uplus v \gtrsim u \uplus w$, we must show that

$$u^\sharp \cup v^\sharp \gtrsim^\sharp u^\sharp \cup w^\sharp \qquad (1)$$

and

$$u^\flat \cup v^\flat \gtrsim^\flat u^\flat \cup w^\flat. \qquad (2)$$

For the former inequation, suppose $x \in u^\sharp \cup w^\sharp$. We must show that there is an $x' \in u^\sharp \cup v^\sharp$ such that $x' \lesssim x$. If $x \in u^\sharp$, then this is immediate since we can take $x' = x$. If $x \in w^\sharp$, then there is an $x' \in v^\sharp$ such that $x' \lesssim x$ because of the mixed powerdomain ordering. This establishes inequation 1; a similar argument may be used to show inequation 2. To show the monotonicity of $\uplus$ in the other argument is also similar. The *mixed powerdomain singleton* is a function $\{|\cdot|\} : A \to \mathcal{M}^0 A$ given by taking

$$\{|x|\} = (\{x\}, \{x\})$$

for each $x \in A$. The proof that this is well defined and monotone is straight-forward. Of course, the union and singleton can be be defined as continuous functions

$$\uplus : \mathcal{M}D \times \mathcal{M}D \to \mathcal{M}D$$
$$\{|\cdot|\} : D \to \mathcal{M}D$$

using Lemma 5 on the basis KD of D.

In some sense, the mixed powerdomain is "larger" than each of the upper, lower and convex powerdomains on those pre-orders A that have an element $\perp$ which satisfies $\perp \lesssim x$ for each $x \in A$. To see this, define $f : A^\sharp \to \mathcal{M}^0 A$ by $f(u) = (u, \{\perp\})$. This function extends to a continuous embedding from the upper powerdomain into the mixed powerdomain. Similarly, $g : A^\flat \to \mathcal{M}^0 A$ extends to a continuous embedding embedding from the upper powerdomain into the mixed powerdomain.

On the other hand, the mixed powerdomain of D may be viewed as a certain kind of open subset of the convex powerdomain of D. To see this, first recall the definition of the Scott topology on a cpo. The following notation is useful:

Notation: Given a pre-order A and a subset $u \subseteq A$, define

$$\uparrow u = \{x \in A \mid x \gtrsim y \text{ for some } y \in u\}$$
$$\downarrow u = \{x \in A \mid x \lesssim y \text{ for some } y \in u\} \blacksquare$$

Definition: Let D be a cpo. A set $U \subseteq D$ is *Scott open* if

1. $U = \uparrow U$ and

2. whenever $M \subseteq D$ is directed and $\bigvee M \in U$, then $M \cap U \neq \emptyset$. $\blacksquare$

The following is a basic fact about the poset of open subsets:

Lemma 7 *Let D be a domain. Then the poset ΩD of Scott open subsets of D ordered by subset inclusion is an algebraic lattice such that $U \in KD$ iff there is a finite set $u \subseteq KD$ such that $U = \uparrow u$.* $\blacksquare$

We can now express the desired property. Recall that an *order-embedding* $f : D \to E$ is a continuous function such that $x = y$ iff $f(x) = f(y)$ for $x, y \in D$.

Proposition 8 *There is an order-embedding from $\mathcal{M}D$ into the Scott open subsets of CD.*

Proof: Let $f : \mathcal{M}^0(KD) \to K\Omega(\mathcal{C}D)$ be given by

$$f : (u,v) \mapsto \{w \mid (u,v) \precsim (w,w)\}$$

By Lemma 7, the value of f on a pair (u,v) is, in fact, a compact open subset because

$$f(u,v) = \uparrow\{w \mid v \subseteq w \subseteq u \cup v\}.$$

Moreover, f is clearly monotone. Now, suppose $f(u,v) = f(u',v')$. We must show that $(u,v) \approx (u',v')$. Since $(u \cup v, u \cup v) \in f(u',v')$, we must have $u' \precsim^\sharp u \cup v$. But $u \cup v \precsim^\sharp u$, so $u' \precsim^\sharp u$. A similar argument shows that $u \precsim^\sharp u'$. We also have $(v,v) \in f(u',v')$ so $v' \precsim^\flat v$ and a similar argument for $v \precsim^\flat v'$. By Lemma 5, the monotone function f extends to a unique continuous function $f' : \mathcal{M}D \to \Omega(\mathcal{C}D)$. The function f' will be an order-embedding since f is. ∎

4 Algebraic characterization of the mixed powerdomain.

One of the most challenging problems for new powerdomain constructions has been the discovery of the appropriate algebraic structures to capture the their essential features. In the case of the convex powerdomain, the first intuitions—as described in [Plo76]—came from the semantics of parallel computation. Although [Plo76] describes all of the relevant algebraic operations, it was only later, in [HP79] that the convex powerdomain was characterized in terms of these operations together a simple set of equational axioms which they satisfy. At the same time, the upper and lower powerdomains were also thus characterized using the same algebraic signature but additional inequational axioms. Such characterizations are now treated as a standard element of the general methodology of semantics (see [Hen88] as an example of this). Unfortunately, no characterization of this kind has yet been found for the sandwiches powerdomain and this remains an open question. However, in this section, I will demonstrate an algebraic characterization of the mixed powerdomain in terms of a kind of structure called a *mix algebra*.

One problem which has arisen in the study of powerdomains for concurrency is how to derive a powerdomain which includes an *emptyset* element. This was missing from our earlier discussion where we always assumed that sets were non-empty. If we were to allow the emptyset as an element of the convex powerdomain, for example, we would have the problem that it is *unrelated* to other elements under the convex ordering. In particular, a powerdomain with emptyset would not have a least element. Given the importance of least elements for the solution of recursive equations, this straight-forward approach to adding an emptyset is unsatisfactory for the semantics of programming languages. The problem is generaly rectified by "adding the empty set onto the side" of the convex powerdomain. So the emptyset element is related only to the least element. This approach seems acceptable in the sense that it makes a reasonable semantics possible, but it makes a mess of the algebraic characterization of the powerdomain. The simple problem is this, if we add an axiom which says that the least element is less than the empty element, the the least element is part of our signature and is therefore preserved by any of the homomorphisms which we construct. But this is not desirable since there may well be terms in the language whose intended interpretation is non-strict (*i.e.* does not send the least element of its domain to the least element of its range). In fact, it can be shown that this problem has no acceptable solution with the simplest signature and axioms; we sketch a proof of this impossibility later.

Another goal of this section is to show how the problems with the algebraic properties of powerdomains with emptyset can resolved by using the *mixed powerdomain with emptyset*. To anticipate the basic idea, consider the nature of the emptyset as a piece of partial information about a set. The information content of the emptyset as *upper* information is quite different from its significance as *lower* information. In the upper powerdomain ordering, the emptyset is totally descriptive—it means that the set being described has no members. On the other hand, in the lower powerdomain ordering, the emptyset is totally nondescriptive—it means that no element is known to be in the set being described. In the case that the underlying domain has a least element $\bot$, even the singleton set $\{\bot\}$ is more informative under the lower ordering than the emptyset. Now, in the mixed powerdomain with emptyset, the mix $(\{\bot\}, \emptyset)$ is the *least* element. Even the element $(\{\bot\}, \{\bot\})$ is more informative, since this latter element describes only *non-empty* sets! In the mixed powerdomain, the emptyset $(\emptyset, \emptyset)$ is a total (maximal) element which describes the unique set with no members.

A *mix algebra* (with unit) is a pre-order N together with a monotone binary operation $* : N \times N \to N$, a monotone unary operation $\Box : N \to N$ and a constant $e \in N$ which satisfy the following nine axioms

1. associativity: $(r * s) * t \approx r * (s * t)$
2. commutativity: $r * s \approx s * r$
3. idempotence: $s * s \approx s$
4. unit: $e * s \approx s * e \approx s$
5. $\Box(s * r) \approx (\Box s) * (\Box r)$

6. $\Box\Box s \approx \Box s$

7. $s * (\Box s) \approx s$

8. $\Box s \lesssim s$

9. $s * (\Box r) \lesssim s$

A *homomorphism* between mix algebras M and N is a monotone function $f : M \to N$ such that $f(r*s) \approx (f(r)) * (f(s))$ and $f(\Box r) \approx \Box f(r)$ and $f(e) \approx e$. A *continuous mix algebra* is a mix algebra $\langle N, *, \Box, e \rangle$ where N is a domain and $*$, $\Box$ are continuous. A homomorphism of continuous mix algebras is a continuous homomorphism of mix algebras.

As the reader is probably aware, the first four axioms are the axioms for a semi-lattice with unit. Given a mix algebra N, the binary operation $*$ on N induces a semi-lattice pre-ordering $\Subset$ given by $r \Subset s$ iff $r * s \approx s$. It is important not to confuse this subset ordering with the ordering $\lesssim$ of partial information since these orderings will rarely coincide. Note, in particular, that axiom (7) says that $\Box$ is a *closure operation* with respect to $\Subset$.

Definition: Let $\langle A, \gtrsim \rangle$ be a pre-order. We define
$$\mathcal{M}_\emptyset^0 A = \{(u,v) \in \mathcal{P}_f A \times \mathcal{P}_f A \mid v \gtrsim^\sharp u\}$$
and define $(u,v) \gtrsim (u',v')$ iff $u \gtrsim^\sharp u'$ and $v \gtrsim^\flat v'$. Let us refer to $\langle \mathcal{M}_\emptyset^0 A, \gtrsim \rangle$ as the mixed powerdomain *with empty-set*. ∎

Given a domain D, define $\Box : \mathcal{M}_\emptyset^0(KD) \to \mathcal{M}_\emptyset^0(KD)$ as $\Box : (u,v) \mapsto (u, \emptyset)$. We show that $\langle KD, \uplus, \Box, (\emptyset,\emptyset) \rangle$ is a mix algebra. Axioms (1)-(4) are immediate consequences of the definition of $\uplus$. To prove (5), let (u,v) and (u',v') be elements of $\mathcal{M}_\emptyset^0(KD)$. Then $\Box((u,v) \uplus (u',v')) \approx \Box(u \cup u', v \cup v') \approx (u \cup u', \emptyset) \approx (u,\emptyset) \uplus (u',\emptyset) \approx \Box(u,v) \uplus \Box(u',v')$. Axiom (6) is immediate from the definition of $\Box$. For axiom (7), $(u,v) \uplus (\Box(u,v)) \approx (u \cup u, v \cup \emptyset) \approx (u,v)$. To see axiom (8), note that $\emptyset \lesssim^\flat v$ for any v. For axiom (9), $(u,v) \uplus (\Box(u',v')) \approx (u \cup u', v) \lesssim (u,v)$ since $u \cup u' \lesssim^\sharp u$.

From this proof that $\langle KD, \uplus, \Box, (\emptyset,\emptyset) \rangle$ is a mix algebra, it follows that $\langle D, \uplus, \Box, e \rangle$ is a continuous mix algebra, where $\uplus$ and $\Box$ are the unique continuous extensions of the corresponding operations on KD and e is the principal ideal generated by $(\emptyset,\emptyset)$.

Theorem 9 *Let A be a pre-order. Suppose N is a mix algebra. For any monotone $f : A \to N$, there is a unique homomorphism $f^+ : \mathcal{M}_\emptyset^0 A \to N$ which completes the following diagram:*

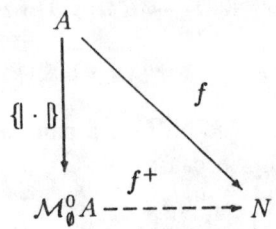

Proof: See [Gun89]. ∎

Corollary 10 *Let D be a domain. Suppose N is a continuous mix algebra. For any continuous $f : D \to N$, there is a unique homomorphism $f^+ : \mathcal{M}D \to N$ which completes the following diagram:*

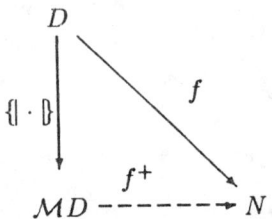

Proof: Let f_0 be the restriction of f to KD. By Theorem 9, there is a homomorphism $f_0^+ : \mathcal{M}_\emptyset^0 D \to N$ of mix algebras such that $f_0^+ \circ \{|\cdot|\} = f_0$. By Lemma 5, this homomorphism has a unique extension to a continuous function $f^+ : \mathcal{M}D \to N$ which satisfies the desired diagram. This map will be a homomorphism. ∎

The reader familiar with category theory will naturally recognize that Corollary 10 can be restated as follows: *The mixed powerdomain is left adjoint to the forgetful functor from the category of continuous mix algebras and continuous homomorphisms to the category of domains and continuous functions.* Several other results such as this are known for powerdomains. The most interesting of these is Theorem 11 below.

Definition: A *continuous semi-lattice* is a domain N together with a binary operation $*$ which satisfies the axioms (1)–(3) for mix algebras. A *homomorphism* of continuous semi-lattices M, N is a continuous function $h : M \to N$ such that $h(r * s) \approx h(r) * h(s)$. ∎

The following Theorem is proved in [HP79]:

Theorem 11 (Hennessy and Plotkin) *The convex powerdomain is left adjoint to the forgetful functor from the category of continuous semi-lattices (with bottom) and homomorphisms to the category of domains (with bottom) and continuous functions.* ∎

Definition: A continuous semi-lattice *with unit* is a continuous semi-lattice with a constant e which satisfies axiom (4) for mix algebras. A homomorphism of continuous semi-lattices M, N with unit is a homomorphism of continuous semi-lattices which sends the unit of M to the unit of N. ∎

The following proposition appears as an exercise in [Plo82] (see Exercise 101 on page 52 of the chapter *Nondeterminism and Parallelism*):

Proposition 12 (Plotkin) *There is no left adjoint to the forgetful functor from continuous semi-lattices with unit and bottom to that of domains with bottom.*

Proof: Suppose that there is a left adjoint to the forgetful functor and let D be the free continuous semi-lattice with unit generated by the poset $\{x\}$ with one element x. Let I be the semi-lattice with unit that has two elements $\bot, x$ with $\bot \precsim x$ and $\bot * x = \bot$. Let f be the map from $\{x\}$ to I which sends x to $\bot$. We demonstrate a contradiction by showing that for no map u is there a unique homomorphism f^+ which completes the diagram

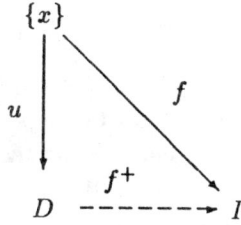

Now, let T be the poset with three distinct elements $e, x, \bot$ with $\bot \precsim e$ and $\bot \precsim x$. This poset can be given the structure of a semi-lattice with unit e by defining $x * \bot = \bot$. Since D is freely generated by $\{x\}$, there is a homomorphism $g : D \to T$ which sends the image of x under u to $x \in T$. If e is the unit of D, then $g(e) = e$. Since g is monotone, this means $u(x)$ is incomparable to e in D and, consequently, $g(\bot) = \bot$. Now, consider the map $h : T \to I$ which sends the elements of T constantly to $e = x$ and the map $k : T \to I$ which sends $\bot$ to $\bot$. The situation can be illustrated as follows:

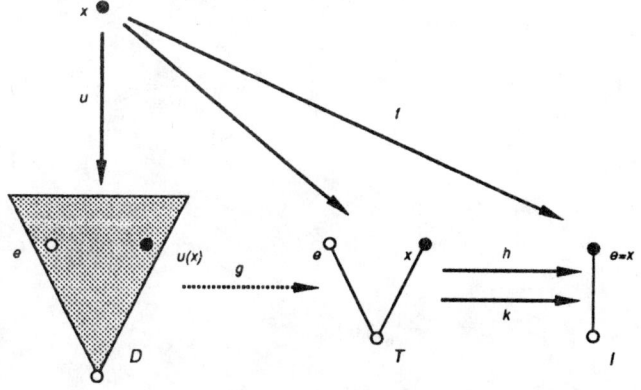

Both of these maps are homomorphisms so we must have $f^+ = h \circ g = k \circ g$. But this is clearly false, since the two compositions are not equal. ∎

Proposition 13 *The mixed powerdomain is left adjoint to the forgetful functor from the category of continuous mix algebras with bottom to the category of domains with bottom.*

Proof: This is immediate from Corollary 10 since the mixed powerdomain of a domain D has a least element given as the principal ideal generated by $(\{\bot\}, \emptyset)$. ∎

The big union function is the unique homomorphism $\uplus$ which completes the following diagram

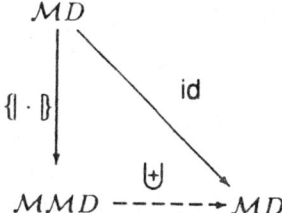

where id is the identity function. It it straight-forward to calculate it using the definitions of the mix algebra operations [Gun89].

5 Semantics using the mixed powerdomain.

In this section I will examine an extension of the sample language from Section 2 to include a new construct suggested by the algebraic structure investigated in the previous section. A denotational semantics using mix algebras will be expressed for the expanded language. The language will be given an operational semantics and a simple relationship between this and the denotational semantics will be expressed.

To motivate the construct which will be added to the language below, consider the following specification question. Would an implementation of the construct e_1 or e_2 which always chose e_1 be considered acceptable? This depends on our attitude toward how the operational rules and denotational equations in Section 2 are to be taken. It is not unusual for a language specification to leave various choices to the implementor. However, when we write the operational rules

$$\frac{e_1 \Rightarrow c}{e_1 \text{ or } e_2 \Rightarrow c} \qquad \frac{e_2 \Rightarrow c}{e_1 \text{ or } e_2 \Rightarrow c}$$

what we probably mean is that e_1 or e_2 *sometimes* evaluates e_1 and *sometimes* evaluates e_2. In other words, each of

$$\lambda x.\, e \Rightarrow \lambda x.\, e \qquad \frac{e \Rightarrow \lambda x.\, e'' \quad e' \Rightarrow c' \quad [c'/x]e'' \Rightarrow c}{e(e') \Rightarrow c}$$

$$\frac{e_1 \Rightarrow \text{true} \quad e_2 \Rightarrow c}{\text{if } e_1 \text{ then } e_2 \text{ else } e_3 \Rightarrow c} \qquad \frac{e_1 \Rightarrow \text{false} \quad e_3 \Rightarrow c}{\text{if } e_1 \text{ then } e_2 \text{ else } e_3 \Rightarrow c}$$

$$\frac{e_1 \Rightarrow c}{e_1 \text{ or } e_2 \Rightarrow c} \qquad \frac{e_2 \Rightarrow c}{e_1 \text{ or } e_2 \Rightarrow c}$$

$$\frac{e_1 \Rightarrow c}{e_1 \,\square\, e_2 \Rightarrow c} \qquad \frac{e_2 \Rightarrow c}{e_1 \,\square\, e_2 \Rightarrow c}$$

$$\frac{e \Rightarrow c}{e \Rrightarrow c} \qquad \frac{[\mu x.\, e/x]e \Rightarrow c}{\mu x.\, e \Rightarrow c}$$

Figure 7: *Operational semantics for the language with the $\square$ operator.*

e_1 and e_2 is actually realized as a possibility in the evaluation. But suppose this is not what is meant, and it is really left to the implementor to decide whether the language defined earlier is truely non-deterministic. How are we to express this distinction? Let us introduce another choice construct written $e_1 \,\square\, e_2$ with the following meaning: any implementation *must* sometimes evaluate the expression e_1, but whether the evaluation of e_2 will sometimes occur is dependent on the particular implementation. But how can we express this kind of distinction operationally and denotationally? It seems that there are basically two kinds of operational rules: those which *must* be implemented and those which *may* be implemented. We can deal with this problem by distinguishing two classes of operational rules: "may rules" and "must rules". As for the denotational equations, such distinctions are not new to research in the semantics of non-determinism; the distinctions between the powerdomains are meant to be used for just this kind of purpose.

The raw terms are those of the language defined earlier, together with a new binary infix operator $\square$ which allows us to form expressions of the form $e_1 \square e_2$ where e_1 and e_2 are raw terms. The new operator obeys the following typing rule:

$$\frac{H \vdash e : s \quad H \vdash e' : s}{H \vdash e \,\square\, e' : s}$$

and its intended denotational semantics can be expressed with the following semantic equation:

$$[\![H \vdash e \,\square\, e' : s]\!]\rho = [\![H \vdash e : s]\!]\rho \uplus \square [\![H \vdash e' : s]\!]\rho$$

The operational rules for the calculus are given in Figure 7.

As an example, consider the program

$$e = (\lambda x : \text{int}.\, \textbf{times}(2)(x) \,\square\, \textbf{plus}(x)(-1))(2 \,\square\, 3)$$

The denotational semantics of e is the following element of $\text{int}^* = \mathcal{M}(\mathbb{Z}_\bot)$:

$$\{\!|4|\!\} \uplus \square\{\!|1|\!\} \uplus \square\{\!|2|\!\} \uplus \square\{\!|6|\!\}$$

The operational semantics has the following relations:

$$e \Rightarrow 4 \qquad e \Rrightarrow 1 \qquad e \Rrightarrow 2 \qquad e \Rrightarrow 6.$$

Recall that $r \in s$ iff $r * s \approx s$. In general we have the following:

Theorem 14 *1. If $e \Rightarrow c$ then $[\![c]\!] \in [\![e]\!]$.*

2. If $e \Rrightarrow c$ then $\square[\![c]\!] \in [\![e]\!]$. ∎

Theorem 14 is somewhat weaker than what one could probably prove about the relationship between the operational and denotational semantics for the language we have presented. However, it does illustrate the basic idea that mix algebras can be used as a tool in semantic descriptions that go beyond what would be possible with the upper, lower and convex powerdomains alone.

6 Acknowledgements.

The research on this paper was supported in part by U.S. Army Research Office Grant DAAG29-84-K-0061 and ONR contract number N00014-88-K-0557.

References

[Abr87] S. Abramsky. Domains in logical form. In D. Gries, editor, *Symposium on Logic in Computer Science*, pages 47–53, IEEE Computer Society Press, Ithaca, New York, June 1987.

[Abr88] S. A. Abramsky. *Domain Theory and the Logic of Observable Properties*. PhD thesis, Queens College, 1988.

[Abr89] S. A. Abramsky. Domain theory in logical form. *Annals of pure and applied logic*, 1989. To appear.

[BDW88] P. Buneman, S. Davidson, and A. Watters. A semantics for complex objects and approximate queries. In *Principles of Database Systems*, ACM, March 1988.

[BJO89] P. Buneman, A. Jung, and A. Ohori. Using powerdomains to generalize relational databases. *Theoretical Computer Science*, 1989. To appear.

[BO86] P. Buneman and A. Ohori. A domain theoretic approach to higher-order relations. In *International Conference on Database Theory*, Springer-Verlag, 1986.

[GS88] C. A. Gunter and D. S. Scott. Semantic domains. In J. van Leeuwen, editor, *Handbook of Theoretical Computer Science*, North Holland. To appear in 1989.

[Gun87] C. A. Gunter. Universal profinite domains. *Information and Computation*, 72:1–30, 1987.

[Gun89] C. A. Gunter. *The mixed powerdomian*. Research Report **Logic and Computation,** University of Pennsylvania, Philadelphia, November 1989.

[Hen88] M. Hennessy. *Algebraic Theory of Processes*. MIT Press, 1988.

[HP79] M. Hennessy and G. D. Plotkin. Full abstraction for a simple parallel programming language. In J. Bečvář, editor, *Mathematical Foundations of Computer Science*, pages 108–120, *Lecture Notes in Computer Science vol. 74*, Springer, 1979.

[Plo76] G. D. Plotkin. A powerdomain construction. *SIAM Journal of Computing*, 5:452–487, 1976.

[Plo77] G. D. Plotkin. LCF considered as a programming language. *Theoretical Computer Science*, 5:223–255, 1977.

[Plo82] G. D. Plotkin. The category of complete partial orders: a tool for making meanings. Postgraduate lecture notes, Department of Computer Science, Edinburgh University, 1982.

[Smy78] M. Smyth. Power domains. *Journal of Computer System Sciences*, 16:23–36, 1978.

[Smy83] M. Smyth. Power domains and predicate transformers: a topological view. In J. Diaz, editor, *International Colloquium on Automata, Languages and Programs*, pages 662–676, *Lecture Notes in Computer Science vol. 154*, Springer, 1983.

[SP82] M. Smyth and G. D. Plotkin. The category-theoretic solution of re¡cursive domain equations. *SIAM Journal of Computing*, 11:761–783, 1982.

[Win85] G. Winskel. On powerdomains and modality. *Theoretical Computer Science*, 36:127–137, 1985.

On Oraclizable Networks and Kahn's Principle

James R. Russell*
Computer Science Department, Cornell University
Ithaca, NY 14853

Abstract

In this paper we investigate generalizations of Kahn's principle to nondeterministic dataflow networks. Specifically, we show that for the class of "oraclizable" networks a semantic model in which networks are represented by certain sets of continuous functions is fully abstract and has the fixed-point property. We go on to show that the oraclizable networks are the largest class representable by this model, and are a proper superclass of the networks implementable with the *infinity fair merge* primitive. Finally, we use this characterization to show that infinity fair merge networks and oraclizable networks are proper subclasses of the networks with Egli-Milner monotone input-output relations.

1 Introduction

Dataflow networks are an important model for asynchronous parallel computation, in which concurrently executing processes communicate by sending streams of tokens along FIFO channels. The well known Kahn's principle [Kah77] gives a semantic model for determinate dataflow networks in which the networks are represented by continuous stream valued functions. This model has the two desirable properties that it is fully abstract and that the denotation of a composite network can be computed from the denotations of its components via a fixed-point construction. In this paper we investigate generalizations of Kahn's principle to nondeterministic dataflow networks.

Recently, there has been much work on the problem of finding semantic models generalizing Kahn's to various kinds of indeterminate dataflow networks. The most common examples of indeterminate networks are those containing the various *merge* primitives, e.g. fair merge, angelic merge, infinity-fair merge, and unfair merge. Recent work of Panangaden, Stark, and others [MPS88,Sta88,PS88,PS87] has shown that these primitives have provably inequivalent expressive power. In particular, they have shown that these primitives form a hierarchy of expressibility, with fair merge at the highest level.

Many semantic models for indeterminate networks have been developed [Pan85,BA81,KP85, Bro83,Pra86,Par82], and only recently have fully abstract models emerged [PS89,Jon89,JK88,Kok88, Rus89]. However, these fully abstract models are based on traces or similar formalisms, and do not have a fixed-point theory. Keller and Panangaden [KP86, Pan85] and Broy [Bro83] have both developed models for the full range of nondeterminism that employ fixed-point constructions, but they are cumbersome and not fully abstract. Misra [Mis89] has described a nice equational system for reasoning about nondeterministic networks in which network meanings are 'smooth' solutions to recursive equations, but he does not consider full abstraction, nor provide fixed-point techniques for computing the smooth solutions. Abramsky [Abr89] has developed a general categor-

---

*Supported in part by an NSF graduate fellowship, NSF grant CCR-8818979, and an IBM graduate fellowship.

ical theory for Kahn-type models for indeterminate dataflow networks.

The approach we take in this paper is to look at a restricted class of nondeterministic dataflow networks, develop a model for this class that is both fully abstract and has a fixed-point theory, and to characterize the representation and expressiveness of this class. The class we consider is that of oraclizable networks. We show that for this class a semantics based on sets of continuous functions is fully abstract and has a simple and general fixed-point principle. We also show that this class is universal for the sets of functions representation, i.e. that it is the largest class describable by sets of functions.

We relate the oraclizable networks to the hierarchy of nondeterministic primitives by noting that they properly contain all networks implementable with infinity-fair merge. One characteristic that separates infinity-fair merge networks from networks at higher levels of the hierarchy is that the input-output relations of the infinity-fair merge networks are monotone in the Egli-Milner ordering, while this is not necessarily the case for networks at higher levels. It has been conjectured that infinity-fair merge is universal for Egli-Milner monotone relations, i.e. that any Egli-Milner monotone relation is the input-output relation of some network implementable with infinity-fair merge. Using the above characterization and semantics we are able to show that this conjecture is false.

2 Dataflow Networks

2.1 Background and Definitions

In this section we briefly review the definitions and terminology of dataflow networks. Since the main point of this paper is to investigate relations between semantic models and observable properties of networks, we only give an informal presentation of the main concepts. See, for example, [Sta89,PS88, Sta87,JK88,Jon89,PS89] for the formal development on which this is based.

The fundamental unit of a network is an *input-output port automaton*. These automata communicate with each other and the outside world by sending and receiving data values on "ports". Each port is either an input or an output port for the automaton, and in each step of its execution an automata may poll or read an input port, write to an output port, or change its internal state (do internal computations).

A *dataflow network* consists of a set of concurrently executing port automata connected together by directed channels. The channels act as perfect, unbounded FIFO queues. Each channel may be connected to at most one input port, and at most one output port. There are three types of channels: *input channels*, which are not connected to an output port of any automaton, and transmit data into the network from outside; *output channels*, which are not connected to an input port of any automaton, and transmit data from the network outside; and *internal channels*, which transmit data between network nodes.

An important feature of dataflow networks is that they can be composed, and larger networks built using smaller networks in place of individual automata. There are two atomic operation of network composition: aggregation and looping. The aggregate of networks M and N, written $M\|N$, is the network formed by combining them 'side-by-side' with no identification of channels. Given a network M, $\mathsf{loop}(a, b, M)$ is the network formed from M by identifying input channel a with output channel b. It is clear that any network can be constructed from these operations.

A *computation* of a network is a sequence of state transitions of the component automata. We define *communication events* as transitions of a computation in which data either arrives on an input channel or is sent along an output channel (*input events* and *output events*, respectively). A *trace* of a network is a sequence of communications events on the external channels of a network. Traces are commonly written as sequences of pairs $\langle channel\_name, data\_value\rangle$, and we write $\mathcal{T}[\![N]\!]$ for the set of traces of a network N. We call the sequence of values of the events on the input (or output) channels the *input* (or *output*) *history* of a trace.

2.2 Operational Semantics

The *input-output relation* of a network N is the set of all pairs of input and output histories for traces in $T[\![N]\!]$. The input-output relation of a network is what we consider to be the "observable" behavior. From the outside, an observer can see the values of the input and output channels, but cannot distinguish the relative order of the input events, output events, and internal events. Note that we consider the full, possibly infinite, streams of values to be observable. Other, more restrictive notions are possible, as in the work of Rabinovich and Trakhtenbrot [RT88], who consider a theory based on finite observations. We write $\mathcal{IO}[\![N]\!]$ for the input-output relation of the network N, and take it as our *operational semantics*.

We now define properties useful in relating abstract semantics to observable operational behavior. We say two networks N_1 and N_2 are *operationally equal* if, for every network context $C[]$, the composite networks $C[N_1]$ and $C[N_2]$ have the same input-output relation, i.e. that $\mathcal{IO}[\![C[N_1]]\!] = \mathcal{IO}[\![C[N_2]]\!]$.

A semantic model $\mathcal{D}[\![\ ]\!]$ is *adequate* if whenever $\mathcal{D}[\![N_1]\!] = \mathcal{D}[\![N_2]\!]$, N_1 and N_2 are operationally equal. A semantic model $\mathcal{D}[\![\ ]\!]$ is *fully abstract* if the converse of adequacy holds as well, i.e. that $\mathcal{D}[\![N_1]\!] = \mathcal{D}[\![N_2]\!]$ if and only if N_1 and N_2 are operationally equal.

3 Kahn's Semantics and Traces

The first major work in the area of dataflow semantics was by Kahn [Kah77], who gave a simple and elegant semantics for dataflow networks in which all the processes are determinate. His semantics describes networks as continuous stream valued functions corresponding to the (functional) input-output relation of the network. This semantics has the desirable properties that it is fully abstract, and the denotation of a composite network can be obtained from the denotations of its components as the least fixed point of the equations describing the network. Specifically, a network M with m input channels and n output channels is represented as a function $f_M : S^m \to S^n$, where S is the domain of streams. If N is a network with m' inputs and n' outputs, then $f_{M\|N} = \langle f_M, f_N \rangle : S^{m+m'} \to S^{n+n'}$, where $\langle f_M, f_N \rangle$ is the function that on input $\langle i, i' \rangle \in S^{m+m'}$ (with $i \in S^m, i' \in S^{m'}$) produces output $\langle f_M(i), f_N(i') \rangle \in S^{n+n'}$. Similarly, $f_{\mathsf{loop}(a,b,M)} = \mathrm{fix}(a, b, f_M)$, where $g = \mathrm{fix}(a, b, f_M)$ is the function in $S^{m-1} \to S^{n-1}$ that computes fixed points of f_M; $g(i) = o$ means that o is the least output on the components other than b such that there exists a stream l with $f_M(i, l) = (o, l)$ (where l is actually the ath component of the input and the bth component of the output). The importance of the semantics having this fixed-point property is that it provides us with a simple method for computing the meaning of a looped network as a limit.

Indeterminate dataflow networks are those for which the input-output relation is not functional. Obviously such networks cannot be represented by a function, and a representation by the (nonfunctional) input-output relation fails to be fully abstract [BA81,Rus89]. Thus, the naive generalizations of Kahn's semantics to the indeterminate setting fail, and different models have to be sought out. In this paper we develop such a model for the class of oraclizable nondeterministic networks.

The work in [Jon89,PS89,Rus89] shows that the trace semantics $T[\![\ ]\!]$ is fully abstract, and in the following sections we compare our semantics to $T[\![\ ]\!]$ rather than directly to the operational semantics. We also employ an alternative shorthand notation for traces which we call *checkpoint sequences*. We define a checkpoint sequence for a network M as a sequence $(i_0, o_0), (i_1, o_1), \ldots (i, o)$ where i_n and o_n are tuples of finite input and output streams (one for each channel), $(i_n, o_n) \sqsubseteq (i_{n+1}, o_{n+1})$ for all n, and $(i, o) = \sqcup (i_n, o_n)$. We regard such a checkpoint sequence as shorthand for a trace t of M consisting of all the input events of i_0, followed by the output events of o_0, followed by the input events of $i_1 - i_0$, followed by the output events of $o_1 - o_0$, etc. Furthermore the entire input history of t must be i, and the output history of t must be o. Note that a given checkpoint sequence actually represents a family of traces related by the permutation of adjacent input (or output) events on different channels, since trace sets are closed under such permutations.

4 Semantics of Oraclizable Networks

In this section we investigate semantic models that generalize Kahn's to the class of oraclizable networks. In the first subsection we define oraclizable networks and present our first semantic model. This model is a straightforward extension of Kahn's in which oraclizable networks - which can be thought of as nondeterministic networks choosing among many different determinate behaviors - are represented by *sets* of stream valued functions, corresponding to the sets of possible determinate behaviors. With this representation the fixed-point property of Kahn's semantics extends directly to this model, by applying it to each of the possible equations.

Unfortunately, this straightforward representation fails to be fully abstract. In the second subsection we modify the model of the first and represent oraclizable networks by sets of functions that are closed in a certain sense. With this modification, we show that this second semantics becomes fully abstract, and preserves the fixed-point property of the first.

4.1 The Direct Semantics

Definition 1. A nondeterministic network M is *oraclizable* if it is operationally equal to a nondeterministic network M_O without input channels (the "oracle"), connected to some inputs of a determinate network M_D.

It is easily seen that the class of oraclizable networks is closed under composition.

Given an oraclizable network M, we can identify its oracle part M_O with the set of possible outputs of M_O. Additionally, we can regard its determinate part M_D, which we know acts as a function f_{M_D} from oracle inputs and external inputs to outputs, as function from oracle inputs to functions from external inputs to outputs. This view leads naturally to our first semantic model.

Definition 2. Given an oraclizable network M, we represent it by its set of possible functional behaviors

$$\mathcal{F}_1[\![M]\!] \stackrel{\text{def}}{=} \bigcup_{o \in M_O} f_{M_D}(o).$$

Lemma 1.

$$\mathcal{F}_1[\![M||N]\!] = \{g | g = \langle f, f' \rangle, f \in \mathcal{F}_1[\![M]\!], f' \in \mathcal{F}_1[\![N]\!]\}$$
$$\mathcal{F}_1[\![\text{loop}(a,b,M)]\!] = \{f | f = \text{fix}(a,b,f'), f' \in \mathcal{F}_1[\![M]\!]\}$$

Proof: These follow directly from the definitions.

$\mathcal{F}_1[\![\cdot]\!]$ is an attractive semantic model, since the network composition operations of aggregation and looping correspond to function aggregation and least fixed point applied to each of the functions in the representation, as we desire. Now we compare the semantics $\mathcal{F}_1[\![\cdot]\!]$ to the fully abstract trace semantics $\mathcal{T}[\![\cdot]\!]$.

Lemma 2.

$$\mathcal{T}[\![M]\!] = \{(i_0, o_0), (i_1, o_1), \ldots (i, o) | $$
$$\exists f \in \mathcal{F}_1[\![M]\!], f(i) = o, f(i_n) \sqsupseteq o_n \text{ for all } n\}$$

Proof: Direct from the definition of $\mathcal{F}_1[\![M]\!]$ and the observation that for a determinate network D,

$$\mathcal{T}[\![D]\!] = \{(i_0, o_0), (i_1, o_1), \ldots (i, o) | $$
$$f_D(i) = o, f_D(i_n) \sqsupseteq o_n \text{ for all } n\}$$

From lemma 2 we conclude that $\mathcal{F}_1[\![M]\!] = \mathcal{F}_1[\![N]\!]$ implies $\mathcal{T}[\![M]\!] = \mathcal{T}[\![N]\!]$, and hence $\mathcal{F}_1[\![\cdot]\!]$ is adequate. It is not, however, fully abstract, as can be seen in the example in figure 1.

4.2 A Fully Abstract Variation

Intuitively, $\mathcal{F}_1[\![M]\!]$ fails to be fully abstract because it only includes the functional behaviors explicit in M, while there may be other functions inherent in the behavior of M, though not corresponding to any single oracle value. In order to be fully abstract, the representation must identify networks differing only by such functions.

Definition 3. Given a set of functions F, $Cl(F)$ is the closure of F under the addition of functions not finitely distinguishable from F. These are the functions inherent in the behavior of F.

$Cl(F) \stackrel{\text{def}}{=}$
$\{f | \forall$ chains of finite inputs
$\quad i_0 \sqsubseteq i_1 \sqsubseteq \cdots, i = \bigsqcup i_n,$ and
$\quad \forall$ chains of finite outputs
$\quad\quad o_0 \sqsubseteq o_1 \sqsubseteq \cdots, f(i) = \bigsqcup o_n, o_n \sqsubseteq f(i_n)$ for each n,
$\quad \exists f' \in F$ with $f'(i) = f(i), f'(i_n) \sqsupseteq o_n$ for each $n\}$

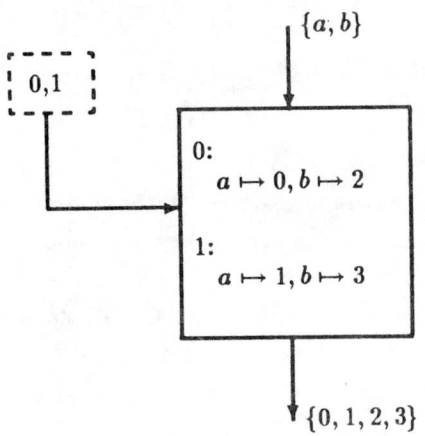 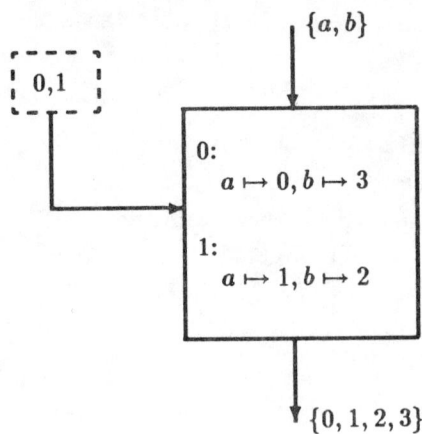

Both the above processes take as input a single token, either a or b, and if it is an a produce either 0 or 1, and if it is a b produce either 2 or 3. However, the left process uses its oracle to choose between the functions $a \mapsto 0, b \mapsto 2$ and $a \mapsto 1, b \mapsto 3$, while the right process uses its oracle to choose between the two different functions $a \mapsto 0, b \mapsto 3$ and $a \mapsto 1, b \mapsto 2$.

Figure 1: Two indistinguishable processes with different sets of functions.

Definition 4. Given an oraclizable network M, we represent it by the closure of its set of functional behaviors.

$$\mathcal{F}_2[\![M]\!] \stackrel{\text{def}}{=} Cl(\mathcal{F}_1[\![M]\!])$$

Clearly $\mathcal{F}_2[\![M]\!] \supseteq \mathcal{F}_1[\![M]\!]$ for any M.

As justification for the claim that the additional functions were inherent in M we have the following:

Lemma 3. Given an oraclizable network M, suppose M' is an oraclizable network whose functional behaviors are all those in $\mathcal{F}_2[\![M]\!]$ (i.e. $\mathcal{F}_1[\![M']\!] = \mathcal{F}_2[\![M]\!]$). Then M and M' are operationally indistinguishable.

Proof: We will show $\mathcal{T}[\![M']\!] = \mathcal{T}[\![M]\!]$. Using lemma 2 and the definition of $\mathcal{F}_2[\![\,]\!]$ we have

$$\mathcal{T}[\![M']\!] = \{(i_0, o_0), (i_1, o_1), \ldots (i, o) | \exists f \in \mathcal{F}_1[\![M']\!],$$
$$f(i) = o, f(i_n) \sqsupseteq o_n \text{ for all } n\}$$
$$= \{(i_0, o_0), (i_1, o_1), \ldots (i, o) | \exists f \in Cl(\mathcal{F}_1[\![M]\!]),$$
$$f(i) = o, f(i_n) \sqsupseteq o_n \text{ for all } n\}$$
$$= \{(i_0, o_0), (i_1, o_1), \ldots (i, o) | \exists f' \in \mathcal{F}_1[\![M]\!],$$
$$f'(i) = f(i) = o, f'(i_n) \sqsupseteq o_n \text{ for all } n\}$$
$$= \mathcal{T}[\![M]\!]$$

Thus, the sets $\mathcal{F}_2[\![M]\!]$ and $\mathcal{F}_1[\![M]\!]$ represent the same operational behavior. However, $\mathcal{F}_2[\![\,]\!]$ is general enough that it is fully abstract.

Theorem 1. (Full Abstraction for Oraclizable Networks) Given oraclizable networks M and N,

$$\mathcal{F}_2[\![M]\!] = \mathcal{F}_2[\![N]\!] \iff \mathcal{T}[\![M]\!] = \mathcal{T}[\![N]\!]$$

Proof: $\Leftarrow$: It is clear from lemma 2 and the definition of $\mathcal{F}_2[\![\,]\!]$ that

$$\mathcal{F}_2[\![M]\!] = \{f | \forall \text{ chains } i_0 \sqsubseteq i_1 \sqsubseteq \cdots, i = \bigsqcup i_n, \text{ and}$$
$$\forall \text{ chains } o_0 \sqsubseteq o_1 \sqsubseteq \cdots, f(i) = \bigsqcup o_n,$$
$$o_n \sqsubseteq f(i_n) \text{ for each } n,$$
$$\text{the checkpoint sequence}$$
$$(i_0, o_0), (i_1, o_1), \ldots (i, f(i)) \text{ is in } \mathcal{T}[\![M]\!]\}$$

Hence $\mathcal{T}[\![M]\!]$ determines $\mathcal{F}_2[\![M]\!]$, and the result follows.

$\Rightarrow$: Say $(i_0, o_0), (i_1, o_1), \ldots (i, o) \in \mathcal{T}[\![M]\!]$. Then by lemma 2 we know there exists $f \in \mathcal{F}_1[\![M]\!]$ with $f(i) = o, f(i_n) \sqsupseteq o_n$ for each n. But $f \in \mathcal{F}_1[\![M]\!] \subseteq \mathcal{F}_2[\![M]\!] = \mathcal{F}_2[\![N]\!]$, so from the above equality we conclude $(i_0, o_0), (i_1, o_1), \ldots (i, o) \in \mathcal{T}[\![N]\!]$.

Thus, $\mathcal{F}_2[\![\,]\!]$ is a modification of $\mathcal{F}_1[\![\,]\!]$ that is fully abstract. We now verify that $\mathcal{F}_2[\![\,]\!]$ preserves the desirable composition and fixed-point properties of $\mathcal{F}_1[\![\,]\!]$.

Theorem 2. $\mathcal{F}_2[\![]\!]$ has the same composition and fixed-point properties as $\mathcal{F}_1[\![]\!]$. Specifically,

$$\mathcal{F}_2[\![M\|N]\!] = \{g|g = \langle f, f'\rangle, f \in \mathcal{F}_1[\![M]\!], f' \in \mathcal{F}_2[\![N]\!]\}$$
$$\mathcal{F}_2[\![\mathsf{loop}(a,b,M)]\!] = Cl(\{g|g = \mathsf{fix}(a,b,g'), g' \in \mathcal{F}_2[\![M]\!]\}).$$

Proof: The aggregation property follows directly from the definitions.

We see directly the containment $\mathcal{F}_2[\![\mathsf{loop}(a,b,M)]\!] \subseteq Cl(\{g|g = \mathsf{fix}(a,b,g'), g' \in \mathcal{F}_2[\![M]\!]\})$, since

$$\mathcal{F}_2[\![\mathsf{loop}(a,b,M)]\!] = Cl(\mathcal{F}_1[\![\mathsf{loop}(a,b,M)]\!])$$
$$= Cl(\{f|f = \mathsf{fix}(a,b,f'), f' \in \mathcal{F}_1[\![M]\!]\})$$

and $\mathcal{F}_1[\![M]\!] \subseteq \mathcal{F}_2[\![M]\!]$.

Finally, we show $\{g|g = \mathsf{fix}(a,b,g'), g' \in \mathcal{F}_2[\![M]\!]\} \subseteq Cl(\mathcal{F}_1[\![\mathsf{loop}(a,b,M)]\!])$ via an intricate construction that we only outline here.

Given $g' \in \mathcal{F}_2[\![M]\!], g = \mathsf{fix}(a,b,g')$, choose chains $i_0 \sqsubseteq i_1 \sqsubseteq \cdots i$, and $o_0 \sqsubseteq o_1 \sqsubseteq \cdots o$, with $g(i_n) \sqsupseteq o_n, g(i) = o$. Now we know that $g(i_n) = p_n$ means that p_n is the least tuple of output streams such that there exists a stream l (the 'looped' input) with $g'(i_n, l) = (p_n, l)$ (where l is actually the ath component of the input and the bth component of the output).

Using approximations to the fixed point, we are able to construct chains of finites

$$(i_0, \epsilon) \sqsubseteq (i_0, l_1) \sqsubseteq \cdots (i_0, l_{k_0}) \sqsubseteq (i_1, l_{k_0+1}) \sqsubseteq \cdots (i, l)$$
$$(p_0, l_1) \sqsubseteq (p_1, l_2) \sqsubseteq \cdots (p_{k_0}, l_{k_0+1}) \sqsubseteq$$
$$(p_{k_0+1}, l_{k_0+2}) \sqsubseteq \cdots (p, l)$$

with $p_{k_n} \sqsupseteq o_n \forall n$, $p = o$, $g'(i_n, l_k) \sqsupseteq (p_k, l_{k+1}) \forall n, k$, and $g'(i, l) = (p, l)$.

Then, since $g' \in \mathcal{F}_2[\![M]\!]$, there exists $f' \in \mathcal{F}_1[\![M]\!]$ with $f'(i_n, l_k) \sqsupseteq (p_k, l_{k+1}) \forall n, k$, and $f'(i, l) = (p, l)$. Finally, we let $f = \mathsf{fix}(a, b, f') \in \mathcal{F}_1[\![\mathsf{loop}(a,b,M)]\!]$, and we have $f(i_n) \sqsupseteq p_{k_n} \sqsupseteq o_n \forall n$ and $f(i) = p = o$. Hence, $g \in Cl(\mathcal{F}_1[\![\mathsf{loop}(a,b,M)]\!])$.
∎

Thus, we have succeeded in finding what we want: A semantic model for the class of oraclizable networks that is fully abstract and that comes equipped with a fixed-point principle, thereby generalizing both aspects of Kahn's principle to this class. In the next section we investigate characterizations of this class in terms of this model and its expressibility.

5 The Universality of Oraclizable Networks

In the previous section we restricted ourselves to the class of oraclizable networks and discovered that the representation by certain sets of functions was fully abstract. In this section we show that the oraclizable networks are universal for this representation; i.e. that the oraclizable networks are the largest class of networks representable by sets of functions. We go on to show that all networks constructible using the *infinity-fair merge* primitive are oraclizable, and that the infinity-fair merge networks are a proper subclass of the oraclizable networks.

Finally, we use these characterizations to show that another tempting conjecture fails to hold. Namely, that although the input-output relations of infinity-fair merge networks (and of all oraclizable networks) are monotone in the Egli-Milner ordering, the class of oraclizable networks (which includes infinity-fair merge networks) is a proper subset of the Egli-Milner monotone networks.

Theorem 3. The oraclizable networks are exactly the whose behavior can be described by a set of functions

Proof: By lemmas 4 and 5.

Lemma 4. The behavior of any oraclizable network is representable by a set of functions.

Proof: This is the semantics of the previous section.

Lemma 5. Given any set of functions F, there is an oraclizable network M implements F (i.e. $\mathcal{F}_1[\![M]\!] = F$).

Proof: Given F, we explicitly construct the network M, with determinate part M_D, and oracle part M_O.

The idea behind M_D is that F can be organized into a countably branching tree indexed by infinite integer sequences. For a stream i we define the notation $[i]_n$ to denote the prefix of i of length at most n; similarly for $[f(i)]_n$. Given functions $f, f' \in F$, we write $f \equiv_n f'$ iff for all i,

$$[f([i]_n)]_n = [f'([i]_n)]_n.$$

Now we note that there are only countably many equivalence classes of F modulo $\equiv_1$. Hence we can index them by integers and denote them C_{k_1}. Similarly, for every integer k_1, we index the equivalence classes of C_{k_1} modulo $\equiv_2$ by integers and denote them $C_{k_1 k_2}$. Proceeding in this way, we can define C_s for any finite sequence s of integers. For s infinite, C_s is the intersection of all $C_{s'}$ with s' a prefix of s, and hence is either empty or contains a single function from F. We will let S be the set of infinite sequences s for which C_s is not empty.

Now we define a function P such that given input i and a sequence of integers s, we have

$$P(s,i) \stackrel{\text{def}}{=} \begin{cases} [f([i]_n)]_n, f \in C_s & \text{if } s \text{ finite of length } n \\ \bigsqcup \{P(s',i) | s' \text{ a finite prefix of } s\} & \text{o.w.} \end{cases}$$

It is easy to see that P is continuous, and that for infinite s with C_s not empty, P computes the unique function $f \in F$ indexed by s. We take M_D to be the determinate process that computes P.

Finally, we take M_O to be an oracle process that produces exactly the streams $s \in S$. Clearly, with this definition of M, M can behave like any and all the functions in F – that is, $\mathcal{F}_1[\![M]\!] = F$. Note that although M_D is defined for infinite streams not in S (and may not compute a function in F on such streams), restricting the oracle M_O to the set S assures that the "extra" functions are not possible behaviors for M. ∎

Theorem 4. The class of all networks constructible with infinity-fair merge is a proper subclass of the oraclizable networks.

Proof: By the following two lemmas.

Lemma 6. All networks constructible with infinity-fair merge and determinate processes are oraclizable.

Proof: Infinity-fair merge is oraclizable, since it is equivalent to an oracle that produces fair bit streams connected to a deterministic merge that uses the oracle input to decide which channel to read next. Since oraclizable networks are closed under composition, the result follows.

Lemma 7. The set of oraclizable networks has strictly greater cardinality than the set of infinity-fair merge networks.

Proof: As we have already noted, infinity-fair merge is equivalent to an oracle that produces all fair bit streams connected to a determinate merge. Hence any infinity-fair merge network can be implemented as this fair oracle connected to some determinate network. Thus, the number of infinity-fair merge networks is bounded by the number of determinate networks, which by Kahn's principle is the same as the number of continuous stream-valued functions. Since the domain of streams is ω-algebraic, this is the same cardinality as the powerset of ω, $\mathcal{P}(\omega)$.

In general, the oracle part of an oraclizable network may emit *any* set of streams. Hence there are at least as many oraclizable networks as the powerset of the domain of streams, $\mathcal{P}(S)$. Since the domain of streams is as large as $\mathcal{P}(\omega)$, the cardinality of the set of oraclizable networks is at least that of $\mathcal{P}(\mathcal{P}(\omega))$, which is strictly greater than the cardinality of $\mathcal{P}(\omega)$. ∎

Finally, we show that the conjecture that the infinity-fair merge networks are exactly those whose input-output relations are Egli-Milner monotone fails to be true. In fact, we show that even the oraclizable networks fail to capture all of the Egli-Milner monotone input-output relations. Recall that given sets A and B, $A \sqsubseteq_{EM} B$ iff

$$\forall a \in A \, \exists b \in B \text{ s.t. } a \sqsubseteq b \, \& \, \forall b \in B \, \exists a \in A \text{ s.t. } a \sqsubseteq b.$$

We say that the input-output relation of a network M is Egli-Milner monotone iff $i \sqsubseteq i'$ implies

$$\{o|(i,o) \in \mathcal{IO}[\![M]\!]\} \sqsubseteq_{EM} \{o'|(i',o') \in \mathcal{IO}[\![M]\!]\}.$$

Theorem 5. The class of oraclizable networks (and hence the infinity-fair merge networks) is a proper subclass of the class of networks with Egli-Milner monotone input-output relations.

Proof: It is easily seen that all oraclizable networks have Egli-Milner monotone input-output relations. To see that the containment is proper, consider the input-output relation described in figure 2 (lines are

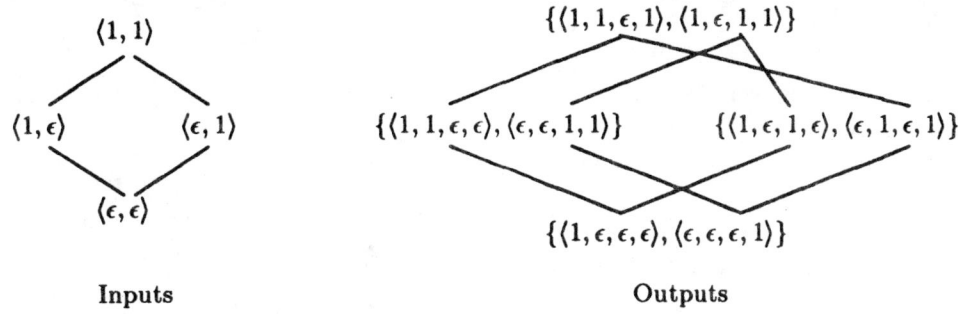

Figure 2: An Egli-Milner monotone input-output relation from S^2 to S^4.

drawn between comparable elements). It is clearly Egli-Milner monotone, but cannot be represented by any set of functions, since the "diamond" of relations among the inputs does not appear in the output. Since we know that sets of functions are universal for infinity-fair merge networks, no such network can implement this relation.

6 Future Work

In the above we have considered the characterization and semantics of oraclizable networks in terms of sets of functions. Another possible representation of this class is on by certain functors relating appropriate categorical powerdomains. An approach along these lines may extend the results of this paper to broader classes of nondeterminism.

Another interesting direction is an investigation of the relations among classes of networks constructed using more powerful merge primitives, such as angelic merge or fair merge, and the oraclizable networks, Egli-Milner monotone networks, or networks with weaker monotonicity properties.

References

[Abr89] S. Abramsky. Unpublished lecture at MFPS, 1989.

[BA81] J. D. Brock and W. B. Ackerman. Scenarios: A model of non-determinate computation. In *Formalization of Programming Concepts*, pages 252–259, 1981. LNCS 107.

[Bro83] M. Broy. Fixed point theory for communication and concurrency. In *Formal Description of Programming Concepts II*, pages 125–148. North-Holland, 1983.

[JK88] B. Jonsson and J. Kok. Comparing dataflow models. Manuscript, 1988.

[Jon89] B. Jonsson. A fully abstract trace model for dataflow networks. In *Proceedings of the Sixteenth Annual ACM Symposium On Principles Of Programming Languages*, 1989.

[Kah77] G. Kahn. The semantics of a simple language for parallel programming. In *Information Processing 74*, pages 993–998. North-Holland, 1977.

[Kok88] J. Kok. Dataflow semantics. Technical Report CS-R8835, Centre for Mathematics and Computer Science, August 1988.

[KP85] R. M. Keller and P. Panangaden. Semantics of networks containing indeterminate operators. In *Proceedings of the 1984 CMU Seminar on Concurrency*, pages 479–496, 1985. LNCS 197.

[KP86] R. M. Keller and P. Panangaden. Semantics of digital networks containing indeterminate operators. *Distributed Computing*, 1(4):235–245, 1986.

[Mis89] J. Misra. Equational reasoning about nondeterministic processes. unpublished manuscript, 1989.

[MPS88] D. McAllester, P. Panangaden, and V. Shanbhogue. Nonexpressibilty of fairness and signaling. In *Proceedings of the 29th Annual Symposium of Foundations of Computer Science*, 1988.

[Pan85] P. Panangaden. Abstract interpretation and indeterminacy. In *Proceedings of the 1984 CMU Seminar on Concurrency*, pages 497–511, 1985. LNCS 197.

[Par82] D. Park. The "fairness problem" and nondeterministic computing networks. In *Proceedings of the Fourth Advanced Course on Theoretical Computer Science, Mathematisch Centrum*, pages 133–161, 1982.

[Pra86] V. Pratt. Modeling concurrency with partial orders. *International Journal Of Parallel Programming*, 15(1):33–71, 1986.

[PS87] P. Panangaden and V. Shanbhogue. On the expressive power of indeterminate primitives. Technical Report 87-891, Cornell University, Computer Science Department, November 1987.

[PS88] P. Panangaden and E. W. Stark. Computations, residuals and the power of indeterminacy. In Timo Lepisto and Arto Salomaa, editors, *Proceedings of the Fifteenth ICALP*, pages 439–454. Springer-Verlag, 1988. Lecture Notes in Computer Science 317.

[PS89] P. Panangaden and V. Shanbhogue. Traces are fully abstract for networks with fair merge. unpublished manuscript, 1989.

[RT88] A. Rabinovich and B. A. Trakhtenbrot. Nets of processes and dataflow. To appear in Proceedings of ReX School on Linear Time, Branching Time and Partial Order in Logics and Models for Concurrency, LNCS, 1988.

[Rus89] J. R. Russell. Full abstraction for nondeterministic dataflow networks. To appear in Proceedings of the 30th Annual Symposium of Foundations of Computer Science, 1989.

[Sta87] E. W. Stark. Concurrent transition system semantics of process networks. In *Proceedings Of The Fourteenth Annual ACM Symposium On Principles Of Programming Languages*, pages 199–210, 1987.

[Sta88] E. W. Stark. On the relations computable by a class of concurrent automata. Manuscript in preparation, 1988.

[Sta89] E. W. Stark. Concurrent transition systems. *Theoretical Computer Science*, 1989.

On the Relations Computable by a Class of Concurrent Automata

Eugene W. Stark*
Department of Computer Science
State University of New York at Stony Brook
Stony Brook, NY 11794 USA

Abstract

We consider *monotone input/output automata*, which model a usefully large class of dataflow networks of indeterminate (or nonfunctional) processes. We obtain a characterization of the relations computable by these automata, which states that a relation $R : X \to 2^Y$ (viewed as a "nondeterministic function") is the input/output relation of an automaton iff there exists a certain kind of Scott domain D, a continuous function $F : X \to [D \to Y]$ and a continuous function $G : X \to \mathcal{P}(D)$, such that $R(x) = F(x)^\dagger(G(x))$ for all inputs $x \in X$. Here $\mathcal{P}$ denotes a certain powerdomain operator, and † denotes the pointwise extension to the powerdomain of a function on the underlying domain. An attractive feature of this result is that it specializes to two subclasses of automata, *determinate* automata, for which G is single-valued, and *semi-determinate* automata, for which G is a constant function. A corollary of the latter result is the impossibility of implementing "angelic merge" by a network of determinate processes and "infinity-fair merge" processes.

1 Introduction

Dataflow networks (see, *e.g.* [3,4,6,7,8]) consist of a collection of concurrently executing sequential processes that communicate by transmitting sequences or "streams" of "value tokens" over FIFO communication channels. Typically, a network is described as a directed graph, whose nodes are processes and whose arcs are communication channels. Each channel serves to connect an "output port" of one process to an "input port" of another process. "Determinate" (or functional) networks were first studied by Kahn [7], who gave an elegant fixed-point principle for determining the function computed by a network from the functions computed by the components. "Indeterminate" (or non-functional) networks remain less well understood, despite extensive study. An interesting class of indeterminate processes are the "merge" processes, which shuffle together sequences of values from two input channels onto a single output channel. *Fair merge* (**fmerge**) guarantees that every value arriving on either of the two inputs will eventually be transmitted to the output. *Angelic merge* (**amerge**) guarantees to transmit all values from one input channel only in case the sequence of values arriving on the *other* channel is finite. *Infinity-fair merge* (**imerge**) guarantees to transmit all values from one input channel only in case the sequence of values arriving on the other channel is *infinite*.

In previous papers [15,21,22], we identified the networks of "monotone" processes as an interesting and particularly well-behaved subclass of the class of indeterminate dataflow networks. The main result of [15] was that, although such networks can be used to perform the "unfair" merging operations **amerge** and **imerge**, no such network can implement **fmerge**. We obtained this result by showing that every network of monotone processes implements a monotone input/output relation, that **amerge** and **imerge** are implementable by networks of monotone processes, but that **fmerge** is not a monotone relation. Now, it is not difficult to see how to use **fmerge** to implement **imerge**, and Panangaden [13] has shown how, using **fmerge**, we can implement **amerge**. Thus the questions left unanswered in [15] are: (1) Can **amerge** be implemented by a network of **imerge** processes and processes with functional behaviors? (2) Can **imerge** be so implemented by **amerge**? Question (1) was answered in the negative by Panangaden and Shanbhogue [14], using *ad hoc* techniques. In this paper, we give an alternative proof by the more general methods of [15]. Contrary to our initial expectations, we have found that question (2) has an affirmative answer, and we exhibit a network with the stated property. This network can be viewed as a demonstration that there can be no notion of "finite indeterminacy" that is preserved by network construction. The three merge primitives, arranged in

---

*Research supported in part by NSF Grant CCR-8702247.

order of their power to implement relations when used in combination with functional processes, thus form a strict hierarchy with **imerge** the weakest of the three primitives, **amerge** strictly stronger, and **fmerge** the strongest.

To obtain the negative answer to question (1), we refine the methods of [15], thereby obtaining a useful characterization of the relations implemented by the class of "monotone input/output automata." Our characterization theorem states that a relation $R : X \to 2^Y$ (viewed as a "nondeterministic function") is the input/output relation of such an automaton iff there exists a certain kind of Scott domain D, a continuous function $F : X \to [D \to Y]$ and a continuous function $G : X \to \mathcal{P}(D)$, such that $R(x) = F(x)^\dagger(G(x))$ for all inputs $x \in X$. Here $\mathcal{P}$ denotes a certain powerdomain operator, and † denotes the pointwise extension to the powerdomain of a function on the underlying domain. This characterization also specializes nicely to the classes of "determinate" and "semi-determinate" automata. For determinate automata, the theorem holds with the restriction that G be single-valued, and for semi-determinate automata, G is restricted to be a constant function. The latter result is interesting, since it shows that semi-determinate automata may be thought of as implementing a collection of continuous functions, indexed by an "oracle set" (the constant value of G). Since **imerge** is representable as such an oracleized set of functions, but **amerge** is not, we conclude that **imerge** is implementable by a semi-determinate automaton, but **amerge** is not. Since the class of semi-determinate automata is closed under network construction, it follows that **amerge** cannot be implemented by a network of **imerge** and functional components.

As in [15], our main tool is the notion of *permutation equivalence* of computation sequences. Intuitively, two finite computation sequences are permutation-equivalent if one can be transformed into the other by a finite sequence of steps in which the order of adjacent "concurrent pairs" of transitions is permuted. We use a result, shown elsewhere [20,23], that the set of equivalence classes of computation sequences of an automaton, under the induced partial order, is a Scott domain whose finite elements are exactly the equivalence classes of finite computation sequences, and which has other useful properties. This result was established in the previous work by using the auxiliary notion of the *residual* of one finite computation sequence by another, to obtain an alternative characterization of permutation equivalence. For this paper, we simply quote the previous result without proof, and this permits us to prove our main result without having to develop the algebra of residuals.

2 Preliminaries

We require some concepts from trace theory [1,12] and domain theory [16,17,18]. In the sequel, all sets whose cardinality is left unspecified are assumed to be at most countable.

2.1 Domains

A (Scott) *domain* is an ω-algebraic, consistently complete cpo. A *subdomain* of D is a subset U of D, which is a domain under the the ordering inherited from D, such that the inclusion of U in D is continuous. A subdomain U of D is *normal* if for every $d \in D$, the set $\{u \in U : u \sqsubseteq d\}$ is directed. Normal subdomains have the following property, which we use in the proof of Lemma 7.

Lemma 1 *Suppose U is a normal subdomain of a domain D. Then any continuous $F : U \to E$ extends to a least continuous $F' : D \to E$.*

Proof – Take $F'(d) = \bigsqcup\{F(u) : u \in U, u \sqsubseteq d\}$. ∎

An *interval* in a domain D is a pair $[d, d']$ with $d \sqsubseteq d'$. An interval $[d, d']$ is *prime* if d' covers d; that is, there does not exist d'' with $d \sqsubset d'' \sqsubset d'$.

2.2 The Fringe Set Powerdomain

Suppose D is a domain. Let $I_D : D \to 2^D$ denote the map that takes d to $\{d\}$. If $F : D \to E$ is any function, then its *pointwise extension* is the function $F^\dagger : 2^D \to 2^E$ defined by: $F^\dagger(U) = \{F(d) : d \in U\}$. Call a subset U of D *closed* if it is downward-closed, closed under lubs of directed subsets, and also closed under lubs of pairs of elements that are consistent in D. The *closure* U^c of U is the least closed set containing U. Define a nonempty subset U of D to be a *fringe set* if U is precisely the set of all maximal elements of U^c. It follows that fringe sets are *pairwise inconsistent*: if d, d' are two distinct elements of a fringe set U, then the set $\{d, d'\}$ has no upper bound in D. Define a binary relation $\sqsubseteq$ on fringe sets of D by defining $U \sqsubseteq V$ iff $U^c \subseteq V^c$. An equivalent characterization of $\sqsubseteq$ is the following: $U \sqsubseteq V$ iff $\forall x \in U\ \exists y \in V(x \sqsubseteq y)$. It is clear from this definition that $\sqsubseteq$ is a preorder, and since U and V are fringe sets, the relation $\sqsubseteq$ is a partial order. In fact, in view of the bijective correspondence between fringe sets and their closures, we have the following:

Lemma 2 *The set $\mathcal{P}(D)$ of all fringe sets of D, equipped with the ordering $\sqsubseteq$, is a domain.*

Indeed, this is nothing more than a slight variant of the "relational," "lower," or "Hoare" powerdomain of D [16,17], whose elements we have chosen to represent by fringe sets, rather than by closed sets as is perhaps more usual. The fringe set representation proves more convenient for our purposes. Usually, the relational powerdomain of a domain D is defined in terms of sets that are closed in the Scott topology on D. The set of maximal elements of a Scott-closed set is pairwise incomparable under the ordering on D, but it is not necessarily pairwise inconsistent. The closed sets defined above are Scott-closed sets with the additional property of being closed under lubs of consistent pairs.

2.3 Traces

A *concurrent alphabet* is a set X, equipped with a symmetric, irreflexive binary relation $\|$ on X, called the *concurrency relation*. The *direct product* of concurrent alphabets X and Y is the concurrent alphabet $X \otimes Y$ whose set of elements is the disjoint union of $X + Y$ of X and Y, and whose concurrency relation $\|_{X \otimes Y}$ is defined to be

$$\|_{X \otimes Y} = \|_X \cup \|_Y \cup (X \times Y) \cup (Y \times X).$$

Suppose X is a concurrent alphabet. Let X^* denote the free monoid generated by X, then there is a least congruence $\sim$ on X^* such that $a\|b$ implies $ab \sim ba$ for all $a, b \in X$. The quotient $X^*/\sim$ is the *free partially commutative monoid* generated by X, and its elements are called *traces*. We use ϵ to denote the identity element (the empty trace). The monoid $X^*/\sim$ is partially ordered, with $x \sqsubseteq y$ iff $\exists z(xz = y)$. Let $\bar{X}$ denote the domain obtained by ideal completion of this poset. We call $\bar{X}$ the *trace domain* generated by the concurrent alphabet X. Notice that since the finite (=isolated=compact) elements of $\bar{X}$ are in bijective correspondence with the elements of $X^*/\sim$, they inherit the monoid operation of $X^*/\sim$, with the bottom element of $\bar{X}$ as the monoid identity. Let $\bar{X}^\circ$ denote the set of finite elements of $\bar{X}$. In the sequel, we identify the elements of $X^*/\sim$ with the corresponding elements of $\bar{X}^\circ$. If $Z \subseteq X$, then the monoid homomorphism from X^* to Z^* that deletes elements of $X \setminus Z$, respects $\sim$, hence induces a monoid homomorphism from $X^*/\sim$ to $Z^*/\sim$ and a continuous map from $\bar{X}$ to $\bar{Z}$. We write $x|Z$ for the application of this map to a trace $x \in \bar{X}$.

Lemma 3 *The following are equivalent statements about a domain D:*

1. *D is isomorphic, by a map that preserves prime intervals, to a normal subdomain of $\bar{X}$ for some concurrent alphabet X.*
2. *E is an event domain in the sense of [5,24].*
3. *D is isomorphic to the domain of configurations of an event structure $(E, \vdash, \#)$, where E is a set of events, $\vdash$ is an enabling relation between finite subsets of E and elements of E, and $\#$ is a binary conflict relation on E.*

The equivalence of (2) and (3) is a theorem of Winskel [5,24]. The equivalence of (1) and (2) is shown in [20]. We shall see that event domains arise naturally as the domains of computations of the kind of automata we consider.

3 Monotone Input/Output Automata

A *monotone input/output automaton* (henceforth simply "automaton") is a tuple

$$A = (E, X, Y, Q, q^I, T),$$

where

- E is a concurrent alphabet of *actions*, and X, Y are disjoint subsets of E, called the sets of *input actions* and *output actions*, respectively. The elements of $E \setminus (X \cup Y)$ are called *internal actions*.
- Q is a set of *states*.
- $q^I \in Q$ is a distinguished *initial state*.
- T is a function that maps each pair of states $q, r \in Q$ to a set $T(q, r) \subseteq E$.

These data are required to satisfy the following conditions:

(Disambiguation) $r \neq r'$ implies $T(q, r) \cap T(q, r') = \emptyset$.

(Commutativity) For all states q and actions a, b, if $a\|b$, $a \in T(q, r)$, and $b \in T(q, s)$, then there exists a state p such that $a \in T(s, p)$ and $b \in T(r, p)$.

(Monotonicity) $a\|b$ whenever $a \in X$ and $b \in E \setminus X$.

(Receptivity) For all states q and input actions a, there exists a state r such that $a \in T(q, r)$.

Intuitively, if $a \in E$, then $a \in T(q, r)$ iff it is possible for A to take a step from state q in which action a occurs and the state changes to r. Input actions represent steps in which input is received from the external environment, and output actions represent steps in which output is transmitted to the external environment. We say that action a is *enabled* in state q if $a \in T(q, r)$ for some r. By the disambiguation condition, if a is enabled in state q, then there is a unique state r such that $a \in T(q, r)$. We sometimes denote this state by qa.

The *transitions* of an automaton are the triples (q, a, r) with $a \in T(q, r)$. We often use the notation $q \xrightarrow{a} r$ or $a : q \to r$ to denote the transition (q, a, r). If t is the transition (q, a, r), then q is called the *domain* $dom(t)$ of t and r is called the *codomain* $cod(t)$ of t. Transitions t and u are called *coinitial* if $dom(t) = dom(u)$.

Monotone input/output automata are closely related to the input/output automata defined by Lynch and Tuttle [10,11]. If we ignore the distinction between input and output actions, and we delete the monotonicity and receptivity conditions, we obtain automata similar to those that have been studied by Bednarczyk [2], Kwiatkowska [9], and Shields [19]. To further motivate the definitions, we describe how monotone input/output automata can be used to model dataflow networks. For this, we use a restricted class of automata called "monotone port automata," which are similar to the monotone port automata defined in [15].

Formally, let us fix in advance countably infinite sets P of *ports* and V of *values*. We call elements of the set $P \times V$ *port actions*, and if e is the port action (p, v), then we write $port(e)$ for its port component p, and $value(e)$ for its value component v. Define an automaton $A = (E, X, Y, Q, q^I, T)$ to be a *port automaton* if $X = P^{\text{in}} \times V$ and $Y = P^{\text{out}} \times V$ for some disjoint finite subsets P^{in} and P^{out} of P, and for all $e, e' \in X \cup Y$ we have $e \| e'$ iff $port(e) \neq port(e')$. Such an automaton models a dataflow process or network with input port set P^{in} and output port set P^{out}. An input (output) action (p, v) corresponds to the receipt (transmission) of value v on port p, and internal actions correspond to internal computation steps in which communication with the environment does not take place. It follows from the definition of $\|$ that the trace domains $\bar{X}$ and $\bar{Y}$ are, up to isomorphism, domains of "port histories" as in [15]. That is, the elements of $\bar{X}$ and $\bar{Y}$ are functions, mapping ports to finite and infinite sequences of values, and ordered argumentwise by prefix.

Notice that, in contrast to more typical models for dataflow networks, our definitions do not specify directly any particular concrete structure for the state sets of port automata, such as the existence of a FIFO "channel buffers" for each input or output port. However, the receptivity, commutativity, and monotonicity axioms can be interpreted as abstract statements about the properties of such buffers. The receptivity condition can be interpreted as stating that arriving input values can always be placed into an input buffer. The commutativity condition, together with the definition of the relation $\|$, captures the notion that distinct ports have separate buffers, The monotonicity condition can be viewed as a restriction on the way input buffers can be accessed: since arriving input cannot disable transitions previously enabled, one can test for the *presence* of input in a buffer, but never for its *absence*.

4 Computations of Automata

A *finite computation sequence* for an automaton is a finite sequence γ of transitions of the form:
$$q_0 \xrightarrow{e_1} q_1 \xrightarrow{e_2} \ldots \xrightarrow{e_n} q_n.$$

The number n is called the *length* $|\gamma|$ of γ. We call the computation sequence of length 0 from state q the *identity* computation sequence, and we denote it by id_q, or just id, when q is clear from the context. Also, it will sometimes be convenient to write $id_q = (q \xrightarrow{\epsilon} q)$. An *infinite computation sequence* is an infinite sequence of transitions:
$$q_0 \xrightarrow{e_1} q_1 \xrightarrow{e_2} \ldots.$$

A computation sequence that contains only input actions is called a *pure-input* computation sequence; one containing no input actions is called a *non-input* computation sequence. The *trace* of γ is the element $\text{tr}(\gamma) = e_1 e_2 \ldots$ of the trace domain $\bar{E}$.

We extend notation and terminology for transitions to computation sequences, so that if γ is a computation sequence, then the *domain* $dom(\gamma)$ of γ is the state q_0, and if γ is finite, then the *codomain* $cod(\gamma)$ of γ is the state q_n. We write $\gamma : q \to r$ to assert that γ is a finite computation sequence with domain q and codomain r. A computation sequence γ is *initial* if $dom(\gamma)$ is the distinguished initial state I. If $\gamma : q \to r$ and $\delta : q' \to r'$ are finite computation sequences, then γ and δ are called *composable* if $q' = r$, and we then define their *composition* to be the finite computation sequence $\gamma\delta : q \to r'$, obtained by concatenating γ and δ and identifying $cod(\gamma)$ with $dom(\delta)$. The operation of composition of finite computation sequences is associative, and identity computation sequences behave as units for it. A finite computation sequence γ is a *prefix* of a computation sequence δ, and we write $\gamma \preceq \delta$, iff there exists a computation sequence ξ with $\gamma\xi = \delta$.

Define *permutation equivalence* to be the least congruence $\sim$, respecting concatenation, on the set of finite computation sequences of A such that:

- Computation sequences $q \xrightarrow{a} r \xrightarrow{b} p$ and $q \xrightarrow{b} s \xrightarrow{a} p$ are $\sim$-related if $a \| b$.

Closely related to permutation equivalence is the *permutation preorder* relation $\sqsubseteq$ on finite computation sequences of A, which is defined to be the transitive closure of $\preceq \cup \sim$. That is, $\gamma \sqsubseteq \delta$ iff there is a way to perform a finite number of permutations of adjacent concurrent transitions in δ, and obtain a computation δ' that has γ as a prefix. It is not difficult to see that $\gamma \sim \delta$ iff $\gamma \sqsubseteq \delta$ and $\delta \sqsubseteq \gamma$. Permutation preorder extends in a straightforward way to infinite computation sequences as well: if γ' and δ' are coinitial finite or infinite computation sequences, then define $\gamma' \sqsubseteq \delta'$ to hold iff for every finite $\gamma \preceq \gamma'$ there exists a finite $\delta \preceq \delta'$, such that $\gamma \sqsubseteq \delta$. We may then extend permutation equivalence to infinite computation sequences by defining $\gamma' \sim \delta'$ iff $\gamma' \sqsubseteq \delta'$ and $\delta' \sqsubseteq \gamma'$.

A *computation* is a $\sim$-equivalence class of computation sequences. Obviously, all finite computation sequences that are representatives of the same $\sim$-equivalence class have the same length, so the notion of the *length* $|\gamma|$ of a finite computation γ makes sense. For each state q, the permutation preorder $\sqsubseteq$ on computation sequences from state q induces a partial order $\sqsubseteq$ on the set of all computations from state q. Coinitial computations γ and γ' are called *consistent* if they have an upper bound with respect to $\sqsubseteq$. For finite γ, γ', this is equivalent to the existence of a pair of finite computations δ, δ' such that $\gamma\delta' = \gamma'\delta$.

The following result, proved in [20], provides a great deal of information about the structure of the partially ordered set of computations of an automaton. Our main theorem is a direct consequence.

Lemma 4 *Suppose A is an automaton. For each state q, the set $\mathrm{Comp}_q(A)$ of computations of A with domain q, partially ordered by $\sqsubseteq$, is an event domain whose finite elements are exactly the equivalence classes of finite computation sequences. Moreover, the map $\mathrm{tr} : \mathrm{Comp}_q(A) \to \bar{E}$ that takes each equivalence class to the corresponding trace, is a prime-interval-preserving embedding of $\mathrm{Comp}_q(A)$ as a normal subdomain of $\bar{E}$.*

Rather than reproving this result here, we merely comment on the method used. It is fairly obvious from the definitions we have given that the map $\mathrm{tr} : \mathrm{Comp}_q(A) \to \bar{E}$ is a monotone injection that preserves prime intervals. To show $\mathrm{Comp}_q(A)$ is a domain, it is necessary to show that all directed subsets have lubs and that all consistent pairs of computations have lubs. To show that the map tr is an embedding of a normal subdomain, we may show that tr is strict, additive, continuous, and reflects consistency. To show these facts, we define the auxiliary notion of the *residual* of one computation sequence "after" another. Formally, we have the following: Suppose γ and γ' are consistent finite computations. Then there exists a unique pair of finite computations $\gamma\backslash\gamma'$ and $\gamma'\backslash\gamma$ (read "γ after γ'" and "γ' after γ"), such that $\gamma(\gamma'\backslash\gamma) = \gamma'(\gamma\backslash\gamma')$, and such that if δ and δ' are any finite computations with $\gamma\delta' = \gamma'\delta$, then there exists a unique finite computation ξ such that $(\gamma\backslash\gamma')\xi = \delta$ and $(\gamma'\backslash\gamma)\xi = \delta'$.

We may think of $\backslash$ as a partial binary operation on coinitial pairs of computations, where $\gamma\backslash\delta$ is defined exactly when γ and δ are consistent, or when they could both be part of the "same concurrent computation." In this case, δ may contain some transitions that "overlap" with γ and some that are "concurrent" with γ. Then $\gamma\backslash\delta$ should be thought of as what is "left" of γ after the part that overlaps with δ has been deleted. The residual $\gamma\backslash\delta$ is undefined exactly when γ contains some indeterminate choice that conflicts with a choice made in δ. A concrete construction of $\gamma\backslash\delta$ for arbitrary consistent finite computations γ and δ is performed by induction on their length.

A similar residual operation can be defined on finite traces (in fact more easily so, since there are no states to worry about). Formally, if x and x' are consistent traces then the *residual* of x after x' is the unique trace $x\backslash x'$ with the property that $x'(x\backslash x') = x \sqcup x'$. From this definition, one can easily see that $x \sqsubseteq y$ iff $x\backslash y = \epsilon$. A similar relation holds for computations: $\gamma \sqsubseteq \delta$ iff $\gamma\backslash\delta = \mathrm{id}$. Thus, the partial ordering on computations has an equivalent characterization in terms of residuals. Using this observation, Lemma 4 may then be proved by using residuals to perform an inductive construction of lubs of directed collections of computations and of consistent pairs, and also to show that the map $\mathrm{tr} : \mathrm{Comp}_q(A) \to \bar{E}$ preserves residuals (hence is continuous) and reflects consistency.

We conclude this section with some additional facts about the computations of monotone input/output automata. We do not use these facts explicitly in this paper, but they are helpful in understanding the behavior of these automata. Proofs can be found (in a somewhat more abstract setting) in [21,22].

Proposition 5 *A monotone automaton A has the following properties:*

1. *For every state q and input trace x, there exists a unique computation $\iota_x(q)$ with $\mathrm{dom}(\iota_x(q)) = q$ and $\mathrm{tr}(\iota_x) = x$. Moreover, the map $\iota : \bar{X} \to \mathrm{Comp}_q(A)$ that takes $x \in \bar{X}$ to $\iota_x \in \mathrm{Comp}_q(A)$, is a prime-interval-preserving embedding of $\bar{X}$ as a normal subdomain of $\mathrm{Comp}_q(A)$.*

2. *Suppose γ is a computation with $\mathrm{dom}(\gamma) = q$, and x is an input trace that is consistent with $\mathrm{tr}(\gamma)|X$. Then γ and $\iota_x(q)$ are consistent.*

3. *Every finite computation γ factors uniquely as $\gamma = \delta\xi$, where δ is a pure-input computation and ξ is a non-input computation. We call the pair (δ,ξ) a pure-input/non-input factorization of γ.*

4. *For every computation γ, there exists a computation δ that is $\sqsubseteq$-maximal among all computations γ' such that $\gamma \sqsubseteq \gamma'$ and $\mathrm{tr}(\gamma)|X = \mathrm{tr}(\gamma')|X$.*

5 Relations Computed by Automata

A computation is called *completed* if it is $\sqsubseteq$-maximal among all computations having the same input trace. In [15] it was shown that this notion coincides with an appropriate notion of "fairness" for monotone automata that are constructed as the parallel composition of a collection of "single-process" components. Specifically, a computation is "fair" if every component process having an enabled non-input action eventually performs some non-input action. Here, we consider a more general situation in which automata need not be networks of single-process components. Although fairness does not generalize directly to this situation, the notion "completed" does, and we therefore adopt it as the appropriate generalization of fairness.

The *input/output relation* of an automaton A is the function $R : \bar{X} \to 2^{\bar{Y}}$ that maps each $x \in \bar{X}$ to the set of all $y \in \bar{Y}$, such that for some some completed initial computation γ of A, we have $x = \text{tr}(\gamma)|X$ and $y = \text{tr}(\gamma)|Y$.

We can now state our main result:

Theorem 1 *A map $R : \bar{X} \to 2^{\bar{Y}}$ is the input/output relation of a monotone input/output automaton iff there exists an event domain D, a continuous function $F : \bar{X} \to [D \to \bar{Y}]$, and a continuous function $G : \bar{X} \to \mathcal{P}(D)$, such that $R(x) = F(x)^\dagger(G(x))$ for all $x \in \bar{X}$.*

Proof – Follows from Lemmas 6 and 7 below. ∎

Before proceeding to the proof, we give the definitions of **fmerge**, **amerge**, and **imerge**, and mention the implications of Theorem 1 for these. Intuitively, each of these relations takes as input finite or infinite sequences of values on two input ports, and produces a finite or infinite sequence of values on one output port. To formalize this, let p_0 and p_1 stand for the two input ports, and let p_2 stand for the single output port. Let V be a countably infinite set of values. Form a concurrent alphabet $X = \{p_0, p_1\} \times V$ with $(p, v)\|(p', v')$ iff $p \neq p'$, and a concurrent alphabet $Y = \{p_2\} \times V$ with $\| = \emptyset$. Then the trace domain $\bar{X}$ is isomorphic to the domain of functions mapping $\{p_0, p_1\}$ to finite or infinite sequences of values with the prefix order; similarly, $\bar{Y}$ is isomorphic to the domain of functions from $\{p_2\}$ to value sequences. It will be convenient notationally to regard $x \in \bar{X}$ as a function on $\{p_0, p_1\}$, and similarly $y \in \bar{Y}$ as a function on $\{p_2\}$.

The three relations are defined as follows:

- **fmerge** is the set of all $(x, y) \in \bar{X} \times \bar{Y}$ such that $y(p_2)$ is a shuffle of $x(p_0)$ and $x(p_1)$.

- **amerge** is the set of all $(x, y) \in \bar{X} \times \bar{Y}$ such that $y(p_2)$ is a shuffle of a prefix x_0 of $x(p_0)$ and a prefix x_1 of $x(p_1)$, such that
  1. If $x(p_0)$ is finite, then $x_1 = x(p_1)$.
  2. If $x(p_1)$ is finite, then $x_0 = x(p_0)$.
  3. If both $x(p_0)$ and $x(p_1)$ are infinite, then either $x_0 = x(p_0)$ or $x_1 = x(p_1)$.

- **imerge** is the set of all $(x, y) \in \bar{X} \times \bar{Y}$ such that $y(p_2)$ is a shuffle of a prefix x_0 of $x(p_0)$ and a prefix x_1 of $x(p_1)$, such that
  1. If $x(p_0)$ is infinite then $x_1 = x(p_1)$.
  2. If $x(p_1)$ is infinite, then $x_0 = x(p_0)$.
  3. If one of $x(p_0)$ and $x(p_1)$ is finite, then both x_0 and x_1 are finite, and either $x_0 = x(p_0)$ or else $x_1 = x(p_1)$.

As a consequence of Theorem 1, if R is the input/output relation of an automaton, then R has the following *monotonicity* property: If $y \in R(x)$, and $x \sqsubseteq x'$, then there exists $y' \in R(x')$ with $y \sqsubseteq y'$. The relation **fmerge** is not monotone (consider $x(p_0) = \epsilon$, $x(p_1) = 555\ldots$, $y(p_2) = 555\ldots$, $x'(p_0) = 7$ and $x'(p_1) = 555\ldots$), hence is not the input/output relation of an automaton. In contrast, **amerge** can be expressed in the form of Theorem 1: assuming that the set of values that arrive on port p_0 is disjoint from those that arrive on p_1, we may take $D = \bar{Y}$, take $G = $ **amerge**, and take $F(x)(y) = y$ for all $x \in \bar{X}$ and $y \in \bar{Y}$. (If the value sets are not disjoint, then we may use a slight modification of this construction, in which we take D to be a "tagged" version of $\bar{Y}$, and the function $F(x)$ removes the tags.) Hence **amerge** is the input/output relation of an automaton. It is slightly more complicated to express **imerge** in the required form, and we postpone this to Section 6.2 below. The results of [15] are therefore a corollary of Theorem 1.

Lemma 6 *Suppose A is an automaton with input/output relation $R : \bar{X} \to 2^{\bar{Y}}$. Then there exists an event domain D, a continuous function $F : \bar{X} \to [D \to \bar{Y}]$, and a continuous function $G : \bar{X} \to \mathcal{P}(D)$, such that $R(x) = F(x)^\dagger(G(x))$ for all $x \in \bar{X}$.*

Proof – Let $D = \text{Comp}_{q_I}(A)$, then D is an event domain by Lemma 4. Define $F : \bar{X} \to [D \to \bar{Y}]$ by:

$$F(x)(\gamma) = \bigsqcup \{\text{tr}(\delta)|Y : \delta \sqsubseteq \gamma, \text{tr}(\delta)|X \sqsubseteq x\}.$$

That is, $F(x)(\gamma)$ is the maximum output that can be produced in a "prefix up to permutation" δ of γ, when the input is constrained to be less than x. It is straightforward to check that F is well-defined and continuous. Define $G : \bar{X} \to 2^D$ to map each $x \in \bar{X}$ to the set of all completed initial computations with input history x. By construction, $R(x) = F(x)^\dagger(G(x))$ for all $x \in \bar{X}$. It remains to be shown that $G : \bar{X} \to \mathcal{P}(D)$ and that G is continuous.

We first claim that $G(x)$ is a fringe set for all $x \in \bar{X}$. But this is clear from the fact that the set $\Gamma(x)$ of all initial computations γ with $\text{tr}(\gamma)|X \sqsubseteq x$ is closed, and $G(x)$ is the set of its maximal elements. Next, we show that G is monotone. This is immediate from the fact that if $x \sqsubseteq x'$, then $\Gamma(x) \subseteq \Gamma(x')$. Finally, we show that G is continuous. Given a directed collection $\{x_i : i \in I\}$ of inputs, with supremum x, let $\Gamma = \bigcup \Gamma(x_i)$, and note that $\Gamma = \Gamma(x)$. Thus, $G(x) = \bigsqcup \{G(x_i) : i \in I\}$. ∎

Lemma 7 *Let $R : \bar{X} \to 2^{\bar{Y}}$ and suppose there exists an event domain D, a continuous function $F : \bar{X} \to [D \to \bar{Y}]$, and a continuous function $G : \bar{X} \to \mathcal{P}(D)$, such that $R(x) = F(x)^\dagger(G(x))$ for all $x \in \bar{X}$. Then R is the input/output relation of a monotone automaton.*

Proof – Since D is an event domain, by Lemma 4 it is isomorphic via a prime-interval-preserving map μ to a normal subdomain of $\bar{Z}$, for some concurrent alphabet Z. Define $C(x) = \mu(G(x)^c)$. Let $F' : \bar{X} \to [\bar{Z} \to \bar{Y}]$ be defined so that for each $x \in \bar{X}$, the map $F'(x) : \bar{Z} \to \bar{Y}$ is the least continuous function (which exists by Lemma 1) with the property that $F(x) = F'(x) \circ \mu$.

Next, we construct an automaton

$$A = (E, X, Y, Q, q^I, T)$$

as follows:

- Let $E = X \otimes Y \otimes Z$.

- Let $Q = \bar{X}^\circ \times \bar{Y}^\circ \times \bar{Z}^\circ$, with $q^I = (\epsilon, \epsilon, \epsilon)$.

- The map T is defined as follows:

  1. If $a \in X$, then $a \in T((x,y,z),(x',y',z'))$ iff $x' = xa$, $y' = y$, and $z' = z$.
  2. If $b \in Y$, then $b \in T((x,y,z),(x',y',z'))$ iff $x' = x$, $y' = yb$, $z' = z$, and $y' \sqsubseteq F'(x)(z)$.
  3. If $c \in Z$, then $c \in T((x,y,z),(x',y',z'))$ iff $x' = x$, $y' = y$, $z' = zc \in C(x)$.

Intuitively, the first component of the state will is used to keep track of the finite input received so far in a computation, the second component keeps track of the finite output issued so far, and the third keeps track of the history of how indeterminate choices have been resolved so far.

It is straightforward to check that the definition of A satisfies the requirements for a monotone input/output automaton. The commutativity property of A follows from the fact that $G(x)$, hence $C(x)$, is closed under lubs of consistent pairs of elements. We also observe, by a straightforward induction, that if γ is any finite initial computation sequence for A, then $\operatorname{tr}(\gamma)|Y \sqsubseteq F'(\operatorname{tr}(\gamma)|X)(\operatorname{tr}(\gamma)|Z))$ and $\operatorname{tr}(\gamma)|Z \in C(\operatorname{tr}(\gamma)|X)$. By continuity, these relationships extend also to infinite γ.

We claim that the automaton A has R as its input/output relation. There are two parts to the proof: (1) show that if $y \in R(x)$, then there exists a completed initial computation sequence γ with $x = \operatorname{tr}(\gamma)|X$ and $y = \operatorname{tr}(\gamma)|Y$; (2) show that if γ is a completed initial computation sequence, then $\operatorname{tr}(\gamma)|Y \in R(\operatorname{tr}(\gamma)|X)$.

(1) Suppose $y \in R(x)$. Then by hypothesis, there exists $z \in \bar{Z}$ such that $z \in \mu(G(x))$ and $y = F'(x)(z)$. Choose sequences $a_1, a_2, \ldots \in X \cup \{\epsilon\}$, $b_1, b_2, \ldots \in Y \cup \{\epsilon\}$, and $c_1, c_2, \ldots \in Z \cup \{\epsilon\}$, such that $x = a_1 a_2 \ldots$, $y = b_1 b_2 \ldots$, and $z = c_1 c_2 \ldots$. These sequences exist by the fact that trace domains are ω-algebraic and *finitary* (there are at most finitely many prefixes of any finite trace). Also, because the map $\mu : D \to \bar{Z}$ preserves prime intervals, we may choose $c_1, c_2, \ldots$ so that $c_1 c_2 \ldots c_k \in C(x)$ for all k.

Next, we use these sequences in a "scheduling argument" to construct a sequence $d_1, d_2, \ldots \in E \cup \{\epsilon\}$ such that if $w = d_1 d_2 \ldots$, then $x = w|X$, $y = w|Y$, and $z = w|Z$. We do this as follows: Suppose we have defined $d_1, d_2, \ldots, d_k$, for some $k \geq 0$. Suppose further that

$$\begin{aligned}
x_k &= a_1 a_2 \ldots a_l = (d_1 d_2 \ldots d_k)|X, \\
y_k &= b_1 b_2 \ldots b_m = (d_1 d_2 \ldots d_k)|Y, \\
z_k &= c_1 c_2 \ldots c_n = (d_1 d_2 \ldots d_k)|Z.
\end{aligned}$$

Define d_{k+1} as follows:

- Suppose $k \bmod 3 = 0$. Then let $d_{k+1} = a_{l+1}$.
- Suppose $k \bmod 3 = 1$. If $y_k b_{m+1} \sqsubseteq F'(x_k)(z_k)$, then let $d_{k+1} = b_{m+1}$, otherwise let $d_{k+1} = \epsilon$.
- Suppose $k \bmod 3 = 2$. If $z_k c_{n+1} \in C(x_k)$, then let $d_{k+1} = c_{n+1}$, otherwise let $d_{k+1} = \epsilon$.

It is clear from the construction that $w|X = x$, $w|Y \sqsubseteq y$, and $w|Z \sqsubseteq z$. Moreover, since the domain $\bar{Z}$ is algebraic, and the function G is continuous, given any finite $z' \sqsubseteq z$, there exists K such that $z' \in C(x_k)$ for all $k \geq K$, thus $z' \sqsubseteq z_k$ for sufficiently large k. Since z' may be arbitrary, we conclude $w|Z = z$. Similar reasoning shows that $w|Y = y$.

Now, it follows from the definition of A and the construction of the sequence $d_1, d_2, \ldots$, that there exist states $q^I = q_0, q_1, \ldots$, such that for each $k \geq 0$ we have $q_k \xrightarrow{d_{k+1}} q_{k+1}$, and thus

$$\gamma = q_0 \xrightarrow{d_1} q_1 \xrightarrow{d_2} \ldots$$

is an initial computation for A. We claim that γ is completed. For if not, then there would exist δ with $\gamma \sqsubseteq \delta$ but $\gamma \neq \delta$, such that $\operatorname{tr}(\delta)|X = x = \operatorname{tr}(\gamma)|X$. By the injectiveness of the map tr, we would have either $\operatorname{tr}(\gamma)|Z \sqsubset \operatorname{tr}(\delta)|Z$ or else $\operatorname{tr}(\gamma)|Y \sqsubset \operatorname{tr}(\delta)|Y$. The former is impossible because $z = \operatorname{tr}(\gamma)|Z$ is maximal in $C(x) = \mu(G(x)^c)$, and then the latter is also impossible because $\operatorname{tr}(\delta)|Y$ is functionally determined (via F') by $\operatorname{tr}(\delta)|X = x$ and $\operatorname{tr}(\delta)|Z = z$.

(2) Suppose γ is a completed initial computation. Let $x = \operatorname{tr}(\gamma)|X$, $y = \operatorname{tr}(\gamma)|Y$, and $z = \operatorname{tr}(\gamma)|Z$. As previously observed, we know that $y \sqsubseteq F'(x)(z)$ and $z \in C(x)$. We claim that in fact $y = F'(x)(z)$ and $z \in \mu(G(x))$. First, suppose $y \sqsubset F'(x)(z)$. Then there is some finite $y'' \sqsubseteq F'(x)(z)$, such that $y'' \not\sqsubseteq y$. Assume y'' is chosen to be of minimal length, then $y'' = y'b$ where $y' \sqsubseteq y$ and b is an output action. Using the algebraicity of $\bar{Y}$ and the continuity of F', we can obtain finite $x' \sqsubseteq x$ and $z' \sqsubseteq z$ such that $y'b \sqsubseteq F'(x')(z')$. Choose a finite prefix γ' of γ such that $x' \sqsubseteq \operatorname{tr}(\gamma')|X$, $y' \sqsubseteq \operatorname{tr}(\gamma')|Y$, and $z' \sqsubseteq \operatorname{tr}(\gamma')|Z$. By the definition of A, and the monotonicity of F', we must have b enabled in state $cod(\gamma')$. If $r = cod(\gamma')$ and t is the transition

$r \xrightarrow{b} rb$, then $\text{tr}(\gamma)$ and $\text{tr}(\gamma' t)$ are consistent, hence γ and $\gamma' t$ are consistent, and they have a $\sqsubseteq$-upper bound $\delta \neq \gamma$. Since this contradicts the assumption that γ is completed, we conclude that $y = F'(x)(z)$.

Finally, suppose $z \notin \mu(G(x))$. Because $z \in C(x) = \mu(G(x)^c)$, we have $z \sqsubset \mu(d)$ for some $d \in G(x)$. Therefore, there must exist some finite $z'' \in C(x)$, such that $z'' \not\sqsubseteq z$, but with z and z'' consistent and $z \sqcup z'' \sqsubseteq \mu(d)$. The argument then proceeds for z'' similarly to the above for y'', contradicting the assumption that γ is completed, and concluding that $z \in \mu(G(x))$. ∎

6 Specializations of the Main Result

Our result specializes to two interesting subclasses of automata: "determinate" automata and "semi-determinate" automata. In the case of determinate automata, we restrict G to be single-valued in Theorem 1. The theorem then becomes the statement that the determinate automata compute exactly the class of continuous functions from input to output. Although this result has perhaps been known in various forms for a long time, the interesting point here is how we obtain it as a specialization of a general result. In the case of semi-determinate automata, we restrict G to be a constant function in Theorem 1. The theorem then states that semi-determinate automata compute exactly those relations R such that $R(x) = \{F_i(x) : i \in G(\epsilon)\}$, where the F_i are continuous and $G(\epsilon)$ may be thought of as an "oracle set."

An interesting consequence of the latter result is that there are relations (*e.g.* **amerge**) that are implementable by monotone automata, but cannot be represented in oracleized form as above, hence cannot be implemented by semi-determinate automata. Since **imerge** can be implemented by a semi-determinate automaton, this gives us a separation in expressive power between **amerge** and **imerge**.

6.1 Determinate Automata

An automaton is *determinate* if it satisfies the following condition:

(**Determinacy**) Suppose $b : q \to r$ and $b' : q \to r'$, where b and b' are distinct non-input actions. Then $b \| b'$.

Intuitively, a determinate automaton exhibits no "internal nondeterminism"—the only possible nondeterministic choices are those that occur between input transitions. The determinacy property may also be seen as a kind of Church-Rosser or "diamond" property for non-input actions.

Call coinitial computations γ and δ *input-consistent* if their input traces $\text{tr}(\gamma)|X$ and $\text{tr}(\delta)|X$ are consistent.

The following lemma gives the characteristic property of determinate automata:

Lemma 8 *Suppose A is a determinate automaton. Then two coinitial computations γ and δ of A are consistent iff they are input-consistent.*

Proof – The proof may be accomplished by an inductive argument in which residuals are used to construct the lub of two coinitial input-consistent computations γ and δ. (See [21].) ∎

Theorem 2 *For determinate automata, Theorem 1 holds if we restrict G to be single-valued.*

Proof – Suppose $R(x) = F(x)^\dagger(G(x))$ for all $x \in \bar{X}$, where G is single-valued and F and G are as in Theorem 1. It is straightforward to check that application of the construction in the proof of Lemma 7 yields a determinate automaton.

Conversely, suppose A is a determinate automaton with input/output relation R. Lemma 4 and Lemma 8, together with an application of Zorn's Lemma, show that for each $x \in \bar{X}$, there is a unique completed computation γ_x with $\text{tr}(\gamma_x)|X = x$. Hence G is single-valued. ∎

Corollary 9 *Suppose $R : \bar{X} \to 2^{\bar{Y}}$. Then R is the input/output relation of a determinate automaton iff $R = I_Y \circ H$, where $H : \bar{X} \to \bar{Y}$ is continuous.*

Proof – Given H, we may take D to be a one-element domain, and G to be the identically $\bot$ function, which is clearly single-valued. ∎

Since there exist nonfunctional relations (*e.g.* **imerge** and **amerge**) that are computable by monotone automata, it follows from the previous theorem that the class of determinate automata is strictly weaker in expressive power than the class of all monotone automata.

6.2 Semi-Determinate Automata

An automaton A is *semi-determinate* if it satisfies the following condition:

(**Semi-Determinacy**) There exists a collection $C \subseteq E \setminus (X \cup Y)$ of *choice actions*, such that:

1. Whenever $q \xrightarrow{a} r$ and $r \xrightarrow{c} s$, where $c \in C$ and $a \notin C$, then $a \| c$ and c is enabled in state q.

2. The automaton, formed from A by deleting all elements of C from each set $T(q, r)$, is determinate.

It is not difficult to see from this definition that if there exists a set C with these properties, then there is a unique largest such set. When we speak of *the set C*

of choice actions for a particular semi-determinate automaton, we refer to the largest such set. A *pure-choice computation* will be a computation in which only choice actions occur.

Lemma 10 *Suppose A is semi-determinate. Then every finite computation γ of A can be factored uniquely as $\gamma = \gamma'\gamma''$, where γ' contains only choice actions, and γ'' contains no choice actions. Moreover, if $\gamma = \gamma'\gamma''$ and $\delta = \delta'\delta''$ are two such factorizations, where γ and δ are input-consistent, then γ and δ are consistent iff γ' and δ' are consistent.*

Proof – The required factorization is obtained by using property (1) in the definition of semi-determinacy, and the commutativity property in the definition of automata, to "permute all choice actions to the front." The consistency assertion then follows using property (2) in the definition of semi-determinacy. A formal proof may be carried out by induction on the length of a computation sequence. ∎

Theorem 3 *For semi-determinate automata, Theorem 1 holds if we restrict G to be a constant function.*

Proof – Given D, F, and constant function G, let A be constructed as in the proof of Lemma 7. Because the enabling of actions in Z depends only on the $\bar{Z}^\circ$ component of the state, it follows that A is semi-determinate with $C = Z$.

Conversely, given A, we use a slight modification of the construction in the proof of Lemma 6. Let D be the domain of all initial pure-choice computations. For each $x \in \bar{X}$, let $G(x)$ be the set of all maximal initial pure-choice computations. Then $G(x)$ is obviously a fringe set, and G is constant, hence continuous. Now, the fact that deleting the choice transitions from A yields a determinate automaton implies that for each $x \in \bar{X}$ and for each initial pure-choice computation δ, there exists a unique completed initial computation $\gamma_{x,\delta}$ of A such that $\text{tr}(\gamma_{x,\delta})|X = x$ and such that δ is the greatest pure-choice computation with $\delta \sqsubseteq \gamma_{x,\delta}$. Let $F(x)$ be the function that takes each $\delta \in D$ to the trace $\text{tr}(\gamma_{x,\delta})|Y$. It is straightforward to see from this definition that $F(x)$ is continuous for each $x \in \bar{X}$, and that F itself is continuous as a function of x. Finally, observe that $R(x) = F(x)^\dagger(G(x))$ for all $x \in \bar{X}$. ∎

Corollary 11 *The relation* **imerge** *is the input/output relation of a semi-determinate automaton, but* **amerge** *is not.*

Proof – We may express **imerge** = $F(x)^\dagger(G(x))$, where D is the domain of finite and infinite sequences of natural numbers with the prefix order, $G(x)$ is the set of all infinite sequences, and $F(x)$ uses its argument as an oracle to schedule the selection of values from the two input ports. More formally, let X_0 be the subset of X consisting of the actions (p_0, m), and similarly for X_1. Define recursively,

$$F(x)(\epsilon) = \epsilon$$
$$F(x)(nd) = H_0(x|X_0, x|X_1, n+1, d)$$
$$H_0(x, x', 0, \epsilon) = \epsilon$$
$$H_0(x, x', 0, nd) = H_1(x, x', n+1, d)$$
$$H_0(\epsilon, x', k+1, d) = \epsilon$$
$$H_0((p_0, m)x, x', k+1, d) = (p_2, m)H_0(x, x', k, d)$$
$$H_1(x, x', 0, \epsilon) = \epsilon$$
$$H_1(x, x', 0, nd) = H_0(x, x', n+1, d)$$
$$H_1(x, \epsilon, k+1, d) = \epsilon$$
$$H_1(x, (p_1, m)x', k+1, d) = (p_2, m)H_1(x, x', k, d).$$

In contrast, if we could express **amerge** in a similar form, then for any given $d \in D$, the function F_d defined by $F_d(x) = F(x)(d)$ would be a monotone function with the property $F_d(x) \in \textbf{amerge}(x)$ for all $x \in \bar{X}$. However, no such function can exist. To see this, observe that we must have $F_d((p_0, 5)) = (p_2, 5)$ and $F_d((p_1, 7)) = (p_2, 7)$, so there is no possible value for $F((p_0, 5)(p_1, 7))$ that will make F_d monotone. Hence, **amerge** is not the input/output relation of a semi-determinate automaton. ∎

7 Networks of Automata

So far, we have avoided entirely the issue of how automata may be composed into networks of communicating, concurrently executing components. What we have established so far is the existence of a hierarchy of monotone input/output automata, consisting of the determinate automata, the semi-determinate automata, and all the monotone automata, and we have established some separation results for this hierarchy. The results so far may be summarized by saying that semi-determinate automata compute a strictly larger class of input/output relations than do determinate automata, and compute a strictly smaller class of input/output relations than do arbitrary monotone input/output automata. However, we would like to say more. We would like our results to imply something about the "implementability" of various relations in terms of networks of "primitive components." To do this, we need to define an operation of parallel composition, by which a collection of automata is combined into a network, and we must show that the various classes of automata are closed under this operation.

7.1 Parallel Composition

Although it would be possible to define parallel composition on collections of unrestricted monotone input/output automata, the definitions are more transparent if we restrict our attention to "monotone port automata," which we defined in Section 3.

Formally, suppose $\mathcal{A} = \{A_i : i \in I\}$ is a collection of port automata, where $A_i = (E_i, X_i, Y_i, Q_i, q_i^I, T_i)$. We say that $\mathcal{A}$ is *compatible* if for all $i, j \in I$, if $i \neq j$ then $E_i \cap (E_j \setminus X_j) \subseteq X_i \cap Y_j$.

If $\mathcal{A}$ is compatible, then its *parallel composition* is the automaton $\prod A_i = (E, X, Y, Q, q^I, T)$, where

- $E = \bigcup E_i$, with $a \| b$ iff $a \|_i b$ for all $i \in I$ such that both a and b are in E_i.

- $Y = \bigcup Y_i$ and $X = (\bigcup X_i) \setminus Y$.

- $Q = \prod_{i \in I} Q_i$,

- $q^I = (q_i^I : i \in I)$,

- $e \in T((q_i : i \in I), (r_i : i \in I))$ iff for all $i \in I$, either $e \notin E_i$ and $r_i = q_i$, or else $e \in E_i$ and $e \in T_i(q_i, r_i)$.

Intuitively, component automata in a network communicate by transmitting values on shared ports. The outputting of a value v on port p by one component automaton occurs simultaneously with the inputting of value v from port p by all other automata that share port p. The compatibility condition states that only input or output actions may be shared between components, and that each shared action (port) may be an output action (port) for at most one component automaton in a network. It is not our purpose here to further justify this particular definition of parallel composition. The reader may refer to the papers [10,11,15] for additional motivation and discussion. Here we wish merely to observe the following:

Theorem 4 *The parallel composition of a compatible collection of port automata is a port automaton. Moreover, the classes of determinate port automata and semi-determinate port automata are closed under parallel composition of compatible collections.*

Proof – The disambiguation, receptivity, and commutativity properties are immediate from the definition and the corresponding properties of the A_i. To show monotonicity, suppose $a \in X$ and $b \in Y$. Then a and b are both port actions, and $port(a) \neq port(b)$. Hence whenever both $a, b \in E_i$, we have $a\|_i b$, so $a\|b$.

Now, assume the A_i are determinate, and suppose $a, b \in E \setminus X$ are both enabled in state q. If both $a, b \in E_i$, then there are four cases:

1. If both $a, b \in E_i \setminus X_i$, then $a\|_i b$ by the determinacy of A_i.

2. If $a \in X_i$ and $b \in E_i \setminus X_i$, then $a\|_i b$ by monotonicity of A_i.

3. If $a \in E_i \setminus X_i$ and $b \in X_i$, then $a\|_i b$ by monotonicity of A_i.

4. If both $a, b \in X_i$, then $port(a) \neq port(b)$. This is because if $port(a) = port(b)$, then for some $j \in I$ we would have both $a, b \in E_j \setminus X_j$, hence not $a\|_j b$, contradicting the determinacy of A_j. Since $port(a) \neq port(b)$, we have $a\|_i b$.

Since $a\|_i b$ in all four cases, we conclude that $a\|b$ and $\prod A_i$ is determinate.

Finally, assume the A_i are semi-determinate, and let C_i be the largest set of choice actions for A_i. We claim that $\prod A_i$ is semi-determinate, with $C = \bigcup C_i$ as a set of choice actions. For each $i \in I$, let A_i' be the determinate automaton obtained from A_i by deleting all elements of C_i from each $T(q, r)$. Similarly, let A' be the automaton from $\prod A_i$ obtained by deleting all elements of C from each $T(q, r)$. Then $A' = \prod A_i'$, so A' is determinate. Now suppose

$$(q_i : i \in I) \xrightarrow{a} (r_i : i \in I) \xrightarrow{c} (s_i : i \in I),$$

where $a \in E \setminus C$ and $c \in C$. Since each C_i is a set of internal actions, by compatibility we have $c \in C_i$ for precisely one $i \in I$. There are two cases: either $a \in E_i \setminus C_i$ or else $a \notin E_i$. If $a \in E_i \setminus C_i$, then since A_i is semi-determinate we know that $a\|_i c$ and that c is enabled for A_i in state q_i. Since $c \notin C_j$ for $j \neq i$ it follows that $a\|c$ and that c is enabled for A in state $(q_i : i \in I)$. If $a \notin E_i$, then $a\|c$ by definition of $\|$. Since $q_i = r_i$ we know that c is enabled for A_i in state q_i. Then c is also enabled for A in state $(q_i : i \in I)$. ∎

Now, we can interpret our results as saying something about the implementability of relations in terms of networks of "primitives." For each continuous input/output function, let us choose a "standard" determinate port automaton that computes that function. For example, we may choose the automata that result from the construction of Lemma 7. Similarly, we may choose a particular semi-determinate port automaton that computes **imerge**, and a port automaton that computes **amerge**. Then our results imply:

1. the impossibility of implementing **fmerge** by any network of our standard primitives.

2. the impossibility of implementing **amerge** by any network of our standard functional primitives and our standard **imerge** automaton.

3. the impossibility of implementing **imerge** or **amerge** by any network of our standard functional primitives.

7.2 Finite Indeterminacy

We have not yet answered the question of whether **imerge** can be implemented in terms of our standard functional primitives and our standard **amerge** automaton. Although the answer to this question is "yes,"

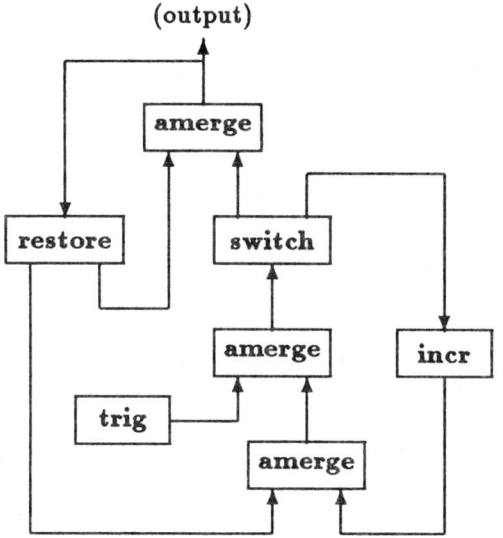

Figure 1: Implementation of Iterated Unbounded Choice by **amerge**.

for a long time it seemed likely to the author that one could prove the opposite by trying to define a class of automata with a property of "finite indeterminacy," and showing that no such automaton could compute **imerge**. This was to be accomplished by proving a version of Theorem 1 for automata with finite indeterminacy in which the sets $G(x)$ were required to have a topological compactness property. After a number of failed attempts, the author realized that it is possible to construct a finite network of standard functional and **amerge** processes that computes **imerge**. One way to interpret this result is that there is can be no definition of "finite indeterminacy" that is satisfied by some standard automaton that computes **amerge**, is not satisfied by any automaton that computes **imerge**, and that is preserved under parallel composition.

Figure 1 shows how **amerge** can be used together with functional processes to construct a network that outputs an arbitrary infinite sequence of nonnegative integers. Once one has such a network, it is straightforward to use it as an "oracle" (as suggested by the proof of Corollary 11) to construct an implementation of **imerge**.

We give only an informal description of the operation of the network, rather than a formal definition and correctness proof. All processes other than the **amerge** processes are functional. All tokens that traverse the channels contain either numeric values or a special "trigger" value, used by the node **switch**. The process **trig** generates an infinite sequence of trigger values. The process **incr** repeatedly reads numeric values from its input, increments them and then issues the incremented values at the output. The process **switch** reads numeric values and outputs them to the right-hand output until a trigger value is read. Once this has happened, the next numeric value is output to the left, and the cycle repeats. Multiple trigger values arriving in succession at the input are treated identically to a single trigger value. The process **restore** initially outputs a zero on its right-hand output and a one on its left-hand output. Once this is done, it repeats the following forever: Read a numeric value from the input; if the value read is zero, output a zero on the right-hand output, otherwise output a one on the left-hand output.

The network operates as follows: Initially, the **restore** process supplies a zero token at one input of the top **amerge** and a one token to the bottom **amerge**, which injects it into the loop. The nonzero token cycles an indeterminate number of times (possibly forever) around the loop, getting its value incremented each time. If a trigger token ever makes it through the middle **amerge** to the **switch**, then the loop will be terminated, however we can't guarantee that this will ever happen. What we do know, though, is that *either* the zero token will make it through the top **amerge**, or a nonzero token will exit the loop and pass through the top **amerge**. Thus, eventually a token will pop out the top, and it is easy to see that any nonnegative integer value is possible.

Once a token has been output, it is the function of the **restore** process to reinitialize the network. If a zero was output, then the **restore** process supplies another zero token to the top **amerge**. If a nonzero value was output, then the **restore** process injects another "one" token into the loop via the bottom **amerge**. Note that it is *not* necessary (and it is in fact impossible) to remove the token still circulating around the loop in the case that a zero was output. Since the circulating token might have any value, simply restoring a zero token to the top **amerge** is sufficient to reinitialize the network.

8 Conclusion

We have defined a class of concurrent automata that can be used to model indeterminate dataflow networks, we have defined two subclasses of automata in terms of their transition structure, and we have obtained a characterization of the input/output relations computed by each class. We have also defined an operation of parallel composition, and observed that each of the three classes of automata is closed under this operation. The three classes (determinate, semi-determinate, and unrestricted) automata form a strict hierarchy with respect to their power to compute relations.

An interesting direction for future research would be to obtain a version of Theorem 1 that characterizes the relations that are computable by automata that are parallel compositions of single-process components. Formally, we may define an automaton to be *single-process* if it satisfies the following condition:

(**Single-Process**) Suppose $b : q \to r$ and $b' : q \to r'$, where b and b' are distinct non-input actions. Then not $b \| b'$.

Define a *network automaton* to be an automaton of the form $\prod A_i$, where $\{A_i : i \in I\}$ is a compatible collection of single-process automata. The problem is then to find conditions under which we can "decompose" an automaton into a network of single-process automata, and to relate these conditions to the structure of the domain of computations. One condition that does permit us to perform such a decomposition is the to require that the complement # of the concurrency relation $\|$ on actions be an equivalence relation. We can then recover the "processes" as the equivalence classes of #. At the moment, though, it is not clear how this equivalence relation condition on an automaton is reflected in the structure of its domain of computations.

References

[1] I. J. Aalbersberg and G. Rozenberg. Theory of traces. *Theoretical Computer Science*, 60(1):1–82, 1988.

[2] M. Bednarczyk. *Categories of Asynchronous Systems*. PhD thesis, University of Sussex, October 1987.

[3] J. D. Brock and W. B. Ackerman. Scenarios: a model of non-determinate computation. In *Formalization of Programming Concepts*, pages 252–259, Springer-Verlag. Volume 107 of *Lecture Notes in Computer Science*, 1981.

[4] M. Broy. Nondeterministic data-flow programs: how to avoid the merge anomaly. *Science of Computer Programming*, 10:65–85, 1988.

[5] P.-L. Curien. *Categorical Combinators, Sequential Algorithms, and Functional Programming*. Research Notes in Theoretical Computer Science, Pitman, London, 1986.

[6] A. A. Faustini. An operational semantics for pure dataflow. In *Automata, Languages, and Programming, 9th Colloquium*, pages 212–224, Springer-Verlag. Volume 140 of *Lecture Notes in Computer Science*, 1982.

[7] G. Kahn. The semantics of a simple language for parallel programming. In J. L. Rosenfeld, editor, *Information Processing 74*, pages 471–475, North-Holland, 1974.

[8] G. Kahn and D. B. MacQueen. Coroutines and networks of parallel processes. In B. Gilchrist, editor, *Information Processing 77*, pages 993–998, North-Holland, 1977.

[9] M. Kwiatkowska. *Categories of Asynchronous Systems*. PhD thesis, University of Leicester, May 1989.

[10] N. A. Lynch and E. W. Stark. A proof of the Kahn principle for input/output automata. *Information and Computation*, 1989. (to appear).

[11] N. A. Lynch and M. Tuttle. *Hierarchical Correctness Proofs for Distributed Algorithms*. Technical Report MIT/LCS/TR-387, M. I. T. Laboratory for Computer Science, April 1987.

[12] A. Mazurkiewicz. Trace theory. In *Advanced Course on Petri Nets*, GMD, Bad Honnef, September 1986.

[13] P. Panangaden. Implementation of amerge with fmerge. June 1988. (Private communication).

[14] P. Panangaden and V. Shanbhogue. *On the Expressive Power of Indeterminate Network Primitives*. Technical Report 87-891, Cornell University Dept. of Computer Science, December 1987.

[15] P. Panangaden and E. W. Stark. Computations, residuals, and the power of indeterminacy. In *Automata, Languages, and Programming*, pages 439–454, Springer-Verlag. Volume 317 of *Lecture Notes in Computer Science*, 1988.

[16] G. D. Plotkin. Domains: lecture notes. 1979. (unpublished manuscript).

[17] D. A. Schmidt. *Denotational Semantics: A Methodology for Language Development*. Allyn and Bacon, 1986.

[18] D. S. Scott. *Lectures on a Mathematical Theory of Computation*. Technical Report PRG-19, Oxford University Computing Laboratory, Programming Research Group, May 1981.

[19] M. W. Shields. Deterministic asynchronous automata. In *Formal Methods in Programming*, North-Holland. 1985.

[20] E. W. Stark. Compositional relational semantics for indeterminate dataflow networks. In *Category Theory and Computer Science*, pages 52–74, Springer-Verlag. Volume 389 of *Lecture Notes in Computer Science*, Manchester, U. K., 1989.

[21] E. W. Stark. Concurrent transition system semantics of process networks. In *Fourteenth ACM Symposium on Principles of Programming Languages*, pages 199–210, January 1987.

[22] E. W. Stark. Concurrent transition systems. *Theoretical Computer Science*, 64:221–269, 1989.

[23] E. W. Stark. Connections between a concrete and abstract model of concurrent systems. In *Fifth Conference on the Mathematical Foundations of Programming Semantics*, Springer-Verlag. Lecture Notes in Computer Science, New Orleans, LA, 1990. (to appear).

[24] G. Winskel. *Events in Computation*. PhD thesis, University of Edinburgh, 1980.

Higher-Order Modules and the Phase Distinction

Robert Harper [*]
Carnegie Mellon University
Pittsburgh, PA 15213

John C. Mitchell [†]
Stanford University
Stanford, CA 94305

Eugenio Moggi [‡]
University of Cambridge
Cambridge CB2 3QG, UK
(on leave from Univ. of Edinburgh)

Abstract

In earlier work, we used a typed function calculus, XML, with dependent types to analyze several aspects of the Standard ML type system. In this paper, we introduce a refinement of XML with a clear compile-time/run-time *phase distinction*, and a direct compile-time type checking algorithm. The calculus uses a finer separation of types into universes than XML and enforces the phase distinction using a nonstandard equational theory for module and signature expressions. While unusual from a type-theoretic point of view, the nonstandard equational theory arises naturally from the well-known Grothendieck construction on an indexed category.

1 Introduction

The module system of Standard ML [HMM86] provides a convenient mechanism for factoring ML programs into separate but interrelated program units. The basic constructs are *structures*, which are a form of generalized "records" with type, value and structure components, and *functors*, which may be regarded as parameterized structures or functions from structures to structures. The types of structures and functors are called *signatures*. The signature of a structure lists the component names and their types, while the signature of a functor also includes the types of all parameters. Typically, program units are represented as structures that are linked together by functor application. When two structure parameters of a functor must share a common substructure, this is specified using a "sharing" constraint within the functor parameter list. In Standard ML as currently implemented, there are no functors with functor parameters. In this respect, the current language only uses "first-order" modules.

There are two formal analyses of the module system, one operational and the other a syntactic translation leading to a denotational semantics. The structured operational semantics of [HMT87b, HMT87a, Tof87] includes a computational characterization of the type checker. This gives a precise, implementation-independent definition of the Standard ML language that may be used for a variety of purposes. The second formal analysis is a type-theoretic description of ML, which leads to a denotational semantics to the language. The second line of work, beginning with [Mac86] and continued in [MH88], uses dependent sum types $\Sigma x{:}A.B$ to explain structures and dependent function types $\Pi x{:}A.B$ for functors. In addition to providing some insight into the functional behavior of the module constructs, the XML calculus introduced in [MH88] establishes a framework for studying a class of *ML-like* languages. Because variants of Standard ML may be considered as XML theories, the emphasis of this approach is on properties of Standard ML that remain invariant under extensions of the language. In addition, XML is most naturally defined with higher-order modules, suggesting a useful extension of Standard ML. However, some important aspects of Standard ML are not accurately reflected in the XML analysis.

---

[*] Supported by the Office of Naval Research under contract N00014-84-K-0415 and by the Defense Advanced Research Projects Agency (DOD), ARPA Order No. 5404, monitored by the Office of Naval Research under the same contract.

[†] Partially supported by an NSF PYI Award, matching funds from Digital Equipment Corporation, Xerox Corporation and the Powell Foundation and by NSF grant CCR-8814921.

[‡] Supported by ESPRIT Basic Research Action No. 3003, Categorical Logic In Computer Science.

Although ML is designed to allow compile-time type checking, it is not clear how to "statically" type check versions of XML with certain additional type constructors or with higher-order modules. This is particularly unfortunate for higher-order modules, since these seem useful in supporting separate compilation or as an alternative to ML's "sharing" specifications [BL84, Mac86]. In this paper, we redesign XML so that compile-time type checking is an intrinsic part of the type-theoretic framework. Since it is difficult to characterize the difference between compile-time and run-time precisely, we focus on establishing a *phase distinction*, in the terminology of [Car88]. However, to give better intuition, we generally refer to these phases as *compile-time* and *run-time*. The main benefit of our redesign is that type checking becomes decidable, even in the presence of higher-order functors and arbitrary equational axioms between "run-time" expressions.

The main difficulty with higher-order functors may be illustrated by considering an expression e containing a "functor" variable F which maps *type*, *int* pairs (representing structures) to *type*, *int* pairs. Such an expression e might occur as the body of a higher-order functor, with functor parameter F. In type checking e, we might encounter a type expression of the form $Fst(F[int,e_1])$, referring to the type component of the structure obtained by applying the functor parameter F to structure $[int,e_1]$. Since F is a formal parameter, we cannot hope to evaluate this type expression without performing functor application, which we consider a "run-time," or second phase, operation. However, in type checking e, we might need to decide whether two such type expressions, say $Fst(F[int,e_1])$ and $Fst(F[int,e_2])$, are equal. The natural equality to consider involves deciding whether structure components e_1 and e_2 are equal. However, if these are complicated integer expression, perhaps containing recursive functions, then it is impossible to algorithmically compare two such expressions for equality. While it is possible to simplify type checking using syntactic equality of possibly divergent expressions, this is too restrictive in practice.

In this paper, we present a typed calculus λ^{ML} which includes both higher-order modules and a clear separation into "phases" which correspond intuitively to compile-time and run-time. The new calculus is at once a refinement and an extension of XML. The universe structure of XML is refined so that the core language (*i.e.*, the language without modules) possesses a natural phase distinction. Then the language is extended in a systematic way to include dependent types for representing structures and functors. In order to preserve the phase distinction a non-standard formulation of the rules for dependent types is needed. Rather than restrict the syntax of structures and functors, as one might initially expect, we adopt non-standard equational axioms that allow us to simplify each structure or functor into separate "compile-time" and "run-time" parts. Referring back to the example above, we test whether $Fst(F[int,e_1])$ and $Fst(F[int,e_2])$ are equal essentially by simplifying F to a pair of maps, one compile-time and the other run-time. This allows us to compute compile-time (type) values of these expressions without evaluating run-time expressions e_1 or e_2. This approach follows naturally from the development of [Mog89a], which defines the *category of modules* over any suitable indexed category representing a typed language. In categorical terms, the category of modules is the Grothendieck construction on an indexed category, which is proved relatively cartesian closed when certain natural assumptions about the indexed category are satisfied. Our λ^{ML} calculus is a concrete outgrowth of Moggi's categorical development, providing an explicit lambda notation for the category of modules.

Like XML, λ^{ML} may be extended with any typed constants and corresponding equational axioms. In contrast to XML, constants and non-logical λ^{ML} axioms only affect the "run-time" theory of the language and do not interact with type checking. We show that λ^{ML} typing is decidable for any variant of the calculus based on any (possibly undecidable) equational theory for "run-time" expressions. A similar development may be carried out using the computational λ-calculus approach of [Mog89b] in place of equational axioms, but we will not go into that in this paper.

The paper is organized as follows. In Section 2 we introduce the core calculus, λ^{ML}, which we later extend to include modules. λ^{ML} is essentially the HML calculus given in [Mog89a] and closely related to the *Core*-XML calculus given in [MH88]. In Section 3 we introduce λ^{ML}_{mod}, the full calculus of higher-order modules. We prove that λ^{ML}_{mod} is a definitional extension of a simpler "structures-only" calculus and use this result to establish decidability and compile-time type checking for the full calculus of modules. Brief concluding remarks appear in Section 4.

2 Core Calculus

We begin by giving the definition of the λ^{ML} core calculus, λ^{ML}, which is essentially the calculus HML of [Mog89a]. This calculus captures many of the essential features of the ML type system, but omits, for the sake of simplicity, ML's concrete and abstract types (which could be modeled using existential types [MP88]), recursive types (which can be described through a λ^{ML} theory), and record types. We also do not consider pattern matching, or computational aspects such as side-effects and exceptions. A promising approach toward integrating these features is described in [Mog89b].

2.1 Syntactic Preliminaries

There are four basic syntactic classes in λ^{ML}: *kinds, constructors, types* and *terms*. The kinds include T, the collection of all monotypes, and are closed under formation of products and function spaces. The constructors, which include monotypes such as *int*, and type constructors such as *list*, are elements of kinds. The types of λ^{ML}, whose elements are terms, include cartesian products, function spaces and polymorphic types. The terms of the calculus correspond to the basic expression forms of ML, but are written in an explicitly-typed syntax, following [MH88]. It is important to note that our "types" correspond roughly to ML's "type schemes," the essential difference being that we require them to be closed with respect to quantification over all kinds (not just the kind of monotypes) and function spaces. These additional closure conditions for type schemes are needed to make the the category of modules for λ^{ML} relatively cartesian closed (*i.e.*, closed under formation of dependent products and sums).

The organization of λ^{ML} is a refinement of the type structure of *Core*-XML[MH88]. The kind T of monotypes corresponds directly to the first universe U_1 of *Core*-XML. However, the second universe, U_2, of *Core*-XML is separated into distinct collections of kinds and types. For technical reasons, the cumulativity of the *Core*-XML universes is replaced by the explicit "injection" of T into the collection of types, written using the keyword *set*.

2.2 Syntax

The syntax of λ^{ML} raw expressions is given in Table 1. The collection of term variables, ranged over by x, and the collection of constructor variables, ranged over by v, are assumed to be disjoint. The metavariable τ ranges over the collection of monotypes (constructors of kind T). Contexts consist of a sequence of *declarations* of the form $v{:}k$ and $x{:}\sigma$ declaring the kind or type, respectively, of a constructor or term variable. In addition to the context-free syntax, we require that no variable be declared more than once in a context Φ so that we may unambiguously regard Φ as a partial function with finite domain Dom(Φ) assigning kinds to constructor variables and types to term variables.

2.3 Judgement Forms

There are two classes of judgements in λ^{ML}, the *formation judgements* and the *equality judgements*. The formation judgements are used to define the set of well-formed λ^{ML} expressions. With the exception of the kind expressions, there is one formation judgement for each syntactic category. (Every raw kind expression is well-formed.) The equality judgements are used to axiomatize equivalence of expressions. (There is no equality judgement for kinds; kind equivalence is just syntactic identity.) The equality judgements are divided into two classes, the *compile-time* equations and the *run-time* equations, reflecting the intuitive phase distinction: kind and type equivalence are compile-time, term equivalence is run-time. The judgment forms of λ^{ML} are summarized in Table 2. The metavariable $\mathcal{F}$ ranges over formation judgements, $\mathcal{E}$ ranges over equality judgements, and $\mathcal{J}$ ranges over all forms of judgement. We sometimes write $\Phi \gg \alpha$ to stand for an arbitrary judgement when we wish to make the context part explicit.

2.4 Formation Rules

The syntax of λ^{ML} is specified by a set of inference rules for deriving formation judgements. These resemble rules in [MH88, Mog89a] and are essentially standard. Due to space constraints, they are omitted from this conference paper. We write $\lambda^{ML} \vdash \mathcal{F}$ to indicate that the formation judgement $\mathcal{F}$ is derivable using these rules. The formation rules may be summarized as follows. The constructors and kinds form a simply-typed λ-calculus (with product and unit types) with base kind T, and basic constructors $1, \times$, and $\rightarrow$. The collection of types is built from base types 1 and $\mathrm{set}(\tau)$, where τ is a constructor of kind T, using the type constructors $\times$ and $\rightarrow$, and quantification over an arbitrary kind. The terms amount to an explicitly-typed presentation of the ML core language, similar to that presented in [MH88]. (The **let** construct is omitted since it is definable here.)

2.5 Equality rules

The rules for deriving equational judgements also resemble rules in [MH88, Mog89a] and are essentially standard. We write $\lambda^{ML} \vdash \mathcal{E}$ to indicate that an equation $\mathcal{E}$ is derivable in accordance with these rules.

$$
\begin{aligned}
k &\in kind &::=&\ 1 \mid T \mid k_1 \times k_2 \mid k_1 \to k_2 \\
u &\in constr &::=&\ v \mid 1 \mid \times \mid \to \mid * \mid \langle u_1, u_2\rangle \mid \pi_i(u) \mid (\lambda v{:}k.u) \mid u_1\,u_2 \\
\sigma &\in type &::=&\ \mathrm{set}(u) \mid \sigma_1 \times \sigma_2 \mid \sigma_1 \to \sigma_2 \mid (\forall v{:}k.\sigma) \\
e &\in term &::=&\ x \mid * \mid \langle e_1, e_2\rangle \mid \pi_i(e) \mid (\lambda x{:}\sigma.e) \mid e_1\,e_2 \mid (\Lambda v{:}k.e) \mid e[u] \\
\Phi &\in context &::=&\ \emptyset \mid \Phi, v{:}k \mid \Phi, x{:}\sigma
\end{aligned}
$$

Table 1: λ^{ML} raw expressions

$\Phi\ context$	Φ is a context
$\Phi \gg u : k$	u is a constructor of kind k
$\Phi \gg \sigma\ type$	σ is a type
$\Phi \gg e : \sigma$	e is a term of type σ
$\Phi \gg u_1 = u_2\ k$	u_1 and u_2 are equal constructors of kind k
$\Phi \gg \sigma_1 = \sigma_2\ type$	σ_1 and σ_2 are equal types
$\Phi \gg e_1 = e_2 : \sigma$	e_1 and e_2 are equal terms of type schema σ

Table 2: λ^{ML} judgement forms

The λ^{ML} equational rules are formulated so as to ensure that if an equational judgement is derivable, then it is well-formed, meaning that the evident associated formation judgements are derivable. For the sake of convenience we give a brief summary of the equational rules of λ^{ML}.

2.5.1 Compile-Time Equality

Constructors Equivalence of constructor expressions is the standard equivalence of terms in the simply-typed λ-calculus based on the following axioms:

$$(1\ \eta)\quad \dfrac{\Phi \gg u : 1}{\Phi \gg u = * : 1}$$

$$(\times\ \beta)\quad \dfrac{\Phi \gg u_1 : k_1 \quad \Phi \gg u_2 : k_2}{\Phi \gg \pi_i(\langle u_1, u_2\rangle) = u_i : k_i}\ (i=1,2)$$

$$(\times\ \eta)\quad \dfrac{\Phi \gg u : k_1 \times k_2}{\Phi \gg \langle \pi_1(u), \pi_2(u)\rangle = u : k_1 \times k_2}$$

$$(\to\ \beta)\quad \dfrac{\Phi \gg u_1 : k_1 \quad \Phi, v{:}k_1 \gg u_2 : k_2}{\Phi \gg (\lambda v{:}k_1.u_2)\,u_1 = [u_1/v]u_2 : k_2}$$

$$(\to\ \eta)\quad \dfrac{\Phi \gg u : k_1 \to k_2}{\Phi \gg (\lambda v{:}k_1.u\,v) = u : k_1 \to k_2}\ (v \notin \mathrm{Dom}(\Phi))$$

Types The equivalence relation on types includes the following axioms expressing the interpretation of the basic ML type constructors

$$(1\ T=)\quad \dfrac{\Phi\ context}{\Phi \gg \mathrm{set}(1) = 1\ type}$$

$$(\times\ T=)\quad \dfrac{\Phi \gg \tau_1 : T \quad \Phi \gg \tau_2 : T}{\Phi \gg \mathrm{set}(\tau_1 \times \tau_2) = \mathrm{set}(\tau_1) \times \mathrm{set}(\tau_2)\ type}$$

$$(\to\ T=)\quad \dfrac{\Phi \gg \tau_1 : T \quad \Phi \gg \tau_2 : T}{\Phi \gg \mathrm{set}(\tau_1 \to \tau_2) = \mathrm{set}(\tau_1) \to \mathrm{set}(\tau_2)\ type}$$

2.5.2 Run-Time Equality

Terms There are seven axioms corresponding to the reduction rules associated with each of the type constructors:

$$(1\ \eta)\quad \dfrac{\Phi \gg e : 1}{\Phi \gg e = * : 1}$$

$$(\times\ \beta)\quad \dfrac{\Phi \gg e_1 : \sigma_1 \quad \Phi \gg e_2 : \sigma_2}{\Phi \gg \pi_i(\langle e_1, e_2\rangle) = e_i : \sigma_i}\ (i=1,2)$$

$$(\times\ \eta)\quad \dfrac{\Phi \gg e : \sigma_1 \times \sigma_2}{\Phi \gg \langle \pi_1(e), \pi_2(e)\rangle = e : \sigma_1 \times \sigma_2}$$

$$(\to\ \beta)\quad \dfrac{\Phi \gg e_1 : \sigma_1 \quad \Phi, x{:}\sigma_1 \gg e_2 : \sigma_2}{\Phi \gg (\lambda x{:}\sigma_1.e_2)\,e_1 = [e_1/x]e_2 : \sigma_2}$$

$(\to \eta)$ $\dfrac{\Phi \gg e : \sigma_1 \to \sigma_2}{\Phi \gg (\lambda x{:}\sigma_1.e\, x) = e : \sigma_1 \to \sigma_2}$ $(x \notin \mathrm{Dom}(\Phi))$

$(\forall \beta)$ $\dfrac{\Phi \gg u : k \quad \Phi, v{:}k \gg e : \sigma}{\Phi \gg (\Lambda v{:}k.e)[u] = [u/v]e : [u/v]\sigma}$

$(\forall \eta)$ $\dfrac{\Phi \gg e : (\forall v{:}k.\sigma)}{\Phi \gg (\Lambda v{:}k.e[v]) = e : (\forall v{:}k.\sigma)}$ $(v \notin \mathrm{Dom}(\Phi))$

2.6 Theories

The λ^{ML} calculus is defined with respect to an arbitrary *theory* $\mathcal{T} = (\Phi^{\mathcal{T}}, \mathcal{A}^{\mathcal{T}})$ consisting of a well-formed context $\Phi^{\mathcal{T}}$ and a set $\mathcal{A}^{\mathcal{T}}$ of run-time equational axioms of the form $e_1 = e_2 : \sigma$ with $\Phi_0 \gg e_i : \sigma$ derivable for $i = 1, 2$. A theory corresponds to the programming language notion of standard prelude, and might contain declarations such as $int : T$ and $fix : \forall t{:}T.\,\mathrm{set}((t \to t) \to t)$, and axioms such as expressing the fixed-point property of *fix*. For $\mathcal{T} = (\Phi^{\mathcal{T}}, \mathcal{A}^{\mathcal{T}})$, we write $\lambda^{ML}[\mathcal{T}] \vdash \mathcal{J}$ to indicate that the judgement $\mathcal{J}$ is derivable in λ^{ML}, taking the variables declared in $\Phi^{\mathcal{T}}$ as basic constructors and terms, and taking the equations in $\mathcal{E}^{\mathcal{T}}$ as non-logical axioms. We write $\lambda^{ML}[\mathcal{T}] \vdash_{ct} \mathcal{J}$ to indicate that the judgement $\mathcal{J}$ is derivable from theory $\mathcal{T}$ using only the compile-time equational rules and equational axioms of $\mathcal{T}$.

2.7 Properties of λ^{ML}

We will describe the phase distinction in λ^{ML} by separating contexts into sets of "compile-time" and "run-time" declarations. If Φ is a λ^{ML} context, we let Φ^c be the context obtained by omitting all term variable declarations from Φ and let Φ^r be the context obtained by eliminating all constructor variable declarations from Φ. The following lemma expresses the compile-time type checking property of λ^{ML}:

Lemma 2.1 *Let $\mathcal{T}$ be any theory. The following implications hold:*

If $\lambda^{ML}[\mathcal{T}] \vdash$	then $\lambda^{ML}[\Phi^{\mathcal{T}}, \emptyset] \vdash_{ct}$
Φ context	Φ^c, Φ^r context
$\Phi \gg u : k$	$\Phi^c \gg u : k$
$\Phi \gg u_1 = u_2 : k$	$\Phi^c \gg u_1 = u_2 : k$
$\Phi \gg \sigma$ type	$\Phi^c \gg \sigma$ type
$\Phi \gg \sigma_1 = \sigma_2$ type	$\Phi^c \gg \sigma_1 = \sigma_2$ type
$\Phi \gg e : \sigma$	$\Phi^c, \Phi^r \gg e : \sigma$
$\Phi \gg e_1 = e_2 : \sigma$	$\Phi^c, \Phi^r \gg e_i : \sigma$

Since the constructors and kinds form a simply-typed λ-calculus, it is a routine matter to show that equality of well-formed constructors (and, consequently, types) in λ^{ML} is decidable. It is then easy to show that type checking in λ^{ML} is decidable. This is a well-known property of the polymorphic lambda calculus F_ω (*c.f.* [Gir71, Gir72, Rey74, BMM89]), which may be seen as an impredicative extension of the λ^{ML} calculus.

Lemma 2.2 *There is a straightforward one-pass algorithm which decides, for an arbitrary well-formed theory $\mathcal{T}$ and formation judgement $\mathcal{F}$, whether or not $\lambda^{ML}[\mathcal{T}] \vdash \mathcal{F}$.*

The main technical accomplishment of this paper is to present a full calculus encompassing the module expressions of ML which has a compile-time decidable type checking problem.

3 Modules Calculus

3.1 Overview

In the XML account of Standard ML modules [Mac86, MH88] (see also [NPS88, C+86, Mar84] for related ideas), a structure is an element of a *strong sum* type of the form $\Sigma x{:}A.B$. For example, a structure with one type and one value component is regarded as a pair $[\tau, e]$ of type $S = \Sigma t{:}T.\sigma$. Although Standard ML structures bind names to their components, component selection in XML is simplified using the projections *Fst* and *Snd*. Functors are treated as elements of *dependent function* types of the form $\Pi x{:}A.B$. For example, a functor mapping structures with signature S to structures with the same signature would have type $\Pi s{:}(\Sigma t{:}T.\sigma).(\Sigma t{:}T.\sigma)$. In XML, functors are therefore written as λ-terms mapping structures to structures. As discussed in the introduction, the standard use of dependent types conflicts with compile-time type checking since a type expression (which we expect to evaluate a compile time) may depend on an arbitrary (possibly run time) expression. For example, if F is a functor variable of signature $S \to S$ (where S is as above), then $Fst(F[int, 3])$ is an irreducible type expression involving a run-time sub-expression.

In this section we develop a calculus λ^{ML}_{mod} of higher-order modules with a phase distinction based on the categorical analysis of [Mog89a]. We begin with a simpler "structures-only" calculus that is primarily a technical device used in the proofs. The full calculus of higher-order modules has a standard syntax for dependent strong sums and functions, resembling

XML, but a non-standard equational theory inspired by the categorical interpretation of program modules [Mog89a]. The calculus also employs a single non-standard typing rule for structures that we conjecture is not needed for decidable typing, but which allows a more generous (and simple) type-checking algorithm without invalidating the categorical semantics. Although inspired by a categorical construction, we prove our main results directly using only standard techniques of lambda calculus. The non-standard aspects of λ^{ML}_{mod} calculus are justified by showing that this calculus is a definitional extension of the "structures-only" calculus, which itself bears a straightforward relationship to the core calculus. This definitional extension result is used to prove that λ^{ML}_{mod} type equivalence is decidable and that the language therefore has a practical type checking algorithm.

3.2 The Calculus of Structures

In this section, we extend λ^{ML} with structures and signatures. The resulting calculus, λ^{ML}_{str}, has a straightforward phase distinction and forms the basis for the full calculus of modules. We assume we have some set of structure variables that are disjoint from the constructor and term variables, and use $s, s', s_1, \ldots$ as metavariables for structure variables. The additional syntax of λ^{ML}_{str} is given in Table 3. Note that contexts are extended to include declarations of structure identifiers, but structures are required to be in "split" form $[u, e]$. (A variable s is not a structure and there is no need for operations to select the components of a structure.)

The judgement forms of λ^{ML} are extended with two additional formation judgements, and two additional equality judgements, summarized in Table 4. The rules for deriving judgements in λ^{ML}_{str} are obtained by extending the rules of λ^{ML} (taking contexts now in the extended sense) with the obvious rules for structures in "split" form, in particular the following two rules governing the use of structure variables:

$$([\,]\ E_1) \quad \frac{\Phi\ context}{\Phi \gg s^c : k}\ (\Phi(s) = [v{:}k, \sigma])$$

$$([\,]\ E_2) \quad \frac{\Phi\ context}{\Phi \gg s^r : [s^c/v]\sigma}\ (\Phi(s) = [v{:}k, \sigma])$$

The notion of theory and derivability with respect to a theory are the same as in λ^{ML}.

The calculus of structures may be understood in terms of a translation into the core calculus, which amounts to showing that λ^{ML}_{str} may be interpreted into the category of modules of [Mog89a]. For Φ a λ^{ML}_{str} context, define Φ^* to be the λ^{ML} context obtained by replacing all structure variable declarations $s : [v{:}k, \sigma]$ by the pair of declarations $s^c : k$ and $s^r : [s^c/v]\sigma$.

Lemma 3.1 *Let T be a well-formed λ^{ML} theory.*

1. $\lambda^{ML}_{str}[T] \vdash \Phi \gg [v{:}k, \sigma]$ sig iff $\lambda^{ML}[T] \vdash \Phi^*, v{:}k \gg \sigma$ type, and similarly for signature equality.

2. $\lambda^{ML}_{str}[T] \vdash \Phi \gg [u, e] : [v{:}k, \sigma]$ iff $\lambda^{ML}[T] \vdash \Phi^* \gg u : k$ and $\lambda^{ML}[T] \vdash \Phi^* \gg e : [u/v]\sigma$, and similarly for structure equality.

3. $\lambda^{ML}_{str}[T] \vdash \Phi \gg \alpha$ iff $\lambda^{ML}[T] \vdash \Phi^* \gg \alpha$, for any judgement α other than of the four forms considered in items 1. and 2. above.

It is an immediate consequence of this lemma and the decidability of λ^{ML} type equivalence that λ^{ML}_{str} type equivalence is decidable. This will be important for the decidability of type checking in the full modules calculus.

3.3 The Calculus of Modules

The relative cartesian closure of Moggi's category of modules implies that higher-order functors are *definable* in λ^{ML}_{str}. This may seem surprising, since λ^{ML}_{str} is a rather minimal calculus of structures, with nothing syntactically resembling lambda abstraction over structures. The key idea in understanding this phenomenon is to regard *all* modules as "mixed-phase" entities, consisting of a compile-time part and a run-time part. For basic structures of the form $[u, e]$, the partitioning is clear: u, a constructor, may be evaluated at compile-time, while e, a term, is left until run-time. For more complex module expressions such as functors, the separation requires further explanation.

Consider the signature $S = [v{:}T, \text{set}(v)]$, and let $F{:}S \to S$ be a functor. Since this functor lies within the first-order fragment of λ^{ML}, we may rely on Standard ML for intuition. The functor F takes a structure of signature S as argument, and returns a structure, also of signature S. On the face of it, F might compute the type component of the result as a function of *both* the type and term component of the argument. However, no such computation is possible in ML since there are no primitives for building types from terms. Thus we may regard F as consisting of two parts, the compile-time part, which computes the type component of the result as a function of the type component of the argument, and the run-time part, which computes the term component of the result as a function of both the type and term component of the argument. (Since we are working in

$$
\begin{aligned}
k &\in \mathit{kind} & ::= & \ \ldots \\
u &\in \mathit{constr} & ::= & \ \ldots \mid s^c \\
\sigma &\in \mathit{type} & ::= & \ \ldots \\
e &\in \mathit{term} & ::= & \ \ldots \mid s^r \\
S &\in \mathit{sig} & ::= & \ [v{:}k,\sigma] \\
M &\in \mathit{mod} & ::= & \ [u,e] \\
\Phi &\in \mathit{context} & ::= & \ \ldots \mid \Phi, s{:}S
\end{aligned}
$$

Table 3: λ^{ML}_{str} raw expressions

$\Phi \gg S\ sig$ S is a signature
$\Phi \gg M : S$ M is a structure of signature S

$\Phi \gg S_1 = S_2\ sig$ S_1 and S_2 are equal signatures
$\Phi \gg M_1 = M_2 : S$ M_1 and M_2 are equal modules of signature S

Table 4: λ^{ML}_{str} judgement forms

a typed framework with explicit polymorphism, the term component may contain type information that depends on the compile-time functor argument.) For a more concrete example, suppose I is the identity functor $\lambda s{:}S.s$. Separated into compile time and run time parts, I becomes the structure

$$[\lambda s^c{:}T.s^c, \Lambda s^c{:}T.\lambda s^r{:}\mathrm{set}(s^c).s^r]$$

of signature

$$[f{:}T{\to}T, \forall s^c{:}T.\ \mathrm{set}(s^c{\to}fs^c)].$$

In other words, I may be represented by the structure consisting of the identity constructor on types, and the polymorphic identity on terms. (A technical side comment is that the structure corresponding to I has more than one signature, as we shall see.)

With functors represented by structures, functor application becomes a form of "structure application." In keeping with the above discussion, structure application is computed by applying the first component of the functor to the first component of the argument, and the second component of the functor to both components of the argument. More precisely, if $[u,e]$ is a structure of signature $[f{:}k' \to k, \forall v'{:}k'.\sigma' \to [fv'/v]\sigma]$, and $[u',e']$ is a structure of signature $[v'{:}k',\sigma']$, then the application $[u,e][u',e']$ is defined to be the structure $[uu', eue']$ of signature $[v{:}k,\sigma]$. As we shall see below, the appropriate typing conditions are satisfied whenever the first structure is the image of a functor under the translation sketched in the next paragraph. Moreover, both type correctness and equality are preserved under the translation.

Although λ^{ML}_{str} already "has" higher-order modules, the syntax for representing them forces the user to explicitly decompose every functor into distinct compile-time and run-time parts, even for the first-order functors of Standard ML. This is syntactically cumbersome. In keeping with the syntax of Standard ML, and practical programming considerations, we will consider a more natural notation based on [Mac86, MH88]. However, our calculus will nonetheless respect the phase distinction inherent in representing functors as structures. This is achieved by employing a non-standard equational theory that, when used during type checking, makes explicit the underlying "split" interpretation of module expressions, and hence eliminates apparent phase violations. For example, if A is a functor of signature $[t{:}T,\mathrm{set}(int)]{\to}[t{:}T,1]$, then the type expression $\sigma = Fst(A[int,3])$ is equal, using the non-standard rules, to $Fst(A)\ int$, which is free of run-time subexpressions. As a result, if e is a term of type σ, then the application

$$(\lambda x{:}\mathrm{set}(Fst(A[int,5])).x)\ e$$

is type-correct, whereas in the absence of the non-standard equations this would not be so (assuming $3 \neq 5 : int$).

The raw syntax of λ^{ML}_{mod} is an extension of that of λ^{ML}; the extensions are given in Table 5. The judgement forms are the same as for λ^{ML}_{str}, and are axiomatized by standard structure and functor rules, as in [MH88]. The λ^{ML}_{mod} calculus is parametric in a the-

$$
\begin{aligned}
k &\in kind & ::= &\ \ldots \\
u &\in constr & ::= &\ \ldots \mid Fst(M) \\
\sigma &\in type & ::= &\ \ldots \\
e &\in term & ::= &\ \ldots \mid Snd(M) \\
S &\in sig & ::= &\ [v{:}k,\sigma] \mid 1 \mid (\Sigma s{:}S_1.S_2) \mid (\Pi s{:}S_1.S_2) \\
M &\in mod & ::= &\ s \mid [u,e] \mid * \mid \langle M_1, M_2 \rangle \mid \pi_i(M) \mid (\lambda s{:}S.M) \mid M_1\,M_2 \\
\Phi &\in context & ::= &\ \ldots \mid \Phi, s{:}S
\end{aligned}
$$

Table 5: λ_{mod}^{ML} raw expressions

ory, defined as in λ^{ML} (*i.e.*, we do not admit module constants, or axioms governing module expressions.)

The formation rules of λ_{mod}^{ML} are essentially the standard rules for dependent strong sums and dependent function types. The equational rules include the expected rules for dependent types, together with the non-standard rules summarized in Table 6.

Beside the non-standard equational rules (and "orthogonal" to them), there is also a non-standard typing rules for structures:

$$
\frac{\Phi \gg M : [v{:}k, \sigma] \qquad \Phi, v{:}k \gg \sigma' \ type \qquad \Phi \gg Snd\,M : [Fst\,M/v]\sigma'}{\Phi \gg M : [v{:}k, \sigma']}
$$

The non-standard typing rule is *consistent* with the interpretation in the category of modules [Mog89a], but (we conjecture that) without it the main properties of λ_{mod}^{ML}, namely the compile-time type checking theorem and the decidability of typing judgements, would still hold. The reason for having such rule is mainly pragmatic: to have a simple type checking algorithm (see Definition 3.9). Moreover, this additional typing rule captures a particularly natural property of Σ-types (once uniqueness of type has been abandoned), namely that a structure M should be *identified* with its expansion $[Fst\,M, Snd\,M]$. A typical example of typing judgement derivable by the non-standard typing rule is $s{:}[v{:}k, \sigma] \gg s : [v{:}k, [Fst\,s/v]\sigma]$.

3.4 Translation of λ_{mod}^{ML} into λ_{str}^{ML}

The non-standard equational theory used in the definition of λ_{mod}^{ML} is justified by proving that λ_{mod}^{ML} is a *definitional extension* of λ_{str}^{ML}, in a sense to be made precise below. This definitional extension result will then play an important role in establishing the decidability and compile-time type checking property of λ_{mod}^{ML}.

We begin by giving a translation $\_^\flat$ from raw λ_{mod}^{ML} expressions into raw λ_{str}^{ML} expressions. This translation is defined by induction on the structure of λ_{mod}^{ML} expressions. Apart from the cases given in Table 7, the translation is defined to commute with the expression constructors. For the basis we associate with every module variable s a constructor variable s^c and a term variable s^r in λ_{str}^{ML}. For convenience in defining the translation we fix a constructor variable $\mathbf{v}$ that may occur in expressions of λ_{mod}^{ML}, but not in expressions of λ_{mod}^{ML}. Signatures of λ_{mod}^{ML} will be translated to λ_{str}^{ML} signatures of the form $[\mathbf{v}{:}k, \sigma]$. The translation is extended "declaration-wise" to contexts: $\Phi^\flat$ is obtained from Φ by replacing declarations of the form $x{:}\sigma$ by $x{:}\sigma^\flat$, and declarations of the form $s{:}S$ by $s{:}S^\flat$. Note that the translation leaves λ^{ML} expressions fixed; consequently, the translation need not be extended to theories.

Lemma 3.2 (Substitutivity) *The translation $\_^\flat$ commutes with substitution.*
In particular if $M^\flat = [u, e]$, then $([M/s]\_)^\flat = [u, e/s^c, s^r](\_^\flat)$.

Theorem 3.3 ($\_^\flat$ interpretation) *Let $\mathcal{T}$ be a well-formed theory, and let $\mathcal{J}$ be a λ_{mod}^{ML} judgement. If $\lambda_{mod}^{ML}[\mathcal{T}] \vdash \mathcal{J}$, then $\lambda_{str}^{ML}[\mathcal{T}] \vdash \mathcal{J}^\flat$.*

Conversely, λ_{str}^{ML} is essentially a sub-calculus of λ_{mod}^{ML}, differing only in the treatment of structure variables. To make this precise, define the embedding $\_^e$ of λ_{str}^{ML} raw expressions into λ_{mod}^{ML} raw expressions by replacing all occurrences of s^c by $Fst(s)$, and all occurrences of s^r by $Snd(s)$.

Theorem 3.4 ($\_^e$ interpretation) *Let $\mathcal{T}$ be a well-formed theory, and let $\mathcal{J}$ be a λ_{str}^{ML} judgement. If $\lambda_{str}^{ML}[\mathcal{T}] \vdash \mathcal{J}$, then $\lambda_{mod}^{ML}[\mathcal{T}] \vdash \mathcal{J}^e$.*

Theorem 3.5 (Definitional extension) *Let $\mathcal{T}$ be a well-formed theory.*

- *For any formation judgement $\mathcal{F}$ of λ_{str}^{ML}, if $\lambda_{str}^{ML}[\mathcal{T}] \vdash \mathcal{F}$, then $(\mathcal{F}^e)^\flat$ is syntactically equal to $\mathcal{F}$, modulo the names of bound variables.*

Non-standard equational rules for signatures

$(1 >)$ $$\frac{\Phi \; context}{\Phi \gg 1 = [v{:}1, 1] \; sig}$$

$(\Sigma >)$ $$\frac{\Phi, v_1{:}k_1 \gg \sigma_1 \; type \quad \Phi, v_1{:}k_1, v_2{:}k_2 \gg \sigma_2 \; type}{\Phi \gg (\Sigma s{:}[v_1{:}k_1, \sigma_1].[v_2{:}k_2, [Fst(s)/v_1]\sigma_2]) = [v{:}k_1 \times k_2, [\pi_1 v/v_1]\sigma_1 \times [\pi_1 v, \pi_2 v/v_1, v_2]\sigma_2] \; sig}$$

$(\Pi >)$ $$\frac{\Phi, v_1{:}k_1 \gg \sigma_1 \; type \quad \Phi, v_1{:}k_1, v_2{:}k_2 \gg \sigma_2 \; type}{\Phi \gg (\Pi s{:}[v_1{:}k_1, \sigma_1].[v_2{:}k_2, [Fst(s)/v_1]\sigma_2]) = [v{:}k_1 \to k_2, (\forall v_1{:}k_1.\sigma_1 \to [v\, v_1/v_2]\sigma_2)] \; sig}$$

Non-standard equational rules for modules

$(1\, I >)$ $$\frac{\Phi \; context}{\Phi \gg * = [*, *] \; [v{:}1, 1]}$$

$(\Sigma\, I >)$ $$\frac{\begin{array}{c}\Phi, v_1{:}k_1 \gg \sigma_1 \; type \quad \Phi, v_1{:}k_1, v_2{:}k_2 \gg \sigma_2 \; type \\ \Phi \gg u_1 : k_1 \quad \Phi \gg e_1 : [u_1/v_1]\sigma_1 \\ \Phi \gg u_2 : k_2 \quad \Phi \gg e_2 : [u_1, u_2/v_1, v_2]\sigma_2 \end{array}}{\Phi \gg \langle [u_1, e_1], [u_2, e_2] \rangle = [\langle u_1, u_2 \rangle, \langle e_1, e_2 \rangle] : [v{:}k_1 \times k_2, [\pi_1 v/v_1]\sigma_1 \times [\pi_1 v, \pi_2 v/v_1, v_2]\sigma_2]}$$

$(\Sigma\, E_1 >)$ $$\frac{\Phi, v_1{:}k_1 \gg \sigma_1 \; type \quad \Phi, v_1{:}k_1, v_2{:}k_2 \gg \sigma_2 \; type \\ \Phi \gg u : k_1 \times k_2 \quad \Phi \gg e : [\pi_1 u/v_1]\sigma_1 \times [\pi_1 u, \pi_2 u/v_1, v_2]\sigma_2}{\Phi \gg \pi_1[u, e] = [\pi_1 u, \pi_1 e] : [v_1{:}k_1, \sigma_1]}$$

$(\Sigma\, E_2 >)$ $$\frac{\Phi, v_1{:}k_1 \gg \sigma_1 \; type \quad \Phi, v_1{:}k_1, v_2{:}k_2 \gg \sigma_2 \; type \\ \Phi \gg u : k_1 \times k_2 \quad \Phi \gg e : [\pi_1 u/v_1]\sigma_1 \times [\pi_1 u, \pi_2 u/v_1, v_2]\sigma_2}{\Phi \gg \pi_2[u, e] = [\pi_2 u, \pi_2 e] : [v_2{:}k_2, [\pi_1 u/v_1]\sigma_2]}$$

$(\Pi\, I >)$ $$\frac{\begin{array}{c}\Phi, v_1{:}k_1 \gg \sigma_1 \; type \quad \Phi, v_1{:}k_1, v_2{:}k_2 \gg \sigma_2 \; type \\ \Phi, v_1{:}k_1 \gg u : k_2 \quad \Phi, v_1{:}k_1, x{:}\sigma_1 \gg e : [u/v_2]\sigma_2\end{array}}{\begin{array}{c}\Phi \gg (\lambda s{:}[v_1{:}k_1, \sigma_1].[Fst\, s, Snd\, s/v_1, x][u, e]) = [(\lambda v_1{:}k_1.u), (\Lambda v_1{:}k_1.\lambda x{:}\sigma_1.e)] : \\ \; [v{:}k_1 \to k_2, (\forall v_1{:}k_1.\sigma_1 \to [v\, v_1/v_2]\sigma_2)]\end{array}}$$

$(\Pi\, E >)$ $$\frac{\begin{array}{c}\Phi, v_1{:}k_1 \gg \sigma_1 \; type \quad \Phi, v_1{:}k_1, v_2{:}k_2 \gg \sigma_2 \; type \\ \Phi \gg u_1 : k_1 \quad \Phi \gg e_1 : [u_1/v_1]\sigma_1 \\ \Phi \gg u : k_1 \to k_2 \quad \Phi \gg e : (\forall v_1{:}k_1.\sigma_1 \to [v\, v_1/v_2]\sigma_2)\end{array}}{\Phi \gg [u, e][u_1, e_1] = [u\, u_1, e[u_1]\, e_1] : [v_2{:}k_2, [u_1/v_1]\sigma_2]}$$

Table 6: Non-standard equations

expression	translation	induction hypotheses
$Fst(M)$	u	where $M^\flat = [u, e]$
$Snd(M)$	e	where $M^\flat = [u, e]$
s	$[s^c, s^r]$	
$[v{:}k, \sigma]$	$[\mathbf{v}{:}k, [\mathbf{v}/v]\sigma^\flat]$	
1	$[\mathbf{v}{:}1, 1]$	
$(\Sigma s{:}S_1.S_2)$	$[\mathbf{v}{:}(k_1 \times k_2), ([\pi_1\mathbf{v}/\mathbf{v}]\sigma_1 \times [\pi_1\mathbf{v}, \pi_2\mathbf{v}/s^c, \mathbf{v}]\sigma_2)]$	where $S_i^\flat = [\mathbf{v}{:}k_i, \sigma_i]$
$(\Pi s{:}S_1.S_2)$	$[\mathbf{v}{:}(k_1 \to k_2), \forall s^c{:}k_1.[s^c/\mathbf{v}]\sigma_1 \to [\mathbf{v}\, s^c/\mathbf{v}]\sigma_2]$	where $S_i^\flat = [\mathbf{v}{:}k_i, \sigma_i]$
$*$	$[*, *]$	
$\langle M_1, M_2 \rangle$	$[\langle u_1, u_2 \rangle, \langle e_1, e_2 \rangle]$	where $M_i^\flat = [u_i, e_i]$
$\pi_i M$	$[\pi_i u, \pi_i e]$	where $M^\flat = [u, e]$
$(\lambda s{:}S.M)$	$[(\lambda s^c{:}k.u), (\Lambda s^c{:}k.\lambda s^r{:}[s^c/\mathbf{v}]\sigma.e)]$	where $S^\flat = [\mathbf{v}{:}k, \sigma]$ and $M^\flat = [u, e]$
$M_1 M_2$	$[u_1 u_2, e_1[u_2] e_2]$	where $M_i^\flat = [u_i, e_i]$

Table 7: Translation of λ_{mod}^{ML} into λ_{str}^{ML}

- If $\lambda_{mod}^{ML}[\mathcal{T}] \vdash \Phi \gg M : S$, then the following equality judgements are derivable in $\lambda_{mod}^{ML}[\mathcal{T}]$:

  - $\Phi_s \gg \Phi(s) = (\Phi(s)^\flat)^e$ sig, for all $s \in$ Dom(Φ), where $\Phi \equiv \Phi_s, s{:}\Phi(s), \Phi^s$ (and similarly for x and v in Dom(Φ))
  - $\Phi \gg S = (S^\flat)^e$ sig
  - $\Phi \gg M = (M^\flat)^e : S$

(and similarly for the other formation judgements.)

Corollary 3.6 (Conservative extension) *Let $\mathcal{T}$ be an arbitrary well-formed theory. For any λ_{str}^{ML} judgement $\mathcal{J}$, $\lambda_{mod}^{ML}[\mathcal{T}] \vdash \mathcal{J}^e$ iff $\lambda_{str}^{ML}[\mathcal{T}] \vdash \mathcal{J}$.*

3.5 Compile-Time Type Checking for λ_{mod}^{ML}

The compile-time equational theory of λ_{mod}^{ML} and λ_{str}^{ML} is determined using a restricted equational proof system, defined as follows.

Definition 3.7 (Compile-time calculus)
Compile-time provability in λ_{mod}^{ML} and λ_{str}^{ML} is defined by disallowing the use of all β and η rules for term equivalence, and all β and η rules for module equivalence, apart from those related to "basic" signatures $[v{:}k, \sigma]$.

Let us designate the β and η axioms for terms of λ^{ML} by $\beta\eta$, then the full λ_{mod}^{ML} calculus may be recovered by working in the theory $(\emptyset, \beta\eta)$, since the β and η axioms for modules are derivable in such a theory.

It may be easily verified that the variants of Theorems 3.3, 3.4 and 3.5 obtained by considering compile-time derivability hold.

Theorem 3.8 (Compile-time type checking)
Given any well-formed theory $\mathcal{T} = (\Phi^\mathcal{T}, \mathcal{A}^\mathcal{T})$, the following implications hold:

If $\lambda_{mod}^{ML}[\mathcal{T}] \vdash$	then $\lambda_{mod}^{ML}[\Phi^\mathcal{T}, \emptyset] \vdash_{ct}$
Φ context	Φ context
$\Phi \gg \sigma$ type	$\Phi \gg \sigma$ type
$\Phi \gg S$ sig	$\Phi \gg S$ sig
$\Phi \gg u : k$	$\Phi \gg u : k$
$\Phi \gg e : \sigma$	$\Phi \gg e : \sigma$
$\Phi \gg M : S$	$\Phi \gg M : S$

If $\lambda_{mod}^{ML}[\mathcal{T}] \vdash$	then $\lambda_{mod}^{ML}[\Phi^\mathcal{T}, \emptyset] \vdash_{ct}$
$\Phi \gg \sigma_1 = \sigma_2$ type	$\Phi \gg \sigma_1 = \sigma_2$ type
$\Phi \gg S_1 = S_2$ sig	$\Phi \gg S_1 = S_2$ sig
$\Phi \gg u_1 = u_2 : k$	$\Phi \gg u_1 = u_2 : k$
$\Phi \gg e_1 = e_2 : \sigma$	$\Phi \gg e_i : \sigma$
$\Phi \gg M_1 = M_2 : S$	$\Phi \gg M_i : S$
	$\Phi \gg [Fst\, M_1, Snd\, M_1]$
	$\quad = [Fst\, M_2, Snd\, M_1] : S$

3.6 Decidability of λ_{mod}^{ML}

The decidability of λ_{mod}^{ML} is proved by giving an algorithm that "flattens" structures and signatures during type checking. As a result, checking signature equivalence is reduced to checking type equivalence in λ_{str}^{ML}, and this is, as we have already argued, decidable. The main complication in the algorithm stems from the failure of unicity of types. For example, the structure $[int, 3]$ has both of the inequivalent signatures $[t{:}T, \mathsf{set}(t)]$ and $[t{:}T, int]$. Our approach is to compute the "most specific" signature for a structure (in the foregoing example this would be the second)

350

which will always have the form $[v{:}k, \sigma]$ where v does not occur free in σ. As a notational convenience, we will usually omit explicit designation of the non-occurring variable, and write such signatures in the form $[{:}k, \sigma]$. The algorithm defined below takes as input a raw context Φ and, for instance, a raw module expression M of λ_{mod}^{ML} and produces one of the following results:

- The context $\Phi^\flat$ and $M^\flat \equiv [u, e]{:}[{:}k, \sigma]$, meaning that $\Phi \gg M : [{:}k, \sigma]$ is derivable in λ_{mod}^{ML}.

- An error, meaning that Φ *context* is not derivable in λ_{mod}^{ML} or that $\Phi \gg M : S$ is not derivable in λ_{mod}^{ML} for any S.

Definition 3.9 (Type-checking algorithm) *The type-checking algorithm TC is given by a deterministic set of inference rules to derive judgements of the following form:*

input		output
Φ	$\twoheadrightarrow$	$\Phi^\flat$ context
$\Phi \gg \sigma$	$\twoheadrightarrow$	$\Phi^\flat \gg \sigma^\flat$ type
$\Phi \gg S$	$\twoheadrightarrow$	$\Phi^\flat \gg S^\flat$ sig
$\Phi \gg u$	$\twoheadrightarrow$	$\Phi^\flat \gg u^\flat : k$
$\Phi \gg e$	$\twoheadrightarrow$	$\Phi^\flat \gg e^\flat : \sigma$
$\Phi \gg M$	$\twoheadrightarrow$	$\Phi^\flat \gg M^\flat : [{:}k, \sigma]$

In the last three cases TC not only computes the translation, but also a kind/type/signature. A sample of the inference rules that constitute the algorithm is given in Table 8.

TC is parametric in a theory $\mathcal{T}$, and we write $TC[\mathcal{T}]$ for the instance of the algorithm in which the constants declared in $\Phi^\mathcal{T}$ are regarded as variables. More precisely, $\Phi \twoheadrightarrow \Phi^\flat$ *context* in $TC[\mathcal{T}]$ iff $\Phi^\mathcal{T}, \Phi \twoheadrightarrow \Phi^\mathcal{T}, \Phi^\flat$ *context* in TC.

Theorem 3.10 (Soundness) *Let $\mathcal{T}$ be a well-formed theory. The following implications hold:*

If $TC[\mathcal{T}] \vdash$	then $\lambda_{mod}^{ML}[\mathcal{T}] \vdash_{ct}$
$\Phi \twoheadrightarrow \Phi^\flat$ context	Φ context
$\Phi \gg \sigma \twoheadrightarrow \Phi^\flat \gg \sigma^\flat$ type	$\Phi \gg \sigma$ type
$\Phi \gg S \twoheadrightarrow \Phi^\flat \gg S^\flat$ sig	$\Phi \gg S$ sig
$\Phi \gg u \twoheadrightarrow \Phi^\flat \gg u^\flat : k$	$\Phi \gg u : k$
$\Phi \gg e \twoheadrightarrow \Phi^\flat \gg e^\flat : \sigma$	$\Phi \gg e : \sigma^{\mathsf{e}}$
$\Phi \gg M \twoheadrightarrow \Phi^\flat \gg [u,e] : [{:}k, \sigma]$	$\Phi \gg M : [{:}k, \sigma^{\mathsf{e}}]$

Theorem 3.11 (Completeness) *Let $\mathcal{T}$ be any well-formed theory. The following implications hold:*

If $\lambda_{mod}^{ML}[\mathcal{T}] \vdash_{ct}$	then $TC[\mathcal{T}] \vdash$ & $\lambda_{str}^{ML}[\mathcal{T}] \vdash_{ct}$
Φ context	$\Phi \twoheadrightarrow \Phi^\flat$ context
$\Phi \gg \sigma$ type	$\Phi \gg \sigma \twoheadrightarrow \Phi^\flat \gg \sigma^\flat$ type
$\Phi \gg S$ sig	$\Phi \gg S \twoheadrightarrow \Phi^\flat \gg S^\flat$ sig
$\Phi \gg u : k$	$\Phi \gg u \twoheadrightarrow \Phi^\flat \gg u^\flat : k$
$\Phi \gg e : \sigma$	$\Phi \gg \sigma \twoheadrightarrow \Phi^\flat \gg \sigma^\flat$ type $\Phi \gg e \twoheadrightarrow \Phi^\flat \gg e^\flat : \sigma'$ $\Phi^\flat \gg \sigma^\flat = \sigma'$ type
$\Phi \gg M : S$	$\Phi \gg S \twoheadrightarrow \Phi^\flat \gg [\mathbf{v}{:}k, \sigma]$ sig $\Phi \gg M \twoheadrightarrow \Phi^\flat \gg [u, e] : [{:}k, \sigma']$ $\Phi^\flat \gg \sigma' = [u/\mathbf{v}]\sigma$ type

If $\lambda_{mod}^{ML}[\mathcal{T}] \vdash_{ct}$	then $TC[\mathcal{T}] \vdash$ & $\lambda_{str}^{ML}[\mathcal{T}] \vdash_{ct}$
$\Phi \gg \sigma_1 = \sigma_2$ type	$\Phi \gg \sigma_i \twoheadrightarrow \Phi^\flat \gg \sigma_i^\flat$ type $\Phi^\flat \gg \sigma_1^\flat = \sigma_2^\flat$ type
$\Phi \gg S_1 = S_2$ sig	$\Phi \gg S_i \twoheadrightarrow \Phi^\flat \gg S_i^\flat$ sig $\Phi^\flat \gg S_1^\flat = S_2^\flat$ sig
$\Phi \gg u_1 = u_2 : k$	$\Phi \gg u_i \twoheadrightarrow \Phi^\flat \gg u_i^\flat : k$ $\Phi^\flat \gg u_1^\flat = u_2^\flat : k$
$\Phi \gg e_1 = e_2 : \sigma$	$\Phi \gg \sigma \twoheadrightarrow \Phi^\flat \gg \sigma^\flat$ type $\Phi \gg e_i \twoheadrightarrow \Phi^\flat \gg e_i^\flat : \sigma_i$ $\Phi^\flat \gg \sigma^\flat = \sigma_i$ type $\Phi^\flat \gg e_1^\flat = e_2^\flat : \sigma^\flat$
$\Phi \gg M_1 = M_2 : S$	$\Phi \gg S \twoheadrightarrow$ $\quad \Phi^\flat \gg [\mathbf{v}{:}k, \sigma]$ sig $\Phi \gg M_i \twoheadrightarrow$ $\quad \Phi^\flat \gg [u_i, e_i] : [{:}k, \sigma_i]$ $\Phi^\flat \gg u_1 = u_2 : k$ $\Phi^\flat \gg \sigma = [u_i/\mathbf{v}]\sigma_i$ type $\Phi^\flat \gg e_1 = e_2 : \sigma$

Theorem 3.12 (Decidability) *It is decidable whether a raw type-checking judgement lhs $\twoheadrightarrow$ rhs is derivable using the inference rules in Definition 3.9.*

Corollary 3.13 *Given any well-formed theory $\mathcal{T}$, the derivability of formation judgements in $\lambda_{mod}^{ML}[\mathcal{T}]$ is decidable and does not depend on run-time axioms nor the axioms in $\mathcal{T}$.*

4 Conclusion

Although the relatively straightforward ML-like function calculus XML of [MH88] illustrates some important properties of ML-like languages, it does not provide an adequate basis for the design of a compile-time type checker. Similar problems arise in other programming language models based on dependent

$(\Phi, s:S)$ $\quad\dfrac{\Phi \gg S \twoheadrightarrow \Phi^{\flat} \gg S^{\flat} \ sig}{\Phi, s:S \twoheadrightarrow \Phi^{\flat}, s:S^{\flat} \ context}\ (s \notin \mathrm{Dom}(\Phi))$

$([\ ]\ sig)$ $\quad\dfrac{\Phi, v:k \gg \sigma \twoheadrightarrow \Phi^{\flat}, v:k \gg \sigma^{\flat} \ type}{\Phi \gg [v:k, \sigma] \twoheadrightarrow \Phi^{\flat} \gg [v:k, \sigma^{\flat}] : sig}$

$([\ ]\ I)$ $\quad\dfrac{\Phi \gg u \twoheadrightarrow \Phi^{\flat} \gg u^{\flat} : k \quad \Phi \gg e \twoheadrightarrow \Phi^{\flat} \gg e^{\flat} : \sigma}{\Phi \gg [u, e] \twoheadrightarrow \Phi^{\flat} \gg [u, e] : [:k, \sigma]}$

$([\ ]\ E_1)$ $\quad\dfrac{\Phi \gg M \twoheadrightarrow \Phi^{\flat} \gg [u, e] : [:k, \sigma]}{\Phi \gg Fst(M) \twoheadrightarrow \Phi^{\flat} \gg u : k}$

$([\ ]\ E_2)$ $\quad\dfrac{\Phi \gg M \twoheadrightarrow \Phi^{\flat} \gg [u, e] : [:k, \sigma]}{\Phi \gg Snd(M) \twoheadrightarrow \Phi^{\flat} \gg e : \sigma}$

(var) $\quad\dfrac{\Phi \twoheadrightarrow \Phi^{\flat} \ context}{\Phi \gg s \twoheadrightarrow \Phi^{\flat} \gg [s^{c}, s^{r}] : [:k, [s^{c}/\mathbf{v}]\sigma]}\ (\Phi^{\flat}(s) = [\mathbf{v}:k, \sigma])$

$(1\ I)$ $\quad\dfrac{\Phi \ context \twoheadrightarrow \Phi^{\flat} \ context}{\Phi \gg * \twoheadrightarrow \Phi^{\flat} \gg [*, *] : [:1, 1]}$

$(\Sigma\ I)$ $\quad\dfrac{\Phi \gg M_1 \twoheadrightarrow \Phi^{\flat} \gg [u_1, e_1] : [:k_1, \sigma_1] \quad \Phi \gg M_2 \twoheadrightarrow \Phi^{\flat} \gg [u_2, e_2] : [:k_2, \sigma_2]}{\Phi \gg \langle M_1, M_2 \rangle \twoheadrightarrow \Phi^{\flat} \gg [\langle u_1, u_2\rangle, \langle e_1, e_2\rangle] : [:k_1 \times k_2, \sigma_1 \times \sigma_2]}$

$(\Sigma\ E_i)$ $\quad\dfrac{\Phi \gg M \twoheadrightarrow \Phi^{\flat} \gg [u, e] : [:k_1 \times k_2, \sigma_1 \times \sigma_2]}{\Phi \gg \pi_i M \twoheadrightarrow \Phi^{\flat} \gg [\pi_i u, \pi_i e] : [:k_i, \sigma_i]}$

$(\Pi\ I)$ $\quad\dfrac{\Phi, s:S_1 \gg M \twoheadrightarrow \Phi^{\flat}, s:[\mathbf{v}:k_1, \sigma_1] \gg [u, e] : [:k_2, \sigma_2]}{\begin{array}{l}\Phi \gg (\lambda s:S_1.M) \twoheadrightarrow \Phi^{\flat} \gg [(\lambda s^c:k_1.u), (\Lambda s^c:k_1.\lambda s^r:[s^c/\mathbf{v}]\sigma_1.e)] : \\ \qquad [:k_1 \to k_2, \forall s^c:k_1.[s^c/\mathbf{v}]\sigma_1 \to \sigma_2]\end{array}}$

$(\Pi\ E)$ $\quad\dfrac{\begin{array}{c}\Phi \gg M \twoheadrightarrow \Phi^{\flat} \gg [u, e] : [:k_1 \to k_2, \forall v:k_1.\sigma_1 \to \sigma_2] \\ \Phi \gg M_1 \twoheadrightarrow \Phi^{\flat} \gg [u_1, e_1] : [:k_1, \sigma] \\ \hline \Phi \gg M\ M_1 \twoheadrightarrow \Phi^{\flat} \gg [u\ u_1, e[u_1]\ e_1] : [:k_2, [u_1/v]\sigma_2]\end{array}}{}\ \lambda^{ML}_{str} \vdash \Phi^{\flat} \gg \sigma = [u_1/v]\sigma_1\ type$

Table 8: Type checking algorithm (selected rules)

types. To address this pragmatic issue, we have developed an alternate form of the XML calculus in which there is a clear compile-time/run-time distinction. Essentially, our technique is to add equational axioms that allow us to decompose structures and functors into separate compile-time and run-time components. While the phase distinction in λ^{ML} reduces to the syntactic difference between types and their elements, the general technique seems applicable to other forms of phase distinction.

The basis for our development is the "category of modules" over an indexed category, which is an instance of the Grothedieck construction. General properties of the category of modules are explained in the companion paper [Mog89a]. In the specific case of λ^{ML}, our non-standard equational axioms lead to a calculus which bears a natural relationship to the category of modules. In future work, it would be interesting to explore the exact connection between our calculus and the categorical construction, and to develop phase distinctions for languages whose type expressions may contain "run-time" subexpressions in more complicated ways.

References

[BL84] R. Burstall and B. Lampson. A kernel language for abstract data types and modules. In *Proc. Int. Symp. on Semantics of Data Types, Sophia-Antipolis (France), Springer LNCS 173*, pages 1–50, 1984.

[BMM89] K. B. Bruce, A. R. Meyer, and J. C. Mitchell. The semantics of second-order lambda calculus. *Information and Computation*, 1989. (to appear).

[C+86] Constable et al. *Implementing Mathematics with the Nuprl Proof Development System*, volume 37 of *Graduate Texts in Mathematics*. Prentice-Hall, 1986.

[Car88] L. Cardelli. Phase distinctions in type theory. Manuscript, 1988.

[Gir71] J.-Y. Girard. Une extension de l'interpretation de Gödel à l'analyse, et son application à l'élimination des coupures dans l'analyse et la théorie des types. In J.E. Fenstad, editor, *2nd Scandinavian Logic Symposium*, pages 63–92. North-Holland, 1971.

[Gir72] J.-Y. Girard. Interpretation fonctionelle et elimination des coupures de l'arithmetique d'ordre superieur. These D'Etat, Universite Paris VII, 1972.

[HMM86] R. Harper, D.B. MacQueen, and R. Milner. Standard ml. Technical Report ECS-LFCS-86-2, Lab. for Foundations of Computer Science, University of Edinburgh, March 1986.

[HMT87a] R. Harper, R. Milner, and M. Tofte. The semantics of standard ML. Technical Report ECS-LFCS-87-36, Lab. for Foundations of Computer Science, University of Edinburgh, August 1987.

[HMT87b] R. Harper, R. Milner, and M. Tofte. A type discipline for program modules. In *TAPSOFT '87*, volume 250 of *LNCS*. Springer-Verlag, March 1987.

[Mac86] D.B. MacQueen. Using dependent types to express modular structure. In *Proc. 13-th ACM Symp. on Principles of Programming Languages*, pages 277–286, 1986.

[Mar84] P. Martin-Löf. *Intuitionistic Type Theory*. Bibliopolis, Napoli, 1984.

[MH88] J.C. Mitchell and R. Harper. The essence of ML. In *Proc. 15-th ACM Symp. on Principles of Programming Languages*, pages 28–46, January 1988.

[Mog89a] E. Moggi. A category-theoretic account of program modules. In *Summer Conf. on Category Theory and Computer Science*, pages 101–117, 1989.

[Mog89b] E. Moggi. Computational lambda calculus and monads. In *Fourth IEEE Symp. Logic in Computer Science*, pages 14–23, 1989.

[MP88] J.C. Mitchell and G.D. Plotkin. Abstract types have existential types. *ACM Trans. on Programming Languages and Systems*, 10(3):470–502, 1988. Preliminary version appeared in *Proc. 12-th ACM Symp. on Principles of Programming Languages*, 1985.

[NPS88] B. Nordstrom, K. Peterson, and J. Smith. Programming in martin-löf's type theory. University of Gothenburg / Chalmers Instiue of Technology, Book draft of Midsummer 1988.

[Rey74]　J.C. Reynolds. Towards a theory of type structure. In *Paris Colloq. on Programming*, pages 408–425. Springer-Verlag LNCS 19, 1974.

[Tof87]　M. Tofte. *Operational Semantics and Polymorphic Type Inference*. PhD thesis, University of Edinburgh, 1987.

Safe Run-time Overloading

François Rouaix
INRIA*
B.P.105 78153 Le Chesnay Cedex, France

Abstract

We present a functional language featuring a form of dynamic overloading akin to message passing in object oriented languages. We give a dynamic semantics describing a non-deterministic evaluation, as well as a type discipline (static semantics) supporting type inference. The type system ensures that a well-typed program has a correct execution, unique up to a semantic equivalence relation, and allows this execution to proceed deterministically, while resolving overloading at run-time.

1 Presentation

1.1 Motivation

When analyzing the history of relations between language design and types, we can point out two different uses of types in a language. The first one has for purpose the guarantee of correct execution of a well-typed program. A static type-checker ensures an execution free of type-errors. This concept is mainly popular in languages designed as formal systems, such as ML. The second one is to help gaining efficiency, and design facility for programs. Using type information, one may be able to compile some features of the language with optimizations, or to provide tools for program maintenance [SchaCoo 86, MeyNM 87, Johnson 86]. While formal systems need new constructs (such as abstraction from implementation), object-oriented languages need formalization and types. We present a system which incorporates concepts from the two worlds.

*This work has been partially supported by the Eureka Software Factory (ESF) project

1.2 Intuitive Overview

One of the ideas underlying the system presented here is that these two points of view (formal types vs. efficient implementation) are to be treated separately, following ideas in CLU [Liskov 81], Emerald [RajLev 89] or Duo-Talk [Lunau 89]. If we take inheritance, we think that it should be split in two distinct issues: the first aspect is property inheritance (or behavior inheritance), which says that, for example, "a child has more properties than its parent". It should concern only the type-system. The second aspect is sharing data representation or primitive functions between child and parent, and this is an implementation issue.

In ML's interpretation of types, a functional value is said polymorphic if it has many types. Now, reversing this definition, one may understand a polymorphic function (or object such as nil) as a description of a set of monomorphic values (one for each instance) sharing the same implementation. The idea here is to extend the notion of parametric polymorphism by qualifying type variables with sets of properties. These properties will be used to constrain the set of permitted implementations for the entity having a "qualified polymorphic type". Although this extension is similar to *ad-hoc* polymorphism [CarWeg 86, WadBlo 89], it behaves like parametric polymorphism. In particular, function types are covariant with argument types, with respect to our definition of type inclusion.

We introduce a restricted form of overloading, that can be typed with usual polymorphism, and we argue that it addresses a wide range of programming issues, such as object-oriented languages or code reuse.

Let us describe what kind of overloading mechanism we want for our language.

1. Resolution may be done at run-time. That is, the value denoted by an overloaded symbol is not necessarily determined statically from the program.

2. Resolution of overloading does not fail at run-time. The (correct) solutions are the values that

will not cause a type-error.

3. When multiple solutions are found, all possible solutions are "equivalent".

The idea is to delay the resolution of an overloaded symbol to its occurrence where the context provides enough information to choose a safe value. This mechanism is very close to the "call by name" of Algol 60. Like call by name, the suspension may yield different values at each evaluation. However, here the changes are due to contextual typing constraints instead of side-effects since our language is purely applicative. The syntactic construct in the language that introduces this form of evaluation is the *let in* construct. If we take the example

$$let\ double = \lambda x.(x+x)\ in\ (double\ 3, double\ \pi)$$

where + is overloaded with addition of *Integer* and addition of *Float*, we see intuitively that lazy expansion for *double* allows a safe choice for both occurrences of +.

Informally, we consider a set of specifications (i.e. types) of overloaded symbols, a set of specifications of implementations (resolution values of overloaded symbols), and want to determine if the code we write is compatible with these specifications. This is achieved by interpreting types of objects as sets of properties, sometimes called classes.

The typing may be found very flexible when comparing with other systems. The way the typing is designed makes that highly overloaded code is almost always typable (the only errors detected are applications of non-functional objects). It just means that the code may be executed provided there exists a proper implementation of the primitives that are used. In a way, the type inference computes the minimal constraints on the code, imposed by some specifications, such that fulfilling these constraints ensure a proper execution. The advantage of minimal constraints is that they give maximum re-use.

In terms of object-oriented programming, overloaded symbols are methods, but more powerful, since the selection is not necessarily on the first argument, and they are first-class citizens of the functional language (which is also the choice in CLOS [DeMGab 87]). Polymorphic functions or objects may be seen as methods associated to meta-classes[1].

---
[1] Meta-classes are entities for grouping common method definitions among different classes

2 Comparison with current solutions

We are interested in existing solutions for functional languages implementing run-time overloading and type inference.

Kaes work

The formalism presented in [Kaes 88] has the same basis: qualified type variables and overloading schemes. The enhancements presented here are mainly: dynamic semantics for an *untyped* functional language featuring overloading, a known framework for operations on types, and more general overloading schemes.

Haskell

Haskell proposes a class system with similar goals. However, the approach is different on some points. We will go into certain details because they enlighten some aspects of our system.

- The first essential difference is that Haskell imposes the declaration of classes. This strongly influences the type-inference by forcing computed types to belong to a predefined hierarchy of types. This is an argument for readability of types and strictness of programming, but tends to be a drawback in the areas of object-oriented programming and reusability. For example, modifying the hierarchy of classes (while keeping the same definitions of overloaded symbols) greatly changes the typing. The advantage we have here is that we compute types in a larger set with a more convenient structure. There are cases where Haskell would produce a type-error because it tries to infer a class which is not pre-declared. Our choice is that any inferred "class" is legitimate. The matter that there exists an implementation for this "class" may or may not be relevant depending on the context. If it is relevant, then the user-interface may inform the user of what actual implementations exists and which primitive they lack to match the "class".

- A second important difference is the notion of principal type. In Haskell, static resolution when ambiguity arises is considered as a failure because there is no principal types. In our point of view, the principal type still exists before static resolution. Static resolution consists in an arbitrary choice, but all choices have to be equivalent from a semantic point a view. We certainly do not have a principal type property after static resolution, but we don't consider this as a failure. The point here is that in our system, we may not be able to translate a well-typed term into an ML term by following Haskell technique ([HudWad 88],p. 64).

SML

SML provides another form of overloading, that should be solved statically. Expressions such as $\lambda x.(x + x)$ where $+$ is overloaded are not typable. However, in the spirit of giving tools for program maintenance, SML provides modules. These modules also provide a form of overloading, that must be solved with aid of the user, using explicit qualifiers to select primitives from a structure previously opened. If we consider only this aspect of modules, then we may say by analogy that we infer the minimal "open" statements (we infer the signature of the module as well), and the qualifiers are now implicit[2]. The same issue of declaring or not structures appears here.

Work on OO languages

There has been considerable work in the OO community to design type systems for safe object-oriented languages. The mechanisms involved are delegation and inheritance (from the language approach), subtyping and subclassing (from the type approach). The system presented here relies mainly on a covariant subclass relation, coded by polymorphism. The separation of the hierarchies allows a separate treatment for the subtyping hierarchy.

3 Formal Language definition

To formalize these concepts, we define a simple language, its dynamic and static semantics and then show how they interact[3]. This language has only the minimum constructions to express that it is functional and has overloading. Detailed examples are given in an appendix.

If Id is a denumerable set of non-overloaded symbols and Oid a finite set of overloaded symbols, we

---

[2] provided primitives with the same name in different structures are defined homogeneously

[3] All semantics are written with Natural Semantics [CleDDK 86], this choice being justified later

note e an expression ranging over $OExp$ defined by:

$$\begin{array}{rlll} e & := & b & \text{basic constant} \\ & | & x & \text{where } x \in Id \\ & | & o & \text{where } o \in Oid \\ & | & \lambda x.e & \text{abstraction} \\ & | & e\ e' & \text{application} \\ & | & let\ x = e\ in\ e' & \text{lazy expansion} \end{array}$$

3.1 Dynamic Semantics

The semantical objects of the langage are:

- basic values (constants) in predefined sets $B_1, \ldots, B_n$ and built-in primitives (closures)

- closures, composed of a symbol name (formal parameter), a body expression and an environment, for λ-abstractions.

- thunks, composed of an expression and an environment, for *let* expressions.

There are two kinds of environments, E used in closures and thunks and a global environment O, which describes the values associated to each overloaded symbol. Formally,

$$\begin{array}{rl} b \in & BaseValues = B_1 \cup \ldots \cup B_n \\ [x,e,E] \in & Closures = Id \times OExp \times Env \\ \langle e, E \rangle \in & Thunks = OExp \times Env \\ v \in & Val = BaseValues + Closures \\ E \in & Env = Id \to (Val + Thunks) \\ O \in & OEnv = Oid \to \mathcal{P}(Val) \end{array}$$

The dynamic semantics (Figure 1) is a set of inference rules, describing evaluation of expressions in $OExp$. Sequents are of the form $E \vdash_d e \longrightarrow v$, meaning that v can be derived from e in environment E (O is global).

An evaluation is a proof in this system. This semantics is clearly non-deterministic, since the evaluation of an overloaded symbol may yield any of its possible values (cf. rule OID_d). There is no rule defining a wrong execution, nor a specific *wrong* value. Failure is expressed by the fact that no rule is available to interpret an expression or by type-errors in application of built-in closures. Besides non-determinism, another important point is the interpretation of the *let* construct. The object $\langle e, E \rangle$ *freezes* the source code just like in a closure. The purpose is to delay the actual evaluation of the binding value until it is really used, possibly with different evaluations for each occurrence. The ID_d rule describes this evaluation, by calling a small subsystem $REAL_{d'}$ and $TAUT_{d'}$

Figure 1: Dynamic semantics

$$OID_d \quad \frac{o \in Dom(O) \qquad v \in O(o)}{E \vdash_d o \longrightarrow v}$$

$$ID_d \quad \frac{x \in Dom(E) \qquad \vdash_{d'} E(x) \longrightarrow v}{E \vdash_d x \longrightarrow v}$$

$$REAL_{d'} \quad \frac{E \vdash_d e \longrightarrow v}{\vdash_{d'} \langle e, E \rangle \longrightarrow v}$$

$$TAUT_{d'} \quad \frac{}{\vdash_{d'} v \longrightarrow v}$$

$$ABS_d \quad \frac{}{E \vdash_d \lambda x.e \longrightarrow [x, e, E]}$$

$$APP_d \quad \frac{E \vdash_d e \longrightarrow [x'', e'', E''] \qquad E \vdash_d e' \longrightarrow v' \qquad E'' \cup \{x'' \mapsto v'\} \vdash_d e'' \longrightarrow v}{E \vdash_d e\, e' \longrightarrow v}$$

$$LET_d \quad \frac{E \cup \{x \mapsto \langle e, E \rangle\} \vdash_d e' \longrightarrow v'}{E \vdash_d let\ x = e\ in\ e' \longrightarrow v'}$$

which says how to *realize* a *thunk*. Strict deterministic evaluation would force the resolution of overloading statically. Non-determinism was the significant argument for choosing Natural Semantics over Denotational Semantics. It is totally implicit in Natural Semantics.

3.2 Correct programs

As a program (a closed expression of $OExp$) may have different executions, we need a notion of *correctness* for program execution.

Definition 3.1 *Let S be some equivalence relation on the set Val of values that we call semantic equivalence. Execution of a term $e \in OExp$ is correct for S iff*

- *there is a proof of $\vdash_d e \longrightarrow v$ in $\vdash_d$, $\vdash_{d'}$ for some v.*
- *all such v are equivalent in S*

These definitions do not imply the use of a type-system. Naturally this is a formal reference semantics, and the typing algorithm will allow us to transform the original term in a term that can be executed deterministically according to one of the safe computations.

3.3 Static semantics

Our goal is to provide an algorithm that, given a term in $OExp$ and an overloading environment, will determine statically if there exists a correct execution in the former system. For this purpose, we will use a type-system derived from ML. If we examine our requirements on overloading, we reasonably choose that

- the type expression for an overloaded symbol in the environment should be polymorphic.

- the actual value of an occurrence of an overloaded symbol depends on its type at this occurrence, this type reflecting somehow the context of application of this overloaded symbol. We then need a new syntactic form for types of overloaded symbols.

- This new syntactic form should have some properties we can use when defining our semantic equivalence

An overloaded symbol acts like a polymorphic object, the values of which are chosen from its type instance when it is used. This interpretation extends to polymorphic functions, which are now abstract functions, "realized" when they are used.

We have chosen a language of sorted and rational terms[4] for the types. The following consists in its definition and many useful notations. Most of this is borrowed from Rémy's extension to ML types for records and variants.

Expressions are of two sorts *Type* and *Field*. Signatures of function symbols are written as usual with $\Rightarrow$ and $\otimes$ operators. Given

- B a set of basic constants of sort *Type*
- L a finite ordered set of symbols[5] of cardinality l.
- the constructors $\mathcal{C} = \{\rightarrow, \triangle, \triangledown, \Theta\}$ with signatures:

$$\begin{array}{rcl} \rightarrow & :: & Type \otimes Type \Rightarrow Type \\ \triangle & :: & Type \Rightarrow Field \\ \triangledown & :: & Field \\ \Theta & :: & \underbrace{Field \otimes Field \otimes \ldots Field}_{l} \Rightarrow Type \end{array}$$

- two denumerable sets of variables $\mathcal{V}^t, \mathcal{V}^f$ of respective sorts *Type*, *Field*, their union is denoted by $\mathcal{V} = \mathcal{V}^t \cup \mathcal{V}^f$
- two denumerable sets of generic variables $\mathcal{V}_g^t, \mathcal{V}_g^f$ of respective sorts *Type*, *Field*, their union is denoted by $\mathcal{V}_g = \mathcal{V}_g^t \cup \mathcal{V}_g^f$,

we define

- $\mathcal{R}$ as the set of first order sorted regular trees constructed over the set of variables $\mathcal{V}$, constants in B and constructors in $\mathcal{C}$. Elements of R of sort *Type* are called *types*. Their subset is noted $\mathcal{T}$.
- $\mathcal{R}_g$ as the set of first order sorted regular trees constructed over the set of variables $\mathcal{V}_g \cup \mathcal{V}$, constants in B and constructors in $\mathcal{C}$. Elements of $\mathcal{R}_g$ of sort *Type* are called *generic types*. Their subset is noted $\mathcal{T}_g$.
- A (non-generic) *graft*[6] μ is a mapping from $\mathcal{V}$ to $\mathcal{R}$ respecting the sorts.
- A *total* graft is a *total* mapping from $\mathcal{V}$ to $\mathcal{R}$ respecting the sorts.
- A *generic graft* μ_g is a mapping from $\mathcal{V}_g$ to $\mathcal{R}_g$ respecting the sorts.
- A *monotype* (or ground type) is a type with no variables (noted ι).
- A graft is *ground* if it ranges in monotypes.

In the following we use the notations: α (resp. α_g) for type (resp. generic type) variables ; σ, τ for types; σ_g, τ_g for generic types ; ϕ for field variables (i.e. variables of sort *Field*). We will note $\tau\mu$ (resp. $A\mu$) the application of the graft μ to τ (resp. A).

To help understanding what follows, here is an intuitive interpretation of these new constructions. A non-functional type is denoted by a Θ-term. The fields correspond to the possible properties (e.g. primitive functions) of the type. The construction $\triangle(\tau)$ means that the field is present with the type τ. The construction $\triangledown$ means that the field is absent. An *abstract data type* (ADT) may be seen as an open set of properties. "Open" means that this set may be extended during unification for example. Such an extension restricts the possible implementations of this ADT.

In our formalism, an ADT is a type constructed with Θ such that all fields are either variables or constructed with $\triangle$, (not all being $\triangle$ since ADTs are open)[7].

An *implementation* is a type constructed with Θ with no field variable. It is a non-expandable set of properties. We will be using the name of the implementation as a special label because we must be able to tell between two implementations of a same ADT. This label also acts as a discriminant when unifying two implementations.

Definition 3.2 (Abstract,Real) *By extension, we will say that a type σ_g is abstract if at least one subterm of σ_g is an ADT. Otherwise σ_g is said to be real.*

3.4 Overloading scheme and implementations

This section shows how we are going to use these new type constructs. The overloading environment is a set of overloading schemes, which intuitively, describe the type of an overloaded symbol, together with a set of implementation descriptions.

For any set V of symbols, we define the language $Simple(V)$ by

$$\begin{array}{rcl} s & := & v \in V \\ & | & s \rightarrow s \end{array}$$

---

[4] Intuitively, a rational term may be seen as an infinite term with a regular structure.

[5] These symbols in L are intended for field names in Θ-terms (see below). Since each Θ-term has a field for each of the symbols in L, they are left implicit, and the correspondance is based on field order and L order

[6] In non-rational terms, a graft is a substitution

[7] see appendix for examples

Figure 2: Examples of overloading schemes

$$
\begin{aligned}
+ &\rightsquigarrow (\omega \to \omega \to \omega, \{\}) \\
fst &\rightsquigarrow (\omega \to \alpha_g, \{\ left\ :\ \alpha_g\ \}) \\
snd &\rightsquigarrow (\omega \to \alpha_g, \{\ right\ :\ \alpha_g\ \}) \\
hd &\rightsquigarrow (\omega \to \alpha_g, \left\{ \begin{array}{ll} elem & : \alpha_g \\ tl & : \omega \to \omega \\ cons & : \alpha_g \to \omega \to \omega \end{array} \right\}) \\
cons &\rightsquigarrow (\alpha_g \to \omega \to \omega, \left\{ \begin{array}{ll} elem & : \alpha_g \\ tl & : \omega \to \omega \\ hd & : \omega \to \alpha_g \end{array} \right\}) \\
nil &\rightsquigarrow (\omega, \{\})
\end{aligned}
$$

$$
\begin{aligned}
Oid &= \{+, fst, snd, hd, cons, nil\} \\
Qualifiers &= \{left, right, elem\} \\
\alpha_g &\in \mathcal{V}_g^t
\end{aligned}
$$

Let $Qualifiers$ be a finite set of symbols, and ω be a special symbol[8]. Let $\mathcal{I}$ be a set of symbols to be used as implementation names.

Definition 3.3 (Implementation description) *An implementation description is a binding $i \sim \rho$ where*

- $i \in \mathcal{I}$ is the implementation name.
- ρ is a mapping from $Qualifers \cup Oid$ to $Simple(\mathcal{V}_g^t \cup \{\omega\} \cup \{B_1, \ldots, B_n\} \cup (\mathcal{I} - i))$

ρ describes what primitives the implementation provides, and eventually what properties it has. A minimal implementation of natural numbers could be described by

$$
num_0 \sim \left\{ \begin{array}{ll} natural & : \omega \\ 0 & : \omega \\ succ & : \omega \to \omega \end{array} \right\}
$$

An implementation description $i \sim \rho$ is expanded in a Θ-type, built from ρ, using the following rules:

- the set L is defined as $Qualifiers \cup \mathcal{I} \cup Oid$
- ω denotes an occurrence of the Θ-type we are building (i.e. it expresses recursion in the type).

---
[8] one may think of ω denoting *self* in object-oriented languages

- the fields of the Θ-type are $\triangle(\rho(q))$ when q is defined in ρ, $\triangle(\omega)$ for the field corresponding to i, and $\triangledown$ for other fields.

As expected, the generated type is an *implementation*, according to our terminology. It has a field corresponding to its name, to be used as a discriminant with other implementations with the same primitives and properties.

Definition 3.4 (Overloading scheme) *An overloading scheme is a binding $o \rightsquigarrow (s, \rho)$ where*

- $o \in Oid$
- $s \in Simple(\mathcal{V}_g^t \cup \{\omega\} \cup \{B_1, \ldots, B_n\} \cup \mathcal{I})$ such that ω appears in s
- ρ is a mapping from $Qualifiers \cup Oid$ to $Simple(\mathcal{V}_g^t \cup \{\omega\} \cup \{B_1, \ldots, B_n\} \cup \mathcal{I})$, such that $\rho(o) = s$.[9]

Examples of overloading schemes are given in Figure 2.

An overloading scheme $o \rightsquigarrow (s, \rho)$ is expanded in a type, built from s, using the following rules:

- the set L is defined as $Qualifiers \cup \mathcal{I} \cup Oid$
- ω denotes an occurrence of an Θ-type which fields are built using ρ: the fields are $\triangle(\rho(q))$ when q is defined in ρ, $\triangle(s)$ for the field corresponding to o, and a fresh generic field variable $\phi_g \in \mathcal{V}_g^f$ for each other field.

Intuitively, ω can be considered as a type variable which instantiation is restricted by the presence of properties described in ρ. Polymorphism appears in the field variables ϕ_g which provide the possibility of later instantiation that changes the status of the Θ type from an ADT to an implementation. The recursion on ω (i.e. the presence of $o : s$ in the Θ construction, implicit in the figure examples) shows where we will take the actual value of o: when the Θ-type becomes an implementation, then this implementation will provide the specific adequate value for o in its primitives. One can read the example hd in Figure 2 as $hd : \theta \to \alpha$, such that θ has properties $hd : \theta \to \alpha$, and also $elem : \alpha$, $tl : \theta \to \theta$, $cons : \alpha \to \theta \to \theta$.

Although the description of an implementation is syntactically similar to an overloading scheme, it is expanded into a "closed tree", rather than an "open" tree (i.e. ADT) for overloading schemes.

---
[9] For conciseness, the value $\rho(o)$ is not given in the description of ρ

Figure 3: Typing rules

$$
\begin{array}{ll}
OID_s & \dfrac{o \in Oid \qquad \sigma \in \lfloor A(o) \rfloor}{A \vdash_s o : \sigma} \\[2ex]
ID_s & \dfrac{x \in Id \qquad \sigma \in \lfloor A(x) \rfloor}{A \vdash_s x : \sigma} \\[2ex]
ABS_s & \dfrac{A_x \cup \{x \mapsto \sigma\} \vdash_s e : \tau}{A \vdash_s \lambda x.e : \sigma \to \tau} \\[2ex]
APP_s & \dfrac{A \vdash_s e : \sigma \to \tau \qquad A \vdash_s e' : \sigma}{A \vdash_s ee' : \tau} \\[2ex]
LET_s & \dfrac{A \vdash_s e : \sigma \qquad A_x \cup \{x \mapsto \lceil A, \sigma \rceil\} \vdash_s e' : \tau}{A \vdash_s \text{let } x = e \text{ in } e' : \tau}
\end{array}
$$

3.5 Typing rules

Static semantic rules use sequents of the form

$$A \vdash_s e : \tau$$

where :

$$
\begin{array}{rcl}
\tau, \sigma & \in & \mathcal{T} \\
\sigma_g & \in & \mathcal{T}_g \\
A & \in & TEnv = (Id \cup Oid) \to \mathcal{T}_g
\end{array}
$$

Following [CleDDK 86, Rémy 89], we define a modified version of the original typing rules [Milner 78, DamMil 82] in Figure 3, where[10]

- $\lfloor \sigma_g \rfloor$ is the set of instances of σ_g, i.e. types obtained from σ_g by grafting all generic variables in σ_g by trees in $\mathcal{R}$

- Generalization $\lceil A, \sigma \rceil$ is the grafting of all non-generic variables in σ which do not appear in A by new generic variables.

- A_x denotes A where the binding $x \mapsto A(x)$ has been removed if it exists.

Remark 3.1 *Since Id and Oid are disjoint, the mapping $A \downarrow Oid$* [11] *is never modified in $\vdash_s$.*

As proved in [Rémy 89], there exists an algorithm (W), sound and complete, that computes a principal type for expressions in $OExp$. Basically, we are re-using here Rémy's result that the original W algorithm designed by Milner may be extended to rational types, with Huet's unification algorithm[Huet 76]. Types are also simpler than in Rémy's system since we don't consider records as objects of the language, so that operations on types do not introduce the problem of forgetting fields. Note that this part of the type-checking is really syntactic work on the language. Our special interpretation of the *let in* construct does not change the typing. Also, since recursive types in W allow the typing of expressions such as $\lambda x.(x\,x)$ or the Y combinator, we must be careful when interpreting types. In this presentation, we forbid recursive types which are not Θ-types.

It should be noted that the algorithm W, as well as computing a principal type[12] for an expression, annotates (deterministically) each node of the expression by its type. We remind here an essential property of the static semantics:

Lemma 3.1 (Sub) $A \vdash_s e : \tau \Rightarrow A\mu \vdash_s e : \tau\mu$
(where μ is a non-generic graft.)

Remark 3.2 *In the inference system defined above, generic types appear only in type-environments A.*

3.6 Safety and static resolution

We now need to prove the consistency of static and dynamic semantics, which is that a well-typed term has a correct execution. The first point is that the type computed by W is not sufficient to determine

---

[10] the rule for basic constants is omitted, since we can treat them as identifiers in Id

[11] $A \downarrow Oid$ (resp. $A \downarrow Id$) denotes the restriction of A to to Oid (resp. Id).

[12] which, in this presentation, is a type, not a generic type as noted by Tofte[Tofte 87]

if there exists an execution. Using the overloading environment described in Figure 2, the term

$$\lambda x.\ hd(cons\ x\ nil)$$

would be typed by $\alpha \to \alpha$. Typing does not guarantee that we have compatible values for hd, cons and nil. The problem comes from variables of sort *Field* that are created by ID_s or OID_s, and eliminated during APP_s rule. These *Field* variables may be thought of as variables that delay the choice of an implementation.

Definition 3.5 (Safety) We need a caracterization of types and grafts that takes in account the interpretation of *Field* variables.

- *A type σ_g is safe if either σ_g is real or all field variables in σ_g are generic.*
- *A type environment A is safe if $\forall x \in A$, $A(x)$ is safe.*
- *A graft μ is safe for τ if $\tau\mu$ is safe*
- *A graft μ is safe for A if $A\mu$ is safe*

Static Resolution: We define here an algorithm which purpose is to complete W to get the consistency, while keeping some overloading resolution at run-time. We consider an expression e decorated by τ, (noted $e :: \tau$), where τ is the type inferred by W (i.e. the principal type τ such that $A \vdash_s e : \tau$), and where each subexpression of e is decorated in the same fashion. Let-bindings[13] are decorated with their generalized types rather than the simple type during this algorithm. Let $OFree$ be the set of *non-generic field variables* in all types decorating e. Find a ground graft SR on $OFree$, safe for A and all types in $e :: \tau$. If we can't find SR then the typing fails. If we find SR, then SR is applied on the proof tree of W in the following, and we note the sequents in the proof $A \vdash_s^{W+SR} e : \tau$.

Lemma 3.2 (Static resolution) *All types in $(e :: \tau)SR$ are safe. Sequents $A \vdash_s^{W+SR} e : \tau$ with τ abstract only appear in the proof under application of the LET_s rule.*

Proof: by construction, since the SR removes all non-generic field variables. Abstract types are now necessarily generic.
Example:(following previous specifications of overloaded symbols) $\lambda x.hd(cons\ x\ nil)$ is typed with

$$\alpha \to \alpha$$

---
[13]i.e. the e expression in $let\ x = e\ in\ e'$

with SR forcing the choice of compatible values for hd, cons and nil.

Finding the ground graft SR implies an arbitrary choice when there are multiple implementations for a same ADT. We must remind this when we will examine the relation between static resolution and our definition of correct execution.

Another remark concerns the implications of static resolution on a real implementation of this system in a language. If we consider a closed term (i.e. a term as defined in the formalism $OExp$), then static resolution may be seen as a two-step operation, which consists in macro-expansion[14] of *let* expressions, and then full resolution of overloaded symbols. However, in a toplevel loop for example, which consists in "open lets", such as $let\ x = e;;$ (expression that does *not* belong to OExp), there is no macro-expansion. As said before, the identification of overloaded symbols in e will be delayed until the typing of an occurrence of x provides enough information. The purpose of SR in this case is to identify overloaded symbols that do **not** depend on future instantiations of the type of x, and to solve them immediately.

3.7 Consistency

The object of this section is to give the semantic interpretation of types in our system. This interpretation[15] is given by a relation $\models$ between $v \in Val + Thunks$ and $\sigma_g \in \mathcal{T}_g$.

We first define the relation on $BaseValues$ and monotypes. Note that *implementations* are not necessarily monotypes. They may contain generic variables of sort *Type*. The point is that implementations types do not contain *field* variables.

- $\models b : \iota_B \in \{B_1, \ldots, B_n\}$ by definition of the built-in environment

- $\models v : \iota_I \in \mathcal{I}$ where ι_I is a ground type, by definition of the built-in environment

- $\models [x, e, E] : \iota_1 \to \iota_2$ if for all v such that $\models v : \iota_1$, there exists r such that

  - $E \cup \{x \mapsto v\} \vdash_d e \longrightarrow r$
  - $\models r : \iota_2$

A type environment A is said *closed* and noted $\overline{A}$ when all variables (of sort *Field* or *Type*) in types on the range of $\overline{A}$ are generic.

---
[14]in fact redex elimination, with eventual renamings
[15]based on [Tofte 87]

The semantic relation $\models$ is extended on types, generic types and environments. We need a definition for environment with non-generic variables (i.e. not closed) for the proofs.

- $\models v : \sigma$ if for all total, ground, safe graft μ, $\models v : \sigma\mu$

- $\models v : \sigma_g$ if for all safe generic grafts μ_g, $\models v : \sigma_g\mu_g$

- $\models \langle e, E\rangle : \sigma_g$ if for all safe instance σ_0, of σ_g there exists v such that $\vdash_{d'} \langle e, E\rangle \longrightarrow v$ and $\models v : \sigma_0$,

- $\models O : \overline{A} \downarrow Oid$, if $\forall o \in O, \forall v \in O(o),$ (with $\models v : \sigma_g$), σ_g is real and $\exists \mu_g, \sigma_g = \overline{A}(o)\mu_g$

- $\models E : \overline{A} \downarrow Id$ if $\forall x \in Dom(E), \models E(x) : \overline{A}(x)$

- $\models E : \overline{A}$ if $Dom(E) \cup Dom(O) = Dom(\overline{A})$, $\models O : \overline{A} \downarrow Oid$, $\models E : \overline{A} \downarrow Id$.

- $\models E : A$ if for all total, ground, safe graft μ, $\models E : A\mu$

Theorem 3.1 (Consistency) If $\models E : A$, $A \vdash_s^{W+SR} e : \tau$, and A is safe, then

$$\exists r, E \vdash_d e \longrightarrow r, \text{ such that } \models r : \tau$$

Sketch of Proof: by structural induction on e. The game consists in using the premises of static rules to prove (by induction) the premises of the dynamic rules, thus finding a safe derivation [16]. Note that when A is not safe, the theorem does not hold (non-generic field variables in types potentially means unresolved overloading with possible failure). We need the following lemma:

Lemma 3.3 (Realization) If $\models E : A$ and $A \vdash_s^{W+SR} e : \tau$ then for all total, ground, safe graft μ,

$$\exists r, E \vdash_d e \longrightarrow r, \text{ such that } \models r : \tau\mu$$

This lemma does not give unicity of the result r. However, we may now write the proof of the Consistency theorem, using the static resolution lemma. All inductions but for let-bound symbols are done on the theorem itself, and for these symbols we use the Realization lemma. The important point is that during induction on the theorem itself, A and types are always safe.

---

[16] For a given term structure in $OExp$, there is only one possible rule for static semantics and for dynamic semantics

3.8 Correctness

Static resolution may involve an arbitrary choice of implementations to transform the non-deterministic program in a deterministic one. We need to be sure that this choice is compatible with our correctness definition. Intuitively, the typing inferred by W gives the observable behaviour of the values derived in the program. The minimum semantic equivalence between different values derivable from the same term is defined by the set of operations[17] that can be applied to these values. The type inferred by W is exactly this set of properties. SR as defined above is then seen as the choice of a set of implementations satisfying these properties. Therefore, any valid choice from SR is compatible with the equivalence relation defined by the type inferred in W.

4 Recursion

We already said that we considered recursive types as invalid (except those cycling on Θ). Static semantics supports them (syntactically) but we have no interpretation of these types in the $\models$ relation. We still can add recursion in $OExp$, using rec rules in static and dynamic semantics to provide the same kind of extension as for ML, with the Y combinator for example. The type of Y is simply declared in the built-in environment. From a practical point of view, it is easy to add recursion both in the language and in the typing. We believe that the definition of correctness of execution with recursion could be a step-by-step equivalence of possible executions.

Note also that we don't have "polymorphic recursion". We then know that overloading resolution will be the same in each recursive call, since the resolution happens at instantiation time.

5 A real language

The previous sections deal only with the formal presentation of the language. It is clear that a real implementation is not a non-deterministic language, and that we do not want to re-compute completely thunks when they are used. However, we are able to use the information gathered during type-inference to produce a compiled code for thunks. The occurrence of overloaded symbols that depend on the type of the instance may be replaced by a look-up function call to their corresponding property in the type. This means that the evaluation of a thunk needs a new argument

---

[17] possibly extended with properties

which is the type of its instance. This new evaluation mechanism becomes deterministic, with respect to the arbitrary choices during static resolution. Note that tagging values with their implementation type does not help, since we may have to select a value from the result type.

The construction above neither describes how implementations are managed, nor details the static resolution. As noted in the introduction, this issue belongs to a different topic. Some issues are:

- when dealing with polymorphic implementations during static resolution, it should be noted that only field variables are grafted. The implementation is *not* an instance of the unresolved type.

- relying in structural equivalence of implementation types as semantic equivalence if not sufficient. However, as our types are compatible with record types, it seems natural to use formalisms such as [CooHC 90] to code implementations with records. Stronger semantic relations may be enforced by direct operations on the primitives of implementations.

In fact, the whole hierarchy dealing with code inheritance, or delegation, has to be managed in the implementation's world.

There are still some major limitations in our approach, due to the very simplicity of the instantiation relation considered as a "subclass" relation. It is not possible to have more than one occurrence of a primitive symbol in a Θ type. This makes impossible to overload, for example, matrix multiplications by a matrix and by a scalar and use them simultaneously in a program. However, this kind of overloading is more a syntactical facility than a conceptual notion of abstraction or code reuse.

Conclusion

We presented in this paper a new approach for overloading that can reconciliate functional programming and object-oriented concepts (abstraction, subclassing, overloading) using familiar techniques such as call-by-name and polymorphism, while keeping useful properties of strong static typing. The formalism presented here is not only an extension of existing type-checkers but rather an attempt for a full system with adequate semantics. The definition of overloading schemes being rather flexible, a wide range of programming methodologies may be modelled by this system. We believe that this formalism can be turned into a real language, with more work on implementation management and new constructs for manipulating the overloading environment. Future work includes also generalization of overloading schemes and run-time extensions of the overloading environment.

Acknowledgements. I am grateful to B. Lang for initiating this work as a formalisation of the implicit typing used in the VTP [Lang 86], and for his support. D. Rémy explained to me many key points in ML typing. B. Lang, V. Donzeau-Gouge and J.-J. Lévy helped in choosing the dynamic semantics.

References

[BorIng 82] A.H. Borning, D.H.H Ingalls: "A type declaration and inference system for SmallTalk", *Proc. of the ACM Conf. on Principles of Programming Languages 1982.*

[CarWeg 86] L. Cardelli, P. Wegner: "On Understanding Types, Data Abstraction, and Polymorphism", *ACM Computing Surveys*, Vol.17, No.4, pp.471-522, December 1986.

[CleDDK 86] D. Clément, J. Despeyroux, T. Despeyroux, G. Kahn: "A Simple Applicative Language: Mini-ML", *Proc. of the ACM Symp. on Lisp and Functional Programming 1986*,13-27.

[CooHC 90] W. Cook, W. Hill, P. Canning: "Inheritance is not Subtyping" to appear in *Proc. of the ACM Conf. on Principles of Programming Languages 1990.*

[DamMil 82] L. Damas, R. Milner: "Principal type-schemes for functional programs", *Proc. of the ACM Conf. on Principles of Programming Languages 1982*

[DeMGab 87] L.G. DeMichiel, R.P. Gabriel: "CLOS Overview", *Proceedings of ECOOP 87.*

[HudWad 88] P. Hudak, P. Wadler et al.: "Report on the Functional Programming Language Haskell, Draft proposed standard", Research report, Yale University, Dec. 88.

[Huet 76] G. Huet: "Résolution d'équations dans les langages d'ordre $1, 2, \ldots, \omega$", Thèse de doctorat d'état, Université Paris 7, 1976.

[Johnson 86] R.E. Johnson: "Type-Checking SmallTalk" in OOPSLA '86 Proceeding *ACM SIGPLAN* Vol 21., No. 11, pp.315-321, November 86.

[Kaes 88] S. Kaes: " Parametric Overloading in Polymorphic Programming Languages", *Proc. of the 2nd European Symp. on Programming 88* LNCS 300,Springer-Verlag.

[Lang 86] B. Lang "The Virtual Tree Processor" *Esprit Project GIPE, Third review report*,September 1986.

[Liskov 81] B.H. Liskov: "Clu Reference Manual", *Lecture Notes in Computer Science* 114,Springer-Verlag 1981.

[MeyNM 87] B. Meyer, J-M. Nerson, M. Matsuo: "Eiffel: Object-oriented design for software engineering", *Proc. of the 1st European Software Engineering Conference* Sept.87, AFCET.

[Milner 78] R. Milner: "A Theory of Type Polymorphism in Programming", *J. Comput. Syst. Sci* 17 (1978), pp.348-375.

[Lunau 89] C. Pii Lunau: "Separation of Hierarchies in Duo-Talk", *Journal of Object-Oriented Programming Jul/Aug 1989*.

[RajLev 89] R.K. Raj, H.M. Levy : "A Compositional Model for Software Reuse", *Conf. Proceedings of ECOOP '89*.

[Rémy 89] D. Rémy: "Typechecking records and variants in a natural extension of ML", *Proc. of the ACM Symp. on Principles of Programming Languages 1989*

[SchaCoo 86] C. Schaffert, T. Cooper et al. : "An Introduction to Trellis/Owl", *Conf. Proceedings of OOPSLA '86*

[Suzuki 81] N. Suzuki: "Inferring Types in SmallTalk", *Proc. of the ACM Symp. on Principles of Programming Languages 1981*.

[Tofte 87] M. Tofte: "Operational Semantics and Polymorphic Type Inference", *Ph.D. Thesis* University of Edinburgh, 1987.

[WadBlo 89] P. Wadler, S. Blott: "How to make ad-hoc polymorphism less ad-hoc", *Proc. of the ACM Symp. on Principles of Programming Languages 1989*

Figure 4: Overloading schemes

$$
\begin{aligned}
0, 1, \ldots &\rightsquigarrow (\omega, \{ num : \omega \}) \\
"a", \ldots &\rightsquigarrow (\omega, \{ str : \omega \}) \\
= &\rightsquigarrow (\omega \to \omega \to Bool), \{\}) \\
+ &\rightsquigarrow (\omega \to \omega \to \omega, \{\}) \\
hd &\rightsquigarrow (\omega \to \alpha_g, \{ elem : \alpha_g \}) \\
tl &\rightsquigarrow (\omega \to \omega, \{\}) \\
cons &\rightsquigarrow (\alpha_g \to \omega \to \omega, \{ elem : \alpha_g \}) \\
nil &\rightsquigarrow (\omega, \{\}) \\
null? &\rightsquigarrow (\omega \to Bool, \{\})
\end{aligned}
$$

A Examples

The examples given below are samples of what a prototype of the system (with recursion and a toplevel) produces. As announced, the readability of inferred types is not good. Θ-types looks like $\omega = \{p_1 : \sigma_1, p_2 : \sigma_2 \ldots p_n : \sigma_n; \phi\}$ for ADTs. Field names (symbols in L) are here explicitly given. ▽ fields are omitted. Field variables are grouped in a unique extension variable, noted ϕ. Generic variables are prefixed with the quote character(e.g. $'a$). In the following, they are written, for example:

`SA={+:SA->SA->SA ; 'u}`

Implementations are denoted by their unique name. The environment used in the following examples contains

- a basic type for booleans (*Bool*)

- a built-in implementation of integers, with primitives: addition (+), equality (=), and property *num*. All integer constants are overloaded, and we use the property *num* for this purpose.

- a built-in implementation of strings, with primitives: concatenation (+), equality (=), and property *str* to overload all string tokens.

- a built-in implementation of lists, with usual primitives: $hd, tl, cons, nil, null?$

The formal definition of this environment is given in Figure 4 and Figure 5.

Figure 5: Implementations descriptions

$$Integer \sim \left\{ \begin{array}{lll} = & : & \omega \to \omega \to Bool \\ + & : & \omega \to \omega \to \omega \\ num & : & \omega \end{array} \right\}$$

$$String \sim \left\{ \begin{array}{lll} = & : & \omega \to \omega \to Bool \\ + & : & \omega \to \omega \to \omega \\ str & : & \omega \end{array} \right\}$$

$$List \sim \left\{ \begin{array}{lll} hd & : & \omega \to \alpha_g \\ tl & : & \omega \to \omega \\ cons & : & \alpha_g \to \omega \to \omega \\ nil & : & \omega \\ null? & : & \omega \to Bool \\ elem & : & \alpha_g \end{array} \right\}$$

Each example is chosen to exhibit a feature or a property of the type system.

Example 1 : Simple overloading

```
#let double = fun x -> x + x ;;
(* SR is happy *)
double : SA -> SA
with
SA={+:SA->SA->SA ; 'u}
```

Double may be used on any data type providing a + operation, so here

```
#(double 3, double "foo") ;;
(* SR finds Integer, String *)
(6,"foofoo") : (Integer & String)
```

Note that lexical tokens 3 and "foo" are overloaded though here only one implementation is provided for each. Static resolution had to find an implementation for the ADTs $\omega = \{num : \omega; + : \omega \to \omega \to \omega; \phi_1\}$ and $\omega = \{str : \omega; + : \omega \to \omega \to \omega; \phi_2\}$.

Example 2 : Static resolution at work

```
#fun x -> hd (cons x nil) ;;
(* SR finds List *)
fun : 'a -> 'a
```

In this example, the overloaded symbols $hd, cons, nil$ have been statically resolved since the inference determined that their resolution do not depend on the type of x.

Example 3 : Constructor/Destructor dissociation

```
#letrec map =
# fun f ->
#   (fun l ->
#      if (null? l)
#      then nil
#      else (cons (f (hd l))
#                 (map f (tl l)))) ;;
(* SR is happy *)
map : ('a -> 'b) -> SA -> SB
with
SA={hd:SA->'a , tl:SA->SA, elem:'a,
    null?:SA->Bool ; 'u}
SB={nil:SB, cons:'b->SB->SB, elem:'b, 'v}
```

The fact that the list primitives are dissociated in our environment explains this typing, where constructors and destructors of the list have been separated in the two types. A remarkable consequense is that the result list may not have the same implementation as the input list.

Example 4 : More on implementation independance

```
#letrec append =
# fun l1 ->
#   (fun l2 ->
#      if (null? l1)
#      then l2
#      else (cons (hd l1)
#                 (append (tl l1) l2))) ;;
(* SR is happy *)
append : SA->SB->SB
with
SA={hd:SA->'a, tl:SA->SA, null:SA->Bool,
    elem: 'a}
SB={cons:'a->SB->SB, elem:'a}
```

Although the input lists must contain elements of the same type, their implemention might be different. However, by construction of the program, the result list has the same implementation as the second input list.

Quasi-static Typing
(Preliminary Report)

Satish R. Thatte[*]
Department of Mathematics and Computer Science
Clarkson University, Potsdam, NY 13676.

Abstract

We present a new approach to dynamic typing in a static framework. Our main innovation is the use of structural subtyping for dynamic types based on the idea that possible dynamic typing as a property should be *inherited* by objects of all types. Two properties of our system set it apart from existing systems which combine static and dynamic typing: all tagging and checking takes place via implicit coercions, and the semantics of dynamic typing is representation independent. The latter property leads to a significant increase in expressive power—for instance it allows us to define a *general* call-by-value fixpoint operator.

The resulting system—which we call quasi-static typing—is a seamless merger of static and dynamic typing. The system divides programs into three categories: well-typed, ill-typed and ambivalent programs. Ill-typed programs contain expressions that are *guaranteed* to go wrong. Run-time checking is limited to doubtful function applications in ambivalent programs. Conceptually, quasi-static typing takes place in an unusual two-phase process—a first phase infers types and coercions and a second *plausibility checking* phase identifies ill-typed programs. The typing rules allow minimal typing judgements and plausibility checking can be characterized as simplification via a canonical set of rewrite rules. The two phase process can therefore be implemented with a one pass algorithm.

1 Introduction

In programming language design, the choice between static and dynamic typing is often seen as a fundamental choice between two opposing ideologies. In reality, there are many situations where it is desirable to combine the two approaches. For instance, it has been shown convincingly [ABC+83, ACPP89] that efficient and type secure use of persistent data—such as database files or just data exchanged beween different programs—requires type information for such objects to be saved and checked at run-time. Languages which subscribe to this idea (PS-Algol [ABC+83], Amber [Car86]) often allow any data object to be persistent, including those which involve complex pointer structures such as sharing and circularities. If such a language is otherwise statically typed (like Amber), it needs to provide dynamic typing as an option in an orthogonal way. An orthogonal combination of static and dynamic typing has other interesting applications. For instance, during program development, it is sometimes more convenient to use LISP-like heterogeneous data structures—which require dynamic typing—instead of "homogeneous" structures of variant types because the exact shapes of some

---

[*]This work was started while the author was at the University of California, San Diego.

Permission to copy without fee all or part of this material is granted provided that the copies are not made or distributed for direct commercial advantage, the ACM copyright notice and the title of the publication and its date appear, and notice is given that copying is by permission of the Association for Computing Machinery. To copy otherwise, or to republish, requires a fee and/or specific permission.

© 1990 ACM 089791-343-4/90/0001/0367 $1.50

variant types may not be clear at the early stages of design.

Several practical statically typed languages (CLU, Mesa, Amber, Modula-3) address this issue by making special provisions for dynamic typing. In a recent paper, Abadi, Cardelli, Pierce and Plotkin [ACPP89] survey the history of these ideas and describe an elegant general combination of static and dynamic typing based on existing features in Amber and Modula-3 [CDJ+89]. The system they describe disguises dynamically typed objects with a special "static" type Dynamic, and provides special operations to the user for explicit attachment and checking of run-time type-tags. The main shortcoming of this system is that the semantics of dynamic typing is closely tied to the underlying representation—an object in effect "remembers" the history of tagging steps through which it has passed and a successful run-time check must look for the exact tagging pattern reflecting this history. This can have counterintuitive semantic consequences, as we argue in Section 2. Moreover, when programmers must explicitly manage the static-dynamic interface, the need to keep track of tagging patterns represents a considerable burden if dynamic typing is used extensively.

We describe a new approach to dynamic typing in static languages that gives representation-independent semantics to dynamically typed objects while at the same time eliminating the need for explicit management of the static-dynamic interface. We use the general framework of [ACPP89] as our starting point. The key new idea in our approach is to treat dynamic typing as a property that is *inherited* by all types from the type Dynamic through a natural subtype structure. The subtype structure is given a *coercive* interpretation. Positive coercions (from static to dynamic types) are tagging operations. We also need *negative* coercions (from supertypes to subtypes, *i.e.*, from dynamic to static types) to account for run-time checks. The idea of automatic negative coercions is new, as far as we know. Much of the theory developed here is in fact independent of the specific subtype structure induced by Dynamic and could be presented much more abstractly as a theory of type inference involving positive and negative coercions for a class of *injective* subtype structures.

Using the ideas outlined above, we achieve (for the user) a seamless merger of static and dynamic typing which we call *quasi-static typing*. Its practical characteristics are qualitatively different from those of purely static and purely dynamic systems. Static systems traditionally attempt to prove that a program is (or can be) well-typed, rejecting those for which no such proof is possible within the system. In most static systems there is no way to prove that a program is *ill*-typed in the sense that it contains an expression that necessarily goes wrong at run-time. Given the undecidability of "semantically complete" typechecking for most languages, a system that permits ill-typing proofs has to make a three way division of programs into well-typed, ill-typed, and ambivalent ones. Such a system can combine some of the advantages of static and dynamic typing by using run-time checking only in ambivalent programs, or better yet, only at the ambivalent *applications* in ambivalent programs. Quasi-static typing is a system of this kind. The version in this paper is limited to simply typed dialects of the λ-calculus, but it should be possible to construct more general systems based on the same principles along the lines of other systems which combine subtyping with parametric polymorphism [CW85, BTCGS89]. We have elsewhere [Tha88] described constraint resolution algorithms that may be useful for improving the degree of type inference in such a generalized system.

Conceptually, quasi-static typing is a two phase process. The first phase makes typing (and coercion) judgements. A program that would normally be considered statically well-typed is accepted by this phase without any *negative* coercions and *all* other programs are accepted *with* some negative coercions. One way to understand the reason for this excessive lenience is to think of quasi-static typing as a system which matches the liberality of dynamic typing while restricting tagging and checking operations to those that are actually found to be required based on compile-time analysis. The typing/coercion judgements express the results of this analysis. The information gained through the analysis makes it possible to identify many ill-typed programs at compile-time. This is accomplished by a novel *plausibility checking* phase that preevaluates the coercions introduced by typing. Strictly speaking, the programs rejected during plausibility checking are not *statically* ill-typed—they contain dynamic type errors that can be statically detected. It is easy to modify quasi-static typing to reintroduce the possibility of static type errors in the formal sense. This is actually highly desirable for methodological reasons. Some ideas for such modifications are discussed in Section 8.

Our typing rules allow the derivation of minimal typing/coercion judgements (see below) and plausibility checking can be characterized as a simplification process specified by a canonical (confluent terminating) set of rewrite rules. This permits a complete one pass implementation of the two phases described above.

An interesting theoretical point to note in connection with the notion of minimal judgements is that certain design decisions (discussed in Section 3) lead us to abandon coherence of typing judgements—the property that the meaning of an expression depends only on its typing judgement, not on the specific proof for that judgement (see [BTCGS89] for a discussion). The possibility of dependence on the proof is created by the fact that the coercions introduced during typing depend on the proof rather than on the typing judgement. Such a dependence on proof is clearly unacceptable. Among other things, it calls into question the notion of a minimal typing/coercion judgement, since the coercion part may not be "minimal" in any reasonable sense if it is nondeterministically related to the typing part. Fortunately, our type system does possess a weaker property—which we call *convergence*—which ensures that there is a "minimal" proof for each typing judgement which gives the "least error-prone" (and therefore canonical) semantics. The notion of a minimal typing/coercion judgement in our system is therefore defined in two steps. A minimal judgement has a minimal typing part, and a coercion part corresponding to a minimal proof for the typing part. These ideas are made precise in Sections 3 and 7.

In expressive power, our system is not directly comparable to that of [ACPP89]. Besides automation of tagging and checking, the semantics of dynamic typing in our system is significantly more abstract. For instance, a general call-by-value fixpoint operator can be expressed in our framework. The analogous construction (with explicit tagging and checking) in the language of [ACPP89] fails due to their representation oriented interpretation of dynamic typing. Our system is *less* general in one respect. The typecase construct of [ACPP89] (which can coexist with quasi-static typing) uses multiple patterns and has conditional branching on both success and failure of dynamic checks. It is hard to see how an *implicit* check can produce anything other than a run-time error on failure. Examples like the general purpose print function of [ACPP89] are therefore beyond our system.

The next section motivates and describes our interpretation of dynamic typing. Typing and plausibility checking rules are described in Sections 3 and 4. A complete type inference algorithm is given in Section 5. Operational and denotational semantics is described in Sections 6 and 7. We conclude with a discussion of some pragmatic issues and concluding remarks in Sections 8 and 9.

2 Partial Types and Cumulative Coercions

In this section we motivate and explain our interpretation of dynamic typing and the corresponding coercion scheme. General familiarity with existing work in the area is assumed (see [ACPP89] for a brief survey and formal treatment). For convenience of explanation, we use simple objects such as integers and booleans in examples, but it should be clear that we could have used complex objects like bitmaps and relations instead.

The type structure used in this section includes basic types Nat and Bool, and the usual type constructors for product ($\times$), list([ ]), and function($\rightarrow$) types. The formal part of the paper leaves out list types for brevity. The static type of dynamically typed objects is denoted by Ω instead of Dynamic for reasons to be explained shortly. The subtype order is based on the scheme $\tau \leq \Omega$ for all types τ, which expresses the basic inheritance relationship we wish to capture. This extends monotonically over the type constructors except for the usual antimonotonic behavior of the first argument of "$\rightarrow$". For instance we have [Nat] $\leq$ [Ω] and [Ω] $\rightarrow$ Nat $\leq$ [Nat] $\rightarrow$ Ω. "More" in this order is just "more dynamic". The order relates all (and only) pairs $\tau_1 \leq \tau_2$ such that an object x of type τ_1 can be converted to one of type τ_2 by applying or composing tagging operations with either the whole or parts of x.

Programs are written in a "user language" which is just Church's typed λ-calculus. There are no tagging or checking constructs such as, for instance, Amber's dynamic and coerce. Analogous but somewhat different constructs are used by the type system as *implicit* coercions. One reason why Amber-like constructs cannot be used is that their semantics is too closely tied to the underlying representation—different tagging patterns lead to semantically different objects even when the underlying untagged objects and the types of their tagged versions are identical. Using these constructs as coercions (with their current semantics) would result in loss of coherence for subsumption judgements. Given $\tau_1 \leq \tau_2 \leq \tau_3$, an object x of type τ_1 would be converted to semantically distinct objects of type τ_3 depending on whether or not an intermediate conversion to type τ_2 occurs. It would be impossible to construct unique coercions for every subtype relationship as one usually expects. A very simple example illustrates the problems and suggests a solution. Suppose l is a list of type [Nat];

$\text{emb}_{\text{Nat}} = \lambda x . \text{dynamic } x : \text{Nat}$

$l_0 = \text{map emb}_{\text{Nat}} \; l$

$l_1 = \text{dynamic } l_0 : [\Omega]$

$l_2 = \text{dynamic } l : [\text{Nat}]$

Recall that the result of the expression "dynamic $x : \tau$" is an object of type Ω which is just the dynamically typed version of x (assuming that x has type τ). Clearly, l_0 converts l to an object of type [Ω], and l_1, l_2 both define tagged versions of l of type Ω. The only difference between l_1 and l_2 is that the conversion in l_1 takes place in two steps rather than one. Nonetheless, l_1 and l_2 are *observably* different objects in the system of [ACPP89]. This is not just a theoretical difficulty. The semantic distinction may cause spurious run-time errors. For instance, coerce l_1 to [Nat] (to use the Amber notation for run-time checks) fails. The more direct tagging in l_2 causes coerce l_2 to [Ω] to fail. In each case, substituting the "other" version leads to success. This is not a fatal problem when tagging is explicit because the programmer is then responsible for knowing the tagging pattern and checking it appropriately, although it does represent a greater burden than is generally recognized. When both tagging and checking are implicit, this kind of uncertainty would make the system unusable.

We conclude that the recasting of dynamic typing as an inherited property forces a change in its interpretation. In place of a representation oriented semantics we need a more abstract "information" oriented semantics in which types involving Dynamic are viewed as *partial* static types, in analogy with Wadsworth's partial terms [Wad76]. Tagging and checking clearly obey a "law of conservation of type information" which decrees that a loss of static type information is accompanied by an identical gain in dynamic type information and *vice versa*. The transitivity of our subtype order for dynamic types implies that gains and losses in type information are *cumulative*. The increments in which they occur should not affect the end result. Hence the expectation that l_1 and l_2 should behave in an identical way. To emphasize this shift in perspective, we use Wadsworth's Ω symbol—which represents lack of information—in place of Dynamic. To make tagging and checking free from representation bias, we take it as a principle that a runtime check should succeed whenever it is possible to convert the object of the check (by untagging) to a value that belongs to a *subtype* of the required type. This may require the check to be propagated to components of a structure. Under this regime, **coerce** l_1 **to** [Nat] succeeds, and l_1 and l_2 are *observably equivalent* at run-time.

It is possible to achieve these semantic changes by simply changing the interpretation of **coerce** appropriately. Although this would eliminate the semantic problem in using **dynamic** and **coerce** as implicit coercions, *static* detection of type errors in the resulting system would be all but impossible. As we describe in Section 4, statically detected errors in our system correspond to cases where tagging and checking operations are combined in an *implausible* way, *i.e.*, in a way that ensures a dynamic type error. For instance, the expression 1+true is coerced by the typing phase to (the equivalent of) 1+**coerce** (**dynamic** true:Bool) **to** Nat, which is rejected as implausible at compile-time. The effectiveness of this technique depends on statically manifest tagging at the outermost level possible. For instance, **coerce** l_0 **to** [Bool] is *not* statically implausible, even though the type of the underlying value l is incompatible with [Bool]. There is no way to coerce l to the type [Ω] with direct (outermost) tagging using **dynamic**. The difficulty is caused by the fact that **dynamic** and **coerce** can only do limited conversions—those for subsumptions of the form $\tau \leq \Omega$. The obvious solution is to generalize these operations to arbitrary subsumptions. We use a family $\uparrow^\sigma_\tau$, $\downarrow^\sigma_\tau$ of postfix operators (one for each pair $\tau \leq \sigma$) for generalized tagging and checking; $e \uparrow^\sigma_\tau$ means e belongs to type τ and is being coerced to a more dynamic type σ by tagging, and $e \downarrow^\sigma_\tau$ means e belongs to type σ and is being coerced to a less dynamic type τ by checking. Thus emb$_{Nat}$ is redefined as $\lambda x :$ Nat. $x \uparrow^\Omega_{Nat}$ and $l_3 = l \uparrow^{[\Omega]}_{[Nat]}$ is equivalent to $l_4 =$ map emb$_{Nat}$ l at run-time, but *not* at compile-time. For instance, given a function $f :$ [Bool] $\to$ Bool, the application $f\, l_3$ is coerced by the typing phase to $f(l \uparrow^{[\Omega]}_{[Nat]} \downarrow^{[\Omega]}_{[Bool]})$ but $l \uparrow^{[\Omega]}_{[Nat]} \downarrow^{[\Omega]}_{[Bool]}$ is rejected as ill-typed by the plausibility checking phase at compile-time. The application $f\, l_4$ is coerced to $f\, (l_4 \downarrow^{[\Omega]}_{[Bool]})$ which is considered plausible and leads to a type error at run-time.

Heterogeneous data structures can be typed using partial types. If $[x_1, \ldots, x_n]$ denotes the list containing items $x_1, \ldots, x_n$, then [1, 2, 3, true] may be coerced to the list $z = [1\uparrow^\Omega_{Nat}, 2\uparrow^\Omega_{Nat}, 3\uparrow^\Omega_{Nat}, \text{true}\uparrow^\Omega_{Bool}]$ of type [Ω]. Given a function $sum :$ [Nat] $\to$ Nat, the application $sum\, z$ is coerced to the plausible form $sum\, (z \downarrow^{[\Omega]}_{[Nat]})$. The dynamic check implied by the coercion is carried out when sum is called and the error is caught at that time, rather than being delayed until true is actually encountered during the execution of sum. In general, dynamic type errors in this scheme are caught much earlier and at more "logical" points than in LISP-like pure dynamic typing under which only illegal applications of primitive functions are caught and it is often hard to find the *programming* error that led to the type error. A technique for improving the *efficiency* of generalized checks—such as $z \downarrow^{[\Omega]}_{[Nat]}$ in the sum application above—is discussed in Section 8.

In the next section, we give additional examples including a general call-by-value fixpoint operator.

3 Typing Rules

Throughout the formal part of the paper, our notation largely follows [ACPP89]. The set of all type expressions (described in Section 2) will be denoted by *Typecode*. Letting the metavariable e range over expressions in the user language, x over identifiers and τ over type expressions, we have:

$$e ::= \quad x \qquad\qquad\qquad identifiers$$
$$\mid \lambda x : \tau. e_{body} \qquad typed\ abstractions$$
$$\mid e_{fun}\ e_{arg} \qquad\qquad applications$$
$$\mid e_{left}, e_{right} \qquad\qquad pairs$$

The internal language of the system also has the coercion operators $\uparrow^\sigma_\tau$ and $\downarrow^\sigma_\tau$ as described in Section 2. For brevity, we assume that the environment contains a family of primitives for elimination of tupling. In practice, one would need additional constructs for this, for conditional expressions, and so forth.

One rather unusual aspect of our inference rules for typing judgements is that we need to insert run-time checks which are *negative* coercions (from a supertype to a subtype). The insertion of positive coercions is often left implicit as a side-effect of a subtyping rule. A similar implicit rule for the insertion of negative coercions would be equivalent to adding the relationship $\Omega \leq \tau$ which would collapse the subtype order and destroy both semantic consistency and minimal typing. We therefore make the insertion of coercions explicit in typing judgements. The general form of a judgement is "$TE \vdash e \Rightarrow e_{new} : \tau$" which may be read as: "given the set TE of typing assumptions for free variables, the (user language) expression e can be coerced to the (internal language) expression e_{new} which has the type τ". The first four rules are standard:

$$\frac{x \in Dom(TE)}{TE \vdash x \Rightarrow x : TE(x)}$$

$$\frac{TE \vdash e \Rightarrow e_{new} : \tau \quad \tau \leq \sigma}{TE \vdash e \Rightarrow (e_{new} \uparrow_\tau^\sigma) : \sigma}$$

$$\frac{TE[x \leftarrow \tau] \vdash e_{body} \Rightarrow e_{newbody} : \sigma}{TE \vdash \lambda x : \tau.\, e_{body} \Rightarrow \lambda x : \tau.\, e_{newbody} : \tau \rightarrow \sigma}$$

$$\frac{TE \vdash e_{left} \Rightarrow e_{newleft} : \sigma \quad TE \vdash e_{right} \Rightarrow e_{newright} : \tau}{TE \vdash (e_{left}, e_{right}) \Rightarrow (e_{newleft}, e_{newright}) : \sigma \times \tau}$$

The insertion of run-time checks takes place under two circumstances, both in the context of an application. The first case is the more common one where the type of the argument demanded by a function is a subtype of the type of the actual argument.

$$\frac{TE \vdash e_{fun} \Rightarrow e_{newfun} : \sigma \rightarrow \mu \quad TE \vdash e_{arg} \Rightarrow e_{newarg} : \tau \quad \tau \geq \sigma}{TE \vdash e_{fun}\, e_{arg} \Rightarrow e_{newfun}\, (e_{newarg} \downarrow_\sigma^\tau) : \mu}$$

The second case for applications occurs when the function part is of type Ω. This roughly resembles the situation in ML-style typechecking where the type of the function part is a type variable. The solution is roughly similar, except that a check instead of a unification is invoked:

$$\frac{TE \vdash e_{fun} \Rightarrow e_{newfun} : \Omega \quad TE \vdash e_{arg} \Rightarrow e_{newarg} : \tau}{TE \vdash e_{fun}\, e_{arg} \Rightarrow (e_{newfun} \downarrow_{\tau \rightarrow \Omega}^\Omega)\, e_{newarg} : \Omega}$$

The form of the rules for application together with the semantics of run-time checks for function values is the central design issue in quasi-static typing. The engineering problem is a tradeoff between expressive power and static detection of errors, while attempting to maintain certain desirable "invariants" such as coherence. Expressive power is enhanced by defering checks to run-time. For instance, the semantics of checking for function values defined in Sections 6 and 7 is quite lenient: an implied check on the argument of a function is defered to run-time. Tightening the semantics of checking for functions by treating implied checks on arguments as errors would improve static detection of errors at the cost of causing the *apply* and *fix* operators defined later in this section to fail. The other choice is in the typing rules: when the actual type of an argument in an application is a supertype of the required type, the required check could be applied to either the function or the argument part. With a strict semantics of checking for functions, this choice would be immaterial, but given our lenient semantics it is significant. Applying the check to the function part yields the rule

$$\frac{TE \vdash e_{fun} \Rightarrow e_{newfun} : \sigma \rightarrow \mu \quad TE \vdash e_{arg} \Rightarrow e_{newarg} : \tau \quad \tau \geq \sigma}{TE \vdash e_{fun}\, e_{arg} \Rightarrow (e_{newfun} \downarrow_{\tau \rightarrow \mu}^{\sigma \rightarrow \mu})\, e_{newarg} : \mu}$$

Using this rule would make the system "semantically complete" in the sense that no program would be rejected unless its *untyped version* is guaranteed to lead to type error at run-time. However, this seriously damages the ability of the system to detect type errors statically because the lenient semantics of checking for function values makes all checks on them plausible. For this reason, the first rule above applies the check to the argument part. But this is not consistent with coherence—the property that the same typing judgement for an expression, arrived at by different proofs, should correspond semantically to the same coerced value. The problem can be seen with a simple example. The function part of the application $(\lambda x : \Omega.\, x)$ 3 can be coerced using the subtyping rule to $(\lambda x : \Omega.\, x) \uparrow_{\Omega \to \Omega}^{\text{Bool} \to \Omega}$. The argument 3 must then be coerced to $3 \uparrow_{\text{Nat}}^{\Omega} \downarrow_{\text{Bool}}^{\Omega}$ to satisfy the rule above. The coerced expression is implausible; it is guaranteed to lead to error at run-time. However, the original application $(\lambda x : \Omega.\, x)$ 3 can also be coerced by subtyping to $(\lambda x : \Omega.\, x)\, (3 \uparrow_{\text{Nat}}^{\Omega})$ which evaluates without error.

To summarize the design issue, there are three alternatives with increasing expressive power and decreasing detection of static errors:

1. A strict semantics for checking of function values.

2. A lenient semantics with checks caused by applications applied to arguments.

3. A lenient semantics with checks caused by applications applied to functions.

Alternatives (1) and (3) are coherent while (2) is not. However, (2) is not ruled out because the system it implies does possess a "minimal judgement" property (Theorem 7 below) which not only guarantees minimal typing but also a "least error-prone" conversion of the original expression. In other words, the lack of coherence only permits introduction of spurious dynamic errors. We use alternative (2) in this paper, partly to demonstrate its viability and also because it provides an attractive balance of expressive power and static error detection. For many languages, applications such as *apply* and *fix* (see below) would be irrelevant, and alternative (1) might be the preferred choice.

The typing rules possess soundness and completeness properties. In the following, the notation $[\![e]\!]\rho$ denotes the denotation of expression e in environment ρ, and $[\![TE]\!]$ denotes a set of possible environments corresponding to the set TE of typing assumptions for free variables. The denotational semantics of types and expressions is discussed in Section 7. In stating the semantic soundness of the typing rules, Theorem 1 below explicates the semantic role of typing judgements: the intended semantics of an expression in the user language is the just the ordinary semantics of its coerced version.

Theorem 1 (Soundness of Typing Rules) $TE \vdash e \Rightarrow e' : \tau$ implies $\forall \rho \in [\![TE]\!].\, [\![e']\!]\rho \in [\![\tau]\!]$.

In the theorem below, $ClosedExp(TE)$ denotes the set of expressions that are closed relative to TE, *i.e.*, those whose free variables have typing assumptions in TE.

Theorem 2 (Completeness of Typing Rules) $\forall TE.\, \forall e \in ClosedExp(TE).\, \exists e', \tau.\, TE \vdash e \Rightarrow e' : \tau$.

Theorem 2 implies that *all* expressions are statically well-typed in the formal sense. The purpose of the typing process is to insert enough tagging and checking operations to make the expression *prima facie* meaningful. A judgement "$TE \vdash e \Rightarrow e' : \tau$" is a well-typing judgement in the usual sense only if e' does not contain any run-time checks. The detection of ill-typed expressions takes place in the plausibility checking process described in Section 4.

As an example of the use of these typing rules, consider an example from [ACPP89]—a function that applies its first argument to its second argument. The coerced form is shown following a "$\Rightarrow$".

$$\begin{aligned} apply &= \lambda f : \Omega.\, \lambda x : \Omega.\, f\, x \\ &\Rightarrow \lambda f : \Omega.\, \lambda x : \Omega.\, (f \downarrow_{\Omega \to \Omega}^{\Omega})\, x \end{aligned}$$

Using the evaluation rules of Section 6, it is easy to show that the application *apply* $((\lambda y : \text{Nat}.\, y) \uparrow_{\text{Nat} \to \text{Nat}}^{\Omega})$, for instance, is equivalent to $\lambda x : \Omega.\, (x \downarrow_{\text{Nat}}^{\Omega} \uparrow_{\text{Nat}}^{\Omega})$. The details of a related evaluation are described in Section 6.

A nice demonstration of the expressive power of the system is given by the next example, which shows that in contrast to the system of [ACPP89]—which can only allow *specialized* fixpoint operators—we can express a general call-by-value fixpoint operator in a very straightforward way:

$$\begin{aligned} \mathit{fix} &= \lambda f : \Omega \to \Omega.\, d\, d,\ \text{where} \\ d &= \lambda x : \Omega.\, \lambda z : \Omega.\, (f\, (x\, x))\, z \\ &\Rightarrow \lambda f : \Omega \to \Omega.\, d\, (d \uparrow_{\Omega \to (\Omega \to \Omega)}^{\Omega}),\ \text{where} \\ d &= \lambda x : \Omega.\, \lambda z : \Omega.\, ((f\, ((x \downarrow_{\Omega \to \Omega}^{\Omega})\, x)) \downarrow_{\Omega \to \Omega}^{\Omega})\, z \end{aligned}$$

The type of *fix* is $(\Omega \to \Omega) \to (\Omega \to \Omega)$ which seems unusual but, with the semantics for coercions given in Sections 6 and 7, works properly. The details are left as an exercise for the reader. It is interesting to note that the coercions in this example are similar to those needed to provide a coercion-based semantics for the untyped λ-calculus [BTCGS89, pages 113-114 (with $D=\Omega$)].

4 Plausibility Checking

Plausibility checking is a kind of simplification. The process is most naturally specified by a canonical—confluent terminating—set of conditional rewrite rules meant to be used at compile-time. In the rules below, we use the unusual arrow "$\rightsquigarrow$" for the rewrite relation to avoid confusion with the constructor for function types. The notation $\tau \sqcap \sigma$ denotes the GLB of the type expressions τ and σ. Algorithms for GLB and LUB are self-evident. When a rule is conditional, the condition is given above a line like a hypothesis in an inference rule. The symbol *wrong* represents dynamic type-error. It is more formally described in the denotational semantics given in Section 7. Since the tagging and checking operators are only introduced internally by the typing phase and are not available to users, we assume that their occurrences are always "well-formed". An expression such as $\text{true} \downarrow_{\text{Bool}}^{\text{Nat}}$ will never be encountered since the typing rules—by the soundness property—never produce an expression of the form $e \downarrow_\tau^\sigma$ unless $\sigma \geq \tau$ and $[\![e]\!]\rho \in [\![\sigma]\!]$ for an appropriate environment ρ. Similar remarks apply to tagging.

$$e \downarrow_\tau^\tau \rightsquigarrow e \qquad e \uparrow_\tau^\tau \rightsquigarrow e$$

$$e \downarrow_\sigma^\tau \downarrow_\mu^\sigma \rightsquigarrow e \downarrow_\mu^\tau \qquad e \uparrow_\mu^\sigma \uparrow_\sigma^\tau \rightsquigarrow e \uparrow_\mu^\tau$$

$$\frac{\mu = \tau \sqcap \nu}{e \uparrow_\tau^\sigma \downarrow_\nu^\sigma \rightsquigarrow e \downarrow_\mu^\tau \uparrow_\mu^\nu} \qquad \frac{\not\exists \mu.\ \mu = \tau \sqcap \nu}{e \uparrow_\tau^\sigma \downarrow_\nu^\sigma \rightsquigarrow \text{wrong}}$$

The first four of these rules are simple and require no explanation. The last two (conditional) rules embody the essence of plausibility checking. The idea is that a run-time check is plausible only if the known type of the expression being checked and the type required by the check have a *common subtype*. The possibility that this is not so arises when the best (least) known type is not a supertype of the required type. In this case, the typing phase creates a tagging operation followed by a checking operation—this is the pattern addressed by the last two rules. The rules state that, for instance, the check in $e \uparrow_{\text{Nat} \times \Omega}^{\Omega \times \Omega} \downarrow_{\Omega \times \text{Bool}}^{\Omega \times \Omega}$ can only be successful if the untagged value of e belongs to $\text{Nat} \times \text{Bool}$. The first rule therefore changes the expression to $e \downarrow_{\text{Nat} \times \text{Bool}}^{\text{Nat} \times \Omega} \uparrow_{\text{Nat} \times \text{Bool}}^{\Omega \times \text{Bool}}$. Such a simplification is not possible for $e \uparrow_{\text{Bool} \times \Omega}^{\Omega \times \Omega} \downarrow_{\text{Nat} \times \Omega}^{\Omega \times \Omega}$—a type conflict is guaranteed in the first component of the product. The situation is very much like a failure in unifying the known and required type of an expression in ML-like type inference (with a new variable substituted for each occurrence of Ω). The only difference occurs for function types: the types $\text{Nat} \to \text{Nat}$ and $\text{Bool} \to \text{Nat}$ have the common subtype $\Omega \to \text{Nat}$, but they are not unifiable. The semantic justification for these ideas is expressed Theorem 3.

Theorem 3 (Characterization of Implausibility)
If $\not\exists \mu.\ \mu = \tau \sqcap \sigma$ then for any well-formed expression $e \uparrow_\tau^\sigma \downarrow_\nu^\sigma$ and any environment ρ, $[\![e \uparrow_\tau^\sigma \downarrow_\nu^\sigma]\!]\rho = \text{wrong}$.

Given Theorem 3, it is easy to show that plausibility checking is *meaning preserving*. In the following, $ENV(e)$ is the set of all environments which define the free variables of e.

Theorem 4 (Soundness of Plausibility Checking)
$\vdash e \triangleright e'$ *implies* $\forall \rho \in ENV(e).\ [\![e]\!]\rho = [\![e']\!]\rho$.

It is easy to see how the six rewrite rules for plausibility checking can be incorporated in an algorithm. However, such an algorithm is forced to make some arbitrary choices since these rules are *nondeterministic* in the sense that more than one rule may be applicable to a given expression. It is therefore reassuring to note that the set of rules as a whole has pleasant syntactic properties that ensure the deterministic nature of plausibility checking:

Theorem 5 (Canonicity of Plausibility Checking) *If $\leadsto$ is taken to denote an abstract rewrite relation in the sense of [Hue80], then the relation defined by the six rules above is confluent and terminating, i.e., canonical, and therefore produces* unique *normal forms.*

Any algorithm that implements these rewrite rules must therefore compute the same abstract function for deriving the normal forms guaranteed by Theorem 5. We use the symbol **Simplify** to denote this function. The notation "$\vdash e \triangleright e'$" is used to express the *simplification* judgement that "*e is reduced by plausibility checking to the expression e'*". Simplification judgements are derived via the single obvious rule:

$$\vdash e \triangleright \mathbf{Simplify}(e)$$

5 The Algorithm Type

The type inference algorithm **Type** is given in Figure 1. The algorithm is straightforward and efficient. The only opaque spot is the call **Simplify**($e_a \uparrow_{\tau_a}^{\Omega} \downarrow_{\tau_{fa}}^{\Omega}$) in the application case. However, since e_a is already in normal form, the action of this call is very similar—except for the argument parts of function types—to a unification of τ_a and τ_{fa}. Note that this call on **Simplify** may *fail* (produce *wrong*), in which case the application is implausible and the algorithm **Type** returns with failure as well. **Type** is faithful to the typing rules in that when successful it returns a valid typing (and coercion) judgement.

Theorem 6 (Correctness of Type) *If the call* **Type**(TE, e) *succeeds and returns* (τ, e_1), *then for some e_2, $TE \vdash e \Rightarrow e_2 : \tau$ and* **Simplify**$(e_2) = e_1$.

It is very desirable that a typing algorithm have a *completeness* property in the sense that any judgement in the corresponding logic can be factored uniquely into the "minimal" judgement rendered by the algorithm and a simple additional inference step. In a pure typing logic, this translates to the property that the algorithm derives the *principle* type, which in our case is the *minimal* type. When the judgement also involves coercion, an additional *coherence* property of the logic—which asserts that the semantics of the coercion part of a judgement is a function of the typing part—ensures that the factoring via the minimal type works for the coercion part as well. As we explained in Section 3, we choose to abandon coherence in order to find a balance between expressive power and static detection of type-errors. Instead of coherence, we use a weaker but practically sufficient *convergence* property which preserves the notion of a canonical judgement discovered by **Type**. The basis of this property is a partial order relation "$\sqsupseteq$" on semantic values: $v_1 \sqsupseteq v_2$ means that either v_1 is *wrong* or v_1 is "more error-prone" than v_2. This is defined extensionally in roughly the same way as the approximation relation in Scott-domains. A precise definition is given in Section 7. Convergence asserts that corresponding to each typing judgement, there is a *minimal* proof which derives the *least error-prone* coerced version of the given expression. For lack of space, we leave the formal statement of convergence as simply one of the corollaries of the following theorem.

Theorem 7 (Completeness of Type) *If $TE \vdash e \Rightarrow e_1 : \tau$ and* **Simplify**$(e_1) \neq$ *wrong, then* **Type**(TE, e) *succeeds and returns (σ, e_2) such that $\tau \geq \sigma$ and $\forall \rho \in [\![TE]\!]. [\![e_1]\!]\rho \sqsupseteq [\![e_2 \uparrow_\sigma^\tau]\!]\rho$.*

Corollary 8 *For any TE, any $e \in ClosedExp(TE)$ and any type τ, if there are derivations of the form $TE \vdash e \Rightarrow e_1 : \tau$, then there is an expression e_0 such that $TE \vdash e \Rightarrow e_0 : \tau$, and for all $\rho \in [\![TE]\!]. [\![e_1]\!]\rho \sqsupseteq [\![e_0]\!]\rho$ for all such e_1.*

Proof (sketch) The only cases not covered by Theorem 7 are those in which all e_1 are semantically equivalent to *wrong*. The corollary in that case is trivial. ⊣

$$
\begin{aligned}
\textbf{Type}(TE, e) = \ &\text{case } e \text{ of}\\
&x: \ TE(x), x\\
&e_{left}, e_{right}: \ \text{let } \tau_l, e_l = \textbf{Type}(TE, e_{left}) \text{ and } \tau_r, e_r = \textbf{Type}(TE, e_{right})\\
&\qquad \text{in} \quad \tau_l \times \tau_r, \ (e_l, e_r)\\
&\lambda x: \tau.\, e_{body}: \ \text{let } \tau_b, e_b = \textbf{Type}(TE[x \leftarrow \tau], e_{body})\\
&\qquad \text{in} \quad \tau \to \tau_b, \ \lambda x: \tau.\, e_b\\
&e_{fun} \ e_{arg}: \ \text{let } \tau_f, e_f = \textbf{Type}(TE, e_{fun}) \text{ and } \tau_a, e_a = \textbf{Type}(TE, e_{arg})\\
&\qquad \text{in if } \tau_f = \tau_{fa} \to \tau_{fr} \text{ then}\\
&\qquad\qquad \text{let } e_{na} = \textbf{Simplify}(e_a \uparrow^\Omega_{\tau_a} \downarrow^\Omega_{\tau_{fa}}) \text{ in} \quad \tau_{fr}, \ (e_f \ e_{na})\\
&\qquad \text{else if } \tau_f = \Omega \text{ then} \quad \Omega, \ (e_f \downarrow^\Omega_{\tau_a \to \Omega} e_a)\\
&\qquad \text{else fail}
\end{aligned}
$$

Figure 1: *Algorithm* **Type**

6 Operational Semantics

The operational semantics is given in the "natural semantics" style following [ACPP89]. The idea of evaluation is to reduce an expression to a unique normal form. The evaluation judgement "$\vdash e \Rightarrow v$" is read "the expression e reduces to the normal form v". Evaluation is only defined for closed expressions. The call-by-value interpretation is used for evaluation of applications. Non-terminating computations do not have a normal form, and therefore do not have an operational meaning. It is worth noting that the normal forms derived in the operational semantics do *not* always correspond directly to the semantic values used in the denotational semantics, although the two are related by the soundness property stated in Theorem 9. This point and its implications are discussed in Section 8.

Evaluation preserves *wrong*. The role of *wrong* is a bit tricky. This constant represents run-time error, and belongs to all types rather than none. As such, it can be derived as the result of a statically well-typed and plausible expression. It in effect plays two roles in the rules below—it may be the result of evaluating an absurd expression such as (3 true) which would never be produced by the typing phase, or it may be the result of a failed run-time check. It would be more appropriate to use two different constants for these purposes. One could then show that the former case never occurs in "well-typed" expressions. This separation is absent in the rules below.

The semantics of constants, λ-expressions, applications and pairs is similar to [ACPP89]:

$$\vdash \textit{wrong} \Rightarrow \textit{wrong}$$

$$\vdash \lambda x : \tau.\, e \Rightarrow \lambda x : \tau.\, e$$

$$\frac{\vdash e_{fun} \Rightarrow \lambda x : \tau.\, e_{body} \quad \vdash e_{arg} \Rightarrow w \ (w \neq \textit{wrong}) \quad \vdash e_{body}[x \leftarrow w] \Rightarrow v}{\vdash e_{fun} \ e_{arg} \Rightarrow v}$$

$$\frac{\vdash e_{fun} \Rightarrow w \quad (w \neq \lambda x : \tau.\, e_{body})}{\vdash e_{fun} \ e_{arg} \Rightarrow \textit{wrong}}$$

$$\frac{\vdash e_{arg} \Rightarrow \textit{wrong}}{\vdash e_{fun} \ e_{arg} \Rightarrow \textit{wrong}}$$

$$\frac{\vdash e_{left} \Rightarrow l \ (l \neq \textit{wrong}) \quad \vdash e_{right} \Rightarrow r \ (r \neq \textit{wrong})}{\vdash e_{left}, e_{right} \Rightarrow l, r}$$

$$\frac{\vdash e_{left} \Rightarrow \textit{wrong}}{\vdash e_{left}, e_{right} \Rightarrow \textit{wrong}}$$

$$\frac{\vdash e_{right} \Rightarrow \textbf{wrong}}{\vdash e_{left}, e_{right} \Rightarrow \textbf{wrong}}$$

The simplifications performed in plausibility checking are operationally sound:

$$\frac{\vdash e \triangleright e' \qquad \vdash e' \Rightarrow v}{\vdash e \Rightarrow v}$$

There are three cases for evaluating tagging operations. If the value being tagged in not *wrong*, and the *result* type in the tagging operation is not a function type, then the tagged version is in normal form. Note that tagging is not propagated to the components of pairs, although checking (see below) is. Cases where a check is applied to a tagged pair are handled by the simplification judgement used in the rule above.

$$\frac{\vdash e \triangleright e' \uparrow_\tau^\sigma \quad (\sigma \neq \sigma_1 \to \sigma_2) \qquad \vdash e' \Rightarrow w \quad (w \neq \textbf{wrong})}{\vdash e \Rightarrow w \uparrow_\tau^\sigma}$$

Tagging of function values is resolved by applying the implied tagging operations to the argument and result.

$$\frac{\vdash e \Rightarrow \lambda x : \tau_1.\, e_{body}}{\vdash e \uparrow_{\tau_1 \to \tau_2}^{\sigma_1 \to \sigma_2} \Rightarrow \lambda y : \sigma_1.\, (e_{body}[x \leftarrow (y \uparrow_{\sigma_1}^{\tau_1})]) \uparrow_{\tau_2}^{\sigma_2}}$$

The notation $e[x \leftarrow e']$ denotes the expression obtained by replacing the variable x in e by e' avoiding capture of free variables in the usual sense. Finally, tagging preserves *wrong*.

$$\frac{\vdash e \Rightarrow \textbf{wrong}}{\vdash e \uparrow_\tau^\sigma \Rightarrow \textbf{wrong}}$$

An expression with a *check* is obviously never in normal form. When the checked value is a pair, for instance, the check must be propagated to the components.

$$\frac{\vdash e \Rightarrow l, r \qquad \vdash l \downarrow_{\sigma_1}^{\tau_1}, r \downarrow_{\sigma_2}^{\tau_2} \Rightarrow v}{\vdash e \downarrow_{\sigma_1 \times \sigma_2}^{\tau_1 \times \tau_2} \Rightarrow v}$$

Checks on function values are resolved by applying the implied checking operations to the argument and result. The object of a (nontrivial) check on a function value often does not belong to a subtype of the required type. This is the only case in which a check nonetheless succeeds under such circumstances.

$$\frac{\vdash e \Rightarrow \lambda x : \sigma_1.\, e_{body}}{\vdash e \downarrow_{\tau_1 \to \tau_2}^{\sigma_1 \to \sigma_2} \Rightarrow \lambda y : \tau_1.\, (e_{body}[x \leftarrow (y \downarrow_{\sigma_1}^{\tau_1})]) \downarrow_{\tau_2}^{\sigma_2}}$$

All checks which remain *after simplification* but do not match the two rules above fail. There is no need to specify the behavior of checks on atomic values such as 1 or **true** because successful checks on such values are always resolved by simplification.

$$\frac{\vdash e \triangleright e' \downarrow_\tau^\sigma \qquad \vdash e' \Rightarrow w \quad (w \neq \lambda x : \tau.\, e,\ w \neq l, r)}{\vdash e \Rightarrow \textbf{wrong}}$$

As an application of these evaluation rules, consider the evaluation of the expression z defined as

$$z = (apply\, ((\lambda y : \textsf{Nat}.\, y) \uparrow_{\textsf{Nat} \to \textsf{Nat}}^{\Omega}))\, (3 \uparrow_{\textsf{Nat}}^{\Omega})$$

The function part of the application in z is not in normal form. By first rule for applications, the function part reduces to the normal form

$$\lambda x : \Omega.\, ((\lambda y : \textsf{Nat}.\, y) \uparrow_{\textsf{Nat} \to \textsf{Nat}}^{\Omega}) \downarrow_{\Omega \to \Omega}^{\Omega}\, x$$

Note that the *bodies* of λ-expressions do not have to be in normal form. By the definition of *apply* and the first rule for applications, the normal form of z therefore reduces to the normal form of

$$((\lambda y : \textsf{Nat}.\, y) \uparrow_{\textsf{Nat} \to \textsf{Nat}}^{\Omega} \downarrow_{\Omega \to \Omega}^{\Omega})\, (3 \uparrow_{\textsf{Nat}}^{\Omega})$$

The simplified version of the function part of this application (using the simplification judgement rule) is

$$(\lambda y : \textsf{Nat}.\, y) \downarrow_{\Omega \to \textsf{Nat}}^{\textsf{Nat} \to \textsf{Nat}} \uparrow_{\Omega \to \textsf{Nat}}^{\Omega \to \Omega}$$

Applying the rules for checking and tagging for function values, this reduces to the normal form

$$\lambda y : \Omega.\, y \uparrow_\Omega^\Omega \downarrow_{\textsf{Nat}}^\Omega \downarrow_{\textsf{Nat}}^{\textsf{Nat}} \uparrow_{\textsf{Nat}}^\Omega$$

which is equivalent to (but does not need to be reduced to) the form $\lambda y : \Omega.\, y \downarrow_{\textsf{Nat}}^{\Omega} \uparrow_{\textsf{Nat}}^{\Omega}$ mentioned in Section 3. The normal form of z therefore reduces to the normal form of

$$(\lambda y{:}\Omega.\, y \uparrow^\Omega_\Omega \downarrow^\Omega_{\text{Nat}} \downarrow^{\text{Nat}}_{\text{Nat}} \uparrow^\Omega_{\text{Nat}})\ (3 \uparrow^\Omega_{\text{Nat}})$$

which by the first application rule, and simplification, reduces to just $3 \uparrow^\Omega_{\text{Nat}}$ as expected.

7 Denotational Semantics

The value domain used for semantics is defined by the following domain equation, in which B is the flat domain of booleans, N is the flat domain of natural numbers, and W is the type-error domain $\{w\}_\bot$.

$$V \cong B + N + (V \to V) + (V \times V) + (V \times \textit{Typecode}) + W$$

The semantics of type expressions—given in Figure 2—is almost identical to that of [ACPP89]. The only difference is that *wrong* ($= w$ in V) in our semantics represents run-time type error—the only kind there is. It belongs to *every* type rather than none. This is left implicit in the equations below. The ideal *Dynamic* used as the meaning of Ω is defined as the solution of a recursive domain equation. The details including the argument for the existence of the solution are given in [ACPP89].

$[\![\textbf{Bool}]\!] = B$ $[\![\textbf{Nat}]\!] = N$ $[\![\Omega]\!] = \textit{Dynamic}$

$[\![\tau \to \sigma]\!] = \{c \mid c([\![\tau]\!]) \subseteq [\![\sigma]\!]\}$

$[\![\tau \times \sigma]\!] = \{\langle a, b \rangle \mid a \in [\![\tau]\!] \text{ and } b \in [\![\sigma]\!]\}$

Figure 2: **Semantics of Type Expressions**

The most important constructions in the notation used for the semantics of object expressions are:

- d in V (where $d \in D$ and D is a summand of V) is the injection of d into V. Therefore we always have $(d \text{ in } V) \in V$.

- *wrong* is just w in V.

- $v \in D$ (where $v \in V$ and D is a summand of V) yields $\bot_B$ if $v = \bot_V$, true if $v = d$ in V for some $d \in D$, and false otherwise.

$tag(x, \tau, \sigma)$

$= \textit{if } \tau = \sigma \textit{ then } x$

   $\textit{else if } \sigma = \Omega \textit{ then } \langle x, \tau \rangle \text{ in } V$

   $\textit{else if } x \in V \to V \textit{ then}$

      $\textit{let } \tau_1 \to \tau_2 = \tau \textit{ and } \sigma_1 \to \sigma_2 = \sigma$

      $\textit{in } (\lambda y.\, tag(x|_{V \to V}(tag(y, \sigma_1, \tau_1))), \tau_2, \sigma_2) \text{ in } V$

   $\textit{else if } x \in V \times V \textit{ then}$

      $\textit{let } \langle x_1, x_2 \rangle = x|_{V \times V},\ \tau_1 \times \tau_2 = \tau$

      $\textit{and } \sigma_1 \times \sigma_2 = \sigma$

      $\textit{in } \langle tag(x_1, \tau_1, \sigma_1), tag(x_2, \tau_2, \sigma_2) \rangle \text{ in } V$

$\textit{else wrong}$

Figure 3: **Semantics of Tagging**

- $v|_D$ (where $v \in V$ and D is a summand of V) yields d if $v = d$ in V for some $d \in D$, and $\bot_D$ otherwise.

Using this notation, the "more error-prone" ordering ($\sqsupseteq$) used in Theorem 7 is defined as:

- $\forall v \in V.\ \textit{wrong} \sqsupseteq v$.

- If $f, g \in V \to V$, then $f \sqsupseteq g \iff \forall v \in V.\ f|_{V \to V}(v) \sqsupseteq g|_{V \to V}(v)$.

- If $x, y \in V \times V$, $x|_{V \times V} = \langle x_1, x_2 \rangle$ and $y|_{V \times V} = \langle y_1, y_2 \rangle$, then $x \sqsupseteq y \iff x_1 \sqsupseteq y_1$ and $x_2 \sqsupseteq y_2$.

The semantic equations for object expressions use two auxiliary functions which describe the semantics of tagging and checking. Of these, the tagging function is given in Figure 3 and the function for checking is given in Figure 4. The clause for function values in the latter is the only situation in which a check succeeds even if the type of the underlying value does not belong to a subtype of the required type. The semantic equations for object expressions are given in Figure 5. All cases except those for tagging and checking operations are standard. The latter assume as before that the expressions involved are well-formed.

$$
\begin{aligned}
&check(x, \tau, \sigma) \\
&= \textbf{if } \tau = \sigma \textbf{ then } x \\
&\quad \textbf{else if } \tau \leq \sigma \textbf{ then } tag(x, \tau, \sigma) \\
&\quad \textbf{else if } x \in V \times Typecode \textbf{ then} \\
&\quad\quad let\ \langle y, \mu \rangle = x|_{V \times Typecode}\ in\ check(y, \mu, \sigma) \\
&\quad \textbf{else if } x \in V \to V \textbf{ then} \\
&\quad\quad let\ \tau_1 \to \tau_2 = \tau\ and\ \sigma_1 \to \sigma_2 = \sigma \\
&\quad\quad in\ (\lambda y.\ check(x|_{V \to V}(check(y, \sigma_1, \tau_1))), \tau_2, \sigma_2) \\
&\quad \textbf{else if } x \in V \times V \textbf{ then} \\
&\quad\quad let\ \langle x_1, x_2 \rangle = x|_{V \times V},\ \tau_1 \times \tau_2 = \tau \\
&\quad\quad\quad and\ \sigma_1 \times \sigma_2 = \sigma \\
&\quad\quad in\ \langle check(x_1, \tau_1, \sigma_1), check(x_2, \tau_2, \sigma_2) \rangle \\
&\quad \textbf{else wrong}
\end{aligned}
$$

Figure 4: **Semantics of Checking**

The connection between the operational and denotational semantics is expressed in the following theorem, which simply asserts that operational evaluation preserves denotational meaning.

Theorem 9 (Soundness of Evaluation) *Given an arbitrary expression e and a normal form expression v, $\vdash e \Rightarrow v$ implies that $[\![e]\!]\emptyset = [\![v]\!]\emptyset$.*

It is important to note that the operational semantics is less abstract than the denotational semantics (otherwise the implication in Theorem 9 would be an equivalence) and the denotational semantics itself is not fully abstract. For instance, the values $\langle\langle 2, \text{true}\rangle, \text{Nat} \times \text{Bool}\rangle$ and $\langle\langle\langle 2, \text{Nat}\rangle, \text{true}\rangle, \Omega \times \text{Bool}\rangle$ are derived for the expressions $(2, \text{true}) \uparrow_{\text{Nat} \times \text{Bool}}^{\Omega}$ and $(2 \uparrow_{\text{Nat}}^{\Omega}, \text{true}) \uparrow_{\Omega \times \text{Bool}}^{\Omega}$ respectively, but these values cannot be observably distinguished. It does not seem worth while to complicate the semantics to avoid this quirk but the necessary modification is easily made if needed.

$$
\begin{aligned}
&[\![e \downarrow_\sigma^\tau]\!]\rho = let\ x = [\![e]\!]\rho\ in\ check(x, \tau, \sigma) \\
&[\![e \uparrow_\tau^\sigma]\!]\rho = let\ x = [\![e]\!]\rho\ in\ tag(x, \tau, \sigma) \\
&[\![e_{fun}\ e_{arg}]\!]\rho = let\ f = [\![e_{fun}]\!]\rho\ and\ x = [\![e_{arg}]\!]\rho\ in \\
&\quad\quad if\ f \not\in V \to V\ then\ \textbf{wrong}\ else\ f|_{V \to V}(x) \\
&[\![e_{left},\ e_{right}]\!]\rho = let\ l = [\![e_{left}]\!]\rho\ and\ r = [\![e_{right}]\!]\rho \\
&\quad\quad in\ \langle l, r \rangle \\
&[\![\lambda x : \tau.\ e]\!]\rho = \lambda v.\ [\![e]\!](\rho[x \leftarrow v])
\end{aligned}
$$

Figure 5: **Semantics of Object Expressions**

8 Pragmatic Issues

The implementation of our system does not present any fundamentally new problems (see [ACPP89] for a discussion of relevant techniques). Type matching in our system clearly requires Amber-like structural representation of types at run-time since the subtyping scheme is based on structural matching.

From a pragmatic viewpoint, the differences between the operational and denotational semantics raise interesting questions about the details of an implementation. For instance, tagging of pair values is propagated to components in the latter but not in the former. Propagation in the denotational semantics is forced because the ideal representing tagged values makes no provision for the "result type" tag $\Omega \times \Omega$ in a normal form such as $(2, \text{true}) \uparrow_{\text{Nat} \times \text{Bool}}^{\Omega \times \Omega}$. Similar remarks apply to other data structures. For instance, the tagging in the example $l_3 = l \uparrow_{[\text{Nat}]}^{[\Omega]}$ used in Section 2 must be propagated to components in the denotational semantics. There is essentially a tradeoff between time and space here. An implementation according to the operational semantics must often provide space for two tags per tagged value instead of one, but both tagging and checking would on average be faster than in an implementation according to the denotational semantics.

A related issue is raised by applications such as

$sum\ ([1\uparrow^{\Omega}_{\text{Nat}}, 2\uparrow^{\Omega}_{\text{Nat}}, 3\uparrow^{\Omega}_{\text{Nat}}, 4\uparrow^{\Omega}_{\text{Nat}}]\downarrow^{[\Omega]}_{[\text{Nat}]})$. A straightforward implementation of such checks would involve two passes over the list: one to carry out the check and another to carry out the sum (since the check is successful). A possible method to avoid this is to make checks on data structures "lazy"—propagated when the structure is eliminated. This would seem to erase our advantage—over LISP-like languages—of early detection of type errors. However, information about the *origin* of the check can be propagated along with the check, and used to pinpoint the actual source of the error if a propagated check fails. Although the detection of the error would be delayed, the reported error would be the same as in the straightforward implementation, at the cost of some overhead in carrying the information about the source of a check.

A system with automatic transitions from static to dynamic typing raises some serious methodological issues. Cardelli [Car89] points out that automatic generation of run-time *checks* could be dangerous since users might not be aware of the points where they are being used. A slight change to a statically well-typed program may unwittingly cause a whole set of automatic dynamic checks to be inserted. This could reduce the robustness of the program below the programmer's intentions. One solution would be to modify our system to require the user's "written permission" (through a dialog box, for instance) for insertion of checks. The denial of such permission is equivalent to a static type error. Such interaction may become tedious if intended checks are numerous. A better solution is to provide two different constructs for function application—a strict one which prohibits checks and a permissive one which allows them. The programmer would then retain responsibility for insertion of checks without the burden of writing the corresponding code. The language we consider in this paper does not have these safeguards, but their introduction does not seem to pose any technical problems.

9 Concluding Remarks

We have described a system that merges static and dynamic typing with very little added complexity at the user level. The interpretation of dynamic typing we use is more abstract than existing static systems which allow some dynamic typing and is closer in spirit to that in LISP-like pure dynamic systems.

Two underlying themes in the paper are worth recalling. One is the use of coercive structural subtyping as a way of specifying simple kinds of program synthesis. This technique is very promising as a way of adding expressive power to a language at relatively little cost in semantic complexity. An application of the technique to APL-like implicit scaling is described in [Tha89]. Robinson and Tennent [RT88] have suggested an application to the record update problem.

A related theme is the idea of negative coercions and plausibility checking. This is clearly applicable in many subtyping situations, both inclusive and coercive. A simple example is automatic generation (and plausibility) of bounds checks for subranges. More complex examples might involve labeled records or explicitly declared inheritance relationships among abstract types. As we mentioned in the introduction, much of the theory presented above can be generalized to account for a large class of such examples.

The coercion based interpretation of inheritance used in this paper is similar in spirit to the framework of [BTCGS89]. We hope to explore this connection to generalize the present system to polymorphic and recursive types.

10 Acknowledgements

I would like to thank Luca Cardelli for a discussion which clarified some basic ideas for me, and Jens Dill, Uwe Pleban and Fritz Ruehr for helpful comments on a previous version of this paper.

References

[ABC+83] M.P. Atkinson, P.J. Bailey, K.J. Chisholm, P.W. Cockshott, and R. Morrison. An approach to persistent programming. *The Computer Journal*, 26(4):360–365, 1983.

[ACPP89] Martin Abadi, Luca Cardelli, Benjamin Pierce, and Gordon Plotkin. Dynamic typing in a statically typed language. In *Proc. of Sixteenth POPL Symposium*. ACM, January 1989.

[BTCGS89] V. Breazu-Tannen, T. Coquand, C. Gunter, and A. Scedrov. Inheritance and explicit coercion. In *Proc. of Fourth LICS Symposium*. IEEE, June 1989.

[Car86] Luca Cardelli. Amber. In Guy Cousineau, Pierre-Louis Curien, and Bernard Robinet, editors, *Combinators and Functional Programming Languages*. Springer Verlag, 1986. Lecture Notes in Computer Science, Vol. 242.

[Car89] Luca Cardelli, January 1989. Personal Communication.

[CDJ+89] Luca Cardelli, James Donahue, Mick Jordan, Bill Kaslow, and Greg Nelson. The modula-3 type system. In *Proc. of Sixteenth POPL Symposium*. ACM, January 1989.

[CW85] L. Cardelli and P. Wegner. On understanding types, data abstraction and polymorphism. *Computing Surveys*, 17(4), 1985.

[Hue80] G. Huet. Confluent reductions: Abstract properties and applications to term rewriting. *J. Assoc. Comp. Mach.*, 27(4):797–821, 1980.

[RT88] Edmund Robinson and Robert Tennent, October 1988. Note sent to "Types" E-mail forum.

[Tha88] Satish R. Thatte. Type inference with partial types. In Timo Lepisto and Arto Salomaa, editors, *Automata, languages and programming : 15th International Colloquium*, pages 615–629. Springer-Verlag, July 1988. Lecture Notes in Computer Science, Vol. 317.

[Tha89] Satish R. Thatte. Type inference and implicit scaling, 1989. To Appear.

[Wad76] C. Wadsworth. The relation between computational and denotational properties for Scott's D_∞ models of the λ-calculus. *SIAM J. Comput.*, 5(3):488–520, 1976.

Deciding ML Typability is Complete for Deterministic Exponential Time

HARRY G. MAIRSON
Department of Computer Science
Brandeis University
Waltham, Massachusetts 02254

Abstract. A well known but incorrect piece of functional programming folklore is that ML expressions can be efficiently typed in polynomial time. In probing the truth of that folklore, various researchers, including Wand, Buneman, Kanellakis, and Mitchell, constructed simple counterexamples consisting of typable ML programs having length n, with principal types having $\Omega(2^{cn})$ distinct type variables and length $\Omega(2^{2^{cn}})$. When the types associated with these ML constructions were represented as directed acyclic graphs, their sizes grew as $\Omega(2^{cn})$. The folklore was even more strongly contradicted by the recent result of Kanellakis and Mitchell that simply deciding whether or not an ML expression is typable is PSPACE-hard.

We improve the latter result, showing that deciding ML typability is DEXPTIME-hard. As Kanellakis and Mitchell have shown containment in DEXPTIME, the problem is DEXPTIME-complete. The proof of DEXPTIME-hardness is carried out via a generic reduction: it consists of a very straightforward simulation of any deterministic one-tape Turing machine M with input x running in $O(c^{|x|})$ time by a polynomial-sized ML formula $\Phi_{M,x}$, such that M accepts x iff $\Phi_{M,x}$ is typable. The simulation of the transition function δ of the Turing Machine is realized uniquely through terms in the lambda calculus *without* the use of the polymorphic *let* construct. We use *let* for two purposes only: to generate an exponential amount of blank tape for the Turing Machine simulation to begin, and to compose an exponential number of applications of the ML formula simulating state transition.

It is purely the expressive power of ML polymorphism to succinctly express function composition which results in a proof of DEXPTIME-hardness. We conjecture that lower bounds on deciding typability for extensions to the typed lambda calculus can be regarded precisely in terms of this expressive capacity for succinct function composition.

To further understand this lower bound, we relate it to the problem of proving equality of type variables in a system of type equations generated from an ML expression with let-polymorphism. We show that given an oracle for solving this problem, deciding typability would be in PSPACE, as would be the actual computation of the principal type of the expression, were it indeed typable.

1 Introduction.

ML [Mi78][HMM86] is a well known functional programming language incorporating a variety of novel features, and prominent in its contributions to programming language design is its polymorphic typing system. A strongly typed language like Pascal is completely type checked at compile time, obviating the need for runtime type checking; the penalty is that code which has been written in a largely "type independent" style (stacks, trees, or even the identity function) must be repeated with only changes in type declarations. On the other hand, a naive Lisp compiler will do no compile time type checking, allowing Lisp code to be freely reused on different data types, but the

Permission to copy without fee all or part of this material is granted provided that the copies are not made or distributed for direct commercial advantage, the ACM copyright notice and the title of the publication and its date appear, and notice is given that copying is by permission of the Association for Computing Machinery. To copy otherwise, or to republish, requires a fee and/or specific permission.

© 1990 ACM 089791-343-4/90/0001/0382 $1.50

price paid is run time type checking.

The ML idea of type polymorphism is a successful attempt to get part of the best of both worlds. Given an ML expression, a precisely defined *type discipline* automatically infers the functional type of the expression, or rejects the expression as untypable. The simplest example of this type polymorphism in action is the identity function. In the ML expression *let $I = \lambda x.x$ in $\langle body \rangle$*, the identifier I is thought to have functional type $t \to t$ for *any* type t, and separate (so-called "let-bound") instances of the identifier I in the expression $\langle body \rangle$ do not further constrain each other in terms of inferring their types. This contrasts with "lambda-bound" variables, where each instance in the body must have *identical* and not merely isomorphic type. A Lisp-like interpretation of the ML expression *let $I = \lambda x.x$ in II* would be as syntactic sugar for $(\lambda I.II)(\lambda x.x)$, but the ML interpretation is better thought of as $(\lambda y.y)(\lambda x.x)$, which would infer that $\lambda x.x$ was of type $t \to t$, that $\lambda y.y$ was of type $(t \to t) \to (t \to t)$, and that the entire expression was then of type $t \to t$. The Lisp-like interpretation $(\lambda I.II)(\lambda x.x)$ would be rejected by the ML type discipline, however, since the lambda-bound variable I is forced to have both type $t \to u$ (in its "function" incarnation in the body) as well as type t in its "argument" incarnation. The type discipline insists via unification that $t = t \to u$, and on the basis of this positive *occur check*, the subexpression $\lambda I.II$ is declared untypable. The fact that, of course, this example does *not* cause a type error motivates the search for more robust type disciplines.

In embedding such polymorphic type inference in a programming language, there are natural concerns that the inference mechanism be *decidable* so that the compiler can terminate, and *efficient* so that termination is within a reasonable amount of time. In his original paper, Milner made it clear that the former was true, and straightforward termination and correctness proofs (for example, [W87], which is actually a correctness proof for typing pure lambda terms, but works for ML with trivial changes) have since been published.

Certainly in practice, the inference system has been efficient, which led to the belief that this efficiency was a polynomial time one, i.e., that typing an ML expression of length n could be done in time polynomial in n. Upon closer scrutiny, however, this putative folk theorem turned out instead to be unsubstantiated folk lore.

First, it was observed by several researchers, including Buneman, Kanellakis, Mitchell, and Wand, that there exist pathological ML expressions whose principal type is of vastly larger size than the original expression.

Example 1.1.

$$\begin{aligned}&let\ x_0 = \lambda z.z \\ &in\ let\ x_1 = \langle x_0, x_0 \rangle \\ &\quad in\ let\ x_2 = \langle x_1, x_1 \rangle \\ &\quad\quad in\ ... \\ &\quad\quad\quad in\ let\ x_n = \langle x_n, x_n \rangle \\ &\quad\quad\quad\quad in\ x_n\end{aligned}$$

Example 1.2.

$$\begin{aligned}&let\ x_1 = \lambda y.\langle y, y \rangle \\ &in\ let\ x_2 = \lambda y.x_1(x_1(y)) \\ &\quad in\ ... \\ &\quad\quad in\ let\ x_n = \lambda y.x_{n-1}(x_{n-1}(y)) \\ &\quad\quad\quad in\ x_n(\lambda z.z)\end{aligned}$$

(We use $\langle x, y \rangle$ as an abbreviation for $\lambda z.zxy$, the familiar lambda calculus implementation of pairing.)

In Example 1.1, we have a construction for ML expressions of length n which include $\Omega(2^{cn})$ distinct type variables. Even more pathological is the construction of Example 1.2, based on repeated function composition: it has a principal type which is of length $\Omega(2^{2^{cn}})$ when printed as a string, and has a representation as a directed acyclic graph with $\Omega(2^{cn})$ nodes. The author type checked the expression when $n = 5$ using Standard ML running on a Sun 3/160 workstation, a computation which consumed over 2 minutes of processor time, 60 megabytes of memory, and output 173 printed pages of the principal type until output summarily aborted. [1] This experiment places many comments about typing and software engineering in a curious light, for instance, the (by no means unusual) remark in [Pf88] that "[Types]...provide a succinct and formal documentation and thus help the programmer read, debug, and maintain his programs."

Secondly, a more sophisticated and more damning blow was struck at the folklore of efficiency of ML typing by Kanellakis and Mitchell [KM89], who showed that simply *deciding whether or not an ML expression is indeed typable* is PSPACE-hard, indicating that the difficulty of typing expressions is not merely intractible because of the size of the output, but because of complexities of a more intrinsic nature. An upper bound is given by them that the typability question (and indeed, the actual computation of the principal type) can be answered in DEXPTIME. They mention the resolution of the complexity of this decision problem as an outstanding open question, leaving speculation that its difficulty might be greater than that computable in polynomial space.

After all this bad news, some good news is in order. Unfortunately, this paper only gives more bad news: we show here that deciding ML typability for the "Core ML" language treated by Kanellakis and Mitchell is actually DEXPTIME-hard. As a consequence, deciding ML typability is complete for deterministic exponential time. We note that a simultaneous proof [KTU89a] has been announced, using altogether different methods.

This bound is of obvious relevance to the understanding the typing mechanisms of a variety of functional languages which have been built in part around the ML type discipline, e.g., Miranda, Orwell, Haskell, etc. It also provides interesting insights into problems in software engineering concerning reusable code, because let-polymorphism is precisely a mechanism for specifying that code, and ensuring that its subsequent use will not generate run-time type errors.

1.1 Lower bounds.

Lower bounds proofs relating to complexity classes generally fall into two categories: reductions from problems of known and proven difficulty, and generic reductions. For example, the PSPACE-hardness proof in [KM89] is a reduction from Quantified Boolean Formulas (QBF), already known to be complete for PSPACE. The intuition of Kanellakis and Mitchell was primarily derived from Example 1.1 above: they realized that the use of ML polymorphism essentially described in this example could also be used to simulate truth tables. Even though a truth table on n variables is of exponential size, their insight was that a short (i.e., polynomial in n) ML program could "expand" exponentially via *let*-reduction (the *let*-equivalent of β-reduction) to simulate the table.

We present in contrast a *generic* reduction: given any deterministic one-tape Turing machine M with input x running in $O(c^{|x|})$ time, we show how to construct an ML formula $\Phi_{M,x}$, such that M accepts x iff $\Phi_{M,x}$ is typable, where the length of $\Phi_{M,x}$ is polynomial in the length of the description of M and x. Since every language L in DEXPTIME has a deterministic Turing Machine M_L which can decide if $x \in L$ for input x in $O(c^{|x|})$ time, this reduction shows that the difficulty of deciding typability of ML expressions is (within a polynomial factor) as hard as deciding membership in the "hardest" languages in DEXPTIME. We note that there are languages in DEXPTIME requiring exponential time and space infinitely often, for example, deciding if a *semiregular* expression (regular operators plus intersection) over some alphabet Σ denotes Σ^* [AHU][Hu73].

The simple intuition providing the foundation of the DEXPTIME-hardness proof presented here is motivated by the above Example 1.2. The intuition is the following: note that the function x_n in the example is equivalent to the lambda term

---

[1] Space limitations naturally restrict a full report on this experiment; we include a summary in Appendix A. A serious question is motivated by this little test: if a decidable type system can output 50 unreadable pages of principal type with huge computational overhead, does it really make any difference if the type system is decidable?

$\lambda y.x_0^{2^{n-1}}(y)$, namely, a function which applies the x_0 function an exponential number of times to its argument. If y was a piece of Turing Machine tape, and x_0 was a function which added a tape square to the tape, x_n would be a good function for constructing exponential-sized Turing Machine IDs. If y was a Turing Machine ID, and x_0 was its transition function δ, x_n would be a good way to "turn the transition crank" and apply δ an exponential number of times to the initial machine ID. Of course, there are many technical details to work out, but the inspiration is simply that the "exp" in "exponential function composition" is the same "exp" in "DEXPTIME." It is uniquely the expressive power of ML polymorphism to succinctly express function composition which results in a proof of DEXPTIME-hardness. We conjecture that stronger lower bounds on deciding typability for extensions to the ML typing system—or, for that matter, extensions to the typed lambda calculus— can be regarded precisely in terms of this capacity for succinct function composition.

In our proof, the technical mechanics simulating the transition function δ of the Turing Machine are realized purely through terms in the lambda calculus *without* the use of the polymorphic *let* construct. The transition function can be represented in a straightforward manner by a Boolean circuit, where the inputs are variables q_i set to *true* iff the machine is in state i, and variables z and o indicate whether the tape head is reading a 0 or a 1. The output of the circuit indicates the new state, what is written on the tape cell, and the head direction. As we will show, all of this circuitry can be realized by lambda terms, using the Boolean gadgets of Kanellakis and Mitchell, originally proposed in their paper on the inherent sequentiality of unification [DKM84], and recycled most recently as lambda terms in their PSPACE-hardness proof. We add a Boolean "fanout" gate to their logical menagerie in the interest of facilitating our proof.

We present the proof in "bottom up" form, showing first how to encode Boolean values as lambda terms, adding Boolean logic, Turing machine state encoding, tape encoding, proceding piece by piece to build up the entire simulation. It may come as a shock to some more practical functional programming language enthusiasts that this rather arcane lower bound *is just a computer program*, where we are interested in the *type* produced by the program instead of the *value*. The generic reduction, as one of my colleagues with more applied interests put it, is just a compiler: namely, how to compile Turing Machines into ML types. Since our "object code" is ML, we have endeavored to follow the gospel of [AS85] wherever possible, using modularization and data abstraction to make the program and proof more understandable.

1.2 Polymorphic unification.

We then proceed from this lower bound to a further understanding why deciding typability is so difficult, focusing our attention on the kind of type equations which must be solved (using unification) to decide whether an ML expression is typable. Given such a set of type equations, and two type variables chosen from this set, a natural question is to ask whether the variables must have the same value in the unification solution. Were this solvable efficiently (e.g., by an oracle), we show that deciding typability, and in addition the computation of the actual type, can be done in polynomial space. It is, therefore, this particular question about unification which is the bottleneck in deciding typability. It turns out that there is a natural correspondence between this question and the encoding of Boolean logic which is integral to our Turing Machine simulation.

2 The DEXPTIME-hardness bound.

We present the ML program constructed from a Turing Machine M and input x as a series of equations which are meant to be nested as a series of *let*-expressions. The program is written in "Core ML," i.e. the language defined as:

$$E ::= x \mid \lambda x.E \mid EE \mid \text{let } x = E \text{ in } E$$

In some instances, we also give the principal type of the expression to clarify its significance. In the ML "type hacking" which follows, we acknowledge an obvious debt to the authors of [KM89], who introduced many of the techniques; the contribution of this paper is to use them more expressively. The coding tricks used here allow types to simulate calculations by exploiting the power of polymorphism to drive the inference engine of unification, in the same spirit that Church showed how the values of lambda terms could, via β-reduction, simulate computation.

2.1 Notation. Miscellaneous combinators.

$$\begin{aligned} I &= \lambda z.z \\ K &= \lambda x.\lambda y.x \\ Eq &= \lambda x.\lambda y.K\ x\ \lambda z.K\ (z\,x)(z\,y): \\ & a \longrightarrow a \longrightarrow a \end{aligned}$$

$$\langle \phi_1, \phi_2, \ldots, \phi_n \rangle = \\ \lambda z.z\phi_1\phi_2\ldots\phi_n : \\ (t_1 \longrightarrow t_2 \longrightarrow \cdots \longrightarrow t_n \longrightarrow u) \longrightarrow u$$

$$pair = \\ \lambda x.\lambda y.\lambda x'.\lambda y'.\lambda z.K\ z \\ (K\ Eq(x,x')\ Eq(y,y')) : \\ a \longrightarrow b \longrightarrow a \longrightarrow b \longrightarrow c \longrightarrow c$$

We typically write $Eq(x, y)$ instead of $Eq\ x\ y$. The importance of the Eq combinator is that for ML to correctly type $Eq(\phi, \psi)$, the ML expressions ϕ and ψ are constrained to have identical type. When ϕ and ψ are lambda-bound variables, this constraint can affect the types of other expressions: it is this phenomenon which permits us to carry out the reduction. If the constraint is impossible (i.e., causing a positive occur check), a mistyping occurs and the entire expression is rejected.

Notice that in the definition of $\langle \phi_1, \ldots, \phi_n \rangle$, we imagine the formula ϕ_i to have principal type t_i, and in the entire expression, the types t_i do not necessarily constrain each other. When an ML formula $\lambda w.Kw\langle \phi_1, \ldots, \phi_n \rangle$ is typed, it has the same principal type as the I combinator, *provided* that the type constraints introduced by the ϕ_i can be satisfied. This construct allows a transparent means of introducing constraints on types of subexpressions.

The definition of *pair* introduces the type equivalent of the Lisp **cons**. Instead of *pair x y* we usually write $[x; y]$. When applied to two terms x and y, the term $[x; y]$ has type $a \longrightarrow b \longrightarrow c \longrightarrow c$, where a is the type of x and b is the type of y. If u and v are ML lambda-bound variables and we need to type the function application $[x; y]\ u\ v$, then the types of x and u must be the same, as must be the types of y and v.

2.2 Boolean values: *true* and *false*.

$$\begin{aligned} true &= \lambda x.\lambda y.\lambda z.K\ z\ Eq(x,y): \\ & a \longrightarrow a \longrightarrow b \longrightarrow b \\ false &= \lambda x.\lambda y.\lambda z.z: \\ & a \longrightarrow b \longrightarrow c \longrightarrow c \end{aligned}$$

The types of *true* and *false* are virtually identical. If we regard them as functions, the only difference is that the first two (curried) arguments of *true* must be of the same type. If *true* is applied to two arguments whose types cannot be unified, for example I and Eq, then a mistyping occurs; on the other hand, *false I Eq* can be typed. In the innermost *let* in our ML simulation of a Turing Machine, then, we produce a Boolean value indicating if the machine rejected its input, and apply that value to two non-unifiable arguments; the whole formula types properly iff the machine accepts. (For more details, see Section 2.12.)

2.3 Zero and One (Tape Symbols).

$$zero = [true; false]$$
$$= \lambda x.\lambda y.\lambda z.K\,z$$
$$\langle Eq(x, true), Eq(y, false)\rangle$$
$$one = [false; true]$$
$$= \lambda x.\lambda y.\lambda z.K\,z$$
$$\langle Eq(x, false), Eq(y, true)\rangle$$

Now we define predicates telling if a cell holds a zero or a one:

$$zero? = \lambda cell.\lambda x.\lambda y.\lambda z.K z$$
$$\lambda p.\langle cell\ p,\ p\ x\ y\rangle$$

Observe that *cell p* causes p to unify with the "first" component in the cell, and then $p\,x\,y$ "loads" the right "type bindings" for x and y in the "answer" $\lambda x.\lambda y.\lambda z.z$, possibly unifying x and y if p encodes *true*.

The definition of *zero?* also demonstrates a general style for using ML to compute with types. Note first the declarations of "inputs" and "outputs," though in the relational calculus of unification they are really one and the same—it matters only which of the two you choose to constrain! The $\lambda z.Kz$ marks the end of the inputs and outputs; next comes the "local declarations," of which we have only one, for p. In the brackets, we have the "body" of the procedure. It is intuitively useful for us to think of the instructions in the body being executed from top to bottom, even if they represent a set of constraints which are being realized "simultaneously."

$$one? = \lambda cell.\lambda x.\lambda y.\lambda z.Kz$$
$$\lambda p.\lambda q.\langle cell\ pq,\ q\ x\ y\rangle$$

The importance of this encoding scheme for zero and one is that we simulate the Boolean circuitry in the finite state control of the Turing Machine using only the *monotone* functions *and* and *or*. By encoding zero and one as these pairs of Boolean values, we do not need to simulate negation, because we have encoded whether the tape symbol is a zero in the type bound to x, and the negation in the type bound to y.

2.4 Boolean operators *and* and *or*. Fanout.

We implement these monotone Boolean operators using the gadgets introduced in [DKM84]. We add yet another gadget to implement multiple fanout, indicating why such an addition is necessary.

$$and =$$
$$\lambda in_1.\lambda in_2.\lambda u.\lambda v.\lambda z.Kz$$
$$\lambda x_1.\lambda y_1.\lambda x_2.\lambda y_2.\lambda w.$$
$$\langle in_1 x_1 y_1,\ in_2 x_2 y_2,$$
$$x_1 u,\ y_1 w,\ x_2 w,\ y_2 v\rangle$$

Observe that if $u : a$, $v : b$, and $w : c$, then the subterms $x_1 u$, $y_1 w$, $x_2 w$, $y_2 v$ get typed as

$$x_1^a \xrightarrow{f} u^a \quad y_1^c \xrightarrow{g} w^c \quad x_2^c \xrightarrow{h} w^c \quad y_2^b \xrightarrow{k} v^b.$$

If the type of x_1 equals the type of y_1, then $a \longrightarrow f = c \longrightarrow g$ and $a = c$. If the type of x_2 equals the type of y_2, similarly $b = c$, and $a = b$ follows—namely, that the "output" variables u and v are forced into having the same type.

Now for disjunction:

$$or =$$
$$\lambda in_1.\lambda in_2.\lambda u.\lambda v.\lambda z.Kz$$
$$\lambda x_1.\lambda y_1.\lambda x_2.\lambda y_2.$$
$$\langle in_1 x_1 y_1,\ in_2 x_2 y_2,$$
$$x_1 u,\ y_1 v,\ x_2 u,\ y_2 v\rangle$$

In typing this term, we have the constraints

$$x_1^a \xrightarrow{f} u^a \quad y_1^b \xrightarrow{g} v^b \quad x_2^a \xrightarrow{h} u^a \quad y_2^b \xrightarrow{k} v^b.$$

If the type of x_i equals the type of y_i, $i = 1, 2$, then $a = b$, and the type of u equals the type of v.

An anomaly

Note that, however strong the temptation may be, these logic gates cannot be used in a "free" functional style if the simulation of Boolean logic is to be faithful. For example, we find (rather oddly) that

$$(\lambda p.\lambda q.\lambda r.[or\ p\ q;\ or\ q\ r])\ true\ false\ false$$
$$= [true;\ true]$$

when we would have expected the answer to be [*true*; *false*]. What happened? Imagine we have for $1 \leq i \leq 3$ pairs of *let*-bound variables (x_i, y_i), where the type of x_1 and y_1 are constrained to be identical in simulation of our encoding of the Boolean "true." We let (u_j, v_j), $1 \leq j \leq 2$ encode the Boolean *or* of the first two and last two pairs. The encoding of the *or* operator enforces the following constraints:

$$x_1^a \xrightarrow{f} u_1^a \quad y_1^a \xrightarrow{f} v_1^a \quad x_2^a \xrightarrow{g} u_1^a \quad y_2^a \xrightarrow{h} v_1^a$$
$$x_2^a \xrightarrow{g} u_2^a \quad y_2^a \xrightarrow{h} v_2^a \quad x_3^a \xrightarrow{k} u_2^a \quad y_3^a \xrightarrow{\ell} v_2^a$$

Note that the type equality of x_1 and y_1 naturally forces the equality of the types of u_1 and v_1, but this forces the "argument" part of the types of x_2 and y_2 to be equal. This equality in turn forces the equality of the types of u_2 and v_2.

What has been ignored in the Boolean simulation is that the second input has multiple fanout: if we introduced constraints by typing the terms $\{x_2 u_1 u_2, y_2 v_1 v_2\}$ instead of typing $\{x_2 u_1, x_2 u_2, y_2 v_1, y_2 v_2\}$, then everything works out properly:

$$x_1^a \xrightarrow{f} u_1^a \qquad y_1^b \xrightarrow{g} v_1^b$$
$$x_2^{a \to c} \xrightarrow{h} u_1^a u_2^c \qquad y_2^{b \to d} \xrightarrow{k} v_1^b v_2^d$$
$$x_3^c \xrightarrow{\ell} u_2^c \qquad y_3^d \xrightarrow{m} v_2^d$$

If the types of x_2 and y_2 are equal in this example, we get $a \longrightarrow c \longrightarrow h = b \longrightarrow d \longrightarrow k$, so $a = b$ and $c = d$—both outputs are true. But if only the types of x_1 and y_1 are equal, we derive $a \longrightarrow f = b \longrightarrow g$, hence $a = b$, but we cannot derive $c = d$, the latter equality necessary to make the second output true.

These examples motivate the introduction of another gadget—not to do Boolean logic, but fanout. We observe that as long as we use the fanout gate to ensure that no input is used in two different Boolean calculations, the simulation will be faithful.

$$fanout =$$
$$\lambda in.\lambda out_1.\lambda out_2.\lambda z.K\ z$$
$$\lambda u.\lambda v.\lambda x_1.\lambda y_1.\lambda x_2.\lambda y_2.$$
$$\langle in\ u\ v,$$
$$out_1\ x_1\ y_1, Eq(out_1, false),$$
$$out_2\ x_2\ y_2, Eq(out_2, false),$$
$$u\ x_1\ x_2,$$
$$v\ y_1\ y_2 \rangle$$

Viewed as a dag in the style of [DKM84] (see Figure 1(a)), the *fanout* gate is just an upside-down *or* gate. Do not be misled by the *Eq* above: its use only constrains the types of the out_1 (and similarly, out_2) to have type $a \longrightarrow b \longrightarrow c \longrightarrow c$ ("false until proven true"); further constraints may force $a = b$. Figure 1(b) shows the type of *fanout* as a type dag.

By using *fanout*, we can also replicate the types of lambda terms $\lambda x_1.\lambda x_2.\cdots \lambda x_k.\lambda z.z$ where the x_i have Boolean types associated with them:

$$copy_k =$$
$$\lambda in.\lambda out_1.\lambda out_2.\lambda z.K\ z$$
$$\lambda u_1.\lambda u_2.\cdots \lambda u_k.$$
$$\lambda v_1.\lambda v_2.\cdots \lambda v_k.$$
$$\lambda w_1.\lambda w_2.\cdots \lambda w_k.$$
$$\langle in\ u_1\ u_2 \cdots u_k,$$
$$fanout\ u_1\ v_1\ w_1,$$
$$fanout\ u_2\ v_2\ w_2,$$
$$\cdots$$
$$fanout\ u_k\ v_k\ w_k,$$
$$Eq(out_1, \lambda x_1.\lambda x_2.\cdots \lambda x_k.\lambda y.y),$$
$$Eq(out_2, \lambda x_1.\lambda x_2.\cdots \lambda x_k.\lambda y.y),$$
$$out_1\ v_1\ v_2 \cdots v_k,$$
$$out_1\ w_1\ w_2 \cdots w_k \rangle$$

This definition can be used to copy tape symbols:

$$copy\text{-}cell\ =\ copy_2$$

In addition, we can use the definition of $copy_k$ to construct more than two copies of some type structure:

$$copy_{k,j} =$$
$$\lambda in.\lambda out_1.\lambda out_2.\cdots\lambda out_j.\lambda z.Kz$$
$$\lambda u_1.\lambda u_2.\cdots\lambda u_j.$$
$$\langle copy_k\ in\ u_1\ out_1,$$
$$copy_k\ u_1\ u_2\ out_2,$$
$$copy_k\ u_2\ u_3\ out_3,$$
$$\ldots$$
$$copy_k\ u_{j-1}\ u_j\ out_j\rangle$$

Notice that copying or fanning-out a type tends to "corrupt" it via unification, so that using it again as an input can cause problems with the simulation of the logic. To avoid this complication in the above definition, we use the "temporary" types u_i, so that $copy_k\ u_i\ u_{i+1}\ out_{i+1}$ uses u_i to copy the type structure into out_{i+1} as well as u_{i+1}; the latter uncorrupted type is then used to continue copying.

2.5 Machine states. Testing for acceptance or rejection.

Now we commence in earnest the coding of a Turing Machine. Let its states be

$$Q = \{q_1, q_2, \ldots, q_n\}$$

where q_1 is the initial state, and the accepting and rejecting states are (respectively):

$$A = \{q_{\ell+1}, q_{\ell+2}, \ldots, q_m\}$$
$$R = \{q_{m+1}, q_{m+2}, \ldots, q_n\}$$

We now code up the ML simulation of the initial state, and how states can be replicated:

$$initial\text{-}state =$$
$$\lambda q_1.\lambda q_2.\cdots\lambda q_n.\lambda z.Kz$$
$$\langle Eq(q_1, true), Eq(q_2, false),$$
$$Eq(q_3, false), \ldots, Eq(q_n, false)\rangle$$
$$copy\text{-}state = copy_n$$

Note that in a type faithfully encoding a machine state, only *one* of the q_i has the type of *true*, and the rest have the type of *false*. We now define a predicate giving the type output of *true* when applied to a state coding acceptance:

$$accept? =$$
$$\lambda state.\lambda x.\lambda y.\lambda z.Kz$$
$$\lambda q_1.\lambda q_2.\cdots\lambda q_n.\lambda acc.$$
$$\langle state\ q_1\ q_2\ \cdots\ q_n,$$
$$Eq(acc, or\ q_{\ell+1}(or\ q_{\ell+2}(or\cdots$$
$$(or\ q_{m-1}\ q_m)\cdots))),$$
$$acc\ x\ y\rangle$$

The type of the "answer," i.e., the functional application $accept?\ state$, is the type of the ML term $\lambda x.\lambda y.\lambda z.Kz$, subject to the constraints that follow. The expression $state\ q_1\ q_2\ \cdots\ q_n$ forces the types of the q_i to unify with Boolean values encoded in the type of $state$. The type of acc is then constrained to be that of *true* or *false*, depending on the type of the Boolean expression. The final constraint $acc\ x\ y$ forces x and y in the "answer" to unify if the Boolean formula typed as *true*.

A predicate $reject?$ is defined similarly.

2.6 Generating an exponential amount of blank tape.

In coding up an initial ID of the Turing Machine in ML, we need to generate the exponential space in which the exponential time machine can run. Here's how: first, for lack of anything better, we define

$$nil = \lambda z.z$$

Now we use function composition to generate an exponential amount of tape using a polynomial-sized expression. Let c be a positive integer; in the following, we explicitly include the *let* syntax to emphasize the power of polymorphism needed.

let $zero_0 = \lambda tape.[zero; tape]$
in let $zero_1 = \lambda tape.zero_0(zero_0\ tape)$
  in let $zero_2 = \lambda tape.zero_1(zero_1\ tape)$
    in ...
  in let $zero_{cn} = \lambda tape.zero_{cn-1}(zero_{cn-1}\ tape)$
  in $zero_{cn}$ nil

The nested *let*-expression then *let*-reduces to the ML term

[zero; [zero; [zero; [zero; $\cdots$ [zero; nil] $\cdots$]]]]

where we have 2^{cn} zeroes. By composing the $zero_i$ functions, we can code up a list (i.e., tape) of k zeroes for $0 \leq k \leq 2^{cn}$ using an ML expression of size polynomial in n. We can then "hand code" more symbols at the end of the tape, e.g., a binary encoding for tape endmarkers.

2.7 State transition function.

Computing the next state of the Turing Machine is simply a Boolean function

$$\sigma(q_1, q_2, \ldots, q_n, z, o) = (t_1, t_2, \ldots, t_n),$$

where exactly one of the q_i is *true*, indicating that the machine is in state q_i, and either z or o is true, indicating what value is being read. A circuit to compute σ would form all the conjuncts $q_i \wedge z$, $q_i \wedge o$, partition the Boolean outputs of these $2n$ *and* gates into disjoint sets S_i, $1 \leq i \leq n$, and *disjoin* each S_i to generate the value of t_i. Viewed as a circuit, each input q_i has outdegree 2, the outdegree of z and o is n, and the outdegree of each conjunct is 1. Our simulation of σ thus uses the *fanout* gate to generate that many copies of each variable to realize the circuit faithfully.

next-state =
  $\lambda state.\lambda cell.$
    $\lambda t_1.\lambda t_2.\cdots \lambda t_n.\lambda w.Kw$
      $\lambda state_1.\lambda state_2.$
      $\lambda cell_1.\lambda cell_2.\cdots \lambda cell_n.$
      $\lambda q_1^{(1)}.\lambda q_2^{(1)}.\cdots \lambda q_n^{(1)}.$
      $\lambda q_1^{(2)}.\lambda q_2^{(2)}.\cdots \lambda q_n^{(2)}.$
      $\lambda z_1.\lambda z_2.\cdots \lambda z_n.$
      $\lambda o_1.\lambda o_2.\cdots \lambda o_n.$
        $\langle$copy-state state $state_1$ $state_2$,
        $copy_{2,n}$ cell $cell_1$ $cell_2$ $\cdots$ $cell_n$,
        $state_1\ q_1^{(1)}\ q_2^{(1)}\ \cdots\ q_n^{(1)}$,
        $state_2\ q_1^{(2)}\ q_2^{(2)}\ \cdots\ q_n^{(2)}$,
        $cell_1\ z_1\ o_1$,
        $cell_2\ z_2\ o_2$,
        ...
        $cell_n\ z_n\ o_n$,
        $Eq(t_1, \phi_1), Eq(t_2, \phi_2), \ldots,$
        $Eq(t_n, \phi_n)\rangle$

The formula ϕ_i computes whether state q_i is reached at the next transition: it is just a Boolean expression using *or* and *and* gates, where we write the conjunction of the Boolean variables q_i and z (respectively, o) as *and* $q_i^{(1)}\ z_i$ (respectively, *and* $q_i^{(2)}\ o_i$). Note that just the right number of copies of each input have been provided via state and cell copying, and that *state* and *cell* are only used for replication, and not Boolean calculation.

2.8 Computing the new value of the tape cell being read.

The construction of the ML expression giving the new value written on the currently-read tape cell is virtually identical to the expression for giving the next state, detailed above. The only difference is that we have fewer Boolean outputs.

new-cell =
  $\lambda state.\lambda cell.$
    $\lambda f.\lambda g.\lambda h.Kh$
      $\lambda state_1.\lambda state_2.$
      $\lambda cell_1.\lambda cell_2.\cdots \lambda cell_n.$
      $\lambda q_1^{(1)}.\lambda q_2^{(1)}.\cdots \lambda q_n^{(1)}.$

$\lambda q_1^{(2)}.\lambda q_2^{(2)}.\cdots.\lambda q_n^{(2)}.$
$\lambda z_1.\lambda z_2.\cdots \lambda z_n.$
$\lambda o_1.\lambda o_2.\cdots \lambda o_n.$

$\langle$ copy-state state state$_1$ state$_2$,
copy$_{2,n}$ cell cell$_1$ cell$_2 \cdots$ cell$_n$,
state$_1$ $q_1^{(1)}$ $q_2^{(1)}$ $\cdots$ $q_n^{(1)}$,
state$_2$ $q_1^{(2)}$ $q_2^{(2)}$ $\cdots$ $q_n^{(2)}$,
cell$_1$ z_1 o_1,
cell$_2$ z_2 o_2,
$\cdots$
cell$_n$ z_n o_n,
$Eq(f, \phi_{\text{zero?}}), Eq(g, \phi_{\text{one?}})\rangle$

The expressions $\phi_{\text{zero?}}$ and $\phi_{\text{one?}}$ are Boolean formulas indicating whether a zero or a one is written in the tape cell. Again, care must be taken to use each input "copy" once.

2.9 Turing Machine IDs.

We represent a Turing Machine ID by a type

$$state \longrightarrow left \longrightarrow right \longrightarrow a \longrightarrow a,$$

where *state*, *left*, and *right* are type metavariables representing more complicated type structures encoding, respectively, the state of the machine (as described in Section 2.5), and *left* and *right* are lists constructed with *pair* representing the contents of the tape to the left and right of the tape head of the machine. We imagine that the tape head is currently reading the first cell on the list *right* (see Figure 2).

$initial\text{-}ID =$
  $\lambda state.\lambda left.\lambda right.\lambda z.Kz$
  $\langle Eq(state, initial\text{-}state),$
  $Eq(left, nil),$
  $Eq(right, \Phi)\rangle$

where Φ is an exponential tape formula as described in Section 2.6.

2.10 Some notes on the simulation.

Let M be a Turing Machine which accepts or rejects an input $x \in \{0,1\}^*$ in $2^{c|x|}$ state transitions, for some positive integer c. We have already considered how to simulate M's state changes and its writing on the tape, but not its head movements. The reason is that it does not seem obvious (at least to this author!) how to simulate the head movements if at every state transition, the machine might move left or right. Instead, we simulate an equivalent machine having *uniform* movement of the tape head. We now clarify what the term "uniform" precisely means.

Instead of simulating M on input x, we simulate an M^* which sweeps its tape head right $2^{c|x|}$ times and then sweeps its tape head left $2^{c|x|}$ times in order to simulate *one* transition of M. It repeats this loop $2^{c|x|}$ times to simulate M's computation on x. The running time of M^* is then slower than M by an exponential factor, but is still running in exponential time.

Suppose then that M has states Q, alphabet $\Sigma = \{0,1\}$, and is running on input x. We construct another Turing Machine M'_x with states Q' and alphabet

$\Sigma' = \{0, 1, \$, blank\} \cup$
  $\{\langle \sigma, q, mode \rangle \mid \sigma \in \Sigma, q \in Q,$
  $mode \in \{left, OK\}\}.$

M'_x simulates M on input x as follows:

1. M'_x writes a \$ on the tape, moves $2^{c|x|}$ tape cells to the right, and writes another \$. It then returns to the left \$ mark, writing blanks as it moves left, writes x in the left of the marked out region, again returning to the leftmost \$. We assume without loss of generality that M never moves to the left of its input $x = x_1 x_2 \cdots x_t$. M'_x now replaces x_1 by the symbol $\langle x_1, q_1, OK \rangle$, indicating M to be in its initial state reading the tape square with x_1 in it.

2. M'_x now begins the simulation of M's computation on x.

(i) M'_x advances its head towards the right until it encounters a tape cell labelled $\langle \sigma, q, OK \rangle$.

(ii) If $\delta_M(\sigma, q) = (q', \sigma', R)$, then M'_x replaces $\langle \sigma, q, OK \rangle$ by σ', moves 1 cell to the right, replaces the next tape symbol τ by $\langle \tau, q', OK \rangle$, and moves its read head all the way to the rightmost \$ on the tape.

(iii) If M wants to move left, on the other hand, i.e., $\delta_M(\sigma, q) = (q', \sigma', L)$, then M'_x replaces $\langle \sigma, q, OK \rangle$ by $\langle \sigma', q', left \rangle$, and moves to the rightmost \$.

(iv) Now for the return journey: M'_x moves its tape head left until it sees a \$ or a $\langle \sigma, q, left \rangle$. If it sees a $\langle \sigma, q, left \rangle$ symbol, let τ be the contents of the neighboring cell to the left: M'_x replaces $\langle \sigma, q, left \rangle$ by σ, moves one tape cell left, replaces τ by $\langle \tau, q, OK \rangle$, and then moves to the leftmost \$.

By executing (i)-(iv), M'_x simulates one state transition of M. M'_x codes accepting states of M by remembering in its finite state memory, when sweeping left from the cell labelled $\langle \sigma, q, OK \rangle$ to \$, if q is an accepting state of M, and stays in an accepting state itself during this tape traversal.

Finally, we simulate M'_x by another Turing Machine M^*, where the alphabet of M^* is just $\{0, 1\}$, coding up tape symbols in Σ' by $\log_2 |\Sigma'|$ bits. Deriving M^* from M'_x is tedious but straightforward; see any decent book on automata theory (e.g., [HU79]) for details. It is clear that M^* runs in exponential time and space, and reaches an accepting state iff M'_x does.

It should be noticed that the tape endmarkers \$ are really not needed, but the price paid is a complication of the ML simulation. In presenting the proof, we have taken care to present the ML code so that it looks as much as possible like a Turing Machine. An alternative is to reconfigure the code so that it computes a function mapping IDs to IDs; in this case the endmarkers could be removed.

2.11 Transition function for a "uniform" Turing Machine.

First, we code a transition of M^* moving right:

$$
\begin{aligned}
&delta\text{-}right = \\
&\quad \lambda old\text{-}ID. \\
&\qquad \lambda new\text{-}state.\lambda new\text{-}left.\lambda new\text{-}right.\lambda z.K\ z \\
&\qquad \lambda state.\lambda left.\lambda right.\lambda cell. \\
&\qquad \lambda state_1.\lambda state_2.\lambda cell_1.\lambda cell_2. \\
&\qquad \langle old\text{-}ID\ state\ left\ right, \\
&\qquad\quad right\ cell\ new\text{-}right, \\
&\qquad\quad copy\text{-}state\ state\ state_1\ state_2, \\
&\qquad\quad copy\text{-}cell\ cell\ cell_1\ cell_2, \\
&\qquad\quad Eq(new\text{-}state, \\
&\qquad\qquad next\text{-}state\ state_1\ cell_1), \\
&\qquad\quad Eq(new\text{-}left, \\
&\qquad\qquad [new\text{-}cell\ state_2\ cell_2;\ left])\rangle
\end{aligned}
$$

Notice that the term *right cell new-right* simulates the breaking of the right hand side of the tape into the cell being read (*cell*) and the rest of the tape to the right (*new-right*). We now generate an exponential number of "move right" transitions:

$$
\begin{aligned}
&let\ \delta_0^R = delta\text{-}right \\
&in\ let\ \delta_1^R = \lambda ID.\delta_0^R(\delta_0^R\ ID) \\
&\quad in\ let\ \delta_2^R = \lambda ID.\delta_1^R(\delta_1^R\ ID) \\
&\quad\quad in\ \ldots \\
&\quad\quad\quad in\ let\ \delta_{cn}^R = \lambda ID.\delta_{cn-1}^R(\delta_{cn-1}^R\ ID)
\end{aligned}
$$

The functions *delta-left* and δ_{cn}^L can be defined similarly. Note carefully how the rightward movement of the tape head is coded into *delta-right*: the *left* list representing the tape to the left of the read head grows, and the *right* list decreases.

2.12 The simulation: Finale.

The innermost sequence of *let* expressions brings the simulation to its conclusion:

$$\text{let } loop_0 = \lambda ID.\delta_{cn}^L(\delta_{cn}^R \, ID)$$
$$\text{in let } loop_1 = \lambda ID.loop_0(loop_0 \, ID)$$
$$\text{in let } loop_2 = \lambda ID.loop_1(loop_1 \, ID)$$
$$\text{in } \ldots$$
$$\text{in let } loop_{cn} = \lambda ID.loop_{cn-1}(loop_{cn-1} \, ID)$$
$$\text{in}$$
$$\lambda state.\lambda z. K \, z$$
$$\langle (loop_{cn} \text{ initial-ID}) \text{ state},$$
$$(\text{reject? state}) \text{ Eq } I \rangle$$

In the above expression, we note that while *initial-ID* is indeed the initial instantaneous description of the *simulation*, it is *not* the initial configuration of the Turing Machine. The latter begins its computation by marking off an exponential amount of tape, writing the input, and returning to the leftmost endmarker; it is this state of the computation where we begin our simulation.

Remember that (*reject? state*) returns *true* : $a \longrightarrow a \longrightarrow b \longrightarrow b$ or *false* : $a \longrightarrow b \longrightarrow c \longrightarrow c$; in the case of the former, $Eq : a \longrightarrow a \longrightarrow a$ and $I : a \longrightarrow a$ will be forced to be unified, causing a mistyping.

Theorem 2.1. *Deciding whether an ML expression is typable is DEXPTIME-hard.*

2.13 Some comments on the lower bound.

The only place in the above construction where ML polymorphism is absolutely necessary is where we use exponential function composition: in constructing the exponential tape of zeroes, and in the construction of the transition function, detailed in Sections 2.6, 2.11, and 2.12. The other uses of *let* are mere notational conveniences: we could remove them by *let*-reduction (i.e., reinstantiating several copies of the code) without the resulting ML formula blowing up exponentially, so that we no longer have a polynomial reduction.

Observe that since the transition function can be polynomially realized by typed lambda terms, generic reductions showing PTIME-hardness and PSPACE-hardness follow easily by relaxing our use of *let* polymorphism. The simple reason that we get merely DEXPTIME-hardness (and DEXPTIME-completeness, via the upper bound in [KM89]) has nothing to do directly with Turing Machines; rather, is that we cannot compose function application any more succinctly. Since Church numerals are just function composition, we are tempted to say that ML typability is DEXPTIME-complete because we cannot count high enough, fast enough.

Because of the generic reduction detailed here, lower bounds on typability of extensions to the ML type discipline—or extensions to the expressive power of the typed lambda calculus—can probably be established merely by considering how succinctly functions can be composed. Since the lambda-calculus part of the proof encodes Turing Machines as well as simpler computing media (automata, for instance), it may well be generalizable in other ways, e.g., automata- or regular expression-based lower bounds for Girard's System F [GLT89], for example. Of course at the moment this is wishful thinking.

3 Polymorphic unification.

We have now seen that deciding typability is DEXPTIME-complete. What is it *about* deciding typability, however, that makes the problem so difficult? We now identify a certain problem concerning unification to be the root cause of the intractability of the decision problem.

A standard algorithm (whose correctness has been succinctly proven in [W87]) to decide if a lambda calculus term is typable is to use the term to generate a series of type equations over a set of type variables with a binary function symbol $\longrightarrow$. The equations are of the form $U = V$ or $U = V \longrightarrow W$. This set of equations, whose size is linear in the size of the original lambda term, is then given to a unification algorithm, which closes the set of equations over a simple *unification logic*. The closure groups type variables having the same solution into equivalence classes. These equivalence classes then can be thought of as the nodes of a special kind of directed graph, where the out-degree of every node is either 0 or 2; in the latter case, an equation $U = V \longrightarrow W$ can be interpreted as $[U] = [V] \longrightarrow [W]$, namely that $[U]$ is an equivalence class (node) with two labelled children nodes $[V]$ and $[W]$. A certain subgraph of this structure can be identified with the putative type of the original lambda term, and this term is typable iff the subgraph is acyclic.

The problem of typing Core ML expressions is virtually identical, except for the *let* polymorphism. In this case, certain subsets of type equations can be thought of as being *polymorphically reinstantiated* in the set of equations to be unified. For example, in typing *let* $x = E$ *in* B, where E is a closed lambda term, the set of type equations to be unified contains a "copy" of the type equations associated with E (reinstantiated with new type variables) for *each* free occurance of x in B. As in the case of lambda terms, the expression is typable if the graph induced by the equivalence classes created by unification is acyclic.

Given a set of type equations generated by a Core ML expression E, and two type variables U and V from the system, we may ask: in the unification solution of the system, do U and V have the same value? That is, are they in the same equivalence class? If this question can be answered, say, by an oracle requiring no computing resources, then the typability of E can be decided in PSPACE. Furthermore, if E is indeed typable, then its principal type can be output as a directed acyclic graph in polynomial space. (The careful reader will note that at this point, an earlier, failed proof that typability is in PSPACE is being recycled.) While the details of our DEXP-TIME-hardness bound have been spelled out in full, we limit ourselves to a sketch of the important features of this analysis.

3.1 A canonical-form transformation.

We begin by showing how an arbitrary Core ML expression E can be transformed into another expression E' in a certain *canonical form* which preserves the principal type iff there is one. We write $|E|$ to refer to the *length* of an ML expression E, defined without loss of generality as the size of its parse tree. The length of a type is defined similarly as the size of its tree (or where relevant, dag) representation.

The canonical form we compute has the following structure:

$C_n \equiv$
let $x_0 = E_0$ in
let $x_1 = (\lambda \ell_1.\lambda \ell_2.\cdots \lambda \ell_{i_1}.E_1)\ x'_{1,1}\ x'_{1,2}\ \cdots\ x'_{1,i_1}$
 in
let $x_2 = (\lambda \ell_1.\lambda \ell_2.\cdots \lambda \ell_{i_2}.E_2)\ x'_{2,1}\ x'_{2,2}\ \cdots\ x'_{2,i_2}$
 in
 $\ldots$
let $x_n = (\lambda \ell_1.\lambda \ell_2.\cdots \lambda \ell_{i_n}.E_n)\ x'_{n,1}\ x'_{n,2}\ \cdots\ x'_{n,i_n}$
 in
x_n

The salient features of the canonical form are:

- Its length is polynomial in the length of the original expression.

- All the let-expressions are nested in a single chain.

- E_0 and each $\lambda \ell_1.\lambda \ell_2.\cdots \lambda \ell_{i_j}.E_j$ are all let-free and are closed lambda terms.

We now describe how this transformation can be made in polynomial time. First, we α-convert all λ- and let-bindings to be unique identifiers, so that subsequent transformation of the expression does not result in any unwanted name clashes. The initial ML expression E is then transformed using the following rule we call *let-lifting*, since each *let* is "lifted" as far "outside" of the expression as possible:

$$\lambda x.\text{let } y = F \text{ in } M \implies$$
$$\text{let } y' = \lambda x.F \text{ in } \lambda x.M[y'x/y]$$

Repeatedly applying the above transformation to E results in an expression where no let-binding occurs in a lambda body, and preserves the principal type. The resulting expression has length at most quadratic in $|E|$.

Next, we arrange the let-bindings so that they form a uniform chain. To do so, we use the following simple type-preserving transformations until they can no longer be applied:

$$\Phi \ (let\ x = E\ in\ B) \implies$$
$$let\ x = E\ in\ \Phi\ B$$
$$(let\ x = E\ in\ B)\ \Phi \implies$$
$$let\ x = E\ in\ B\ \Phi$$
$$let\ x = (let\ y = F\ in\ N)\ in\ M \implies$$
$$let\ y = F$$
$$in\ let\ x = N$$
$$in\ M$$

The result of applying all these transformations is an expression having a single chain of let-bindings, each of which is let-free.

Theorem 3.1. *An arbitrary ML expression can be reduced to canonical form with only a quadratic increase in expression size.*

3.2 Deciding typability: the type tree.

We now use the canonical form to define an exponential-sized data structure called the *type tree*. We can then essentially dispense with the original ML expression E as well as its canonical form, and use a compact representation of the type tree to derive whether or not E is typable.

3.3 The type tree.

Notice that in the canonical form, each expression bound to x_k is defined in terms of two polymorphic copies of some set of x_j, $j < k$, imitating the structure of a tree where the nodes have different branching factors (outdegree). If the expression is typable, each x_k has a principal type derived from taking polymorphic copies of the principal types for each x_j, $j < k$, and merging them modulo a small (i.e., polynomial) set of constraints. This set of constraints is defined from the type of the closed lambda term $\lambda\ell_1.\lambda\ell_2.\cdots\lambda\ell_{i_k}.E_k$.

We use Example 1.2 in the Introduction to illustrate this point: bindings to each x_k can be written as

$$let\ x_k = (\lambda\ell_1.\lambda\ell_2.\lambda y.\ell_1(\ell_2 y))\ x_{k-1}\ x_{k-1}\ in\ \ldots,$$

and we may type the closed λ-term as

$$\lambda\ell_1^{b \to c}.\lambda\ell_2^{a \to b}.\lambda y^a.(\ell_1^{b \to c}(\ell_2^{a \to b}y^a)^b)^c :$$
$$(b \to c) \to (a \to b) \to a \to c.$$

Suppose x_{k-1} has a principal type τ, and separate copies of τ are bound to ℓ_1 and ℓ_2: the constraint that the definition of x_k places on these types is that the "output" of the type of ℓ_2 must equal the "input" of the type of ℓ_1.

Definition 3.2. *The type tree $\mathcal{T}_n$ of the canonical expression $\mathcal{C}_n$ is tree, where the root contains type equations derived from the closed lambda term*

$$\lambda\ell_1.\lambda\ell_2.\cdots\lambda\ell_{i_n}.E_n,$$

with a particular type variable X_n in the root denoting the type of x_n. The children of the root are also type trees, one for each free occurance of a let-bound variable x_j appearing in the definition of x_n. The root also contains an equation $X_{s,j} = Y_{s,j}$ where $Y_{s,j}$ is a type variable in the subtree associated with the type of the sth free occurance of x_j in the definition of x_n, and $X_{s,j}$ is the type variable associated with that free occurance in the root.

The type tree enjoys the following friendly properties:

- While the type tree has size exponential in the size of the canonical ML expression, each node in the type tree takes only polynomial space to store. Furthermore, the variables appearing in a constraint equation always appear in adjacent type tree nodes.

- Variables can be uniquely identified as to what tree node they come from, where the variable names have polynomial length encoding the path to the node, and which variable in the node is being referenced.

- The unification solution of the constraints in the tree contains the solution for the principal type of the canonical expression, if there is such a type.

The idea of the type tree is very similar to a variety of other representation schemes for describing the exponential number of type equations generated by *let* polymorphism, in particular Kanellakis' *pointer dags* [Ka] and Kfoury's *acyclic semi-unification*[Kf].

An important consequence of the above properties on which the PSPACE result (with oracle) rests is the following: even though the type tree has exponential size, it can be virtually represented in polynomial space by simply storing type equation representations of the closed lambda terms. The type equations at any node can be regenerated in polynomial time by taking the virtual "master copy" of the node, and simply renaming variables based on the path to the node.

The last point above—that the solution S of the constraints determines the principal type—provides insight into the core of our polynomial space algorithm. Given two variables U and V from the type tree, we want to determine in polynomial space if $U = V$ in S, a relation we will write as $U \equiv V$ to distinguish it from the $=$ constraints in the type tree. The solution S defines an obvious equivalence relation among the variables which is given by $\equiv$, but we may further associate a relation $\Rightarrow$ among these equivalence classes as $[U] \Rightarrow [V]$ if $A = B \to C$ is a constraint in the type tree, $A \in [U]$, and $B \in [V]$ or $C \in [V]$. The type tree $\mathcal{T}_n$ then induces a graph $\mathcal{G}_n$, where the nodes are the equivalence classes, and the directed edges are the $\Rightarrow$ relation. The relation $\Rightarrow$ naturally encodes the idea of "type substructure," from which we have the following lemma, stating that a core ML expression is untypable iff an *occur check* returns positive.

Lemma 3.3. *The ML expression E is typable iff $\mathcal{G}_n$ is acyclic, equivalently, iff the transitive closure of $\Rightarrow$ is irreflexive.*

We now sketch some of the important features of our polynomial space solution. We are assuming that the $\equiv$ relation is computed by an oracle at no cost, from which we can compute the $\Rightarrow$ relation in polynomial space. A consequence of these assumptions is that deciding typability can also be computed in polynomial space by a simple nondeterministic algorithm. Let R be a type tree variable associated with the putative principal type of the ML expression E. Beginning with R, our algorithm simply *guesses* a *path*, i.e., a set of relations $V_0 = R \Rightarrow V_1 \Rightarrow \cdots \Rightarrow V_j$, and guesses as well to remember some V_i where $i < j$; it then checks if $V_i \equiv V_j$. If the answer is "yes," the ML expression is not typable, because a cycle was discovered. The ML expression is clearly not typable if it is possible to make a series of correct guesses leading to a "yes." A crucial reason *why* this computation is in PSPACE is that the number of V_k which must be guessed along the path is merely exponential, and thus in polynomial space we may maintain a sort of *clock* initialized to a value exponential in $|E|$, and decreased by one after each V_k is guessed; if there is a path leading to an acyclicity, it must be guessed before the clock runs to zero. By Savitch's Theorem [Sa70], we know that this algorithm can be simulated by a deterministic one with only a quadratic blowup in space, resulting in a polynomial-space algorithm.

How can the lower bound presented in Section 2 and this oracular PSPACE upper bound be understood together? First, they indicate that the bottleneck in deciding typability can be understood in terms of proving equality of type variables in the context we have detailed above. Secondly, given the oracle, deciding if our Turing Machine simulation codes an accepting computation can be decided in constant time: observe that acceptance or rejection is expressed by a Boolean variable coded as (*reject? state*). The Boolean simulation of *true* and *false* each use two type variables which may or may not be constrained to be equal; being able to test in constant time this type variable equality is analogous to examining the exponential sized Boolean "circuits" defined by ML let-polymorphism, and being allowed to test any "output wire" in constant time to see if it is a 0 or 1. In other words, the lower bound, in its simulation of Boolean values via pairs of type variables, exploits *precisely* the computational intractability of proving equivalence of type variables, the problem which the oracle was specifically intended to solve.

3.4 How to output the principal type as a directed acyclic graph

Given that we can decide if an ML expression is typable, how can we indeed output its type, and assuming that we have a $\equiv$-oracle, can this be done in polynomial space? Since the principal type can have exponential size, we clearly cannot compute and store the entire type in polynomial space; instead we ask if we can construct an output device having polynomial space which will output the principal type into an external file. We begin with the following simple observation:

Lemma 3.4. *The principal type of an ML expression E cannot be output as a string in space polynomial in $|E|$.*

Proof. Let $|E| = n$. If the output device is allowed some polynomial $p(n)$ space, it can only encode $c^{p(n)}$ states. By a simple counting argument just like the pumping lemma for finite automata, if the output device is required to generate a principal type represented as a string of length $2^{2^{cn}}$, it must either abort prematurely or loop. ⋈

Instead, we show how to output the principal type as a directed acyclic graph, and in this case, such counting arguments will not work, since the dag size is at most a single exponential in $|E|$.

Definition 3.5. *A type tree variable V has structure if $V = P \to Q$ is a constraint in the type tree.*

Definition 3.6. *Type tree variable P is a parent of Q if $W = R \to S$ is a constraint in the type tree, $P \equiv W$, and either $Q \equiv R$ or $Q \equiv S$. P is an ancestor of R if either P is a parent of R, or P is a parent of Q and Q is an ancestor of R.*

Definition 3.7. *A path is a sequence $\langle U_1, \ldots, U_k \rangle$ of type variables where U_i is a parent of U_{i+1}, $1 \leq i < k$. A path $\mathcal{P}_1 = \langle U_1, \ldots, U_k \rangle$ appears to the left of a path $\mathcal{P}_2 = \langle V_1, \ldots, V_\ell \rangle$, written $\mathcal{P}_1 \prec \mathcal{P}_2$, if $U_1 \equiv V_1$, and either $U_1 \equiv U_2 \longrightarrow V_2$, or $U_2 \equiv V_2$ and $\mathcal{P}_1 = \langle U_2, \ldots, U_k \rangle$ appears to the left of $\mathcal{P}_2 = \langle V_2, \ldots, V_\ell \rangle$. A type tree variable U appears to the left of type tree variable V, written $U \prec V$, if there exist leftmost paths $\mathcal{P}_1 = \langle U_1, \ldots, U_k \rangle$ and $\mathcal{P}_2 = \langle V_1, \ldots, V_\ell \rangle$ where $\mathcal{P}_1 \prec \mathcal{P}_2$, $U \equiv U_k$ and $V \equiv V_\ell$.*

Lemma 3.8. *Given type tree variables P and Q, we can determine if $P \prec Q$ in polynomial space.*

Definition 3.9. *We associate with every type tree variable V a canonical type tree variable $\chi(V)$ defined as follows: let $E(V) = \{W \mid W \equiv V\}$. The $W \in E(V)$ have a lexicographic ordering. Define $E_s(V) = \{W \in E(V) \mid W \text{ has structure}\}$. If $E_s(V) \neq \emptyset$, we define $\chi(V)$ to be the lexicographically minimal element of $E_s(V)$. Otherwise, we define $\chi(V)$ to be the lexicographically minimal element of $E(V)$.*

Lemma 3.10. *For any type tree variable V, we can compute $\chi(V)$ in polynomial space.*

If an ML expression E is typable, then the solution to its associated set of equational constraints contains no positive occur checks. This means precisely that the "graph encoding" of the solution (modulo $\equiv$-equivalence of variables) is acyclic. Hence we follow the following strategy: beginning with the root variable R, we depth-first search the graph following children in left to right order: if $V \equiv P = Q \to R$, we visit the node (equivalence class) associated with V, then in turn output the structures associated with Q and R. When we are about to explore such a structure, we first compute whether it has already been output, this the intent of the definition of $\prec$. Since the node of every output structure has a unique parent via the use of depth-first search, we do not need a stack to implement the tree recursion, although the space savings is at a rather prohibitive time cost. To compute the address pointers associated with nodes is easy: since each node in the graph corresponds to an equivalence class of type variables in $\mathcal{T}_n$, we choose as node pointer the canonical representative of the class (see Definition 3.9 above).

procedure *outdag* $(V : type\ variable)$:
  { only called on structures that have
    not yet been output }
  $U := \chi(V)$;
  if U has structure $\longrightarrow$
    { say, $U = A \to B$ }
    output internal node U;
    if $\exists\ W \prec U$ where $W \Rightarrow A \longrightarrow$
      output pointer $\chi(A)$;
      if $\exists\ W \prec U$ where $W \Rightarrow B \longrightarrow$
        output pointer $\chi(B)$;
        backup(U)
      [] **else** $\longrightarrow$ *outdag*(B)
      fi
    [] **else** $\longrightarrow$ *outdag*(A)
    fi
  [] **else** $\longrightarrow$
    { U doesn't have structure;
      we've reached a leaf }
    output leaf U;
    backup(U)
  fi
erudecorp;

Remark. When *outdag*(V) is only called on "new" structures, the leftmost parent of V is unique up to $\equiv$-isomorphism.

procedure *backup* $(V : type\ variable)$:
  if $V \equiv R \longrightarrow$ **return**
  [] **else** $\longrightarrow$
    $U := \chi(V)$;
    if $\exists$ *leftmost* parent $P = A \to B$ where
      $A \equiv B \equiv U \longrightarrow$
      { The second "copy" of U should
        be generated by a dag pointer }
      output pointer $\chi(U)$;
      backup(P)
    [] $\exists$ *leftmost* parent $P = A \to B$ where
      $A \equiv U, B \not\equiv U \longrightarrow$
      if $\exists\ W \prec B$ where $W \equiv B \longrightarrow$
        { B already generated }
        output pointer $\chi(B)$;
        backup(P)
      [] **else** $\longrightarrow$ *outdag*(B)
      fi
    [] $\exists$ *leftmost* parent $P = A \to B$ where
      $A \not\equiv U, B \equiv U \longrightarrow$
      backup(P)
    fi
  fi
erudecorp;

4 Conclusions.

In this paper, we have provided a simple proof that deciding ML typability is DEXPTIME-complete. The proof was just a computer program written in ML, whose principal type simulated an exponential number of moves by an arbitrary Turing Machine; by changing the program slightly, we could force a mistyping precisely when the Turing Machine rejected its input. We identified a closely related problem in the logic of unification, namely deciding the equality of two type variables in an exponential set of type equations derived from a Core ML expression, and showed that the lower bound comes precisely from this problem. Were it solvable in polynomial space, deciding typability would be in PSPACE, and computation of the principal type would also be possible in polynomial space.

One question immediately comes to mind: given the oracle we have postulated for solving the type variable equality problem described above, is deciding typability PSPACE-hard? We conjecture this is the case: an argument based on transitive closure will probably bear this out. Can the DEXPTIME-hardness proof be reworked to get an undecidability result for the Milner/Mycroft type system? We conjecture that it should be possible to use their FIX rule to code up an unbounded amount of blank tape, as well as an ML simulation of a Turing Machine which generates an unbounded number of IDs. This might provide some alternative intuitions to the proof of [KTU89b]. Finally, we propose using the basic Turing Machine simulation in typed lambda calculus as a tool for studying other more complex type systems.

The significance of the lower bound presented in this paper is not at all mitigated by the fact that programmers do not typically code up Turing Machines in their types. The importance of the result is that *a priori* one cannot set a *reasonable* upper bound on the amount of computation that goes on during polymorphic type checking. The Turing Machine simulation is merely an example of a particular kind of huge computation.

The question remains why everyone has believed ML polymorphic type checking to be efficient, when in the worst case it is clearly not so. Bounding the amount of nested uses of *let*, the notion of *let depth* as proposed in [KM89], is one syntactic means of assuring polynomial-time type inference, but this restriction seems arbitrary; indeed, its main virtue is that it facilitates an inductive argument in proving the upper bound. Some sort of average-case analysis would be very nice, but it is not at all clear what probabilistic distribution on programs would be convincing or realistic. Certainly distributions on trees (e.g., branching, depth) simulating the canonical form could be used to produce a result, but whether such an analysis would produce an answer of practical relevance is not obvious.

Acknowledgments. Paris Kanellakis was kind enough to send me his unpublished notes on details of the PSPACE-hardness construction sketched in his paper with John Mitchell, which allowed me to understand how the proof really worked. I would especially like to thank Paris for detailed reading of several earlier versions of this paper, some of which were truly flawed beyond belief, and for his merciless cross-examination and verification of the final DEXPTIME-hardness bound. John Mitchell also read an exposition of the lower bound, and checked many of its details by implementing them in Standard ML. I am indeed fortunate to have benefited from their advice and scrutiny, but even more fortunate to have written a proof that could practically have been checked by a computer!

I would also like to thank Dennis Kfoury for his patience and invaluable role as sounding board and critic during a feverish period in April and May of 1989, when I began thinking that the work described in [KM89] was worthy of a sequel. The opportunity to present that paper at the BU/Northeastern type theory seminar motivated my interest in this subject.

5 References.

[AS85] Harold Abelson and Gerald Sussman, Structure and Interpretation of Computer Programs. MIT Press, 1985.

[AHU74] Alfred V. Aho, John E. Hopcroft, and Jeffrey D. Ullman. The Design and Analysis of Computer Algorithms. Addison-Wesley, 1974.

[DKM84] Cynthia Dwork, Paris Kanellakis, and John Mitchell, On the Sequential Nature of Unification. J. Logic Programming 1(1):35-50.

[GLT89] Jean-Yves Girard, Yves Lafont, and Paul Taylor, Proofs and Types. Cambridge University Press, 1989.

[HMM86] Robert Harper, David MacQueen, and Robin Milner, Standard ML. Research Report ECS-LFCS-86-2, Computer Science Department, University of Edinburgh, March 1986.

[HU79] John E. Hopcroft and Jeffrey D. Ullman, Introduction to Automata Theory, Languages, and Computation. Addison-Wesley, 1979.

[Hu73] Harry B. Hunt, The equivalence problem for regular expressions with intersection is not polynomial in tape. TR 73-156, Computer Science Department, Cornell University, 1973.

[Ka] Paris Kanellakis, personal communication.

[KM89] Paris Kanellakis and John Mitchell, Polymorphic unification and ML typing, POPL 1989.

[Kf] Dennis Kfoury, personal communication.

[KTU89a] Dennis Kfoury, Jerzy Tiuryn, and Pavel Urzyczyn, An analysis of ML typability. Preprint.

[KTU89b] Dennis Kfoury, Jerzy Tiuryn, and Pavel Urzyczyn, Undecidability of the semi-unification problem. Preprint.

[Mi78] Robin Milner, A theory of type polymorphism in programming, JCSS 17 (1978), pp. 348–375.

[Sa70] Walter Savitch, Relationship between non-deterministic and deterministic tape complexities, JCSS 4:2 (1970), pp. 177–192.

[Pf88] Frank Pfenning, Partial polymorphic type inference and higher-order unification. 1988 Conference on Lisp and Functional Programming.

[W87] Mitch Wand, A simple algorithm and proof for type inference. Fundamenta Informaticae 10 (1987).

A A pathological example

```
Standard ML of New Jersey,
Version 0.24, 22 November 1988
val it = () : unit
- fun pair x y=fn z=> z x y;
val pair = fn :
  'a -> 'b -> ('a -> 'b -> 'c) -> 'c
- let val x1=fn y=> pair y y
  in let val x2=fn y=> x1(x1(y))
     in let val x3=fn y=> x2(x2(y))
        in let val x4=fn y=> x3(x3(y))
           in let val x5=fn y=> x4(x4(y))
              in x5(fn z=> z) end end end end end;
[Major collection...
   97% used (375228/385108), 1280 msec]
   [Increasing heap to 1104k]
[Major collection...
   88% used (504800/568000), 1940 msec]
   [Increasing heap to 1480k]
[Major collection...
   [Increasing heap to 2288k]
   99% used (824308/825248), 3200 msec]
   [Increasing heap to 2416k]
[Major collection...
   [Increasing heap to 3816k]
   99% used (1313348/1314312), 5140 msec]
   [Increasing heap to 3848k]
[Major collection...
   99% used (2057024/2058152), 8400 msec]
   [Increasing heap to 6032k]
[Major collection...
   99% used (3185268/3186408), 12680 msec]
   [Increasing heap to 9336k]
[Major collection...
   99% used (4887136/4888160), 20540 msec]
   [Increasing heap to 14320k]
[Major collection...
   99% used (7394828/7395948), 31020 msec]
   [Increasing heap to 21672k]
[Major collection...
   [Increasing heap to 35016k]
   99% used (12274372/12351328), 49780 msec]
   [Increasing heap to 35968k]
[Major collection...
   99% used (19176936/19179460), 79040 msec]
   [Increasing heap to 56184k]
[Major collection...
  -48% used (28902440/28906544), 119580 msec]
   [Increasing heap to 57960k]
[Major collection...
   [Increasing heap to 58936k]
   [Increasing heap to 59192k]
   [Increasing heap to 59320k]
  -35% used (31712940/31713380), 129880 msec]
   [Increasing heap to 59352k]

val it = fn : (((((((((((((((((((((((((((
((('a -> 'a) -> ('a -> 'a) -> 'b) -> 'b) ->
((('a -> 'a) -> ('a -> 'a) -> 'b) -> 'b) ->
'c) -> 'c) -> ((((('a -> 'a) -> ('a -> 'a) ->
'b) -> 'b) -> ((('a -> 'a) -> ('a -> 'a) ->
'b) -> 'b) -> 'c) -> 'c) -> 'd) -> 'd) -> ((
((((('a -> 'a) -> ('a -> 'a) -> 'b) -> 'b) ->
((('a -> 'a) -> ('a -> 'a) -> 'b) -> 'b) ->
'c) -> 'c) -> ((((('a -> 'a) -> ('a -> 'a) ->
'b) -> 'b) -> ((('a -> 'a) -> ('a -> 'a) ->
'b) -> 'b) -> 'c) -> 'c) -> 'd) -> 'd) -> 'e)
-> 'e) -> (((((((('a -> 'a) -> ('a -> 'a) ->
'b) -> 'b) -> ((('a -> 'a) -> ('a -> 'a) ->
'b) -> 'b) -> 'c) -> 'c) -> ((((('a -> 'a) ->
('a -> 'a) -> 'b) -> 'b) -> ((('a -> 'a) ->
('a -> 'a) -> 'b) -> 'b) -> 'c) -> 'c) -> 'd)
-> 'd) -> ((((((('a -> 'a) -> ('a -> 'a) ->
'b) -> 'b) -> ((('a -> 'a) -> ('a -> 'a) ->
'b) -> 'b) -> 'c) -> 'c) -> ((((('a -> 'a) ->
('a -> 'a) -> 'b) -> 'b) -> ((('a -> 'a) ->
('a -> 'a) -> 'b) -> 'b) -> 'c) -> 'c) -> 'd)
-> ... and so on for hundreds of pages! ...
```

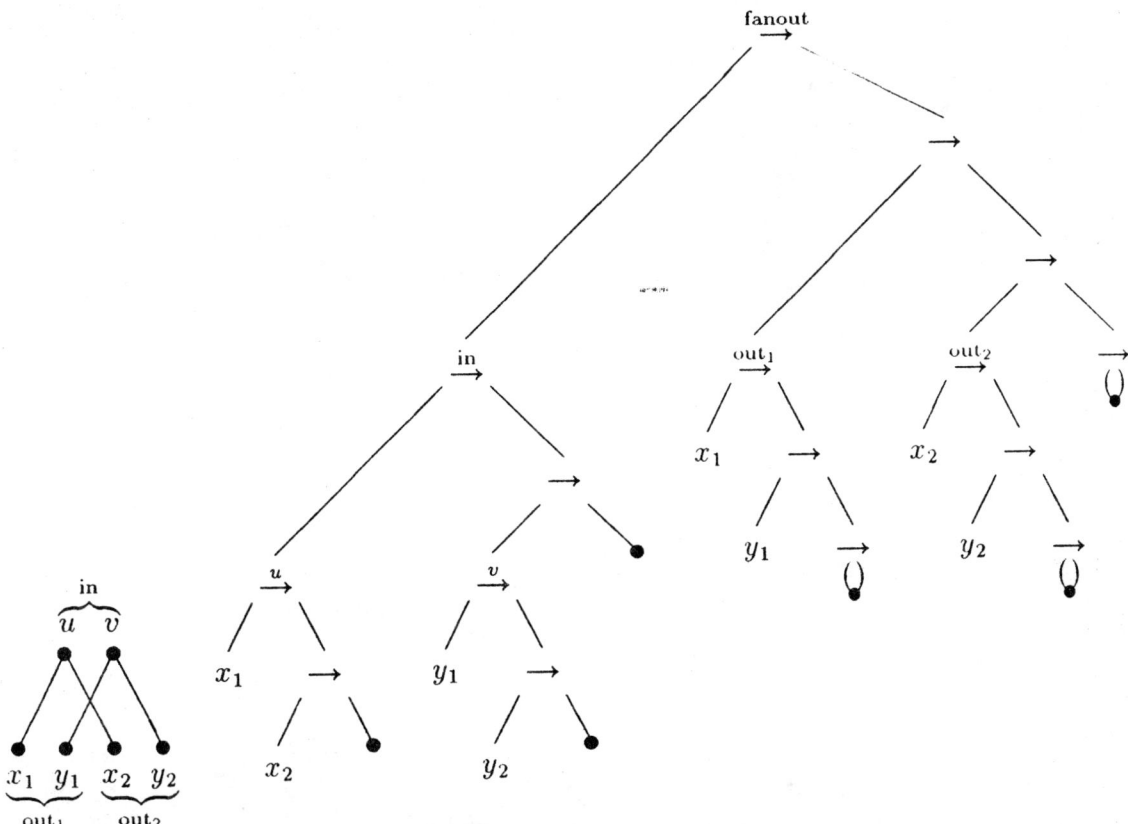

Figure 1: Implementing *fanout* as (a) a dag; (b) a type.

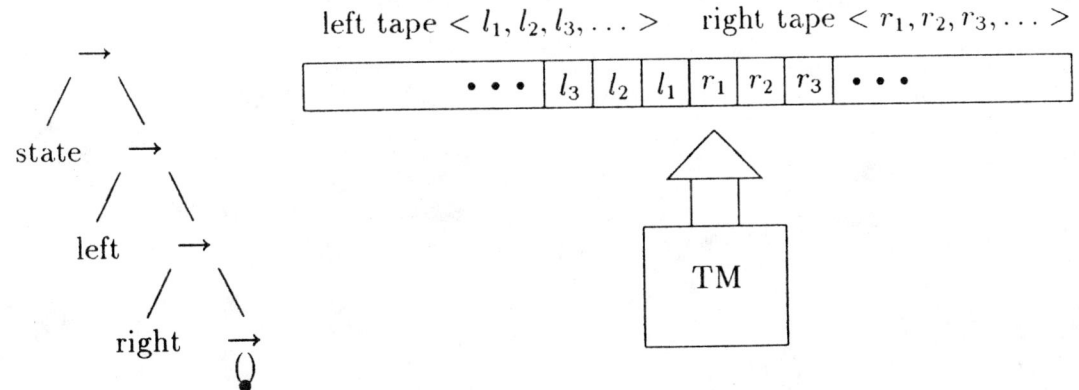

Figure 2: Turing Machine IDs.

NOTES